Arizona
New Mexico

Published by:
AAA Publishing
1000 AAA Drive
Heathrow, FL 32746-5063
Copyright AAA 1999

Send Written Comments to:
AAA Member Comments
1000 AAA Drive, Box 61
Heathrow, FL 32746-5063

Advertising Rate and Circulation Information
Call: (407) 444-8280

Printed in the USA by Quebecor Printing, Buffalo, NY

 Printed on recyclable paper.
Please recycle whenever possible.

Stock #4602

Arizona
New Mexico

TourBook Navigator

Follow our simple guide to make the most of this member benefit 7-26

Comprehensive City Index
Alphabetical list for the entire book 472

■ *Arizona*

Historical Timeline 30

Fast Facts 33

AAA Starred Attractions 34

Recreation Areas Chart 38

Temperature Chart 39

POINTS OF INTEREST 40-118

    Phoenix 70-87

    Tucson 100-112

MAPS

Arizona Orientation 37

Grand Canyon National Park 53

Phoenix Destination Area 73

Phoenix 74

Tucson Destination Area 103

Tucson 104

ACCOMMODATIONS 171-361

    Phoenix 216

    Tucson 319

MAPS

Phoenix Destination Area 216

Phoenix-Sun City 224

Phoenix-Glendale 225

Scottsdale-Paradise Valley 226

Tempe-Mesa-Chandler 227

Tucson Destination Area 319

Downtown Tucson 323

Tucson and Vicinity 324

■ *New Mexico*

Historical Timeline 122

Fast Facts 125

AAA Starred Attractions 126

Temperature Chart 128

Recreation Areas Chart 128

POINTS OF INTEREST 131-169

    Albuquerque 132

    Santa Fe 158

    MAPS

    New Mexico Orientation 127

    Albuquerque 133

    Santa Fe 159

ACCOMMODATIONS 363-457

    Albuquerque 365

    Santa Fe 425

    MAPS

    Albuquerque 369

    Santa Fe 428

Featured Information

Offices 458

Driving Distances Map 459

NEW Bed & Breakfast Advertising
    Section 460

    Bed & Breakfast Lodgings
        Index 460

    Country Inns Index 461

    Historical Lodgings & Restaurants
        Index 461

    Resorts Index 461

    Points of Interest Index 463

SAVE Attraction Admission Discount
        Index 471

Comprehensive City Index 472

Photo Credit Index 474

© 1999, Promus Hotels, Inc.

You don't have to travel back in

time for old-fashioned hospitality.

Just across America.

Whether it's our free breakfast, clean, comfortable rooms, fair rates or our 100% Satisfaction Guarantee, there's nothing we like more than seeing a smile on your face. For reservations call 1-800-HAMPTON or visit us at www.hampton-inn.com.

One of the few nice places still around.℠

When it comes to personal trip planning, nobody beats trained AAA travel counselors.

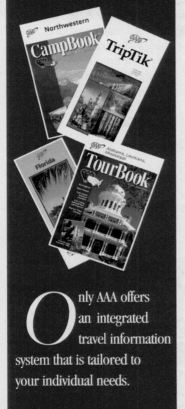

Only AAA offers an integrated travel information system that is tailored to your individual needs.

Our highly trained counselors can assist you with all facets of planning your trip, from designing the route to making reservations. In addition, only AAA travel counselors can provide our exclusive collection of travel materials selected especially for you.

TourBook® guides are comprehensive travel guides listing AAA Approved attractions, lodgings and restaurants. In addition to the coveted Diamond Ratings, you'll find descriptions of towns and cities and information on discounts available only to AAA members. TourBooks are updated annually and cover every state and province in the United States and Canada.

TripTik® routings trace your route mile-by-mile and are clearly marked with the vital information you need while on the road, such as highway exits and rest stops. These handy maps are custom-configured by your AAA travel counselor and can highlight the quickest, shortest or most scenic routes, as well as highway construction projects along the way.

Sheet maps are updated annually and cover every state and province, plus regional areas throughout North America. An extensive network of road reporters and club staff works with AAA cartographers to ensure that AAA maps are the most detailed and accurate maps available.

CampBook® guides list AAA Approved camping and RV facilities, both public and private, throughout the United States and Canada.

So the next time you're planning a trip, remember to visit your local AAA travel counselor.

Travel With Someone You Trust®

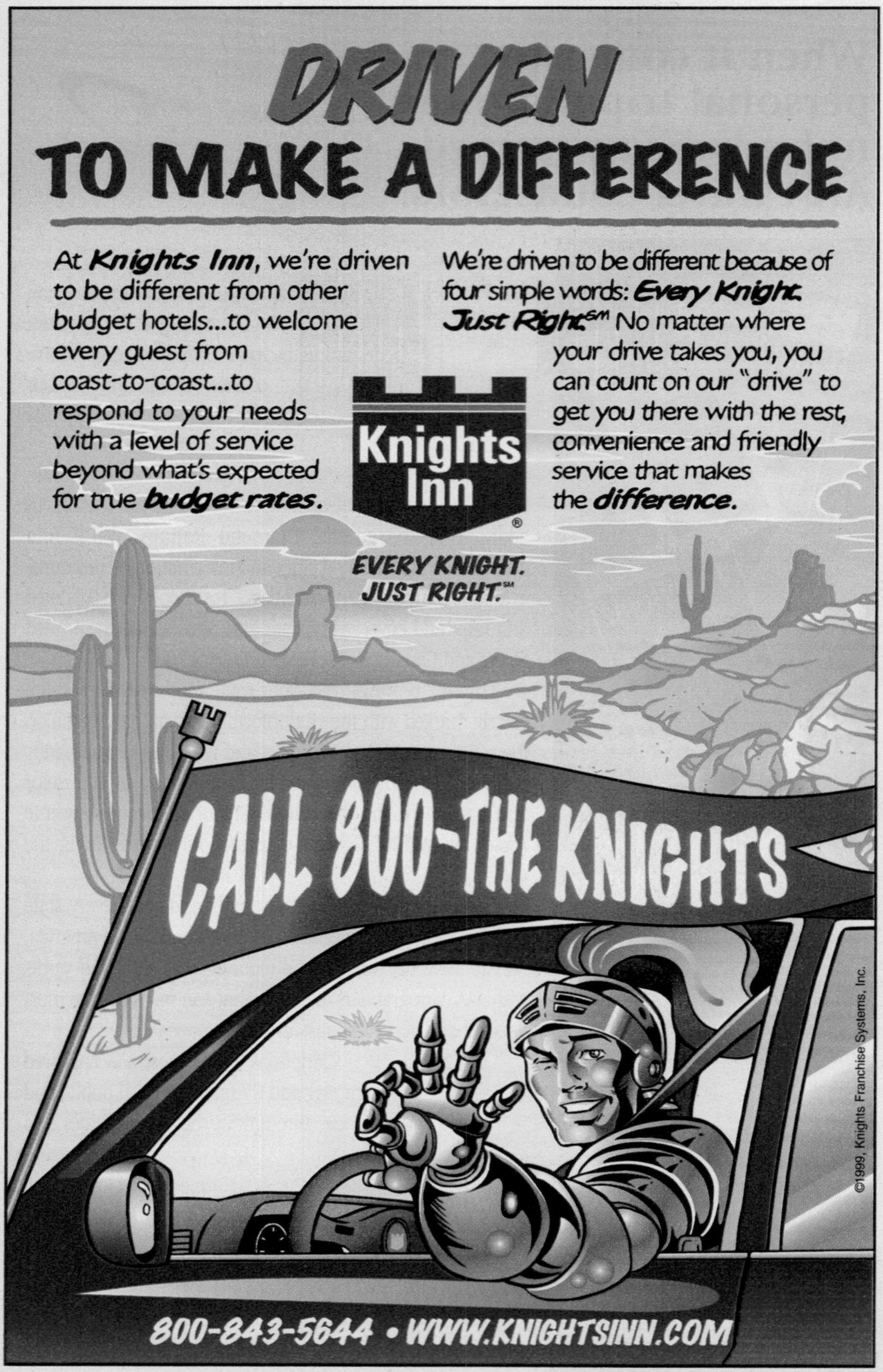
DRIVEN
TO MAKE A DIFFERENCE
At Knights Inn, we're driven to be different from other budget hotels...to welcome every guest from coast-to-coast...to respond to your needs with a level of service beyond what's expected for true budget rates.
We're driven to be different because of four simple words: Every Knight. Just Right.SM No matter where your drive takes you, you can count on our "drive" to get you there with the rest, convenience and friendly service that makes the difference.
Knights Inn®
EVERY KNIGHT. JUST RIGHT.SM
CALL 800-THE KNIGHTS
800-843-5644 • WWW.KNIGHTSINN.COM
©1999, Knights Franchise Systems, Inc.

Trust

the AAA TourBook
for objective travel information.
Follow the pages of TourBook Navigator to thoroughly
understand this unique member benefit.

Making Your Way Through the AAA Listings

Attractions, lodgings and restaurants are listed on the basis of
merit alone after careful evaluation, approval and rating by one of our full-time inspectors or, in rare
cases, a designated representative. Annual lodging inspections are unannounced and conducted on
site by random room sample.

Those lodgings and restaurants listed with an [fyi] icon have not gone through the same
inspection process as other rated properties. Individual listings will denote the reason why this icon
appears. Bulleted attraction listings are not inspected but are included for member information.

An establishment's decision to advertise in the TourBooks has no bearing on its inspection,
evaluation or rating. Advertising for services or products does not imply AAA endorsement.

All information in this TourBook was reviewed for accuracy before publication. However, since
changes inevitably occur between annual editions, we suggest you contact establishments directly
to confirm prices and schedules.

How the TourBook is

Organized

Geographic listing is used for accuracy and consistency. This means attractions, lodgings and
restaurants are listed under the city in which they physically are located—or in some cases under
the nearest recognized city. A comprehensive TourBook City Index located in the back of the book
contains an A-to-Z list of cities. Most listings are alphabetically organized by state or province, city,
and establishment name. A color is assigned to each state so that you can match the color bars at
the top of the page to switch from Points of Interest to Lodgings and Restaurants.

Destination Cities and Destination Areas

The TourBook also groups information by destination city and destination area. If a city is grouped in a
destination vicinity section, the city name will appear at
its alphabetical location in the book, and a handy cross
reference will give the exact page on which listings for
that city begin. Maps are placed at the beginning of
these sections to orient you to the destinations.

Destination cities, established based on
government models and local expertise, are comprised of metropolitan areas plus nearby vicinity
cities.

Destination areas are regions with broad
tourist appeal. Several cities will comprise
the area.

Points of Interest Section

Orientation maps

near the start of each Attractions section show only those places we call points of interest. Coordinates included with the city listings depict the locations of those cities on the map. Stars accent towns with "must see" attractions. And the black ovals with white numerals locate items listed in the nearby Recreation Areas chart.

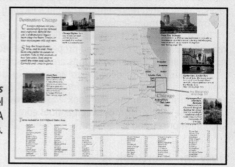

Destination area maps

illustrate key travel areas defined by local travel experts. Communities shown have listings for AAA approved attractions.

National park maps

represent the area in and around the park. Some campground sites and lodges spotted on the maps do not meet AAA/CAA criteria, but are shown for members who nevertheless wish to stay close to the park area.

Walking or self-guiding tour maps

correspond to specific routes described in TourBook text.

City maps

show areas where numerous points of interest are concentrated and indicate their location in relation to major roads, parks, airports and other landmarks.

Featured Information Section

Driving distance maps

are intended to be used only for trip-distance and driving-time planning.

Lodgings & Restaurants Section

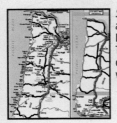

State or province orientation maps appear before the property listings in the Lodgings & Restaurants section of selected TourBooks and show the relative positions of major metropolitan areas and the vicinity towns in those areas.

Area maps denote large geographical areas in which there are many towns containing lodgings and/or restaurants. Due to these maps' small scale, lodgings and restaurants are not shown; towns with lodgings and/or restaurants are printed in magenta type.

Destination area maps illustrate key travel areas defined by local travel experts. Communities shown have listings for AAA-RATED® lodgings and/or restaurants.

Spotting maps show the location of lodgings and restaurants. Lodgings are spotted with a black-background (**22** for example); restaurants are spotted with a white-background (**23** for example). Spotting map indexes have been placed after the main city heading to provide the user with a convenient method to identify what an area has to offer at a glance. The index references the map page number where the property is spotted, indicates if a property is an Official Appointment and contains an advertising reference if applicable. It also lists the property's diamond rating, high season rate range and listing page number.

Downtown/city spotting maps are provided when spotted facilities are very concentrated. Starred points of interest also appear on these maps.

Vicinity spotting maps spot those properties that are outside the downtown or city area. Major roads, landmarks, airports and starred points of interest are shown on vicinity spotting maps as well. The names of suburban communities that have AAA-RATED® accommodations are shown in magenta type.

Sample Attraction Listing

> [SAVE] ★ **RED OAK** is off I-95 exit 4A, then 2 mi. e. to 610 Magnolia St. The restored 1812 house has eight 60-foot columns and is furnished in period. Allow 1 hour minimum. Daily 9-5, Apr. 1-Labor Day; Thurs.-Sun. 9-5, mid-Feb. through Mar. 31 and day after Labor Day-Nov. 30; by appointment rest of year. Closed holidays. Admission $4; over 65 and ages 6-12, $3; ages 2-5, $2; family rate $10. MC, VI ($10). Phone (601) 222-2222 or (800) 222-3333.

1 2   3   4

[SAVE] ★   off I-95 exit   year. Closed
                           0. MC, VI ($

                                    5

gh Mar. 31 and day after Labor Day-Nov. 30;
Admission $4; over 65 and ages 6-12, $3; a
(601) 222-2222   (800) 222-3333.

1   [SAVE] Participating attractions offer AAA/CAA cardholders or holders of a AAA MasterCard or AAA Visa Card and up to six family members at least 10% off admission for the validity period of the TourBook. Present your card at the admissions desk. A list of participating attractions appears in the Indexes section of the book. The SAVE discount may not be used in conjunction with other discounts. Discounts may not apply during special events or particular days or seasons.

2   ★ Attraction is of exceptional interest and quality.

3   Unless otherwise specified, directions are given from the center of town, using the following highway designations: I (interstate highway), US (federal highway), Hwy. (Canadian highway), SR (state route), CR (county road), FM (farm to market road), FR (forest road), MM (mile marker)

4
AE=American Express	JC=Japanese Credit Bureau
CB=Carte Blanche	MC=MasterCard
DI=Diners Club	VI=VISA
DS=Discover	

Minimum amounts that may be charged appear in parentheses when applicable.

5   Admission prices are quoted without sales tax. Children under the lowest age specified are admitted free when accompanied by an adult. Days, months and age groups written with a hyphen are inclusive. Prices pertaining to attractions in the United States are quoted in U.S. dollars; Canadian province and territory attraction prices are quoted in Canadian dollars.

Bulleted Listings: Casino gambling establishments not contained within hotels are visited by club personnel to ensure safety. Recreational activities of a participatory nature (requiring physical exertion or special skills) are not inspected. Both are presented in a bulleted format for informational purposes.

Attraction Partners

These Show Your Card & Save® attraction partners provide the listed member benefits. Admission tickets that offer greater discounts may be available for purchase at the local AAA club. A maximum of six tickets is available at the discount price.

Universal Studios Escape
Universal Studios Hollywood

SAVE Save $3 on 1-day admission, $4 on 2-day admission, and $5 on 3-day admission at the gate (Universal Studios Florida and Hollywood)

SAVE Save 10% on selected souvenirs and dining

SeaWorld/Busch Gardens

Save at SeaWorld, Busch Gardens, Sesame Place, Water Country USA and Adventure Island.

SAVE Save 10% on general admission

Six Flags Adventure Parks

SAVE Save $4 on admission at the gate

SAVE Save $12 on admission at the gate each Wednesday

SAVE Save 10% on selected souvenirs and dining

Citizens or permanent residents of the United States who are 62 and older can obtain Golden Age Passports for a one-time $10 fee. Golden Access Passports are free to citizens or permanent residents of the United States (regardless of age) who are medically blind or permanently disabled. Both cover entrance fees for the holder and accompanying private party to all national parks, historic sites, monuments and battlefields within the U.S. national park system, plus half off camping and other fees. Apply in person at most federally operated areas.

The Golden Eagle Passport is available to everyone, despite country of origin. It costs $50 annually and covers entrance fees for the holder and accompanying private party to all federally operated areas. Obtain the pass in person at any national park or regional office of the U.S. park service or forest service.

Golden Passports

Sample Lodging Listing

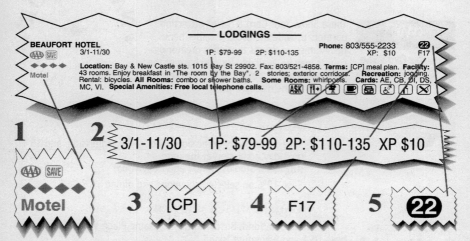

1 🔶 or 🔶 indicates our Official Appointment (OA) lodgings. The OA Program permits properties to display and advertise the 🔶 or 🔶 emblem. We highlight these properties with red diamonds and classification. Some OA listings include special amenities such as free breakfast; early check-in/late check-out; free room upgrade or preferred room, such as ocean view or poolside (subject to availability); free local phone calls; and free daily newspaper. This does not imply that only these properties offer these amenities. The 🔶 or 🔶 sign helps traveling members find accommodations that want member business.

◆◆◆ or ◆◆◆ The number of diamonds—not the color—informs you of the overall level of quality in a lodging's amenities and service. More diamond details appear on page 14.

Motel or Motel: Diamond ratings are applied in the context of lodging type, or classification. See pages 20-21 for our Lodging Classifications.

Discounts

🔲 Official Appointment properties guarantee members a minimum 10% discount off the published TourBook rates.

🔲 AAA's Show Your Card & Save® chain partners provide special values to our members: Select Choice Hotels, Days Inn, Hilton, Hyatt, and La Quinta . Individual properties in these chains appearing in the TourBook have been inspected and approved by AAA. Be sure to read How to Get the Best Room Rates on page 19.

🔲 Establishments offer a minimum senior discount of 10% off the listed rates. This discount is available to members 60 or older.

🔲 Many TourBook properties offer discounts to members even though the lodgings do not participate in a formal discount program. The 🔲 is another reminder to inquire about available discounts when making your reservations or at check-in.

> **Discounts normally offered at some lodgings may not apply during special events or holiday periods. Special rates and discounts may not apply to all room types.**

To obtain published rates or discounts, you must identify yourself as a AAA or CAA member and request AAA rates when making reservations. The SAVE or senior discount may not be used in conjunction with other discounts. Be sure to show your card at registration and verify the room rate.

The rates listed for approved properties are provided to AAA by each lodging and represent the regular (rack) rate for a standard room. Printed rates, based on rack rates and last room availability, are rounded to the nearest dollar. Rates do not include taxes and discounts. U.S. rates are in U.S. dollars; rates for Canadian lodgings are in Canadian dollars.

2 Rate Lines

Shown from left to right: dates the rates are effective; rates for 1 person or 2 persons; extra person charge (XP); and any applicable family plan indicator.

Rates Guaranteed

AAA members are guaranteed that they will not be charged more than the maximum regular rate printed in each rate range for a standard room. Rates may vary within the range depending on season and room type. Listed rates are based on last standard room availability.

Exceptions

Lodgings may temporarily increase room rates, not recognize discounts or modify pricing policies during special events. Examples of special events range from Mardi Gras and Kentucky Derby (including pre-Derby events) to college football games, holidays, holiday periods and state fairs. Although some special events are listed in AAA TourBook guides, it is always wise to check, in advance, with AAA travel counselors for specific dates.

Discounts

Member discounts will apply to rates quoted, within the rate range, applicable at the time of booking. Special rates used in advertising, and special short-term, promotional rates lower than the lowest listed rate in the range, are not subject to additional member discounts.

3 Meal Plan Indicators

The following types of meal plans may be available in the listed room rate:

AP = American Plan of three meals daily
BP = Breakfast Plan of full hot breakfast
CP = Continental Plan of pastry, juice and another beverage
ECP = Expanded Continental Plan, which offers a wider variety of breakfast items
EP = European Plan, where rate includes only room
MAP = Modified American Plan of two meals daily

> Check-in times are shown in the listing only if they are after 3 p.m.; check-out times are shown only if they are before 10 a.m. Parking is on the premises and free unless otherwise noted.

4 Family Plan Indicators

F17 = Children 17 and under stay free (age displayed will reflect property's policy)
D17 = Discount for children 17 and under
F = Children stay free
D = Discounts for children

5 Lodging Locators

Numerals are used to locate, or "spot," lodgings on maps we provide for larger cities.

The few lodgings with **fyi** in place of diamonds are included as an "informational only" service for members. The icon indicates that a property has not been rated for one or more of the following reasons: too new to rate; under construction; under major renovation; not inspected; or may not meet all AAA requirements. Listing prose will give insight as to why the **fyi** rating was assigned.

The Lodging Diamond Ratings

AAA field inspectors evaluate and rate each lodging based on the overall quality and services offered at a property. The size, age and overall appeal of an establishment are considered as well as regional decorating and architectural differences.

While guest services are an important part of all diamond ratings, they are particularly critical at the four and five diamond levels. A property must provide a high level of service, on a consistent basis, to obtain and support the four and five diamond rating.

Properties are world-class by definition, exhibiting an exceptionally high degree of service as well as striking, luxurious facilities and many extra amenities. Guest services are executed and presented in a flawless manner. The guest is pampered by a professional, attentive staff. The properties' facilities and operation help set industry standards in hospitality and service.

Properties are excellent and display a high level of service and hospitality. They offer a wide variety of amenities and upscale facilities in the guest rooms, on the grounds and in the public areas.

Properties offer a degree of sophistication. Additional amenities, services and facilities may be offered. There is a noticeable upgrade in physical attributes, services and comfort.

Properties maintain the attributes offered at the one diamond level, while showing marked enhancements in decor and furnishings. They may be recently constructed or older properties, both targeting the needs of a budget-oriented traveler.

Properties offer good but modest accommodations. Establishments are functional, emphasizing clean and comfortable rooms. They must meet the basic needs of comfort and cleanliness.

Guest Safety

Room Security

In order to be approved for listing in AAA/CAA TourBook® guides for the United States and Canada, all lodgings must comply with AAA's guest room security requirements.

In response to AAA/CAA members' concern about their safety at properties, AAA-RATED® accommodations must have deadbolt locks on all guest room entry doors and connecting room doors.

If the area outside the guest room door is not visible from inside the room through a window or door panel, viewports must be installed on all guest room entry doors. Bed and breakfast properties and country inns are not required to have viewports. Ground floor and easily accessible sliding doors must be equipped with some other type of secondary security locks.

Field inspectors view a percentage of rooms at each property since it is not feasible to evaluate every room in every lodging establishment. Therefore, AAA cannot guarantee that there are working locks on all doors and windows in all guest rooms.

Fire Safety

Because of the highly specialized skills needed to conduct professional fire safety inspections, AAA/CAA inspectors cannot assess fire safety.

All U.S. and Canadian lodging properties must be equipped with an operational, single-station smoke detector, and all public areas must have operational smoke detectors or an automatic sprinkler system. A AAA/CAA inspector has evaluated a sampling of the rooms to verify this equipment is in place.

For additional fire safety information read the page posted on the back of your guest room door, or write:

**National Fire Protection Association
1 Batterymarch Park, P.O. Box 9101
Quincy, MA 02269-9101**

Access for Travelers with Disabilities

Qualified properties listed in this book have symbols indicating they are fully accessible, semi-accessible or meet the needs of the hearing-impaired. This two-tiered mobility standard was developed to meet members' varying degrees of accessibility needs.

(&) Fully accessible properties meet the needs of those that are significantly disabled and utilize a wheelchair or scooter. A fully accessible lodging will provide at least one guest room meeting the designated criteria. A traveler with these disabilities will be able to park and access public areas, including restrooms, check-in facilities and at least one food and beverage outlet. A fully accessible restaurant indicates that parking, dining rooms and restrooms are accessible.

(f) Semi-accessible properties meet the needs of those that are disabled but do have some mobility. Such travelers would include people using a cane or walker, or a disabled individual with good mobility but a limited arm or hand range of motion. A Semi-accessible lodging will provide at least one guest room meeting the designated criteria. A traveler with these disabilities will be able to park and access public areas, including restrooms, check-in facilities and at least one food and beverage outlet. A semi-accessible restaurant indicates that parking, dining rooms and restrooms are accessible.

(🔊) This symbol indicates a property with the following equipment available for hearing impaired travelers: TDD at front desk or switchboard; visual notification of fire alarm, incoming telephone calls, door knock or bell; closed caption decoder available; text telephone or TDD available for guest room use; telephone amplification device available, with shelf and electric outlet next to guest room telephone.

The criteria used by AAA/CAA do not represent the full scope of the Americans With Disabilities Act of 1990 Accessibility Guidelines (ADAAG); they are, however, consistent with the ADAAG. Members can obtain from their local AAA/CAA club the AAA brochure, "AAA Accessibility Criteria for Travelers with Disabilities", which describes the specific criteria pertaining to the fully accessible, semi-accessible and hearing-impaired standards.

The Americans With Disabilities Act (ADA) prohibits businesses that serve the public from discriminating against persons with disabilities who are aided by service animals. Some businesses have mistakenly denied access to their properties to persons with disabilities who use service animals. ADA has priority over all state and local laws, as well as a business owner's standard of business, that might bar animals from the premises. Businesses must permit guests and their service animal entry, as well as allow service animals to accompany guests to all public areas of a property. A property is permitted to ask whether the animal is a service animal or a pet, or whether a guest has a disability. The property may not, however, ask questions about the nature of a disability or require proof of one.

No fees or deposits (even those normally charged for pets) may be charged for the service animal.

AAA/CAA urges members with disabilities to always phone ahead to fully understand the accommodation's offerings. Some properties do not fully comply with AAA/CAA's exacting accessibility standards but may offer some property design standards that meet the needs of some guests with disabilities.

AAA/CAA does not evaluate recreational facilities, banquet rooms or convention and meeting facilities for accessibility. Call a property directly to inquire about your needs for these areas.

What The Icons Mean

Member Values

AAA or AA Official Appointment

SAVE Offers minimum 10% discount

SAVE SYC&S chain partners

ASK May offer discount

S/D Offers senior discount

fyi Informational listing only

Member Services

Airport transportation

Pets allowed

Restaurant on premises

Restaurant off premises
(walking distance)

24-hour room service

Cocktail lounge

Special Features

Business services

Valet parking

Laundry service

Child care

Fully accessible

Semi-accessible

Roll-in showers

Hearing impaired

In-Room Amenities

Non-smoking rooms

No air conditioning

No telephones

No cable TV

Movies

VCR

Radio

Coffee maker

Microwave

Refrigerator

Data port/modem line

Sports/Recreation

Outdoor pool

Indoor pool

Indoor/outdoor pool

Fitness center

Recreational facilities

Please see listing prose for specific details regarding any item represented by an icon.

Additional Fees

Fees may be charged for some of the services represented by the icons listed here; please refer to the listing text and inquire when making reservations.

If a pet icon is not present, assume that the property does not accept pets; although deposits and fees are stated in the listing, check policies and restrictions when making reservations.

Preferred Lodging Partners

 Call the member-only toll-free numbers below or your club to get these member benefits. Have your membership card on hand when calling.

GUARANTEED RATES - Lowest public rate available for dates of stay when booked in advance via the toll-free numbers listed below.

SATISFACTION GUARANTEE - If you're not satisfied with your stay, it's free. *Member must provide opportunity for lodging to correct any problem.*

Save 10%.   Save 10%.   Save 10%.   Save 20%.*   Save 10%.   Save 10%.

Satisfaction Guarantee. Children under 18 stay free.   *(most Clarion & Carriage House Inns)

(800) 228-1222

Guaranteed Rates. Satisfaction Guarantee. Children under 12 stay free.

(800) 432-9755

Guaranteed Rates. Satisfaction Guarantee. Children under 18 and spouse stay free.

(800) 221-4731

**Guaranteed Rates. Satisfaction Guarantee. Children under 18 stay free.
Receive second entree at half price when staying in hotel.**

(800) 532-1496

Hilton
Guaranteed Rates. Satisfaction Guarantee. Children under 18 stay free. Save up to 25%

(800) 916-2221

Lowest Public Rate. Satisfaction Guarantee. Children 18 and under stay free.

(800) 456-7793

Special rates and discounts may not apply to all room types. Not available to groups and cannot be combined with other discounts. Restrictions apply to satisfaction guarantees and free children stays. Valid AAA/CAA membership card must be presented at check-in. Offers good at time of publication; chains and offers may change without notice.

Making Reservations

Give Proper Identification

When making reservations, you must identify yourself as a AAA/CAA member. Give all pertinent information about your planned stay. Request written confirmation to guarantee: type of room, rate, dates of stay, and cancellation and refund policies. Note: Age restrictions may apply.

Confirm Deposit, Refund and Cancellation Policies

Most establishments give full deposit refunds if they have been notified at least 48 hours before the normal check-in time. Listing prose will note if more than 48 hours notice is required for cancellation. However, when making reservations, confirm the property's deposit, cancellation and refund policies. Some properties may charge a cancellation or handling fee.

When this applies, "cancellation fee imposed" will appear in the listing. If you cancel too late, you have little recourse if a refund is denied.

When an establishment requires a full or partial payment in advance, and your trip is cut short, a refund may not be given.

When canceling reservations, call the lodging immediately. Make a note of the date and time you called, the cancellation number if there is one, and the name of the person who handled the cancellation. If your AAA/CAA club made your reservation, allow them to make the cancellation for you as well so you will have proof of cancellation.

Review Charges for Appropriate Rates

When you are charged more than the maximum rate listed in the TourBook, question the additional charge. If management refuses to adhere to the published rate, pay for the room and submit your receipt and membership number to AAA/CAA within 30 days. Include all pertinent information: dates of stay, rate paid, itemized paid receipts, number of persons in your party, the room number you occupied, and list any extra room equipment used. A refund of the amount paid in excess of the stated maximum will be made if our investigation indicates that unjustified charging has occurred.

Get the Room You Reserved

When you find your room is not as specified, and you have written confirmation of reservations for a certain type of accommodation, you should be given the option of choosing a different room or finding one elsewhere. Should you choose to go elsewhere and a refund is refused or resisted, submit the matter to AAA/CAA within 30 days along with complete documentation, including your reasons for refusing the room and copies of your written confirmation and any receipts or canceled checks associated with this problem.

How to Get the Best Room Rates

You'll find the best room rate if you book your reservation in advance with the help of a travel counselor or agent at your local AAA/CAA office.

If you're not yet ready to make firm vacation plans or if you prefer a more spontaneous trip, take advantage of the partnerships that preferred hotel chains have arranged with AAA. Call the toll-free numbers on the previous page that have been set up exclusively for members for the purpose of reserving with these Show Your Card & Save® chain partners.

Even if you were unable to make a reservation, be sure to show your membership card at the desk and ask if you're being offered the lowest rate available for that time. Many lodgings offer reduced rates to members.

Lodging Classifications

AAA inspectors evaluate lodgings based on classification, since all lodging types by definition do not provide the same level of service and facilities. Thus, hotels are rated in comparison to other hotels, resorts to other resorts—and so on. A lodging's classification appears beneath its diamond rating in the listing.

Hotel — *full service*
Usually high-rise establishments, offering a wide range of services and on-premise food/beverage outlets, shops, conference facilities and recreational activities.

Motel — *limited service*
Low-rise or multi-story establishment offering limited public and recreational facilities.

Country Inn — *moderate service*
Similar in definition to a bed and breakfast, but usually larger in size, with a dining facility that serves at least breakfast and dinner.

Resort — *full service*
Offers a variety of food/beverage outlets, and an extensive range of recreational and entertainment programs - geared to vacation travelers.

Bed & Breakfast — *limited service*
Usually smaller, owner-operated establishments emphasizing an "at home" feeling. A continental or full, hot breakfast is served and included in the room rate.

Condominium — *limited service*
Apartment-style units or homes primarily owned by individuals and available for rent. A variety of room styles and décor treatments, as well as limited housekeeping service, is typical.

Motor Inn — *moderate service*
Single or multi-story establishment offering on-premise food/ beverage service, meeting and banquet facilities and some recreational facilities.

Complex — *service varies*
A combination of two or more types of lodging classifications.

Lodge — *moderate service*
Typically two or more stories with all facilities in one building. Rustic décor is common. Usually has food/beverage service.

Apartment — *limited service*
Primarily offers temporary guest accommodations with one or more bedrooms, a living room, a full kitchen and an eating area. Studio apartments may combine the sleeping and living areas into one room.

Cottage — *limited service*
Primarily individual housing units that may offer one or more separate sleeping areas, a living room and cooking facilities.

Ranch — *moderate service*
Often offers rustic décor treatments and food/beverage facilities. Entertainment and recreational activities are geared to a Western theme.

Subclassifications

The following are subclassifications that may appear along with the classifications listed above to provide a more specific description of the lodging.

Suite
One or more bedrooms and a living room/sitting area, closed off by a full wall. Note: May not have a partition bedroom door.

Extended Stay
Properties catering to longer-term guest stays. Will have kitchens or efficiencies and may have a separate living room area, evening office closure and limited housekeeping services.

Historic
Accommodations in restored structures built prior to 1920, with décor reflecting the ambiance of yesteryear. Rooms may lack some modern amenities and may have shared bathrooms.

Classic
Renowned and landmark properties, older than 50 years, known for their unique style and ambiance.

Sample Restaurant Listing

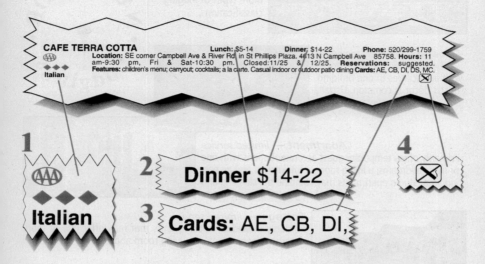

CAFE TERRA COTTA Lunch: $5-14 Dinner: $14-22 Phone: 520/299-1759
Location: SE corner Campbell Ave & River Rd in St Phillips Plaza. 4613 N Campbell Ave 85758. **Hours:** 11 am-9:30 pm, Fri & Sat-10:30 pm. Closed:11/25 & 12/25. **Reservations:** suggested. **Features:** children's menu; carryout; cocktails; a la carte. Casual indoor or outdoor patio dining **Cards:** AE, CB, DI, DS, MC.
Italian

1 (AAA) ◆◆◆ **Italian**

2 Dinner $14-22

3 Cards: AE, CB, DI,

4 [X]

1 ⊕ or ⊕ indicates our Official Appointment (OA) restaurants. The OA Program permits properties to display and advertise the ⊕ or ⊕ emblem. We highlight these properties with red diamonds and cuisine type. The ⊕ or ⊕ sign helps traveling members find restaurants that want member business.

◆◆◆ or ◆◆◆ The number of diamonds—not the color—informs you of the overall level of quality for food and presentation, service and ambiance. Restaurants also are classified by cuisine type.

2 The dinner price range is approximate and includes a salad or appetizer, an entrée, a vegetable and a non-alcoholic beverage for one person. Taxes and tip are not included. Some listings include additional information such as the availability of a senior citizen menu, children's menu or "early bird specials," if offered at least 5 days a week.

3 AE=American Express   JC=Japanese Credit Bureau
CB=Carte Blanche   MC=MasterCard
DI=Diners Club   VI=VISA
DS=Discover

Minimum amounts that may be charged appear in parentheses when applicable.

4 This icon indicates that the restaurant has a designated non-smoking section or is entirely smoke-free.

The restaurants with [fyi] in place of diamonds are included as an "informational only" service for members. This designation indicates that the restaurant has not been inspected.

The Restaurant Diamond Ratings

AAA field inspectors evaluate and rate each restaurant on the overall quality of food, service, décor and ambiance—with extra emphasis given to food and service.

The ratings represent a range of member dining needs and expectations. A one diamond rating indicates simple, family or specialty meals, while a five diamond rating indicates an ultimate dining experience that is truly a memorable occasion.

A memorable occasion—the ultimate in adult dining. Food shows the highest culinary skills, evident in all areas of preparation and presentation. An extensive wine list is available. A professional staff—often in formal attire—provides flawless and pampering service. The decor has classic details, often formal, and reflects comfort and luxury.

A high degree of sophistication, thus creating an adult dining experience. Complex food is creatively presented. An extensive wine list is offered. The service staff, often formally attired, is professionally trained. The decor is distinctive, stylish and elegant; some establishments are casual while still offering refinement or formality.

An upscale or special family dining experience. Food is cooked to order and creatively prepared with quality ingredients. A wine list is available. A skilled, often uniformed staff provides service. The usually professional and inviting decor projects a trendy, upbeat, casual or formal atmosphere.

More extensive menus for family or adult dining. Food is prepared with standard ingredients. Service is attentive but may be informal, casual, limited or self-serve. The decor presents a unified theme that is comfortable but also may be trendy, casual or upbeat.

Provides a simple, family or specialty meal in clean, pleasant surroundings. Food is basic and wholesome. Service is casual, limited or self-serve. Decor is informal.

Note: Major restaurant chains are not listed due to their widespread recognition.

The Smart Choice for Your Family's Financial Future

*Y*our family's financial needs change throughout life. Now you can trust AAA to bring you a full array of financial products and services to meet those financial needs at every stage. With AAA Financial Services' great rates and hassle-free service, you're covered for life. Call us today!

Exclusively for AAA members

- AAA *Platinum Plus*[sm] Visa® Credit Card

1-800-523-7666

- Market Rate Checking
- Money Market Accounts
- Auto Loans & Leases
- Home Equity Loans & Lines of Credit[1]
- Certificates of Deposit[2]
- Education Loans

1-800-680-AAA4

Financial Services

Make The Most Of Your Membership.[SM]

24 Hours A Day. 7 Days A Week.

www.financial.aaa.com

If You Like This Book ...
You'll Love Our Others

You already understand the value of using AAA's TourBook® guides. But did you know that AAA publishes a wide variety of other travel materials including:

- *AAA World Atlas*
- *AAA Europe, Britain, France, Caribbean and Mexico TravelBooks*
- *AAA Europe, Britain and France Road Atlases*
- *AAA Guide to the National Parks*
- *AAA Guide to North America's Theme Parks*
- *AAA Guide to North American Bed & Breakfasts, Country Inns and Historical Lodgings*
- *AAA Britain and France Bed & Breakfast Guides*
- *Traveling With Your Pet– The AAA PetBook®*
- *The AAA New Car & Truck Buying Guide*
- *AAA North American Road Atlas*

Plus, AAA offers travel videos and other products to make your trip more enjoyable. To purchase these items at discounted prices, contact your local AAA office.

Travel With Someone You Trust®

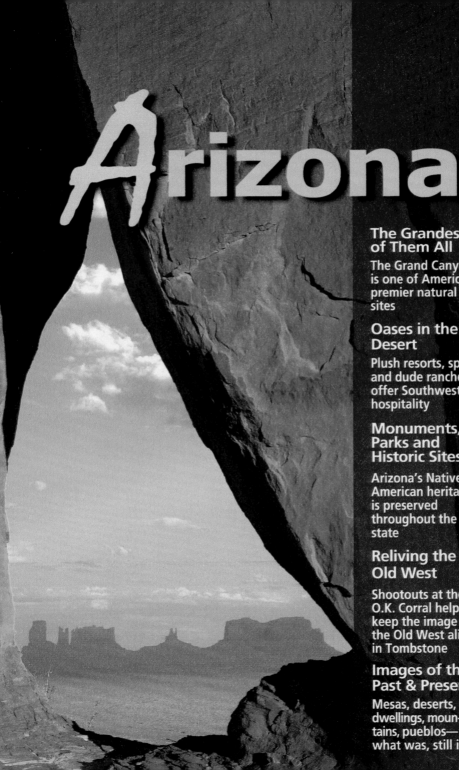

Arizona

The Grandest of Them All

The Grand Canyon is one of America's premier natural sites

Oases in the Desert

Plush resorts, spas and dude ranches offer Southwestern hospitality

Monuments, Parks and Historic Sites

Arizona's Native American heritage is preserved throughout the state

Reliving the Old West

Shootouts at the O.K. Corral help keep the image of the Old West alive in Tombstone

Images of the Past & Present

Mesas, deserts, cliff dwellings, mountains, pueblos— what was, still is

the past
lives
in the
present

Take a minute. Close your eyes and think about Arizona. What do you see? Chances are the images that first come to mind are those of the Old West—cowboys, Indians, deserts, cacti—stuff straight out of TV Westerns. You half expect Wyatt Earp or Cochise to emerge from behind a wagon train.

Cowboys still do exist here, but they are more likely to be found assisting city slickers at modern guest ranches than lassoing cattle on a trail drive.

Native Americans, the first Arizonans, though a small percentage of today's population, are a major influence in everyday life. Reminders of their heritage are evident in national monuments, tribal parks and historic sites that preserve their ancient dwellings, customs and crafts.

As for the deserts, well, the sand and the intricate rock formations are still there, but their expanse is now broken by major metropolitan areas such as Phoenix and Tucson and golf courses that seem strangely out of place. And rare species of cactus, such as the organ pipe and saguaro, are protected in their own preserves.

Wagon trains no longer cross Arizona's plains. Adventure now comes courtesy of four-wheel-drive vehicles and week-end hikes in the state's hills and mountains. Mr. Earp and Cochise would be amazed.

"Did the government build it?"

More than one flabbergasted visitor has asked this upon first seeing Arizona's Grand Canyon. Although it may sound preposterous, it's a question you're sure to find less naive after gazing at these myriad erosion-carved columns, arches and windows—a virtual cityscape of landforms that would make a Manhattanite feel at home.

Thank You, Father Time

No doubt politicians would love to claim responsibility for the Grand Canyon, but only Father Time can take credit for this natural wonder. Over millions of years geologic upheaval forced a former sea bottom into the sky, allowing wind and water to work their rock-sculpting magic. The result is a spectacle so awesome that at least 5 million people from all over the world visit every year and walk away struggling for words to describe it.

Theodore Roosevelt remarked that it was "the one great sight which every American should see." And while Uncle Sam can't take credit for building the canyon, he does protect it for future generations as part of the national park system.

Like most visitors, you'll probably want to begin your canyon experience at the South Rim, site of the park's visitor center. This area boasts many of the best vantage points from which to gape at the canyon in all its multihued glory. What's more, the tall pine trees here hide the great chasm from view until you are almost at its edge. Abruptly confronting this breathtaking scene as you emerge from the forest is an experience you won't want to miss.

Visit during the early morning or late afternoon when colors dance along canyon walls in the rapidly changing sunlight. And if a storm comes your way, don't despair: Shadows of drifting rain clouds can create striking patterns of darkness as they move across the canyon's depths.

But even after visiting the Grand Canyon, don't think you've seen it all. An equally spectacular play of color and light awaits you at Monument Valley Navajo Tribal Park. Visitors are less likely to suspect the government's hand in constructing these weathered monoliths, but you just might feel like you're walking through a Hollywood set, and with good reason: This valley has served as backdrop for numerous

Franciscan friar Marcos de Niza searches unsuccessfully for the fabled Seven Cities of Cíbola throughout the Southwest.
1539

The Gadsden Purchase brings the rest of the area that is currently Arizona and New Mexico under U.S. control.
1853

The railroad reaches Arizona, bringing prosperity in the form of ranchers, prospectors and farmers.
1883

Phoenix is chosen as the territorial capital.
1889

1848
Following the Mexican War the Treaty of Guadalupe-Hidalgo cedes the Territory of New Mexico, which includes part of Arizona, to the expanding United States.

Arizona Historical Timeline

1911
The completion of the Roosevelt Dam on the Salt River delivers much-needed water to the area.

classic Westerns and countless car commercials. Ask someone to imagine "the West" and they'll likely describe the immense, rose-tinted buttes and mesas of this picturesque land.

Grand Canyon visitors frequently overlook another Arizona jewel—the red rock territory around Sedona. Though not as large as the big gorge to the north, Sedona's Oak Creek Canyon has its own collection of buttes, spires and sheer rock walls that shimmer with shades of beige, ocher, salmon and scarlet. And if you get too hot, you can go with Oak Creek's flow at Slide Rock State Park, where a waterslide—natural, not man-made—splashes from pool to pool.

And it's not just Arizona's rocky terrain that evokes comparisons to unnatural objects; the Canyon State's plant life does so as well. Cactuses at Organ Pipe Cactus National Monument appear as if they could produce music, and the saguaros dotting Saguaro National Park resemble a crowd of captured bank robbers, arms raised in a perpetual gesture of surrender.

"Married to the Ground"

Arizona's inhabitants also have blurred the line between natural and artificial. Ancient cliff dwellings at Montezuma Castle, Canyon de Chelly and Navajo national monuments blend with their surroundings so well, they seem to have sprouted from the precipices they are perched upon.

Centuries after these towns in the sky were abandoned, architect Frank Lloyd Wright designed buildings according to his belief that they should harmoniously coexist with their surroundings. Taliesin West, Wright's former home and studio in Scottsdale, illustrates how a modern house can be integrated into its environment, not unlike Arizona's venerable cliff dwellings.

Wright once summed up his design philosophy by saying his buildings were "married to the ground." It's easy to see why he chose Arizona as his studio's setting. Here the terrain seems a willing companion to man's handiwork: mesas rise from the desert like skyscrapers and pinnacles soar like church spires. Although these "buildings" took billions of years to construct, you'll have to admit they were worth waiting for.

Arizona enters the Union as the 48th state.

1912

In Miranda vs. Arizona, the U.S. Supreme Court decides that police must inform arrested persons of their rights, including the right to remain silent, before they are questioned.

1966

Native son, U.S. senator and 1964 Republican presidential candidate Barry Goldwater dies at the age of 89.

1998

1974

Work begins on the Central Arizona Project to bring Colorado River water to dry parts of the state.

1981

Arizonan Sandra Day O'Connor is appointed as the first woman member of the U.S. Supreme Court.

1991

Eight scientists begin living in the glass-enclosed biomes of Biosphere 2 near Oracle to provide information about the sustainability of Earth's ecosystems.

Recreation

Canyons. Mountains. Forests. Lakes. The extensive Colorado River. Arizona, derived from the Native American word meaning "little spring," is a veritable fountain of fun for outdoor types.

Hopefully you packed your putter. With more than 225 **golf** courses to choose from, people drive from all over the country to chip and putt. But watch out for hazards—Mesa, Phoenix, northern Scottsdale and Tucson are chock-full of challenging fairways. Contact Golf Arizona, (800) 942-5444, for a detailed list of courses.

Simply Gorges!

Then there's *the* Canyon, the grandest of them all. Peer off the edge while **hiking** along the South Rim Trail—the view from the top will simply knock your socks off.

If you're more adventurous, a whole new world awaits below the rim—numerous corridor trails beginning at the South Rim provide access to the depths of the gorge. Begin with the Bright Angel Trail—established in the 1890s as the canyon's first hiking path, it's a day hike that remains one of the best for beginners. The South Kaibab and North Kaibab trails (departing from the popular South and sylvan North rims, respectively) also are good treks on foot or on hoof: **Mule rides** are available for 2-day jaunts. Advanced reservations are required before you saddle up.

Since it takes a full day to descend to the bottom, **camping** is a popular option on the canyon floor. Be sure to acquire a backcountry permit for overnight travel by contacting Trip Planner, Grand Canyon National Park, P.O. Box 129, Grand Canyon, AZ 86023; phone (520) 638-7888.

Rafting trips on the Colorado River, which weaves through the canyon, can be arranged at Page, Lees Ferry or in Grand Canyon National Park. Trips range from 3 days to 3 weeks. For a bird's-eye view, try a **helicopter** or **airplane tour** across the gaping chasm; trips depart from the Grand Canyon Airport south of Tusayan.

Ah, Agua . . .

Despite Arizona's arid landscape, there are plenty of places to find refreshment. Water buffs will want to dip their toes, jet skis, sailboards and speedboats into the waves on Lake Powell in Glen Canyon National Recreation Area and lakes Mead and Mojave in Lake Mead National Recreation Area.

Water-skiers and **swimmers** play on—and in—these lakes, where views of the surrounding colorful cliffs are astounding. Or you might choose to soak in the view from the deck of a houseboat. Canoes and sailboats often drift on Lake Havasu, and inner tubes float lazily along the Colorado River as it flows through Yuma.

Take to the air in a giant hot air balloon, where you'll become part of a striking panorama as you ascend over Oak Creek Canyon in Sedona's spectacular Red Rock area. Experience this reddish region while hanging onto the roll bar of a **jeep;** you can pilot yourself or ride along with a guide. At Monument Valley on the Navajo Indian Reservation, Navajo guides relate tribal legends while ushering passengers on **four-wheel-drive tours** amid the stark, fantastic rock formations.

If **fishing** is your sport, head for the Black River in the White Mountains area, where you can hook all sorts of trout—native Apache, brook, brown, cutthroat and rainbow are a few varieties—as well as bass, crappie, arctic grayling, northern pike and catfish. For information about **hunting** trophy elk or other game, phone the Arizona Game and Fish Department.

When it gets chilly, **skiing** at the Arizona Snowbowl, just north of Flagstaff in the Coconino National Forest, is the cool thing to do. In summer, ski runs are converted to trails for hiking and **mountain biking.** Other places to catch a chairlift are Sunrise Park, in central Arizona's White Mountains; Mount Lemmon, north of Tucson; and Williams Ski Area in Williams. North Rim Nordic Center near the North Rim of the Grand Canyon has **cross-country skiing** trails.

Throughout the TourBook, you may notice a Recreational Activities heading with bulleted listings of recreation-oriented establishments listed underneath. Since normal AAA inspection criteria cannot be applied, these establishments are presented for information only. Age, height and weight restrictions may apply. Reservations are often recommended and sometimes required. Visitors should phone or write the attraction for additional information, and the address and phone number are provided for this purpose.

Fast Facts

POPULATION: 4,555,000.

AREA: 113,909 square miles; ranks 6th.

CAPITAL: Phoenix.

HIGHEST POINT: 12,643 ft., Humphreys Peak.

LOWEST POINT: 70 ft., Colorado River.

TIME ZONE: Mountain. DST on Navajo Reservation only.

MINIMUM AGE FOR DRIVERS: 18; 16 with parental consent.

MINIMUM AGE FOR GAMBLING: 18.

SEAT BELT/CHILD RESTRAINT LAWS: Seat belts required for driver and front-seat passengers; child restraints required for under 6.

HELMETS FOR MOTORCYCLISTS: Required for rider and passenger if under 18.

RADAR DETECTORS: Permitted.

FIREARMS LAWS: Vary by state and/or county. Contact the Law Library of Arizona, 1501 W. Washington St., Phoenix, AZ 85007; phone (602) 542-5297.

HOLIDAYS: Jan. 1; Martin Luther King Jr.'s Birthday, Jan. (2nd Mon.); Lincoln's Birthday, Feb. (2nd Mon.); Washington's Birthday, Feb. (3rd Mon.); Memorial Day, May (last Mon.); July 4; Labor Day, Sept. (1st Mon.); Columbus Day, Oct. (2nd Mon.); Veterans Day, Nov. 11; Thanksgiving, Nov. (4th Thurs.); Dec. 25.

TAXES: Arizona's statewide sales tax is 5 percent, with local options to impose additional increments on goods and services, including lodgings.

STATE INFORMATION CENTERS: Welcome centers that provide details about state attractions, accommodations, historic sites, parks and events are at Flagstaff, Kearny, Painted Cliffs, Phoenix, Scottsdale, Sedona/Oak Creek, Tempe and Verde Valley.

DAYLIGHT-SAVING TIME: The Navajo Reservation is the only area in the state to observe daylight-saving time.

INDIAN RESERVATIONS: Indian reservations are regarded as sovereign nations, making and enforcing laws regarding their land. The following rules are the most relevant to visitors to the reservations: alcoholic beverages are prohibited (including transportation and use); leaving established roadways and hiking cross-country is prohibited unless permission is obtained from the local tribal office; seat belts must be worn by motorists; helmets must be worn by motorcyclists. For further information contact the Native American Travel Service; phone (480) 945-0771.

FURTHER INFORMATION FOR VISITORS:

Arizona Office of Tourism
2702 N. 3rd St., Suite 4015
Phoenix, AZ 85004-4608
(602) 230-7733 or (888) 520-3434
(allow 4 weeks for receipt of mailings)

RECREATION INFORMATION:

Arizona State Parks Board
1300 W. Washington
Phoenix, AZ 85007
(602) 542-4174

FISHING AND HUNTING REGULATIONS:

Game and Fish Department
2222 W. Greenway Rd.
Phoenix, AZ 85023
(602) 942-3000

NATIONAL FOREST INFORMATION:

Southwestern Region
Public Affairs Office
517 Gold Ave. S.W.
Albuquerque, NM 87102
(505) 842-3292 or 842-3898
(877) 444-6777 (reservations)

AAA Starred Attractions
EXCEPTIONAL INTEREST AND QUALITY

Canyon de Chelly National Monument (A-6)

CANYON DE CHELLY NATIONAL MONU-MENT—Ruins from a succession of Native American villages provide insights into the cultures of the tribes that lived in the caves and at the base of these red sandstone cliffs from 2500 B.C. to the present-day Navajo residents. See p. 44.

Casa Grande Ruins National Monument (E-4)

CASA GRANDE RUINS NATIONAL MONU-MENT—The remains of the four-story "big house," built by the Hohokam about 1350, leave no clue to its purpose or the reason for the tribe's sudden disappearance a century later. See p. 44.

Chiricahua National Monument (F-6)

CHIRICAHUA NATIONAL MONUMENT—This homeland of Cochise and the Chiricahua Apaches is accented with precariously balanced boulders, spires and fantastic rock formations. See p. 45.

Dragoon (F-5)

AMERIND FOUN-DATION MU-SEUM—True to its name, a contraction of American and Indian, the museum is the repository of a world-class collection of Native American artifacts spanning 10,000 years. See p. 48.

Glen Canyon National Recreation Area (A-4)

GLEN CANYON NATIONAL RECREATION AREA—Shared with Utah, man-made Lake Powell is the main attraction of this 1.25-million-acre recreation area along the Colorado River; boating, fishing, water skiing, hiking and camping are a few of the activities to be enjoyed here. See p. 50.

Grand Canyon National Park (B-3)

GRAND CANYON NATIONAL PARK—They just don't come any grander than this immense, awe-inspiring chasm; spectacular vistas and overlooks along the canyon's rim are accessible by automobile and foot. See p. 52.

TUSAYAN RUIN AND MUSEUM—Remains of a pueblo built by the Anasazi about 1185 provide a glimpse of what life was like at their agrarian village. See p. 57.

VISITOR CENTER—An information center and a museum housed here are prerequisites before beginning a visit to the Grand Canyon; dioramas, exhibits and an audiovisual presentation explain the park's history. See p. 55.

Lake Mead National Recreation Area (B-1)

HOOVER DAM—As an alternative to the standard guided tours of the dam and power plant, "hard hat" tours allow a close-up look at what makes the turbines operate. See p. 62.

LAKE MEAD NATIONAL RECREATION AREA—A year-round recreation mecca, Lake Mead beckons boaters, fishermen, hikers and water skiers as well as those simply in search of scenic drives. See p. 61.

Montezuma Castle National Monument (C-4)

MONTEZUMA CASTLE NATIONAL MONU-MENT—This five-story Sinagua Indian cliff dwelling, built during the 12th and 13th centuries, was originally reached only by ladders; too fragile for visitors, the ruins can be seen from a self-guiding trail. See p. 63.

Monument Valley Navajo Tribal Park (A-5)

MONUMENT VALLEY NAVAJO TRIBAL PARK—Self-guiding tours of this park, which is entirely within the Navajo Indian Reservation, provide insights into tribal culture; tours on horseback or in four-wheel-drive vehicles also are available. See p. 63.

(continued on next page)

Navajo National Monument (A-4)

NAVAJO NATIONAL MONUMENT—Reservations are needed for ranger-led tours to two remarkably preserved 13th-century Anasazi cliff dwellings, both reachable by strenuous hikes during summer months only; a visitor center compensates with a videotape and displays of prehistoric pottery and other artifacts. See p. 64.

Organ Pipe Cactus National Monument (E-2)

ORGAN PIPE CACTUS NATIONAL MONUMENT—The national monument preserves the habitat and inhabitants of this section of the Sonoran Desert, in particular its namesake, an immense cactus found only in this area. See p. 66.

Petrified Forest National Park (C-5)

PAINTED DESERT—Stained multiple hues over the ages by various minerals, the badlands of the Painted Desert seem to change colors as shadows progressively move across the hills. See p. 69.

PETRIFIED FOREST NATIONAL PARK—Horizontal fragments of petrified logs and fossils of long-departed dinosaurs and plants dot the multicolored, rugged landscape along a 28-mile drive through the park. See p. 68.

Phoenix (D-4)

ARIZONA STATE CAPITOL MUSEUM—The old state capitol building, completed in 1900, now houses a museum dedicated to Arizona's history; restored offices contain memorabilia, documents and artifacts. See p. 76.

DESERT BOTANICAL GARDEN—Specializing in plants indigenous to desert areas, the garden is a must-see for those interested in cacti and other flora common to arid climates. See p. 77.

HALL OF FLAME MUSEUM OF FIREFIGHTING—Anything and everything relating to firefighting can be found in this museum's collections, including horse-drawn pumpers, hook-and-ladder wagons, helmets, uniforms and badges. See p. 76.

HEARD MUSEUM—There is no better place to learn about Native American art, culture and heritage than the Heard Museum; innovative displays of baskets, ceramics, jewelry and kachina dolls are enhanced by examples of typical lodgings and audiovisual presentations. See p. 76.

Prescott (C-3)

SHARLOT M. HALL MUSEUM—Pioneer artifacts and documents collected by author and territorial historian Sharlot M. Hall are displayed in the old governor's mansion she helped restore; an amphitheater, other period buildings and extensive gardens are part of the complex. See p. 89.

Saguaro National Park (E-5)

SAGUARO NATIONAL PARK—Separated into two divisions east and west of Tucson, the park protects the saguaro cactus and its Sonoran Desert environment; scenic drives and trails lead to stands of these giant, many-armed plants. See p. 111.

Sedona (C-4)

OAK CREEK CANYON—The 16-mile-long, narrow canyon, which can be explored along a scenic stretch of SR 89A, is noted for the outcroppings of juniper, cypress and pine on its multicolored cliffs and for the trout-filled creek that flows through it. See p. 94.

Supai (B-3)

HAVASU CANYON—On the Havasupai Reservation, the canyon floor and sparkling waterfalls are remote and reachable only by a precipitous 8-mile trip by foot, horseback or helicopter and an arduous return climb. See p. 97.

Superior (J-6)

BOYCE THOMPSON ARBORETUM STATE PARK—This garden in the desert is home to plants and trees native to arid regions around the world; scenic walkways meander through the park. See p. 97.

Boyce Thompson Southwestern Arboretum

AAA Starred Attractions (continued)

EXCEPTIONAL INTEREST AND QUALITY

Tombstone (F-5)

TOMBSTONE—"The town too tough to die" is alive and well; the O.K. Corral, Boothill Graveyard, the *Tombstone Epitaph* building, saloons, the 1882 courthouse and dance halls attest to this old mining boomtown's Wild West atmosphere. See p. 97.

Tucson (F-4)

ARIZONA-SONORA DESERT MUSEUM—A hybrid combination of zoo and garden, the animals and plants that thrive here in natural settings are all natives of Arizona's Sonoran Desert region. See p. 104.

ARIZONA STATE MUSEUM—On the campus of the University of Arizona, the museum is known for its collections of prehistoric Hohokam and Mogollon artifacts and for its exhibits about Native American tribes of the Southwest, both historic and contemporary. See p. 105.

MISSION SAN XAVIER DEL BAC—Founded by Jesuits in the 1600s, the present Spanish mission-style structure was built 1783-97 by the Franciscans; this "White Dove of the Desert" continues to serve its Tohono O'odham parishioners. See p. 106.

TUCSON MOUNTAIN PARK—Come to this park in the Tucson Mountains not only to hike and to ride horses, but also to see one of the Southwest's largest saguaro forests. See p. 107.

Tumacacori National Historical Park (F-4)

TUMACACORI NATIONAL HISTORICAL PARK—The ruins of the never-completed Mission San Jose de Tumacacori, begun by the Franciscans, date to the early 1800s; the adobe church is partially restored. See p. 113.

Tuzigoot National Monument (C-3)

TUZIGOOT NATIONAL MONUMENT—The site preserves the ruins of a Sinagua Indian pueblo occupied approximately 1100-1425; a visitor center contains artifacts uncovered from its 110 rooms. See p. 113.

Walnut Canyon National Monument (B-4)

WALNUT CANYON NATIONAL MONUMENT—Filled with centuries-old ruins, artifacts and petroglyphs, this archeological site boasts more than 300 pre-Columbian dwellings scattered along the rim and within wall niches of a 400-foot-deep gorge. See p. 113.

Wupatki National Monument (B-4)

WUPATKI NATIONAL MONUMENT—Well-preserved ruins of hundreds of pueblos and cliff dwellings allow a look into the agricultural lifestyles of the Native Americans who lived here more than 700 years ago. See p. 116.

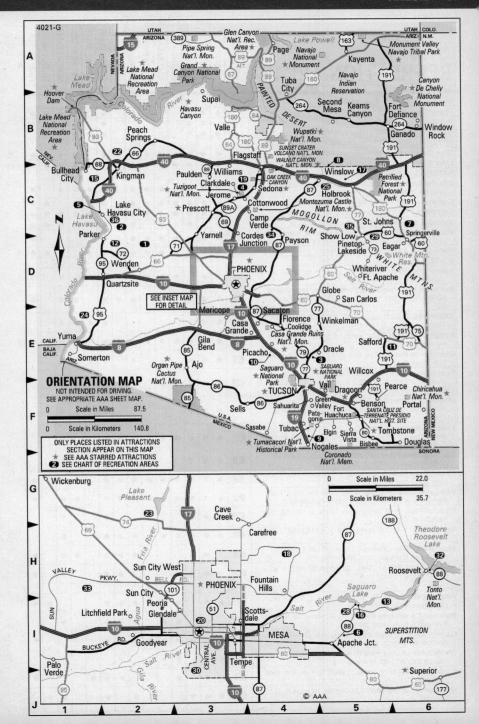

ORIENTATION MAP

NOT INTENDED FOR DRIVING.
SEE APPROPRIATE AAA SHEET MAP.

Scale in Miles 87.5

Scale in Kilometers 140.8

ONLY PLACES LISTED IN ATTRACTIONS
SECTION APPEAR ON THIS MAP
SEE AAA STARRED ATTRACTIONS
SEE CHART OF RECREATION AREAS

4021-G

RECREATION AREAS

	MAP LOCATION	CAMPING	PICNICKING	HIKING TRAILS	BOATING	BOAT RAMP	BOAT RENTAL	FISHING	SWIMMING	PETS ON LEASH	BICYCLE TRAILS	NATURE PROGS.	VISITOR CENTER	LODGE/CABINS	FOOD SERVICE
NATIONAL PARKS *(See place listings)*															
Grand Canyon (B-3) 1,218,376 acres.		•	•	•				•		•		•	•	•	•
Petrified Forest (C-5) 93,533 acres.			•	•						•			•		•
Saguaro (E-5) 91,000 acres.		•	•	•						•	•	•	•		
NATIONAL RECREATION AREAS *(See place listings)*															
Glen Canyon (A-4) North-central Arizona.		•	•	•	•	•	•	•	•	•		•	•	•	•
Lake Mead (B-1) Northwest Arizona. Scuba diving.		•	•	•	•	•	•	•	•	•		•	•	•	•
NATIONAL FORESTS *(See place listings)*															
Apache-Sitgreaves 2,008,308 acres. East-central Arizona. Horse rental.		•	•	•	•	•	•	•	•	•		•	•		•
Coconino 1,821,495 acres. Northern Arizona.		•	•	•	•	•	•	•	•	•		•	•		•
Coronado 1,780,196 acres. Southeastern Arizona.		•	•	•	•	•	•	•	•	•		•	•		•
Kaibab 1,556,432 acres. North-central Arizona.		•	•	•	•	•		•		•		•	•	•	•
Prescott 1,238,154 acres. Central Arizona. Electric boat motors only. Horse rental.		•	•	•	•	•	•	•		•					•
Tonto 2,900,000 acres. Central Arizona.		•	•	•	•	•	•	•	•	•				•	•
STATE															
Alamo Lake (D-2) 5,642 acres 38 mi. n. of US 60 via a paved road. *(See Wenden p. 114)*	❶	•	•		•	•	•	•	•	•			•		
Buckskin Mountain State Park & River Island Unit (C-2) 1,677 acres 11 mi. n. off SR 95. *(See Parker p. 66)*	❷	•	•	•	•	•	•	•	•	•			•		•
Catalina (E-5) 5,511 acres 9 mi. n. off SR 77. *(See Tucson p. 105)*	❸	•	•	•						•	•		•		
Cattail Cove (C-1) 5,520 acres off SR 95. *(See Lake Havasu City p. 61)*	❺	•	•	•	•	•	•	•	•	•			•		
Dead Horse Ranch (C-4) 866 acres off 10th St. *(See Cottonwood p. 47)*	❹	•	•	•	•			•		•			•		
Fool Hollow Lake Recreation Area (C-5) 850 acres 2 mi. n. of US 60 off SR 260, then e. on Old Linden Rd. to 32nd Ave. *(See Show Low p. 96)*	㉟	•	•	•	•	•		•		•			•	•	
Homolovi Ruins (B-5) 4,000 acres 3 mi. e. on I-40 to exit 257, then 1 mi. n. on SR 87. *(See Winslow p. 116)*	❽	•	•	•						•			•	•	
Lake Havasu State Park (C-1) 6,200 acres n. of London Bridge off London Bridge Rd. *(See Lake Havasu City p. 61)*	㊱	•	•	•	•	•	•		•	•	•				
Lost Dutchman (I-5) 320 acres 5 mi. n.e. off SR 88. *(See Apache Junction p. 82)*	❻	•	•	•						•	•	•	•		
Lyman Lake (C-6) 1,180 acres 11 mi. s. off US 191. *(See St. Johns p. 92)*	❼	•	•	•	•	•	•	•	•	•			•	•	•
Patagonia Lake (F-4) 640 acres 7 mi. s.w. on SR 82, then 5 mi. w. following signs. *(See Patagonia p. 67)*	❾	•	•	•	•	•	•	•	•	•			•		
Picacho Peak (E-4) 3,600 acres 12 mi. s. off I-10. *(See Picacho p. 88)*	❿	•	•	•						•			•		
Roper Lake (E-6) 319 acres 4 mi. s. off US 191. *(See Safford p. 91)*	⓫	•	•	•	•			•	•	•			•		
Slide Rock (C-4) 43 acres 7 mi. n. off SR 89A within Oak Creek Canyon. *(See Sedona p. 95)*	⓳		•	•				•	•	•		•	•		•
Tonto Natural Bridge (C-4) 160 acres 13 mi. n.w. off SR 87. *(See Payson p. 67)*	㉞		•	•					•	•			•		
OTHER															
Apache Lake (I-5) 2,656 acres 30 mi. n.e. on SR 88. *(See Apache Junction p. 81)*	⓭	•	•		•	•	•	•	•	•				•	•
Bullhead Community Park (C-1) 20 acres .25 mi. s. of Bullhead City. No tent camping.	⓯		•		•	•		•	•	•			•		
Canyon Lake (I-5) 950 acres 16 mi. n.e. on SR 8. *(See Apache Junction p. 82)*	⓰	•	•		•	•	•	•	•	•					•
Cholla Lake County Park (C-5) 360 acres 2 mi. e. of Joseph City on I-40. Water skiing.	⓱	•	•		•	•		•							
Encanto Park (I-3) 66 acres at 2605 N. 15th Ave. Golf (nine and 18 holes). *(See Phoenix p. 76)*	⓴		•	•					•	•	•	•			•
Hualapai Mountain (B-2) 2,200 acres 10 mi. s.e. of Kingman.	㉒	•	•	•				•		•			•	•	

RECREATION AREAS

	MAP LOCATION	CAMPING	PICNICKING	HIKING TRAILS	BOATING	BOAT RAMP	BOAT RENTAL	FISHING	SWIMMING	PETS ON LEASH	BICYCLE TRAILS	NATURE PROGS.	VISITOR CENTER	LODGE/CABINS	FOOD SERVICE
Lake Pleasant (G-2) 24,500 acres 30 mi. n. via I-17, then 10 mi. w. on SR 74. *(See Peoria p. 84)*	23	•	•		•	•	•	•	•	•			•		•
La Paz County Park (D-2) 165 acres 8 mi. n. of Parker via SR 95. *(See Parker p. 66)*	12	•	•		•	•		•	•	•			•		
Martinez Lake (E-1) 600 acres 25 mi. n. of Yuma. Water skiing.	24	•	•		•	•		•	•	•				•	•
McDowell Mountain (H-4) 20,941 acres 15 mi. n.e. of Scottsdale.	18	•	•	•											
McHood Park (C-5) 160 acres 5 mi. s.e. of Winslow off SR 99.	25	•			•	•		•	•	•					
Saguaro Lake (I-5) 1,280 acres 25 mi. n.e. of Mesa via US 60 and Bush Hwy.	28		•		•	•	•	•	•					•	•
Show Low Lake (C-5) 100 acres 5.5 mi. s.e. of Show Low via SR 260.	29	•	•	•	•	•		•	•	•					
South Mountain Park (J-3) 16,500 acres 8 mi. s. on S. Central Ave. Horse rental, playground. *(See Phoenix p. 78)*	30		•	•						•	•		•		
Theodore Roosevelt Lake (H-6) 17,315 acres 29 mi. n.w. of Globe via SR 88.	32	•	•	•	•	•	•	•	•	•				•	•
White Tanks Mountain (H-1) 26,337 acres 15 mi. w. of Peoria via Dunlap/Olive aves.	33	•	•	•	•					•					

Arizona Temperature Averages
Maximum/Minimum
From the records of the National Weather Service

	JAN	FEB	MAR	APR	MAY	JUN	JUL	AUG	SEP	OCT	NOV	DEC
Grand Canyon	41 / 17	45 / 20	51 / 24	59 / 30	69 / 37	81 / 45	83 / 52	80 / 51	75 / 45	64 / 34	53 / 26	44 / 17
Phoenix	65 / 38	69 / 41	74 / 45	84 / 52	93 / 60	101 / 68	105 / 77	102 / 76	98 / 70	88 / 57	75 / 45	66 / 38
Springerville	47 / 15	51 / 18	55 / 22	63 / 30	71 / 37	80 / 46	80 / 52	78 / 49	75 / 42	68 / 32	58 / 21	48 / 14
Tucson	63 / 38	67 / 40	71 / 44	81 / 50	90 / 57	98 / 66	98 / 74	95 / 72	93 / 67	84 / 56	72 / 49	65 / 39
Yuma	68 / 43	73 / 46	78 / 50	86 / 57	93 / 64	101 / 71	106 / 81	104 / 81	100 / 74	90 / 62	76 / 50	68 / 44

Summer Temperatures

Summer temperatures can cause the air inside a closed vehicle to expand enough to shatter a windshield, so consider leaving one of the side windows open a crack to allow air to escape.

Temperatures inside a closed vehicle can exceed 160 degrees Fahrenheit, so **never leave children or pets in an unattended vehicle.**

Points of Interest

AJO (E-3) pop. 2,900, elev. 1,747′

Home to the first copper mine in the state, Ajo did not boom until ore-refining methods made the mining of low-grade ore profitable in the early 1900s. In 1906 Col. John Greenway formed the New Cornelia Copper Co., which was eventually purchased by one of the nation's largest copper companies, Phelps Dodge Corp., in 1921. Visitors to the town can view the New Cornelia Open Pit Mine on Indian Village Road. Nearly 2 miles in diameter and 1,000 feet deep, the mine has a visitor center and observation area.

The name Ajo comes either from the Papago word for "paint" or the Spanish name for "garlic." As in much of the southwest, the Spanish and American Indian influence can be seen in Ajo's Spanish Colonial Revival town square, which is surrounded by a park, mission churches and Southwestern-style buildings. Historic buildings include the 1919 Curley School and the Greenway Mansion on Indian Village Road.

Ajo Stage Lines offers historical and ecological tours to the remote areas of the Sonoran Desert. Phone (520) 387-6467, 387-6559 or (800) 942-1981.

Ajo District Chamber of Commerce: 321 Taladro St., Ajo, AZ 85321; phone (520) 387-7742.

CABEZA PRIETA NATIONAL WILDLIFE REFUGE, 1611 N. Second Ave., was created in 1939 for the conservation and development of natural wildlife resources and to protect the diminishing population of desert bighorn sheep. The 860,000-acre refuge protects desert wildlife, including, kangaroo rats, pocket gophers, jack rabbits, lizards and bats. In addition, such endangered species as the Sonoran pronghorn antelope and the lesser longnose bat inhabit the refuge.

During migration periods warblers, swallows, phoebes, prairie falcons and quails can be seen. Because part of the Barry Goldwater Air Force Range airspace is over the refuge, an entry permit must be obtained at the visitor center. A four-wheel-drive vehicle is required. Firearms are prohibited and campfires are limited; check with the refuge for regulations. Mon.-Fri. 7:30-4:30. Free. Phone (520) 387-6483.

APACHE JUNCTION—
see Phoenix p. 81.

APACHE-SITGREAVES NATIONAL FORESTS

Elevations in the forests range from 3,500 ft. in the Upper Sonoran Desert to 11,300 ft. at Mt. Baldy. Refer to AAA maps for additional elevation information.

The Apache-Sitgreaves national forests comprise 2,008,308 acres along the south rim of the Colorado Plateau in east-central Arizona. They are named, respectively, for the Apaches and for Lt. Lorenzo Sitgreaves, who in 1851 led the first military topographical mapping expeditions across Arizona. The forests include the Mount Baldy, Bear Wallow and Escudilla wilderness areas and the Blue Range Primitive Area.

Hunting is permitted in season. Numerous lakes and streams offer trout fishing. Boats with motors larger than 8 horsepower are prohibited; on some lakes only electric motors are permitted. Trails are available for varying interests, including horseback riding, mountain biking, and hiking as well as for off-road vehicles. Picnic facilities are available in summer. Winter activities include cross-country skiing, snowmobiling, showshoeing and ice fishing.

Visitor centers are at Big Lake and on the Mogollon Rim near Heber. Visitor information also is available in summer from attendants at developed campgrounds in the forests and district ranger offices.

The Coronado Trail Scenic Byway (SR 191), 5,000 feet high and 127 miles long, connects the cities of Clifton/Morenci to Springerville/Eagar. The present Coronado Trail (US 191) commemorates portions of the historic route followed by Francisco Vásquez de Coronado when he sought the fabled Seven Cities of Cíbola in 1540. The road traverses areas that remain much as they were more than 450 years ago.

From Clifton the road climbs a corkscrew grade up Rose Peak to an elevation of 8,550 feet. Near this point a Forest Service lookout tower affords a magnificent panorama. Continuing northward, the trail rises 650 feet in 7 miles to an elevation of 9,200 feet at K.P. Cienega. The steep, narrow road is not recommended for vehicles pulling trailers more than 20 feet long.

The White Mountains Scenic Byway is a series of connecting roads that forms a loop through the White Mountains of the Apache-Sitgreaves national forests. The 123-mile loop includes parts of SRs 73, 260, 273 and 373.

From the rim northward the road is noted for its spectacular autumn coloring. The named portion of the trail ends at Springerville, where US 191 joins US 60.

For more information contact the Forest Supervisor's Office, Apache-Sitgreaves National Forests, 309 S. Mountain Ave., P.O. Box 640, Springerville, AZ 85938; phone (520) 333-4301. *See Recreation Chart and the AAA Southwestern CampBook.*

BENSON (F-5)
pop. 3,800, elev. 3,576'

Benson/San Pedro Valley Chamber of Commerce: 226 4th St., Benson, AZ 85602; phone (520) 586-2842.

SAN PEDRO & SOUTHWESTERN RAILROAD, I-10 exit Milepost 303, takes visitors on guided tours along the San Pedro River in open-air and enclosed train cars. Departures year-round. Times and dates vary; phone ahead. Fare $28; over 60, $25; ages 5-18, $19; family rate $88. MC, VI. Phone (800) 269-6314.

BISBEE (F-5) pop. 6,300, elev. 5,300'

Bisbee became internationally renowned during the 1880s mining rush, with the discovery of the Copper Queen Lode. Bisbee mines, nestled in the foothills of the Mule Mountains in southeast Arizona, have produced more than $2 billion in copper, gold, lead, silver and zinc. By 1900 Bisbee was the largest cosmopolitan center between St. Louis and San Francisco. Besides operating several stock exchanges, the town was a major venue for rodeos, circus, vaudeville, theater and lectures.

By the early 1970s most of the mines had closed, and artists' studios replaced the miner's shacks. Bisbee is now home to 27 art galleries and studios and serves as an enclave for more than 100 resident artists and artisans as well as actors, dancers, writers, musicians and photographers. Events and cultural activities are held throughout the year; contact the chamber of commerce for further information.

Artifacts and period furnishings of early Bisbee are displayed at the Muheim Heritage House at 207 Youngblood Hill. The house was completed in 1914 by a prominent local businessman. Another museum that preserves Bisbee's past through artifacts, clothing and memorabilia is the Bisbee Restoration Museum at 37 Main St.

Greater Bisbee Chamber of Commerce: Copper Queen Plaza, P.O. Drawer BA, Bisbee, AZ 85603; phone (520) 432-5421. *See color ad p. 42*

Shopping areas: The downtown section known as Old Bisbee has several specialty shops that sell antiques, assorted crafts, gifts, jewelry, turquoise and Western items.

BISBEE MINING AND HISTORICAL MUSEUM, 5 Copper Queen Plaza between Main St. and Brewery Gulch, is in the building that served as the headquarters of the Copper Queen Consolidated Mining Company. The museum examines local history and culture through its exhibit "Bisbee: Urban Outpost on the Frontier." The display depicts the history of the town 1877-1917.

The museum's Shattuck Memorial Archival Library contains photographs, manuscripts, documents and research books about Arizona and Bisbee's copper mining history. Daily 10-4; closed Jan. 1 and Dec. 25. Admission $4, under 18 free. Phone (520) 432-7071.

QUEEN MINE, on SR 80 next to The Lavender Pit mine, offers 1.25-hour tours by mine car into an underground copper mine. The tours are conducted by former miners. Sweaters or jackets are recommended. Tours depart daily at 9, 10:30, noon, 2 and 3:30; closed Thanksgiving and Dec. 25. Admission $10; ages 7-11, $3.50; ages 3-6, $2. Reservations are suggested. MC, VI. Phone (520) 432-2071.

SURFACE MINE AND HISTORIC DISTRICT VAN TOUR departs from the Queen Mine Tour Office on SR 80. The tour visits an inactive $25 million open-pit copper mine from which 41 million tons of concentrated ore were mined. It is 1.25 miles long, nearly a mile wide and 950 feet deep and can be viewed from SR 80, which traverses a bench of the pit. An 11-mile, 1.25-hour van tour departs daily at 10:30, noon, 2 and 3:30; closed Thanksgiving and Dec. 25. Fare $7. Reservations are suggested. MC, VI. Phone (520) 432-2071.

Naco, Mexico

Approximately 11 miles south of Bisbee, Naco is a small border town in the state of Sonora. U.S. and Canadian visitors must carry proof of citizenship; a valid U.S. or Canadian passport is the most convenient, since it serves as a photo ID and facilitates many transactions such as cashing traveler's checks. The U.S., Canadian and Mexican governments also recognize a birth certificate (must be a certified copy from the government agency that issued it). A driver's license or baptismal certificate is *not* proof of citizenship.

All persons who plan to visit the interior or stay in the border area more than 72 hours also must obtain a *tarjeta de turista* (Mexican government tourist card). Tourist cards can be obtained from any AAA Arizona office. Before driving into Mexico check with a AAA office for documentation and insurance requirements. The border is open daily 24 hours. The Mexican Customs office is usually open daily 8-5, while the U.S. Customs office is open daily 8:30-4:30.

BULLHEAD CITY (C-1)
pop. 22,000, elev. 540'

Established originally as a supply and support base for builders of the Davis Dam, which impounds Lake Mojave in the Lake Mead National Recreation Area, Bullhead City has evolved into a vacation community. Sailing, water-skiing and fishing are available on the Colorado River, Lake Mohave and Lake Mead National Recreation Area *(see place listing p. 61)*. The city's accommodations industry thrives on the thousands of visitors drawn to the casinos across the river in Laughlin, Nev. Two bridges connect the towns, while the casinos and hotels operate a free river ferry.

Bullhead Area Chamber of Commerce: 1251 SR 95, Bullhead City, AZ 86429; phone (520) 754-4121.

CAMP VERDE (C-4)
pop. 6,200, elev. 3,160'

Camp Verde was founded as Camp Lincoln in 1866 by Arizona Volunteers to defend pioneers from Apache raids. The fort was renamed Fort Verde a few years later by the U.S. Army. As the area became more peaceful, residents turned their energies toward cattle raising and farming, the two major industries in the broad Verde Valley.

Camp Verde Chamber of Commerce: 435 Main St., P.O. Box 3520, Camp Verde, AZ 86322; phone (520) 567-9294.

FORT VERDE STATE HISTORIC PARK is 3 mi. e. of I-17. In one of the four restored structures of the old fort are Native American, pioneer and military artifacts. Officers' quarters, married housing and the doctor's quarters are furnished in period. Living history programs are presented on Saturdays during the winter months. Allow 1 hour minimum. Daily 8-5; closed Dec. 25. Admission $2; ages 7-13, $1. Phone (520) 567-3275.

RECREATIONAL ACTIVITIES
White-water Rafting
• **AAE's Mild to Wild Rafting**, across the street from the Camp Verde Chamber of Commerce. Write 11 Rio Vista Cir., Durango, CO 81301. Daily late Feb.-late May. Phone (888) 567-7238.

★CANYON DE CHELLY NATIONAL MONUMENT (A-6)

Reached from Gallup or Shiprock, N.M., and Chambers, Holbrook, Winslow or Tuba City, Ariz., the Canyon de Chelly (d'-SHAY) National Monument is in the Navajo Reservation, 3 miles east of Chinle. Five periods of Native American culture (Archaic, Basketmakers, Anasazi, Hopi and Navajo), dating from 2500 B.C. to present, are represented within the 83,849-acre monument.

Archaic, Basketmakers and Anasazi successively occupied the canyons until a reduction in population in A.D. 1350. During the 14th and 15th centuries the Hopis utilized the canyons. The Navajo arrived sometime in the 17th century and continue to live in the canyons, growing corn and peaches and herding livestock.

The 26-mile-long Canyon de Chelly is joined by the 25-mile-long Canyon del Muerto; red sandstone walls rise from 30 to 1,000 feet in a sheer, remarkably smooth ascent. Pictographs painted on the walls date from the earliest occupation to the Navajo era.

The principal area ruins are White House, Antelope House, Standing Cow and Mummy Cave. White House was first explored in 1848, and its architecture may indicate connections with Chaco Canyon. Antelope House is named for the large pictograph of running antelopes that appears there. Mummy Cave, in which some well-preserved human remains were discovered, has a three-story tower and is said to be one of the largest cliff dwellings in the United States. It is considered spiritual by Native Americans, and there is no access granted to visitors.

Authorized Navajo guides are available for canyon trips; park rangers' hours vary. The Thunderbird Lodge near the monument headquarters conducts trips into the canyon daily, depending on high water conditions, with four- and six-wheel-drive vehicles. All-day tour (including lunch) $57.50. Half-day tour $35.75; under 13, $27.50; phone (520) 674-5841.

For individuals with their own four-wheel-drive vehicles, guides are available for $10 per hour (3-hour minimum); each additional four-wheel-drive vehicle costs $1 per hour. Other regulations apply; *see the Fast Facts box.* Guided tours on horseback also are available.

Except for a self-guiding trail from White House Overlook to the White House Ruin, all visitors within the canyons *must* be accompanied by a park ranger or an authorized guide.

Scenic drives traverse both sides of the canyon, affording views of most major ruins from overlooks. Allow 2 hours for each drive if stopping at all of the overlooks. The visitor center is open daily 8-6, May-Sept.; 8-5, rest of year. The Navajo Reservation observes daylight-saving time, unlike the rest of the state; times listed reflect this when applicable. Monument admission free. For further information contact the Superintendent, Canyon de Chelly National Monument, P.O. Box 588, Chinle, AZ 86503; phone (520) 674-5500.

CAREFREE—*see Phoenix p. 82.*

CASA GRANDE (E-3)
pop. 19,100, elev. 1,387'

Casa Grande, founded in 1879, was named for the Hohokam Indian ruins *(see Casa Grande Ruins National Monument)* 20 miles northeast of town. The town, once dependent on agriculture and mining, is now a diversified community.

Greater Casa Grande Chamber of Commerce: 575 N. Marshall, Casa Grande, AZ 85222; phone (520) 836-2125 or (800) 916-1515.

CASA GRANDE VALLEY HISTORICAL SOCIETY AND MUSEUM, 110 W. Florence Blvd., has more than 3,000 items relating to life in the desert and regional history. Included are three period rooms, Native American artifacts, mining and agricultural exhibits, a 1929 fire engine, an antique doll house and an historical diorama. Mon.-Sat. 1-5, Sept. 15-May 15; closed major holidays. Admission $2, under 18 free. Phone (520) 836-2223.

★CASA GRANDE RUINS NATIONAL MONUMENT (E-4)

Casa Grande Ruins National Monument is within the city limits of Coolidge off SR 87/287 *(see place listing p. 46).* The Casa Grande (Big

House) was built by prehistoric peoples called Hohokam prior to 1350 A.D. Partially ruined, the four-story structure is constructed of layers of caliche mud and represents the height of Hohokam architecture. Around the main building are the remains of a walled village. A viewing platform overlooking a ball court is behind the picnic area.

The Hohokam lived in the area for many centuries prior to the construction of Casa Grande. Some time around 1450 Casa Grande was abandoned for unknown reasons after the Hohokam had used it for only a century. The ruins were seen and named in 1694 by Father Eusebio Francisco Kino, a missionary who was led to the site by local Pima Indians.

The visitor center features a museum. Self-guiding tours and picnic facilities are available. Allow 1 hour minimum. Monument open daily 8-5; closed Dec. 25. Admission $2 per person or $4 per private vehicle, under 17 free. For further information contact the Superintendent, Casa Grande Ruins National Monument, 1100 Ruins Dr., Coolidge, AZ 85228; phone (520) 723-3172.

CAVE CREEK—*see Phoenix p. 82.*

★ CHIRICAHUA NATIONAL MONUMENT (F-6)

Chiricahua (cheer-ee-KAH-wah) National Monument, the "Wonderland of Rocks," is in the Chiricahua Mountains at an elevation ranging from 5,100 to 7,800 feet. It lies 70 miles northeast of Douglas via US 191 and SR 181; it is 36 miles southeast of Willcox via SR 186 and SR 181. The county road that runs 21 miles south from Bowie across Apache Pass to SR 186 is unpaved and rough in places. Unseasoned mountain drivers and cars pulling trailers should avoid the narrow, winding route from Portal; it is closed in winter.

The 12,000-acre area encompasses lands once controlled by the Chiricahua Apaches under Cochise, who led the Native Americans' resistance to the white man during the 1860s.

The Chiricahua Mountains rise above the surrounding grasslands, providing shady forests and glens that harbor Mexican chickadees, raccoon-like coatimundis, javelinas and a number of other wildlife species. Among the monument's outstanding features are gigantic, erosion-sculptured monoliths of volcanic rock.

Current research indicates that about 27 million years ago violent eruptions from the nearby Turkey Creek caldera took place, covering the area with white-hot ash. After the ash fused and cooled into an almost 2,000-foot layer of rock, the forces of erosion sculpted it into the odd array of shapes that can be seen.

Formations include the Totem Pole, 137 feet high and only a yard thick at its narrowest point;

the Mushroom; and Big Balanced Rock, weighing 1,000 tons and resting on a base about 4 feet thick. In some places canyon walls rise as much as 1,000 feet. Many areas can be reached only on foot.

Among the first pioneers to settle in the area were Ja Hu Stafford and Neil and Emma Erickson. By the 1920s one of the Erickson daughters, Lillian, and her husband, Ed Riggs, had turned the homestead into a guest ranch, built trails into the rocks and were the driving force in the creation of Chiricahua National Monument. Today the ranch is preserved as an historic site with daily tours *(see attraction listing).*

Picnicking, camping and parking areas are available near the headquarters in Bonita Canyon. Reached from the visitor center by 6 miles of paved mountain road, 7,000-foot Massai Point offers an overlook and a geology exhibit building. Trails lead to all parts of the monument. Campfire programs are conducted at designated times every week from early April to mid-September; contact the visitor center for a schedule of evening programs.

A visitor center containing exhibits and an audiovisual display is 2 miles inside the monument entrance. A hiker's shuttle departs to the high country daily at 8:30. Visitor center daily 8-5; closed Dec. 25. The entrance fee is $6 per private vehicle or $3 per person arriving by other means. Shuttle $2. Campers must register at the campground; an $8 per night fee is charged. Campgrounds will not accommodate travel trailers more than 26 feet long; most motor homes are acceptable.

For further information contact the Superintendent, Chiricahua National Monument, HCR 2, Box 6500, Willcox, AZ 85643; phone (520) 824-3560, ext. 104.

FARAWAY RANCH, 1.5 mi. w. of the monument visitor center, is the restored homestead of pioneers Neil and Emma Erickson. The home was built in 1888 and additions were made through 1917. By the 1920s the Ericksons' daughter Lillian and her husband had turned the homestead into a working cattle and guest ranch.

Allow 1 hour minimum. Homestead site accessible daily dawn-dusk. Guided tours of the home are given Mon.-Fri. at 10:30 and 2:30, Sat.-Sun. at 10:30, 2:30 and 3:30. Admission $2 (tickets sold at ranch) in addition to entrance fee to Chiricahua National Monument. Phone (520) 824-3560, ext. 104.

CLARKDALE (C-3)
pop. 2,100, elev. 3,545'

VERDE CANYON RAILROAD, 300 N. Broadway, offers a 4-hour scenic ride through the North Verde River Canyon and Sycamore Wilderness Area near Sedona. Visitors can view Sinagua Indian ruins and desert flora and fauna including bald eagles, blue herons and deer. Climate-controlled and open-air cars are available.

Departures vary, depending on season; phone ahead. First-class fare $54.95 (all ages). Regular fare $35.95; over 65, $32.95; ages 2-12, $20.95. Reservations are required. AE, DS, MC, VI. Phone (520) 639-0010 or (800) 293-7245.

COCONINO NATIONAL FOREST

Elevations in the forest range from 2,600 ft. at Fossil Creek in the Verde Valley to 12,643 ft. at the San Francisco Peaks. Refer to AAA maps for additional elevation information.

The 1,821,495 acres of Coconino National Forest range in altitude from 2,600 feet to 12,643 feet. In the south the forest is cut by deep canyons; in the north the San Francisco Peaks attain the highest elevation in Arizona. These peaks, including Mount Humphreys, the state's highest point, and Mount Agassiz, are some of the places in Arizona where alpine conditions exist. Many roads provide scenic drives.

Outstanding features include Oak Creek Canyon (see Sedona p. 92) and the Mogollon Rim, at an altitude of 7,600 feet. Among the recreational facilities within the forest is the Snowbowl winter sports area (see Flagstaff p. 49). Lake Mary offers good fishing, boating, snowmobiling and waterfowl hunting. Limited camping facilities are available in the area Memorial Day-Labor Day; a $10-$12 per night fee is charged.

For additional information contact the Forest Supervisor, 2323 East Greenlaw Ln., Flagstaff, AZ 86004; phone (520) 527-3600. See Recreation Chart and the AAA Southwestern CampBook.

COOLIDGE (E-4)
pop. 6,900, elev. 1,430'

SAVE **GOLDEN ERA TOY AND AUTO MUSEUM,** off SR 87 at 297 W. Central Ave., features a collection of antique toys, dolls and model trains as well as restored automobiles. Fri.-Sun. 11-5, mid-Oct. to late May. Admission $5; under 13, $2. Phone (480) 948-9570 or (520) 723-5044.

CORDES JUNCTION (D-4)
elev. 2,825'

Cordes Junction is a good access point for trips into the Bradshaw Mountains, where there are several deserted mining camps and ghost towns. The mountains are popular with rockhounds. Some unpaved roads are very rough; check locally for road conditions.

ARCOSANTI is 2.5 mi. e. of I-17 on a dirt road, following signs; the road may be rough due to

weather conditions. The town is architect Paolo Soleri's prototype urban design based on his philosophy of arcology (architecture plus ecology). The town, which will occupy only 25 acres of a 4,000-acre preserve, will be a pedestrian-oriented city with a goal of reducing urban sprawl and its impact on the environment. Visitors to Arcosanti should keep in mind that the area is still in the midst of construction.

Workshops and elderhostel programs are held throughout the year. Monthly concerts take place in the Colly Soleri Music Center, except in winter; phone for schedule. Visitor center daily 9-5. One-hour tours are conducted on the hour daily 10-4; closed Thanksgiving and Dec. 25. Tour $5. Visitor center free. AE, DS, MC, VI. Phone (520) 632-7135.

CORONADO NATIONAL FOREST

Elevations in the forest range from 2,800 ft. in the Santa Catalina Mountains to 10,720 ft. in the Pinaleno Mountains. Refer to AAA maps for additional elevation information.

Coronado National Forest's 12 widely scattered sections cover 1,780,196 acres in southeastern Arizona and southwestern New Mexico. Named for Spanish explorer Francisco Vásquez de Coronado who journeyed through southern Arizona in 1540, the forest's varied plant and animal life reflects the area's extremes of elevation: Flat deserts of cactuses and paloverde give way to rugged, heavily forested mountains covered with oak, juniper, pine, fir and spruce, depending on the elevation.

Within the forest's boundaries are five fishing lakes and one of the southernmost ski areas in the country. More than 1,100 miles of trails offer hiking opportunities. Scenic drives include Sky Island Scenic Byway to Mount Lemmon, Swift Trail in the Pinaleno Mountains (Mt. Graham), Ruby Road in the Tumacacori Mountains, Onion Saddle Road and Rucker Canyon Road in the Chiricahua Mountains and SRs 82 and 83.

Further information can be obtained at district offices in Douglas, Nogales, Safford, Sierra Vista and Tucson, or contact the Supervisor, Coronado National Forest, Federal Building, 300 W. Congress St., Tucson, AZ 85701; phone (520) 670-4552. See Recreation Chart and the AAA Southwestern CampBook.

WHIPPLE OBSERVATORY is atop Mount Hopkins in the Santa Rita Mountains. The visitor center is accessible from I-19 exit 56 (Canoa Rd.); from Canoa Rd. turn e. to Frontage Rd., 3 mi. s. to Elephant Head Rd., 1 mi. e. to Mt. Hopkins Rd., then 7 mi. s.e. The observatory houses one of the world's largest multi-mirror telescopes for conducting interstellar investigations. A visitor center has exhibits about astronomy, astrophysics and natural science as well as scenic views. A 6-hour guided tour of the observatory is available by appointment; phone for more information.

Visitor center open Mon.-Fri. 8:30-4:30. Tour departs Mon., Wed. and Fri. at 9; closed holidays. Visitor center free. Observatory tour $7; ages 6-12, $2.50. AE, MC, VI. Phone (520) 670-5707.

CORONADO NATIONAL MEMORIAL (F-5)

Coronado National Memorial is 22 miles south of Sierra Vista, 5 miles off SR 92. The memorial was established to commemorate Francisco Vásquez de Coronado's exploration of the Southwest. The expedition, the first European venture across what is now the U.S.-Mexican border, began in February 1540 when the viceroy of Mexico sent young Coronado northward in search of gold from the fabled Seven Cities of Cíbola.

Coronado led an expedition of more than 1,400 soldiers and natives as well as 1,500 animals. Five months of hard travel brought the party not to the gold of the fabled cities but to the rock and adobe pueblos of the Zuni Indians near Zuni, N.M. After traveling as far east as central Kansas, the expedition gave up its search and retraced the route to Mexico in 1542.

Although they never found the city of gold, Coronado and his men found the Grand Canyon as well as the many Hopi, Zuni and other villages scattered along the Rio Grande and into northern New Mexico. Besides paying tribute to Coronado's journey, the memorial's 4,750 acres provide a natural habitat for a variety of plants and animals.

The park, at the southern end of the Huachuca Mountains, is mostly oak woodland sprinkled with yucca, cholla and beargrass, which bloom from April to August. The mountains and canyons harbor wildlife ranging from bobcats to golden eagles. A sweeping view of the area extends from Montezuma Pass, 3.5 miles west of the visitor center.

An alternative to driving to the pass is a 3-mile trail that begins near the visitor center. A half-mile hiking trail, with benches for resting and markers bearing quotations from Coronado's journals, extends from the pass to Coronado Peak. The visitor center has a 14-foot-long window wall for viewing wildlife. Picnic facilities are available dawn-dusk.

The visitor center is open daily 8-5; closed Thanksgiving and Dec. 25. Free. For further information write the Superintendent, Coronado National Memorial, 4101 E. Montezuma Canyon Rd., Hereford, AZ 85615; phone (520) 366-5515.

CORONADO CAVE is accessible via a steep .75-mi. trail from the visitor center. The cave, which remains in its natural state with no lighting or guardrails, features two chambers connected by a narrow passageway. Several tunnels branch from the main cavern and require some crawling. Daily 8-5. Visitors must obtain a free permit at the visitor center and be equipped with one flashlight per person.

CORONADO TRAIL—
see Apache-Sitgreaves National Forests p. 40.

COTTONWOOD (C-4)
pop. 5,900, elev. 3,314′

One of two Arizona towns called Cottonwood, this Cottonwood is located in the center of the 1,500-square-mile Verde Valley, which contributed to its development as a commerce center for the area. In 1874 soldiers from nearby Camp Verde were quartered in town. Settlers eventually arrived and named the community for a nearby stand of 16 large cottonwood trees. Cottonwood is about 2 miles southeast of Tuzigoot National Monument *(see place listing p. 113).*

Hot air balloon rides over Prescott National Forest *(see place listing p. 90)* are available in the morning (weather permitting). For information and reservations contact Sky High Balloon Adventures, (520) 204-1395 or (800) 551-7597.

Cottonwood/Verde Valley Chamber of Commerce: 1010 S. Main St., Cottonwood, AZ 86326; phone (520) 634-7593.

DEAD HORSE RANCH STATE PARK, off 10th St., was named for a large horse skeleton found in the area by local children. Once the stomping grounds of Native Americans and Spanish conquistadors, the park now features Quetta Seed Pine Orchard, a stocked fishing pond, hiking trails and picnic areas overlooking the Verde River. Camping is available. Daily 8-8. Admission $4 per private vehicle. Camping $10-$15 per private vehicle. Phone (520) 634-5283. *See Recreation Chart.*

DOUGLAS (F-6)
pop. 13,100, elev. 3,955′

Douglas, on the Mexican border, began as the site of annual roundups for surrounding ranches. The town was founded in 1901 by a copper-smelting company and is now a center for commerce, manufacturing, agriculture and tourism.

The Gadsden Hotel, 1046 G Ave., was built in 1906 and has a high-ceilinged lobby with a mural of leaded stained glass and a curving staircase. Of interest in the vicinity are the many ghost towns and mining camps.

Douglas Chamber of Commerce: 1125 Pan American Ave., Douglas, AZ 85607; phone (520) 364-2477. *See color ad p. 42.*

Self-guiding tours: Maps detailing self-guiding historical tours of Douglas are available at the chamber of commerce.

⊞ **SAN BERNARDINO RANCH NATIONAL HISTORIC LANDMARK (SLAUGHTER RANCH MUSEUM),** 16 mi. e. on 15th St. (which turns into Geronimo Tr.), was the home of John Slaughter. The former Texas Ranger and sheriff of Cochise County developed the property he purchased in 1884 into a vast cattle ranch. Now restored to its turn-of-the-20th-century opulence, the main house contains many original family photographs and furnishings. Also on the ranch are a car shed, granary, barn and cook's ice and wash houses. Near the ranch is an early 1900s military outpost that was occupied during Mexican and Native American uprisings.

Geronimo Trail is accessible only under dry conditions. Picnic facilities are available. Allow 2 hours minimum. Wed.-Sun. 10-3. Admission $3, under 12 free. Phone (520) 558-2474.

Agua Prieta, Mexico

Adjoining Douglas in the state of Sonora is Agua Prieta. U.S. and Canadian visitors must carry proof of citizenship; a valid U.S. or Canadian passport is the most convenient, since it serves as a photo ID and facilitates many transactions such as cashing traveler's checks. The U.S., Canadian and Mexican governments also recognize a birth certificate (must be a certified copy from the government agency that issued it). A driver's license or baptismal certificate are *not* proof of citizenship.

All persons who plan to visit the interior or stay in the border area more than 72 hours also must obtain a *tarjeta de turista* (Mexican government tourist card). Tourist cards can be obtained from any AAA Arizona office. Before driving into Mexico check with a AAA office for documentation and insurance requirements. Mexican and U.S. customs are open daily 24 hours.

DRAGOON (F-5) elev. 4,615'

⊞ ★ **AMERIND FOUNDATION MUSEUM,** off Dragoon Rd. at 2100 N. Amerind Rd., is an archeological research facility and museum. More than 25,000 items span 10,000 years of cultural history in the Americas, focusing primarily on the native cultures of the Southwest, the Pacific Northwest, the Arctic and the high native civilizations of Mexico and South America.

An art gallery contains the works of Native Americans and such well-known artists as Frederic Remington. Hopi art is featured. Picnicking is permitted. Allow 1 hour, 30 minutes minimum. Daily 10-4, Sept.-May; Wed.-Sun. 10-4, rest of year. Closed major holidays. Admission $3; over 60 and ages 12-18, $2. Phone (520) 586-3666.

EAGAR (D-6) pop. 4,000, elev. 7,114'

THE LITTLE HOUSE MUSEUM, 4 mi. w. on SR 260, then 3 mi. s. on Southfork Rd., is situated on landscaped grounds next to the Little Colorado River. Narrated tours of the museum offer colorful anecdotes about former residents and visitors of the area, including pioneers, cattle rustlers and author Zane Grey. Exhibits feature local artifacts and memorabilia, including antique automatic musical instruments. Trout fishing is available.

Allow 1 hour minimum. Guided tours are given Thurs.-Mon. at 1:30, Fri.-Sat. at 11 and 1:30, May 15-Labor Day; by appointment rest of year. Admission $4. Phone (520) 333-2286.

ELGIN (F-5) elev. 4,700'

WINERIES

• **Sonoita Vineyards,** 3 mi. s. on Canelo Rd. (a graded gravel road). Daily 10-4; closed holidays. Phone (520) 455-5893.

FLAGSTAFF (B-3)
pop. 45,900, elev. 6,905'

It is believed that Flagstaff's name came from the discovery of a lone pine tree in an open valley. The pine was stripped of its branches and used as a flagstaff during Fourth of July celebrations in 1876. The flagstaff remained and served as a landmark for wagon trains bound for California. The pines also have continued to provide the town with a wood products industry.

Within the boundaries of Coconino County, the second largest in the country, are the Grand Canyon *(see place listing p. 52)*, Wupatki National Monument *(see place listing p. 116)*, Sunset Crater Volcano National Monument *(see place listing p. 96)*, Oak Creek Canyon *(see Sedona p. 94)*, Walnut Canyon National Monument *(see place listing p.113)*, Meteor Crater *(see Winslow p. 116)* and the San Francisco Peaks.

⊞ Gray Line bus tours to the Grand Canyon, Oak Creek Canyon, Montezuma Castle National Monument *(see place listing p. 63)* and other nearby points of interest are available; reservations are required. Check with the Flagstaff airport for information about airplane rides to the Grand Canyon. Scenic flights of the Grand Canyon are available from the Grand Canyon Airport *(see Grand Canyon National Park p. 52)*.

A 54-mile-long scenic stretch of SR 89A begins in Flagstaff, winds its way south through Oak Creek Canyon *(see Sedona p. 94)* and ends in Jerome. The steep, narrow road is not recommended for vehicles pulling trailers more than 20 feet long. The nearby mountains are ideal for camping, fishing and hunting.

Flagstaff Visitor Center: 1 E. SR 66, Flagstaff, AZ 86001; phone (520) 774-9541 or (800) 842-7293.

Self-guiding tours: A map outlining a walking tour of Flagstaff's historic downtown area is available at the visitor center.

Shopping areas: Flagstaff Mall, 6 miles east at 4650 US 89N, has more than 60 stores, including Dillard's, JCPenney and Sears. Flagstaff's downtown historic district also offers shopping opportunities.

SAVE **LOWELL OBSERVATORY,** 1 mi. w. of downtown via Santa Fe Ave. to 1400 W. Mars Hill Rd., following signs, was founded in 1894 by scientist Percival Lowell. Some of the best-known discoveries made at the observatory include Lowell's observations about the planet Mars, the basis for the theory of the expanding universe and the discovery of the ninth planet, Pluto, in 1930. Research continues at the observatory, enhanced by the operation of nine telescopes, including the 24-inch Clark refracting telescope.

A guided tour begins with a multimedia presentation documenting the history of the observatory and its founder. Interactive exhibits are featured as well as the Pluto Walk, a model of the planets in sequential order. Open daily 9-5, Apr.-Oct.; noon-5, rest of year. Nightly viewings are available; phone for details. Admission $3.50; senior citizens and university students with ID $3; ages 5-17, $1.50. AE, MC, VI. Phone (520) 774-2096.

SAVE **MUSEUM OF NORTHERN ARIZONA** is 3 mi. n. to 3101 N. Fort Valley Rd. (US 180). The museum contains displays about the archeology, biology, ethnology, geology, anthropology and fine art of northern Arizona. A reproduction of a kiva—a circular meeting place and ceremonial room—also is featured in addition to exhibits about native peoples.

Daily 9-5; closed Jan. 1, Thanksgiving and Dec. 25. Admission $5; over 55, $4; students with ID $3; ages 7-17, $2. Phone (520) 774-5213.

★ **OAK CREEK CANYON**—*see Sedona p. 94.*

RIORDAN MANSION STATE HISTORIC PARK, .5 mi. n. of jct. I-17 and I-40 (off Main St. and Milton Rd.) at 409 Riordan Ranch St., features the 40-room Riordan Mansion. Built in 1904, the structure was home to prominent lumbermen Timothy and Michael Riordan and their families. The rustic exterior incorporates log-slab siding, volcanic stone arches and hand-split wood shingles. The lavish interior contains handcrafted furniture, stained-glass windows and personal items of the Riordan families.

The park's visitor center has exhibits, a slide program and a children's "touch table." Picnicking is permitted. Allow 1 hour minimum. Grounds open daily 8:30-5, May-Sept.; 11:30-5, rest of year. Closed Dec. 25. Guided tours of the mansion are given daily on the hour, beginning 1 hour after opening. Admission $4; under 13, $2.50. Phone (520) 779-4395.

SCHULTZ PASS ROAD leads n. off US 180, then circles n.e. to join US 89. The dirt road is a scenic drive through Schultz Pass between the San Francisco Peaks and the Elden Mountains. Check locally for road conditions. A scenic portion of SR 89/89A extends from the I-40 junction in Flagstaff 54 miles southeast to Jerome.

RECREATIONAL ACTIVITIES
Skiing
- **Snowbowl**, in the San Francisco Peaks, is 7 mi. n. on Fort Valley Rd. (US 180), then 7 mi. n. on Snow Bowl Rd. Other activities are offered. Skiing is available daily 9-4, mid-Dec. to mid-Apr. (weather permitting). Phone (520) 779-1951.

FLORENCE (E-4)
pop. 7,500, elev. 1,493′

One of Arizona's oldest towns, Florence was founded by Levi Ruggles in 1866. Naming the town at the settlers' request, Territorial Governor Richard McCormick chose the name of his sister. Florence is now the seat of Pinal County; many old homes and other buildings perpetuate its frontier atmosphere.

Scenic desert highways from Florence include Kelvin Highway, a county road running east to Kelvin, and the Pinal Pioneer Parkway, a part of SR 79 leading southeast to Oracle Junction. The former might be rough; check locally for road conditions. Markers along the parkway identify desert wildlife.

Pinal County Development Board Visitors Center: 330 E. Butte, P.O. Box 967, Florence, AZ 85232; phone (520) 868-4331.

McFARLAND STATE HISTORIC PARK, Main St. and Ruggles Ave., features the first Pinal County courthouse, which was built in 1878. The adobe building includes museum exhibits about the jail, courthouse and hospital once housed there. The World War II Florence POW Camp exhibit portrays life at what was reportedly the largest POW camp in Arizona, housing more than 5,600 prisoners. Photographs, movies, aerial views, uniforms and German and Italian memorabilia from 1942 are on display. Allow 1 hour minimum. Thurs.-Mon. 8-5; closed Dec. 25. Admission $2; ages 7-13, $1. Phone (520) 868-5216.

PINAL COUNTY HISTORICAL MUSEUM, 715 S. Main St., displays Indian artifacts from Mexico and the Southwest, blacksmith equipment, antique woodworking tools, more than 100 varieties of barbed wire and documents relating to the county's history. A restored and furnished homesteader's shack also is displayed.

Allow 1 hour minimum. Wed.-Sat. 11-4, Sun. noon-4, Sept. 1-July 14; closed Jan. 1, Easter, Thanksgiving and Dec. 25. Free. Phone (520) 868-4382.

FORT APACHE (D-5)
FORT APACHE HISTORIC PARK, s. off SR 73, is a 288-acre site containing more than 20 buildings

dating 1870-1930 as well as pre-Columbian and historic petroglyphs, the Apache Culture Center and a re-created Apache village. Among the buildings that can be seen are the commanding officer's, captain's and officer's quarters, the guardhouse, stables and magazine. Mon.-Sat. 8-5, Memorial Day-Labor Day; daily 9-4, rest of year. Admission $3; senior citizens, students with ID and ages 5-12, $2. Phone (520) 338-4625.

FORT DEFIANCE (B-6)
pop. 4,500, elev. 6,862'

Fort Defiance lies at the mouth of Canyon Bonito, or Blue Canyon, in the Navajo Reservation. In some places sheer walls overhang the canyon floor. Established in 1851, Fort Defiance saw action in the Navajo wars that occurred during the 1860s. For many years it has been the headquarters of the Bureau of Indian Affairs, Fort Defiance Agency.

Navajos on the reservation maintain much of their traditional way of life. They engage in agriculture, stock raising, employment on the reservation and seasonal off-reservation work. Many still dwell in hogans, circular log and earth huts. Distinctive Navajo blankets, rugs and silver and turquoise jewelry are crafted.

FORT HUACHUCA (F-5)

Fort Huachuca (wa-CHOO-ka), covering 73,272 acres, was founded in 1877 to combat raids by Native Americans and outlaws. In 1954 the fort became the site of the Army Electronic Proving Ground. The fort is headquarters of the U.S. Army Information Systems Command, the U.S. Army Intelligence Center and various other military organizations. The Old Post retains many of the original buildings constructed in the late 19th century.

FORT HUACHUCA MUSEUM, 3.6 mi. n.w. of Fort Huachuca's main gate in the Old Post area at Boyd and Grierson aves., depicts the history of the Southwest and the U.S. Army's activities in the area. A visitor's pass must be obtained at the main gate; present your driver's license, vehicle registration and proof of insurance. Mon.-Fri. 9-4, Sat.-Sun. 1-4; closed Jan. 1, Thanksgiving and Dec. 25. Free. Phone (520) 533-5736 or 533-3638.

FOUNTAIN HILLS—
see Phoenix p. 82.

FOUR CORNERS MONUMENT—
see Window Rock p. 115.

GANADO (B-6)
pop. 1,300, elev. 6,386'

Ganado is one of the traditional meeting and trading centers of the Pueblo Colorado Valley.

For centuries the valley has been a favored Native American gathering place, first for the Anasazi and now for the Navajo. When John Hubbell bought the original trading post, he christened it Ganado to honor his Navajo friend Ganado Mucho and to distinguish the community from Pueblo, Colo.

Visitors to the reservation should be aware of certain travel restrictions; see the Fast Facts box.

HUBBELL TRADING POST NATIONAL HISTORIC SITE, 1 mi. w. via SR 264, is the oldest continuously operated trading post in the Navajo Nation. In 1878 John L. Hubbell bought the trading post and established himself as one of the leading traders of his time. Hubbell also collected Western art and Native American crafts, which are displayed in his furnished house on the site.

The trading post and the Hubbell home depict the role of trading in the history of the Southwest and the life of a trader's family. The trading post conducts business much as it did during the 89 years when the Hubbell family ran it. Members of the Navajo, Hopi, Zuni and other tribes sell and trade such crafts as hand-woven rugs, jewelry, baskets and pottery.

Rangers offer guided tours of the trading post compound and the Hubbell home; hours vary. The visitor center holds weaving demonstrations and distributes self-guiding tour booklets about the site. For further information contact the Superintendent, Hubbell Trading Post National Historic Site, P.O. Box 150, Ganado, AZ 86505. Allow 1 hour minimum. Daily 8-6, May-Sept.; 8-5, rest of year. Closed Jan. 1, Thanksgiving and Dec. 25. Free. Phone (520) 755-3475.

GILA BEND (E-3)
pop. 1,700, elev. 735'

Gila Bend is the center for a prosperous stock-raising and farming region in the Gila River Valley. The first farms were established in 1699 by Jesuit missionary Father Eusebio Francisco Kino. Just west of town is the site of the infamous 1851 Oatman Massacre, where all but three children of a westward-bound family were killed by Apaches.

Gila Bend Chamber of Commerce: 644 W. Pima, P.O. Drawer CC, Gila Bend, AZ 85337; phone (520) 683-2002.

★ GLEN CANYON NATIONAL RECREATION AREA (A-4)

Glen Canyon National Recreation Area extends along the Colorado River from Grand Canyon National Park (see place listing p. 52) in far north-central Arizona to Canyonlands National Park in southeastern Utah. One of the highest in the United States and part of the Colorado River storage project, the Glen Canyon Dam generates hydroelectric power that is distributed to cities and industries throughout the West; the dam's main purpose is water storage.

Reaching out to hidden canyons, sandy coves and inlets, and winding through towering red cliffs, 186-mile-long Lake Powell presents an ever-changing array of scenery and such recreational opportunities as water skiing, boating and fishing. Amenities include campsites, marinas and boat rentals and tours. A copy of fishing regulations can be obtained at park ranger stations, the Carl Hayden Visitor Center, the Navajo Bridge Interpretive Center, the Bullfrog Visitor Center or at the administration offices in Page.

The Bullfrog Visitor Center, at the Bullfrog Marina in Utah, exhibits the natural and cultural history of Glen Canyon and includes a life-size slot canyon model. The Navajo Bridge Interpretive Center, on US 89A near Lees Ferry, features a pedestrian bridge over the Colorado River at Marble Canyon and outdoor exhibits highlighting the area's historic river crossings.

Exhibits in the Carl Hayden Visitor Center, next to US 89, Glen Canyon Dam and Glen Canyon Bridge in Page, illustrate the construction of the dam and bridge and include a relief model of the canyon country. Guided tours of the dam are available throughout the year. The center is open daily 8-7, Memorial Day-Sept. 30; 8-5, rest of year. Closed Jan. 1, Thanksgiving and Dec. 25.

Free evening programs are given at Wahweap campground, 7 miles northwest of Page off US 89, Memorial Day-Labor Day; phone or stop by the visitor center for a list of scheduled performance days and times.

Arrangements for boat tours on Lake Powell can be made at Wahweap Lodge and Marina (*see color ad*); facilities, including public launching ramps, boat rentals, camping and boat and automobile fuel, are provided at Wahweap and at four other marinas on the lake. A boat ramp providing access to 15 miles of the Colorado River below Glen Canyon Dam is available at Lees Ferry, 5 miles north of Marble Canyon.

Boat excursions, which last from 1 hour to all day, are available; phone (602) 278-8888 in Phoenix, or (800) 528-6154. One-day raft trips on the Colorado River below the dam can be arranged in Page. Half-day and full-day trips are available to Rainbow Bridge National Monument, Utah, which is about 50 miles from Wahweap. Trips on the San Juan River leave from Mexican Hat and Bluff, Utah.

Park admission is $5 per private vehicle, or $3 per individual on foot or bicycle (both valid for up to 7 days). An additional entrance fee is charged for each motorized vessel. For further information contact the Superintendent, Glen Canyon National Recreation Area, Box 1507, Page, AZ 86040; phone (520) 608-6404 or

608-6200. *See Recreation Chart and the AAA Southwestern CampBook.*

GLENDALE—*see Phoenix p. 83.*

GLOBE (D-5) pop. 6,100, elev. 3,517'

Named for a globe-shaped piece of almost pure silver reputedly found nearby, Globe has a colorful history punctuated by mining discoveries. It began as a mining community in 1876. The town's first boom was silver; the second was copper, which is still mined in large quantities. Globe also serves as a trading center for the San Carlos Apache Reservation *(see San Carlos p. 92)* 4 miles east.

Salt River Canyon, traversed by US 60 about 45 miles northeast, is 1,500 to 2,000 feet deep. About 5 miles wide at the top, the vertical-walled canyon winds for many miles with sedimentary rock layers visible from the road. At the foot of the canyon is a state roadside park. Running westward from Globe, scenic US 60 traverses Devil's Canyon before reaching Superior *(see place listing p. 97).*

Globe is the eastern terminus of yet another scenic highway, the Apache Trail (SR 88). The road runs northwest to Roosevelt and Theodore Roosevelt Lake Recreation Area *(see Recreation Chart)* before turning southwest toward Apache Junction *(see place listing p. 81 for an advisory about driving this route).*

Greater Globe-Miami Chamber of Commerce: 1360 N. Broad St., P.O. Box 2539, Globe, AZ 85502; phone (520) 425-4495 or (800) 804-5623.

BESH-BA-GOWAH ARCHAEOLOGICAL PARK, 1.5 mi. s. via Jess Hayes Rd., is a 300-room pueblo inhabited 1225-1400 by Salado Indians. Several rooms are restored and furnished in period. Artifacts from the ruins are displayed in the museum, and an ethnobotanical garden illustrating how native plants were used by the Salado is featured. Daily 9-5; closed Jan. 1, Thanksgiving and Dec. 25. Admission $3; over 64, $2; under 12 free with an adult. Phone (520) 425-0320.

COBRE VALLEY CENTER FOR THE ARTS, 101 N. Broad St., is housed in the Old Gila County Courthouse. The center presents sculptures, photography, paintings, ceramics, jewelry, hand weaving and other art forms created by local artists. The Copper City Community Players present live performance pieces; phone for schedule. Allow 30 minutes minimum. Mon.-Sat. 10-5, Sun. and holidays noon-5; closed Jan. 1, Easter, Thanksgiving and Dec. 25. Donations. Phone (520) 425-0884.

DEVIL'S CANYON, w. on US 60, is noted for its sharp ridges, rock strata and cathedral-like tower formations that illustrate the enormous geological pressures exerted on the region. The mineral wealth of the area is credited mainly to these forces. The Queen Creek Gorge, Bridge and Tunnel are on the drive through the canyon.

THEODORE ROOSEVELT DAM AND LAKE— *see Roosevelt p. 91.*

RECREATIONAL ACTIVITIES
White-water Rafting

- **AAE's Mild to Wild Rafting,** 40 mi. n. off US 60/SR 77, following signs, P.O. Box 2771, Globe, AZ 85502. Daily late Feb.-late May. Phone (888) 567-7238.

- SAVE **Far Flung Adventures,** through the Salt River Canyon, P.O. Box 2804, Globe, AZ 85502. Feb.-May. Phone (520) 425-7272 or (800) 231-7238.

GOODYEAR—*see Phoenix p. 83.*

★ GRAND CANYON NATIONAL PARK (B-3)

Elevations in the park range from 1,200 ft. in the lower part of the canyon to 9,000 ft. at the North Rim. Refer to AAA maps for additional elevation information.

The Grand Canyon of the Colorado River is one of the world's most outstanding spectacles. In form, glowing color and geological significance, it is unsurpassed. The canyon is 277 miles long and averages 10 miles in width from rim to rim; it is 5,700 feet deep at the North Rim, which averages about 1,200 feet higher than the South Rim.

The park's eastern border is bounded by lofty, multicolored walls; beyond lies the Painted Desert. The western portion of the canyon includes the broad Havasu Canyon, part of the Havasupai Reservation *(see Supai p. 97).* This small agricultural tribe was present before the first European explorers arrived in 1540. Some 250 tribal members still live in the canyon.

The region possesses five of the seven life zones ascribed to the Northern Hemisphere. The geological aspect of the Grand Canyon is of great scientific importance. At no other place in the world is such a vast view of time displayed so clearly. Each stratum of rock distinctly marks a period of the Earth's history from 2 billion to 250 million years ago.

The first recorded viewing of the canyon by a European was in 1540 when a member of Francisco Vásquez de Coronado's expedition in

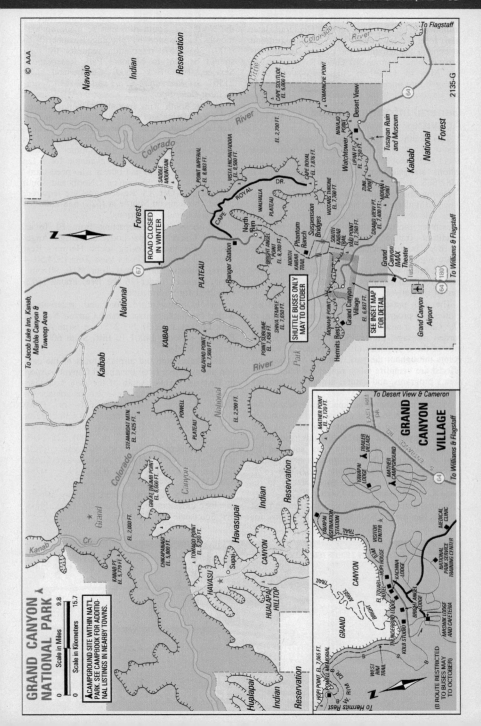

search of the Seven Golden Cities of Cíbola stumbled upon the great gorge. Centuries later Maj. John Wesley Powell led the first expedition to explore the length of the canyon. He and his party of nine boatmen left Green River, Wyo., in late May of 1869; on Aug. 30 six of them emerged into open country at the Virgin River on the western end of the canyon.

General Information and Activities

The South Rim is open all year; however, heavy snows close the North Rim roads from about late October until mid-May. For road conditions and weather information phone (520) 638-7888.

During the winter snow accumulates in the pine and juniper forests along the South Rim, but trails into the canyon are usually open. Anyone attempting the trails should be in good physical condition. Trail conditions should be verified at the Backcountry Office or park headquarters. Since nights are cool even in summer, visitors should bring warm clothing. However, be prepared for high summer temperatures at the bottom of the canyon.

The park presents a variety of scheduled activities and programs. All are outlined in detail in *The Guide*, a newsprint publication, and in a recorded message; phone (520) 638-7888. Schedules of these activities also are posted at various points throughout the park. Among the programs offered are campfire talks, ranger-led hikes, children's programs, and nature, history and geology walks.

Visitors planning to backpack anywhere in the park or camp below the canyon rim must obtain a permit from the Backcountry Office, Box 129, Grand Canyon, AZ 86023. Permits and backcountry camping reservations are accepted by mail or in person. For information about backpacking below the rim phone (520) 638-7875, Mon.-Fri. 1-5; or write the park directly to request a "Backcountry Trip Planner."

Several campgrounds are near the rim and just outside the park's boundaries. Reservations for National Park Service-operated campgrounds on the North and South rims can be made up to 5 months in advance by phoning Biospherics at (800) 365-2267; reservation requests by mail should be sent to National Park Reservations Service, P.O. Box 1600, Cumberland, MD 21501. *See Recreation Chart and the AAA Southwestern CampBook.*

At the South Rim free shuttle service along West Rim Drive and around Grand Canyon Village is available from about mid-March to mid-October. Passenger vehicles are not permitted on West Rim Drive during the summer months. Shuttle bus transportation is available for a fee for rim-to-rim hikers and others who need transportation between the canyon's North and South rims May 15-Oct. 15. Reservations are required; phone Transcanyon Shuttle at (520) 638-2820 for information and reservations.

Sightseeing buses departing from El Tovar, Maswik Lodge, Yavapai Lodge and Bright Angel Lodge offer the following tours: Hermit's Rest Tour ($13, 2 hours); Desert View Tour ($24.50, 4 hours); Sunrise and Sunset Tour ($10, 90 minutes). Children under 16 are free. Phone (502) 638-2631 for information.

For lodging information and reservations within the park, contact Grand Canyon National Park Lodges at (303) 297-2757, or write AmFac Parks & Resorts, 14001 E. Iliff, Suite 600, Aurora, CO 80014.

Both helicopter and airplane tours of the canyon are available from the Grand Canyon Airport in Tusayan, 5 miles south of the park headquarters. For information and reservations contact Air Grand Canyon (520) 638-2686 or (800) 247-4726; Airstar Helicopters, (520) 638-2622 or (800) 962-3869; SAVE Grand Canyon Airlines (*see color ad*), (520) 638-2463 or (800) 528-2413; Kenai Helicopters Grand Canyon, (520) 638-2764 or (800) 541-4537; and Papillon Grand Canyon Helicopters, (520) 638-2419 or (800) 528-2418.

Flight tours also are offered at many airports in other cities, including Flagstaff, Page, Phoenix, Scottsdale and Williams.

Another way to see the Grand Canyon is by tours conducted in four-wheel-drive vehicles. These back road sightseeing trips are led by guides well-versed in the ecology of the canyon, its history, wildlife and legends. Contact Grand Canyon Jeep Tours & Safaris at (520) 638-5337 or (800) 320-5337.

ADMISSION to the park area is $20 per private vehicle or $10 per individual on foot or by bicycle (both valid for up to 7 days). Admission includes both rims.

PETS are permitted in the park only if they are leashed, crated or otherwise physically restrained at all times. Pets are excluded entirely from back-country areas and are not allowed below the rim; kennels are available.

ADDRESS inquiries to the Superintendent, Grand Canyon National Park, P.O. Box 129, Grand Canyon, AZ 86023; phone (520) 638-7888. Information also is available from the Grand Canyon Chamber of Commerce, P.O. Box 3007, Grand Canyon, AZ 86023; phone (520) 638-2901.

GRAND CANYON RAILWAY—
see Williams p. 115.

MULEBACK TRIPS are available from the South and North rims. The trips are strenuous and should be undertaken only by those in good physical condition; pregnant women are not permitted on the trips. For safety purposes, riders must be fluent in English, over 4 feet 7 inches tall, and weigh less than 200 pounds when fully dressed (including equipment).

South Rim: One-day guided mule trips along the Bright Angel Trail to Plateau Point or overnight trips to Phantom Ranch in the bottom of the canyon can be arranged. Reservations must be made well in advance, particularly during summer and holidays. For reservations contact the Reservation Dept., Grand Canyon National Park Lodges, P.O. Box 699, Grand Canyon, AZ 86023. Rates for 1-day and overnight trips vary; phone ahead. Phone (303) 297-2757.

North Rim: Both half- and all-day muleback trips into the canyon are offered daily when the Grand Canyon Lodge is open. For reservations contact Grand Canyon Trail Rides, Box 128, Tropic, UT 84776. Full-day trip $95; half-day trip $40. Phone (435) 679-8665.

★ **VISITOR CENTER**, 6 mi. n. of the South Entrance Station and 1 mi. e. of Grand Canyon Village, is at an altitude of 6,950 feet and houses exhibits and an information center; ranger-naturalists are on duty. Exhibits and a 17-minute slide presentation explain the natural and human history of the Grand Canyon. Inquire at the center about local road conditions. Center open daily

at 8, June-Aug. (closing time varies); 8-5, rest of year. Free. Phone (520) 638-7888.

RECREATIONAL ACTIVITIES
Horseback Riding

- **Apache Stables**, .25 mi. s. of the s. entrance to the park at Moqui Lodge in Tusayan. Schedule and ride times vary, depending on weather and season. Phone (520) 638-2891 or 638-2424.

White-water Rafting

- **Raft Trips**, on the Colorado River. Write River Subdistrict Office, Grand Canyon National Park, P.O. Box 129, Grand Canyon, AZ 86023, or Rivers & Oceans, P.O. Box 40321, Flagstaff, AZ 86004. Trips operate Apr.-Oct. Phone (520) 526-4575 or (800) 473-4576. *See ad.*

Points of Interest—South Rim

Covering approximately 35 miles on well-paved roads, the drives on the South Rim afford a series of incomparable views. The West Rim Drive passes Powell Memorial and Hopi, Mohave and Pima points—all superb observation points—on the way to Hermit's Rest; it is closed to private vehicles mid-March to mid-October.

East Rim Drive passes many points, including Yaki, Grandview, Moran and Lipan, on its way to Desert View, 25 miles from Grand Canyon Village. The Hopi House, opposite El Tovar Hotel, is a reproduction of a Hopi dwelling.

Kolb Studio, in Grand Canyon Village near Bright Angel Lodge, was built as a photography studio in 1904; it now serves as an exhibit hall with changing art displays.

BRIGHT ANGEL TRAIL starts just w. of Bright Angel Lodge and descends 4,460 feet to the river. Only experienced hikers in the soundest physical condition should attempt this or any of the park trails on foot because the climbs back out of the canyon are arduous. Before attempting a trip, hikers should check *The Guide*, the park's newsprint publication, for the latest information about the trail. Overnight hikers must obtain a camping permit.

The trail leads 9 miles to the Colorado River and Phantom Ranch. From Indian Garden a branch trail leads 3 miles across the Tonto Platform to Plateau Point, offering a magnificent view of the Colorado River 1,300 feet below. Water must be carried on all canyon trails. If hikers choose to view the depths from the rim, telescopes are available near the Bright Angel Lodge and at Desert View Watchtower.

GRAND CANYON IMAX THEATER, 8.5 mi. s. of Grand Canyon Village on SR 64 in Tusayan, is

equipped with a seven-story screen and a six-track sound system. The theater presents "Grand Canyon—The Hidden Secrets," a film that depicts the history and captures the beauty of this geologic formation. The film is shown every hour on the half-hour 8:30-8:30, Mar.-Oct.; 10:30-6:30, rest of year. Admission $8; under 12, $5.50. Phone (520) 638-2468. *See color ad p. 56.*

★ **HAVASU CANYON**—*see Supai p. 97.*

LIPAN POINT, at an elevation of 7,250 feet, offers a fine view of the river, Unkar delta and the San Francisco Peaks.

PHANTOM RANCH, in Bright Angel Canyon, is reached by hiking *(see Bright Angel Trail)* or muleback trips *(see attraction listing).* It provides dormitory accommodations and a dining room. Reservations are required for both; contact the Bright Angel Transportation Desk, or phone (303) 297-2757.

RIM TRAIL extends along the rim of the canyon between Maricopa Point on the West Rim to Yavapai Museum. Relatively flat, the 3.5-mile paved rim trail is better for children and casual hikers than the park's other more strenuous canyon trails. A portion extending from the visitor center is a self-guiding nature trail. Free pamphlets about the biology and geology of the canyon can be obtained from boxes along the trail.

SOUTH KAIBAB TRAIL begins near Yaki Point, 3.5 mi. e. of Grand Canyon Village. This is a steep, 7-mile trail to a Colorado River suspension bridge. Hikers can descend the Kaibab Trail and return by the River and Bright Angel trails; the trip is recommended only for hardy individuals. The Kaibab Trail is extremely strenuous and is not recommended for hiking out of the canyon. Park officials strongly recommend that visitors do not attempt to hike from the South Rim to the river and back in 1 day.

A good 1.5-mile day hike leads from the head of Kaibab Trail to Cedar Ridge. Conducted hikes to Cedar Ridge are scheduled in summer. Hikers should carry water (1 gallon per person per day), since none is available along the trail.

★ **TUSAYAN RUIN AND MUSEUM** is 22 mi. e. of Grand Canyon Village on a short spur leading off East Rim Dr. The museum traces the development of the Native American culture at the canyon. Tusayan Ruin is a small prehistoric pueblo. Guided walks are offered. Daily 9-5. Seasonal closures in winter; phone for schedule. Free. Phone (520) 638-2305.

WATCHTOWER is at Desert View, 26 mi. e. of Grand Canyon Village. Built in 1932 as a rest stop for Grand Canyon visitors, the 70-ft. tower built of stone and mortar is a re-creation of the prehistoric towers found throughout the southwest. From the brink of the canyon wall, the tower commands views of the river, the canyon,

the Painted Desert and Kaibab National Forest *(see place listing p. 59);* telescopes extend the view far into the Navajo Reservation and to the Colorado River.

Also at Desert View are food concessions, a ranger station, gas station, general store and campground. Daily 8-5:30. Tower admission 25c, under 7 free.

YAVAPAI OBSERVATION STATION, 1.5 mi. e. of Grand Canyon Village, offers exhibits and programs that explain the geologic history of the region. A panoramic view of the canyon is visible through the building's windows. Daily 8-8, June-Aug.; 8-6 in Sept. and May; 8-5, rest of year. Free.

Points of Interest—North Rim

Less visited than the South Rim, the North Rim is not as extensively developed. The views from the North and South rims differ considerably. Observers at Bright Angel Point on the North Rim can see the San Francisco Peaks, which are 80 miles south of the South Rim.

From Grand Canyon Village on the South Rim, it is 220 miles to Grand Canyon Lodge via SR 64 to Cameron, US 89 to its junction with US 89A, US 89A to Jacob Lake and scenic SR 67 to the North Rim Entrance Station. The 5-hour drive passes through the Navajo reservation, the Painted Desert and Kaibab National Forest.

A road runs 22 miles southeast from the Grand Canyon Lodge road to Point Imperial, Vista Encantada and Cape Royal. Point Imperial, at 8,803 feet, is the highest point on the canyon rim. These points all afford splendid views. Reservations for the North Rim Campground can be made by phoning Biospherics at (800) 365-2267. *See Recreation Chart and the AAA Southwestern CampBook.*

MARBLE CANYON, at the n.e. end of the park, is traversed by US 89A via the Navajo Bridge, which is 616 feet long and 467 feet high. The Colorado River lies in a 500-foot-deep gorge that cuts across the level plain on which the highway sits. A herd of wild bison inhabits House Rock Valley, about 22 miles west on a rough dirt road off US 89A.

NORTH KAIBAB TRAIL starts at the head of Roaring Springs Canyon. This 14.2-mile trail descends 5,850 feet to the river and Phantom Ranch, following Bright Angel Creek. Only experienced hikers in good physical condition should use the trail. Be sure to obtain a copy of the Bright Angel and Kaibab trails pamphlet before embarking and check *The Guide*, the park's newsprint publication, for the latest information about the trail. Overnight hikers must obtain a camping permit and make camping reservations.

TUWEEP AREA, in the n.w. corner, embraces 40 miles of the Grand Canyon between Kanab Creek and the Pine Mountains. The remote area can be reached via SR 389 and a 60-mile dirt road west of Fredonia, Ariz.; the road is impassable when wet. Due to a lack of accommodations, the trip should not be attempted without adequate preparation and equipment.

No water, gasoline or camping supplies are available. Limited camping is offered south of the Tuweep Ranger Station. From Toroweap Overlook there are exceptional views of the inner gorge of the Grand Canyon and of geologically recent lava flows; at this point the canyon is 3,000 feet deep and averages less than a mile in width. Vulcan's Throne, a cinder cone, is on the Esplanade just west of Toroweap Overlook.

GREEN VALLEY—
see Tucson p. 111.

HOLBROOK (C-5)
pop. 4,700, elev. 5,080'

Holbrook was founded in 1881 when the Atlantic and Pacific Railroad reached this point. Once called the "town too tough for women and churches," the community was named for Henry R. Holbrook, chief engineer of the railroad project. The seat of Navajo County, Holbrook is close to Petrified Forest National Park *(see place listing p. 68)* and several reservations.

The Little Colorado River's sweeping turns traverse westward through town, and the terrain consists of flat plains, rugged hills and small buttes. Official U.S. mail is delivered to Scottsdale in late January when the Pony Express rides from Holbrook.

Holbrook Chamber of Commerce: 100 E. Arizona, Holbrook, AZ 86025; phone (520) 524-6558 or (800) 524-2459. *See ad.*

Self-guiding tours: A self-guiding tour including the Navajo County Courthouse/Museum is available. Brochures can be obtained at the chamber of commerce.

JEROME (C-3) pop. 400, elev. 5,435'

In 1582 Spanish missionaries exploring the Verde Valley recorded that natives were using the copper mines near what is now Jerome. The missionaries' description of the mines was identical to the workings found in 1883 by the United Verde Co. Eugene Jerome of New York agreed to finance the mining project on condition the camp be named for him. In 1886 a smelter arrived by rail from Ash Fork and operations began in earnest.

Once a city with a population of 15,000, Jerome became a virtual ghost town when the United Verde Branch copper mines of the Phelps Dodge Corp. closed in 1953. Since then, shops,

galleries, studios and museums have been established in the restored town. Some of the restored homes are open during the Home Tour in May.

A 54-mile-long scenic stretch of SR 89A begins in Flagstaff and winds its way south through Oak Creek Canyon (see Sedona p. 94) and ends in Jerome. The steep, narrow road is not recommended for vehicles pulling trailers more than 20 feet long. The nearby mountains are ideal for camping, fishing and hunting.

Jerome Chamber of Commerce: 310 Hull St., Drawer K, Jerome, AZ 86331; phone (520) 634-2900.

JEROME STATE HISTORIC PARK is off SR 89A. The park museum in the 1916 adobe brick Douglas Mansion traces the history of local mining and the family of James S. Douglas, developer of the rich United Verde Extension Mine in the early 1900s. A movie highlighting the history of Jerome is shown continuously. Picnicking is permitted. Allow 1 hour minimum. Daily 8-5; closed Dec. 25. Admission (including museum) $2.50; ages 7-13, $1. Phone (520) 634-5381.

MINE MUSEUM, 200 Main St., depicts Jerome's history through mine artifacts and equipment. Daily 9-4:30; closed Thanksgiving and Dec. 25. Admission $1, under 12 free. Phone (520) 634-5477.

KAIBAB NATIONAL FOREST

Elevations in the forest range from 5,500 ft. in the southwest lowlands to 10,418 ft. at Kendrick Peak. Refer to AAA maps for additional elevation information.

Kaibab National Forest covers 1,556,432 acres in three districts north and south of Grand Canyon National Park (see place listing p. 52). The portion north of the canyon includes Grand Canyon National Game Preserve, a thickly forested, domed limestone plateau. The north Kaibab Plateau is the only known home of the Kaibab squirrel, a dark gray squirrel with a white tail and tufted ears. The southernmost of the three districts contains volcanic cones and scattered forested peaks.

Big game animals can be seen in roadside meadows and throughout the forest. Fishing can be enjoyed at several lakes. Recreational opportunities within the national forest include hiking, mountain biking, horseback riding and cross-country skiing.

The Kaibab Plateau-North Rim Scenic Byway has been described as the most beautiful 44 miles in the United States. The scenic parkway begins at Jacob Lake and winds through dense forests and alpine meadows to culminate at the North Rim of the Grand Canyon; the road is

closed mid-October through May. For further information contact the Kaibab Plateau Visitor Center, US 89 and SR 67, Jacob Lake, AZ 86022, phone (520) 643-7298; or the Williams and Forest Service Visitor Center, 200 W. Railroad Ave., Williams, AZ 86046; phone (520) 635-4061 or (800) 863-0546. See Recreation Chart and the AAA Southwestern CampBook.

KAYENTA (A-5)
pop. 4,400, elev. 5,641'

Kayenta grew from a trading post that John Wetherill established in 1910. He first called it Oljeto, but eventually changed the name to Kayenta after a deep spring nearby. The area's uranium and coal deposits are important in the town's economy. Scenic US 163, beginning at US 160, passes through Kayenta before running 22 miles north to the Utah border and the entrance to Monument Valley Navajo Tribal Park (see place listing p. 63).

Crawley's Monument Valley Tours offers back-country trips into areas of the park. For further information about the tours and the area contact Crawley's Monument Valley Tours, P.O. Box 187, Kayenta, AZ 86033; phone (520) 697-3463.

KEAMS CANYON (B-5)
pop. 400, elev. 6,184'

Keams Canyon is within the Hopi Reservation that occupies a large tract in the center of the vast Navajo Reservation of northeastern Arizona. The reservation is crossed by SR 264, which runs between US 666, 8 miles north of Gallup, N.M., and US 160 at Tuba City. Noted for weaving, pottery and jewelry, the Hopi also farm and raise livestock. Information about Hopi ceremonies can be obtained from the Hopi Indian Agency in Keams Canyon, (520) 738-2222, or from the Hopi tribal headquarters in Kykotsmovi, (520) 734-2441.

Of particular interest are the villages of Old Oraibi and Walpi on First Mesa. High on a narrow, rocky mesa, Old Oraibi is possibly the oldest of the present Hopi villages; it is thought to be one of the oldest continuously inhabited cities in the country. A trading post and schools are in each village, and the main tribal headquarters is at nearby Kykotsmovi. Walpi occupies the end of a high mesa, where ancestors of the present inhabitants began building about 1680.

No photography, painting, recording or sketching are permitted while on the Hopi Reservation. Primitive campgrounds are at Second Mesa, next to the Hopi Cultural Center; phone (520) 734-2401.

KINGMAN (C-2)
pop. 12,700, elev. 3,334'

The seat of Mohave County, Kingman was founded in 1880 when the railroad was built through the area.

Kingman's popularity is maintained as the main stop on the longest existing stretch of Historic Route 66—the first completely paved transcontinental highway in the country. Linking hundreds of towns and cities between Chicago and Los Angeles, Route 66 formed the main street of towns along its route, thus its nickname "Main Street of America." Today travelers can traverse some 140 miles of historic roadway beginning west of Ashfork, continuing from Seligman through Peach Springs to Kingman and through Oatman and Goldroad to Topock. For a self-guiding driving tour brochure contact the Historic Route 66 Association, P.O. Box 66, Kingman, AZ 86402; phone (520) 753-5001.

At the junction of I-40 and US 93, Kingman is an access point to lakes Mead, Mohave and Havasu. Ghost towns surround this former goldmining community. One such town is Oatman, a business and social center for surrounding mining camps during the early 20th century. With many of its original buildings still standing, Oatman draws both filmmakers and tourists. From Kingman, Oatman is reached by SR 66 (Old Route 66).

Hualapai Mountain Park, 12 miles southeast, is named for the Native Americans who inhabited the mountains until the 1870s. Mountain elevations range from 5,000 to 8,500 feet. A variety of native wildlife lives here, including deer, eagles, elk, foxes, hawks, rabbits and squirrels. *See Recreation Chart.*

Kingman Powerhouse Visitor Center: 120 W. Andy Devine Ave., Kingman, AZ 86401; phone (520) 753-6106. *See ad.*

MOHAVE MUSEUM OF HISTORY AND ARTS is .25 mi. s.e. of US 93 exit off I-40 at 400 W. Beale St. The museum depicts the history of northwestern Arizona with collections of turquoise, re-created Mohave and Hualapai dwellings and local artifacts and artwork. There also is an exhibit about Mohave County ranching history. Andy Devine memorabilia and Lawrence Williams' portraits of presidents and first ladies are featured. Mon.-Fri. 9-5, Sat.-Sun. 1-5; closed

major holidays. Admission $3; under 12, 50c (free when accompanied by adult). Phone (520) 753-3195.

LAKE HAVASU CITY (C-2)
pop. 24,400, elev. 482'

Lake Havasu City takes its name from the lake by which it lies. Formed by the impoundment of Parker Dam in 1938, Lake Havasu is fed by the Colorado River. The 45-mile-long lake has a maximum width of 3 miles and supplies water to Arizona, Los Angeles and intermediate cities. Paved roads cross the lake at Topock on the north end and Parker Dam at the south end.

Originally an Army Air Corps landing strip and rest camp, the land was purchased by industrialist Robert P. McCulloch Sr. in 1963 and turned into a planned recreational and retirement community.

The town captured the world's attention in 1968 when McCulloch bought the London Bridge. Originally built in 1831 by architect John Rennie, the multi-arch bridge resided over the Thames River until 1962, when it began to sink into the river. Dismantled stone by stone, the bridge was brought over from London and reconstructed over a man-made inlet on the Colorado River.

Lake Havasu provides a setting for all types of water sports. The London Bridge is a center for boat tours of Lake Havasu and Topock Gorge. Operators offering a variety of excursions dock their boats under the celebrated span. Colorado River adventures aboard sit-down personal watercraft are offered by SAVE London Bridge Watercraft Tours; phone (520) 453-8883 or (800) 732-3665. Narrated cruises aboard various types of watercraft are offered through Blue Water Charters, (520) 855-7171 or (888) 855-7171. Numerous companies rent canoes, houseboats, personal watercraft, outboards, pontoon boats and sailboats for use on the lake; consult a telephone directory for vendors.

Fishing is excellent, especially for striped and large-mouth bass, bluegill and crappie. Open stretches of water make Lake Havasu an ideal spot for national outboard, sailing, water skiing and personal watercraft championships.

Lake Havasu Tourism Bureau: 314 London Bridge Rd., Lake Havasu City, AZ 86403; phone (520) 453-3444 or (800) 242-8278. *See color ad.*

Shopping areas: The English Village, Island Fashion Mall, London Shopping Center and Shambles Villages all provide shopping opportunities in the London Bridge area.

BILL WILLIAMS RIVER NATIONAL WILDLIFE REFUGE is 25 mi. s. at the delta of the Bill Williams River at its confluence with the Colorado River. A 9-mile corridor along the river encompasses more than 6,000 acres of desert riparian and upland habitat. Named after trapper Bill Williams, who explored the area in the 1800s, the refuge is dedicated to preserving some of the last remaining riparian habitat in the Lower Colorado River Valley.

The refuge is home to beavers, bobcats, foxes, mule deer, bighorn sheep and raccoons as well as some 275 species of birds. Fishing and limited hunting are permitted (in season). Camping is prohibited. For further information contact the Refuge Manager, Bill Williams River National Wildlife Refuge, 60911 SR 95, Parker, AZ 85344. Office open Mon.-Fri. 8-4. Free. Phone (520) 667-4144.

CATTAIL COVE STATE PARK, 15 mi. s. off US 95, is named after the numerous cattails located in the park's cove. Water activities abound in the park; hiking and camping also are available. Food is available. Daily 8-5. Admission $7 per private vehicle. Camping $10-$15 per private vehicle. Phone (520) 855-1223. *See Recreation Chart.*

HAVASU NATIONAL WILDLIFE REFUGE consists of two units. The largest is Topock Gorge, south of the junction of I-40 and the Colorado River; it is accessible only by boat or on foot. Also included is the 18,000 acre Havasu Wilderness Area. The second unit, Topock Marsh, begins north of I-40 on the Arizona side of the Colorado River and continues for 11 miles.

The 37,515-acre refuge is the home of some of America's rarest birds, the Southwestern willow flycatcher and the Yuma clapper rail. Other species sheltered at the refuge include migratory birds, beavers and bighorn sheep. Hunting and fishing (in season) are permitted, as are boating and camping in designated areas. The refuge headquarters is in Needles, Calif. Refuge open daily 8-4. Free. Phone (760) 326-3853.

LAKE HAVASU STATE PARK, n. of London Bridge off US 95 and London Bridge Rd., stretches along the river. Camping and hiking are available. Daily 8 a.m.-10 p.m. Admission $7 per private vehicle. Camping $12 per vehicle. Phone (520) 855-2784. *See Recreation Chart.*

LONDON BRIDGE, off US 95 along the Colorado River, once the famed span on the Thames River in London, now crosses a man-made channel of the Colorado River in the Arizona desert. The channel created an island that contains recreational facilities, including a golf course, marina and campground. Transported block by block from England and reassembled at this location in its original form, the bridge is a striking landmark in this community.

RECREATIONAL ACTIVITIES

Jeep Tours

- **Outback Off-Road Adventures Inc.,** 1350 McCulloch Blvd., P.O. Box 1969, Lake Havasu City, AZ 86405-1969. Tours depart daily at 7:45 and 1. Reservations are required. Phone (520) 680-6151.

Parasailing, Water Skiing

- SAVE **Water Sport Center Inc.,** at the Nautical Inn, 1000 McCulloch Blvd., Lake Havasu City, AZ 86403. Mon.-Fri. 9-5, Sat.-Sun. 8-6. Phone (520) 453-6212.

★LAKE MEAD NATIONAL RECREATION AREA (B-1)

Extending about 140 miles along the Colorado River from Grand Canyon National Park, Ariz.,

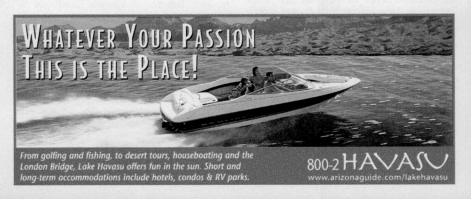

to Bullhead City, Ariz., Lake Mead National Recreation Area embraces 1.5 million acres in western Arizona and southern Nevada. Included are Lake Mohave and Lake Mead as well as an isolated pocket of land north of the lower portion of Grand Canyon National Park.

Three of America's four desert ecosystems—the Mojave, the Great Basin and the Sonoran deserts—meet in Lake Mead National Recreation Area. Therefore the area is home to numerous plants and animals, including bighorn sheep, mule deer, coyotes, foxes and bobcats as well as lizards and snakes. Such threatened and endangered species as the desert tortoise and peregrine falcon also live here.

Fishing is popular in both lakes all year; licenses are required. Largemouth bass, striped bass and catfish are the chief catches in Lake Mead, while rainbow trout and bass are plentiful in Lake Mohave. The recreation area can be enjoyed year-round and is a prime destination for swimming, boating and skiing as well as fishing.

Area open daily 24 hours. Free. For further information contact the Superintendent, Lake Mead National Recreation Area, 601 Nevada Hwy., Boulder City, NV 89005; phone (702) 293-8906. *See the Recreation Chart and the AAA Southwestern CampBook.*

★ **HOOVER DAM**, on SR 93, stands 726 feet high and is one of the highest concrete dams ever constructed. Completed in 1936 for flood control and water storage, it impounds Lake Mead, one of the largest man-made lakes in the United States by volume of water. Although the dam originally was intended to be built in Boulder Canyon, the more structurally sound Black Canyon was used when construction began in 1931.

Visitors can view a 25-minute film presentation at the Hoover Dam Visitor Center; phone (702) 294-3523. A scenic overlook atop the center provides views of the dam, Lake Mead and Black Canyon. Thirty-five-minute guided tours of the dam and power plant are featured. Elevators descend 520 feet through the rock wall of Black Canyon to the bottom of the dam, where visitors can view several hydroelectric generators. The Exhibit Building at the west end of the dam houses a model of the river basin; a recorded lecture can be played.

A 1-hour Hard Hat tour goes behind the scenes where visitors can see the inner workings of the dam. Visitor center daily 8:30-6; closed Thanksgiving and Dec. 25. Admission $8; over 62, $7; ages 6-16, $2. Hard Hat tour $25, under 6 are not permitted. AE, DS, MC, VI. Phone (702) 294-3523 for visitor center, or 294-3524 for Hard Hat tour reservations.

LAKE MEAD is 110 miles long and averages 200 feet in depth (500 ft. at its deepest point). The 550-mile shoreline encircles 157,900 acres of water (*see Lake Mead National Recreation Area*

for fishing information). There are six major recreational centers with marinas and launch facilities. Temple Bar in Arizona is about 80 miles north of Kingman. In Nevada are Boulder Beach, 6 miles northeast of Boulder City; Las Vegas Wash, 13 miles northeast of Boulder City; Callville Bay, 22 miles east of North Las Vegas; and the Overton Beach and Echo Bay areas, both south of Overton.

Films and exhibits about natural and cultural history are offered at the Alan Bible Visitor Center, 4 miles east of Boulder City at US 93 and Lakeshore Road, overlooking Lake Mead. A botanical garden surrounding the visitor center has desert flora. Visitor center daily 8:30-4:30; closed Jan. 1, Thanksgiving and Dec. 25. Free. Phone (702) 293-8990. *See Recreation Chart and the AAA California/Nevada CampBook.*

Information also is available at district ranger stations and the headquarters office, 601 Nevada Hwy., Boulder City, NV 89005; phone (702) 293-8907.

Desert Princess departs from the Lake Mead Cruises Landing on Lakeshore Rd. (SR 166). Excursion cruises on a paddlewheeler include a narration about area history and the construction of Hoover Dam. Breakfast, dinner and dance cruises also are available. Ninety-minute round-trip excursion cruises depart daily at 10, noon, 2 and 4. Fare $16; ages 2-12, $6. Reservations are recommended. AE, DS, MC, VI. Phone (702) 293-6180.

LAKE MOHAVE extends 67 mi. s. from Hoover Dam to Davis Dam. Recreational developments offering launching ramps, trailer sites, refreshment concessions, boat rentals and overnight accommodations are available at Katherine Landing, about 35 miles west of Kingman, Ariz., and at Cottonwood Cove, 14 miles east of Searchlight, Nev. Other accommodations are available a short distance away in Needles, Calif., and Bullhead City, Ariz.

Willow Beach, 28 miles east of Boulder City on US 93, offers a launch ramp and concession facilities. Information regarding recreational facilities is available at all three sites (*see Lake Mead National Recreation Area for fishing information*). Davis Dam is open daily 7:30-3:30 (Mountain Standard Time) for self-guiding tours.

LAKE POWELL—
see Glen Canyon National Recreation Area p. 51.

LAKESIDE—
see Pinetop-Lakeside p. 88.

LITCHFIELD PARK—
see Phoenix p. 83.

MARICOPA (E-3) elev. 1,177'

A prevalence of clear blue skies beckons fans of soaring to Maricopa. This area at the foot of the Sierra Estrella Mountains is noted for its thermal conditions. The Estrella Sailport, (520) 568-2318, is on SR 238W.

Maricopa Community Chamber of Commerce: P.O. Box 711, Maricopa, AZ 85239; phone (520) 568-2844.

CASINOS

- **Harrah's Phoenix Ak-Chin Casino**, 1 mi. s. on SR 347 to 15406 Maricopa Rd. Daily 24 hours. Phone (800) 427-7247.

MESA—*see Phoenix p. 83.*

METEOR CRATER—
see Winslow p. 116.

★ MONTEZUMA CASTLE NATIONAL MONUMENT (C-4)

Montezuma Castle National Monument, off I-17 exit 289 on Montezuma Castle Hwy., contains ruins of an early cliff dwelling. Built in the 12th and 13th centuries, it is among the best preserved dwellings of its type. The foundation is in a vertical cliff 46 feet above the talus slope. The five-story castle, believed to be inhabited by Sinagua Indians, contains 20 rooms and was once accessible only by ladders. Other ruins dot the cliffs and hilltops around Beaver Creek.

As a preservative measure, tours into Montezuma Castle are not allowed, but a self-guiding trail offers good views of the castle and displays a scale model of its interior. The visitor center contains artifacts found in the area as well as exhibits featuring local flora and fauna. Picnicking is permitted in designated areas. Allow 1 hour minimum. Visitor center and monument open daily 8-7, Memorial Day-Labor Day; 8-5, rest of year. Admission $2, under 17 free. Phone (520) 567-3322.

MONTEZUMA WELL, about 11 mi. n.e., is a detached portion of the monument. The limestone sinkhole, 470 feet wide and 55 feet deep, is rimmed by pueblos and cliff dwellings. A source of water to the fields of ancient peoples, some of the ditches dug A.D. 1200-1300 are still visible. Picnic facilities and a self-guiding trail are available. Allow 1 hour minimum. Daily 8-7, June-Aug.; 8-5, rest of year. Free. Phone (520) 567-5276.

★ MONUMENT VALLEY NAVAJO TRIBAL PARK (A-5)

A colorful region covering several thousand square miles, Monument Valley Navajo Tribal Park lies within the Navajo Indian Reservation in Arizona and Utah. The park contains Mystery Valley, where isolated monoliths of red sandstone tower as much as 1,000 feet above the valley floor. It is reached via scenic US 163 from Kayenta, Ariz., and from Gouldings and Mexican Hat, Utah.

The visitor center, 4 miles southeast of US 163, provides information about self-guiding tours. Guided tours from the center are offered daily; camping and picnicking are permitted. Horseback and four-wheel-drive trips through Monument Valley can be arranged through agencies in Kayenta and in Utah at Bluff, Mexican Hat and Monument Valley. Overnight accommodations also are available; reservations are recommended.

Visitors should not photograph the Native Americans, their homes or their possessions without asking permission; a gratuity is usually requested. Other restrictions apply; *see the Fast Facts box.* For more information contact the Navajo Parks and Recreation Department, P.O. Box 360289, Monument Valley, UT 84536.

The park and visitor center are open daily 7-7, May-Sept.; 8-5, rest of year (weather permitting); Thanksgiving 8-noon. Closed Dec. 25. Last admission 30 minutes before closing. Admission $2.50; over 59, $1; under 8 free. Phone (435) 727-3287.

★ NAVAJO NATIONAL MONUMENT (A-4)

Navajo National Monument preserves some of the largest and most intact of Arizona's known cliff dwellings in perhaps the most awe-inspiring area in the Southwest. There are two areas that can be visited by ranger guided tours, each of which contains a remarkable 13th-century Pueblo ruin. The monument lies within the Navajo Indian Reservation. A 9-mile paved road (SR 564) leads from US 160 to the monument headquarters. Most of the other roads on the reservation are dirt surfaced; inquire locally about road conditions before starting. Traveling off paved roads is not recommended.

At an elevation of approximately 7,300 feet, the visitor center at the monument headquarters offers exhibits of ancestral Native American artifacts, a 20-minute videotape tour of the Betatakin ruins, a 25-minute videotape about the prehistoric culture and summer campfire programs. Free year-round camping and picnicking are permitted near the monument headquarters. The 30 campsites are available on a first-come first-served basis and are usually filled by dusk during the summer; vehicles must be no longer than 25 feet in length.

Accommodations are available at Kayenta; reservations are recommended. Gas and grocery services are not available in the park; the nearest services are 9 miles south at the junction of SR 564 and US 160. Visitors should be aware of certain restrictions; *see the Fast Facts box.*

Note: In summer the Navajo Reservation observes daylight-saving time, which is an hour later than outside the reservation.

BETATAKIN AREA, the most accessible area, contains the monument headquarters. Betatakin Ruin is 2.5 miles from headquarters by way of a strenuous trail (5 miles round trip). The ruin can be visited on ranger-guided tours once daily from May through September (weather permitting). Hikers should arrive early in the day to ensure a spot on this popular tour, which is limited to 25 people per day. Sturdy shoes and 2 quarts of water are recommended; the high altitude, heat and steep grade of the trail make good physical condition a requirement.

The cliff dwelling also can be viewed across the canyon from the end of the Sandal Trail year-round via a 1-mile round-trip self-guiding walk. Mon.-Sat. 8-5. For information and schedule updates phone (520) 672-2366.

KEET SEEL AREA is accessible by several means; check with headquarters. The trail is a difficult 17-mile round-trip. The area contains the largest and best preserved of the cliff dwellings in the vicinity, which date from around 1250-1300. To protect these fragile ruins there is a daily limit of 20 people. This trip is not recommended for inexperienced hikers or riders. Primitive campgrounds are available for hikers.

Check with rangers at the visitor center for reservations; they can and should be made within 2 months of the date of the trip and be confirmed 1 week prior. Permits must be picked up by 9 a.m. on the day of the trip.

Trail open Memorial Day-Labor Day. Schedules for tours of the ruins vary. Free. Reservations are required. For reservations, information and schedule updates phone (520) 672-2366, or 672-2367 Mon.-Fri. 8-5.

NAVAJOLAND (A-5) pop. 100,000

Encompassing some 27,000 square miles, Navajoland includes parts of Arizona, Utah and New Mexico. Larger than the state of West Virginia, the sovereign nation is the largest Native American nation in the country.

From the stark monoliths of Monument Valley Navajo Tribal Park *(see place listing p. 63)* and the sheer walls of Canyon de Chelly National Monument *(see place listing p. 44)* to the ancient ruins of Navajo National Monument *(see place listing p. 64)*, Navajoland is home to more than a dozen national monuments. The area also contains the Petrified Forest National Park *(see place listing p. 68)*, 186-mile-long Lake Powell and various tribal parks and historic sites.

Heritage is important to the Navajo, and powwows and dances give the Navajo a chance to wear their traditional attire. Tribal dress includes knee-high moccasins, velvet vests, concho belts and silver and turquoise jewelry for both men and women. Powwows often are performed throughout the Navajo nation and visitors are invited to observe.

The Navajo, or Dineh, consider themselves an extension of Mother Earth and therefore treat nature with great respect. Not only rich in culture, the Navajo live in an area rich in minerals; oil, gas, coal and uranium lie beneath the arid desert. The discovery of oil in the 1920s prompted the Navajo to form their own tribal government to help handle the encroachment of mining companies. Reorganized in 1991, the Navajo government consists of an elected president, vice president and 88 council delegates representing 110 local units of government. Council meetings take place four times a year in Window Rock *(see place listing p. 115);* visitors are welcome.

Tradition also can be seen in the Navajo's arts and crafts. Famous for their distinct style of rugs and blankets, the Navajo also are excellent silversmiths, sandpainters and basketweavers. Visitors to the area can purchase Navajo wares at various shops throughout the area.

The following places in Navajoland are listed separately under their individual names: Fort Defiance, Ganado, Kayenta, Keams Canyon, Page, Second Mesa, Tuba City and Window Rock.

Visitors should be aware of certain restrictions while in Navajoland; *see the Fast Facts box.*

Navajo Tourism Department: P.O. Box 663, Window Rock, AZ 86515; phone (520) 871-6436, ext. 7371.

NOGALES (F-4) pop. 19,500, elev. 3,865'

Nogales (noh-GAH-lehs) is rich in Spanish history; Franciscan missionary Fray Marcos de Niza entered Santa Cruz County as early as 1539.

Mexico's Pacific Highway, a four-lane divided highway, starts in Nogales and continues through Guadalajara, Mexico, with connecting roads to Mexico City. Nogales is a popular port of entry for U.S. travelers as well as for some 75 percent of winter fruits and vegetables shipped throughout the United States and Canada. Retail and wholesale trade with Northern Mexico also is an important industry in the town.

Nogales-Santa Cruz County Chamber of Commerce: 123 W. Kino Park, Nogales, AZ 85621; phone (520) 287-3685.

Self-guiding tours: Walking-tour brochures of downtown Nogales are available from the Pimeria Alta Historical Society.

WINERIES

• **Arizona Vineyards**, 2 mi. e. on SR 82. Daily 10-5; closed Dec. 25. Phone (520) 287-7972.

Nogales, Mexico

Nogales, Mexico, is just across the international border from Nogales, Ariz. U.S. and Canadian visitors must carry proof of citizenship; a valid U.S. or Canadian passport is the most convenient, since it serves as a photo ID and facilitates many transactions such as cashing traveler's checks. The U.S., Canadian and Mexican governments also recognize a birth certificate (must be a certified copy from the government agency that issued it). A driver's license or baptismal certificate are *not* proof of citizenship.

All persons who plan to visit the interior or stay in the border area more than 72 hours also must obtain a *tarjeta de turista* (Mexican government tourist card). Tourist cards can be obtained from any AAA Arizona office. Before driving into Mexico check with the Tucson AAA office for temporary vehicle importation and insurance requirements; phone (520) 885-0694 or 296-7461. Mexican and U.S. Customs offices are open daily 24 hours.

With several good restaurants and an array of shops selling everything from cheap curios to high-quality handicrafts, Nogales is a popular day-trip destination. Since almost all of the tourist-oriented shopping is within easy walking distance of the border, it is easiest to park on the Arizona side, where guarded lots are available, and head into Mexico on foot.

The shops and markets catering to tourists are concentrated near the border along Avenida Obregón. They offer pottery, baskets, leather goods, glassware,

Cactus

An indelible symbol of the Great American Desert, the cactus embodies the evolutionary theory of survival of the fittest. Withering to most other plant life, the desert brings out the best in cactuses. Their brilliantly colored blossoms all but vanquish any image of the desert as a drab and barren place.

A type of succulent, cactuses can live for long periods without water. Their stems act as storage chambers for the precious rainwater absorbed by their shallow roots. The thorny spines that adorn most species are  actually highly modified leaves, trimmed down to prevent transpiration. These spines also shield the plants from wildlife, especially non-native cattle that have all but wiped out smooth-textured varieties.

Sadly, the cactus' needles are no match for the threats posed by encroaching civilization. Research teams at the University of Arizona seek means to control decay caused by disease, worms and pollution. Greatly diminished populations of coyote and other predators have led to an overabundance of desert rodents, which feed on and nest in cactuses, often causing irreparable damage.

Because cactuses have become increasingly popular houseplants, poaching has become a serious problem. State laws now impose heavy fines on those who willfully damage or attempt to remove free-growing specimens. The federal government has set aside large portions of the Sonoran Desert as the Organ Pipe Cactus National Monument *(see place listing p. 65)* and Saguaro National Park *(see place listing p.111).*

furniture, rugs, jewelry and more. Where prices are not fixed, bargaining is acceptable and even expected. The more exclusive establishments carry crafts and items from all over Mexico. When buying at stalls or from street vendors, always check for quality.

★ OAK CREEK CANYON—
see Sedona p. 94.

ORACLE—see Tucson p. 111.

ORAIBI—see Keams Canyon p. 59.

★ ORGAN PIPE CACTUS NATIONAL MONUMENT (E-2)

Of particular interest to desert aficionados, Organ Pipe Cactus National Monument preserves a diverse and relatively undisturbed sample of the Sonoran Desert. The organ pipe cactus thrives within the United States primarily in this 516-square-mile preserve. The spectacular saguaro cactuses, along with the paloverde, ironwood and ocotillo, also contribute to the desert landscape.

The monument contains two graded dirt park roads: the 21-mile Ajo Mountain Drive and the 53-mile Puerto Blanco Drive. Both begin near the visitor center, and conditions are generally good for car travel. The drives are closed occasionally because of rain. Phone in advance for road conditions. No trailers or recreational vehicles over 25 feet are permitted on these park roads.

The visitor center, 17 miles south of the park entrance on scenic SR 85, is open daily 8-5; closed Dec. 25. Exhibits interpret the flora, fauna and cultural history of the monument. A 15-minute introductory slide program is shown every half-hour. Self-guiding interpretive trails are near the visitor center and the campground area. The campground ($8 per night) and back-country primitive camping are available to those with permits, which are distributed at the visitor center.

Admission $4 per private vehicle. For further information contact the Superintendent, Organ Pipe Cactus National Monument, Rte. 1, Box 100, Ajo, AZ 85321; phone (520) 387-6849. See the AAA Southwestern CampBook.

PAGE (A-4) pop. 6,600, elev. 4,281′

Established to provide housing and facilities for workers on the Glen Canyon Dam project, Page was named for John Chatfield Page, the commissioner of reclamation who devoted many years to the development of the upper Colorado River. The town is a center for outfitters who provide trips into the Glen Canyon National Recreation Area (see place listing p. 50).

Scenic flights over Lake Powell and the surrounding Indian country as well as to the Grand Canyon depart from the Page airport. Lake Powell boat trips and Glen Canyon raft trips can be arranged through the chamber of commerce.

Page-Lake Powell Chamber of Commerce: 644 N. Navajo, Suite C, P.O. Box 727, Page, AZ 86040; phone (520) 645-2741 or (888) 261-7243.

GLEN CANYON NATIONAL RECREATION AREA—see place listing p. 50.

JOHN WESLEY POWELL MUSEUM AND VISITOR INFORMATION CENTER, Lake Powell Blvd. and N. Navajo Dr., contains exhibits relating to Native American culture, geology, the Colorado River and John Wesley Powell, the river's first modern scientist-explorer. Videotapes are shown upon request and highlight popular destinations and historical figures of the surrounding area. The museum staff can book Lake Powell, Colorado River and scenic air tours.

Ground excursions are available into nearby slot canyons. Travel into the canyons is by guided tour only, available at the museum. Daily 8-6, May-Sept.; hours vary rest of year. Free. Phone (520) 645-9496.

★ PAINTED DESERT—
see Petrified Forest National Park p. 69.

PALO VERDE—see Phoenix p. 84.

PARKER (C-1) pop. 2,900, elev. 1,642′

Parker, founded in 1908, was named for Eli Parker, the first Native American to fight in the Spanish-American War. The city originally was located south of its current location but was moved to accommodate the Santa Fe Railroad. Parker is a trade center for the surrounding Native American communities. The Parker Dam and Power Plant, 17 mi. n. on SR 95, is considered the world's deepest because 65 percent of its structural height is below the riverbed. Overlooks on top of the dam provide views of Lake Havasu and the Colorado River. Just north of town on SR 95 is La Paz County Park (see Recreation Chart).

Parker Area Chamber of Commerce: 1217 California Ave., Parker, AZ 85344; phone (520) 669-2174.

BUCKSKIN MOUNTAIN STATE PARK & RIVER ISLAND UNIT, 11 mi. n. off SR 95, is the state's "water playground" on the Colorado River. Activities include hiking, swimming, boating and fishing. Food is available. Daily 8 a.m.-10 p.m. Admission $6 per private vehicle. Camping fees $12-$20. Phone (520) 667-3231. See Recreation Chart.

COLORADO RIVER INDIAN TRIBES MUSEUM AND LIBRARY is 2 mi. s. via SR 95 at 2nd and Mohave sts. The museum houses the Beebee Brown Basket Collection, excavations from the restoration of the nearby ghost town of La Paz, and historical and modern material about local tribes. The adjacent library contains books, original manuscripts, records and tapes pertaining to various Native American cultures. Mon.-Fri. 8-5; closed holidays. Donations. Phone (520) 669-9211, ext. 1335.

PATAGONIA (F-5) pop. 900, elev. 4,057'

PATAGONIA LAKE STATE PARK, 7 mi. s.w. on SR 82, then 5 mi. w. following signs, is home to southeastern Arizona's largest lake. Boating, fishing, camping and swimming are available. Bird-watching is a popular activity. Daily 8 a.m.-10 p.m. Admission $5 per private vehicle (up to 4 passengers, $1 for each additional passenger). Camping $10-$15 per private vehicle. Phone (520) 287-6965. *See Recreation Chart.*

PATAGONIA-SONOITA CREEK PRESERVE, w. off SR 82 onto 4th St., then 1.7 mi. s. on Pennsylvania Ave., is home to many species of birds as well as mountain lions, bobcats, deer, javelinas, coyotes, turtles and rattlesnakes. The preserve also protects the cottonwood-willow riparian forest containing some of the largest and oldest Fremont cottonwood trees in the world. A self-guiding nature trail and a visitor center are available. Wed.-Sun. 7:30-4. Guided walks Sat. at 9. Admission $5. Phone (520) 394-2400.

PAULDEN (C-3) elev. 4,407'

RECREATIONAL ACTIVITIES
Horseback Riding
• **Double D Ranch And Wagon Train Co.,** off SR 89N, P.O. Box 334, Paulden, AZ 86334-0334. Phone (520) 636-0418.

PAYSON (D-4) pop. 8,400, elev. 4,887'

Known by such names as Green Valley, Long Valley, Big Valley and Union City, Payson was first settled by prospectors who came to the area seeking wealth. Payson's mines provided little, and cattle and lumber soon became the community's livelihood. With the help of Senator Payson of Chicago, the early residents help establish a post office and named it and the town in his honor.

Surrounded by the lakes and dense woodlands of Tonto National Forest *(see place listing p. 98)* and the nearby Mogollon Rim, Payson has become a convenient getaway for visitors, with Phoenix only 2 hours away.

Rim Country Regional Chamber of Commerce: 100 W. Main St., P.O. Box 1380, Payson, AZ 85547; phone (520) 474-4515 or (800) 672-9766.

PAYSON ZOO, e. on SR 260 to Lion Spring Rd., features more than 40 animals. African lions, baboons, bears, bobcats, coyotes, deer, lemurs, servals and wolves are represented. Allow 1 hour minimum. Fri.-Wed. 10-3 (weather permitting). Admission $4; under 12, $1. Phone (520) 474-5435.

TONTO NATURAL BRIDGE STATE PARK, 13 mi. n.w. off SR 87, is bordered by Tonto National Forest. The

Dust Storms

Dust storms can strike without warning and make driving conditions hazardous. Reddish-brown walls of dust can seriously limit a driver's view. Areas especially prone to storms include I-10 between Phoenix and Tucson and I-8 from Gila Bend to Casa Grande. Dust storm alert signs with changeable messages are posted along I-10 and I-8. During normal driving conditions the signs contain directional information. The message "Dust Storm Alert" appears, however, when dust activity is detected in the area. Storm warnings also are issued

on radio stations KOY (550 AM), KTAR (620 AM) and KFYI (910 AM).

Dust storms usually last only a few minutes, but drivers should follow established procedures to reduce the possibility of accident or injury.

If a dense dust cloud is observed, do not enter the area. Pull off the roadway as far as possible, stop, turn any lights off and set the emergency brake. Make sure your foot does not rest on the brake pedal when you are stopped—other cars will follow your brake lights thinking that you are moving and an accident could ensue. If the car is engulfed on the roadway, do not stop on the pavement, but instead try to pull the car off the roadway as far as possible. If conditions prevent pulling off the roadway, proceed at a slow speed with the lights on, using the center line as a guide. Under no circumstances should a motorist stop on the roadway.

bridge, among the world's largest natural travertine structures, reaches a height of 183 feet; the opening beneath is 150 feet wide and 400 feet long. A historic lodge (not available for overnight stays) is furnished with antiques that were lowered into the canyon using ropes and mules. Tours are available by reservation.

The trail from the top of the bridge into the canyon below is steep and difficult for many persons to negotiate. Pets are not permitted on canyon trails. Daily 8-5, May-Sept.; 11-5, rest of year. Closed Dec. 25. Admission $5 per private vehicle (up to four persons), $1 per pedestrian, children under 12 free with adult. Phone (520) 476-4202. *See Recreation Chart.*

CASINOS

• **Mazatzal Casino**, .5 mi. s. on SR 87 (Beeline Hwy.). Daily 24 hours. Phone (520) 474-6044 or (800) 777-7529.

PEACH SPRINGS (B-2)
pop. 800, elev. 4,788′

Peach Springs is the trading center and headquarters for the Hualapai Indian Reservation, which covers nearly a million acres between the town and the Colorado River. The town also serves as the transportation corridor to the western parts of the Grand Canyon *(see place listing p. 52).* Fishing is allowed on the river and at small ponds on the reservation. Primitive camping also is available.

[SAVE] **GRAND CANYON CAVERNS**, 12 mi. e. on SR 66, is reached by a 21-story elevator descent. The temperature is 56 degrees Fahrenheit throughout the year. Nearly a mile of trails highlights colorful mineral formations; 45-minute guided tours are offered. An abbreviated tour is available for the physically challenged. Daily 8-6, Memorial Day-Labor Day; 9-5, rest of year. Closed Dec. 25. Admission $8.50; ages 4-12, $5.75. AE, DS, MC, VI. Phone (520) 422-3223.

PEARCE (F-5) elev. 4,400′

Pearce at the end of the 19th century was a booming mining town. Following the gold strike by John Pearce in 1894 people swarmed to the area, all but depopulating nearby Tombstone, whose mines were no longer productive. The Commonwealth Mine, Pearce's claim, maintained full operation until 1904, when an impeding water level and a cave-in reduced activities. It was worked sporadically until the late 1930s.

Pearce-Sunsites Chamber of Commerce: 133 Frontage Rd., P.O. Box 308, Pearce, AZ 85625; phone (520) 826-3535.

PEORIA—*see Phoenix p. 84.*

★ PETRIFIED FOREST NATIONAL PARK (C-5)

> Elevations in the park range from 5,300 ft. at the Puerco River to 6,235 ft. at Pilot Rock. Refer to AAA maps for additional elevation information.

The 93,533-acre Petrified Forest National Park contains an abundance of petrified logs. Most of the brilliantly colored trees are prone, and many are in fragments. Early dinosaurs once roamed the area, and numerous fossil bones and fossil plants have been discovered in the park.

About 225 million years ago trees growing in nearby highlands were transported by swollen streams to this wet, swampy lowland. The trees were submerged in water and buried under volcanic ash sediments rich in silica; a replacement process began to take place. Silica replaced the wood until the logs were virtually turned to stone. Iron oxide and other minerals stained the silica to produce rainbow colors.

Later the region was uplifted, and erosion exposed part of the logs; many remain buried to a depth of 300 feet. There are five areas with heavy concentrations of petrified wood in the park: Blue Mesa, Jasper Forest, Crystal Forest, Rainbow Forest (comprising Long Logs and Giant Logs near US 180) and Black Forest. The first four are accessible by the park road. Black Forest can be reached from the parking lot at Kachina Point, down a switchback unimproved trail to the desert floor. The Long Logs area contains the most colorful concentration of petrified wood.

General Information and Activities

The park is open daily 8-5; closed Dec. 25. Hours may be extended May-Sept. Phone to confirm schedule.

The 28-mile drive through the park offers breathtaking views from Pintado Point and Kachina Point. Other scenic overlooks include Nizhoni, Tawa, Tiponi and Whipple points.

Westbound motorists on I-40 should use the northern entrance to avoid backtracking. Visitors can view the Painted Desert *(see attraction listing),* ancient pueblos and petroglyphs, petrified log deposits and the Rainbow Forest Museum *(see attraction listing).* Motorists should exit on US 180 and continue west to Holbrook. Eastbound motorists can use the southern (Rainbow Forest) entrance off US 180, 19 miles from Holbrook, to see the same attractions in reverse order, then exit onto I-40 east. Allow 2 hours minimum.

Within the park it is unlawful to gather plants, sand, rocks or specimens of petrified wood of any size whatsoever; archeological material is likewise protected. Violations are punishable by heavy fines and imprisonment. Curio stores sell a variety of polished specimens collected from privately owned land outside the park.

There are no overnight accommodations in the park; backpack camping is allowed by permit only for hikers staying overnight in the Painted Desert wilderness area. Picnic sites are near the Rainbow Forest Museum and on the Painted Desert rim at Chinde Point. Gas, oil and food services are available adjacent to the Painted Desert Visitor Center. *See Recreation Chart.*

ADMISSION to the park is $10 per private vehicle, $5 per person arriving by other means.

PETS are permitted in the park only if they are leashed, crated or otherwise physically restricted at all times. Pets are excluded entirely from back-country buildings and wilderness areas.

ADDRESS inquiries to the Superintendent, Petrified Forest National Park, P.O. Box 2217, Petrified Forest National Park, AZ 86028; phone (520) 524-6228.

Points of Interest

AGATE BRIDGE is a petrified log that spans a 40-foot-wide ravine; 111 feet of the concrete-supported log are exposed.

NEWSPAPER ROCK bears prehistoric petroglyphs that can be viewed from an overlook. Parking is off a short side road a mile south of the Puerco River.

★ **PAINTED DESERT**, partially contained in the northern part of the park, is an area of badlands that displays a variety of hues. Overlooks with an especially scenic view include Chinde Point, Kachina Point, Pintado Point, Tawa Point and Tiponi Point. The Painted Desert Visitor Center, open during park hours, offers a 20-minute film every 30 minutes that explains how wood is petrified. Free. Phone (520) 524-6228.

PUERCO PUEBLO, s. of the Puerco River, is the remains of an ancient Indian pueblo. It was abandoned more than 6 centuries ago. Petroglyphs can be seen in this area; a summer solstice calendar is interpreted in June.

RAINBOW FOREST MUSEUM, near the s. entrance, contains polished petrified wood, fossil leaves, fossil casts and exhibits telling the story of the early dinosaurs and the petrified forest. Allow 30 minutes minimum. Daily 8-5; hours may be extended May-Sept. Free. Phone (520) 524-6822 or 524-6823.

Phoenix

Bold and sophisticated, vigorous and vital, a medley of Mexican American, Native American and American West cultures, home of the cowboy and the cosmopolitan, cultural and industrial center of the new Southwest—Phoenix generates the spirit of its heritage.

Scientific discoveries and tribal legends indicate that prehistoric Hohokam Indians mastered the Salt River Valley desert by building irrigation ditches, and then mysteriously disappeared about 1450. On the ancient Hohokam site John Smith established a hay camp in 1864 and contracted to supply forage to Camp McDowell, an Army outpost 30 miles away. During this time the name Phoenix was suggested, as a new city could be expected to rise from the remnants of the vanished civilization, just as the mythical phoenix rose from its own ashes.

By 1879 the village was the supply point for the north-central Arizona Territory, with its rich mining districts and hundreds of prospectors. Stagecoaches began to roll in; saloons and gambling palaces sprang up; soldiers, miners and cowboys frequented the town; and outlawry was rampant. The 1800s ended abruptly with two public hangings in an attempt to regain law and order in this raucous, rapidly growing frontier town.

In the 20th century four milestones marked Phoenix's rapid progress. In 1911 the Roosevelt Dam on the Salt River was completed, converting desert into farmland and supplying power for industrial development. In 1926 population growth received its first great impetus when the Southern Pacific Railroad connected Phoenix with the East, enabling the less adventurous to journey west in relative comfort and safety.

The advent of air conditioning catalyzed industrial growth and brought even more people. Finally water supplied by the Central Arizona Project's system of aqueducts spurred the tremendous growth that has made Phoenix the country's ninth largest city.

Phoenix is the thriving capital of Arizona. Countless suburbs, sprawling shopping centers and rambling ranch-style homes retain a Western look, while high-rise office buildings stand as gleaming symbols of Eastern influence. Spanish Colonial and Native American pueblo architecture add color and variety.

The city displays enthusiasm and pride in the many athletic and cultural activities it supports. The arts are pursued at excellent theaters, numerous museums and lectures at colleges and universities. The Civic Plaza downtown houses a state-of-the-art convention center and a symphony hall. Greyhound races, horse races, golf tournaments and rodeos add to the city's entertainment scene.

Phoenix is an agricultural, industrial and service center. Cotton as well as dates, olives, citrus and other subtropical fruits and vegetables are grown in the area. The dry climate and natural beauty have attracted companies in the fields of electronics, high-tech research and development, communications and aerospace; tourism also is big business, with an increasing number of visitors enjoying the city's quality of life.

Approaches

By Car

Major highways make Phoenix readily accessible from all directions. The main route from Flagstaff and other points north is I-17, while the main route from the south and southeast is I-10. US 60, coming from the east, joins I-10 just north of Baseline Road.

In Phoenix I-10 intersects I-17 at 20th Street and leads west to Los Angeles. West of Phoenix, SR 85 intersects with I-10 and continues south to Gila Bend; I-8 can then be followed to Yuma and San Diego.

Getting Around

Street System

The streets in Phoenix form an orderly grid. Numbered streets run north and south, intersected by named streets going east and west. The axis is formed by Washington Street, which divides the city north and south, and Central Avenue, which determines the east and west sections. All avenues run west of Central; all streets, east.

Unless otherwise posted the speed limit on most streets is 25 mph. A right turn on red after a complete stop is legal unless otherwise posted. During rush hours the center turn lanes of 7th Avenue and 7th Street are reverse traffic flow lanes: morning rush hour one way into the city and evening rush hour one way out of the city. Try to avoid rush hours, 7-9 a.m. and 4-6 p.m.

Parking

Parking is regulated by meters. During business hours and in the downtown area certain one-way streets have restricted parking hours. Rates at public lots start at $1.50 per hour.

What To See

ARIZONA HALL OF FAME, 1101 W. Washington St., is in the former Carnegie Public Library building, completed in 1908. The museum honors those who have made significant contributions to Arizona. Changing exhibits focus on the famous, the not yet famous and the perhaps infamous. Among the highlights are exhibits showcasing the oil paintings of Lon Megargee, whose work has hung in the state capitol and "My Name is Arizona." Allow 30 minutes minimum. Mon.-Fri. 8-5; closed holidays. Free. Phone (602) 255-2110.

(continued on page 76)

The Informed Traveler

City Population: 983,400

Elevation: 1,092 ft.

SALES TAX: Arizona's statewide sales tax is 5 percent; an additional 1.8 percent is added in Maricopa County. There is a hotel/motel tax of 10.35 percent. Rental cars incur a 13.8 percent tax, plus a 10 percent concession fee.

WHOM TO CALL

Emergency: 911

Police (non-emergency): (602) 262-6151

Time and Weather: (602) 265-5550

Hospitals: John C. Lincoln-North Mountain, (602) 943-2381; Maricopa Medical Center, (602) 344-5011; Maryvale Samaritan Medical Center, (623) 848-5000; Phoenix Memorial, (602) 258-5111; Phoenix Regional Medical Center, (602) 650-7600; St. Joseph's, (602) 406-3000.

WHERE TO LOOK

Newspapers

The city's daily newspaper is the *Arizona Republic,* published in the morning.

Radio and TV

Phoenix radio station KTAR (620 AM) is an all-news/weather station; KJZZ (91.5 FM) is a member of National Public Radio.

The major TV channels are 5 (CBS), 8 (PBS), 10 (FOX), 12 (NBC) and 15 (ABC). For a complete list of radio and television programs, consult the daily newspapers.

Visitor Information

Distributing the helpful *Visitors Guide* is the Phoenix & Valley of the Sun Convention and Visitors Bureau with its main office at One Arizona Center, 400 E. Van Buren #600, Phoenix, AZ 85004; a second office is in Biltmore Fashion Park, 24th Street and Camelback Road; phone (602) 254-6500, or 252-5588 for the Automated Visitors Information Line.

TRANSPORTATION

Air Travel

Sky Harbor International Airport, 4 miles southeast of downtown, is served by major airlines. SuperShuttle, is a 24-hour shared-ride service. Phone (602) 244-9000 in metro Phoenix, or (800) 331-3565 outside Arizona. ExecuCar also is available from SuperShuttle; phone (602) 232-4630 or (888) 473-9227.

Airport limousine service, independent of the hotels, costs $60-$150. Some companies that serve the airport and certain downtown hotels are Arizona Limousines, (602) 267-7097 or (800) 678-0033; Carey Limousine, (602) 996-1955; and Desert Rose Limousine Service, (623) 780-0159 or (800) 716-8660.

Rental Cars

Several rental car companies serve the Phoenix metropolitan area. Located at the airport, Hertz, (602) 267-8822 or (800) 654-3080, offers discounts to AAA members. Check the telephone directory for additional listings.

Buses

Greyhound Lines Inc. has terminals at 2115 Buckeye Rd., (602) 389-4200, and 2647 W. Glendale Ave., (602) 246-9855.

Taxis

Taxi companies serving the greater Phoenix area are Checker Cab, (602) 257-1818; Citywide Cab, (602) 277-7100; Statewide Cab, (480) 994-1616; and Yellow Cab, (602) 252-5071.

Public Transport

Phoenix Transit System buses serve Glendale, Mesa, Phoenix, Scottsdale and Tempe. Most routes operate 6 a.m.-6:30 p.m. The Bus Book, which outlines available routes, can be obtained at Phoenix metropolitan libraries.

Destination Phoenix

*B*asking in sunshine more than 300 days a year, sprawling Phoenix is centered within the aptly named Valley of the Sun.

*A*lthough renowned for its warm, dry climate, Arizona's capital city offers much more than great weather. Phoenix, one of the ten largest urban areas in America, abounds with museums, art galleries and theaters.

Encanto Park.
A paddleboat jaunt around the lagoon is just one of many diversions offered at Encanto Park, downtown Phoenix's lush oasis. (See listing page 76)

Phoenix Zoo.
Children see the world from a new perspective as they ride atop a camel, one of the zoo's many exotic denizens. (See listing page 77)

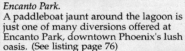

Arizona State Capitol, Phoenix.
Completed in 1900, the State Capitol now houses historical displays, including one about the USS *Arizona*, sunk by the Japanese in Pearl Harbor. (See listing page 76)

Rosson House, Phoenix.
Built by the city's mayor in 1895, this Victorian mansion is the centerpiece of Heritage Square, a collection of restored 19th-century buildings. (See listing page 77)

See Vicinity map page 74

See Downtown map page 75

Cave Creek
Carefree
Phoenix
Fountain Hills
Surprise
Youngstown
Sun City
Peoria
Glendale
Litchfield Park
Goodyear
Tolleson
Scottsdale
Mesa
Apache Junction
Palo Verde
Tempe
Chandler

*P*laces included in this AAA Destination City:

Apache Junction 81	Mesa 83
Carefree 82	Palo Verde 84
Cave Creek 82	Peoria 84
Fountain Hills 82	Scottsdale 85
Glendale 83	Sun City/Sun City
Goodyear 83	West 86
Litchfield Park 83	Tempe 86

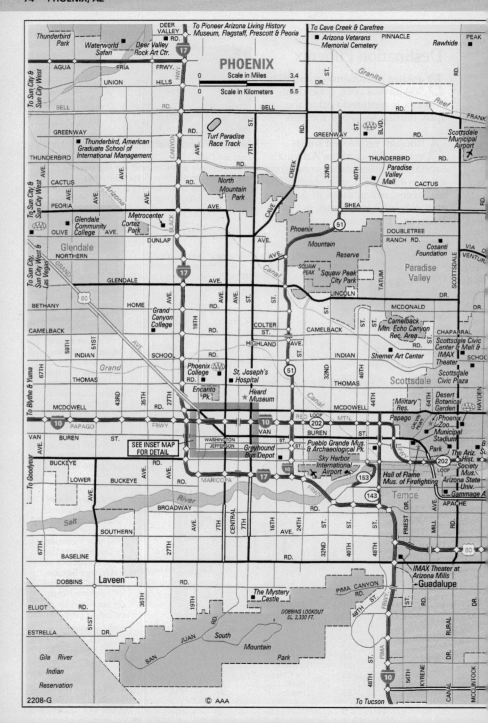

PHOENIX

Scale in Miles 0 — 3.4

Scale in Kilometers 0 — 5.5

To Pioneer Arizona Living History Museum, Flagstaff, Prescott & Peoria

To Cave Creek & Carefree

Thunderbird Park

Waterworld Safari

Deer Valley Rock Art Ctr.

Arizona Veterans Memorial Cemetery

PINNACLE PEAK

Rawhide

To Sun City & Sun City West

AGUA FRIA UNION HILLS

DEER VALLEY

Granite Reef

FRANK

BELL

GREENWAY

Thunderbird, American Graduate School of International Management

Turf Paradise Race Track

GREENWAY

Scottsdale Municipal Airport

THUNDERBIRD

CACTUS

PEORIA

North Mountain Park

SHEA

Paradise Valley Mall

CACTUS

OLIVE

Glendale Community College

Metrocenter Cortez Park

Phoenix Mountain Reserve

DOUBLETREE

Cosanti Foundation

VIA DE VENTURA

DUNLAP

Glendale NORTHERN

GLENDALE

SQUAW PEAK

Squaw Peak City Park

LINCOLN

RANCH RD.

Paradise Valley

BETHANY

HOME

Grand Canyon College

MCDONALD

CAMELBACK

Camelback Mtn. Echo Canyon Rec. Area

CHAPARRAL

INDIAN

SCHOOL

COLTER ST.

HIGHLAND

CAMELBACK

INDIAN

Shemer Art Center

Scottsdale Civic Center & Mall & IMAX Theater

Grand

THOMAS

Phoenix College

St. Joseph's Hospital

Encanto Pk.

Heard Museum

THOMAS

Scottsdale

Scottsdale Civic Plaza

MCDOWELL

PAPAGO

VAN BUREN

MCDOWELL

Military Res.

Papago Park

Desert Botanical Garden

Phoenix Zoo

Phoenix Municipal Stadium

The Ariz. Hist. Society Mus.

SEE INSET MAP FOR DETAIL

WASHINGTON JEFFERSON

Greyhound Bus Depot

Pueblo Grande Mus. & Archaeological Pk.

Sky Harbor International Airport

Hall of Flame Mus. of Firefighting

Arizona State Univ.

Gammage A

BUCKEYE

LOWER BUCKEYE

MARICOPA

River

BROADWAY

Tempe

APACHE

Salt

SOUTHERN

BASELINE

IMAX Theater at Arizona Mills Guadalupe

DOBBINS

Laveen

The Mystery Castle

PIMA CANYON

ELLIOT

ESTRELLA

DOBBINS LOOKOUT EL 2,330 FT.

SAN JUAN

South Mountain Park

Gila River Indian Reservation

To Tucson

2208-G

© AAA

To Sun City & Sun City West

To Sun City & Sun City West & Las Vegas

To Blythe & Yuma

To Goodyear

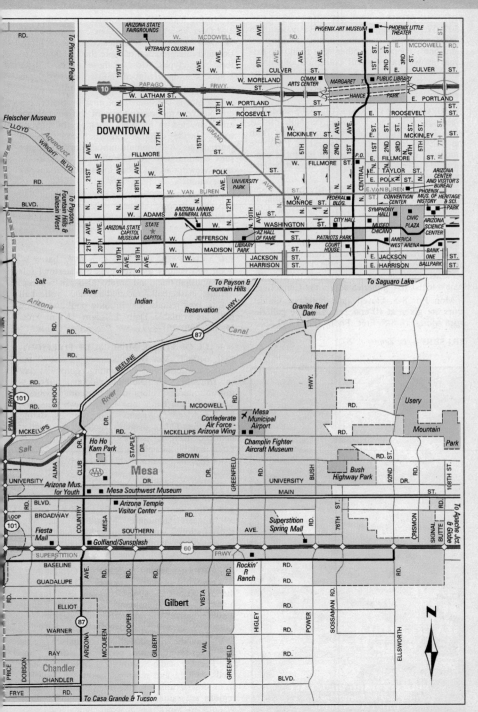

ARIZONA MINING AND MINERAL MUSEUM, 1502 W. Washington St., displays more than 3,000 specimens, including industrial minerals, gemstones, copper and other ores found in Arizona, as well as a small collection of mining equipment. Mon.-Fri. 8-5, Sat. 11-4; closed state holidays. Free. Phone (602) 255-3791 for the Department of Mines and Mineral Resources.

★**ARIZONA STATE CAPITOL MUSEUM,** W. Washington St. and 17th Ave., is built of tuff stone from Kirkland Junction and granite from the Salt River Mountains. Opened in 1900, the four-story building served as the territorial capitol until statehood came in 1912 when it became the state capitol.

The restored wings exhibit artifacts and documents of early Arizona; political memorabilia, including the restored offices of the governor, mine inspector and secretary of state; the restored House and Senate chambers; an exhibit about the USS *Arizona;* and a wax figure of the first governor of Arizona, George Hunt. Behind the building is a newer structure built in 1974 that now contains the state executive branch offices. The state's legislative galleries adjoin the Capitol.

Mon.-Fri. 8-5; closed state holidays. Guided tours are given at 10 and 2. Legislative galleries open Mon.-Fri. 8-5. Free. Phone (602) 542-4675.

BIG SURF—see Tempe p. 87.

SAVE **DEER VALLEY ROCK ART CENTER,** I-17 exit Deer Valley Road W., then 2 mi. w. to 3711 W. Deer Valley Rd., is dedicated to the preservation and interpretation of more than 1,500 prehistoric petroglyphs. Most of these are on hillside boulders at the Hedgpeth Hills; the petroglyphs can be viewed from the base of the hills.

The site is considered spiritual by Southwestern Native Americans; some of the petroglyphs are connected to religious teachings of existing tribes. Inside exhibits explain the history of petroglyphs. A 15-minute introductory videotape runs continuously. A .25-mile trail leads to the main viewing area. Guided tours are available by reservation.

Allow 1 hour, 30 minutes minimum. Tues.-Sat. 9-5, Sun. noon-5. Hours may vary mid-May through Sept. 1; phone ahead. Admission $4; senior citizens and students with ID $2; ages 6-12, $1. Phone (623) 582-8007.

ENCANTO PARK, 2605 N. 15th Ave., has a lagoon and islands that serve as a waterfowl refuge; unusual trees and shrubs also can be seen. Tennis, basketball, racquetball and volleyball courts, boat rentals, a swimming pool and nature trails are available. Daily 5:30 a.m.-11 p.m. Free. Phone (602) 261-8991. *See Recreation Chart.*

★**HALL OF FLAME MUSEUM OF FIREFIGHTING,** 6101 E. Van Buren St., houses one of the largest collections of firefighting equipment dating from 1725. A 10-minute videotape presentation introduces visitors to the museum's exhibits, which include hand- and horse-drawn pumpers, hook-and-ladder wagons and vehicles dating 1800-1969. Other displays include fire marks, helmets, badges, patches, an interactive fire safety exhibit and play area for children, and artwork depicting major events in the history of fire service.

The National Firefighting Hall of Heroes recognizes firefighters who died in the line of duty and were decorated for bravery. Allow 2 hours, 30 minutes minimum. Mon.-Sat. 9-5, Sun. noon-4; closed Jan. 1, Thanksgiving and Dec. 25. Admission $5; over 62, $4; ages 6-17, $3; ages 3-5, $1.50. MC, VI. Phone (602) 275-3473.

SAVE ★**HEARD MUSEUM,** 2301 N. Central Ave., is a museum of native cultures and art. Among the exhibits in its 10 galleries are ethnological, historical and contemporary materials of Southwestern Native Americans; Native American basketry, jewelry and pottery; and kachina dolls.

Visitors are greeted with sounds and images as they enter the museum's permanent exhibit "Native Peoples of the Southwest." The architecture, foods, culture and religious beliefs of 23 tribes from desert, uplands and the Colorado Plateau regions are examined. Interactive exhibits allow visitors to work on a bead loom and walk through a pueblo. Changing exhibits and audio-visual presentations also are featured. Guided tours are offered daily. Food is available.

Allow 1 hour minimum. Daily 9:30-5; closed holidays. Admission $7; over 65, $6; ages 4-12, $3; Native Americans free. AE, DS, MC, VI. Phone (602) 252-8840.

HERITAGE AND SCIENCE PARK is on Monroe St. between 6th and 7th sts. The park's main sites include Heritage Square, comprised of eight structures from the late 19th century that were part of the original site of Phoenix. The restored buildings contain a variety of exhibits, a museum and restaurants. Except for the Rosson, Silva and Stevens houses, the buildings are open on an irregular basis. Other sites within this historic area are the Arizona Science Center and the Phoenix Museum of History *(see attraction listings)*. Also in the square the modern Lath House Pavilion serves as a community meeting area, botanical garden and festival site. Phone (602) 262-5071 for hours.

Arizona Doll and Toy Museum, in the Stevens House at 602 E. Adams, exhibits antique dolls and toys from around the world. One exhibit is devoted to a late 19th-century schoolroom, featuring the dolls as students. Allow 30 minutes minimum. Tues.-Sat. 10-4, Sun. noon-4, Sept.-July. Admission $2.50, children $1. Phone (602) 253-9337.

SAVE **Arizona Science Center,** 600 E. Washington St., offers some 350 changing interactive exhibits for all ages. Hands-on displays allow visitors to explore aerospace, geology, computers, weather, biology, psychology and physics in a fun environment. A giant screen theater and planetarium also are featured. Daily 10-5; closed Thanksgiving and Dec. 25. Admission $8; over 64 and under 13, $6. Planetarium and theater shows are additional. MC, VI. Phone (602) 716-2000.

SAVE **Phoenix Museum of History** is at 105 N. 5th St. Interactive exhibits include telegraphy, wagon loading for a cross-country trek and design of a Victorian mansion. Visitors can discover how time and place have influenced the development of Phoenix from a dusty desert town to a modern metropolis. Allow 1 hour, 30 minutes minimum. Mon.-Sat. 10-5, Sun. noon-5; closed Jan. 1, Thanksgiving and Dec. 25. Admission $5; senior citizens and students with ID $3.50; ages 6-12, $2.50. MC, VI. Phone (602) 253-2734.

SAVE **Rosson House,** 6th and Monroe sts. at 139 N. 6th St., was built in 1895 for Dr. Roland Lee Rosson, mayor of Phoenix 1895-96. The restored Victorian mansion, constructed in 6 months at a cost of $7,525, features lathe-worked posts on the veranda, pressed-tin ceilings, parquet floors, an elaborately carved staircase and period furnishings. Various events are presented throughout the year.

Guided tours are given every half-hour Wed.-Sat. 10-3:30, Sun. noon-3:30, day after Labor Day-July 31; otherwise varies. Closed major holidays. Admission $3; over 62, $2; ages 6-13, $1. Phone (602) 262-5071.

MUSEO CHICANO (CHICANO MUSEUM), 147 E. Adams St., displays various artworks dedicated to the Chicano heritage. Changing exhibits, seminars and special events also are offered. Tues.-Sat. 10-4. Admission $2, senior citizens and students with ID $1. AE, CB, DS, MC, VI. Phone (602) 257-5536.

SAVE **THE MYSTERY CASTLE,** near South Mountain Park, is s. on Central Ave. then w. to 800 E. Mineral Rd. Built 1930-45 by Boyce Luther Gulley as his dream castle for his daughter, the house is constructed of native stone and a conglomeration of scavenged materials such as recycled bottles and old bricks. The 8,000-square-foot home is furnished with Native American artifacts and antiques.

Gulley's daughter Mary Lou displays her works and other arts and crafts by Southwestern artists. Allow 30 minutes minimum. Thurs.-Sun. 11-4, Oct.-June. Admission $5; senior citizens $4; ages 6-15, $2. Phone (602) 268-1581.

NORTH MOUNTAIN PARK, 9 mi. n. at 10600 N. 7th St., accesses more than 7,000 acres of the Phoenix Mountain Preserve. Nature trails traverse the park. Guided trail rides are available nearby at the Pointe at Tapatio Cliffs, 11111 N. 7th St.; for time and rate schedules phone (800) 723-3538. Park open daily 5:30 a.m.-11 p.m. Free. Phone (602) 262-7901.

OUT OF AFRICA WILDLIFE PARK— *see Fountain Hills p. 82.*

PAPAGO PARK, jct. Galvin Pkwy. and Van Buren St., covers 1,200 acres and features fishing lagoons, bicycle paths, nature trails, picnic areas and a golf course. Daily 6 a.m.-11 p.m. Free. Phone (602) 256-3220.

SAVE ★ **Desert Botanical Garden,** 1201 N. Galvin Pkwy., covers more than 145 acres in Papago Park. The garden is devoted exclusively to arid land plants of the world. The paved Desert Discovery Trail leads visitors through the garden; other walkways include the Plants and People of the Sonoran Desert Trail, the Sonoran Desert Nature Trail and the Center for Desert Living Trail. The majority of the garden's plants are succulents, such as cactuses, aloes and century plants. The height of the wildflower blooming season is March through May.

Summer evening programs are offered May through August; call for event schedule. Allow 2 hours minimum. Daily 7 a.m.-8 p.m., May-Sept.; 8-8, rest of year. Admission $7.50; senior citizens $6.50; ages 5-12, $1.50. AE, DS, MC, VI. Phone (480) 941-1225.

Phoenix Zoo, off Galvin Pkwy. in Papago Park, exhibits more than 1,300 mammals, birds and reptiles on 125 acres. Of special note are the zoo's four main trails: the Arizona Trail, featuring plants and animals of the Southwest; the Africa Trail, home to meerkats, lions, a warthog and dozens of other species; the Discovery Trail, presenting small animals from around the world and a barnyard petting area where children can groom goats and sheep; and the Tropics Trail, home to creatures of the rain forests as well as the Forest of Uco, habitat of the spectacled bear.

Harmony Farm provides insight into farm life through interactive exhibits. "Feel the Difference" allows visually-impaired visitors the chance to explore the differences between various animals with sculptures, artifacts and live animals. Other features include Baboon Kingdom, the Tropical Flights Rain Forest and a 30-minute narrated Safari Train. Food and picnic facilities are available.

Allow 2 hours minimum. Daily 7-4, May 1-Labor Day; 9-5, rest of year. Closed Dec. 25. Admission $8.50; over 60, $7.50; ages 3-12, $4.25. Safari Train tours $2. AE, DS, MC, VI. Phone (602) 273-1341.

PHOENIX ART MUSEUM, 1625 N. Central Ave., features a collection of American, European, Asian, Latin American, Western American and Contemporary art, as well as Fashion Design. The museum presents international exhibitions by renowned artists, and also contains an interactive Artworks Gallery for children and the Thorne Miniature Rooms of Historic Interiors. Guided tours are offered daily. Food is available.

Allow 1 hour minimum. Tues.-Sun. 10-5 (also Thurs.-Fri. 5-9); closed major holidays. Admission $7; senior citizens and students with ID $5; ages 6-18, $2; free to all Thurs. Phone (602) 257-1222.

[SAVE] **PIONEER ARIZONA LIVING HISTORY MUSEUM** is off I-17 exit 225 (Pioneer Rd.). More than 20 original and reconstructed buildings, spread over a wide area, replicate the Southwest as it was in the 1880s. Costumed living-history interpreters re-enact life in territorial Arizona and are available for questions. Melodramas and other theater performances are staged in the Opera House daily, and themed special events change monthly.

Allow 2 hours minimum. Wed.-Sun. 9-5, Oct.-Aug.; closed Dec. 25. Admission $5.75; over 60 and students with ID $5.25; ages 6-12, $4. MC, VI. Phone (623) 465-1052.

[SAVE] **PUEBLO GRANDE MUSEUM AND ARCHAEOLOGICAL PARK,** 4619 E. Washington St., contains a prehistoric Hohokam ruin that includes a platform mound, ball court and irrigation canals. Displays center on archeology and the life of the Hohokam. Changing exhibits and tours also are available. Allow 1 hour minimum. Mon.-Sat. 9-4:45, Sun. 1-4:45; closed Memorial Day, July 4, Labor Day, Thanksgiving and Dec.

25. Admission $2; senior citizens $1.50; ages 6-17, $1; free to all Sun. Phone (602) 495-0900 or 495-0901.

SHEMER ART CENTER, 5005 E. Camelback Rd., is in the first house built in the Arcadia section of Phoenix; the house was completed in the early 1920s. The restored Santa Fe Mission-style building with adobe walls contains changing exhibits of crafts and fine art. A highlight is a miniature doll house. An orchard and gardens are at the rear of the building. Mon.-Fri. 10-5 (also Tues. 5-9), Sat. 9-1; closed major holidays. Donations. Phone (602) 262-4727.

SOUTH MOUNTAIN PARK, 8 mi. s. on S. Central Ave., contains 16,500 acres of peaks, canyons and strange rock formations as well as trees, shrubs and cactuses native to Arizona. There is a drive to the crest of South Mountain. The Environmental Education Center just inside the park entrance features displays about the park and offers visitor information. Dobbins Lookout affords an excellent view; phone ahead for hours, as road closing times vary. A rock on Pima Canyon Road bears a Spanish inscription that reads: "Marcos de Niza; where he passed from Mexico to Aycos (Acoma) in the Year of Our Lord 1539." Daily 5 a.m.-10:30 p.m. Environmental Education Center daily 9-5. Free. Phone (602) 495-0222. *See Recreation Chart.*

WATERWORLD SAFARI, 4243 W. Pinnacle Peak Rd., features 20 acres of water slides and wave pools, including the Endless River Ride. Changing rooms and showers are on the premises; lockers and tubes can be rented. Food is available. Mon.-Thurs. 10-8, Sun. 11-7, Memorial Day-Labor Day. Admission $14.95; ages 4-11, $12.50. AE, MC, VI. Phone (623) 581-8446.

What To Do

Sightseeing

Four-wheel-drive and Van Tours

A tour is the best way to get an overall view of the city, and a variety are available. Several companies offer four-wheel-drive or van tours of the desert, including: Arizona Desert Mountain Jeep Tours, (480) 860-1777; Big Red Jeep Tours, (602) 263-5337; Grand Canyon Tours, (602) 971-1381 or (800) 513-1381; and Wayward Wind Tours Inc., (602) 867-8162 or (800) 804-0480.

Plane Tours

Sunrise Airlines provides air transportation to the Grand Canyon, ground tours and helicopter tours. Arrangements for flights can be made at the Scottsdale Municipal Airport; phone (480) 991-8252.

Sports and Recreation

Phoenix's mild winters make it an all-year sports paradise. The Fiesta Bowl **football** classic at the Arizona State University stadium is a January highlight. For spectators the winter months also mean **horse racing** at Turf Paradise from October through early May; phone (602) 942-1101. **Dog racing** at Phoenix Greyhound Park takes place daily all year; phone (602) 273-7181.

Note: Policies vary concerning admittance of children to pari-mutuel betting facilities. Phone for information.

In spring **baseball** arrives as the Oakland Athletics begin their training at Phoenix Municipal Stadium, (602) 392-0217. Other teams with spring training sites in the Phoenix area include the Anaheim Angels at Tempe Diablo Stadium in Tempe, (480) 350-5205; Chicago Cubs at Ho Ho Kam Park in Mesa, (480) 964-4467; the Milwaukee Brewers at Maryvale Sports Complex in Phoenix, (623) 245-5500; the San Diego Padres at Peoria Sports Complex in Peoria, (623) 878-4337; the San Francisco Giants at Scottsdale Stadium in Scottsdale, (480) 990-7972; and the Seattle Mariners at Peoria Sports Complex in Peoria, (623) 412-9000. The Arizona Diamondbacks, one of Major League Baseball's newest teams, play ball at the domed Bank One Ballpark in downtown Phoenix; phone (602) 514-8400.

The America West Arena is the site of many of Phoenix's sporting events. It is the home court of the NBA Phoenix Suns **basketball** team October through March; phone (602) 379-7867. The WNBA's Phoenix Mercury take over the arena's court May through August; phone (602) 252-9622. April through August the arena also houses the Arizona Rattlers, Phoenix's professional **arena football** team, (602) 514-8383. September through April America West Arena is the home of the Phoenix Coyotes, the city's National **Hockey** League team; phone (602) 379-7800.

Professional **football** is played in Tempe, where the NFL Arizona Cardinals take the field at Arizona State University's Sun Devil Stadium; phone (602) 379-0101. The Arizona Veteran's Memorial Coliseum is home ice to the Phoenix Mustangs of the West Coast **Hockey** League. The hockey season runs from October to April; phone (602) 340-0001.

National Hot Rod Association **drag racing** as well as **dragboat racing** are at Firebird Raceway, about 8 miles south of Phoenix at Maricopa Road and I-10; phone (602) 268-0200. Indy cars as well as NASCAR **stock cars** race at Phoenix International Raceway, S. 115th Avenue and Baseline Road; phone (602) 252-3833.

Licensed drivers can experience race car driving at Bob Bondurant School of High Performance Driving, (520) 796-1111, I-10 and Maricopa Road.

A round of **golf** in a panorama of mountain peaks and blue skies entices not only Arizona residents but visitors too. Golfing is a year-round activity in Arizona. There are more than 200 golf courses in the state, both public and private, ap-

pealing to all levels of proficiency—Phoenix has nearly 120. Among the courses in Phoenix are Club West, (480) 460-4400, 16400 S. 14th Ave.; Encanto, (602) 253-3963, at 2745 N. 15th Ave.; The Foothills, (480) 460-4653, at 2201 E. Clubhouse Dr.; Maryvale, (623) 846-4022, at 5902 W. Indian School Rd.; Papago, (602) 275-8428, in Papago Park at 5595 E. Moreland St.; Lookout Mountain, (602) 866-6356, at 11111 N. 7th St.; Phantom Horse, (602) 431-6480, at 7777 S. Pointe Pkwy. W.; and Stonecreek, (602) 953-9110, at 4435 E. Paradise Village Pkwy. S.

Golf courses in nearby Mesa include: Dobson Ranch, (602) 644-2291, at 2155 S. Dobson Rd.; Red Mountain Ranch, (480) 985-0285, at 6425 E. Teton St.; and Superstition Springs, (602) 985-5555, at 6542 E. Baseline Rd. Courses in Scottsdale include: Marriott's Camelback, (480) 596-7050, at 7847 N. Mockingbird Ln.; Marriott's Mountain Shadows Resort, (480) 948-7111, at 5641 E. Lincoln Dr.; McCormick Ranch, (480) 948-0260, at 7505 E. McCormick Pkwy.; Scottsdale Country Club, (480) 948-6000, at 7702 E. Shea Blvd.; TPC Scottsdale, (480) 585-3600, at 17020 N. Hayden Rd.; and Troon North, (480) 585-5300, at 10320 E. Dynamite Blvd.

Other area courses include: Gold Canyon, (480) 982-9449, at 6100 S. Kings Ranch Rd. in Apache Junction; Ocotillo, (480) 917-6660, at 3751 S. Clubhouse Dr. in Chandler; The Legend at Arrowhead, (623) 561-0953, at 21027 N. 67th Ave. in Glendale; The Wigwam Resort, (602) 272-4653, at 451 N. Litchfield Rd. in Litchfield Park; Hillcrest, (623) 584-1500, at 20002 Star Ridge Dr. in Sun City West; Karsten, (480) 921-8070, at 1125 E. Rio Salado Pkwy. in Tempe; and Ken McDonald, (480) 350-5250, at 800 E. Divot Dr. in Tempe.

Tennis courts open to the public are plentiful at several high schools and park areas, including Granada Park, 6505 N. 20th St., and Encanto Park, 15th Avenue and Encanto Drive. The Phoenix Tennis Center, (602) 249-3712, at 6330 N. 21st Ave., has 22 lighted courts and reasonable rates; reservations are accepted.

The valley's beautiful desert country lends itself to **horseback riding**. The Ponderosa and South Mountain Stables, (602) 268-1261, at 10215 S. Central Ave., offers trail rides. Weekend or longer excursions on horseback are available throughout Arizona through Don Donnelly Horseback Vacations and Stables (*see Apache Junction p. 81*).

Trails for **hiking** and **bicycling** are plentiful. A favorite hike is the 1-mile scenic trek to the summit of Squaw Peak. The Phoenix Parks and Recreation Department, (602) 262-6861, operates a number of parks; some have municipal **swimming** pools. Saguaro Lake and Canyon Lake offer **water skiing, boating** and **fishing**. The Salt River is popular with **tubing** enthusiasts. Salt River Tubing & Recreation (*see Mesa p. 84*),

(480) 984-3305, rents tubes and also provides shuttle-bus service along the Salt River.

For the **shooting** enthusiast, the Ben Avery Shooting Range, (623) 582-8313, 25 miles north of Phoenix off I-17 exit 223, offers pistol, rifle and archery ranges and trap and skeet fields.

The suburb of Tempe boasts inland **surfing** at Big Surf *(see Tempe p. 87)*, (480) 947-7873, **roller skating** at Surfside Skateland, (480) 968-9600, and **ice skating** at the Oceanside Ice Arena, (480) 947-2470, at 1520 N. McClintock Dr. Phoenix also offers ice skating at The Ice Chalet, (602) 267-0591, at 3853 E. Thomas Rd.

Hot air balloon rides over the metropolitan area and the Sonora Desert are available through several companies. Balloon rides average 1 hour and are usually followed by a champagne brunch. Many companies operate October through May, but some offer flights year-round. Prices range from $115 to $135 per person. Companies include: SAVE A AeroZona Adventure Inc., (480) 991-4260 or (888) 991-4260; SAVE Hot Air Expeditions, (480) 502-6999 or (800) 831-7610; and SAVE Unicorn Balloon Co., (480) 991-3666 or (800) 468-2478. **Soaring** is available at Turf Soaring School, (602) 439-3621, at 8700 W. Carefree Hwy. in Peoria.

Shopping

Shopping in Phoenix can be diverse and exciting. Dolls, Native American handicrafts, jewelry, rugs, and Western fashions are only a few of the temptations. Shopping malls such as Metrocenter, 9617 Metro Pkwy. W., and Paradise Valley Mall, 4568 E. Cactus Rd., incorporate innovative architecture with a colorful array of shops.

Malls and centers include Arcadia Crossing, 4469 E. Thomas Rd.; the Arizona Center, Van Buren between 3rd and 5th streets; Arrowhead Towne Center, 7700 W. Arrowhead Towne Center; Chris-Town Shopping Center, 1703 W. Bethany Home Rd.; Desert Sky Mall, 7611 W. Thomas Rd.; Tower Plaza, 3735 E. Thomas Rd.; and Town & Country Shopping Center, 2021 E. Camelback Rd. Anchor stores include Dillard's, JCPenney, Macy's, Robinson-May, Saks Fifth Avenue (Biltmore Fashion Park only) and Sears.

For shoppers interested in a bargain, the Park 'n' Swap, 40th Street and E. Washington, offers garage sale-style shopping on 54 acres; Swapmart, 5115 N. 27th Ave., also offers bargains. Southwest of the city in Goodyear is Wigwam Outlet Stores, 1400 N. Litchfield Rd., with more than 30 stores and restaurants to choose from. Northwest of Phoenix is Arizona Factory Shops at 4250 W. Honda Bow Rd.

There are many Native American handicraft stores that sell everything from jewelry to Navajo rugs. Among the best in Phoenix are the Heard Museum Shop, 22 E. Monte Vista Rd. and Gilbert Ortega's, at several locations including 122 N. 2nd St. In Scottsdale Native American handicrafts are sold at Atkinson's Herman Indian Trading Post, 3957 N. Brown Ave.; Gilbert Ortega's, 7237 E. Main St.; and Grey Wolf, 7239 E. First Ave.

Theater and Concerts

Phoenix's rapid growth has been cultural as well as industrial. The following theaters present a mix of classic and contemporary drama: Herberger Theater, (602) 252-8497, 222 E. Monroe; Phoenix Theatre, (602) 254-2151, 100 E. McDowell Rd.; Stagebrush Theater, (480) 990-7405, 7020 E. 2nd St. in Scottsdale; and TheaterWorks, (623) 815-7930, at 9850 W. Peoria in Peoria. The Arizona Theater Co., (602) 256-6995, Arizona's professional state theater group, performs at the Herberger Theater during its October to June season.

The historic Orpheum Theatre, 203 W. Adams St., was originally built for vaudeville acts and movies in 1929. Scheduled to be condemned, the city bought the theater and in 1997 reopened it as a 1,400-seat performing arts center. Self-guiding tours of the Spanish Baroque Revival building are available; phone (602) 252-9678.

For music lovers, the Arizona Opera, Arizona State University Lyric Opera, Phoenix Boys Choir, Phoenix Chamber Music Society and Phoenix Symphony offer concerts throughout the year. The symphony performs in the striking Phoenix Symphony Hall, Phoenix Civic Plaza, (602) 262-7272, 225 E. Adams St.

Cabarets, special concerts, big-name entertainment, shows and lectures are presented at the Herberger Theater in Phoenix, (602) 252-8497; the SunDome Center for the Performing Arts, (623) 975-1900, 19403 R.H. Johnson Blvd. in Sun City West; and the Grady Gammage Auditorium, (480) 965-3434, on the campus of Arizona State University in Tempe. Other special performance areas include America West Arena, (602) 379-7800, 201 E. Jefferson St.; Arizona Veteran's Memorial Coliseum, (602) 258-6711, 1826 W. McDowell Rd.; Desert Sky Pavilion, (602) 254-7200, 2121 N. 83rd Ave.; and the Mesa Amphitheater, (480) 644-2560, in Mesa.

Special Events

New Year's in Tempe begins with the Fiesta Bowl and all its pregame activities; the Fiesta Bowl Parade ranks among the largest parades in the country. Also in January Scottsdale hosts the Parada del Sol and the Phoenix Open Golf Tournament.

The month of February is highlighted by a popular event among equestrians, the All-Arabian Horse Show. February also is when the American Hot Rod Association holds the Winternationals. March events include the LPGA Standard Register Ping and the Maricopa County Fair. In March visitors to Phoenix also can attend the Valley of the Sun Annual Square and Round Dance Festival, in addition to the Indian Fair and Market, held at the Heard Museum. The Cinco de Mayo Festival corresponds to other Mexican celebrations that occur in early May.

Various fall festivals take place in the Phoenix area from October into November. The Arizona State Fair and the Cowboy Artists of America Exhibition in October draw crowds. In November the Thunderbird Balloon Classic and Air Show is held at Westworld of Scottsdale, 16601 N. Pima Rd.

The Pueblo Grande Museum Auxiliary Indian Market is held the second weekend in December at the Pueblo Grande Museum. The year's festivities conclude with *posadas,* Mexican neighborhood celebrations that take place during the 9 days preceding Christmas.

The Phoenix Vicinity

APACHE JUNCTION (I-5)
pop. 18,100, elev. 1,715'

As its name implies, Apache Junction—the western terminus of the Apache Trail—is at the junction of US 60 and SR 88. The surrounding desert, lakes and mountains make Apache Junction a natural recreation site. Hiking, horseback riding, picnicking, rockhounding and water sports facilities are available.

At the junction of Old West Highway and SR 88 stands a monument to the memory of Jacob Waltz, purported discoverer of the Lost Dutchman Gold Mine, which is said to be in the nearby Superstition Mountains.

For eight consecutive weekends from the first Saturday in February through the last Sunday in March, the Arizona Renaissance Festival is held 9 miles east on US 60. Beginning at 10 a.m. and ending at 6 p.m., activities during this re-creation of a 16th-century European village at play during a market fair include jousting tournaments, wandering musicians, theatrical events and demonstrations of period crafts. For more information phone (520) 463-2700.

Apache Junction Chamber of Commerce: 112 E. 2nd Ave., P.O. Box 1747, Apache Junction, AZ 85219-1747; phone (480) 982-3141.

APACHE LAKE, 30 mi. n.e. on SR 88, is part of the Salt River chain of lakes. A popular recre-ation area, it is surrounded by the Tonto National Forest *(see place listing p. 98).* To the south lies the Superstition Wilderness. *See Recreation Chart.*

APACHE TRAIL was created in 1905 to transport supplies from Phoenix and Globe to the construction site of Roosevelt Dam. This 78-mile road parallels the ancient route of the Apaches through the canyons of the Salt River with its desert scenery. The present Apache Trail (SR 88) starts at Apache Junction, climbs past the famed Superstition Mountains, passes through Fish Creek Canyon and skirts the southern edges of Apache, Saguaro, Canyon and Roosevelt lakes and ends at Globe.

The 25-mile portion of Apache Trail between Tortilla Flat and Roosevelt is a narrow, winding gravel road. Although the route is well-maintained, it is not recommended during rainy weather for inexperienced drivers or for vehicles more than 35 feet. A west-to-east journey, from Apache Junction to Globe, is advisable: Travel in this direction will put you on the inside lane of the road and grant all passengers the security of rock walls rather than the steep cliffs on the other side.

Fish Creek Canyon is noted for massive, vividly colored walls rising as much as 2,000 feet above the highway.

CANYON LAKE, 16 mi. n.e. on SR 88, is one of a series of lakes on the Salt River. Impounded by the Mormon Flat Dam, Canyon Lake twists for 10 miles through a magnificent gorge to Horse Mesa Dam. *See Recreation Chart.*

[SAVE] **GOLDFIELD GHOST TOWN & MINE TOURS**, 3.5 mi. n. on SR 88 at 4650 N. Mammoth Mine Rd., offers mine tours, gold panning, a large exhibit of antique mining equipment, gunfights and specialty shops within view of the spectacular Superstition Mountains. A scenic narrow-gauge railroad also encompasses the town. Daily 10-5. Town free. Mine tour $4; over 55, $3.50; ages 6-12, $2. Railroad $4; over 55, $3.50; under 12, $2. Phone (480) 983-0333.

LOST DUTCHMAN STATE PARK, 5 mi. n.e. off SR 88 to 6109 N. Apache Tr., offers 320 acres of hiking trails, camping and picnicking areas. Special moonlight hikes are offered monthly. Guided hikes and campfire programs are offered weekly November through April. Daily 8-5. Admission $5 per private vehicle. Camping $10 per private vehicle. Phone (480) 982-4485. *See Recreation Chart.*

SUPERSTITION MOUNTAINS, e. of town, were named for the many legends surrounding them. The fabled Lost Dutchman Gold Mine lies somewhere in these mountains. Whether the mine really exists is uncertain, but at least eight men were killed because of it and many others died searching for it. Monuments at Roosevelt Dam and Apache Junction commemorate Jacob Waltz, who allegedly discovered the mine.

RECREATIONAL ACTIVITIES
Horseback Riding
• [SAVE] **Don Donnelly Horseback Vacations and Stables**, 6010 S. Kings Ranch Rd., Gold Canyon, AZ 85219. Daily year-round; closed Dec. 25. Phone (480) 982-7822 or (800) 346-4403.

CAREFREE (G-4)
pop. 1,700, elev. 2,389'

Clinging to the base of Black Mountain, Carefree began as a planned community in the 1950s. With such street names as Easy Street, Wampum Way and Ho and Hum streets, Carefree is a laid-back town set amid a desert landscape. One of the largest sundials in the Western Hemisphere—90 feet in diameter—is found off Cave Creek Road.

Carefree-Cave Creek Chamber of Commerce: 6710 E. Cave Creek Rd., Cave Creek, AZ 85331; phone (480) 488-3381.

Shopping areas: El Pedregal, 34505 Scottsdale Rd., combines shopping, dining and entertainment in an outdoor marketplace. Located on Ho and Hum streets, the Spanish Village features specialty shops and restaurants in a courtyard atmosphere. Other shopping areas in Carefree include Los Portales and the Warren Mall.

RAWHIDE LAND AND CATTLE COMPANY JEEP TOURS offers pick-up service from local hotels and provides guided Jeep tours through Arizona's backcountry along old stagecoach routes with views of a Native American ruin. Nature walks and a chance at six-gun target shooting also are available. Narratives provide information about area history, wildlife and plant life.

Departures are offered daily in the morning and in the afternoon. Fare $65-$70; under 13, $32.50-$35. AE, DS, MC, VI. Phone (480) 488-0023 or (800) 294-5337.

CAVE CREEK (G-3)
pop. 2,900 elev. 2,129'

Cave Creek was originally home to the Hohokam, who irrigated their fields with water from Cave Creek. In 1870 a road was built to link the newly formed town of Cave Creek to Fort McDowell on the Verde River. The late 1800s saw the establishment of numerous mining camps in the surrounding mountains and was followed by permanent settlers who took to ranching and farming.

Recreational activities abound in Cave Creek with the Tonto National Forest *(see place listing p. 98)* as its neighbor. Six lakes in the forest offer numerous opportunities for swimming, fishing and boating.

FOUNTAIN HILLS (H-4)
pop. 10,000, elev. 1,600'

Fountain Hills is named for its rolling terrain and celebrated fountain. The community provides a number of recreation and vacation opportunities.

Fountain Hills Chamber of Commerce: 16837 E. Palisades, P.O. Box 17598, Fountain Hills, AZ 85269; phone (480) 837-1654.

THE FOUNTAIN, is off Saguaro Blvd. in Fountain Park. Within a 28-acre lake, the 560-foot-tall white jet of water shoots above the town for 15 minutes every hour on the hour daily 10-9. Wind gusts over 12 miles per hour may prevent operation. The surrounding park is open daily dawn-11 p.m. Free.

OUT OF AFRICA WILDLIFE PARK, 2 mi. n. of Shea Blvd. and SR 87 to 9736 N. Ft. McDowell Rd., features a variety of wildcats within their natural settings, including spotted, black and snow leopards; mountain lions; and Bengal and Siberian tigers. Of particular interest among the seven animal shows is "Tiger Splash," where lions, tigers, jaguars and cougars swim with humans. Food is available.

Allow 2 hours, 30 minutes minimum. Park open Tues.-Sun. 9:30-5, early Oct.-early June;

Wed.-Fri. 4:30-9:30, Sat.-Sun. 9:30-9:30, rest of year. Closed Thanksgiving and Dec. 25. Admission $13.95; over 65, $12.95; ages 4-11, $4.95. AE, MC, VI. Phone (480) 837-7779.

GLENDALE (I-3)
pop. 147,900, elev. 1,154′

Established in 1892, Glendale retains much of its turn-of-the-20th-century charm. Its tree-lined town square, red brick sidewalks and gaslights form an appropriate setting for the abundance of antique shops around shady Murphy Park in the city's historic downtown.

In a more modern vein, Glendale also is home to Thunderbird, The American Graduate School of International Management and the jet fighter wing at Luke Air Force Base.

City of Glendale Tourism Division: 5850 W. Glendale Ave., Glendale, AZ 85301-2599; phone (623) 930-2960.

Shopping areas: Known as the Antique Capital of Arizona, more than 90 antique stores, specialty shops and restaurants are concentrated around Glendale's town square, a four-block area around Murphy Park and the city hall complex at the intersection of Glendale and 58th avenues. The two major antique districts are Old Towne Glendale and the Historic Catlin Court Shops District, both specializing in oak furniture, dolls, jewelry, period clothing and Western memorabilia.

THE BEAD MUSEUM, 5754 W. Glenn Dr., preserves and displays beads from ancient and ethnic cultures. Displays of adornment from Africa, China, Colombia, Italy and New Guinea are featured. Mon.-Sat. 10-5 (also Thurs. 5-8), Sun. 11-4; closed Jan. 1, Thanksgiving and Dec. 25. Admission $3. Phone (623) 931-2737.

GOODYEAR (I-2)
pop. 6,300, elev. 1,000′

In the early 1900s Goodyear Tire & Rubber Company obtained tracts of land in the Salt River Valley, with the intent of growing Egyptian cotton, a component in tire cords. The small farms established on this land evolved into company towns, including one named for its originator. Just 14 miles west of Phoenix, the town is now a suburban residential community.

Tri-City West Chamber of Commerce: 501 W. Van Buren St., Suite K, Avondale, AZ 85323; phone (623) 932-2260.

ESTRELLA MOUNTAIN REGIONAL PARK, off I-10 Estrella Pkwy. S. exit, contains 19,840 acres of rugged desert terrain, riding trails and an 18-hole golf course. Equestrian and rodeo events are held throughout the year. Park open Mon.-Fri. 6 a.m.-8 p.m., Sat.-Sun. 6 a.m.-10 p.m. Admission $2 per private vehicle. Phone (623) 932-3811.

LITCHFIELD PARK (I-2)
pop. 3,300

WILDLIFE WORLD ZOO, 16501 W. Northern Ave., presents more than 320 rare and exotic species of animals. Camels, giraffes, jaguars, rhinoceroses and tigers can be viewed. Visitors walk through a net-enclosed aviary that includes more than 40 species of tropical birds, many curassow birds from South America and other species not commonly found in American zoos. Of special interest is the lory parrot feeding exhibit and a safari train ride through animal exhibits.

The Waters of the World exhibit features sharks, piranhas and electric eels, while the Tropics of the World reptile exhibit is home to pythons, crocodiles and iguanas. Daily 9-5. Admission $10.95; over 60 (Tues. only) $9.95; ages 3-12, $4.95. Phone (623) 935-9453.

MESA (I-4) pop. 288,100, elev. 1,234′

Mesa (Spanish for "tabletop") is in the center of the Salt River Valley on a plateau. The area has long been inhabited by Native Americans, including the Hohokam, or "the Departed Ones." The resourceful tribe realized the need for water for irrigation and dug some 125 miles of canals around 700 B.C. Some of these irrigation ditches are still in use and can be seen at the Park of the Canals and Mesa Grande Ruins.

In 1883 the founding Mormon community discovered the ancient canal system and used it to irrigate the thousands of fertile acres of farmland above the Salt River. Alfalfa, cotton, wheat and grapes were the major crops; citrus was introduced in 1897. Agriculture carried the town into the 20th century and now tourism plays a big role in Mesa's economy.

Recreational areas east and north of the city are easily accessible from Mesa. Rafting and other water sports on the Salt River are popular, as are varied activities available within the Apache, Canyon and Roosevelt Lake recreational areas *(see Apache Junction p. 81)* and Saguaro Lake.

Mesa Convention and Visitors Bureau: 120 N. Center St., P.O. Box 5529, Mesa, AZ 85201-5529; phone (480) 827-4700 or (800) 283-6372.

Shopping areas: The largest shopping centers in the city are Fiesta Mall, US 60 and Alma School Road, which offers Dillard's, Macy's, Robinson's and Sears; and Superstition Springs Center, at US 60 and Superstition Springs Boulevard, which offers Dillard's, JCPenney, Mervyn's and Sears.

Bargain hunters can find discounted namebrand merchandise at VF Factory Outlet Mall, a half-mile south of US 60 at Power and Baseline roads. The Mesa Market Place and Swap Meet offers produce and new and used merchandise at its indoor facility at 10550 E. Baseline Rd.

SAVE **ARIZONA MUSEUM FOR YOUTH,** 35 N. Robson St., offers children the opportunity to view, create and explore various forms of art. Three new exhibitions are introduced each year, and workshops teach a variety of skills from papermaking to clay sculpturing. Allow 1 hour minimum. Tues.-Sat. 9-5, Sun. 1-5, June-Sept.; Tues.-Fri. and Sun. 1-5, Sat. 10-5, rest of year. Closed periodically for exhibit installation. Admission $2.50, under 2 free. Phone (480) 644-2467.

ARIZONA TEMPLE VISITOR CENTER is at 525 E. Main St. The center presents dioramas and an audiovisual program that explains the purpose of the temple and the history of the Mormon religion. Free 30-minute guided tours of the visitor center end in a religious question-and-answer session. A Passion Play is presented during the week before Easter, and a Christmas lights display is featured in December. Allow 1 hour minimum. Daily 9-9. Guided tours are given daily every quarter-hour. Free. Phone (480) 964-7164.

SAVE **CHAMPLIN FIGHTER AIRCRAFT MUSEUM,** 4636 Fighter Aces Dr. at Falcon Field, houses exhibits which showcase artifacts and memorabilia from fighter pilots in World Wars I and II, Korea and Vietnam. The museum also features 34 American, British, French, Russian and German fighter aircraft from 1914 to the present. Videotapes about the evolution of fighters and combat footage are continuously shown.

Allow 1 hour, 30 minutes minimum. Daily 10-5, Sept. 15-Apr. 14; 8:30-3:30, rest of year. Closed Easter, Thanksgiving and Dec. 25. Admission $6.50; ages 5-12, $3. MC, VI. Phone (480) 830-4540.

SAVE **CONFEDERATE AIR FORCE—ARIZONA WING,** adjoining Falcon Field at 2017 N. Greenfield Rd., is dedicated to the preservation of World War II warplanes. Displays include such war artifacts as flight equipment and ration coupons. Of special interest is *Sentimental Journey,* a restored World War II B-17 bomber in flying condition. Allow 1 hour minimum. Daily 10-4; closed Thanksgiving and Dec. 25. Admission $5; ages 6-14, $2. MC, VI. Phone (480) 924-1940.

GOLFLAND/SUNSPLASH, 155 W. Hampton Ave., is a 12-acre miniature golf and water park complex featuring three miniature golf courses, 10 water slides including the Master Blaster, a wave pool, bumper boats, go-carts, a children's pool, a video arcade and a river for tubing. Changing rooms, lockers and food are available.

Mon.-Thurs. 10-8, Fri.-Sat. 10-9, Sun. 11-7, Memorial Day-Labor Day. Admission $14.95; ages 4-11, $12.50; senior citizens $7. Reduced rates after 4 p.m. Separate fees for golf, go-carts and bumper boats. AE, MC, VI. Phone (480) 834-8319.

SAVE **MESA SOUTHWEST MUSEUM,** 53 N. Macdonald St., covers the history of Arizona from the days of the dinosaurs to the growth period of the 20th century. Permanent exhibits focus on Arizona's prehistoric life, featuring animated dinosaurs, dinosaur skeletons and other models and fossil specimens. Archeology displays highlight the life of Arizona's ancient Hohokam people, while reminders of old Mesa's past include territorial jail cells and the Dutchman's Treasure Mine.

Note: The museum is in the midst of an expansion project scheduled for completion in 2000. Some areas of the museum may be temporarily closed during this process.

Allow 1 hour minimum. Tues.-Sat. 10-5, Sun. 1-5; closed major holidays. Admission $4; over 55 and students with ID $3.50; ages 3-12, $2. Phone (480) 644-2230 or 644-2169.

SAVE **ROCKIN' R RANCH,** 6136 E. Baseline Rd., is a re-creation of a Western town where you can pan for gold. All-you-can-eat chuckwagon suppers are served cowboy style. A stage show has songs and humor of the Old West; a gunfight is staged after the show.

Days and hours vary; phone ahead. Admission $21; over 65, $19; ages 13-18, $15; ages 3-12, $10. Reservations are requested. AE, DI, MC, VI. Phone (480) 832-1539.

RECREATIONAL ACTIVITIES
Tubing

- **Salt River Recreation,** 10 mi. s.e. of SR 87 on Bush Hwy., P.O. Box 6568, Mesa, AZ 85216. Daily 9-4, May 1 to mid-Sept. Last rental is 1 hour before closing. Phone (480) 984-3305.

PALO VERDE (I-1) elev. 845'

PALO VERDE NUCLEAR GENERATING STATION is off I-10 exit 98 on Wintersburg Rd. The Energy Information Center has hands-on displays illustrating various energy sources. Guided tours or narrated bus tours of a nuclear generating station are available by reservation. Tues.-Fri. 9-3:30. Free. Phone (623) 393-5757.

PEORIA (I-2) pop. 50,600, elev. 1,122'

LAKE PLEASANT REGIONAL PARK, 30 mi. n. via I-17 and 10 mi. w. via SR 74, encompasses more than 25,000 acres. A 10-lane boat ramp is available at the main entrance and a four-lane ramp is at the north entrance. Admission $5 per private vehicle, $7 per private vehicle with watercraft or $2 per motorcycle. Phone (623) 780-9875. *See Recreation Chart.*

Waddell Dam impounds Lake Pleasant. On the Agua Fria River the earthen dam completed in 1992 is 4,700 feet long and 300 feet high.

SCOTTSDALE (I-4)
pop. 130,100, elev. 1,259′

Scottsdale was named for Chaplain Winfield Scott, Civil War veteran and retired military man who purchased some farmland in 1888. Throughout his travels, Scott promoted the fertile land and encouraged settlement, and in 1896 there were enough children in the town to form School District #48.

Known for its more than 100 art galleries, Scottsdale also is home to craft shops, specialty stores, golf courses, resorts and torchlit swimming pools.

McCormick-Stillman Railroad Park, 7301 E. Indian Bend Rd., (480) 312-2312, offers 1-mile rides on a ⁵⁄₁₂ scale train. Several full-size railroad cars, two train depots, a 1907 locomotive, two Navajo hogans and an operating 1950s carousel are in the park. Picnic facilities are available.

A return to the good old days of the West takes place at Scottsdale's Rawhide *(see attraction listing)* for 4 days in March during the US West National Festival of the West. Western music; a Western film festival; a cowboy trade show, featuring everything from horse gear to art to furniture; rodeo and shooting competitions; cowboy poetry; a mountainman encampment; a chuckwagon cook-off; special children's activities; and period costumes recall the glory days of early Western settlement.

Scottsdale Chamber of Commerce: 7343 Scottsdale Mall, Scottsdale, AZ 85251-4498; phone (480) 945-8481 or (800) 877-1117.

Self-guiding tours: Maps detailing self-guiding walking tours of Scottsdale's Old Town are available from the chamber of commerce.

Shopping areas: Borgata of Scottsdale, an elegant shopping and dining complex designed after San Gimignano (Town of Towers) in Italy, is .25 miles south of Lincoln Drive on Scottsdale Road. Many specialty and gift shops can be found along Fifth Avenue between Marshall Way and Main Street as well as in Old Town, where Western storefronts recreate an aura of the past.

Other shopping areas include Fashion Square at Scottsdale and Camelback roads, with more than 165 merchants, including Banana Republic, Dillard's, Neiman Marcus, Nordstrom, Robinsons-May and Tiffany & Co., specialty stores and restaurants.

COSANTI FOUNDATION, 6433 Doubletree Ranch Rd., is the headquarters and workshop of architect-craftsman Paolo Soleri. Displays include sculptures, windbells and photographs of the models for the city of Arcosanti *(see Cordes Junction p. 46)*, Soleri's prototype urban design. Allow 1 hour minimum. Daily 9-5; closed major holidays. Donations. Phone (480) 948-6145.

FLEISCHER MUSEUM is at 17207 N. Perimeter Dr., on the n.w. corner of E. Bell and Pima rds.

The museum contains American Impressionist paintings from the California School dating 1890-1930 and Russian/Soviet Impressionists dating from 1930s-80s. Sculptures also are displayed throughout the gallery. Cameras are not permitted. Allow 30 minutes minimum. Daily 10-4; closed holidays. Free. Phone (480) 585-3108 or (800) 528-1179.

IMAX THEATER, 4343 N. Scottsdale Rd. at jct. Civic Center Blvd., is equipped with a screen that measures 6 stories high and 78 feet wide. Single and double features are offered in the afternoon; schedule varies. Double features are offered in the evening. Theater open daily 11-9. Double features daily at 7 and 9 p.m. Closed Dec. 25. Admission $7; over 60, $6; under 12, $5. Double feature admission $9.75; over 60, $8.50; under 12, $7.50. AE, MC, VI. Phone (480) 945-4629 or 949-3105 to charge tickets by phone.

RAWHIDE, 4 mi. n. of Bell Rd. at 23023 Scottsdale Rd., is a re-creation of an 1880s Western town. Craftsmen create and sell their wares in 20 antique buildings and shops, which include a photography studio, general store, blacksmith shop and ice cream parlor. Live six gun shootouts and stunt shows occur hourly.

Other highlights include an area for panning for fool's gold; a shooting gallery; a petting zoo; hayrides; and burro, camel, stagecoach and train rides. There is a 140-pound weight limit for burro rides.

Mon.-Thurs. 5-10 p.m., Fri.-Sun. 11-10, Oct.-May; daily 5-10 p.m., rest of year. Closed Dec. 25. Free. Ride fees vary. Phone (480) 502-1880.

SCOTTSDALE CIVIC CENTER AND MALL adjoins the Civic Center Plaza. The center houses a library and municipal buildings. The mall features a park, concrete walkways, fountains, sculptures, a pond, and landscaped lawns and flower beds. The SAVE Scottsdale Center for the Arts, (480) 994-2787, located on the mall, is a forum for the visual and performing arts. Changing exhibits are featured. Various outdoor events are scheduled throughout the year. Mon.-Sat. 10-5, Sun. noon-5. Free. Center for the Arts $5, students with ID $3, under 16 free, free to all Tues. Phone (480) 945-8481.

Scottsdale Historical Museum, 7333 E. Civic Center Mall, is housed in a 1909 red brick grammar school furnished in period. A replica of a barbershop, complete with a barber chair and tools, and an old-fashioned kitchen are featured. Other exhibits include a display of town memorabilia and a replica of a 1900 schoolroom. Allow 30 minutes minimum. Wed.-Sat. 10-5, Sun. noon-4, Sept.-June. Donations. Phone (480) 945-4499.

TALIESIN WEST, 114th St. (Frank Lloyd Wright Blvd.) and Cactus Rd., was the winter home and architectural studio of renowned architect Frank

Lloyd Wright. Located on 600 acres of Sonoran Desert at the foothills of the McDowell Mountains, the site includes a complex of buildings connected by walkways, gardens and terraces that showcase Wright's ability to integrate indoor and outdoor areas. Taliesin West is the international headquarters for the Frank Lloyd Wright Foundation, which offers a broad range of tours of the site.

Tours include the 1-hour Panorama Tour, which provides a basic introduction to the complex and Wright's theories of architecture. The 90-minute Insights Tour encompasses the famed Living Room. A 3-hour Behind the Scenes Tour includes tea in the colorful dining room, and the 90-minute Desert Walk introduces visitors to the environment surrounding the complex. Other tours are available.

Allow 1 hour minimum. Panorama Tours depart daily 10-4, Oct.-May; 9-11 a.m., rest of year. Insights Tours depart daily at noon, 1, 2 and 3, June-Sept.; at 9 and 9:30, rest of year. Behind the Scenes Tours depart Tues. and Thurs. at 9, Oct.-May; Mon. and Thurs. at 9, rest of year. Desert Walks depart at 11:15, Oct.-May. Closed Jan. 1, Easter, Thanksgiving and Dec. 25.

Panorama Tour Oct.-May $14.50; over 65 and students with ID $12; ages 4-12, $3. Fee rest of year $10; over 65 and students with ID $8; ages 4-12, $3. Insights Tour Oct.-May $20; over 65, students with ID and ages 4-12, $16. Fee rest of year $14; over 65, students with ID and ages 4-12, $12. Behind the Scenes Tour Oct.-May $35; fee rest of year $25. Desert walk $20. Combination rates are available. Tours not recommended for children under 4. Reservations are recommended for some tours. AE, MC, VI. Phone (480) 860-2700, or 860-8810 for recorded tour information.

RECREATIONAL ACTIVITIES

Jeep Tours (Self-driving)

- [SAVE] **Scottsdale Jeep Rentals**, 8820 N. 86th St., Scottsdale, AZ 85258. Daily 8-5. Phone (480) 951-2191. *See ad.*

SUN CITY/SUN CITY WEST
(I-2) pop. 38,100, elev. 1,140'

Twelve miles northwest of Phoenix but part of the metropolitan area of the capital city, Sun City is one of the largest and most popular retirement communities in the country. By 1978 it had reached its population goal of more than 40,000, with most residential property in use. Sun City West, 2.5 miles west via Grand Avenue, offers a similar array of golf courses, stores, restaurants, recreation areas and other services.

The Sundome presents concerts with nationally known entertainers. For a schedule of events contact The Sundome, 19403 R.H. Johnson Blvd., Sun City West, AZ 85375; phone (623) 975-1900.

Sun City Visitors Center: 9903 W. Bell Rd., Sun City, AZ 85351; phone (623) 977-5000.

TEMPE (I-3) pop. 141,900, elev. 1,159'

Founded as Hayden's Ferry in 1872, the town originally was named for Charles Trumbull Hayden who owned a flour mill and operated a ferry across the Salt River; Hayden Flour Mill is purportedly the oldest continuously operating industry in the state. The town was renamed Tempe (Tem-PEE) in 1878 for the area's alleged resemblance to the Vale of Tempe in ancient Greece.

In 1886 the dusty cow town became the home of the Arizona Territorial Normal School, later to become Arizona State University. The town grew with education and farming as its mainstays.

One of the last major buildings designed by Frank Lloyd Wright, the Gammage Center for the Performing Arts is on the campus of Arizona State University. Depending on the special events scheduled, free guided tours of the center depart from the box office on the half-hour Mon.-Fri. 1-4, Aug.-May.

Tempe kicks off Arizona's calendar of events on New Year's with the Fiesta Bowl Football Classic, one of the largest college bowl games. The game is played at Arizona State University's

Sun Devil Stadium, which also is the home stadium for the Arizona Cardinals professional football team.

Tempe Convention and Visitors Bureau: 51 W. Third St., Suite 105, Tempe, AZ 85281; phone (480) 894-8158 or (800) 283-6734.

Shopping areas: Specialty shops are scattered throughout Old Town Tempe, the four-block segment of Mill Avenue between 3rd and 7th streets.

THE ARIZONA HISTORICAL SOCIETY MUSEUM, in Papago Park at 1300 N. College Ave., portrays the history of the state through exhibits, hands-on displays and films. Visitors can view a 35-foot reconstructed section of the Roosevelt Dam, use a kiosk to learn about the development of the area and visit a turn-of-the-20th-century saloon and general store. Changing exhibits, guided tours and a research library and archives are available. Mon.-Sat. 10-4, Sun. noon-4; closed Jan. 1, July 4, Thanksgiving and Dec. 25. Free. Phone (480) 929-0292.

ARIZONA STATE UNIVERSITY is at University Dr. and Mill Ave. Located in the heart of Tempe, the university's main campus includes distinctive Gammage Memorial Auditorium, a concert hall designed by Frank Lloyd Wright that is one of his last completed nonresidential designs. A 1-hour campus tour departs from the Student Services Building Amphitheater Mon.-Fri. at 10:30 and 2, late Aug. through mid-May; Mon.-Fri. at 9, rest of year. Phone (602) 965-9011 for general information, or (602) 965-7788 for tour reservations.

Arizona State University Art Museum, housed in the Nelson Fine Arts Center at 10th St. and Mill Ave., displays American and European prints from the 15th century through present-day and American paintings and sculptures from the 19th century to the present. The museum's primary focus is on contemporary art, American ceramic crafts and a collection of art by Latino artists. Changing exhibitions also are presented. Nelson Fine Arts Center open Tues.-Sat. 10-5 (also Tues. 5-9, Sept.-Apr.), Sun. 1-5. Free. Phone (480) 965-2787.

Arizona State University Museum of Geology is in the Physical Sciences Building, F Wing, near the intersection of University Dr. and McAllister St. Displays include a working seismograph; a six-story Foucault pendulum demonstrating the Earth's rotation; minerals, gemstones and fossils. Attendants are present to answer questions. Hours vary; phone for schedule. Closed major holidays. Free. Phone (480) 965-7065 or 965-5081.

BIG SURF, 1500 N. McClintock Rd., provides man-made waves in a wave pool and beaches. There also are 15 water slides, several volleyball courts and three activity pools. Mon.-Sat. 10-6, Sun. 11-7, Memorial Day-Labor Day. Admission $14.95; ages 4-11, $12.50. Reduced rates after 3 p.m. MC, VI. Phone (480) 947-2477.

SAVE **IMAX THEATER AT ARIZONA MILLS,** off I-10 Baseline Rd. exit at the mall, presents films that are based on both IMAX and IMAX 3D technology. IMAX 3D films require the use of 3D headsets. The lifelike images are projected on a screen that is 6 stories high. Both types of films are shown daily. Hours vary; phone ahead. Admission for IMAX 3D films $8.50; over 60, $7.50; under 13, $6.50. Admission for IMAX films $7; over 60, $6; under 13, $5. Double feature prices are available. AE, MC, VI. Phone (480) 945-4629.

This ends listings for the Phoenix Vicinity.
The following page resumes the alphabetical listings of cities in Arizona.

PICACHO (E-4) elev. 1,607'

PICACHO PEAK STATE PARK, 12 mi. s. off I-10 exit 219, is the site of Arizona's westernmost Civil War battle. On April 15, 1862, a dozen Union soldiers overtook and defeated 17 Confederate cavalrymen. The park is home to the 1,500-foot peak that was used as a landmark for settlers traveling between New Mexico and California. The Mormon Battalion constructed the road that was used by the forty-niners and the Butterfield Overland Stage. Today the trails meander throughout the park as well as to the top of the peak. A variety of activities are offered, including camping, hiking and picnicking.

A Civil War re-enactment is held each spring. Daily 8-5. Admission $5 per private vehicle, $1 per person. Camping fees $10-$15. Phone (520) 466-3183. *See Recreation Chart.*

PINETOP-LAKESIDE (D-5)

pop. 2,400, elev. 6,960'

Lakeside originally was named Fairview in 1880 by Mormon pioneers. Pinetop, also founded by Mormons, began in 1878 with a sawmill and ranching on the open range of the White Mountains. Before tourism, logging and ranching were the mainstays of the area. The twin towns were incorporated in 1984 as a resort area.

Pinetop-Lakeside, on the edge of the White Mountain Apache Reservation, is 10 miles southeast of Show Low on SR 260 on the edge of Mogollon Rim. The elevation makes the area cool in summer for trout fishing, camping and other activities. Winter sports such as snowmobiling, skiing and ice fishing are popular in the Apache-Sitgreaves National Forests *(see place listing p. 40)* and on the reservation. Fishing also is permitted by fee on the reservation.

DID YOU KNOW

Although most people think of Arizona as being desert, mountains and plateaus comprise more than half the land.

Pinetop-Lakeside Chamber of Commerce: 674 E. White Mountain Blvd., P.O. Box 4220, Pinetop, AZ 85935; phone (520) 367-4290 or (800) 573-4031.

CASINOS

- **Hon-Dah Resort Casino and Conference Center**, 3 mi. e. at jct. SRs 260 and 73. Daily 24 hours. Phone (520) 369-0299.

RECREATIONAL ACTIVITIES

Skiing

- **Sunrise Ski Area**, off SR 273, McNary, AZ 85930. Daily 9-4 Dec.-Apr. Phone (520) 735-7669.

PIPE SPRING NATIONAL MONUMENT (A-3)

Pipe Spring National Monument, within the Kaibab-Paiute Indian Reservation off SR 389, is 14 miles west of Fredonia. The monument is a tribute to the pioneers who explored, settled and developed large portions of the Southwest. It preserves an 1870 cattle ranch consisting of the ranch house and two exterior buildings used as barracks.

Pipe Spring received the first telegraph in Arizona and also served as a way station for weary travelers. Allow 1 hour minimum. Daily 8-4:30; closed Jan. 1, Thanksgiving and Dec. 25. Admission $2, under 17 free. Phone (520) 643-7105.

PORTAL (F-6) elev. 4,773'

Portal received its name because it is at the entrance to Cave Creek Canyon. The town became a popular summer vacation spot for those seeking cool, high altitudes and such recreational pastimes as camping, fishing, hiking and hunting.

CAVE CREEK CANYON, s.w. via a paved road, displays brilliant colors and rugged towering cliffs of red rhyolite rising from the canyon floor. The Southwestern Research Station of the American Museum of Natural History in New York City is at the upper end of the canyon; its laboratories are closed to the public. Camping and hiking opportunities are available.

PRESCOTT (C-3)

pop. 26,500, elev. 5,346'

The area around Prescott was first settled in 1864 by miners prospecting for gold. It was the presence of gold that prompted the cash-poor Union to designate Arizona as a territory in 1863. President Abraham Lincoln chose an area just north of Prescott as the first seat of government because the gold fields were nearby and because Southern sympathizers dominated Tucson. In 1867 the capitol was moved south to Tucson. However, Prescott briefly became capital again in 1877, a title it lost to Phoenix in 1889.

Named to honor historian William Hickling Prescott, the town was incorporated in 1883. Because of the surrounding pine forests, wooden structures rather then the typical adobe buildings populated the town. Fire devastated the town in 1900, but determined townsfolk rebuilt and developed a water system utilizing Del Rio Springs.

Surrounded by mountain ranges, Prescott is now a resort community. Nearly encircled by the Prescott National Forest, outdoor enthusiasts can indulge in camping, horseback riding, hiking, fishing, rockhounding and picnicking.

Prescott Downs offers Thoroughbred and quarterhorse races Saturday through Tuesday, Memorial Day weekend through Labor Day weekend. Phone (520) 445-0220.

Note: Policies concerning admittance of children to pari-mutuel betting facilities vary. Phone for information.

Prescott Chamber of Commerce: 117 W. Goodwin St., P.O. Box 1147, Prescott, AZ 86302; phone (520) 445-2000 or (800) 266-7534.

Self-guiding tours: A leaflet outlining a self-guiding walking tour of Prescott's Victorian-era neighborhoods can be obtained at the chamber of commerce.

Shopping areas: Whiskey Row/Courthouse Square, downtown off SR 89 and Cortez Street, offers antique, souvenir and clothes shopping opportunities as well as several eateries.

BUCKY O'NEILL MONUMENT, on Courthouse Plaza, was created by Solon H. Borglum. It pays tribute to the First U.S. Volunteer Cavalry (Roosevelt's Rough Riders) and Capt. William O'Neill, the first volunteer in the Spanish-American War and organizer of the Rough Riders.

GRANITE BASIN, just inside Prescott National Forest about 12 mi. n.w., is a 10-acre lake lying at the foot of Granite Mountain. A recreation area offers hiking, camping and fishing.

GRANITE DELLS (Point of Rocks), 4 mi. n. on SR 89, is a summer playground on Watson Lake. Granite formations line the highway for 2 miles.

[SAVE] **HERITAGE PARK ZOO,** 6 mi. n. via SR 89, off Willow Creek Rd. in Heritage Park, presents exotic and native wild animals in their natural settings. Guided tours are available by appointment. Daily 9-5, May-Oct.; 10-4, rest of year. Admission $4; over 62, $3.50; ages 3-12, $1.50. Phone (520) 778-4242.

[SAVE] **PHIPPEN MUSEUM,** 6 mi. n.e. at 4701 SR 89N, displays a collection of historical artifacts and works by prominent Western artists, together with contemporary artwork depicting the Ameri-

can West. Allow 30 minutes minimum. Mon. and Wed.-Sat. 10-4, Sun. 1-4. Admission $3; over 60, $2. MC, VI. Phone (520) 778-1385.

★**SHARLOT M. HALL MUSEUM,** downtown at 415 W. Gurley St., contains 3.5 acres of galleries and gardens. The museum is in the Territorial Mansion, which had been restored by poet and one-time state historian Sharlot M. Hall. Hall filled the mansion with Arizona pioneer artifacts donated to her for use in the museum, which opened in 1927. Six historic buildings and two modern exhibits trace the heritage of the area.

Also on the grounds are an amphitheater that hosts plays during the summer; herb and rose gardens; and Fort Misery, the first cabin built in Prescott. The buildings were constructed 1864-1937. The Museum Center contains archives and a library for research.

Allow 1 hour minimum. Mon.-Sat. 10-5, Sun. 1-5, Apr.-Oct.; Mon.-Sat. 10-4, Sun. 1-5, rest of year. Closed Jan. 1, Thanksgiving and Dec. 25. Donations. Phone (520) 445-3122.

Governor's Mansion was completed in 1864 for John N. Goodwin, Arizona's first territorial governor. The mansion's furnishings and artifacts depict the period 1864-67. Exhibits include "Arizona Goes to War, 1898" and "View from Thumb Butte—The Changing Townscape."

John C. Fremont House was built in 1875 and served as the home of the celebrated "Pathfinder" during his term as fifth territorial governor of Arizona. The furnishings and artifacts depict the period 1875-81.

William C. Bashford House, built in 1877, represents the late Victorian style. The home is furnished in period.

SMOKI MUSEUM, n. of Gurley St. at 147 N. Arizona St., is patterned after early Pueblo structures both in architecture and interior design. The museum contains artifacts and documents pertaining to Native American pre-history and history with emphasis on the Prescott region. Ceramics, baskets, beaded ornaments, clothing, jewelry and paintings are among the items displayed. Mon.-Sat. 10-4, Sun. 1-4, May-Sept.; Fri.-Sat. 10-4, Sun. 1-4, in Oct. Admission $2, under 12 free. Phone (520) 445-1230.

THUMB BUTTE, 4 mi. w., is a rugged outcropping of granite. Extensive views are offered from the summit, which can be reached on foot. Picnic facilities are available. Parking $2.

CASINOS

• **Bucky's Casino,** 530 E. Merritt at jct. SRs 89 and 69. Daily 24 hours. Phone (502) 776-5695.

Petroglyphs And Pictographs

As forerunners of true writing, Native Americans used petroglyphs and pictographs as a way to communicate with each other as well as to record history. A petroglyph is a symbol that is scratched or carved into the veneer of a rock with another rock. Scientists believe that veneer is created by

years of accumulated dirt slowly building—clay dust and minerals are cemented to the surface by bacteria living in the rocks. After the veneer is chipped away and a petroglyph is created, a new layer of veneer slowly begins to build over the carving. Over time, the petroglyphs darken as the veneer thickens. While petroglyphs are carved, pictographs are painted on the surface of a rock. Visitors to Arizona can view the historic and prehistoric symbols in various sites throughout the state.

PRESCOTT NATIONAL FOREST

Elevations in the forest range from 3,071 ft. in the Verde Valley to 7,971 ft. at Mount Union. Refer to AAA maps for additional elevation information.

Covering 1,238,154 acres in central Arizona, Prescott National Forest encompasses two long mountain ranges with varying elevations. Major access routes include SR 89, SR 89A and SR 69 off I-17. Other scenic but primitive roads not recommended for low-clearance vehicles penetrate the forest. Check locally for road conditions.

Developed recreation areas are at Mingus Mountain and in Prescott Basin. Camping, picnicking, hiking and backpacking are popular recreational pursuits; many trails can be enjoyed year-round. Some popular day-use areas in Prescott have a $2 parking fee. Hunting is permitted in season with the appropriate state game license; phone (520) 692-7700.

For further information contact Prescott National Forest, 344 S. Cortez St., Prescott, AZ 86303; phone (520) 771-4700 Mon.-Fri. 8-4:30, or TDD (520) 771-4792. *See Recreation Chart and the AAA Southwestern CampBook.*

QUARTZSITE (D-2)
pop. 1,900, elev. 876′

A settler named Charles Tyson built a fort on this site in 1856 for protection against Native Americans. Because of a good water supply it soon became a stagecoach stop on the Ehrenburg-to-Prescott route. As the stage lines vanished, Fort Tyson, or Tyson's Wells (as it became known), was abandoned. A small mining boom in 1897 revitalized the area, and the settlement revived as Quartzsite.

The winter population of this desert town swells to 1 million during January and February because of the gem and mineral shows in the area. The Pow Wow Rock and Mineral Show began the rockhound winter migration to town in 1965; now eight major shows entice gem enthusiasts, collectors and jewelers to Quartzsite to buy and sell. In an event that has attained international scope, thousands of dealers offer raw and handcrafted merchandise over the weekends in January and February.

Quartzsite Chamber of Commerce: 1490 Main Event Ln., P.O. Box 85, Quartzsite, AZ 85346; phone (520) 927-5600.

HI JOLLY MEMORIAL, e. on I-10 in the old cemetery, honors Hadji Ali. Nicknamed Hi Jolly by soldiers and pioneers, the Arab came to Arizona in 1856 with an Army consignment of camels. The camels adapted well to their new environment but were never used successfully, partly because the sight of them caused horses, mules and cattle to stampede.

KOFA NATIONAL WILDLIFE REFUGE, encompassing the Kofa and Castle Dome mountains, preserves the habitat of the desert bighorn sheep. Access is primarily limited to four-wheel-drive and high-clearance vehicles. Firearms are prohibited in the refuge except during special hunting seasons.

Remote Palm Canyon is 20 miles south of Quartzsite on US 95, then 9 miles east on a maintained gravel road. It is one of the few places in Arizona where native palms grow. They can be seen from a point 200 yards away via a .25-mile hike up a moderately steep trail. The last 200 yards to the palms present a strenuous climb. Refuge and canyon accessible daily 24 hours. Free. Phone (520) 783-7861.

ROOSEVELT (H-6) elev. 2,215'

THEODORE ROOSEVELT DAM AND LAKE is reached via SR 88 (the Apache Trail). Two centuries before Christ, natives of the region built 150 miles of stone-lined canals to irrigate their fields. Modern Arizona's reclamation of the Salt River Valley began with the completion of the Roosevelt Dam in 1910. Unlike other dams, the Roosevelt was made with thousands of hand-hewn stones and is considered the world's highest all-masonry dam.

As the first major federal reclamation project, the dam provides water and power to one of the state's richest agricultural regions. Many recreational opportunities are available on the lake.

For further information contact the Tonto Basin Ranger District, HC 02, Box 4800, Roosevelt, AZ 85545; phone (520) 467-3200. *See Recreation Chart.*

SACATON (E-4)
pop. 1,500, elev. 1,127'

Sacaton, first visited by Spanish missionaries in 1696, was even then an ancient Pima Indian settlement; currently the town is the headquarters for the Pima Reservation. American pioneers noted the abundance of very tall grass, from which they derived the town name.

GILA RIVER CULTURAL CENTER, next to I-10 exit 175 on Casa Blanca Rd., contains a park with reconstructed Indian homes from various tribes that depict more than 2,000 years of Native American life in the Gila River Basin. The communities represent the Akimel, Apache, Hohokam, Pee-Posh and Tohono O'odham cultures. A museum and craft center adjoin the park. Food is available. Allow 1 hour minimum. Daily 8-5; closed major holidays. Free. Phone (520) 315-3411.

SAFFORD (E-5)
pop. 7,400, elev. 2,920'

The first American colony in the Gila Valley, Safford was founded in 1874 by farmers whose previous holdings had been washed away by the Gila River. From Safford the Swift Trail winds 36 miles to the top of 10,720-foot Mount Graham. En route the trail traverses five of the seven ecological zones in Western North America. Camping, hiking and picnicking are permitted. Gila Box Riparian National Conservation Area, 15 miles northeast, offers seasonal river floating opportunities.

The region south of Safford is known for its hot mineral water baths. Information about area spas is available from the chamber of commerce.

For seekers of fire agates and other semiprecious stones, there are two rockhound areas administered and maintained by the U.S. Bureau of Land Management. Black Hills Back Country Byway is a 21-mile scenic drive through the Black Hills. The drive is a graded dirt road with sharp turns and steep drops.

Round Mountain Rockhound Area, featuring chalcedony roses and fire agates, is 12 miles south of Duncan on US 70, west at Milepost 5.6, 7.1 miles to BLM sign, then 2.5 miles south to the first collection area. A second collection area is 4.5 miles south using the left fork in the road. **Note:** The road is not maintained and is very rough. Because of the area's remote location, visitors should bring along plenty of water and gasoline. Phone ahead for road conditions. Information about these areas can be obtained by contacting the Bureau of Land Management, 711 14th Ave., Safford, AZ 85546; phone (520) 348-4400.

Graham County Chamber of Commerce: 1111 Thatcher Blvd., Safford, AZ 85546; phone (520) 428-2511.

ROPER LAKE STATE PARK, 4 mi. s. off US 191, is at the base of Mt. Graham. Camping, swimming and picnicking are available. Daily 6 a.m.-8 p.m. Admission $4 per private vehicle. Camping $10-$15 per private vehicle. Phone (520) 428-6760. *See Recreation Chart.*

★SAGUARO NATIONAL PARK—*see Tucson p. 111.*

SAHUARITA—*see Tucson p. 112.*

ST. JOHNS (C-5)
pop. 3,300, elev. 5,650'

APACHE COUNTY HISTORICAL SOCIETY MUSEUM, .25 mi. w. of jct. US 191 and SR 61 at 180 W. Cleveland St., displays pioneer artifacts, mammoth bones, Native American artifacts, miniature replicas of early St. Johns homes and antique guns and slot machines. Allow 30 minutes minimum. Mon.-Fri. 9-5; other times by appointment. Closed holidays. Donations. Phone (520) 337-4737.

LYMAN LAKE STATE PARK, 11 mi. s. on US 191, offers acres of rolling grassland that provide a home to a small herd of buffalo and other wildlife. A water ski course is set up on the lake during the summer months. Tours of Native American ruins and prehistoric rock art are available. Daily 8-5. Admission $4 per private vehicle. Camping $10-$15 per private vehicle. Phone (520) 337-4441. *See Recreation Chart.*

SAN CARLOS (D-5)
pop. 2,900, elev. 2,432'

San Carlos, north of Coolidge Dam, is a trading center and headquarters for the San Carlos Indian Agency. The Apaches operate one of the largest cattle ranches in this area. The reservation offers some of the best trophy-hunting and fishing in the state; permits are required. For permit information contact the San Carlos Recreation and Wildlife Department, P.O. Box 97, San Carlos, AZ 85550; phone (520) 475-2343 or (888) 275-2653.

Coolidge Dam, about 9 miles southeast on the Gila River, impounds the waters that irrigate the Casa Grande Valley. Construction of the dam was delayed until a solution satisfactory to the Apache Indians was found concerning the disturbance of tribal burial grounds. Once it was agreed that a concrete slab would cover the cemetery, construction resumed.

SANTA CRUZ DE TERRENATE PRESIDIO NATIONAL HISTORIC SITE
(F-5)

Located within the San Pedro Riparian National Conservation Area, Santa Cruz de Terrenate Presidio National Historic Site is 4 mi. n. of Tombstone on SR 80, 6 mi. w. on SR 82 to Fairbank, .75-mi. w. to Kellar Rd., then 2 mi. n. Established by the Spanish in 1776 on the banks of the San Pedro River, the presidio was built to protect the overland route east of Tucson. Because of the frequent Apache raids as well as the lack of proper supplies, Terrenate was abandoned less than 5 years after its establishment.

The site, once consisting of seven structures built around a central courtyard, contains signs showing what each of the structures originally looked like. Many of the adobe walls that surrounded the presidio are eroded and only a few remain. Although the walls were planned to be built to a height of 15 feet, the highest they got was 12 feet due to lack of funds. In addition, the bastion/gunpowder storehouse was never completed, and less than one-fourth of the planned barracks were not constructed because of insufficient funding.

The historic site is fragile and visitors are instructed by signs to stay on the trails and not to touch the remaining structures. A 1.2-mile dirt trail leads from the parking lot to the presidio. Visitors should bring their own food and water as no facilities are available. Free. Phone (520) 458-3559.

SASABE (F-4) elev. 3,560'

BUENOS AIRES NATIONAL WILDLIFE REFUGE, 7 mi. n. off SR 286, is a 117,000-acre refuge established to preserve the endangered masked bobwhite quail. The refuge contains extensive grasslands and seasonal streams and a lake. It also is home to 300 species of birds, including hawks, herons, grayhawks, vermilion fly catchers and golden eagles (during migration). Other wildlife include coyotes, deer, foxes, mountain lions, bobcats and pronghorn antelopes.

Popular trails are located on the eastern side near the town of Arivaca. Guided tours to Brown Canyon are offered on Saturdays. Allow 4 hours minimum. Daily dawn-dusk. Refuge free. Guided tours $3; reservations are required. Phone (520) 823-4251.

SCOTTSDALE—*see Phoenix p. 85.*

SECOND MESA (B-5)
pop. 900, elev. 5,680'

Second Mesa, near the junction of SRs 264 and 87, is within a Hopi Reservation that occupies a large tract in the center of the vast Navajo Reservation of northeastern Arizona. Special permission is required for photographing, painting or sketching while on the Hopi Reservation.

HOPI CULTURAL CENTER MUSEUM, 5 mi. w. of SR 87 on SR 264, displays basketry, weaving, jewelry and other artifacts depicting the history of the Hopi. Kachina dolls, representations of divine ancestral spirits, also are featured. Allow 1 hour minimum. Mon.-Fri. 8-5, Sat.-Sun. 9-3. Admission $3; under 13, $1. Phone (520) 734-6650.

SEDONA (C-4)
pop. 7,700, elev. 4,400'

Sedona is situated amid the red-hued rocks of Oak Creek Canyon. Overlooking Oak Creek, the monoliths and buttes provide a startling contrast to the surrounding lush vegetation and forest. At the southern end of Oak Creek Canyon, Sedona is a center for contemporary and traditional arts, and a relatively upscale retirement and tourism area. Galleries and boutiques are found throughout the city and in Tlaquepaque, a Mexican/Spanish-style village. Specialty shops feature pottery, sculptures, painting, jewelry and imported wares.

Sedona is purportedly home to several vortexes, electromagnetic energy fields emitting upward from the earth. These fields of energy are thought to energize and inspire visitors. Some of the more popular sites include the Airport Hill, Bell Rock, Boynton Creek and Cathedral Rock vortexes.

Oak Creek Canyon Drive (SR 89A) began as a cattle trail across Oak Creek Canyon's east wall. The trail was transformed to a rough wagon road by Jim Munds, when he used it as a shortcut to Flagstaff. From the vista point on the Mogollon Rim to Sedona the drive offers a continuous and changing display of natural beauty. The dramatic drop in altitude brings sudden changes in vegetation and colored rock formations. Oak Creek flows between 1,200-foot canyon walls toward the red rock of Sedona.

Sedona is the starting point for scenic drives through the rugged Red Rocks area. [SAVE] Great Ventures Charter Tours offers a variety of excursions from Sedona; phone (520) 282-4451 or (800) 578-2643. Guided jeep tours of the back country are offered by Pink Jeep Tours, (520) 282-5000 or (800) 873-3662; [SAVE] Sedona Adventures, (520) 282-3500 or (800) 888-9494; and Sedona Red Rock Jeep Tours, (520) 282-6826 or (800) 848-7728.

The Sedona Trolley can be boarded at various signed trolley stops around town. Drivers provide sightseeing narration. For schedule information and fares phone (520) 282-5400.

Information about hiking trails, scenic flights and various sightseeing tours can be obtained at the chamber of commerce.

Hot air balloon rides over the Sedona and Oak Creek Canyon areas are available in the morning (weather permitting). For information and reservations contact Northern Light Balloon Expeditions (*see color ad*), (520) 282-2274 or (800) 230-6222; or Red Rock Balloon Adventures (*see*

color ad p. 94), (520) 284-0040 or (800) 258-3754.

Sedona-Oak Creek Canyon Chamber of Commerce: Forest Road and SR 89A, P.O. Box 478, Sedona, AZ 86339; phone (520) 282-7722 or (800) 288-7336.

Shopping areas: Art galleries and restaurants intermingle with specialty shops at Tlaquepaque, a half mile south of town on SR 179. Oak Creek Factory Outlet, 7 mi. s. on SR 179, offers more than 30 outlet stores. Other areas featuring galleries and shops are Hillside, Hozho and Sinagua.

[SAVE] **ARIZONA HELICOPTER ADVENTURES**, departing from the Sedona Airport, offers a variety of in-flight, narrated sightseeing tours of Sedona and environs, including the Native American ruins of Boynton Canyon and the area's scenic red rock formations. Daily 9-5; closed Dec. 25. Length of tours varies. Fare $48-$128. Reservations are recommended. AE, DS, MC, VI. Phone (520) 282-0904 or (800) 282-5141.

CHAPEL OF THE HOLY CROSS, 3 mi. s. off SR 179 on Chapel Rd., stands on a small mountain that provides scenic views. The contemporary Catholic shrine is constructed on the area's noted red rock. Built in 1956, the chapel is situated between two large red sandstone peaks with a ramp leading to the entrance. A 90-foot cross dominates the structure. Allow 30 minutes minimum. Mon.-Sat. 9-5, Sun. 10-5. Free. Phone (520) 282-4069.

GRAND CANYON WILD WEST TOURS, with pick-up from local hotels, offers narrated coach tours to the Grand Canyon. Highlights include

the Painted Desert, the Navajo Indian Reservation and lunch at the 1916 Trading Post in Cameron (not included in fare). A 3.5-hour tour along the east and south rim of the canyon includes the Grand Canyon IMAX Theater (*see color ad p. 56*) (*see attraction listing in Grand Canyon National Park p. 56*) and park entry fee. Mon.-Thurs. 8-6:30; closed Thanksgiving and Dec. 25. Fare $79. AE, MC, VI. Phone (520) 284-1123 or (800) 201-9453.

★ OAK CREEK CANYON, n. on SR 89A, is traversed by a scenic stretch of that road. About 16 miles long and rarely more than 1 mile wide, the canyon is known for its spectacularly colored white, yellow and red cliffs dotted with pine, cypress and juniper. Rocky gorges, unusual rock formations and buttes add interest to the drive.

Oak Creek is noted for trout fishing; throughout the canyon are Forest Service camping and picnicking grounds. Area maps are available from the chambers of commerce in Flagstaff and Sedona.

PAGE SPRINGS FISH HATCHERY is 12 mi. s. on Page Springs Rd. Nature trails are available. Daily 7-4. Free. Phone (520) 634-4805.

[SAVE] RED ROCK BI-PLANE TOURS AND AIR SAFARI, 1 mi. w. on SR 89A, then s. to 1225 Airport Rd., offers guided bi-plane tours over Sedona. Passengers can view from the air ancient American Indian dwellings not accessible by foot or vehicle. Daily 8-dusk. Fare $36-$139. Two-passenger minimum. AE, DS, MC, VI. Phone (520) 204-5939 or (888) 866-7433. *See color ad p. 95.*

RED ROCK STATE PARK, 4 mi. s. off US 89A on Lower Red Rock Loop Rd., features 286 acres of a diminishing riparian ecosystem. Oak Creek runs through the park creating a diverse riparian habitat that abounds with plants and wildlife. Displays in the visitor center highlight the ecology and conservation of Oak Creek. Nature hikes, bird walks, theater presentations and other planned activities are offered; phone for schedule.

Park open daily 8-6, May-Sept.; 8-5, rest of year. Visitor Center open daily 9-5. Admission $5 per private vehicle (up to four persons), $1 per pedestrian. Phone (520) 282-6907. *See Recreation Chart.*

[SAVE] **SEDONA SUPERVUE THEATER**, 7 mi. s. on SR 179 at Prime Outlets, presents motion pictures, shown on a giant screen, that draw viewers into the sights and sounds of the film. Shows begin daily on the hour 10-7. Admission $7; ages 3-11, $5; under 3 free with adult. MC, VI. Phone (520) 284-3214.

SLIDE ROCK STATE PARK, 7 mi. n. off SR 89A within Oak Creek Canyon, developed around a natural 70-foot-long waterslide. The park is the site of the historic Pendley homestead and an apple orchard. Activities include swimming and picnicking. Daily 8-7, May-Sept.; 8-6, Mar.-Apr. and in Oct.; 8-5, rest of year. Admission $5 per private vehicle (up to four passengers), $1 for each additional passenger over age 11. Phone (520) 282-3034. *See Recreation Chart.*

RECREATIONAL ACTIVITIES

Jeep Tours (Self-driving)

- **Sedona Jeep Rentals**, 235 Air Terminal Dr., Sedona, AZ 86336-5837. Daily 8-5. Phone (520) 282-2227 or (800) 879-5337. *See ad p. 94.*

- **Desert Jeep and Bike Rentals**, 75 Bell Rock Plaza, Suite 3, Sedona, AZ 86351. Other activities are offered. Mon.-Sat. 8-5. Phone (520) 284-1099 or (888) 464-5337. *See color ad.*

SELLS (F-3) pop. 2,800, elev. 2,379'

Originally known as Indian Oasis, Sells was renamed in 1918 in honor of Indian commissioner Cato Sells. The dependable water supply made the area a popular stop for travelers, even in prehistoric times.

Sells is the headquarters of the Tohono O'odham Indian Reservation. In addition to this vast reservation west of Tucson, a smaller tract is

south of Tucson at the site of Mission San Xavier del Bac *(see Tucson p. 106)*. Mainly farmers and ranchers, the Tohono O'odham are known for their handcrafted baskets and pottery.

SHOW LOW (C-5)
pop. 5,000, elev. 6,347'

Show Low took its name from the winning hand in a poker game between Native American scout Col. Croyden E. Cooley and his friend Marion Clark. The town's main street, Deuce of Clubs, was named after the winning card.

Situated on the edge of the Mogollon Rim, the town offers numerous recreational pursuits, including fishing, camping, hiking and horseback riding.

Show Low Chamber of Commerce: 951 W. Deuce of Clubs, P.O. Box 1083, Show Low, AZ 85902; phone (520) 537-2326 or (888) 746-9569.

FOOL HOLLOW LAKE RECREATION AREA, 2 mi. n. of US 60 off SR 260, then e. on Old Linden Rd. to park entrance, offers fishing, swimming and boating in a lake covering the old town site of Adair. Camping among the 100-foot-tall pine trees also is available. Daily 8-5. Admission $5 per private vehicle. Camping $10-$15 per private vehicle. Phone (520) 537-3680. *See Recreation Chart.*

SIERRA VISTA (F-5)
pop. 33,000, elev. 4,600'

Sierra Vista has been built upon the historic past of Fort Huachuca *(see place listing p. 50)*, established in 1877. The fort is now the largest single employer in southern Arizona, and most of its personnel live in the area. The scenery makes Sierra Vista special: The city is nestled on the eastern slopes of the Huachuca Mountains and overlooks the San Pedro River Valley. Nature lovers are attracted to nearby Coronado National Memorial *(see place listing p. 47)*, San Pedro Riparian Conservation Area (24 miles west) and Ramsey Canyon Preserve.

Sierra Vista Area Chamber of Commerce: 21 E. Wilcox Dr., Sierra Vista, AZ 85635; phone (520) 458-6940. *See color ad p. 42.*

FORT HUACHUCA MUSEUM— *see Fort Huachuca p. 50.*

SOMERTON (E-1)
pop. 5,300, elev. 103'

CASINOS
- **Cocopah Casino,** jct. US 95 (Ave. B) and 15th St. Daily 24 hours. Phone (520) 726-8066.

SPRINGERVILLE (C-6)
pop. 1,800, elev. 6,862'

Springerville is in a cattle-ranching area of eastern Arizona. Created by shield volcanoes, the town is a gateway to the White Mountains, where visitors can enjoy outdoor activities year-round. In a wing of the Latter-day Saints Church on Apache Street is a collection of European artworks and furniture dating from the Renaissance to the early 20th century. The Renee Cushman Art collection is shown by appointment; phone (520) 333-4514.

Round Valley Chamber of Commerce: 318 E. Main St., P.O. Box 31, Springerville, AZ 85938; phone (520) 333-2123.

CASA MALPAIS PUEBLO, 318 Main St., is a 15-acre restoration project of Mogollon and ancient pueblo ruins occupied 1250-1400. Pottery, food and baskets unearthed at the project are displayed at the visitor center. After watching an orientation film, visitors drive to the site for a guided walking tour.

Allow 1 hour, 30 minutes minimum. Center open daily 8-5. Guided tours depart the visitor center at 9, 11 and 2. Fee $4; over 55 and ages 12-18, $3. Phone (520) 333-5375.

SAVE **RAVEN SITE RUIN,** 12 mi. n. on US 180/191, .5 mi. e. on Tucson Electric Power Plant Rd., then 1 mi. s. on a dirt road, is a field school and research center. The two Raven Site Ruin pueblos with 800 rooms and two kivas are on a 5-acre knoll overlooking the Little Colorado River and were occupied from about 700 to about 1550. Two hundred rooms are currently open to the public.

Guided hiking tours of the nearby petroglyphs and shrine sites are offered. Also featured are tours of a laboratory, museum and archeological excavation sites, where visitors can view artifacts and a collection of unusual Amazonian insects. Available by reservation are 1-day and multi-day hands-on excavation programs for adults and children over age 9. For reservations contact White Mountain Archaeological Center, HC 30, Box 30, St. Johns, AZ 85936.

Daily 10-5, May 1 to mid-Oct. Site tour $4; over 62 and ages 12-17, $3. One-day excavation fee $55; ages 9-17, $35. Reservations are required for guided petroglyph tours. Phone (520) 333-5857.

SUN CITY/SUN CITY WEST—
see Phoenix p. 86.

SUNSET CRATER VOLCANO NATIONAL MONUMENT (B-4)

The truncated cone of Sunset Crater Volcano, a 1,000-foot-high cinder cone, dominates the surrounding fields of cinders, lava flows and spatter cones. The monument is 12 miles north of Flagstaff via US 89, then 2 miles east on Sunset Crater-Wupatki Loop Road. The bright-reddish hues of the decomposed, water-stained sulfuric rock at the summit are in stark contrast with the black basalt of the adjacent rocks. From a distance the mountain appears to be on fire. Dark at the base, the volcano also has shades of red, orange and yellow leading to the summit and takes on a rosy tint during the hour before sunset. In 1892 John Wesley Powell noted the phenomenon and purportedly gave the cone its name.

Sunset Crater Volcano first erupted A.D. 1064-65 and was active intermittently for nearly 200 years. A self-guiding trail leads over the Bonito lava flow; sturdy walking shoes are recommended. A paved road crosses the lava flow and connects the monument with Wupatki National Monument *(see place listing p. 116).* Picnic facilities are available.

Allow 30 minutes minimum. The visitor center is open daily 8-6; closed Dec. 25. In winter the monument may be closed by snow. Admission $3 (includes Wupatki National Monument), under 17 free. Phone (520) 526-0502.

SUPAI (B-3) pop. 400, elev. 3,195′

★HAVASU CANYON is accessible from Hualapai Hilltop, which is reached from SR 66 via a turnoff 5 miles e. of Peach Springs. There are no services after the turnoff. Most of the 65-mile road from Peach Springs is in good condition. Havasu Canyon is home to the village of Supai, which serves as the governmental center of the Havasupai Indian Reservation.

Automobiles must be left at Hualapai Hilltop; the 8 mile journey to the canyon floor and Havasu Falls can be covered on horseback, helicopter or on foot down a precipitous trail. Anyone attempting the trail must carry at least one gallon of water. The trail is only recommended for experienced hikers in good physical condition. Summer temperatures should be taken into account when planning daytime trips. The return climb out of the canyon is very arduous.

Camping is permitted; no open fires are allowed. Horse rental is available. Reservations for horses, helicopter and campgrounds are required and can be made by writing Havasupai Tourist Enterprise, P.O. Box 160, Supai, AZ 86435.

Office hours daily 8-5. Entrance fee $20. Campground fee $10 per person. Helicopter fee $65 per person. MC, VI. Phone (520) 448-2121 or (602) 516-2790 for helicopter schedule.

SUPERIOR (J-6) pop. 3,500, elev. 2,730′

Although it began as a silver-mining town, Superior owes its existence to its proximity to some of the deepest and richest copper lodes in the country. Near Superior is Apache Leap Cliff, where, according to legend, 75 Apache warriors leaped to their deaths rather than be captured by the cavalry. The town also is near the southern terminus of US 60 (Gila/Pinal Scenic Drive), which travels northward through Tonto National Forest, Salt River Canyon and the Fort Apache Indian Reservation.

Superior Chamber of Commerce: 151 Main St., P.O. Box 95, Superior, AZ 85273; phone (520) 689-2441.

★BOYCE THOMPSON ARBORETUM STATE PARK, 3 mi. w. on US 60, has more than 300 acres of desert plants collected from all over the world; 50 acres are accesible for viewing. Founded in the 1920s by mining magnate Col. William Boyce Thompson, the arboretum has nature paths leading past towering trees, cacti, mountain cliffs, a streamside forest, a desert lake, hidden canyon and panoramic views.

An interpretive center has educational displays and two greenhouses housing cacti and succulents. Picnicking is available. Allow 1 hour minimum. Daily 8-5; closed Dec. 25. Admission $5; ages 5-12, $2. Phone (520) 689-2811.

RAY MINE, 18 mi. s. on SR 177, is an open-pit copper mine. An overlook is open daily dawn-dusk. Phone (520) 356-7811.

TEMPE—*see Phoenix p. 86.*

★TOMBSTONE (F-5)
pop. 1,220, elev. 4,540′

"The Town Too Tough To Die," Tombstone was perhaps the most renowned of Arizona's old mining camps. When Ed Schieffelin came to Camp Huachuca with a party of soldiers and left the fort to prospect, his comrades told him that he would find his tombstone rather than silver. Thus, in 1877 Schieffelin named his first claim Tombstone, and rumors of rich strikes made a boomtown of the settlement that adopted this name.

Days of lawlessness and violence climaxed with the infamous Earp-Clanton battle, fought at the rear entrance to the O.K. Corral. Over the course of 7 years the mines produced millions of dollars in silver and gold before rising underground waters forced suspension of operations.

Many of Tombstone's historic buildings are within an area bounded by Fremont, 6th, Toughnut and 3rd streets. Among them are St. Paul's Episcopal Church, built in 1882; the Crystal Palace, one of the most luxurious saloons in the West; and the *Tombstone Epitaph* building, where the oldest continuously published paper in Arizona is still being printed. Western printing history exhibits in the front office are free to the public.

Tombstone Office of Tourism: P.O. Box 917, Tombstone, AZ 85638; phone (800) 457-3423. *See color ad p. 42.*

BIRD CAGE THEATRE, 6th and Allen sts., was built in 1881 and remains virtually unchanged, with the original fixtures, furnishings and interior still intact. A combination theater, saloon and dance hall, the theater was known in its heyday as the bawdiest nightspot between Basin Street and the Barbary Coast. The refrain from the song "Only a Bird in a Gilded Cage" was inspired by this opera house saloon. Allow 1 hour minimum. Daily 8-6; closed Dec. 25. Admission $4.50; senior citizens $4; ages 8-18, $3; family rate $12.50. Phone (520) 457-3421.

BOOTHILL GRAVEYARD, at the n. city limits off SR 80, contains 300 marked graves of early citizens as well as graves of some of the town's famous and infamous residents. This is reportedly the first cemetery to be called "Boot Hill." Allow 1 hour minimum. Daily 7:30-6. Donations. Phone (520) 457-9344.

HISTORAMA is next to the main entrance of the O.K. Corral. A 30-minute multimedia presentation narrated by actor Vincent Price offers a look at Tombstone's history. This is a good starting point for a tour of the town. Shows begin on the hour daily 9-4. Admission $2.50, under 6 free. Combination ticket with O.K. Corral (including a copy of the *Tombstone Epitaph* reporting the gunfight) $5, gunfight re-enactment $1.50. Phone (520) 457-3456.

O.K. CORRAL, between 3rd and 4th sts. on Allen St., includes the site where the Earp-Clanton gunfight took place on Oct. 26, 1881. A re-enactment of the gunfight takes place daily at 2 p.m. Allow 30 minutes minimum. Daily 9-5. Admission (including Camillus Fly Studio) $2.50, under 6 free. Gunfight re-enactment $2. Combination ticket with Historama (including a copy of the *Tombstone Epitaph* reporting the gunfight) $5, gunfight re-enactment $1.50. Phone (520) 457-3456.

Camillus Fly Studio, between 3rd and 4th sts. on Fremont St., is entered only through the O.K. Corral. This is the re-created studio and boardinghouse of the pioneer photographer. Photographs of early Tombstone and its personalities are displayed. Allow 30 minutes minimum. Daily 9-5.

[SAVE] **ROSE TREE MUSEUM AND BOOKSTORE,** 116 S. 4th St. at the corner of 4th and Toughnut sts., features the world's largest rosebush, which now covers more than 8,000 square feet; the size of the bush is verified by "The Guinness Book of World Records" yearly. The white-blossomed shrub was planted as a cutting sent from Scotland about 1885. Rose slips may be purchased. Exhibits include antique furniture brought to Tombstone by covered wagon in 1880.

Allow 30 minutes minimum. Daily 9-5; closed Thanksgiving and Dec. 25. Admission $2, under 14 free when accompanied by adult. MC, VI. Phone (520) 457-3326.

SCHIEFFELIN HALL, 4th and Fremont sts., a theatrical and civic center of early Tombstone, is

one of the largest adobe structures in the West. It is closed to the public.

TOMBSTONE COURTHOUSE STATE HISTORIC PARK, 219 E. Toughnut St., was built in 1882. The building contains displays pertaining to the history of Tombstone and Cochise County, using antiques and artifacts to present the lives of former citizens. Allow 1 hour minimum. Daily 8-5; closed Dec. 25. Admission $2.50; ages 7-13, $1. Phone (520) 457-3311.

TONTO NATIONAL FOREST

Elevations in the forest range from 1,300 ft. at Apache Junction to 7,900 ft. at the Mogollon Rim in the Payson District. Refer to AAA maps for additional elevation information.

Stretching some 90 miles south from the scenic Mogollon Rim to the city of Scottsdale, the Tonto National Forest encompasses 2.9 million acres of spectacular pine, brush and cactus country, making it one of the largest national forests. Elevations range from 1,300 feet to almost 7,900 feet in the northern pine country. Eight regions have been designated as wilderness areas; the entire forest offers more than 860 miles of trails for backpacking, hiking and horse travel.

Scenic roadways in the area include the Apache Trail (SR 88) *(see Apache Junction p. 81)*, Beeline Highway (SR 87) and Young Highway (SR 288). Some unpaved roads are very rough, so check locally for road conditions.

Six lakes offer recreational areas for boating, swimming and fishing; Saguaro, Bartlett, Canyon, Apache and Theodore Roosevelt lakes have marina facilities. Tubing is a popular pastime in the summer on the lower Salt River. Campgrounds, picnic sites and other recreational opportunities also are available throughout the forest. A map showing roads, recreation sites and tourist services can be obtained from the local Forest Service office for $4.

For further information contact the Forest Supervisor's Office, Tonto National Forest, 2324 E. McDowell Rd., Phoenix, AZ 85006; phone (602) 225-5200. *See Recreation Chart and the AAA Southwestern CampBook.*

TONTO NATIONAL MONUMENT (H-6)

Tonto National Monument, east of Roosevelt Dam on SR 88/188, preserves the most accessible of south-central Arizona's prehistoric cliff dwellings. The remains of a two-story pueblo built in a natural cave are visible from the headquarters parking area. A .5-mile paved foot trail ascends 350 feet and leads to cliff dwellings that were occupied by the Salado culture in the 13th and 14th centuries. Summer temperatures are high; wear a hat and suitable shoes and carry sufficient water.

Ranger-conducted, 3-hour tours to the less accessible 40-room Upper Cliff Dwelling are available from November through April; reservations are required. Write Tonto National Monument, HC 02, Box 4602, Roosevelt, AZ 85545.

A visitor center and museum contain artifacts from the Salado culture, including examples of the pottery and woven textiles for which they are noted. Allow 1 hour, 30 minutes minimum. Park and visitor center open daily 8-5; closed Dec. 25. Trail closes to the Lower Cliff Dwelling at 4. Picnic area 8-4:45. Admission $4 per private vehicle or $2 per person on foot, motorcycle or bicycle. Phone (520) 467-2241.

TUBA CITY (A-4)
pop. 7,300, elev. 4,936'

Tuba City was named after Tuve, a Hopi leader. Natural springs attracted generations of Hopi, Navajo and Paiute Indians to the area. In 1875 the city was laid out and settled by Mormons, who used blocks of dressed stone from nearby prehistoric sites to build structures, some of which still stand.

The town lies on US 160, 10 miles east of US 89 within Arizona's northeastern Indian country, which encompasses the Navajo and Hopi Indian reservations. A variety of Native American crafts are produced, including baskets, pottery and silver products.

TUBAC (F-4) elev. 3,200'

Tubac, meaning "sinking water," was a Pima village when Jesuit Eusebio Francisco Kino visited the area in 1691. A presidio and mission were established in 1752 (the first military base in Arizona) shortly after the Pima revolted against Spanish encroachment. Between 1752 and 1856 some 500 people lived at Tubac, but in 1776 the presidio was moved to help fortify the strategically important Tucson. With the Gadsden Purchase in 1853, the town became a part of the United States.

The Mexican War, The California Gold Rush of 1849 and the raiding Apaches depopulated the town throughout much of the 19th century. However, in 1859 Arizona's first newspaper was printed by a local mining company who revived the town. By 1860 Tubac was the largest town in Arizona, but the Civil War left the town unprotected, and it was deserted once again. Once the Apaches ceded control of the area in the late 1800s, Tubac began to grow, but it never regained its earlier importance.

Modern Tubac is a small community of writers and artists located next to the old presidio; many of the shops and galleries in town sell the local art.

Tubac Chamber of Commerce: P.O. Box 1866, Tubac, AZ 85646; phone (520) 398-2704. *See color ad.*

TUBAC PRESIDIO STATE HISTORIC PARK is off I-19. Arizona's first state park encompasses the Spanish military site that made Tubac Arizona's first European settlement in 1752. An underground exhibit reveals portions of the captain's house.

The visitor center and museum contain Native American, Spanish, Mexican and territorial artifacts as well as a restored 1885 schoolhouse and the press that printed Arizona's first newspaper in 1859. A living-history program, depicting life in Tubac 1752-76, is presented Sun. 1-4, Oct.-Mar. Allow 1 hour minimum. Daily 8-5; closed Dec. 25. Admission $2; ages 7-13, $1. Phone (520) 398-2252.

Tucson

Sunshine, dry air, mountains and rich desert vegetation are Tucson's drawing cards. The city boasts an average of 3,800 hours of sunshine a year, placing it high on any list of health and winter resorts. More than just a vacation destination, Tucson also is a culturally active city. In addition to the visual arts, all areas of the performing arts—dance, opera, theater, music—are well represented.

The 321-acre University of Arizona is a major asset both culturally and economically—the needs of its 31,000 students create diverse jobs. Davis-Monthan Air Force Base, which contains a large aircraft storage facility, is another leading employer. Such large private companies as IBM, Garrett AiResearch and Hughes Aircraft have operations in Tucson.

Tucson is in a high desert valley, once the floor of an ancient inland sea. It is surrounded by four mountain ranges: the Santa Catalinas to the north, the Rincons to the east, the Santa Ritas to the south and the Tucsons to the west. These protective mountains and the Santa Cruz River attracted humans approximately 12,000 years ago. The Native American name for the ancient settlement was *stjukshon*, pronounced like Tucson, which loosely translates into "spring at the foot of the black hill," a reference to the springs that once lined the banks of the Santa Cruz.

In 1700 Spanish Jesuit Eusebio Francisco Kino established the San Xavier Mission at the nearby village of Bac. Spanish ranchers and miners soon penetrated the valley, forcing the natives (particularly the Apaches) to protect their territory. After numerous Indian attacks, a garrison was built near the mission in Tubac *(see place listing p. 99)* and moved in 1776 to a new walled presidio in Tucson. The city's nickname "The Old Pueblo" refers to these walls.

When Mexico shook off Spanish rule in 1821, Tucson came under Mexican jurisdiction. The American flag was first raised over Tucson in 1846 by the commander of the Mormon Battalion during the Mexican War. The wagon road the Mormons built to California became a major east-west corridor that was used by thousands of homesteaders and miners during the California gold rush. Disputes over right-of-way through this corridor prompted the Gadsden Purchase in 1853, which joined southern Arizona and Tucson with the rest of the Arizona Territory.

Overland stage service to San Diego from San Antonio began in 1857, and Tucson gained a certain notoriety as a stage stop. A stay in Tucson usually meant sleeping in the infamous Tucson bed, which the traveler made by lying on his stomach and covering himself with his back. Despite its no-frills reputation, the

village remained a major outpost, offering protection against the Apaches and supplies for travelers.

The Civil War interrupted travel along this southern route to California. After the war Tucson continued as a supply and distribution point, first for the Army and then for miners. From 1867 through 1877 Tucson was the territorial capital. The "Old Pueblo" began to shed its outpost image with the arrival of the Southern Pacific Railroad in 1880 and the founding of the University of Arizona in 1885. Tucson entered the 20th century as Arizona's largest city and remained so until 1920, when it was surpassed by Phoenix.

Tucson's Native American and Mexican roots are ever present. Mexican-Americans make up a substantial portion of the population. Spanish is widely spoken and Native American dialects are occasionally heard. Mexican restaurants abound, serving the neighboring country's spicy cuisine. Architecturally, low, Pueblo-style buildings with adobe walls and flat, tiled roofs predominate. Interiors are decorated with Navajo rugs and Pueblo pottery, and many festivals celebrate the cultures of the city's original inhabitants.

In the 1950s dude ranches were Tucson's main attractions. Now these guest ranches are complemented by elaborate resorts, and renovations have given the downtown business district a new look. La Placita Village incorporates fountains, territorial architecture and modern buildings in a contemporary blend; the adjoining Community Center has facilities for conventions, sports, theater and entertainment.

These complexes, connected by plazas, parks, walkways and bridges, and combined with a sprinkling of 19th-century houses, form an inviting and compact downtown area. While a Western atmosphere has been preserved, Tucson has emerged as a cosmopolitan city. The walls of "The Old Pueblo" have yielded to new structures that no longer defend but welcome.

Approaches
By Car

Tucson's major approach and through-route is I-10, the nation's southernmost transcontinental highway. Primarily an east-west route, it angles into the city from the southeast and the northwest. Northbound, I-10 intersects with I-19 in south Tucson and then continues along the west side of the city, providing access to the downtown area. Once I-10 leaves the city, it proceeds northwest to Phoenix, 120 miles away.

A major approach from the west is I-8, which originates in San Diego and joins with I-10 about midway between Phoenix and Tucson. Because both I-10 and I-8 traverse desert country, some of their sections are subject to dust storms, particularly in spring and early summer. Local radio stations broadcast advisories during these fluctuating weather conditions, and interstate signs with changeable messages warn motorists.

(continued on p. 104)

The Informed Traveler

City Population: 405,400

Elevation: 2,389 ft.

SALES TAX: Arizona's statewide sales tax is 5 percent; an additional 2 percent is levied in Tucson. The tax on a hotel room in Tucson is 9.5 percent, plus $1 per room per night; the tax is 7.5 percent elsewhere in Pima County. There is a rental car tax of 10 percent, plus a concession fee of 10 percent if the car is picked up at the airport; the tax is 12 percent if the car is picked up off airport property, but within the Tucson city limits. Pima County imposes a car rental fee of $3.50.

WHOM TO CALL

Emergency: 911

Police (non-emergency): (520) 791-4444

Time and Temperature: 1-676-1676 (toll 75c)

Hospitals: Carondelet St. Joseph's, (520) 296-3211; Carondelet St. Mary's, (520) 622-5833; University Medical Center, (520) 694-0111.

WHERE TO LOOK

Newspapers

The two major newspapers are the *Arizona Daily Star,* published in the morning, and the *Tucson Citizen,* which is published in the afternoon. These papers are supplemented by local journals.

Radio and TV

Tucson radio station KTUC (1400 AM) is an all-news/weather station; KUAT (90.5 FM and 1550 AM) is a member of National Public Radio. There are two Spanish-language radio stations.

The major TV channels are 4 (NBC), 6 (PBS), 9 (ABC), 11 (FOX) and 13 (CBS). For a complete list of radio and television programs, consult the daily newspapers.

Visitor Information

The Metropolitan Tucson Convention & Visitors Bureau, 130 S. Scott Ave., Tucson, AZ 85701, can provide a variety of information, including the *Official Visitors Guide to*
Metropolitan Tucson; the guide is available in English and in Spanish. The bureau's visitor center is open Mon.-Fri. 8-5, Sat.-Sun. 9-4; closed major holidays. Phone (520) 624-1817 or (800) 638-8350.

TRANSPORTATION

Air Travel

Ten miles south of downtown, Tucson International Airport is served by many major passenger airlines. Short-term airport parking costs $1.25 per hour; long-term parking costs $5.50 for 24 hours.

The Arizona Stage Coach, (520) 889-1000, provides van service throughout the Tucson area; prices range from $9-$32. Sunset Limousine, (520) 573-9418 or (800) 266-8059, provides limousine service throughout the Tucson area; prices range $50-$70 per hour. Cab service to downtown averages 20 minutes and costs $17-$25.

Rental Cars

Hertz, (520) 294-7616 or (800) 654-3080, offers discounts to AAA members. Check the telephone directory for listings of other agencies.

Rail Service

The Amtrak Station, 400 E. Toole, accommodates Amtrak rail lines. For ticket and schedule information phone (520) 623-4442 or (800) 872-7245.

Buses

The terminal for Greyhound Lines Inc. is at 2 S. 4th Ave.; phone (800) 231-2222.

Taxis

There are many independent taxi companies in Tucson. Rates are not regulated by the city. One company that serves the area is Yellow Cab, (520) 624-6611.

Public Transport

Sun Tran operates buses throughout the metropolitan area. The fare is 85c to all points. Passes are available for students, senior citizens and the physically impaired. For schedule and route information phone (520) 792-9222.

Destination Tucson

*T*he heritage of the Old West meets trendy Southwestern chic in this dynamic Sunbelt city, home to both Spanish colonial adobes and high-tech facilities.

*L*a Casa Cordova, Tucson's oldest house, testifies to the city's Spanish and Mexican background, while Old Tucson Studios dramatizes its history as a wild frontier outpost. On the flip side are the Biosphere 2 Center in Oracle and Kitt Peak National Observatory: both renowned, cutting-edge research institutions.

Arizona-Sonora Desert Museum, Tucson. Come face-to-face with mountain lions and 300 other species of animals at this zoo, natural history museum and botanical garden rolled into one. (See listing page 104)

Tucson Museum of Art and Historic Block At this downtown cultural space, modern museum buildings contrast strikingly with the restored homes of Tucson's El Presidio Historic District. (See listing page 107)

Oracle

*P*laces included in this *AAA Destination City:*

Green Valley.............111
Oracle......................111
Sahuarita.................112
Vail.........................112

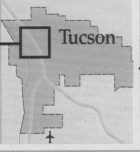

See Downtown map page 104

Tucson

See Vicinity map page 104

10

19

10

Saharita

Vail

Sabino Canyon, Tucson. Hikers and swimmers have it made at this lovely desert oasis, part of the Coronado National Forest. (See listing page 106)

Green Valley

Mission San Xavier del Bac, Tucson. Known as the "White Dove of the Desert," this splendid example of Spanish mission architecture represents 200 years of Arizona history. (See listing page 106)

A well-known route reaching Tucson from the north is SR 77. One of the area's oldest two-lane routes, it is especially scenic. South of Tucson, Bus. Rte. 19 parallels sections of I-19, which is the more recent link with the Mexican border at Nogales.

Getting Around

Street System

Tucson is laid out in a grid pattern. Numbered streets run east-west to the south of Speedway Boulevard, and numbered avenues run north-south to the west of Euclid Avenue. Address numbers start at the intersection of Broadway, the north-south divider, and Stone, the east-west divider. Unless otherwise posted the speed limit on most streets is 25 to 30 mph.

During rush hours the center turn lanes of Broadway, 22nd Street, Grant Road and Speedway Boulevard are reverse traffic flow lanes: morning rush hour one way into the city and evening rush hour one way out of the city. Rush-hour traffic, 7-9 a.m. and 4-6 p.m., should be avoided.

Parking

Metered parking is available on many downtown streets, but be sure to check signs and meters for restricted times and limits. There also are a number of commercial garages and lots. Rates are $2 per hour or $5 per day.

What To See

ARIZONA HISTORICAL SOCIETY/TUCSON MUSEUM, near the entrance to the University of Arizona campus off Park Ave. at 949 E. 2nd St., houses a museum documenting Arizona's cultural history, a research library and an Arizona mining exhibit. The society also administers the Fort Lowell Museum and the Sosa-Carillo-Fremont House *(see attraction listings).*

Allow 1 hour minimum. Open Mon.-Sat. 10-4, Sun. noon-4; closed major holidays. Library open Mon.-Fri. 10-4, Sat. 10-1. Donations. Phone (520) 628-5774.

★**ARIZONA-SONORA DESERT MUSEUM,** 14 mi. w. in Tucson Mountain Park at 2021 N. Kinney Rd., exhibits more than 300 live animal species, including mountain lions, prairie dogs, Gila

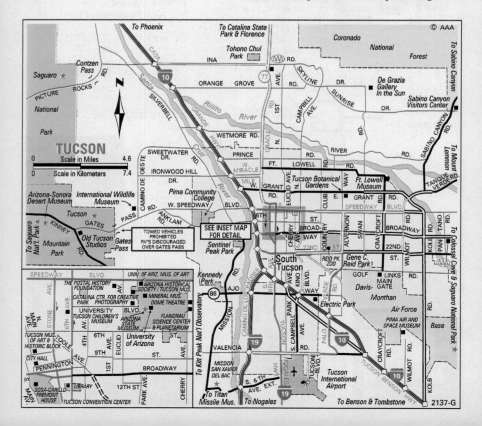

monsters, hawks, bighorn sheep and humming-birds, in natural habitats. Almost 2 miles of paths lead visitors through landscapes containing more than 1,300 species of plants indigenous to the Sonoran Desert region; included are desert grass-lands and cactus and desert gardens.

A pollination gardens complex consists of seven gardens that show crucial interactions be-tween insects, birds, bats and plants, and a fence-less enclosure allows javelinas to explore hillsides and take mud baths in a shady arroyo.

A simulated walk-through limestone cave fea-tures a collection of regional gems and minerals. A display about how the planet has evolved with explanations of erosion, volcanic and seismic ac-tivity and plate tectonics also is featured. Food is available. Allow 2 hours minimum. Daily 7:30-6, Mar.-Sept.; 8:30-5, rest of year. Admission $8.95; ages 6-12, $1.75. MC, VI. Phone (520) 883-2702.

★ **ARIZONA STATE MUSEUM,** on the University of Arizona campus at Park Ave. and University Blvd. in Buildings 26 and 30, emphasizes the archeology and ethnology of Arizona. Its collec-tions of artifacts from prehistoric Hohokam and Mogollon Native Americans are considered the most comprehensive in existence.

The newest exhibit, "Paths of Life—American Indians of the Southwest," specializes in the his-torical and contemporary cultures of Southwest-ern Native Americans. Tribes emphasized include the southern Paiutes, the Pais of the northern Colorado plateau, the Apaches, Navajos, Hopis, Yumans, Akimels and Tohono O'odhams.

Modern and ancient Native American lifestyles are contrasted, and the works of modern Native American artists are displayed. Included are ex-amples of Apache beadwork and Navajo blan-kets, as well as pieces by Nampeyo, the noted Hopi potter credited with combining traditional and contemporary designs into her works of art. Temporary exhibits depict the culture of the Southwest.

The research library contains 30,000 volumes; phone (520) 621-4695 for information. The an-thropological archives, which includes 200,000 photographs, documents the archeology and eth-nology of the Greater Southwest; phone (520) 621-2970. Allow 1 hour minimum. Museum open Mon.-Sat. 10-5, Sun. noon-5; closed major holidays. Library open Mon.-Fri. 8-12:30 and 2-4:30. Archives open by appointment. Dona-tions. Phone (520) 621-6302.

BIOSPHERE II—see Oracle p. 111.

CATALINA STATE PARK, 9 mi. n. off SR 77 Milepost 81 to 11570 N. Oracle Rd., is home to 5,511 acres of desert plants. Situated at the base of the Santa Catalina Mountains, the park's ac-tivities include bird-watching, hiking, camping and horseback riding. Daily dawn-10 p.m. Ranger station 8-5. Admission $5 per private ve-hicle (up to four passengers), $1 for bicycles and each additional passenger. Camping $10-$15 per private vehicle. Phone (520) 628-5798. *See Rec-reation Chart.*

DE GRAZIA GALLERY IN THE SUN is 1 mi. n. of Sunrise Rd. in the Santa Catalina Mountains at 6300 N. Swan Rd. Paintings, bronzes and ce-ramics by artist Ted De Grazia are displayed. Next to the gallery is the Mission in the Sun, an open-air chapel De Grazia built and decorated with frescoes. Daily 10-4; closed Easter, Thanks-giving and Dec. 25. Donations. Phone (520) 299-9191 or (800) 545-2185.

FORT LOWELL MUSEUM, Fort Lowell and Craycroft rds. in Fort Lowell Park, embraces the ruins of the old fort which played a major role in the Apache Indian wars. The building, a recon-struction of the commanding officer's quarters, contains exhibits relating to military life at Fort Lowell, with a room furnished in period. Military equipment and changing photography exhibits are displayed. Allow 1 hour minimum. Wed.-Sat. 10-4; closed holidays. Free. Phone (520) 885-3832.

GENE C. REID PARK, 22nd St. and Country Club Rd., is a 160-acre park offering picnic areas, ten-nis courts, a fishing lake and Hi Corbett Field, where the Colorado Rockies professional base-ball team holds spring training. Fishing is al-lowed for those under 14. The park is open daily 7 a.m.-10 p.m. Free. Phone (520) 791-4873.

Reid Park Zoo, off 22nd St. just e. of Country Club Rd. in Gene C. Reid Park, houses more than 550 animals representing 150 species, in-cluding bears, baboons, giraffes, zebras and os-triches. Each habitat and species is fully described. Allow 2 hours minimum. Daily 9-4; closed Dec. 25. Admission $4; senior citizens $3; ages 5-14, 75c. Phone (520) 791-4022.

SAVE **INTERNATIONAL WILDLIFE MUSEUM** is 5 mi. w. of I-10 on Speedway Blvd. Tucson's inter-active natural history museum contains dioramas depicting more than 400 species of mammals, in-sects, birds and prehistoric animals from around the world. Hands-on exhibits and interactive dis-plays are found throughout the 38,000-square-foot museum.

A 98-seat theater offers hourly natural history films. Food is available. Mon.-Fri. 9-5, Sat.-Sun. 9-6. Admission $6; over 62 $4.75; ages 6-12, $2. AE, DI, MC, VI. Phone (520) 617-1439.

KITT PEAK NATIONAL OBSERVATORY, 56 mi. s.w. off SR 86, is located on the Tohono O'odham reservation in the Quinlan Mountains of the Sonoran Desert. Reputed to be the largest optical telescope facility, the observatory con-tains 24 major research instruments, including the world's largest solar telescope as well as the Mayall 4-meter telescope.

The three-building research facility, part of the National Optical Astronomy Observatories, monitors solar, stellar and extragalactic activities. Exhibits, videotaped programs and nightly stargazing utilizing a 16-inch telescope also are featured. Picnic facilities are available. Travelers are advised to check on weather and road conditions.

Open daily 9-3:45; closed Jan. 1, Thanksgiving and Dec. 25. Guided tours of the facility are offered daily at 10, 11:30 and 1:30. Donations. Reservations required for night observation program. Phone (520) 318-8726.

★ MISSION SAN XAVIER DEL BAC is 9 mi. s. off I-19 exit 92, on San Xavier Rd. in the Tohono O'odham Indian Reservation. Though founded by Jesuit Father Eusebio Francisco Kino before 1700, the present structure was built 1783-97 by the Franciscans. The missionaries were forced to leave San Xavier in 1828 but returned in 1911, and since that time have maintained old San Xavier as the main church and school of the Tohono O'odham.

This is the only Kino mission in the nation still active in preaching to the Tohono O'odham. Called the "White Dove of the Desert," the structure is an impressive example of Spanish mission architecture. The domes, carvings, arches and flying buttresses distinguish it from other missions. The interior murals and the altar are especially noteworthy.

A continuous video presentation is shown in the museum and a self-guiding tour is available. Daily 9:30-5:30. Donations. Phone (520) 294-2624.

SAVE OLD TUCSON STUDIOS is 12 mi. w. via Speedway Blvd. or Ajo Way in Tucson Mountain Park; follow signs. This replica of 1860s Tucson, erected in 1939 by Columbia Pictures for the filming of "Arizona," was the location decades later for the movie "Tombstone." The television series "High Chaparral" and "The Young Riders" were filmed at the studios as well as more than 300 films, TV episodes and commercials.

Visitors can ride in stagecoaches or descend into a dark mine. Live gunfights, stunt demon-

strations and Western musical revues, Storyteller Theater and Family Carousel Theater are highlights. Thirty-minute trail rides also are featured. Rio Lobo Stage offers concerts featuring national acts. Food is available.

Daily 10-6; closed Thanksgiving and Dec. 25. Admission $14.95; ages 4-11, $9.95. Prices may vary; phone ahead. AE, DS, MC, VI. Phone (520) 883-0100, ext. 1. See color ad.

SAVE PIMA AIR AND SPACE MUSEUM is at 6000 E. Valencia Rd.; from I-10 eastbound exit to Valencia and from I-10 westbound exit to Wilmot Rd. More than 200 vintage aircraft depicting the nation's aviation history are displayed; many are still being restored.

The DC-6 used by Presidents John F. Kennedy and Lyndon B. Johnson is open for touring 9-3:30. Additional aircraft are displayed in hangars and along pathways, including a replica 1903 Wright Flyer and a SR-71 Blackbird. The Tucson Challenger Learning Center features interactive, hands-on science exhibits designed to simulate a space mission. Food is available. Daily 9-5; closed Thanksgiving and Dec. 25. Last admission 1 hour before closing. Admission $7.50; over 62 and military with ID $6.50; ages 10-17, $4. MC, VI. Phone (520) 574-0462.

THE POSTAL HISTORY FOUNDATION, 920 N. First Ave., features stamps, postmarks and books tracing the history of the U.S. Postal Service and caters to serious philatelists and postal historians. Original equipment from the Naco, Ariz., post office as well as antique file cabinets and other memorabilia are on display. Allow 1 hour minimum. Mon.-Fri. 8-3; closed holidays. Donations. Phone (520) 623-6652.

SABINO CANYON, 17 mi. e. via Tanque Verde Rd. and Sabino Canyon Rd., lies in the Santa Catalina Mountains and is part of the Coronado National Forest (see place listing p. 46). Among the recreational activities available at this desert oasis are swimming, hiking, bird-watching and picnicking. Sabino Canyon Tours offers narrated excursions into the canyon aboard shuttle buses;

phone (520) 749-2327. Pets and motor vehicles are not allowed in the canyon.

Allow 1 hour minimum. Visitor reception area open daily 8-4:30. Free. Shuttle tours $6; ages 3-12, $2.50. Phone (520) 749-8700.

SAGUARO NATIONAL PARK—
see place listing p. 111.

SENTINEL PEAK PARK, off Broadway w. of I-10 on Cuesta, contains the peak more popularly known as "A Mountain" because of the big "A" annually whitewashed on it by University of Arizona freshmen. It affords an excellent view of Tucson and surrounding mountains. At night the city's lights are particularly captivating from this vantage point. Daily 6 a.m.-10:30 p.m.

SOSA-CARILLO-FREMONT HOUSE is at 151 S. Granada Ave. in the Convention Center Complex. Restored to its 1880 appearance, the Mexican-American adobe *casa* was John Fremont's residence during part of his term as territorial governor. Period furnishings and changing exhibits are displayed.

Two-hour guided walking tours of the historic districts begin at the house Sat. at 10 a.m. Nov.-Mar.; reservations are recommended. Allow 30 minutes minimum. Wed.-Sat. 10-4; closed holidays. House free. Walking tours $5. Phone (520) 622-0956.

TITAN MISSILE MUSEUM—
see Green Valley p. 111.

TOHONO CHUL PARK is at 7366 N. Paseo del Norte. Tohono O'odham for "desert corner," Tohono Chul Park is a 50-acre desert preserve set amid a rapidly growing urban area. The park features nature trails, a Geology Wall, a Children's Garden and changing art exhibits. Displays educate visitors about water conservation, arid lands and the traditions and cultures of the Southwest. Guided and self-guiding tours are available. Park open daily 7-dusk. Exhibit building open Mon.-Sat. 9:30-5, Sun. 11-5. Admission $2. Phone (520) 575-8468 or 742-6455.

[SAVE] **TUCSON BOTANICAL GARDENS,** 2150 N. Alvernon Way, covers 5.5 acres and features backyard bird-watching, cactus, children's, herb, historical, iris, sensory and xeriscape gardens as well as Native American crop gardens. Exhibits include useful plants of tropical forests and a Native American round house. A self-guiding tour and guided tours are available. Daily 8:30-4:30; closed Jan. 1, July 4, Thanksgiving and Dec. 25. Admission $4; over 62, $3; ages 5-11, $1. Phone (520) 326-9255.

[SAVE] **TUCSON CHILDREN'S MUSEUM,** 200 S. 6th Ave., encourages learning through hands-on exhibits and programs for ages 2-11 that include a grocery store, health center, electricity and optic exhibits, a firehouse and dress up room. Sat.10-5, Sun noon-5. Weekday and holidays hours vary;

phone ahead. Last admission 1 hour before closing. Admission $5.50; over 62, $4.50; ages 2-16, $3.50. Phone (520) 792-9985.

★ **TUCSON MOUNTAIN PARK,** 8 mi. w. on Speedway Blvd. and Kinney Rd., encompasses approximately 17,000 acres of the Tucson Mountains and adjoining mesa land and embraces one of the largest areas of saguaro and natural desert growth in the Southwest. Foot and horse trails as well as picnic facilities are available. Camping is available at the Gilbert Ray Campground *(see the AAA Southwestern CampBook).* Park open daily 7 a.m.-10 p.m. Park free. Camping $6-$9.50 per night. For campground information phone (520) 883-4200 or 740-2690.

TUCSON MUSEUM OF ART AND HISTORIC BLOCK is at 140 N. Main Ave. in an historical arts complex. Collections include pre-Columbian, Spanish Colonial and Western American art pieces. Changing exhibits of historical and contemporary art also are presented. Art lectures and classes are offered in the education center auditorium; a library, photographs and memorabilia also are featured.

Surrounding the museum in the El Presidio Historic District are five of Tucson's early homes. Presently the Leonardo Romero House serves as a museum school. The Hiram S. Stevens House, La Casa Cordova, the restored 1906 Corbett House and the John K. Goodman Pavilion of Western Art are open to the public. Walking tours of the historic district are offered Oct. 1-May 1. Museum open Mon.-Sat. 10-4, Sun. noon-4, Labor Day-Memorial Day; Tues.-Sat. 10-4, Sun. noon-4, rest of year. Closed major holidays. Admission $2; over 65 and students $1; under 12 free; free to all Tues. Phone (520) 624-2333.

La Casa Cordova, on N. Meyer Ave., was built about 1850 and is one of the oldest buildings in Tucson. The home contains the Presidio History Room. Mon.-Sat. 10-4, Sun. noon-4, Labor Day-Memorial Day; Tues.-Sat. 10-4, Sun. noon-4, rest of year. Closed holidays. Free.

UNIVERSITY OF ARIZONA, bounded by Euclid Ave., E. Helen St., Campbell Ave. and E. 7th St., was founded in 1885 as the state's first institution of higher learning. Classes, dorms, offices and the library were all located in one building, Old Main. Today the campus encompasses 345 acres and is one of the nation's top research universities. A 1.5-hour walking tour of the campus is offered Thurs. and Sat. at 9:30, Sept.-May. A bus tour departs the first Sat. of each month at 9:30, Sept.-May. Free. Phone (520) 621-5130.

Center for Creative Photography is at Olive Rd. n. of 2nd St. Metered public parking is available in the visitor section of the Park Avenue Garage, just n. of Speedway Blvd., with direct pedestrian access to the center's front door. The center houses one of the most comprehensive photographic collections in the world. More than 60,000 photographs representing the work of about 1,400 photographers can be seen in a print-viewing room. Displayed in the center's galleries are temporary exhibitions from its collection and elsewhere.

The center's library contains more than 10,000 monographs, catalogs, books and periodicals. Videotaped interviews and lectures are available for viewing. The photographic archives of several dozen major artists also are displayed. Building open daily 8-5. Library open Mon.-Fri. 10-5, Sun. noon-5. Gallery Mon.-Fri. 9-5, Sat.-Sun. noon-5. Free. Reservations are recommended for the print-viewing room. Phone (520) 621-7968.

Dome Theater, in the planetarium on the first floor of the Flandrau Science Center, has elaborate projection and sound systems. The 1-hour programs are of a historical and educational nature. Tickets go on sale the day of the show. Planetarium admission $5; over 55, military with ID and ages 13-18, $4.50; ages 3-12, $4. For schedule information phone (520) 621-7827.

Flandrau Science Center & Planetarium, at University Blvd. and Cherry Ave., has interactive science exhibits dealing with topics such as sound, light, optical illusions, magnetism and astronomy. Displays also highlight scientific research being conducted at the university as well

as current scientific issues. The multimedia planetarium theater presents science, cultural and laser light shows. In the public observatory a 16-inch telescope is available for night viewing (weather permitting).

Daily 9-5 (also Wed.-Sat. 7-9 p.m.); closed major holidays. Exhibits (includes Mineral Museum) $3; under 13, $2 (free with theater ticket). Theater tickets $4-$6. Phone (520) 621-7827, or 621-4515 for schedule.

Mineral Museum, on the lower level of the Flandrau Science Center, displays fine gems, meteorites and mineral specimens from around the world. The museum specializes in minerals from Arizona and Mexico. Visitors can use a microscope to see micro-size specimens. Daily 9-5; closed major holidays. Admission included with Flandrau Science Center & Planetarium. Phone (520) 621-4227.

University of Arizona Museum of Art, s.w. corner of Park Ave. and Speedway Blvd. in the Fine Arts Complex, displays the Kress Collection of more than 50 European paintings from the Renaissance through the 17th century, including the "Retablo of the Ciudad Rodrigo" by Fernando Gallego and works by Giovanni Piazetta, Jacopo Pontormo and Tintoretto.

Among the museum's 20th-century paintings and sculpture are a large collection of sketches

and models by Jacques Lipchitz as well as works by Henry Moore, Pablo Picasso, Auguste Rodin and Andrew Wyeth. Changing exhibits also are featured. Hourly rate parking is available. Allow 1 hour minimum. Mon.-Fri. 9-5, Sun. noon-4, late Aug. to mid-May; Mon.-Fri. 9-3, Sun. noon-4, rest of year. Closed major holidays. Free. Phone (520) 621-7567.

CASINOS

- **Casino of the Sun**, I-19 exit Valencia, 4.5 mi. w., then .5 mi. s. to 7406 S. Camino de Oeste. Daily 24 hours. Phone (520) 883-1700 or (800) 344-9435. *See color ad p. 108.*

- **Desert Diamond Casino**, I-19 exit Valencia, 1 mi. e., then 1 mi. s. to 7350 S. Old Nogales Hwy. Daily 24 hours. Phone (520) 294-7777.

What To Do

Sightseeing

Bus Tours

[SAVE] Gray Line Tours, (520) 622-8811, offers sightseeing tours to Tucson's major sites as well as trips to Nogales, Mexico, and the Grand Canyon. Overnight and multiple-day tours are available. Reservations are advised.

Bus tours of Davis-Monthan Air Force Base are available at the main gate near the intersection of South Craycroft and Golf Links roads. For schedule and information phone (520) 228-3358.

From April through June and September through December an evening trip takes passengers into Upper Sabino Canyon after dark, when nocturnal wildlife is active. Phone (520) 749-2861 for schedule information.

[SAVE] **OLD PUEBLO TOURS**, with pick ups available from local hotels, offers 6.5-hour guided tours of Tucson with stops for sightseeing and shopping. Departures Mon.-Sat. at 9:30, Sept.-May. Fare $40; under 16, $15. Reservations are required. Phone (520) 795-7448. *See ad.*

Walking Tours

For those who prefer to explore the city and its environs on their own, the Metropolitan Tucson Convention and Visitors Bureau, 130 S. Scott Ave., distributes walking and driving tour brochures; phone (520) 624-1817 or (800) 638-8350. The bureau is open Mon.-Fri. 8-5, Sat.-Sun. 9-4. Guided group 2-hour walking tours of the downtown historic districts depart the Sosa-Carillo-Fremont House *(see attraction listing p. 107)* Sat. at 10, Nov.-Mar.; phone (520) 622-0956.

Sports and Recreation

Tucson's city parks and Pima County parks offer facilities for almost any activity. A number of **swimming** pools and **tennis, racquetball** and **handball** courts are available as well as picnic areas, playgrounds and ball fields. For information about facilities and reservations for their use contact the Pima County Parks and Recreation office at 1204 W. Silverlake Rd.; phone (520) 740-2680.

Tucson's climate is made to order for **golf** addicts. More than 40 courses are in the vicinity. The courses offer everything from world-renowned resorts to public access courses; some of them have been designed by such top course designers as Robert Cupp, Tom Fazio, Arthur Hill, Robert Trent Jones, Jack Nicklaus and other noted architects. Among the courses in Tucson are: Randolph Municipal, (520) 791-4336, at 600 S. Alvernon Way; Santa Rita, (520) 762-5620, at 16461 S. Houghton Rd.; Sheraton El Conquistador, (520) 544-1770 or 544-1800, at 10000 N. Oracle Rd. and 10555 N. La Cañada Dr.; Tucson National, (520) 575-7540, at 2727 W. Club Dr.; and Ventana Canyon, (520) 577-4061, at 6200 N. Clubhouse Ln. Also in the area is Canoa Hills, (520) 648-1880, in Green Valley

For those who prefer the more rugged outdoors, the Tucson Convention and Visitors Bureau distributes a brochure that describes all the **camping** areas in Arizona; phone (520) 624-1817 or (800) 638-8350.

Hiking is probably the best way to discover the flora and fauna of this desert environment. Trails are abundant in Tucson Mountain Park. The Santa Catalina Mountains also are accessible and offer many areas of unspoiled beauty. Trails into the Catalinas can be found at the north end of Alvernon Way, the north end of Campbell Road, and at 1st Avenue and Magee Road. Hiking permits are required for these areas. Empty vehicles will be towed if a permit is not displayed.

Permits can be obtained from Pima County Parks and Recreation, (520) 740-2688. Catalina State Park *(see attraction listing, the Recreation Chart and the AAA Southwestern CampBook),* (520) 628-5798, has trails that can challenge the experienced hiker but not intimidate the novice; two longer trails begin at the end of the park's paved road. For more information about hiking phone the county's recreation office at (520) 740-2690.

Another great way to see the countryside is on a trail ride. Several stables offer half-day, full-day and overnight **horseback riding** trips into the mountains and desert. Check the telephone directory for listings. **Skiing** is available at Mount Lemmon Ski Valley, a scenic 30-mile drive northeast from Tucson. The southernmost ski area in the nation, Mount Lemmon offers both downhill and cross-country skiing. A sky ride on the ski lift is offered during the off season. For information about snow conditions phone (520) 576-1400.

For fans of the national pastime, several Major League **Baseball** teams are participants in the Cactus League. The National League's Arizona Diamondbacks conduct spring training at Tucson Electric Park, 2500 E. Ajo Way. A different field at this same sporting complex is used by the American League's Chicago White Sox. Phone (520) 325-8601 or (888) 683-3900 for information about either team. The Colorado Rockies practice at the U S West Sports Complex at Hi Corbett Field, in Gene C. Reid Park off E. Broadway; for ticket information phone (520) 327-9467. The Tucson Toros of the AAA Pacific Coast League also play their games at Hi Corbett Field from April through September; phone (520) 325-2621.

The University of Arizona's Wildcats excite crowds during the **football** and **basketball** seasons. Home football games are played at Arizona Stadium, and basketball teams square off at McKale Center. **Soccer** is played all year by two area leagues. Matches are held most Sundays at Jacobs, Reid and Udall parks.

Greyhound racing is available at Tucson Greyhound Park, (520) 884-7576, 2601 S. 3rd Ave. at 36th Street. The dogs race Wednesday through Sunday, year-round; closed Dec. 24-25.

Note: Policies concerning admittance of children to pari-mutuel betting facilities vary. Phone for information.

Shopping

Tucson is filled with specialty shops containing Mexican and Native American handmade items. Among the featured items are baskets, cactuses, feathered and furred kachina dolls, silver and gold jewelry, moccasins, Pueblo pottery, Navajo rugs and Western wear. A popular place to find such purchases is Old Town Artisans, 201 N. Court Ave. and 186 N. Meyer Ave.; phone (520) 623-6024 or (800) 782-8072.

Within a one-block adobe restoration area the works of more than 150 local artists are displayed, along with Native American and Latin folk art. El Mercado de Boutiques, Broadway and Wilmot, encompasses 20 shops with similar offerings as well as Oriental works. The Old Pueblo Museum in the Foothills Mall, 7401 N. La Cholla Blvd., features exhibits and items for sale from gems and minerals to African-American art and sculpture.

Downtown Tucson's shopping district stretches along 4th Avenue between 4th and 7th streets, where everything from antiques to the latest fashions can be purchased. Lovers of flea markets will find varied goods at the Tanque Verde Swap Meet, Palo Verde Road just south of Ajo. The swap meet is open to visitors for bargaining Thurs.-Fri. 3-11 p.m. and Sat.-Sun. 7 a.m.-11 p.m.

University of Arizona fans will find an array of items bearing the school's name at Arizona Wildwear, 813 N. Park Ave. Souvenirs and T-shirts are popular items.

For one-stop shopping in air-conditioned comfort, Tucson offers four shopping malls: El Con Mall, near downtown at 3601 E. Broadway at Alvernon; Foothills Mall, 7401 N. La Cholla Blvd. at Ina Road; Park Mall, east at 5870 E. Broadway at Wilmot; and Tucson Mall, 4500 N. Oracle Rd. The major department stores in these malls are Dillard's, Foley's and Macy's.

Theater and Concerts

When it comes to theater, Tucson offers many choices. Top billing is given to the Arizona Theatre Company, (520) 622-2823, Arizona's professional state theater. This premier company performs six plays during its September through May season at the Temple of Music and Art. A forum for experimental theater is The Invisible Theatre, (520) 882-9721, 1400 N. 1st Ave., which stages six plays between September and June.

Entertainment for the entire family is available at the Gaslight Theatre, (520) 886-9428, 7010 E. Broadway, where melodramas encourage audience participation; reservations are required. The University of Arizona adds to Tucson's theater offerings. The school's resident company, (520) 621-1162, presents its offerings of musicals and serious drama in spring, summer and fall.

No bit players, Tucson's opera company plays a major part in the performing arts arena. Accompanied by a full orchestra in the Tucson Convention Center from October through March, members of the Arizona Opera Company, (520) 293-4336, present five operas.

Completing the cultural scene are the city's orchestras. The Tucson Symphony Orchestra, (520) 882-8585, plays both classical and pop music in the Tucson Convention Center September to May. Under the desert skies at the Reid Park Bandshell, the Tucson Pops Orchestra, (520) 791-4873, entertains audiences in the spring and fall. From September through May the University of Arizona's Centennial Hall resounds with sounds from jazz to chamber music performed by guest artists and student musicians.

Special Events

The Southern Arizona Square and Round Dance Festival begins the year's activities in January. In February the city boasts another superlative: the world's largest gem and mineral show. During the 14-day Tucson International Gem & Mineral Show the Tucson Convention Center is filled with hundreds of dealers selling to both wholesalers and the public. Many hotels and motels feature rock and mineral shows; visitors should note that rooms are booked well in advance. Special museum exhibits also are featured.

If you like horses and cowboys, Tucson is the place to be in late February during La Fiesta de los Vaqueros Rodeo at the rodeo grounds. This classic event begins with a "cowboy breakfast" and a 3-hour parade, with people afoot, on horseback and in every size and shape of horse-drawn vehicle. The fiesta ends 4 days later with the rodeo finals in which some of the best riders and ropers on the circuit compete. In March the Randolph Golf Course is the site of the Touchstone Energy Championship LPGA Tucson Open.

The Yaqui Easter Ceremony combines old Yaqui traditions with Christian beliefs in a week-long celebration. In April and again in December Tucson's 4th Avenue transforms into a street fair filled with artisans selling and demonstrating their crafts. Enhanced by music and an abundance of food and drink, these weekends attract visitors and residents alike. The Pima County Fair is held in mid-April.

Tucson's fall activities begin in late September and early October as Mount Lemmon Ski Valley plays host to Octoberfest. Luminaria Night is held at the Tucson Botanical Gardens, and the intercollegiate Insight.com Bowl football game is played in December.

The Tucson Vicinity

GREEN VALLEY (F-5)
pop. 13,200, elev. 2,900′

Green Valley, nestled at the foot of the Santa Rita Mountains, is a popular retirement community located 25 miles south of Tucson on I-19. Camping, hiking, golfing and bird-watching are favorite pastimes.

Green Valley Chamber of Commerce: 270 W. Continental, #100, P.O. Box 5661, Green Valley, AZ 85622; phone (520) 625-7575 or (800) 858-5872.

SAVE **TITAN MISSILE MUSEUM**, .75 mi. w. of I-19 exit 69 off Duval Mine Rd., is a formerly active Intercontinental Ballistic Missile (ICBM) complex preserved as a museum. Of the 54 Titan ICBM sites in the United States weapon system, all except the missile museum have been destroyed.

Allow 1 hour minimum. Guided tours daily 9-5, Nov.-Apr.; Wed.-Sun. 9-5, rest of year. Closed Thanksgiving and Dec. 25. Last tour begins 1 hour before closing. Admission $7.50; over 62 and military with ID $6.50; ages 10-17, $4. Reservations are strongly advised. MC, VI. Phone (520) 625-7736.

Note: The tour includes descending/ascending 55 steps and might be cumbersome for the physically challenged and those with a heart condition. Arrangements may be made for the use of an elevator for the physically challenged.

ORACLE (E-5) pop. 3,000, elev. 4,513′

SAVE **BIOSPHERE 2 CENTER**, 5 mi. n.e. of jct. SRs 79 and 77 to Biosphere 2 Rd., encompasses five biomes: rain forest, ocean, savanna, desert and marsh. The glass and steel structure dominates the landscape and is a learning, teaching and research center for determining an ecosystem's ability to recycle air, water and nutrients in order to sustain plant and animal life.

A guided tour begins with a film presentation at the center, where a model is on display, and includes a .75-mile walking tour inside the Biosphere 2 human habitat. Comfortable walking shoes and sunscreen are recommended. Allow 2 hours minimum. Daily 8:30-6; closed Dec. 25. Admission $12.95; ages 13-17, $8.95; ages 6-12, $6. AE, DI, DS, MC, VI. Phone (520) 896-6200.

★ SAGUARO NATIONAL PARK (E-5)

Saguaro National Park is divided into two districts. The Rincon Mountain District (Saguaro East) is about 15 miles east of central Tucson via

Old Spanish Trail, and the Tucson Mountain District (Saguaro West) is 15 miles west of Tucson via Speedway Boulevard. Both typify the Sonoran arboreal desert and contain stands of saguaro cactuses, known for their sometimes human-like shapes.

The saguaro grows only in southern Arizona, in California along the Colorado River and in the northern Mexican state of Sonora. It can live more than 200 years, attaining heights of 30 to 40 feet; a few exceptional ones exceed 50 feet. Its blossom, the state flower, appears in May and June. Native Americans use its fruit for food and as a beverage base.

In addition to protecting the saguaro and other desert vegetation of the Sonoran Desert, the park's Tucson Mountain District has rock formations decorated with Native American petroglyphs and designs.

At the park headquarters in the Rincon Mountain District a visitor center contains plant and animal exhibits and offers nature programs in the winter; phone (520) 733-5153. The 8-mile Cactus Forest Drive begins at the visitor center parking lot. Picnic facilities are available. The 6-mile Bajada Loop Drive winds through the Tucson Mountain District. A visitor center has exhibits; phone (520) 733-5158.

Both districts open daily dawn-dusk. Visitor centers open daily 8:30-5; closed Dec. 25. Admission to the Rincon Mountain District is by 7-day or annual permit; 7-day permits cost $4 per private vehicle or $2 for persons arriving by other means. The Tucson Mountain District is free. For additional information contact the Superintendent, Saguaro National Park, 3693 S. Old Spanish Tr., Tucson, AZ 85730-5601; phone (520) 733-5153. *See Recreation Chart.*

SAHUARITA (F-4)
pop. 1,600, elev. 2,702'

ASARCO MINERAL DISCOVERY CENTER, off I-19 exit 80 to 1421 W. Pima Mine Rd., features hands-on exhibits about mining and minerals. A theater offers presentations about mining, mineral resources and reclamation. A 1-hour tour provides a look inside an operating open-pit copper mine. Allow 1 hour, 30 minutes minimum. Tues.-Sat. 9-5. Last tour departs 1 hour, 30 minutes before closing. Center free. Mine tour $6; over 62, $5; ages 5-12, $4. AE, DS, MC, VI. Phone (520) 625-7513.

VAIL (F-5) pop. 200, elev. 3,225'

COLOSSAL CAVE, off I-10 exit 279, then n. on SR 83 to 16711 E. Colossal Cave Rd., is considered by some to be the world's largest dry cavern. Only partially explored, it has chambers and lighted passageways. Allow 1 hour minimum. Guided 45-minute tours Mon.-Sat. 8-6, Sun. and holidays 8-7, Mar. 15-Sept. 15; daily 9-5, rest of year. Fee $7.50; ages 6-12, $4. DS, MC, VI. Phone (520) 647-7275.

WINERIES
• Dark Mountain Brewery and Winery, 1 mi. e. off I-10 exit 279 on Frontage Rd., Vail, AZ 85641. Mon.-Sat. 10-5 (also Sat. 5-11), Sun. noon-6. Phone (520) 762-5777.

This ends listings for the Phoenix Vicinity.
The following page resumes the alphabetical listings of cities in Arizona.

★ TUMACACORI NATIONAL HISTORICAL PARK (F-4)

Tumacacori National Historical Park, 19 miles north of Nogales on I-19 exit 29, preserves the abandoned Mission San Jose de Tumacacori. Once a Pima Indian village, Tumacacori was visited by Jesuit Eusebio Francisco Kino in 1691. In 1767 the Jesuits were expelled from Tumacacori by the King of Spain and replaced by Franciscans. The Franciscans began building the present massive adobe church about 1800, but it was never completed. Apache raids, neglect and a terrible winter contributed to its abandonment in 1848, yet afterward people continued to visit the site.

Americans of European extraction first visited the site in 1849, but Apache raids forced the settlers to leave. The area became a national monument in 1908. The 1990 addition of two Spanish mission sites, Guevavi and Calabazas, increased the total acreage to 47. Guevavi and Calabazas can presently be visited by reservation only on Wednesday, September through April. A historic museum distinguished by architectural features of the Sonora missions unfolds local history and describes mission life.

A self-guiding tour includes the church and cemetery, mortuary chapel, portions of the convento area, a patio garden and a visitor center/museum. Picnic facilities are available. Allow 1 hour minimum. Daily 8-5; closed Thanksgiving and Dec. 25. Admission $2 per person or $4 per private vehicle, under 17 free. Phone (520) 398-2341.

★ TUZIGOOT NATIONAL MONUMENT (C-3)

About 2 miles northwest of Cottonwood, Tuzigoot National Monument preserves the ruins of a pueblo that was occupied by the Sinagua Indians from about 1000 until it was abandoned in 1425. From more than 110 rooms archeologists have recovered stone and bone tools, textiles, pottery, shell beads and bracelets, which are displayed in the visitor center.

Allow 1 hour minimum. Daily 8-7, Memorial Day-Labor Day; 8-5, rest of year. Admission $2, under 17 free. Phone (520) 634-5564.

VAIL—*see Tucson p. 112.*

VALLE (B-3)

AIR MUSEUM PLANES OF FAME is at the Valle Airport near the jct. of SR64 and US 180. Covering aviation history from World War I through the supersonic jet age, the museum's collection includes Gen. Douglas MacArthur's personal transport plane *Bataan*, a Lockheed C-121A Constellation. Other aircraft include a 1928 Ford Trimotor, a DeHavilland Vampire, a 1944 Messerschmitt BF109G-10, a Grumman F-11F Tiger formerly used by the Navy's Blue Angels and many others. Allow 1 hour minimum. Daily 9-6, Apr.-Sept.; 9-5, rest of year. Closed Thanksgiving and Dec. 25. Admission $5; ages 5-12, $1.95. AE, CB, DI, MC, VI. Phone (520) 635-1000.

★ WALNUT CANYON NATIONAL MONUMENT (B-4)

Walnut Canyon National Monument, off I-40 exit 204, 7.5 miles east of Flagstaff, preserves the remains of more than 300 pre-Columbian dwellings built on a series of ledges in the 400-foot-deep gorge. Inhabited by the Sinagua Indians about 1000-1200, these single-family dwellings are visible from the visitor center on the canyon rim. The self-guiding Island Trail, which descends 185 feet over the course of a half mile, is an interesting but arduous paved path that leads past 25 of the cliff dwelling rooms. The Rim Trail, a pleasant .75 mile round trip, features two overlooks into the canyon, as well access to a small pueblo and pit house. Snow and ice might close both trails at times in winter and spring. Interpretive programs are available from June through August. A museum and picnic facilities are available, however, food is not available. Pets are not allowed on park trails, in buildings or tied to fixed objects.

Note: The Island Trail includes descending/ascending 240 steps and might be cumbersome for the physically challenged and those with heart conditions.

Allow 1 hour, 30 minutes minimum. Daily 8-6, June-Aug.; 8-5, Sept.-Nov. and Mar.-May; 9-5, rest of year. Closed Dec. 25. Last admittance to main trail is 1 hour before closing. Admission $3 per person, under 17 free. For further

---

DID YOU KNOW

Monument Valley in northeastern Arizona has served as the setting for many Western films.

information contact the District Ranger, Walnut Canyon National Monument, Walnut Canyon Road #3, Flagstaff, AZ 86004; phone (520) 526-3367.

WALPI—see *Keams Canyon p. 59.*

WENDEN (D-2) elev. 1,869'

ALAMO LAKE STATE PARK, 38 mi. n. of US 60 via a paved rd., offers views of the Buckskin and Rawhide mountains from its site on the Bill Williams River. Activities include fishing, camping, boating and hiking. Daily 7-5. Admission $4 per private vehicle. Camping $8-$15 per private vehicle. Phone (520) 669-2088. *See Recreation Chart.*

WHITERIVER (D-5) pop. 3,800

Center of the Fort Apache Reservation fishing, camping and recreation area, Whiteriver also is the administrative headquarters of the 1,664,874-acre reservation. Four miles south is Fort Apache *(see place listing p. 49)*, an active post during the Indian wars; it is now the site of the Theodore Roosevelt Indian School.

Seven miles west of town via a dirt road are the Kinishba Ruins, a partially restored village inhabited 1050-1350; check locally to confirm road and weather conditions. Visitors are welcome at both the Alchesay National Fish Hatchery, (520) 338-4901, 8 miles north via SR 73, and the Williams Creek Hatchery, (520) 334-2346, 16 miles n. via SR 73 following signs.

WICKENBURG (G-1)
pop. 4,500, elev. 2,071'

Nineteen miles southwest of Wickenburg is the Vulture Gold Mine, which yielded more than $20 million in gold during the hectic period following its discovery by Henry Wickenburg in 1863. Allegedly Wickenburg found the gold in one of the rocks he was hurling at his escaping mule.

The gold rush that ensued reached such proportions that by 1866 Wickenburg was the third largest city in Arizona and missed becoming the territorial capital by only two votes. Still standing in the center of town is the old mesquite jail tree to which lawmen chained their prisoners during the early boom years; no one wanted to take time from mining to build a proper jail.

The Hassayampa River, running through town, was called "the river which flows upside down" by Native Americans because its main flow is 20 feet below the surface. It is one of the last and greatest natural riparian areas in the state.

Wickenburg, known for its Old West atmosphere and many dude ranches, brings the past to life in April, when the Desert Caballeros begin their ride into the Bradshaw Mountains, where they spend several days under the stars; the whole town gathers to bid the horsemen farewell as they ride off into the mountains.

Wickenburg Chamber of Commerce: 216 N. Frontier St., Wickenburg, AZ 85390; phone (520) 684-5479 or (800) 942-5242.

SAVE DESERT CABALLEROS WESTERN MUSEUM, 21 N. Frontier St., contains dioramas depicting the town's history, a re-creation of an early Wickenburg street scene, ancient native artifacts and collections of gems and minerals. A gallery displays works by noted Western artists. Allow 1 hour minimum. Mon.-Sat. 10-5, Sun. noon-4; closed Jan. 1, Easter, July 4, Thanksgiving and Dec. 25. Admission $5; over 55, $4; ages 6-16, $1. Phone (520) 684-2272.

WILLCOX (E-5)
pop. 3,100, elev. 4,156'

Willcox, which began as a small cow town, was one of the country's major cattle-shipping centers. In days past the large cattle ranches in the surrounding hills and valleys were notorious as refuges for fugitive gunslingers. Raising cattle is still important today, but added to the contemporary economic mix are cultivation of pistachios, onions, tomatoes and for their distinctive leather: ostriches.

Southeast of town at Apache Pass is the isolated Old Fort Bowie National Historic Site. The fort was built in 1862 to guard the Butterfield Overland Trail and to protect pioneers from Apache raids and skirmishes with Native Americans led by Cochise and Geronimo. The site can only be reached by traveling the last 1.5 miles on foot. The high elevation and temperature extremes might make this hike unsuitable for some. Water is available at the fort, but hikers should bring their own canteen. Beware of flash floods, mountain lions and rattlesnakes. All historic items and natural features are strictly protected; metal detectors, digging tools, guns and hunting are prohibited.

Willcox Chamber of Commerce: 1500 N. Circle I Rd., Willcox, AZ 85643; phone (520) 384-2272 or (800) 200-2272. *See color ad p. 42.*

REX ALLEN ARIZONA COWBOY MUSEUM, 150 N. Railroad Ave., honors the career of Western star Rex Allen, who was born in Willcox in 1920. Allen's life is depicted from his ranching and homesteading years through his radio, television and film career. Through photographs, storyboards, clothing and ranch implements the museum also highlights the pioneers and ranchers who shaped the West. Daily 10-4; closed Jan. 1, Thanksgiving and Dec. 25. Admission $3 per couple, $2 per person, family rate $5. MC, VI. Phone (520) 384-4583 or (877) 234-4111.

WILLIAMS (C-3)
pop. 2,500, elev. 6,752'

Williams was named after Bill Williams, the early mountain man who guided trapping parties and expeditions through the wilderness.

Principally a resort town, Williams marks the beginning of the major entrance route to Grand Canyon National Park *(see place listing p. 52)*. The town is at the base of Bill Williams Mountain, which boasts a ski area offering both downhill and cross-country skiing. Cross-country skiing also is popular in the surrounding Kaibab National Forest *(see place listing p. 59)*. Cataract, Kaibab Dog Trail and White Horse lakes offer camping, picnicking and fishing *(see the AAA Southwestern CampBook)*.

Williams and Forest Service Visitor Center: 200 West Railroad Ave., Williams, AZ 86046; phone (520) 635-4061 or (800) 863-0546.

[SAVE] **GRAND CANYON DEER FARM,** 6752 E. Deer Farm Rd. off I-40, has several varieties of deer and other animals. Visitors are permitted to walk among the deer and feed them. Daily 8-7, June-Aug.; 9-6, Mar.-May and Sept.-Oct.; 10-5, rest of year. Closed Thanksgiving and Dec. 25. Admission $5.50; over 62, $4.50; ages 3-13, $3.25. AE, DS, MC, VI. Phone (520) 635-4073 or (800) 926-3337.

[SAVE] **GRAND CANYON RAILWAY,** .5 mi. s. of I-40 exit 163 (Grand Canyon Blvd.), offers round-trip excursions through grassy plains and ponderosa pine forests to the south rim of the Grand Canyon aboard authentically restored 1923 Harriman coaches pulled by turn-of-the-20th-century steam engines (Memorial Day weekend through September) or vintage diesel locomotives (rest of year). On-board strolling musicians, Western characters and refreshments are provided. Five classes of train service are available, including luxury parlor class. For an additional fee, bus tours of the south rim with and without lunch are available.

A museum at the restored 1908 Williams Depot contains railroad, mining, ranching and logging artifacts as well as photographs. The Grand Canyon Depot was constructed in 1910 of ponderosa pine logs and is the only working log depot in the country. A Wild West show takes place daily at 9 (weather permitting).

Train departs daily at 9:30 and returns at 5:30, with a 3.5-hour stopover at the canyon; closed Dec. 24-25. Schedule is subject to change; phone ahead. Round-trip coach fare $49.95; under 17, $24.95. One-way fare available; upgraded seats are available for an additional fee. Fare does not include admission to Grand Canyon National Park. Reservations are recommended. AE, DS, MC, VI. Phone (800) 843-8724. *See ad p. 55.*

WINDOW ROCK (B-6) pop. 3,300

Window Rock is the capital of the Navajo nation and seat of its tribal government. The elected tribal council meets in the council house at least four times a year. Window Rock also contains the U.S. government's Bureau of Indian Affairs, Navajo Area Office.

The headquarters of the Navajo Arts and Crafts Enterprises is just east of the junction of SR 264 and Navajo Route 12. The Navajo Nation Museum, several blocks east at SR 264 and Loop Road, contains items relating to the history and culture of the Navajo and to the prehistoric cultures of the Four Corners region. A re-created

trading post of the 1870-1930 period and changing exhibits by Navajo craftsmen and artists are featured. Phone (520) 871-6673.

Navajo Land Tourism Department: P.O. Box 663, Window Rock, AZ 86515; phone (520) 871-6436 or 871-7371.

FOUR CORNERS MONUMENT, in Navajo Tribal Park e. on SR 264, n. on US 666, w. on US 64 to E. US 160, is the only place in the country where four states meet. The juncture of Arizona, Utah, Colorado and New Mexico is marked by a concrete monument bearing the seal of each state. The Hopi, Navajo and Ute sell their wares near the site. Daily 7-7, May-Aug.; 8-5 rest of year. Admission $2. Phone (520) 871-6647.

ST. MICHAELS HISTORICAL MUSEUM, 24 Mission Rd. off SR 264 in the St. Michaels Mission complex, features permanent displays chronicling the work of the Franciscan Friars on the Navajo Nation. Temporary exhibits include examples of Navajo life and culture. The museum is housed in the original mission building, restored to its 1898 appearance. Allow 30 minutes minimum. Mon.-Sat. 9-5, Sun. 10-6, Memorial Day-Labor Day. Donations. Phone (520) 871-4171.

WINKELMAN (E-5)
pop. 700, elev. 1,928'

A mining and agricultural center, Winkelman is near the 8.5-mile Aravaipa Canyon, a wilderness retreat that was once the headquarters of the Apache Indians. The canyon's abundant vegetation, nourished by the year-round flow of Aravaipa Creek, contrasts with the surrounding desert terrain. Off SR 77, then 13 miles east on a paved and gravel road, the canyon is within the 4,044-acre Aravaipa Canyon Primitive Area. Permits are required to enter the area; contact the

DID YOU KNOW

The only place where four states meet is at Four Corners—a monument marks the spot where Arizona, Colorado, New Mexico and Utah touch.

Bureau of Land Management's District Office in Safford; phone (520) 348-4400. Visitation to the area is limited; reservations are required.

WINSLOW (C-5)
pop. 9,100, elev. 4,856'

Winslow was named after Gen. Edward Francis Winslow, a president of the Atlantic and Pacific Railroad. This railroad center is an important shipping and trading site. The Apache-Sitgreaves National Forests *(see place listing p. 40)* lie south of town.

Winslow Chamber of Commerce: 300 W. North Rd., P.O. Box 460, Winslow, AZ 86047; phone (520) 289-2434.

HOMOLOVI RUINS STATE PARK, 3 mi. e. on I-40 to exit 257, then 1.5 mi. n. on SR 87, is 4,000 acres containing more than 300 archeological sites ranging from smaller sites to large pueblo ruins and petroglyphs. Sunset Cemetery, all that remains of an 1876 Mormon settlement, also is on the site. The visitors center/museum provides interpretive information about the Anasazi as well as the park. Picnic facilities and campsites are available. It is illegal to damage or remove any pre-Columbian or historic site, artifact or rock art within the park.

Visitor center 8-5; closed Dec. 25. Park dawndusk. Admission $4 per private vehicle. Phone (520) 289-4106 for camping information. *See Recreation Chart.*

METEOR CRATER, 22 mi. w. on I-40, then 6 mi. s. off exit 233, was formed nearly 50,000 years ago when a meteorite estimated to have been 150 feet across and weighing several hundred thousand tons, slammed into the rocky plain.

The meteorite left a crater 700 feet deep and more than 4,000 feet across. Today it is 550 feet deep, 2.4 miles in circumference and nearly 1 mile across. Because the terrain of the crater is very similar to that of the moon, NASA once trained Apollo astronauts here. The site's visitor center includes the Museum of Astrogeology, which houses interactive displays, a large-screen theater, the Astronaut Wall of Fame, an Apollo Space Capsule and an overview of the history of astronaut training at the crater.

Guided trail tours of the rim are offered (weather permitting). Appropriate footwear is required. Food is available. Allow 2 hours minimum. Tours depart daily 9-2. Admission $9; over 60, $8; ages 6-17, $4. DS, MC, VI. Phone (520) 289-2362 or (800) 289-5898. *See ad p. 63.*

★ WUPATKI NATIONAL MONUMENT (B-4)

With the increased rainfall after the late 11th-century eruption of Sunset Crater Volcano, south of Wupatki National Monument, farming became productive enough that at one time the region may have been one of the more densely populated sections of northern Arizona. The original inhabitants of Wupatki are believed to have been ancestors of the Hopi Indians.

Hundreds of ruins are within the 35,253-acre monument north of Flagstaff off US 89. The largest and among the most impressive is Wupatki, or "Tall House," containing more than 100 rooms. Nearby are a ceremonial amphitheater, ball court and "blow hole." Other important ruins are the Citadel, Nalakihu, Lomaki and the three-story Wukoki, all reachable by short, self-guiding trails. Most of the ruins were inhabited from about 1100-1225. Picnicking is available.

Allow 1 hour minimum. Visitor center open daily 8-5; closed Dec. 25. Extended hours are available during summer; phone ahead. Ruins open daily dawn-dusk. Admission $3 per person, under 17 free. Admission includes Sunset Crater Volcano National Monument *(see place listing p. 96)*. Phone (520) 679-2365.

YARNELL (C-3) elev. 4,800′

Yarnell sprang up as a gold-mining town after a prospector named Harrison Yarnell struck gold on a nearby mountain peak in 1863. Some active mines still produce silver, gold and copper; however, the area's primary industries are cattle raising and tourism. Many vacationers visit Yarnell in the summer to escape the desert heat and to enjoy the many recreational pursuits the area offers.

Yarnell/Peeples Valley Chamber of Commerce: P.O. Box 275, Yarnell, AZ 85362; phone (520) 427-3301.

SHRINE OF ST. JOSEPH OF THE MOUNTAINS, .5 mi. w. off SR 89, is an open-air mountainside shrine with statues that depict scenes of The Last Supper, Garden of Gethsemane, The Way of the Cross and the Risen Christ. Information is available at the shrine or by writing P.O. Box 1027, Yarnell, AZ 85362. Open daily 24 hours. Donations.

YUMA (E-1) pop. 57,000, elev. 200′

Although he was not the first white man to visit the area, Father Eusebio Francisco Kino was the first to recognize the Yuma Crossing as the gateway to California. Yet Kino's discovery would not be used for almost a century until another priest, Father Francisco Garces, followed it in his own search for a land route to California.

In 1779 two missions were founded at the crossing by Father Garces, who, along with all the colonists, was later killed during the last major uprising of the Yuma Indians. With the destruction of the colony the crossing again faded from memory. Fifty years passed before it was rediscovered, this time by Kit Carson. It finally became a permanent settlement during the California gold rush.

Lutes Casino on Main Street, the oldest continuous pool hall and domino parlor in the state, began as a grocery store in 1901. Today visitors can play dominos and pool or just browse around the room filled with eclectic memorabilia.

Yuma is host to a number of outdoor events as well as being the spring training headquarters of the Yakult Swallows, a professional baseball team from Japan. The town becomes flooded with hunters when the hunting season opens over Labor Day weekend.

Yuma Convention and Visitors Bureau: 377 Main St., Yuma, AZ 85364; phone (520) 783-0071 or (800) 293-0071.

Self-guiding tours: The Colorado River crossing in Yuma is the site of several historical and cultural buildings, most of which are open to the public. Brochures about self-guiding tours are available from the convention and visitors bureau.

ARIZONA HISTORICAL SOCIETY CENTURY HOUSE MUSEUM AND GARDENS, 240 Madison Ave., was the home of pioneer merchant E.F. Sanguinetti. The house contains late 19th-century period rooms and exhibits about Yuma history. The surrounding gardens and aviaries are maintained as they were in the early 1900s. Tues.-Sat. 10-4; closed holidays. Free. Phone (520) 782-1841.

IMPERIAL NATIONAL WILDLIFE REFUGE encompasses 25,125 acres along the Colorado River. The Arizona section of the refuge is 40 mi. n. off US 95 via Martinez Lake Rd., following signs. The remainder of the refuge can be reached only by boat. Canadian geese, ducks, egrets and eagles gather at the refuge. Hiking, hunting, fishing and boating are permitted in designated areas. Maps and public-use regulations are available upon request.

For further information contact the Refuge Manager, Imperial National Wildlife Refuge, P.O. Box 72217, Yuma, AZ 85365. Daily dawn-dusk. Visitor center open Mon.-Fri. 7:30-4, Sat.-Sun. 9-4, Nov. 15-Apr. 1; Mon.-Fri. 7:30-4, rest of year. Closed federal holidays. Free. Phone (520) 783-3371.

KOFA NATIONAL WILDLIFE REFUGE—
see Quartzsite p. 91.

SAHATI CAMEL FARM AND DESERT ANIMAL BREEDING CENTER is at 15672 S. Ave 1E; go 5 mi. s. on Ave. 3E, then 2 mi. w. on CR 16 to jct. Ave. 1E. This facility for the conservation and propagation of the wildlife of the Arabian deserts displays camels, Asian water buffaloes, ibexes, oryxes and desert foxes among its many exotic species.

Allow 1 hour minimum. Guided tours are given Mon.-Sat. at 10 and 2, Oct.-May; closed Thanksgiving and Dec. 25. Fee $3, under 3 free. Reservations are suggested. Phone (520) 627-2553.

YUMA CROSSING STATE HISTORICAL PARK,
I-8 4th Ave. exit to 201 N. 4th Ave., is on a 20-
acre site on the s. side of the Colorado River.
The park salutes 5 centuries of transportation
across the Colorado River. From 1864 through
1883 the U.S. Army Quartermaster Depot stored
and distributed supplies for military posts
throughout the Southwest. Five restored buildings stand on the site that once comprised the
depot. The depot office was built in 1871. Daily
10-5, Nov.-Apr.; Thurs.-Mon. 10-5, rest of year.
Closed Dec. 25. Admission $3; ages 7-13, $2.
Phone (520) 329-0471.

**YUMA TERRITORIAL PRISON STATE HIS-
TORIC PARK,** 4th St. exit off I-8, is on a bluff
on the s. side of the Colorado River "meander"
(where the river bends). Erected in 1876, the
building was a prison until 1909. The adobe
walls, which no longer stand, were 8 feet thick at
the base and 5 feet thick at the top, and at full
capacity confined 3,000 prisoners. Of interest are
the cellblocks, the "hole" and a museum. Guided
tours are available by request. Open daily 8-5;
closed Dec. 25. Admission $3; ages 7-13, $2.
Phone (520) 783-4771.

New Mexico

Spectacular Carlsbad Caverns

Colorful limestone formations create a subterranean wonderland

Ancient Pueblos

Continuing native traditions and culture at centuries-old dwellings

Birthplace of the Nuclear Age

White gypsum sands mark the site of the first atomic weapon

The Wild West

Outlaw legends once ravaged the old Southwest

The Santa Fe Trail

Wagon wheel ruts lead past dazzling mountain and desert scenery

a land of legends

New Mexico is a mosaic of azure skies, adobe architecture and red rock cliffs.

A coyote, silhouetted by a glorious desert sunset, sings a mysterious song. A roadrunner pauses near a cactus—then with a clatter of his bill, he races away.

It is enchanting scenes like these that inspired such artisans as author D.H. Lawrence and artist Georgia O'Keeffe.

But New Mexico's scenic grandeur reveals more than mere beauty. Its landscape tells the stories of ancient civilizations who carved dwellings from the rocks and cliffs, of desperados who gave rise to the term "Wild West," of cattle barons who tamed the southeast plains and traded along the Santa Fe Trail.

Indeed, people like Billy the Kid and

Pat Garrett and places such as Cimarron and Taos have been immortalized in movies and books. But ghost towns, rugged mountains, gypsum sands and wild rivers stimulate the imagination as well.

Pueblos, built thousands of years ago and still functioning today, demonstrate the continuity of culture and spirit of the American Indians who dwell here.

The state is a saga of many chapters. Whether the story is that of prehistoric cliff-dwellers or the birthplace of the nuclear age, New Mexico is legendary.

"Beware: Hot Stuff" warns the label on a jar of spicy green chile salsa. Welcome to New Mexico, deemed the home of the world's finest chile peppers, where you can fire up your taste buds with more than 10 varieties—most in the "extra hot" category.

Ristras, colorful strings of sun-dried chile peppers, drape café entryways and residential doorways. They are said to ward off evil, welcome visitors and alert guests to the fiery delicacies served there. Start with chile con queso, then move to chorizo (spicy pork sausage) or green chile stew. Locals know one thing about chile: It's the hottest ingredient in any dish, and that's putting it mildly.

Feeling Hot, Hot, Hot

But chile isn't the only thing that heats things up. The radiant symbol that has come to represent New Mexico (found on its license plate and flag) is the Zia Indian sign for sun. Four rays extend from the center, signifying directions, seasons, periods of the day and stages of life.

Under the glow of the sun, hundreds of rainbow-colored gentle giants fill the sky with hot air during balloon festivals held across the state. The selection is anything but ordinary at the Albuquerque International Balloon Fiesta: It's common to see such diverse shapes as a castle, parrot, spare tire, cola can, corncob, dragon and yes, even Dumbo, everyone's favorite flying elephant.

From the basket of a balloon you may catch a glimpse of centuries-old, flat-roofed houses and cliff dwellings, which remain quintessential elements of New Mexico. Constructed of adobe—sun-dried bricks of earth, sand, charcoal and grass—they blend into the landscape in color and cast. Sunny weather and lack of rainfall were fundamental in the establishment of adobe due to its ability to keep cool in summer and warm in winter. This mixture served as the primary building material for pueblos, communal settlements established by the Spanish in the 16th century.

Nineteen working pueblos remain at Taos and other locations in north-central New Mexico. Each retains an independent government, social order and religious practice as well as a distinct artistic flair. Artisans produce traditional art individual to their own pueblo: Turquoise jewelry, storyteller dolls, pottery, drums, carvings, Navajo rugs and

Cabeza de Vaca and other explorers cross New Mexico to reach Mexico, spreading rumors of the Seven Cities of Cibola.

1536

The Mexican-American War is fought. New Mexico becomes a U.S. territory.

1846-48

The Long Walk begins when Navajos and Apaches are ousted from their homeland. Thousands die of starvation and disease.

1863-67

1680

The Pueblo Indian Rebellion is victorious in expelling Spanish rule.

1862

Key Civil War battles are fought at Glorieta Pass and Valverde in New Mexico territory.

New Mexico Historical Timeline

weavings are coveted by visitors and collectors alike.

Some pueblos welcome guests to experience their heritage at annual festivals held in honor of the pueblo's patron saint. Corn, deer or buffalo dances are executed according to strict standards, culminating in a flamboyant display of colorful costumes.

While native traditions at the pueblos continue, only stark adobe walls remain at the uninhabited Chaco Culture National Historical Park, and at Aztec Ruins and Bandelier national monuments. Explore what were once thriving Anasazi communities; multistory cliff dwellings with remnants of hundreds of rooms, kivas (ceremonial meeting halls) and petroglyphs offer a warm welcome into the state's rich cultural past.

Sizzling Secrets

Southeastern New Mexico was a hotbed of controversy when, in 1947, a farmer discovered exotic metal debris on a sheep ranch. Some are convinced it was the wreckage of a flying saucer, while others believe it to be the result of tests performed by the U.S. Air Force.

The mysteries surrounding what was dubbed the "Roswell Incident" make the International UFO Museum & Research Center all the more intriguing. Here you can purchase your very own alien (stuffed, magnetic or featured on a rubber doormat). And don't pass up the annual Roswell UFO Encounter Festival: Here, aliens are the hot ticket.

Or you can learn more about another top secret scientific development—the Manhattan Project. Los Alamos was chosen as the hot spot for a weapons laboratory that developed and tested the atomic bomb during World War II. Visit the Bradbury Science Museum and peruse some 500 artifacts from the project.

If you can't stand the heat, pack a parka and head for the cool solace of Carlsbad Cavern. At 750 feet below the surface, the three-level limestone cave begs exploration. Arguably the biggest underground cavern in the world, it measures 1,500 feet long and 300 feet tall—and at a chilly 56 F, it's definitely cool.

Spicy food, sunny skies, intriguing history, warmhearted residents and even hot springs—New Mexico knows how to put a spark in any itinerary.

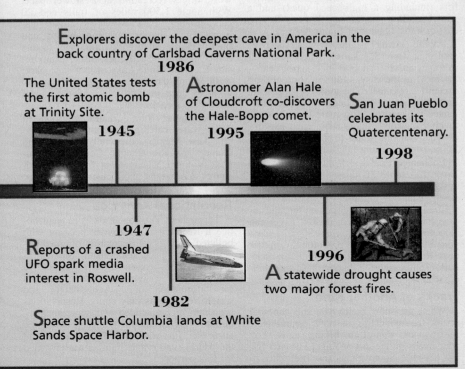

Explorers discover the deepest cave in America in the back country of Carlsbad Caverns National Park.
1986

The United States tests the first atomic bomb at Trinity Site.
1945

Astronomer Alan Hale of Cloudcroft co-discovers the Hale-Bopp comet.
1995

San Juan Pueblo celebrates its Quatercentenary.
1998

1947
Reports of a crashed UFO spark media interest in Roswell.

1996
A statewide drought causes two major forest fires.

1982
Space shuttle Columbia lands at White Sands Space Harbor.

Recreation

From snow-clad mountains and sandy desert lowlands to rusty looking canyons and verdant timbered forests, the New Mexico landscape is a tapestry of colors and shapes that can be enjoyed to the fullest in any season.

Drawing the Line

North-central New Mexico is the place to go for **snow skiing**. Sandia Peak Ski Area, just east of Albuquerque in the Cibola National Forest, packs a variety of trails, bowls and catwalks into a wedge of mountain. A 55-passenger aerial tramway ascends the western slope of the mountain to the 10,378-foot summit, but the ski runs from this height are recommended only for experienced skiers; a novice ski area on the eastern slope can be accessed by private vehicle.

The Sangre de Cristo Mountain Range supports a cluster of ski resorts open mid-December to mid-March. Santa Fe Ski Area, north of Santa Fe off US 285, attracts families and first-timers to its groomed slopes for downhill skiing; this resort's Chipmunk Corner teaches children to swish safely on powder. With 58 runs for beginning and intermediate skiers as well as six lifts (including a high-speed quad) and a **snowboarding** park, Angel Fire Resort, east of Taos, is another family favorite.

Alpine skiing is the winter sport of choice at Taos Ski Valley, where snowfall averages more than 300 inches per year—the most in the state—and the vertical drop exceeds 2,600 feet. The toughest slopes are long and steep, just begging to be challenged by experts. With more than 72 trails to choose from, skiers who are "less inclined" will find a hill to match their skill. Sorry, snowboarding is not permitted.

Enchanted Forest, 3.5 miles east of Red River, has some 21 miles of groomed trails designed for cross-country skiing. You'll surely catch a glimpse of wildlife while striding over forested slopes or through alpine meadows. Outfitters in Red River can help you prepare for the trek. Sugarite Canyon State Park, on the Colorado border near Raton, and Manzano Mountain State Park, southeast of Albuquerque, also welcome cross-country skiers.

Tracks of Another Kind

When the snow melts, you still can soar across the mountains of north-central New Mexico—on **mountain biking** trails. Lay your treads on the dirt at Angel Fire and follow 23-mile South Boundary Trail through Carson National Forest to Taos. The scenery is spectacular, but you'll have to be in shape to see it; this daylong trip starts with a 4-mile climb and tops out at 10,800 feet.

Trails in southern New Mexico are as varied as the terrain. Fresnal Canyon Loop traverses the Sacramento Mountains foothills, just northeast of Alamogordo, passing through villages as well as cherry and apple orchards. Riding time depends on how many glasses of cider you stop to sample. Race the jack rabbits on a 4.5-mile loop around Tortugas Mountain, 1 mile southeast of Las Cruces. The riding surface in this desertlike area comes in three textures: rocky, sandy and smooth.

Bicycling on paved surfaces can be a family event at Chaco Culture National Historical Park, in the northwest. An easy 8-mile circle tour begins at the visitor center and offers stops at several archeological ruins that you can tour at your leisure. The king of the road-rides may well be a 70-mile round-trip excursion via state and forest roads from Carlsbad to Sitting Bull Falls, in Lincoln National Forest; a rest beside the waterfall will rejuvenate you for the return trip.

The Gila National Forest, in the southwest, offers recreation at a slower pace. With some 1,500 miles of trails and 20 campgrounds, New Mexico's largest national forest invites **camping, hiking** and **backpacking**. State parks, too, cater to this trinity of outdoor activities. Strike camp beside Elephant Butte Lake in that state park; walk among the aspens in Hyde Memorial; or press deep into primitive Morphy Lake State Park's backwoods.

The spring thaw creates a flood of **white-water rafting** opportunities in northern New Mexico, especially on the Rio Grande and Rio Chama. Contact the Bureau of Land Management for maps, brochures and details about rules and permits; phone (505) 758-8851.

Recreational Activities

Throughout the TourBook, you may notice a Recreational Activities heading with bulleted listings of recreation-oriented establishments listed underneath. Since normal AAA inspection criteria cannot be applied, these establishments are presented for information only. Age, height and weight restrictions may apply. Reservations are often recommended and sometimes required. Visitors should phone or write the attraction for additional information, and the address and phone number are provided for this purpose.

Fast Facts

POPULATION: 1,729,800.

AREA: 121,666 square miles; ranks 5th.

CAPITAL: Santa Fe.

HIGHEST POINT: 13,161 ft., Wheeler Peak.

LOWEST POINT: 2,817 ft., Red Bluff Reservoir.

TIME ZONE: Mountain. DST.

MINIMUM AGE FOR DRIVERS: 16.

MINIMUM AGE FOR GAMBLING: 21

SEAT BELT/CHILD RESTRAINT LAWS: Seat belts required for driver and front-seat passengers; child restraints required for under 11.

HELMETS FOR MOTORCYCLISTS: Required for under 18.

RADAR DETECTORS: Permitted.

FIREARMS LAWS: Vary by state or county. Contact the Office of the Attorney General, P.O. Box 1508, Santa Fe, NM 87504; phone (505) 827-6000.

HOLIDAYS: Jan. 1; Lincoln's Birthday, Feb. 12; Washington's Birthday, Feb. (3rd Mon.); Memorial Day, May (last Mon.); July 4; Labor Day, Sept. (1st Mon.); Veterans Day, Nov. 11; Thanksgiving; Dec. 25.

TAXES: New Mexico's statewide sales tax is 5.75 percent, with local option for additional increments of up to 1.5 percent.

STATE INFORMATION CENTERS: Welcome centers that provide maps, weather information, brochures and information about state attractions, accommodations, historic sites, parks and events are at I-10W near Anthony, SR 544 near Aztec, US 64/84 at Chama, I-40W near Glenrio, I-10E at Lordsburg, I-25 near Raton, I-25 near Santa Fe and at U.S. 84 near Texico.

FURTHER INFORMATION FOR VISITORS:
New Mexico Department of Tourism
Lamy Building, Room 106
491 Old Santa Fe Tr.
Santa Fe, NM 87503
(505) 827-7400 or (800) 545-2040

RECREATION INFORMATION:
State Park and Recreation Division
408 Galisteo St.
P.O. Box 1147
Santa Fe, NM 87504-1147
(505) 827-7173
(888) 667-2757

FISHING AND HUNTING REGULATIONS:
Department of Game and Fish
Villagra Building
State Capitol
Santa Fe, NM 87503
(505) 827-7911

NATIONAL FOREST INFORMATION:
Southwestern Region
517 Gold Ave. S.W.
Albuquerque, NM 87102
(505) 842-3292
(800) 444-6777 (reservations)

SPECIAL NOTE: PLAGUE BACILLI, A CONDITION PROMOTED BY FLEAS, IS ENDEMIC TO NEW MEXICO. PET OWNERS ARE ADVISED TO KEEP THEIR PETS DUSTED WITH FLEA POWDER.

AAA Starred Attractions

EXCEPTIONAL INTEREST AND QUALITY

Alamogordo (E-4)

SPACE CENTER—This large complex includes Stapp Air and Space Park, Astronaut Memorial Garden and Shuttle Camp. An outdoor display features launch vehicles and spacecraft. See p. 132.

Albuquerque (C-3)

NEW MEXICO MUSEUM OF NATURAL HISTORY & SCIENCE—Origins and geographical history of the Southwest are explored. A naturalist center and saltwater aquarium also are featured. See p. 135.

OLD TOWN—The site presents a visible record of Albuquerque's evolution from small town to big city. American Indians and artisans vend their handicrafts around the plaza. See p. 135.

RIO GRANDE ZOOLOGICAL PARK—More than 1,300 animals representing some 300 species are housed here. See p. 135.

Angel Fire (B-4)

VIETNAM VETERANS NATIONAL MEMORIAL—A curvilinear structure is dedicated to Vietnam War casualties. The hilltop vantage affords views of the Sangre de Cristo Mountains and the Moreno Valley. See p. 136.

Aztec Ruins National Monument (A-2)

AZTEC RUINS NATIONAL MONUMENT—A monument marks one of the largest and best preserved Anasazi ruins in the Southwest. See p. 137.

Bandelier National Monument (B-3)

BANDELIER NATIONAL MONUMENT—Remnants of an Anasazi community established centuries ago include pueblo and cliff ruins as well as cave rooms hewn out of soft tuff rock. See p. 137.

Capulin Volcano National Monument (A-5)

CAPULIN VOLCANO NATIONAL MONUMENT—Created about 10,000 years ago when ash and cinders piled up around a volcano vent, this is one of the best examples of a volcanic cinder cone in the nation. See p. 139.

Carlsbad Caverns National Park (F-4)

CARLSBAD CAVERN—More than 30 miles of surveyed subterranean corridors and chambers feature beautiful limestone formations. See p. 140.

CARLSBAD CAVERNS NATIONAL PARK—In the rugged foothills of the Guadalupe Mountains, the park's exhibits depict the geology, biology, history and archeology of the area. See p. 139.

Chama (A-3)

CUMBRES AND TOLTEC SCENIC RAILROAD—Ride on the narrow gauge railroad to explore the territory along the rugged San Juan and Sangre de Cristo mountain ranges. See p. 142.

Cibola National Forest

SANDIA PEAK AERIAL TRAMWAY—Visitors are transported above the deep canyons of the Sandia Mountains. Balloonists and hang gliders launch from Sandia Peak. See p. 144.

Los Alamos (B-3)

BRADBURY SCIENCE MUSEUM—Exhibits interpret the depth of science and engineering capabilities, including that of the Manhattan Project. See p. 154.

Roswell (D-5)

ROSWELL MUSEUM AND ART CENTER—Historical art and artifacts of Southwestern culture are displayed. See p. 156.

Santa Fe (B-4)

MISSION OF SAN MIGUEL OF SANTA FE—One of the country's oldest churches, the mission is adorned with priceless ornaments and paintings. See p. 161.

MUSEUM OF INTERNATIONAL FOLK ART—Exhibits include miniature buildings, streets and marketplaces in village scenes from 100 countries. Also featured is Spanish colonial folk art. See p. 161.

PALACE OF THE GOVERNORS—Built in 1610, the adobe structure was the seat of government under Spanish, American Indian, Mexican and U.S. territorial rule until 1909, when it became the state history museum. See Santa Fe p. 161.

Santa Teresa (F-3)

WAR EAGLES AIR MUSEUM—Featured are restored aircraft from World War II and jet fighters from the Korean War. See p. 164.

White Sands National Monument (E-3)

WHITE SANDS NATIONAL MONUMENT—Source of white gypsum sands and dunes that rise up to 60 feet above the Tularosa Valley, the site features a visitor center and interpretive programs. See p. 169.

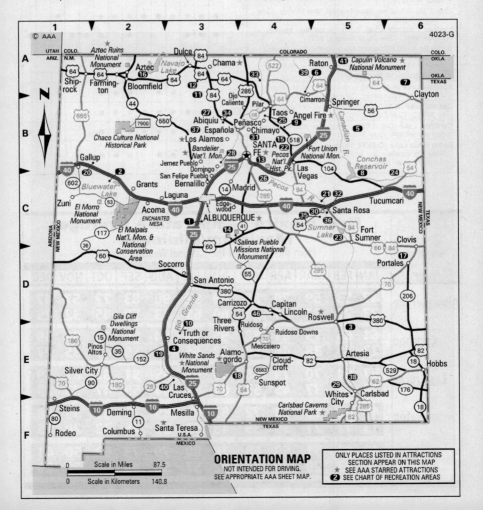

ORIENTATION MAP
NOT INTENDED FOR DRIVING.
SEE APPROPRIATE AAA SHEET MAP.

ONLY PLACES LISTED IN ATTRACTIONS
SECTION APPEAR ON THIS MAP
★ SEE AAA STARRED ATTRACTIONS
❷ SEE CHART OF RECREATION AREAS

RECREATION AREAS

	MAP LOCATION	CAMPING	PICNICKING	HIKING TRAILS	BOATING	BOAT RAMP	BOAT RENTAL	FISHING	SWIMMING	PETS ON LEASH	BICYCLE TRAILS	WINTER SPORTS	VISITOR CENTER	LODGE/CABINS	FOOD SERVICE
NATIONAL PARKS															
Carlsbad Caverns (F-4) 46,776 acres. Southeast New Mexico. *(See place listing p. 139)*			•	•									•		•
Chaco Culture (B-2) 33,974 acres. Northwest New Mexico. *(See place listing p. 142)*		•	•	•						•	•		•		
NATIONAL CONSERVATION AREA															
El Malpais (C-2) 376,000 acres. Central New Mexico. *(See Grants p. 150)*		•	•	•									•		
NATIONAL FORESTS															
Carson 1,500,000 acres. North-central New Mexico. *(See place listing p. 141)*		•	•	•				•		•	•	•	•		
Cibola 1,630,221 acres. Central New Mexico. *(See place listing p. 144)*		•	•	•	•	•		•	•	•	•	•	•	•	•
Gila 3,321,000 acres. Southwestern New Mexico. *(See place listing p. 149)*		•	•	•	•	•	•	•	•	•		•	•		
Lincoln 1,103,466 acres. South-central New Mexico. Horse rental. *(See place listing p. 153)*		•	•	•				•		•	•	•	•	•	•
Santa Fe 1,568,820 acres. North-central New Mexico between the San Pedro Mountains and the Sangre de Cristo Mountains. *(See place listing p. 163)*		•	•	•				•		•	•	•	•		
ARMY CORPS OF ENGINEERS															
Abiquiu Lake (B-3) 4,015 acres 7 mi. n.w. of Abiquiu via US 84. Water skiing. *(See Abiquiu p. 131)*	27	•	•		•	•		•	•	•			•		
Cochiti Lake (B-3) 1,200 acres 5 mi. n. of Peña Blanca on SR 22. *(See Domingo p. 146)*	28	•	•	•	•	•	•	•	•	•			•		
Conchas Lake (C-5) 1,557 acres 31 mi. n.w. of Tucumcari via SR 104. *(See Tucumcari p. 168)*	8	•	•	•	•	•	•	•	•	•			•	•	•
Santa Rosa Lake (C-5) 14,000 acres 7 mi. n. of Santa Rosa via access road. Water skiing; nature trail. *(See Santa Rosa p. 164)*	21	•	•	•	•	•	•	•		•	•		•		

New Mexico Temperature Averages
Maximum/Minimum
From the records of the National Weather Service

	JAN	FEB	MAR	APR	MAY	JUN	JUL	AUG	SEP	OCT	NOV	DEC
Albuquerque	47/23	53/27	59/32	70/41	80/51	89/60	92/65	90/63	83/58	72/45	57/32	47/25
Carlsbad	61/27	65/31	73/38	81/46	88/54	95/63	95/66	94/65	89/59	79/47	69/35	59/27
Las Cruces	57/28	64/31	70/37	79/45	88/53	96/61	97/67	95/66	91/59	82/47	67/33	59/29
Raton	45/13	49/17	55/21	63/30	72/39	83/48	87/53	85/51	79/45	69/33	55/20	48/15
Santa Fe	40/19	43/23	51/29	59/35	68/43	78/52	80/57	79/56	73/49	62/39	50/28	41/20

RECREATION AREAS

Recreation Area	Map Location	Camping	Picnicking	Hiking Trails	Boating	Boat Ramp	Boat Rental	Fishing	Swimming	Pets on Leash	Bicycle Trails	Winter Sports	Visitor Center	Lodge/Cabins	Food Service
STATE															
Bluewater Lake (C-2) 2,105 acres 29 mi. n.w. of Grants off I-40.	2	•	•	•	•	•	•	•	•	•			•		•
Bottomless Lakes (E-5) 1,611 acres 16 mi. s.e. of Roswell via US 380, then 6 mi. s. on SR 409. *(See Roswell p. 156)*	3	•	•	•	•		•	•	•	•			•		
Brantley Dam (E-5) 3,000 acres 12 mi. n. of Carlsbad off US 285.	38	•	•		•	•		•		•					
Caballo Lake (E-3) 11,610 acres 14 mi. s. of Truth or Consequences off I-25. *(See Truth or Consequences p. 168)*	4	•	•	•	•	•		•	•	•			•		•
Chicosa Lake (B-5) 640 acres 9 mi. n.e. of Roy on SR 120.	5	•	•	•				•		•			•		
Cimarron Canyon (A-5) 33,000 acres 12 mi. e. of Eagle Nest via US 64.	6	•	•	•				•		•		•			
Clayton Lake (A-6) 417 acres 15 mi. n. of Clayton on SR 370. *(See Clayton p. 145)*	7	•	•	•	•			•		•			•		
Coyote Creek (B-4) 80 acres 14 mi. n.e. of Mora on SR 434.	9	•	•					•					•		
Elephant Butte Lake (E-3) 40,056 acres 5 mi. e. of Truth or Consequences off I-25. *(See Truth or Consequences p. 168)*	10	•	•	•	•	•	•	•	•	•			•	•	•
El Vado Lake (A-3) 113 acres 4 mi. n.e. of El Vado off SR 112.	11	•	•	•	•	•	•	•	•	•			•	•	•
Fenton Lake (B-3) 700 acres 38 mi. w. of Los Alamos via SRs 4 and 126. Canoeing, cross-country skiing.	37	•	•	•				•		•		•			
Heron Lake (A-3) 4,107 acres 11 mi. w. of Tierra Amarilla via US 84 and SR 95.	12	•	•	•	•	•		•		•		•	•		
Hyde Memorial (B-4) 350 acres 8 mi. n.e. of Santa Fe on Hyde Park Rd. *(See Santa Fe p. 160)*	13	•	•	•						•		•	•		
Leasburg Dam (E-3) 140 acres 15 mi. n.w. of Las Cruces via I-25 and SR 185. Canoeing; playground.	40	•	•					•		•					
Manzano Mountains (C-3) 160 acres 13 mi. n.w. of Mountainair via SR 55.	14	•	•	•						•			•		
Morphy Lake (B-4) 65 acres 11 mi. n. of Las Vegas off SR 518. *(See Las Vegas p. 152)*	15	•	•					•		•					
Navajo Lake (A-2) 13,300 acres 23 mi. n.e. of Bloomfield on SR 511. *(See Bloomfield p. 138)*	16	•	•	•	•	•	•	•	•	•			•	•	•
Oasis (D-6) 193 acres 5.7 mi. n. of Portales off SR 467. *(See Portales p. 155)*	17	•	•					•		•					
Oliver Lee Memorial (E-3) 180 acres 10 mi. s. on US 54, then 5 mi. e. on Dog Canyon Rd. *(See Alamogordo p. 132)*	18	•	•	•						•			•		
Percha Dam (E-2) 84 acres 21 mi. s. of Truth or Consequences via I-25. Playground.	19	•	•	•	•			•	•	•					
Red Rock (C-1) 640 acres 8 mi. e. of Gallup on I-40. Museum. *(See Gallup p. 149)*	20	•	•							•			•		•
Sen. Willie M. Chavez (C-3) 150 acres on the Rio Grande at Belen.	1	•	•	•				•		•	•		•		
Storrie Lake (B-4) 83 acres 5 mi. n. of Las Vegas off SR 518. Windsurfing. *(See Las Vegas p. 152)*	22	•	•	•	•	•		•	•	•			•		
Sugarite Canyon (A-5) 9,500 acres 10 mi. n.e. of Raton via SR 72. Historic. Canoeing, cross-country skiing, mountain climbing, snowmobiling. *(See Raton p. 156)*	41	•	•	•	•			•		•		•	•		
Sumner Lake (C-5) 5,425 acres 16 mi. n. of Fort Sumner on US 84.	23	•	•	•	•	•		•	•	•					•
Ute Lake (C-6) 633 acres 2 mi. s.w. of Logan on SR 540. *(See Tucumcari p. 168)*	24	•	•	•	•	•	•	•	•	•			•	•	
Villanueva (C-4) 1,679 acres 31 mi. s.w. of Las Vegas via I-25 and SR 3.	26	•	•	•				•	•	•			•		
OTHER															
Blue Hole (C-4) 50 acres .5 mi. w. of Park Lake on La Pradira Ln. in Santa Rosa. Scuba diving. *(See Santa Rosa p. 163)*	35		•	•				•	•				•		

RECREATION AREAS

	MAP LOCATION	CAMPING	PICNICKING	HIKING TRAILS	BOATING	BOAT RAMP	BOAT RENTAL	FISHING	SWIMMING	PETS ON LEASH	BICYCLE TRAILS	WINTER SPORTS	VISITOR CENTER	LODGE/CABINS	FOOD SERVICE
Fort Stanton (D-4) 23,000 acres 5 mi. w. of Lincoln on US 380. Caving; horse trails.	46	•	•	•				•							
Janes-Wallace Memorial (C-5) 1 mi. s. of Santa Rosa on SR 91. *(See Santa Rosa p. 164)*	32	•	•					•					•		
Lake Carlsbad (E-5) In Carlsbad on Park Dr. Water skiing. *(See Carlsbad p. 139)*	29	•	•		•	•		•	•				•		•
Orilla Verde (B-4) 2,840 acres 6 mi. n of Pilar on SR 570.	25	•	•	•	•			•						•	
Park Lake (C-5) In Santa Rosa. *(See Santa Rosa p. 164)*	30		•	•				•	•	•	•				
Perch Lake (C-5) 22 acres 2 mi. s. of Santa Rosa on SR 91. Scuba diving. *(See Santa Rosa p. 164)*	36		•	•				•	•						
Santa Clara Canyon (B-3) 730 acres 4 mi. s.w. of Española on SR 30, then 10 mi. w. on SR 5.	34	•	•	•				•							
Santa Cruz Lake (B-4) 2,543 acres 14 mi. e. of Española via SRs 76 and 4. Mountain bicycling. *(See Española p. 147)*	31	•	•	•	•	•	•	•							
Valle Vidal (A-4) 100,000 acres 4 mi. n. on US 64, then 21 mi. n.w. on Valle Vidal Rd. following signs. *(See Cimarron p. 144)*	39	•	•	•				•		•					
Wild Rivers (A-4) 20,300 acres 5 mi. w. of Questa off SR 378.	33	•	•	•				•						•	

Rules of the Road Can Change at State Borders

Speed limits are usually posted at state lines, but adherence to less known traffic regulations also is important for safe and enjoyable travel between states.

To assist traveling motorists, AAA publishes the *Digest of Motor Laws*—a comprehensive description of the laws that govern motor vehicle operation in the United States and Canada.

Examples of laws that differ in neighboring states include:

- In Oklahoma, police can only cite motorists for not wearing seat belts if they are stopped for another infraction. In neighboring Texas—and in 12 other states—police can stop motorists solely for failure to wear a seat belt.

- Drivers in Michigan are permitted to wear headsets, but not when they cross the border into Ohio or travel to 14 other states.

- Radar detectors are legal in Maryland—and 48 other states—but can't be used in Virginia and Washington, D.C.

To obtain a copy of the *Digest of Motor Laws*, contact your local AAA club or the traffic safety department of AAA's national office at 1000 AAA Drive, Heathrow, FL 32746-5063. The glove-compartment size book retails for $8.95.

Points of Interest

ABIQUIU (B-3) elev. 5,930'

In the mid-18th century Abiquiu was one of several settlements the Spanish government provided for *Genízaros,* people of mixed blood who were either the Spaniards' own prisoners or captives ransomed from the Comanches or Apaches and later released from slavery. By 1778 the community was a stop on the Old Spanish Trail, which led westward to an infant coastal hamlet called Los Angeles.

Abiquiu was the birthplace of Padre Antonio José Martínez, the priest credited with the establishment of the Southwest's first coeducational school. His lifelong crusade to educate his people took him to Taos in 1826, then into politics.

Abiquiu Lake *(see Recreation Chart and the AAA Southwestern CampBook),* 7 miles northwest via US 84, provides opportunities for water sports while controlling downstream flooding and sedimentation. The Carson and Santa Fe national forests *(see place listings p. 141 and 163)* surround the lake.

GHOST RANCH LIVING MUSEUM is 14 mi. n.w. on US 84. The center stresses conservation education through displays of geology, native animals and plants, a miniature forest and a beaver museum. Another exhibit area explores the cultural history of the Rio Chama region. The outreach branch of New Mexico Museum of Natural History & Science *(see Albuquerque p. 135)* schedules exhibits periodically. Allow 30 minutes minimum. Tues.-Sun. 9-4. Admission $3; $1.50; ages 6-18, $1; Golden Eagle and Golden Age pass holders free. Phone (505) 685-4312.

ACOMA (SKY CITY) (C-2)

One of the oldest continuously inhabited sites in the country—evidence dates it from at least 1150—Acoma was well established when Francisco Vasquez de Coronado explored New Mexico in 1540. Inhabitants worked fields on the plains 357 feet below their village and climbed back atop the mesa each night. The Sky City afforded protection through nearly a century of warfare, but the numerical superiority of the Spaniards proved too much, resulting in the community's surrender.

Visitors bound for Sky City, 14 miles southwest of the junction of I-40 and Reservation Roads 30 and 32, must register at the visitor center at the base of the mesa. A 90-minute guided tour of Sky City and San Esteban del Rey Mission is $8 per person. There is a $10 charge for still-camera use, and video cameras are not permitted.

About 3 miles northeast is Enchanted Mesa, which looms 430 feet above the surrounding plain. According to legend, this was an ancestral dwelling, but access to it was wiped out by a violent storm, leaving an old woman and her granddaughter to starve on the mesa top.

SAN ESTEBAN DEL REY MISSION, at the top of the mesa, dates from 1629 and is the largest early Southwestern mission. Every grain of sand used in construction was carried to the mesa top; the great log beams were hand-cut and carried from Mount Taylor, more than 30 miles away. Within the mission are religious paintings, an unusual altar and images of saints. Sky City guided tours include the mission and leave from the visitor center; a guide must accompany visitors on the mesa top. Some restrictions apply to taking photographs. Food is available.

Allow 1 hour minimum. Daily 8-7, Apr. 1 to mid-Oct.; 8-4:30, rest of year. Closed July 10-13, the first or second weekend in Oct. and other days without notice. Tour $8; over 59, $7; ages 6-17, $6. Phone (505) 470-4966 or (800) 747-0181.

ALAMOGORDO (E-4)
pop. 27,600, elev. 4,335'

On July 16, 1945, in a remote section of White Sands Missile Range, the first man-made atomic explosion sent a huge multicolored cloud surging to an altitude of 40,000 feet. The resultant sloping crater at Trinity Site is mute evidence of man's transition to the Atomic Age.

Trinity Site is open the first Saturdays in April and in October. Contact the Public Affairs Office, Bldg. 122, White Sands Missile Range, NM 88002; phone (505) 678-1134.

The Air Force Missile Development Center at Holloman Air Force Base conducts rocket and allied research. The work done at National Solar Observatory *(see Sunspot p. 166)* is an integral part of Holloman and the missile range.

A ready water supply from the looming Sacramento Mountains prompted the town's founding as a railroad division point in 1898. Alamogordo—Spanish for "fat cottonwood"—grew quickly as ranching, lumber production, farming and tourism were added to its assets. Nevertheless, modern development has been due primarily to the air force base. Diversified industry, much of it related to space, also contributes to the economy.

Tularosa Basin Historical Society Museum, 1301 N. White Sands Blvd., focuses on local history; phone (505) 434-4438. Leading eastward to Cloudcroft *(see place listing p. 145),* US 82 passes through the state's only highway tunnel.

Alamogordo Chamber of Commerce: 1301 White Sands Blvd., P.O. Box 2828, Alamogordo, NM 88311-0518; phone (505) 437-6120.

ALAMEDA PARK AND ZOO, jct. US 54 and 10th St., features American and exotic wildlife including herd animals, cougars, bears and birds. Shaded lawns are available for picnicking and recreation. Daily 9-5; closed Jan. 1 and Dec. 25. Admission $2.25; over 59 and ages 3-11, $1.25. Phone (505) 439-4290.

OLIVER LEE MEMORIAL STATE PARK, 8 mi. s. on US 54, then 4 mi. e. on Dog Canyon Rd., is at the mouth of Dog Canyon in the western face of the Sacramento Mountains. Year-round springs have attracted man for some 6,000 years. In the 1880s Frenchy Rochas homesteaded at the canyon mouth; remnants of his rock walls, cabin, orchard and an irrigation ditch still stand. A ranch house built by Lee has been reconstructed and furnished with period antiques. Visitor center exhibits explain the canyon's natural and historical significance.

Park open daily 24 hours. One-hour house tours are given Sat.-Sun. at 3. Visitor center open daily 9-4. Admission $4 per private vehicle. Phone (505) 437-8284. *See Recreation Chart and the AAA Southwestern CampBook.*

★ **SPACE CENTER**, 2 mi. n.e. of US 54, is a large complex including Stapp Air and Space Park, Astronaut Memorial Garden, International Space Hall of Fame and Shuttle Camp. Exhibits honor pioneers from many nations and include international space program items. An outdoor display features launch vehicles and spacecraft.

Allow 2 hours minimum. Daily 9-5; closed Dec. 25. Hall of fame $2.50; over 59 and military with ID $2.25; ages 6-17, $2. Phone (505) 437-2840 or (800) 545-4021.

Clyde W. Tombaugh IMAX Dome Theater and Planetarium features a 70-millimeter movie projector. Films are projected onto a 40-foot wraparound screen.

Show times are daily on the hour 10-4 and at 7 p.m., Memorial Day-Labor Day; Mon.-Fri. at 10, noon, 2 and 4 (also 7 p.m. on Fri.), Sat.-Sun. on the hour 10-4 and at 7 p.m., rest of year.

Admission $5.50; over 60 and military with ID $5; ages 13-17, $4.50; ages 6-12, $3.50. Admission for two films $9; over 60 and military with ID $8; ages 13-17, $7.50; ages 6-12, $5.50.

TOY TRAIN DEPOT, 1 mi. n. on US 70/54 to 1991 N. White Sands Blvd., features hundreds of models and toy train displays housed in an old depot. Built in 1898, a 16-inch gauge train ride runs outdoors through adjacent Alameda Park. Allow 30 minutes minimum. Wed.-Sun. noon-5. Admission $2; under 12, $1.50. Train fare $2; under 12, $1.50. DS, MC, VI. Phone (505) 437-2855.

ALBUQUERQUE (C-3)
pop. 384,600, elev. 5,000'

Commanding the wide valley between the Sandia Mountains and the sweeping plateau country paralleling the Rio Grande, metropolitan Albuquerque is New Mexico's big city. Many residents work at Sandia National Laboratories or other research and development firms.

Albuquerque offers just about everything: a genuine casual elegance; big business, high-tech and metropolitan growing pains; and the sometimes fiery and always interesting juxtaposition of American Indian, Spanish and Anglo cultures. Omnipresent in the city's architecture, art and ecological concern is the kernel of everything New Mexican—the elusive but binding sense of the land.

Once the home of wealthy Spanish families, Albuquerque was abandoned during the Pueblo Rebellion of 1680. Reclaimed by Spanish general Don Diego de Vargas in 1692, the land attracted 30 families from Bernalillo in search of greener pastures. Soon their flocks and crops were flourishing.

Wide bottomlands and a central location attracted a steady stream of settlers. By 1790 its population neared 6,000. Except for the 1880s, when Socorro surpassed it, Albuquerque has been the state's largest city. From the beginning it has benefited from the flow of commerce between Santa Fe and Mexico City, Mexico.

It became a military town as well after Gen. Stephen Kearny raised the U.S. flag over the plaza in 1846 and established an Army post. This made Albuquerque a prize during the Civil War; it was under Confederate occupation for 2 months early in 1862.

The coming of the railroad in 1880 created a modern, more vigorous Albuquerque 2 miles east. Although the old city languished, it did not lose its character and the new city soon engulfed and later annexed Old Town *(see attraction listing p. 135).*

Nearby reservations represent the spirit of the American Indian. Seven miles north is Sandia Reservation; its Bien Mur Indian Market Center, 1 mile east of I-25 exit 234, is one of the largest in the Southwest. Isleta Indian Reservation, 13 miles south of town, features pottery and other traditional crafts as well as fresh bread. Rock carvings are the focus of Petroglyph National Monument, 8 miles northwest via SR 448 and Atrisco Drive.

Other important factors in Albuquerque's makeup are the University of New Mexico *(see attraction listing p. 136),* and Kirtland Air Force Base.

Ideal wind and weather conditions have made this a favorite locale for hot-air ballooning. The multicolored globes are seen frequently but never so dramatically as in the mass ascensions that highlight the 9-day Kodak Albuquerque International Balloon Fiesta in October.

A 62-mile scenic loop follows I-40 east to Tijeras, SR 14 north to San Antonito, SR 44 west to Bernalillo and returns to Albuquerque via I-25. The section between San Antonito and Bernalillo crosses the crest of the Sandias, but because the most rugged 8 miles are unpaved, large trucks, trailers and RVs are prohibited. Drivers should heed posted signs.

Another scenic route, Turquoise Trail, runs along the east side of the Sandias between Cedar Crest and La Cienega near Santa Fe on SRs 14

and 536; highlights include mountain scenery, a few ghost towns, thick pine and aspen forests and Sandia Crest *(see Cibola National Forest p. 144)*.

Albuquerque Convention and Visitors Bureau: 20 First Plaza N.W., Suite 20, Albuquerque, NM 87102; phone (505) 842-9918 or (800) 733-9918.

Self-guiding tours: Brochures of driving tours through Albuquerque and nearby communities are available from the convention and visitors bureau.

Shopping areas: Coronado Center, 6600 Menaul St. N.E., counts Macy's, JCPenney, Foley's,

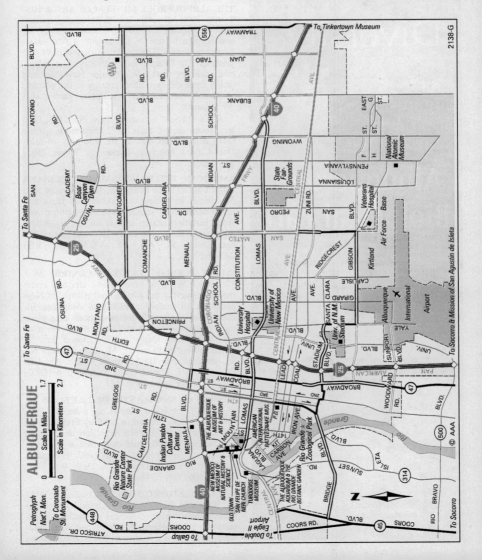

Explore the
Mystery
and
Diversity
...of living organisms 362 days a year at the

Albuquerque Biological Park

The Albuquerque Aquarium and Rio Grande Botanic Garden are located at 2601 Central NW; Rio Grande Zoo at 903 Tenth Street SW. Open daily 9:00am - 5:00pm; Summer Weekend hours 9:00am - 6:00pm Website: www.cabq.gov/biopark

For special assistance, call BioPark Admissions at 505.764.6200 or by TTY 505.764.6297 at least three days before you visit.

Albuquerque Biological Park

City of Albuquerque

Mervyn's and Sears among its 160 stores. Cottonwood Mall, 10000 Coors Blvd. N.W., features Dillard's, JCPenney, Foley's and Mervyn's California.

THE ALBUQUERQUE AQUARIUM, 2601 Central Ave., displays marine life and habitats of the Gulf of Mexico. Tanks contain stingrays, jellyfish, eels, sharks and other fish. A short orientation film also is shown. Food is available. Allow 1 hour minimum. Mon.-Fri. 9-5 (also Sat.-Sun. 9-6, June-Aug.); closed Jan. 1, Thanksgiving and Dec. 25. Admission $4.50; over 64 and ages 3-15, $2.50. Phone (505) 764-6200. *See color ad.*

THE ALBUQUERQUE MUSEUM OF ART & HISTORY, 2000 Mountain Rd. N.W., houses temporary and permanent exhibits about history, art and science in one of the country's first solar-heated museums. The central display depicts 400 years of Rio Grande Valley history. The collection includes works from major New Mexican artists from the early 20th century to the present. Children's exhibits and a sculpture garden also are featured.

Allow 2 hours minimum. Tues.-Sun. 9-5. Gallery tours depart daily at 2. Sculpture garden tours depart Tues.-Fri. at 10, mid-May to mid-Oct. Closed holidays. Donations. Phone (505) 243-7255.

AMERICAN INTERNATIONAL RATTLESNAKE MUSEUM, 202 San Felipe St., features more than 30 species of rattlesnakes as well as films and information about snakes and other reptiles. Artwork featuring snakes also is on display. Allow 30 minutes minimum. Daily 10-6. Admission $2; ages 3-16, $1. AE, DS, VI. Phone (505) 242-6569.

INDIAN PUEBLO CULTURAL CENTER, 2401 12th St. N.W., is a museum and arts and crafts market depicting the history and culture of New Mexico's 19 pueblos. Traditional American Indian dances and craft demonstrations take place on weekends. Food is available. Allow 30 minutes minimum. Daily 9-5:30; closed Jan. 1, Thanksgiving and Dec. 25. Museum $4; over 62, $3; students with ID $1; under 4 free. AE, CB, DS, MC, VI. Phone (505) 843-7270 or (800) 766-4405. *See color ad p. 135.*

MISSION OF SAN AGUSTIN DE ISLETA, 16 mi. s. via I-25 in Isleta Pueblo, is a heavily buttressed structure erected in 1613 by Fray Juan de Salas. During the Pueblo Rebellion the mission was burned partially and then used as a corral. The church, restored after the 1692 reconquest, has been in constant use since. Daily 9-6. Free. Phone (505) 869-3398.

NATIONAL ATOMIC MUSEUM, Building 20358 on Wyoming Blvd. S.E. at Kirtland Air Force Base, traces the development of nuclear weaponry through photographs, films and such hardware as an original hydrogen bomb, missiles and artillery pieces. Aircraft, including an F-105 fighter, a B-52 bomber and a B-29 bomber, are displayed outdoors. A 53-minute documentary about the Manhattan Project is shown daily at 10:30, 11:30, 2 and 3. Allow 30 minutes minimum.

Daily 9-5; closed Jan. 1, Easter, Thanksgiving and Dec. 25. A free shuttle runs from the base's Wyoming and Gibson entrance gates to the museum every 30 minutes. Admission $2; over 54, active military and ages 7-18, $1. Phone (505) 284-3243.

★NEW MEXICO MUSEUM OF NATURAL HISTORY & SCIENCE is .5 mi. s. of I-40 on Rio Grande Blvd., then 2 blks. e. to 1801 Mountain Rd. N.W. The origins and geological history of the Southwest are explored through full-scale dinosaur models, a walk-through volcano, an ice age cave replica, a time machine and a naturalist center. A saltwater aquarium as well as zoological and botanical exhibits are featured.

Allow 1 hour minimum. Daily 9-5. Dynamax shows, which last 45 minutes, are shown on the hour. Museum $5.25; over 59 and students with ID $4.20; ages 3-11, $2.10. Dynamax $5.25; over 59 and students with ID $4.20; ages 3-11, $2.10. Combination ticket $8.40; over 59 and students with ID $6.30; ages 3-11, $3.15. Phone (505) 841-2800.

★OLD TOWN, 1 blk. n. of the 2000 blk. of Central Ave. N.W. (US 66) and .5 mi. s. of the I-40 Rio Grande Blvd. exit, is the site of the city's original settlement, founded in 1706 and named in honor of the Duke of Albuquerque. Old Town is a visible record of Albuquerque's evolution from small village to big city. The shops and galleries surrounding Old Town Plaza offer arts, crafts and edible delicacies. American Indians and artisans also vend their handicrafts around the plaza; bargaining is in order.

The 1706 San Felipe de Neri Church, on the northern corner of the plaza, is a mix of Victorian and basic adobe architecture. An information booth across the street provides free maps of Old Town. Free guided 1-hour walking tours of Old Town depart Tues.-Sun. at 11, mid-May to mid-

Dec., from The Albuquerque Museum of Art & History *(see attraction listing p. 134).*

THE RIO GRANDE BOTANIC GARDEN, 2601 Central Ave., features displays that emphasize the Southwest and the desert climate. Highlights include the Mediterranean and desert conservatories, formal gardens, water and plant exhibits and changing demonstration gardens. Food is available. Allow 1 hour minimum. Mon.-Fri. 9-5 (also Sat.-Sun. 9-6, June-Aug.); closed Jan. 1, Thanksgiving and Dec. 25. Admission $4.50; over 64 and ages 3-15, $2.50. MC, VI. Phone (505) 764-6200. *See color ad p. 134.*

RIO GRANDE NATURE CENTER STATE PARK, 2901 Candelaria Rd. N.W., comprises a wildlife refuge with walking trails along the Rio Grande and a visitor center with exhibits explaining area geology, wildlife and plant life. Allow 30 minutes minimum. Daily 10-5; closed Jan. 1, Thanksgiving and Dec. 25. Admission $1; under 17, 50c. Phone (505) 344-7240.

★**RIO GRANDE ZOOLOGICAL PARK,** 903 Tenth St. S.W., houses more than 1,000 animals representing some 250 species in exhibit areas ranging from the African plains to the New Mexico prairie. Featured are Komodo dragons, Bengal tigers, polar bears, lowland gorillas and bison, among others. Seal and sea lion feedings take place daily in a 350,000-gallon tank. Koala Creek features Australian wildlife. Concerts, bird shows and other programs are scheduled during summer. Food is available.

Mon.-Fri. 9-5 (also Sat.-Sun. 9-6, June-Aug.); closed Jan. 1, Thanksgiving and Dec. 25. Admission $4.50; over 64 and ages 3-15, $2.50. Under 13 must be with an adult. MC, VI. Phone (505) 764-6200.

SANDIA CREST—
see Cibola National Forest p. 144.

★**SANDIA PEAK AERIAL TRAMWAY—**
see Cibola National Forest p. 144.

TINKERTOWN MUSEUM is 20 mi. n. off I-40, 6 mi. n. on SR 14, then 1.5 mi. w. on SR 536 to

121 Sandia Crest Rd. The museum displays a miniature Western town and circus, complete with mechanical people and moving vehicles, all carved from wood. A fence made of 48,000 glass bottles and cement surrounds the museum. Daily 9-6, Apr.-Oct. Admission $2.50; ages 4-16, $1. Phone (505) 281-5233.

THE TURQUOISE MUSEUM, 2107 Central Ave. N.W., features rare turquoise specimens from around the world. Mon.-Sat. 9:30-5:30; closed Jan. 1, Thanksgiving and Dec. 25. Admission $2; over 59 and ages 7-18, $1.50. Phone (505) 247-8650.

UNIVERSITY OF NEW MEXICO occupies a 640-acre campus 2 mi. e. on Central Ave. (US 66). Its buildings are of modified Pueblo style; of particular interest is Hodgin Hall. Popejoy Hall is the home of the New Mexico Symphony Orchestra as well as a setting for ballet, musicals and other programs; for performance information phone (505) 277-3824. Points of interest include the Art and Art History and Thompson galleries and Centennial Museum. Phone (505) 277-5813 for events information.

Center for the Arts is at Cornell St. and Redondo Dr. N.E. Changing exhibits present paintings, prints and photography from the 19th century through contemporary periods as well as Southwestern artworks and artifacts. Tues.-Fri. 9-4, Sun. 1-4 (also Tues. 5-8 and Fri.-Sat. evenings during performances at Popejoy Hall); closed holidays. Free. Phone (505) 277-4001.

Geology Museum of the University of New Mexico, 200 Yale Blvd. (Northrup Hall) in the Earth and Planetary Sciences Building, contains 22 exhibits explaining the constitution of a mineral, various types of minerals, the geology of the earth and geological time periods. Self-guiding tour brochures explain each exhibit. Allow 30 minutes minimum. Mon.-Fri. 8-noon and 1-4:30; closed holidays. Donations. Phone (505) 277-4204.

Jonson Gallery, 1909 Las Lomas N.E., houses the works of Raymond Jonson and other major modernist painters. Jonson created the gallery as a residence, gallery, archive and repository for contemporary art. His works are displayed June through August; other artists' works are displayed the rest of the year. Allow 30 minutes minimum. Tues.-Fri. 9-4 (also Tues. 5-8); closed holidays. Free. Phone (505) 277-4967.

Maxwell Museum of Anthropology, on University Blvd. just n. of Martin Luther King Ave., emphasizes native cultures of the American Southwest—including such ancestral groups as the Anasazi—in its collections about early man. Changing exhibits also are presented. Tues.-Fri. 9-4, Sat. 10-4; closed holidays. Donations. Phone (505) 277-4404.

Meteorite Museum, part of the Institute of Meteoritics on the first floor of the Earth and Plan-

etary Sciences Building at 200 Yale Blvd. (Northrup Hall), exhibits meteorites discovered throughout the world. The institute also is concerned with the teaching and research of space and planetary sciences. A self-guiding tour brochure, available at the entrance, explains all specimens. Allow 30 minutes minimum. Mon.-Fri. 8-noon and 1-4:30; closed holidays. Donations. Phone (505) 277-2747.

CASINOS

- **Isleta Gaming Palace,** 11000 Broadway S.E. Fri.-Sun. 24 hours, Mon.-Thurs. 9 a.m.-5 a.m. Phone (505) 869-2614.

WINERIES

- **Anderson Valley Vineyards,** 4920 Rio Grande Blvd. N.W. Tours are given daily on the hour noon-5:30. Closed holidays. Phone (505) 344-7266.

- **Sandia Shadows Vineyard and Winery,** 7 mi. n. on Tramway Blvd. to San Rafael, then .5 mi. w. to 11704 Coronado N.E. Daily noon-5; closed holidays. Phone (505) 856-1006.

ANGEL FIRE (B-4) pop. 100

In the Moreno Valley of the Sangre de Cristo Mountains, Angel Fire is a year-round resort offering water sports, hunting, golf, hiking, mountain bicycling and horseback riding in summer, and snowmobiling and downhill and cross-country skiing in winter.

Angel Fire Chamber of Commerce: P.O. Box 547, Angel Fire, NM 87710; phone (505) 377-6661 or (800) 446-8117.

★ **VIETNAM VETERANS NATIONAL MEMORIAL,** on US 64, is a curvilinear structure originally built as one family's memorial to a young loved one, killed in an enemy ambush in Vietnam. President Ronald Reagan proclaimed it a national memorial in November 1987. The chapel is dedicated to Vietnam War casualties. Its hilltop vantage affords views of the Sangre de Cristo Mountains and the broad Moreno Valley. Chapel open daily 24 hours. Visitor center open daily 9-7, Memorial Day weekend-Labor day; 9-5, rest of year. Free. Phone (505) 377-6900.

APACHE-SITGREAVES NATIONAL FOREST—

see Arizona p. 40.

ARTESIA (E-5)
pop. 10,600, elev. 3,377'

Artesia was named for its huge underground water supply, which is pumped to the surface via numerous artesian wells. The water irrigates thousands of acres of area farmland.

Another underground resource—oil—was discovered in 1923. This, coupled with reserves of natural gas, has bolstered Artesia's economy and made it one of New Mexico's most productive oil centers. The city also claims what was once the first underground school in the country, built to shelter about 500 students and 2,000 other citizens in the event of a nuclear attack.

Greater Artesia Chamber of Commerce: 408 W. Texas St., P.O. Box 99, Artesia, NM 88211-0099; phone (505) 746-2744.

HISTORICAL MUSEUM AND ART CENTER, 505 W. Richardson Ave., occupies two preserved houses built at the beginning of the 20th century. The museum, devoted to local history, displays equipment used in industrial development as well as such Western paraphernalia as saddles, barbed wire and clothing. The art center next to the museum offers works by area artists. Allow 30 minutes minimum. Tues.-Sat. 8-5; closed holidays. Free. Phone (505) 748-2390.

AZTEC (A-2) pop. 5,500, elev. 5,590′

Pioneers founded the city in 1890 along the Animas River across from ancient Pueblo ruins.

Aztec Chamber of Commerce: 110 N. Ash St., Aztec, NM 87410; phone (505) 334-9551.

AZTEC MUSEUM AND PIONEER VILLAGE, 125 N. Main St., exhibits American Indian artifacts, a collection of rocks and minerals, antique drilling equipment and pioneer furnishings, clothing and memorabilia. The outdoor oil and gas exhibit depicts the history of the industry. Farm and ranch equipment used by early settlers also is displayed. Mon.-Sat. 9-5, May 1-Sept. 1; Mon.-Sat. 10-4, rest of year. Closed Thanksgiving and Dec. 25. Donations. Phone (505) 334-9829.

★ AZTEC RUINS NATIONAL MONUMENT (A-2)

In the northwest corner of New Mexico, just north of Aztec via a spur off US 550, is one of the largest and best preserved ancient pueblo ruins in the Southwest. The misnomer Aztec was applied by early settlers who incorrectly inferred the builders' identity. The largest of these sandstone pueblos, the West Ruin, was built about 1100; it contained nearly 500 rooms, some of which remain intact. Several smaller structures adjoin the main ruin.

A large ceremonial building, the Great Kiva, is the only restoration of its kind in North America. The visitor center features artifacts found during excavations. Daily 8-6, Memorial Day-Labor Day; 8-5, rest of year. Closed Jan. 1, Thanksgiving and Dec. 25. Admission $4, under 17 free. MC, VI. Phone (505) 334-6174.

★ BANDELIER NATIONAL MONUMENT (B-3)

On the Pajarito Plateau in the rugged canyon and mesa country of northern New Mexico, Bandelier National Monument lies 50 miles northwest of Santa Fe; the 32,727-acre monument can be reached via US 285 to Pojoaque, then west on SR 502 and south on SR 4. Remnants of an Anasazi community established 7 or 8 centuries ago include pueblo and cliff ruins.

The most accessible ruins consist of cave rooms hewn out of the soft tuff rock, houses built on the talus slopes and a circular community village. Bandelier also contains 23,267 acres of designated wilderness, including 70 miles of hiking trails. Free permits, required for overnight back-country travel, can be obtained at the visitor center. Pets are not permitted on any trails in the monument.

An introductory slide program and a small museum in the visitor center provide orientation to and interpretation of the area. A 1-hour self-guiding walking tour of the principal ruins starts at the visitor center. Monument open daily dawn-dusk. Visitor center open daily 8-6, Memorial Day-Labor Day; 8-4:30, rest of year. Closed Jan. 1 and Dec. 25. Admission $10 per private vehicle; $5 per person arriving by bicycle, bus, motorcycle or on foot. Visitor center free. Phone

(505) 672-3861. *See the AAA Southwestern CampBook.*

BERNALILLO (C-3)
pop. 6,000, elev. 5,050'

Still essentially a Spanish and American Indian farming community and livestock shipping point, Bernalillo nevertheless is growing as the Albuquerque metropolitan area expands northward along the Rio Grande. The first settlers—descendants of Bernal Díaz del Castillo, chronicler of Hernando Cortés' conquest of Mexico—arrived in 1698.

Remnants of times past remain. Northwest of Bernalillo are the pueblos of Zía and Santa Ana and the Spanish-American village of San Ysidro. At Santa Ana is one of the oldest missions in the United States. Closed to visitors, it is believed to have been built by Fray Juan de Rosas, who accompanied Juan de Oñate on his expedition to New Mexico in 1598.

Greater Bernalillo Chamber of Commerce: P.O. Box 1776, Bernalillo, NM 87004; phone (505) 867-1185.

CORONADO STATE MONUMENT, 485 Kuaua Rd., 2 mi. n.w. on Hwy. 44, includes partially reconstructed ruins of Kuaua, a Tiwa village. One kiva yielded a rare find: polychrome murals of animal and human forms. The restored kiva is painted with symbols illustrating historical figures and ceremonial activities; original murals are on display in the visitor center museum, where another exhibit traces the cultural changes wrought by the arrival of the Spaniards. Daily 8:30-5; closed Jan. 1, Easter, Thanksgiving and Dec. 25. Admission $3, under 17 free. Phone (505) 867-5351.

ZIA PUEBLO AND MISSION, 16 mi. n.w. on SR 44, stands on a barren mesa. The mission was established in the early 17th century, but old traditions remain strong. An ancient Zía sun symbol can be seen on the New Mexico state flag. The pueblo's feast day, Aug. 15, features a corn dance. Visitors are not permitted to take still or motion pictures, to make video- or audiotapes, or to sketch or paint. Daily dawn-dusk. Museum open Mon.-Fri. 8-5. Closed during some religious and ceremonial events. Free. Museum by donation. Phone (505) 867-3304.

BLOOMFIELD (A-2)
pop. 5,200, elev. 5,400'

Bloomfield was settled about 1876 and quickly became a classic Wild West town, complete with a gang of rustlers headed by its own ex-sheriff. The gang operated openly, marketing stolen beef through its own butcher shop. After the gang's decline, outlawry found haven at Blancett's Saloon, which attracted gunmen from throughout the San Juan Basin.

That violent era passed unmourned. By the early 20th century residents were more interested in stimulating agriculture through irrigation, an endeavor that persists. Navajo Reservoir, 25 miles northeast via US 64 and SR 511, is the source of much of the area's irrigation water. Navajo Lake State Park, surrounding the reservoir in Navajo Dam, offers recreational opportunities. *See Recreation Chart and the AAA Southwestern CampBook.*

Bloomfield Chamber of Commerce: 224 W. Broadway St., Bloomfield, NM 87413; phone (505) 632-0880.

SALMON RUIN, covering 2 acres 2.5 mi. w. on US 64, was built in the late 11th century by people from the Chaco culture *(see Chaco Culture National Historical Park p. 142).* The C-shaped masonry complex measures 450 feet along the back wall and 150 feet along the arms. Some of the more than 1 million artifacts recovered are displayed in San Juan County Archaeological Research Center and Library, next to the ruin. A slide show is offered.

Mon.-Sat. 9-5, Sun. noon-5; closed Jan. 1, Thanksgiving and Dec. 25. Admission (includes Heritage Park) $3; over 65, $2; ages 6-16, $1. Phone (505) 632-2013.

Heritage Park offers a glimpse into the lifestyles and cultures of San Juan Valley people. Visitors can enter a Basketmaker pithouse—a semi-underground house that conserved heat in winter and remained cool in summer; examine ancient figures pecked into stone; or view the unusual construction of the Salmon homestead, built about 1900. Picnicking is permitted.

CAPITAN (D-4) pop. 800, elev. 7,398'

Capitan began to flourish in 1897 when the El Paso and Northeastern Railway built a line to nearby coal reserves. After the mines were depleted and the railroad abandoned its branch, Capitan became a business center for farmers, ranchers and visitors to the recreation lands of Lincoln National Forest *(see place listing p. 153).*

Capitan Chamber of Commerce: Hwy. 380, P.O. Box 441, Capitan, NM 88316; phone (505) 354-2273.

SMOKEY BEAR HISTORICAL STATE PARK, on US 380, is dedicated to forest conservation. Visitor center exhibits trace the history of Smokey Bear and the government's efforts to combat forest fires; a 20-minute film is shown by request. Having survived a devastating fire in 1950, Smokey was found clinging to a burned tree on the outskirts of Lincoln National Forest and became the national symbol for wildfire prevention. He died in 1976.

A half-mile interpretive trail winds through gardens representing New Mexico vegetation zones. Picnicking is permitted. Daily 9-5; closed Jan. 1, Thanksgiving and Dec. 25. Admission $1; ages 7-12, 50c. Phone (505) 354-2748.

★CAPULIN VOLCANO NATIONAL MONUMENT (A-5)

Within Capulin Volcano National Monument, 3 miles north of US 64/87 and Capulin on SR 325, is one of the best examples of a volcanic cinder cone in the nation. About 60,000 years ago ash, cinders and lava erupted and formed a classic cinder cone that stands more than 1,000 feet above the surrounding prairie. Today, a 2-mile road winds up the volcano, and trails lead into the crater and around the rim. The view from the summit includes the Rocky Mountains, volcanic features of the Raton-Clayton Volcanic Field, and the distant horizons of Colorado, Oklahoma and Texas.

The visitor center offers information and an audiovisual program. Road to the crater rim, park and visitor center open daily 7:30-6:30, Memorial Day weekend-Labor Day; 8-4, rest of year. Closed Jan. 1, Thanksgiving and Dec. 25. Admission $4 per private vehicle; $2 per person arriving by bus or motorcycle. Phone (505) 278-2201.

CARLSBAD (E-5)
pop. 25,000, elev. 3,110′

The fields of cotton, alfalfa and vegetables that surround Carlsbad are made possible by the U.S. Bureau of Reclamation's system of dams and canals, which irrigates 25,000 acres. The city also benefits from the rich neighboring oil and gas fields and potash mines as well as its proximity to Carlsbad Caverns National Park *(see place listing)*. Lake Carlsbad *(see Recreation Chart)* offers fishing, boating and water sports.

Carlsbad Convention and Visitors Bureau: 302 S. Canal St., P.O. Box 910, Carlsbad, NM 88220; phone (505) 887-6516 or (800) 221-1224. *(See color ad)*

CARLSBAD MUSEUM AND ART CENTER, 1 blk. w. of Canal St. at 418 W. Fox St., exhibits minerals, archeological specimens, Southwestern art, American Indian pottery and pioneer ranching artifacts. McAdoo Room features paintings by the founders of the Taos Colony, a group of artists who arrived in town at the turn of the 20th century and were inspired by the area's light, scenery and American Indian culture. Allow 1 hour minimum. Mon.-Sat. 10-5; closed holidays. Free. Phone (505) 887-0276.

LIVING DESERT ZOO & GARDENS, atop the Ocotillo Hills off US 285, is a zoological and botanical state park exhibiting plants and animals of the Chihuahuan Desert in their native habitat. Species that can be viewed include the mountain lion, bobcat, golden eagle and roadrunner. A greenhouse displays succulents from around the world. The visitor center houses interactive exhibits and mineral displays. Daily 8-8, Memorial Day weekend-Labor Day; 9-5, rest of year. Closed Dec. 25. Last admission is 90 minutes before closing. Admission $4; ages 7-12, $2. Phone (505) 887-5516.

★CARLSBAD CAVERNS NATIONAL PARK (F-4)

Elevations in the park range from 3,596 ft. in the southeastern corner to 6,368 ft. in the southwestern region. Refer to AAA maps for additional elevation information.

Twenty miles southwest of Carlsbad on US 62/180, Carlsbad Caverns National Park lies in the rugged foothills of the Guadalupe Mountains. Within its 46,776 acres is Carlsbad Cavern, a series of enormous rooms that forms one of the world's largest caves. The cavern was created in a limestone fossil reef by percolating ground water, a process thought to have begun some 2 million to 4 million years ago.

Formations range from small, delicate growths resembling plants to massive stalagmites, stalactites and columns. Many are tinted by iron and other minerals present in the limestone.

Every evening from mid-May to mid-September, hundreds of thousands of bats emerge from the uppermost chamber of the cavern at dusk to feed on flying insects. The flight outward may last a half-hour or more; the bats return near dawn. During the day they hang head down from the walls and ceilings of a portion of the cavern not open to visitors.

General Information and Activities

The park is open all year, except Dec. 25. Near the entrance to the cave are the visitor center and observation tower. Exhibits depict the geology, biology, history and archeology of the cavern and surrounding area. Interpretive programs about bats are given at dusk at the cave entrance amphitheater from late May to mid-October. A half-mile self-guiding desert nature trail begins near the cave entrance. Guided tours are available by reservation; phone (800) 967-2283.

The 9.5-mile Walnut Canyon Desert Drive, a one-way loop drive over a graded gravel road, offers views of Rattlesnake Canyon and upper Walnut Canyon. A permit is required for overnight back-country trips; inquire at the visitor center for hiking information.

The visitor center is open daily 8-7, Memorial Day to mid-Aug.; 8-5:30, rest of year. Closed Dec. 25. Free. Phone (505) 785-2232 for recorded information. *See Recreation Chart.*

ADMISSION to the park area without a visit to the caves is free.

DID YOU KNOW

Carlsbad Caverns has a year-round temperature of 56 degrees.

PETS, except Seeing Eye dogs, are not permitted inside the cavern. The visitor center provides kennels for $3.75 per pet.

ADDRESS inquiries to the Superintendent, Carlsbad Caverns National Park, 3225 National Parks Hwy., Carlsbad, NM 88220; phone (505) 785-2232.

Points of Interest

★**CARLSBAD CAVERN** has more than 30 miles of surveyed subterranean corridors and great chambers. The natural entrance is 90 feet wide and 40 feet high. Leading into the cave is a paved but mostly steep trail, making flat-heeled shoes with rubber soles the safest and most comfortable footwear. Because the temperature underground is a constant 56 F, a sweater is recommended. Food is available.

Visitors can view the caverns at their own pace; return to the surface is by elevator. Flash and time-exposure photography is permitted, but all photographs must be taken from paved trails. Alternative activities—including ranger talks, self-guiding nature trails and a desert automobile drive—are available for early arrivals. A CD-ROM guide, triggered by electronic signals, provides descriptive commentary. Interpretive signs explain cavern features, history and geology. Visitors must attend a brief orientation before they begin the tour.

Admission, which is valid 3 days and includes self-guiding tours of Big Room and Natural Entrance, $6; ages 6-15, $3. CD-ROM guide rental $3.

Big Room, one of the most impressive chambers, is in the shape of a cross, 1,800 feet in one direction and 1,100 feet in the other. The ceiling arches 255 feet in one area. Among the most interesting features are clear pools lined with masses of limestone resembling lily pads and graceful stalagmites reminiscent of totem poles. Other formations evoke an atmosphere of snow-banked forests, adding to the tranquil beauty of the cavern.

Big Room is recommended for those short on time and for those who prefer a less strenuous walk; a portion of the tour is wheelchair accessible. Big Room may be toured daily 8:30-5, Memorial Day weekend-third Sun. in Aug.; 8:30-3:30, rest of year.

Natural Entrance descends 750 feet over a distance of 1 mile. Highlights include Bat Cave, Devil's Spring, Iceberg Rock, Green Lake Overlook and the Boneyard, a maze of limestone rock reminiscent of Swiss cheese. Natural Entrance may be toured daily 8:30-3:30, Memorial Day weekend-third Sun. in Aug.; 8:30-2, rest of year.

GUIDED CAVE TOURS, most of which depart from the visitor center, are led by park rangers and cover a broad range of difficulties. Reservations are required for all tours. Phone (800) 967-2283.

Hall of the White Giant, a strenuous tour, leads to a remote chamber. Participants must crawl long distances, squeeze through crevices such as the tight Matlock's Pinch and climb a slippery passage. Sturdy shoes and four AA batteries are required; knee pads, gloves and long pants are recommended. Tours depart Sat. at 1. Under 12 not permitted. Fee $20; ages 12-15, $10. The fee is in addition to cavern admission.

King's Palace is toured via an almost circular route. Cave decorations include helectites, draperies, columns and soda straws. Tours are given daily on the hour 9-3, Memorial Day weekend-third Sun. in Aug.; every two hours 9-3, rest of year. Fee $8; ages 6-15, $4. The fee is in addition to cavern admission. Under 4 are not permitted on the tour.

Left Hand Tunnel highlights cavern history and geology via a .5-mile lantern tour. Sights along the easy tour include cave pools and fossils. Lanterns are provided; walking shoes are required. Tours depart daily at 9. Under 6 not permitted. Fee $7; ages 6-15, $3.50. The fee is in addition to cavern admission.

Lower Cave offers cave pools, beautiful formations and evidence of early exploration. The Rookery is a showcase for cave pearls. The moderately strenuous tour includes ladders. Sturdy shoes and four AA batteries are required. Tours depart Mon.-Fri. at 1. Under 12 not permitted. Fee $20; ages 12-15, $10. The fee is in addition to cavern admission.

Slaughter Canyon Cave is 25 mi. s.w. on US 62/180, then 11 mi. w. on CRs 418, 422 and 423. The last mile is unpaved. A 1-mile trail leads from the parking area to the cave and climbs 500 feet. This undeveloped cave contains dramatic formations. Sturdy shoes, a flashlight and water are required. Admission is only by a 2-hour guided lantern/flashlight tour, which is given daily at 10 and 1, Memorial Day weekend-third Sun. in Aug.; Sat.-Sun. at 10 and 1, rest of year. Reservations are required. Under 6 not permitted. Tour $15; ages 6-15, $7.50.

Spider Cave, the most strenuous tour, is a three-dimensional maze that includes tight crawlways, canyonlike passages and bizarre formations. Highlights include the Mace and Medusa rooms and Cactus Spring. Sturdy shoes and four AA batteries are required; knee pads, gloves, long pants and water are recommended. Tours depart Sun. at 1. Under 12 not permitted. Fee $20; ages 12-15, $10.

CARRIZOZO (D-3)
pop. 1,100, elev. 5,426'

Once a shipping and commercial center for area ranches, Carrizozo is now a busy county seat and tourist center. In addition to its own parks and recreational facilities, it offers easy access to the northern portion of Lincoln National Forest *(see place listing p. 153)*. Established in 1899 as a division point on the El Paso & Northeastern Railroad, the community takes its name from *carrizo,* a regional grass.

Nine miles northeast via US 54 and SR 349 is the ghost town of White Oaks. For 20 years after the original gold strike on nearby Baxter Mountain in 1880 White Oaks was a substantial community with stone buildings, two banks and two newspapers. Although White Oaks faded with the gold market in the 20th century, one of the first strikes—the Old Abe Mine—produced $3 million in gold until it closed around 1960.

Carrizozo Chamber of Commerce: P.O. Box 567, Carrizozo, NM 88301; phone (505) 648-2732.

VALLEY OF FIRES RECREATION AREA, 4 mi. w. on US 380, covers 463 acres of *mal país*—bad country—and was named for a Mescalero account of ancient volcanic eruptions creating a valley of fires. The magma flowed from Little Black Peak 1,500 to 2,000 years ago and covered about 44 miles. A nature trail winds through the park; trail guides are available at the trailhead. Camping is available. Pets on leashes are permitted.

Daily 24 hours. Admission $3-$5 per private vehicle; $3 per person arriving by bicycle, motorcycle or on foot. Admission is half-price for Golden Access and Golden Eagle pass holders. Further information is available from Carrizozo Travel Information Center; phone (505) 648-2241. *See the AAA Southwestern CampBook.*

CARSON NATIONAL FOREST

Elevations in the park range from 6,000 ft. in the Pinon Juniper Tree region to 13,161 ft. at Wheeler Peak. Refer to AAA maps for additional elevation information.

Carson National Forest encompasses 1,500,000 acres. Its scenic and recreational focus is in the districts that encompass the Sangre de Cristo and the San Juan mountains flanking the upper Rio Grande Valley.

Five wilderness areas—Wheeler Peak, Latir Peak, Cruces Basin, the northern portion of the Pecos and Chama wildernesses and an 8-mile-long section of the Rio Grande Wild River—preserve the region's pristine beauty. Wildlife abounds in the 100,000-acre Valle Vidal Unit.

Enchanted Circle Scenic Byway is an 84-mile driving loop offering a panorama of the southern Rocky Mountains from Taos east to Eagle Nest, then north to Questa via SR 38, and south on SR 522 back to Taos.

The curved cliff side of Echo Amphitheater, 3 miles north of the museum off US 84, is a prime spot for photography. Summer and winter recreation is available. Trails for cycling, hiking, horseback riding, snowmobiling and cross-country skiing traverse the forest.

For further information contact Carson National Forest, 208 Cruz Alta Rd., Taos, NM 87571; phone (505) 758-6200. *See Recreation Chart.*

CHACO CULTURE NATIONAL HISTORICAL PARK (B-2)

Chaco Culture National Historical Park preserves the ruins of 13 major great houses, called pueblos, and several thousand smaller sites that exemplify the development of the ancestral Pueblo people A.D. 850-1150. Located in northwestern New Mexico, the park can be reached via Hwy. 44 (550), exit at CR 7900—entry is about 3 miles southeast of Nageezi and approximately 50 miles west of Cuba. Follow signs to the park for 21 miles. (This route has 5 miles of paved road and 16 miles of dirt road.)

Because the park is accessible only over dirt roads that are rough, towing trailers more than 30 feet long is not advised. Some sections of road may become impassable during inclement weather; phone (505) 786-7014 for current weather conditions. There are no services, food, gas or lodging available in the park. Campers must bring their own wood or charcoal. Drinking water and dump station facilities are available.

By about A.D. 500 the ancestral Pueblo people gradually exchanged their nomadic ways for agriculture and permanent settlements. They began to build Pueblo Bonito at the base of the northern canyon wall, 4 miles west of the headquarters area, during the mid-9th century. By the late 12th century Pueblo Bonito had attained a height of at least 4 stories and contained more than 600 rooms and kivas (ceremonial rooms).

In addition to the large public buildings, numerous smaller village sites in the canyon attest to the settlement's sizable and diverse populations, which were greater than those found in the area today. It is one of the most imposing ruins in the Southwest.

Not content with building great public buildings and an elaborate irrigation system of gates and canals that diverted runoff from summer storms into their cornfields, the Chacoans also constructed a vast road network. These straight, 20- to 30-foot-wide corridors linked the canyon settlements with the more than 150 outliers (satellite communities), some as distant as Arizona, Colorado and Utah.

One route, the Great North Road, runs from Pueblo Alto near Pueblo Bonito to a point near Salmon Ruin *(see Bloomfield p. 138)* and may continue to Aztec Ruins National Monument *(see place listing p. 137).*

Another major achievement of the Chaco is a highly sophisticated solstice marker. High on the isolated Fajada Butte a sliver of noontime sunlight slashes between stone slabs onto two spiral petroglyphs, precisely timing the equinoxes and solstices by which the Chacoans planted their crops and scheduled their ceremonies. The Butte is closed to the public due to its fragile condition.

Eventually Chaco's influence waned and new centers emerged at Aztec and Mesa Verde—by 1200 only the wind whispered among the colossal masonry walls of Pueblo Bonito and its sister cities. The people were assimilated into the existing populations in the Zuni, Hopi, Acoma, Rio Grande and Mesa Verde regions. Descendents continue to return to honor these sacred places.

Self-guiding trails explore seven major sites, including Pueblo Bonito, Chetro Ketl, Pueblo del Arroyo, Casa Rinconada and three village sites. Allow 1 hour minimum per trail. Four other trails for day hiking lead into the back country; free permits, available at the visitor center, are required.

Camping and picnicking are permitted only in designated areas. Rangers conduct tours of the major Chacoan sites. An observatory provides a view of the evening sky.

VISITOR CENTER is 1.5 mi. from the s. entrance. A museum traces the history of the canyon and the cultures that developed it. Displays include artifacts of the Pueblo and Navajo tribes as well as various forms of pottery. Short films about the area are shown. Daily 8-6, Memorial Day-Labor Day; 8-5, rest of year. Admission $8 per private vehicle; $4 per person arriving by bicycle, motorcycle or on foot; under 16 free. Phone (505) 786-7014.

CHAMA (A-3) pop. 1,000, elev. 7,900'

Like the railroad that is its most popular attraction, Chama grew during the silver mining boom of the 1880s. The old railroad yards, shops, a roundhouse and one of the last coal tipples in the nation are relics of that era. In addition to tourism, lumber and outdoor recreation contribute to the town economy.

Chama Valley Chamber of Commerce: P.O. Box 306, Chama, NM 87520; phone (505) 756-2306 or (800) 477-0149.

★**CUMBRES AND TOLTEC SCENIC RAILROAD,** on SR 17, operates the New Mexico Express from Chama to Osier, Colo., where it connects with the Colorado Limited, which continues to Antonito, Colo. All-day trips on the old, narrow-gauge coal-burning trains afford spectacular views of the rugged San Juan and Sangre de Cristo mountain ranges.

Osier, inaccessible by automobile, is the transfer point for those making the complete trip and returning by van as well as the turnaround point for passengers making the round trip to their point of origin. Food is available. An overnight trip can be arranged. For information and reservations contact Cumbres and Toltec Scenic Railroad, P.O. Box 789, Chama, NM 87520, or P.O. Box 668, Antonito, CO 81120. AAA offices in New Mexico and Colorado can make reservations.

The train departs daily at 10:30 from Chama and at 10 from Antonito, mid-May to mid-Oct. Excursions return to Chama about 4:30 and to Antonito about 5. Round trip between either terminal and Osier $34; under 11, $17. Through fare with van return $52; under 12, $27. Reservations are suggested. DI, MC, VI. Phone (505) 756-2151 in N.M. or (719) 376-5483 in Colo. *See color ad.*

CHIMAY (B-4) pop. 1,400

The Spanish village of Chimayó is the home of the softly colored Chimayó blankets and rugs woven by Ortega family members, who have pursued the craft for eight generations. Throughout the village winding dirt roads lead past adobe homes. A vibrant mix of colors decorates the village each autumn as the golden foliage of cottonwood trees provides a backdrop for garlands of red chili peppers that drape houses while the popular spice dries in the air.

Chimayó was settled in 1598 and for the next 100 years was the easternmost outpost of the Province of New Mexico, the frontier place of banishment. The reconquest of the rebellious Pueblo and Apache in 1692 initiated a new settlement in the western foothills of the Sangre de Cristo Mountains, and Spaniards were granted permission to settle along the Santa Cruz River.

In 1696 San Buenaventura de Chimayó—Chimayó of the Good Venture—was built. The plaza is one of the oldest of Spanish colonial origin surviving in the Southwest; many surrounding structures are homes of the settlers' descendants.

East of Chimayó on SR 76—a route known as the High Road to Taos—are two other well-known craft villages. Cordova maintains a tradition of excellence in woodcarving, in which the Lopez family is most prominent. Beyond Cordova, Truchas is the home of the Cordova family of master weavers. Visitors are welcome to browse during daylight hours in the workshops scattered throughout the villages.

Shopping areas: Galleria Plaza del Cerro, in the town center, offers crafts and other goods.

EL SANTUARIO DE NUESTRO SEÑOR DE ESQUIPULAS is at the s.e. end of town. In 1810 Bernardo Abeyta, a farmer, was praying and claimed to see a light emanating from the soil. Upon investigation he found a cross, which is know kept inside the chapel. Legend maintains that the earth surrounding this cross has healing power. Many pilgrims come to touch the supposedly curative earth found in a pit inside the

chapel, which is lined with castoff crutches and braces. Daily 9-5. Free. Phone (505) 351-4889.

CIBOLA NATIONAL FOREST

Elevations in the park range from 6,500 ft. in the Magdalena district to 11,301 ft. at Mt. Taylor. Refer to AAA maps for additional elevation information.

The forest comprises scattered mountain ranges rising from the desert east and south of Albuquerque and stretching west to Arizona. The forest's 1,630,221 acres encompass four wilderness areas: Sandia, Manzano, Apache Kid and The Withington. Recreational opportunities include camping, fishing and hiking.

The rugged Canadian River Canyon west of Roy provides another type of beauty within Kiowa National Grassland. The forest also administers Black Kettle National Grassland, in neighboring western Oklahoma and the Texas panhandle. Camping and fishing center on the grassland's five lakes. Hunting is available in season, and there is skiing at Sandia Peak Ski Area. *See Recreation Chart.*

SANDIA CREST, which rises 10,678 feet, is 16 mi. e. of Albuquerque on I-40, 6 mi. n. on SR 14, then 13 mi. n.w. on SR 536. Paved and all-weather roads lead to the observation deck, where a panorama encompasses 15,000 square miles. Hiking trails cover 80 miles. Sandia Crest Road Scenic Byway, an 11-mile stretch of SR 536, is on the Turquoise Trail, the 61-mile scenic stretch of SRs 14 and 536 that links Albuquerque and Santa Fe. Volcanic rock formations, ghost towns and old turquoise and gold mines are found along the way.

A self-guiding nature trail begins at the crest and loops for .2 mile. Cross-country skiing is offered during winter. Food is available. Phone (505) 281-3304.

★SANDIA PEAK AERIAL TRAMWAY is off I-25 exit 234, then 4.5 mi. e. on Tramway Rd. The 2.7-mile tramway, one of the world's longest, transports visitors above the deep canyons and spectacular terrain of the Sandia Mountains. A Forest Service visitor center is in the upper tram terminal. Restaurants operate at the launch site and at the summit; special tram rates accompany dinner reservations. The tram is closed for 2 weeks each April for maintenance.

Sandia Peak is a popular recreation spot. Skiers frequent the 10,378-foot peak from mid-December to mid-March. Mountain bicycle rentals are available Memorial Day weekend to mid-October; helmets are required. Hang gliders launch from Sandia Peak. A chairlift to the northeast face of the peak leaves from a terminal on SR 536 Thursday through Sunday 10-4 in summer; rides are $6. Phone (505) 242-9052.

Trams make the 18-minute ascent up the west side of Sandia Peak daily 9 a.m.-10 p.m., Memorial Day-Labor Day; Thurs.-Tues. and holidays 9-8, Wed. 5-8, mid-Mar. to day before Memorial Day and day after Labor Day to mid-Dec.; Mon.-Tues. and Thurs.-Fri. 9-8, Wed. 5-8, Fri.-Sat. and holidays 9-9, rest of year.

Round trip $14; over 62 and ages 5-12, $10. Combination tram and chairlift ticket (available Thurs.-Sun., Memorial Day weekend to mid-Oct.) $18; over 62 and ages 5-12, $14. Parking $1. AE, DS, MC, VI. Phone (505) 856-6419 or 856-7325.

CIMARRON (B-4)
pop. 800, elev. 6,430'

Meaning "wild" or "untamed," Cimarron was fitting for both the brawling stream and the settlement that developed on its banks. Although Eagle Nest Lake ultimately tamed the river, nothing could contain the activities in town from the late 1860s to about 1880. The Las Vegas *Gazette* once reported, "Things are quiet in Cimarron; nobody has been killed in three days."

Billy the Kid, Bob Ford, Clay Allison and Black Jack Ketchum were among notorious part-time residents. Gunfights killed 16 men, and New Mexico's first printing press was dumped into the Cimarron River before the range wars ended and the town ceased to be a magnet for every outlaw in the Southwest.

Cimarron languished after losing the county seat to Springer in 1880 but revived in the early 1900s with the arrival of two railroads and the lumber industry. A quiet community, it serves nearby ranches, some logging operations and a lively tourist trade. St. James Hotel, where Annie Oakley joined Buffalo Bill Cody's Wild West Show, and the old jail are among the buildings that stand as reminders of a boisterous past.

The 3,600-acre Maxwell National Wildlife Refuge, 30 miles east off I-25, supports sizable populations of eagles, hawks and falcons around its grasslands, lakes and farmland. Valle Vidal Park *(see Recreation Chart)*, 100,000 acres of rugged back country used for backpacking, hunting and fishing, is 4 miles north on scenic US 64, then 21 miles northwest on Valle Vidal Road, following signs.

Cimarron Chamber of Commerce: P.O. Box 604, Cimarron, NM 87714; phone (505) 376-2417.

OLD AZTEC MILL MUSEUM, s. of US 64 in Old Town on SR 21, is in an 1864 building housing four floors of artifacts relating to county history. Included are American Indian arts and crafts, furnishings, historic items, vintage clothing and books. Placards explain the mill's original workings, which are partially intact. Allow 1 hour minimum. Mon.-Wed. and Fri.-Sat. 9-5, Sun. 1-5, June-Aug.; Sat. 9-5, Sun. 1-5 in May and Sept.

Admission $2; over 62 and under 12, $1. Phone (505) 376-2913.

PHILMONT SCOUT RANCH, 5 mi. s. off SR 21, is a 137,493-acre national camping center operated by the National Council of the Boy Scouts of America. More than 18,000 teenagers from nearly every state as well as from other countries visit Philmont each summer. A museum at headquarters exhibits items relevant to the history and art of the Southwest. Seton Memorial Library in the museum houses the art of Ernest T. Seton, the first chief scout of the Boy Scouts of America. Museum and library open daily 8-5, June-Aug. Donations. Phone (505) 376-2281.

CLAYTON (B-6)
pop. 2,500, elev. 5,054'

So numerous were the herds of cattle driven through this small farming community in the mid-1880s that the Denver & Fort Worth Railroad established the settlement as a division point. As a railhead and trading center, Clayton underwent a Wild West phase. Celebrated train robber Black Jack Ketchum was hanged from a gallows enclosed in a stockade to foil yet another rescue by his gang.

Clayton, at the foot of the Rabbit Ear Mountains, is still a cattle town; some of the largest feedlots in the region are just to the north. It also is one of the world's largest producers of carbon dioxide, which is used for recovering oil in the Permian Basin in New Mexico and Texas.

Livestock studies are conducted at Clayton Livestock Research Center, 5 miles east in Kiowa Rita Blanca National Grasslands. The University of New Mexico and the U.S. Forest Service investigate problems related to the health, nutrition and management of cattle. Tours of the facility are available by appointment; phone (505) 374-2566.

Recreational opportunities abound at Clayton Lake State Park *(see Recreation Chart and the AAA Southwestern CampBook)*, known for its excellent trout, walleye and bass fishing. Dinosaur tracks were discovered on the spillway of the dam in 1982; more than 500 such tracks have been plotted.

Clayton-Union County Chamber of Commerce: 1103 S. First St., P.O. Box 476, Clayton, NM 88415; phone (505) 374-9253.

CLOUDCROFT (E-4)
pop. 600, elev. 8,650'

A flourishing resort and recreation center at the summit of the Sacramento Mountains, Cloudcroft offers skiing in winter and varied summer activities, especially in Lincoln National Forest *(see place listing p. 153).*

This high, wide country was settled when the Southern Pacific Railroad ran a spur from Alam-

ogordo to tap the timber reserves in the Sacramento Mountains. The railroad built an elaborate lodge and resort for its excursion customers; the lodge still serves its original purpose. Lumber remains an important factor in Cloudcroft's economy.

Sacramento Mountains Historical Museum on US 82 recalls the town's settlement days. In the museum complex Cloudcroft Pioneer Village features historic buildings furnished in period, a granary, a barn and antique farm equipment.

Cloudcroft Chamber of Commerce: P.O. Box 1290, Cloudcroft, NM 88317; phone (505) 682-2733.

CLOVIS (C-6)
pop. 31,000, elev. 4,270'

Clovis, begun in 1906 as a sidetrack, grew rapidly after the Atchison, Topeka & Santa Fe Railway transferred its shops to the area. Clovis continues to thrive on an economy based on the railroad, stock raising and bountiful crops of wheat, sugar beets and alfalfa as well as related light industry. Cannon Air Force Base is 6 miles west.

Hillcrest Park, at 10th and Sycamore streets, encompasses a sunken garden, picnic areas and Hillcrest Park Zoo.

Clovis/Curry County Chamber of Commerce: 215 N. Main St., Clovis, NM 88101; phone (505) 763-3435.

COLUMBUS (F-2)
pop. 600, elev. 4,001'

Just before dawn on March 9, 1916, the revolutionary activities of Pancho Villa and his 1,000 guerrillas spilled over the international border into drowsy Columbus and its military outpost. Though quickly repulsed, the attackers took 18 American lives and elicited immediate retaliation.

Within a week Gen. John "Black Jack" Pershing marched his 6,000 troops, accompanied by motorized vehicles and airplanes, into Mexico to mark the first mechanized U.S. military action. Artifacts from the raid are on display at Columbus Historical Society's museum, on SR 11 in the restored Southern Pacific Depot.

PANCHO VILLA STATE PARK, 32 mi. s. at jct. SRs 9 and 11, was the site of Pancho Villa's raid into American territory. A visitor center and restored relics from the attack, along with a few remaining buildings from Camp Furlong, where Pershing began his retaliatory campaign, recount the conflict. This 58-acre park also highlights nature trails, a playground and a botanical garden with some 500 varieties of cactuses. Daily 8-5. Admission $4 per private vehicle. Phone (505) 531-2711. *See the AAA Southwestern CampBook.*

CORONADO NATIONAL FOREST—*see Arizona p. 46.*

DEMING (F-2)
pop. 11,000, elev. 4,335'

Fields of cotton and grain flourish in the seemingly riverless valley around Deming. The water that sustains them is the subsurface flow of the Mimbres River, which vanishes into the earth north of the city and reappears in a lake in the Mexican state of Chihuahua. Stock raising and some manufacturing augment the economy of this busy county seat, which also is a growing retirement center. Southeast the Little Florida (flo-REE-da) Mountains yield an abundance of agate, fire opal, jasper and semiprecious stones.

Deming-Luna County Chamber of Commerce: 800 E. Pine, P.O. Box 8, Deming, NM 88031; phone (505) 546-2674.

CITY OF ROCKS STATE PARK covers 680 acres 30 mi. n.w. via US 180, then 3 mi. n.e. on SR 61. Wind and water have carved welded tuff—compressed layers of volcanic ash—into rows of massive monoliths. A small desert botanical garden contains cactuses and other native plants. Camping and picnicking are permitted. Daily 7 a.m.-9 p.m. Admission $4 per private vehicle. Phone (505) 536-2800. *See the AAA Southwestern CampBook.*

DEMING LUNA MIMBRES MUSEUM, 301 S. Silver St., exhibits items pertaining to Southwest history. Included are pioneer artifacts, military items, early railroad and photographic equipment, gems and minerals, a cowboy display and a Mimbres Indian exhibit with pottery and baskets. In the transportation annex, 10 street scenes with antique automobiles depict historic Deming. A 53-foot mural illustrates county history. Mon.-Sat. 9-4, Sun. 1:30-4; closed Jan. 1, Easter, Thanksgiving and Dec. 25. Donations. Phone (505) 546-2382.

ROCKHOUND STATE PARK covers 250 acres 14 mi. s.e. off SR 11. Rock and mineral hunters can find agate, jasper, opal, chalcedony, quartz crystals and carnelian- and amethyst-filled geodes in the rhyolitic matrix that is Rockhound State Park. Camping and picnicking are permitted. Daily 7:30-5. Admission $4 per private vehicle. Camping fee $10-$14. Phone (505) 546-6182. *See the AAA Southwestern CampBook.*

DOMINGO (B-3) pop. 2,100

Once known as La Bajada, Domingo was a stopover on the way to Peña Blanca during Spanish colonial times. It later served as a stage stop on the road between Albuquerque and Santa Fe. The 1883 Santo Domingo Trading Post is one of the largest in the area.

About 9 miles north near Peña Blanca is Cochiti Lake *(see Recreation Chart),* where a recreation area offers fishing, nature trails, a visitor center, a swimming pool and water sports. Co-

chiti Pueblo lies west of the Rio Grande River, a few miles southwest of Cochiti Dam. Visitors are welcome dawn to dusk; no drawing, painting, photography or tape recording of any kind is permitted.

Tent Rocks, 20 miles northwest via SR 22 and BIA 92, are tepeelike formations created by the effects of erosion on lava.

SANTO DOMINGO PUEBLO is several miles w. on I-25 exit 259. Artisans are noted for their fine heishe beads of turquoise and other stones. Daily 8-5. Free. Phone (505) 465-2214.

Church of the Pueblo of Santo Domingo dates from 1886 and replaced a mission that had been carried away by Rio Grande floodwaters. Records as well as paintings by American Indian artists can be seen. No photography of any kind, sketching, painting or recording is permitted. Phone (505) 465-2214.

DULCE (A-3) elev. 6,767'

Dulce is the capital and principal town of Jicarilla Apache Indian Reservation. The Jicarillas, whose name means "little baskets," are renowned for woven baskets and other ornate craftwork. Visitors can watch artisans at work at Arts and Craft Museum on the reservation.

The town, at the northeastern corner of the reservation, is a popular provision point with hunters and anglers.

Jicarilla Apache Tribe, Public Relations Department: P.O. Box 507, Dulce, NM 87528; or phone Travel Headquarters of Dulce at (505) 759-3242.

★VIETNAM VETERANS NATIONAL MEMO-RIAL—*see Angel Fire p. 136.*

EDGEWOOD (C-3)
pop. 3,300, elev. 6,774'

WILD WEST NATURE PARK, I-40 exit 187 to 87 W. Frontage Rd., is a 122-acre habitat park containing animals and plants native to New Mexico. Trails allow visitors to see elk, whitetail deer, pronghorn antelope, ducks and birds. Allow 1 hour, 30 minutes minimum. Daily 10-6, Apr.-Oct.; noon-4, rest of year. Closed Dec. 25-Jan. 1. Admission $3; over 59 and ages 6-16, $2. Phone (505) 281-7655.

EL MALPAIS NATIONAL MONUMENT AND NATIONAL CONSERVATION AREA—
see Grants p. 150.

EL MORRO NATIONAL MONUMENT (C-1)

El Morro National Monument is 43 miles southwest of Grants via SR 53. The central features of the 1,278-acre monument are 200-foot-high Inscription Rock and the water hole fed by rainfall pouring off the rock. The Spanish called the sandstone mesa *El Morro,* meaning "the bluff" or "the headland."

Carved into the soft rock are centuries-old petroglyphs. The first known European inscription was left in 1605 by Juan de Oñate, governor and colonizer of New Mexico. Others include those of Gov. Manuel de Silva Nieto in 1629, a soldier in 1632, and Don Diego de Vargas, leader of the reconquest, in 1692. Later settlers making their way west added their names and dates.

Two Anasazi villages once thrived atop this mesa. Remains of what may have been a 300- to 500-room dwelling from about the 13th century have been excavated.

Self-guiding tours are available. A .5-mile trail and a 2-mile trail take about 45 minutes and 1.5 hours, respectively. A campground is available on a first-come-first-served basis. For further information contact the Superintendent, El Morro National Monument, Rt. 2, P.O. Box 43, Ramah, NM 87321.

Daily 9-7 (trails close at 6), Memorial Day-Labor Day; 9-5 (trails close at 4), rest of year. Closed Jan. 1 and Dec. 25. Admission $4 per private vehicle; $2 per person arriving by bicycle, bus, motorcycle or on foot; under 17 free. Phone (505) 783-4226.

ESPAÑOLA (B-3)
pop. 8,400, elev. 5,590′

In the northern Rio Grande Valley between the Jemez Mountains and the Truchas Peaks, Española was founded in 1598 by the Spaniards as the first capital of New Mexico.

The town assumed its present role as a trading and distribution center when the Denver and Rio Grande Western Railroad built its Chili Line between Española and Antonito, Colo., in the late 1870s. Part of the old narrow-gauge railway still functions. In late summer garlands of *ristras*—strings of scarlet chilies drying in the sun—decorate houses and fences.

Santa Cruz Lake *(see Recreation Chart and the AAA Southwestern CampBook)* is 14 miles east via SRs 76 and 4.

Española Valley Chamber of Commerce: 1 Calle de las Españolas, Española, NM 87532; phone (505) 753-2831.

POJOAQUE AND NAMBÉ PUEBLOS are 8 mi. s.w. on US 84; Nambé is 8 mi. e. of Pojoaque on SR 4. Pojoaque was abandoned during a small-pox epidemic in 1890, and today is inhabited by fewer than 40 descendants of the original tribe. Visitors may tour the museum, cultural center and tourist information center daily; permission is required to tour the rest of the pueblo. Dances are held some Saturdays.

Nambé is known for pottery made from micaceous clay and also for Nambé Falls, east of the pueblo. Nambe Falls Recreation Area is popular for fishing, hiking, picnicking and boating. Pueblo open Mon.-Fri. 8-5. Recreation area open daily 6 a.m.-8 p.m. Phone (505) 455-2278 for Pojoaque, or for Nambe (505) 455-2036 or 455-2304.

PUYE CLIFF DWELLINGS AND COMMUNAL HOUSE RUINS, 11 mi. w. via SRs 30 and 5, are remnants of the Anasazi culture that settled the Puye (Poo-YAY) Cliffs late in the 12th century. A drought prompted the abandonment of the Puye area around the late 1500s. Ruins extend more than a mile along the south mesa wall; caves hollowed from the soft stone rise one to three stories. The mesa top is reached by driving on a gravel road or climbing a strenuous path. Guided tours are available by reservation. Mon.-Fri. 9-6, Sat.-Sun. 8-8. Admission $5; over 64 and ages 7-14, $4. Phone (505) 753-7326.

SAN ILDEFONSO PUEBLO, 13 mi. s. at San Ildefonso and reached via SR 30/4, is best known as the home of Maria Martinez, celebrated potter and creator of the black-on-black pottery so highly acclaimed by artists. Family members and other potters continue her tradition. Several regionally known painters also are residents. Daily 8-5; closed holidays. Admission $3 per private vehicle. Fees for still-camera photography $10; painting or drawing $25; videotaping $20. Phone (505) 455-3549.

SAN JUAN PUEBLO is 4 mi. n.e. off SR 68. In 1598 Juan de Oñate named this pueblo San Juan de los Caballeros for the friendly Tewa Indians. Some 700 inhabitants of San Juan Pueblo—headquarters for the Eight Northern Indian Pueblos Council—maintain farms and produce red pottery, beadwork and embroidery. The remains of its sister pueblo, San Gabriel de los Españoles, comprise mounds, and a cross and a stone marker on SR 74. Dance of the Matachines is performed Dec. 25. Daily dawn-dusk. Fee for photography $5. Phone (505) 852-4400.

SANTA CLARA INDIAN PUEBLO, 2 mi. s. on SR 30, is inhabited by people believed to be descendants of the Pajarito Plateau Indians. Artists are noted for glossy black and red pottery with meticulously incised designs as well as for paintings and sculpture. The pueblo operates Santa Clara Canyon Recreation Area *(see Recreation Chart).* Daily dawn-dusk. Fees for still-camera photography $5. Phone (505) 753-7326.

FARMINGTON (A-2) pop. 34,000

Orchards have replaced outlaws, and coal mines have ousted card sharks from dominance over Farmington, the major industrial and retail center of the Four Corners region in northwestern New Mexico.

Navajo Mine, west of town, is one of the largest coal mining operations in the world; its output fuels the adjacent Four Corners Power Plant.

The power plant borders Morgan Lake and heats the lake waters used by windsurfers. Anglers favor the San Juan River and nearby Farmington and Jackson lakes.

West of town the vast Navajo Indian Reservation extends into Arizona. The convention and visitors bureau distributes a list of trading posts.

Forty miles south via SR 371 is the Bisti/De-Na-Zin Wilderness, a barren of weirdly eroded hoodoos and slate-topped *mesitas*—geological formations made up of sandstone and shale that have become eroded by wind and rain. Angel Peak Recreation Area *(see the AAA Southwestern CampBook)* lies 35 miles southeast via SR 44. Once considered by the Navajos as the dwelling place of sacred ones, the colorful sandstone formations crowning the peak were shaped over millions of years.

Gateway Museum and Visitors Center, 3041 E. Main St., offers exhibits, lectures and demonstrations by local artists. Changing exhibits by area artists are displayed at Farmington Civic Center and at San Juan College Fine Arts Center.

The drama "Black River Traders," is performed mid-June to mid-August in The Lion's Wilderness Park, a natural sandstone amphitheater.

Farmington Convention and Visitors Bureau: 3041 E. Main St., Farmington, NM 87402; phone (505) 326-7602 or (800) 448-1240. *See color ad.*

FORT SUMNER (C-5)
pop. 1,300, elev. 4,060'

The agricultural potential of the Pecos River bottomlands surrounding this quiet farming and ranching center so impressed Maj. James Carleton that in 1852 he recommended the site for an Army post. A decade later, as brigadier general, he realized his dream. He established Fort Sumner and made it the core of a permanent reservation for the Navajos and Apaches, whose resettlement was being supervised by Col. Kit Carson.

In 1864 Carson forced more than 8,600 Navajos to make the 400-mile Long Walk from Fort Defiance, Ariz., to the 1,024,000-acre reservation at Fort Sumner. The fort was abandoned in 1869, and the Navajos returned to their tribal lands.

De Baca/Ft. Sumner County Chamber of Commerce: 707 N. 4th St., P.O. Box 28, Fort Sumner, NM 88119; phone (505) 355-7705.

FORT SUMNER STATE MONUMENT is about 3 mi. e. on US 60, then 3 mi. s. on Billy the Kid Rd. The complex of buildings that housed the infantry and cavalry troops who guarded the Navajos no longer exists. Fort history is recounted on a marker. A visitor center houses American Indian, military and archeological exhibits. Old Fort Sumner Museum, a quarter-mile east, displays photographs and memorabilia relating to fort history. The gravesite of Billy the Kid is behind the museum.

Daily 8:30-5, May 1-Sept. 15; 8:30-4:30, rest of year. Closed winter holidays. Monument $1, under 17 free. Museum $3; ages 8-14, $2. Phone (505) 355-2573, or (505) 355-2942 for museum.

FORT UNION NATIONAL MONUMENT (B-4)

Ranks of chimneys 8 miles northwest of Watrous on SR 161 are stark reminders of the days when Fort Union was the largest military post on the Southwestern frontier. Fort Union was the chief quartermaster depot 1851-1891 for all garrisons throughout the region as well as the primary station for troops assigned to protect settlers and Santa Fe Trail travelers.

The site was well chosen, for the two branches of the Santa Fe Trail—the Mountain Branch and the Cimarron Cutoff—converged about 6 miles south. In addition the remote location put the soldiers closer to the tribes and farther from Santa Fe, then considered a sink of vice and extravagance.

A group of log buildings west of Wolf Creek constituted the first Fort Union. For a decade it served as a way station on the Santa Fe Trail and as a headquarters for battling the Utes, Jicarilla Apaches, Comanches and Kiowas.

The outbreak of the Civil War abruptly turned the Army's attention away from these conflicts. The second Fort Union, an earthwork defense bastion, was built east of the creek in late 1861. It was constructed by 1,660 New Mexican Army volunteers just before Confederate forces from Texas, eager to control Colorado's mineral resources and Fort Union's supplies, swept up the Rio Grande Valley. After their supply train was destroyed in the Battle of Glorieta, the Confederate troops withdrew.

The third fort and the large supply depot, the ruins of which stand today, date from the mid-1860s. For the next 15 years the Indian wars again occupied the military, while tons of goods flowed through the depot. Gradually local tribes were subdued, and when the Santa Fe Railway reached New Mexico it ended the post's usefulness. Fort Union was abandoned in 1891.

A self-guiding 1.2-mile tour trail explores 100 acres of adobe ruins. A visitor center with a museum relates fort history. People in period clothing demonstrate aspects of fort life during summer. Daily 8-6, Memorial Day-Labor Day; 8-5, rest of year. Closed Jan. 1 and Dec. 25. Admission $2 per person; $4 per private vehicle. Phone (505) 425-8025.

FOUR CORNERS MONUMENT—

see Window Rock, Ariz., p. 115.

GALLUP (B-1)

pop. 19,200, elev. 6,510'

The Atchison, Topeka & Santa Fe Railway pushed into this red rock mesa region in 1881 to use area coal deposits for its engines. Until then mostly stockmen had lived in the area; Gallup was a stage stop consisting of a saloon/general store called the Blue Goose. Coal mining and the presence of the railroad attracted settlers from other nations, giving the city an especially cosmopolitan heritage.

The city is best known as the main trading center for most Navajos, whose vast reservation extends north and west into Arizona, as well as for the residents of the nearby Zuni Pueblo (see Zuni p. 169). At many trading posts handmade articles ranging from rugs and baskets to turquoise jewelry are sold.

Gallup Convention and Visitors Bureau: 701 Montoya Blvd., P.O. Box 600, Gallup, NM 87305; phone (505) 863-3841 or (800) 242-4282.

RED ROCK STATE PARK is 8 mi. e. on I-40. Its focal point is the 6,800-seat rodeo arena in a natural amphitheater at the base of red sandstone cliffs. Red Rock Museum traces Southwestern American Indian culture through displays of artwork and crafts. Two nature trails are available. Daily 8-6, Memorial Day-Labor Day; 8-4:30,

rest of year. Park free. Museum admission is by donation. Phone (505) 722-3839. See Recreation Chart and the AAA Southwestern CampBook.

GILA CLIFF DWELLINGS NATIONAL MONUMENT (E-2)

Gila (HEE-la) Cliff Dwellings National Monument is in rough and desolate country, a 2-hour drive 42 miles north of Silver City via SR 15. About 175 feet above the floor of the canyon, near the west fork of the Gila River, seven natural cavities indent the face of the cliff. Five of them contain rooms constructed during the late 13th century by people of the Mogollon culture—these remain the focus of the monument.

A 1-mile loop trail leads from the parking area to the dwellings. Gila Visitor Center (see Gila National Forest) is 1.5 miles from the entrance.

The dwellings tour is self-guiding. There are weekend activity programs in summer; a park ranger is on duty all year. Pets are not permitted on the monument trail; free kennels are available. Vehicles pulling trailers 20 feet or longer should use SR 35 north from San Lorenzo. Daily 8-6, Memorial Day-Labor Day; 9-4, rest of year. Closed Jan. 1 and Dec. 25. Admission $3, under 12 free. Trail guide brochures are available for 50c. Phone (505) 536-9461.

GILA NATIONAL FOREST

Elevations in the park range from 4,000 ft. in the desert to 11,000 ft. at Whitewater Baldy. Refer to AAA maps for additional elevation information.

Gila National Forest occupies 3,321,000 acres of forest and rangeland in southwestern New Mexico. The smaller of its two units extends north from Lordsburg along the Big Burro Mountains. The main unit, north of Silver City (see place listing p. 165), embraces the Black, Mogollon, Tularosa and Diablo mountains. These wild ranges and remote canyons were the stronghold of such Apache warriors as Geronimo and Mangas Coloradas.

Much of the Mogollon Mountains lies within the Gila Wilderness, the first area in the nation to be so designated. Instrumental in its 1924 establishment was Aldo Leopold, the forester and naturalist whose "Sand County Almanac" and other writings have become classics of environmental literature.

A plaque 8 miles south of Pleasanton on US 180 marks Leopold Vista Historical Monument. The Gila, Blue Range and Aldo Leopold wilderness areas as well as Gila Cliff Dwellings National Monument (see place listing), lie north of Silver City.

In the 1870s the region was the center of a mining boom, of which ghost towns and old mine structures are silent reminders. The Catwalk, a metal grillwork suspended between the walls of Whitewater Canyon, is about 20 feet above the creek that once provided water to a nearby mill. Now a popular Forest Service recreation site, it is reached via FR 95 from Glenwood on US 180.

The 110-mile Inner Loop/Gila Cliff Dwellings Scenic Byway travels from Silver City east to San Lorenzo, through the Mimbres Valley, down Sapillo Creek, past Clinton P. Anderson Vista to Gila Cliff Dwellings National Monument, and returns to Silver City over the Pinos Altos Range. Overlooks along the byway provide perspective on the magnitude of the cliffs and the surrounding countryside.

There are numerous developed recreation areas in the forest. Stream and lake fishing and big game hunting are available in season. *See Recreation Chart.*

GILA VISITOR CENTER, 44 mi. n. of Silver City via SR 15, has exhibits pertaining to Gila Cliff Dwellings. A natural history audiovisual program is offered. Daily 8-5, Memorial Day weekend-Labor Day; 8-4:30, rest of year. Closed Jan. 1 and Dec. 25. Free. Phone (505) 536-9461.

GRANTS (C-2)
pop. 8,600, elev. 6,460'

Navajo rancher Paddy Martinez's curiosity about the odd yellow rock he found on Haystack Mountain about 10 miles west had far-reaching effects. The rock was uranium, and within months of the day he happened upon it in 1950, Grants was transformed from a farming community to a mining town.

With huge contracts from the Atomic Energy Commission for all the uranium they could produce, mining companies rushed to the area, which soon proved to be one of the largest uranium reserves in the world. A 1982-83 recession forced the closure of mills and mines, bringing to an end a prosperous era.

Grants/Cibóla County Chamber of Commerce: 100 Iron Ave., P.O. Box 297, Grants, NM 87020; phone (505) 287-4802 or (800) 748-2142.

EL MALPAIS NATIONAL MONUMENT AND NATIONAL CONSERVATION AREA is 25 mi. s. of I-40 via SRs 53 and 117. The 114,000-acre monument is surrounded by a 376,000-acre conservation area, which preserves lava beds, sandstone cliffs, a large sandstone arch, lava tubes, two wilderness areas and ancient pueblo ruins. Recreational opportunities include camping, hiking, bicycling and horseback riding; free backcountry camping permits are available at the ranger station. Ranger stations are 9 mi. s. on SR 117 and 23 mi. s. on SR 53.

Daily 24 hours; closed Jan. 1, Thanksgiving and Dec. 25. Both ranger stations are open daily 8:30-4:30; closed Jan 1, Thanksgiving and Dec. 25. Free. Phone (505) 240-0300 or 783-4774. *See Recreation Chart.*

Note: Use heavy footgear and extreme care when walking on the sharp lava: The Spanish did not call the region *mal país*—bad country—unjustly.

Ice Cave and Bandera Volcano, at an elevation of 8,000 feet, are s.w. on SR 53, the park's Zuni-Cibola Trail. Some 5,000 years ago an erupting volcano created caverns that now contain perpetual formations of ice. Nearby, inactive Bandera Volcano rises 500 feet above the mountain valley. Self-guiding tours depart from the trading post south of SR 53; wear comfortable shoes. Picnicking is permitted. Allow 1 hour minimum. Daily 8-7, June-Sept.; 8-1 hour before dusk, rest of year. Admission $7; ages 5-11, $3.50. AE, DS, MC, VI. Phone (505) 783-4303.

NEW MEXICO MINING MUSEUM, 1 mi. w. off I-40 exit 85 at 100 N. Iron Ave., contains exhibits about the 1950 uranium discovery. Reached by elevator, beneath the museum is a replica of a mine—complete with equipment. One-hour guided tours are available by reservation. Allow 1 hour minimum. Mon.-Sat. 9-5, Sun. 9-4, May-Sept.; closed Jan. 1, Easter, Thanksgiving and Dec. 25. Admission $3; over 59 and ages 7-18, $2. Phone (505) 287-4802 or (800) 748-2142.

HOBBS (E-6) pop. 29,100, elev. 3,625'

Oil and water mix in the economy of Hobbs, a modern city on the western edge of the flat Llano Estacado. Grasslands first attracted farmers and cattlemen to this streamless region in the early 20th century; one of them, James Hobbs, gave his name to the community. A vast underground reserve of water brought bountiful crops of cotton, alfalfa, vegetables and grain as well as a thriving cattle industry.

In 1928, however, the discovery of another kind of well changed pastoral Hobbs into a boomtown. Within a decade the city was the home of some 10,000 citizens, most associated with tapping the oilfield that still produces 90 percent of the state's petroleum supply. Many oil companies operating in the area have headquarters in Hobbs.

World War II aircraft from the New Mexico Wing of the Confederate Air Force are displayed in the Flying Museum at Lea County and Hobbs Airport. For history buffs, the Thelma Webber Southwest Heritage Room in Scarborough Memorial Library at the College of the Southwest on SR 18 contains prehistoric American Indian artifacts, art pieces and pioneer collectibles.

Hobbs Chamber of Commerce: 400 N. Marland Blvd., Hobbs, NM 88240; phone (505) 397-3202 or (800) 658-6291.

LEA COUNTY COWBOY HALL OF FAME AND WEST-ERN HERITAGE CENTER, about 4 mi. n. on Lovington Hwy. (SR 18) on the New Mexico Junior College campus, honors well-known ranchers and rodeo performers of Lea County. Exhibits depict the cultures—American Indian to pioneer—that shaped the area for 150 years. Allow 30 minutes minimum. Mon.-Fri. 10-5, Sat. 1-5; closed holidays. Free. Phone (505) 392-1275.

JEMEZ PUEBLO (B-3)
pop. 1,500, elev. 5,479′

Jemez Pueblo resulted from the Spaniards' efforts to convert and control the American Indians of Jemez (HAY-mehs) Canyon. Tribe members bitterly opposed this domination, and frequent rebellions resulted in onslaughts by the Spanish military. Some defenders escaped; the remainder gathered in what is now Jemez Pueblo. After holding off the Spaniards for 4 years, their defenses—but not their traditions—were broken by gunpowder.

The Jemez continue to farm, fashion pottery and observe ancient rituals. Tribal ceremonial dances are held in early August and mid-November. Admission is free; photography, tape recording, sketching or painting is not permitted. For further information contact the office of the Governor of the Pueblo, P.O. Box 100, Jemez Pueblo, NM 87024; phone (505) 834-7359.

About 5 miles north of Jemez Springs are the Soda Dam and Battleship Rock formations; there are picnic facilities at Battleship Rock, and trout fishing is available. SR 44 is a scenic highway that runs through the Jemez and Zía reserves between Cuba and San Ysidro.

JEMEZ STATE MONUMENT, 18 mi. n. on SR 4 near Jemez Springs, preserves the San Jose de los Jemez Mission and Guisewa Pueblo ruins. Franciscans, directing the converts, built the fortresslike mission about 1621. There is a visitor center and museum. Daily 8:30-5; closed Jan. 1, Easter, Thanksgiving and Dec. 25. Admission $3, under 16 free. Phone (505) 829-3530.

LAGUNA (C-3) elev. 5,794′

Rich in American Indian history, Laguna Pueblo is divided into six villages, with Old Laguna Village having served as the capital since the early 1300s. Agriculture, craftwork and some manufacturing form the pueblo's economic base.

The establishment of the pueblo in the late 1600s was followed, as was typical, by the construction of a mission. Built in 1699, the Mission of the Pueblo of Laguna is a long, narrow stone structure notable for its bright and unusual interior design.

The pueblo can be visited dawn-dusk on weekdays, although religious ceremonies are closed to the public during the summer. Photographing, sketching, painting or recording pueblo ceremonies is not permitted.

High-Altitude Health

Temples throbbing, gasping for breath and nauseated, you barely notice the scudding clouds or the spectacular view.

You might be suffering from Acute Mountain Sickness (AMS). Usually striking at around 8,000 feet (2,450 m) in altitude, AMS is your body's way of coping with the reduced oxygen and humidity of high altitudes. Among the symptoms are headaches, shortness of breath, loss of appetite, insomnia and lethargy. Some people complain of temporary weight gain

or swelling in the face, hands and feet.

If your AMS is severe, you should stop ascending; you will recover in a few days. If the AMS is mild, a quick descent will end the suffering immediately.

You can reduce the effect of high altitude by being in top condition. If you smoke or suffer from heart or lung ailments, consult your physician. Alcohol and certain drugs will intensify the symptoms.

A gradual ascent with a couple days of acclimatization is best if you have time. On the way up, eat light, nutritious meals and drink plenty of water. A spicy, high-carbohydrate diet may mitigate the effects of low oxygen and encourage you to drink more.

Other high-altitude health problems include sunburn and hypothermia. Dress in layers to protect yourself from the intense sun and wide fluctuations in temperature.

Finally, after you lounge in the sauna or whirlpool bath at your lodgings, remember to stand up carefully, for the heat has relaxed your blood vessels and lowered your blood pressure.

Governor of the Pueblo: P.O. Box 194, Laguna, NM 87026; phone (505) 552-6654 or 552-6655.

LAS CRUCES (E-3)
pop. 62,100, elev. 3,896'

A little forest of crosses marking the graves of members of a caravan ambushed by Mescalero Apaches soon came to identify this spot on the Camino Real at the foot of the Organ Mountains. By the mid-19th century Las Cruces—the crosses—was a major supply point for mining operations and Fort Selden and other posts that protected the trade routes to Santa Fe and points west.

The town's real foundation, however, is agriculture. Irrigated by the Rio Grande River, the surrounding Mesilla Valley is a leading producer of alfalfa, chilies, cotton and pecans. With a growing roster of manufacturers broadening the economic picture, the city is now the largest business center in southern New Mexico.

Las Cruces, home of New Mexico State University, balances agriculture and industry with education and the Space Age. About 24 miles northeast on US 70/82, then 4 miles south, is White Sands Missile Range, where experimental rockets are tested. The facility is open Monday through Friday 8-4:30; phone (505) 678-2250.

Las Cruces Convention and Visitors Bureau: 211 N. Water St., Las Cruces, NM 88001; phone (505) 541-2444 or (800) 343-7827.

BRANIGAN CULTURAL CENTER, at the north end of Downtown Mall at 500 N. Water St., features the works of area artists. A small permanent collection of Victorian furniture and clothing is displayed. Allow 30 minutes minimum. Mon.-Fri. 8-5, Sat. 9-3; closed holidays. Free. Phone (505) 541-2155.

FORT SELDEN STATE MONUMENT is 15 mi. n. to I-25 exit 19, then .2 mi. w. The fort was established in 1865 to protect travelers and residents in the Mesilla Valley from raids by local tribes. As a child Gen. Douglas MacArthur lived at the fort. A museum displays military uniforms, photographs and hardware. Daily 8:30-5. Living-history demonstrations are given Sat.-Sun. 1-4, May 1-Sept. 15. Closed holidays. Admission $2, under 17 free. Phone (505) 526-8911.

LAS CRUCES MUSEUM OF NATURAL HISTORY, in Mesilla Valley Mall at 700 S. Telshor Blvd., has permanent and temporary exhibits relating to the area's natural history. Some live animals and hands-on displays are included. Allow 30 minutes minimum. Mon.-Thurs. noon-5, Fri. noon-9, Sat.-Sun. 10-6; closed holidays. Donations. Phone (505) 522-3120.

UNIVERSITY MUSEUM is on the New Mexico State University campus in Kent Hall at Solano Dr. and University Ave. The museum presents changing exhibits about the archeology, history and culture of southern New Mexico and northern Mexico. Lectures, workshops and guided tours are available. Allow 30 minutes minimum. Tues.-Sat. noon-4; closed holidays. Donations. Phone (505) 646-3739.

LAS VEGAS (C-4)
pop. 14,800, elev. 6,371'

The faint wagon wheel ruts still visible outside Las Vegas attest to the town's era as a mercantile center on the Santa Fe Trail. Las Vegas also was a military post until Fort Union (see Fort Union National Monument p. 148) was built. During the 1880s it was known as one of the roughest towns on the frontier, with such desperadoes as Billy the Kid and Doc Holliday frequenting the area.

The arrival of the Santa Fe Railroad in 1879 ushered in commercial activity and prosperity. Las Vegas soon became a major retail center. The townspeople embarked on a flurry of building and rebuilding, using previously unavailable materials in Eastern architectural styles.

Las Vegas has structures that represent nearly every popular style of the Victorian period. Old adobe buildings in the Old Town Plaza Park district, the core of the original settlement, remain intact.

Outdoor recreation is available at Storrie Lake and Mora's Morphy Lake state parks (see Recreation Chart and the AAA Southwestern CampBook), 5 and 25 miles north, respectively, off SR 518; and in the Sangre de Cristo Mountains, which rise to the west (see Santa Fe National Forest p. 163).

Las Vegas-San Miguel Chamber of Commerce: 727 Grand Ave., P.O. Box 128, Las Vegas, NM 87701; phone (505) 425-8631 or (800) 832-5947.

Self-guiding tours: Brochures of walking and driving tours are available from the chamber of commerce.

CITY OF LAS VEGAS MUSEUM AND ROUGH-RIDER MEMORIAL COLLECTION, just n. of I-25 exit 345 at 725 N. Grand Ave., commemorates the Rough Riders, a volunteer cavalry regiment organized by President Theodore Roosevelt for service in the Spanish-American War. Displayed are local historical items and mementos and relics belonging to regiment members. Allow 30 minutes minimum. Mon.-Fri. 8-5; closed holidays. Donations. Phone (505) 454-1401.

LAS VEGAS NATIONAL WILDLIFE REFUGE, 6 mi. s.e. via SRs 104 and 281, covers 8,672 acres of prairie land bordered by the timbered canyons of the Gallinas River and Vegosa Creek. The refuge has more than 300 species of wildlife—including 239 species of birds—and is noted for its diversity of birds of prey. In season golden and bald eagles, rough-legged and Swainson's hawks, burrowing owls and kestrels abound.

Area bird lists, interpretive leaflets outlining a 7-mile driving tour, and permits for walking on a self-guiding nature trail can be obtained at the refuge office until 2 p.m. (weather permitting). Allow 1 hour minimum for the driving tour, 2 hours minimum for the nature trail. Refuge office open Mon.-Fri. 8-4:30. Free. Phone (505) 425-3581.

LINCOLN (D-4) elev. 5,710′

Lincoln's main street is lined with adobe houses and commercial structures dating from the late 19th century, when stock raising, farming, mining and the status of a frontier county seat sustained the village. But Lincoln's notoriety as the fulcrum of Billy the Kid lore is by far the town's most well-known aspect.

Billy was tried, convicted and sentenced to hang as retribution for a life of rustling and murder, but instead he killed his guards and escaped from Lincoln County Courthouse. Sheriff Pat Garrett tracked him to Fort Sumner, where two shots from his pistol ended the outlaw's story July 14, 1881.

LINCOLN STATE MONUMENT, along the two-block stretch of town, immortalizes the memory of the 5-day gun battle that was fought in 1878 for control of the area's economy. The locale comprises Tunstall Museum, a general store furnished in period, the Montaño Store Museum, the 1887 Mission of San Juan and Lincoln County Courthouse. Allow 1 hour minimum. Daily 8:30-5; closed Jan. 1, Easter, Thanksgiving and Dec. 25. Admission $7 Mar.-Nov., $5 rest of year; under 17 free. Phone (505) 653-4372.

LINCOLN NATIONAL FOREST

Elevations in the park range from 4,440 ft. at Grapevine Canyon to 11,580 ft. at Lookout Mountain. Refer to AAA maps for additional elevation information.

Most of the Sacramento, Jicarilla, Guadalupe and Capitan mountains, with pine, juniper and fir timber, lie within the 3 units of Lincoln National Forest. Covering 1,103,466 acres, the forest ranges from desert to subalpine terrain. The northern units of the White and Capitan mountain wildernesses offer pristine back country for horseback riding or hiking trips, while Ruidoso (see place listing p. 157) is a popular recreation and resort center.

Cloudcroft (see place listing p. 145) is another recreation complex. The southern unit embraces the relatively little-traveled, semiarid Guadalupe Mountains. A waterfall, uncommon in this region, is the focus of Sitting Bull Falls Picnic Area, 49 miles southwest of Carlsbad via US

285, SR 130 and FR 236. There also are more than 100 area caves that can be entered with a free permit, available by mail.

Five Points Vista, 74 miles north of Carlsbad on FR 540, then about 11 miles south of its junction with SR 137, offers a panorama of Dog Canyon and the Brokeoff Mountains. Commonly called Sunspot Highway, SR 6563 offers spectacular views of the Tularosa Basin as well as of the dunes of White Sands National Monument (see place listing p. 169). Hunting is good throughout the forest.

For further information contact the Supervisor, Lincoln National Forest, Federal Bldg., 1101 New York Ave., Alamogordo, NM 88310; phone (505) 434-7200. See Recreation Chart.

LOS ALAMOS (B-3)
pop. 19,000, elev. 7,410′

In 1942 the federal government selected Los Alamos Ranch School for Boys as the top secret, maximum security site for the Manhattan Project, an atomic bomb research and testing program where Little Boy and Fat Man—the atomic bombs that ended World War II—were built. By 1945, when the first atomic device was detonated at Trinity Site (see Alamogordo p. 131), more than 3,000 civilian and military personnel were working at the laboratory.

Los Alamos National Laboratory continues to apply science to issues of national security, economic strength and energy security. Its staff of more than 7,000 conducts extensive research about technology associated with nuclear weapons, deterrence and other defense applications, energy production, health, safety and environmental concerns, astrophysics and life sciences.

Explosions of another sort helped to create the setting that was so necessary for the Manhattan Project. About a million years ago the volcanic vents that had built the Jemez Mountains issued 100 cubic miles of ash and pumice, then collapsed. The result is Valle Grande, one of the largest measured calderas on earth. Covering 175 square miles, with a rim averaging 500 feet above its floor, it scars privately owned ranchland.

SR 4, about 15 miles west of Los Alamos, outlines the crater's southern curve and permits views into its vast, grassy bowl. The erupted ash hardened into a layer of tuff, the Pajarito Plateau, characterized by a remoteness that is protected by the finger canyons that serrate its edges. Within the plateau Bandelier National Monument (see place listing p. 137) contains extensive Anasazi ruins.

Los Alamos County Chamber of Commerce: 109 Central Park Sq., P.O. Box 460, Los Alamos, NM 87544; phone (505) 662-8105.

Self-guiding tours: A guidebook available at Los Alamos County Historical Museum (see attraction listing) outlines a walking tour of sites related to stages in area history.

★ **BRADBURY SCIENCE MUSEUM** is at 15th St. and Central Ave. The museum features exhibits interpreting the Los Alamos National Laboratory's history as well as the depth of its science and engineering capabilities. The Manhattan Project history and the laboratory's defense, technology and basic research projects are detailed in 40 interactive exhibits. Science demonstrations and educational and community programs are presented. Tues.-Fri. 9-5, Sat.-Mon. 1-5; closed Jan. 1, Thanksgiving and Dec. 25. Free. Phone (505) 667-4444.

FULLER LODGE ART CENTER, 2132 Central Ave., occupies the west wing of the lodge that served first as a dining and recreation hall for Los Alamos Ranch School for Boys and then for wartime scientists. Featured are works by northern New Mexico artists; artist displays change every 5-6 weeks. The center occasionally shows exhibits from other parts of the United States, but its focus is on local talent. Allow 1 hour minimum. Mon.-Sat. 10-4; closed Jan. 1, Thanksgiving and Dec. 25. Donations. Phone (505) 662-9331.

LOS ALAMOS COUNTY HISTORICAL MUSEUM, next to Fuller Lodge on Central Ave., occupies a restored log and stone cottage that once served as the infirmary for Los Alamos Ranch School for Boys. The museum details area history. Newspaper articles, military uniforms, photographs recording bomb testing and changing exhibits are displayed. A Tiwa ruin dating from the 13th century and a relocated homesteader's cabin are other highlights. Pamphlets for self-guiding tours of the area are available.

Mon.-Sat. 9:30-4:30, Sun. 11-5, May-Sept.; Mon.-Sat. 10-4, Sun. 1-4, rest of year. Closed Jan. 1, Easter, Thanksgiving and Dec. 25. Donations. Phone (505) 662-6272 or 662-4493.

MADRID (C-4)

Once a ghost town, Madrid is coming back to life as artists and merchants transform abandoned buildings into studios, galleries and shops. For nearly a century Madrid prospered as a coal mining town, supplying the military in Santa Fe and Las Vegas during the Civil War and producing commercially after the Santa Fe Railway reached neighboring Cerillos in 1880.

Madrid continued as a coal center until the 1950s, when the development of cheaper and cleaner fuels marked the beginning of its decline. Many restored buildings are incorporated in Old Coal Mine Museum. Exhibits include the locomotive repair shop, now home to the Engine House Theatre Melodrama, the original town jail and displays of antique and modern mining equipment. During the summer Madrid is host to bluegrass and jazz concerts.

MESCALERO (E-4) pop. 1,300

Mescalero is the largest town on and headquarters of Mescalero Apache Reservation. The 463,000-acre tract embraces the Sierra Blanca Mountains and their wealth of timber, grazing lands and scenic beauty. Among the last American Indians to lay down arms against the U.S. government, the tribe now operates as a federally chartered corporation.

Capitalizing on their land's recreational potential, the Mescaleros have developed a ski area and a major resort near Ruidoso (see place listing p. 157). Information about ceremonials and recreational facilities is available from the community center; phone (505) 671-4494.

MESILLA (F-3)
pop. 2,000, elev. 3,865'

Mesilla had its official beginning in 1850, when some residents of a nearby community that had become part of the United States by the Treaty of Guadalupe Hidalgo elected to move to the town in order to retain Mexican citizenship. They received a Mexican land grant in 1853, but in 1854 the Gadsden Purchase transferred nearly 30,000 square miles west of the Rio Grande River to the United States.

The combination of excellent farmland and strategic location spurred Mesilla's growth. By the time the Butterfield Trail Overland mail route established a major stage stop in 1858, Mesilla was the largest town in the southern part of New Mexico Territory, which then included present-day Arizona. By contrast, El Paso, Texas, and neighboring Las Cruces (see place listing p. 152) were mere hamlets. Billy the Kid was tried and sentenced in Mesilla, a former territorial capital.

La Mesilla State Monument consists of the plaza and surrounding buildings, which have been restored to their 19th-century appearance and now house shops and businesses.

GADSDEN MUSEUM is just e. of SR 28 on Boutz/Barker Rd. Collections depict American Indian, Spanish and Anglo cultures in the Southwest through artifacts, paintings and carvings. Allow 1 hour minimum. Daily 9-11 and 1-5; closed holidays. Admission $2; ages 6-10, $1. Phone (505) 526-6293.

OJO CALIENTE (B-3) elev. 6,292'

First enjoyed by American Indians, then by Spaniards, the five mineral springs at Ojo Caliente are still the target of many who seek their purported therapeutic properties. The springs contain iron, sodium sulphate, lithia, soda and arsenic; the last is thought to be the only arsenic spring outside Baden-Baden, Germany. Numerous bath facilities and swimming pools harness the waters; phone (800) 222-9162.

Perhaps additional qualities are lent to the springs by virtue of their being, according to Tiwa tradition, the home of the grandmother of sacred spiritual figure Poseyemo, who returns each year to visit her. The springs themselves were considered to be the windows between the outer world and the below world, where the people originated.

PECOS NATIONAL HISTORICAL PARK (B-4)

Two miles south of Pecos on SR 63, Pecos National Historical Park preserves the ruins of one of the largest ancient pueblos as well as two mission churches built by Franciscans in the 17th and 18th centuries. The American Indian population dwindled over the years because of famine, diseases, emigration and the changing needs of the mission. In 1838 the remaining Pecos people moved to Jemez Pueblo (see place listing p. 151).

Visitors can walk through the ruins on a 1.2-mile self-guiding trail; guided tours are available on request. A visitor center offers a film depicting Pecos' history and displays hand-carved furniture, artifacts from excavations, tin chandeliers and original artwork. Picnic facilities are available.

Allow 1 hour, 30 minutes minimum. Daily 8-6, Memorial Day weekend-Labor Day; 8-5, rest of year. Closed Jan. 1, Dec. 25. Entry fee $4 per private vehicle; $2 per person arriving by bicycle, bus, motorcycle or on foot. Phone (505) 757-6414.

PEÑASCO (B-4) elev. 7,452'

PICURIS PUEBLO is about 7 mi. n.w. off SR 75. Believed to have been established 1250-1300, the pueblo was a site of unrest during the revolts of the late 17th century. Mission of San Lorenzo, erected after the 1692 reconquest, has been in use for more than 2 centuries. A free museum displays artifacts excavated from the pueblo. Food is available. Pueblo and museum open daily 9-6. Self-guiding tour $1.75. Fees for still-camera photography $5; sketching, painting or videotaping $10. Phone (505) 587-2519.

PILAR (B-4) pop. 100, elev. 6,082'

RECREATIONAL ACTIVITIES
White-water Rafting
• **Far Flung Adventures** departs from Pilar Cafe. Write P.O. Box 707, El Prado, NM 87529. Daily late Apr.-Sept. 30. Phone (505) 758-2628 or (800) 359-2627.
• **Rio Grande Rapid Transit** departs from the Rio Grande Gorge Visitors Center at jct. SRs 68 and 570. Write P.O. Box A, Pilar, NM 87531. Daily mid-May through Labor Day. Phone (505) 758-9700 or (800) 222-7238. See ad p. 160.

PINOS ALTOS (E-2) elev. 6,845'

When John Birch bent to drink from Bear Creek in 1860, he found that the stream would satisfy more than just thirst—the gold glimmering in the water would assuage a hunger for wealth. News of riches spread quickly, and within 3 months Birchville, renamed Pinos Altos in 1866, emerged as a camp of 700 miners. In 1868 it was designated the seat of newly formed Grant County.

Pinos Altos, with a small population descended from its founders, retains the atmosphere of a 19th-century frontier town. The dirt streets, saloon, opera house and store have been restored or remain essentially as they existed in the 1860s. Pinos Altos Historical Museum, housed in an 1866 log cabin, preserves many items from the town's mining era.

Silver City-Grant County Chamber of Commerce: 201 N. Hudson St., Silver City, NM 88061; phone (505) 538-3785 or (800) 548-9378.

PORTALES (D-6)
pop. 10,700, elev. 4,002'

The discovery of shallow ground water in 1890 ensured the prosperity of Portales. Wells irrigate the thousands of acres of peanuts, sorghum, cotton and other crops that surround this commercial center. Dairying, hog raising and petroleum production also are important.

Blackwater Draw Archaeological Site, 7 miles northeast via US 70 on SR 467, has yielded evidence of paleo-Indian habitation stretching back more than 11,000 years. Eastern New Mexico University, which occupies a 550-acre campus off US 70 at the south edge of town, maintains Blackwater Draw Museum on US 70. Roosevelt County Museum on campus traces more recent area history, focusing on the late 19th and early 20th centuries.

Various recreational pursuits are available at Oasis State Park (see Recreation Chart and the AAA Southwestern CampBook), 5.7 miles north on SR 467, then 2 miles west.

Roosevelt County Chamber of Commerce: 200 E. Seventh St., Portales, NM 88130; phone (505) 356-8541 or (800) 635-8036.

RATON (A-5) pop. 7,400, elev. 6,640'

In 1866 Uncle Dick Wootton, an enterprising man, completed 27 miles of road over Raton Pass, set up a tollgate at his ranch near the summit and charged $1.50 per wagon to use his improvement. As the Santa Fe Trail was the main route between the East and Southwest, he did well. It is said that his bank deposits consisted of whiskey kegs full of silver dollars.

By 1880 this pleasant watering hole 7 miles south of the summit of Raton Pass evolved into a thriving community. Named for the pass, Raton bases its economy on the railroad, commerce, cattle ranching and, later, the development of nearby coal reserves. These industries, along with outdoor recreation and the tourism generated by the ease of traveling I-25, continue to sustain Raton.

The Victorian architecture along First Street preserves the atmosphere of Raton's 19th-century mining and railroad heyday. The 1890s Palace Hotel is at First and Cook streets.

Sugarite Canyon State Park *(see Recreation Chart and the AAA Southwestern CampBook),* 10 miles northeast via SR 72, provides lakes and picnic sites. A winter sports area is 2 miles farther.

Raton Chamber of Commerce: 100 Clayton Rd., P.O. Box 1211, Raton, NM 87740; phone (505) 445-3689.

NRA WHITTINGTON CENTER, 4 mi. w. of I-25 exit 446 on US 64, is the National Rifle Association's 33,300-acre shooting facility. A 10-mile gravel road connects several shooting ranges, including black powder and police pistol combat areas. An unaltered section of the Santa Fe Trail cuts through the complex. Allow 1 hour minimum. Daily 8-5; closed Dec. 25. Free. Phone (505) 445-3615.

RATON MUSEUM, 216 S. First St., contains photographs, household articles, railroad memorabilia and other items that depict life in Raton during the 19th century. Tues.-Sat. 9-5, Memorial Day-Labor Day; Wed.-Sat. 10-4, rest of year. Closed holidays. Free. Phone (505) 445-8979.

RODEO (F-1) elev. 4,118′

CHIRICAHUA GALLERY, on SR 80, exhibits works by local artists and artisans. Works include paintings, photographs, ceramics, basketry, woodwork, quilted items, leather work, silver jewelry, pottery and regional foods. Allow 30 minutes minimum. Mon.-Sat. 10-4; closed Thanksgiving and Dec. 25. Free. Phone (505) 557-2225.

ROSWELL (D-5)
pop. 44,700, elev. 3,570′

Roswell, established as a crossroads in the 1870s, had several large springs within a few miles that sustained cattle herds and were exploited for irrigation. In 1891 residents realized that beneath the surface lay an artesian basin fed by precipitation in the mountains to the west. With this increased knowledge, agriculture—especially the raising of apples, alfalfa and cotton—supplanted livestock as the backbone of the economy.

Roswell kept pace; by 1910 it was one of the most prosperous, fastest growing towns in New Mexico. Dr. Robert Goddard conducted rocketry experiments on the nearby prairie 1930-1945; his work ultimately made possible man's venture into space.

Roswell's economy is based on agriculture, shipping, manufacturing and oil production. A branch of Eastern New Mexico University and New Mexico Military Institute add to the cultural life; Roswell also has a symphony orchestra, theater, concert series and library programs.

Ten miles east on US 380, Bottomless Lakes State Park *(see Recreation Chart and the AAA Southwestern CampBook)* offers water recreation.

Roswell Chamber of Commerce: 131 W. Second St., P.O. Drawer 70, Roswell, NM 88202; phone (505) 623-5695.

BITTER LAKE NATIONAL WILDLIFE REFUGE, 8 mi. e. via US 380, occupies more than 24,000 acres of grassland, ponds and desert shrubs. Wintering waterfowls, sandhill cranes, roadrunners, quails and pheasants are among the 300 species of birds that use the area. Salt Creek Wilderness can be entered only on foot or horseback. An 8-mile self-guiding driving tour on the south unit allows for bird and wildlife observation. The best months to visit are October through February; hunting is available in season. Picnicking is permitted.

A tour leaflet and other information can be obtained at the refuge headquarters or by writing P.O. Box 7, Roswell, NM 88202. Refuge open daily 1 hour before dawn-1 hour after dusk, weather permitting. Free. Phone (505) 622-6755.

INTERNATIONAL UFO MUSEUM & RESEARCH CENTER, 114 N. Main St., is dedicated to the study of Unidentified Flying Objects (UFOs) thought to be from other planets. Exhibits include paintings, murals and dioramas depicting the purported 1947 crash of a UFO in Roswell along with other legendary sightings of alien beings and their spacecraft. Allow 1 hour, 30 minutes minimum. Daily 10-5. Free. Phone (505) 625-9495.

LT. GEN. DOUGLAS L. McBRIDE MUSEUM is at W. College Blvd. and N. Main St., on the campus of New Mexico Military Institute. Displays examine methods of waging war and preserving peace. Exhibits emphasize the services of New Mexicans and the Institute's graduates throughout American history. Tues.-Fri. 8:30-11:30 and 1-3; closed holidays. Admission $2; under 13, $1. Phone (505) 624-8220.

★ **ROSWELL MUSEUM AND ART CENTER,** 11th and Main sts., contains historical art and artifacts of Southwestern culture as well as works by Southwestern artists. Among the last are a painting by Georgia O'Keeffe and a major group of paintings by landscape artist Peter Hurd, who was born in Roswell.

The Goddard wing has a re-creation of Dr. Robert Goddard's early laboratory with displays about rocketry and space materials. Traveling exhibits are shown regularly. There also is a planetarium. Mon.-Sat. 9-5, Sun. and holidays 1-5; closed Thanksgiving and Dec. 25. Free. Phone (505) 624-6744.

SPRING RIVER PARK AND ZOO, 1 mi. e. on College Blvd. or n. on Atkinson Rd. off US 70 and US 285, exhibits more than 100 animals and birds from 40 different species. Also occupying the 36-acre zoo are a wintering Canada goose flock, wooden-horse carousel, miniature train ride, children's fishing lake and picnic facilities. Allow 1 hour minimum. Daily 10-dusk; closed Dec. 25. Free; rides 25c. Phone (505) 624-6760.

RUIDOSO (D-4) pop. 4,600

With skiing in winter, golfing, riding, hiking and fishing in spring and summer, and the gilded beauty of the aspen highlighting autumn, Ruidoso is among the state's premier year-round mountain playgrounds. So popular is it during the summer that prospective visitors are advised to make reservations several months in advance for holiday weekends.

The town's setting is the timbered Sacramento Mountains within Lincoln National Forest *(see place listing p. 153).* The community that now extends 10 miles along the Ruidoso River began in the 1890s as a tin-roofed trading post. The post's old water wheel still stands on the main street.

Ruidoso Valley Chamber of Commerce and Visitors Center: 720 Sudderth Dr., P.O. Box 698, Ruidoso, NM 88345; phone (505) 257-7395 or (800) 253-2255.

RECREATIONAL ACTIVITIES
Skiing

- **Ski Apache** is 18 mi. n.w. at the end of SR 532. Write P.O. Box 220, Ruidoso, NM 88355. Daily 8:45-4, late Nov.-early Apr. Phone (505) 336-4356 or 257-9001 for ski conditions.

RUIDOSO DOWNS (E-4) pop. 900

One of the Ruidoso area's major attractions, and the one that led to its development as a resort, is the quarter horse and Thoroughbred racing at Ruidoso Downs.

One of the sport's biggest events, the All-American Futurity, is held on Labor Day, the final day of the racing season. Tagged the world's richest quarter horse race—the purse exceeds $2 million—it is the final leg of quarter horse racing's Triple Crown. The first two, the Ruidoso Quarter Horse Futurity and the Rainbow Futurity, take place at Ruidoso Downs in May and July, respectively. Phone (505) 378-4431 or 378-4140.

Note: Policies concerning admittance of children to pari-mutuel betting facilities vary. Phone for information.

HUBBARD MUSEUM OF THE AMERICAN WEST, 1 mi. e. of the racetrack off US 70, displays horse-related items from the Anne C. Stra-

dling Collection. Included are life-size models, saddles, wagons and carriages, harnesses, crops and paintings. Guided tours are available. Allow 1 hour minimum. Daily 9-5:30, May 1-Labor Day; 10-5, rest of year. Closed Thanksgiving and Dec. 25. Admission $6; over 60 and active military $5; under 17 free with adult. AE, DS, MC, VI. Phone (505) 378-4142.

SALINAS PUEBLO MISSIONS NATIONAL MONUMENT (D-4)

Within Salinas Pueblo Missions National Monument, near Mountainair, are three geographically and historically related pueblos and 17th-century Spanish Franciscan missions. The 1,071-acre park includes the former Gran Quivira National Monument and two former state monuments, Abó and Quarai.

The abandonment of the Salinas Jurisdiction by both the Tompiro and Tiwa Indians and the Spaniards in the late 17th century, due to cultural and environmental pressures, and the lack of resettlement have left the masonry ruins remarkably intact. All three sites are open daily 9-6, Memorial Day weekend-Labor Day; 9-5, rest of year. Free.

A visitor center on US 60 a block west of SR 55 offers a 15-minute orientation film and an art exhibition depicting regional history. The center is open daily 8-5. Phone (505) 847-2585.

ABO, 9 mi. w. of Mountainair on US 60, then .7 mi. n. on SR 513, was a Tompiro Indian village. Once one of the largest pueblos in the Southwest, the village was abandoned in the 1670s. The 1620 church of San Gregorio de Abo was remodeled in the 1650s. It has a 40-foot buttressed curtain wall and is one of few surviving examples of medieval architecture in the United States. A self-guiding tour pamphlet, which includes the pueblo and mission ruins, can be obtained at the visitor center. Picnicking is permitted. Allow 1 hour minimum.

GRAN QUIVIRA, 26 mi. s. of Mountainair on SR 55, was one of the most populous pueblos of Salinas Province, with more than 1,500 inhabitants. The 21 limestone house mounds date 1300-1670; 300 rooms and six kivas can be viewed. Also preserved are the ruins of the churches and convents of San Isidro, begun in 1629, and San Buenaventura, begun in 1659. A visitor center displays artifacts and interpretive exhibits and shows 10- and 40-minute videotapes on request. A leaflet for a self-guiding trail is available. Picnicking is permitted. Allow 1 hour minimum.

QUARAI, 8 mi. n. of Mountainair on SR 55 and 1 mi. w. on a hard-surface road, preserves 10 large unexcavated pueblo house mounds and the remains of the 1630 church and convent of Nuestra Señora de La Purísima Concepción de

Cuarac. The sandstone church has walls about 40 feet high. Another small church may date from 1820 or earlier. A museum displays a scale model of the older church and a small collection of pottery and other artifacts. A leaflet outlines a short self-guiding trail. Picnicking is permitted.

SAN ANTONIO (D-3) elev. 4,500'

Founded in 1629 as a mission, San Antonio is a trading center for nearby farms and ranches. Corn and alfalfa thrive in the fields along the Rio Grande Valley. To the southeast, beyond the river valley, lies a 35-mile-wide, 90-mile-long stretch of merciless desert. In the days of the Camino Real the desert earned the name Jornada del Muerto—Journey of the Dead.

Some 21 miles south across the river from San Marcial is Valverde Battlefield, scene of the first Civil War engagement in New Mexico. Confederate forces led by Gen. H.H. Sibley beat back Union troops from nearby Fort Craig in a day-long battle in February, 1862, and went on to occupy Albuquerque. Remnants of the fort survive and are accessible to the public; however, the battlefield is not.

San Antonio is the birthplace of famed hotelier Conrad Hilton. The ruins of the Hilton family's mercantile boardinghouse and home is 1 mile south of US 380 west of SR 1.

BOSQUE DEL APACHE NATIONAL WILDLIFE REFUGE, 8 mi. s. of I-25 exit 139 at US 380 and SR 1, occupies marsh, grasslands and desert uplands that are a habitat for whooping and sandhill cranes, snow geese, ducks and more than 300 other bird species; mammals, reptiles and amphibians also are present. A 12-mile automobile route and several interpretive trails thread through the area. Wildlife viewing is best late November through early February. Fishing and hunting are permitted in designated areas; restrictions apply.

Allow 1 hour. 30 minutes minimum. Refuge open daily 1 hour before dawn-1 hour after dusk. A visitor center with exhibits is open Mon.-Fri. 7:30-4, Sat.-Sun. 8-4:30. Entrance fee for the automobile route $3 per private vehicle. DS, MC, VI. Phone (505) 835-1828.

SAN FELIPE PUEBLO (C-3)
pop. 1,600, elev. 5,007'

Founded in 1706, San Felipe Pueblo is the most conservative Keresan village. Services take place only during ceremonials; crafts booths bustle near San Felipe Church at these times.

CASINOS

- **San Felipe's Casino Hollywood,** 25 Hagan Rd. Mon.-Thurs. 8 a.m.-4 a.m., Fri.-Sun. 24 hours. Phone (505) 867-6700.

SANTA FE (B-4)
pop. 55,900, elev. 7,000'

Santa Fe is the city where opposing strands of the enduring weave of New Mexico converge. American Indian, Spanish and Anglo cultures; church and state; past and future remain unmerged but firmly linked in Santa Fe. As these differences are the essence of the state, they also are the soul and charm of its capital city.

The link with the past is particularly strong. Excavations regularly unearth relics of unknown age; modern technology is merely window dressing on the efficient architectural designs devised by the Pueblo Indians in the first millennium.

The past was evident at the site that newly appointed governor Don Pedro de Peralta chose for the provincial capital 1609-10. The Spanish penchant for long titles did not fail Peralta, who named his city La Villa Real de Santa Fé de San Francisco de Asis—the Royal City of the Holy Faith of St. Francis of Assisi. By late 1610 the Plaza, governor's palace and some city walls were tangible proof of the beginning of what would become the oldest continuous seat of government in the United States.

That same year the Mission of San Miguel of Santa Fe (see attraction listing p. 161) was established to serve as headquarters for a second power in the region: the church. Franciscan fathers quickly fanned out to usher the local tribe members into the Christian fold; a 1617 report stated that 14,000 souls had been converted. Santa Fe has been a major Catholic stronghold since.

Time mercifully has shortened the city's name to Santa Fe, but the core of the original settlement—the Plaza—remains essentially intact. At its north edge Peralta's palacio—a monument to continuity of rule, if not of rulers—still stands. Four flags have flown over the building as a governmental center under Spain, Mexico, the Confederate States of America and the United States.

As it has been for nearly 4 centuries, the Plaza, the square block bounded by Lincoln Avenue, E. Palace Avenue and San Francisco Street, is a vital center of commerce, festivals and history. Guided walking tours of the city regularly depart from the blue gate of the Palace of the Governors (see attraction listing p. 161) Monday through Saturday at 10:15. Museum of New Mexico offers walking tours of historic downtown; phone (505) 827-7941.

Santa Fe's cultural scene is as richly varied. In addition to dance and theater, the city features the Santa Fe Symphony, which performs at Sweeney Center, and the Santa Fe Opera (see attraction listing p. 162).

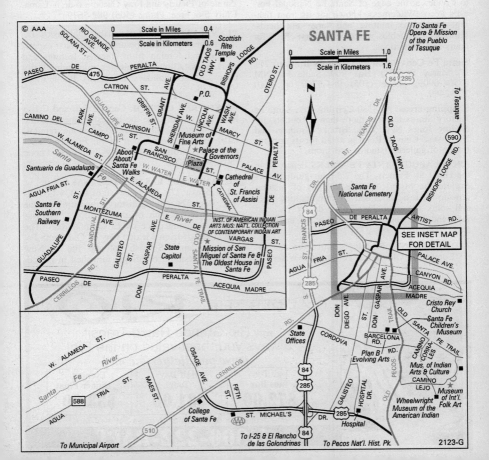

A re-enactment of the most important battle of the Civil War fought in the Southwest, the Battle of Glorieta Pass, is staged southeast of Santa Fe. The Union victory is depicted on Father's Day at Pigeon's Ranch.

The Santa Fe Scenic Byway follows SR 475 northeast through Little Tesuque Canyon to Hyde Memorial State Park *(see Recreation Chart and the AAA Southeastern CampBook)* and continues to the Santa Fe Ski Area winter sports area. The loop is completed via FR 102 through Pacheco Canyon and SR 22, which ends at Tesuque, about 6 miles north. Forest roads are not paved; check road conditions before starting.

Turquoise Trail, SRs 14 and 536, runs along the east side of the Sandias between Cedar Crest and La Cienega; highlights along this route include spectacular mountain scenery, a few ghost towns, thick pine and aspen forests and Sandia Crest *(see Cibola National Forest p. 144).*

Another interesting trip follows I-25 through Glorieta Pass to Pecos. There, SR 63 turns north to Cowles at the edge of Santa Fe National Forest's Pecos Wilderness, known for its trout fishing, big game hunting and large elk herds. Various area pueblos welcome visitors; check for hours and restrictions.

Santa Fe Convention and Visitors Bureau: 201 W. Marcy St., P.O. Box 909, Santa Fe, NM 87504-0909; phone (505) 984-6760 or (800) 777-2489.

Shopping areas: At 8380 Cerrillos Rd., Santa Fe Factory Stores features more than 40 outlets, including Jones New York, Brooks Brothers and Nine West. Canyon Road is noted for its concentration of galleries, studios and shops.

ABOOT ABOUT/SANTA FE WALKS depart from the Hotel St. Francis. The 2.5-hour guided tours explore the history, culture and art of historic downtown, residential and art communities. Special tours are available. Tours depart daily at 9:45 and 1:45. Fee $10; over 64, $9; under 16 free. Phone (505) 988-2774.

AFOOT IN SANTA FE tours depart from the Hotel Loretto at Old Santa Fe Tr. and Water St.

These guided walking tours include commentary about the city's history and architecture, Anasazi ruins, museums and art galleries. Allow 2 hours minimum. Tours depart daily at 9:30. Fee $10, under 16 free. Parking fee is $5 for all day. Phone (505) 983-3701.

Loretto Line, 2 blks. e. of the Plaza at jct. Old Santa Fe Tr. and E. Alameda St., offers guided tours on open-air trams. Allow 1 hour, 30 minutes minimum. Tours depart daily at 10, noon, 2 and 4, Apr.-Nov. Fare $9; under 12, $4. Parking fee is $5 for all day.

CATHEDRAL OF ST. FRANCIS OF ASSISI is 1 blk. e. of the Plaza on Cathedral Pl. Built to serve Santa Fe's Spanish community, it was the first church between Durango, Mexico, and St. Louis to attain the status of cathedral. Archbishop J.B. Lamy, the model for the main character of Willa Cather's novel "Death Comes for the Archbishop," is buried beneath the main altar. Others interred in the cathedral are Fray Zarate of Picuris and Fray Gerónimo de la Lama. Daily 6-6. Free. Phone (505) 982-5619.

PLAN B EVOLVING ARTS, 1050 Old Pecos Tr., is a forum for contemporary art exhibits, experimental and foreign films, theater, lectures and workshops. Allow 30 minutes minimum. Daily noon-7; closed holidays. Donations. Phone (505) 982-1338.

CRISTO REY CHURCH, Canyon Rd. and Cristo Rey St., is said to be the largest adobe structure in the country. Its hand-carved stone reredos, taken from the older part of St. Francis Cathedral, dates from 1761. Daily 7-7. Free. Phone (505) 983-8528.

EL RANCHO DE LAS GOLONDRINAS is 3 mi. w. off I-25 exit 276, following signs to 334 Los Pinos Rd. The living-history museum's name means "The Ranch of the Swallows." It was once a stopping place on El Camino Real (The Royal Road) from Mexico City to Old Santa Fe. Exhibits depict Spanish colonial life in New Mexico. Restored buildings, furnished in period,

include an 18th-century *placita* house with defensive tower as well as a mill, smithy, schoolhouse and church. A 1.5-mile path leads to the buildings.

Allow 1 hour, 30 minutes minimum. Wed.-Sun. 10-4, June-Sept.; by appointment, Apr.-May and in Oct. Admission $4; over 62 and ages 13-18, $3; ages 5-12, $1.50. Prices may increase during special events. AE, MC, VI. Phone (505) 471-2261.

INSTITUTE OF AMERICAN INDIAN ARTS MUSEUM: NATIONAL COLLECTION OF CONTEMPORARY INDIAN ART is at 108 Cathedral Pl. Displays contain paintings, sculpture, pottery, ceramics, beadwork and textiles of alumni, students and faculty of the Institute of American Indian Arts as well as new art forms created in Indian Country. Allow 1 hour minimum. Daily 9-5, June-Sept.; 10-5, rest of year. Closed Jan. 1, Easter, Thanksgiving and Dec. 25. Admission $4; over 62, $2; students with ID and under 16 free. Phone (505) 988-6281.

MISSION OF THE PUEBLO OF TESUQUE is 9 mi. n. on US 84/285. With the exception of the sacristy, which has been remodeled into a house of worship, little remains of the once beautiful mission. The Pueblos, who have retained the traditions of their ceremonials, hold a traditional Corn Dance and fiesta Nov. 12. Mon.-Fri. 8-noon and 1-5. Free. No photographs, video, sketches or recordings are permitted. Phone (505) 983-2667.

★**MISSION OF SAN MIGUEL OF SANTA FE** is 3 blks. s. of the Plaza at Old Santa Fe Tr. and E. De Vargas St. The mission is one of the country's oldest churches. It was begun in 1610, and although records of its early history were burned during the Rebellion of 1680, the thick, sturdy adobe walls remained unharmed. Stone buttresses later were added to strengthen the walls, remodeled tower and modern facade.

A bell cast in Spain in 1356 is displayed in an anteroom. It was used in churches in Spain and Mexico before being brought to Santa Fe by ox-cart in the early 19th century. Priceless ornaments and paintings adorn the interior of the mission.

A 6-minute audio presentation is given continuously. Recorded tours Mon.-Sat. 9-4:30, Sun. 2-4:30, May-Oct.; Mon.-Sat. 10-4, Sun. 2-4:30, rest of year. Closed Jan. 1, Good Friday, Easter, Thanksgiving and Dec. 25. Admission $1, under 7 free. Phone (505) 983-3974.

The Oldest House in Santa Fe, across from the church at 215 E. DeVargas St., is considered the earliest remaining house in Santa Fe. The house contains the remains of a Spanish warrior, who according to legend, was killed by two witches who lived in the house during the 1600s. There also is a small weaving display. Daily 11-3; closed Jan. 1 and Dec. 25. Donations.

MUSEUM OF NEW MEXICO, in five museums and five monuments at 113 Lincoln Ave., deals with various phases and periods of Southwestern and international culture. Tues.-Sun. 10-5; closed Jan. 1, Easter, Thanksgiving and Dec. 25. Admission $5, under 17 free. Four-day pass $10. Phone (505) 476-5060, or 827-6463 for recorded information.

Museum of Fine Arts is across from Palace of the Governors at 107 W. Palace Ave. The museum, completed in 1917, houses contemporary and traditional American art. Changing exhibitions focus on Southwestern artists from the 19th century to the present, including the Santa Fe and Taos masters. Allow 1 hour minimum. Phone (505) 476-5072.

Museum of Indian Arts and Culture, 710 Camino Lejo, interprets Southwest American Indian culture. Artifacts from the Laboratory of Anthropology Collection include pottery, basketry, woven fabrics, jewelry and contemporary crafts. An exhibit details the comprehensive story of the Southwest's Navajo, Apache and Pueblo peoples in their own words and voices. Allow 1 hour minimum. Phone (505) 827-6344.

★**Museum of International Folk Art** is at 706 Camino Lejo, off Old Santa Fe Tr. Of the museum's 120,000 objects, the Girard Foundation Collection contains more than 106,000, including miniature buildings, streets and marketplaces in village scenes from 100 countries. The Hispanic Heritage Wing features Spanish colonial art; the Neutrogena Wing contains 2,600 textiles and other art objects; and Lloyd's Treasure Chest contains interactive pieces. Allow 2 hours minimum. Phone (505) 827-6350.

★**Palace of the Governors,** on the n. side of the Plaza at 105 W. Palace Ave., is said to be one of the oldest public buildings in the United States. Built in 1610, the long, low adobe structure with massive walls was the seat of government under Spanish, American Indian, Mexican and U.S. territorial rule until 1909, when it became the state history museum. Exhibits reflect the history of New Mexico and its varied cultures. The Palace Print Shop and Bindery features 19th-century printing presses and other equipment, all of which still operate.

The *portal*—porch—is a gathering place for American Indian artisans. Guided tours of the museum are available. Allow 2 hours minimum. Phone (505) 827-6483.

SANTA FE CHILDREN'S MUSEUM, 1 mi. s. of the Plaza at 1050 Old Pecos Tr., is geared to children ages 2-12. Interactive exhibits focus on the arts, sciences and humanities. Among highlights are an outdoor garden learning environment, four bubble exhibits, a rock climbing wall and water works. Hands-on activities are conducted by artists on Saturdays and scientists on Sundays. Wed.-Sat. 10-5, Sun. noon-5, June 1-Labor Day; Thurs.-Sat. 10-5, Sun. noon-5, rest of year. Closed holidays. Admission $3; under 12, $2. MC, VI. Phone (505) 989-8359.

SANTA FE NATIONAL CEMETERY, 1.5 mi. n. of the Plaza on US 285, originally was the military post cemetery. It contains the graves of soldiers from the Indian wars as well as those killed in the battles of Pigeon's Ranch and Valverde during the Civil War. Daily 8-dusk. Free. Phone (505) 988-6400.

SANTA FE OPERA, 7 mi. n. on US 84/285, features well-known artists in an open-air theater. Inquire about weather policies. Write P.O. Box 2408, Santa Fe, NM 87504-2408. Operas are presented Mon.-Sat. evenings in Aug.; Wed., Fri. and Sat. evenings in July. Tickets $20-$114 on weekdays, $28-$122 on weekends. Prices are higher on opening nights. AE, DS, MC, VI. Phone (505) 986-5900 or (800) 280-4654.

SANTA FE SOUTHERN RAILWAY, which departs from Santa Fe Depot at 410 S. Guadalupe St., offers 4.5-hour train rides through the picturesque New Mexico landscape on a working freight train in vintage coaches. The train makes a 1.5-hour lunch layover in historic Lamy. High Desert Highball and Campfire Barbecue rides also are available. Food is available.

Scenic day trains depart Tues.,Thurs. and Sat.-Sun. at 10:30, Apr.-Oct.; Tues., Thurs. and Sat. at 10:30 in Mar.; Thurs. and Sat. at 10:30, rest of year. Day train $25-$45; over 59, $20-$30; ages 3-13, $13-$28. Reservations are recommended. MC, VI. Phone (505) 989-8600 or (888) 989-8600. *See color ad.*

SANTUARIO DE GUADALUPE, 4 blks. w. of the Plaza at Agua Fria and Guadalupe sts., is the nation's oldest shrine dedicated to Our Lady of Guadalupe. A 1783 oil-on-canvas reredo of Guadalupe by Mexican baroque artist José de Alzibar graces the altar. Also included are the meditation chapel with religious woodcarvings, a pictorial history room and the Plants of the Holy Land botanical garden. An 18th-century mission is at the end of El Camino Real. Guided tours are available Mon.-Sat. 9-4, May-Oct.; Mon.-Fri. 9-4, rest of year. Donations. Phone (505) 988-2027.

SCOTTISH RITE TEMPLE is on Washington Ave., 3 blks. n. of the Plaza. Part of the building was inspired by the Alhambra in Granada, Spain. Mon.-Fri. 9-noon and 1:30-4; closed holidays. Free. Phone (505) 982-4414.

SOUTHWEST SAFARIS, which departs from and returns to Santa Fe by airplane, offers air/land combination tours to the Grand Canyon, Monument Valley, Canyon de Chelly, Arches/Canyonlands and Mesa Verde. The expeditions include exploration of landmarks and ruins and on-site

explanations of the region's geology, archeology and history. Scenic flights also are available. Write P.O. Box 945, Santa Fe, NM 87504. Most tours last about 8 hours; some include lunch. Prices start at $199 per person. Reservations are required. AE, DS, MC, VI. Phone (505) 988-4246 or (800) 842-4246. *See ad p. 162.*

STATE CAPITOL, Old Santa Fe Tr. and Paseo de Peralta, 4 blks. s. of the Plaza, has a round kiva-like design that resembles the Zía sun symbol, the official emblem of New Mexico. Guided tours, which begin in the rotunda and end in the governor's office, feature a collection of artworks and furnishings handcrafted by New Mexico natives. The informational tours also present an overview of state government. Mon.-Sat. 8-5, Memorial Day-Labor Day; Mon.-Fri. 8-5, rest of year. Tours are given at 10 and 2. Free. Phone (505) 986-4589.

WHEELWRIGHT MUSEUM OF THE AMERICAN INDIAN, 2 mi. s.e. of the plaza on Camino Lejo, is reminiscent of a Navajo hogan. The museum offers exhibits of historic and contemporary American Indian art with emphasis on the Southwest. Mon.-Sat. 10-5, Sun. 1-5; closed Jan. 1, Thanksgiving and Dec. 25. Donations. Phone (505) 982-4636.

RECREATIONAL ACTIVITIES
White-water Rafting

- **New Wave Rafting Co.,** Route 5, Box 302A, Santa Fe, NM 87501. Daily May-Labor Day. Phone (505) 984-1444 or (800) 984-1444. *See ad p. 158.*

- **Santa Fe Rafting Co.,** 1.5 mi. s.w. of the Plaza on Cerrillos Rd. Write P.O. Box 23525, Santa Fe, NM 87502-3525. Daily Apr.-Oct. Phone (505) 988-4914 or (800) 467-7238. *See color ad.*

SANTA FE NATIONAL FOREST

Elevations in the park range from 7,300 ft. to 13,101 ft. at Truchas Peak. Refer to AAA maps for additional elevation information.

Some 1,568,820 acres of forest and rangeland lie within Santa Fe National Forest. The southern Sangre de Cristo Range, with several 12,000- to 13,000-foot peaks, dominates the eastern half. Within the forest are Pecos Wilderness, the headwaters of the Pecos River and the Santa Fe Basin winter sports area. The 18-mile trip along SR 63 between Cowles and Pecos provides outstanding views of the forest's eastern section.

In the portion west of the Rio Grande are the Jemez Mountains, San Pedro Parks Wilderness, Chama Wilderness and Dome Wilderness. Developed recreation sites and day-use picnic areas are near streams, trailheads and other scenic highlights. Recreational opportunities include hiking, fishing, horseback riding and such winter sports as cross-country skiing and snowshoeing. Fees are required for some developed areas.

For information and maps contact the Supervisor, Santa Fe National Forest, P.O. Box 1689, Santa Fe, NM 87504; phone the Public Information Officer at (505) 438-7840. *See Recreation Chart.*

SANTA ROSA (C-5)
pop. 2,300, elev. 4,615'

Santa Rosa is surrounded by parcels of land with property lines that were established by Spanish land grants. Many residents are descendents of the men who accompanied Francisco Vasquez de Coronado on his explorations of the area in 1540.

The town is in a semidesert area with artesian springs and lakes. Blue Hole, an artesian spring

87 feet deep and 60 feet in diameter, is a half-mile west of Park Lake on La Pradira Lane. Stocked with goldfish, its 65-degree waters attract scuba divers; a diving permit is required. A city park at Perch Lake also offers scuba diving. *See Recreation Chart.*

Other nearby lakes, such as Park Lake and the lake in Janes-Wallace Memorial Park, yield large catches of trout, crappie and walleye *(see Recreation Chart).* Channel cat are taken from the Pecos River. Rock Lake Trout Hatchery, 2 miles south of town on River Road, propagates rainbow trout and walleye.

Scenic SR 91 follows the Pecos River south for 10 miles to Puerto de Luna, one of several abandoned Spanish settlements in the area. A marker indicates where Coronado encamped to build a bridge across the river. Another pleasant drive leads to Santa Rosa Lake State Park *(see Recreation Chart and the AAA Southwestern CampBook),* 7 miles north off Eighth Street. A .7-mile nature trail and other recreational facilities border the dam and reservoir.

Santa Rosa Chamber of Commerce: 486 Parker Ave., Santa Rosa, NM 88435; phone (505) 472-3763.

SANTA TERESA (F-3)

Due to its southwestern location, Santa Teresa offers access to nearby Cuidad Juárez, Mex. Just west of El Paso, Tx., the town contains a border crossing station; this port of entry offers easy access to Mexico and also can process the paperwork necessary for travel into the interior.

Ciudad Juárez also can be reached by several bridges. The Zaragoza Bridge (toll) on Zaragoza Avenue enters Mexico east of Ciudad Juárez; the Cordoba Bridge (Bridge of the Americas or the "free bridge") enters the suburb of San Lorenzo just east of the city; the Stanton Street Bridge (toll) is one way into downtown Ciudad Juárez. Toll fees are $2 per vehicle; pedestrians 30c. **Note:** The Cordoba Bridge is the only city crossing that processes the paperwork necessary for vehicle travel beyond the border area.

Motorists returning to the United States from downtown Juárez must use the northbound-only Paseo del Norte Bridge (toll) via Avenida Juárez or the free Cordoba Bridge (Bridge of the Americas) via Avenida Lincoln. Toll fees are $2 per vehicle; pedestrians 70c. Dollars or pesos are accepted when entering or departing Mexico or the United States. Baggage must be inspected at the customs offices. Both Mexican and U.S. customs and immigration offices are open 24 hours daily.

U.S. and Canadian visitors must carry proof of citizenship. A valid U.S. or Canadian passport is the most convenient, since it serves as a photo ID and facilitates many transactions, such as cashing traveler's checks. The U.S., Canadian and Mexican governments also recognize a birth certificate, which must be a certified copy from the government agency that issued it. A driver's license or baptismal certificate is **not** proof of citizenship.

All who plan to visit the interior or stay in the border area more than 72 hours also must obtain a **tarjeta de turista** (Mexican government tourist card). Tourist cards normally can be obtained from any AAA Texas office. Before driving into Mexico, check with the El Paso AAA office for documentation and insurance requirements; phone (915) 778-9521. For a more detailed explanation of border crossing procedures and the requirements for temporary importation of vehicles, *see the Arriving in Mexico section in the AAA Mexico TravelBook.*

In July 1999 Mexico began collecting a visitor entry fee of 150 pesos (about $15) from each person entering the country. By land, the fee is collected at designated highway checkpoints or at branches of any bank operating in Mexico. Upon collection of the fee an official "Fee Paid" stamp is affixed to your tourist card. Since verification of payment may be required by Mexican officials, the tourist card should be carried with you at all times while in Mexico. Exemptions to the visitor entry include those staying in Mexico less than 72 hours and those traveling within the 16-mile (26-kilometer) border zone.

★ **WAR EAGLES AIR MUSEUM** is off I-10 exit 11, 3 mi. w. on Mesa Dr., 2 mi. n. on SR 273, then 4 mi. w. on Airport Rd. at Santa Teresa Airport. The 54,000-square-foot museum features restored aircraft from the World War II era and jet fighters used in the Korean Conflict. Fighters include the P-51 Mustang, the P-38 Lightning, the P-40 Warhawk, a twin-engine Invader bomber, a Fieseler Storch and a German observation aircraft.

Among the 1950s jets is a F-86 Sabre, a T-33 Silver star and MIG-15s. Additional exhibits include equipment used by pilots, a display about women in aviation and the role they played in World War II as well as a collection of 12 vintage automobiles. Allow 1 hour minimum. Tues.-Sun. 10-4; closed holidays. Admission $5; over 64, $4; under 12 free. Phone (505) 589-2000.

SHIPROCK (A-1)
pop. 7,200, elev. 7,192'

The geological formation Shiprock is 15 miles southwest via US 666 and Red Rock Road, from which it can be viewed. The basalt core of an old volcano, the rock rises more than 1,700 feet above the desert. At sunset it appears to shimmer and float.

Because the Navajo consider Shiprock to be a sacred place, the tribe does not permit climbers to scale it. Scenic Indian Route 33 runs between Shiprock and Red Rock on the Arizona border.

FOUR CORNERS MONUMENT—
see Window Rock, Ariz., p. 115.

SILVER CITY (E-1)
pop. 10,700, elev. 5,900'

Silver City burgeoned with the discovery of silver in the late 1860s. Growth was reinforced by additional discoveries in the area, and the city became the county seat in late 1871. A lumber mill was set up to take advantage of nearby timberland; the mill and other businesses based on supplying the proliferating mines ensured that Silver City's existence would not be the brief, single-minded one of the typical mining town.

Permanence was declared with the establishment of Western New Mexico University in 1893—the same year the bottom dropped out of the silver market. As the mines closed and mining towns faded into history throughout the region, Silver City's economy regrouped around shipping and cattle ranching. The city is remembered as the boyhood home of William Bonney, who later gained notoriety as outlaw Billy the Kid.

Mining processes can be viewed from an open pit copper mine 15 miles east on SR 152. The huge pit, 1.7 miles across and 1,000 feet deep, has produced mountains of ore since the discovery of the deposits in 1800. One of the largest operations of its type in the United States, Chino Mine shows evidence of Spanish and Mexican workings. Chino Mines Co. provides an observation point and a picnic area.

Twelve miles south on SR 90, another vast open-pit mine yields some 50,000 tons of copper ore a day from the original site of Tyrone. Built in 1915 by Phelps-Dodge Corp. to house miners and their families, it was a beautifully designed city until declining markets caused the closure of the mine in 1921. Reactivation in the mid-1960s resulted in a new Tyrone 4.5 miles south of Silver City. A viewpoint on SR 90 overlooks the mine pit.

Silver City provides access to the 110-mile Inner Loop/Gila Cliff Dwellings Scenic Byway, which leads to Gila Cliff Dwellings National Monument *(see place listing p. 149)* via US 180 and SRs 152, 35 and 15, then crosses the Piños Altos Range back to Silver City. Guided tours are available. Reservations are required; contact the visitor center at Gila National Forest *(see place listing p. 149)* at (505) 536-9344.

Grant County Silver City Chamber of Commerce: 1103 N. Hudson St., Silver City, NM 88061; phone (505) 538-3785 or (800) 548-9378.

SILVER CITY MUSEUM, 312 W. Broadway St., is in a mansard mansion built in 1881. Collections include 19th- and 20th-century local articles and photographs, Southwestern American Indian artifacts and items concerning the town of Tyrone. Allow 1 hour minimum. Tues.-Fri. 9-4:30, Sat.-Sun. 10-4; closed Jan. 1, Thanksgiving and Dec. 24-25. Free. Phone (505) 538-5921.

WESTERN NEW MEXICO UNIVERSITY MUSEUM, .5 mi. s.w. of US 180 at 10th and West sts. in Fleming Hall, displays an extensive permanent exhibit of prehistoric Mimbres pottery. Also displayed are Casa Grande prehistoric pottery, stone tools, ancient jewelry, photographs, Southwestern oral history recordings and military and mining artifacts. Mon.-Fri. 9-4:30, Sat.-Sun. 10-4; closed Labor Day weekend. Donations. Phone (505) 538-6386.

SOCORRO (D-3)
pop. 8,200, elev. 4,617'

Socorro was the biggest—and wildest—city in New Mexico during the 1880s. After the Panic of 1893 sent silver prices plunging, local mines produced zinc and other ores until these reserves became depleted. After most miners left, the remaining townspeople turned their energies to farming and stock raising.

A natural outgrowth of the mining era was the 1889 founding of the New Mexico School of Mines, later renamed New Mexico Institute of Mining and Technology.

Socorro County Chamber of Commerce: 103 Francisco de Avondo, P.O. Box 743, Socorro, NM 87801; phone (505) 835-0424.

Self-guiding tours: A brochure outlining a walking tour of historic buildings and places, most within walking distance of the central plaza, is available from the chamber.

MINERAL MUSEUM, at Bullock Ave. and Canyon Rd. at the Institute of Mining and Technology, contains an extensive mineral collection. Displayed are more than 12,000 specimens indigenous to the region and from around the world as well as artifacts and memorabilia related to mining and minerals. Exhibits change periodically. Mon.-Fri. 8-noon and 1-5, Sat.-Sun. 10-3; closed Thanksgiving and Dec. 25-Jan. 1. Free. Phone (505) 835-5420.

SAN MIGUEL MISSION is n. of the plaza at 403 Camino Real. The twin-steeple church, built 1819-21, is still in use. Its predecessor, constructed in the 1620s after an earlier mission was abandoned, was destroyed in the Pueblo Rebellion of 1680. A portion of one wall dates from the 1598 mission; hand-carved ceiling beams highlight the interior. Artifacts are displayed in the adjoining church office. Daily 7-6. Free. Phone (505) 835-1620.

VERY LARGE ARRAY (VLA)—RADIO TELESCOPE, 52 mi. w. on US 60, consists of 27 antennas, each weighing 230 tons and measuring 82 feet in diameter, distributed along railroad tracks arranged in a Y-shape. Two branches of the Y are about 13 miles long; the other is more than 11 miles long. Antennas aim at a celestial body and produce an image of it. A visitor center provides exhibits, a slide show and self-guiding tours. Allow 1 hour minimum. Daily 8:30-dusk. Free. Phone (505) 835-7000.

SPRINGER (B-5)
pop. 1,300, elev. 5,810′

Springer was named for Frank Springer, who came to New Mexico from Iowa in 1873. Having settled in Cimarron, Springer was a prominent lawyer and paleontologist. His most lasting legacy is the Museum of New Mexico's Museum of Fine Arts (see Santa Fe p. 161), of which he was a founder.

The Santa Fe Trail Museum, housed in the old county courthouse at US 56 and US 85, displays household items, clothing, period furniture and the only electric chair used in New Mexico.

Springer Chamber of Commerce and Visitor Center: 806 Maxwell St., P.O. Box 323, Springer, NM 87747; phone (505) 483-2998.

STEINS (F-1)

STEINS RAILROAD GHOST TOWN, off I-10 exit 3, comprises more than 15 pioneer buildings— including remnants of Hotel Steins, saloons, a bordello stand and several adobe and stone structures—restored to their original appearance. Many rooms, including the pioneer kitchen, are furnished in period. A bottle collection and pioneer artifacts dating to the 1800s are among the historic displays. Antique corrals hold farm animals. A 30-minute guided tour is offered. Picnicking is permitted.

Allow 30 minutes minimum. Daily 9-7, late May-late Oct.; 8-5, rest of year. Closed Thanksgiving and Dec. 25. Admission $2.50, under 12 free. Phone (505) 542-9791.

SUNSPOT (E-4) elev. 9,200′

NATIONAL SOLAR OBSERVATORY, on Sacramento Peak, is a facility for solar research. The observatory also offers a view of the Tularosa Basin. Self-guiding tours include the hilltop dome, vacuum tower and grain bin dome. Allow 1 hour minimum. Daily 10-6, May-Oct.; 10-4, rest of year. Admission $2; over 55, $1; under 6 free. Phone (505) 434-7000.

TAOS (B-4) pop. 4,100, elev. 6,965′

Spanish, American Indian and Anglo influences mingle yet remain distinct in Taos, which is actually three villages. Taos proper—legally Don Fernando de Taos—is the original Spanish town that is now a center of art and tourism. Pueblo de Taos (San Gerónimo de Taos), home of the conservative Taos Indians, remains as it was before the Spanish conquest. Ranchos de Taos is the farming community; its mission church is one of the most frequently depicted structures in the state.

This cultural mix and a dramatic setting on a plateau between the Rio Grande and the western foot of the Sangre de Cristo Range have lured artists and writers since the mid-19th century. The Taos Society of Artists is noteworthy for the distinctive mark it has made on art in the United States. Artists and artisans, writers and musicians continue to uphold the city's reputation as a center of creativity.

Galleries, studios and shops occupy the brown stucco buildings that surround the town plaza. The people who gather are as diverse as those who came to trade in the 19th century.

Taos Historic Walks, 1.5-hour guided walking tours of the town, depart regularly from the Mabel Dodge Luhan House, 2 blocks east of Taos Plaza, June through September. For reservations phone (505) 758-4020.

Eight miles northwest on US 64 is one of the highest highway bridges in the nation. The three-span, continuous-truss bridge crosses Rio Grande Gorge some 650 feet above the river. Raised sidewalks and observation platforms permit views. Until its junction with I-25, US 64 also provides outstanding views of the region.

Farther north and east the mountainous skyline, extolled by author D.H. Lawrence as the most beautiful he had ever encountered, beckons recreationists to Carson National Forest (see place listing p. 141). Lawrence is enshrined on a knoll on his Kiowa Ranch, now a facility of the University of New Mexico, 15 miles north on scenic SR 522, then 5 miles east. The shrine can be visited only during daylight hours; check road conditions during or after inclement weather.

Eight miles south on SR 518 is Fort Burgwin Research Center of Southern Methodist University (SMU). The 1st Dragoons of the U.S. Cavalry had their headquarters 1852-1860 at Fort Burgwin, which is now restored.

Chamber music concerts are presented at Taos Community Auditorium and Hotel St. Bernard at Taos Ski Valley from late June through early August. Phone (505) 776-2388.

The region's natural assets provide recreational opportunities. The proximity of the Rio Grande River makes Taos a popular starting point for river rafting. Outfitters are based in Taos and Santa Fe. Ski resorts are south and northeast of town. Wheeler Peak Wilderness Area is open in summer for camping, fishing and hiking. Phone (505) 776-2916 for snow conditions.

Taos County Chamber of Commerce: 1139 Paseo del Pueblo Sur, P.O. Drawer I, Taos, NM 87571; phone (505) 758-3873 or (800) 732-8267.

ERNEST L. BLUMENSCHEIN HOME, 2 blks. w. of historic Taos Plaza on Ledoux St., is the restored home of the artist and co-founder of the original Taos Society of Artists. Portions of the adobe house were built in 1797; other sections were added when Blumenschein purchased it in

1919. The house, which contains original antique furnishings, now serves as a showcase for paintings by other Taos painters as well as the work of Ernest and Mary Blumenschein and their daughter, Helen.

Daily 9-5, Apr.-Oct.; 10-4, rest of year. Closed Jan. 1, Thanksgiving and Dec. 25. Admission $5; ages 6-15, $2.50; family rate $10. A combination ticket is available with Kit Carson Home and Museum and Martinez Hacienda. Two houses $7.50; ages 6-15, $4; family rate $15. Three houses $10; ages 6-15, $5; family rate $20. Phone (505) 758-0505.

THE FECHIN HOUSE AND STUDIO, 227 Paseo del Pueblo Norte, is a showplace for the woodcarvings, paintings and, charcoal drawings of Russian-born Nicolai Fechin. The Institute, home and studio of the artist 1928-55, is intricately carved throughout and serves as a cultural center for the Southwest. Changing exhibits, including pieces acquired in barter for his own works, are displayed, and concerts, lectures and other programs are offered. Allow 30 minutes minimum. Wed.-Sun. 10-2. Admission $4. Phone (505) 758-1710.

HARWOOD FOUNDATION, 238 Ledoux St., has Taos art from the 19th century to the present, including paintings, sculpture and Hispanic religious art. Changing exhibits are presented. Tues.-Sat. 10-5, Sun. noon-5; closed holidays. Admission $5, under 13 free. Phone (505) 758-9826.

KIT CARSON HOME AND MUSEUM, .5 blk. e. of the historic Taos Plaza on Kit Carson Rd., housed the frontiersman 1843-68. Rooms are furnished in period; guns, saddles, wearing apparel, household utensils, American Indian artifacts and Mountain Men paraphernalia are displayed.

Daily 8-6, June-Oct.; 9-5, rest of year. Closed Jan. 1, Thanksgiving and Dec. 25. Admission $5; ages 6-15, $2.50; family rate $10. A combination ticket is available with Blumenschein Home and Martinez Hacienda. Two houses $7.50; ages 6-15, $4; family rate $15. Three houses $10; ages 6-15, $5; family rate $20. AE, DS, MC, VI. Phone (505) 758-4741.

KIT CARSON PARK, 2 blks. n. of the plaza, includes the cemetery where Kit Carson, Padre Martinez and other historic figures are buried. Picnicking is permitted. Daily 8-5. Free. Phone (505) 758-8234.

MARTINEZ HACIENDA, 2 mi. w. of Taos Plaza at 708 Ranchitos Rd., is thought to be the only restored *hacienda* open to the public. It was built in 1804 by Don Antonio Severino Martinez, a merchant and *alcalde*—mayor—of Taos. The fortresslike house has 21 rooms built around two large *placitas*, or patios. Furnished in period, it contains exhibits of Spanish colonial life and culture. Living-history demonstrations are presented.

Daily 9-5, Apr.-Oct.; 10-4, rest of year. Closed Jan. 1, Thanksgiving and Dec. 25. Admission $5; ages 6-15, $2.50; family rate $10. A combination ticket is available with Blumenschein Home and Kit Carson Home and Museum. Two houses $7.50; ages 6-15, $4; family rate $15. Three houses $10; ages 6-15, $5; family rate $20. Phone (505) 758-1000.

MILLICENT ROGERS MUSEUM, an adobe house 4 mi. n. of Taos Plaza near US 64, displays the art, history and culture of the Southwest, focusing on the American Indians, Hispanics and Anglos of Taos and northern New Mexico. Allow 1 hour minimum. Daily 10-5, Apr.-Oct.; Tues.-Sun. 10-5, rest of year. Closed Jan. 1, Easter, Sept. 30, Thanksgiving and Dec. 25. Admission $6; over 60 and students with ID $5; New Mexico residents $4; ages 6-16, $1; family rate $12. Phone (505) 758-2462.

PICURIS PUEBLO—
see Peñasco p. 155.

SAN FRANCISCO DE ASIS CHURCH, 4 mi. s. on SR 68, is one of the Southwest's most splendid Spanish churches. Built 1710-55, the heavily buttressed structure is 120 feet long. The interior is adorned with art, images of saints, a large Christ figure and a pictorial rederos that probably dates from the church's founding. Henri Ault's painting "The Shadow of the Cross," which in some lighting shows Christ carrying a cross and in others makes the cross invisible, is in the parish hall.

Allow 1 hour minimum. Church open Mon.-Sat. 9-4; closed first 2 weeks of June. Rectory open 9-noon and 1-4. Admission $2. Phone (505) 758-2754.

STABLES ART GALLERY, 135 Paseo del Pueblo Norte, displays changing exhibits by local artists. Each exhibition, sponsored by the Taos Art Association, lasts 4-6 weeks. Allow 30 minutes minimum. Mon.-Sat. 10-5, Sun. noon-5; closed Thanksgiving and Dec. 25. Donations. Phone (505) 758-2036.

TAOS PUEBLO is 2.5 mi. n. of Taos Plaza. Two five-story terraced communal dwellings, flat-topped adobe houses, barred windows and narrow, winding streets reflect a culture hundreds of years old. This picturesque pueblo is the tallest in the Southwest. Electricity and running water are banned. Men wear blankets around their heads.

Guided tours are included with admission. Allow 30 minutes minimum. Mon.-Sat. 8:30-4:30, Sun. 8:30-4, May-Feb. Admission $10. Fees charged for using still-cameras $10, video or movie cameras $20. Parking $6. Phone (505) 758-1028.

Note: Taos Pueblo is closed to the public during funerals and other ceremonies that can occur without notice. Phone ahead. Photography is not permitted on certain days, and no cameras are permitted in the area during ceremonial dances; check with the officer on duty. Commercial photographers must obtain permission from the office of the governor of the pueblo. There is no admittance to private homes and other restricted areas.

Ruins of the Mission San Gerónimo de Taos are near the entrance to the pueblo. Sections of the massive walls and a portion of an original bell tower are all that remain. Established about 1598, the mission was burned by the Pueblos in their 1680 rebellion, restored 25 years later and finally destroyed by U.S. troops during a revolt in 1847.

RECREATIONAL ACTIVITIES
Skiing

- **Taos Ski Valley**, in the Sangre de Cristo Mountains in Carson National Forest *(see place listing p. 141)*. Write Taos Ski Valley, NM 87525. Other activities are offered. Daily Thanksgiving to mid-Apr. Phone (505) 776-2291.

White-water Rafting

- **Los Rios River Runners**, P.O. Box 2734, Taos, NM 87571. Daily Mar.-Oct. Phone (505) 776-8854 or (800) 544-1181.

- **Native Sons Adventures** departs from 1033A Paseo de Pueblo Sur (US 68) or from Pilar, 14 mi. s. on US 68. Write Box 6144, Taos, NM 87571. Daily May-Sept. Phone (800) 753-7559.

THREE RIVERS (D-3) elev. 4,562′

Watered by runoff from the surrounding mountains, the grazing lands of the upper Tularosa Valley attracted cattle barons in the 1870s. Three Rivers, once a railroad shipping point, maintains a ranching and farming economy.

THREE RIVERS PETROGLYPH SITE, 5 mi. e. on a paved road from US 54 following signs, contains a large group of prehistoric picture writings, with more than 21,000 individual petroglyphs. The Jornada branch of the Mogollon culture is thought to have inscribed them A.D. 900-1400. A trail links many petroglyphs. Camping and picnicking are permitted. Daily 24 hours. Admission $2 per private vehicle. Phone (505) 525-4300.

TRUTH OR CONSEQUENCES
(E-3) pop. 6,200, elev. 4,260′

Playing host to a live broadcast of the radio program "Truth or Consequences" changed not only Hot Springs' future but also its name. So pleased were residents with the publicity engendered by Ralph Edwards' popular show that they adopted the program's name in 1950.

The fire of the chilies—one of the Rio Grande Valley's major crops—is nearly matched by the 110 degrees Fahrenheit of the thermal springs that bubble to the surface in Truth or Consequences. The mineral springs have been enjoyed for their legendary curative properties since the days when only the Apaches knew of them. Inevitably, popular bathhouses grew up around the springs in the early 20th century.

Elephant Butte Lake *(see Recreation Chart and the AAA Southwestern CampBook)* and Caballo Lake state parks *(see Recreation Chart)* offer water activities.

Truth or Consequences/Sierra County Chamber of Commerce: 201 S. Foch St., P.O. Box 31, Truth or Consequences, NM 87901; phone (505) 894-3536 or (800) 831-9487.

GERONIMO SPRINGS MUSEUM, 211 Main St., houses American Indian artifacts, prehistoric Mimbres pottery, ranching and mining items, paleontological and geological finds, a reconstructed log cabin, Southwestern art and mementos of Ralph Edwards, originator of the "Truth or Consequences" radio show. Allow 1 hour, 30 minutes minimum. Mon.-Sat. 9-5; closed Jan. 1, July 4, Thanksgiving and Dec. 25. Admission $2, students with ID $1. MC, VI. Phone (505) 894-6600.

TUCUMCARI (C-5)
pop. 6,800, elev. 4,085′

Established with the Rock Island Railroad in 1901, Tucumcari supposedly takes its name from the 4,999-foot Tucumcari Mountain once used by the Comanches as a lookout point, or *tucumcari*.

A more sentimental theory, however, traces the origin of the name to the legend of an ill-fated romance between the Apache warrior Tocom and Kari, the daughter of an Apache chief. When Tocom died in a fight for Kari's hand, Kari stabbed the victor, then herself. Witness to the tragic scene, her father also ended his life with a dagger, crying out "Tocom-Kari."

The two Canadian River reservoirs that irrigate 45,000 acres around the city also provide water sports and other recreation. Conchas Lake is 31 miles northwest via SR 104; Ute Lake is 23 miles northeast via SR 54 at Logan. *See Recreation Chart and the AAA Southwestern CampBook.*

Tucumcari-Quay County Chamber of Commerce: 404 W. Tucumcari Blvd., P.O. Box E, Tucumcari, NM 88401; phone (505) 461-1694.

TUCUMCARI HISTORICAL MUSEUM, 416 S. Adams St., displays American Indian and frontier artifacts. Mon.-Sat. 9-6, June 2-Labor Day; Tues.-Sat. 9-5, rest of year. Closed holidays. Admission $2; ages 6-15, 50c. Phone (505) 461-4201.

★ WHITE SANDS NATIONAL MONUMENT (E-3)

About 15 miles southwest of Alamogordo *(see place listing p. 131)* on US 70/82, the 146,535-acre White Sands National Monument is the source of rare gypsum sands that form snow-white dunes rising up to 60 feet above the Tularosa Basin floor. Water from rain and melting snow convey tons of gypsum from the mountains into Lake Lucero, in the southwestern portion of the monument.

Dry winds evaporate the *playa* and carry the broken pieces of crystalline gypsum to the northeast, gradually reducing the fragile pieces to sand and piling it into dunes. Much of the wide sea of dunes is bare of vegetation. However, a few species of plants exhibit remarkable adaptation to their peculiar surroundings by resisting burial under the constantly shifting sands. Plants with stems extending through the sand more than 30 feet have been found.

Drinking water is available only at the visitor center; covered picnic sites and restrooms are in the heart of the dunes area. Information about park facilities is broadcast continuously within 6 miles of the monument over AM 1610.

A visitor center presents the story of the origin and history of White Sands through exhibits and a sound and light program. The center is open daily 8-7, Memorial Day-Labor Day; 8-4:30, rest of year. Closed Dec. 25.

Summer programs include guided walks from marked locations in the dunes daily at 7 p.m. and slide-illustrated talks in the picnic area daily at 8:30 p.m.—earlier in August and September. Brochures describing four self-guiding walking tours also are available. Full-moon nights featuring guest speakers are held at 8:30 p.m., 2 days per month during the full moon, May through September. In addition, an orientation video is presented every 30 minutes at the visitor center.

The scenic 16-mile round-trip Dunes Drive can be taken daily 7 a.m.-9 p.m., Memorial Day-Labor Day; 7 a.m.-dusk, rest of year. Closed Dec. 25. Admission $3; under 17 free. Phone (505) 479-6124 or 679-2599.

WHITES CITY (F-5) elev. 3,648'

MILLION DOLLAR MUSEUM is at 25 Carlsbad Caverns Hwy., on SR 7 at entrance to Carlsbad Caverns National Park. The museum's 10 rooms contain exhibits about area history and include European doll houses, doll collections, a 1905 car, pioneer items, rifles, jukeboxes and American Indian artifacts. Antique furniture is displayed throughout the house. Daily 7 a.m.-9 p.m., May 15-Sept. 14; 7 a.m.-8 p.m., rest of year. Admission $3; over 61, $2.50; under 13, $2. Phone (505) 785-2291.

ZUNI (C-1) pop. 5,600, elev. 6,283'

About 30 miles south of Gallup *(see place listing p. 149)* via SRs 602 and 53, Zuni is the only surviving settlement of the Seven Cities of Cibola sought by Francisco Vasquez de Coronado in his quest for gold. It is among the largest of existing live pueblos. Fray Marcos de Niza, bringing the first contact with Europeans in 1539, was followed by Coronado, Juan de Oñate and Franciscan padres, who found the Zuni people unresponsive to Christianity.

Ancient rites and traditions still are preserved. Ceremonial dances are held throughout the year; outsiders may view most of the masked dances, a privilege not extended in many other pueblos. Visitors are asked to observe strict rules of etiquette, however, and permission must be obtained from the governor of Zuni for privileges, including all photography.

Long considered master carvers, the Zuni are renowned for their quality inlay jewelry of silver, jet, shell and turquoise, including needlepoint work of finely cut turquoise in silver, and for carved animal fetishes. In addition, some Zunis have gained international reputations as marathon runners, others as dancers. Visitors are welcome daily dawn-dusk. Phone (505) 782-4481.

LOOK FOR THE RED

*N*ext time you pore over a AAA TourBook® guide in search of a lodging or restaurant, take note of the vibrant red AAA logo just under the property's name! These properties place a high value on the business they receive from dedicated AAA travelers.

As a member, you already turn to TourBooks for quality travel information. Now look for lodging and dining establishments that display the red AAA logo beside their listing for experiences you'll long remember!

Travel With Someone You Trust®

Arizona

Flagstaff........ 178

Grand Canyon
National
Park............. 192

Phoenix 216

Sedona 297

Tucson.......... 319

AJO pop. 2,900

────── LODGINGS ──────

THE GUEST HOUSE INN
◆◆◆
Bed &
Breakfast
2/1-5/31 & 9/1-1/31 | 1P: $69 | 2P: $79 | XP: $10
6/1-8/31 | 1P: $59 | 2P: $69 | XP: $10
Phone: 520/387-6133
Location: 0.5 mi sw of SR 85; from town plaza, take La Mina Ave and Hospital Dr. 700 Guest House Rd 85321. **Terms:** [BP] meal plan; 3 day cancellation notice. **Facility:** 4 rooms. Originally built in 1925, rooms are reminiscent of early Arizona. Desert view from attractive deck area at rear of house. 1 story; interior corridors; designated smoking area. **All Rooms:** combo or shower baths. **Cards:** DI, MC, VI.
⊠ ☎

LA SIESTA MOTEL
◆
Motel
2/1-5/1 & 12/1-1/31 | 1P: $36-$50 | 2P: $54-$58 | XP: $4 | F13
5/2-11/30 | 1P: $34-$36 | 2P: $42-$54 | XP: $4 | F13
Phone: 520/387-6569
Location: 1.8 mi n on SR 85. 2561 N Ajo-Gila Bend Hwy 85321 (PO Box 384). Fax: 520/387-7343. **Terms:** 3 day cancellation notice; pets. **Facility:** 11 rooms. 1 story; exterior corridors; 1 tennis court. **All Rooms:** combo or shower baths. **Some Rooms:** Fee: VCR. **Cards:** AE, DI, DS, MC, VI.
🛒 🏊 ⊠ VCR 💻 📶 ⊠

MARINE MOTEL
ⒶⒶⒶ SAVE
◆
Motel
2/1-4/20 | 1P: $44-$54 | 2P: $54-$65 | XP: $6 | F12
4/21-5/31 | 1P: $42-$49 | 2P: $49-$59 | XP: $6 | F12
10/21-1/31 | 1P: $38-$49 | 2P: $44-$54 | XP: $6 | F12
6/1-10/20 | 1P: $35-$38 | 2P: $40-$44 | XP: $6 | F12
Phone: (520)387-7626
Location: 1 mi n on SR 85. 1966 N 2nd Ave 85321. Fax: 520/387-3835. **Terms:** Pets. **Facility:** 21 rooms. 1 story; exterior corridors. **All Rooms:** combo or shower baths. **Cards:** AE, DI, DS, MC, VI. **Special Amenities:** Free local telephone calls.
S🅳 🛒 ⊠ 📺 📶

THE MINE MANAGER'S HOUSE INN
◆◆◆
Historic Bed
& Breakfast
All Year | 1P: $79-$105 | 2P: $79-$105 | XP: $10
Phone: (520)387-6505
Location: 0.7 mi s of SR 85; from town plaza take La Mina Ave, Hospital Dr and Greenway Dr. 601 W Greenway Dr 85321. Fax: 520/387-6508. **Terms:** [BP] meal plan; 3 day cancellation notice. **Facility:** 5 rooms. 1919 Craftsman House on hill overlooking the town. 1 story; interior/exterior corridors; designated smoking area. **All Rooms:** combo or shower baths. **Some Rooms:** color TV. **Cards:** MC, VI.
ASK S🅳 🏊 ⊠ 🖨

AMADO pop. 100

────── LODGING ──────

AMADO TERRITORY INN
ⒶⒶⒶ SAVE
◆◆◆
Bed &
Breakfast
2/1-6/30 & 11/1-1/31 | 1P: $105-$135 | 2P: $105-$135
7/1-10/31 | 1P: $90-$105 | 2P: $90-$105
Phone: (520)398-8684
Location: E side of I-19, exit 48. 3001 E Frontage Rd 85645 (PO Box 81). Fax: 520/398-8186. **Terms:** [BP] meal plan; age restrictions may apply; 7 day cancellation notice. **Facility:** 10 rooms. Charming rooms in a 2-story ranch house. 2 stories; interior corridors; designated smoking area. **Dining:** Adjacent restaurant serves lunch & dinner. **All Rooms:** combo or shower baths. **Some Rooms:** kitchen, color TV. **Cards:** AE, DS, MC, VI. **Special Amenities:** Free breakfast and free local telephone calls.
⊠ ☎ 🖨 🖥 📶

────── RESTAURANT ──────

AMADO CAFE
◆◆
American
Lunch: $6-$12 | **Dinner:** $12-$19
Phone: 520/398-9211
Location: E side of I-19, exit 48. 3001 E Frontage Rd 85645. **Hours:** 11:30 am-2 & 5-8 pm. Closed: 1/1, 12/25, Mon; Tues in summer. **Features:** casual dress; cocktails. Nicely decorated. Good selection of sandwiches, steak and pasta. Smoke free premises. **Cards:** AE, DS, MC, VI.
⊠

APACHE JUNCTION —See Phoenix p. 255.

BENSON pop. 3,800

────── LODGINGS ──────

BEST WESTERN QUAIL HOLLOW INN
ⒶⒶⒶ SAVE
◆◆◆
Motel
2/1-5/1 & 10/1-1/31 | 1P: $40-$65 | 2P: $45-$70 | XP: $5 | F18
5/2-9/30 | 1P: $38-$58 | 2P: $40-$60 | XP: $5 | F18
Phone: (520)586-3646
Location: Adjacent to I-10, exit 304. 699 N Ocotillo St 85602. Fax: 520/586-7035. **Terms:** 7 day cancellation notice; small pets only. **Facility:** 89 rooms. 2 stories; exterior corridors; heated pool, whirlpool. **Dining:** Restaurant nearby. **All Rooms:** combo or shower baths, extended cable TV. **Some Rooms:** Fee: VCR. **Cards:** AE, CB, DI, DS, MC, VI. **Special Amenities:** Free local telephone calls.
S🅳 🛒 🍽 🏊 ⊠ VCR 🖨 💻 📶 DATA PORT 🚗

DAYS INN
◆◆
Motel
All Year | 1P: $40-$65 | 2P: $45-$70 | XP: $5 | F17
Phone: (520)586-3000
Location: Adjacent to I-10, exit 304. 621 Commerce Dr 85602. Fax: 520/586-7000. **Terms:** [CP] meal plan. **Facility:** 61 rooms. 2 stories; interior corridors; heated pool. **Cards:** AE, CB, DI, DS, JC, MC, VI.
SAVE S🅳 🍽 🏊 ⊠ 🎬 🖥 📶 DATA PORT 🚗

HOLIDAY INN EXPRESS
Phone: (520)586-8800

(AAA) (SAVE)

	1P: $69-$89	2P: $69-$89	XP: $10	F19
10/1-1/31	1P: $69-$89	2P: $69-$89	XP: $10	F19
2/1-4/29	1P: $89	2P: $89	XP: $10	F19
4/30-9/30	1P: $59	2P: $59	XP: $10	F19

Motel
Location: SR 90, at jct I-80, exit 302. 630 S Village Loop 85602. Fax: 520/586-1370. **Terms:** [CP] meal plan; small pets only. **Facility:** 62 rooms. Attractive Western decor. 1 viewroom with whirlpool tub, $99; whirlpool room, $69-$99; suites, $79-$109; 2 stories; interior corridors; heated pool. **Dining:** Restaurant nearby. **All Rooms:** combo or shower baths, extended cable TV. **Cards:** AE, CB, DI, DS, JC, MC, VI. **Special Amenities:** Free breakfast and free local telephone calls. *(See color ad below)*

SUPER 8 MOTEL
Phone: 520/586-1530

◆◆

| 2/1-5/31 & 10/1-1/31 | 1P: $43 | 2P: $45 | XP: $6 | F16 |
| 6/1-9/30 | 1P: $39 | 2P: $44 | XP: $6 | F16 |

Motel
Location: Just n of I-10, exit 304. 855 N Ocotillo Rd 85602. Fax: 520/586-1534. **Terms:** Pets, $10 dep req. **Facility:** 40 rooms. Exterior corridors; heated pool. **Some Rooms:** Fee: refrigerators. **Cards:** AE, DI, DS, MC, VI.

BISBEE pop. 6,300

—— LODGING ——

SAN JOSE LODGE
Phone: (520)432-5761

(AAA) (SAVE)

| All Year | 1P: $49-$55 | 2P: $55-$75 | XP: $10 | D12 |

◆◆

Motel
Location: Jct SR 92 and 80, take SR 92 2.5 mi sw, 1.5 mi s on Naco Hwy. 1002 Naco Hwy 85603. Fax: 520/432-4302. **Terms:** Pets, $10 extra charge. **Facility:** 43 rooms. 1 story; exterior corridors. **Dining:** Restaurant; 7 am-9 pm, Sun-8 pm; $6-$12; cocktails. **All Rooms:** extended cable TV. **Some Rooms:** 6 efficiencies. **Cards:** AE, DI, DS, MC, VI. **Special Amenities:** Early check-in/late check-out and free local telephone calls.

—— RESTAURANTS ——

CAFE ROKA   Historical
Dinner: $12-$18
Phone: 520/432-5153

◆◆◆

American
Location: In Historic Downtown Bisbee. 35 Main St 85603. **Hours:** 5 pm-10 pm. Closed major holidays, Sun & Mon. **Reservations:** suggested. **Features:** cocktails & lounge; street parking. Located in a restored 1907 building. Italian and California cuisine excellently prepared using seasonal ingredients. Vegetarian entrees offered. Smoke free premises. **Cards:** AE, MC, VI.

COPPER QUEEN HOTEL DINING ROOM
Lunch: $6-$9   **Dinner:** $13-$22   Phone: 520/432-2216

◆◆

American
Location: Howell St, just n of SR 80, in Historic Downtown Bisbee. **Hours:** 7 am-10:30, 11-2:30 & 5:30-9 pm. **Features:** casual dress; cocktails & lounge; street parking. Charming Victorian decor. Patio dining in season. Smoke free premises. **Cards:** AE, DI, DS, MC, VI.

BUCKEYE —See Phoenix p. 255.

BULLHEAD CITY pop. 22,000

—— LODGINGS ——

BEST WESTERN BULLHEAD CITY INN
Phone: (520)754-3000

(AAA) (SAVE)

| All Year | 1P: $45-$69 | 2P: $45-$69 | XP: $5 | F17 |

◆◆◆

Motel
Location: 1.8 mi s of Laughlin Bridge on SR 95, then just e on 3rd St. 1126 Hwy 95 86429. Fax: 520/754-5234. **Terms:** [ECP] meal plan; weekly & monthly rates avail; pets, $5 extra charge, also $25 dep req. **Facility:** 88 rooms. Pool at center of property. Rooms decorated in light contemporary colors. 2 stories; exterior corridors; whirlpool. **All Rooms:** Fee: safes. **Cards:** AE, CB, DI, DS, JC, MC, VI. **Special Amenities:** Free breakfast and free newspaper.

FIRST CHOICE INN
◆   All Year   1P: $50-$150   2P: $150-$250   Phone: (520)758-1711
Motel   **Location:** 3.5 mi s of Laughlin Bridge on SR 95, then just e. 2200 Rancho Colorado 86442.   XP: $10   F13
Fax: 520/758-7937. **Terms:** [CP] meal plan; cancellation fee imposed; small pets only, $100 dep req, $20 extra charge. **Facility:** 70 rooms. Rooms are decorated in light colors. 3 stories; interior corridors; heated pool. **All Rooms:** combo or shower baths. **Some Rooms:** 17 efficiencies. **Cards:** AE, CB, DI, DS, JC, MC, VI.   🐾 🛏 ✕ 📹 🖥 🛗 🏊

LAKE MOHAVE RESORT
(AAA) (SAVE)   All Year   1P: $70-$100   Phone: (520)754-3245
◆   **Location:** 3 mi n of SR 68 and Davis Dam, in Lake Mead National Recreation Area. Katherine Landing 86430.   XP: $6   F10
Resort   Fax: 520/754-1125. **Terms:** 72 day cancellation notice; cancellation fee imposed; pets, $5. **Facility:** 52 rooms. Rooms furnished in western theme. Restaurant at Lake Mohave, across from establishment. 2 stories; exterior corridors; beach; boat ramp, marina. **Dining:** Restaurant; 8 am-8 pm, Fri & Sat-9 pm; $9-$14; cocktails. **Recreation:** swimming, fishing, waterskiing. Fee: houseboats. Rental: boats. **All Rooms:** combo or shower baths. **Some Rooms:** 14 efficiencies. **Cards:** DS, MC, VI.   🐾 🍴 🖥 🛗 ✕

LODGE ON THE RIVER
◆◆   Property failed to provide current rates   Phone: 520/758-8080
Motel   **Location:** On SR 95, 3.8 mi s of Laughlin Bridge. 1717 Hwy 95 86442. Fax: 520/758-8283. **Terms:** Pets, $20 dep req. **Facility:** 64 rooms. At the Colorado River. Contemporary style rooms in light pastel colors, housed in a modern-colored territorial-style building. 2 stories; exterior corridors; heated pool. **All Rooms:** combo or shower baths. **Cards:** AE, CB, DI, DS, MC, VI.   🐾 🛏 ✕ 🖥 🛗 🏊

SHANGRI-LA LODGE/VILLAGER LODGE
◆◆   All Year   1P: $30-$60   2P: $30-$60   Phone: (520)758-1117
Extended   **Location:** 2 mi s of Laughlin Bridge. 1767 Georgia Ln 86442. Fax: 520/758-5975. **Terms:** 3 day cancellation   XP: $10   F12
Stay Motel   notice; small pets only. **Facility:** 28 rooms. 2 stories; exterior corridors. **All Rooms:** kitchens. **Cards:** DS, MC, VI.   (ASK) 🐾 🛏 ✕ 📹 🖥

SUNRIDGE HOTEL & CONFERENCE CENTER
(AAA) (SAVE)   All Year   1P: $49-$89   2P: $49-$89   Phone: (520)754-4700
◆◆◆   **Location:** 3 mi n on SR 95, 1.3 mi e on SR 68, just s on Landon Dr. 839 Landon Dr 86429. Fax: 520/754-1225.   XP: $5   F18
Motor Inn   **Terms:** [CP] meal plan; weekly rates avail; small pets only, $100 dep req. **Facility:** 148 rooms. On quiet hillside off highway. 4 stories; exterior corridors; whirlpool. **All Rooms:** extended cable TV. **Cards:** AE, CB, DI, DS, MC, VI. **Special Amenities:** Early check-in/late check-out and free breakfast.   🅂🄳 🐾 🦮 🖥 ✕ 🛗 🖥 🛗 🏊 👥

────── **RESTAURANT** ──────

TOWNE'S SQUARE CAFE   **Lunch:** $5-$7   **Dinner:** $7-$12   Phone: 520/763-2477
◆◆   **Location:** 3.6 mi s of Laughlin Bridge on SR 95. 1751 W Hwy 95, Ste 25 86442. **Hours:** 6 am-10 pm.
American   Closed: 12/25. **Features:** casual dress; children's menu; senior's menu; carryout; beer & wine only. Good selection of sandwiches, beef, chicken and seafood entrees. Nice family style restaurant with homey decor and atomosphere. **Cards:** AE, DI, DS, MC, VI.   ✕

CAMP VERDE pop. 6,200

──── LODGINGS ────

BEST WESTERN CLIFF CASTLE LODGE & CASINO
◆
Motor Inn
All Year   1P: $40-$50   **Phone:** 520/567-6611
Location: On Middle Verde Rd, just e of I-17, exit 289. 333 Middle Verde Rd 86322 (PO Box 4667). **Fax:** 520/567-9455. **Terms:** Cancellation fee imposed. **Facility:** 82 rooms. 2 mi s of Montezuma Castle National Monument. 2 stories; exterior corridors; heated pool. **All Rooms:** combo or shower baths. **Cards:** AE, CB, DI, DS, JC, MC, VI.

COMFORT INN
AAA SAVE
◆◆◆
Motel
All Year   1P: $49-$69   2P: $54-$79   XP: $5   F18
Phone: (520)567-9000
Location: Adjacent to I-17, exit 287. 340 N Industrial Dr 86322 (PO Box 4692). **Fax:** 520/567-1828. **Terms:** [ECP] meal plan; pets, $10 fee. **Facility:** 85 rooms. 3 stories; interior corridors; heated pool, whirlpool, seasonal pool. **All Rooms:** combo or shower baths. **Some Rooms:** Fee: refrigerators, microwaves. **Cards:** AE, CB, DI, DS, JC, MC, VI.

MICROTEL INN & SUITES OF CAMP VERDE
AAA SAVE
◆◆
Motel
3/1-11/30	1P: $49-$79	2P: $54-$84	XP: $5	F15
12/1-1/31	1P: $49-$69	2P: $54-$74	XP: $5	F15
2/1-2/29	1P: $39-$59	2P: $44-$64	XP: $5	F15

Phone: (520)567-3700
Location: Adjacent to I-17, exit 287. 504 Industrial Dr 86322. **Fax:** 520/567-1822. **Terms:** Pets, $10 extra charge. **Facility:** 63 rooms. 3 stories; interior corridors; heated pool, whirlpool, seasonal pool. **All Rooms:** combo or shower baths. **Cards:** AE, CB, DI, DS, JC, MC, VI. **Special Amenities:** Free breakfast and free local telephone calls. *(See color ad below)*

SUPER 8 MOTEL-CAMP VERDE
AAA SAVE
◆◆
Motel
All Year   1P: $49-$64   2P: $54-$84   XP: $5   F12
Phone: (520)567-2622
Location: Adjacent to I-17, exit 287 then 0.2 mi e. 1550 W Hwy 260 86322 (PO Box 2838). **Fax:** 520/567-2622. **Terms:** [CP] meal plan; 3 day cancellation notice; cancellation fee imposed. **Facility:** 46 rooms. 2 stories; interior corridors; heated pool, whirlpool. **Dining:** Restaurant nearby. **Cards:** AE, CB, DI, DS, JC, MC, VI. **Special Amenities:** Free breakfast and free local telephone calls. *(See color ad below)*

CAREFREE —See Phoenix p. 256.

CASA GRANDE pop. 19,100

------ LODGINGS ------

BEST WESTERN CASA GRANDE SUITES
Phone: (520)836-1600

◆◆◆	1/1-1/31	1P: $62-$100	2P: $67-$110	XP: $5	F12
Motel	2/1-4/30	1P: $60-$99	2P: $65-$105	XP: $5	F12
	10/1-12/31	1P: $55-$75	2P: $60-$80	XP: $5	F12
	5/1-9/30	1P: $50-$62	2P: $55-$65	XP: $5	F12

Location: On SR 287, 1 mi w of jct I-10, exit 194. 665 Via Del Cielo 85222. Fax: 520/836-7242. **Terms:** [CP] meal plan; 3 day cancellation notice; pets, $25 dep req. **Facility:** 81 rooms. 0.8 mi w of factory outlet center, across from Regional Medical Center. 1 two-bedroom unit. 2 stories; exterior corridors; heated pool. **Some Rooms:** kitchen. **Cards:** AE, CB, DI, JC, MC, VI.

HOLIDAY INN
Phone: (520)426-3500

◆◆◆	2/1-4/30 & 1/1-1/31	1P: $74-$87	2P: $74-$87	XP: $6	F18
Motor Inn	9/1-12/31	1P: $68-$75	2P: $68-$75	XP: $6	F18
	5/1-8/31	1P: $60-$66	2P: $60-$66	XP: $6	F18

Location: Center of town, at jct SR 84 and 287. 777 N Pinal Ave 85222. Fax: 520/836-4728. **Terms:** Pets. **Facility:** 176 rooms. 4 stories; interior corridors; heated pool. **Services:** gift shop. **Some Rooms:** Fee: refrigerators. **Cards:** AE, CB, DI, DS, JC, MC, VI.

MOTEL 6 - 1263
Phone: 520/836-3323

(AAA)	2/1-4/23	1P: $44-$54	2P: $50-$60	XP: $3	F17
	5/25-1/31	1P: $34-$44	2P: $40-$50	XP: $3	F17
◆	4/24-5/24	1P: $32-$42	2P: $38-$48	XP: $3	F17

Motel   **Location:** Adjacent to I-10, exit 200. 4965 N Sunland Gin Rd 85222. Fax: 520/421-3094. **Terms:** Small pets only. **Facility:** 97 rooms. Located in Eloy area. 2 stories; exterior corridors; heated pool. **Dining:** Restaurant nearby. **All Rooms:** combo or shower baths. **Cards:** AE, CB, DI, DS, MC, VI.

SUPER 8 MOTEL
Phone: (520)836-8800

◆◆	2/1-3/31	1P: $65-$120	2P: $70-$120	XP: $5	F12
Motel	1/1-1/31	1P: $59-$85	2P: $62-$85	XP: $5	F12
	4/1-12/31	1P: $45-$65	2P: $49-$69	XP: $5	F12

Location: SR 287, 0.6 mi w of jct I-10, exit 194. 2066 E Florence Blvd 85222. Fax: 520/836-8800. **Terms:** [CP] meal plan. **Facility:** 41 rooms. Just w of Factory Outlet shopping. 2 stories; interior corridors; heated pool. **Cards:** AE, CB, DI, DS, MC, VI.

------ RESTAURANT ------

BEDILLON'S CACTUS GARDEN RESTAURANT   **Lunch:** $6-$10   **Dinner:** $8-$18   **Phone:** 520/836-2045
American   **Location:** Downtown area, just e of Pinal Ave (SR 387), just n of Florence Blvd (SR 287). 800 N Park Ave 85222. **Hours:** 11:30 am-2 & 5-9 pm, Fri & Sat-9:30 pm. Closed major holidays, Sun & Mon. **Features:** casual dress; carryout; cocktails & lounge. Dining in an 80 year-old restored home. Also a western museum and cactus garden. **Cards:** AE, DI, DS, MC, VI.

CAVE CREEK —See Phoenix p. 256.

CHAMBERS pop. 450

------ LODGING ------

BEST WESTERN CHIEFTAIN
Phone: (520)688-2754

(AAA) [SAVE]	6/1-9/30	1P: $56-$60	2P: $61-$65	XP: $5	F17
	1/1-1/31	1P: $51-$55	2P: $56-$60	XP: $5	F17
◆◆	10/1-12/31	1P: $49-$53	2P: $54-$58	XP: $5	F17
Motor Inn	2/1-5/31	1P: $48-$52	2P: $53-$57	XP: $5	F17

Location: Adjacent to I-40, exit 333, at jct US 191. (PO Box 39, 86502). Fax: 520/688-2754. **Terms:** Small pets only, $10 extra charge. **Facility:** 52 rooms. Convenient, interstate highway location. 2 stories; exterior corridors; heated pool open 5/30-9/30. **Dining:** Restaurant; 6 am-9 pm; $7-$14. **Services:** gift shop. **Cards:** AE, CB, DI, DS, MC, VI. **Special Amenities:** Early check-in/late check-out and free local telephone calls.

CHANDLER —See Phoenix p. 256.

CHINLE pop. 5,100

------ LODGINGS ------

BEST WESTERN CANYON DE CHELLY INN
Phone: (520)674-5875

(AAA) [SAVE]	5/1-10/31	1P: $85-$112	2P: $85-$112	XP: $10	F13
◆◆◆	2/1-4/30, 11/1-12/31 & 1/1-1/31	1P: $56-$62	2P: $60-$66	XP: $10	F13

Motor Inn   **Location:** Just e of US 191; 3 mi w of Canyon de Chelly National Monument. 100 Main St, Rt #7 86503 (PO Box 295). Fax: 520/674-3715. **Terms:** 7 day cancellation notice; cancellation fee imposed. **Facility:** 99 rooms. Nicely decorated, southwestern-style decor. 2 stories; exterior corridors; heated pool. **Dining:** Restaurant; 6:30 am-9 pm; $6-$10. **Services:** gift shop. **Cards:** AE, DI, DS, MC, VI. **Special Amenities:** Early check-in/late check-out and free local telephone calls.

HOLIDAY INN CANYON DE CHELLY
Phone: (520)674-5000
◆◆◆ 5/1-10/31   1P: $89-$119   2P: $89-$119   XP: $10   F19
Motor Inn   2/1-4/30 & 11/1-1/31   1P: $69-$89   2P: $69-$89   XP: $10   F19
Location: 2.5 mi e of US 191 at entrance to Canyon de Chelly National Monument. Indian Rt 7 86503 (PO Box 1889). Fax: 520/674-8264. **Terms:** Cancellation fee imposed. **Facility:** 108 rooms. 0.5 mile w of Visitor Center. 2 stories; interior corridors; heated pool. **Services:** gift shop. **All Rooms:** combo or shower baths. **Cards:** AE, CB, DI, DS, MC, VI.

THUNDERBIRD LODGE
Phone: (520)674-5841
◆◆◆ 4/1-10/31   1P: $92-$97   2P: $96-$101   XP: $7
Motor Inn   2/1-3/31   1P: $59   2P: $65   XP: $7
    11/1-1/31   1P: $69-$87   XP: $7
Location: 3.5 mi e of US 191, in Canyon de Chelly National Monument; just e of Visitor Center. (PO Box 548, 86503-0548). Fax: 520/674-5844. **Terms:** Cancellation fee imposed. **Facility:** 72 rooms. Attractive location in a grove of cottonwood trees. Some small rooms in the original stone buildings. 1 story; exterior corridors. **Services:** gift shop. **Cards:** AE, CB, DI, DS, MC, VI.

COTTONWOOD pop. 5,900

——— LODGINGS ———

BEST WESTERN COTTONWOOD INN
Phone: (520)634-5575
AAA SAVE   3/1-10/31   1P: $69-$99   2P: $69-$99   XP: $6   F13
◆◆◆ 2/1-2/29 & 11/1-1/31   1P: $59-$99   2P: $59-$99   XP: $6   F13
Motor Inn   **Location:** On SR 89A at jct SR 260. 993 S Main 86326. Fax: 520/634-5776. **Terms:** [CP] meal plan; cancellation fee imposed; small pets only, in smoking rooms only. **Facility:** 77 rooms. Across from shopping center. 13 spacious, attractively furnished units with king bed, refrigerator and private patio, 4 with whirlpool. 1 two-bedroom unit. 4 whirlpool rooms; 1-2 stories; exterior corridors; whirlpool. **Dining:** Restaurant; 6 am-10 pm; $5-$8; cocktails. **All Rooms:** combo or shower baths. **Cards:** AE, CB, DI, DS, MC, VI. **Special Amenities:** Free breakfast and free local telephone calls.

COTTONWOOD PINES MOTEL
Phone: 520/634-9975
◆ All Year   1P: $35-$46   2P: $39-$52   XP: $3   F12
Motel   **Location:** 0.9 mi s of jct SR 89, just w of Main St. 920 S Main 86326. **Terms:** Small pets only, $20 dep req. **Facility:** 14 rooms. 2 stories; exterior corridors. **Cards:** AE, JC, VI.

QUALITY INN
Phone: (520)634-4207
AAA SAVE   3/1-10/31   1P: $59-$89   2P: $59-$89   XP: $5   F18
◆◆ 2/1-2/29 & 11/1-1/31   1P: $50-$89   2P: $50-$60   XP: $5   F18
Motor Inn   **Location:** 1.5 mi sw. 301 W Hwy 89A 86326. Fax: 520/634-5764. **Terms:** [CP] meal plan. **Facility:** 51 rooms. 2 stories; exterior corridors; whirlpool. **Dining:** Coffee shop; 7 am-9 pm, Sat 8 am-9 pm, Sun 8 am-7 pm; $6-$10; cocktails. **Cards:** AE, DI, DS, MC, VI. **Special Amenities:** Free local telephone calls and free room upgrade (subject to availability with advanced reservations).

SUPER 8 COTTONWOOD
Phone: (520)639-1888
AAA SAVE   All Year   1P: $49-$74   2P: $54-$79   XP: $5   F12
◆◆◆ **Location:** 0.8 mi s of jct 89A and SR 260. 800 S Main St 86326. Fax: 520/639-2285. **Terms:** [CP] meal plan.
Motel   **Facility:** 52 rooms. 1-large apartment with kitchen, extra charge; 2 stories; exterior corridors; heated pool, whirlpool. **All Rooms:** extended cable TV. **Cards:** AE, CB, DI, DS, MC, VI. **Special Amenities:** Free breakfast and free local telephone calls.

THE VIEW MOTEL
Phone: (520)634-7581
AAA SAVE   All Year   1P: $34-$46   2P: $38-$48   XP: $3
◆ **Location:** Just w of jct SR 260/SR 89A. 818 S Main St 86326. Fax: 520/639-2101. **Terms:** Weekly rates avail, 11/15-2/15; pets, $3-$5 extra charge, dogs only. **Facility:** 34 rooms. Hillside location with view of Verde Valley. 4
Motel   small rooms. 1 story; exterior corridors; whirlpool. **All Rooms:** combo or shower baths. **Some Rooms:** 8 efficiencies. **Cards:** MC, VI. **Special Amenities:** Early check-in/late check-out and free local telephone calls.

WILLOW TREE INN
Phone: 520/634-3678
◆◆ 3/1-11/1   1P: $42-$48   2P: $48-$58   XP: $5   F12
Motel   2/1-2/29 & 11/2-1/31   1P: $40-$50   2P: $42-$48   XP: $5   F12
Location: Just e of jct SR 89A. 1089 Hwy 260 86326. Fax: 520/639-0407. **Terms:** Cancellation fee imposed. **Facility:** 30 rooms. Across from shopping center. 2 stories; exterior corridors. **All Rooms:** combo or shower baths. **Some Rooms:** 2 efficiencies. **Cards:** AE, CB, DI, DS, MC, VI.

——— RESTAURANT ———

THE KRAMERS AT THE MANZANITA RESTAURANT   **Lunch:** $4-$9   **Dinner:** $9-$20   **Phone:** 520/634-8851
◆◆ **Location:** In Cornville, 6.5 mi e via SR 89A and Cornville Rd. 11425 E Cornville Rd 86325. **Hours:** 11 am-2
American   & 4:30-8 pm, Sun-7 pm. Closed major holidaysMon & Tues. **Reservations:** suggested. **Features:** casual dress; cocktails & lounge. Popular restaurant in a country location. **Cards:** MC, VI.

EAGAR pop. 4,000

——— LODGING ———

BEST WESTERN SUNRISE INN
Phone: (520)333-2540
◆◆◆ All Year   1P: $53-$89   2P: $59-$99   XP: $5   F12
Motel   **Location:** Just n of SR 260, 1.5 mi s of Springerville and US 60. 128 N Main St 85925 (PO Box 1590, 85925-1590). Fax: 520/333-4700. **Terms:** [ECP] meal plan; small pets only, dogs & cats. **Facility:** 40 rooms. 2 stories; exterior corridors. **Cards:** AE, CB, DI, DS, MC, VI.

EHRENBERG pop. 1,200

------ LODGING ------

BEST WESTERN FLYING J MOTEL   Phone: (520)923-9711
(AAA) (SAVE)   2/1-2/29 & 12/31-1/31   1P: $79-$99   2P: $85-$109   XP: $5   F12
◆ ◆   3/1-12/30   1P: $42-$55   2P: $49-$63   XP: $5   F12
Motor Inn   **Location:** Adjacent to I-10, exit 1. (PO Box 260, 85334). Fax: 520/923-8335. **Terms:** [CP] meal plan; pets.
Facility: 86 rooms. 0.5 mi e of the Colorado River at Flying J Travel Plaza. 2 stories; interior corridors; heated pool,
whirlpool. **Dining:** Restaurant; 24 hrs; $7-$11; wine/beer only. **Cards:** AE, DI, DS, MC, VI. **Special Amenities:**
Free breakfast and free local telephone calls. [icons]

ELOY pop. 7,200

------ LODGING ------

SUPER 8 MOTEL   Phone: (520)466-7804
(AAA) (SAVE)   2/1-3/31   1P: $55   2P: $60   XP: $4   F12
◆   12/1-1/31   1P: $48   2P: $53   F12
Motel   10/1-11/30   1P: $42   2P: $47   XP: $4   F12
          4/1-9/30   1P: $37   2P: $43   XP: $4   F12
Location: Adjacent to I-10 at Toltec Rd; 4 mi se of jct I-8. 3945 W Houser Rd 85231. Fax: 520/466-3431.
Terms: Pets, $5 dep req. **Facility:** 42 rooms. 2 stories; exterior corridors; heated pool. **Cards:** AE, DI, DS, MC, VI.
Special Amenities: Early check-in/late check-out and free breakfast. [icons]

FLAGSTAFF pop. 45,900—See also GRAND CANYON NATIONAL PARK.

> Federal regulations require all trains to sound their whistles at street level crossings day
> or night. Freight train traffic has increased in Flagstaff. Steps have been taken by lodg-
> ings to minimize the train noise levels in your room. However, you may still experience
> some whistle noise.

------ LODGINGS ------

AMERISUITES   Phone: (520)774-8042
(AAA) (SAVE)   5/1-9/30   1P: $89-$149   2P: $89-$159   XP: $10   F17
◆ ◆ ◆   2/1-4/30 & 10/1-1/31   1P: $69-$109   2P: $69-$119   XP: $10   F17
Motel   **Location:** Nw of jct I-17 and I-40; from I-40 exit 195B, just n to Forest Meadows, w to Beulah Blvd, then just s on
Beulah Blvd. 2455 S Beulah Blvd 86001. Fax: 520/774-5524. **Terms:** [ECP] meal plan; weekly rates avail; package
plans; pets, $10. **Facility:** 117 rooms. 6 business suites, $79-$129; 5 stories; interior corridors; heated pool, whirl-
pool. **Dining:** Restaurant nearby. **All Rooms:** extended cable TV. **Cards:** AE, CB, DI, DS, MC, VI. **Special Amenities:** Free
breakfast and free newspaper. *(See color ad opposite title page)* [icons]

BEST WESTERN KINGS HOUSE MOTEL

Phone: (520)774-7186

6/1-9/15	1P: $60-$70	2P: $70-$80	XP: $5	F17
2/1-5/31 & 9/16-1/31	1P: $42-$52	2P: $50-$65	XP: $5	F17

Location: On US 89, 180 and I-40 business loop; from I-40 exit 198, 1 mi n to Route 66. 1560 E Route 66 86001. Fax: 520/774-7188. **Terms:** [CP] meal plan; pets, in smoking rooms only. **Facility:** 57 rooms. On busy commercial street along railroad tracks. Some small units. 1 two-bedroom unit. 2 stories; exterior corridors; heated pool, pool open summer season only. **Dining:** Restaurant nearby. **All Rooms:** extended cable TV. **Cards:** AE, CB, DI, DS, JC, MC, VI. **Special Amenities:** Free breakfast and free local telephone calls.

BEST WESTERN PONY SOLDIER MOTEL

Phone: (520)526-2388

5/1-10/31	1P: $69-$79	2P: $79-$99	XP: $5	F18
2/1-4/30	1P: $49-$69	2P: $69-$79	XP: $5	F18
11/1-1/31	1P: $49-$69	2P: $59-$79		

Location: on US 89, 180 and I-40 business loop; from I-40 exit 201, then 1.7 mi w. 3030 E Route 66 86004. Fax: 520/527-8329. **Terms:** [CP] meal plan. **Facility:** 90 rooms. Cozy rooms decorated in a southwest motif. Located on historic Route 66 along railroad tracks. 1 two-bedroom unit. 2 stories; interior corridors; heated pool, whirlpool. **Dining:** Restaurant; 11 am-9 pm; closed Mon, in winter; $6-$11; cocktails. **All Rooms:** extended cable TV. **Cards:** AE, CB, DI, DS, JC, MC, VI. **Special Amenities:** Free breakfast and free newspaper. *(See color ad below)*

BUDGET HOST SAGA MOTEL

Phone: 520/779-3631

5/5-9/10	1P: $38-$46	2P: $38-$46	XP: $4
2/1-5/4 & 9/11-1/31	1P: $28-$34	2P: $28-$38	XP: $4

Location: I-40, westbound exit 195B, 1.5 mi n, then just w on Rt 66; eastbound exit 191. 820 W Route 66 86001. **Facility:** 29 rooms. Cozy, nicely furnished units. Located across from NAU. 1 story; exterior corridors; heated pool 5/1-10/31. **Dining:** Restaurant nearby. **All Rooms:** extended cable TV. **Cards:** AE, DI, DS, MC, VI. *(See color ad p 194)*

CANYON INN

Phone: (520)774-7301

5/1-8/31	1P: $60-$75	2P: $70-$100	XP: $10	F
9/1-10/31	1P: $50-$70	2P: $60-$80	XP: $10	F
2/1-4/30	1P: $33-$43	2P: $40-$45	XP: $10	F
11/1-1/31	1P: $29-$39	2P: $29-$39	XP: $10	F

Location: Just e jct Milton Rd and US 66. 500 S Milton Rd 86001. Fax: 520/774-7301. **Terms:** Weekly rates avail; small pets only, $10 extra charge. **Facility:** 21 rooms. 1 story; exterior corridors. **Cards:** AE, DS, MC, VI. *(See color ad p 180)*

COMFORT INN

Phone: (520)774-7326

5/5-9/3	1P: $49-$109	2P: $49-$109	XP: $5	F18
9/4-11/2	1P: $43-$99	2P: $46-$99	XP: $5	F18
2/1-5/4	1P: $42-$64	2P: $45-$64	XP: $5	F18
11/3-1/31	1P: $43-$59	2P: $46-$59	XP: $5	F18

Location: 1.2 mi n of jct I-17 and I-40; from I-40, exit 195B. 914 S Milton Rd 86001. Fax: 520/774-7328. **Terms:** [CP] meal plan; pets. **Facility:** 67 rooms. Units decorated in attractive southwestern colors. 2 stories; exterior corridors; heated pool open 5/15-9/15. **Dining:** Restaurant nearby. **Cards:** AE, CB, DI, DS, MC, VI. **Special Amenities:** Free breakfast and free local telephone calls. *(See color ad p 181)*

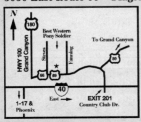

CRYSTAL INN

Phone: (520)774-4581

5/1-10/31	1P: $60-$75	2P: $75-$95	XP: $10	F12
2/1-4/30	1P: $33-$43	2P: $40-$60	XP: $10	F12
11/1-1/31	1P: $29-$39	2P: $34-$50	XP: $10	F12

Motel
Location: 1.5 mi n of jct I-17 and I-40, exit 195B, just w of Milton Rd. 602 W Rt 66 86001. Fax: 520/774-4581.
Terms: [CP] meal plan; pets, $10 extra charge. **Facility:** 66 rooms. Near Northern Arizona University. 3 whirl-pool rooms; 1-2 stories; exterior corridors; heated pool, whirlpool. **Cards:** AE, DI, DS, JC, MC, VI. **Special Amenities:** Free local telephone calls. *(See color ad below)*

DAYS INN EAST

Phone: (520)527-1477

5/5-9/4	1P: $54-$99	2P: $59-$110	XP: $5	F18
3/10-5/4	1P: $39-$69	2P: $44-$74	XP: $5	F18
9/5-1/31	1P: $35-$59	2P: $39-$69	XP: $5	F18
2/1-3/9	1P: $30-$39	2P: $35-$44	XP: $5	F18

Motel
Location: US 89, 180 and I-40 business loop; from I-40 exit 201, then 0.5 mi w, just n of Route 66. 3601 E Lockett Rd 86004. Fax: 520/527-0228. **Terms:** [CP] meal plan. **Facility:** 54 rooms. Located along historic Rt 66 next to rail-road tracks. 2 two-bedroom units. 3 stories; interior corridors; heated pool, indoor whirlpool. **Dining:** Restaurant nearby. **All Rooms:** safes. **Cards:** AE, CB, DI, DS, JC, MC, VI. *(See color ad p 178)*

DAYS INN FLAGSTAFF HWY 66

Phone: (520)774-5221

5/1-8/31	1P: $59-$119	2P: $59-$119	XP: $10 F18
9/1-10/31	1P: $44-$79	2P: $44-$79	XP: $10 F18
2/1-4/30	1P: $39-$79	2P: $44-$79	XP: $10 F18
11/1-1/31	1P: $29-$49	2P: $29-$49	XP: $10 F18

Motor Inn

Location: From I-40, exit 195B, 1.5 n, then just w on Rt 66. 1000 W Hwy 66 86001. Fax: 520/774-4977.
Terms: 3 day cancellation notice; cancellation fee imposed; small pets only, in smoking rooms only. **Facility:** 157 rooms. 2 stories; exterior corridors; heated pool. **Dining:** Restaurant; 6 am-10 & 5-9 pm; in winter 7 am-10 & 5-9 pm; $4-$7; cocktails. **Services:** gift shop. **Recreation:** in room video games. **Cards:** AE, CB, DI, DS, JC, MC, VI. *(See color ad below & p 192)*

DAYS INN-I-40

Phone: (520)779-1575

5/4-9/4	1P: $49-$109	2P: $49-$109	XP: $5 F13
9/5-10/28	1P: $45-$69	2P: $45-$69	XP: $5 F13
2/1-5/3 & 10/29-1/31	1P: $35-$59	2P: $35-$59	XP: $5 F13

Motel

Location: NW of jct I-40 and I-17; from I-40 exit 195B, just n to Forest Meadows, w to Beulah Blvd, then just s on Woodlands Village Blvd. 2735 S Woodlands Village Blvd 86001. Fax: 520/779-0044. **Terms:** [CP] meal plan; 7 day cancellation notice; pets, with credit card only. **Facility:** 57 rooms. Across from shopping center and restaurants. 2 stories; interior corridors; indoor whirlpool. **All Rooms:** safes. **Cards:** AE, DI, DS, MC, VI. *(See color ad p 183 & p 197)*

ECONO LODGE I-40 & I-17

Phone: (520)774-2225

(AAA) [SAVE]	5/26-9/3	1P: $60-$120	2P: $60-$120	XP: $5	F18
◆ ◆	9/4-10/29	1P: $60-$90	2P: $60-$90	XP: $5	F18
	10/30-1/31	1P: $50-$90	2P: $50-$90	XP: $5	F18
Motel	2/1-5/25	1P: $50-$90	2P: $50-$90	XP: $5	F18

Location: Nw of jct I-40 and I-17; from I-40 exit 195B, 0.2 mi n to Forest Meadows, then w 1 blk. 2355 S Beulah Blvd 86001. Fax: 520/774-2225. **Terms:** [CP] meal plan; weekly rates avail; cancellation fee imposed; small pets only, $5 fee. **Facility:** 85 rooms. Spacious, attractive lobby area. 2 stories; interior corridors; whirlpools, small heated pool 6/1-9/1. **Dining:** Restaurant nearby. **Some Rooms:** 20 efficiencies. **Cards:** AE, CB, DI, DS, JC, MC, VI. **Special Amenities:** Free breakfast and free local telephone calls. *(See color ad p 183)*

ECONO LODGE LUCKY LANE

Phone: (520)774-7701

(AAA) [SAVE]	4/1-9/6	1P: $49-$69	2P: $69-$99	XP: $10	F14
◆ ◆	9/7-12/31	1P: $39-$49	2P: $49-$69	XP: $10	F14
	1/1-1/31	1P: $30-$40	2P: $49-$69	XP: $10	F14
Motel	2/1-3/31	1P: $30-$40	2P: $40-$50	XP: $5	F14

Location: N side of I-40, Butler Ave exit 198, e on Lucky Ln. 2480 E Lucky Ln 86004. Fax: 520/774-7855. **Terms:** [CP] meal plan; small pets only, $10 extra charge. **Facility:** 68 rooms. 3 stories; interior corridors; heated pool, whirlpool. **Cards:** AE, CB, DI, DS, MC, VI. **Special Amenities:** Free breakfast and free local telephone calls.

EMBASSY SUITES/FLAGSTAFF-GRAND CANYON GATEWAY

Phone: (520)774-4333

◆ ◆ ◆	5/1-10/31	1P: $114-$199	2P: $124-$209	XP: $10	F18
Suite Motel	2/1-4/30 & 11/1-1/31	1P: $79-$169	2P: $89-$199	XP: $10	F18

Location: 1.5 mi n of jct I-17 and I-40, exit 195B. 706 S Milton Rd 86001. Fax: 520/774-0216. **Terms:** [BP] meal plan; cancellation fee imposed; package plans; pets, $25 extra charge. **Facility:** 119 rooms. Adjacent to Northern Arizona University. Spacious 1-bedroom suites. 3 stories; interior corridors; heated pool. **Some Rooms:** Fee: VCR. **Cards:** AE, CB, DI, DS, JC, MC, VI. *(See ad p 184)*

FAIRFIELD INN BY MARRIOTT
◆◆
Motel

5/1-8/31	1P: $55-$79	2P: $55-$79
2/1-4/30	1P: $45-$65	2P: $45-$66
9/1-10/31	1P: $50-$65	2P: $50-$65
11/1-1/31	1P: $45-$65	2P: $45-$65

Phone: (520)773-1300

Location: 0.5 mi n of jct I-17 and I-40; from I-40 exit 195B. 2005 S Milton Rd 86001. **Fax:** 520/773-1462. **Terms:** [CP] meal plan. **Facility:** 135 rooms. 3 stories; interior/exterior corridors; heated pool. **Cards:** AE, CB, DI, DS, MC, VI.

HAMPTON INN
Phone: (520)526-1885

	5/26-9/4	1P: $69-$119	2P: $69-$119
	3/1-5/25	1P: $59-$119	2P: $59-$119
	9/5-1/31	1P: $55-$109	2P: $55-$109
Motel	2/1-2/29	1P: $55-$75	2P: $55-$75

Location: On US 180, 89 and I-40 business loop; from I-40 exit 201, then 0.5 mi w. Just n of Route 66. 3501 E Lockett Rd 86004. Fax: 520/526-9885. **Terms:** [CP] meal plan; 7 day cancellation notice. **Facility:** 50 rooms. Near Flagstaff Mall. 3 stories; interior corridors; heated pool, whirlpool. **All Rooms:** combo or shower baths. **Cards:** AE, CB, DI, DS, JC, MC, VI. *(See color ad p 182)*

HAMPTON INN & SUITES
Phone: (520)913-0900

	5/26-9/4	1P: $89-$129	2P: $89-$139
	9/5-1/31	1P: $69-$129	2P: $69-$139
	4/1-5/25	1P: $79-$119	2P: $79-$129
Motel	2/1-3/31	1P: $59-$99	2P: $69-$109

Location: Adjacent to I-40 and I-27; from I-40, exit 195B, from I-17, exit Milton Rd. 2400 S Beulah Blvd 86001. Fax: 520/913-0800. **Terms:** [ECP] meal plan. **Facility:** 126 rooms. 6 whirlpool rooms, $99-$149; 5 stories; interior corridors; heated pool, whirlpool. **Dining:** Restaurant nearby. **Recreation:** in-room video games. **All Rooms:** combo or shower baths. **Cards:** AE, CB, DI, DS, JC, MC, VI. **Special Amenities:** Free breakfast and free local telephone calls.

HILTON GARDEN INN
Phone: (520)226-8888

| | 5/1-10/31 | 1P: $89-$129 | 2P: $89-$129 | XP: $10 | F17 |
| | 2/1-4/30 & 11/1-1/31 | 1P: $79-$109 | 2P: $79-$109 | XP: $10 | F17 |

Location: 0.5 mi n of jct I-17 and I-40 from I-40 exit 195B. 350 W Forest Meadows St 86001. Fax: 520/556-9059. **Terms:** [CP] meal plan. **Facility:** 90 rooms. 3 stories; interior corridors; heated pool, sauna, whirlpool. **Recreation:** TV's with video game systems. **Cards:** AE, CB, DI, DS, MC, VI. **Special Amenities:** Free newspaper. *(See color ad p 41 & below)*

HOLIDAY INN FLAGSTAFF/GRAND CANYON
Phone: (520)526-1150

| | 6/1-9/30 | 1P: $70-$100 | 2P: $70-$100 |
| Motor Inn | 2/1-5/31 & 10/1-1/31 | 1P: $60-$100 | 2P: $60-$100 |

Location: N side of I-40, Butler Ave exit 198. 2320 E Lucky Ln 86004. Fax: 520/779-2610. **Terms:** Pets. **Facility:** 157 rooms. 5 stories; interior corridors; heated pool. **All Rooms:** combo or shower baths. **Cards:** AE, CB, DI, DS, JC, MC, VI.

HOWARD JOHNSON HOTEL

Phone: (520)779-6944

4/1-10/31	1P: $69-$129	2P: $69-$129	XP: $10 F17
2/1-3/31 & 11/1-1/31	1P: $49-$79	2P: $49-$79	XP: $10 F17

Motor Inn

Location: Just nw of I-40, exit 198. 2200 E Butler Ave 86004. Fax: 520/774-3990. **Terms:** Weekly & monthly rates avail; pets, $50 dep req. **Facility:** 100 rooms. 3 stories; interior corridors; heated pool, saunas, whirlpool. **Dining:** Coffee shop; 24 hrs; $5-$10; cocktails. **All Rooms:** extended cable TV. **Some Rooms:** Fee: VCR.
Cards: AE, CB, DI, DS, JC, MC, VI.

HOWARD JOHNSON INN

Phone: (520)526-1826

5/16-9/15	1P: $49-$59	2P: $54-$69	XP: $5 F17
4/1-5/15	1P: $44-$54	2P: $49-$59	XP: $5 F17
2/1-3/31 & 9/16-1/31	1P: $35-$49	2P: $44-$49	XP: $5 F17

Motor Inn

Location: I-40, exit 201, then 1.7 mi w. 3300 E Rt 66 86004. Fax: 520/527-1872. **Terms:** Pets. **Facility:** 56 rooms. 2 stories; exterior corridors. **Dining:** Restaurant; 6 am-10 pm; 6 am-9 pm in winter; $5-$10.
All Rooms: combo or shower baths, extended cable TV. **Cards:** AE, CB, DI, DS, MC, VI. **Special Amenities:** Early check-in/late check-out and free local telephone calls. *(See color ad below)*

THE INN AT 410 BED & BREAKFAST

Phone: (520)774-0088

All Year	1P: $125-$175	2P: $125-$175	XP: $10

Historic Bed & Breakfast

Location: Downtown 4 blks n of Rt 66. 410 N Leroux St 86001. Fax: 520/774-6354. **Terms:** [BP] meal plan; check-in 4 pm. **Facility:** 9 rooms. Charming 1907 Craftsman home comfortably furnished with antiques and touches of the southwest. Guest rooms distinctively decorated. Quiet garden gazebo. Walking distance to historic downtown Flagstaff. Some rooms w/fireplace. 3 whirlpool rooms; 2 stories; interior/exterior corridors; smoke free premises. **Services:** complimentary evening beverages. **All Rooms:** combo or shower baths.
Cards: MC, VI. **Special Amenities:** Free breakfast.

THE INN AT NAU

Phone: 520/523-1616

5/9-9/7	1P: $79-$89	2P: $79-$89	XP: $10 F5
3/14-5/8 & 9/8-1/31	1P: $69	2P: $69	XP: $10 F5
2/1-3/13	1P: $54	2P: $54	XP: $10 F5

Motel

Location: I-40 exit 195B and I-17 exit 341 to McConnell, 1.5 mi via McConnell and San Francisco St to Bldg 33 NAU campus. San Francisco Bldg 33 NAU 86011 (PO Box 5606). Fax: 520/523-1625. **Terms:** [ECP] meal plan. **Facility:** 19 rooms. Nicely decorated rooms with workstations. 1 story; interior corridors; smoke free premises; 8 tennis courts. **Recreation:** sports court.
All Rooms: combo or shower baths, safes. **Cards:** AE, MC, VI.

INN SUITES HOTEL

Phone: (520)774-7356

5/28-9/6	1P: $67-$195	2P: $67-$195	XP: $5	F18
9/7-1/31	1P: $49-$145	2P: $49-$145	XP: $5	F18
2/1-5/27	1P: $44-$145	2P: $44-$145	XP: $5	F18

(AAA) (SAVE) ◆◆
Motel

Location: On US 89, 180 and I-40 business loop; from I-40 exit 198, 1 mi n to Rte 66. 1008 E Route 66 86001. Fax: 520/556-0130. **Terms:** [BP] meal plan; weekly & monthly rates avail; pets, $25 dep req. **Facility:** 134 rooms. Complimentary barbecue for guests-Wed. Guest rooms and suites avail. Across from railroad tracks. Breakfast buffet included in room rate. 2 two-bedroom units. 16 larger suites with kitchenettes & whirlpool, $79-$139; 2 stories; exterior corridors; heated pool, seasonal pool, indoor whirlpool; playground. **Services:** complimentary evening beverages. **Recreation:** televisions with video game systems. **Some Rooms:** 15 efficiencies. **Cards:** AE, CB, DI, DS, MC, VI. **Special Amenities: Free breakfast and free local telephone calls.** *(See color ad p 185)*

JEANETTE'S BED & BREAKFAST

Phone: (520)527-1912

2/1-4/30 & 11/1-1/31	1P: $79	2P: $85-$130	XP: $20
5/1-10/31	1P: $89	2P: $99	XP: $20

(AAA) (SAVE) ◆◆◆
Bed & Breakfast

Location: Acc From US 180, 89 and I-40 business loop; from I-40 at exit 201, then 0.5 mi w, just n of Rte 66. 3380 E Lockett Rd 86004. Fax: 520/527-1713. **Terms:** [BP] meal plan; check-in 4 pm; 7 day cancellation notice; cancellation fee imposed. **Facility:** 4 rooms. Stately Victorian style two-story home. Bathrooms with vintage claw foot tubs and showers featuring hand made toiletry soap. Rooms with fireplace or porch avail. Smoke free premesis. 2 stories; interior corridors; smoke free premises. **Services:** complimentary evening beverages. **Cards:** AE, DS, MC, VI. **Special Amenities: Free breakfast and free local telephone calls.**

LA QUINTA INN & SUITES

Phone: (520)556-8666

All Year   1P: $65-$85   2P: $65-$85

(AAA) (SAVE) ◆◆◆
Motel

Location: Nw of jct I-40 and I-17, from I-40 exit 195B, just n to Forest Meadow, then just w. 2015 S Beulah Blvd 86001. Fax: 520/214-9140. **Terms:** [ECP] meal plan; package plans, winter; small pets only. **Facility:** 128 rooms. Attractively decorated rooms and public areas. Near Northern Arizona University. 4 suites with workstation; 3-4 stories; interior corridors; heated pool, whirlpool. **Recreation:** TV's have video game systems. **All Rooms:** combo or shower baths. **Cards:** AE, CB, DI, DS, JC, MC, VI. **Special Amenities: Free breakfast and free local telephone calls.**

LITTLE AMERICA HOTEL

Phone: (520)779-2741

5/1-10/31	1P: $119-$129	2P: $119-$129	XP: $10	F10
3/10-4/30 & 11/1-1/31	1P: $89-$99	2P: $89-$99	XP: $10	F10
2/1-3/9	1P: $79-$89	2P: $79-$89	XP: $10	F10

(AAA) (SAVE) ◆◆◆
Hotel

Location: Adjacent to I-40, exit 198. 2515 E Butler Ave 86004 (PO Box 3900, 86003). Fax: 520/779-7983. **Terms:** Check-in 4 pm. **Facility:** 246 rooms. Tree-shaded grounds. Large luxurious rooms. 2 two-bedroom apartments; 2 stories; interior corridors; heated pool, pool open 5/1-10/31; playground. **Dining:** Dining room, coffee shop; 6 am-11 pm; $8-$25; cocktails; also, Western Gold Dining Room, see separate listing; entertainment. **Services:** gift shop. **Recreation:** jogging, video game systems on TV's. **All Rooms:** extended cable TV. **Some Rooms:** Fee: VCR. **Cards:** AE, CB, DI, DS, MC, VI. **Special Amenities: Free newspaper.** *(See color ad below)*

MOUNTAIN COUNTRY CONDOS
◆◆◆   All Year   Phone: 520/526-4287
Condominium   **Location:** I-40, exit 201; 0.7 mi s on Country Club Dr to Oakmont, then just w. 2380 N Oakmont Dr 86004. Fax: 520/526-4910. **Terms:** Check-in 4 pm; 3 day cancellation notice; cancellation fee imposed. **Facility:** 19 rooms. A variety of 1, 2 and 3-bedroom condos situated throughout a residential area. 8 two-bedroom units, 2 three-bedroom units. 1 story; exterior corridors; 10 lighted tennis courts. Fee: 18 holes golf. **Services:** Fee: massage. **All Rooms:** kitchens. **Cards:** AE, DS, MC, VI.

QUALITY INN
(AAA) (SAVE)   Phone: (520)774-8771
        5/1-9/4   1P: $69-$129   2P: $69-$129   XP: $5   F18
        9/5-10/31   1P: $59-$119   2P: $59-$119   XP: $5   F18
◆◆◆   2/1-4/30 & 11/1-1/31 1P: $49-$109   2P: $49-$109   XP: $5   F18
Motel   **Location:** 0.5 mi n of jct I-17 and I-40; exit 195B. 2000 S Milton Rd 86001. Fax: 520/773-9382. **Facility:** 96 rooms. Attractively decorated contemporary-style rooms. 2 stories; interior corridors. **Dining:** Restaurant nearby. **Recreation:** pool open 5/1-10/1. **All Rooms:** combo or shower baths, extended cable TV. **Cards:** AE, CB, DI, DS, JC, MC, VI. **Special Amenities: Free local telephone calls and free newspaper.**

RADISSON WOODLANDS HOTEL FLAGSTAFF
◆◆◆   Phone: (520)773-8888
        5/1-10/31   1P: $119-$139   2P: $119-$139   XP: $10
Hotel   1/1-1/31   1P: $99-$129   2P: $99-$129   XP: $10
        11/1-12/31   1P: $99-$119   2P: $99-$119   XP: $10
        2/1-4/30   1P: $99   2P: $99   XP: $10
Location: 1.8 mi nw of jct I-40 and I-17. From I-40 westbound, exit 195B, 1.5 mi n, then 0.5 mi w on Rt 66, Eastbound use exit 191, then 2 mi e. 1175 W Route 66 86001. Fax: 520/773-0597. **Terms:** 3 day cancellation notice; cancellation fee imposed; package plans. **Facility:** 183 rooms. Beautifully decorated public areas and guest rooms. Oriental motif. 3-4 stories; interior corridors; heated pool. **Services:** gift shop. **All Rooms:** combo or shower baths. **Some Rooms:** Fee: VCR. **Cards:** AE, CB, DI, DS, JC, MC, VI. *(See color ad below & p 196)*

RAMADA LIMITED
◆◆◆   Phone: (520)773-1111
        4/1-9/30   1P: $69   2P: $89   XP: $10   F17
Motel   10/1-10/31   1P: $59   2P: $69   XP: $10   F17
        2/1-3/31 & 11/1-1/31 1P: $49   2P: $59   XP: $10   F17
Location: NW of jct I-40 and I-17. From I-40 exit 195B, just n to Forest Meadows St, then w to Beulah Rd, then just s. 2755 Woodlands Village Blvd 86001. Fax: 520/774-1449. **Terms:** [ECP] meal plan; 30 day cancellation notice; cancellation fee imposed; pets, $25 dep req. **Facility:** 89 rooms. Across from shopping center. 2 stories; exterior corridors; heated pool. **Cards:** AE, CB, DI, DS, JC, MC, VI.

RAMADA LIMITED-LUCKY LANE
(AAA) (SAVE)   Phone: (520)779-3614
        5/16-9/15   1P: $59-$69   2P: $65-$75   XP: $10   F17
        4/1-5/15   1P: $44-$54   2P: $49-$59   XP: $10   F17
◆◆   2/1-3/31 & 9/16-1/31 1P: $35-$49   2P: $44-$49   XP: $10   F17
Motel   **Location:** Adjacent to I-40, exit 198. 2350 E Lucky Ln 86004. Fax: 520/774-5834. **Terms:** [CP] meal plan; pets, $5 extra charge. **Facility:** 102 rooms. 2-3 stories, no elevator; exterior corridors; heated pool, pool closed 10/1-4/30. **Dining:** Restaurant nearby. **Cards:** AE, CB, DI, DS, JC, MC, VI. **Special Amenities: Free breakfast and free local telephone calls.** *(See color ad p 188)*

RED ROOF INN
Phone: (520)779-5121

	5/1-8/31	1P: $39-$69	2P: $44-$74	XP: $5	F18
	9/1-10/31	1P: $34-$54	2P: $39-$59	XP: $5	F18
	2/1-4/30 & 11/1-1/31	1P: $29-$49	2P: $34-$54	XP: $5	F18

Motel   **Location:** I-40 exit 198, just e on Lucky Ln. 2520 E Lucky Ln 86004. Fax: 520/774-3809. **Terms:** [CP] meal plan; 14 day cancellation notice; small pets only. **Facility:** 139 rooms. In a motel and commercial area next to freeway. 2 stories; exterior corridors; heated pool, seasonal pool, indoor whirlpool. **Cards:** AE, CB, DI, DS, JC, MC, VI.

RESIDENCE INN BY MARRIOTT
Phone: (520)526-5555

5/1-9/30	2P: $160
2/1-4/30 & 10/1-1/31	2P: $130

Apartment   **Location:** Just s of I-40, exit 201. 3440 N Country Club Dr 86004. Fax: 520/527-0328. **Terms:** [ECP] meal plan; check-in 4 pm; cancellation fee imposed; small pets only, $10 extra charge. **Facility:** 102 rooms. Nicely decorated studio and 2-bedroom suites with kitchen. Many with fireplace. 24 two-bedroom units. 2 stories; exterior corridors. **Recreation:** sports court. **All Rooms:** combo or shower baths. **Cards:** AE, CB, DI, DS, MC, VI.

SLEEP INN
Phone: (520)556-3000

5/16-9/6	1P: $59-$89	2P: $69-$99	XP: $10	F18
9/7-1/31	1P: $55-$65	2P: $65-$85	XP: $5	F18
2/1-5/15	1P: $49-$59	2P: $59-$79	XP: $5	F18

Motel   **Location:** Nw of jct I-40 and I-17. From I-40 exit 195B, just n to Forest Meadows St, then w to Beaulah Rd, then just s. 2765 S Woodlands Village Blvd 86001. Fax: 520/774-1901. **Terms:** [CP] meal plan. **Facility:** 58 rooms. 2 stories; interior corridors; heated pool. **All Rooms:** combo or shower baths. **Cards:** AE, CB, DI, DS, JC, MC, VI.

SUPER 8 MOTEL
Phone: (520)526-0818

6/1-9/30	1P: $54-$64	2P: $54-$74	XP: $5	F18
4/1-5/31	1P: $49-$59	2P: $49-$69	XP: $5	F18
2/1-3/31 & 10/1-1/31	1P: $44-$54	2P: $44-$59	XP: $5	F18

Motel   **Location:** US 180, 89 and I-40 Business Loop, 0.5 mi w of jct I-40, exit 201. 3725 N Kasper Ave 86004. Fax: 520/526-8786. **Terms:** Pets. **Facility:** 90 rooms. 0.5 mi w of Flagstaff Mall, on busy commercial street across from railroad tracks. 2 stories; interior corridors. **All Rooms:** combo or shower baths. **Cards:** AE, CB, DI, DS, MC, VI.

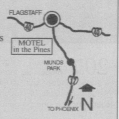

UNIVERSITY/GRAND CANYON TRAVELODGE   Phone: (520)774-3381

(AAA) (SAVE)   5/1-9/20   1P: $45-$80   2P: $45-$80
◆   2/1-4/30 & 9/21-1/31   1P: $30-$40   2P: $30-$40
Motel   **Location:** I-40 exit 191 then 2 mi e. 801 W Highway 66 86001. **Fax:** 520/774-1648. **Terms:** Pets, $25 dep req.
                     Facility: 49 rooms. 8 two-bedroom units. 8 family units, $39-$89; 2 stories; exterior corridors; sauna, whirlpool.
                     All Rooms: combo or shower baths. **Some Rooms:** Fee: refrigerators. **Cards:** AE, CB, DI, DS, MC, VI.
Special Amenities: Free breakfast and free newspaper.

--------- **RESTAURANTS** ---------

BEAVER STREET BREWERY & WHISTLE STOP CAFE   **Lunch:** $7-$9   **Dinner:** $7-$15   **Phone:** 520/779-0079
◆◆   **Location:** Downtown, just s of railroad tracks. 11 S Beaver St 86001. **Hours:** 11:30 am-midnight; in winter,
American   11:30 am-11 pm. Closed: 1/1, 11/23, 12/25. **Features:** children's menu; cocktails & lounge. Casual
                     atmosphere. Menu features soups, fondues, salads, sandwiches and wood-fired pizzas. A selection of
entrees also availiable at dinner. Several ales and beers brewed on premises. Smoke free premises. **Cards:** AE, DS,
MC, VI.

BLACK BART'S STEAK HOUSE & MUSICAL REVUE   **Dinner:** $11-$25   **Phone:** 520/779-3142
◆◆   **Location:** Adjacent to I-40 at exit 198 e 0.5 mi. 2760 E Buner Ave 86004. **Hours:** 5 pm-9 pm, Fri & Sat to
Steakhouse   10 pm. Closed: 11/23, 12/24 & 12/25. **Features:** children's menu; cocktails; entertainment. Oak broiled steak,
                     seafood, chicken and prime rib in a unique atmosphere. Musical revue provided nightly while you dine.
Smoke free premises. **Cards:** AE, DI, DS, MC, VI.

BUSTER'S   **Lunch:** $5-$9   **Dinner:** $9-$18   **Phone:** 520/774-5155
◆◆   **Location:** 0.5 mi n of jct I-40 and I-17 on e side of Milton Rd; In Green Tree Village. 1800 S Milton Rd
American   86001. **Hours:** 11:30 am-10 pm. Closed: 11/23 & 12/25. **Reservations:** accepted. **Features:** casual dress;
                     children's menu; early bird specials; cocktails & lounge. Casual dining in a lively atmosphere. Salad,
sandwiches and entrees. Daily selection of fresh seafood. Smoke free premises. **Cards:** AE, CB, DI, DS, MC, VI.

CHEZ MARC BISTRO   **Lunch:** $8-$15   **Dinner:** $20-$30   **Phone:** 520/774-1343
◆◆◆   **Location:** On US 180 (Humphreys St), just n of Rt 66. 503 Humphreys St 86001. **Hours:** 5 pm-9 pm;
French   10/1-5/30 Thur-Sun 11:30 am-2:30 pm. **Reservations:** suggested. **Features:** semi-formal attire; Sunday
                     brunch; children's menu; carryout; cocktails & lounge; a la carte. Fine dining in a charming, historic house.
Cuisine excellently prepared and served. Smoke free premises. **Cards:** AE, CB, DI, DS, MC, VI.

COTTAGE PLACE RESTAURANT   **Dinner:** $15-$25   **Phone:** 520/774-8431
(AAA)   **Location:** Just s of Downtown, just w of Beaver St. 126 W Cottage Ave 86001. **Hours:** 5 pm-9:30 pm.
◆◆◆   Closed: Mon. **Reservations:** suggested. **Features:** No A/C; casual dress; children's menu; beer & wine only;
Continental   street parking. Fine dining in a restored 1909 bungalow. Classical background music. Nice selection of
                     International entrees. Smoke free premises. **Cards:** AE, MC, VI.

DOWN UNDER NEW ZEALAND RESTAURANT   **Lunch:** $6-$11   **Dinner:** $12-$25   **Phone:** 520/774-6677
◆◆◆   **Location:** Downtown, s of Rt 66, cross street Leroux. 6 E Aspen Ave 86001. **Hours:** 7:30 am-10 pm, to 9
English   pm, off season, Sat 9 am-10 pm, Sun 10 am-9 pm. **Features:** Sunday brunch; children's menu; carryout;
                     cocktails & lounge; fee for parking. Casual fine dining featuring New Zealand lamb and venison. Kangaroo,
rabbit, seafood, beef and pork. Vegetarian dishes and specialty desserts. Seasonal patio dining. Smoke free premises.
Cards: AE, MC, VI.

HORSEMEN LODGE   **Dinner:** $11-$18   **Phone:** 520/526-2655
(AAA)   **Location:** On US 89; 3.5 mi n of I-40 exit 201. 8500 Hwy 89 N 86004. **Hours:** 5 pm-10 pm. Closed major
                     holidays11/23 & 12/25, Sun & Mon in winter, Sun in summer. **Reservations:** suggested. **Features:** casual
◆◆   dress; children's menu; carryout; salad bar; cocktails & lounge. Old West atmosphere. Oak-smoked
American   barbecue ribs and chicken. Also steaks, veal and trout. **Cards:** MC, VI.

JAKE'S EAST SIDE BAR & GRILL   **Lunch:** $4-$9   **Dinner:** $10-$20   **Phone:** 520/526-4840
◆◆   **Location:** On US 89N, at interchange I-40, exit 201. 4217 N Hwy 89 86004. **Hours:** 11 am-9 pm. Closed:
American   1/1, 11/23, 12/25 & Sun 2/1-3/31. **Features:** casual dress; children's menu; carryout; cocktails & lounge.
                     Casual family dining. Specializing in St. Louis barbecue pork baby back ribs. Fresh seafood. Locally owned.
Smoke free premises. **Cards:** AE, MC, VI.

KELLY'S CHRISTMAS TREE   **Lunch:** $4-$12   **Dinner:** $9-$24   **Phone:** 520/526-0776
◆◆   **Location:** Just s of I-40, exit 201 via Country Club Rd; in Continental Shopping Plaza. 5200 E Cortland Blvd
American   86004. **Hours:** 11:30 am-3 & 5-10 pm, Sun from 5 pm. Closed: 1/1 & 12/25. **Reservations:** suggested.
                     Features: casual dress; children's menu; early bird specials; carryout; cocktails & lounge. Festive Early
American decor. Prime rib, lamb, steak, seafood and house specialty of chicken and dumplings. Home-made pastries.
Smoke free premises. **Cards:** AE, MC, VI.

MAMMA LUISA   **Dinner:** $8-$17   **Phone:** 520/526-6809
◆◆   **Location:** On US 180 and 89, just n of E Route 66, in Kachina Square Shopping Center. 2710 N Steves
Italian   Blvd 86004. **Hours:** 5 pm-10 pm. Closed: 11/23 & 12/25. **Reservations:** suggested. **Features:** casual dress;
                     children's menu; carryout; cocktails. Small, cozy restaurant with a nice selection of pasta, veal, seafood and
chicken. Vegetarian dishes avail. Smoke free premises. **Cards:** AE, DI, DS, MC, VI.

MARC'S CAFE AMERICAN   **Lunch:** $7-$11   **Dinner:** $9-$19   **Phone:** 520/556-0093
◆◆◆   **Location:** 801 S Milton Rd 86001. **Hours:** 11 am-2:30 & 4:30-9 pm. **Features:** casual dress; children's
American   menu; carryout; cocktails. Nice selection of appetizers, meat, poultry, seafood, steaks and pastas with a
                     French brasserie accent. Extensive wine selection. Smoke free premises. **Cards:** AE, DI, DS, MC, VI.

SAKURA RESTAURANT   **Lunch:** $5-$9   **Dinner:** $11-$17   **Phone:** 520/773-9118
◆◆◆   **Location:** 1.8 mi nw of jct I-40 and I-17. From I-40 westbound, exit 195B, 1.5 mi n, then 0.5 mi w on Rt 66,
Ethnic   Eastbound use exit 191, then 2 mi e; in Radisson Woodlands Hotel Flagstaff. 1175 W Rt 66 86001.
         Hours: 11:30 am-2 & 5-10 pm, Sun 5 pm-10 pm. Closed: 11/23. **Reservations:** suggested.
Features: casual dress; cocktails. Attractive restaurant with Teppanyaki style cooking. Smoke free premises. **Cards:** AE, CB,
DI, DS, JC, MC, VI. *(See color ad p 187)*
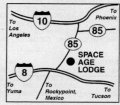

WESTERN GOLD DINING ROOM   **Lunch:** $7   **Dinner:** $15-$22   **Phone:** 520/779-2741
◆◆◆   **Location:** Adjacent to I-40, exit 198, in Little America Hotel. 2515 E Butler Ave 86004. **Hours:** 11 am-2 &
American   5-10 pm, Sat & Sun from 5 pm. **Reservations:** suggested. **Features:** casual dress; Sunday brunch; cocktails
         & lounge; entertainment; a la carte. Attractive dining room with nice selection of American and continental
cuisine, including rack of lamb and Chateaubriand. Luncheon buffet. Smoke free premises. **Cards:** AE, CB, DI, DS, MC, VI.

FLORENCE pop. 7,500

──── LODGINGS ────

BLUE MIST MOTEL   **Phone:** (520)868-5875
AAA [SAVE]   All Year   1P: $35-$45   2P: $50-$60   XP: $10
◆   **Location:** On SR 79 at jct SR 287. 40 S Pinal Pkwy 85232. Fax: 520/868-0660. **Terms:** 3 day cancellation no-
Motel   tice. **Facility:** 22 rooms. 7 kitchens, $5 extra; 1 story; exterior corridors. **All Rooms:** combo or shower baths.
         Cards: AE, CB, DI, DS, JC, MC, VI. **Special Amenities:** Early check-in/late check-out and free local tele-
         phone calls.

RANCHO SONORA INN   **Phone:** 520/868-8000
◆◆   2/1-4/30 & 1/1-1/31   1P: $69   2P: $74   XP: $10   F10
Motel   10/1-12/31   1P: $64   2P: $69   XP: $10   F10
         5/1-9/30   1P: $54   2P: $59   XP: $10   F10
Location: On SR 79, 5 mi s of SR 287. 9198 N Hwy 79 85232. Fax: 520/868-8000. **Terms:** [CP] meal plan; 7 day cancella-
tion notice; pets. **Facility:** 9 rooms. Located in a quiet desert location. Adobe style buildings face into a charming patio area.
Also, one 1-bedroom and one 2-bedroom cottage with kitchen. 1 two-bedroom unit. 1 story; exterior corridors; designated
smoking area; putting green; heated pool. **All Rooms:** combo or shower baths. **Some Rooms:** 4 efficiencies. **Cards:** AE, CB,
DI, MC, VI.

FOREST LAKES pop. 350

──── LODGING ────

FOREST LAKES LODGE   **Phone:** (520)535-4727
AAA [SAVE]   5/7-9/30   1P: $41-$69   2P: $49-$69   XP: $10   F12
         10/1-1/31   1P: $41-$59   2P: $49-$59
◆◆   2/1-5/6   1P: $41-$59   2P: $49-$59   XP: $10   F12
Motel   **Location:** SR 260, 16 mi w of Heber. 85931 (PO Box 1947). **Terms:** [CP] meal plan; pets, $10 extra charge.
         Facility: 20 rooms. In an attractive forest setting. 2 stories; exterior corridors. **Recreation:** Limited TV viewing.
Cards: AE, MC, VI. **Special Amenities:** Free breakfast and free local telephone calls.

FOUNTAIN HILLS —*See Phoenix p. 259.*

GILA BEND pop. 1,700

──── LODGINGS ────

BEST WESTERN SPACE AGE LODGE   **Phone:** (520)683-2273
AAA [SAVE]   2/1-3/31 & 12/16-1/31   1P: $64-$74   2P: $69-$79   XP: $5   F17
◆◆◆   4/1-12/15   1P: $49-$59   2P: $54-$64   XP: $5   F17
Motor Inn   **Location:** Business Loop I-8, in center of town. 401 E Pima St 85337 (PO Box C). Fax: 520/683-2273.
         Terms: Pets. **Facility:** 41 rooms. Contemporary space age decor. 1 story; exterior corridors; whirlpool.
         Dining: Coffee shop; 24 hours; $5-$10. **Services:** gift shop. **Cards:** AE, CB, DI, DS, MC, VI.
Special Amenities: Free local telephone calls and preferred room (subject to availability with advanced reserva-
tions). *(See ad below)*

SUPER 8 MOTEL

◆

Motel

			Phone: 520/683-6311
2/1-2/29	1P: $59	2P: $62	XP: $5 F12
8/16-9/30	1P: $50	2P: $50	XP: $5 F12
3/1-5/15	1P: $45	2P: $50	XP: $5 F12
5/16-8/15	1P: $41	2P: $45	XP: $4 F12

Location: Just w of I-8, exit 119. 2888 Butterfield Tr 85337 (PO Box 993). Fax: 520/683-2120. **Terms:** Open 2/1-9/30; 10 day cancellation notice; pets, $10 extra charge. **Facility:** 63 rooms. 3 stories; interior corridors. **Cards:** AE, CB, DI, DS, MC, VI.

⟦ASK⟧ ⟦S/D⟧ ⟦🛏⟧ ⟦¶↑⟧ ⟦✕⟧ ⟦🎬⟧ ⟦🏊⟧

GLENDALE —See Phoenix p. 260.

GLOBE pop. 6,100

—— LODGINGS ——

COMFORT INN

◆◆

Motel

Phone: 520/425-7575

Property failed to provide current rates

Location: 1 mi e on US 60. 1515 South St 85501. Fax: 520/425-4062. **Terms:** [CP] meal plan; pets. **Facility:** 52 rooms. 2 stories; exterior corridors; heated pool. **Cards:** AE, CB, DI, DS, JC, MC, VI.

⟦S/D⟧ ⟦🛏⟧ ⟦¶↑⟧ ⟦✕⟧ ⟦🎬⟧ ⟦🖨⟧ ⟦▤⟧ ⟦📁⟧ ⟦DATA PORT⟧ ⟦🏊⟧

COPPER MANOR MOTEL

◆

Motel

Phone: (520)425-7124

All Year   1P: $36-$40   2P: $39-$45

Location: 0.5 mi e on US 60. 637 E Ash St 85501. Fax: 520/425-5266. **Facility:** 39 rooms. Modest rooms. 2 stories; exterior corridors; heated pool. **Cards:** AE, CB, DI, DS, MC, VI.

⟦ASK⟧ ⟦¶↑⟧ ⟦✕⟧ ⟦🎬⟧ ⟦🖨⟧ ⟦📁⟧ ⟦🏊⟧

DAYS INN

⟦AAA⟧ ⟦SAVE⟧

◆◆◆

Motel

Phone: (520)425-5500

All Year   1P: $49-$65   2P: $52-$69   XP: $5   F17

Location: 1.3 mi e on US 60. 1630 E Ash St 85501. Fax: 520/425-4146. **Terms:** [CP] meal plan; cancellation fee imposed. **Facility:** 42 rooms. 2 stories; exterior corridors; whirlpool; pool heated 11/1-3/15. **Dining:** Restaurant nearby. **Cards:** AE, CB, DI, DS, MC, VI.

⟦S/D⟧ ⟦¶↑⟧ ⟦🐕⟧ ⟦✕⟧ ⟦🎬⟧ ⟦🖨⟧ ⟦▢⟧ ⟦📁⟧ ⟦DATA PORT⟧ ⟦🏊⟧

HOLIDAY INN EXPRESS-GLOBE

◆◆

Motel

			Phone: (520)425-7008
9/1-1/31	1P: $68	2P: $68	
2/1-4/30	1P: $65	2P: $65	
5/1-8/31	1P: $60	2P: $60	

Location: 4 mi w on US 60. 2119 Hwy 60 85501 (PO Box 1043, 85502). Fax: 520/425-6410. **Terms:** [CP] meal plan; small pets only. **Facility:** 45 rooms. 2 stories; interior corridors. **Cards:** AE, CB, DI, DS, MC, VI. *(See ad below)*

⟦ASK⟧ ⟦S/D⟧ ⟦🛏⟧ ⟦🐕⟧ ⟦♨⟧ ⟦✕⟧ ⟦🎬⟧ ⟦🖨⟧ ⟦📁⟧ ⟦DATA PORT⟧

RAMADA LIMITED

⟦AAA⟧ ⟦SAVE⟧

◆◆◆

Motel

Phone: (520)425-5741

All Year   1P: $47-$59   2P: $52-$75   XP: $10   F18

Location: 1.3 mi e on US 60. 1699 E Ash St 85501 (PO Box 85502). Fax: 520/402-8466. **Terms:** 14 day cancellation notice; pets, $20 extra charge. **Facility:** 80 rooms. Minimal landscaping. 3 two-bedroom units. 2 room suite with 3-4 beds $62-85 for up to 6 persons; 10 whirlpool rooms, $60-$65; 2 stories; interior/exterior corridors; heated pool, whirlpool. **Cards:** AE, CB, DI, DS, MC, VI. **Special Amenities:** Free breakfast and free local telephone calls.

⟦S/D⟧ ⟦🛏⟧ ⟦🐕⟧ ⟦♨⟧ ⟦✕⟧ ⟦🎬⟧ ⟦🖨⟧ ⟦📁⟧ ⟦🏊⟧

GOLD CANYON

―――― LODGING ――――

―――― *The following lodging was either not inspected or did not* ――――
meet AAA rating requirements but is listed for your information only.

BEST WESTERN GOLD CANYON INN & SUITES | | | **Phone:** 480/671-6000
(fyi)
	2/1-4/15	1P: $129-$149	2P: $129-$149	XP: $10	F12
	1/1-1/31	1P: $109-$129	2P: $109-$129	XP: $10	F12
Motel	10/16-12/31	1P: $69-$99	2P: $69-$99	XP: $10	F12
	4/16-10/15	1P: $59-$89	2P: $59-$89	XP: $10	F12

Too new to rate, opening scheduled for September 1999. **Location:** 7 mi e of Apache Junction, on ne corner of Hwy 60 and Kings Ranch Rd. 8333 E Sunrise Sky 85219. Fax: 480/671-0013. **Amenities:** 68 rooms, radios, coffeemakers, microwaves, refrigerators, pool, exercise facilities. **Cards:** AE, CB, DI, DS, MC, VI.

GOODYEAR —*See Phoenix p. 260.*

GRAND CANYON NATIONAL PARK —*See also FLAGSTAFF & WILLIAMS.*

―――――――――――――――――――――――――――――――
GRAND CANYON NATIONAL PARK-South Rim
―――――――――――――――――――――――――――――――
―――― LODGINGS ――――

BEST WESTERN GRAND CANYON SQUIRE INN | | | **Phone:** (520)638-2681
(AAA) (SAVE)
♦♦♦
	4/2-11/18	1P: $105-$175	2P: $105-$175	XP: $10	F12
	3/21-4/1	1P: $75-$125	2P: $75-$125	XP: $10	F12
Hotel	2/1-3/20 & 11/19-1/31	1P: $60-110	2P: $60-110	XP: $10	F12

Location: On SR 64 in Tusayan; 9 mi s of Grand Canyon Village, outside park boundary. 86023 (PO Box 130, Hwy 64). Fax: 520/638-0162. **Terms:** Check-in 4 pm. **Facility:** 250 rooms. Large, attractive lobby. A variety of accommodations from standard to spacious. Attractively decorated rooms and suites. Suites, $200-$225; 2-3 stories; interior/exterior corridors; wading pool, sauna, heated pool in summer; 2 tennis courts. **Dining:** Coffee shop; other limited food service avail in recreation center; $7-$18; cocktails; also, Coronado Room-In Best Western Grand Canyon Squire Inn, see separate listing. **Services:** gift shop. Fee: massage. **Recreation:** indoor whirlpool; bowling, recreation center. **All Rooms:** combo or shower baths, extended cable TV. **Cards:** AE, DI, DS, MC, VI. *(See color ad p 194)*

⊡ ✈ 🍴 🍸 🐾 🛁 👧 🔌 ✕ 💻 [DATA PORT] 🏊 👷 ✕

EL TOVAR HOTEL | | | **Phone:** 303/297-2757
♦♦♦
| | All Year | 1P: $118-$199 | 2P: $118-$199 | XP: $9 | F16 |
| Historic Hotel | | | | | |

Location: At Grand Canyon Village South Rim. 86023 (PO Box 699). Fax: 303/297-3175. **Terms:** Check-in 4 pm; cancellation fee imposed; kennels avail $10-$12.50. **Facility:** 78 rooms. Historic hotel on the rim, built in 1905. A variety of nicely furnished rooms, from small to spacious. 4 one-bedroom suites with canyon view. Limited parking. 3 stories, no elevator; interior corridors. **Services:** gift shop. **Cards:** AE, CB, DI, DS, JC, MC, VI. *(See ad p 195)*

🍴 🍸 ✕

GRAND CANYON QUALITY INN & SUITES | | | **Phone:** (520)638-2673
♦♦♦
| | 4/1-10/21 | 1P: $118-$188 | 2P: $118-$188 | XP: $10 | F18 |
| Motor Inn | 2/1-3/31 & 10/22-1/31 | 1P: $73-$98 | 2P: $73-$98 | XP: $10 | F18 |

Location: Just w of SR 64 in Tusayan; 9 mi s of Grand Canyon Village outside park boundary. 86023 (PO Box 520, GRAND CANYON). Fax: 520/638-9537. **Terms:** Cancellation fee imposed. **Facility:** 232 rooms. Located behind the Imax Theatre. Large enclosed atrium. 3 stories; interior/exterior corridors; heated pool. **Services:** gift shop. **All Rooms:** combo or shower baths. **Some Rooms:** honor bars. **Cards:** AE, CB, DI, DS, JC, MC, VI.

[SAVE] ⊡ 🍴 🐾 👧 🔌 ✕ 🎾 💻 📷 🛗 [DATA PORT] 🏊

GRAND CANYON SUITES

Motel

			Phone: (520)638-3100
8/1-10/15	1P: $129-$159	2P: $129-$159	XP: $10 F19
4/1-7/31	1P: $119-$129	2P: $119-$129	XP: $10 F19
2/1-3/31 & 10/16-1/31	1P: $79-$109	2P: $79-$109	XP: $10 F19

Location: 2 mi s of South Rim entrance. (PO Box 3251, GRAND CANYON, 86023). Fax: 520/638-2747. **Terms:** [CP] meal plan; 3 day cancellation notice; cancellation fee imposed. **Facility:** 32 rooms. 2 two-bedroom units. Interior corridors; smoke free premises. **Dining:** Restaurant nearby. **Cards:** AE, MC, VI. **Special Amenities:** Free breakfast and free local telephone calls. *(See color ad below)*

GRAND HOTEL & CANYON STAR

Hotel

			Phone: (520)638-3333
6/17-10/20	1P: $119-$138	2P: $119-$138	XP: $10 F18
3/25-6/16	1P: $89-$110	2P: $89-$110	XP: $10 F18
2/1-3/24	1P: $69-$89	2P: $69-$89	XP: $10 F18
10/21-1/31	1P: $69-$89	2P: $89	XP: $10 F18

Location: SR 64; 9 mi s of Grand Canyon Village, outside park boundary. (P O Box 3319, GRAND CANYON, 86023). Fax: 520/638-3131. **Terms:** Check-in 4 pm; 14 day cancellation notice; cancellation fee imposed. **Facility:** 121 rooms. 3 stories; interior corridors; heated pool, whirlpool. **Dining:** Restaurant; 6:30 am-10 pm, 7 am-10 pm in winter; $14-$22; cocktails; entertainment. **Services:** gift shop. **Cards:** AE, DS, MC, VI. *(See color ad below)*

HOLIDAY INN EXPRESS GRAND CANYON

	8/1-10/15	1P: $119-$139	2P: $119-$139	XP: $10	F19
	4/1-7/31	1P: $99-$129	2P: $99-$129	XP: $10	F19
	2/1-3/31 & 10/16-1/31	1P: $59-$95	2P: $59-$95	XP: $10	F19

Phone: (520)638-3000

Motel   **Location:** On SR 64; 7 mi s of Grand Canyon Village, outside park boundary. (PO Box 3245, GRAND CANYON, 86023). Fax: 520/638-0123. **Terms:** [ECP] meal plan; check-in 4 pm; 3 day cancellation notice; cancellation fee imposed. **Facility:** 165 rooms. 3 stories; interior corridors. **Dining:** Restaurants nearby. **All Rooms:** combo or shower baths. **Cards:** AE, CB, DI, DS, JC, MC, VI. **Special Amenities:** Free breakfast and free local telephone calls.
(See color ad p 193)

KACHINA LODGE

	All Year	1P: $124	2P: $124	XP: $9	F16

Phone: 303/297-2757

Motel   **Location:** At Grand Canyon Village South Rim. (PO Box 699, 86023). Fax: 303/297-3175. **Terms:** Check-in 4 pm; cancellation fee imposed; kennels avail $10-$12.50 extra charge. **Facility:** 49 rooms. Registration at El Tovar Hotel. A modern lodge building at the rim. Many rooms face the canyon. Limited parking. 2 stories; interior corridors. **Cards:** AE, CB, DI, DS, JC, MC, VI.

MASWIK LODGE
◆◆   2/1-11/5   1P: $118   2P: $118   Phone: 303/297-2757
Motor Inn   11/6-1/31   1P: $65   2P: $65   XP: $9   F16
XP: $9   F16
Location: (PO Box 699, 86023). Fax: 303/297-3175. **Terms:** Check-in 4 pm; cancellation fee imposed; kennels avail $8-$13. **Facility:** 278 rooms. In southwest area of village. Modern motel units and quad cabins on several acres of grounds. 2 stories; exterior corridors. **Services:** gift shop. **All Rooms:** combo or shower baths. **Cards:** AE, CB, DI, DS, JC, MC, VI. (See ad below)

MOQUI LODGE
◆◆   4/1-11/1   1P: $94   2P: $94   Phone: 303/297-2757
Motor Inn   **Location:** On SR 64, 8 mi s of Grand Canyon Village, 0.5 mi s of entrance station. (PO Box 369, 86023).   XP: $12   F14
Fax: 303/297-3175. **Terms:** Open 4/1-11/1; [BP] meal plan; check-in 4 pm; 48 day cancellation notice; cancellation fee imposed. **Facility:** 136 rooms. Rustic buildings. Located just north of Tusayan. 2 stories; exterior corridors. **Services:** gift shop. **Recreation:** Fee: horseback riding. **All Rooms:** combo or shower baths. **Cards:** AE, CB, DI, DS, JC, MC, VI. (See ad below)

RODEWAY INN-RED FEATHER LODGE
Phone: (520)638-2414

	5/21-10/14	1P: $79-$119	2P: $79-$119	XP: $10	F18
	3/19-5/20	1P: $69-$109	2P: $69-$109	XP: $10	F18
	2/1-3/18 & 10/15-1/31	1P: $59-$89	2P: $59-$89	XP: $10	F18

Motel **Location:** On SR 64 in Tusayan; 9 mi s of Grand Canyon Village, outside Park Boundary. 86023 (PO Box 1460, GRAND CANYON). Fax: 520/638-9216. **Terms:** Check-in 3:30 pm; small pets only, $50 dep required, in designated rooms. **Facility:** 231 rooms. New building has more upscale decor. Older wing is more basic in appearance. 3 stories; interior/exterior corridors; heated pool, whirlpool, seasonal pool. **Dining:** Restaurant nearby. **Recreation:** video game room. **Cards:** AE, DI, DS, MC, VI. **Special Amenities:** Free local telephone calls. (See color ad p 197)

THUNDERBIRD LODGE
◆◆ All Year   1P: $124   2P: $124   XP: $9   F16
Motel   **Location:** At Grand Canyon Village South Rim. (PO Box 699, 86023). Fax: 303/297-3175. **Terms:** Check-in 4 pm; cancellation fee imposed; kennels avail $10-$22. **Facility:** 55 rooms. Registration at Bright Angel Lodge. A modern lodge building at the rim. Many rooms face the canyon. Limited parking. 2 stories; interior corridors. **Cards:** AE, CB, DI, DS, JC, MC, VI. *(See ad p 195)*

Phone: 303/297-2757

YAVAPAI LODGE
◆◆ 3/16-11/25   1P: $89   XP: $9   F16
Motor Inn   2/18-3/15   1P: $63   XP: $9   F16
     Location: 1 mi e of village, opposite Visitor Center. (PO Box 699, 86023). Fax: 303/297-3175. **Terms:** Open 2/18-11/25; check-in 4 pm; kennels avail $8-$13. **Facility:** 358 rooms. On several acres of wooded terrain. 2 stories; exterior corridors. **Services:** gift shop. **Cards:** AE, CB, DI, DS, JC, MC, VI. *(See ad p 195)*

Phone: 303/297-2757

──────── *The following lodging was either not inspected or did not* ────────
meet AAA rating requirements but is listed for your information only.

BRIGHT ANGEL LODGE & CABINS   Phone: 303/297-2757
[fyi]   Not inspected; located in remote area. **Location:** At Grand Canyon Village South Rim. 86023 (PO Box 699).
               Facilities, services, and decor characterize a basic property. *(See ad p 195)*

──────── **RESTAURANTS** ────────

ARIZONA STEAKHOUSE   **Dinner:** $12-$19   Phone: 520/638-2631
◆◆   **Location:** At Grand Canyon Village South Rim, between Bright Angel Lodge and Thunderbird Lodge. 86023.
American   **Hours:** Open 3/1-12/31; 4:30 pm-10 pm. **Features:** casual dress; cocktails & lounge. Popular restaurant with
            windows looking toward the canyon. Menu features a selection of steak, barbecue, chicken and seafood.
Smoke free premises. **Cards:** AE, CB, DI, DS, JC, MC, VI.   ✕

CORONADO ROOM-IN BEST WESTERN GRAND CANYON SQUIRE INN   **Dinner:** $12-$23   Phone: 520/638-2681
◆◆   **Location:** On SR 64 in Tusayan,9 mi s of Grand Canyon Village, outside park boundary; in Best Western
American   Grand Canyon Squire Inn. **Hours:** 5 pm-10 pm. **Features:** casual dress; children's menu; cocktails & lounge.
            Nice selection of steak, seafood, pastas and Mexican dishes. **Cards:** AE, CB, DI, DS, MC, VI.   ✕

EL TOVAR HOTEL DINING ROOM   Historical   **Lunch:** $5-$15   **Dinner:** $16-$27   Phone: 520/638-2631
◆◆◆   **Location:** In El Tovar Hotel. 86023. **Hours:** 6:30-11 am, 11:30-2 & 5-10 pm. **Reservations:** suggested.
Continental **Features:** casual dress; cocktails & lounge; a la carte. Very attractive dining room serving a nice selection of
            veal, beef, seafood, chicken and vegetarian entrees. Smoke free premises. **Cards:** AE, CB, DI, DS, JC,
MC, VI.

MOQUI LODGE RESTAURANT   **Dinner:** $10-$19   Phone: 520/638-2424
◆◆   **Location:** On SR 64, 8 mi s of Grand Canyon Village, 0.5 mi s of entrance station; in Moqui Lodge. 86023.
Mexican   **Hours:** Open 4/1-10/31; 6:30 am-10 am & 5-10 pm. Closed: 11/1-3/31. **Features:** casual dress; children's
            menu; carryout; cocktails & lounge. Attractive dining room. Smoke free premises. **Cards:** AE, CB, DI, DS,
MC, VI.   ✕

GREEN VALLEY —*See Tucson p. 348.*

HEBER pop. 1,500

──────── **LODGING** ────────

BEST WESTERN SAWMILL INN   Phone: (520)535-5053
(AAA) [SAVE]   5/1-10/31   1P: $60-$68   2P: $60-$68   XP: $5   F12
               2/1-4/30 & 11/1-1/31   1P: $54-$62   2P: $54-$62   XP: $5   F12
◆◆◆   **Location:** 0.5 mi e on SR 260. 1877 Hwy 260 85928 (PO Box 730). Fax: 520/535-4164. **Terms:** [CP] meal
Motel   plan; weekly rates avail; pets, $5 extra charge, $25 dep req. **Facility:** 42 rooms. 3 large rooms with king bed,
            refrigerator & microwave, $70-$80; 2 stories; exterior corridors; indoor whirlpool. **Recreation:** video rentals.
All Rooms: combo or shower baths, extended cable TV. **Some Rooms:** Fee: refrigerators, microwaves, VCR. **Cards:** AE, CB,
DI, DS, MC, VI. **Special Amenities:** Free breakfast and free local telephone calls.

HOLBROOK pop. 4,700

──────── **LODGINGS** ────────

BEST WESTERN ADOBE INN   Phone: (520)524-3948
(AAA) [SAVE]   6/1-9/30   1P: $45-$55   2P: $45-$55   XP: $4   F19
               5/1-5/31   1P: $40-$50   2P: $40-$50   XP: $2   F19
◆◆   2/1-4/30 & 10/1-1/31   1P: $35-$45   2P: $40-$50   XP: $2   F19
Motel   **Location:** On US 180, 1 mi e of jct I-40, exit 285. 615 W Hopi Dr 86025. Fax: 520/524-3612. **Terms:** [CP] meal
            plan; pets, $25 dep req. **Facility:** 54 rooms. 0.5 mi west of downtown and historic courthouse. 2 stories; ex-
terior corridors; heated pool. **All Rooms:** extended cable TV. **Cards:** AE, CB, DI, DS, MC, VI. **Special Amenities:** Free breakfast and free local telephone calls. *(See color ad p 200)*

BEST WESTERN ARIZONIAN INN   Phone: (520)524-2611
(AAA) [SAVE]   5/1-8/31   1P: $52-$64   2P: $58-$70   XP: $4   F17
               9/1-10/31   1P: $52-$58   2P: $58-$64   XP: $4   F17
◆◆◆   11/1-1/31   1P: $41-$48   2P: $47-$54   XP: $4   F17
Motor Inn   2/1-4/30   1P: $41-$47   2P: $47-$53   XP: $4   F17
            Location: I-40, exit 289, then 0.5 mi w. 2508 E Navajo Blvd 86025. Fax: 520/524-2611. **Terms:** [CP] meal plan;
            pets, $30 dep req. **Facility:** 70 rooms. Nicely furnished and decorated units. 2 stories; exterior corridors; heated pool, seasonal
pool. **Dining:** 24 hrs; $5-$10; restaurant nearby. **All Rooms:** extended cable TV. **Cards:** AE, CB, DI, DS, MC, VI.
Special Amenities: Free breakfast and free local telephone calls. *(See color ad p 200)*

BUDGET HOST HOLBROOK INN
Phone: (520)524-3809

(AAA) (SAVE)   3/1-10/31   1P: $22-$26   2P: $26-$30   XP: $4   F10
◆   2/1-2/29 & 11/1-1/31   1P: $20-$24   2P: $24-$28   XP: $4   F10
Motel   **Location:** On US 180, just w of downtown; from I-40 use exit 285. 235 W Hopi Dr 86025. Fax: 520/524-3072.
Terms: [CP] meal plan; weekly rates avail; pets, $4 extra charge, $10 dep req. **Facility:** 25 rooms. Modest accommodations in downtown area. 2 stories; exterior corridors. **All Rooms:** extended cable TV.
Some Rooms: 8 efficiencies, no utensils. **Cards:** AE, CB, DI, DS, JC, MC, VI. **Special Amenities:** Free local telephone calls. *(See color ad p 194)*

COMFORT INN
Phone: (520)524-6131

◆◆◆   5/1-9/30   1P: $46-$65   2P: $50-$70   XP: $5   F18
Motor Inn   10/1-1/31   1P: $38-$48   2P: $42-$55   XP: $5   F18
2/1-4/30   1P: $38-$48   2P: $42-$52   XP: $5   F18
Location: Just w of I-40, exit 289. 2602 E Navajo Blvd 86025. Fax: 520/524-2281. **Terms:** [CP] meal plan; pets, $25 dep req. **Facility:** 60 rooms. 2 stories; exterior corridors; heated pool. **Cards:** AE, CB, DI, DS, MC, VI.

DAYS INN
Phone: (520)524-6949

(AAA) (SAVE)   5/16-10/31   1P: $42-$70   2P: $48-$70   XP: $6   F12
◆◆◆   4/1-5/15   1P: $42-$62   2P: $48-$62   XP: $6   F12
Motel   2/1-3/31 & 11/1-1/31   1P: $34-$48   2P: $48-$58   XP: $6   F12
Location: I-40, exit 289, then 0.3 mi w. 2601 Navajo Blvd 86025. Fax: 520/524-6665. **Terms:** [CP] meal plan.
Facility: 54 rooms. Contemporary-style units with nice view of desert. 3 whirlpool rms, extra charge; 2 stories; exterior corridors; heated pool, whirlpool. **Dining:** Restaurant nearby. **Recreation:** video rentals. **All Rooms:** extended cable TV. **Some Rooms:** Fee: VCR. **Cards:** AE, CB, DI, DS, JC, MC, VI. **Special Amenities:** Free breakfast and free local telephone calls. *(See color ad p 201)*

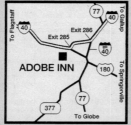

ECONO LODGE
◆◆
Motel

All Year

Phone: (520)524-1448
XP: $5   F18

1P: $30-$45   2P: $38-$55

Location: Just w of I-40, exit 289. 2596 E Navajo Blvd 86025. Fax: 520/524-1493. **Terms:** Small pets only, $25 dep req. **Facility:** 63 rooms. 2 stories; exterior corridors; heated pool. **Cards:** AE, CB, DI, DS, JC, MC, VI.

HOLBROOK HOLIDAY INN EXPRESS
◆◆◆
Motel

5/21-10/31   1P: $67   2P: $67
3/1-5/20   1P: $61   2P: $61
2/1-2/29 & 11/1-1/31 1P: $56   2P: $56

Phone: (520)524-1466

Location: Just n of I-40, exit 286. 1308 E Navajo Blvd 86025. Fax: 520/524-1788. **Terms:** [ECP] meal plan; small pets only, $10 dep req. **Facility:** 59 rooms. 2 stories; interior corridors; heated pool. **Cards:** AE, CB, DI, DS, MC, VI.

RAMADA LIMITED
◆◆◆
Motel

5/23-8/20   1P: $50   2P: $59
2/1-5/22 & 8/21-1/31 1P: $39   2P: $46

Phone: (520)524-2566
XP: $7   F12
XP: $5   F12

Location: Just w of I-40, exit 289. 2608 E Navajo Blvd 86025. Fax: 520/524-6427. **Terms:** Cancellation fee imposed; small pets only, in smoking rooms, $5 extra charge. **Facility:** 40 rooms. 2 stories; exterior corridors; heated pool. **Some Rooms:** Fee: VCR. **Cards:** AE, DI, DS, MC, VI.

RELAX INN
◆◆
Motel

5/23-8/20   1P: $35   2P: $40
2/1-5/22 & 8/21-1/31 1P: $30   2P: $35

Phone: (520)524-6815
XP: $5   F12
XP: $5   F12

Location: I-40, exit 289; 0.4 mi w. 2418 E Navajo Blvd 86025. Fax: 520/524-2328. **Terms:** Cancellation fee imposed; pets, $5 extra charge. **Facility:** 33 rooms. 2 stories; exterior corridors. **Cards:** AE, DI, DS, MC, VI.

——— *The following lodging was either not inspected or did not* ———
meet AAA rating requirements but is listed for your information only.

BEST INN   Phone: (520)524-2654
AAA SAVE   6/1-9/30   1P: $45-$49   2P: $50-$57   XP: $5   F14
     5/1-5/31   1P: $41-$45   2P: $46-$53   XP: $5   F14
fyi   2/1-4/30 & 10/1-1/31   1P: $39-$41   2P: $44-$49   XP: $5   F14
Motel   Under major renovation, scheduled to be completed December 1999. **Last rated:** ◆ **Location:** 1 mi w on Navajo Blvd from I-40, exit 289. 2211 E Navajo Blvd 86025. Fax: 520/524-2654. **Terms:** Pets, $25 dep req. **Facility:** 40 rooms. 2 stories; exterior corridors. **All Rooms:** extended cable TV. **Cards:** AE, CB, DI, DS, MC, VI. **Special Amenities:** Free breakfast and free local telephone calls. *(See color ad p 201)*

——— **RESTAURANT** ———

MESA ITALIANA RESTAURANT   **Lunch:** $5-$9   **Dinner:** $6-$14   **Phone:** 520/524-6696
◆◆   **Location:** I-40 exit 286, 1.3 mi e on Navajo Blvd. 2318 E Navajo Blvd 86025. **Hours:** 11 am-9 pm. **Closed:**
Italian   11/23, 12/25 & Mon. **Features:** casual dress; cocktails & lounge. Nice selection of traditional Italian dishes. Friendly atmosphere. Smoke free premises. **Cards:** AE, DS, MC, VI.

KAYENTA pop. 4,400

——— **LODGINGS** ———

BEST WESTERN WETHERILL INN   Phone: (520)697-3231
AAA   5/1-10/15   1P: $98   2P: $98   XP: $6   F12
◆◆◆   2/1-4/30   1P: $55-$70   2P: $55-$70   XP: $5   F12
     10/16-11/15   1P: $70   2P: $70   XP: $5   F12
Motel   11/16-1/31   1P: $55   2P: $55   XP: $5   F12
Location: US 163, 1 mi n of jct US 160. (PO Box 175, 86033). Fax: 520/697-3233. **Facility:** 54 rooms. On road to Monument Valley. 2 stories; exterior corridors. **Dining:** Restaurant nearby. **Services:** gift shop. **Cards:** AE, CB, DI, DS, JC, MC, VI.

HOLIDAY INN-MONUMENT VALLEY   Phone: (520)697-3221
◆◆◆   5/1-10/31   1P: $119-$169   2P: $119-$169   XP: $10   F18
Motor Inn   2/1-4/30   1P: $89-$129   2P: $89-$129   XP: $10   F18
     11/1-1/31   1P: $69-$109   2P: $69-$109   XP: $10   F18
Location: Jct of US 160 and 163. (PO Box 307, 86033). Fax: 520/697-3349. **Terms:** 3 day cancellation notice. **Facility:** 164 rooms. 2 stories; interior/exterior corridors; heated pool. **Services:** gift shop. **Cards:** AE, DI, DS, JC, MC, VI.

KINGMAN pop. 12,700

——— **LODGINGS** ———

BEST WESTERN A WAYFARER'S INN   Phone: (520)753-6271
AAA SAVE   4/1-10/31   1P: $56-$65   2P: $63-$72   XP: $5   F12
◆◆◆   2/1-3/31 & 11/1-1/31   1P: $49-$53   2P: $54-$58   XP: $5   F12
Motel   **Location:** On I-40 business loop; 0.5 mi sw of I-40, exit 53. 2815 E Andy Devine 86401. Fax: 520/753-9608. **Terms:** [ECP] meal plan; pets, $20 dep req. **Facility:** 100 rooms. Spacious rooms decorated in light contemporary colors. 4 two-bedroom units. 2 stories; exterior corridors; heated pool, indoor whirlpool, pool heated 4/1-10/31. **Dining:** Coffee shop nearby. **Cards:** AE, CB, DI, DS, JC, MC, VI. **Special Amenities:** Free breakfast and free room upgrade (subject to availability with advanced reservations). *(See color ad p 203)*

BEST WESTERN KING'S INN   Phone: (520)753-6101
AAA SAVE   4/1-10/31   1P: $57-$65   2P: $63-$72   XP: $5   F17
◆◆◆   2/1-3/31 & 11/1-1/31   1P: $51   2P: $57   XP: $5   F17
Motel   **Location:** On I-40 business loop; 0.3 mi sw of jct I-40, exit 53. 2930 E Andy Devine 86401. Fax: 520/753-6192. **Terms:** [CP] meal plan; 7 day cancellation notice, 5/1-9/30; pets. **Facility:** 101 rooms. 3 two-bedroom units. 5 whirlpool rooms, $57-$92; suites, $78-$92; 2 stories; exterior corridors; sauna, indoor whirlpool. **Dining:** Restaurant nearby. **Recreation:** pool heated 4/15-10/15. **All Rooms:** combo or shower baths, extended cable TV. **Some Rooms:** 3 kitchens. **Cards:** AE, CB, DI, DS, MC, VI. **Special Amenities:** Free breakfast and free local telephone calls.

BRUNSWICK HOTEL   Phone: (520)718-1800
AAA SAVE   All Year   1P: $25-$60   2P: $25-$60   XP: $10   F10
◆◆   **Location:** Downtown Historic district on Rt 66. 315 E Andy Devine 86401. Fax: 520/718-1801. **Terms:** Cancellation fee imposed; 2 night min stay; package plans; small pets only, $10 extra charge, in limited rooms.
Hotel   **Facility:** 24 rooms. 3 stories; interior corridors; designated smoking area. **Dining:** Restaurant, $9-$17; cocktails. **All Rooms:** extended cable TV. **Some Rooms:** kitchen, combo or shower baths, shared bathrooms, color TV. **Cards:** AE, DS, MC, VI. **Special Amenities:** Free breakfast and free room upgrade (subject to availability with advanced reservations).

COMFORT INN
◆◆◆
Motel

	1P: $55-$75	2P: $59-$79	XP: $10	F18
5/10-8/31	1P: $49-$69	2P: $49-$69	XP: $10	F18
2/1-5/9 & 9/1-10/31	1P: $49-$59	2P: $49-$59	XP: $10	F18
11/1-1/31				

Phone: (520)718-1717

Location: I-40 exit 53, adjacent to w side of I-40 just n of Andy Devine. 3129 E Andy Devine 86401. Fax: 520/718-5668. **Terms:** Package plans. **Facility:** 38 rooms. 3 stories; interior corridors; heated pool. **All Rooms:** combo or shower baths. **Cards:** AE, CB, DI, DS, JC, MC, VI.

DAYS INN EAST
(AAA) (SAVE)
◆◆
Motel

	1P: $35-$45	2P: $45-$75	XP: $10	F12
4/1-10/31	1P: $32-$42	2P: $39-$50	XP: $10	F12
2/1-3/31 & 11/1-1/31				

Phone: (520)757-7337

Location: SR 66; 0.5 mi ne of jct I-40, exit 53. 3381 E Andy Devine 86401. Fax: 520/757-5591. **Terms:** 3 day cancellation notice; small pets only, $10 extra charge. **Facility:** 42 rooms. 9 whirlpool rooms; 2 stories; exterior corridors; seasonal pool, indoor whirlpool. **Cards:** AE, CB, DI, DS, JC, MC, VI. **Special Amenities:** Free breakfast and free local telephone calls.

DAYS INN WEST
(AAA) (SAVE)
◆◆◆
Motel

	1P: $45-$55	2P: $55-$75	XP: $10	F12
4/1-10/31	1P: $35-$49	2P: $45-$55	XP: $10	F12
2/1-3/31 & 11/1-1/31				

Phone: (520)753-7500

Location: On I-40 business loop, just sw of jct I-40, exit 53. 3023 E Andy Devine 86401. Fax: 520/757-4686. **Terms:** [CP] meal plan; 3 day cancellation notice; small pets only, $10 extra charge. **Facility:** 60 rooms. 2 stories; exterior corridors; heated pool, indoor whirlpool. **Dining:** Restaurant nearby. **Cards:** AE, CB, DI, DS, JC, MC, VI. **Special Amenities:** Free breakfast and free local telephone calls.

HIGH DESERT INN
(AAA) (SAVE)
◆
Motel

| All Year | 1P: $25-$45 | 2P: $35-$75 | XP: $10 | D12 |

Phone: (520)753-2935

Location: On I-40 business loop; 0.5 mi sw of jct I-40, exit 53. 2803 E Andy Devine 86401. **Terms:** Weekly rates avail; small pets only, $10 dep req. **Facility:** 15 rooms. Modest accommodations. 2 two-bedroom units. 1 story; exterior corridors. **All Rooms:** combo or shower baths. **Cards:** MC, VI. **Special Amenities:** Free local telephone calls.

HILL TOP MOTEL
(AAA) (SAVE)
◆
Motel

	1P: $24-$42	2P: $25-$48	XP: $5
5/1-9/16	1P: $24-$36	2P: $24-$39	XP: $5
9/17-10/31	1P: $22-$36	2P: $24-$39	XP: $5
2/1-4/30	1P: $22-$34	2P: $22-$36	XP: $5
11/1-1/31			

Phone: (520)753-2198

Location: On I-40 business loop; 2 mi sw of I-40, exit 53; 2.3 mi e, exit 48. 1901 E Andy Devine 86401. Fax: 520/753-5985. **Terms:** 3 day cancellation notice; pets, dogs only. **Facility:** 29 rooms. View of the Hualapai Mountains. Attractive cacti display. Some small rooms. 1 story; exterior corridors; pool heated 4/1-10/1. **All Rooms:** combo or shower baths, extended cable TV. **Some Rooms:** Fee: refrigerators, microwaves. **Cards:** DS, MC, VI. **Special Amenities:** Free local telephone calls.

HOLIDAY INN
◆◆
Motor Inn

| All Year | 1P: $39-$79 | 2P: $39-$99 | XP: $5 | F19 |

Phone: (520)753-6262

Location: On I-40 business loop; 0.3 mi w of I-40, exit 53. 3100 E Andy Devine 86401. Fax: 520/753-7137. **Terms:** 3 day cancellation notice; small pets only. **Facility:** 116 rooms. 2 stories; exterior corridors. **Cards:** AE, CB, DI, DS, JC, MC, VI.

KINGMAN TRAVEL INN

AAA SAVE

◆ ◆

Motel

			Phone: (520)757-7878
4/1-9/30	1P: $30-$39	2P: $35-$45	XP: $5 F18
2/1-3/31 & 10/1-1/31	1P: $25-$30	2P: $35-$40	XP: $5 F18

Location: On SR 66, 0.3 mi ne of jct I-40, exit 53. 3421 E Andy Devine 86401. Fax: 520/692-6539. **Facility:** 28 rooms. 4 whirlpool rooms; 2 stories; exterior corridors; heated pool, seasonal pool. **Cards:** AE, CB, DI, DS, MC, VI. **Special Amenities:** Free local telephone calls and free room upgrade (subject to availability with advanced reservations).

MOTEL 6 - 1114

AAA

◆

Motel

			Phone: 520/753-9222
5/25-9/27	1P: $42-$52	2P: $48-$58	XP: $3 F17
9/28-1/31	1P: $38-$48	2P: $44-$54	XP: $3 F17
2/1-5/24	1P: $36-$46	2P: $42-$52	XP: $3 F17

Location: Just s of I-40, exit 48. 424 W Beale St 86401. Fax: 520/753-4791. **Terms:** Small pets only. **Facility:** 80 rooms. 2 stories; exterior corridors; seasonal pool. **Dining:** Restaurant nearby. **All Rooms:** combo or shower baths. **Cards:** AE, CB, DI, DS, MC, VI.

QUALITY INN

AAA SAVE

◆ ◆

Motel

			Phone: (520)753-4747
5/1-9/30	1P: $50-$70	2P: $70-$90	XP: $10 F18
2/1-4/30 & 10/1-1/31	1P: $40-$50	2P: $50-$60	XP: $10 F18

Location: On I-40 business loop; 2.3 mi sw of I-40, exit 53; 2 mi e of exit 48. 1400 E Andy Devine 86401. Fax: 520/753-4747. **Terms:** [CP] meal plan; small pets only. **Facility:** 97 rooms. Interesting display of historic Rt 66 memorabilia in lobby. 2 stories; exterior corridors; heated pool, sauna, seasonal pool, indoor whirlpool. **Dining:** Restaurant nearby. **All Rooms:** extended cable TV. **Some Rooms:** 13 efficiencies. Fee: VCR. **Cards:** AE, DI, DS, JC, MC, VI. **Special Amenities:** Free breakfast and free local telephone calls.

RAMBLIN' ROSE MOTEL

AAA SAVE

◆

Motel

			Phone: (520)753-5541
1/1-1/31	1P: $22	2P: $65-$85	XP: $5 F15
2/1-12/31	1P: $22	2P: $65	XP: $5 F15

Location: On I-40 business loop; 2.5 mi sw of I-40 exit 53; 1.5 mi e of exit 48. 1001 E Andy Devine 86401. Fax: 520/753-4344. **Terms:** Weekly rates avail; cancellation fee imposed. **Facility:** 35 rooms. 2 two-bedroom units. 2 stories; exterior corridors. **All Rooms:** combo or shower baths. **Cards:** AE, CB, DI, DS, MC, VI. **Special Amenities:** Free local telephone calls and preferred room (subject to availability with advanced reservations).

SUPER 8 MOTEL

AAA SAVE

◆ ◆

Motel

			Phone: (520)757-4808
4/1-10/31	1P: $36-$49	2P: $49-$59	XP: $10 F12
2/1-3/31 & 11/1-1/31	1P: $32-$39	2P: $35-$49	XP: $10 F12

Location: On SR 66, 0.3 mi ne of jct I-40, exit 53. 3401 E Andy Devine 86401. Fax: 520/757-4808. **Terms:** 3 day cancellation notice; small pets only, $10 daily fee. **Facility:** 61 rooms. 3 stories; interior corridors. **Cards:** AE, CB, DI, DS, JC, MC, VI. **Special Amenities:** Free local telephone calls and preferred room (subject to availability with advanced reservations).

TRAVELODGE

AAA SAVE

◆ ◆

Motel

			Phone: (520)757-1188
All Year	1P: $55-$65	2P: $60-$70	XP: $5 F17

Location: On Rt 66; just e of jct I-40, exit 53. 3275 E Andy Devine 86401. Fax: 520/757-1010. **Terms:** 10 day cancellation notice. **Facility:** 65 rooms. Slump stone exterior. 2 stories; exterior corridors; heated pool, whirlpool. **Dining:** Restaurant nearby. **Cards:** AE, CB, DI, DS, JC, MC, VI. **Special Amenities:** Free local telephone calls and free newspaper.

──── RESTAURANTS ────

DAMBAR STEAKHOUSE

AAA

◆ ◆

Steakhouse

Lunch: $7-$10   **Dinner:** $8-$18   **Phone:** 520/753-3523

Location: I-40 Business Loop; 1.2 mi sw of jct I-40, exit 53. 1960 E Andy Devine 86401. **Hours:** 11 am-10 pm, Fri & Sat-11 pm. Closed: 12/25, day after Labor Day. **Reservations:** suggested; weekends. **Features:** casual dress; children's menu; early bird specials; carryout; cocktails & lounge. Good selection of steak, ribs, sandwiches and salad. **Cards:** AE, DS, MC, VI.

PORTOFINO RISTORANTE ITALIANO

◆ ◆

Italian

Lunch: $4-$7   **Dinner:** $8-$16   **Phone:** 520/753-7504

Location: Downtown, at jct of 2nd and 3rd. 318 Oak St 86401. **Hours:** 11 am-3 & 5-9 pm, Sat from 5 pm. Closed major holidays & Sun. **Features:** carryout; beer & wine only. Smoke free premises. **Cards:** MC, VI.

LAKE HAVASU CITY pop. 24,400

──── LODGINGS ────

BEST WESTERN LAKE PLACE INN

AAA SAVE

◆ ◆

Motel

			Phone: (520)855-2146
All Year	1P: $50-$90	2P: $50-$90	XP: $6 F12

Location: 1 mi e of SR 95 via Swanson Ave. 31 Wing's Loop 86403. Fax: 520/855-3148. **Terms:** Weekly rates avail; pets, $5 extra charge. **Facility:** 40 rooms. Large units. Desert-landscaped courtyard. 1-2 stories; exterior corridors; heated pool. **Dining:** Restaurant nearby. **All Rooms:** extended cable TV. **Cards:** AE, CB, DI, DS, MC, VI. *(See ad p 205)*

HAVASU TRAVELODGE   Phone: (520)680-9202

(AAA) (SAVE)   2/1-11/30   1P: $59-$135   2P: $64-$165   XP: $10   F18
                12/1-1/31   1P: $55-$100   2P: $59-$100   XP: $10   F18
◆ ◆   **Location:** 1 mi n of London Bridge. 480 London Bridge Rd 86403. Fax: 520/680-1511. **Terms:** Weekly &
Motel   monthly rates avail; 14 day cancellation notice, 30 day notice 10/1-10/31. **Facility:** 40 rooms. Near Windsor
               Beach State Park. 2 stories; interior corridors; indoor whirlpool. **Dining:** Restaurant nearby.
Some Rooms: kitchen. Fee: refrigerators, microwaves. **Cards:** AE, CB, DI, DS, MC, VI. **Special Amenities:** Free local tele-
phone calls and free room upgrade (subject to availability with advanced reservations). (See color ad below)

🖥 ⤒ ✕ ⛾ 🖥 🛢

HIDDEN PALMS ALL SUITE INN   Phone: (520)855-7144

(AAA) (SAVE)   All Year   1P: $59-$99   2P: $59-$99   XP: $5   F18
◆ ◆   **Location:** 1 mi e of London Bridge on SR 95, just s on Swanson Ave. 2100 Swanson Ave 86403.
Motel   Fax: 520/855-2620. **Terms:** Weekly & monthly rates avail; 3 day cancellation notice, determined by length of
               stay. **Facility:** 22 rooms. 2 stories; exterior corridors; heated pool. **Dining:** Restaurant nearby.
               All Rooms: kitchens, extended cable TV. **Cards:** AE, DS, MC, VI. **Special Amenities:** Free local telephone
calls and preferred room (subject to availability with advanced reservations).

⤒ ⛱ ✕ 🖥 🖥 🛢 🏊

HOLIDAY INN   Phone: (520)855-4071

◆ ◆ ◆   All Year   1P: $60-$80   2P: $60-$80   XP: $8   F19
Motor Inn   **Location:** 0.5 mi n of London Bridge. 245 London Bridge Rd 86403. Fax: 520/855-2379. **Terms:** Package
               plans; small pets only. **Facility:** 162 rooms. Many units with balcony. 4 stories; interior/exterior corridors;
heated pool. **Dining:** entertainment. **All Rooms:** combo or shower baths. **Some Rooms:** Fee: VCR. **Cards:** AE, CB, DI, DS,
JC, MC, VI.

(ASK) 🖥 🛏 🍽 🎣 ⛱ ♿ 🚭 ✕ ⛾ (VCR) 🖥 🖥 🛢 (DATA PORT) 🏊

HOWARD JOHNSON EXPRESS INN & SUITES   Phone: (520)453-4656

(AAA) (SAVE)   1/15-1/31   1P: $85-$90   2P: $90-$95   XP: $6   F12
◆ ◆ ◆   2/1-11/30   1P: $80-$90   2P: $85-$95   XP: $6   F12
Motel   12/1-1/14   1P: $70-$75   2P: $75-$80   XP: $6   F12
               Location: 0.8 mi n of London Bridge. 335 London Bridge Rd 86403. Fax: 520/680-4561. **Terms:** Weekly &
               monthly rates avail. **Facility:** 47 rooms. Some units with balcony and view of lake. Suites, $70-$105; 2 stories;
interior corridors; heated pool, whirlpool. **Dining:** Restaurant nearby. **All Rooms:** combo or shower baths. **Some Rooms:** 6
efficiencies. **Cards:** AE, CB, DI, DS, MC, VI. **Special Amenities:** Free newspaper and free room upgrade (subject to availability with advanced reservations). (See color ad p 206)

🖥 ⤒ ⛱ ✕ ⛾ 🖥 🖥 🖥 🛢 (DATA PORT) 🏊

INN AT TAMARISK
Phone: (520)764-3033

[AAA] [SAVE] All Year ◆◆ Motel
1P: $34-$43 2P: $39-$55 XP: $4

Location: 4.2 mi n of London Bridge, on London Bridge Rd. 3101 London Bridge Rd 86404. Fax: 520/764-3046. **Terms:** Weekly & monthly rates avail; 7 day cancellation notice; cancellation fee imposed; 2 night min stay, holidays. **Facility:** 17 rooms. Some 1-2 bedroom suites; some have lake view. Tastefully furnished. 5 two-bedroom units. 2 stories; exterior corridors; heated pool. **Recreation:** horseshoe pit, shuffleboard. **All Rooms:** shower baths, extended cable TV. **Some Rooms:** 9 kitchens. **Cards:** AE, CB, DI, DS, MC, VI. **Special Amenities:** Free local telephone calls and preferred room (subject to availability with advanced reservations).

ISLAND INN HOTEL
Phone: (520)680-0606

[AAA] [SAVE]
3/1-10/31	1P: $65-$85	2P: $70-$90	XP: $10 F16
2/1-2/29	1P: $49-$59	2P: $55-$75	
11/1-1/31	1P: $49-$59	2P: $55-$75	XP: $10 F16

◆◆◆ Motor Inn

Location: 0.5 mi sw of SR 95, over London Bridge. 1300 W McCulloch Blvd 86403. Fax: 520/680-4218. **Terms:** Weekly & monthly rates avail; small pets only, $10 extra charge. **Facility:** 117 rooms. 0.5 mi from London Bridge and Island Fashion Mall Shops. Many rooms with balcony. Coffee makers, microwaves and refrigerators avail upon request. 4 stories; interior corridors; heated pool, whirlpool. **Dining:** 7 am-10 pm; $8-$11. **Cards:** AE, CB, DI, DS, MC, VI.

LAKE HAVASU CITY SUPER 8
Phone: (520)855-8844

◆ Motel
All Year 1P: $36-$46 2P: $46-$56 XP: $5 F12

Location: Just w of SR 95, exit Palo Verde. 305 London Bridge Rd 86403. Fax: 520/855-7132. **Terms:** 4 day cancellation notice; small pets only, $50 dep req. **Facility:** 60 rooms. Some lakeview units. 0.5 mile from London Bridge and English Village. 3 stories, no elevator; interior corridors; heated pool. **Cards:** AE, CB, DI, DS, MC, VI.

LONDON BRIDGE RESORT
Phone: 520/855-0888

◆◆◆ Hotel
Property failed to provide current rates

Location: At London Bridge. 1477 Queens Bay 86304. **Terms:** Check-in 4 pm. **Facility:** 122 rooms. 60 two-bedroom units. Putting green; 3 heated pools; 1 lighted tennis court; boat dock; playground. Fee: 9 holes golf. **Dining:** entertainment. **Services:** gift shop. Fee: massage. **Recreation:** charter fishing, fishing. Fee: boating, scuba diving, snorkeling, waterskiing. **All Rooms:** kitchens. **Cards:** AE, CB, DI, DS, JC, MC, VI.

NAUTICAL INN RESORT & CONFERENCE CENTER   Phone: (520)855-2141

(AAA) [SAVE]
◆◆
Motel

3/13-4/30	1P: $199	2P: $285	XP: $10 F16
5/1-9/30	1P: $99	2P: $119-$199	XP: $10 F16
2/1-3/12 & 10/1-1/31	1P: $69	2P: $89-$109	XP: $10 F16

Location: 1000 McCulloch Blvd 86403. Fax: 520/453-5808. **Terms:** Weekly rates avail; check-in 4 pm; package plans. **Facility:** 120 rooms. Deluxe 2 bedroom condos $136-$325; 2 stories; exterior corridors; heated pool, whirlpool; boat dock. **Dining:** Restaurant; 7 am-10 pm; $12-$23; cocktails. **Services:** gift shop. **Recreation:** Fee: sailboating; bicycles. **All Rooms:** extended cable TV. **Some Rooms:** 22 efficiencies. **Cards:** AE, DI, MC, VI. **Special Amenities:** Free room upgrade and preferred room (each subject to availability with advanced reservations).

RAMADA INN   Phone: (520)855-1111

◆◆◆
Motor Inn

All Year   1P: $65   2P: $75   XP: $10   F18

Location: Off of Hwy 95, Cross Streets SmokeTree and Swanson. 271 S Lake Havasu Ave 86403. Fax: 520/855-6228. **Terms:** Package plans. **Facility:** 120 rooms. 3 stories; exterior corridors; heated pool. **All Rooms:** combo or shower baths. **Some Rooms:** Fee: refrigerators, microwaves. **Cards:** AE, CB, DI, DS, JC, MC, VI.

SANDS VACATION RESORT   Phone: (520)855-1388

◆◆
Suite Motel

All Year   1P: $80-$150   2P: $80-$150   XP: $10

Location: 1 mi e of SR 95, just n of McCulloch Blvd. 2040 Mesquite Ave 86403. Fax: 520/453-1802. **Terms:** 3 day cancellation notice; package plans. **Facility:** 42 rooms. All suites nicely furnished and decorated. 6 two-bedroom units. 2 stories; exterior corridors; heated pool; 1 lighted tennis court. **All Rooms:** kitchens. **Cards:** AE, DI, DS, MC, VI.

——— **RESTAURANTS** ———

CITY OF LONDON ARMS PUB, RESTAURANT & BREWERY   **Lunch:** $5-$8   **Dinner:** $8-$15   **Phone:** 520/855-8782
◆◆
American

Location: In English Village. 422 English Village 86403. **Hours:** 11 am-9 pm, Sun 8 am-noon & 4-9 pm. Closed: 11/23 & 12/25. **Features:** casual dress; Sunday brunch; children's menu; early bird specials; senior's menu; health conscious menu; carryout; cocktails & lounge; fee for parking. Nice variety of English and American appetizers, entrees and ale. English high tea served daily. Patio dining, brewery on site with a gift shop. Smoke free premises. **Cards:** AE, CB, DI, DS, JC, MC, VI.

KRYSTAL'S FINE DINING   **Dinner:** $10-$20   **Phone:** 520/453-2999
◆◆
Steak and
Seafood

Location: Just e of London Bridge Rd. 460 El Camino Way 86403. **Hours:** 4 pm-10 pm, Fri & Sat-11 pm. **Reservations:** suggested. **Features:** casual dress; early bird specials; carryout; cocktails & lounge. Extensive variety of seafood and limited meat selections. **Cards:** AE, MC, VI.

MONTANA STEAK HOUSE   **Dinner:** $7-$22   **Phone:** 520/855-3736
◆
American

Location: 4 mi s of London Bridge; just n of SR 95 and Oro Grande, on Maricopa Ave. 3301 Maricopa Ave 86406. **Hours:** 3:30 pm-9 pm, Fri & Sat-10 pm. Closed: 11/23 & 12/25. **Reservations:** suggested. **Features:** casual dress; early bird specials; cocktails. Good selection of steak, seafood and chicken. Steak is the house specialty. Casual family atmosphere. **Cards:** AE, MC, VI.

SHUGRUE'S   **Lunch:** $6-$9   **Dinner:** $10-$24   **Phone:** 520/453-1400
◆◆
Steak and
Seafood

Location: W end of London Bridge. 1425 McCulloch Blvd 86403. **Hours:** 11 am-10 pm, Sun from 11 am-9 pm. Closed: 12/25. **Features:** semi-formal attire; children's menu; carryout; cocktails & lounge. Overlooks channel to Lake Havasu and London Bridge. Pastries and bread baked on premises. Fresh seafood daily. Sushi avail Thurs eve. **Cards:** AE, MC, VI.

LAKE MONTEZUMA pop. 1,800

——— **LODGING** ———

BEAVER CREEK INN   Phone: 520/567-4475
◆
Motel

All Year   1P: $57-$68   2P: $57-$68   XP: $5

Location: 3 mi ne on Lake Montezuma Ave; I-17 exit 293. 4225 S Montezuma Ave 86342 (PO Box 5546). **Terms:** Cancellation fee imposed; package plans. **Facility:** 22 rooms. Across from Beaver Creek Golf Course. 2 stories; exterior corridors. **Cards:** AE, DS, MC, VI.

LITCHFIELD PARK —See Phoenix p. 260.

MESA —See Phoenix p. 261.

MIAMI pop. 2,000

——— **LODGING** ———

COPPER HILLS INN & SUITES   Phone: (520)425-7151
◆◆
Motor Inn

All Year   1P: $42   2P: $45   XP: $4   F12

Location: US 60; 0.3 mi w of jct SR 88. 4805 E Hwy 60 85539. Fax: 520/425-2504. **Terms:** [CP] meal plan; small pets only, $5 extra charge. **Facility:** 68 rooms. Rooms decorated in traditional and contemporary styles. 2 two-bedroom units. 2 stories; exterior corridors. **Services:** gift shop. **Some Rooms:** efficiency. **Cards:** AE, CB, DI, DS, MC, VI.

MONUMENT VALLEY, UTAH pop. 225

———— LODGING ————

GOULDING'S TRADING POST & LODGE
Phone: (435)727-3231

(AAA) | 4/17-10/15 | 1P: $98-$145 | 2P: $98-$145 | XP: $8 | F8
◆◆◆ | 4/1-4/16 & 10/16-3/31 | 1P: $62-$98 | 2P: $62-$98 | XP: $8 | F8
Motor Inn **Location:** Just n of Arizona border, 2 mi w of US 163. 1000 Main 84536 (PO Box 360001, MONUMENT VALLEY, UT). Fax: 435/727-3344. **Terms:** 3 day cancellation notice; package plans. **Facility:** 62 rooms. Panoramic view of Monument Valley. Hillside rooms at foot of cliffs, all with patio or balcony. 2 cabins; 2 stories; exterior corridors; designated smoking area; indoor heated pool 4/15-10/15. **Dining:** Restaurant; 7 am-9:30 pm, limited hours 12/1-2/28; $8-$20. **Services:** gift shop. **Recreation:** Fee: multi-media theatre, museum, tours & air tours in Monument Valley. **Cards:** AE, CB, DI, DS, JC, MC, VI.

MORMON LAKE

———— RESTAURANT ————

MORMON LAKE LODGE STEAK HOUSE & SALOON **Lunch:** $5-$7 **Dinner:** $9-$20 **Phone:** 520/354-2227
◆◆ **Location:** 30 mi s of Flagstaff via Lake Mary and Mormon Lake rds. **Hours:** 8 am-9 pm, Fri & Sat-10 pm;
Steakhouse 1/1-4/30 Fri 4 pm-9 pm, Sat from 9 am, Sun 9 am-6 pm. **Features:** No A/C; children's menu; early bird specials; carryout; cocktails & lounge. **Cards:** AE, DS, MC, VI.

MUNDS PARK pop. 1,000

———— LODGING ————

MOTEL IN THE PINES
Phone: (520)286-9699

(AAA) SAVE | 4/1-10/31 | 1P: $40-$60 | 2P: $45-$65 | XP: $5 | F12
◆◆ | 2/1-3/31 & 11/1-1/31 | 1P: $30-$50 | 2P: $35-$55 | XP: $5 | F12
Motel **Location:** Just e of I-17, exit 322. 17 mi s of Flagstaff. 80 W Pinewood Rd 86017 (PO Box 18171). Fax: 520/286-2552. **Terms:** Weekly rates avail; small pets only; $30 cash dep req, $3 extra charge. **Facility:** 22 rooms. Pine-shaded grounds. 0.3 mi from Pinewood Country Club Golf Course. 4 mini suites with fireplace, refrigerator, microwave & coffeemaker, $65-$85; 2 stories; exterior corridors. **Dining:** Restaurant nearby. **Cards:** AE, DS, MC, VI. **Special Amenities:** Free local telephone calls and free room upgrade (subject to availability with advanced reservations). *(See color ad p 188)*

NOGALES pop. 19,500

———— LODGINGS ————

AMERICANA MOTOR HOTEL
Phone: (520)287-7211

(AAA) SAVE | 2/1-4/30 | 1P: $45-$55 | 2P: $53-$63 | XP: $5 | F12
◆ | 9/1-1/31 | 1P: $42-$52 | 2P: $49-$57 | XP: $5 | F12
Motor Inn | 5/1-8/31 | 1P: $39-$49 | 2P: $45-$55 | XP: $5 | F12
Location: 1 mi n of International Border on I-19 business loop, 0.6 mi s of jct SR 82. 639 N Grand Ave 85621. Fax: 520/287-5188. **Terms:** Weekly rates avail; 3 day cancellation notice; cancellation fee imposed; small pets only, $5 extra charge. **Facility:** 97 rooms. 2 stories; interior corridors; heated pool. **Dining:** Dining room; 6 am-9 pm; $7-$15; cocktails. **All Rooms:** extended cable TV. **Cards:** AE, DI, DS, MC, VI. **Special Amenities:** Early check-in/late check-out and free local telephone calls.

BEST WESTERN SIESTA MOTEL
Phone: (520)287-4671

(AAA) SAVE | 2/1-2/29 | 1P: $70-$80 | 2P: $80-$90 | F12
◆◆ | 3/1-1/31 | 1P: $58-$70 | 2P: $58-$70 | XP: $3 | F12
Motel **Location:** 1 mi n of International Border on Business Loop 19, 0.6 mi s of jct SR 82. 673 N Grand Ave 85621. Fax: 520/287-9616. **Terms:** [CP] meal plan; pets. **Facility:** 50 rooms. 2 stories; exterior corridors; heated pool, whirlpool. **Dining:** Restaurant nearby. **All Rooms:** extended cable TV. **Some Rooms:** color TV. **Cards:** AE, CB, DI, DS, MC, VI. **Special Amenities:** Free breakfast and free local telephone calls.

SUPER 8 MOTEL
Phone: 520/281-2242
◆◆ Property failed to provide current rates
Motor Inn **Location:** Just e of I-19, exit 4, Mariposa Rd. 547 W Mariposa Rd 85621. Fax: 520/281-2242. **Terms:** Small pets only, $5 extra charge. **Facility:** 117 rooms. 3 stories; interior/exterior corridors. **Cards:** AE, DI, DS, MC, VI.

TRAVELODGE
Phone: (520)287-4627

◆◆ | 11/16-1/31 | 1P: $40-$48 | 2P: $42-$54 | XP: $3 | F12
Motel | 2/1-5/31 | 1P: $40-$48 | 2P: $42-$52 | XP: $3 | F12
| 6/1-11/15 | 1P: $34-$40 | 2P: $36-$44 | XP: $3 | F12
Location: 1.3 mi n of International Border on Business Loop 19, just s of jct SR 82. 921 N Grand Ave 85621. Fax: 520/287-6949. **Terms:** [CP] meal plan; small pets only. **Facility:** 43 rooms. 2 stories; exterior corridors; heated pool. **Cards:** AE, CB, DI, DS, MC, VI.

—— **RESTAURANT** ——

MR. C'S SUPPER CLUB   **Lunch:** $6-$13   **Dinner:** $14-$25   **Phone:** 520/281-9000
◆◆   **Location:** 0.5 mi e of I-19, exit 4, Mariposa Rd, s on Mastick to Viewpoint Dr. 282 W Viewpoint Dr 85621.
American   **Hours:** 11:30 am-11 pm. Closed major holidays and Sun. **Reservations:** suggested. **Features:** casual
dress; salad bar; cocktails & lounge. A hilltop restaurant featuring a variety of steak, seafood and chicken
entrees. **Cards:** DI, DS, MC, VI.

ORACLE —See Tucson p. 349.

PAGE pop. 6,600

—— **LODGINGS** ——

BEST WESTERN ARIZONAINN   **Phone:** 520/645-2466
◆◆   Property failed to provide current rates
Motor Inn   **Location:** 0.7 mi e of US 89 via SR 89L, Lake Powell Blvd. 716 Rimview Dr 86040 (PO Box 250).
Fax: 520/645-2053. **Terms:** Pets, $10 extra charge. **Facility:** 103 rooms. Hillside location, some units with pan-
oramic view. 3 stories; interior corridors; heated pool. **Cards:** AE, DI, DS, MC, VI.

BEST WESTERN AT LAKE POWELL   **Phone:** (520)645-5988
(AAA) (SAVE)   4/1-10/31   1P: $69-$99   2P: $69-$99   XP: $6   F12
               2/1-3/31 & 11/1-1/31   1P: $49-$69   2P: $49-$69   XP: $6   F12
◆◆◆   **Location:** 0.8 mi e of US 89, via SR 89 L. 208 N Lake Powell Blvd 86040 (PO Box 4899). Fax: 520/645-2578.
Motel   **Terms:** [BP] meal plan; check-in 3:30 pm; package plans. **Facility:** 132 rooms. Some rooms with view. 3-4
stories; interior corridors; heated pool, whirlpool, seasonal pool. **Dining:** 6:30-9:30 am, to 8:30 am in winter;
breakfast extra charge; restaurant nearby. **All Rooms:** extended cable TV. **Cards:** AE, DI, DS, MC, VI. *(See ad below)*

COMFORT INN-PAGE/LAKE POWELL   **Phone:** (520)645-5858
◆◆◆   5/1-9/30 Dly   1P: $59-$109   2P: $59-$119   XP: $10   F17
Motel   3/1-4/30 Dly   1P: $45-$59   2P: $45-$59   XP: $5   F17
         10/1-1/31 Dly   1P: $39-$59   2P: $39-$59   XP: $5   F17
         2/1-2/29 Wkly   1P: $39-$49   2P: $39-$49   XP: $5   F17
Location: Just e of SR 89, on SR 89L (Lake Powell Blvd). 649 S Lake Powell Blvd 86040 (PO Box 4450). Fax: 520/645-0335.
Terms: [ECP] meal plan; 3 day cancellation notice. **Facility:** 101 rooms. 3 stories; interior corridors; heated pool.
All Rooms: combo or shower baths. **Cards:** AE, CB, DI, DS, JC, MC, VI.

COURTYARD BY MARRIOTT   **Phone:** (520)645-5000
◆◆◆   7/16-8/31   1P: $139-$159   2P: $139-$159
Motor Inn 9/1-10/31   1P: $99-$109   2P: $99-$109
         2/1-7/15   1P: $69-$109   2P: $69-$109
         11/1-1/31   1P: $69-$89   2P: $69-$89
Location: On SR 89L at jct US 89. 600 Clubhouse Dr 86040 (PO Box 4150). Fax: 520/645-5004. **Terms:** Package plans.
Facility: 153 rooms. Attractive Sante Fe/Southwestern style motif. Adjacent to public golf course. 2-4 stories; interior corridors.
Fee: 18 holes golf. **Services:** gift shop. **All Rooms:** combo or shower baths. **Cards:** AE, CB, DI, DS, JC, MC, VI.

ECONO LODGE

Phone: (520)645-2488

5/1-9/30	1P: $55-$69	2P: $59-$69	XP: $5	F17
3/1-4/30 & 10/1-1/31	1P: $39-$49	2P: $39-$55	XP: $5	F17
2/1-2/29	1P: $35-$45	2P: $39-$49	XP: $5	F17

Motel

Location: 1.3 mi e on Lake Powell Blvd from US 89/SR 89L. 121 S Lake Powell Blvd 86040 (PO Box 4450). Fax: 520/645-9472. **Terms:** 3 day cancellation notice; small pets only, $20 dep req. **Facility:** 63 rooms. 8 two-bedroom units. 11 rms with 3 queen beds, $10 extra charge; 1-2 stories; exterior corridors; small pool, seasonal pool. **Dining:** Restaurant nearby. **All Rooms:** extended cable TV. **Cards:** AE, CB, DI, DS, JC, MC, VI. **Special Amenities:** Free local telephone calls.

HOLIDAY INN EXPRESS

Phone: 520/645-9000

5/1-9/30	1P: $59-$109	2P: $65-$119	XP: $10
3/1-4/30	1P: $45-$59	2P: $49-$59	XP: $5
10/1-1/31	1P: $39-$59	2P: $45-$59	XP: $5
2/1-2/29	1P: $39-$49	2P: $39-$49	XP: $5

Motel

Location: On SR 89L, 1.5 mi e of US 89. 751 S Navajo Dr 86040 (PO Box 4450). Fax: 520/645-1605. **Terms:** [ECP] meal plan; 3 day cancellation notice. **Facility:** 74 rooms. 3 stories; interior corridors; heated pool. **All Rooms:** combo or shower baths. **Some Rooms:** 2 kitchens. **Cards:** AE, CB, DI, DS, JC, MC, VI.

LAKE POWELL DAYS INN & SUITES

Phone: (520)645-2800

6/1-10/31	1P: $79-$89	2P: $89-$99	XP: $5	F18
4/1-5/31	1P: $59-$69	2P: $59-$79	XP: $5	F18
2/1-3/31 & 11/1-1/31	1P: $39-$49	2P: $49-$69	XP: $5	F18

Motel

Location: On US 89. 961 N Hwy 89 86040 (PO Box 3910). Fax: 520/645-2604. **Terms:** [CP] meal plan; cancellation fee imposed; package plans; small pets only, $150 dep req. **Facility:** 82 rooms. 3 stories; interior corridors; heated pool. **Services:** gift shop. **All Rooms:** combo or shower baths. **Cards:** AE, CB, DI, DS, JC, MC, VI.

LAKE POWELL MOTEL

Phone: (520)645-2433

5/12-10/15	1P: $79-$99	2P: $79-$99	XP: $10	F18

Motel

Location: On US 89; 4 mi n of Glen Canyon Dam, 3 mi w of Wahweap Marina, at north entrance to marina. US 89 86040 (PO Box 1597). Fax: 520/645-1031. **Terms:** Open 5/12-10/15; 3 day cancellation notice; cancellation fee imposed; small pets only, $10 dep req. **Facility:** 25 rooms. Located in a quiet area with a distant view of Lake Powell. 2 stories; exterior corridors. **Services:** area transportation, Page. **Cards:** AE, DI, DS, MC, VI.

LINDA'S LAKE POWELL CONDOS

Phone: (520)645-3222

5/1-10/1	1P: $95-$105	2P: $95-$115
10/2-1/31	1P: $69	2P: $69-$79
2/1-4/30	1P: $68	2P: $68-$78

Cottage

Location: 1019 Tower Butte 86040 (1019 Tower Butte, GREENHAVEN MOBILE PARK). Fax: 520/353-4200. **Terms:** Check-in 4 pm; 3 day cancellation notice; cancellation fee imposed; small pets only, $100 extra charge, limited rooms. **Facility:** 40 rooms. 2 stories; exterior corridors; smoke free premises. **All Rooms:** efficiencies. **Cards:** AE, DS, MC, VI.

MOTEL 6 - PAGE/LAKE POWELL - 4013 Phone: 520/645-5888

◆◆ Motel

	5/1-9/30	1P: $55-$64	2P: $55-$70	XP: $6	F17
	3/1-4/30	1P: $39-$49	2P: $39-$55	XP: $6	F17
	10/1-1/31	1P: $30-$49	2P: $30-$55	XP: $6	F17
	2/1-2/29	1P: $30-$39	2P: $30-$39	XP: $6	F17

Location: Just e of SR 89, on Business Loop 89A (Lake Powell Blvd). 637 S Lake Powell Blvd 86040 (PO Box 4450). **Fax:** 520/645-0009. **Terms:** 3 day cancellation notice; small pets only. **Facility:** 111 rooms. 3 stories; interior corridors; heated pool. **All Rooms:** combo or shower baths. **Cards:** AE, CB, DI, DS, MC, VI.

RAMADA INN PAGE/LAKE POWELL Phone: (520)645-8851

(AAA) SAVE
◆◆◆ Motor Inn

	5/1-9/30	1P: $69-$99	2P: $69-$99	XP: $7	F18
	10/1-10/31	1P: $69	2P: $69	XP: $7	F18
	2/1-4/30 & 11/1-1/31	1P: $49	2P: $49	XP: $7	F18

Location: US 89/SR 89L, 0.8 mi e on Lake Powell Blvd. 287 N Lake Powell Blvd 86040 (PO Box 1867). **Fax:** 520/645-2523. **Terms:** Package plans; small pets only. **Facility:** 129 rooms. Many rooms with balcony or patio providing area panoramic views. 3 stories; interior corridors; heated pool, seasonal pool. **Dining:** Dining room; 6 am-1 & 5:30-9:30 pm; 10/1-4/30 6 am-1 & 5:30-9 pm; $7-$16; cocktails. **Services:** gift shop. **Recreation:** golf and lake activities avail. **All Rooms:** extended cable TV. **Cards:** AE, CB, DI, DS, JC, MC, VI. **Special Amenities:** Free local telephone calls and free newspaper.

SUPER 8 MOTEL Phone: 520/645-2858

◆ Motel

	5/1-9/30	1P: $55-$69	2P: $59-$69	XP: $5	F17
	3/1-4/30 & 10/1-1/31	1P: $39-$49	2P: $39-$55	XP: $5	F17
	2/1-2/29	1P: $39-$45	2P: $39-$49	XP: $5	F17

Location: 1 mi e of US 89, via SR 89L; just n of Lake Powell Blvd. 75 S 7th Ave 86040 (PO Box 4450). **Fax:** 520/645-2890. **Terms:** 3 day cancellation notice. **Facility:** 39 rooms. 2 stories; exterior corridors. **Cards:** AE, CB, DI, DS, MC, VI.

WAHWEAP LODGE Phone: (520)645-2433

(AAA) SAVE
◆◆◆ Resort

	5/19-10/14	1P: $169-$189	2P: $169-$189	XP: $10	F18
	4/1-5/18	1P: $109-$149	2P: $109-$149	XP: $10	F18
	10/15-1/31	1P: $69-$99	2P: $69-$99	XP: $10	F18
	2/1-3/31	1P: $69-$89	2P: $69-$89	XP: $10	F18

Location: 4 mi n of Glen Canyon Dam via US 89 and Lakeshore Dr. 100 Lakeshore Dr 86040 (PO Box 1597). **Fax:** 520/645-1031. **Terms:** 3 day cancellation notice; cancellation fee imposed; small pets only, $10 dep req. **Facility:** 350 rooms. Overlooking Wahweap Basin and Lake Powell. Balconies and patios. 2 stories; interior corridors; 2 heated pools, whirlpool; boat ramp. Fee: boat dock, marina. **Dining:** Dining room; 6 am-10 pm; 7 am-9 pm, in winter; $14-$18; cocktails; entertainment. **Services:** gift shop; area transportation, Page. **Recreation:** Fee: waterskiing, boat trips, river rafting, houseboats. Rental: boats. **All Rooms:** combo or shower baths. **Cards:** AE, DI, DS, MC, VI. *(See color ad p 51 & p 210)*

RESTAURANTS

BELLA NAPOLI **Dinner:** $7-$15 Phone: 520/645-2706

◆◆ Italian

Location: 1 mi s of US 89/SR 89L and just e of Lake Powell Blvd. 810 N Navajo Dr 86040. **Hours:** 5/1-10/31 5 pm-9 pm, Fri & Sat-10 pm. Closed major holidays, Sun, in winter. **Features:** casual dress; children's menu; carryout; beer & wine only. Charming restaurant featuring a nice selection of pasta and pizza. Fresh fish or seafood special Fri. Outdoor patio dining available. Smoke free premises. **Cards:** AE, DS, MC, VI.

THE DAM BAR & GRILLE **Lunch:** $5-$9 **Dinner:** $10-$24 Phone: 520/645-2161

◆◆ American

Location: 0.6 mi n of SR 89 and just n of Lake Powell Blvd; in shopping center. 644 N Navajo Blvd 86040. **Hours:** 4/1-10/15-11 am-midnight, 10/16-3/31-11 am-9 pm. Closed: 12/25 & Sun in off season. **Features:** casual dress; children's menu; carryout; cocktails & lounge. Nice selection of steak, chicken, seafood, pasta, and assortment of sandwiches. **Cards:** AE, MC, VI.

KEN'S OLD WEST RESTAURANT & LOUNGE **Dinner:** $9-$20 Phone: 520/645-5160

◆◆ Steakhouse

Location: Just e of Hwy 89 C. 718 Vista Ave 86040. **Hours:** 4 pm-10 pm; Fri & Sat to 11 pm. Closed: 1/1, 12/25, Sun & Mon in winter. **Features:** No A/C; casual dress; carryout; salad bar; cocktails & lounge; entertainment. Nice selection of steak, seafood and prime rib entrees. Live country and western music daily. **Cards:** AE, MC, VI.

PEPPER'S **Lunch:** $7-$20 **Dinner:** $9-$20 Phone: 520/645-1247

◆◆ Southwest American

Location: On SR 89 L at jct US 89; in Courtyard by Marriott. 600 Clubhouse Dr 86040. **Hours:** 6 am-2 & 5-10 pm. **Features:** casual dress; children's menu; carryout; cocktails & lounge. Very comfortable hotel restaurant featuring Southwest decor and nice variety of Southwestern and American entrees. **Cards:** AE, CB, DI, DS, JC, MC, VI.

PARADISE VALLEY —*See Phoenix p. 265.*

PARKER pop. 2,900

——— LODGINGS ———

BEST WESTERN PARKER INN   Phone: (520)669-6060
AAA SAVE   12/31-1/31   1P: $59-$89   2P: $69-$99   XP: $5   F12
◆◆◆   2/1-4/30 & 8/31-12/30   1P: $59-$79   2P: $59-$99   XP: $5   F12
Motel   5/1-8/30   1P: $49-$69   2P: $49-$89   XP: $5   F12
           Location: E of US 95. 1012 Geronimo Ave 85344. Fax: 520/669-6204. **Terms:** Weekly rates avail; cancella-
           tion fee imposed; small pets only, in limited rooms. **Facility:** 44 rooms. 2 stories; interior corridors.
All Rooms: combo or shower baths. **Cards:** AE, CB, DI, DS, JC, MC, VI. **Special Amenities: Free local telephone calls
and free room upgrade (subject to availability with advanced reservations).** *(See color ad below)*

BLUE WATER RESORT & CASINO   Phone: (520)669-7000
◆◆◆   2/1-5/15   1P: $109-$129   2P: $109-$129
Resort   5/16-9/5   1P: $99-$119   2P: $99-$119
           9/6-1/31   1P: $79-$99   2P: $79-$99
Location: 1.5 mi e of SR 95. 11300 Resort Dr 85344. Fax: 520/669-6381. **Terms:** Cancellation fee imposed. **Facility:** 200
rooms. All rooms with balcony and marina view. 5 stories; exterior corridors; 4 heated pools. Fee: miniature golf; boat dock,
marina. **Services:** gift shop. **Cards:** AE, DS, MC, VI.

STARDUST MOTEL   Phone: (520)669-2278
AAA SAVE   2/1-3/31 & 1/1-1/31   1P: $40   2P: $50   XP: $10   F8
◆   4/1-12/31   1P: $35   2P: $40   XP: $10   F8
Motel   **Location:** W end of town. 700 California Ave 85344. Fax: 520/669-6658. **Facility:** 23 rooms. 4 two-bedroom
           units. 2 stories; exterior corridors. **Cards:** AE, DI, DS, MC, VI. **Special Amenities: Free local telephone calls
           and preferred room (subject to availability with advanced reservations).**

Savings at Your Fingertips

When you have a AAA TourBook® guide in your hand, you have a world of savings right at your fingertips. Lodgings that display the bright-red AAA emblem beside their listing want AAA member business, and many of them offer special amenities and discounts.

Also, keep your eye out for the familiar SAVE symbol. This icon represents a 10 percent savings off published room rates to AAA members.

So, when planning your next vacation, be sure to consult your AAA TourBook.

Travel With Someone You Trust®

PAYSON pop. 8,400

—— LODGINGS ——

BEST WESTERN PAYSONGLO LODGE
Phone: (520)474-2382

4/7-10/28	1P: $75-$140	2P: $75-$140	XP: $10	D10
10/29-1/31	1P: $75-$114	2P: $75-$114	XP: $10	D10
2/1-4/6	1P: $72-$114	2P: $72-$114	XP: $10	D10

Motel **Location:** On SR 87, 1 mi s of jct SR 260. 1005 S Beeline Hwy 85541. Fax: 520/474-1937. **Terms:** [ECP] meal plan; small pets only, $30 dep req, in smoking rooms. **Facility:** 47 rooms. Nicely furnished units, 16 with fireplace. Some small units. 1-2 stories; exterior corridors; heated pool, whirlpool. **Dining:** Coffee shop nearby. **All Rooms:** extended cable TV. **Cards:** AE, CB, DI, DS, MC, VI. *(See color ad below)*

DAYS INN & SUITES
Phone: (520)474-9800

6/1-8/31	1P: $69-$149	2P: $69-$149	XP: $6	F12
2/1-5/31 & 9/1-1/31	1P: $39-$99	2P: $39-$99	XP: $6	F12

Motel **Location:** On SR 87 just s of jct SR 260. 301 A S Beeline Hwy 85541. Fax: 520/474-9700. **Terms:** [CP] & [ECP] meal plans; weekly rates avail; 24 day cancellation notice; small pets only, $10 extra charge, in smoking rooms. **Facility:** 48 rooms. 3 whirlpool rooms; $79-$149; 2 stories; interior corridors; heated pool, whirlpool. **All Rooms:** extended cable TV. **Cards:** AE, CB, DI, DS, JC, MC, VI. **Special Amenities:** Free breakfast and free newspaper.

THE FOUNTAIN INN
Phone: (520)474-0622

All Year	1P: $95-$165	2P: $95-$165

Bed & Breakfast **Location:** 0.2 mi e of jct SR 260 and SR 87, just se on Granite Dell Rd. 801 E Granite Dells Rd 85541. Fax: 520/474-0622. **Terms:** Check-in 4 pm; 14 day cancellation notice; cancellation fee imposed; 2 night min stay, weekends. **Facility:** 5 rooms. Beautifully decorated rooms in different theme. 1 room with private patio and whirlpool; 3 rooms with fireplace. 2 persons max in each room. Walking path and creek. 2 stories; interior/exterior corridors. **Some Rooms:** color TV. **Cards:** MC, VI.

HOLIDAY INN EXPRESS

Phone: (520)472-7484

6/1-8/31	1P: $79-$149	2P: $79-$149	XP: $5 F19
9/1-1/31	1P: $49-$119	2P: $49-$119	XP: $5 F19
2/1-5/31	1P: $49-$99	2P: $49-$99	XP: $5 F19

Motel
Location: SR 87, just s of jct SR 260. 206 S BeeLine 85541 (PO Box 279, 85547). Fax: 520/472-6283. **Terms:** [ECP] meal plan; small pets only, $25 dep req, in limited rooms. **Facility:** 44 rooms. 19 whirlpool rooms, $89-$159; 3 stories; interior corridors; heated pool, whirlpool. **Services:** area transportation, Shuttle to Casino. **Recreation:** video rentals. **Some Rooms:** Fee: VCR. **Cards:** AE, DI, DS, JC, MC, VI. **Special Amenities:** Free breakfast and free newspaper.

INN OF PAYSON

Phone: (520)474-3241

5/1-10/31	1P: $89	2P: $89	XP: $10 F15
2/1-4/30 & 11/1-1/31	1P: $79	2P: $79	XP: $10 F15

Motel
Location: .3 mi n of SR 260 on SR 87. 801 N Beeline Hwy 85541 (PO Box 399). Fax: 520/472-6564. **Terms:** [ECP] meal plan; small pets only, $10 fee. **Facility:** 99 rooms. 2 stories; exterior corridors; heated pool. **All Rooms:** combo or shower baths. **Cards:** AE, DI, DS, MC, VI. *(See color ad below)*

MAJESTIC MOUNTAIN INN

Phone: 520/474-0185

5/27-9/4	1P: $56-$99	2P: $62-$99	XP: $6
9/5-1/31	1P: $50-$85	2P: $58-$85	
2/1-5/26	1P: $50-$85	2P: $58-$85	XP: $6

Motel
Location: On SR 260. 0.5 mi e of jct SR 87. 602 E Hwy 260 85541. Fax: 520/472-6097. **Terms:** Pets, $6 extra charge, designated rooms. **Facility:** 50 rooms. Pine-shaded lawn area with picnic tables and barbecue. 1-2 stories; exterior corridors; heated pool. **Cards:** AE, CB, DI, DS, MC, VI.

PAYSON PUEBLO INN

Phone: (520)474-5241

5/1-9/30	1P: $54-$99	2P: $59-$159	XP: $5 F3
2/1-4/30 & 10/1-1/31	1P: $44-$79	2P: $49-$135	XP: $5 F3

Motel
Location: On SR 260; 0.8 mi e of SR 87. 809 E Hwy 260 85541. Fax: 520/472-6919. **Terms:** [CP] meal plan; weekly rates avail; small pets only, $50 dep req, $10 fee. **Facility:** 39 rooms. Attractive pueblo style building. 7 large units with whirlpool, 6 with gas fireplace $79-$159; 2 stories; exterior corridors. **Dining:** Coffee shop nearby. **All Rooms:** extended cable TV. **Cards:** AE, CB, DI, DS, MC, VI. **Special Amenities:** Free breakfast and free local telephone calls.

RIM COUNTRY INN

Phone: (520)474-4526

5/1-10/31	1P: $39-$79	2P: $44-$89	XP: $6 F12
2/1-4/30 & 11/1-1/31	1P: $35-$64	2P: $39-$69	XP: $6 F12

Motel
Location: SR 87, 1.3 mi s of jct SR 260. 101 West Phoenix St 85541. Fax: 520/474-0263. **Terms:** Small pets only, $6 extra charge. **Facility:** 39 rooms. Located on Beeline Hwy, at south edge of town. 2 stories; interior corridors. **Cards:** AE, CB, DI, DS, JC, MC, VI.

TRAILS END MOTEL   Phone: (520)474-2283

5/1-11/1	1P: $39-$99	2P: $39-$99	XP: $5	F12
2/1-4/30 & 11/2-1/31	1P: $29-$79	2P: $29-$79	XP: $5	F12

Motel   **Location:** 0.5 mi s of jct SR 260 and SR 87. 811 S Beeline Hwy 85541. **Fax:** 520/474-5448. **Terms:** Cancellation fee imposed; pets, $5 extra charge. **Facility:** 24 rooms. 2 stories; interior/exterior corridors. **All Rooms:** combo or shower baths, extended cable TV. **Cards:** AE, CB, DI, DS, JC, MC, VI. **Special Amenities:** Free local telephone calls and free room upgrade (subject to availability with advanced reservations).

----- **RESTAURANTS** -----

MARIO'S RESTAURANT & LOUNGE   **Lunch:** $4-$14   **Dinner:** $4-$14   **Phone:** 520/474-5429

◆◆
Italian   **Location:** On SR 260, 0.5 mi e of jct SR 87 and 260. 600 E Hwy 260 85541. **Hours:** 10:30 am-9 pm, Fri & Sat-10 pm. Closed: 11/23 & 12/25. **Features:** casual dress; children's menu; carryout; salad bar; cocktails. Casual family dining. Homemade fresh bread daily. Catering and off track betting. **Cards:** AE, DS, MC, VI.

THE OAKS RESTAURANT   **Lunch:** $5-$9   **Dinner:** $11-$18   **Phone:** 520/474-1929

◆◆◆
American   **Location:** 0.3 mi w of SR 87. 302 W Main St 85541. **Hours:** 11 am-2 & 5-8 pm, Fri & Sat-9 pm. Closed: 12/25, Mon & Tues. **Reservations:** suggested. **Features:** casual dress; Sunday brunch; cocktails & lounge. Charming, homelike atmosphere. Outdoor patio dining avail during warm weather. Nice selection of prime rib, steak, seafood, veal and chicken. Smoke free premises. **Cards:** AE, DS, MC, VI.

PEACH SPRINGS

----- **LODGING** -----

HUALAPAI LODGE   Phone: (520)769-2230

◆◆
5/29-9/27	1P: $75-$85	2P: $75-$85	XP: $10	F18
2/1-5/28 & 9/28-1/31	1P: $50-$60	2P: $55-$65	XP: $10	F18

Motor Inn   **Location:** I-40, exit 53 in Kingman, then 49 mi n on Historic Rt 66. 900 Rt 66 86434 (PO Box 538). **Fax:** 520/769-2372. **Terms:** Package plans. **Facility:** 60 rooms. 2 stories; interior corridors. **Services:** gift shop. **All Rooms:** combo or shower baths. **Cards:** AE, DS, MC, VI. *(See color ad p 196)*

PEORIA —*See Phoenix p. 265.*

PHOENIX —*See Phoenix p. 230.*

Take a Step
Back in Time

*B*ring a little of the past into the present. Make your next vacation stay at a Bed & Breakfast. Look for the new ***Bed & Breakfast Ad Index*** in this TourBook® guide and discover the charming B&Bs located along your way.

Travel With Someone You Trust®

Destination Phoenix

*R*ising from the centuries-old ashes of a once-thriving Hohokam Indian community, modern Phoenix is a city of diverse architectural styles.

*F*rom prehistoric ruins at the Pueblo Grande Museum, to Heritage Square's Victorian homes, to Frank Lloyd Wright's paragon of modernism Taliesin West, you can witness Phoenix's heritage manifested in timber, brick and stone.

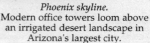

Phoenix skyline.
Modern office towers loom above an irrigated desert landscape in Arizona's largest city.

Golf course.
Pack your clubs when you visit Phoenix; the city is home to some of the best golf courses in the nation.

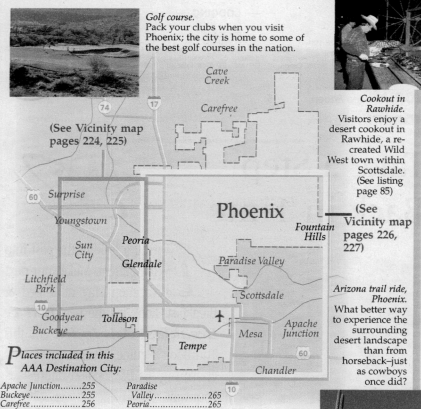

Cookout in Rawhide.
Visitors enjoy a desert cookout in Rawhide, a recreated Wild West town within Scottsdale. (See listing page 85)

(See Vicinity map pages 224, 225)

(See Vicinity map pages 226, 227)

Arizona trail ride, Phoenix.
What better way to experience the surrounding desert landscape than from horseback–just as cowboys once did?

*P*laces included in this AAA Destination City:

Apache Junction	255	Paradise Valley	265
Buckeye	255	Peoria	265
Carefree	256	Scottsdale	266
Cave Creek	256	Sun City/Sun City West	280
Chandler	256	Surprise	280
Fountain Hills	259	Tempe	281
Glendale	260	Tolleson	289
Goodyear	260	Youngtown	289
Litchfield Park	260		
Mesa	261		

Phoenix *pop. 983,400*

This index helps you "spot" where approved accommodations are located on the detailed maps that follow. Rate ranges are for comparison only and show the property's high season. Turn to the listing page for more detailed rate information and consult display ads for special promotions. Restaurant rate range is for dinner unless only lunch (L) is served.

✈ Airport Accommodations

Spotter/Map Page Number	OA	PHOENIX	Diamond Rating	Rate Range High Season	Listing Page
149 / p. 225	⊕	Best Western Airport Inn, 1 mi s of w airport entrance	◆ ◆	$99-$119 [SAVE]	230
155 / p. 225		Courtyard by Marriott Phoenix Airport, 0.5 mi s of e airport entrance	◆ ◆ ◆	$169	235
140 / p. 225		Doubletree Guest Suites at the Phoenix Gateway Cen, 1.3 mi n of e airport entrance	◆ ◆ ◆	$119-$144	236
156 / p. 225		Fairfield Inn by Marriott Phoenix Airport, 0.5 mi s of e airport entrance	◆ ◆	$119	238
151 / p. 225		Hilton Phoenix Airport, 0.5 mi s of e airport entrance	◆ ◆ ◆	$85-$110	240
148 / p. 225	⊕	Holiday Inn-Select Airport, 1 mi n of e airport entrance	◆ ◆ ◆	$99-$149 [SAVE]	241
154 / p. 225	⊕	Radisson Phoenix Airport Hotel, 3 mi se of west airport entrance; use I-10 east	◆ ◆ ◆	$169-$199 [SAVE]	246
152 / p. 225		Sleep Inn Sky Harbor Airport, 0.5 mi s of e airport entrance	◆ ◆	$89-$129	249
133 / p. 225	⊕	Wyndham Garden Hotel Phoenix Airport, 1.3 mi n of e airport entrance	◆ ◆ ◆	$184 [SAVE]	252
408 / p. 227	⊕	La Quinta Inn, 1 mi s of e airport entrance	◆ ◆ ◆	$89-$109 [SAVE]	285

SUN CITY/SUN CITY WEST

Spotter/Map Page Number	OA	SUN CITY/SUN CITY WEST - Lodgings	Diamond Rating	Rate Range High Season	Listing Page
3 / p. 224	⊕	Best Western Inn & Suites of Sun City - see color ad p 238	◆ ◆ ◆	$80-$95 [SAVE]	280

PHOENIX

Spotter/Map Page Number	OA	PHOENIX - Lodgings	Diamond Rating	Rate Range High Season	Listing Page
50 / p. 225	⊕	Days Inn-North Phoenix	◆ ◆ ◆	$70-$90 [SAVE]	236
52 / p. 225	⊕	Wyndham Garden Hotel North Phoenix - see color ad p 251	◆ ◆ ◆	$139 [SAVE]	250
53 / p. 225		Homestead Village North/Deer Valley	◆ ◆ ◆	$59	241
54 / p. 225		Sleep Inn Phoenix North	◆ ◆	$79-$99	249
55 / p. 225		Super 8 Motel	◆ ◆ ◆	$70-$85	249
57 / p. 225	⊕	Red Roof Inn-Phoenix	◆ ◆	$50-$85	247
58 / p. 225	⊕	Best Western Bell Hotel - see color ad p 231	◆ ◆ ◆	$93-$109 [SAVE]	230
61 / p. 225		Fairfield Inn by Marriott Phoenix North	◆ ◆	$119	238
62 / p. 225	⊕	Comfort Inn Turf Paradise	◆ ◆	$46-$100 [SAVE]	233
63 / p. 225	⊕	La Quinta Phoenix North - see color ad p 242	◆ ◆ ◆	$79-$99 [SAVE]	242
65 / p. 225	⊕	Embassy Suites Phoenix North - see color ad p 238	◆ ◆ ◆	$143-$153 [SAVE]	238
67 / p. 225		Candlewood Suites - see ad p 232	◆ ◆ ◆	$60-$105	233
68 / p. 225		Ramada Plaza Hotel Metrocenter	◆ ◆ ◆	$119	247
69 / p. 225	⊕	Wellesley Inn & Suites Phoenix/Metrocenter	◆ ◆ ◆	$65-$110 [SAVE]	250
70 / p. 225	⊕	Pointe Hilton Tapatio Cliffs Resorts - see color ad p. 41 & ad p 245	◆ ◆ ◆ ◆	$189-$239 [SAVE]	244
71 / p. 225	⊕	AmeriSuites-Phoenix Metro Center - see color ad opposite title page	◆ ◆ ◆	$89-$126 [SAVE]	230
72 / p. 225	⊕	Crowne Plaza Phoenix-Metrocenter - see ad p 234	◆ ◆ ◆	$119 [SAVE]	236
73 / p. 225	⊕	Royal Suites - see color ad p 248	◆ ◆ ◆	$85 [SAVE]	248

Spotter/Map Page Number	OA	PHOENIX - Lodgings (continued)	Diamond Rating	Rate Range High Season	Listing Page
75 / p. 225		Comfort Suites	◆◆◆	$99-$109	234
76 / p. 225		Homewood Suites Hotel - see color ad p 241	◆◆◆	$99	241
77 / p. 225		Wyndham Metrocenter Hotel - see color ad p 251	◆◆◆	$169	252
79 / p. 225	⊕	Premier Inns	◆◆	$50-$100 🆂🆅🅴	244
80 / p. 225		Courtyard by Marriott Phoenix North	◆◆◆	$99-$129	235
82 / p. 225		Sierra Suites Hotel-Phoenix/Metro Center	◆◆◆	$119	248
83 / p. 225		TownePlace Suites-Phoenix	◆◆◆	$39-$85	249
84 / p. 225		Sheraton Crescent Hotel	◆◆◆◆	$119-$250	248
85 / p. 225		Spring Hill Suites-Phoenix/Metro Center	◆◆◆	$99-$119	249
86 / p. 225	⊕	Residence Inn By Marriott - see color ad p 247	◆◆◆	$119-$139 🆂🆅🅴	247
87 / p. 225		Homestead Village/Guest Suites/Phoenix Metro	◆◆◆	$59	241
88 / p. 225	⊕	Super 8 Motel	◆◆	$54-$81 🆂🆅🅴	249
90 / p. 225		Hampton Inn I-17	◆◆◆	$94	239
91 / p. 225	⊕	Best Western InnSuites Hotel Phoenix - see color ad p 232	◆◆◆	$89-$189 🆂🆅🅴	232
92 / p. 225	⊕	Pointe Hilton Squaw Peak Resort - see color ad p 41 & ad p 245	◆◆◆	$239 🆂🆅🅴	244
93 / p. 225	⊕	Phoenix Inn	◆◆◆	$129-$149 🆂🆅🅴	244
94 / p. 225	⊕	Comfort Inn Black Canyon - see color ad p 229	◆◆	$76-$109 🆂🆅🅴	233
95 / p. 225		Ramada Hotel-Camelback	◆◆	$99-$109	246
96 / p. 225		Maricopa Manor Bed & Breakfast Inn	◆◆◆	$129-$249	243
98 / p. 225		Sierra Suites Hotel-Phoenix/Camelback	◆◆◆	$129-$159	248
99 / p. 225	⊕	Embassy Suites-Biltmore - see color ad p 237	◆◆◆	$239 🆂🆅🅴	237
102 / p. 225		Royal Palms Hotel & Casitas	◆◆◆◆	$315	248
104 / p. 225		Ritz Carlton-Phoenix	◆◆◆◆	$209	248
105 / p. 225	⊕	Howard Johnson-Grand Ave - see color ad p 368	◆◆	$109 🆂🆅🅴	242
106 / p. 225		Courtyard by Marriott Camelback	◆◆◆	$179	234
107 / p. 225	⊕	Ramada Limited Suites	◆◆◆	$99-$109 🆂🆅🅴	247
108 / p. 225	⊕	Wellesley Inn & Suites Phoenix Airport	◆◆◆	$80-$100 🆂🆅🅴	250
109 / p. 225	⊕	Lexington Hotel at City Square	◆◆◆	$99-$139 🆂🆅🅴	243
110 / p. 225		Les Jardins Hotel & Suites	fyi	$89-$99	252
112 / p. 225	⊕	Holiday Inn Midtown Phoenix	◆◆◆	$95-$149 🆂🆅🅴	240
113 / p. 225	⊕	Quality Suites - see color ad p 246	◆◆	$119-$139 🆂🆅🅴	246
114 / p. 225	⊕	Red Roof Inn	◆◆	$50-$85	247
115 / p. 225		Ramada Limited I-10 West	◆◆◆	$69-$109	247
116 / p. 225	⊕	Holiday Inn West	◆◆◆	$99-$129 🆂🆅🅴	241
118 / p. 225	⊕	Days Inn-I-17 & Thomas - see color ad p 231	◆	$73-$99 🆂🆅🅴	236
119 / p. 225	⊕	Country Suites by Carlson - Phoenix/West - see color ad p 234	◆◆◆	$59-$125 🆂🆅🅴	234
120 / p. 225	⊕	La Quinta Inn-Coliseum - see color ad p 242	◆◆◆	$69-$89 🆂🆅🅴	242
121 / p. 225	⊕	Quality Hotel & Resort	◆◆	$109-$129 🆂🆅🅴	244
122 / p. 225		Hilton Suites-Phoenix - see color ad p 41 & ad p 240	◆◆◆	$157	240
123 / p. 225	⊕	Wellesley Inn & Suites Phoenix/Park Central	◆◆◆	$100 🆂🆅🅴	250
124 / p. 225		Embassy Suites Hotel Airport West - see color ad p 237	◆◆◆	$149-$180	237
125 / p. 225	⊕	Embassy Suites Airport at 44th St - see color ad p 237	◆◆◆	$149-$189 🆂🆅🅴	237
126 / p. 225		Fairfield Inn Phoenix West	◆◆◆	$69-$79	238
128 / p. 225		Hampton Inn Phoenix I-10 West - see ad p 239	◆◆◆	$79-$99	239
129 / p. 225	⊕	Days Inn I-10 West	◆◆	$80-$130 🆂🆅🅴	236
130 / p. 225	⊕	Travelers Inn	◆◆	$43-$70 🆂🆅🅴	249
132 / p. 225		Best Western Executive Park Hotel	◆◆◆	$101	231

Spotter/Map Page Number	OA	PHOENIX - Lodgings (continued)	Diamond Rating	Rate Range High Season	Listing Page
133 / p. 225	◆	Wyndham Garden Hotel Phoenix Airport - see color ad p 251	◆◆◆	$184 ⬛	252
134 / p. 225	◆	Los Olivos Hotel & Suites - see ad p 243	◆◆	$99-$129	243
135 / p. 225		Holiday Inn Express Hotel & Suites	◆◆◆	$109-$189	240
136 / p. 225	◆	Crowne Plaza Downtown Phoenix - see ad p 235	◆◆◆	$183-$229 ⬛	235
137 / p. 225	◆	Days Inn-Airport	◆◆	$72-$105 ⬛	236
139 / p. 225		Hampton Inn Phoenix Airport North	◆◆◆	$119-$129	239
140 / p. 225		Doubletree Guest Suites at the Phoenix Gateway Center - see ad p 236	◆◆◆	$119-$144	236
142 / p. 225	◆	Hyatt Regency Phoenix	◆◆◆	$189-$214 ⬛	242
146 / p. 225	◆	Super 8-Airport	◆	$89 ⬛	249
148 / p. 225	◆	Holiday Inn-Select Airport	◆◆◆	$99-$149 ⬛	241
149 / p. 225	◆	Best Western Airport Inn - see color ad p 230	◆◆	$99-$119 ⬛	230
150 / p. 225		Holiday Inn Express Hotel and Suites	◆◆◆	$139	240
151 / p. 225		Hilton Phoenix Airport - see color ad p 41	◆◆◆	$85-$110	240
152 / p. 225		Sleep Inn Sky Harbor Airport - see color ad p 231	◆◆	$89-$129	249
154 / p. 225	◆	Radisson Phoenix Airport Hotel	◆◆◆	$169-$199 ⬛	246
155 / p. 225		Courtyard by Marriott Phoenix Airport	◆◆◆	$169	235
156 / p. 225		Fairfield Inn by Marriott Phoenix Airport	◆◆	$119	238
158 / p. 225		Hampton Inn Airport/Tempe	◆◆◆	$99-$119	239
159 / p. 225	◆	Pointe Hilton South Mountain Resort - see color ad p 41 & ad p 245	◆◆◆◆	$209 ⬛	244
160 / p. 225		Quality Inn-South Mountain - see color ad p 246	◆◆◆	$99-$119	246
161 / p. 225	◆	Best Western Grace Inn At Ahwatukee	◆◆◆	$129-$169 ⬛	232
163 / p. 225	◆	Wellesley Inn & Suites Phoenix/Chandler	◆◆	$99-$109 ⬛	250
164 / p. 225	◆	La Quinta Inn & Suites-Chandler - see color ad p 242	◆◆◆	$85-$105 ⬛	242
165 / p. 225	◆	Travelodge-Fairgrounds	◆	$50-$70 ⬛	249
166 / p. 225	◆	Comfort Inn I-10 West/Central	◆◆◆	$70-$100 ⬛	233
		PHOENIX - Restaurants			
20 / p. 225		Pointe in Tyme Restaurant at Tapatio Cliffs	◆◆	$10-$20	254
21 / p. 225		Different Pointe of View	◆◆◆◆	$24-$35	253
22 / p. 225		Our Gang Cafe	◆◆	$5-$15	254
24 / p. 225		Aunt Chiladas	◆◆	$7-$14	252
26 / p. 225		Lantana Grille	◆	$10-$21	253
28 / p. 225		Christo's	◆◆◆	$10-$18	253
29 / p. 225		Eddie Matney's	◆◆◆	$17-$30	253
30 / p. 225		The Fish Market & Top of The Market	◆◆	$13-$30	253
31 / p. 225		Omaha Steakhouse	◆◆	$11-$34	253
32 / p. 225		Sam's Cafe	◆◆	$6-$15	254
33 / p. 225		Vincent Guerithault	◆◆◆	$20-$22	255
34 / p. 225		Tarbell's	◆◆◆	$11-$20	254
36 / p. 225		Havana Cafe	◆◆	$10-$17	253
37 / p. 225		T. Cook's	◆◆◆	$17-$39	254
39 / p. 225		Ed Debevic's Short Orders Deluxe	◆	$4-$8	253
40 / p. 225		Bistro 24	◆◆◆	$8-$23	253
41 / p. 225		RoxSand	◆◆◆	$16-$22	254
43 / p. 225		The Bamboo Club	◆◆	$6-$18	252
46 / p. 225		Ristorante Pronto	◆◆◆	$10-$16	254
47 / p. 225		Anna's Cafe	◆	$11-$16	252
48 / p. 225		Macayo	◆◆	$10-$12	253
49 / p. 225		The Roman Table	◆	$8-$20	254
50 / p. 225		Rose's	◆◆	$9-$18	254
52 / p. 225		Compass Restaurant	◆◆◆	$10-$21	253
53 / p. 225		Stockyards Restaurant	◆	$14-$30	254
54 / p. 225		Rennicks	◆◆	$10-$19	254

Spotter/Map Page Number	OA	PHOENIX - Restaurants (continued)	Diamond Rating	Rate Range High Season	Listing Page
55 / p. 225		Rustler's Rooste	◆◆	$13-$31	254
57 / p. 225		Another Pointe in Tyme at South Mountain	◆◆◆	$15-$25	252
61 / p. 225		T-Bone Steakhouse	◆	$14-$25	254

GLENDALE

Spotter/Map Page Number	OA	GLENDALE - Lodgings	Diamond Rating	Rate Range High Season	Listing Page
180 / p. 225		SpringHill Suites by Marriott	◆◆◆	$39-$99	260
181 / p. 225		Holiday Inn Express Arrowhead	◆◆◆	$89-$109	260

SCOTTSDALE

Spotter/Map Page Number	OA	SCOTTSDALE - Lodgings	Diamond Rating	Rate Range High Season	Listing Page
256 / p. 226		Springhill Suites	◆◆◆	$139	277
258 / p. 226		Courtyard By Marriott/Scottsdale North	◆◆◆	Failed to provide	267
259 / p. 226		Scottsdale Princess	◆◆◆◆◆	$449-$569	276
261 / p. 226	(AAA)	Sleep Inn	◆◆	$85-$103 🛏	276
262 / p. 226	(AAA)	Holiday Inn Hotel & Suites - see color ad p 271	◆◆◆	$159-$169 🛏	271
264 / p. 226		Scottsdale Fairfield Inn	◆◆	$135	275
265 / p. 226		Sierra Suites Hotel	◆◆◆	$109-$169	276
267 / p. 226		Country Inn & Suites By Carlson - see color ad p 229	◆◆◆	$109-$129	267
268 / p. 226	(AAA)	Doubletree Paradise Valley Resort - see ad p 269	◆◆◆	$225-$245 🛏	268
269 / p. 226	(AAA)	La Quinta Inn & Suites - see color ad p 242	◆◆◆	$99-$125 🛏	273
270 / p. 226		Courtyard by Marriott Scottsdale/Mayo Clinic	◆◆◆	$129-$169	267
271 / p. 226	(AAA)	Hampton Inn Scottsdale - see ad p 270	◆◆◆	$109-$160 🛏	270
273 / p. 226	(AAA)	Comfort Inn of Scottsdale - see ad p 267	◆◆◆	$109-$146 🛏	267
274 / p. 226		Homewood Suites Hotel Phoenix/Scottsdale	◆◆◆	$130	272
275 / p. 226		Gainey Suites Hotel	◆◆◆	$139-$212	269
276 / p. 226		Hyatt Regency Scottsdale at Gainey Ranch	◆◆◆	$390-$400	272
277 / p. 226	(AAA)	The Scottsdale Plaza Resort	◆◆◆◆	$350	276
279 / p. 226	(AAA)	Radisson Resort & Spa Scottsdale - see color ad p 277	[fyi]	$199 🛏	278
280 / p. 226	(AAA)	Regal McCormick Ranch	◆◆◆	$245-$319 🛏	274
282 / p. 226	(AAA)	Scottsdale Pima Inn & Suites - see color ad p 276	◆◆	$99-$154 🛏	276
283 / p. 226	(AAA)	Marriott's Camelback Inn Resort, Golf Club & Spa	◆◆◆◆◆	$255-$469 🛏	273
285 / p. 226		Holiday Inn Sunspree Resort - see ad p 272	◆◆◆	$145-$179	272
286 / p. 226		Marriott's Mountain Shadows Resort and Golf Club	◆◆◆	$199-$229	273
288 / p. 226	(AAA)	Doubletree La Posada Resort - Scottsdale - see ad p 269	◆◆◆	$210 🛏	268
289 / p. 226		Residence Inn by Marriott	◆◆◆	$149-$179	275
290 / p. 226	(AAA)	Renaissance Cottonwoods Resort	◆◆◆	$149-$279 🛏	275
291 / p. 226	(AAA)	Hilton Scottsdale Resort & Villas - see color ad p 41	[fyi]	$294-$404 🛏	278
294 / p. 226	(AAA)	The Phoenician	◆◆◆◆	$525-$655	274
295 / p. 226	(AAA)	Fairfield Inn-Downtown Scottsdale - see color ad p 270	◆◆	$88-$108 🛏	268
296 / p. 226		The Ivy at the Waterfront	◆◆	$189-$425	273
297 / p. 226	(AAA)	Days Inn, Scottsdale Fashion Square Resort - see color ad p 268	◆◆	$89-$215 🛏	267
298 / p. 226		Scottsdale Downtown Courtyard	◆◆◆	$169	275
299 / p. 226		SunBurst Resort	◆◆◆	$165-$205	277
300 / p. 226		Homestead Village	◆◆	$85-$100	272
301 / p. 226	(AAA)	AmeriSuites-Scottsdale/Civic Center - see color ad opposite title page	◆◆◆	$125-$179 🛏	266
302 / p. 226		Econo Lodge - Scottsdale	◆◆	$89-$109	268

Spotter/Map Page Number	OA	SCOTTSDALE - Lodgings (continued)	Diamond Rating	Rate Range High Season	Listing Page
303 / p. 226		Hampton Inn-Oldtown Scottsdale	◆◆◆	$89-$109	270
305 / p. 226	⊕	Holiday Inn Old Town Scottsdale - see color ad p 271	◆◆◆	$130-$145 ⬛	271
306 / p. 226		Ramada Valley Ho Resort - see color ad p 274	◆◆	$99-$129	274
308 / p. 226		Marriott Suites Scottsdale	◆◆◆	$89-$229	274
309 / p. 226		Comfort Suites-Scottsdale	◆◆	$119-$149	267
311 / p. 226	⊕	Rodeway Inn of Scottsdale - see ad p 275	◆◆	$89-$121 ⬛	275
312 / p. 226		Quality Inn and Suites	◆◆◆	$119-$139	274
314 / p. 226	⊕	Best Western Papago Inn & Resort - see color ad p 266	◆◆◆	$109-$129 ⬛	266
316 / p. 226		InnSuites Hotel Scottsdale - see color ad p 273	◆◆	$79-$99	273
317 / p. 226		Summerfield Suites Hotel	◆◆◆	$159-$189	277
319 / p. 226	⊕	Hospitality Suite Resort	◆◆◆	$129-$159 ⬛	272
320 / p. 226	⊕	Hampton Inn & Suites	◆◆◆	$119-$139 ⬛	270
		SCOTTSDALE - Restaurants			
115 / p. 226		Rawhide Steakhouse & Saloon	◆	$10-$23	279
116 / p. 226		La Hacienda	◆◆◆◆	$25-$32	278
117 / p. 226		The Grill	◆◆◆	varies	278
118 / p. 226		Marquesa	◆◆◆◆◆	$32-$40	279
119 / p. 226		Golden Swan	◆◆◆	$24-$35	278
121 / p. 226		Sandolo Ristorante	◆◆	$14-$22	280
122 / p. 226		Remington's	◆◆◆	$16-$22	279
123 / p. 226		Pinon Grill	◆◆	$18-$26	279
124 / p. 226		The Chaparral	◆◆◆◆	$28-$45	278
125 / p. 226		El Chorro Lodge Restaurant	◆◆◆	$16-$36	278
126 / p. 226		Roy's Pacific Rim Cuisine	◆◆◆	$17-$28	280
127 / p. 226		The Other Place	◆◆	$9-$20	279
128 / p. 226		The Quilted Bear	◆◆	$9-$18	279
129 / p. 226		Cafe Terra Cotta	◆◆	$8-$23	278
130 / p. 226		Mancuso's Restaurant	◆◆◆	$12-$27	279
131 / p. 226		Rancho Pinot Grill	◆◆◆	$17-$28	279
133 / p. 226		Voltaire's	◆◆	$18-$28	280
134 / p. 226		P F Chang's China Bistro	◆◆	$8-$13	279
136 / p. 226		Windows on the Green	◆◆◆	$25-$40	280
137 / p. 226		The Terrace Dining Room	◆◆◆◆	$17-$25	280
139 / p. 226		Mary Elaine's	◆◆◆◆◆	$27-$50	279
140 / p. 226		Malee's Thai On Main	◆◆	$9-$19	279
141 / p. 226		Russell's on 2nd	◆◆	$12-$22	280
142 / p. 226		Pepin	◆◆	$13-$25	279

TEMPE

Spotter/Map Page Number	OA	TEMPE - Lodgings	Diamond Rating	Rate Range High Season	Listing Page
370 / p. 227	⊕	Ramada Suites Tempe/Scottsdale	◆◆	$117-$179 ⬛	286
371 / p. 227		Hampton Inn & Suites	◆◆◆	$105-$125	284
372 / p. 227		Country Inn & Suites by Carlson	◆◆◆	$109	283
373 / p. 227	⊕	Best Western Inn of Tempe - see color ad p 282	◆◆◆	$112-$132 ⬛	281
374 / p. 227		Tempe Mission Palms Hotel - see color ad p 250	◆◆◆	$209-$299	287
376 / p. 227	⊕	Sumner Suites Tempe/Phoenix Airport	◆◆◆	$159-$169 ⬛	287
377 / p. 227		Microtel Inn & Suites	◆◆	$59-$89	286
379 / p. 227		Courtyard by Marriott-Downtown Tempe	◆◆◆	$179	283
380 / p. 227		Tempe Super 8	◆◆	$69-$99	287
382 / p. 227	⊕	Econo Lodge/Tempe ASU - see color ad p 284	◆	$45-$85 ⬛	283
383 / p. 227		Sheraton Plaza Hotel-Phoenix Airport	◆◆◆	$235	286
384 / p. 227	⊕	Mainstay Suites-Tempe - see color ad p 281	◆◆◆	$110-$130 ⬛	286

Spotter/Map Page Number	OA	TEMPE - Lodgings (continued)	Diamond Rating	Rate Range High Season	Listing Page
385 / p. 227	⚑	Rodeway Inn Phoenix Airport East - see color ad p 281	◆◆	$59-$79 ⚏	286
386 / p. 227	⚑	Twin Palms Hotel At ASU	◆◆	$95-$169 ⚏	288
387 / p. 227	⚑	Red Roof Inn Phoenix Airport	◆◆	$49-$84	286
388 / p. 227		Howard Johnson Express	◆◆	$80-$90	285
389 / p. 227	⚑	The Buttes-A Wyndham Resort - see ad p 233	fyi	$240 ⚏	288
391 / p. 227	⚑	Fiesta Inn	◆◆◆	$165-$185 ⚏	283
392 / p. 227		Holiday Inn	◆◆◆	$154-$164	284
394 / p. 227	⚑	Tempe/University Travelodge - see color ad p 287	◆◆	$69-$89 ⚏	287
395 / p. 227		Residence Inn by Marriott	◆◆◆	$99-$179	286
396 / p. 227		Comfort Inn/Rio Salado ASU - see color ad p 282	◆◆◆	$159	283
397 / p. 227		Homestead Village	◆◆	$59	284
398 / p. 227	⚑	AmeriSuites/Arizona Mills Mall - see color ad opposite title page	◆◆◆	$99-$129 ⚏	281
399 / p. 227		Candlewood Suites - see ad p 232	◆◆◆	$110-$145	283
400 / p. 227	⚑	Embassy Suites Phoenix-Tempe - see color ad p 237	◆◆◆	$149-$183	283
401 / p. 227	⚑	InnSuites Tempe/Phoenix Airport - see color ad p 285	◆◆◆	$99-$109 ⚏	285
402 / p. 227		Springhill Suites by Marriott	◆◆◆	$89-$109	287
403 / p. 227	⚑	Red Roof Inn	◆◆	$55-$82 ⚏	286
404 / p. 227		Holiday Inn Express/Tempe - see color ad p 285 , p 235	◆◆	$99-$129	284
406 / p. 227		Country Inn & Suites By Carlson - see color ad p 229	◆◆	$59-$109	283
408 / p. 227	⚑	La Quinta Inn - see color ad p 242	◆◆◆	$89-$109 ⚏	285
		TEMPE - Restaurants			
192 / p. 227		Los Sombreros	◆	$8-$11	288
195 / p. 227		Macayo Depot Cantina	◆	$6-$12	288
196 / p. 227		Top of the Rock Restaurant	◆◆◆	$19-$30	289
197 / p. 227		Mike Pulo's Spaghetti Company	◆	$7-$11	288
198 / p. 227		Alcatraz Brewing Company	◆	$9-$20	288
199 / p. 227		Rusty Pelican Restaurant	◆	$12-$21	289
201 / p. 227		John Henry's	◆◆	$12-$24	288

MESA

Spotter/Map Page Number	OA	MESA - Lodgings	Diamond Rating	Rate Range High Season	Listing Page
418 / p. 227	⚑	Best Western Mezona Inn	◆◆	$85-$100 ⚏	261
419 / p. 227	⚑	Quality Inn Royal Mesa - see ad p 263	◆◆	$79-$109 ⚏	264
421 / p. 227	⚑	Sheraton Mesa Hotel - see color ad p 264	◆◆◆	$99 ⚏	264
424 / p. 227		Fairfield Inn Phoenix/Mesa	◆◆	$99-$109	262
425 / p. 227	⚑	Best Western Mesa Inn	◆◆	$70-$99 ⚏	261
426 / p. 227		Residence Inn by Marriott Mesa	◆◆◆	$149	264
427 / p. 227		Courtyard by Marriott	◆◆◆	$79-$139	261
428 / p. 227	⚑	La Quinta Inn & Suites-Mesa	◆◆◆	$95-$115 ⚏	263
430 / p. 227	⚑	Motel 6 - 1030	◆	$42-$61	263
431 / p. 227		Days Inn	◆	$86-$106	261
433 / p. 227		Hilton Mesa Pavilion - see color ad p 41, p 262	◆◆◆	$129-$149	263
434 / p. 227	⚑	Dobson Ranch Inn Resort-Best Western	◆◆◆	$137-$157 ⚏	262
436 / p. 227		Homestead Village	◆◆◆	$59	263
437 / p. 227		Holiday Inn Hotel & Suites - see color ad p 262	◆◆	$99	263
438 / p. 227	⚑	Ramada Inn Suites	◆◆	$86-$155 ⚏	264
439 / p. 227		Hampton Inn	◆◆◆	$99-$109	262
440 / p. 227		Travelodge Suites Mesa	◆◆	$84-$124	265
441 / p. 227	⚑	Days Inn-East Mesa	◆◆	$80-$95 ⚏	261

Spotter/Map Page Number	OA	**MESA - Lodgings (continued)**	Diamond Rating	Rate Range High Season	Listing Page
444 / p. 227	⊕	Arizona Golf Resort & Conference Center	◆ ◆ ◆	$149-$169 SAVE	261
445 / p. 227	⊕	Sleep Inn of Mesa	◆	$39-$109 SAVE	264
447 / p. 227		Best Western Superstition Springs Inn & Suites	◆ ◆ ◆	$65-$135	261
448 / p. 227		Country Inn & Suites By Carlson - see color ad p 229	◆ ◆ ◆	$129-$199	261
450 / p. 227	⊕	La Quinta Inn & Suites-Superstition Springs - see color ad p 242	◆ ◆ ◆	$95-$115 SAVE	263
		MESA - Restaurants			
212 / p. 227	⊕	The Landmark Restaurant	◆ ◆ ◆	$10-$20	265
213 / p. 227		The American Grill	◆ ◆	$14-$22	265
215 / p. 227		Monti's at the Ranch	◆	$9-$16	265
216 / p. 227	⊕	The Weather Vane Restaurant	◆ ◆	$7-$14	265

Phoenix Vicinity

Spotter/Map Page Number	OA	**SURPRISE - Lodgings**	Diamond Rating	Rate Range High Season	Listing Page
8 / p. 224		Country Inn & Suites By Carlson	◆ ◆ ◆	$89-$99	280
9 / p. 224	⊕	Windmill Inn at Sun City West - see ad p 243	◆ ◆ ◆	$149 SAVE	281
10 / p. 224		Quality Inn & Suites	◆ ◆ ◆	$99-$119	280
		YOUNGTOWN - Lodgings			
15 / p. 224	⊕	Motel 6 - 22	◆	$56-$72	289
		LITCHFIELD PARK - Lodgings			
17 / p. 224		The Wigwam Resort	◆ ◆ ◆ ◆	$330-$475	260
		LITCHFIELD PARK - Restaurant			
8 / p. 224		Arizona Kitchen	◆ ◆ ◆ ◆	$20-$32	260
		GOODYEAR - Lodgings			
20 / p. 224		Holiday Inn Express	◆ ◆ ◆	Failed to provide	260
21 / p. 224	⊕	Best Western Phoenix Goodyear Inn	◆ ◆	Failed to provide	260
		TOLLESON - Lodgings			
24 / p. 224	⊕	Econo Lodge - see color ad p 229	◆	$80-$90 SAVE	289
		PEORIA - Lodgings			
190 / p. 225	⊕	Hampton Inn	◆ ◆ ◆	$109-$129 SAVE	266
191 / p. 225		Residence Inn by Marriott	◆ ◆ ◆	$219	266
192 / p. 225		Comfort Suites of Peoria	◆ ◆ ◆	$99-$134	265
193 / p. 225	⊕	La Quinta Inn & Suites - see color ad p 242	◆ ◆ ◆	$99-$119 SAVE	266
		PARADISE VALLEY - Lodgings			
334 / p. 226		Hermosa Inn	◆ ◆ ◆	$260-$330	265
		PARADISE VALLEY - Restaurant			
155 / p. 226		Lon's at the Hermosa	◆ ◆ ◆	varies	265
		FOUNTAIN HILLS - Lodgings			
345 / p. 226	⊕	Comfort Inn	◆ ◆	$85-$105 SAVE	259
348 / p. 226	⊕	Southwest Inn at Eagle Mountain - see color ad p 259	◆ ◆ ◆ ◆	$99-$295 SAVE	259
		FOUNTAIN HILLS - Restaurant			
170 / p. 226		La Piazza	◆ ◆	$7-$16	259
		CHANDLER - Lodgings			
464 / p. 227	⊕	Best Western Inn & Suites	◆ ◆	Failed to provide	256
465 / p. 227		Fairfield Inn-Phoenix/South	◆ ◆	Failed to provide	257
467 / p. 227	⊕	Hampton Inn - see color ad p 256	◆ ◆ ◆	$99 SAVE	257
468 / p. 227		Hawthorn Suites Ltd	◆ ◆ ◆	$99-$109	257
470 / p. 227		Holiday Inn Express Hotel & Suites - see color ad p 257	◆ ◆ ◆	$99-$119	257
471 / p. 227		Homewood Suites	◆ ◆ ◆	$159-$209	257
474 / p. 227		Microtel Inn	◆	$59-$69	258
475 / p. 227	⊕	Red Roof Inn-Chandler	◆ ◆	$50-$85	258

Spotter/Map Page Number	OA	CHANDLER - Lodgings (continued)	Diamond Rating	Rate Range High Season	Listing Page
477 / p. 227	⚍	Sheraton San Marcos Resort	◆◆◆	$99-$199 [SAVE]	258
478 / p. 227	⚍	Windmill Inn of Chandler - see ad p 258	◆◆◆	$116-$134 [SAVE]	258
480 / p. 227	⚍	Wyndham Garden Hotel	◆◆◆	$159 [SAVE]	258
		CHANDLER - Restaurants			
228 / p. 227		The Pasta House	◆◆	$9-$20	258

PHOENIX/ SUN CITY AREA ACCOMMODATIONS

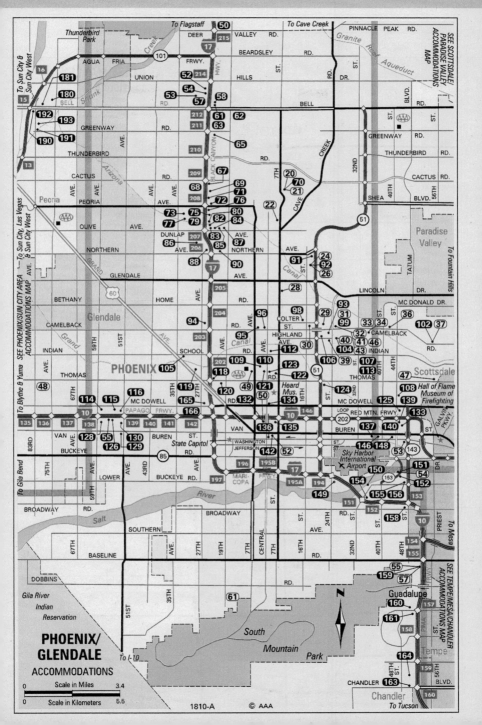

PHOENIX/GLENDALE ACCOMMODATIONS

Scale in Miles 0 — 3.4
Scale in Kilometers 0 — 5.5

1810-A © AAA

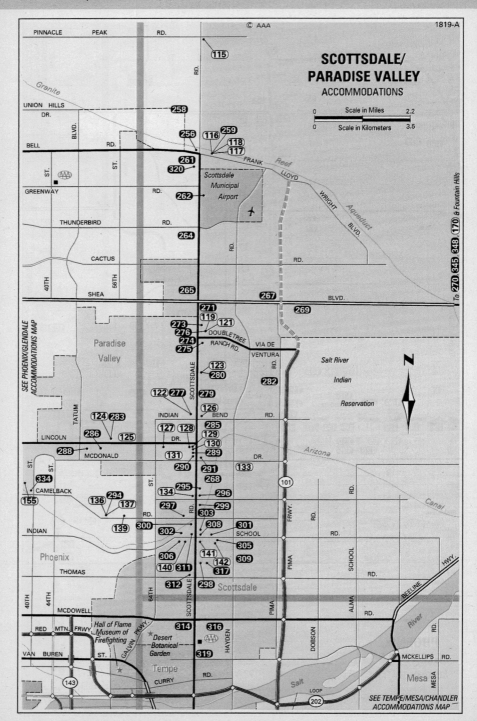

SCOTTSDALE/
PARADISE VALLEY
ACCOMMODATIONS

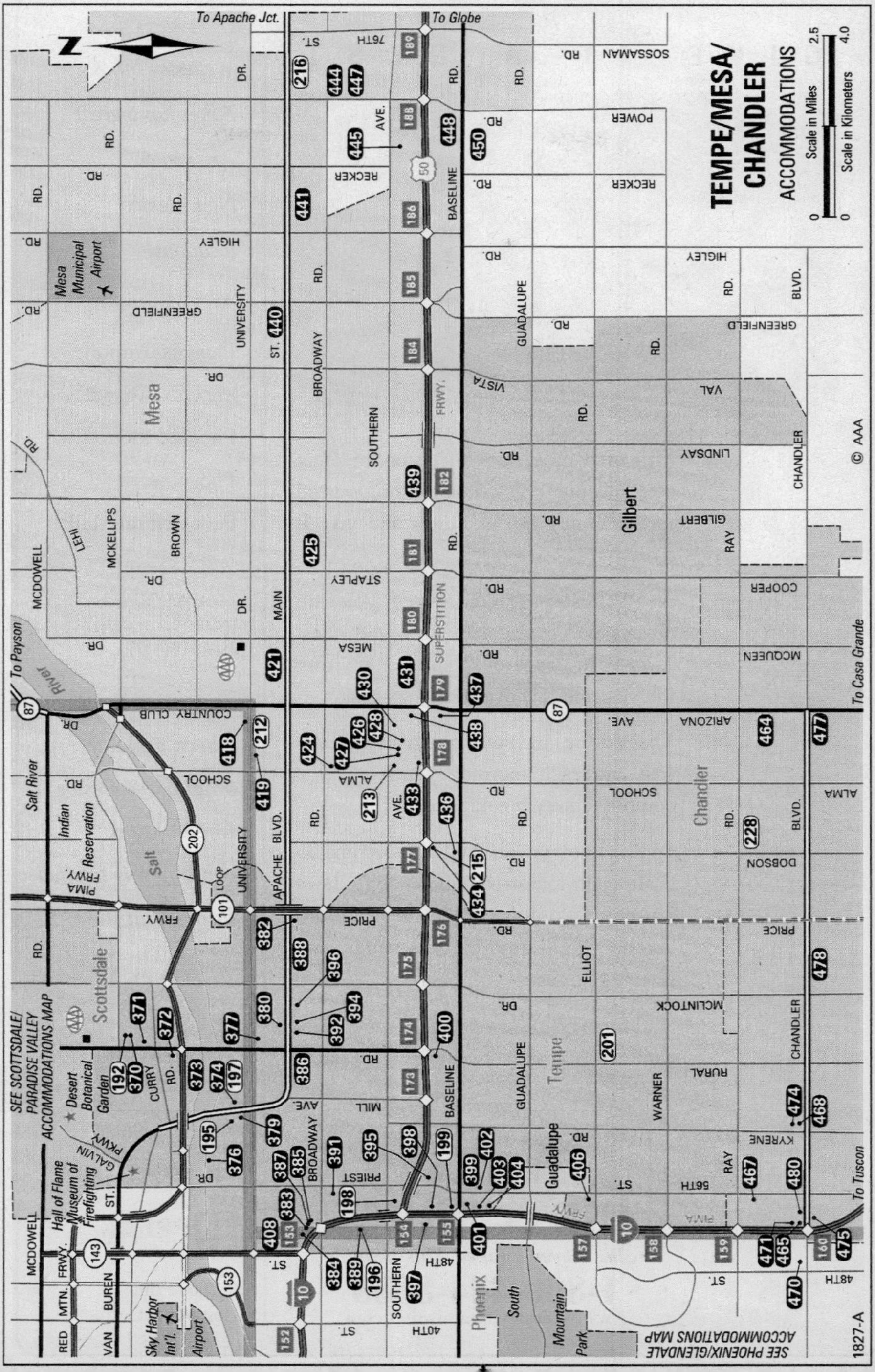

TEMPE/MESA/
CHANDLER
ACCOMMODATIONS
Scale in Miles
Scale in Kilometers
0
2.5
0
4.0
© AAA
1827-A
To Apache Jct.
To Globe
To Payson
To Casa Grande
To Tuscon
SEE SCOTTSDALE/
PARADISE VALLEY
ACCOMMODATIONS MAP
SEE PHOENIX/GLENDALE
ACCOMMODATIONS MAP
Mesa
Municipal
Airport
Mesa
Gilbert
Chandler
Tempe
Scottsdale
Guadalupe
Phoenix
South
Mountain
Park
Salt River
Indian
Reservation
Salt
River
Sky Harbor
Int'l.
Airport
Hall of Flame
Museum of
Firefighting
Desert
Botanical
Garden
MCDOWELL
RD.
MCKELLIPS
BROWN
UNIVERSITY
DR.
MAIN
ST.
BROADWAY
SOUTHERN
AVE.
BASELINE
GUADALUPE
ELLIOT
WARNER
RAY
CHANDLER
BLVD.
SUPERSTITION
FRWY.
PIMA
FRWY.
LOOP
APACHE
BLVD.
CURRY
GALVIN
PKWY.
VAN
BUREN
RED
MTN.
40TH
ST.
48TH
56TH
KYRENE
MILL
PRIEST
RURAL
MCLINTOCK
PRICE
DOBSON
ALMA
SCHOOL
ARIZONA
COUNTRY CLUB
MESA
STAPLEY
GILBERT
LINDSAY
VAL
VISTA
GREENFIELD
HIGLEY
RECKER
POWER
SOSSAMAN
LEHI
COOPER
MCQUEEN
76TH
HIGLEY
192
370
371
372
373
374
197
377
380
386
388
382
396
392
394
400
195
376
379
387
385
383
384
389
196
391
198
395
398
199
397
408
401
399
402
403
404
406
201
418
212
419
424
427
426
428
430
213
433
436
215
434
431
437
438
421
425
439
440
441
445
448
450
444
447
216
228
464
477
474
468
478
467
480
471
465
470
475
10
87
101
143
153
202
50
152
153
154
155
157
158
159
160
173
174
175
176
177
178
179
180
181
182
184
185
186
188
189

PHOENIX   pop. 983,400   (See map p. 225; index p. 217)

———— LODGINGS ————

AMERISUITES-PHOENIX METRO CENTER   **Phone:** (602)997-8800   **71**

⏣ 🅂🄰🅅🄴	2/1-3/31	1P: $89-$116	2P: $99-$126	XP: $10 F18
	9/16-1/31	1P: $80-$89	2P: $90-$99	XP: $10 F18
◆◆◆	4/1-9/15	1P: $62-$71	2P: $72-$81	XP: $10 F18

Motel   **Location:** 10838 N 25th Ave 85029. Fax: 602/997-4218. **Terms:** [CP] meal plan; small pets only. **Facility:** 128 rooms. 4 stories; interior corridors; heated pool. **Services:** area transportation, within 5 mi. **Recreation:** video games. **Cards:** AE, DI, DS, JC, MC, VI. **Special Amenities: Free breakfast and free newspaper.** *(See color ad opposite title page)*

🆂🅳 🐾 〼 ♿ ⌲ ✕ 🎥 VCR 🖨 🖥 🍽 🚪 DATA PORT 🐕 👥

BEST WESTERN AIRPORT INN   **Phone:** (602)273-7251   **149**

⏣ 🅂🄰🅅🄴	2/1-5/31 & 1/1-1/31	1P: $99-$119	2P: $99-$119	XP: $5 F17
	9/1-12/31	1P: $79-$99	2P: $79-$99	XP: $5 F17
◆◆	6/1-8/31	1P: $59-$79	2P: $59-$79	XP: $5 F17

Motor Inn   **Location:** Just s of I-10 airport exit (24th St); eastbound travel to University Dr, re-enter I-10 westbound. 2425 S 24th St 85034. Fax: 602/273-7180. **Terms:** Cancellation fee imposed; small pets only. **Facility:** 114 rooms. 2 stories; interior/exterior corridors; heated pool, saunas, whirlpool. **Dining:** Dining room; 6 am-10 pm; $10-$15; cocktails. **Services:** area transportation, bus depots. **All Rooms:** combo or shower baths. **Cards:** AE, CB, DI, DS, JC, MC, VI. **Special Amenities: Free local telephone calls and free room upgrade (subject to availability with advanced reservations).** *(See color ad below)*

🆂🅳 ♨ 🐾 🍽 🍸 ♿ 🛎 🏊 ✕ 🎥 🖨 🚪 DATA PORT 🐕

BEST WESTERN BELL HOTEL   **Phone:** (602)993-8300   **58**

⏣ 🅂🄰🅅🄴	2/1-4/15 & 1/1-1/31	1P: $93-$99	2P: $99-$109	XP: $5 F17
◆◆◆	4/16-12/31	1P: $59-$69	2P: $59-$69	XP: $5 F17

Motel   **Location:** Adjacent to I-17, exit Bell Rd E, just n on frontage road. 17211 N Black Canyon Hwy 85023. Fax: 602/863-2163. **Terms:** [CP] meal plan; small pets only, $25 extra charge. **Facility:** 103 rooms. All rooms with hair dryer, iron and ironing board. 1 bedroom efficiency for up to 4 persons, $79.50-$99.50; 2 stories; exterior corridors; heated pool, whirlpool. **Dining:** Restaurant nearby. **Cards:** AE, CB, DI, DS, MC, VI. **Special Amenities: Free breakfast and free local telephone calls.** *(See color ad p 231)*

🆂🅳 🐾 🍽 🏊 🎥 ✕ 🖨 🖥 🍽 🚪 DATA PORT 🐕

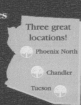

(See map p. 225)

BEST WESTERN EXECUTIVE PARK HOTEL   **Phone:** (602)252-2100   132

◆◆◆

	2/1-5/15	1P: $101	2P: $101	XP: $10
Hotel	9/16-1/31	1P: $88	2P: $88	XP: $10
	5/16-9/15	1P: $71	2P: $71	XP: $10

F17
F17
F17

Location: On Central Ave just s of McDowell Rd on w side of Central Ave. 1100 N Central Ave 85004. Fax: 602/340-1989.
Facility: 107 rooms. Spacious, attractively decorated units. Adjacent to the Margaret T. Hance Park. 2 mi n of America West Arena. 8 stories; interior corridors; heated pool. **All Rooms:** combo or shower baths. **Cards:** AE, DI, DS, MC, VI.

(See map p. 225)

BEST WESTERN GRACE INN AT AHWATUKEE   **Phone:** (480)893-3000   161

2/1-5/16 & 1/1-1/31	1P: $129-$159	2P: $169	XP: $10	F17
9/16-12/31	1P: $119-$139	2P: $149	XP: $10	F17
5/17-9/15	1P: $99-$109	2P: $109	XP: $10	F17

Motor Inn   **Location:** Adjacent to w side of I-10, exit 157 (Elliot Rd). 10831 S 51st St 85044. Fax: 480/496-8303. **Terms:** Cancellation fee imposed. **Facility:** 160 rooms. In planned residential community, with easy access to nearby business parks. 8 one-bedroom suites with refrigerators & microwave, $114-$167 for up to 2 persons; 6 stories; interior corridors; heated pool, whirlpool; 1 lighted tennis court. **Dining:** Restaurant; 6 am-10 pm; $10-$17; cocktails; entertainment. **Services:** gift shop; area transportation, within 2 mi. **Recreation:** basketball court, shuffleboard. **Some Rooms:** 8 efficiencies. **Cards:** AE, CB, DI, DS, MC, VI. **Special Amenities:** Free room upgrade and preferred room (each subject to availability with advanced reservations).

BEST WESTERN INNSUITES HOTEL PHOENIX   **Phone:** (602)997-6285   91

9/20-1/31	1P: $89-$189	2P: $89-$189	XP: $5	F
2/1-3/27	1P: $99-$139	2P: $99-$139	XP: $5	F
3/28-5/15	1P: $79-$99	2P: $79-$99	XP: $5	F
5/16-9/19	1P: $59-$79	2P: $59-$79	XP: $5	F

Motel   **Location:** On s side of Northern Ave just e of 16th St. 1615 E Northern Ave 85020. Fax: 602/943-1407. **Terms:** [BP] meal plan; weekly & monthly rates avail. **Facility:** 123 rooms. At the foothills of the Phoenix Mountains. 4 whirlpool rooms, $99-$189; suites, $99-$189; 2 stories; exterior corridors; heated pool, whirlpool; playground. **Services:** complimentary evening beverages. **Some Rooms:** 4 kitchens. **Cards:** AE, CB, DI, DS, MC, VI. **Special Amenities:** Free breakfast and free local telephone calls. *(See color ad below)*

(See map p. 225)

CANDLEWOOD SUITES
◆◆◆
Motel

	1P: $60-$105	2P: $60-$105
2/1-4/18 & 1/1-1/31	1P: $60-$105	2P: $60-$105
9/27-12/31	1P: $55-$99	2P: $55-$99
4/19-9/26	1P: $35-$79	2P: $35-$79

Phone: (602)861-4900   67

Location: E side of I-17, exit Peoria Ave, 0.5 mi n. 11411 N Black Canyon Hwy 85029. Fax: 602/861-4940. **Terms:** Check-in 4 pm; cancellation fee imposed. **Facility:** 98 rooms. Studio and 1-bedroom with kitchen and CD player. 3 stories; interior corridors; heated pool. **Cards:** AE, DI, DS, MC, VI. (See ad p 232)

[ASK] [S/D] [♨] [△] [✕] [♫] [VCR] [🖨] [DATA PORT] [⊃] [♿]

COMFORT INN BLACK CANYON
(AAA) [SAVE]
◆◆
Motel

	1P: $76-$106	2P: $79-$109	XP: $10	F17
2/1-4/1	1P: $76-$106	2P: $79-$109	XP: $10	F17
4/2-5/6 & 12/31-1/31	1P: $56-$79	2P: $59-$85	XP: $10	F17
5/7-12/30	1P: $45-$55	2P: $49-$59	XP: $10	F17

Phone: (602)242-8011   94

Location: W side of I-17, Camelback Rd exit. 5050 N Black Canyon Hwy 85017. Fax: 602/242-0467. **Terms:** [CP] meal plan; pets, limited rooms avail. **Facility:** 153 rooms. Suites avail; 3 stories; exterior corridors; heated pool, whirlpool. **Dining:** Restaurant nearby. **Cards:** AE, CB, DI, DS, JC, MC, VI. **Special Amenities:** Early check-in/late check-out. (See color ad p 229)

[S/D] [🛏] [♨] [🐾] [△] [✕] [♫] [▣] [🖨] [🛗] [DATA PORT] [⊃]

COMFORT INN I-10 WEST/CENTRAL
(AAA) [SAVE]
◆◆◆
Motel

	1P: $70-$100	2P: $70-$100	XP: $10	F18
2/1-4/30 & 1/15-1/31	1P: $70-$100	2P: $70-$100	XP: $10	F18
5/1-1/14	1P: $50-$80	2P: $50-$80	XP: $10	F18

Phone: (602)415-1623   166

Location: Just s of McDowell Rd, I-10 westbound exit 27th Ave, n on 27th Ave; I-10 eastbound exit 35th Ave, n on 35th Ave, 1 mi e on McDowell Rd, then s. 1344 N 27th Ave 85009. **Terms:** [CP] meal plan. **Facility:** 65 rooms. 3 stories; interior corridors; heated pool, whirlpool. **Cards:** AE, CB, DI, DS, MC, VI. **Special Amenities:** Free breakfast and free local telephone calls.

[S/D] [△] [✕] [♫] [🖨] [▣] [🛗] [DATA PORT] [⊃]

COMFORT INN TURF PARADISE
(AAA) [SAVE]
◆◆
Motel

All Year	1P: $46-$90	2P: $50-$100	XP: $10	F18

Phone: (602)866-2089   62

Location: 1.3 mi e of I-17, Bell Rd East exit, on s side of Bell Rd. 1711 W Bell Rd 85023. Fax: 602/789-7669. **Terms:** [CP] meal plan. **Facility:** 163 rooms. Adjacent to Turf Paradise Racetrack. Some units with patio or balcony. 24 two-bedroom units. 1- & 2-bedroom suites, $65-$130; 3 stories; exterior corridors; heated pool, whirlpool. **Dining:** Restaurant nearby. **Some Rooms:** Fee: microwaves. **Cards:** AE, CB, DI, DS, JC, MC, VI. **Special Amenities:** Early check-in/late check-out.

[S/D] [♨] [△] [🏊] [✕] [♫] [▣] [🖨] [🛗] [DATA PORT] [⊃]

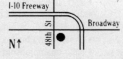

(See map p. 225)

COMFORT SUITES
◆◆◆   Phone: (602)861-3900 **75**
Motel

	2/1-5/1 & 12/2-1/31	1P: $99-$109	2P: $99-$109
	10/1-12/1	1P: $79-$99	2P: $79-$99
	5/2-9/30	1P: $59-$69	2P: $59-$69

Location: I-17, Peoria Ave exit. 10210 N 26th Dr 85021. Fax: 602/681-9300. **Terms:** [CP] meal plan; 7 day cancellation notice; small pets only, $50 dep req, in smoking rooms rooms. **Facility:** 60 rooms. 42 two-bedroom units. 3 stories; interior corridors; heated pool. **Cards:** AE, CB, DI, DS, MC, VI.

COUNTRY SUITES BY CARLSON - PHOENIX/WEST   Phone: (602)279-3211 **119**
Suite Hotel

	2/1-4/23 & 9/16-1/31	1P: $59-$125	2P: $59-$125	XP: $10	F18
	4/24-5/31	1P: $65	2P: $65	XP: $10	F18
	6/1-9/15	1P: $59	2P: $59	XP: $10	F18

Location: On US 60, 0.5 mi s of Indian School Rd; 1.3 mi w of I-17; on the se side of Grand Ave. 3210 NW Grand Ave 85017. Fax: 602/230-2145. **Terms:** [BP] meal plan; check-in 4 pm; 2 night min stay. **Facility:** 167 rooms. 1-bedroom suites with living room and efficiency. Landscaped courtyard. 2 rooms with exercise cycle. 4 stories; exterior corridors; heated pool, whirlpool. **Dining:** Restaurant; 11 am-2 & 5-10 pm, closed Sun; $10-$18; cocktails. **Services:** complimentary evening beverages. **Recreation:** in-room video games. **Cards:** AE, CB, DI, DS, JC, MC, VI. **Special Amenities:** Free breakfast and free newspaper. (See color ad below and p 229)

COURTYARD BY MARRIOTT CAMELBACK   Phone: (602)955-5200 **106**
Motor Inn

	2/1-4/16	1P: $169-$179
	9/16-1/31	1P: $149-$179
	4/17-6/14	1P: $139-$159
	6/15-9/15	1P: $69-$149

Location: In Town and Country Shopping Center; 20th St and Camelback Rd, on s side of Camelback Rd. 2101 E Camelback Rd 85016. Fax: 602/955-1101. **Facility:** 155 rooms. Many units with patio and balcony. Landscaped courtyard. Commercial area. 4 stories; interior corridors; heated pool. **Cards:** AE, CB, DI, DS, MC, VI.

(See map p. 225)

COURTYARD BY MARRIOTT PHOENIX AIRPORT   **Phone:** (480)966-4300   [155]
◆◆◆   2/1-4/14   1P: $149-$169
Motor Inn   9/10-1/31   1P: $129-$149
          4/15-5/18   1P: $119-$139
          5/19-9/9   1P: $79-$99
Location: 0.7 mi n of I-10 exit SR 143N, just nw of University Dr exit. 2621 S 47th St 85034. Fax: 480/966-0198.
Terms: Check-in 4 pm. **Facility:** 145 rooms. Landscaped courtyard. 4 stories; interior corridors; heated pool. **Cards:** AE, DI,
DS, MC, VI.

COURTYARD BY MARRIOTT PHOENIX NORTH   **Phone:** (602)944-7373   [80]
◆◆◆   9/10-1/31   1P: $99-$129   2P: $99-$129
Motor Inn   2/1-4/15   1P: $129   2P: $129
          4/16-5/13   1P: $89   2P: $89
          5/14-9/9   1P: $59   2P: $59
Location: Just s of Peoria Ave exit on e side of I-17. 9631 N Black Canyon Hwy 85021. Fax: 602/944-0079. **Facility:** 146
rooms. 3 stories; interior corridors; heated pool. **Cards:** AE, CB, DI, DS, MC, VI.

CROWNE PLAZA DOWNTOWN PHOENIX   **Phone:** (602)333-0000   [136]
(AAA) (SAVE)   2/1-5/31 & 9/20-1/31   1P: $183-$229   2P: $183-$229   XP: $20   F18
◆◆◆   6/1-9/19   1P: $97-$129   2P: $97-$129   XP: $20   F18
Hotel   **Location:** 1st St and Adams, downtown, just n of Washington; on w side of 1st St. 100 N 1st St 85004.
Fax: 602/254-7926. **Terms:** Weekly & monthly rates avail; check-in 4 pm. **Facility:** 532 rooms. Spacious lobby.
18 stories; interior corridors; heated pool. Fee: parking. **Dining:** Dining room, coffee shop; 6 am-1 am; $9-$22;
cocktails. **Services:** gift shop. Fee: massage. **All Rooms:** combo or shower baths. **Some Rooms:** Fee: refrigerators, microwaves, VCR. **Cards:** AE, DI, DS, MC, VI. **Special Amenities:** Free newspaper. *(See ad below)*

(See map p. 225)

CROWNE PLAZA PHOENIX-METROCENTER   **Phone:** (602)943-2341   72
(AAA) [SAVE]
Hotel
- 2/1-3/31 & 10/1-1/31   1P: $119
- 4/1-9/30   1P: $59

Location: Adjacent to I-17, exit Peoria Ave, ne corner. 2532 W Peoria Ave 85029. Fax: 602/371-8470. **Terms:** Package plans; pets, $25 dep req. **Facility:** 250 rooms. 4 stories; interior corridors; 2 heated pools, sauna, whirlpools; 1 lighted tennis court. **Dining:** Dining room, coffee shop; 6 am-11 pm; $7-$19; cocktails. **Services:** gift shop; area transportation, within 5 mi. **Recreation:** sand volleyball. **All Rooms:** combo or shower baths. **Some Rooms:** honor bars. **Cards:** AE, DI, DS, MC, VI. **Special Amenities:** Free newspaper. *(See ad p 234)*

DAYS INN-AIRPORT   **Phone:** (602)244-8244   137
(AAA) [SAVE]
Motel

2/1-4/24	1P: $72-$95	2P: $77-$105	XP: $10 F12
9/29-11/5	1P: $62-$89	2P: $62-$89	XP: $10 F12
11/6-1/31	1P: $39-$89	2P: $39-$89	XP: $10 F12
4/25-9/28	1P: $39-$59	2P: $39-$59	XP: $10 F12

Location: I-10 exit Washington, e to 32nd St, n to Van Buren just e. 3333 E Van Buren 85008. Fax: 602/244-8240. **Terms:** Check-in 4 pm; small pets only, $25 dep req. **Facility:** 216 rooms. 2 whirlpool rooms; 3 stories; interior/exterior corridors; heated pool, whirlpool. **Dining:** Restaurant; 6 am-10 pm; $7-$10; entertainment. **Services:** gift shop; area transportation, hospital, train, bus. **All Rooms:** Fee: safes. **Some Rooms:** 2 kitchens. **Cards:** AE, DI, DS, MC, VI. **Special Amenities:** Early check-in/late check-out and preferred room (subject to availability with advanced reservations).

DAYS INN-I-17 & THOMAS   **Phone:** (602)257-0801   118
(AAA) [SAVE]
Motel

2/1-4/15	1P: $73-$89	2P: $79-$99	XP: $10 F17
4/16-1/31	1P: $49-$69	2P: $59-$79	XP: $10 F17

Location: I-17, Thomas Rd exit, at ne corner of junction. 2420 W Thomas Rd 85015. Fax: 602/258-5336. **Terms:** [CP] meal plan; small pets only, $25 extra charge. **Facility:** 150 rooms. 2 stories; interior corridors; heated pool, whirlpool. **Dining:** Restaurant nearby. **Some Rooms:** 69 efficiencies. **Cards:** AE, DI, DS, MC, VI. **Special Amenities:** Free local telephone calls and free room upgrade (subject to availability with advanced reservations). *(See color ad p 231)*

DAYS INN I-10 WEST   **Phone:** (602)484-9257   129
(AAA) [SAVE]
Motel

2/1-3/31	1P: $80-$130	2P: $80-$130	XP: $12 F12
10/1-1/31	1P: $70-$130	2P: $70-$130	XP: $12 F12
4/1-9/30	1P: $55-$120	2P: $55-$120	XP: $12 F12

Location: I-10 exit 51st Ave, n to McDowell Rd, just w. 1550 N 52nd Dr 85043. Fax: 602/484-9257. **Terms:** [CP] meal plan. **Facility:** 56 rooms. Exterior corridors; small pool. **All Rooms:** safes. **Cards:** AE, DS, MC, VI. **Special Amenities:** Free breakfast and free local telephone calls.

DAYS INN-NORTH PHOENIX   **Phone:** (623)434-5500   50
(AAA) [SAVE]
Motel

2/1-4/15	1P: $70-$80	2P: $80-$90	XP: $5 F14
4/16-5/31	1P: $50-$60	2P: $60-$70	XP: $5 F14
6/1-1/31	1P: $40-$50	2P: $50-$60	XP: $5 F14

Location: Just w of I-17, Deer Valley Rd exit 217B. 21636 N 26th Ave 85027. Fax: 623/434-5500. **Terms:** [CP] meal plan; 10 day cancellation notice; cancellation fee imposed. **Facility:** 70 rooms. 2 whirlpool rooms, $80-$99; 2 stories; interior corridors; small pool. **Dining:** Coffee shop nearby. **All Rooms:** combo or shower baths. **Cards:** AE, DS, MC, VI. **Special Amenities:** Early check-in/late check-out and free breakfast.

DOUBLETREE GUEST SUITES AT THE PHOENIX GATEWAY CENTER   **Phone:** (602)225-0500   140
Suite Hotel

2/1-4/20	1P: $119-$144	2P: $119-$144	XP: $10 F17
4/21-5/18 & 10/2-1/31	1P: $109-$124	2P: $109-$124	XP: $10 F17
5/19-10/1	1P: $64-$84	2P: $64-$84	XP: $10 F17

Location: 5 mi e; 0.3 mi s of SR 202 (Red Mountain Frwy), 44th St exit. 320 N 44th St at Van Buren 85008. Fax: 602/225-0957. **Terms:** [BP] meal plan; cancellation fee imposed. **Facility:** 242 rooms. Oasis amid busy streets. 6 stories; exterior corridors; heated pool. **Services:** gift shop; area transportation. **All Rooms:** honor bars. **Some Rooms:** Fee: VCR. **Cards:** AE, CB, DI, DS, JC, MC, VI. *(See ad below)*

(See map p. 225)

EMBASSY SUITES AIRPORT AT 44th ST

				Phone: (602)244-8800	**125**
ⒶⒶⒶ SAVE	2/1-4/20	1P: $149-$179	2P: $149-$189	XP: $10	F18
◆◆◆	9/5-1/31	1P: $99-$149	2P: $99-$159	XP: $10	F18
Suite Hotel	4/21-5/25	1P: $99-$139	2P: $99-$149	XP: $10	F18
	5/26-9/4	1P: $69-$99	2P: $69-$109	XP: $10	F18

Location: SE corner McDowell Rd and 44th St. 1515 N 44th St 85008. **Fax:** 602/244-8114. **Terms:** [BP] meal plan. **Facility:** 229 rooms. 1-bedroom suites with living room and efficiency. Landscaped courtyard. 4 stories; exterior corridors; heated pool, whirlpool. **Dining:** Restaurant; 11:30 am-10 pm, Sat & Sun from 5 pm; $8-$18. **Services:** gift shop; complimentary evening beverages. **Recreation:** in-room video games. **All Rooms:** efficiencies. **Cards:** AE, DI, DS, JC, MC, VI. **Special Amenities:** Free breakfast and free newspaper. *(See color ad below)*

⬛⬛⬛⬛⬛⬛⬛⬛⬛⬛⬛⬛

EMBASSY SUITES-BILTMORE

				Phone: (602)955-3992	**99**
ⒶⒶⒶ SAVE	2/1-5/22 & 1/1-1/31	1P: $239	2P: $239	XP: $20	F18
◆◆◆	9/5-12/31	1P: $199	2P: $199	XP: $20	F18
Suite Hotel	5/23-9/4	1P: $120	2P: $120	XP: $20	F18

Location: Just n of Camelback Rd on 24th St, adjacent to Biltmore Fashion Park. 2630 E Camelback Rd 85016. **Fax:** 602/955-6479. **Terms:** [BP] meal plan; small pets only, $25 extra charge. **Facility:** 233 rooms. 5 stories; interior corridors; heated pool, whirlpool. **Dining:** Omaha Steakhouse, see separate listing; entertainment. **Services:** complimentary evening beverages. **All Rooms:** efficiencies. **Cards:** AE, CB, DI, DS, JC, MC, VI. **Special Amenities:** Early check-in/late check-out and free breakfast. *(See color ad below)*

⬛⬛⬛⬛⬛⬛⬛⬛⬛⬛⬛⬛⬛⬛

EMBASSY SUITES HOTEL AIRPORT WEST

				Phone: (602)957-1910	**124**
◆◆◆	2/1-4/21	1P: $149-$170	2P: $149-$180	XP: $10	F18
Suite Hotel	9/5-1/31	1P: $109-$129	2P: $109-$139		
	4/22-5/25	1P: $109-$119	2P: $109-$129		
	5/26-9/4	1P: $69-$75	2P: $69-$85		

Location: Just w of 24th St. 2333 E Thomas Rd 85016. **Fax:** 602/955-2861. **Terms:** [BP] meal plan; cancellation fee imposed; pets, $10 extra charge. **Facility:** 183 rooms. 1-bedroom suites with living room. 4 stories; exterior corridors; heated pool. **Services:** gift shop; area transportation. **All Rooms:** efficiencies. **Cards:** AE, CB, DI, DS, JC, MC, VI. *(See color ad below)*

ASK ⬛⬛⬛⬛⬛⬛⬛⬛⬛⬛⬛⬛⬛

(See map p. 225)

EMBASSY SUITES PHOENIX NORTH   Phone: (602)375-1777   65

(AAA) (SAVE)	2/1-4/30	1P: $143	2P: $153	XP: $20	F18
	10/1-1/31	1P: $90	2P: $100	XP: $20	F18
◆ ◆ ◆	5/1-9/30	1P: $59	2P: $69	XP: $20	F18

Suite Hotel   **Location:** Just e of I-17, Greenway Rd exit. 2577 W Greenway Rd 85023. Fax: 602/375-4012. **Terms:** [BP] meal plan; cancellation fee imposed. **Facility:** 314 rooms. 1-bedroom suites with living room. Landscaped courtyard with pool, whirlpool and wading pool. Whirlpool room, $235-$300; 3 stories; exterior corridors; heated pool, wading pool, sauna, whirlpool; 2 lighted tennis courts, lighted sand volleyball court. **Dining:** Restaurant; 6:30 am-10 pm, Sat & Sun from 7 am; $7-$20; cocktails. **Services:** gift shop. **All Rooms:** combo or shower baths. **Cards:** AE, CB, DI, DS, JC, MC, VI. **Special Amenities:** Free breakfast and free newspaper. *(See color ad below)*

FAIRFIELD INN BY MARRIOTT PHOENIX AIRPORT   Phone: 480/829-0700   156

◆ ◆	2/1-3/31	1P: $89-$119
Motel	9/1-1/31	1P: $79-$119
	4/1-4/30	1P: $79-$99
	5/1-8/31	1P: $59-$74

Location: 0.7 mi n of I-10, SR 143N, just nw of University Dr exit. 4702 E University Dr 85034. Fax: 480/829-8068. **Terms:** [CP] meal plan; cancellation fee imposed. **Facility:** 90 rooms. 3 stories; interior corridors; heated pool. **Cards:** AE, CB, DI, DS, MC, VI.

FAIRFIELD INN BY MARRIOTT PHOENIX NORTH   Phone: (602)548-8888   61

◆ ◆	2/1-5/1	1P: $69-$119
Motel	10/2-1/31	1P: $59-$109
	5/2-10/1	1P: $39-$89

Location: Adjacent to I-17, Bell Rd E exit; just n on frontage road. 17017 N Black Canyon Hwy 85023. Fax: 602/548-9553. **Terms:** [CP] meal plan. **Facility:** 66 rooms. 3 stories; interior corridors. **Cards:** AE, CB, DI, DS, MC, VI.

FAIRFIELD INN PHOENIX WEST   Phone: (602)269-1919   126

| ◆ ◆ ◆ | 2/1-4/18 & 1/1-1/31 | 1P: $69 | 2P: $79 |
| Motel | 4/19-12/31 | 1P: $39-$49 | 2P: $49-$52 |

Location: Adjacent to I-10; 0.3 mi sw via Latham St, 51st Ave exit. 1241 N 53rd Ave 85043. Fax: 602/269-1919. **Terms:** [CP] meal plan. **Facility:** 126 rooms. Landscaped grounds. 3 stories; exterior corridors; heated pool. **Cards:** AE, CB, DI, DS, MC, VI.

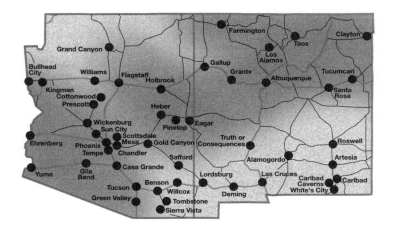

66 ways to take you from the state of Arizona or New Mexico to the state of bliss.

Wherever you're headed in the Southwest, chances are you're headed in our direction. With 66 hotels located throughout Arizona and New Mexico, most of which are rated AAA three diamond, you'll never have to stray far from your path to find a good night's sleep. Not to mention a great deal. Just present this ad at any participating Best Western in Arizona or New Mexico and get 15% off the published room rate.

for reservations 1.888.827.8298
to enroll in Gold Crown Club International 1.888.438.7234
www.bestwesternarizona.com

BEST WESTERN
GOLD CROWN CLUB®
I N T E R N A T I O N A L

ARIZONA

Benson
Best Western Quail Hollow Inn

Bullhead City
(Laughlin, NV Area)
Best Western Bullhead City Inn

Casa Grande
Best Western Casa Grande Suites

Chandler
Best Western
Inn & Suites of Chandler

Cottonwood
Best Western Cottonwood Inn

Eagar (Springerville Area)
Best Western Sunrise Inn

Ehrenberg (Blythe Area, CA)
Best Western Flying J Motel

Flagstaff (2)
Best Western Kings House Motel
Best Western Pony Soldier

Gila Bend
Best Western Space Age Lodge

Gold Canyon
Best Western
Gold Canyon Inn & Suites

Grand Canyon
Best Western
Grand Canyon Squire Inn

Green Valley
Best Western Green Valley

Heber
Best Western Sawmill Inn

Holbrook (2)
Best Western Adobe Inn
Best Western Arizonian Inn

Kingman (2)
Best Western A Wayfarer's Inn
Best Western Kings Inn & Suites

Mesa (4)
Best Western
Dobson Ranch Inn & Resort
Best Western Mesa Inn
Best Western Mezona Inn
Best Western
Superstition Springs Inn & Suites

Phoenix (3)
Best Western Airport Inn
Best Western
Grace Inn At Ahwatukee
Best Western
InnSuites Hotels Phoenix

Pinetop
Best Western Inn of Pinetop

Prescott
Best Western Prescottonian

Safford
Best Western Desert Inn

Scottsdale
Best Western
Papago Inn & Resort

Sierra Vista
Best Western Mission Inn

Sun City
Best Western
Inn & Suites of Sun City

Tempe
Best Western Inn of Tempe

Tombstone
Best Western Lookout Lodge

Tucson (4)
Best Western
A Royal Sun Inn and Suites
Best Western Executive Inn
Best Western Inn at the Airport
Best Western
InnSuites Hotels Tucson

Wickenburg
Best Western Rancho Grande

Willcox
Best Western Plaza Inn

Williams
Best Western Inn of Williams

Yuma
Best Western Coronado Hotel

NEW MEXICO

Alamogordo
Best Western
Desert Aire Motor Inn

Albuquerque (3)
Best Western
American Motor Inn
Best Western Rio Grande Inn
Best Western Winrock Inn

Albuquerque Area
(Rio Rancho)
Best Western Inn at Rio Rancho

Artesia
Best Western Pecos Inn

Carlsbad
Best Western Stevens Inn

Carlsbad Caverns Area
(Whites City)
Best Western Cavern Inn

Clayton
Best Western Kokopelli Lodge

Deming
Best Western Mimbres Valley Inn

Farmington
Best Western Inn and Suites

Gallup
Best Western Inn and Suites

Grants
Best Western Inn & Suites

Las Cruces (2)
Best Western Mesilla Valley Inn
Best Western Mission Inn

Lordsburg
Best Western
American Motor Inn

Los Alamos
Best Western
Hilltop House Hotel

Roswell (2)
Best Western
El Rancho Palacio Motor Lodge
Best Western
Sally Port Inn & Suites

Santa Rosa
Best Western Adobe Inn

Taos
Best Western Kachina Lodge
& Meetings Center

Truth or Consequences
Best Western
Hot Springs Motor Inn

Tucumcari (2)
Best Western Discovery Inn
Best Western Pow Wow Inn

Whites City
(Carlsbad Caverns Area)
Best Western Guadalupe Inn

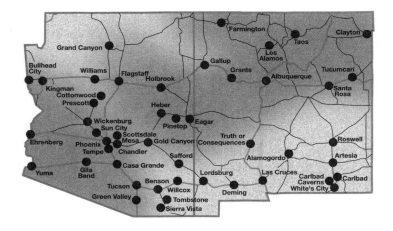

66 ways to take you from the state of Arizona or New Mexico to the state of bliss.

Wherever you're headed in the Southwest, chances are you're headed in our direction. With 66 hotels located throughout Arizona and New Mexico, most of which are rated AAA three diamond, you'll never have to stray far from your path to find a good night's sleep. Not to mention a great deal. Just present this ad at any participating Best Western in Arizona or New Mexico and get 15% off the published room rate.

for reservations 1.888.827.8298

to enroll in Gold Crown Club International 1.888.438.7234

www.bestwesternarizona.com

BEST WESTERN
GOLD CROWN CLUB®
I N T E R N A T I O N A L

ARIZONA

Benson
Best Western Quail Hollow Inn

Bullhead City
(Laughlin, NV Area)
Best Western Bullhead City Inn

Casa Grande
Best Western Casa Grande Suites

Chandler
Best Western
Inn & Suites of Chandler

Cottonwood
Best Western Cottonwood Inn

Eagar (Springerville Area)
Best Western Sunrise Inn

Ehrenberg (Blythe Area, CA)
Best Western Flying J Motel

Flagstaff (2)
Best Western Kings House Motel
Best Western Pony Soldier

Gila Bend
Best Western Space Age Lodge

Gold Canyon
Best Western
Gold Canyon Inn & Suites

Grand Canyon
Best Western
Grand Canyon Squire Inn

Green Valley
Best Western Green Valley

Heber
Best Western Sawmill Inn

Holbrook (2)
Best Western Adobe Inn
Best Western Arizonian Inn

Kingman (2)
Best Western A Wayfarer's Inn
Best Western Kings Inn & Suites

Mesa (4)
Best Western
Dobson Ranch Inn & Resort
Best Western Mesa Inn
Best Western Mezona Inn
Best Western
Superstition Springs Inn & Suites

Phoenix (3)
Best Western Airport Inn
Best Western
Grace Inn At Ahwatukee
Best Western
InnSuites Hotels Phoenix

Pinetop
Best Western Inn of Pinetop

Prescott
Best Western Prescottonian

Safford
Best Western Desert Inn

Scottsdale
Best Western
Papago Inn & Resort

Sierra Vista
Best Western Mission Inn

Sun City
Best Western
Inn & Suites of Sun City

Tempe
Best Western Inn of Tempe

Tombstone
Best Western Lookout Lodge

Tucson (4)
Best Western
A Royal Sun Inn and Suites
Best Western Executive Inn
Best Western Inn at the Airport
Best Western
InnSuites Hotels Tucson

Wickenburg
Best Western Rancho Grande

Willcox
Best Western Plaza Inn

Williams
Best Western Inn of Williams

Yuma
Best Western Coronado Hotel

NEW MEXICO

Alamogordo
Best Western
Desert Aire Motor Inn

Albuquerque (3)
Best Western
American Motor Inn
Best Western Rio Grande Inn
Best Western Winrock Inn

Albuquerque Area
(Rio Rancho)
Best Western Inn at Rio Rancho

Artesia
Best Western Pecos Inn

Carlsbad
Best Western Stevens Inn

Carlsbad Caverns Area
(Whites City)
Best Western Cavern Inn

Clayton
Best Western Kokopelli Lodge

Deming
Best Western Mimbres Valley Inn

Farmington
Best Western Inn and Suites

Gallup
Best Western Inn and Suites

Grants
Best Western Inn & Suites

Las Cruces (2)
Best Western Mesilla Valley Inn
Best Western Mission Inn

Lordsburg
Best Western
American Motor Inn

Los Alamos
Best Western
Hilltop House Hotel

Roswell (2)
Best Western
El Rancho Palacio Motor Lodge
Best Western
Sally Port Inn & Suites

Santa Rosa
Best Western Adobe Inn

Taos
Best Western Kachina Lodge
& Meetings Center

Truth or Consequences
Best Western
Hot Springs Motor Inn

Tucumcari (2)
Best Western Discovery Inn
Best Western Pow Wow Inn

Whites City
(Carlsbad Caverns Area)
Best Western Guadalupe Inn

(See map p. 225)

HAMPTON INN AIRPORT/TEMPE   **Phone:** (602)438-8688   158
◆◆◆   2/1-4/24   1P: $99-$109   2P: $109-$119
Motel   8/25-1/31   1P: $65-$109   2P: $75-$119
             4/25-6/1   1P: $59-$75   2P: $69-$85
             6/2-8/24   1P: $49-$59   2P: $59-$69
Location: Eastbound, adjacent to s side I-10 at exit 153, 48th St/Broadway; westbound exit 153B, 52nd St/Broadway, 0.4 mi nw. 4234 S 48th St 85040. Fax: 602/431-8339. **Terms:** [CP] meal plan. **Facility:** 134 rooms. Landscaped courtyard. 4 stories; interior corridors; heated pool. **Services:** area transportation. **Cards:** AE, DI, DS, MC, VI.

HAMPTON INN I-17   **Phone:** 602/864-6233   90
◆◆◆   2/1-4/1   1P: $79-$94
Motel   9/17-1/31   1P: $79-$84
             4/2-5/31   1P: $59-$64
             6/1-9/16   1P: $49
Location: Adjacent to I-17, Northern Ave exit. 8101 Black Canyon Hwy 85021. Fax: 602/995-7503. **Terms:** 48 day cancellation notice; cancellation fee imposed; pets. **Facility:** 149 rooms. Twelve small rooms. 3 stories; exterior corridors; heated pool. **Cards:** AE, DI, DS, MC, VI.

HAMPTON INN PHOENIX AIRPORT NORTH   **Phone:** (602)267-0606   139
◆◆◆   2/1-4/20   1P: $119   2P: $129
Motel   9/8-1/31   1P: $89   2P: $99
             4/21-6/8   1P: $79   2P: $89
             6/9-9/7   1P: $59   2P: $69
Location: Just n of Van Buren; just s of Loop 202 (Red Mountain Frwy). 601 N 44th St 85008. Fax: 602/267-9767. **Terms:** [ECP] meal plan; cancellation fee imposed. **Facility:** 106 rooms. Across from Chinese Cultural Center. 3 stories; interior corridors; heated pool. **Services:** gift shop; area transportation. **Cards:** AE, DI, DS, JC, MC, VI.

HAMPTON INN PHOENIX I-10 WEST   **Phone:** (602)484-7000   128
◆◆◆   2/1-4/1   1P: $79-$99   2P: $79-$99
Motel   4/2-6/1 & 10/1-1/31   1P: $59-$79   2P: $59-$79
             6/2-9/30   1P: $54-$69   2P: $54-$69
Location: I-10 51st Ave exit. 5152 W Latham St 85043. Fax: 602/484-4377. **Terms:** [CP] meal plan; 3 day cancellation notice. **Facility:** 123 rooms. 3 stories; interior corridors; heated pool. **Cards:** AE, CB, DI, DS, MC, VI. *(See ad below)*

(See map p. 225)

HILTON PHOENIX AIRPORT

◆◆◆
Hotel

	9/5-1/31	1P: $85-$95	2P: $100-$110	XP: $15	F18
	2/1-3/30	1P: $95	2P: $110	XP: $15	F18
	3/31-5/25	1P: $85	2P: $100	XP: $15	F18
	5/26-9/4	1P: $60	2P: $75	XP: $15	F18

Phone: (480)894-1600 〔151〕

Location: 0.7 mi n of I-10, southbound exit 153, westbound exit 153A; just nw of University Dr exit. 2435 S 47th St 85034. Fax: 480/921-7844. **Terms:** Cancellation fee imposed. **Facility:** 255 rooms. Most units with patio or balcony. 4 stories; interior corridors; smoke free premises; heated pool. **Services:** gift shop. Fee: massage. **All Rooms:** honor bars. **Some Rooms:** Fee: VCR. **Cards:** AE, CB, DI, DS, JC, MC, VI. *(See color ad p 41)*

HILTON SUITES-PHOENIX

◆◆◆
Suite Hotel

	2/1-6/1 & 11/24-1/31	1P: $157	2P: $157	XP: $15	F18
	10/1-11/23	1P: $117	2P: $117	XP: $15	F18
	5/26-9/30	1P: $81	2P: $81	XP: $15	F18

Phone: (602)222-1111 〔122〕

Location: On Thomas Rd just e of Central Ave, in Phoenix Plaza. 10 E Thomas Rd 85012. Fax: 602/265-4841. **Terms:** [BP] meal plan; check-in 4 pm; package plans; pets, $50 dep req. **Facility:** 226 rooms. Atrium lobby with restaurant, plants and ponds. 11 stories; interior corridors; heated pool. Fee: parking. **Services:** gift shop; area transportation. **All Rooms:** combo or shower baths. **Cards:** AE, CB, DI, DS, JC, MC, VI. *(See color ad p 41 & ad below)*

HOLIDAY INN EXPRESS HOTEL AND SUITES

◆◆◆
Motel

	1/1-1/31	1P: $149-$199	2P: $149-$199	XP: $10	F18
	2/1-5/31	1P: $139-$179	2P: $139-$179	XP: $10	F18
	10/1-12/31	1P: $109-$159	2P: $109-$159	XP: $10	F18
	6/1-9/30	1P: $79-$129	2P: $79-$129	XP: $10	F18

Phone: (602)452-2020 〔150〕

Location: 0.5 mi s of I-10, exit 7th St. 620 N 6th St 85004. Fax: 602/252-2909. **Terms:** 21 day cancellation notice; pets. **Facility:** 90 rooms. All rooms with hair dryer, iron, ironing board, voice mail and 2 phones. 3 stories; interior corridors; heated pool. **Services:** area transportation. **Recreation:** sports court. **All Rooms:** combo or shower baths. **Cards:** AE, DI, DS, JC, MC, VI.

HOLIDAY INN EXPRESS HOTEL & SUITES

◆◆◆
Motor Inn

	2/1-4/13	1P: $109-$179	2P: $119-$189	XP: $10	F18
	9/10-1/31	1P: $89-$159	2P: $99-$169	XP: $10	F18
	4/14-5/25	1P: $89-$139	2P: $99-$149	XP: $10	F18
	5/26-9/9	1P: $59-$99	2P: $69-$109	XP: $10	F18

Phone: (602)453-9900 〔135〕

Location: Adjacent to I-10, University Dr exit. 3401 E University Dr 85034. Fax: 602/453-0090. **Terms:** [ECP] meal plan; small pets only. **Facility:** 114 rooms. 4 stories; interior corridors; heated pool. **Services:** gift shop; area transportation. **Cards:** AE, CB, DI, DS, JC, MC, VI.

HOLIDAY INN MIDTOWN PHOENIX

AAA SAVE
◆◆◆
Hotel

	1/8-1/31	1P: $95-$139	2P: $149	XP: $10	F18
	2/1-4/20	1P: $90-$134	2P: $144	XP: $10	F18
	9/19-1/7	1P: $78-$114	2P: $124	XP: $10	F18
	4/21-9/18	1P: $66-$102	2P: $112	XP: $10	F18

Phone: (602)200-8888 〔112〕

Location: 0.3 mi n of Indian School Rd. 4321 N Central Ave 85012. Fax: 602/200-8800. **Terms:** Weekly & monthly rates avail; cancellation fee imposed. **Facility:** 185 rooms. 3-4 stories; exterior corridors; heated pool, whirlpool. **Dining:** Restaurant; 6 am-10 pm, Fri & Sat-11 pm; $7-$13; cocktails. **Services:** area transportation, within 5 mi. **Cards:** AE, CB, DI, DS, MC, VI. **Special Amenities:** Early check-in/late check-out and free newspaper.

(See map p. 225)

HOLIDAY INN-SELECT AIRPORT

Phone: (602)273-7778 148

AAA SAVE
◆◆◆
Hotel

9/17-1/31	1P: $99-$139	2P: $109-$149	XP: $10	F19
2/1-4/20	1P: $139	2P: $149	XP: $10	F19
4/21-5/31	1P: $99	2P: $109	XP: $10	F19
6/1-9/16	1P: $69	2P: $79	XP: $10	F19

Location: Nw corner of Washington and 44th Sts. 4300 E Washington St 85034. Fax: 602/275-5616. **Terms:** Weekly rates avail; small pets only, $200 dep req. **Facility:** 298 rooms. Large lobby. Landscaped grounds. 10 stories; interior corridors; heated pool, whirlpool. **Dining:** Restaurant; 6 am-11 pm; $10-$20; cocktails; entertainment. **Services:** gift shop. **Recreation:** in-room video games. **Some Rooms:** Fee: VCR. **Cards:** AE, CB, DI, DS, JC, MC, VI.

HOLIDAY INN WEST

Phone: (602)484-9009 116

AAA SAVE
◆◆◆
Hotel

2/1-4/30	1P: $99-$129	2P: $99-$129	XP: $10	F19
9/11-1/31	1P: $89-$109	2P: $89-$109	XP: $10	F19
5/1-9/10	1P: $69-$89	2P: $69-$89	XP: $10	F19

Location: Adjacent to n side of I-10 W, exit 51st Ave. 1500 N 51st Ave 85043. Fax: 602/484-0108. **Terms:** [BP] meal plan; pets. **Facility:** 144 rooms. Atrium lobby. 4 one-bedroom suites, $250; 3 whirlpool rooms, $250; suites avail; 4 stories; interior corridors; heated pool, sauna, whirlpool. **Dining:** Restaurant; 6 am-10 pm; $9-$17; cocktails. **Services:** gift shop. **Cards:** AE, CB, DI, DS, JC, MC, VI.

HOMESTEAD VILLAGE/GUEST SUITES/PHOENIX METRO

Phone: (602)944-7828 87

◆◆◆
Extended
Stay Motel

2/1-4/15	1P: $59	2P: $59	XP: $10	F18
4/16-1/31	1P: $39	2P: $39	XP: $10	F18

Location: 0.6 mi e of I-17, exit Dunlap Ave. 2102 W Dunlap Ave 85021. Fax: 602/944-7831. **Terms:** Pets, $100 dep req. **Facility:** 141 rooms. 2 stories; exterior corridors. **All Rooms:** kitchens, combo or shower baths. **Cards:** AE, DI, DS, JC, MC, VI.

HOMESTEAD VILLAGE NORTH/DEER VALLEY

Phone: (602)843-1151 53

◆◆◆
Extended
Stay Motel

2/1-4/15	1P: $59	2P: $59	XP: $10	F18
4/16-1/31	1P: $39	2P: $39	XP: $10	F18

Location: W side of I-17, Union Hills Dr exit. 18405 N 27th Ave 85023. Fax: 602/843-6302. **Terms:** Pets, $100 dep req. **Facility:** 141 rooms. 2 stories; exterior corridors. **All Rooms:** kitchens. **Cards:** AE, DI, DS, JC, MC, VI.

HOMEWOOD SUITES HOTEL

Phone: 602/674-8900 76

◆◆◆
Extended
Stay Motel

2/1-4/30 & 9/12-1/31	1P: $99
5/1-9/11	1P: $49

Location: E side of I-17, Peoria Ave exit. 2536 W Beryl Ave 85021. Fax: 602/674-1004. **Terms:** [CP] meal plan; pets, $50 per stay, $200 dep req. **Facility:** 126 rooms. 9 two-bedroom units. 5 stories; interior corridors; heated pool. **Services:** gift shop; area transportation. **All Rooms:** kitchens. **Cards:** AE, CB, DI, DS, JC, MC, VI.
(See color ad below)

(See map p. 225)

HOWARD JOHNSON-GRAND AVE   Phone: (602)264-9164   **105**
AAA SAVE   2/1-4/15 & 1/1-1/31   1P: $109   2P: $109   XP: $10   F18
           9/17-12/31   1P: $79   2P: $79   XP: $10   F18
◆◆   4/16-9/16   1P: $59   2P: $59   XP: $10   F18
Motel   **Location:** 3400 Grand Ave 85017. Fax: 602/264-7633. **Terms:** Small pets only, $10 dep req. **Facility:** 132
rooms. 12 two-bedroom units. 2 stories; heated pool, whirlpool. **Dining:** Restaurant nearby. **All Rooms:** combo
or shower baths. Fee: safes. **Cards:** AE, CB, DI, DS, JC, MC, VI. **Special Amenities: Free breakfast and free newspaper.**
(See color ad p 371)   🚬 🐕 🍴 📶 🏊 ✕ 🎦 📺 🖥 💾 📠 🏃

HYATT REGENCY PHOENIX   Phone: (602)252-1234   **142**
AAA SAVE   All Year   1P: $189   2P: $214   XP: $25   F18
◆◆◆   **Location:** Just e of Washington St and Central Ave; on the w side of 2nd St. 122 N 2nd St 85004.
Hotel   Fax: 602/254-9472. **Terms:** Cancellation fee imposed. **Facility:** 712 rooms. Located at the Civic Plaza. Spa-
cious lobby. Many balconies. 24 stories; interior corridors; heated pool, whirlpool. Fee: parking. **Dining:** Coffee
shop; 6 am-10 pm; $7-$16; cocktails; also, Compass Restaurant, see separate listing. **Services:** gift shop.
Some Rooms: Fee: VCR. **Cards:** AE, CB, DI, DS, JC, MC, VI.
🍴 24 📶 🅿️ 🏊 ♿ 🐕 🐾 ✕ 🎦 VCR 📠 🖥 💾 🏃 🏋️

LA QUINTA INN & SUITES-CHANDLER   Phone: (480)961-7700   **164**
AAA SAVE   All Year   1P: $85-$105   2P: $85-$105
◆◆◆   **Location:** Just w of I-10, exit 160, Chandler Blvd. 15241 S 50th St 85044. Fax: 480/961-7705. **Terms:** [CP]
Motel   meal plan; small pets only. **Facility:** 117 rooms. 2-room suites with microwave & refrigerator; 4 stories; interior
corridors; heated pool, whirlpool. **Services:** area transportation, within 5 mi. **Cards:** AE, CB, DI, DS, JC,
MC, VI. **Special Amenities: Free breakfast and free local telephone calls.** *(See color ad below)*
✈ 🐕 🍴 📶 🏊 ✕ 🎦 📠 🖥 💾 💻 📠 🏃 🏋️

LA QUINTA INN-COLISEUM   Phone: (602)258-6271   **120**
AAA SAVE   2/1-3/31   1P: $69-$89   2P: $69-$89
◆◆◆   10/1-1/31   1P: $65-$85   2P: $65-$85
Motel   4/1-9/30   1P: $55-$75   2P: $55-$75
            Location: Adjacent to I-17, Thomas Rd exit. 2725 N Black Canyon Hwy 85009-1897. Fax: 602/340-9255.
Terms: [CP] meal plan; small pets only. **Facility:** 139 rooms. 2 stories; exterior corridors; heated pool.
Dining: Coffee shop nearby. **Recreation:** in-room video games. **Cards:** AE, CB, DI, DS, JC, MC, VI. **Special Amenities: Free
breakfast and free local telephone calls.** *(See color ad below)*   🐕 🍴 🏊 ✕ 🎦 📠 🖥 💾 📠 🏃

LA QUINTA PHOENIX NORTH   Phone: (602)993-0800   **63**
AAA SAVE   2/1-3/31   1P: $79-$99   2P: $79-$99
◆◆◆   10/1-1/31   1P: $75-$95   2P: $75-$95
Motel   4/1-9/30   1P: $55-$75   2P: $55-$75
            Location: Adjacent to I-17, exit Greenway Rd. 2510 W Greenway Rd 85023. Fax: 602/789-9172. **Terms:** [CP]
meal plan; small pets only. **Facility:** 147 rooms. Landscaped grounds. 2 stories; exterior corridors; heated pool,
wading pool, whirlpool; 2 lighted tennis courts. **Recreation:** in-room video games. **Cards:** AE, CB, DI, DS, JC, MC, VI.
Special Amenities: Free breakfast and free local telephone calls. *(See color ad below)*
🐕 🅿️ 🏊 🐾 ✕ 🎦 📠 💾 📠 🏃 🏋️ ✕

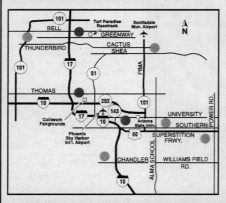

(See map p. 225)

LEXINGTON HOTEL AT CITY SQUARE

Phone: (602)279-9811 **109**

	1/1-1/31	1P: $99-$139	2P: $99-$139	XP: $10	F18
	2/1-3/31	1P: $89-$139	2P: $89-$139	XP: $10	F18
Hotel	4/1-9/15 & 9/16-12/31	1P: $89-$119	2P: $89-$119	XP: $10	F18

Location: Just w of Central Ave, 0.3 mi s of Indian School Rd, on the n side of Clarendon Ave. 100 W Clarendon Ave 85013. Fax: 602/631-9358. **Terms:** Pets, $125 dep req. **Facility:** 180 rooms. Centrally located in a commercial area. 3-7 stories; interior corridors; heated pool, whirlpool. **Dining:** Restaurant; 6 am-10:30 am, 11 am-10 pm, Mon-Sat, closed Sun; $10-$16; cocktails; entertainment, nightclub. **Services:** gift shop. Fee: massage. **All Rooms:** combo or shower baths. **Cards:** AE, DI, DS, MC, VI.

LOS OLIVOS HOTEL & SUITES

Phone: (602)528-9100 **134**

	2/1-4/14	1P: $99-$129	2P: $99-$129	XP: $10	F14
Motor Inn	10/1-1/31	1P: $79-$99	2P: $79-$99	XP: $10	F14
	4/15-9/30	1P: $59-$79	2P: $59-$79	XP: $10	F14

Location: Just e of Central Ave, on n side of McDowell Rd. 202 E McDowell Rd 85004. Fax: 602/258-7259. **Terms:** Pets. **Facility:** 48 rooms. Landscaped courtyard. 3 stories; interior corridors; heated pool. **Some Rooms:** 15 kitchens. Fee: refrigerators, microwaves, VCR. **Cards:** AE, CB, DI, DS, JC, MC, VI. *(See ad below)*

MARICOPA MANOR BED & BREAKFAST INN

Phone: (602)274-6302 **96**

	2/1-5/31 & 9/1-1/31	1P: $129-$229	2P: $149-$249	XP: $25	F6
	6/1-8/31	1P: $89-$129	2P: $89-$149	XP: $25	F6

Bed & Breakfast **Location:** Just n of Camelback Rd and w of Central Ave, on the s side of Pasadena Ave. 15 W Pasadena Ave 85013 (PO Box 7186, 85011). Fax: 602/266-3904. **Terms:** [CP] meal plan; check-in 4 pm. **Facility:** 6 rooms. Refurbished Spanish mission house built in 1928. Orange, lemon, tangerine and pecan trees. Beautifully decorated 1-bedroom suites. 2 whirlpool rooms, $149-$229; 1 story; interior/exterior corridors; designated smoking area; heated pool, whirlpool. **Recreation:** gazebo & spa. **All Rooms:** combo or shower baths. **Some Rooms:** kitchen. **Cards:** AE, CB, DI, DS, MC, VI.

(See map p. 225)

PHOENIX INN
Phone: (602)956-5221   **93**

AAA SAVE	2/1-4/27	1P: $129-$149	2P: $129-$149	XP: $10	F17
◆◆◆	9/11-1/31	1P: $99-$119	2P: $99-$119	XP: $10	F17
Motel	4/28-5/25	1P: $99-$109	2P: $99-$109	XP: $10	F17
	5/26-9/10	1P: $59-$69	2P: $59-$69	XP: $10	F17

Location: Just sw of Camelback Rd and 24th St. 2310 E Highland Ave 85016. Fax: 602/468-7220. **Terms:** [CP] meal plan; cancellation fee imposed. **Facility:** 120 rooms. 10 whirlpool rooms, $99-$209; 4 stories; interior corridors; heated pool, whirlpool. **Dining:** Restaurant nearby. **All Rooms:** extended cable TV. **Cards:** AE, CB, DI, DS, MC, VI. **Special Amenities:** Free breakfast and free local telephone calls.

POINTE HILTON SOUTH MOUNTAIN RESORT
Phone: (602)438-9000   **159**

AAA SAVE	2/1-4/29	1P: $209	2P: $209	XP: $25	F18
◆◆◆◆	4/30-5/24 & 9/10-1/31	1P: $179	2P: $179	XP: $15	F18
Resort	5/25-9/9	1P: $109	2P: $109	XP: $15	F18

Location: Just w of I-10, Baseline Rd exit; on the s side of Baseline Rd. 7777 S Pointe Pkwy 85044. Fax: 602/431-6535. **Terms:** Check-in 4 pm; 3 day cancellation notice; cancellation fee imposed; package plans. **Facility:** 638 rooms. 1-bedroom suites with living room, many overlooking the city. Very spacious grounds. 2-5 stories; exterior corridors; putting green; 6 heated pools, sauna, steamroom, whirlpools. Fee: 36 holes golf; racquetball courts, 10 lighted tennis courts. **Dining:** 4 restaurants; 6 am-1 am; $8-$20; cocktails; also, Another Pointe in Tyme at South Mountain, Rustler's Rooste, see separate listing; entertainment. **Services:** gift shop; complimentary evening beverages. Fee: massage. **Recreation:** hiking trails, jogging. Fee: horseback riding. Rental: bicycles. **All Rooms:** honor bars. **Some Rooms:** Fee: VCR. **Cards:** AE, CB, DI, DS, JC, MC, VI. *(See ad color ad p 41 & ad p 245)*

POINTE HILTON SQUAW PEAK RESORT
Phone: (602)997-2626   **92**

AAA SAVE	2/1-4/29	1P: $239	2P: $239	XP: $25	F18
◆◆◆	4/30-5/24 & 9/10-1/31	1P: $189	2P: $189	XP: $15	F18
Resort	5/25-9/9	1P: $109	2P: $109	XP: $15	F18

Location: 0.5 mi n of Glendale Ave. 7677 N 16th St 85020. Fax: 602/997-2391. **Terms:** Check-in 4 pm; 3 day cancellation notice; cancellation fee imposed. **Facility:** 563 rooms. 1-bedroom suites with living room. Also, 78 1- and 2-bedroom villas. On extensive grounds with tree-shaded, nicely landscaped pool areas and courtyards. Hole In The Wall River Ranch offers a variety of waterslides and water rec. 3-4 stories; exterior corridors; 7 heated pools, saunas, steamroom, waterslide, whirlpools. Fee: putting green; 4 lighted tennis courts. **Dining:** 3 restaurants; 6 am-10 pm; $10-$22; also, Lantana Grille, see separate listing; entertainment. **Services:** gift shop; complimentary evening beverages; area transportation, within 5 mi, shopping ctr. Fee: massage. **Recreation:** in-room video games, jeep rentals. Fee: horseback riding. Rental: bicycles. **All Rooms:** extended cable TV. **Some Rooms:** honor bars. Fee: VCR. **Cards:** AE, CB, DI, DS, JC, MC, VI. *(See ad color ad p 41 & ad p 245)*

POINTE HILTON TAPATIO CLIFFS RESORTS
Phone: (602)866-7500   **70**

AAA SAVE	9/10-1/31	1P: $189-$239	2P: $189-$239	XP: $15	F18
◆◆◆◆	2/1-4/29	1P: $239	2P: $239	XP: $25	F18
Resort	4/30-5/24	1P: $189	2P: $189	XP: $15	F18
	5/25-9/9	1P: $109	2P: $109	XP: $15	F18

Location: 2 mi n of Dunlap Ave. 11111 N 7th St 85020. Fax: 602/993-0276. **Terms:** Check-in 4 pm; 3 day cancellation notice; package plans. **Facility:** 585 rooms. 1-bedroom suites with living room. On extensive, nicely landscaped, hillside grounds. Rooms are in the main buildings and on the hills, some with views. 5 stories; exterior corridors; 9 heated pools, saunas, steamrooms, waterslide, whirlpools. Fee: 18 holes golf; 11 lighted tennis courts. **Dining:** 3 restaurants; 6 am-11 pm; $10-$35; cocktails; also, Different Pointe of View, Pointe in Tyme Restaurant at Tapatio Cliffs, see separate listing; entertainment. **Services:** gift shop; complimentary evening beverages. Fee: massage. **Recreation:** Fee: horseback riding, hayride-cookout. Rental: bicycles. **All Rooms:** honor bars. **Cards:** AE, CB, DI, DS, JC, MC, VI. *(See ad color ad p 41 & ad p 245)*

PREMIER INNS
Phone: (602)943-2371   **79**

AAA SAVE	2/1-4/15 & 1/15-1/31	1P: $50-$100	2P: $50-$100	
◆◆	4/16-1/14	1P: $45-$85	2P: $45-$85	
Motel				

Location: I-17, exit 208, w to 28th Dr, 0.5 mi to Metro Pkwy, e to 27th Ave, then n. 10402 N Black Canyon Hwy 85051. Fax: 602/943-5847. **Terms:** [CP] meal plan; pets. **Facility:** 252 rooms. 2 stories; exterior corridors; 2 pools, 1 heated, whirlpool. **Some Rooms:** Fee: refrigerators. **Cards:** AE, CB, DI, DS, MC, VI. **Special Amenities:** Free breakfast and free local telephone calls.

QUALITY HOTEL & RESORT
Phone: (602)248-0222   **121**

AAA SAVE	2/1-4/30 & 1/1-1/31	1P: $109-$119	2P: $119-$129	XP: $10	F18
◆◆	9/1-12/31	1P: $89-$99	2P: $99-$109	XP: $10	F18
Motor Inn	5/1-8/31	1P: $79-$89	2P: $79-$89	XP: $10	F18

Location: On 2nd Ave just n of Osborn Rd; 0.5 mi s of Indian School. 3600 N 2nd Ave 85013. Fax: 602/265-6331. **Terms:** Check-in 4 pm; cancellation fee imposed; package plans; small pets only, $25 dep req. **Facility:** 280 rooms. Sun deck on the roof top. Sand beach at one pool. 2 whirlpool rooms, $279-$350; 6-10 stories; interior corridors; putting green; 4 heated pools, whirlpool, playground. **Dining:** Restaurant; 6 am-10 pm; $13-$18; cocktails; entertainment. **Services:** gift shop; area transportation, within 3-5 mi. **Recreation:** in-room video games, sand volleyball court. **All Rooms:** combo or shower baths. **Some Rooms:** Fee: refrigerators, VCR. **Cards:** AE, CB, DI, DS, JC, MC, VI. **Special Amenities:** Free local telephone calls and free newspaper.

(See map p. 225)

QUALITY INN-SOUTH MOUNTAIN   Phone: (480)893-3900   160
◆◆◆
	2/1-4/15 & 1/1-1/31	1P: $99-$109	2P: $109-$119	XP: $10	F18
Motor Inn	9/16-12/31	1P: $79-$89	2P: $89-$99	XP: $10	F18
	4/16-9/15	1P: $49-$59	2P: $59-$69	XP: $10	F18

Location: Just w of I-10, exit 157, Elliot Rd. 5121 E La Puente Ave 85044. Fax: 480/496-0815. **Terms:** Cancellation fee imposed; pets, $15 extra charge. **Facility:** 193 rooms. Located in a planned residential community just west of the freeway. Easy access to shopping and golf. 4 stories; exterior corridors; heated pool. **Some Rooms:** Fee: refrigerators, microwaves. **Cards:** AE, CB, DI, DS, MC, VI. *(See color ad below)*

QUALITY SUITES   Phone: (602)956-4900   113
ⒶⒶⒶ SAVE
	2/1-4/15 & 1/1-1/31	1P: $119-$139	2P: $119-$139	XP: $10	F12
◆◆	9/16-12/31	1P: $99-$119	2P: $99-$119	XP: $10	F12
Motel	4/16-9/15	1P: $59-$79	2P: $59-$79	XP: $10	F12

Location: Just n of Thomas Rd. 3101 N 32nd St 85018. Fax: 602/957-6122. **Terms:** [CP] meal plan; weekly & monthly rates avail. **Facility:** 74 rooms. 12 two-bedroom units. 2-bedroom suites $88-$150; 2 stories; exterior corridors; heated pool, whirlpool. **Dining:** Restaurant nearby. **Services:** area transportation, Diamond Back Stadium. **All Rooms:** kitchens, combo or shower baths. **Cards:** AE, DI, DS, MC, VI. **Special Amenities:** Free breakfast and free local telephone calls. *(See color ad below)*

RADISSON PHOENIX AIRPORT HOTEL   Phone: (602)437-8400   154
ⒶⒶⒶ SAVE
	2/1-4/19	1P: $169-$199	2P: $169-$199	
◆◆◆	4/20-5/24 & 9/11-1/31	1P: $139-$169	2P: $139-$169	
Hotel	5/25-9/10	1P: $89-$99	2P: $89-$99	

Location: Adjacent to I-10; University Dr exit. 3333 E University Dr 85034. Fax: 602/470-0998. **Terms:** [BP] meal plan; monthly rates avail. **Facility:** 163 rooms. Atrium lobby includes a six story water fall enclosed in multiple plexiglass rods. 13 whirlpool rooms, $99-$169; 6 stories; interior corridors; heated pool, sauna, whirlpool. **Dining:** Restaurant; 6 am-10 pm, Sat & Sun from 7 am; $8-$16; cocktails. **Services:** gift shop. **Cards:** AE, CB, DI, DS, JC, MC, VI.

RAMADA HOTEL-CAMELBACK   Phone: (602)264-9290   95
◆◆
	2/1-4/30	1P: $99-$109	2P: $99-$109	XP: $10	F16
Motor Inn	10/1-1/31	1P: $79-$89	2P: $89-$99	XP: $10	F16
	5/1-9/30	1P: $59-$69	2P: $59-$69	XP: $10	F16

Location: 1.8 mi e of I-17, Camelback Rd exit, just e of 7th Ave, on n side of Camelback Rd. 502 W Camelback Rd 85013. Fax: 602/264-3068. **Facility:** 166 rooms. 4 stories; interior corridors; heated pool. **Cards:** AE, CB, DI, DS, JC, MC, VI.

(See map p. 225)

RAMADA LIMITED I-10 WEST

◆◆◆ Phone: (602)269-9300 **115**

Motel

2/1-4/30	1P: $69-$99	2P: $79-$109	XP: $10	F17
9/1-1/31	1P: $59-$79	2P: $69-$99	XP: $10	F17
5/1-8/31	1P: $45-$65	2P: $50-$75	XP: $10	F17

Location: I-10, exit 52nd Ave, n to McDowell Rd, just w. 5259 W McDowell Rd 85043. Fax: 602/269-1811. **Terms:** [CP] meal plan; cancellation fee imposed. **Facility:** 63 rooms. 2 stories; interior corridors. **All Rooms:** Fee: safes. **Cards:** AE, DS, MC, VI.

RAMADA LIMITED SUITES

Phone: (602)957-1350 **107**

Suite Motel

2/1-5/1 & 1/1-1/31	1P: $99	2P: $109	XP: $15	F
10/2-12/31	1P: $89	2P: $109	XP: $15	F
5/2-10/1	1P: $69	2P: $79	XP: $15	F

Location: Just n of Thomas. 3211 E Pinchot 85018. Fax: 602/508-0572. **Terms:** 7 day cancellation notice; package plans; small pets only. $25 dep req. **Facility:** 103 rooms. 3 stories, no elevator; exterior corridors; heated pool. **All Rooms:** efficiencies. **Cards:** AE, DI, DS, JC, MC, VI.

RAMADA PLAZA HOTEL METROCENTER

◆◆◆ Phone: (602)866-7000 **68**

Hotel

2/1-4/15	1P: $119	2P: $119	XP: $10	F18
10/1-1/31	1P: $89	2P: $89	XP: $10	F18
4/16-9/30	1P: $69	2P: $69	XP: $10	F18

Location: Adjacent to I-17, exit Cactus Rd, just s on w side of freeway; at Metrocenter. 12027 N 28th Dr 85029. Fax: 602/942-7512. **Terms:** 3 day cancellation notice; cancellation fee imposed. **Facility:** 172 rooms. 4 stories; interior corridors. **Services:** area transportation. **All Rooms:** combo or shower baths. **Some Rooms:** Fee: refrigerators, microwaves. **Cards:** AE, CB, DI, DS, JC, MC, VI.

RED ROOF INN

Phone: (602)233-8004 **114**

Motel

2/1-3/31	1P: $50-$85	2P: $55-$85	XP: $5	F18
10/1-1/31	1P: $40-$70	2P: $45-$75	XP: $5	F18
4/1-9/30	1P: $40-$60	2P: $45-$65	XP: $5	F18

Location: I-10, 51st Ave exit, just n. 5215 W Willetta 85043. Fax: 602/233-2360. **Terms:** Pets, in designated rooms. **Facility:** 133 rooms. 4 stories; interior corridors; heated pool. **Recreation:** in-room video games. **Cards:** AE, CB, DI, DS, MC, VI.

RED ROOF INN-PHOENIX

Phone: (602)866-1049 **57**

Motel

2/1-3/31	1P: $50-$80	2P: $55-$85	XP: $5	F18
10/1-1/31	1P: $40-$70	2P: $45-$75	XP: $5	F18
4/1-9/30	1P: $40-$60	2P: $45-$65	XP: $5	F18

Location: I-17 at Bell Rd, exit 212 N on Frontage Rd w side. 17222 N Black Cyn Fwy 85023. Fax: 602/866-1834. **Terms:** [CP] meal plan; pets, in smoking rooms only. **Facility:** 125 rooms. 3 stories; interior corridors; heated pool. **Dining:** Restaurant nearby. **Recreation:** in-room video games. **All Rooms:** combo or shower baths. **Cards:** AE, CB, DI, DS, MC, VI.

RESIDENCE INN BY MARRIOTT

◆◆◆ Phone: (602)864-1900 **86**

Suite Motel

2/1-4/17 & 1/1-1/31	1P: $119-$139	2P: $119-$139
10/1-12/31	1P: $89-$119	2P: $89-$119
4/18-9/30	1P: $59-$99	2P: $59-$99

Location: W side of I-17; exit Dunlap Ave, 0.5 mi s. 8242 N Black Canyon Hwy 85051. Fax: 602/995-8251. **Terms:** Monthly rates avail; package plans; pets, $50 extra charge, $150 dep req. **Facility:** 168 rooms. 1- and 2-bedroom suites with living rooms. 40 two-bedroom units. 2 stories; interior/exterior corridors; heated pool, whirlpool; playground. **Services:** complimentary evening beverages. **Recreation:** sports court. **All Rooms:** kitchens, combo or shower baths. **Some Rooms:** Fee: VCR. **Cards:** AE, CB, DI, DS, JC, MC, VI. **Special Amenities:** Free breakfast and free local telephone calls. *(See color ad below)*

(See map p. 225)

RITZ CARLTON-PHOENIX   **Phone: (602)468-0700**   104
◆◆◆◆   2/1-4/19 & 9/6-1/31   1P: $209   2P: $209
Hotel   4/20-9/5   1P: $99   2P: $99
       Location: Southeast corner Camelback Rd and 24th St. 2401 E Camelback Rd 85016. Fax: 602/468-0793.
Terms: Cancellation fee imposed. **Facility:** 281 rooms. An elegant hotel with beautiful guest rooms. Across the street from The Biltmore Fashion Park, in The Esplanade. 11 stories; interior corridors; heated pool. Fee: 1 lighted tennis court. **Dining:** entertainment. **Services:** gift shop. Fee: massage. Rental: bicycles. **All Rooms:** safes, honor bars. **Some Rooms:** Fee: VCR. **Cards:** AE, CB, DI, DS, JC, MC, VI.

ROYAL PALMS HOTEL & CASITAS   **Phone: (602)840-3610**   102
◆◆◆◆   2/1-5/31 & 1/1-1/31   1P: $315   2P: $315   XP: $50   F18
Hotel   9/6-12/31   1P: $255   2P: $255   XP: $50   F18
   6/1-9/5   1P: $115   2P: $115   XP: $50   F18
Location: Just e of 52nd St. 5200 E Camelback Rd 85018. Fax: 602/840-0233. **Terms:** 7 day cancellation notice; cancellation fee imposed; $16 service charge. **Facility:** 116 rooms. Extensive landscape grounds. Mediterranean-style rooms and casitas, many with private patio and fireplace. 2 stories; interior/exterior corridors; designated smoking area; heated pool; 1 tennis court. **Services:** Fee: massage. **All Rooms:** safes, honor bars. **Cards:** AE, CB, DI, DS, MC, VI.

ROYAL SUITES   **Phone: (602)942-1000**   73
(AAA) (SAVE)   2/1-4/15   1P: $85   2P: $85
   10/15-1/31   1P: $65   2P: $65
◆◆◆   4/16-10/14   1P: $60   2P: $60
Suite Motel   **Location:** 1 mi w of I-17 and just s of Peoria Ave; exit Peoria Ave. 10421 N 33rd Ave 85051.
Fax: 602/993-2965. **Terms:** Cancellation fee imposed; package plans, extended stays. **Facility:** 80 rooms. Landscaped courtyard. 13 one bedroom suites-seasonal rates apply; 2 stories; exterior corridors; heated pool, whirlpool. **Dining:** Restaurant nearby. **All Rooms:** kitchens, combo or shower baths, extended cable TV. **Cards:** AE, CB, DI, DS, MC, VI. **Special Amenities:** Free local telephone calls and preferred room (subject to availability with advanced reservations). *(See color ad below)*

SHERATON CRESCENT HOTEL   **Phone: (602)943-8200**   84
◆◆◆◆   2/1-5/18 & 1/1-1/31   1P: $119-$250   2P: $119-$250   XP: $10   F17
Hotel   9/11-12/31   1P: $109-$195   2P: $109-$195   XP: $10   F17
   5/19-9/10   1P: $65-$135   2P: $65-$135   XP: $10   F17
Location: Adjacent to I-17, exit Dunlap Ave, ne corner of intersection. 2620 W Dunlap Ave 85021. Fax: 602/371-2856. **Terms:** 2 night min stay; package plans; pets. **Facility:** 342 rooms. Landscaped grounds. Fenced heated pool and whirlpool. 8 stories; interior corridors; heated pool; racquetball courts, 2 lighted tennis courts. **Services:** gift shop; area transportation. Fee: massage. **Recreation:** sports court. **All Rooms:** combo or shower baths, safes. **Some Rooms:** honor bars. Fee: refrigerators, VCR. **Cards:** AE, DI, DS, JC, MC, VI.

SIERRA SUITES HOTEL-PHOENIX/CAMELBACK   **Phone: (602)265-6800**   98
◆◆◆   2/1-4/30   1P: $129-$159   2P: $129-$159
Extended   9/16-10/31   1P: $99-$119   2P: $99-$119
Stay Motel   5/1-9/15   1P: $79-$99   2P: $79-$99
   11/1-1/31   1P: $69-$89   2P: $69-$89
Location: Just n of Camelback Rd. 5235 N 16th St 85016. Fax: 602/265-1114. **Terms:** Cancellation fee imposed. **Facility:** 113 rooms. 3 stories; interior corridors; heated pool. **All Rooms:** kitchens. **Cards:** AE, DI, DS, MC, VI.

SIERRA SUITES HOTEL-PHOENIX/METRO CENTER   **Phone: (602)395-0900**   82
◆◆◆   2/1-4/30   1P: $99-$119
Extended   9/16-1/31   1P: $79-$89
Stay Motel   5/1-9/15   1P: $49-$59
       Location: Adjacent to e side of I-17, Dunlap Ave exit, just n of intersection. 9455 N Black Canyon Hwy 85021. Fax: 602/395-1900. **Facility:** 89 rooms. 3 stories; interior corridors; heated pool. **All Rooms:** kitchens. **Cards:** AE, MC, VI.

(See map p. 225)

SLEEP INN PHOENIX NORTH
◆◆   Phone: (602)504-1200   54

Motel	2/1-4/2	1P: $79-$99	2P: $79-$99	XP: $10	F18
	10/2-1/31	1P: $60-$99	2P: $60-$99	XP: $10	F18
	4/3-4/30	1P: $55-$75	2P: $55-$75	XP: $10	F18
	5/1-10/1	1P: $44-$55	2P: $44-$55	XP: $5	F18

Location: W side of I-17, Union Hill Dr exit, 0.3 mi s. 18235 N 27th Ave 85023. Fax: 602/504-6100. **Terms:** [CP] meal plan. **Facility:** 61 rooms. 2 stories; interior corridors; small heated pool. **All Rooms:** shower baths. **Cards:** AE, CB, DI, DS, JC, MC, VI.

SLEEP INN SKY HARBOR AIRPORT
◆◆   Phone: (480)967-7100   152

Motel	10/1-1/31	1P: $89-$129	2P: $89-$129
	2/1-9/30	1P: $89-$119	2P: $89-$119
	5/1-9/30	1P: $39-$89	2P: $39-$89

Location: 0.7 mi n of I-10, southbound exit 153, westbound exit 153A; just nw of University Dr exit on 48th St/SR 143 (Hohokam Expressway). 2621 S 47th Pl 85034. Fax: 480/921-7400. **Terms:** [CP] meal plan; small pets only, $25 extra charge. **Facility:** 105 rooms. 3 stories; interior corridors; heated pool. **All Rooms:** shower baths. **Cards:** AE, DI, DS, JC, MC, VI.
(See color ad p 231)

SPRING HILL SUITES-PHOENIX/METRO CENTER
◆◆◆   Phone: (602)943-0010   85

Motel	2/1-6/4	1P: $99-$119	2P: $99-$119
	9/5-1/31	1P: $69-$109	2P: $69-$109
	6/5-9/4	1P: $49-$59	2P: $49-$59

Location: Adjacent to e side I-17, Dunlap Ave exit, just n of intersection. 9425 N Black Canyon Hwy 85021. Fax: 602/943-0010. **Terms:** [CP] meal plan; cancellation fee imposed. **Facility:** 81 rooms. 3 stories; interior corridors; heated pool. **Cards:** AE, CB, DI, DS, MC, VI.

SUPER 8-AIRPORT
Phone: (602)244-1627   146

Motel	2/1-4/23 & 1/17-1/31	1P: $62-$89
	10/1-1/16	1P: $49-$69
	4/24-9/30	1P: $45-$52

Location: 3401 E Van Buren 85008. Fax: 602/275-1126. **Terms:** [CP] meal plan; weekly rates avail; check-in 4 pm; pets, $25 dep req. **Facility:** 80 rooms. 2 stories; interior/exterior corridors; heated pool. **Dining:** Restaurant nearby. **Services:** area transportation, hospital, Amtrak. **Recreation:** spa. **All Rooms:** combo or shower baths. **Cards:** AE, DI, DS, MC, VI. **Special Amenities:** Early check-in/late check-out and preferred room (subject to availability with advanced reservations).

SUPER 8 MOTEL
Phone: (602)995-8451   88

Motel	2/1-4/15 & 1/1-1/31	1P: $54-$74	2P: $61-$81	XP: $4	F18
	4/16-12/31	1P: $43-$63	2P: $50-$70	XP: $4	F18

Location: W side of I-17; between Northern and Dunlap aves. 8130 N Black Canyon Hwy 85051. Fax: 602/995-8496. **Terms:** Cancellation fee imposed. **Facility:** 123 rooms. 2 stories; exterior corridors; heated pool, whirlpool. **Dining:** Cafeteria nearby. **Cards:** AE, CB, DI, DS, MC, VI. **Special Amenities:** Early check-in/late check-out and free local telephone calls.

SUPER 8 MOTEL
◆◆◆   Phone: (602)415-0888   55

Motel	2/1-3/30	1P: $70-$80	2P: $76-$85	XP: $5	F12
	10/1-1/31	1P: $44-$80	2P: $49-$85	XP: $5	F12
	3/31-4/30	1P: $52-$57	2P: $57-$62	XP: $5	F12
	5/1-9/30	1P: $42-$52	2P: $47-$57	XP: $5	F12

Location: Adjacent to I-10, exit 51st Ave. 1242 N 53rd Ave 85043. Fax: 602/455-4888. **Terms:** Cancellation fee imposed; pets, $50 dep req. **Facility:** 67 rooms. 2 stories; interior corridors; heated pool. **Cards:** AE, DI, DS, MC, VI.

TOWNEPLACE SUITES-PHOENIX
◆◆◆   Phone: (602)943-9510   83

Extended Stay Motel	All Year	1P: $39-$85	2P: $39-$85

Location: Adjacent to e side of I-17, Dunlap Ave exit, just n of intersection. 9425-B N Black Canyon Hwy 85021. Fax: 602/943-7654. **Terms:** 10 day cancellation notice; cancellation fee imposed; pets, $100 dep req, $50 fee, $10 extra charge. **Facility:** 95 rooms. 3 stories; interior corridors; heated pool. **All Rooms:** kitchens, combo or shower baths. **Cards:** AE, CB, DI, DS, JC, MC, VI.

TRAVELERS INN
◆◆   Phone: (602)233-1988   130

Motel	All Year	1P: $43-$63	2P: $50-$70	XP: $4	F18

Location: Adjacent to I-10W, 51st Ave exit. 5102 W Latham St 85043. Fax: 602/278-4598. **Terms:** Cancellation fee imposed. **Facility:** 128 rooms. Commercial area. 3 stories; exterior corridors; heated pool, whirlpool. **Dining:** Restaurant nearby. **Cards:** AE, CB, DI, DS, MC, VI. **Special Amenities:** Early check-in/late check-out and free local telephone calls.

TRAVELODGE-FAIRGROUNDS
◆   Phone: (602)269-6281   165

Motel	2/1-4/15	1P: $50-$60	2P: $65-$70	XP: $6	F12
	10/1-1/31	1P: $50-$55	2P: $55-$60	XP: $6	F12
	4/16-6/30	1P: $40-$50	2P: $50-$60	XP: $6	F12
	7/1-9/30	1P: $40-$45	2P: $45-$50	XP: $6	F12

Location: Adj to I-17, just n of jct I-10 & I-17. 1624 N Black Canyon Hwy 85009. Fax: 602/278-3715. **Terms:** [CP] meal plan; weekly rates avail; small pets only. **Facility:** 93 rooms. 2 stories; exterior corridors. **Cards:** AE, CB, DI, DS, JC, MC, VI. **Special Amenities:** Free breakfast and free local telephone calls.

(See map p. 225)

WELLESLEY INN & SUITES PHOENIX AIRPORT Phone: (602)225-2998 [108]
(AAA) [SAVE]   2/1-4/30   1P: $80-$90   2P: $90-$100   XP: $10   F17
◆◆◆   10/1-1/31   1P: $70-$80   2P: $80-$90   XP: $10   F17
   5/1-9/30   1P: $60-$70   2P: $70-$80   XP: $10   F17
Extended Stay   **Location:** 0.4 mi s of Thomas Rd on 44th St. 4357 E Oak St 85008. Fax: 602/275-7607. **Terms:** Daily &
Motel   monthly rates avail; pets, $150 dep req. **Facility:** 138 rooms. 2 stories; exterior corridors.
   All Rooms: kitchens, combo or shower baths. **Cards:** AE, DI, DS, JC, MC, VI. **Special Amenities: Free
breakfast and free newspaper.**

WELLESLEY INN & SUITES PHOENIX/CHANDLER Phone: (480)753-6700 [163]
(AAA) [SAVE]   2/1-5/1 & 1/11-1/31   1P: $99   2P: $109   XP: $10   F18
◆◆   9/4-1/10   1P: $79   2P: $89   XP: $10   F18
Motel   5/2-9/3   1P: $59   2P: $69   XP: $10   F18
   Location: Just w of I-10, exit 160, Chandler Blvd. 5035 E Chandler Blvd 85044. Fax: 480/753-6800.
   Terms: Weekly & monthly rates avail; pets, $250 dep req, $150 refundable. **Facility:** 131 rooms. 2 stories; ex-
terior corridors; heated pool. **Dining:** Restaurant nearby. **All Rooms:** efficiencies. **Cards:** AE, CB, DI, DS, JC, MC, VI.
Special Amenities: Free breakfast and free newspaper.

WELLESLEY INN & SUITES PHOENIX/METROCENTER Phone: (602)870-2999 [69]
(AAA) [SAVE]   2/1-4/15 & 1/15-1/31   1P: $65-$100   2P: $65-$110   XP: $10   F15
◆◆◆   9/15-1/14   1P: $54-$89   2P: $54-$99   XP: $10   F15
   4/16-9/14   1P: $39-$69   2P: $39-$79   XP: $10   F15
Extended Stay   **Location:** Just n of Peoria Ave on e side of I-17. 11211 N Black Canyon Hwy 85029. Fax: 602/870-2992.
Motel   **Terms:** Daily & monthly rates avail; cancellation fee imposed; pets, $250, $150 non-refundable dep req.
   Facility: 134 rooms. 2 stories; exterior corridors; small pool. **Dining:** Restaurant nearby.
All Rooms: kitchens, combo or shower baths. **Cards:** AE, CB, DI, DS, MC, VI. **Special Amenities: Free breakfast and free
newspaper.**

WELLESLEY INN & SUITES PHOENIX/PARK CENTRAL Phone: (602)279-9000 [123]
(AAA) [SAVE]   2/1-5/15   1P: $100   2P: $100   XP: $10   F12
◆◆◆   5/16-1/31   1P: $65   2P: $65   XP: $10   F12
   Location: 0.7 mi s of Indian School Rd. 217 W Osborn Rd 85013. Fax: 602/277-0900. **Terms:** [CP] meal plan;
Extended Stay   weekly rates avail; check-in 4 pm; pets, $250 dep req. **Facility:** 129 rooms. 1 deluxe apartment, extra charge;
Motel   3 stories; interior corridors; heated pool. **Recreation:** in-room video games. **All Rooms:** kitchens. **Cards:** AE,
CB, DI, DS, JC, MC, VI. **Special Amenities: Free breakfast and free newspaper.**

WYNDHAM GARDEN HOTEL NORTH PHOENIX Phone: (602)978-2222 [52]
(AAA) [SAVE]   All Year   1P: $59-$139   XP: $20   F18
◆◆◆   **Location:** W side of I-17, Union Hills Dr exit; s side of Union Hills Dr. 2641 W Union Hills Dr 85027.
Motor Inn   Fax: 602/978-9139. **Terms:** [BP] meal plan; cancellation fee imposed. **Facility:** 166 rooms. 16 2-room units; 2
   stories; interior corridors; heated pool, whirlpool. **Dining:** Restaurant; 6:30 am-10 pm, Sat 7 am-noon; Sun 7
am-2 pm; $7-$18; cocktails. **Cards:** AE, CB, DI, DS, JC, MC, VI. **Special Amenities: Early check-in/late
check-out and preferred room (subject to availability with advanced reservations).** *(See color ad p 251)*

Wyndham
is known for
pleasant surprises.
15% off,
for example.

- AAA members receive 15% off our lowest available rate at the time of booking (discount to be applied at check-in).
- Includes complimentary breakfast on weekends.
- In-room coffee makers, shower massagers, *Bath & Body Works* toiletries.
- 3 p.m. late checkout.
- Over 125 convenient locations throughout North America.

Wyndham Buttes Resort*† 602-225-9000
Wyndham Metrocenter* 602-997-5900
Wyndham Garden Hotel–Chandler 602-961-4444
Wyndham Garden Hotel–North Phoenix 602-978-2222
Wyndham Garden Hotel–Phoenix Airport 602-220-4400

WYNDHAM
HOTELS & RESORTS
The Right Way. The Wyndham Way.

800-WYNDHAM www.wyndham.com

(See map p. 225)

WYNDHAM GARDEN HOTEL PHOENIX AIRPORT
All Year   1P: $59-$184   **Phone:** (602)220-4400   133
                                                                                         XP: $20   F18
Hotel   **Location:** Just n of Van Buren; 0.3 mi s of SR 202 (Red Mountain Frwy). 427 N 44th St 85008.
            Fax: 602/231-8703. **Terms:** Cancellation fee imposed; package plans. **Facility:** 210 rooms. Large nicely fur-
            nished lobby lounge. 24 one-bedroom suites with living room. 7 stories; interior corridors; heated pool, whirl-
            pool. **Dining:** Restaurant; 6:30 am-2:30 & room service available from 5-10 pm; $9-$15; cocktails.
Some Rooms: Fee: refrigerators. **Cards:** AE, CB, DI, DS, JC, MC, VI. **Special Amenities: Early check-in/late check-out
and preferred room (subject to availability with advanced reservations).** *(See color ad p 251)*

WYNDHAM METROCENTER HOTEL   **Phone:** (602)997-5900   77
            All Year   1P: $64-$169   XP: $20   F18
Hotel   **Location:** I-17, Peoria Ave exit, just w to 28th Dr, then just se; on w side. 10220 N Metro Pkwy East 85051.
            Fax: 602/943-6156. **Terms:** Cancellation fee imposed; package plans. **Facility:** 284 rooms. At Metrocenter.
Landscaped courtyard. 5 stories; interior corridors; heated pool. 1 lighted tennis court. **Services:** gift shop. Fee: massage.
All Rooms: shower baths. **Some Rooms:** Fee: refrigerators, microwaves. **Cards:** AE, DI, DS, JC, MC, VI.
(See color ad p 251)

———— *The following lodgings were either not inspected or did not* ————
meet AAA rating requirements but are listed for your information only.

COUNTRY INN & SUITES BY CARLSON   **Phone:** 623/879-9000
[fyi]   Under construction, scheduled to open January 2000. **Location:** From I-17, exit 217 (Rose Garden Ln), w, 27th
            Ave s, just w on Beardsley. 20221 N 29th Ave 85227. **Planned Amenities:** 126 rooms, radios, coffeemakers,
Motel   microwaves, refrigerators, pool, exercise facilities.

EMBASSY SUITES PARADISE VALLEY   **Phone:** 602/569-0888
[fyi]   Under construction, scheduled to open March 2000. **Location:** Adjacent to Stonecrest Golf Club. 4415 E Para-
            dise Village Pkwy S 85032. **Planned Amenities:** 274 rooms, radios, coffeemakers, microwaves, refrigera-
Suite Hotel tors. *(See color ad p 237)*

HAMPTON INN-PHOENIX/MIDTOWN   **Phone:** 602/200-0990
[fyi]   2/1-4/30 & 1/1-1/31   1P: $129-$149   2P: $139-$159
            9/16-12/31   1P: $89-$99   2P: $99-$109
Motel   5/1-9/15   1P: $69-$79   2P: $79-$89
            Too new to rate, opening scheduled for August 1999. **Location:** 0.3 mi w of Central Ave, on ne corner of Cat-
alina Dr & 3rd Ave. 160 W Catalina Dr 85013. Fax: 602/200-0999. **Amenities:** 99 rooms, radios, coffeemakers, microwaves,
refrigerators, pool, exercise facilities. **Cards:** AE, DI, DS, MC, VI.

LES JARDINS HOTEL & SUITES   **Phone:** (602)234-2464   110
[fyi]   2/1-4/30 & 12/27-1/31   1P: $89-$99   2P: $89-$99   XP: $10   F16
            10/1-12/26   1P: $79-$89   2P: $79-$89   XP: $10   F16
Hotel   5/1-9/30   1P: $53-$63   2P: $53-$63   XP: $10   F16
            Under major renovation, scheduled to be completed August 1999. **Last rated:** ◆ ◆ **Location:** Just n of Os-
born Rd and w of Central Ave, on the sw corner of Clarendon and 4th aves. 401 W Clarendon Ave 85013. Fax: 602/277-2602.
Terms: [CP] meal plan; 3 day cancellation notice. **Facility:** 106 rooms. 4 stories; interior/exterior corridors; heated pool.
Cards: AE, CB, DI, DS, JC, MC, VI.

———— **RESTAURANTS** ————

ANNA'S CAFE   **Dinner:** $11-$16   **Phone:** 480/945-4503   47
◆   **Location:** Scottsdale Rd to Thomas, then 3.5 mi w. 5618 E Thomas Rd 85018. **Hours:** Open 2/1-6/25 &
American   9/22-1/31; 5:30-8:30 pm. **Closed:** Sun, Mon & Tues. **Features:** casual dress; wine only; a la carte. Unique
            selection of pasta, seafood, chicken and beef. Extensive selection of wine. Smoke free premises.

ANOTHER POINTE IN TYME AT SOUTH MOUNTAIN   **Dinner:** $15-$25   **Phone:** 602/431-6472   57
◆ ◆ ◆   **Location:** Just w of I-10, Baseline Rd exit; on the s side of Baseline Rd; in Pointe Hilton South Mountain
American   Resort. 7777 S Pointe Pkwy 85044. **Hours:** 5:30 pm-10 pm, Sat 5 pm-11 pm. **Closed:** Sun, Mon in summer.
            Reservations: suggested. **Features:** semi-formal attire; children's menu; health conscious menu; cocktails &
lounge; entertainment; a la carte. Attractively furnished and decorated. Seafood, steak and lamb chops. **Cards:** AE, CB, DI,
DS, JC, MC, VI.

AUNT CHILADAS   **Lunch:** $7-$14   **Dinner:** $7-$14   **Phone:** 602/944-1286   24
◆ ◆   **Location:** 0.5 mi n of Glendale Ave on the e side of 16th St; at the Pointe Hilton Resort at Squaw Peak.
Mexican   7330 N Dreamy Draw Dr 85020. **Hours:** 11 am-10 pm, Fri & Sat-11 pm. **Features:** casual dress; children's
            menu; health conscious menu; carryout; cocktails & lounge. Nicely decorated dining room. Large selection of
Mexican cuisine. **Cards:** AE, CB, DI, DS, MC, VI.

THE BAMBOO CLUB   **Lunch:** $6-$18   **Dinner:** $6-$18   **Phone:** 602/955-1288   43
◆ ◆   **Location:** Just e of 24th St in the Biltmore Fashion Park, 2nd level, e end. 2596 E Camelback Rd 85016.
Ethnic   **Hours:** 11:30 am-11 pm, Fri & Sat-midnight, Sun 5 pm-10 pm. **Closed:** 1/1, 11/23 & 12/25. **Features:** casual
            dress; children's menu; cocktails & lounge. Excellent variety of Pacific Rim Asian specialties. **Cards:** AE, CB,
DI, DS, MC, VI.

(See map p. 225)

BISTRO 24
◆◆◆
French
Lunch: $6-$13   **Dinner:** $8-$23   **Phone:** 602/952-2424   ㊵
Location: Southeast corner Camelback Rd and 24th St; in Ritz Carlton-Phoenix. 2401 E Camelback Rd 85016. **Hours:** 6:30 am-midnight. **Reservations:** suggested. **Features:** casual dress; Sunday brunch; children's menu; health conscious menu; carryout; cocktails & lounge; valet parking; a la carte. Smoke free premises. **Cards:** AE, CB, DI, DS, JC, MC, VI.   ✕

CHRISTO'S
◆◆◆
Italian
Lunch: $5-$9   **Dinner:** $10-$18   **Phone:** 602/264-1784   ㉘
Location: Just s of Maryland Ave on e side of 7th St. 6327 N 7th St 85014. **Hours:** 11:30 am-2:30 & 5:30-10 pm, Sat 5:30-10:30 pm. Closed: 1/1, 11/23, 12/25 & Sun. **Reservations:** suggested. **Features:** semi-formal attire; carryout; cocktails. Excellent variety of traditional Italian dishes. Wonderful dining experience. Smoke free premises. **Cards:** AE, DI, DS, MC, VI.   ✕

COMPASS RESTAURANT
◆◆◆
American
Lunch: $9-$15   **Dinner:** $10-$21   **Phone:** 602/252-1234   ㊵
Location: Just e of Washington St and Central Ave; on the w side of 2nd St; in Hyatt Regency Phoenix. 122 N 2nd St 85004. **Hours:** 11:30 am-2:30 & 5:30-10:30 pm, Sun 10 am-2:30 & 5:30-10:30 pm. **Features:** semi-formal attire; Sunday brunch; children's menu; health conscious menu; carryout; cocktails & lounge; fee for parking & valet parking; a la carte. Salads, chicken, seafood, pork, lamb and prime rib. Sun brunch 10 am-2:30 pm. Revolving restaurant on 24th floor with panoramic view of the city of Phoenix. **Cards:** AE, CB, DI, DS, JC, MC, VI.   ♿ ✕

DIFFERENT POINTE OF VIEW
◆◆◆◆
Regional
American
Dinner: $24-$35   **Phone:** 602/863-0912   ㉑
Location: 2 mi n of Dunlap Ave; in Pointe Hilton Tapatio Cliffs Resorts. 11111 N 7th St 85020. **Hours:** 6 pm-10 pm, Sun 10:30 am-2 & 6-10 pm. Closed: Sun-Mon, 6/22-9/30. **Reservations:** suggested. **Features:** semi-formal attire; Sunday brunch; health conscious menu; cocktails & lounge; entertainment; valet parking; a la carte. Elegant dining featuring haute cuisine in grand manner. Panoramic view of Phoenix. International award winning wine list. **Cards:** AE, CB, DI, DS, JC, MC, VI.   ✕

ED DEBEVIC'S SHORT ORDERS DELUXE
◆
American
Lunch: $4-$8   **Dinner:** $4-$8   **Phone:** 602/956-2760   ㊲
Location: Just w of 24th St and on the n side of Highland Ave; s side of Town and Country Shopping Center. 2102 E Highland Ave 85016. **Hours:** 11 am-9 pm, Fri & Sat-10 pm. Closed: 11/23 & 12/25. **Features:** casual dress; children's menu; carryout; cocktails; entertainment. Re-creation of a 1950's roadside diner. Informal, noisy, family oriented restaurant featuring burgers, sandwiches, chili, and daily specials. **Cards:** AE, DI, DS, MC, VI.   ✕

EDDIE MATNEY'S
◆◆◆
French
Lunch: $8-$17   **Dinner:** $17-$30   **Phone:** 602/957-3214   ㉙
Location: NW corner of Camelback Rd and 24th St, 1st floor of Northern Trust Bank Tower. 2398 E Camelback Rd 85016. **Hours:** 11 am-10 pm, Sat & Sun 5 pm-10 pm. Closed major holidays. **Reservations:** suggested. **Features:** semi-formal attire; cocktails; valet parking; a la carte. Selections of chicken, seafood, steaks, veal and salads. Contemporary French cuisine. Patio dining. Extensive wine list. **Cards:** AE, CB, DI, DS, MC, VI.   ✕

THE FISH MARKET & TOP OF THE MARKET
◆◆
Seafood
Lunch: $7-$18   **Dinner:** $13-$30   **Phone:** 602/277-3474   ㉚
Location: On the n side of Camelback Rd, just e of 16th St. 1720 E Camelback Rd 85016. **Hours:** 11 am-9:30 pm, Fri & Sat-10 pm, Sun from noon. Closed: 11/23 & 12/25. **Reservations:** suggested. **Features:** casual dress; children's menu; carryout; cocktails; a la carte. Casual dining downstairs in Fish Market with take out of fresh fish avail. Menu printed daily based on market availibility of fish. **Cards:** AE, DI, DS, MC, VI.   ✕

HAVANA CAFE
◆◆
Ethnic
Lunch: $6-$12   **Dinner:** $10-$17   **Phone:** 602/952-1991   ㊱
Location: 0.5 mi w of 42nd St, on the s side of Camelback Rd. 4225 E Camelback Rd 85018. **Hours:** 11 am-10 pm, Sun 4 pm-9 pm. Closed major holidays. **Reservations:** accepted. **Features:** casual dress; health conscious menu; carryout; cocktails. Excellent variety of Cuban, Spanish and South American dishes, patio dining. Smoke free premises. **Cards:** AE, CB, DI, DS, MC, VI.   ✕

LANTANA GRILLE
◆
Specialty
Lunch: $6-$11   **Dinner:** $10-$21   **Phone:** 602/997-5850   ㉖
Location: 0.5 mi n of Glendale Ave; in Pointe Hilton Squaw Peak Resort. 7677 N 16th St 85020. **Hours:** 6 am-10 pm, Fri & Sat-11 pm. **Features:** casual dress; children's menu; health conscious menu; carryout; cocktails & lounge. Very popular, attractive restaurant featuring foods of the sun from the equatorial regions of the world. **Cards:** AE, CB, DI, DS, JC, MC, VI.   ✕

MACAYO
◆◆
Mexican
Lunch: $6-$8   **Dinner:** $10-$12   **Phone:** 623/873-0313   ㊽
Location: 0.5 mi w of 75th Ave; on s side of Thomas Rd adjacent to Westridge Mall. 7829 W Thomas Rd 85033. **Hours:** 11 am-11 pm, Fri & Sat-midnight. Closed: 11/23 & 12/25. **Features:** casual dress; children's menu; health conscious menu items; carryout; cocktails & lounge; a la carte. Colorful, casual atmosphere. Nice selection of entrees. **Cards:** AE, DI, DS, MC, VI.   ✕

OMAHA STEAKHOUSE
◆◆
Southwest
Ethnic
Lunch: $9-$17   **Dinner:** $11-$34   **Phone:** 602/955-3992   ㉛
Location: Just n of Camelback Rd on 24th St, adjacent to Biltmore Fashion Park; in Embassy Suites-Biltmore. 2630 E Camelback Rd 85016. **Hours:** 11 am-11 pm, Fri & Sat to midnight. **Features:** casual dress; children's menu; cocktails & lounge; a la carte. Semi-casual atmosphere. Traditional steakhouse with certified Mid-Western corn fed beef. Pasta, seafood, lamb and pork are also featured. **Cards:** AE, CB, DI, DS, MC, VI.   ✕

(See map p. 225)

OUR GANG CAFE **Dinner:** $5-$15 **Phone:** 602/870-4122 ㉒

◆◆

Italian

Location: Just n of Dunlap Ave on the w side of 7th St. 9832 N 7th St 85020. **Hours:** 4:30-10 pm, Sun 5-9 pm, Fri-11 pm. Closed: 1/1 & 12/25, Mon. **Features:** casual dress; children's menu; carryout; cocktails; a la carte. Nice variety of veal, chicken and pasta dishes in addition to traditional Italian dishes. Patio dining avail where smoking is permitted. Coffee and espresso. **Cards:** AE, MC, VI.

POINTE IN TYME RESTAURANT AT TAPATIO CLIFFS **Lunch:** $5-$10 **Dinner:** $10-$20 **Phone:** 602/866-6348 ⑳

◆◆

American

Location: 2 mi n of Dunlap Ave; in Pointe Hilton Tapatio Cliffs Resorts. 11111 N 7th St 85020. **Hours:** 6:30 am-10 pm, Fri & Sat-11 pm. **Reservations:** suggested. **Features:** casual dress; children's menu; early bird specials; health conscious menu; carryout; cocktails & lounge; valet parking; a la carte. Attractively furnished and decorated. Seafood, steak, chicken and pasta. **Cards:** AE, CB, DI, DS, JC, MC, VI.

RENNICKS **Lunch:** $7-$9 **Dinner:** $10-$19 **Phone:** 480/894-1600 (54)

◆◆

American

Location: 0.7 mi n of I-10, southbound exit 153, westbound exit 153A; just nw of University Dr exit; in Hilton Phoenix Airport. 2435 S 47th St 85034. **Hours:** 6 am-2 & 5-10 pm, Sun-9 pm. **Features:** children's menu; health conscious menu; carryout; cocktails & lounge. Southwestern decor. Selections of steak, chicken, seafood and pasta. Limited menu in lounge 11 am-midnight. **Cards:** AE, CB, DI, DS, JC, MC, VI.

RISTORANTE PRONTO **Lunch:** $7-$11 **Dinner:** $10-$16 **Phone:** 602/956-4049 ㊻

◆◆◆

Regional Italian

Location: 0.5 mi s of Camelback Rd; just w of 40th St on the s side of Campbell Ave. 3950 E Campbell Ave 85018. **Hours:** 11:30 am-2:30 & 5:30-10:30 pm, Sat from 5:30 pm. Closed: 7/4, 11/23, 12/25 & Sun. **Reservations:** suggested. **Features:** semi-formal attire; carryout; cocktails; valet parking. Small, charming, nicely decorated restaurant. Valet parking Fri and Sat. **Cards:** AE, CB, DI, DS, MC, VI.

THE ROMAN TABLE **Lunch:** $8-$15 **Dinner:** $8-$20 **Phone:** 602/234-0333 ㊾

◆

Italian

Location: 2.2 mi n of I-10, exit #144, 7th Ave. 4221 N 7th Ave 85013. **Hours:** 11 am-2 & 5-11 pm, Sat 5 pm-11 pm, Sun 4 pm-9 pm. **Features:** casual dress; carryout; cocktails. Entrees include pizza, pasta and chicken. **Cards:** AE, CB, DI, DS, MC, VI.

ROSE'S **Lunch:** $6-$10 **Dinner:** $9-$18 **Phone:** 602/252-2100 ㊿

◆◆

American

Location: On Central Ave just s of McDowell Rd on w side of Central Ave; in Best Western Executive Park Hotel. 1100 North Central 85004. **Hours:** 6:30 am-2 pm & 5-10 pm; light menu in lounge 3 pm-5 pm. **Features:** casual dress; children's menu; senior's menu; carryout; salad bar; cocktails & lounge. Fish, steak, pork chops, chicken, pasta and vegetable plate. Smoke free premises. **Cards:** AE, CB, DI, DS, MC, VI.

ROXSAND **Lunch:** $5-$10 **Dinner:** $16-$22 **Phone:** 602/381-0444 ㊶

◆◆◆

Continental

Location: Just e of 24th St; in Biltmore Fashon Park, 2nd level, e end. 2594 E Camelback Rd 85016. **Hours:** 11 am-4 & 5-10 pm, Fri & Sat-11 pm, Sun noon-4 & 5-9:30 pm. Closed major holidays. **Reservations:** suggested. **Features:** casual dress; health conscious menu; carryout; cocktails & lounge. Intercontinental cuisine, blending dishes from around the world by use of foreign and local sauce, spices and preparation styles to create cross-regional fare. **Cards:** AE, DI, MC, VI.

RUSTLER'S ROOSTE **Dinner:** $13-$31 **Phone:** 602/438-9000 (55)

◆◆

Steakhouse

Location: Just w of I-10, Baseline Rd exit; on the s side of Baseline Rd; in Pointe Hilton South Mountain Resort. 7777 S Pointe Pkwy 85044. **Hours:** 5 pm-10 pm, Fri & Sat-11 pm. **Reservations:** suggested. **Features:** casual dress; children's menu; health conscious menu; carryout; cocktails & lounge; entertainment; valet parking. Popular Western restaurant overlooking the city. Nice selection of steak, seafood and barbecue specialties. Live band nightly. **Cards:** AE, CB, DI, DS, JC, MC, VI.

SAM'S CAFE **Lunch:** $6-$13 **Dinner:** $6-$15 **Phone:** 602/954-7100 ㉜

◆◆

American

Location: Just e of 24th St; in Biltmore Fashion Park, 2nd level, e end. 2566 E Camelback Rd 85016. **Hours:** 11 am-10 pm. Fri & Sat-11 pm. Closed: 1/1, 11/23 & 12/25. **Reservations:** suggested. **Features:** casual dress; Sunday brunch; children's menu; carryout; cocktails & lounge. Nice selection of Southwestern style entrees. **Cards:** AE, CB, DI, DS, MC, VI.

STOCKYARDS RESTAURANT **Lunch:** $8-$14 **Dinner:** $14-$30 **Phone:** 602/273-7378 (53)

◆

American

Location: 0.5 mi e of 48th St on s side of Washington Ave. 5001 E Washington Ave 85034. **Hours:** 11 am-2 & 5-10 pm, Sat from 5 pm, Sun 4:30 pm-9 pm. Closed: 7/4, 11/23, 12/24 & 12/25. **Reservations:** suggested. **Features:** casual dress; children's menu; carryout; cocktails & lounge. Turn-of-the-century western decor. Nice selection of steak, prime rib and other entrees. **Cards:** AE, DI, DS, MC, VI.

TARBELL'S **Dinner:** $11-$20 **Phone:** 602/955-8100 ㉞

◆◆◆

Continental

Location: 3213 E Camelback Rd 85018. **Hours:** 5 pm-11 pm, Sun 5 pm-10 pm. **Reservations:** suggested. **Features:** casual dress; cocktails. Creative food presentation offering a variety of poultry, fish and beef. **Cards:** AE, CB, DI, DS, MC, VI.

T-BONE STEAKHOUSE **Dinner:** $14-$25 **Phone:** 602/276-0945 (61)

◆

Steakhouse

Location: 1.05 mi s of Baseline Rd. 10037 S 19th Ave 85041. **Hours:** 5 pm-10 pm. Closed: 11/23, 12/24 & 12/25. **Features:** casual dress; cocktails. View of city lights. Mesquiute-broiled steaks and chicken. **Cards:** AE, DI, MC, VI.

T. COOK'S **Lunch:** $10-$16 **Dinner:** $17-$39 **Phone:** 602/808-0766 ㊲

◆◆◆

Specialty

Location: Just e of 52nd St; in Royal Palms Hotel & Casitas. 5200 E Camelback Rd 85018. **Hours:** 6 am-2 & 5:30-10 pm. **Reservations:** required. **Features:** dressy casual; Sunday brunch; cocktails & lounge; entertainment; valet parking; a la carte. Nice selection of Mediterranean entrees offered. Wood-burning rotisserie. Patio dining available. **Cards:** AE, CB, DI, DS, MC, VI.

(See map p. 225)

VINCENT GUERITHAULT   **Lunch:** $9-$11   **Dinner:** $20-$22   **Phone:** 602/224-0225   33
◆◆◆   **Location:** Just w of 40th St on the n side of Camelback Rd. 3930 E Camelback Rd 85018. **Hours:** 11:30
Southwest   am-2:30 & 6-10:30 pm, Sat 5:30-10:30 pm, Sun 6 pm-10:30 pm. Closed major holidays & Sun 5/26-10/31.
French   **Reservations:** suggested. **Features:** semi-formal attire; children's menu; health conscious menu items;
carryout; cocktails; valet parking; a la carte. Mesquite grilled breast of pheasant, veal, duck confit, rack of
lamb, beef, cornish hen, fresh seafood and lobster. Service in an intimate atmosphere. **Cards:** AE, DI, MC, VI.   ⊠

The Phoenix Vicinity

APACHE JUNCTION pop. 18,100

—— LODGINGS ——

APACHE JUNCTION MOTEL   **Phone:** (480)982-7702
AAA SAVE   2/1-4/7   1P: $54-$59   2P: $60-$66   XP: $6
◆   12/22-1/31   1P: $41-$47   2P: $47-$53   XP: $6
Motel   10/1-12/21   1P: $35-$40   2P: $40-$45   XP: $5
       4/8-9/30   1P: $29-$34   2P: $34-$38   XP: $5
Location: 2 mi n of US 60, exit Ironwood Dr, just w of Ironwood Dr. 1680 W Apache Tr 85220.
Terms: Weekly rates avail; 7 day cancellation notice; cancellation fee imposed; small pets only, $20 extra charge.
Facility: 15 rooms. 1 story; exterior corridors. **All Rooms:** shower baths, extended cable TV. **Cards:** AE, DS, MC, VI.
Special Amenities: Free local telephone calls and preferred room (subject to availability with advanced
reservations).

APACHE JUNCTION SUPER 8   **Phone:** (480)288-8888
◆◆   2/1-3/31   1P: $74-$85   2P: $76-$88   XP: $3   F12
Motel   11/1-1/31   1P: $57-$69   2P: $60-$69   XP: $3   F12
       4/1-4/30   1P: $54-$62   2P: $57-$65   XP: $3   F12
       5/1-10/31   1P: $49-$57   2P: $52-$60   XP: $3   F12
Location: From US 60 exit Idaho Rd 0.3 mi ne. 251 E 29th Ave 85219. Fax: 480/288-0648. **Terms:** [CP] meal plan; 10 day
cancellation notice; pets, in designated rooms. **Facility:** 60 rooms. 2 stories; interior/exterior corridors; heated pool.
All Rooms: combo or shower baths. **Cards:** AE, DI, DS, MC, VI.

HOLIDAY INN EXPRESS   **Phone:** (480)982-9200
◆◆◆   2/1-4/12   1P: $89-$109   2P: $89-$109   XP: $10   F18
Motel   10/1-1/31   1P: $69-$89   2P: $69-$89   XP: $10   F18
       4/13-9/30   1P: $49-$59   2P: $49-$59   XP: $10   F18
Location: 2 mi n of US 60, Ironwood Dr exit, 0.4 mi e of Ironwood Dr. 1101 W Apache Trail 85220. Fax: 480/671-6183.
Terms: Cancellation fee imposed. **Facility:** 40 rooms. 2 stories; interior/exterior corridors; heated pool. **Cards:** AE, CB, DI, DS,
JC, MC, VI.

—— RESTAURANT ——

BARLEEN FAMILY COUNTRY MUSIC DINNER THEATRE   **Dinner:** $9-$16   **Phone:** 480/982-7991
◆◆   **Location:** from US 60, exit Tomahawk Rd, 1 mi n, then 0.5 mi e on Old West Hwy. 2275 Old West Hwy
American   85219. **Hours:** Tues-Sat 11/1-5/1, seating at 6:30 pm. Closed major holidays, Sun, Mon & 5/2-10/31.
       Reservations: suggested. **Features:** casual dress; children's menu. Three generations performing
country-style entertainment and serving roast beef dinners. Smoke free premises. **Cards:** MC, VI.   ⊠

BUCKEYE pop. 5,000

—— LODGING ——

DAYS INN-BUCKEYE   **Phone:** (623)386-5400
◆◆◆   2/1-4/1 & 9/2-1/31   1P: $89-$99   2P: $109   XP: $10   F12
Motel   4/2-7/1 & 7/2-9/1   1P: $69-$79   2P: $89   XP: $10   F12
       Location: Adjacent to I-10, exit 114 (Miller Rd). 25205 W Yuma Rd 85326. Fax: 623/386-4988. **Terms:** Can-
cellation fee imposed. **Facility:** 60 rooms. 2 stories; exterior corridors. **All Rooms:** Fee: safes. **Cards:** AE, DS, MC, VI.

CAREFREE pop. 1,700

------ LODGING ------

THE BOULDERS RESORT   Phone: (480)488-9009

AAA

	2/1-4/29	1P: $545	2P: $545	XP: $16	F16
	9/10-1/31	1P: $250-$425	2P: $250-$425	XP: $16	F16
◆◆◆◆	4/30-5/25	1P: $425	2P: $425	XP: $16	F16
Resort	5/26-9/9	1P: $145-$185	2P: $145-$185	XP: $16	F16

Location: Scottsdale, on Scottsdale Rd 11 mi n of Bell Rd to Carefree Hwy, then just n; 12.7 mi e of jct I-17 and SR 74, then just n. 34631 N Tom Darlington Rd 85377 (PO Box 2090). Fax: 480/488-4118. **Terms:** [MAP] meal plan; check-in 4 pm; 21 day cancellation notice; cancellation fee imposed; package plans; $20 service charge; pets, $100 fee. **Facility:** 160 rooms. Beautiful location in the desert foothills, built within the natural topography of giant granite boulders. Overlooks Sonoran high desert and lush green golf courses. Spacious rooms in adobe style buildings. Fireplace and patio. 1, 2 & 3 bedroom villas $325-$1100; 1-2 stories; exterior corridors; 2 heated pools, sauna, steamrooms, whirlpools. Fee: 36 holes golf; 8 tennis courts. **Dining:** 2 dining rooms, 2 restaurants, deli; 6:30 am-10 pm; $16-$45; cocktails; also, La Tilla Dining Room, see separate listing; entertainment. **Services:** gift shop. Fee: massage, area transportation. **Recreation:** hiking trails, jogging. Fee: balloon rides, bi-plane rides, aerobics, guided hiking, rock climbing. Rental: bicycles. **All Rooms:** safes, honor bars. **Cards:** AE, CB, DI, MC, VI.

------ RESTAURANT ------

LA TILLA DINING ROOM   **Dinner:** $30-$45   **Phone:** 480/488-9009

◆◆◆

American

Location: Scottsdale, on Scottsdale Rd 11 mi n of Bell Rd to Carefree Hwy, then just n; 12.7 mi e of jct I-17 and SR 74, then just n; in The Boulders Resort. 34631 N Tom Darlington Rd 85377. **Hours:** 6 pm-10 pm. **Reservations:** suggested. **Features:** semi-formal attire; children's menu; health conscious menu; cocktails & lounge; entertainment; valet parking; a la carte. Salad, chicken, seafood, beef, ostrich, pasta with lobster and rack of lamb. Smoke free premises. **Cards:** AE, CB, DI, MC, VI.

CAVE CREEK pop. 2,900

------ LODGING ------

GOTLAND'S INN CAVE CREEK   Phone: 480/488-9636

◆◆◆

	2/1-4/30 & 12/31-1/31	1P: $140-$199	2P: $140-$199	XP: $25
Bed &	9/22-12/30	1P: $120-$169	2P: $120-$169	XP: $25
Breakfast	5/1-9/21	1P: $110-$150	2P: $110-$150	XP: $25

Location: Scottsdale Rd/Tom Darlington, w/b on Cave Creek Rd 1.3 mi, then 0.3 mi n on Schoolhouse Rd. 38555 N Schoolhouse Rd 85331 (PO Box 4948, 85327). Fax: 480/488-6879. **Terms:** [CP] meal plan; check-in 4 pm; 30 day cancellation notice; cancellation fee imposed; package plans. **Facility:** 4 rooms. Located in a desert foothills area. Old west ambiance with southwest decor in guestrooms. Small menagerie of domestic animals on property. 1 story; interior corridors; smoke free premises. **Services:** Fee: area transportation. **Some Rooms:** kitchen. **Cards:** AE, DS, MC, VI.

CHANDLER pop. 90,500   (See map p. 227; index p. 223)

------ LODGINGS ------

BEST WESTERN INN & SUITES   **Phone:** (480)814-8600   464

AAA SAVE

	2/1-4/15 & 1/1-1/31	1P: $89-$109	2P: $89-$109
◆◆	10/1-21/31	1P: $69-$79	2P: $69-$79
Motel	4/16-9/30	1P: $49-$59	2P: $49-$59

Location: Just s of Ray Rd. 950 N Arizona Ave 85224. Fax: 480/814-1198. **Terms:** [CP] meal plan; 4 day cancellation notice. **Facility:** 48 rooms. 4 whirlpool rooms, $80-$125; 2 stories; exterior corridors; whirlpool. **All Rooms:** combo or shower baths. **Cards:** AE, DI, DS, MC, VI. **Special Amenities:** Free breakfast and free local telephone calls.

(See map p. 227)

FAIRFIELD INN-PHOENIX/SOUTH
◆◆
Motel
Phone: (480)940-0099   **465**
Property failed to provide current rates
Location: I-10 exit 160 (Chandler Blvd), 0.4 mi e, s on Southgate. 7425 W Chandler Bvld 85226.
Fax: 480/940-7336. **Terms:** [CP] meal plan. **Facility:** 66 rooms. 3 stories; interior corridors; heated pool.
Cards: AE, DI, DS, MC, VI.

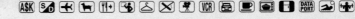

HAMPTON INN
[AAA] [SAVE]
◆◆◆
Motel
Phone: (480)753-5200   **467**

2/1-4/30	1P: $99	2P: $99	XP: $10 F19
10/1-1/31	1P: $69	2P: $69	XP: $10 F19
5/1-9/30	1P: $59	2P: $59	XP: $10 F19

Location: I-10 exit 160 (Chandler Blvd), 0.4 mi e, n on 54th. 7333 W Detroit St 85226. Fax: 480/753-5100.
Terms: [CP] meal plan; cancellation fee imposed. **Facility:** 101 rooms. 8 whirlpool rooms; 6 stories; interior
corridors; heated pool, whirlpool. **Services:** area transportation, within 5 mi. **All Rooms:** combo or shower baths, extended
cable TV. **Cards:** AE, CB, DI, DS, MC, VI. **Special Amenities:** Free breakfast and free local telephone calls.
(See color ad p 256)

HAWTHORN SUITES LTD
◆◆◆
Suite Motel
Phone: 480/705-8881   **468**

2/1-4/30 & 1/11-1/31	1P: $99-$109	2P: $99-$109
9/1-1/10	1P: $89-$99	2P: $89-$99
5/1-8/31	1P: $59-$69	2P: $59-$69

Location: I-10 exit 160 (Chandler Blvd), 1.5 mi e. 5858 W Chandler Blvd 85226. Fax: 480/785-1451. **Terms:** [BP] meal plan;
cancellation fee imposed; small pets only, $50 fee. **Facility:** 100 rooms. 10 two-bedroom units. 2 stories; interior corridors;
heated pool. **All Rooms:** kitchens. **Cards:** AE, CB, DI, DS, JC, MC, VI.

HOLIDAY INN EXPRESS HOTEL & SUITES
◆◆◆
Motel
Phone: (480)785-8500   **470**

10/1-1/31	1P: $99-$119	2P: $99-$119
2/1-4/15	1P: $99-$109	2P: $99-$109
4/16-9/30	1P: $59-$79	2P: $59-$79

Location: Just w of I-10, exit 160 (Chandler Blvd). 15221 S 50th St 85044. Fax: 480/785-7377. **Terms:** [CP] meal plan; small
pets only. **Facility:** 125 rooms. 4 stories; interior corridors; 2 pools, 1 heated, 1 small. **Cards:** AE, CB, DI, DS, JC, MC, VI.
(See color ad below)

HOMEWOOD SUITES
◆◆◆
Motel
Phone: (480)753-6200   **471**

1/1-1/31	1P: $159-$209	2P: $159-$209	XP: $10 F18
2/1-5/31	1P: $149-$199	2P: $149-$199	XP: $10 F18
10/1-12/31	1P: $129-$179	2P: $129-$179	XP: $10 F18
6/1-9/30	1P: $99-$149	2P: $99-$149	XP: $10 F18

Location: From I-10, exit 160 (Chandler Blvd), 0.4 mi e, n on 54th. 7373 W Detroit St 85226. Fax: 480/753-6222.
Terms: [CP] meal plan; cancellation fee imposed; pets, non-refundable fee. **Facility:** 83 rooms. 5 two-bedroom units. 3 stories; interior corridors; heated pool. **Services:** area transportation. **All Rooms:** efficiencies. **Cards:** AE, CB, DI, DS, MC, VI.

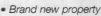

(See map p. 227)

MICROTEL INN
Phone: (480)705-8882   **474**

9/16-1/31	1P: $59	2P: $69
2/1-4/30	1P: $49	2P: $59
5/1-9/15	1P: $39	2P: $49

Motel

Location: I-10 exit 160 (Chandler Blvd), 1.5 mi e, just n. 255 N Kyrene 85226. Fax: 480/705-6697. **Terms:** 3 day cancellation notice; small pets only. **Facility:** 70 rooms. 3 stories; interior corridors; heated pool. **Cards:** AE, CB, DI, DS, JC, MC, VI.

RED ROOF INN-CHANDLER
Phone: (480)857-4969   **475**

2/1-3/31	1P: $50-$80	2P: $55-$85	XP: $5	F18
10/1-1/31	1P: $40-$70	2P: $45-$75	XP: $5	F18
4/1-9/30	1P: $40-$60	2P: $45-$65	XP: $5	F18

Motel

Location: I-10 exit 160 (Chandler Blvd), 0.4 mi e, s on Southgate. 7400 W Boston St 85226. Fax: 480/857-4979. **Terms:** [CP] meal plan; small pets only, in smoking rooms. **Facility:** 131 rooms. 4 stories; interior corridors; heated pool. **Cards:** AE, CB, DI, DS, MC, VI.

SHERATON SAN MARCOS RESORT
Phone: (480)963-6655   **477**

All Year   1P: $99-$189   2P: $109-$199

Hotel

Location: Just s of Chandler Blvd on Arizona Ave. 1 San Marcos Pl 85224. Fax: 480/963-6777. **Terms:** Pets. **Facility:** 294 rooms. Extensive landscaped grounds. Balconies or patios. 4 stories, no elevator; exterior corridors; putting green; 2 heated pools, whirlpool. Fee: 18 holes golf; 2 lighted tennis courts. **Dining:** 2 restaurants; $7-$21; cocktails. **Services:** gift shop; area transportation, Fiesta Mall, AZ Mills. **Recreation:** water basketball, water volleyball. **Cards:** AE, CB, DI, DS, JC, MC, VI.

WINDMILL INN OF CHANDLER
Phone: (480)812-9600   **478**

2/1-4/15	1P: $116-$134	2P: $116-$134	XP: $6	F18
4/16-5/31	1P: $89-$125	2P: $89-$125	XP: $6	F18
9/16-1/31	1P: $99-$116	2P: $99-$116	XP: $6	F18
6/1-9/15	1P: $62-$80	2P: $62-$80	XP: $6	F18

Motel

Location: I-10 exit 160, 3.9 mi e, corner of Country Club Way. 3535 W Chandler Blvd 85226. Fax: 480/812-8911. **Terms:** [CP] meal plan; check-in 4 pm; pets. **Facility:** 126 rooms. Interior corridors; heated pool, whirlpool. **Services:** area transportation, within 5 mi. **Recreation:** bicycles. **All Rooms:** extended cable TV. **Cards:** AE, CB, DI, MC, VI. **Special Amenities:** Free breakfast and free local telephone calls. *(See ad below)*

WYNDHAM GARDEN HOTEL
Phone: (480)961-4444   **480**

All Year   1P: $64-$159   XP: $20   F18

Motor Inn

Location: I-10 exit 160 (Chandler Blvd), 0.4 mi e, s on Southgate. 7475 W Chandler Blvd 85226. Fax: 480/940-0269. **Terms:** [BP] meal plan; cancellation fee imposed. **Facility:** 159 rooms. Landscaped courtyard. Well-appointed guest rooms and public areas. 4 stories; interior corridors; heated pool, whirlpool. **Dining:** Restaurant; 6:30 am-2 & 5-10 pm; $8-$20; cocktails; complimentary evening hors d'oeuvres. **All Rooms:** extended cable TV. **Cards:** AE, CB, DI, DS, JC, MC, VI. **Special Amenities:** Early check-in/late check-out and preferred room (subject to availability with advanced reservations). *(See color ad p 251)*

--- **RESTAURANT** ---

THE PASTA HOUSE   **Lunch:** $6-$9   **Dinner:** $9-$20   Phone: 480/812-1502   **228**

Italian

Location: Se corner Ray and Dobson rds. 1949 W Ray Rd #18 85224. **Hours:** 11 am-10 pm. Closed: 1/1, 11/23 & 12/25. **Reservations:** suggested; Fri & Sat. **Features:** casual dress; children's menu; carryout; cocktails & lounge. Nice selection of steak, chicken, seafood, pasta and pizza. Dessert made fresh daily. Lakeside patio dining available. **Cards:** AE, DI, DS, MC, VI.

FOUNTAIN HILLS pop. 10,000   (See map p. 226; index p. 223)

──── LODGINGS ────

COMFORT INN   Phone: (480)837-5343 345
(AAA) (SAVE) 2/1-4/15 & 1/1-1/31 1P: $85-$89 2P: $95-$105 XP: $10 F18
     9/1-12/31   1P: $59-$64 2P: $69-$75 XP: $10 F18
◆◆ 4/16-8/31   1P: $44-$49 2P: $55-$59 XP: $10 F18
Motel **Location:** 0.5 mi w of SR 87 (BeeLine Hwy) on Shea Blvd. 17105 E Shea Blvd 85268. Fax: 480/837-9146.
Terms: [CP] meal plan. **Facility:** 43 rooms. Located 5 mi east of Mayo Clinic. 2 stories; interior corridors;
heated pool, whirlpool. **Dining:** Restaurant nearby. **Services:** gift shop; area transportation; Mayo Clinic & casino.
All Rooms: extended cable TV. **Cards:** AE, DI, DS, MC, VI. **Special Amenities:** Free breakfast and free local telephone
calls.

SOUTHWEST INN AT EAGLE MOUNTAIN   Phone: (480)816-3000 348
(AAA) (SAVE) All Year   1P: $99-$295 2P: $99-$295 XP: $10 F12
◆◆◆◆ **Location:** 9 mi e of Scottsdale Rd on Shea Blvd, 0.5 s on Eagle Mountain Pky. 9800 N Summer Hill Blvd
Motel 85268. Fax: 480/816-3090. **Terms:** [CP] meal plan; cancellation fee imposed. **Facility:** 42 rooms. Adjacent to
Eagle Mountain Golf Course. All rooms and suites with fireplace and 2-person whirlpool tub. 42 whirlpool
rooms; exterior corridors; designated smoking area; heated pool, whirlpool. **Dining:** Restaurant nearby.
Services: gift shop. **Recreation:** Fee: bicycles. **All Rooms:** shower baths. **Cards:** AE, DI, DS, MC, VI. **Special Amenities:**
Free breakfast and free newspaper. (See color ad below)

────── *The following lodging was either not inspected or did not* ──────
meet AAA rating requirements but is listed for your information only.

INN AT COPPERWYND   Phone: 480/333-1900
(fyi) Under construction, scheduled to open November 1999. **Location:** From Scottsdale Rd, n on Shea Blvd, n on
Motor Inn Palisades, then just w. 13225 N EagleRidge Dr 85268. Fax: 480/333-1901. **Planned Amenities:** 32 rooms,
restaurant, radios, coffeemakers, pool, exercise facilities, golf, tennis.

──── RESTAURANT ────

LA PIAZZA   **Dinner:** $7-$16   **Phone:** 480/837-1878 170
◆◆ **Location:** From Scottsdale Rd, 13 mi e on Shea, then 1.3 mi n. 11865 N Saguaro Blvd 85268. **Hours:** 5
Italian pm-9:30 pm, Sun 4 pm-9 pm. Closed: 1/1, 11/23, 12/25 & Mon. **Features:** cocktails; a la carte. Selections of
chicken, seafood, steak, veal, pork, pasta and salad. Homemade desserts and Tuscan peasant bread. Patio
dining. Bar and patio smoking areas. Smoke free premises. **Cards:** AE, MC, VI.

GLENDALE pop. 147,900 (See map p. 225; index p. 220)

——— LODGINGS ———

HOLIDAY INN EXPRESS ARROWHEAD　　　　　　　　　　　**Phone:** (623)412-2000　181

◆◆◆	2/1-3/31 & 1/1-1/31	1P: $89-$109	2P: $89-$109	XP: $5	F12
Motel	10/16-12/31	1P: $69-$99	2P: $69-$99	XP: $5	F12
	4/1-10/15	1P: $49-$89	2P: $49-$89	XP: $5	F12

Location: Just n of Bell on 79th Ave, on the grounds of Arrowhead Towne Mall. 7885 W Arrowhead Towne Ctr Dr 85308. Fax: 623/412-5522. **Terms:** [CP] meal plan; 3 day cancellation notice; 2 night min stay; small pets only, $25 fee. **Facility:** 60 rooms. 2 stories; exterior corridors; heated pool. **All Rooms:** combo or shower baths. **Cards:** AE, CB, DI, DS, MC, VI.

SPRINGHILL SUITES BY MARRIOTT　　　　　　　　　　　**Phone:** (623)878-6666　180

◆◆◆	4/1-8/31	1P: $39-$79	2P: $99
Motel	2/1-3/31 & 1/1-1/31	1P: $99-$149	
	9/1-12/31	1P: $49-$99	

Location: 0.3 mi e of Loop 101, Bell Rd exit. 7810 W Bell Rd 85308. Fax: 623/878-6611. **Terms:** [CP] meal plan. **Facility:** 89 rooms. At entrance to Arrowhead Towne Center. 4 stories; interior corridors; heated pool. **Cards:** AE, DI, DS, JC, MC, VI.

GOODYEAR pop. 6,300 (See map p. 224; index p. 223)

——— LODGINGS ———

BEST WESTERN PHOENIX GOODYEAR INN　　　　　　　　　**Phone:** (623)932-3210　21

◆◆◆ SAVE	2/1-5/1	1P: $89	2P: $89	XP: $10	F18
	9/1-10/31	1P: $79	2P: $89	XP: $10	F18
◆◆	11/1-1/31	1P: $69	2P: $89	XP: $10	F18
Motor Inn	5/1-8/31	1p: $59	2P: $69	XP: $10	F18

Location: I-10, exit 128; 0.8 mi s. 55 N Litchfield Rd 85338. Fax: 623/932-3210. **Terms:** Check-in 4 pm; 3 day cancellation notice; small pets only, $10 extra charge. **Facility:** 85 rooms. 1 deluxe suite, $99-$139 for up to 4 persons; 2 stories; interior/exterior corridors; heated pool. **Dining:** Coffee shop; 5:30 am-10 pm; $6-$12; cocktails. **Some Rooms:** Fee: VCR. **Cards:** AE, DI, DS, MC, VI. **Special Amenities:** Free breakfast and free local telephone calls.

HOLIDAY INN EXPRESS　　　　　　　　　　　　　　　　**Phone:** 623/535-1313　20

◆◆◆
Motel

	2/1-4/19	1P: $129-$149	2P: $129-$149	XP: $10	F18
	9/15-1/31	1P: $99-$149	2P: $99-$149	XP: $10	F18
	4/20-6/1	1P: $99-$119	2P: $99-$119	XP: $10	F18
	6/2-9/14	1P: $89-$109	2P: $89-$109	XP: $10	F18

Location: Just n of I-10, exit 128, Litchfield Rd. 1313 Litchfield Rd 85338. Fax: 623/535-0950. **Terms:** [ECP] meal plan; 3 day cancellation notice; cancellation fee imposed; pets. **Facility:** 90 rooms. 3 stories; interior corridors; heated pool. **Cards:** AE, CB, DI, DS, JC, MC, VI.

——— *The following lodging was either not inspected or did not* ———
meet AAA rating requirements but is listed for your information only.

HAMPTON INN & SUITES　　　　　　　　　　　　　　　**Phone:** 623/536-1313

fyi　　Under construction, scheduled to open October 1999. **Location:** 0.5 n of I-10, exit 128 (Litchfield Rd). 2000 N
Suite Motel　　Litchfield Rd 85338. **Planned Amenities:** 110 rooms, pool, exercise facilities.

LITCHFIELD PARK pop. 3,300 (See map p. 224; index p. 223)

——— LODGING ———

THE WIGWAM RESORT　　　　　　　　　　　　　　　　**Phone:** (623)935-3811　17

◆◆◆◆	2/1-5/1	1P: $330-$475	2P: $330-$475	XP: $25	F18
Resort	9/7-1/31	1P: $245-$475	2P: $245-$475	XP: $25	F18
	5/2-6/20	1P: $245-$380	2P: $245-$380	XP: $25	F18
	6/21-9/6	1P: $145-$225	2P: $145-$225	XP: $25	F18

Location: I-10 west; exit Litchfield Rd; 2 mi n. 300 Wigwam Blvd 85340 (PO Box 278). Fax: 623/935-3737. **Terms:** Check-in 4 pm; 14 day cancellation notice; cancellation fee imposed; package plans; small pets only, $25 dep req. **Facility:** 331 rooms. A popular, long established resort. Adobe-style buildings on extensive, beautifully landscaped grounds. Authentic, early Arizona decor. 34 units with gas fireplace. 2 stories; exterior corridors; putting green; 2 heated pools; playground. Fee: 54 holes golf; 9 lighted tennis courts. **Dining:** entertainment. **Services:** gift shop; area transportation. Fee: massage. **Recreation:** Fee: bicycles, horseback riding. **All Rooms:** safes, honor bars. **Some Rooms:** Fee: refrigerators. **Cards:** AE, CB, DI, DS, MC, VI. A Preferred Hotel.

——— RESTAURANT ———

ARIZONA KITCHEN　　　　　　**Dinner:** $20-$32　　　　　　**Phone:** 623/935-3811　8

◆◆◆◆　**Location:** I-10 west; exit Litchfield Rd; 2 mi n; in The Wigwam Resort. 300 Wigwam Blvd 85340.
Southwest　**Hours:** Open 2/1-6/30 & 8/31-1/31; 6 pm-10:30 pm. Closed: Sun, Mon & 7/1-8/31.
American　**Reservations:** suggested. **Features:** semi-formal attire; cocktails & lounge; valet parking; a la carte. An
attractive dining room with Arizona territorial decor. Serves an imaginative selection of cuisine. Display
cooking. Smoke free premises. **Cards:** AE, CB, DI, DS, MC, VI.

MESA pop. 288,100   (See map p. 227; index p. 222)

------ LODGINGS ------

ARIZONA GOLF RESORT & CONFERENCE CENTER   Phone: (480)832-3202   **444**

(AAA) (SAVE)	2/1-4/23	1P: $149-$169	2P: $149-$169	XP: $15	F16
◆◆◆	10/1-1/31	1P: $119-$159	2P: $119-$159	XP: $10	F16
	4/24-5/31	1P: $109-$129	2P: $109-$129	XP: $10	F16
Resort	6/1-9/30	1P: $79-$99	2P: $79-$99	XP: $10	F16

Location: 1.3 mi n of US 60 (Superstition Frwy) exit Power Rd; se corner of Broadway and Power rds, entrance on Broadway Rd. 425 S Power Rd 85206. Fax: 480/981-0151. **Terms:** [BP] & [CP] meal plans; pets. **Facility:** 186 rooms. Spacious grounds. 2-bedroom kitchen suites, $109-$199; 2 stories; exterior corridors; putting green; 2 heated pools, whirlpools; 4 tennis courts (2 lighted). Fee: 18 holes golf. **Dining:** Restaurant; 7 am-10 pm, snack bar 6 am-5 pm; $8-$20. **Services:** gift shop. **Recreation:** bicycles, half-court basketball, volleyball net. **All Rooms:** safes. **Some Rooms:** 96 efficiencies, 72 kitchens. **Cards:** AE, DI, DS, JC, MC, VI. **Special Amenities:** Free breakfast and free newspaper.

BEST WESTERN MESA INN   Phone: (480)964-8000   **425**

(AAA) (SAVE)	2/1-4/14	1P: $70-$89	2P: $80-$99	XP: $5	F12
	1/1-1/31	1P: $60-$79	2P: $70-$89	XP: $5	F12
◆◆	12/1-12/31	1P: $49-$59	2P: $59-$79	XP: $5	F12
Motel	4/15-11/30	1P: $43-$53	2P: $49-$69	XP: $5	F12

Location: 2 mi n of US 60 (Superstition Frwy) Stapley Dr exit; 0.5 mi e on Main St. 1625 E Main St 85203. Fax: 480/835-1272. **Terms:** [CP] meal plan; weekly rates avail; small pets only, $5 extra charge. **Facility:** 99 rooms. 2 stories; exterior corridors; heated pool, whirlpool. **Dining:** Restaurant nearby. **Services:** complimentary evening beverages, Mon-Fri. **Some Rooms:** Fee: microwaves. **Cards:** AE, DI, DS, MC, VI. **Special Amenities:** Free breakfast and free local telephone calls.

BEST WESTERN MEZONA INN   Phone: (480)834-9233   **418**

(AAA) (SAVE)	2/1-4/15	1P: $85-$95	2P: $90-$100	XP: $5	F18
	1/1-1/31	1P: $76-$87	2P: $80-$90	XP: $5	F18
◆◆	10/1-12/31	1P: $57-$67	2P: $62-$72	XP: $5	F18
Motor Inn	4/16-9/30	1P: $53-$63	2P: $57-$67	XP: $5	F18

Location: Just w of Center St. 250 W Main St 85201. Fax: 480/844-7920. **Facility:** 136 rooms. 2 stories; exterior corridors; heated pool, whirlpool. **Cards:** AE, CB, DI, DS, JC, MC, VI. **Special Amenities:** Free local telephone calls and free newspaper.

BEST WESTERN SUPERSTITION SPRINGS INN & SUITES   Phone: (480)641-1164   **447**

◆◆◆	2/1-3/31 & 1/1-1/31	1P: $65-$125	2P: $75-$135	XP: $5	F12
Motel	10/16-12/31	1P: $55-$95	2P: $65-$105		
	4/1-10/15	1P: $49-$79	2P: $59-$89	XP: $5	F12

Location: Just n of US 60 (Superstition Frwy) Power Rd exit, on the nw corner of Power Rd and Hampton Ave at Superstition Springs Mall. 1342 S Power Rd 85206. Fax: 480/641-7253. **Terms:** [CP] meal plan; 3 day cancellation notice; pets, $25 fee. **Facility:** 59 rooms. Attractively furnished units. Conveniently located just s of Leisure World. 2 stories; exterior corridors; heated pool. **All Rooms:** combo or shower baths. **Cards:** AE, CB, DI, DS, JC, MC, VI.

COUNTRY INN & SUITES BY CARLSON   Phone: (480)641-8000   **448**

◆◆◆	2/1-4/30	1P: $129-$199	2P: $129-$199	XP: $10	F18
Motel	5/1-5/31	1P: $99-$159	2P: $99-$159	XP: $10	F18
	9/1-1/31	1P: $89-$139	2P: $89-$139	XP: $10	F18
	6/1-8/31	1P: $69-$109	2P: $69-$109	XP: $10	F18

Location: Just s of US 60 (Superstition Freeway) Power Rd exit, just sw. 6650 E Superstition Springs Blvd 85206. Fax: 480/854-4409. **Terms:** [CP] meal plan; check-in 4 pm; cancellation fee imposed. **Facility:** 126 rooms. 4 stories; interior corridors; heated pool. **Services:** area transportation. **Cards:** AE, CB, DI, DS, JC, MC, VI. *(See color ad p 229)*

COURTYARD BY MARRIOTT   Phone: (480)461-3000   **427**

◆◆◆	2/1-4/1	1P: $79-$139	2P: $79-$139		
Motor Inn	4/2-6/1 & 9/16-1/31	1P: $69-$119	2P: $69-$119		
	6/2-9/15	1P: $49-$89	2P: $49-$89		

Location: 0.5 mi n of US 60 (Superstition Frwy), Alma School Rd exit, se corner of Southern and Westwood Aves. 1221 S Westwood Ave 85210. Fax: 480/461-0179. **Facility:** 149 rooms. 3 stories; interior corridors; heated pool. **Cards:** AE, CB, DI, DS, MC, VI.

DAYS INN   Phone: (480)844-8900   **431**

◆	2/1-4/30 & 10/1-1/31	1P: $86-$106	2P: $86-$106	XP: $6	F17
Motel	5/1-9/30	1P: $59-$79	2P: $59-$79	XP: $6	F17

Location: 0.5 mi se of US 60, exit Country Club Dr. 333 W Juanita 85210. Fax: 480/844-0973. **Terms:** [CP] meal plan; pets, $25 dep req. **Facility:** 124 rooms. 3 stories; interior corridors; heated pool. **Cards:** AE, CB, DI, DS, JC, MC, VI.

DAYS INN-EAST MESA   Phone: (480)981-8111   **441**

(AAA) (SAVE)	2/1-4/15 & 1/16-1/31	1P: $80-$90	2P: $85-$95	XP: $5	F13
	10/1-1/15	1P: $50-$60	2P: $60-$70	XP: $5	F13
◆◆	4/16-9/30	1P: $45-$55	2P: $50-$60	XP: $5	F13
Motel					

Location: 0.5 mi e of Higley Rd. 5531 E Main St 85205. Fax: 480/396-8027. **Terms:** [CP] meal plan; cancellation fee imposed. **Facility:** 61 rooms. 2 stories; exterior corridors; heated pool, whirlpool. **Cards:** AE, CB, DI, DS, JC, MC, VI. **Special Amenities:** Free breakfast and free local telephone calls.

(See map p. 227)

DOBSON RANCH INN RESORT-BEST WESTERN   Phone: (480)831-7000   434

	2/1-4/30 & 1/1-1/31	1P: $137	2P: $147-$157	XP: $10	F12
	9/16-12/31	1P: $95	2P: $105	XP: $10	F12
	5/1-9/15	1P: $54-$68	2P: $59-$73	XP: $10	F12

Motor Inn   **Location:** Adjacent to US 60 (Superstition Frwy) Dobson Rd exit. 1666 S Dobson Rd 85202. Fax: 480/831-7000. **Terms:** [BP] meal plan; cancellation fee imposed. **Facility:** 213 rooms. 12 1-bedroom suites; whirlpool room; 2 stories; interior/exterior corridors; heated pool, whirlpools. **Dining:** Restaurant; also, Monti's at the Ranch, see separate listing. **Services:** gift shop. **Cards:** AE, CB, DI, DS, JC, MC, VI. **Special Amenities: Free breakfast and free local telephone calls.**

FAIRFIELD INN PHOENIX/MESA   Phone: (480)668-8000   424

	2/1-4/30	1P: $99-$109	2P: $99-$109
	12/31-1/31	1P: $79-$89	2P: $79-$89
	9/2-12/30	1P: $59-$69	2P: $59-$69
	5/1-9/1	1P: $49-$59	2P: $49-$59

Motel   **Location:** 0.5 mi n of US 60 (Superstition Frwy) Alma School Rd exit, just ne on Southern Ave to Westwood Ave. 1405 S Westwood Ave 85210. Fax: 480/668-7313. **Terms:** [CP] meal plan. **Facility:** 66 rooms. 3 stories; interior corridors; heated pool. **All Rooms:** combo or shower baths. **Cards:** AE, DI, DS, MC, VI.

HAMPTON INN   Phone: (480)926-3600   439

	2/1-3/31	1P: $99	2P: $109
	10/1-1/31	1P: $89	2P: $99
	4/1-5/31	1P: $79	2P: $89
	6/1-9/30	1P: $59	2P: $69

Motel   **Location:** Adjacent to n side of US 60 (Superstition Frwy) Gilbert Rd exit. 1563 S Gilbert Rd 85204. Fax: 480/926-4892. **Facility:** 116 rooms. 4 stories; interior corridors; heated pool. **Cards:** AE, CB, DI, DS, MC, VI.

(See map p. 227)

HILTON MESA PAVILION   Phone: (480)833-5555
◆◆◆
Hotel

2/1-4/19	1P: $129-$149	2P: $129-$149	XP: $15	F18
4/20-5/4 & 9/5-1/31	1P: $115-$135	2P: $115-$135	XP: $15	F18
5/5-9/4	1P: $69-$89	2P: $69-$89	XP: $15	F18

Location: Just n of US 60 (Superstition Frwy) Alma School Rd exit; just e of Alma School Rd on s side of Holmes Ave. 1011 W Holmes Ave 85210. Fax: 480/649-1886. **Facility:** 263 rooms. Beautifully decorated lobby and atrium area. Contemporary decor. Adjacent to Fiesta Lakes Executive 9-Hole Golf Course. 8 stories; interior corridors; heated pool. **Dining:** entertainment. **Services:** gift shop; area transportation. **Some Rooms:** Fee: VCR. **Cards:** AE, CB, DI, DS, MC, VI.
(See color ad p 41 & p 262)

HOLIDAY INN HOTEL & SUITES   Phone: (480)964-7000 437
◆◆
Motor Inn

2/1-4/30 & 1/1-1/31	1P: $99	2P: $99	XP: $10	F18
5/1-12/31	1P: $59	2P: $59	XP: $10	F18

Location: US 60, Superstition Frwy, Country Club Dr exit. 1600 S Country Club Dr 85210. Fax: 480/833-6419. **Terms:** Pets, $100 fee. **Facility:** 246 rooms. 6 stories; interior/exterior corridors; heated pool. **Services:** gift shop; area transportation. **Cards:** AE, CB, DI, DS, MC, VI. *(See color ad p 262)*

HOMESTEAD VILLAGE   Phone: (480)752-2266 436
◆◆◆
Extended
Stay Motel

2/1-4/15	1P: $59	2P: $59	XP: $10	F18
4/16-1/31	1P: $39	2P: $39	XP: $10	F18

Location: Just s of US 60, Dobson Rd exit. 1920 W Isabella 85202. Fax: 480/752-7865. **Terms:** Check-in 4 pm; pets, $100 fee. **Facility:** 123 rooms. Studio units with fully equipped kitchens. 2 stories; exterior corridors. **All Rooms:** kitchens. **Some Rooms:** Fee: VCR. **Cards:** AE, DI, DS, JC, MC, VI.

LA QUINTA INN & SUITES-MESA   Phone: (480)844-8747 428
AAA SAVE
◆◆◆
Motel

2/1-4/30	1P: $95-$115	2P: $95-$115	
10/1-1/31	1P: $89-$109	2P: $89-$109	
5/1-9/30	1P: $65-$85	2P: $65-$85	

Location: US 60 Alma School Rd exit , 0.5 mi n to Southern Ave, 0.5 mi e to Extension Rd, then just s to Grove Ave. 902 W Grove Ave 85210. Fax: 480/844-8850. **Terms:** [CP] meal plan; small pets only. **Facility:** 125 rooms. 7 stories; interior corridors; heated pool, whirlpool. **Cards:** AE, CB, DI, DS, JC, MC, VI. **Special Amenities:** Free breakfast and free local telephone calls.

LA QUINTA INN & SUITES-SUPERSTITION SPRINGS   Phone: (480)654-1970 450
AAA SAVE
◆◆◆
Motel

2/1-4/30	1P: $95-$115	2P: $95-$115
5/1-1/31	1P: $75-$95	2P: $75-$95

Location: Just s US 60 Power Rd exit. 6530 E Superstition Springs Blvd 85208. Fax: 480/654-1973. **Terms:** [CP] meal plan; small pets only. **Facility:** 107 rooms. 6 stories; interior corridors; heated pool, whirlpool. **Cards:** AE, CB, DI, DS, JC, MC, VI. **Special Amenities:** Free breakfast and free local telephone calls. *(See color ad p 242)*

MOTEL 6 - 1030   Phone: 480/834-0066 430
AAA
◆
Motel

2/1-4/24	1P: $42-$55	2P: $48-$61	XP: $3	F17
12/14-1/31	1P: $42-$52	2P: $48-$58	XP: $3	F17
4/25-12/13	1P: $40-$50	2P: $46-$56	XP: $3	F17

Location: SR 60, exit 179 (Country Club Dr), just n. 1511 S Country Club Dr 85210. Fax: 480/969-6313. **Terms:** Small pets only. **Facility:** 91 rooms. Adjacent to Golf Land Amusement Park. 2 stories; exterior corridors; heated pool. **Cards:** AE, CB, DI, DS, MC, VI.

(See map p. 227)

QUALITY INN ROYAL MESA
Phone: (480)833-1231 **419**

2/1-4/15 & 1/1-1/31	1P: $79-$99	2P: $89-$109	XP: $10	F12
10/1-12/31	1P: $59-$69	2P: $69-$79	XP: $10	F12
4/16-9/30	1P: $49-$59	2P: $49-$59	XP: $10	F12

Motel **Location:** 1 mi w of Center St. 951 W Main St 85201. Fax: 480/833-1231. **Terms:** [CP] meal plan. **Facility:** 96 rooms. Balcony or patio. 2 stories; interior corridors; heated pool, saunas, indoor whirlpool.
Cards: AE, DI, DS, JC, MC, VI. **Special Amenities:** Free breakfast and free local telephone calls. *(See ad p 263)*

RAMADA INN SUITES
Phone: (480)964-2897 **438**

2/1-4/30	1P: $86-$155	2P: $86-$155	XP: $5	F
10/1-1/31	1P: $65-$110	2P: $65-$110	XP: $5	F
5/1-9/30	1P: $49-$88	2P: $49-$88	XP: $5	F

Motel **Location:** 0.5 mi n of US 60 (Superstition Frwy), Country Club Dr exit. 1410 S Country Club Dr 85210. Fax: 480/461-0801. **Terms:** [CP] meal plan; weekly & monthly rates avail; check-in 4 pm. **Facility:** 120 rooms. Studios and 1- to 2-bedroom suites with living room and kitchen. Poolside rooms, $10 extra charge; 2 stories, no elevator; exterior corridors; heated pool, whirlpool. **Dining:** Restaurant nearby. **Cards:** AE, CB, DI, DS, MC, VI. **Special Amenities:** Free breakfast and free local telephone calls.

RESIDENCE INN BY MARRIOTT MESA
Phone: (480)610-0100 **426**

2/1-4/2	1P: $99-$149
4/3-5/20 & 9/10-1/31	1P: $69-$109
5/21-9/9	1P: $49-$79

Motel
Location: 941 W Grove Ave 85210. Fax: 480/610-6490. **Terms:** [CP] meal plan; pets, $35 fee. **Facility:** 117 rooms. 37 two-bedroom units. 3 stories; interior corridors; heated pool. **Services:** area transportation. **Recreation:** sports court. **Some Rooms:** 68 efficiencies, 49 kitchens. **Cards:** AE, CB, DI, DS, JC, MC, VI.

SHERATON MESA HOTEL
Phone: (480)898-8300 **421**

2/1-4/30	1P: $99	2P: $99	XP: $10	F12
10/1-1/31	1P: $85	2P: $85	XP: $10	F12
5/1-5/31	1P: $75	2P: $75	XP: $10	F12
6/1-9/30	1P: $55	2P: $55	XP: $10	F12

Hotel **Location:** 2 mi n of US 60 (Superstition Frwy), Mesa Dr exit, just n and w of Mesa Dr. 200 N Centennial Way 85201. Fax: 480/964-9279. **Terms:** 3 day cancellation notice; cancellation fee imposed. **Facility:** 273 rooms. Landscaped courtyard with fountain. 12 stories; interior corridors; heated pool, whirlpool. **Dining:** Dining room, restaurant; 6 am-2 & 4-10 pm; $8-$15; cocktails. **Services:** gift shop; area transportation, within 5 mi. **Cards:** AE, CB, DI, DS, JC, MC, VI. **Special Amenities:** Free newspaper and free room upgrade (subject to availability with advanced reservations). *(See color ad below)*

SLEEP INN OF MESA
Phone: (480)807-7760 **445**

All Year	1P: $39-$99	2P: $49-$109	XP: $5	F18

Location: 6347 E Southern Ave 85206. Fax: 480/807-2646. **Terms:** 7 day cancellation notice; pets, $50 dep req, in designated rooms. **Facility:** 84 rooms. Located at the west end of Superstition Springs Mall. 3 stories; Motel interior corridors; heated pool, whirlpool. **Dining:** Coffee shop nearby. **All Rooms:** combo or shower baths. **Cards:** AE, CB, DI, DS, JC, MC, VI. **Special Amenities:** Free breakfast and free local telephone calls.

(See map p. 227)

TRAVELODGE SUITES MESA
◆◆
Motel

	2/1-4/15 & 1/1-1/31	1P: $84-$124	2P: $84-$124	XP: $5	F12
	10/1-12/31	1P: $64-$84	2P: $64-$84	XP: $5	F12
	4/16-9/30	1P: $49-$69	2P: $49-$69	XP: $5	F12

Phone: (480)832-5961 440

Location: From I-60, exit Greenfield Rd, 2 mi n, just w. 4244 E Main St 85205. Fax: 480/830-9274. **Terms:** Pets, $10 fee, in designated rooms. **Facility:** 75 rooms. 2 stories; exterior corridors; heated pool. **Some Rooms:** 16 efficiencies, 28 kitchens. **Cards:** AE, DS, JC, MC, VI.

──── RESTAURANTS ────

THE AMERICAN GRILL   Lunch: $6-$9   Dinner: $14-$22   Phone: 480/844-1918 213
◆◆
Steakhouse
Location: 0.5 mi n of US 60 (Superstition Frwy); exit Alma School Rd; on e side of Alma School Rd. 1233 S Alma School Rd 85202. **Hours:** 11 am-4 pm & 5-10 pm, Sat noon-3 & 5-10 pm, Sun 5-9 pm. **Reservations:** suggested. **Features:** children's menu; early bird specials; carryout; cocktails & lounge; entertainment. Entrees include beef, chicken, fish and pasta. Attractively decorated in dark woods and brass. Smoke free premises. **Cards:** AE, CB, DI, DS, MC, VI.

THE LANDMARK RESTAURANT   Lunch: $6-$11   Dinner: $10-$20   Phone: 480/962-4652 212
AAA
◆◆◆
American
Location: 0.5 mi e of Alma School Rd on s side of Main St. 809 W Main St 85201. **Hours:** 11 am-9 pm, Sun 11 am-7 pm. Closed: 7/4, 11/23 & 12/25. **Features:** children's menu; salad bar; cocktails. Enjoyable dining in restored church building. Victorian decor. Varied menu, large soup and salad bar with more than 100 selections. Extensive display of Mesa historical photographs. Smoke free premises. **Cards:** AE, CB, DI, DS, MC, VI.

MONTI'S AT THE RANCH   Lunch: $6-$9   Dinner: $9-$16   Phone: 480/831-8877 215
◆
Steakhouse
Location: Adjacent to US 60 (Superstition Frwy) Dobson Rd exit; in Dobson Ranch Inn Resort-Best Western. 1644 S Dobson Rd 85202. **Hours:** 6:30 am-10:30 pm. **Features:** casual dress; children's menu; carryout; cocktails & lounge. Attractive southwest decor. Specializing in prime rib, steak and chicken. Smoke free premises. **Cards:** AE, CB, DI, DS, JC, MC, VI.

THE WEATHER VANE RESTAURANT   Lunch: $6-$10   Dinner: $7-$14   Phone: 480/830-2721 216
AAA
◆◆
American
Location: 0.7 mi e of Power Rd on s side of Main St, in Nevada Bob's Plaza. 7303 E Main St 85207. **Hours:** 11 am-9 pm. Closed: 11/23 & 12/25. **Features:** casual dress; children's menu; carryout; cocktails. Informal family atmosphere. Chicken, pork, seafood, sandwiches and prime rib. Smoke free premises. **Cards:** DS, MC, VI.

PARADISE VALLEY pop. 11,800   (See map p. 226; index p. 223)

──── LODGING ────

HERMOSA INN
◆◆◆
Motor Inn

	2/1-4/9	1P: $260-$330	2P: $260-$330	XP: $25	F7
	9/6-1/31	1P: $210-$265	2P: $210-$265	XP: $25	F7
	4/10-5/21	1P: $170-$210	2P: $170-$210	XP: $25	F7
	5/22-9/5	1P: $95-$140	2P: $95-$140	XP: $25	F7

Phone: (602)955-8614 334

Location: 1 mi s of Lincoln Dr, corner of Stanford Dr. 5532 N Palo Cristi Rd 85253. Fax: 602/955-8299. **Terms:** [CP] meal plan; 7 day cancellation notice, in season; cancellation fee imposed; package plans. **Facility:** 35 rooms. 4 two-bedroom units. 1 story; exterior corridors; designated smoking area; heated pool; 3 tennis courts. **All Rooms:** combo or shower baths, honor bars. **Some Rooms:** 4 kitchens. **Cards:** AE, CB, DI, DS, MC, VI.

──── RESTAURANT ────

LON'S AT THE HERMOSA   Phone: 602/955-7878 155
◆◆◆
American
Location: Located at the Hermosa Inn. 5532 N Palo Cristi Rd 85253. **Hours:** 11 am-2 & 6-10 pm, Sat 6 pm-10 pm, Sun 10 am-2 & 6-10 pm. Closed: 5/29 & 9/4. **Reservations:** suggested. **Features:** semi-formal attire; Sunday brunch; cocktails; valet parking. **Cards:** AE, CB, DI, MC, VI.

PEORIA   (See map p. 225; index p. 223)

──── LODGINGS ────

COMFORT SUITES OF PEORIA
◆◆◆
Motel

	2/16-3/31	1P: $99-$129	2P: $104-$134	
	2/1-2/15 & 10/1-1/31	1P: $69-$79	2P: $74-$84	
	4/1-9/30	1P: $59-$69	2P: $64-$74	

Phone: (623)334-3993 192

Location: Loop 101, Bell Rd exit, then se. 8473 W Paradise Ln 85382. Fax: 623/334-3993. **Terms:** [CP] meal plan; cancellation fee imposed; pets, smoking rooms only. **Facility:** 79 rooms. 3 stories; interior corridors. **Cards:** AE, CB, DI, DS, MC, VI.

(See map p. 225)

HAMPTON INN　　　　　　　　　　　　　　　　　　　　　Phone: (623)486-9918　[190]

AAA SAVE　　3/2-4/5　　　　　1P: $109-$119　　　2P: $119-$129
◆◆◆　　　　2/1-3/1　　　　　1P: $79-$89　　　　2P: $89-$99
Motel　　　　9/1-1/31　　　　1P: $55-$75　　　　2P: $65-$85
　　　　　　4/6-8/31　　　　1P: $45-$55　　　　2P: $49-$65
　　　　Location: Loop 101, Bell Rd exit, then just e. 8408 W Paradise Ln 85382. Fax: 623/486-4842. **Terms:** [CP] meal plan. **Facility:** 112 rooms. Across from Peoria Sports Complex. 5 stories; interior corridors; heated pool, whirlpool. **Dining:** Restaurant nearby. **Recreation:** in-room video games. **Cards:** AE, CB, DI, DS, MC, VI. **Special Amenities:** Free breakfast and free local telephone calls.

LA QUINTA INN & SUITES　　　　　　　　　　　　　　　Phone: (623)487-1900　[193]

AAA SAVE　　2/1-3/31　　　　1P: $99-$119　　　2P: $99-$119
◆◆◆　　　　10/1-1/31　　　1P: $89-$109　　　2P: $89-$109
Motel　　　　4/1-9/30　　　　1P: $65-$85　　　　2P: $65-$85
　　　　Location: Loop 101, Bell Rd exit, then se. 16321 N 83 Ave 85382. Fax: 623/487-1919. **Terms:** Small pets only. **Facility:** 108 rooms. Across from Peoria Sports Complex. 5 stories; interior corridors; heated pool, whirlpool. **Dining:** Restaurant nearby. **Recreation:** in-room video games. **Cards:** AE, CB, DI, DS, JC, MC, VI. **Special Amenities:** Free breakfast and free local telephone calls. *(See color ad p 242)*

RESIDENCE INN BY MARRIOTT　　　　　　　　　　　　Phone: (623)979-2074　[191]
◆◆◆　　　　2/1-4/1　　　　　1P: $99-$219
Motel　　　　4/2-1/31　　　　1P: $79-$159
　　　　Location: Loop 101, Bell Rd exit, then just e. 8435 W Paradise Ln 85382. Fax: 623/979-2074. **Terms:** [CP] meal plan; cancellation fee imposed; pets, $100 dep req. **Facility:** 90 rooms. Across from Peoria Sports Complex, 75 studio and one bedroom units with kitchens; 15 two bedroom units with kitchen. 3 stories; interior corridors; 2 pools, 1 heated, 1 small. **Cards:** AE, DI, DS, JC, MC, VI.

SCOTTSDALE pop. 130,100   (See map p. 226; index p. 220)

—— LODGINGS ——

AMERISUITES-SCOTTSDALE/CIVIC CENTER　　　　　　Phone: (480)423-9944　[301]

AAA SAVE　　2/1-5/15　　　　1P: $125-$179　　2P: $125-$179　　XP: $10　　F16
◆◆◆　　　　9/16-1/31　　　1P: $107-$143　　2P: $107-$143　　XP: $10　　F16
Hotel　　　　5/16-9/15　　　1P: $62-$98　　　2P: $62-$98　　　XP: $10　　F16
　　　　Location: 0.2 mi e of Scottsdale Rd. 7300 E Third Ave 85251. Fax: 480/423-2991. **Terms:** [CP] meal plan; pets, $20 dep req. **Facility:** 128 rooms. 6 stories; interior corridors; heated pool. **Services:** area transportation, within 5 mi. **All Rooms:** efficiencies. **Cards:** AE, DI, MC, VI. **Special Amenities:** Free breakfast and free newspaper. *(See color ad opposite title page)*

BEST WESTERN PAPAGO INN & RESORT　　　　　　Phone: (480)947-7335　[314]

AAA SAVE　　2/1-4/30 & 1/1-1/31　1P: $109-$129　2P: $109-$129　　XP: $10　　F12
◆◆◆　　　　10/1-12/31　　　1P: $89-$99　　　2P: $89-$99　　　XP: $10　　F12
Motor Inn　　5/1-9/30　　　　1P: $79-$99　　　2P: $79-$99　　　XP: $10　　F12
　　　　Location: Sw corner of McDowell and Scottsdale Rds. 7017 E McDowell Rd 85257. Fax: 480/994-0692. **Terms:** [BP] meal plan; weekly rates avail; 7 day cancellation notice. **Facility:** 56 rooms. Located in a busy commercial area. Pool located in garden setting with aviary. Suites, $159-$179; 2 stories; exterior corridors; heated pool, sauna. **Dining:** Dining room; 6 am-10 pm; $6-$15; cocktails. **Services:** complimentary evening beverages. **Some Rooms:** Fee: microwaves. **Cards:** AE, CB, DI, DS, JC, MC, VI. **Special Amenities:** Free breakfast and free newspaper. *(See color ad below)*

(See map p. 226)

COMFORT INN OF SCOTTSDALE Phone: (480)596-6559 **273**

AAA SAVE	2/1-4/15	1P: $109-$139	2P: $116-$146	XP: $7	F18
◆◆◆	4/16-5/13	1P: $89-$109	2P: $96-$116	XP: $7	F18
Motel	9/10-1/31	1P: $69-$109	2P: $76-$116	XP: $7	F18
	5/14-9/9	1P: $49-$69	2P: $56-$76	XP: $7	F18

Location: Just e of Scottsdale Rd and just s of Shea Blvd, on the n side of Gold Dust Ave. 7350 E Gold Dust Ave 85258. Fax: 480/596-0554. **Terms:** [CP] meal plan; weekly rates avail. **Facility:** 124 rooms. 13 whirlpool rooms, $69-$139; 3 stories; interior corridors; heated pool, whirlpool. **Dining:** Restaurant nearby. **Cards:** AE, DI, DS, JC, MC, VI. **Special Amenities:** Free breakfast and free local telephone calls. *(See ad below)*

COMFORT SUITES-SCOTTSDALE Phone: (480)946-1111 **309**

◆◆	2/1-4/30	1P: $119-$139	2P: $129-$149	XP: $10	F18
Motel	1/1-1/31	1P: $119-$129	2P: $129-$139	XP: $10	F18
	9/13-12/31	1P: $69-$79	2P: $79-$99	XP: $10	F18
	5/1-9/12	1P: $59-$79	2P: $69-$89	XP: $10	F18

Location: N of Thomas Rd, just e of Scottsdale Rd. 3275 Civic Center Blvd 85251. Fax: 480/874-1641. **Terms:** [CP] meal plan; cancellation fee imposed. **Facility:** 60 rooms. 3 stories; interior corridors; heated pool. **Cards:** AE, CB, DI, DS, JC, MC, VI.

COUNTRY INN & SUITES BY CARLSON Phone: (480)314-1200 **267**

◆◆◆	2/1-3/31	1P: $109-$119	2P: $119-$129	XP: $10	F18
Motel	9/16-1/31	1P: $99-$109	2P: $109-$119	XP: $10	F18
	4/1-5/15	1P: $89-$99	2P: $99-$109	XP: $10	F18
	5/16-9/15	1P: $59-$69	2P: $69-$89	XP: $10	F18

Location: Just n of Shea Blvd, just e of Pima Rd. 10801 N 89th Pl 85260. Fax: 480/314-7367. **Terms:** [CP] meal plan; check-in 4 pm; small pets only, $50 extra charge, with approval. **Facility:** 163 rooms. 3 stories; interior corridors; heated pool. **Services:** area transportation. **All Rooms:** combo or shower baths. **Some Rooms:** 90 efficiencies. **Cards:** AE, DI, DS, MC, VI. *(See color ad p 229)*

COURTYARD BY MARRIOTT SCOTTSDALE/MAYO CLINIC Phone: (480)860-4000 **270**

◆◆◆	9/12-1/31	1P: $129-$169	2P: $129-$169	
Motor Inn	2/1-4/15	1P: $129-$159	2P: $129-$159	
	4/16-5/22	1P: $129-$149	2P: $129-$149	
	5/23-9/11	1P: $79-$89	2P: $79-$89	

Location: 5.5 mi e of Pima Rd, on n side of Shea Blvd. 13444 E Shea Blvd 85259. Fax: 480/860-4308. **Facility:** 124 rooms. Adjacent to Mayo Clinic, wheelchairs avail. 2 stories; interior corridors; heated pool. **Services:** area transportation. **Cards:** AE, CB, DI, DS, MC, VI.

COURTYARD BY MARRIOTT/SCOTTSDALE NORTH Phone: (480)922-8400 **258**

Property failed to provide current rates

Motor Inn **Location:** Just n of Frank Lloyd Wright Blvd. 17010 N Scottsdale Rd 85255. Fax: 480/948-3481. **Terms:** Check-in 4 pm. **Facility:** 153 rooms. 4 stories; interior corridors; heated pool. **Services:** area transportation. **Cards:** AE, CB, DI, DS, MC, VI.

DAYS INN, SCOTTSDALE FASHION SQUARE RESORT Phone: (480)947-5411 **297**

AAA SAVE	All Year	1P: $89-$195	2P: $89-$215	XP: $20	F12

◆◆ **Location:** Just n of Camelback Rd, on w side of Scottsdale Rd; at the n side of Scottsdale Fashion Square Motel shopping complex. 4710 N Scottsdale Rd 85251. Fax: 480/946-1324. **Terms:** [CP] meal plan. **Facility:** 167 rooms. Nicely landscaped grounds, adjacent to Fashion Square Mall Shopping Center. 2 stories; exterior corridors; putting green; heated pool, whirlpool; 1 lighted tennis court. **Dining:** Beer & wine served at poolside bar noon-10 pm; restaurants nearby. **Services:** area transportation, within 4 mi. **Recreation:** volleyball court. **All Rooms:** Fee: safes. **Some Rooms:** Fee: microwaves. **Cards:** AE, CB, DI, DS, JC, MC, VI. **Special Amenities:** Free breakfast and free room upgrade (subject to availability with advanced reservations). *(See color ad p 268)*

(See map p. 226)

DOUBLETREE LA POSADA RESORT - SCOTTSDALE   Phone: (480)952-0420   288

2/1-5/13	1P: $210	2P: $210	XP: $20 F17
9/17-11/4	1P: $195	2P: $195	XP: $20 F17
11/5-1/31	1P: $162	2P: $162	XP: $20 F17
5/14-9/16	1P: $89	2P: $89	XP: $20 F17

Resort

Location: Se corner of Lincoln Dr and Tatum Blvd, enter from Lincoln Dr. 4949 E Lincoln Dr 85253. Fax: 480/840-8576. **Terms:** Check-in 4 pm; 3 day cancellation notice; cancellation fee imposed; package plans; small pets only. **Facility:** 262 rooms. Attractive, spacious grounds. Patios. Manmade cave and waterfall at pool. Located adjacent to Fiesta Plaza. 9 whirlpool rooms; 1 story; exterior corridors; putting green; 2 heated pools, sauna, whirlpools. Fee: racquetball courts, 6 lighted tennis courts. **Dining:** Dining room, restaurant; 6 am-11 pm, poolside cafe 8 am-6 pm; $10-$20; cocktails; entertainment. **Services:** gift shop. Fee: massage. **Recreation:** horseshoe pit, volleyball court. Rental: bicycles. **All Rooms:** honor bars. **Cards:** AE, CB, DI, DS, JC, MC, VI. **Special Amenities: Free newspaper and preferred room (subject to availability with advanced reservations).** (See ad p 269)

DOUBLETREE PARADISE VALLEY RESORT   Phone: (480)947-5400   268

1/1-1/31	1P: $225-$245	2P: $225-$245	XP: $15 F18
2/1-4/29	1P: $215-$235	2P: $215-$235	XP: $15 F18
9/10-12/31	1P: $175-$195	2P: $175-$195	XP: $15 F18
4/30-9/9	1P: $85-$165	2P: $85-$165	XP: $15 F18

Resort

Location: Just n of Chaparral Rd on e side of Scottsdale Rd. 5401 N Scottsdale Rd 85250. Fax: 480/946-1524. **Terms:** [BP] meal plan; 3 day cancellation notice; cancellation fee imposed. **Facility:** 387 rooms. Balcony or patio. 2 stories; exterior corridors; 2 heated pools, saunas, whirlpools. Fee: racquetball courts, 2 lighted tennis courts. **Dining:** Restaurant; 6:30 am-10 pm; $10-$18; cocktails; entertainment. **Services:** gift shop; area transportation, within 5 mi. Fee: massage. **Recreation:** Fee: bicycles. **All Rooms:** honor bars. **Some Rooms:** Fee: refrigerators, VCR. **Cards:** AE, CB, DI, DS, JC, MC, VI. **Special Amenities: Free newspaper and preferred room (subject to availability with advanced reservations).** (See ad p 269)

ECONO LODGE - SCOTTSDALE   Phone: (480)994-9461   302

2/1-4/15	1P: $89-$109	2P: $89-$109	XP: $10 F17
12/1-1/31	1P: $69-$99	2P: $69-$99	XP: $10 F17
9/1-11/30	1P: $49-$79	2P: $49-$79	XP: $10 F17
4/16-8/31	1P: $49-$69	2P: $49-$69	XP: $10 F17

Motel

Location: Just w of Scottsdale Rd, just n of Indian School Rd, on s side of 5th Ave. 6935 Fifth Ave 85251. Fax: 480/947-1695. **Terms:** [CP] meal plan. **Facility:** 92 rooms. Located close to Fifth Avenue shopping district. 3 stories; exterior corridors; heated pool. **Some Rooms:** Fee: refrigerators. **Cards:** AE, CB, DI, DS, JC, MC, VI.

FAIRFIELD INN-DOWNTOWN SCOTTSDALE   Phone: (480)945-4392   295

2/1-4/30 & 1/1-1/31	1P: $88-$98	2P: $98-$108	XP: $10 F16
9/1-12/31	1P: $59-$79	2P: $59-$79	XP: $10 F16
5/1-8/31	1P: $49	2P: $49	XP: $10 F16

Motor Inn

Location: Just n of Chaparral on e side of Scottsdale Rd. 5101 N Scottsdale Rd 85250. Fax: 480/947-3044. **Terms:** [CP] meal plan; 3 day cancellation notice. **Facility:** 218 rooms. Quiet interior courtyard. 2 stories; exterior corridors; heated pool, whirlpool. **Dining:** Restaurant nearby. **Some Rooms:** Fee: refrigerators, microwaves. **Cards:** AE, CB, DI, DS, MC, VI. **Special Amenities: Early check-in/late check-out and free room upgrade (subject to availability with advanced reservations).** (See color ad p 270)

(See map p. 226)

GAINEY SUITES HOTEL   **Phone:** (480)922-6969   275
◆◆◆   2/1-4/8   1P: $139-$212   2P: $139-$212   XP: $10   F18
Suite Motel   4/9-6/3   1P: $121-$184   2P: $121-$184   XP: $10   F18
               9/17-1/31   1P: $119-$169   2P: $119-$169   XP: $10   F18
               6/4-9/16   1P: $59-$89   2P: $59-$89   XP: $10   F18
Location: Just e of Scottsdale and DoubleTree Ranch rds. 7300 E Gainey Suites Dr 85258. Fax: 480/922-1689. **Terms:** [CP] meal plan; package plans; small pets only, $150 cleaning fee. **Facility:** 164 rooms. Studio rooms and 1-2 bedroom suites. 1-2 stories; interior corridors; heated pool. **Services:** area transportation. **Recreation:** jogging. **All Rooms:** kitchens. **Some Rooms:** Fee: VCR. **Cards:** AE, CB, DI, DS, MC, VI.

ASK SD 🛏 🕭 🖼 ✕ 🍴 VCR 🖨 💻 🖥 🚪 DATA/PORT ➹ 🛠 ✕

A WARM WELCOME.

And sweet savings ahead.

At Doubletree, you'll enjoy special rates for sweet savings, plus first-class amenities and service. Our 22-acre newly renovated Paradise Valley Resort is near great championship golf and premier shopping, while La Posada Resort offers a one million gallon lagoon pool, waterfalls and more in the foothills of Camelback Mountain. Find sanctuary in the heart of red rock country at Sedona's newest all suite, golf & spa resort.

La Posada Resort:
4949 E. Lincoln Drive
602-952-0420
ADID# 15548

Paradise Valley Resort:
5401 N. Scottsdale Road
480-947-5400
ADID# 2933

Sedona Resort:
90 Trail Ridge Drive
520-284-4040

**DOUBLETREE
RESORTS**
SCOTTSDALE • SEDONA

8 0 0 - 2 2 2 - T R E E

Sweet Dreams®

---

*Rates are per room, per night, based on single or double occupancy and subject to availability.

(See map p. 226)

HAMPTON INN & SUITES   Phone: (480)348-9280 320
(AAA) SAVE   2/1-4/15   1P: $119-$129   2P: $129-$139
◆◆◆   9/17-1/31   1P: $89-$129   2P: $99-$139
           4/16-5/20   1P: $89-$99   2P: $99-$109
Motel   5/21-9/16   1P: $59-$69   2P: $69-$79
           Location: Just s of Bell Rd. 16620 N Scottsdale Rd 85254. Fax: 480/348-9281. **Terms:** [CP] meal plan.
Facility: 123 rooms. 4 whirlpool rooms, $109-$179; suites, $99-$169; 3 stories; interior/exterior corridors; heated pool, wading
pool, whirlpool. **Dining:** Restaurant nearby. **Services:** gift shop; area transportation, within 5 mi. **All Rooms:** combo or shower
baths, extended cable TV. **Some Rooms:** 40 kitchens. **Cards:** AE, CB, DI, DS, JC, MC, VI. **Special Amenities:** Free breakfast and free local telephone calls.

HAMPTON INN-OLDTOWN SCOTTSDALE   Phone: (480)941-9400 303
◆◆◆   2/1-4/23   1P: $89-$109   2P: $89-$109
Motel   4/24-5/25 & 10/1-1/31 1P: $69-$99   2P: $69-$99
           5/26-9/30   1P: $59-$69   2P: $59-$69
Location: 0.2 mi e of Scottsdale Rd and just s of Camelback Rd, via 75th St. 4415 N Civic Center Plaza 85251.
Fax: 480/675-5240. **Terms:** Pets, $50 fee. **Facility:** 126 rooms. 5 stories; interior/exterior corridors; heated pool.
All Rooms: combo or shower baths. **Cards:** AE, CB, DI, DS, JC, MC, VI.

HAMPTON INN SCOTTSDALE   Phone: (480)443-3233 271
(AAA) SAVE   2/1-4/13   1P: $109-$160   2P: $119-$160
◆◆◆   9/17-1/31   1P: $79-$160   2P: $79-$160
           4/14-5/20   1P: $79-$129   2P: $89-$129
Motel   5/21-9/16   1P: $49-$89   2P: $49-$89
           Location: Just s of Shea Blvd, on e side of Scottsdale Rd. 10101 N Scottsdale Rd 85253. Fax: 480/443-9149.
Terms: [CP] meal plan. **Facility:** 132 rooms. 4 whirlpool rooms, $99-$160; 2 stories; interior corridors; heated pool, whirlpool.
Dining: Restaurant nearby. **All Rooms:** combo or shower baths, extended cable TV. **Some Rooms:** color TV. **Cards:** AE, DI,
DS, MC, VI. **Special Amenities:** Free breakfast and free local telephone calls. *(See ad below)*

(See map p. 226)

HOLIDAY INN HOTEL & SUITES   **Phone:** (480)951-4000 262

2/1-4/23	1P: $159	2P: $169	XP: $10	F18
9/14-1/31	1P: $129	2P: $139	XP: $10	F18
4/24-5/24	1P: $79	2P: $89	XP: $10	F18
5/25-9/13	1P: $59	2P: $69	XP: $10	F18

Suite Motor Inn **Location:** At Scottsdale Municipal Airport; 0.8 mi n of Thunderbird Rd, 0.5 mi e of Scottsdale Rd, on the s side of Butherus Dr. 7515 E Butherus Dr 85260. Fax: 480/483-9046. **Terms:** [BP] meal plan; small pets only, $25 dep req. **Facility:** 120 rooms. Nicely decorated 2 room suites with microwave and refrigerator. 4 stories; exterior corridors; heated pool, whirlpool. **Dining:** Dining room; 6 am-2 & 5-10 pm; $7-$12; cocktails. **Services:** area transportation, within 5 mi. **Cards:** AE, DI, DS, JC, MC, VI. *(See color ad below)*

HOLIDAY INN OLD TOWN SCOTTSDALE   **Phone:** (480)994-9203 305

2/1-4/15	1P: $130-$145	2P: $130-$145	XP: $10	F18
4/16-5/31 & 9/10-1/31	1P: $99-$120	2P: $99-$120	XP: $10	F18
6/1-9/9	1P: $55-$90	2P: $55-$90	XP: $10	F18

Motor Inn **Location:** Just e of Scottsdale Rd, on s side of Indian School Rd. 7353 E Indian School Rd 85251-3942. Fax: 480/941-2567. **Terms:** Cancellation fee imposed; small pets only. **Facility:** 206 rooms. Located just north of Scottsdale Civic Center. 2-3 stories; exterior corridors; putting green; heated pool, whirlpool; 1 tennis court. **Dining:** Dining room; 6:30 am-10 pm; $12-$18; cocktails. **Services:** gift shop; area transportation, within 3 mi. **Recreation:** Fee: bicycles. **Some Rooms:** Fee: refrigerators. **Cards:** AE, CB, DI, DS, JC, MC, VI. **Special Amenities:** Free newspaper and free room upgrade (subject to availability with advanced reservations). *(See color ad below)*

(See map p. 226)

HOLIDAY INN SUNSPREE RESORT   Phone: (480)991-2400 285
◆◆◆   2/1-4/22   1P: $145-$169   2P: $145-$179   XP: $10   F
Motor Inn 4/23-5/20   1P: $110-$139   2P: $110-$179   XP: $10   F
           9/24-1/31   1P: $110-$139   2P: $110-$139   XP: $10   F
           5/21-9/23   1P: $55-$89   2P: $55-$99   XP: $10   F
Location: 0.5 mi e of Scottsdale Rd, on s side of Indian Bend Rd. 7601 E Indian Bend Rd 85250-4699. Fax: 480/998-2261.
Terms: 7 day cancellation notice. **Facility:** 200 rooms. Located at stretch of Indian Bend Wash. 3 stories; interior corridors;
putting green; heated pool; 2 lighted tennis courts. **Dining:** entertainment. **Services:** gift shop. Fee: massage. **Recreation:** jogging. Fee: bicycles. **Some Rooms:** Fee: VCR. **Cards:** AE, CB, DI, DS, JC, MC, VI. *(See ad below)*

HOMESTEAD VILLAGE   Phone: (480)994-0297 300
◆◆   2/1-3/28   1P: $85-$95   2P: $90-$100   XP: $5   F17
Extended 3/29-5/15 & 9/12-1/31 1P: $44-$54   2P: $49-$59   XP: $5   F17
Stay Motel 5/16-9/11   1P: $35-$45   2P: $40-$50   XP: $5   F17
           Location: Just w of Scottsdale Rd, just s of Goldwater. 3560 N Marshall Hwy 85251. Fax: 480/994-9036.
Terms: Check-in 4 pm; pets, $100 fee. **Facility:** 120 rooms. 2 stories; exterior corridors. **All Rooms:** kitchens. **Cards:** AE, DI,
DS, JC, MC, VI.

HOMEWOOD SUITES HOTEL PHOENIX/SCOTTSDALE   Phone: (480)368-8705 274
◆◆◆   2/1-3/31   1P: $130   2P: $130
Suite Motel 4/1-5/15   1P: $110   2P: $110
           9/16-1/31   1P: $99   2P: $99
           5/16-9/15   1P: $69   2P: $69
Location: 0.5 mi s of Shea Blvd. 9880 N Scottsdale Rd 85253. Fax: 480/368-8725. **Terms:** [CP] meal plan; small pets only,
$100 fee, limit 2. **Facility:** 114 rooms. 3 two-bedroom units. 3 stories; interior corridors; heated pool. **Services:** area transpor-
tation. **All Rooms:** kitchens. **Cards:** AE, DI, DS, MC, VI.

HOSPITALITY SUITE RESORT   Phone: (480)949-5115 319
⬭⬭ SAVE 2/1-3/31   1P: $129-$159   2P: $129-$159
          10/1-1/31   1P: $99-$139   2P: $99-$139
◆◆◆   4/1-4/30   1P: $79-$99   2P: $79-$99
Motor Inn 5/1-9/30   1P: $59-$89   2P: $59-$89
           Location: Just n of McKellips, on e side of Scottsdale Rd. 409 N Scottsdale Rd 85257. Fax: 480/941-8014.
Terms: [BP] meal plan; small pets only, $100 dep req. **Facility:** 210 rooms. Most rooms face the pools. Choice of suites or
studio units. 1 two-bedroom unit. 2-3 stories; exterior corridors; 3 heated pools, whirlpool; 2 lighted tennis courts. **Dining:** Restaurant; 6 am-10 pm; $8-$11; cocktails. **Services:** complimentary evening beverages. **Recreation:** shuffleboard, horseshoe pit
& pool table, ping pong table, basketball court, barbecues. **All Rooms:** kitchens, combo or shower baths. **Cards:** AE, CB, DI,
DS, MC, VI. **Special Amenities:** Early check-in/late check-out and free breakfast.

HYATT REGENCY SCOTTSDALE AT GAINEY RANCH   Phone: (480)991-3388 276
◆◆◆◆   2/1-5/20   1P: $390   2P: $400   XP: $10   F18
Resort   12/25-1/31   1P: $395   2P: $395
           9/11-12/24   1P: $320   2P: $330
           5/21-9/10   1P: $170   2P: $180   XP: $10   F18
Location: 0.7 mi s of Shea Blvd, 0.5 mi e of Scottsdale Rd, on n side of Doubletree Ranch Rd. 7500 E Doubletree Ranch Rd
85258. Fax: 480/483-5550. **Terms:** Check-in 4 pm; 14 day cancellation notice; cancellation fee imposed. **Facility:** 493 rooms.
Beautiful and extensive use of pools, fountains and man-made lakes. Magnificent desert landscaping. Extensive art collection.
Bi-level marbled lobby with open air lounge and live music on lower level. 4 stories; interior/exterior corridors; putting green;
10 heated pools. Fee: 27 holes golf; 8 tennis courts (4 lighted). **Dining:** entertainment. **Services:** gift shop. Fee: massage.
Recreation: bicycles, jogging. **All Rooms:** safes, honor bars. **Some Rooms:** Fee: VCR. **Cards:** AE, CB, DI, DS, JC,
MC, VI.

(See map p. 226)

INNSUITES HOTEL SCOTTSDALE   Phone: (480)941-1202   316
◆◆   9/17-12/31   1P: $79-$99   2P: $79-$99   XP: $10   F17
Motel   2/1-4/8 & 1/1-1/31 1P: $99   2P: $99   XP: $10   F17
                4/9-9/16   1P: $49-$69   2P: $49-$69   XP: $10   F17
Location: Just w of Hayden Rd, on s side of McDowell Rd. 7707 E McDowell Rd 85257. Fax: 480/990-7873. **Terms:** [BP] meal plan; small pets only, $25 extra charge. **Facility:** 121 rooms. Located across from El Dorado Parkway, which extends 10 mi along Indian Bend Wash and contains walkways, lakes and park areas. 2 stories; exterior corridors; heated pool; playground. **Recreation:** bicycles. **Cards:** AE, DI, DS, MC, VI. *(See color ad below)*

THE IVY AT THE WATERFRONT   Phone: (480)994-5282   296
◆◆   2/1-4/15   1P: $189-$425   2P: $189-$425   XP: $10   F12
Motor Inn   10/1-1/31   1P: $139-$319   2P: $139-$319   XP: $10   F12
                4/16-9/30   1P: $99-$219   2P: $99-$219   XP: $10   F12
Location: 0.3 mi e of Scottsdale Rd. 7445 E Chaparral Rd 85250. Fax: 480/994-5625. **Terms:** [BP] meal plan; cancellation fee imposed. **Facility:** 108 rooms. Studio units and 1 & 2-bedroom suites. Located adjacent to the Arizona Canal in a quiet residential area. 30 two-bedroom units. 2 stories; exterior corridors; 5 heated pools; 2 tennis courts; playground. **Recreation:** Fee: bicycles. **All Rooms:** honor bars. **Some Rooms:** 69 kitchens. **Cards:** AE, CB, DI, DS, MC, VI.

LA QUINTA INN & SUITES   Phone: (480)614-5300   269
AAA SAVE   1/16-1/31   1P: $99-$125   2P: $99-$125
◆◆◆   2/1-3/31   1P: $99-$119   2P: $99-$119
Motel   4/1-8/31   1P: $65-$89   2P: $65-$89
                9/1-1/15   1P: $65-$85   2P: $65-$85
Location: Just e of Pima Rd. 8888 E Shea Blvd 85260. Fax: 480/614-5333. **Terms:** [CP] meal plan; small pets only. **Facility:** 140 rooms. 3 stories; interior corridors; heated pool, whirlpool. **Cards:** AE, CB, DI, DS, JC, MC, VI. **Special Amenities:** Free breakfast and free local telephone calls. *(See color ad p 242)*

MARRIOTT'S CAMELBACK INN RESORT, GOLF CLUB & SPA   Phone: (480)948-1700   283
AAA SAVE   9/10-1/31   1P: $255-$469   2P: $255-$469
◆◆◆◆◆   2/1-5/6   1P: $349-$449   2P: $349-$449
Resort   5/7-6/10   1P: $255-$325   2P: $255-$325
                6/11-9/9   1P: $139-$209   2P: $139-$209
Location: 0.5 mi e of Tatum Blvd, on n side of Lincoln Dr. 5402 E Lincoln Dr 85253. Fax: 480/483-3424. **Terms:** [BP] & [MAP] meal plans; check-in 4 pm; 10 day cancellation notice; cancellation fee imposed; package plans, spa, golf & tennis; small pets only. **Facility:** 454 rooms. On 120 acres of beautifully landscaped grounds. Excellent mountain view. Exceptional spa. Extensive recreational facilities. Some units with kitchen, fireplace, private pool and balcony. 1-2 stories; exterior corridors; putting green, 9 hole par 3 golf course; 3 heated pools, saunas, whirlpools; playground. Fee: 36 holes golf; 6 tennis courts (5 lighted). **Dining:** 3 dining rooms, coffee shop, deli; 6:30 am-10 pm; $7-$20; cocktails; also, The Chaparral, see separate listing. **Services:** gift shop. Fee: massage. **Recreation:** hiking trails. Rental: bicycles. **All Rooms:** safes, honor bars. **Some Rooms:** 6 kitchens. **Cards:** AE, CB, DI, DS, JC, MC, VI. **Special Amenities:** Free newspaper and preferred room (subject to availability with advanced reservations).

MARRIOTT'S MOUNTAIN SHADOWS RESORT AND GOLF CLUB   Phone: (480)948-7111   286
◆◆◆   2/1-4/15   1P: $199-$229   2P: $199-$229
Resort   4/16-5/20   1P: $189-$199   2P: $189-$199
                9/10-1/31   1P: $169-$199   2P: $169-$199
                5/21-9/9   1P: $79-$99   2P: $79-$99
Location: 1 mi e of Tatum Blvd, on s side of Lincoln Dr. 5641 E Lincoln Dr 85253. Fax: 480/951-5430. **Terms:** Check-in 4 pm; 5 day cancellation notice; cancellation fee imposed; small pets only. **Facility:** 338 rooms. Spacious, nicely landscaped grounds using native flora. Excellent mountain view. Patio or balcony. 2 stories; exterior corridors; putting green; 3 heated pools; playground. Fee: 54 holes golf; 8 lighted tennis courts. **Services:** gift shop; area transportation. Fee: massage. Rental: bicycles. **All Rooms:** combo or shower baths, honor bars. Fee: safes. **Cards:** AE, DI, DS, JC, MC, VI.

(See map p. 226)

MARRIOTT SUITES SCOTTSDALE   Phone: (480)945-1550   [308]
◆◆◆   All Year   1P: $89-$229   2P: $89-$229
Suite Hotel   **Location:** Just n of Indian School Rd, just e of Scottsdale Rd. 7325 E 3rd Ave 85251. Fax: 480/945-2005.
Terms: Check-in 4 pm. **Facility:** 251 rooms. Walking distance to 5th Ave Shops. 8 stories; interior corridors; heated pool. **Cards:** AE, CB, DI, DS, MC, VI.

THE PHOENICIAN   Phone: (480)941-8200   [294]
(AAA)   12/22-1/31   1P: $525-$655   2P: $525-$655   XP: $50   F17
  2/1-6/1   1P: $475-$625   2P: $475-$625   XP: $50   F17
◆◆◆◆   9/10-12/21   1P: $435-$485   2P: $435-$485   XP: $50   F17
Resort   6/2-9/9   1P: $195-$245   2P: $195-$245   XP: $50   F17
Location: 0.5 mi w of 64th St. 6000 E Camelback Rd 85251. Fax: 480/947-4311. **Terms:** Check-in 4 pm; 7 day cancellation notice; cancellation fee imposed; package plans; small pets only, in Casitas only. **Facility:** 654 rooms. Elegantly furnished units. Tropical lagoon, tiered pools. City, mountain, pool and golf course views. Located at the base of Camelback Mountain. 1- & 2-bedroom suites, some with fireplace. 7 private villas with 2 bedrooms, kitchen, fireplace and garage; 73 whirlpool rooms, $500-$5900; 3-4 stories; interior corridors; putting green; 6 heated pools, wading pools, saunas, waterslide, whirlpools; grass tennis court; playground. Fee: 27 holes golf; 11 lighted tennis courts. **Dining:** Dining room, 3 restaurants, deli; 6 am-10:30 pm; $10-$35; health conscious menu; cocktails; afternoon tea; also, The Terrace Dining Room, Windows on the Green, Mary Elaine's, see separate listing; entertainment. **Services:** gift shop. Fee: massage. **Recreation:** hiking trails, jogging, archery, basketball, lawn bowling, volleyball, croquet court. Rental: bicycles. **All Rooms:** safes, honor bars. **Cards:** AE, CB, DI, DS, JC, MC, VI.

QUALITY INN AND SUITES   Phone: (480)675-7665   [312]
◆◆◆   2/1-4/15   1P: $119-$139   2P: $119-$139   XP: $10   F18
Motel   1/1-1/31   1P: $99-$129   2P: $99-$129   XP: $10   F18
  10/1-12/31   1P: $69-$109   2P: $69-$109   XP: $10   F18
  4/16-9/30   1P: $59-$69   2P: $59-$79   XP: $10   F18
Location: Ne corner of Scottsdale Rd and Earll Dr. 3131 N Scottsdale Rd 85251. Fax: 480/675-8666. **Terms:** [CP] meal plan; small pets only, $50 dep req. **Facility:** 171 rooms. 3 stories; interior corridors; heated pool. **Services:** gift shop. **Cards:** AE, CB, DI, DS, JC, MC, VI.

RAMADA VALLEY HO RESORT   Phone: (480)945-6321   [306]
◆◆   2/1-4/30 & 1/1-1/31   1P: $99-$119   2P: $109-$129   XP: $10   F17
Motor Inn   5/1-11/1   1P: $49-$89   2P: $59-$99   XP: $10   F17
  11/2-12/31   1P: $59-$79   2P: $69-$89   XP: $10   F17
Location: 0.4 mi w of Scottsdale Rd, just s of Indian School Rd, on n side of Main St. 6850 Main St 85251. Fax: 480/947-5270. **Terms:** 3 day cancellation notice; cancellation fee imposed; small pets only, $50 dep req. **Facility:** 292 rooms. Spacious nicely landscaped grounds. Short walk to 5th Ave Shops. 2 stories; exterior corridors; 3 heated pools; 2 lighted tennis courts. **Services:** gift shop; area transportation. **Some Rooms:** Fee: VCR. **Cards:** AE, CB, DI, DS, MC, VI. *(See color ad below)*

REGAL MCCORMICK RANCH   Phone: (480)948-5050   [280]
(AAA) [SAVE]   2/1-4/30   1P: $245-$285   2P: $255-$319   XP: $25   F18
  9/17-1/31   1P: $175-$285   2P: $185-$319   XP: $25   F18
◆◆◆   5/1-5/31   1P: $165-$225   2P: $175-$265   XP: $25   F18
Resort   6/1-9/16   1P: $95-$155   2P: $95-$185   XP: $25   F18
Location: 0.8 mi n of Indian Bend Rd on the e side of Scottsdale Rd. 7401 N Scottsdale Rd 85253. Fax: 480/991-5572. **Terms:** [BP] meal plan; 7 day cancellation notice, 10/1-5/31; cancellation fee imposed. **Facility:** 125 rooms. Located adjacent to small lake; canoes, sailboats and peddleboats available for guest use. All rooms have patio or balcony. 3 stories; interior corridors; heated pool, whirlpool. Fee: 36 holes golf; 3 lighted tennis courts. **Dining:** Dining room; cocktails; entertainment in season; also, Pinon Grill, see separate listing. **Services:** gift shop; area transportation, within 5 mi. **Recreation:** canoeing, paddleboats, sailboating; beach volleyball. **All Rooms:** honor bars. **Some Rooms:** Fee: VCR. **Cards:** AE, CB, DI, DS, MC, VI. **Special Amenities:** Free newspaper and preferred room (subject to availability with advanced reservations).

(See map p. 226)

RENAISSANCE COTTONWOODS RESORT
Phone: (480)991-1414　290

9/10-1/31	1P: $149-$279	2P: $149-$279
2/1-4/15	1P: $199-$259	2P: $199-$259
4/16-5/20	1P: $149-$219	2P: $149-$219
5/21-9/9	1P: $69-$95	2P: $69-$95

Resort

Location: Just n of McDonald Dr, on w side of Scottsdale Rd. 6160 N Scottsdale Rd 85253. Fax: 480/948-2205. **Terms:** Check-in 4 pm; cancellation fee imposed; small pets only, $50 dep req. **Facility:** 171 rooms. Spacious grounds, combining desert landscaping and tree-shaded lawns on 25 acres. Adjacent to the Borrgata Shopping Village. 1 two-bedroom unit. 106 one-bedroom suites with private patio & whirlpool, 34 with fireplace, $85-$399; 1 story; exterior corridors; putting green; 2 heated pools, whirlpools. Fee: water aerobics; 4 tennis courts (2 lighted). **Dining:** Dining room; 7 am-10 pm; $10-$20; cocktails. **Services:** gift shop; area transportation, within 3 mi. **Recreation:** jogging, croquet, ping pong table, shuffleboard. **All Rooms:** combo or shower baths, safes, honor bars. **Some Rooms:** 34 efficiencies. Fee: microwaves, VCR. **Cards:** AE, CB, DI, DS, MC, VI. **Special Amenities:** Free newspaper.

RESIDENCE INN BY MARRIOTT
Phone: (480)948-8666　289

2/1-4/15	1P: $149-$179	2P: $149-$179
9/10-1/31	1P: $99-$159	2P: $99-$159
4/16-5/20	1P: $99-$139	2P: $99-$139
5/21-9/9	1P: $65-$89	2P: $65-$89

Suite Motel

Location: Nw corner Scottsdale Rd and McDonald Dr. 6040 N Scottsdale Rd 85253. Fax: 480/443-4869. **Terms:** [CP] meal plan; pets, $50 dep req, 2 pets max. **Facility:** 122 rooms. 94 one-bedroom units with kitchen, many with a fireplace. 28 two-bedroom units have kitchen and fireplace. Located less than 1 blk from the Borgata Shopping Plaza. 2 stories; interior/exterior corridors; heated pool. **Recreation:** sports court. **Some Rooms:** Fee: VCR. **Cards:** AE, CB, DI, DS, JC, MC, VI.

RODEWAY INN OF SCOTTSDALE
Phone: (480)946-3456　311

2/1-4/15	1P: $89-$113	2P: $97-$121	XP: $8　F18
12/30-1/31	1P: $95-$103	2P: $103-$111	XP: $8　F18
10/1-12/29	1P: $58-$66	2P: $66-$74	XP: $8　F18
4/16-9/30	1P: $37-$59	2P: $45-$67	XP: $8　F18

Motel

Location: Just w of Scottsdale Rd, on n side of Indian School Rd. 7110 E Indian School Rd 85251. Fax: 480/874-0492. **Terms:** [CP] meal plan; weekly rates avail. **Facility:** 65 rooms. Close to Scottsdale 5th Avenue shops, Old Town Scottsdale and civic center. 4 two-bedroom units. 2 stories; exterior corridors; heated pool, whirlpool. **Dining:** Coffee shop nearby. **All Rooms:** extended cable TV. **Cards:** AE, CB, DI, DS, MC, VI. **Special Amenities:** Free breakfast and free local telephone calls. *(See ad below)*

SCOTTSDALE DOWNTOWN COURTYARD
Phone: (480)429-7785　298

12/31-1/31	1P: $169
2/1-5/27	1P: $149
9/7-12/30	1P: $129
5/28-9/6	1P: $89

Motel

Location: Ne corner of Scottsdale Rd & Civic Center Blvd. 3311 N Scottsdale Rd 85251. Fax: 480/429-6320. **Terms:** 14 day cancellation notice; cancellation fee imposed. **Facility:** 180 rooms. 5 stories; interior corridors; heated pool. **Services:** area transportation. **Cards:** AE, CB, DI, DS, JC, MC, VI.

SCOTTSDALE FAIRFIELD INN
Phone: (480)483-0042　264

2/1-3/31	1P: $115-$135
9/1-1/31	1P: $65-$135
4/1-5/31	1P: $59-$95
6/1-8/31	1P: $47

Motel

Location: Just s of Thunderbird Rd, on w side of Scottsdale Rd. 13440 N Scottsdale Rd 85254. Fax: 480/483-3715. **Terms:** [CP] meal plan. **Facility:** 132 rooms. 3 stories; interior/exterior corridors; heated pool. **Some Rooms:** Fee: refrigerators. **Cards:** AE, CB, DI, DS, MC, VI.

(See map p. 226)

SCOTTSDALE PIMA INN & SUITES

Phone: (480)948-3800   282

2/1-4/15 & 12/31-1/31	1P: $99-$149	2P: $109-$154	XP: $10	F17
9/3-12/30	1P: $62-$112	2P: $72-$122	XP: $10	F17
4/16-9/2	1P: $39-$79	2P: $44-$89	XP: $10	F17

Suite Motel   **Location:** 0.4 mi n of Indian Bend Rd, on w side of Pima Rd. 7330 N Pima Rd 85258. Fax: 480/443-3374. **Terms:** [CP] meal plan; weekly & monthly rates avail; package plans; small pets only, $100 dep req. **Facility:** 127 rooms. 2 stories; interior/exterior corridors; heated pool, wading pool, sauna, indoor whirlpool. **Dining:** Restaurant nearby. **Services:** area transportation, within 3 mi. **Some Rooms:** 53 kitchens. **Cards:** AE, CB, DI, DS, MC, VI. **Special Amenities:** Free breakfast and free local telephone calls. *(See color ad below)*

THE SCOTTSDALE PLAZA RESORT

Phone: (480)948-5000   277

9/12-1/31	1P: $255-$350	XP: $15	F17
2/1-4/30	1P: $290-$345	XP: $15	F17
5/1-5/25	1P: $255-$300	XP: $15	F17
5/26-9/11	1P: $160-$180	XP: $15	F17

Resort   **Location:** Just n of Indian Bend Rd, on w side of Scottsdale Rd. 7200 N Scottsdale Rd 85253. Fax: 480/998-5971. **Terms:** 3 day cancellation notice; cancellation fee imposed. **Facility:** 404 rooms. On 40 acres of nicely landscaped grounds. Spacious guest rooms and one-bedroom suites, many with gas fireplace and patio. 4 two-bedroom units. 10 whirlpool rooms; 1-2 stories; exterior corridors; putting green; 5 heated pools, saunas, whirlpools. Fee: racquetball courts, 5 tennis courts (2 lighted). **Dining:** Dining room, restaurant; 6:30 am-2:30 & 5-10 pm; $10-$26; cocktails; also, Remington's, see separate listing; entertainment. **Services:** gift shop; area transportation, within 3 mi radius. Fee: massage. **Recreation:** jogging, croquet. Fee: bicycles. **All Rooms:** honor bars. Fee: safes. **Some Rooms:** 10 kitchens. Fee: refrigerators. **Cards:** AE, CB, DI, DS, MC, VI.

SCOTTSDALE PRINCESS

Phone: (480)585-4848   259

9/5-1/31	1P: $449-$569	2P: $449-$569	XP: $30	F18
2/1-4/15	1P: $429-$539	2P: $429-$539	XP: $30	F18
4/16-6/17	1P: $279-$439	2P: $279-$439	XP: $30	F18
6/18-9/4	1P: $149-$279	2P: $149-$279	XP: $30	F18

Location: 0.6 mi n of Bell Rd and 0.5 e of Scottsdale Rd, on s side of Princess Dr. 7575 E Princess Dr 85255. Fax: 480/585-0086. **Terms:** Check-in 4 pm; 14 day cancellation notice; cancellation fee imposed; package plans, seasonal. **Facility:** 650 rooms. 450-acre luxury resort with southwestern architecture. Balcony or terrace with view of the mountains, pool or golf course. Site of the Phoenix Open at the Tournament of Players championship golf course and ATP Tennis Tournament. 4 stories; interior/exterior corridors; 3 heated pools. Fee: 36 holes golf; racquetball court, 7 tennis courts (6 lighted). **Dining:** entertainment. **Services:** gift shop. Fee: massage. **Recreation:** fishing; hiking trails, jogging. Rental: bicycles. **All Rooms:** safes, honor bars. **Some Rooms:** Fee: refrigerators, VCR. **Cards:** AE, CB, DI, DS, JC, MC, VI.

SIERRA SUITES HOTEL

Phone: (480)483-1333   265

2/1-4/15	1P: $109-$169	2P: $109-$169	
10/1-1/31	1P: $79-$99	2P: $79-$99	
4/16-9/30	1P: $69-$89	2P: $69-$89	

Motel   **Location:** Just n of Shea Blvd. 10660 N 69th St 85254. Fax: 480/483-8811. **Terms:** [CP] meal plan; cancellation fee imposed. **Facility:** 106 rooms. Located in the Agua Caliente Center. 3 stories; interior corridors; heated pool. **All Rooms:** kitchens, combo or shower baths. **Cards:** AE, CB, DI, DS, JC, MC, VI.

SLEEP INN

Phone: (480)998-9211   261

2/1-4/23	1P: $85-$103	2P: $85-$103	XP: $10	F18
9/6-1/31	1P: $62-$94	2P: $62-$99	XP: $10	F18
4/24-5/30	1P: $71-$85	2P: $71-$85	XP: $10	F18
5/31-9/5	1P: $40-$49	2P: $40-$49	XP: $10	F18

Location: Just s of Bell Rd. 16630 N Scottsdale Rd 85254. Fax: 480/607-2893. **Terms:** Small pets only, $50 dep req. **Facility:** 108 rooms. 3 stories; interior corridors; heated pool, whirlpool. **Dining:** Restaurant nearby. **Services:** area transportation, within 5 mi. **All Rooms:** combo or shower baths, extended cable TV. **Cards:** AE, DI, DS, MC, VI. **Special Amenities:** Free breakfast and free local telephone calls.

(See map p. 226)

SPRINGHILL SUITES   **Phone:** (480)922-8700 256

◆◆◆   2/1-4/15   1P: $139   2P: $139
Motel   4/16-5/20 & 9/10-1/31   1P: $99   2P: $99
             5/21-9/9   1P: $55   2P: $55

Location: Just n of Frank Lloyd Wright Blvd. 17020 N Scottsdale Rd 85255. Fax: 480/948-2276. **Terms:** [CP] meal plan; 3 day cancellation notice; cancellation fee imposed. **Facility:** 123 rooms. Well arranged rooms with wetbar, microwave and refrigerator. 4 stories; interior corridors; heated pool. **Services:** area transportation. **Cards:** AE, CB, DI, DS, MC, VI.

SUMMERFIELD SUITES HOTEL   **Phone:** (480)946-7700 317

◆◆◆   1/1-1/31   1P: $159-$189   2P: $159-$189
Suite Motel   2/1-6/16   1P: $119-$179   2P: $119-$179
              9/17-12/31   1P: $119-$149   2P: $119-$149
              6/17-9/16   1P: $69-$99   2P: $69-$99

Location: 0.3 mi e of Scottsdale Rd. 4245 N Civic Center Blvd 85251. Fax: 480/946-7711. **Terms:** [CP] meal plan; check-in 4 pm; 3 day cancellation notice; small pets only, $150-$225 dep req. **Facility:** 164 rooms. 71 two-bedroom units. 3 stories, no elevator; exterior corridors; heated pool. **All Rooms:** kitchens. **Cards:** AE, CB, DI, DS, JC, MC, VI.

SUNBURST RESORT   **Phone:** (480)945-7666 299

◆◆◆   2/1-5/15 & 1/1-1/31   1P: $165-$195   2P: $175-$205
Motor Inn   9/13-12/31   1P: $155-$195   2P: $165-$205
             5/16-9/12   1P: $60-$95   2P: $70-$105

Location: Se corner Scottsdale and Chaparral rds. 4925 N Scottsdale Rd 85251. Fax: 480/946-4056. **Terms:** 10 day cancellation notice. **Facility:** 210 rooms. Spacious grounds. Very attractive southwestern decor. 2 stories; exterior corridors; 2 heated pools. **Dining:** entertainment. **Services:** gift shop; area transportation. **All Rooms:** honor bars. **Cards:** AE, CB, DI, DS, MC, VI.

────── *The following lodgings were either not inspected or did not* ──────
meet AAA rating requirements but are listed for your information only.

FOUR SEASONS RESORT SCOTTSDALE AT TROON NORTH   **Phone:** 480/515-5700

[fyi]   2/1-5/13   2P: $475-$625
            5/14-6/17 & 9/15-1/31   2P: $395-$495
Resort   6/18-9/14   2P: $250-$300

            Too new to rate, opening scheduled for December 1999. **Location:** From Pima Rd, 2.8 mi e on Dynamite Blvd, then 1 mi s on Alma School Pkwy. 10600 E Crescent Moon Dr 85255. Fax: 480/515-5599. **Terms:** 7 day cancellation notice; cancellation fee imposed. **Amenities:** 210 rooms, pets, restaurant, radios, coffeemakers, pool, exercise facilities, golf, tennis. **Dining:** entertainment. **Cards:** AE, DI, DS, JC, MC, VI.

(See map p. 226)

HILTON GARDEN INN SCOTTSDALE   **Phone:** 480/481-0400

(fyi)	9/12-1/31	1P: $89-$188	2P: $132-$188	XP: $10	F18
	2/1-4/20	1P: $124-$174	2P: $124-$174	XP: $10	F18
Hotel	4/21-6/15	1P: $89-$129	2P: $89-$129	XP: $10	F18
	6/16-9/11	1P: $59-$84	2P: $59-$84	XP: $10	F18

Too new to rate, opening scheduled for August 1999. **Location:** Just e of Scottsdale Rd. 7324 E Indian School Rd 85251. Fax: 480/481-0800. **Terms:** [CP] meal plan; cancellation fee imposed. **Amenities:** 200 rooms, restaurant, radios, coffeemakers, microwaves, refrigerators, pool, exercise facilities. **Cards:** AE, DI, DS, MC, VI.

HILTON SCOTTSDALE RESORT & VILLAS   **Phone:** (480)948-7750   [291]

(AAA) (SAVE)	2/1-5/25 & 1/1-1/31	1P: $294-$394	2P: $304-$404	XP: $10	F18
	9/5-12/31	1P: $239-$339	2P: $249-$349	XP: $10	F18
(fyi)	5/26-9/4	1P: $154-$254	2P: $164-$264	XP: $10	F18

Hotel   Under major renovation, scheduled to be completed October 1999. **Last rated:** ◆ ◆ ◆ **Location:** Just s of Lincoln Dr, on e side of Scottsdale Rd. 6333 N Scottsdale Rd 85250. Fax: 480/948-2232. **Terms:** Monthly rates avail; check-in 4 pm; 3 day cancellation notice; cancellation fee imposed. **Facility:** 295 rooms. 1 or 2 bedroom villas have kitchen, washer and dryer, fireplace, private patio, some with whirlpool. 45 villas, $395, $175 off season; 8 whirlpool rooms; 2-3 stories; interior corridors; 2 heated pools, wading pool, sauna, steamroom, whirlpools. Fee: 4 lighted tennis courts. **Dining:** 2 restaurants; 6:30 am-10 pm; $8-$22; cocktails. **Services:** gift shop. Fee: massage. **Recreation:** Tanning Bed. **Cards:** AE, CB, DI, DS, JC, MC, VI. *(See color ad p 41)*

RADISSON RESORT & SPA SCOTTSDALE   **Phone:** (480)991-3800   [279]

(AAA) (SAVE)	2/1-5/6	1P: $199	2P: $199	XP: $15	F18
	9/11-1/31	1P: $165	2P: $165	XP: $15	F18
(fyi)	5/7-6/17	1P: $99	2P: $99	XP: $15	F18
	6/18-9/10	1P: $79	2P: $79	XP: $15	F18

Resort   Under major renovation, scheduled to be completed November 1999. **Last rated:** ◆ ◆ ◆ ◆ **Location:** Just n of Indian Bend Rd on e side of Scottsdale Rd. 7171 N Scottsdale Rd 85253. Fax: 480/948-1381. **Terms:** Weekly & monthly rates avail; check-in 4 pm; cancellation fee imposed; package plans. **Facility:** 275 rooms. Rooms and Suites located on 76 acres of lanscaped grounds. 32 bi-level suites; 2 stories; interior/exterior corridors; 3 heated pools, whirlpool. Fee: 36 holes golf; 21 lighted tennis courts. **Dining:** 2 restaurants, deli; 6 am-10 pm; $10-$25; cocktails. **Services:** gift shop. Fee: massage. **Rental:** bicycles. **Some Rooms:** Fee: coffeemakers. **Cards:** AE, CB, DI, DS, JC, MC, VI. *(See color ad p 277)*

------- **RESTAURANTS** -------

CAFE TERRA COTTA   **Lunch:** $8-$23   **Dinner:** $8-$23   **Phone:** 602/948-8100   [129]
◆ ◆   **Location:** At the Borgata Shopping Center. 6166 N Scottsdale Rd 85253. **Hours:** 11 am-10 pm; 11:30
Southwest   am-2:30 & 5-9:30 pm 6/1-8/31. Closed major holidays. **Reservations:** suggested. **Features:** casual dress;
American   children's menu; carryout; cocktails; a la carte. Variety of meat and fish entrees prepared with fresh
             ingredients. Also innovative selection of pasta, pizza, salad and sandwiches. **Cards:** AE, DI, DS, MC, VI.

THE CHAPARRAL   **Dinner:** $28-$45   **Phone:** 480/948-1700   [124]
◆ ◆ ◆ ◆   **Location:** 0.5 mi e of Tatum Blvd, on n side of Lincoln Dr; in Marriott's Camelback Inn Resort, Golf Club and
Continental Spa. 5402 E Lincoln Dr 85253. **Hours:** 6 pm-10 pm, Fri & Sat-11 pm. **Reservations:** suggested.
             Features: semi-formal attire; cocktails & lounge; valet parking; a la carte. Dining in a relaxed but elegant
setting. Smoke free premises. **Cards:** AE, CB, DI, DS, JC, MC, VI.

EL CHORRO LODGE RESTAURANT   **Lunch:** $9-$16   **Dinner:** $16-$36   **Phone:** 480/948-5170   [125]
◆ ◆ ◆   **Location:** 0.9 mi e of Tatum Blvd on n side of Lincoln Dr. 5550 E Lincoln Dr 85253. **Hours:** 11 am-3 &
Steak and   5:30-11 pm, Sat & Sun 5:30-11 pm. **Reservations:** required. **Features:** casual dress; children's menu; health
Seafood   conscious menu; cocktails & lounge; minimum charge-6.00; valet parking. Small, charming restaurant. Nice
             selection of steak, lamb and fresh seafood. "Sticky Buns" a specialty. Outdoor seating, weather permitting.
Cards: AE, CB, DI, DS, MC, VI.

GOLDEN SWAN   **Dinner:** $24-$35   **Phone:** 480/991-3388   [119]
◆ ◆ ◆   **Location:** 0.7 mi s of Shea Blvd, 0.5 mi e of Scottsdale Rd, on n side of Doubletree Ranch Rd; in Hyatt
American   Regency Scottsdale at Gainey Ranch. 7500 E Doubletree Ranch Rd 85258. **Hours:** 6 pm-10 pm, Sun 9:30
             am-2 & 6-10 pm. Closed: Sun & Mon evenings 7/5-8/30. **Reservations:** suggested. **Features:** Sunday
brunch; cocktails; valet parking; a la carte. Casually elegant restaurant serving regional American cuisines in an open air
environment. Smoking permitted on patio. **Cards:** AE, CB, DI, DS, JC, MC, VI.

THE GRILL   **Phone:** 480/585-4848   [117]
◆ ◆ ◆   **Location:** At the Scottsdale Princess. 7575 E Princess Dr 85253. **Hours:** 6 am-9 pm, Fri & Sat-10 pm.
American   **Reservations:** suggested. **Features:** semi-formal attire; cocktails & lounge. **Cards:** AE, DI, DS, MC, VI.

LA HACIENDA   **Dinner:** $25-$32   **Phone:** 480/585-4848   [116]
◆ ◆ ◆ ◆   **Location:** 0.6 mi n of Bell Rd and just e of Scottsdale Rd, on s side of Princess Dr to Cottage Terrace, then
Traditional 0.3 mi se at Scottsdale Princess. 7575 E Princess Dr 85255. **Hours:** 6 pm-10 pm, Fri & Sat-11 pm. **Re-**
Mexican   **servations:** suggested. **Features:** semi-formal attire; children's menu; cocktails & lounge; entertainment;
             valet parking; a la carte. Selections of lamb, chicken, steak, seafood and signature dish of roast suckling pig.
Strolling mariachis. **Cards:** AE, CB, DI, DS, JC, MC, VI.

(See map p. 226)

MALEE'S THAI ON MAIN
◆◆
Regional
Ethnic

Lunch: $8-$12   **Dinner:** $9-$19   **Phone:** 480/947-6042   140
Location: Just s of Indian School Rd and just w of Scottsdale Rd, on s side of Main St. 7131 E Main St 85251. **Hours:** 11:30 am-2:30 & 5-10 pm, Sat noon-2:30 pm & 5-10 pm, Sun 5 pm-9 pm. Closed major holidays. **Reservations:** suggested. **Features:** casual dress; carryout; cocktails; street parking; a la carte. Casual, popular restaurant with a large selection of Thai food. Patio dining avail. **Cards:** AE, DI, MC, VI. ⊠

MANCUSO'S RESTAURANT
◆◆◆
Italian

Dinner: $12-$27   **Phone:** 480/948-9988   130
Location: Just n of McDonald Dr on w side of Scottsdale Rd in The Borgata Shopping Plaza. 6166 N Scottsdale Rd 85253. **Hours:** 5 pm-10 pm. Closed: 11/23 & 12/25. **Reservations:** suggested. **Features:** casual dress; cocktails & lounge; valet parking. Beautiful restaurant. Also serves a nice selection of Continental cuisine. **Cards:** AE, CB, DI, DS, MC, VI. ⊠

MARQUESA
◆◆◆◆◆
Regional
Ethnic

Dinner: $32-$40   **Phone:** 480/585-4848   118
Location: 0.6 mi n of Bell Rd and just e of Scottsdale Rd, on s side of Princess Dr; in Scottsdale Princess. 7575 E Princess Dr 85255. **Hours:** 6 pm-11 pm, Sun 10:30 am-2:30 & 6-11 pm. **Reservations:** suggested. **Features:** formal attire; Sunday brunch; children's menu; cocktails & lounge; entertainment; valet parking; a la carte. Contemporary Mediterranean cuisine. Fine dining in restaurant with an atmosphere of casual, elegance. Outdoor dining, weather permitting. **Cards:** AE, CB, DI, DS, JC, MC, VI. ⊠

MARY ELAINE'S
◆◆◆◆
French

Dinner: $27-$50   **Phone:** 480/941-8200   139
Location: 0.5 mi w of 64th St; in The Phoenician. 6000 E Camelback Rd 85251. **Hours:** 6:30 am-10 pm. Closed: Sun; 7/1-8/31 Sun & Mon. **Reservations:** suggested. **Features:** semi-formal attire; cocktails; entertainment; a la carte, also prix fixe. Beautifully appointed room with view of the city. Contemporary French food preparation. Smoke free premises. **Cards:** AE, CB, DI, DS, JC, MC, VI. ⊠

THE OTHER PLACE
◆◆
American

Dinner: $9-$20   **Phone:** 480/948-7910   127
Location: Just w of Scottsdale Rd on s side of Lincoln Dr. 7101 E Lincoln Dr 85253. **Hours:** 5-10 pm, Fri & Sat-11 pm. **Features:** casual dress; children's menu; carryout; cocktails & lounge; valet parking. Decorated in Southwest motif. Nice selection of steak, chicken and seafood. **Cards:** AE, DI, DS, MC, VI. ⊠

PEPIN
◆◆
Regional
Ethnic

Lunch: $5-$7   **Dinner:** $13-$25   **Phone:** 480/990-9026   142
Location: Just s of Indian School Rd from Scottsdale Rd, just 0.2 mi e on 2nd St at north end of Wells Fargo Ave. 7363 Scottsdale Mall 85251. **Hours:** 11:30 am-3 & 5-11 pm, Sun 4:30 pm-11 pm. Closed: 1/1, 11/23, 12/25 & Mon. **Reservations:** suggested. **Features:** casual dress; early bird specials; carryout; cocktails & lounge; entertainment. Cuisine represented by various regions in Spain. Authentically prepared with excellent service. Good selection of tapas. Spanish flamenco dancing Thurs-Sat, Spanish guitar Sun and Wed, Latin dancing 9:30 pm-2 am Fri and Sat. **Cards:** AE, CB, DI, DS, MC, VI. ⊠

P F CHANG'S CHINA BISTRO
◆◆
Regional
Chinese

Lunch: $6-$14   **Dinner:** $8-$13   **Phone:** 480/949-2610   134
Location: nw corner of Camelback and Scottsdale rds, in Scottsdale Fashion Square, ground level exterior entrance, s side of mall. 7014 E Camelback Rd 85253. **Hours:** 11 am-11 pm, Fri & Sat-midnight. Closed: 11/23 & 12/25. **Features:** casual dress; health conscious menu; carryout; cocktails; fee for valet parking. Busy restaurant, with excellent variety of regional Chinese dishes. **Cards:** AE, DI, MC, VI. ⊠

PINON GRILL
◆◆
Southwest
American

Lunch: $9-$13   **Dinner:** $18-$26   **Phone:** 480/948-5050   123
Location: 0.8 mi n of Indian Bend Rd on the e side of Scottsdale Rd; in Regal McCormick Ranch. 7401 N Scottsdale Rd 85253. **Hours:** 6:30 am-10:30 pm, Fri & Sat-11 pm. **Features:** casual dress; children's menu; early bird specials; cocktails & lounge. Patio dining with view of lake. Distinctive southwest cuisine serving chicken, seafood, veal, steak and wild game. **Cards:** AE, CB, DI, DS, JC, MC, VI. ⊠

THE QUILTED BEAR
◆◆
American

Lunch: $7-$12   **Dinner:** $9-$18   **Phone:** 480/948-7760   128
Location: Sw corner of Scottsdale Rd and Lincoln Dr, in Lincoln Plaza Shopping Center. 6316 N Scottsdale Rd 85253. **Hours:** 7 am-10 pm, Sun from 8 am. **Features:** casual dress; children's menu; early bird specials; salad bar; cocktails & lounge. Very attractive family restaurant with nice selection of salad, sandwiches and entrees. Cheerful garden atmosphere. **Cards:** AE, DI, DS, MC, VI. ⊠

RANCHO PINOT GRILL
◆◆◆
American

Dinner: $17-$28   **Phone:** 602/468-9463   131
Location: Just s of Lincoln Dr on w side of Scottsdale Rd, in Lincoln Plaza Shopping Center. 6208 N Scottsdale Rd 85253. **Hours:** 5:30 pm-10 pm. Closed: 7/4, 11/23, 12/25, Sun & Mon. **Reservations:** suggested. **Features:** casual dress; cocktails; a la carte. Excellent variety of fresh meat, poultry and seafood. Mesquite grill cooking. Menu changes frequently. Smoke free premises. **Cards:** AE, DS, MC, VI. ⊠

RAWHIDE STEAKHOUSE & SALOON
◆
Steakhouse

Lunch: $6-$10   **Dinner:** $10-$23   **Phone:** 480/502-5600   115
Location: 3.8 mi n of Bell Rd on e side of Scottsdale Rd; just s of Pinnacle Peak Rd. 23023 Scottsdale Rd 85255. **Hours:** 5 pm-10 pm; 10/1-5/31 Fri-Sun 11:30 am-3 & 5-10 pm. Closed: 12/25. **Reservations:** required; for 9 or more. **Features:** casual dress; children's menu; cocktails & lounge; entertainment. Located at Rawhide, a re-creation of an 1880's western town with gift shops and entertainment. Mesquite broiled trout, pork chops, barbeque chicken and ribs, steak and prime rib. **Cards:** AE, DI, DS, MC, VI. ⊠

REMINGTON'S
◆◆◆
American

Lunch: $9-$12   **Dinner:** $16-$22   **Phone:** 480/951-5101   122
Location: Just n of Indian Bend Rd, on w side of Scottsdale Rd; in The Scottsdale Plaza Resort. 7200 N Scottsdale Rd 85253. **Hours:** 11:30 am-2 & 5-10 pm, Fri-10:30 pm, Sat 5 pm-10:30 pm, Sun 5 pm-10 pm. **Reservations:** suggested. **Features:** casual dress; children's menu; early bird specials; cocktails; entertainment; a la carte. New American cuisine with mesquite grilled chops, steak and seafood. Patio dining weather permitting. **Cards:** AE, CB, DI, DS, MC, VI. ⊠

(See map p. 226)

ROY'S PACIFIC RIM CUISINE   **Dinner:** $17-$28   **Phone:** 480/905-1155   [126]
◆ ◆ ◆   **Location:** In Seville Shopping Center ne corner of Indian Bend and Scottsdale Rd. 7001 N Scottsdale Rd
Specialty   85253. **Hours:** 5 pm-10 pm, Fri & SAt-11 pm. Closed major holidays. **Reservations:** suggested.
              Features: casual dress; cocktails & lounge; a la carte. **Cards:** AE, CB, DI, MC, VI.   [X]

RUSSELL'S ON 2ND   **Dinner:** $12-$22   **Phone:** 480/424-7833   [141]
◆ ◆   **Location:** Just e of Scottsdale Rd. 7210 E 2nd St 85251. **Hours:** 5 pm-10 pm, Fri & Sat-11pm. Closed
Italian   major holidays & Sun June-Sept. **Reservations:** suggested. **Features:** casual dress; children's menu;
              carryout; cocktails; a la carte. Casual and intimate restaurant serving excellent Italian cuisine. **Cards:** AE,
CB, DI, DS, MC, VI.

SANDOLO RISTORANTE   **Dinner:** $14-$22   **Phone:** 480/991-3388   [121]
◆ ◆   **Location:** 0.7 mi s of Shea Blvd, 0.5 mi e of Scottsdale Rd, on n side of Doubletree Ranch Rd; in Hyatt
Italian   Regency Scottsdale at Gainey Ranch. 7500 E Doubletree Ranch Rd 85258. **Hours:** 6 pm-10:30 pm.
              Reservations: suggested. **Features:** casual dress; children's menu; cocktails; entertainment; valet parking.
Singing waiters. Dinner includes complimentary gondola ride. Smoking permitted on patio. **Cards:** AE, CB, DI, DS, JC,
MC, VI.   [X]

THE TERRACE DINING ROOM   **Lunch:** $10-$18   **Dinner:** $17-$25   **Phone:** 480/941-8200   [137]
◆ ◆ ◆ ◆   **Location:** 0.5 mi w of 64th St, in The Phoenician. 6000 E Camelback Rd 85251. **Hours:** 6 am-10 pm.
Italian   **Reservations:** suggested. **Features:** semi-formal attire; Sunday brunch; children's menu; health conscious
              menu; cocktails & lounge; entertainment; valet parking; a la carte. Salad, soup, pasta, lamb shank, veal,
steak and fresh seafood. Sunday brunch with live entertainment and dancing. Elegant dining room with indoor and outdoor
covered patio dining. **Cards:** AE, CB, DI, DS, JC, MC, VI.   [X]

VOLTAIRE'S   **Dinner:** $18-$28   **Phone:** 480/948-1005   [133]
◆ ◆   **Location:** 0.4 mi e of Hayden Rd on n side of McDonald Dr. 8340 E McDonald Dr 85250. **Hours:** Open
Traditional   2/1-5/31 & 10/1-1/31; 5:30 pm-10 pm, Fri & Sat-10:30 pm. Closed: 1/1, 12/25 & Sun; Sun & Mon 5/1-5/31.
French   **Reservations:** suggested. **Features:** semi-formal attire; carryout; cocktails & lounge. Nice selection of
              entrees. **Cards:** AE, DI, MC, VI.   [X]

WINDOWS ON THE GREEN   **Lunch:** $20-$30   **Dinner:** $25-$40   **Phone:** 480/941-8200   [136]
◆ ◆ ◆   **Location:** 0.5 mi w of 64th St; in The Phoenician. 6000 E Camelback Rd 85251. **Hours:** 6 pm-10 pm.
Southwest   Closed: Tues; 7/1-8/31 Tues & Wed. **Reservations:** suggested. **Features:** casual dress; health conscious
American   menu items; cocktails & lounge; valet parking; a la carte. Southwestern decor, overlooks the golf course.
              Innovative food preparation. Smoke free premises. **Cards:** AE, CB, DI, DS, JC, MC, VI.   [X]

SUN CITY/SUN CITY WEST pop. 38,100   (See map p. 224; index p. 217)

——— LODGING ———

BEST WESTERN INN & SUITES OF SUN CITY   **Phone:** (623)933-8211   [3]

(AAA) [SAVE]	2/1-5/13	1P: $80-$90	2P: $85-$95	XP: $5	F17
	12/22-1/31	1P: $72-$82	2P: $77-$87	XP: $5	F17
◆ ◆ ◆	10/7-12/21	1P: $63-$73	2P: $68-$78	XP: $5	F17
Motel	5/14-10/6	1P: $49-$56	2P: $55-$62	XP: $5	F17

              Location: Sw side of Grand Ave (US 60), just nw of 111th Ave. 11201 Grand Ave 85363 (PO Box 477, 85372).
Terms: [CP] meal plan; weekly & monthly rates avail; 14 day cancellation notice; cancellation fee imposed; small pets only,
limited rooms. **Facility:** 96 rooms. 2 stories; interior/exterior corridors; heated pool. **Dining:** Coffee shop nearby. **Cards:** AE,
CB, DI, DS, MC, VI. **Special Amenities: Free breakfast and free local telephone calls.** *(See color ad p 238)*

[S/D] [▭] [冊] [⛱] [🔊] [X] [🍴] [🖥] [▯] [🖳] [🔋] [🏊]

SURPRISE pop. 7,100   (See map p. 224; index p. 223)

——— LODGINGS ———

COUNTRY INN & SUITES BY CARLSON   **Phone:** (623)933-4000   [8]

◆ ◆ ◆	2/1-4/15	1P: $89-$99	2P: $89-$99	XP: $10	F17
Motel	10/1-1/31	1P: $79-$89	2P: $79-$89	XP: $10	F17
	4/16-6/1	1P: $69-$79	2P: $69-$79	XP: $10	F17
	6/2-9/30	1P: $59-$69	2P: $59-$69	XP: $10	F17

Location: 0.7 mi e of Dysart Rd, s side of Bell Rd. 12477 W Bell Rd 85374. **Fax:** 623/933-4003. **Terms:** [CP] meal plan; 3 day
cancellation notice. **Facility:** 60 rooms. 3 stories; interior corridors; heated pool. **Cards:** AE, DS, MC, VI.
(See color ad p 229)

[ASK] [S/D] [冊] [X] [🍴] [🖥] [▯] [🖳] [🔋] [DATA PORT] [🏊]

QUALITY INN & SUITES   **Phone:** (623)583-3500   [10]

◆ ◆ ◆	2/1-4/16 & 12/18-1/31	1P: $99-$119	2P: $99-$119	XP: $10	F18
Motel	10/9-12/17	1P: $79-$99	2P: $79-$99	XP: $10	F18
	4/17-10/8	1P: $59-$79	2P: $59-$79	XP: $10	F18

Location: 1 mi e of US 60 (Grand Ave). 16741 N Greasewood St 85374. **Fax:** 623/583-4356. **Terms:** [CP] meal plan; small
pets only, $5 extra charge. **Facility:** 69 rooms. 3 stories; interior corridors; heated pool. **Cards:** AE, DI, DS, MC, VI.

[SAVE] [S/D] [▭] [冊] [🔊] [⛱] [X] [🍴] [🖥] [▯] [🖳] [🔋] [DATA PORT] [🏊] [🏋]

(See map p. 224)

WINDMILL INN AT SUN CITY WEST   Phone: (623)583-0133   **9**

AAA SAVE   2/1-4/30   1P: $125-$149   XP: $8   F18
◆◆◆   11/1-1/31   1P: $103-$123   XP: $8   F18
Suite Motel   9/16-10/31   1P: $79-$96   XP: $8   F18
    5/1-9/15   1P: $64-$85   XP: $8   F18

Location: 0.6 mi e of Dysart Rd, on s side of Bell Rd. 12545 W Bell Rd 85374. **Fax:** 623/583-8366. **Terms:** [CP] meal plan; check-in 4 pm; 14 day cancellation notice; small pets only. **Facility:** 127 rooms. Fronted by small lake with large fountain. 3 stories; interior corridors; heated pool, whirlpool. **Dining:** Restaurant nearby. **Recreation:** bicycles, lending library. **Some Rooms:** 4 efficiencies. **Cards:** AE, DI, DS, MC, VI. *(See ad p 243)*

TEMPE pop. 142,000   (See map p. 227; index p. 221)

———— **LODGINGS** ————

AMERISUITES/ARIZONA MILLS MALL   Phone: (480)831-9800   **398**

AAA SAVE   2/1-5/12   1P: $99-$119   2P: $109-$129   XP: $10   F17
◆◆◆   9/12-1/31   1P: $89-$109   2P: $99-$119   XP: $10   F17
Motel   5/13-9/11   1P: $69-$89   2P: $79-$99   XP: $10   F17

Location: From I-10 exit 155 (Baseline Rd), 0.4 mi e, nw corner Priest Dr. 1520 W Baseline Rd 85283. **Fax:** 480/831-9292. **Terms:** [CP] meal plan; small pets only, $25 fee. **Facility:** 128 rooms. Adjacent to Arizona Mills Mall Outlet center. 6 stories; interior corridors; heated pool. **Services:** area transportation, within 5 mi. **All Rooms:** efficiencies, combo or shower baths. **Cards:** AE, CB, DI, DS, MC, VI. **Special Amenities:** Free breakfast and free newspaper. *(See color ad opposite title page)*

BEST WESTERN INN OF TEMPE   Phone: (480)784-2233   **373**

AAA SAVE   2/1-3/31   1P: $112-$132   2P: $112-$132   XP: $10   F17
◆◆◆   10/1-1/31   1P: $89-$109   2P: $89-$109   XP: $10   F17
Motor Inn   4/1-4/30   1P: $79-$99   2P: $79-$99   XP: $10   F17
    5/1-9/30   1P: $62-$82   2P: $62-$82   XP: $10   F17

Location: Adjacent to s side of SR 202 Loop (Red Mountain Frwy), exit 7 (Scottsdale Rd). 670 N Scottsdale Rd 85281. **Fax:** 480/784-2299. **Terms:** Cancellation fee imposed; small pets only. **Facility:** 103 rooms. 8 whirlpool rooms; 4 stories; interior corridors; 3 indoor whirlpools, 1 outdoor whirlpool, lap pool w/artificial current. **Dining:** Restaurant; 24 hrs; $5-$7. **Services:** area transportation, within 5 mi. **All Rooms:** extended cable TV. **Some Rooms:** Fee: refrigerators. **Cards:** AE, DI, DS, JC, MC, VI. **Special Amenities:** Free room upgrade (subject to availability with advanced reservations). *(See color ad p 282)*

(See map p. 227)

CANDLEWOOD SUITES
◆◆◆   Phone: (480)777-0440   **399**

Motel

2/1-4/14	1P: $110-$145	2P: $110-$145
4/15-6/9	1P: $95-$119	2P: $95-$119
9/23-1/31	1P: $85-$109	2P: $85-$109
6/10-9/22	1P: $75-$89	2P: $75-$89

Location: From I-10, exit Baseline Rd, 0.5 mi e, just e of Priest Dr. 1335 W Baseline Rd 85283. Fax: 480/777-5858. **Facility:** 122 rooms. 3 stories; interior corridors; heated pool. **All Rooms:** kitchens. **Cards:** AE, CB, DI, DS, JC, MC, VI. *(See ad p 232)*

COMFORT INN/RIO SALADO ASU
◆◆◆   Phone: (480)966-7202   **396**

Motel

2/1-5/15 & 1/1-1/31	1P: $99-$159	XP: $10	F18
9/14-12/31	1P: $79-$159		
5/16-9/13	1P: $59-$119	XP: $10	F18

Location: Just e of Rural Rd. 1031 E Apache Blvd 85281. Fax: 480/829-9340. **Terms:** [CP] meal plan; cancellation fee imposed. **Facility:** 72 rooms. 2 two-bedroom units. 3 stories; interior corridors. **Some Rooms:** kitchen. **Cards:** AE, DS, MC, VI. *(See color ad p 282)*

COUNTRY INN & SUITES BY CARLSON
◆◆   Phone: (480)345-8585   **406**

Motel

	1P	2P	XP	
2/1-4/15 & 1/16-1/31	1P: $59-$89	2P: $69-$109	XP: $10	F16
4/16-1/15	1P: $39-$79	2P: $49-$89	XP: $10	F16

Location: Just e of I-10, exit Elliot Rd, on n side of Elliot Rd. 1660 W Elliot Rd 85283. Fax: 480/345-7461. **Terms:** [CP] meal plan; pets, $50-$250 dep req. **Facility:** 139 rooms. Many units with separate bedroom. Attractively landscaped pool area. 3 stories; exterior corridors; heated pool. **Services:** area transportation. **Some Rooms:** 72 efficiencies, 67 kitchens. **Cards:** AE, DI, DS, MC, VI. *(See color ad p 229)*

COUNTRY INN & SUITES BY CARLSON
◆◆◆   Phone: (480)858-9898   **372**

Motel

	1P	2P	XP	
2/1-5/15 & 1/1-1/31	1P: $109	2P: $109	XP: $10	F18
9/16-12/31	1P: $89	2P: $89	XP: $10	F18
5/16-9/15	1P: $65	2P: $65	XP: $10	F18

Location: Adjacent to n side of SR 202 Loop (Red Mountain Frwy), exit 7 (Scottsdale Rd). 808 N Scottsdale Rd 85281. Fax: 480/784-2246. **Terms:** [BP] meal plan; cancellation fee imposed; package plans. **Facility:** 83 rooms. 4 stories; interior corridors; heated pool. **Services:** area transportation. **Cards:** AE, DI, DS, JC, MC, VI. *(See color ad p 229)*

COURTYARD BY MARRIOTT-DOWNTOWN TEMPE
◆◆◆   Phone: (480)966-2800   **379**

Motel

	1P
2/1-4/4	1P: $159-$179
4/5-5/15 & 9/10-1/31	1P: $129-$149
5/16-9/9	1P: $83-$109

Location: Downtown; just w of Mill Ave. 601 S Ash Ave C/5th St 85281. Fax: 480/829-8446. **Facility:** 160 rooms. 3 stories; interior corridors; heated pool. **All Rooms:** combo or shower baths. **Cards:** AE, CB, DI, DS, JC, MC, VI.

ECONO LODGE/TEMPE ASU
SAVE   Phone: (480)966-5832   **382**

Motel

	1P	2P	XP	
2/1-4/14 & 1/1-1/31	1P: $45-$65	2P: $65-$85	XP: $5	F16
10/1-12/31	1P: $40-$45	2P: $55-$65	XP: $5	F16
4/15-9/30	1P: $39-$40	2P: $45-$50	XP: $5	F16

Location: Just w of Price Rd and SR 101 (Pima Frwy), on s side of Apache Blvd. 2101 E Apache Blvd 85281. Fax: 480/966-5832. **Terms:** [CP] meal plan. **Facility:** 40 rooms. 2 stories; exterior corridors; small pool. **Cards:** AE, DI, DS, MC, VI. *(See color ad p 284)*

EMBASSY SUITES PHOENIX-TEMPE
◆◆◆   Phone: (480)897-7444   **400**

Suite Hotel

	1P	2P	XP	
2/1-4/13	1P: $149-$171	2P: $159-$183	XP: $10	F18
4/14-5/25 & 9/11-1/31	1P: $109-$125	2P: $119-$137	XP: $10	F18
5/26-9/10	1P: $89-$109	2P: $88-$95	XP: $10	F18

Location: Adjacent and just s of US 60 (Superstition Frwy), Rural Rd exit, on w side of Rural Rd. 4400 S Rural Rd 85282. Fax: 480/897-6112. **Terms:** [BP] meal plan; cancellation fee imposed. **Facility:** 224 rooms. Nicely furnished. 3 stories; exterior corridors; heated pool, sauna, whirlpool. **Dining:** Restaurant; 11 am-10 pm. **Services:** gift shop; complimentary evening beverages. **Cards:** AE, CB, DI, DS, JC, MC, VI. *(See color ad p 237)*

FIESTA INN
◆◆◆   Phone: (480)967-1441   **391**

Motor Inn

	1P	2P	XP	
1/1-1/31	1P: $165-$175	2P: $175-$185	XP: $10	F18
2/1-5/31	1P: $155-$160	2P: $165-$170	XP: $10	F18
10/1-12/31	1P: $139-$149	2P: $149-$159	XP: $10	F18
6/1-9/30	1P: $88-$95	2P: $88-$95	XP: $5	F18

Location: 0.5 mi e of I-10, at the sw corner of Priest Dr and Broadway Rd, enter from Priest Dr. 2100 S Priest Dr 85282. Fax: 480/967-0224. **Terms:** Cancellation fee imposed; package plans; pets. **Facility:** 270 rooms. Spacious, nicely landscaped pool area with wide variety of flowers, ground cover, shrubs and trees. 3 stories; exterior corridors; lighted golf practice facility includes driving range, practice bunkers, chipping & putting greens; heated pool, whirlpool; 3 lighted tennis courts. **Dining:** Restaurant; 6:30 am-10 pm; $7-$15; cocktails. **Services:** gift shop; area transportation, within 5 mi. **Recreation:** bicycles. **All Rooms:** combo or shower baths. **Cards:** AE, CB, DI, DS, MC, VI. **Special Amenities:** Free local telephone calls and free newspaper.

(See map p. 227)

HAMPTON INN & SUITES					Phone: (480)675-9799	371
◆◆◆	1/1-1/31	1P: $105-$115	2P: $115-$125			
Motel	2/1-3/31	1P: $105-$115	2P: $115-$125		XP: $10	F18
	4/1-9/30	1P: $59-$113	2P: $69-$123		XP: $10	F18
	10/1-12/31	1P: $65-$95	2P: $75-$105			

Location: Just s of McKellips Rd e side of Scottsdale Rd; 0.6 mi n of SR 202 (Red Mountain Frwy). 1429 N Scottsdale Rd 85281. Fax: 480/675-9879. **Terms:** [CP] meal plan; package plans; small pets only, $50 dep req. **Facility:** 160 rooms. Studio units, 2 room suites with microwave, refrigerator and 2 room suites with kitchenette. 1-3 stories; exterior corridors; 2 heated pools; racquetball court, 3 lighted tennis courts. **Services:** gift shop; area transportation. **All Rooms:** combo or shower baths. **Some Rooms:** 40 efficiencies. **Cards:** AE, DI, DS, JC, MC, VI.

ASK ⓢⒹ ⊕ 🐾 🐕 🛇 🖻 🔾 🖉 ✕ 🎥 VCR 🖨 🔲 🗂 🛏 DATA PORT 🛝 ➿ ✕

HOLIDAY INN				Phone: (480)968-3451	392
◆◆◆	2/1-3/25 & 12/24-1/31	1P: $154	2P: $164		
Motor Inn	9/10-12/23	1P: $119	2P: $129		
	3/26-9/9	1P: $84	2P: $94		

Location: Se corner Apache Blvd and Rural Rd. 915 E Apache Blvd 85281. Fax: 480/968-6262. **Terms:** Pets. **Facility:** 190 rooms. Located at southeast area of Arizona State University campus. Many rooms with patio or balcony. 4 stories; interior corridors; heated pool. **Services:** gift shop; area transportation. **Some Rooms:** efficiency. **Cards:** AE, CB, DI, DS, JC, MC, VI.

ASK ⓢⒹ ⊕ 🐕 🍽 🛇 🔾 🖻 🛇 ✕ 🎥 🖨 🔲 🗂 🛏 DATA PORT 🛝 ➿

HOLIDAY INN EXPRESS/TEMPE				Phone: (480)820-7500	404
◆◆	2/1-4/15	1P: $99-$119	2P: $109-$129		
Motel	1/1-1/31	1P: $79-$99	2P: $89-$129		
	10/1-12/31	1P: $79-$99	2P: $79-$109		
	4/16-9/30	1P: $59-$79	2P: $69-$89		

Location: I-10 exit 155 (Baseline Rd), 0.4 mi e, just s on Priest Dr. 5300 S Priest Dr 85283. Fax: 480/730-6626. **Terms:** [CP] meal plan; small pets only. **Facility:** 161 rooms. Large lobby with lounge area. 4 stories; interior corridors; heated pool. **Cards:** AE, CB, DI, DS, JC, MC, VI. *(See color ad p 285 & p 235).*

ASK ⓢⒹ ⊕ 🐕 🍽 🛇 🔾 ✕ 🎥 🖨 🔲 🗂 🛏 DATA PORT 🛝

HOMESTEAD VILLAGE				Phone: (602)414-4470	397
◆◆	2/1-4/15	1P: $59	2P: $59	XP: $10	F18
Motel	4/16-1/31	1P: $39	2P: $39	XP: $10	F18

Location: From I-10 exit 155 (Baseline Rd), 0.4 mi nw. 4909 S Wendler Dr 85282. Fax: 602/414-4466. **Terms:** Pets, $75 fee. **Facility:** 149 rooms. 2 stories; exterior corridors. **All Rooms:** kitchens. **Cards:** AE, DI, DS, JC, MC, VI.

🐕 🛇 ✕ 🎥 🖨 🔲 🗂 🛏 DATA PORT

(See map p. 227)

HOWARD JOHNSON EXPRESS
◆◆
Motel

| | 2/1-3/31 & 10/1-1/31 | 1P: $80 | 2P: $90 | XP: $10 | F12 |
| | 4/1-9/30 | 1P: $50 | 2P: $60 | XP: $10 | F12 |

Phone: (480)736-1700 **388**

Location: 0.4 mi e of McClintock. 1915 E Apache Blvd 85281. Fax: 480/736-9030. **Terms:** [CP] meal plan; 3 day cancellation notice; pets, $25 dep req. **Facility:** 58 rooms. 2 stories; exterior corridors; heated pool. **All Rooms:** Fee: safes. **Cards:** AE, DS, MC, VI.

(ASK) (S⬤) [icons]

INNSUITES TEMPE/PHOENIX AIRPORT
(AAA) (SAVE)
◆◆◆
Motor Inn

	2/1-4/1	1P: $99-$109	2P: $99-$109	XP: $5	F18
	4/2-5/27 & 9/18-1/31	1P: $85-$95	2P: $85-$95	XP: $5	F18
	5/28-9/17	1P: $59-$69	2P: $59-$69	XP: $5	F18

Phone: (480)897-7900 **401**

Location: From I-10 exit 155 (Baseline Rd), just e. 1651 W Baseline Rd 85283. Fax: 480/491-1008. **Terms:** [CP] meal plan; weekly & monthly rates avail; pets, $25 non-refundable fee. **Facility:** 170 rooms. Nicely decorated units, some 2 room suites. 8 whirlpool rooms, $99-$149; 2 stories; exterior corridors; putting green; heated pool, whirlpool; 2 lighted tennis courts; playground. **Dining:** Deli; 6:30 am-2 & 5-10 pm, Sun 6:30 am-11 & 5-9 pm; $5-$11; cocktails. **Services:** complimentary evening beverages; area transportation, within 3 mi. **Recreation:** basketball court, volleyball court. **Some Rooms:** 71 efficiencies, 14 kitchens. **Cards:** AE, CB, DI, DS, MC, VI. **Special Amenities:** Free breakfast and free newspaper. *(See color ad below)*

(S⬤) [icons]

LA QUINTA INN
(AAA) (SAVE)
◆◆◆
Motel

	2/1-4/30	1P: $89-$109	2P: $89-$109
	9/1-1/31	1P: $79-$99	2P: $79-$99
	5/1-8/31	1P: $59-$79	2P: $59-$79

Phone: (480)967-4465 **408**

Location: 0.8 mi n of I-10, eastbound exit 153 (SR 143), westbound exit 153A (SR 143); exit University Dr, on s side of University Dr and e side of SR 143 (Hohokam Expwy). 911 S 48th St 85281. Fax: 480/921-9172. **Terms:** [CP] meal plan; small pets only. **Facility:** 129 rooms. 3 stories; exterior corridors; putting green; heated pool. **Dining:** Restaurant nearby. **Cards:** AE, CB, DI, DS, JC, MC, VI. **Special Amenities:** Free breakfast and free local telephone calls. *(See color ad p 242)*

[icons]

(See map p. 227)

MAINSTAY SUITES-TEMPE
Phone: (480)557-8880   **384**

AAA *SAVE*
♦ ♦ ♦
Extended Stay
Motel

1/1-1/31	1P: $110-$130	2P: $110-$130
2/1-3/31	1P: $100-$120	2P: $100-$120
10/1-12/31	1P: $80-$100	2P: $80-$100
4/1-9/30	1P: $60-$80	2P: $60-$80

Location: 0.3 mi ne of I-10, exit 153, Broadway Rd; then just nw on S 52nd St. 2165 W 15th St 85281. Fax: 480/921-7900. **Terms:** [CP] meal plan; weekly & monthly rates avail; small pets only, $5 extra charge, $100 dep req. **Facility:** 94 rooms. Office hrs 6 am-9 pm weekdays; 8 am-6 pm weekends and holidays. During non-office hrs, check-in requires use of credit card and automated self-serve system. 3 stories; interior corridors; heated pool. **All Rooms:** kitchens. **Cards:** AE, CB, DI, DS, JC, MC, VI. **Special Amenities:** Early check-in/late check-out. *(See color ad p 281)*

MICROTEL INN & SUITES
Phone: (480)774-2500   **377**

♦ ♦
Motel

9/16-1/31	1P: $59-$79	2P: $69-$89
2/1-4/30	1P: $49-$69	2P: $59-$79
5/1-9/15	1P: $39-$59	2P: $49-$69

Location: 0.5 mi e of Rural Rd. 1375 E University Dr 85281. Fax: 480/929-0524. **Terms:** 3 day cancellation notice; pets, $50 dep req, dogs only. **Facility:** 52 rooms. 3 stories; interior corridors; heated pool. **Some Rooms:** 12 efficiencies. **Cards:** AE, CB, DI, DS, JC, MC, VI.

RAMADA SUITES TEMPE/SCOTTSDALE
Phone: (480)947-3711   **370**

AAA *SAVE*
♦ ♦
Suite Motel

2/1-4/30 & 12/29-1/31	1P: $117-$159	2P: $132-$179	XP: $15	F18
10/1-12/28	1P: $79-$105	2P: $89-$115	XP: $15	F18
5/1-9/30	1P: $64-$85	2P: $72-$95	XP: $15	F18

Location: Just s of McKellips Rd, on e side of Scottsdale Rd; 0.8 mi n of SR 202 Loop (Red Mountain Frwy), exit 7 (Scottsdale Rd). 1635 N Scottsdale Rd 85281. Fax: 480/949-7902. **Terms:** [BP] meal plan; cancellation fee imposed. **Facility:** 135 rooms. 1-bedroom suites with living room, microwave and refrigerator. 3 stories, no elevator; exterior corridors; heated pool, whirlpool. **Services:** complimentary evening beverages, Mon-Sat. **Recreation:** barbecues. **All Rooms:** efficiencies, combo or shower baths, safes. **Cards:** AE, CB, DI, DS, MC, VI. **Special Amenities:** Early check-in/late check-out and free breakfast.

RED ROOF INN
Phone: (480)413-1188   **403**

AAA *SAVE*
♦ ♦
Motel

2/1-4/15 & 1/1-1/31	1P: $55-$75	2P: $62-$82	XP: $4	F18
4/16-12/31	1P: $38-$58	2P: $45-$75	XP: $4	F18

Location: I-10 exit 155 (Baseline Rd), just e. 1701 W Baseline Rd 85283. Fax: 480/413-1266. **Terms:** [CP] meal plan; cancellation fee imposed. **Facility:** 121 rooms. Exterior corridors; heated pool, whirlpool. **All Rooms:** combo or shower baths. **Cards:** AE, CB, DI, DS, MC, VI. **Special Amenities:** Early check-in/late check-out and free local telephone calls.

RED ROOF INN PHOENIX AIRPORT
Phone: (480)449-3205   **387**

AAA
♦ ♦
Motel

2/1-4/15	1P: $49-$79	2P: $54-$84	XP: $5	F18
10/1-1/31	1P: $39-$69	2P: $44-$74	XP: $5	F18
4/16-9/30	1P: $39-$49	2P: $44-$54	XP: $5	F18

Location: 0.3 mi ne of I-10, exit 153, Broadway Rd. just nw on s 52nd St. 2135 W 15th St 85281. Fax: 480/449-3235. **Terms:** Pets. **Facility:** 125 rooms. 3 stories; interior corridors; heated pool, whirlpool. **Services:** area transportation, within 3 mi. **Cards:** AE, CB, DI, DS, MC, VI.

RESIDENCE INN BY MARRIOTT
Phone: (480)756-2122   **395**

♦ ♦ ♦
Motel

2/1-4/15	1P: $99-$179	2P: $99-$179
9/10-1/31	1P: $99-$149	2P: $99-$149
4/16-5/20	1P: $89-$149	2P: $89-$149
5/21-9/9	1P: $64-$89	2P: $64-$89

Location: I-10 exit 155 (Baseline Rd), 0.4 mi e, just n on Priest Dr. 5075 S Priest Dr 85282. Fax: 480/345-2802. **Terms:** [CP] meal plan; cancellation fee imposed; pets, $50 fee, $6 daily per pet. **Facility:** 126 rooms. Studio rooms with fully-equipped kitchen and 2-bedroom, 2-bath suites with living room and kitchen. Many suites and studios with fireplace. 32 two-bedroom units. 2 stories; interior/exterior corridors; heated pool. **Recreation:** sports court. **Some Rooms:** Fee: VCR. **Cards:** AE, CB, DI, DS, JC, MC, VI.

RODEWAY INN PHOENIX AIRPORT EAST
Phone: (480)967-3000   **385**

AAA *SAVE*
♦ ♦
Motel

2/1-3/31 & 10/1-1/31	1P: $59-$79	2P: $65-$75	XP: $6	F14
4/1-9/30	1P: $55-$65	2P: $61-$71	XP: $6	F14

Location: 0.3 mi ne of I-10; exit 153, Broadway Rd. 1550 S 52nd St 85281. Fax: 480/966-9568. **Terms:** [CP] meal plan; cancellation fee imposed; pets, $10 extra charge. **Facility:** 100 rooms. Located within business and industrial park area. 2 stories; exterior corridors; heated pool, whirlpool. **Dining:** Restaurant nearby. **Services:** area transportation, within 3 mi. **Some Rooms:** Fee: refrigerators, microwaves. **Cards:** AE, CB, DI, DS, MC, VI. **Special Amenities:** Early check-in/late check-out. *(See color ad p 281)*

SHERATON PLAZA HOTEL-PHOENIX AIRPORT
Phone: (480)967-6600   **383**

♦ ♦ ♦
Motor Inn

1/1-1/31	1P: $235	2P: $235	XP: $10
2/1-5/20	1P: $225	2P: $225	XP: $10
9/6-12/31	1P: $189	2P: $189	XP: $10
5/21-9/5	1P: $139	2P: $139	XP: $10

Location: 0.3 mi ne of I-10, exit 153, Broadway Rd. 1600 S 52nd St 85281. Fax: 480/829-9427. **Terms:** Cancellation fee imposed. **Facility:** 210 rooms. Located within business and industrial park area. Spacious lobby/lounge areas. 4 stories; interior corridors; heated pool. **Services:** gift shop. **Some Rooms:** Fee: refrigerators. **Cards:** AE, CB, DI, DS, JC, MC, VI.

(See map p. 227)

SPRINGHILL SUITES BY MARRIOTT   **Phone:** (480)752-7979   **402**
◆◆◆   2/1-4/30   1P: $89-$109   2P: $89-$109
Motel   5/1-6/17 & 9/10-1/31   1P: $69-$89   2P: $69-$89
        6/18-9/9   1P: $54-$59   2P: $54-$59
Location: Se corner Baseline Rd and Priest Dr. 5211 S Priest Dr 85283. Fax: 480/752-2288. **Terms:** [CP] meal plan.
Facility: 122 rooms. 3 stories; interior corridors; heated pool. **Cards:** AE, CB, DI, DS, MC, VI.

SUMNER SUITES TEMPE/PHOENIX AIRPORT   **Phone:** (480)804-9544   **376**
(AAA) [SAVE]   2/1-4/30   1P: $159-$169   2P: $159-$169   XP: $10   F17
        9/12-1/31   1P: $139-$149   2P: $139-$149   XP: $10   F17
◆◆◆   5/1-5/15   1P: $129-$139   2P: $129-$139   XP: $10   F17
Hotel   5/16-9/11   1P: $99-$109   2P: $99-$109   XP: $10   F17
         Location: Just w of Priest. 1413 W Rio Salado Pkwy 85281. Fax: 480/804-9548. **Terms:** [CP] meal plan; cancellation fee imposed. **Facility:** 125 rooms. 6 stories; interior corridors; heated pool. **Services:** area transportation, within 5 mi.
Cards: AE, DI, DS, MC, VI. **Special Amenities:** Free breakfast and free local telephone calls.

TEMPE MISSION PALMS HOTEL   **Phone:** (480)894-1400   **374**
◆◆◆   1/1-1/31   1P: $209-$299   2P: $209-$299   XP: $10   F17
Hotel   2/1-5/31   1P: $199-$279   2P: $199-$279   XP: $10   F17
        9/1-12/31   1P: $179-$219   2P: $179-$219   XP: $10   F17
        6/1-8/31   1P: $99-$149   2P: $99-$149   XP: $10   F17
Location: Just e of Mill Ave and 0.3 mi n of University Dr. 60 E Fifth St 85281. Fax: 480/968-7677. **Terms:** Cancellation fee imposed; package plans; small pets only, $75 dep req, $25 fee. **Facility:** 303 rooms. Located in the heart of downtown Tempe. Walking distance to food, shopping, entertainment and city government offices. Attractive southwest decor. 4 stories; interior corridors; heated pool; 1 lighted tennis court. **Services:** gift shop; area transportation. **All Rooms:** combo or shower baths. **Some Rooms:** Fee: refrigerators. **Cards:** AE, CB, DI, DS, JC, MC, VI. *(See color ad p 250)*

TEMPE SUPER 8   **Phone:** (480)967-8891   **380**
◆◆   2/1-4/30   1P: $69-$89   2P: $75-$99   XP: $10   F12
Motel   12/31-1/31   1P: $65-$85   2P: $69-$89   XP: $10   F12
        8/16-12/30   1P: $55-$75   2P: $59-$79   XP: $10   F12
        5/1-8/15   1P: $42-$62   2P: $45-$65   XP: $10   F12
Location: Just e of Rural Rd. 1020 E Apache Blvd 85281. Fax: 480/968-7868. **Terms:** [CP] meal plan; cancellation fee imposed; pets, in designated rooms. **Facility:** 55 rooms. Located on a busy commercial strip near Arizona State University. 2 stories; exterior corridors; heated pool. **Cards:** AE, CB, DI, DS, JC, MC, VI.

TEMPE/UNIVERSITY TRAVELODGE   **Phone:** (480)968-7871   **394**
(AAA) [SAVE]   2/1-4/2   1P: $69-$79   2P: $79-$89   XP: $10   F17
        10/1-1/31   1P: $49-$79   2P: $59-$89   XP: $5   F17
◆◆   4/3-5/14   1P: $49-$59   2P: $59-$69   XP: $5   F17
Motel   5/15-9/30   1P: $45-$55   2P: $55-$65   XP: $5   F17
         Location: Just e of Rural Rd, on s side of Apache Blvd. 1005 E Apache Blvd 85281. Fax: 480/968-3991.
Terms: [CP] meal plan; weekly rates avail; small pets only, $4 extra charge, limited rooms. **Facility:** 90 rooms. Located on a busy commercial strip near Arizona State University. 2 stories; exterior corridors; 2 heated pools. **Some Rooms:** Fee: refrigerators, microwaves, VCR. **Cards:** AE, CB, DI, DS, JC, MC, VI. **Special Amenities:** Free local telephone calls and free newspaper. *(See color ad below)*

(See map p. 227)

TWIN PALMS HOTEL AT ASU   Phone: (480)967-9431   386

2/1-4/30 & 1/1-1/31	1P: $95-$159	2P: $105-$169	XP: $10	F16
10/1-12/31	1P: $79-$129	2P: $89-$139	XP: $10	F16
5/1-9/30	1P: $59-$79	2P: $69-$89	XP: $10	F16

Hotel
Location: Just e of Mill Ave. 225 E Apache Blvd 85281. Fax: 480/968-1877. **Terms:** Package plans. **Facility:** 140 rooms. 7 stories; interior corridors; heated pool. **Dining:** Restaurant; 24 hrs; $5-$8; cocktails. **All Rooms:** combo or shower baths. **Cards:** AE, CB, DI, DS, JC, MC, VI. **Special Amenities: Free local telephone calls and free newspaper.**

---
*The following lodging was either not inspected or did not
meet AAA rating requirements but is listed for your information only.*

THE BUTTES-A WYNDHAM RESORT   Phone: (602)225-9000   389

All Year   1P: $89-$240   XP: $20   F18

Resort
Under major renovation, scheduled to be completed July 2000. **Last rated:** ◆ ◆ ◆ **Location:** I-10, westbound exit Broadway Rd, 0.8 mi w to 48th St, 0.3 mi s; eastbound exit 48th St, 0.5 mi s. 2000 Westcourt Way 85282. Fax: 602/438-8622. **Terms:** Cancellation fee imposed; package plans; small pets only, $100 dep req, under 25 lbs. **Facility:** 353 rooms. Hillside location overlooking the valley. Extensive and beautiful desert landscaping. Stream/waterfall fed pool. 4 stories; interior corridors; 2 heated pools, sauna, whirlpools. **Dining:** Dining room, restaurant; 6 am-10 pm; $8-$20; cocktails; also, Top of the Rock Restaurant, see separate listing; entertainment. **Services:** gift shop. Fee: massage. **Recreation:** water slide, 2 volleyball courts. **All Rooms:** honor bars. **Cards:** AE, CB, DI, DS, JC, MC, VI. **Special Amenities: Free newspaper.** *(See ad p 233)*

──── RESTAURANTS ────

ALCATRAZ BREWING COMPANY   **Lunch:** $8-$11   **Dinner:** $9-$20   **Phone:** 480/491-0000   198
◆
American
Location: In Arizona Mills Outlet Mall. 5000 Arizona Mills Circle 85282. **Hours:** 11 am-10:30 pm, Fri & Sat lounge to 1 am. Closed: 11/23 & 12/25. **Reservations:** suggested. **Features:** casual dress; children's menu; carryout; cocktails & lounge. Themed restaurant utilizing photos, news clippings and displays from Alcatraz prison. On-site brewery; good selection of sandwiches, salad, pasta, pizza, and entrees named after former inmates. Limited menu in lounge after hours. **Cards:** AE, DI, DS, MC, VI.

LOS SOMBREROS   **Lunch:** $8-$11   **Dinner:** $8-$11   **Phone:** 480/994-1799   192
◆
Mexican
Location: Se corner McKellips & Scottsdale Rd. 1849 N Scottsdale Rd 85281. **Hours:** 11 am-9 pm, Fri & Sat-10 pm, Sun 4:30-8 pm. Closed major holidays & Mon. **Features:** casual dress; children's menu; carryout; cocktails; a la carte. Small, colorful Mexican restaurant specializing in authentic Mexican marketplace cuisine. **Cards:** AE, DI, DS, MC, VI.

JOHN HENRY'S   **Lunch:** $7-$14   **Dinner:** $12-$24   **Phone:** 480/730-9009   201
◆◆
Italian
Location: 2.5 mi e of I-10, Elliot Rd exit; se corner of Elliot Rd and Rural Rd. 909 E Elliot Rd 85284. **Hours:** 11:30 am-2:30 & 5-10 pm, Fri & Sat 5 pm-11 pm. Closed major holidays. **Reservations:** required. **Features:** casual dress; carryout; cocktails & lounge; entertainment; a la carte. Pasta, chicken, veal, beef and seafood. Homemade dessert. **Cards:** AE, DS, MC, VI.

MACAYO DEPOT CANTINA   **Lunch:** $5-$9   **Dinner:** $6-$12   **Phone:** 480/966-6677   195
◆
Mexican
Location: Just w of Mill Ave via 3rd St; 0.4 mi n of University Dr. 300 S Ash 85281. **Hours:** 11 am-11 pm, Fri & Sat-midnight, football season from 10 am. Closed: 11/23 & 12/25. **Features:** casual dress; children's menu; carryout; cocktails & lounge; entertainment; a la carte. Colorfully decorated and furnished in a Mexican theme. Noisy. Family oriented. **Cards:** AE, DI, DS, MC, VI.

MIKE PULO'S SPAGHETTI COMPANY   **Lunch:** $6   **Dinner:** $7-$11   **Phone:** 480/966-3848   197
◆
American
Location: Just n of University Dr. 414 S Mill Ave 85281. **Hours:** 11 am-10:30 pm, Fri-Sun-11 pm. Closed: 11/23 & 12/25. **Reservations:** suggested. **Features:** casual dress; children's menu; carryout; cocktails & lounge; street parking. Family atmosphere. Eclectic decor. Selection of pasta dishes, burgers and salad. Smoke free premises. **Cards:** MC, VI.

(See map p. 227)

RUSTY PELICAN RESTAURANT   **Lunch:** $6-$11   **Dinner:** $12-$21   **Phone:** 480/345-0972   (199)
◆   **Location:** Just e of I-10 on n side of Baseline Rd, adjacent to Arizona Mills Outlet Mall. 1606 W Baseline Rd
Seafood   85283. **Hours:** 11 am-10 pm, Sat 4:30 pm-11 pm, Sun 4:30 pm-10 pm. **Features:** casual dress; children's
                           menu; early bird specials; carryout; cocktails & lounge. Informal dining in garden-like atmosphere. Also
serving chicken, beef, and pasta. Busy atmosphere. **Cards:** AE, DI, DS, MC, VI.

TOP OF THE ROCK RESTAURANT   **Dinner:** $19-$30   **Phone:** 602/225-9000   (196)
◆ ◆ ◆   **Location:** I-10, westbound exit Broadway Rd, 0.8 mi w to 48th St, 0.3 mi s; eastbound exit 48th St, 0.5 mi s;
American   in The Buttes-A Wyndham Resort. 2000 Westcourt Way 85282. **Hours:** 5 pm-10 pm, Fri & Sat-11 pm, Sun
                           10 am-2 & 5-10 pm. **Reservations:** suggested. **Features:** casual dress; Sunday brunch; children's menu;
cocktails & lounge; valet parking; a la carte. Hilltop location overlooking the valley. **Cards:** AE, CB, DI, DS, JC, MC, VI.

TOLLESON pop. 4,400   (See map p. 224; index p. 223)

—— LODGING ——

ECONO LODGE   **Phone:** (623)936-4667   (24)
(AAA) [SAVE]   2/1-3/31 & 12/1-1/31   1P: $80-$90   2P: $80-$90   XP: $5   F18
               4/1-11/30   1P: $46-$56   2P: $50-$60   XP: $5   F18
◆ ◆   **Location:** Adjacent and just n of I-10, at exit 135(83rd Ave); 0.5 mi n via McDowell St. 1520 N 84th Dr 85353.
Motel   Fax: 623/936-3173. **Terms:** Pets, $10 extra charge, $25 dep req. **Facility:** 120 rooms. 2 stories; interior corri-
               dors; heated pool. **Dining:** Restaurant nearby. **Recreation:** in-room video games. **Cards:** AE, CB, DI, DS, JC,
MC, VI. **Special Amenities:** Early check-in/late check-out. *(See color ad p 229)*

YOUNGTOWN pop. 2,500   (See map p. 224; index p. 223)

—— LODGING ——

MOTEL 6 - 22   **Phone:** 623/977-1318   (15)
(AAA)   12/14-1/31   1P: $56-$66   2P: $62-$72   XP: $3   F17
               2/1-4/23   1P: $52-$62   2P: $58-$68   XP: $3   F17
◆   4/24-12/13   1P: $46-$56   2P: $52-$62   XP: $3   F17
Motel   **Location:** Just w of 111th Ave on Grand Ave (US 60). 11133 Grand Ave 85363. Fax: 623/977-7749.
               Terms: Small pets only. **Facility:** 62 rooms. 2 stories; exterior corridors; heated pool. **Dining:** Restaurant
nearby. **All Rooms:** shower baths. **Cards:** AE, CB, DI, DS, MC, VI.

This ends listings for the Phoenix Vicinity.
The following page resumes the alphabetical listings of
cities in Arizona.

PINETOP-LAKESIDE pop. 2,400

——— LODGINGS ———

BARTRAM'S WHITE MOUNTAIN BED & BREAKFAST
Phone: 520/367-1408
◆◆◆
Property failed to provide current rates
Bed & Breakfast
Location: 1.8 mi s of SR 260, via Woodland and Woodland Lake rds w. 1916 W Woodlake Lake Rd 85929 (Rt 1, Box 1014, LAKESIDE). **Terms:** [BP] meal plan; 14 day cancellation notice; pets. **Facility:** 5 rooms. Quiet, country setting. Very nicely decorated rooms in a restored 1940's ranch style home. 1 story; interior corridors; designated smoking area. **All Rooms:** combo or shower baths.

BEST WESTERN INN OF PINETOP
Phone: (520)367-6667
(AAA) [SAVE]
All Year   1P: $59-$99   2P: $59-$99   XP: $5
◆◆
Motel
Location: On SR 260. 404 S White Mountain Blvd 85935 (PO Box 1006, PINETOP). Fax: 520/367-6672. **Terms:** [ECP] meal plan. **Facility:** 42 rooms. 1 two-bedroom apartment; 1 story. **Recreation:** indoor whirlpool. **Some Rooms:** kitchen. Fee: refrigerators, microwaves, VCR. **Cards:** AE, CB, DI, DS, JC, MC, VI. **Special Amenities:** Free breakfast and free local telephone calls.

COMFORT INN
Phone: (520)368-6600
(AAA) [SAVE]
9/8-11/30   1P: $55-$65   2P: $65-$85
◆◆◆
2/1-6/1   1P: $55-$65   2P: $65-$85   XP: $8   F12
Motel
6/2-9/7 & 12/1-1/31 1P: $65   2P: $85
Location: In Lakeside; on SR 260. 1637 W White Mountain Blvd 85935 (PO Box 1130-D, PINETOP). Fax: 520/368-6600. **Terms:** [CP] meal plan; package plans. **Facility:** 55 rooms. Large rooms, 12 with wood-burning fireplace. 2 stories; interior corridors; indoor whirlpool. **All Rooms:** extended cable TV. **Some Rooms:** Fee: VCR. **Cards:** AE, CB, DI, DS, MC, VI. **Special Amenities:** Free breakfast and preferred room (subject to availability with advanced reservations).

HOLIDAY INN EXPRESS
Phone: (520)367-6077
(AAA) [SAVE]
All Year   1P: $79-$109   2P: $79-$109   XP: $10   F
◆◆◆
Motel
Location: 431 E White Mountain Blvd 85935 (PO Box 1033, PINETOP). Fax: 520/367-3220. **Terms:** [ECP] meal plan; small pets only. **Facility:** 40 rooms. Guest elevator on property. 2 stories; interior corridors; sauna, whirlpool. **All Rooms:** extended cable TV. **Cards:** AE, CB, DI, DS, JC, MC, VI. **Special Amenities:** Free breakfast and free local telephone calls.

LAZY OAKS RESORT
Phone: 520/368-6203
◆◆
All Year   1P: $62-$76   2P: $62-$78   XP: $5   F3
Cottage
Location: 0.8 mi nw of Lakeside via SR 260, 1.3 mi s on Rainbow Lake Dr, then Larson Rd. 1075 Larson Rd 85929 (Rt 2, Box 1215, LAKESIDE). **Terms:** 21 day cancellation notice; cancellation fee imposed; small pets only, with permission. **Facility:** 15 rooms. Shaded grounds on shore of Rainbow Lake. Picnic tables and barbecues. 1 and 2-bedroom housekeeping cabins with fireplace. 1 story; exterior corridors. **Recreation:** fishing; bicycles. Rental: boats. **All Rooms:** kitchens, combo or shower baths.

MOUNTAIN HACIENDA LODGE
Phone: 520/367-4146
◆◆
12/10-1/31   1P: $49-$59   2P: $54-$64
Motel
2/1-3/31   1P: $49-$59   2P: $54-$64   XP: $5   D12
5/21-12/9   1P: $35-$59   2P: $39-$64   XP: $5   D12
4/1-5/20   1P: $35-$45   2P: $39-$49   XP: $5   D12
Location: On SR 260. 1023 E White Mountain Blvd 85935 (PO Box 713, PINETOP). Fax: 520/367-0291. **Terms:** [CP] meal plan; 3 day cancellation notice; cancellation fee imposed. **Facility:** 22 rooms. 2 stories; exterior corridors; playground. Fee: miniature golf. **Recreation:** sports court. **Cards:** AE, DS, MC, VI.

MOUNTAIN HAVEN INN
Phone: (520)367-2101
◆◆
All Year   1P: $49-$59   2P: $49-$69
Motel
Location: E end of town. 1120 E White Moutain Blvd 85935. Fax: 520/367-2101. **Terms:** 7 day cancellation notice; cancellation fee imposed. **Facility:** 10 rooms. 2 two-bedroom units. 1 story; exterior corridors. **Some Rooms:** 4 kitchens. **Cards:** MC, VI.

NORTHWOODS RESORT
Phone: 520/367-2966
◆◆◆
10/1-1/31   1P: $69   2P: $139   XP: $15   F5
Cottage
2/1-5/31   1P: $69-$79   2P: $99-$129   XP: $15   F5
6/1-9/30   2P: $79-$129   XP: $15   F5
Location: On SR 260. 165 E White Mountain Blvd 85935 (PO Box 397A, PINETOP). Fax: 520/367-2969. **Terms:** 14 day cancellation notice; cancellation fee imposed; pets, $12 extra charge, with prior approval. **Facility:** 14 rooms. On several acres of wooded grounds, attractive forest setting. Fire pit area with picnic tables. Nicely decorated studio and 1- 4-bedroom housekeeping cottages with woodburning or gas fireplace. 20 minute walk to Woodland Lake. 5 two-bedroom units, 3 three-bedroom units. 1 story; exterior corridors; playground. **Some Rooms:** efficiency, 13 kitchens. **Cards:** DS, MC, VI.

TIMBER LODGE
Phone: (520)367-4463
(AAA) [SAVE]
2/1-3/31 & 12/16-1/31 1P: $38-$60   2P: $45-$65   XP: $10
◆◆
10/16-12/15   1P: $33-$38   2P: $38-$45
Motel
4/1-10/15   1P: $33-$38   2P: $38-$45   XP: $5
Location: In Pinetop, on SR 260. 1078 E White Mountain Blvd 85935 (PO Box 2959, PINETOP). **Terms:** Weekly rates avail; package plans. **Facility:** 31 rooms. 1-2 stories; exterior corridors. **All Rooms:** combo or shower baths. **Cards:** AE, CB, DI, DS, MC, VI. **Special Amenities:** Free local telephone calls and free room upgrade (subject to availability with advanced reservations).

WOODLAND INN & SUITES
AAA SAVE
◆ ◆
Motel

All Year 1P: $55-$99 2P: $60-$109 XP: $5 F16
Location: On SR 260. 458 E White Mountain Blvd 85935 (PO Box 1226, PINETOP). Fax: 520/367-1543.
Terms: [ECP] meal plan; pets. **Facility:** 42 rooms. 2 stories; exterior corridors; indoor whirlpool. **Cards:** AE, CB, DI, DS, JC, MC, VI. **Special Amenities: Free breakfast and free local telephone calls.**
Phone: (520)367-3636

——— RESTAURANTS ———

THE CHALET RESTAURANT Dinner: $10-$24 Phone: 520/367-1514
◆ ◆
American
Location: On SR 260; in Lakeside. 348 W White Mountain Blvd 85929. **Hours:** 5 pm-9 pm. Closed: Sun; Mon 10/15-5/15. **Features:** casual dress; children's menu; salad bar; cocktails & lounge. Attractive country decor. Nice selection of steak, seafood and chicken. **Cards:** AE, MC, VI.

CHARLIE CLARK'S Dinner: $10-$22 Phone: 520/367-4900
◆ ◆
Steakhouse
Location: On SR 260, e end of Pinetop, on White Mountain Blvd. 1701 E White Mountain Blvd 85935. **Hours:** 5 pm-9 pm, weekends-10 pm. Closed: 4/23. **Reservations:** suggested. **Features:** casual dress; children's menu; cocktails & lounge. Popular, long established restaurant. Informal, western atmosphere. Prime rib, seafood and mesquite broiled steak. Lunch served in bar. **Cards:** AE, CB, DI, DS, MC, VI.

THE CHRISTMAS TREE RESTAURANT Dinner: $13-$35 Phone: 520/367-3107
◆ ◆ ◆
American
Location: In Lakeside; just s of SR 260. 455 N Woodland Rd 85929. **Hours:** 5 pm-9 pm. Closed: Mon & Tues. **Reservations:** suggested. **Features:** No A/C; casual dress; children's menu; cocktails & lounge. Festive holiday decor. Nice variety of entrees; specialty is chicken and dumplings, homemade cinnamon rolls. **Cards:** DS, MC, VI.

PRESCOTT pop. 26,500

——— LODGINGS ———

BEST WESTERN PRESCOTTONIAN MOTEL Phone: (520)445-3096
◆ ◆
Motor Inn
4/1-6/30 & 7/3-9/30 1P: $59-$89 2P: $69-$89 XP: $10 F12
2/1-3/31 & 10/1-1/31 1P: $49-$69 2P: $59-$79 XP: $10 F12
Location: On SR 89 (Gurley St) 1.2 mi e of Montezuma St. 1317 E Gurley St 86301. Fax: 520/778-2976.
Terms: Small pets only, in smoking rooms. **Facility:** 121 rooms. Large units. 2 stories; exterior corridors. **Cards:** AE, CB, DI, DS, MC, VI.

COMFORT INN

Phone: (520)778-5770

(AAA) (SAVE)
◆◆
Motel

4/15-10/28	1P: $88-$108	2P: $88-$108	XP: $10 F11
2/1-4/14 & 10/29-1/31	1P: $65-$95	2P: $65-$95	XP: $10 F11

Location: 1.5 mi s on SR 89 (White Spar Rd/Montezuma St). 1290 White Spar Rd 86303. Fax: 520/776-8404. **Terms:** [CP] meal plan; weekly rates avail; 3 day cancellation notice; cancellation fee imposed. **Facility:** 61 rooms. Located at edge of town in a wooded area. 2 stories; exterior corridors. **Dining:** Restaurant nearby. **All Rooms:** combo or shower baths. **Some Rooms:** 11 efficiencies. **Cards:** AE, CB, DI, DS, MC, VI. **Special Amenities:** Free local telephone calls and free newspaper. *(See color ad p 291)*

THE COTTAGES AT PRESCOTT COUNTRY INN BED & BREAKFAST

Phone: (520)445-7991

◆
Cottage

10/2-1/31	1P: $59-$99	2P: $79-$129	XP: $10 F6
5/1-10/1	1P: $79-$99	2P: $79-$129	XP: $10 F6

Location: Just s on SR 89 (Montezuma St). 503 S Montezuma St 86303. Fax: 520/717-1215. **Terms:** [CP] meal plan; 7 day cancellation notice. **Facility:** 12 rooms. Cozy units decorated in a charming country decor. 9 rooms with gas fireplace. 1 two-bedroom unit. 1 story; exterior corridors; designated smoking area. **All Rooms:** combo or shower baths. **Some Rooms:** 3 efficiencies, 9 kitchens. **Cards:** AE, DS, MC, VI.

DOLLS & ROSES BED & BREAKFAST

Phone: (520)776-9291

◆◆◆
Historic Bed
& Breakfast

All Year	1P: $89-$109	2P: $89-$109	XP: $20

Location: Just n of Gurley St. 109 N Pleasant St 86301. **Terms:** [BP] meal plan; age restrictions may apply; cancellation fee imposed; 2 night min stay. **Facility:** 4 rooms. 2 stories; interior corridors; smoke free premises. **Cards:** MC, VI.

FOREST VILLAS INN

Phone: (520)717-1200

(AAA) (SAVE)
◆◆◆
Motel

4/2-10/31	1P: $85-$175	2P: $95-$185	XP: $10 F12
2/1-4/1 & 11/1-1/31	1P: $69-$145	2P: $79-$155	XP: $10 F12

Location: 2.5 mi e of jct SR 89 on SR 69, just n. 3645 Lee Cir 86301. Fax: 520/717-1400. **Terms:** [CP] meal plan; weekly & monthly rates avail; cancellation fee imposed; 2 night min stay; package plans. **Facility:** 62 rooms. 1 two-bedroom suite with wet bar, whirlpool tub & refrigerator $115-$185.; 15 whirlpool rooms, $95-$135; 2 stories; interior corridors; heated pool, whirlpool, pool & whirlpool closed in winter. **All Rooms:** extended cable TV. **Cards:** AE, CB, DI, DS, MC, VI. **Special Amenities:** Free breakfast and free local telephone calls. *(See ad below)*

HASSAYAMPA INN

Phone: (520)778-9434

◆◆◆
Historic Hotel

5/1-1/31	1P: $155-$175	2P: $155-$175	XP: $15 F6
2/1-4/30	1P: $145-$165	2P: $145-$165	XP: $15 F6

Location: Downtown, just e of Court House Square. 122 E Gurley St 86301. Fax: 520/445-8590. **Terms:** [BP] meal plan; 2 night min stay, 7/4; package plans. **Facility:** 68 rooms. Cozy units with the charm of yesteryear. Circa 1927. Some smaller rooms do not meet all AAA requirements. Lot and street parking. 3-4 stories; interior corridors. **All Rooms:** combo or shower baths. **Cards:** AE, DI, DS, MC, VI. *(See ad p 293)*

HOLIDAY INN EXPRESS PRESCOTT

Phone: (520)445-8900

◆◆◆
Motel

	1P: $89-$169	2P: $89-$169	
4/15-10/14	1P: $89-$169	2P: $89-$169	
10/15-1/31	1P: $79-$149	2P: $79-$149	
2/1-4/14	1P: $79-$149	2P: $79-$149	XP: $10 F17

Location: Corner of Lee Blvd and SR 69. 3454 Ranch Dr 86303. Fax: 520/778-2629. **Terms:** [CP] meal plan. **Facility:** 76 rooms. 3 stories; interior corridors; heated pool. **All Rooms:** combo or shower baths. **Some Rooms:** Fee: refrigerators, microwaves. **Cards:** AE, DI, DS, JC, MC, VI.

HOTEL VENDOME, A CLARION CARRIAGE HOUSE INN

Phone: (520)776-0900

◆◆
Historic Hotel

4/1-10/31	1P: $89-$189	2P: $89-$189	XP: $10 F16
2/1-3/31 & 11/1-1/31	1P: $79-$149	2P: $79-$149	XP: $10 F16

Location: 230 S Cortez St 86303. Fax: 520/771-0395. **Terms:** [CP] meal plan; cancellation fee imposed; 2 night min stay; package plans. **Facility:** 20 rooms. 2 stories; interior corridors. **Cards:** AE, CB, DI, DS, JC, MC, VI.

LYNX CREEK FARM BED & BREAKFAST

Phone: (520)778-9573

◆◆
Bed & Breakfast

3/1-12/31	1P: $85-$155	2P: $85-$155	XP: $20 D15
1/1-1/31	1P: $75-$145	2P: $75-$145	
2/1-2/29	1P: $75-$145	2P: $75-$145	XP: $20 D15

Location: 5.5 mi e on SR 69 from jct SR 69 and SR 89 to Onyx Dr, then 0.5 mi (dirt/gravel road). 5555 Onyx Dr 86302 (PO Box 4301). **Terms:** [BP] meal plan; 14 day cancellation notice; cancellation fee imposed; 2 night min stay, major holidays & Sat; pets, $10 extra charge. **Facility:** 6 rooms. In a quiet, country location. Attractively decorated units in guest house and log cabin. Western and country decor. 1 story; exterior corridors; designated smoking area. **Cards:** AE, DS, MC, VI.

MOTEL 6 - 166

Phone: 520-776-0160

AAA
◆
Motel

6/15-11/1	1P: $42-$52	2P: $48-$58	XP: $3 F17
5/4-6/14 & 11/2-1/31	1P: $38-$48	2P: $44-$54	XP: $3 F17
2/1-5/3	1P: $37-$47	2P: $43-$53	XP: $3 F17

Location: 0.5 mi e of Montezuma St. 1111 E Sheldon St 86301. Fax: 520/445-4188. **Terms:** Small pets only. **Facility:** 79 rooms. 2 stories; exterior corridors; heated pool, pool closed 10/1-5/31. **Dining:** Restaurant nearby. **All Rooms:** shower baths. **Cards:** AE, CB, DI, DS, MC, VI.

PLEASANT STREET INN

Phone: 520/445-4774

◆◆◆
Bed & Breakfast

All Year   1P: $80-$130   2P: $90-$140   XP: $15

Location: Just e of Court House Square via Goodwin St. 142 S Pleasant St 86303. **Terms:** [BP] meal plan; 7 day cancellation notice; cancellation fee imposed. **Facility:** 4 rooms. Victorian house built in 1906 and renovated in 1991. Walking distance to Town Square. 2 stories; interior corridors; designated smoking area. **All Rooms:** combo or shower baths. **Cards:** DS, MC, VI.

PRESCOTT PINES INN BED & BREAKFAST

Phone: 520/445-7270

AAA SAVE
◆◆
Bed & Breakfast

All Year   1P: $65-$110   2P: $65-$110   XP: $10

Location: 1.3 mi s on SR 89 (White Spar Rd/Montezuma St). 901 White Spar Rd 86303. Fax: 520/778-3665. **Terms:** [CP] meal plan; weekly rates avail; 7 day cancellation notice; cancellation fee imposed; 2 night min stay, 7/4. **Facility:** 13 rooms. 1902 Country Victorian inn renovated 1987. Rooms in adjacent cottages and guest houses. 3 gas fireplaces. 1 three-bedroom chalet with fireplace, $229-$249 for up to 8 persons; 1 story; exterior corridors; smoke free premises. **Dining:** Breakfast plan, $5 additional per person. **All Rooms:** combo or shower baths. **Some Rooms:** 5 efficiencies, 3 kitchens. **Cards:** MC, VI.

PRESCOTT RESORT, CONFERENCE CENTER & CASINO

Phone: (520)776-1666

	4/1-10/31	1P: $99-$129	2P: $99-$129	XP: $10	F17
	2/1-3/31 & 11/1-1/31	1P: $89-$119	2P: $89-$119	XP: $10	F17

Hotel   **Location:** Just e of jct SR 89. 1500 Hwy 69 86301. **Fax:** 520/776-8544. **Terms:** Cancellation fee imposed; 2 night min stay, major holidays; package plans, golf & casino. **Facility:** 160 rooms. On top of hill with view of Prescott or valley. Beautifully decorated public areas with many gallery paintings and sculptures. Separate building houses limited casino gaming. 80 one-bedroom suites with living room; 5 stories; interior corridors; heated pool; racquetball court, 1 lighted tennis court. **Dining:** Thumb Butte Dining Room, see separate listing. **Services:** gift shop. Fee: massage. **Recreation:** indoor whirlpool, slot machines, live poker, keno. **Some Rooms:** Fee: VCR. **Cards:** AE, CB, DI, DS, JC, MC, VI. **Special Amenities:** Free room upgrade (subject to availability with advanced reservations).

PRESCOTT SUPER 8 MOTEL

Phone: 520/776-1282

	4/1-1/31	1P: $49-$69	2P: $54-$69	XP: $5	F12
	2/1-3/31	1P: $48-$68	2P: $53-$68	XP: $5	F12

Motel   **Location:** E end of town off Gurley. 1105 E Sheldon St 86301. **Fax:** 520/778-6736. **Terms:** [CP] meal plan; 15 day cancellation notice; small pets only, $10 extra charge, dogs only. **Facility:** 70 rooms. 2 stories; interior corridors; heated pool. **Some Rooms:** Fee: refrigerators. **Cards:** AE, CB, DS, MC, VI.

The following lodging was either not inspected or did not meet AAA rating requirements but is listed for your information only.

SPRINGHILL SUITES BY MARRIOTT

Phone: 520/776-0998

[fyi]	6/1-10/31	1P: $89-$149	2P: $89-$149
	2/1-5/31 & 11/1-1/31	1P: $79-$129	2P: $79-$129

Motel   Too new to rate, opening scheduled for August 1999. **Location:** On US 89, at Marina St. 200 E Sheldon St 86301. **Fax:** 520/776-0998. **Terms:** [CP] meal plan. **Amenities:** 83 rooms, pets, radios, coffeemakers, microwaves, refrigerators, pool, exercise facilities. **Cards:** AE, CB, DI, DS, JC, MC, VI. *(See color ad below)*

--- **RESTAURANTS** ---

GURLEY ST GRILL   Historical

Lunch: $6-$9   Dinner: $9-$14   Phone: 520/445-3388

American   **Location:** Just w of SR 89. 230 W Gurley St 86301. **Hours:** 11 am-midnight. Closed: 12/25. **Reservations:** suggested; for 5 or more. **Features:** casual dress; Sunday brunch; children's menu; carryout; cocktails; street parking. Restored 1901 red brick building. Serves pizza, pasta, burgers, steak and seafood, spit roasted chicken. **Cards:** AE, DS, MC, VI.

MURPHY'S RESTAURANT   Historical

Lunch: $8-$12   Dinner: $12-$25   Phone: 520/445-4044

American   **Location:** Downtown. 201 N Cortez 86301. **Hours:** 11 am-3 & 4:30-10 pm, Fri & Sat-11 pm. Closed: 12/25. **Features:** casual dress; Sunday brunch; children's menu; early bird specials; cocktails & lounge; street parking. Historic 1890 mercantile building. Restored to depict era. Serves mesquite broiled seafood, steak, prime rib and pasta. Breads baked daily on premises. Selection of 60 different domestic and imported beers. **Cards:** AE, DS, MC, VI.

THE PALACE

Lunch: $5-$9   Dinner: $10-$18   Phone: 520/541-1996

American   **Location:** 120 S Montezuma 86301. **Hours:** 11:15 am-2:30 & 4:30-10 pm. Closed: 12/25. **Features:** casual dress; early bird specials; carryout; cocktails & lounge; street parking. Casual, relaxed dining in Arizona's oldest bar. Restored to 1880 decor. **Cards:** AE, MC, VI.

PEACOCK ROOM Historical   **Lunch:** $7-$10   **Dinner:** $14-$22   **Phone:** 520/778-9434
◆◆◆   **Location:** Downtown, just e of Court House Square; in Hassayampa Inn. 122 E Gurley St 86301.
American   **Hours:** 6:30 am-2 & 4:30-9 pm, Fri & Sat-9:30 pm. **Reservations:** suggested. **Features:** casual dress; early
   bird specials; cocktails & lounge. Located in historic 1927 hotel. Fine dining with a selection of pasta, steak,
seafood, veal and other specialities. Desserts made on premises. Smoke free premises. **Cards:** AE, CB, DI, DS, MC, VI.
(See ad p 293)   ⊠

THE PORTERHOUSE   **Dinner:** $8-$25   **Phone:** 520/445-1991
◆◆   **Location:** West end of town off Gurley St. 155 Plaza Dr 86303. **Hours:** 4 pm-10 pm; Fri-Sat-11 pm; Sun 11
Steakhouse   am-8 pm. **Features:** casual dress; Sunday brunch; early bird specials; carryout; cocktails & lounge. Good
   all-American cooking. Patio dining with relaxing sounds from granite creek. Happy hour 4-7 pm. **Cards:** AE,
DS, MC, VI.   ⊠

PRESCOTT BREWING COMPANY   **Lunch:** $6-$15   **Dinner:** $6-$15   **Phone:** 520/771-2795
(AAA)   **Location:** Downtown. 130 W Gurley Suite A 86301. **Hours:** 11 am-10 pm; Fri & Sat-11 pm. Closed: 11/23 &
   12/25. **Features:** casual dress; children's menu; carryout; cocktails & lounge; street parking. Casual dining in
◆◆   a brew pub. Brewery on premises, in house bakery. Smoke free premises. **Cards:** AE, DS, MC, VI.   ⊠
American

THE ROSE RESTAURANT   **Dinner:** $10-$20   **Phone:** 520/777-8308
(AAA)   **Location:** Just s of Gurley St. 234 S Cortez St 86303. **Hours:** 5 pm-9:30 pm. Closed: Mon & Tues.
   Reservations: suggested. **Features:** casual dress; cocktails; a la carte. Restored Victorian house from late
◆◆◆   1890s. Excellent selection of beef, pasta, veal, chicken and vegetarian entrees with unique sauces and
Continental   seasonings. Patio dining available in season. Smoke free premises. **Cards:** AE, CB, DI, DS, MC, VI.   ⊠

TAJ MAHAL   **Dinner:** $6-$15   **Phone:** 520/445-5752
◆◆   **Location:** On Hwy 69 2 mi e, s side in shopping mall. 1781 E Hwy 69 86301. **Hours:** 11 am-2:30 & 5-9 pm.
American   Closed: Tues. **Features:** casual dress; Sunday brunch; carryout; cocktails. East Indian cuisine in an elegant
   atmosphere. Smoke free premises. **Cards:** AE, DS, MC, VI.   ⊠

THUMB BUTTE DINING ROOM   **Lunch:** $7-$10   **Dinner:** $8-$20   **Phone:** 520/776-1666
◆◆◆   **Location:** Just e of jct SR 89; in Prescott Resort, Conference Center & Casino. 1500 Hwy 69 86301.
American   **Hours:** 7 am-10 pm. **Features:** casual dress; cocktails & lounge; entertainment. Hilltop view of Prescott or
   valley. Nice selection of chicken, steak and pasta. **Cards:** AE, CB, DI, DS, JC, MC, VI.   ⊠

ZUMA'S WOODFIRE CAFE   **Lunch:** $5-$8   **Dinner:** $9-$15   **Phone:** 520/541-1400
◆◆   **Location:** Just n of Gurley St. 124 N Montezuma St 86301. **Hours:** 11 am-midnight. Closed: 11/23 & 12/25.
American   **Features:** casual dress; Sunday brunch; children's menu; health conscious menu; carryout; cocktails; a la
   carte. A wide variety of Regional and Southwestern dishes. Pecan wood fired entrees and pizza. Patio dining
avail fireside. **Cards:** AE, DS, MC, VI.   ♿ ⊠

PRESCOTT VALLEY pop. 8,980

——— LODGINGS ———

DAYS INN/PRESCOTT VALLEY   **Phone:** (520)772-8600
(AAA) (SAVE)   All Year   1P: $59-$85   2P: $69-$95   XP: $10   F12
   Location: 0.3 mi w of Robert Rd. 7875 E Hwy 69 86314. Fax: 520/772-0942. **Terms:** [CP] meal plan; pets,
◆◆ $50 dep req. **Facility:** 59 rooms. 2 stories; exterior corridors; whirlpool, pool closed 10/1-4/30. **Dining:** Coffee
Motel   shop nearby. **All Rooms:** extended cable TV. **Some Rooms:** Fee: refrigerators. **Cards:** AE, CB, DI, DS,
MC, VI. **Special Amenities:** Free breakfast and free local telephone calls.

MOTEL 6 - 4048   **Phone:** 520/772-2200
◆◆   5/21-10/19   1P: $46-$66   2P: $52-$72   XP: $6
Motel   3/13-5/20   1P: $44-$54   2P: $50-$60   XP: $6
   2/1-3/12 & 10/20-1/31   1P: $40-$50   2P: $44-$54   XP: $4
Location: 8383 E Hwy 69 86314. Fax: 520/772-7293. **Facility:** 48 rooms. 2 stories; interior corridors; heated pool.
Cards: AE, CB, DI, DS, JC, MC, VI.

SUPER 8 MOTEL   **Phone:** (520)775-5888
◆◆   4/1-9/30   1P: $46-$59   2P: $51-$64   XP: $5   F12
Motel   10/1-1/31   1P: $44-$58   2P: $48-$63
   2/1-3/31   1P: $42-$58   2P: $47-$63   XP: $5   F12
Location: 0.4 mi w of Robert Rd. 7801 E Hwy 69 86314. Fax: 520/772-6939. **Facility:** 59 rooms. 2 stories; interior corridors;
heated pool. **Cards:** AE, CB, DI, DS, MC, VI.

QUARTZSITE pop. 1,800

——— LODGING ———

——— *The following lodging was either not inspected or did not* ———
meet AAA rating requirements but is listed for your information only.

BEST WESTERN QUARTZITE   **Phone:** 520/927-3529
(fyi)   Under construction, scheduled to open October 1999. **Location:** Just s of I-10, exit 17. 1770 Dome Rock Rd
Motel   85346. Fax: 520/927-5337. **Planned Amenities:** 73 rooms, restaurant, coffeemakers, refrigerators, pool.

RIO RICO pop. 1,400

——— LODGING ———

RIO RICO RESORT & COUNTRY CLUB   **Phone:** (520)281-1901
(AAA) [SAVE]   2/1-3/31   1P: $165-$185   2P: $165-$185   XP: $10   F12
◆◆◆◆   4/1-5/31 & 9/1-1/31   1P: $135-$175   2P: $135-$175   XP: $10   F12
Resort   6/1-8/31   1P: $100-$150   2P: $100-$150   XP: $10   F12
Resort   **Location:** 8 mi n of Nogales on I-19, exit 17, Rio Rico Dr; then 0.5 mi w. 1069 Camino Caralampi 85648.
Fax: 520/281-7132. **Terms:** Check-in 4 pm; package plans; small pets only. **Facility:** 180 rooms. Hilltop loca-
tion with nice view of surrounding area. Spacious rooms with balcony or patio. 2 stories; exterior corridors; heated pool, sauna,
whirlpool. Fee: 18 holes golf; 4 lighted tennis courts. **Dining:** Dining room; 6 am-9:30 pm; $11-$27; cocktails. **Services:** gift
shop. Fee: area transportation. **Recreation:** in-room video games. Fee: horseback riding. **All Rooms:** extended cable TV.
Some Rooms: Fee: refrigerators. **Cards:** AE, CB, DI, DS, JC, MC, VI. **Special Amenities: Free newspaper.**
(See ad p 329)   [icons]

SAFFORD pop. 7,400

——— LODGINGS ———

BEST WESTERN DESERT INN   **Phone:** (520)428-0521
(AAA) [SAVE]   All Year   1P: $53-$59   2P: $53-$59   XP: $6   F12
◆◆   **Location:** US 70, 1 mi w of jct US 191. 1391 W Thatcher Blvd 85546. Fax: 520/428-7653. **Terms:** Small pets
Motel   only, $6 extra charge. **Facility:** 70 rooms. 2 one-bedroom suites with efficiency $80; 2 stories; exterior corri-
dors. **Dining:** Restaurant nearby. **All Rooms:** no utensils, extended cable TV. **Cards:** AE, CB, DI, DS, JC,
MC, VI. **Special Amenities: Free local telephone calls and free room upgrade (subject to availability with
advanced reservations).**   [icons]

COMFORT INN   **Phone:** (520)428-5851
◆◆   All Year   1P: $46-$75   2P: $48-$78   XP: $5   F18
Motel   **Location:** On US 70, 1.3 mi w of jct US 191. 1578 W Thatcher Blvd 85546. Fax: 520/428-4968. **Terms:** [CP]
meal plan; pets, in smoking rooms dep req. **Facility:** 44 rooms. 2 stories; exterior corridors; small heated pool.
Cards: AE, CB, DI, DS, JC, MC, VI.   [icons]

DAYS INN   **Phone:** (520)428-5000
◆◆◆   All Year   1P: $65-$120   2P: $80-$120   XP: $15   F18
Motel   **Location:** 0.5 mi e on US 70 and US 171. 520 E Hwy 70 85546. Fax: 520/428-7510. **Terms:** [CP] meal plan;
pets, $20 dep req. **Facility:** 43 rooms. 2 stories; exterior corridors. **All Rooms:** combo or shower baths.
Cards: AE, CB, DI, DS, MC, VI.   [icons]

RAMADA INN-SPA RESORT   **Phone:** (520)428-3200
◆◆◆   All Year   1P: $80-$150   2P: $95-$150   XP: $15   F18
Motor Inn   **Location:** 0.5 mi e on US 70 and US 191. 420 E Hwy 70 85546. Fax: 520/428-3288. **Terms:** [CP] meal plan;
pets, $20 dep req. **Facility:** 102 rooms. Spacious excellently furnished rooms, some with balcony. Smaller
rooms in original section. 1-3 stories; interior/exterior corridors; heated pool. **Services:** gift shop. **Cards:** AE, CB, DI, DS,
MC, VI.   [icons]

ST. JOHNS pop. 3,300

——— LODGING ———

SUPER 8   **Phone:** (520)337-2990
(AAA) [SAVE]   All Year   1P: $36-$40   2P: $38-$44   XP: $2   F17
◆◆   **Location:** Downtown. 75 E Commercial 85936 (PO Box 1920). Fax: 520/337-4487. **Terms:** 7 day cancellation
Motel   notice; pets, $10 dep req. **Facility:** 31 rooms. 2 stories; exterior corridors. **Cards:** AE, CB, DI, DS, MC, VI.
[icons]

ST. MICHAELS pop. 1,100

——— LODGING ———

NAVAJOLAND DAYS INN   **Phone:** (520)871-5690
◆◆◆   All Year   1P: $80-$110   2P: $90-$120   XP: $10   F17
Motel   **Location:** 1.5 mi w of jct SR 12 and SR 264. 392 W Hwy 264 86511 (PO Box 905). Fax: 520/871-5699.
Terms: [CP] meal plan; 10 day cancellation notice. **Facility:** 73 rooms. 2 stories; interior corridors; heated pool.
Services: gift shop. **All Rooms:** combo or shower baths. **Cards:** AE, CB, DI, DS, MC, VI.
[icons]

SCOTTSDALE —See Phoenix p. 266.

SEDONA pop. 7,700

—— LODGINGS ——

ADOBE HACIENDA
♦♦♦
Bed & Breakfast

All Year   2P: $139-$169   XP: $20   D
Phone: (520)284-2020

Location: 7 mi s on SR 179. 10 Rojo Dr 86351. **Terms:** [BP] meal plan; check-in 4 pm; 10 day cancellation notice; cancellation fee imposed; package plans. **Facility:** 5 rooms. Nicely decorated rooms, some with golf course views. TV's and coffeemakers avail upon request. Golf, horseback and health club packages avail. 1 story; exterior corridors; smoke free premises. **Cards:** AE, CB, DI, DS, MC, VI.

ADOBE VILLAGE & THE GRAHAM INN
AAA
♦♦♦♦
Bed & Breakfast

All Year   1P: $154-$354   2P: $169-$369   XP: $20
Phone: (520)284-1425

Location: 6 mi s of SR 89A, just w of SR 179 on Bell Rock Blvd; in Village of Oak Creek. 150 Canyon Circle Dr 86351. Fax: 520/284-0767. **Terms:** [BP] meal plan; 15 day cancellation notice; cancellation fee imposed. **Facility:** 10 rooms. Contemporary southwest inn with views of Red Rocks. Each room beautifully decorated in a different motif. Balconies. 4 luxury casitas with fireplace, waterfall shower, 2 person jacuzzi, bread maker. CD player in all rooms. 9 whirlpool rooms; 2 stories; interior corridors; smoke free premises; heated pool, whirlpool. **Services:** gift shop. Fee: massage. **Recreation:** bicycles. **All Rooms:** combo or shower baths. **Some Rooms:** safes. **Cards:** AE, DS, MC, VI. *(See color ad below)*

ALMA DE SEDONA INN
♦♦♦
Bed & Breakfast

All Year   1P: $149-$215   2P: $149-$215   XP: $25
Phone: (520)282-2737

Location: 3 mi w on SR 89A, then 3 blks nw via Tortilla Dr & Southwest Dr to Hozoni Dr. 50 Hozoni Dr 86336. Fax: 520/203-4141. **Terms:** [BP] meal plan; age restrictions may apply; 15 day cancellation notice; cancellation fee imposed. **Facility:** 12 rooms. All rooms with separate entrance, private patio or balcony and Red Rocks view. 2 stories; exterior corridors; smoke free premises; heated pool. **All Rooms:** combo or shower baths. **Cards:** AE, MC, VI. *(See color ad p 298)*

APPLE ORCHARD INN
Phone: (520)282-5328
All Year   1P: $135-$230   2P: $135-$230   XP: $20

Bed & Breakfast

Location: 656 Jordan Rd 86336. Fax: 520/204-0044. **Terms:** [BP] meal plan; 14 day cancellation notice; cancellation fee imposed; 2 night min stay, weekends in season. **Facility:** 7 rooms. Beautifully decorated contemporary decor. Two rooms with gas fireplaces. 6 whirlpool rooms, $145-$230; 2 stories; interior corridors; smoke free premises; whirlpool, cooling pool. **Services:** complimentary evening beverages. Fee: massage. **Cards:** MC, VI. *(See color ad below)*

A TERRITORIAL HOUSE OLD WEST BED & BREAKFAST
Phone: (520)204-2737
All Year   1P: $100-$150   2P: $115-$165   XP: $20   D

Bed & Breakfast

Location: 3.2 mi w of SR 179, 0.2 mi n on Dry Creek Rd, 0.4 mi w on Kachina Dr to Piki Dr. 65 Piki Dr 86336. Fax: 520/204-2230. **Terms:** [BP] meal plan; check-in 4 pm; 7 day cancellation notice; cancellation fee imposed. **Facility:** 4 rooms. Shaded grounds in a quiet secluded setting. Rooms decorated in a territorial decor. 1 two-bedroom unit. Whirlpool room, $165; 2 stories; interior corridors; designated smoking area; whirlpool. **All Rooms:** combo or shower baths. **Some Rooms:** color TV. **Cards:** AE, DS, MC, VI.

"A TOUCH OF SEDONA"-BED & BREAKFAST
Phone: (520)282-6462
All Year   1P: $99-$149   2P: $109-$159   XP: $15

Bed & Breakfast

Location: In uptown Sedona, just w of SR 89A. 595 Jordan Rd 86336. Fax: 520/282-1534. **Terms:** [BP] meal plan; check-in 4 pm; 10 day cancellation notice; cancellation fee imposed; 2 night min stay, weekends. **Facility:** 5 rooms. In a residential area. Nicely decorated rooms in a modern home. 24 hour beverages and snacks. Check in from 4 pm to 6 pm. 1 story; exterior corridors; smoke free premises. **All Rooms:** combo or shower baths. **Some Rooms:** efficiency. **Cards:** AE, DS, MC, VI.

A "TOUCH OF THE SOUTHWEST" SUITES
Phone: (520)282-4747
All Year   2P: $70-$125

Suite Motel

Location: In uptown Sedona, just w of SR 89A. 410 Jordan Rd 86336. Fax: 520/203-0507. **Terms:** Weekly rates avail; 3 day cancellation notice. **Facility:** 7 rooms. 2-room suites decorated in a Southwestern decor. 2 small rooms. 2 stories; exterior corridors; designated smoking area. **Some Rooms:** 6 kitchens, no utensils. **Cards:** AE, DS, MC, VI. **Special Amenities: Free local telephone calls and free room upgrade (subject to availability with advanced reservations).** *(See color ad p 306)*

BED & BREAKFAST AT SADDLE ROCK RANCH   **Phone:** 520/282-7640
◆◆◆   All Year   1P: $135-$170   2P: $140-$175   XP: $20
Historic Bed   **Location:** 1 mi w on SR 89A, s on Airport Rd to Valley View Dr to Saddle Rock Circle. 255 Rock Ridge Dr
& Breakfast   86336. Fax: 520/282-6829. **Terms:** [BP] meal plan; check-in 4 pm; 10 day cancellation notice; cancellation fee
imposed; 2 night min stay, in and off season. **Facility:** 3 rooms. Located on a hillside with Red Rock vistas.
Historic ranch home built in 1926. Has native rock and adobe walls, massive beamed ceilings and wood and flagstone floors.
1850's working music pump organ. All rooms with CD player. 1 story; interior/exterior corridors; smoke free premises.
Recreation: hiking trails.   ⊠ ☎ [VCR] 🖨 🖦 ⊠

BEST WESTERN ARROYO ROBLE HOTEL   **Phone:** (520)282-4001
AAA SAVE   2/12-10/31   1P: $99-$119   2P: $129   XP: $10   F12
◆◆◆   2/1-2/11 & 11/1-1/31   1P: $69-$89   2P: $109   XP: $10   F12
Motel   **Location:** 0.6 mi n of SR 179. 400 N Hwy 89A 86339 (PO Box NN). Fax: 520/282-4001. **Facility:** 66 rooms.
Units with balcony or patio. Most with view of canyon 1 cottage. 5 suites with wet bar, refrigerator, spa and fireplace. 8 two-bedroom units. 7 two-bedroom creekside condo units with kitchen, VCP, & gas fireplace, $250-
$275 for up to 6 persons; 9 whirlpool rooms, $179-$289; 5 stories; interior corridors; 2 pools, 1 heated indoor/outdoor, sauna,
steamroom, whirlpools. Fee: racquetball courts, 2 lighted tennis courts. **Cards:** AE, CB, DI, DS, MC, VI. **Special Amenities:**
Free local telephone calls and free newspaper. *(See color ad below)*
    🆂 ⊠ ⊠ 🎯 🖨 🖥 🖦 🛏 🖦 🖦 🕴 ⊠

BEST WESTERN INN OF SEDONA
Phone: (520)282-3072

(AAA) [SAVE]
3/17-6/1 & 9/1-1/31   1P: $125   2P: $125   XP: $10   F12
2/1-3/16 & 6/2-8/31   1P: $90   2P: $90   XP: $10   F12

◆◆◆
Motel
Location: 1.2 mi w of SR 179. 1200 W Hwy 89A 86336. Fax: 520/282-7218. **Terms:** [CP] meal plan; cancellation fee imposed; pets, $10 extra charge. **Facility:** 110 rooms. Hilltop location with red rock views. 10 rooms with gas fireplace & VCP, $130; whirlpool room; 3 stories, no elevator; exterior corridors; heated pool, whirlpool. **Cards:** AE, DI, DS, MC, VI. **Special Amenities: Free breakfast and free room upgrade (subject to availability with advanced reservations).** *(See color ad below)*

BOOTS & SADDLES BED & BREAKFAST
Phone: (520)282-1944

◆◆◆
Bed &
Breakfast
All Year   1P: $120-$195   2P: $135-$205   XP: $20   D
Location: 2900 Hopi Dr 86336. Fax: 520/204-2230. **Terms:** [BP] meal plan; check-in 4 pm; 7 day cancellation notice; cancellation fee imposed; 2 night min stay, weekends; package plans. **Facility:** 4 rooms. Casual Western decor. Check-in 4 pm-6 pm. 3 rooms with gas fireplace, whirlpool, patio or balcony. 1 standard room. 2 stories; interior/exterior corridors; designated smoking area. **All Rooms:** combo or shower baths. **Cards:** AE, DS, MC, VI.

BRIAR PATCH INN BED & BREAKFAST
Phone: 520/282-2342

◆◆◆
Cottage
All Year   2P: $149-$295   XP: $25   F4
Location: 3.5 mi n of SR 179, in Oak Creek Canyon. 3190 N Hwy 89A 86336. Fax: 520/282-2399. **Terms:** [BP] meal plan; 10 day cancellation notice; cancellation fee imposed; 2 night min stay, weekends. **Facility:** 17 rooms. On several acres of tree-shaded grounds located on Oak Creek. Comfortable, rustic cottages; many with fireplace. Cassette players and tapes in all rooms. Live classical music in morning 6 days week. Some Sunday concerts in summer. 2 two-bedroom units. 1 story; exterior corridors; designated smoking area. **Recreation:** swimming, fishing. **All Rooms:** combo or shower baths. **Some Rooms:** 4 efficiencies, 9 kitchens, color TV. **Cards:** AE, MC, VI.

CANYON VILLA BED & BREAKFAST INN
Phone: (520)284-1226

(AAA)
◆◆◆◆
Bed &
Breakfast
All Year   1P: $135-$215   2P: $145-$225   XP: $25   D
Location: 6 mi s of SR 89A, just off SR 179 on Bell Rock Blvd; in Village of Oak Creek. 125 Canyon Circle Dr 86351. Fax: 520/284-2114. **Terms:** [BP] meal plan; 14 day cancellation notice; cancellation fee imposed; 2 night min stay, weekends. **Facility:** 11 rooms. A luxurious inn with spectacular Red Rock views from common areas and guest quarters. Beautifully furnished, individually decorated rooms from Victorian to Sante Fe, 4 with gas fireplace. Balcony or patio. Check-in 3 pm-6 pm. 10 whirlpool rooms, $165-$225; 2 stories; interior corridors; smoke free premises; heated pool. **Services:** gift shop; complimentary evening beverages. **Cards:** AE, MC, VI. *(See color ad p 302)*

CASA SEDONA
Phone: (520)282-2938
All Year
1P: $125-$215
2P: $135-$225
XP: $25
Location: 3 mi w on SR 89A, then 3 blks nw via Tortilla Dr, Southwest Dr to Hozoni Dr. 55 Hozoni Dr 86336.
Fax: 520/282-2259. **Terms:** [BP] meal plan; 10 day cancellation notice; cancellation fee imposed. **Facility:** 16
rooms. Southwest style inn with quiet and relaxing atmosphere. Panoramic Red Rock views from a wooded
acre. Each room uniquely decorated. Gas fireplace in all rooms. Check in 3 pm-6 pm. TV/VCP avail upon re-
quest. 16 whirlpool rooms; 2 stories; smoke free premises; whirlpool.
Bed &
Brekfast
Recreation: hiking trails. **Some Rooms:** color TV. **Cards:** AE, MC, VI. *(See color ad below)*

CEDARS RESORT
Phone: 520/282-7010
All Year
1P: $66-$99
2P: $66-$99
XP: $10
Motel
Location: At jct SR 179. 20 W Hwy 89A 86339 (PO Box 292). Fax: 520/282-5372. **Facility:** 39 rooms. Most
units overlooking Oak Creek Canyon. Smoke free premises. Smokers required to pay $100 cash deposit, re-
fundable after room inspection. 1-2 stories; exterior corridors; smoke free premises; heated pool. **All Rooms:** combo or shower
baths. **Cards:** AE, CB, DI, DS, MC, VI.

COMFORT INN

2/1-11/30	1P: $88-$104	2P: $88-$104	XP: $10	F18
12/1-1/31	1P: $66-$84	2P: $66-$84	XP: $10	F18

Phone: (520)282-3132

Motel

Location: 0.8 mi s of jct SR 89A. 725 Hwy 179 86336 (PO Box 180, 86339). **Terms:** [CP] meal plan. **Facility:** 53 rooms. Santa Fe style building. Units and lobby decorated in southwest motif. 2 stories; interior corridors; heated pool, whirlpool. **Dining:** Restaurant nearby. **Cards:** AE, CB, DI, DS, MC, VI.

COZY CACTUS BED & BREAKFAST

Phone: (520)284-0082

3/1-7/5	1P: $95-$115	2P: $105-$125	XP: $15
9/1-1/31	1P: $85-$105	2P: $95-$125	XP: $15
2/1-2/29 & 7/6-8/31	1P: $85-$105	2P: $95-$115	XP: $15

Bed & Breakfast

Location: 6 mi s on SR 179, just w on Bell Rock Blvd; in Village of Oak Creek. 80 Canyon Circle Dr 86351. Fax: 520/284-4210. **Terms:** [BP] meal plan; check-in 4 pm; 14 day cancellation notice; cancellation fee imposed. **Facility:** 5 rooms. Cozy rooms in a ranch style home. Two pairs of rooms share a sitting room with fireplace and kitchen, 1 room in main house. 1 story; interior corridors; designated smoking area. **Cards:** AE, MC, VI. *(See color ad p. 460)*

CREEKSIDE INN AT SEDONA

Phone: (520)282-4992

2/1-5/31 & 8/16-11/14	1P: $175-$275	2P: $175-$275	XP: $25
6/1-8/15 & 11/15-1/31	1P: $125-$225	2P: $125-$225	XP: $25

Bed & Breakfast

Location: Just off Hwy 179, 0.8 mi e of Hwy 89A. 99 Coppercliffs Dr 86339 (PO Box 2161). Fax: 520/282-0091. **Terms:** [BP] meal plan; 10 day cancellation notice; cancellation fee imposed; 2 night min stay, weekends in season. **Facility:** 5 rooms. Elegantly decorated contemporary home with Victorian motif. Creek runs through rear yard. Check in between 4 pm and 6 pm. 1 story; interior/exterior corridors; designated smoking area. **Cards:** AE, DI, MC, VI.

DAYS INN

Phone: (520)282-9166

3/1-10/31	1P: $75-$110	2P: $75-$110
11/1-1/31	1P: $65-$100	2P: $65-$100
2/1-2/29	1P: $65-$92	2P: $65-$92

Motel

Location: 3 mi w of SR179. 2991 W Hwy 89A 86339 (PO Box 1589). Fax: 520/282-6208. **Terms:** [CP] meal plan; cancellation fee imposed. **Facility:** 66 rooms. Many units with balcony or patio. Modest landscaping attractively designed. $100 cash dep req for non-smoking room & refunded after room inspection; 10 one-bedroom suites with microwave, refrigerator & wet bar, $75-$97; 2 stories; exterior corridors; heated pool, whirlpool. **All Rooms:** combo or shower baths. **Cards:** AE, DI, DS, MC, VI. **Special Amenities:** Free breakfast and free local telephone calls.

DESERT QUAIL INN

Phone: (520)284-1433

All Year	1P: $64-$140	2P: $69-$149	XP: $10	F12

Motel

Location: 6.5 mi w of SR 179. 6626 Hwy 179 86351. Fax: 520/284-0487. **Terms:** Cancellation fee imposed; small pets only, $10 extra charge, prior notification req. **Facility:** 41 rooms. Across from factory outlet shopping. Rooms decorated with attractive southwest or lodgepole furniture. 9 rooms with gas fireplace. 4 whirlpool rooms, $89-$150; 2 stories; exterior corridors. **All Rooms:** combo or shower baths. **Cards:** AE, CB, DI, DS, MC, VI. **Special Amenities:** Free local telephone calls and free newspaper. *(See color ad below)*

DOUBLETREE SEDONA RESORT
◆◆◆
Suite Hotel

	1P:	2P:	XP:	
2/1-5/31 & 9/24-12/31	1P: $159-$179	2P: $159-$179	XP: $20	F18
1/1-1/31	1P: $119-$139	2P: $119-$139	XP: $20	F18
6/1-9/23	1P: $109-$119	2P: $109-$119	XP: $20	F18

Phone: (520)284-2949

Location: 7.3 mi s on SR 179; in the Village of Oak Creek. 90 Ridge Trail Dr 86351. Fax: 520/284-6940. **Terms:** 3 day cancellation notice; cancellation fee imposed. **Facility:** 225 rooms. Beautiful Red Rock views. All rooms with fireplaces and private patios. 3 stories; interior corridors; heated pool. Fee: 18 holes golf. **Services:** gift shop. **All Rooms:** safes, honor bars. **Cards:** AE, CB, DI, DS, JC, MC, VI. *(See ad p 269)*

ENCHANTMENT RESORT
(AAA)
◆◆◆◆
Resort

2/11-6/24 & 9/1-1/31	1P: $325-$950		XP: $40	F12
6/25-8/31	1P: $250-$895		XP: $40	F12
2/1-2/10	1P: $195-$755		XP: $40	F12

Phone: (520)282-2900

Location: 3 mi w on SR 89A, 5 mi n on Dry Creek Rd and Forest Rt 152C. 525 Boynton Canyon Rd 86336. Fax: 520/282-9249. **Terms:** Check-in 4 pm; 7 day cancellation notice; cancellation fee imposed; package plans. **Facility:** 222 rooms. Spectacular canyon location. Rooms and 1- to 2-bedroom suites in adobe style casitas. Many with gas fireplace. Patios. 2 two-bedroom guest rooms, $655-$950; 1 story; exterior corridors; putting green, croquet courts, pitch & putt golf course; 4 heated pools, saunas, whirlpools; 7 tennis courts, tennis instruction. **Dining:** Dining room, restaurant; 6:30 am-10 pm; Sun brunch 10:30 am-2:30 pm, reservations req; $8-$26; cocktails. **Services:** gift shop. Fee: massage. **Recreation:** in-room video games. Rental: bicycles. **All Rooms:** honor bars. **Some Rooms:** 45 efficiencies, 11 kitchens. **Cards:** AE, DS, MC, VI.

HAMPTON INN
(AAA) (SAVE)
◆◆◆
Motel

	1P:	2P:	XP:	
9/1-10/31	1P: $109	2P: $99-$109	XP: $10	F19
3/1-8/31	1P: $99	2P: $89-$99	XP: $10	F19
2/1-2/29 & 11/1-1/31	1P: $89	2P: $79-$89	XP: $10	F19

Phone: (520)282-4700

Location: 2 mi s of jct SR 179. 2655 W Hwy 89A 86336. Fax: 520/282-0004. **Terms:** [CP] meal plan; cancellation fee imposed. **Facility:** 56 rooms. 9 whirlpool rooms; 2 stories; interior corridors; heated pool, whirlpool. **Cards:** AE, CB, DI, DS, MC, VI. **Special Amenities:** Free breakfast and free local telephone calls. *(See color ad below)*

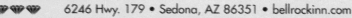

HAWTHORN SUITES LTD BELL ROCK INN

Motor Inn

9/1-1/31	2P: $59-$139	XP: $10 F
2/1-8/31	2P: $59-$99	XP: $10 F

Phone: (520)282-4161

Location: 6 mi s of SR 89A, in Village of Oak Creek. 6246 Hwy 179 86351. Fax: 520/284-0192. **Terms:** [BP] meal plan; cancellation fee imposed; package plans; pets, $10 extra charge, in designated rooms. **Facility:** 96 rooms. Southwestern atmosphere. Rooms and attractive mini-suites. 8 whirlpool rooms, $149; 1-2 stories; interior/exterior corridors; 2 heated pools, whirlpools, guest privileges at Sedona Ridge Spa. **Dining:** Restaurant; 7 am-2 & 5-9 pm, Fri & Sat-9:30 pm; $10-$18; cocktails. **Some Rooms:** safes. **Cards:** AE, MC, VI. **Special Amenities:** Free breakfast. *(See color ad p 304)*

HOLIDAY INN EXPRESS

◆ ◆ ◆
Motel

2/1-5/31 & 9/1-10/31	1P: $99-$129	2P: $99-$129	XP: $10 F17
6/1-8/31 & 11/1-1/31	1P: $89-$119	2P: $89-$119	XP: $10 F17

Phone: (520)284-0711

Location: 6 mi s of SR 89A, in Village of Oak Creek. 6175 Hwy 179 86351. Fax: 520/284-3760. **Terms:** [CP] meal plan; cancellation fee imposed. **Facility:** 104 rooms. 2 stories; interior corridors; heated pool. **Some Rooms:** Fee: VCR. **Cards:** AE, CB, DI, DS, JC, MC, VI. *(See color ad below)*

THE INN ON OAK CREEK

◆ ◆ ◆ ◆
Bed &
Breakfast

All Year	1P: $150-$240	2P: $165-$255	XP: $20

Phone: (520)282-7896

Location: 0.5 mi s of SR 89A. 556 Hwy 179 86336. Fax: 520/282-0696. **Terms:** [BP] meal plan; age restrictions may apply; 7 day cancellation notice; cancellation fee imposed. **Facility:** 11 rooms. Located on Oak Creek with creekside Park, exclusively for guests. Check-in 3-6 pm. Each room uniquely decorated in individual themes. All rooms with fireplaces. Walking distance to shops and galleries. 11 whirlpool rooms; suites, $235-$285; 2 stories; interior corridors; designated smoking area. **Dining:** Restaurant nearby. **Services:** complimentary evening beverages. **Recreation:** hiking trails, jogging, video library. **Cards:** AE, DS, MC, VI. *(See color ad below)*

IRIS GARDEN INN

Phone: (520)282-2552

AAA **SAVE**
◆◆◆
Motel

All Year   1P: $74-$135   2P: $74-$135   XP: $10   F12
Location: In uptown Sedona, just w of SR 89A. 390 Jordan Rd 86336. **Terms:** Weekly rates avail; 3 day cancellation notice; cancellation fee imposed. **Facility:** 8 rooms. 1 story; exterior corridors; designated smoking area; small whirlpool tub. **Dining:** Restaurant nearby. **All Rooms:** extended cable TV. **Some Rooms:** 2 kitchens. **Cards:** AE, DS, MC, VI. **Special Amenities:** Free local telephone calls. *(See color ad below)*

JUNIPINE RESORT

Phone: (520)282-3375

AAA **SAVE**
◆◆◆
Condominium

2/25-11/5   1P: $170-$240   2P: $220-$290   XP: $25   F12
2/1-2/24 & 11/6-1/31   1P: $120-$210   2P: $170-$260   XP: $25   F12
Location: 9 mi n of SR 179. 8351 N Hwy 89A 86336. Fax: 520/282-7402. **Terms:** Weekly & monthly rates avail; 7 day cancellation notice; cancellation fee imposed. **Facility:** 30 rooms. A heavily wooded location in Oak Creek Canyon. Spacious 1 and 2-bedroom condominiums with fireplace and outdoor deck. Some rooms with lofts. 4 whirlpool rooms, $155-$290; 1-2 stories; exterior corridors. **Dining:** Junipine Cafe, see separate listing. **All Rooms:** kitchens. **Cards:** AE, DI, DS, MC, VI. **Special Amenities:** Free newspaper and free room upgrade (subject to availability with advanced reservations).

KOKOPELLI INN

Phone: (520)284-1100

AAA **SAVE**
◆◆◆
Motel

All Year   1P: $65-$130   2P: $65-$130   XP: $10   F12
Location: 7 mi s of SR 89A, in Village of Oak Creek. 6465 Hwy 179 86351. Fax: 520/284-9460. **Terms:** 3 day cancellation notice; cancellation fee imposed. **Facility:** 42 rooms. 8 whirlpool rooms, $150-$160; 2 stories; exterior corridors; heated pool. **All Rooms:** safes. **Cards:** AE, CB, DI, DS, MC, VI. **Special Amenities:** Free breakfast and free newspaper. *(See color ad p 312)*

KOKOPELLI SUITES

Phone: (520)204-1146

AAA **SAVE**
◆◆◆
Motel

All Year   1P: $70-$160   2P: $70-$160   XP: $10   F12
Location: 3.5 mi w of SR 179, in West Sedona. 3119 W Hwy 89A 86336. Fax: 520/204-5851. **Terms:** [CP] meal plan; 3 day cancellation notice; cancellation fee imposed. **Facility:** 46 rooms. 15 whirlpool rooms, $160-$180; suites, $80-$209; exterior corridors; heated pool, whirlpool. **All Rooms:** extended cable TV, safes. **Cards:** AE, DI, DS, JC, MC, VI. **Special Amenities:** Free breakfast and free room upgrade (subject to availability with advanced reservations). *(See color ad p 307 & p 312)*

L'AUBERGE DE SEDONA RESORT

Phone: (520)282-1661

AAA **SAVE**
◆◆◆
Complex

2/28-11/26   1P: $230-$345   2P: $230-$345   XP: $20   F12
2/1-2/27 & 11/27-1/31   1P: $190-$275   2P: $190-$275   XP: $20   F12
Location: From jct SR 89A and SR 179, just n to L'Auberge Ln (e side of SR 89A), just ne down the hill. 301 L'Auberge Ln 86336 (PO Box B, 86339). Fax: 520/282-2885. **Terms:** 14 day cancellation notice; cancellation fee imposed; 2 night min stay, weekends. **Facility:** 59 rooms. In a secluded area along Oak Creek. Lodge and individual cottages on several acres of landscaped and tree-shaded grounds. King canopy beds in most rooms, fireplace in cottages. Country French decor. Rooms with TV have free movies. 2-bedroom cottage, $325-$385; 3 whirlpool rooms, $275-$435; 1-2 stories; interior/exterior corridors; designated smoking area; heated pool, whirlpool. **Dining:** Restaurant, see separate listing. **Services:** gift shop. **Some Rooms:** honor bars. **Cards:** AE, CB, DI, DS, MC, VI. *(See ad p 308)*

THE LODGE AT SEDONA
◆◆◆   All Year   2P: $125-$245   XP: $25   F5
Bed &   **Location:** 1.8 mi w of SR 179 on SR 89A, just s on Kallof PL. 125 Kallof Pl 86336. Fax: 520/204-2128.
Breakfast   **Terms:** [BP] meal plan; 14 day cancellation notice; 2 night min stay, weekends. **Facility:** 13 rooms. Ranch style
home on 2 1/2 acres with secluded privacy. Large comfortable common areas. Rooms individually decorated
and beautifully appointed. 6 with whirlpool tub, 1 with private whirlpool on deck. Some phones avail. 2 stories; interior/exterior
corridors; designated smoking area. **All Rooms:** combo or shower baths. **Cards:** CB, DS, MC, VI. *(See color ad below)*

Phone: (520)204-1942

LO LO MAI LODGE
◆◆   All Year   1P: $50-$90   2P: $55-$95
Motel   **Location:** 1.3 mi w of SR 179, off SR 89A. 50 Willow Way 86336. Fax: 520/282-0535. **Terms:** [CP] meal plan.
Facility: 12 rooms. Garden setting in residential area. Cozy rooms. Guests are permitted to use recreational
facilities at Lo Lo Mai Springs Outdoor Resort, 12 mi sw. 2 stories; exterior corridors; smoke free premises.
All Rooms: combo or shower baths. **Cards:** DS, MC, VI.

Phone: 520/282-2835

MATTERHORN LODGE
ⒶⒶⒶ   2/17-11/30   1P: $74-$104   2P: $74-$104   XP: $5   F5
◆◆◆   2/1-2/16 & 12/1-1/31   1P: $49-$79   2P: $49-$79   XP: $5   F5
Motel   **Location:** Just w of SR 89A in the Uptown Sedona shopping area. 230 Apple Ave 86336. Fax: 520/282-0727.
Terms: 48 day cancellation notice; small pets only, in designated rooms. **Facility:** 23 rooms. Patio or balcony,
overlooking Oak Creek Canyon. 2 stories; exterior corridors; mountain view; heated pool, whirlpool.
Dining: Restaurant nearby. **All Rooms:** extended cable TV. **Cards:** AE, MC, VI. *(See color ad p 309)*

Phone: (520)282-7176

ORCHARDS AT L'AUBERGE
◆◆◆   2/28-11/26   1P: $175-$195   2P: $175-$195   XP: $20   F12
Motor Inn   2/1-2/27 & 11/27-1/31   1P: $160-$180   2P: $160-$180   XP: $20   F12
Location: Just n of SR 179. 301 L'Auberge Ln 86336 (PO Box B, 86339). Fax: 520/282-2885. **Terms:** 14 day
cancellation notice; cancellation fee imposed. **Facility:** 41 rooms. In the uptown Sedona Shopping area. Attractively decorated
guest rooms overlooking Oak Creek Canyon. 3 stories; exterior corridors; designated smoking area; heated pool. **Cards:** AE,
CB, DI, DS, MC, VI.

Phone: (520)282-1661

POCO DIABLO RESORT

Resort
All Year   1P: $135-$245   2P: $135-$245   XP: $20   F16
Phone: (520)282-7333
Location: 2 mi s of SR 179. 1752 S Hwy 179 86339 (PO Box 1709). Fax: 520/282-2090. **Terms:** Cancellation fee imposed. **Facility:** 137 rooms. On several acres of grounds. 41 units with fireplace. Suites $240-$360.; 46 whirlpool rooms, $245; 1-2 stories; exterior corridors; 2 heated pools, whirlpools; playground. Fee: par-3 golf; racquetball court, 4 tennis courts (2 lighted). **Dining:** Dining room; 7 am-9 pm, Fri & Sat-10 pm; $13-$20; cocktails. **Services:** Fee: massage. **Recreation:** half court basketball, in-room video games. **Some Rooms:** Fee: VCR.
Cards: AE, CB, DI, JC, MC, VI. *(See color ad below)*

QUALITY INN-KING'S RANSOM
Motor Inn
3/2-5/31 & 9/2-1/31   1P: $79-$149   2P: $79-$149   XP: $10   F17
2/1-3/1 & 6/1-9/1   1P: $69-$129   2P: $69-$129   XP: $10   F17
Phone: (520)282-7151
Location: 0.8 mi s of SR 89A. 771 Hwy 179 86336 (PO Box 180). Fax: 520/282-5208. **Terms:** 14 day cancellation notice; pets, in smoking rooms only. **Facility:** 101 rooms. Most units with balcony or patio and view of red rock cliffs. Large courtyard area. 2 stories; interior/exterior corridors; heated pool, whirlpool. **Dining:** Restaurant; 7 am-10 pm; $7-$18; cocktails. **All Rooms:** combo or shower baths. **Cards:** AE, CB, DI, DS, MC, VI.
Special Amenities: Free local telephone calls and free newspaper. *(See color ad p 310)*

SEDONA'S Matterhorn LODGE

230 Apple Ave.
Sedona, AZ 86336

Approved

FOR ADVANCE RESERVATIONS:

TEL: (520) 282-7176
FAX: (520) 282-0727

e-mail: mhl@sedona.net

Visit our website at:
http://www.sedona.net/hotel/matterhorn

A Magnificent View From Every Room!

From our hilltop location, all of our rooms offer a large picture window and a private balcony or patio overlooking Sedona's spectacular red rock pinnacles. Conveniently located in the center of Sedona and within walking distance to shopping, restaurants, and recreational activities. Outdoor pool (seasonal) and year-round hot spa.

All rooms also feature the following:

♦ Non-smoking rooms available   ♦ 25" Cable TV
♦ In-room coffee and coffeemaker   ♦ Free local phone calls
♦ Convenient in-room refrigerators   ♦ Some pet rooms avail.
       ♦ Hairdryer and lighted makeup mirror

WINTER VACATION SPECIAL
Stay one night full price, get second night half price, or stay two nights full price, get third night free.

Sun-Thurs nights only, Dec. 4 - Feb. 8 (Holiday periods excluded)
Offer good only with AAA card.   See our listing for rates.

SEDONA'S FAMILY RESORT

- 22 acre resort nestled on famed Oak Creek
- 9 hole par 3 golf course
- Heated pool & spas
- Lighted tennis courts
- Fitness center
- Kids' game room

- Massage therapist
- T. Carl's Restaurant
- Jersey's Bar & Grill
- Refrigerator, wet bar and coffee maker in every room
- Specialty rooms with whirlpool tubs and/or fireplaces

25% OFF Listed Tourbook Rates
Available all year
for AAA members

POCO DIABLO RESORT

1752 S. Hwy 179 at the Gateway to Sedona
Reservations: (800) 528-4275
www.pocodiablo.com

Approved

ROSE TREE INN
Phone: (520)282-2065

	2/17-10/31	1P: $85-$135	2P: $85-$135	XP: $10	D16
	11/1-1/31	1P: $65-$135	2P: $85-$135	XP: $10	D16
	2/1-2/16	1P: $65-$135	2P: $65-$135	XP: $10	D16

Motel

Location: In Uptown Sedona, just w of SR 89A on Apple Ave. 376 Cedar St 86336. **Terms:** Weekly rates avail. **Facility:** 5 rooms. Quiet, garden setting. 2 blks from uptown Sedona shopping area. 1 story; exterior corridors; designated smoking area; whirlpool. **Recreation:** video library. **All Rooms:** shower baths. **Some Rooms:** 4 kitchens. **Cards:** AE, MC, VI. **Special Amenities: Free local telephone calls.** *(See color ad p 306)*

SEDONA MOTEL
Phone: 520/282-7187

| | 3/1-11/30 | 1P: $69-$88 | 2P: $69-$88 | XP: $6 |
| | 2/1-2/29 & 12/1-1/31 | 1P: $49-$69 | 2P: $49-$69 | XP: $6 |

Motel

Location: On SR 179, just s of jct SR 89A. 218 Hwy 179 86339 (PO Box 1450). **Terms:** Cancellation fee imposed. **Facility:** 13 rooms. Covered deck area with Red Rock views. 1 story; exterior corridors. **Dining:** Restaurant nearby. **All Rooms:** extended cable TV, safes. **Cards:** DS, MC, VI. *(See color ad below)*

SEDONA REAL INN
Phone: (520)282-1414

	3/10-11/25	1P: $120-$250	2P: $120-$250	XP: $10	F12
	11/26-1/31	1P: $89-$250	2P: $89-$250	XP: $10	F12
	2/1-3/9	1P: $89-$229	2P: $89-$229	XP: $10	F12

Motel

Location: 3.5 mi w of SR 179 on SR 89A. 95 Arroyo Pinon 86340 (PO Box 4161). Fax: 520/282-0900. **Terms:** [CP] meal plan; cancellation fee imposed. **Facility:** 47 rooms. All rooms with fireplace. 4 whirlpool rooms, $169-$195; exterior corridors; heated pool, whirlpool. **Dining:** Restaurant nearby. **Recreation:** Fee: video rentals. **Some Rooms:** kitchen. **Cards:** AE, DS, MC, VI. **Special Amenities: Free breakfast and free local telephone calls.** *(See color ad p 299)*

SEDONA SUPER 8
◆◆   3/1-11/30   1P: $77-$85   2P: $77-$85   XP: $6   Phone: (520)282-1533
Motel   12/1-1/31   1P: $52-$69   2P: $52-$69   XP: $6   F12
         2/1-2/29   1P: $52-$62   2P: $52-$62   XP: $6   F12
Location: 2.8 mi w of SR 179. 2545 W Hwy 89A 86336. Fax: 520/282-2033. **Facility:** 66 rooms. Lobby decorated in Southwest style. 3 stories; interior corridors; heated pool. **Some Rooms:** efficiency. **Cards:** AE, DI, DS, MC, VI.
(See color ad below)

SKY RANCH LODGE
△△△   All Year   1P: $75-$180   2P: $75-$180   XP: $8   Phone: 520/282-6400
◆◆◆   **Location:** 1 mi w of jct SR 89A and SR 179, 1 mi s on Airport Rd, on w side. Airport Rd 86339 (PO Box 2579).
Motel   Fax: 520/282-7682. **Terms:** Cancellation fee imposed; pets, $10 extra charge. **Facility:** 94 rooms. Beautifully
      landscaped grounds. On a mesa with several rooms overlooking the town. Some rooms with gas fireplace. 1-2
      stories; exterior corridors; heated pool, whirlpool. **Services:** gift shop. **All Rooms:** extended cable TV.
Some Rooms: 20 efficiencies. **Cards:** AE, MC, VI. *(See color ad below)*

SLIDE ROCK LODGE
Phone: (520)282-3531
◆
All Year   1P: $69-$99   2P: $69-$99
Motel   **Location:** 6 mi n of Hwy 179. 6401 N Hwy 89A 86336. Fax: 520/282-2850. **Terms:** 3 day cancellation notice; cancellation fee imposed; 2 night min stay, weekends. **Facility:** 20 rooms. Across the highway from Oak Creek. Some rooms with fireplace. 1 story; exterior corridors. **All Rooms:** shower baths. **Cards:** AE, DS, MC, VI.

(ASK) (SD) (X) (K) (Z)

SOUTHWEST INN AT SEDONA
Phone: (520)282-3344
(AAA) (SAVE)
All Year   1P: $109-$189   2P: $109-$189   XP: $10   F12
◆◆◆◆   **Location:** 3.5 mi sw on SR 89A, in West Sedona. 3250 W Hwy 89A 86336. Fax: 520/282-0267. **Terms:** [CP]
Motel   meal plan; cancellation fee imposed. **Facility:** 28 rooms. Attractive southwestern style rooms with gas fireplace. All with balcony or patio and Red Rock views. 6 whirlpool rooms, $135-$179; 2 stories; exterior corridors; smoke free premises; heated pool, whirlpool. **Cards:** AE, DS, MC, VI. **Special Amenities:** Free breakfast and free local telephone calls. *(See color ad p 299)*

(SD) (X) (📷) (VCR) (🛏) (💻) (🍽) (🛁) (🏊)

VILLAGE LODGE
Phone: (520)284-3626
(AAA) (SAVE)
All Year   1P: $45-$49   2P: $45-$49
◆◆   **Location:** 6 mi s on SR 179, just w of Bell Rock Blvd; in Village of Oak Creek. 78 Bell Rock Blvd 86351 (105
Motel   Bell Rock Plaza). Fax: 520/284-3629. **Terms:** 3 day cancellation notice; small pets only, in designated rooms. **Facility:** 17 rooms. 5 one-bedroom suites with kitchenette & fireplace, $79-$89; 4 whirlpool rooms, $59; suites, $79-$89; 2 stories; interior/exterior corridors; designated smoking area. **Cards:** AE, CB, DI, DS, JC, MC, VI. **Special Amenities:** Free local telephone calls.

(SD) (🐾) (X) (🛏) (💻) (🍽) (🛁) (DATA PORT)

WILDFLOWER INN
Phone: (520)284-3937
(AAA) (SAVE)
All Year   1P: $60-$120   2P: $60-$120   XP: $10   F12
◆◆◆   **Location:** 6 mi s of SR 89A, in Village of Oak Creek. 6086 Hwy 179 86351. Fax: 520/282-9378. **Facility:** 29
Motel   rooms. 2 stories; exterior corridors. **Dining:** Restaurant nearby. **Cards:** AE, DI, DS, MC, VI. **Special Amenities:** Early check-in/late check-out and free room upgrade (subject to availability with advanced reservations). IMA. *(See color ad below)*

(SD) (🍴) (🛌) (X) (🛏) (💻) (🛁)

WISHING WELL BED & BREAKFAST
Phone: (520)282-4914
◆◆◆
All Year   1P: $145-$160   2P: $155-$170
Bed &   **Location:** 0.8 mi from jct SR 179, on top of hill at the end of the driveway. 995 N Hwy 89A 86336.
Breakfast   Fax: 520/204-9766. **Terms:** [CP] meal plan; age restrictions may apply. **Facility:** 5 rooms. Beautifully decorated rooms, all with fireplace. 4 rooms with private whirlpool on patio. Check-in 3-6 pm. 2 stories; interior corridors; smoke free premises. **All Rooms:** shower baths. **Cards:** AE, DS, MC, VI.

(X) (Z) (🛁)

The following lodging was either not inspected or did not
meet AAA rating requirements but is listed for your information only.

A SUNSET CHATEAU B&B INN
Phone: 520/282-2644
(fyi)
All Year   1P: $110-$125   2P: $110-$125   XP: $10   F12
Bed &   Too new to rate, opening scheduled for November 1999. **Location:** 2.1 mi w of jct SR 89A & 179. 665 S Sunset
Breakfast   Dr 86336. Fax: 520/282-9121. **Terms:** [BP] meal plan; age restrictions may apply; 10 day cancellation notice; cancellation fee imposed. **Amenities:** 22 rooms, radios, coffeemakers, microwaves, refrigerators. **Cards:** AE, MC, VI.

─── RESTAURANTS ───

COWBOY CLUB　　　　　　　　Lunch: $8-$10　　　　　　Dinner: $12-$20　　　　Phone: 520/282-4200
Ⓐ　　　　**Location:** From jct SR 89A and SR 179, 0.5 mi n on SR 89A. 241 N Hwy 89A 86336. **Hours:** 11 am-4 &
◆◆　　　5-10 pm. Closed: 12/25. **Reservations:** accepted. **Features:** casual dress; children's menu; cocktails &
American　　lounge; street parking; a la carte. Informal western atmosphere. Selection of southwestern food. Many
　　　　　entrees with buffalo meat. **Cards:** AE, MC, VI.　　　　　　　　　　　　　　　　　　　　☒

DAHL & DILUCA RISTORANTE ITALIANO　　　　　　Dinner: $10-$22　　　　　Phone: 520/282-5219
◆◆◆　　**Location:** 3 mi w of SR 179, in W Sedona. 2321 Hwy 89A 86336. **Hours:** 5 pm-10 pm. Closed major
Italian　　holidays. **Reservations:** suggested. **Features:** casual dress; cocktails. Excellent selection of traditional
　　　　　Italian entrees. Entertainment on weekends. Busy, but friendly atmosphere. **Cards:** AE, DI, DS, MC, VI. ☒

DYLAN'S　　　　　　　　　　Lunch: $7-$14　　　　　　Dinner: $8-$21　　　　Phone: 520/282-7930
◆◆　　　**Location:** In West Sedona, 1 mi w of SR 179. 1405 W Highway 89A 86336. **Hours:** 11 am-9:30 pm. Closed:
American　12/25. **Features:** casual dress; early bird specials; health conscious menu; carryout; cocktails & lounge;
　　　　　minimum charge-$10. Nice selection of meat, poultry and pasta as well as a number of vegetarian
selections. **Cards:** MC, VI.　　　　　　　　　　　　　　　　　　　　　　　　　　　　　　　☒

THE HEARTLINE CAFE　　　　　Lunch: $9-$14　　　　　Dinner: $17-$29　　　Phone: 520/282-0785
◆◆◆　　**Location:** 1.4 mi w of SR 179. 1610 W Hwy 89A 86336. **Hours:** 11:30 am-3 & 5-9:30 pm, Fri & Sat-9:45
American　pm, Sun 5 pm-8:45 pm. Closed: 1/1. **Reservations:** suggested. **Features:** casual dress; carryout; cocktails.
　　　　　Imaginative selection of Southwestern cuisine. Extensive wine list. Smoke free premises. **Cards:** AE, DI, DS,
MC, VI.　　　　　　　　　　　　　　　　　　　　　　　　　　　　　　　　　　　　　　　☒

JUDI'S RESTAURANT　　　　　Lunch: $9-$14　　　　　Dinner: $14-$23　　　Phone: 520/282-4449
◆◆　　　**Location:** 1 mi w on ne corner of SR 89A and Soldier's Pass Rd. 40 Soldier's Pass Rd 86336. **Hours:** 11:30
American　am-9 pm, Sun from 4:30 pm. Closed major holidays. **Reservations:** suggested. **Features:** casual dress;
　　　　　early bird specials; carryout; cocktails & lounge. Comfortable, cozy atmosphere. Menu features chicken,
pasta, seafood and steak. Barbecue baby back ribs a specialty. **Cards:** AE, DI, MC, VI.　　　　　☒

JUNIPINE CAFE　　　　　　　Lunch: $6-$11　　　　　　Dinner: $9-$18　　　Phone: 520/282-7402
◆◆　　　**Location:** 9 mi n in Junipine Resort. 8351 N Hwy 89A 86336. **Hours:** 7:30 am-9 pm.
American　**Reservations:** suggested. **Features:** casual dress; Sunday brunch; children's menu; carryout; cocktails.
　　　　　Cozy restaurant serving nice variety of beef, chicken and pasta. Outdoor dining avail, weather permitting.
Mexican Fiesta dinner on Thurs evening. **Cards:** AE, CB, DI, DS, MC, VI.　　　　　　　　　　☒

L'AUBERGE DE SEDONA RESTAURANT　Lunch: $9-$22　　Dinner: $24-$49　　Phone: 520/282-7131
◆◆◆◆　**Location:** From jct SR 89A and SR 179, just n to L'Auberge Ln (e side of SR 89A), then just ne down the
French　　hill, at L'Auberge de Sedona Resort. 301 L'Auberge Ln 86339. **Hours:** 7-10:30 am, 11:30-2:30 & 5:30-10 pm.
　　　　　Reservations: suggested. **Features:** semi-formal attire; Sunday brunch; cocktails & lounge; a la carte.
Beautiful country French restaurant with elegant surroundings and formal service. Luncheon selection of salad and entrees.
A la carte or prix fixe 6-course meal for dinner. Attractive outdoor creekside dining, weather permitting. Smoke free premises.
Cards: AE, CB, DI, DS, MC, VI.

LOTUS GARDEN　　　　　　　Lunch: $5-$12　　　　　　Dinner: $6-$16　　　Phone: 520/282-3118
◆◆　　　**Location:** 2 mi w on SR 89A, in West Sedona at Bashas' Shopping Center. 164-H Coffee Pot Dr 86336.
Chinese　**Hours:** 11 am-9:30 pm, Fri & Sat-10 pm. Closed: 11/23. **Reservations:** suggested. **Features:** casual dress;
　　　　　carryout; cocktails. An attractive restaurant serving a large selection of a la carte as well as complete
luncheons and dinners. **Cards:** AE, DI, DS, MC, VI.　　　　　　　　　　　　　　　　　　　☒

PIETROS　　　　　　　　　　　　　　Dinner: $13-$24　　　　　　　　　Phone: 520/282-2525
Ⓐ　　　　**Location:** 2.8 mi w of SR 179. 2445 W Hwy 89A 86336. **Hours:** 5:30 pm-9:30 pm. Closed: 12/25.
　　　　　Reservations: suggested. **Features:** casual dress; cocktails. Casual bistro atmosphere serving classic
◆◆◆　　Italian cuisine with a selection of pasta, chicken, seafood, veal and rack of lamb. Children under 6 years old
Italian　　not permitted. Smoke free premises. **Cards:** AE, CB, DI, DS, MC, VI.　　　　　　　　　　☒

RENE AT TLAQUEPAQUE　　　　Lunch: $8-$13　　　　　Dinner: $17-$27　　　Phone: 520/282-9225
Ⓐ　　　　**Location:** On SR 179, just s of jct SR 89A. 86336. **Hours:** 11:30 am-2:30 & 5:30-8:30 pm, Fri & Sat-9 pm.
◆◆◆　　Closed: 11/23 & 12/25. **Reservations:** suggested. **Features:** casual dress; cocktails & lounge; a la carte.
Continental　Elegant dining featuring Continental and American favorites. Smoke free premises. **Cards:** AE, MC, VI. ☒

SASAKI JAPANESE CUISINE & SUSHI BAR　　　Lunch: $6-$10　　Dinner: $11-$23　　Phone: 520/284-1757
Ⓐ　　　　**Location:** 6 mi s of SR 89A, just w of SR 179 on Bell Rock Blvd, in Village of Oak Creek. 65 Bell Rock Blvd
　　　　　86351. **Hours:** 11:30 am-1:30 & 5-9:30 pm. Closed: Tues for lunch. **Reservations:** suggested.
◆◆◆　　**Features:** cocktails & lounge. Contemporary, tasteful Oriental decor. Large selection of authentic Japanese
Specialty　cuisine. Smoke free premises. **Cards:** AE, MC, VI.　　　　　　　　　　　　　　　　　☒

SEDONA SWISS RESTAURANT　　Lunch: $5-$8　　　　　Dinner: $11-$23　　　Phone: 520/282-7959
◆◆◆　　**Location:** In uptown Sedona, just w of SR 89A. 350 Jordan Rd 86336. **Hours:** 11 am-2 & 5:30-9:30 pm.
French　　Closed: Sun & 3 weeks in Jan. **Reservations:** suggested. **Features:** casual dress; children's menu;
　　　　　cocktails. A delightful restaurant serving Swiss-French cuisine. Indoor and outdoor patio dining. Also adjacent
bakery featuring homemade pastries and candies. **Cards:** MC, VI.　　　　　　　　　　　　　☒

SHUGRUE'S
◆ ◆
American
Lunch: $7-$12   **Dinner:** $11-$24   **Phone:** 520/282-2943
Location: 2.5 mi w of SR 179. 2250 W Hwy 89A 86336. **Hours:** 11:30 am-3 & 5-9 pm, Fri & Sat-10 pm, Sun from 10 am. Closed: 12/25. **Reservations:** suggested. **Features:** children's menu; health conscious dinner; carryout; cocktails & lounge. Warm, modern Arizona decor. Nice variety of entrees in casual atmosphere.
Cards: AE, MC, VI.   ☒

SHUGRUE'S HILLSIDE GRILL
◆ ◆ ◆
American
Lunch: $7-$14   **Dinner:** $15-$25   **Phone:** 520/282-5300
Location: 0.8 mi s on SR 179, in Hillside Courtyard and Marketplace. 671 Hwy 179 86336. **Hours:** 11:30 am-3 & 5-9:30 pm, Fri-Sun 11:30 am-3 & 5-9 pm. Closed: 12/25. **Reservations:** suggested.
Features: casual dress; children's menu; early bird specials; health conscious menu; carryout; cocktails & lounge. Hillside location with large picture windows looking towards the mountains. Dining on outside deck in warm weather. Specialty is seafood. Also a selection of beef, lamb and chicken. **Cards:** AE, MC, VI.   ☒

TAKASHI JAPANESE RESTAURANT
◆ ◆
Specialty
Lunch: $9-$15   **Dinner:** $12-$21   **Phone:** 520/282-2334
Location: In downtown Sedona, 0.4 mi e of SR 89A. 465 Jordan Rd 86336. **Hours:** 11:30 am-1:30 & 5 pm. Closed: 11/23, 12/25 & Mon. **Reservations:** suggested. **Features:** casual dress. Excellent selection of Japanese appetizers, entrees and sushi. Attractive Japanese decor. Sakes and Japanese beer. Outdoor dining weather permitting. Smoke free premises. **Cards:** AE, CB, DI, MC, VI.   ☒

WILD TOUCAN RESTAURANT
◆
Mexican
Lunch: $6-$14   **Dinner:** $8-$20   **Phone:** 520/284-1604
Location: 6.2 mi s of SR 89A, in Village of Oak Creek. 6376 Hwy 179 86351. **Hours:** 11 am-9 pm, Fri & Sat-10 pm. Closed: 11/23 & 12/25. **Features:** casual dress; children's menu; senior's menu; carryout; cocktails & lounge. Colorful decor. Features a variety of Mexican and American cuisine. Outdoor patio dining avail. **Cards:** AE, DS, MC, VI.   ☒

SELIGMAN pop. 700

——— LODGING ———

HISTORIC ROUTE 66 MOTEL
◆
Motel
| | All Year | 1P: $47-$57 | 2P: $57-$67 | XP: $10 | F12 |

Phone: 520/422-3204
Location: I-40, exit 121. 500 W Hwy 66 86337 (PO Box 185). Fax: 520/422-3581. **Terms:** Cancellation fee imposed; pets, $25 dep req. **Facility:** 16 rooms. 1 story; exterior corridors. **All Rooms:** combo or shower baths.
Cards: AE, CB, DI, DS, MC, VI.   (ASK) ⓢ ⊟ ☒ 🎥 📞 💻

SHOW LOW pop. 5,000

——— LODGINGS ———

BEST WESTERN PAINT PONY LODGE
AAA SAVE
◆ ◆ ◆
Motor Inn
| | 2/1-4/30 & 10/1-1/31 | 1P: $64 | 2P: $79 | XP: $5 | F12 |
| | 5/1-9/30 | 1P: $69 | 2P: $79 | XP: $5 | F12 |

Phone: (520)537-5773
Location: 1 mi w on SR 60 and 260. 581 W Deuce of Clubs 85901. Fax: 520/537-5766. **Terms:** [CP] meal plan; 3 day cancellation notice. **Facility:** 50 rooms. Attractively decorated. Some rooms with fireplace. Whirlpool room, $89-$130; 2 stories; exterior corridors. **Dining:** Restaurant; 11 am-2 & 5-9 pm; $12-$24; cocktails.
Cards: AE, CB, DI, DS, JC, MC, VI. **Special Amenities:** Free breakfast and free local telephone calls.
ⓢ 🍴 🍸 🛁 ☒ 🎥 📠 💻 🖥 🛏 📶

DAYS INN
AAA SAVE
◆ ◆
Motor Inn
| | 5/16-9/6 | 1P: $57 | 2P: $65 | XP: $10 | F12 |
| | 2/1-5/15 & 9/7-1/31 | 1P: $54 | 2P: $59 | XP: $10 | F12 |

Phone: (520)537-4356
Location: 1.3 mi w on US 60 and SR 260. 480 W Deuce of Clubs Ave 85901. Fax: 520/537-8692. **Terms:** [BP] meal plan; small pets only, $5 extra charge. **Facility:** 122 rooms. 2 stories; interior/exterior corridors; heated pool, enclosed in winter. **Dining:** Restaurant; 6 am-9 pm, Fri & Sat to 11 pm; $6-$9.
All Rooms: combo or shower baths. **Cards:** AE, CB, DI, DS, MC, VI. **Special Amenities:** Free breakfast and free local telephone calls.
ⓢ ⊟ 🍴 🍸 🛁 ♿ ☒ 🎥 📠 🖥 🛏 📶

HOLIDAY INN EXPRESS
AAA SAVE
◆ ◆ ◆
Motel
	4/16-10/31	1P: $69-$99			
	11/1-1/31	1P: $59-$89			
	2/1-4/15	1P: $59-$79			

Phone: (520)537-5115
Location: 0.8 mi w on US 60 and SR 260. 151 W Deuce of Clubs Ave 85901. Fax: 520/537-2929. **Terms:** [ECP] meal plan. **Facility:** 40 rooms. 15 whirlpool rooms, $69-$119; 2 stories; interior corridors; heated pool, whirlpool. **All Rooms:** extended cable TV. **Cards:** AE, DI, DS, JC, MC, VI. **Special Amenities:** Early check-in/late check-out and free breakfast.
ⓢ 🐾 🔒 ☒ 🎥 📠 💻 🖥 🛏 📶 🚗 🏋

K C MOTEL
AAA SAVE
◆ ◆
Motel
| | 5/13-10/16 | 1P: $55-$75 | 2P: $58-$78 | | |
| | 2/1-5/12 & 10/17-1/31 | 1P: $48-$65 | 2P: $52-$68 | | |

Phone: (520)537-4433
Location: 0.8 mi w on US 60 and SR 260. 60 W Deuce of Clubs Ave 85901 (PO Box 175). Fax: 520/537-0106. **Facility:** 35 rooms. Attractively furnished units. Whirlpool room, $95-$125; 1-2 stories; exterior corridors; indoor whirlpool. **Dining:** Restaurant nearby. **All Rooms:** extended cable TV. **Cards:** AE, DI, DS, MC, VI.
🛗 ☒ 🎥 📠 💻 🛏 📶

KIVA MOTEL
Phone: (520)537-4542
AAA SAVE
| | 4/1-9/30 | 1P: $40-$53 | 2P: $46-$59 | XP: $4 | F6 |
| | 2/1-3/31 & 10/1-1/31 | 1P: $36-$40 | 2P: $42 | XP: $6 | F6 |

◆◆
Motel
Location: 0.5 mi w on US 60 and SR 260. 261 E Deuce of Clubs Ave 85901. Fax: 520/537-1024. **Terms:** Pets, $5 extra charge, dogs only. **Facility:** 20 rooms. Close to shopping center. Cozy to large, nicely decorated rooms. Microwave on premises. 3 two-bedroom units. 1 story; exterior corridors; sauna, indoor whirlpool. **Dining:** Restaurant nearby. **Recreation:** exercise equipment. **All Rooms:** combo or shower baths, extended cable TV. **Cards:** AE, CB, DI, DS, MC, VI. **Special Amenities:** Free local telephone calls.

MOTEL 6
Phone: 520/537-7694
◆
Motel
| | 4/1-1/31 | 1P: $46-$56 | 2P: $52-$62 | XP: $3 | F17 |
| | 2/1-3/31 | 1P: $35-$45 | 2P: $41-$51 | XP: $3 | F17 |

Location: US 60, 0.5 mi e of jct SR 260. 1941 E Deuce of Clubs Ave 85901. Fax: 520/537-7694. **Terms:** Pets, $20 dep req. **Facility:** 42 rooms. Some small rooms. 2 stories; exterior corridors. **Cards:** AE, CB, DI, DS, MC, VI.

SLEEP INN-SHOW LOW
Phone: (520)532-7323
◆◆
Motel
| | 2/1-9/30 & 12/1-1/31 | 1P: $57-$135 | 2P: $62-$165 | XP: $10 | F18 |
| | 10/1-11/30 | 1P: $52-$130 | 2P: $57-$165 | XP: $10 | F18 |

Location: 0.5 mi w on Hwy 260. 1751 W Deuce of Clubs Dr 85901. Fax: 520/527-3304. **Terms:** [ECP] meal plan; 10 day cancellation notice. **Facility:** 70 rooms. 3 stories; interior corridors; heated pool. **All Rooms:** combo or shower baths. **Some Rooms:** Fee: VCR. **Cards:** AE, DI, DS, JC, MC, VI.

SNOWY RIVER MOTEL
Phone: (520)537-2926
AAA
| | All Year | 1P: $34 | 2P: $39 | XP: $4 | F5 |

◆
Motel
Location: US 60, just e of jct SR 260. 1640 E Deuce of Clubs Ave 85901. Fax: 520/537-4577. **Terms:** Pets, $5 extra charge, small dogs only. **Facility:** 17 rooms. Small units. 1 story; exterior corridors. **All Rooms:** combo or shower baths, extended cable TV. **Cards:** AE, DI, DS, MC, VI.

SIERRA VISTA pop. 33,000

———— LODGINGS ————

BEST WESTERN MISSION INN
Phone: (520)458-8500
AAA SAVE
| | All Year | 1P: $57-$67 | 2P: $61-$77 | XP: $4 | F18 |

◆◆◆
Motel
Location: Just w of jct SR 90 and 92. 3460 E Fry Blvd 85635. Fax: 520/459-3070. **Terms:** [CP] meal plan; small pets only, one per room. **Facility:** 40 rooms. 2 stories; exterior corridors; pool open Mar-Nov. **All Rooms:** extended cable TV. **Cards:** AE, CB, DI, DS, MC, VI. **Special Amenities:** Free breakfast and free local telephone calls.

GATEWAY STUDIO SUITES
Phone: 520/458-5555
◆◆◆
Motel
| | All Year | 1P: $60 | | XP: $10 | |

Location: Just s of Fry Ave and se of main gate to Ft Hauchula. 203 S Garden Ave 85635. Fax: 520/458-2129. **Terms:** 5 day cancellation notice. **Facility:** 83 rooms. 3 stories; interior corridors; heated pool. **All Rooms:** efficiencies. **Cards:** AE, CB, DI, DS, MC, VI.

SIERRA SUITES
Phone: (520)459-4221
◆◆◆
Motel
| | All Year | 1P: $79 | 2P: $79 | XP: $5 | F12 |

Location: 2.5 mi w of jct SR 90 and SR 92. 391 E Fry Blvd 85635. Fax: 520/459-8449. **Terms:** [CP] meal plan; small pets only, $25 non-refundable dep req. **Facility:** 100 rooms. Most rooms surround small courtyards. 2 stories; exterior corridors; heated pool. **Cards:** AE, DI, DS, MC, VI. *(See color ad below)*

SUN CANYON INN
Phone: (520)459-0610
(AAA) (SAVE)   All Year   1P: $55   XP: $10
◆ ◆
Motor Inn   **Location:** On Garden Ave; just n of Fry Blvd, just e of main gate of Fort Hauchuca. 260 N Garden Ave 85635. Fax: 520/458-5178. **Terms:** [BP] meal plan; 5 day cancellation notice. **Facility:** 80 rooms. Whirlpool room, $100; 4 stories; interior corridors; heated pool, whirlpool. **Dining:** Restaurant; 4:30 pm-9:30 pm; $7-$12. **All Rooms:** combo or shower baths, extended cable TV. **Cards:** AE, CB, DI, DS, MC, VI. **Special Amenities: Free breakfast and free newspaper.**   (icons)

SUPER 8 MOTEL
Phone: 520/459-5380
◆ ◆   4/1-1/31   1P: $49-$69   2P: $54-$69   XP: $5   F12
Motel   2/1-3/31   1P: $45-$65   2P: $50-$65   XP: $5   F12
Location: Just e of main entrance to Fort Huachuca. 100 Fab Ave 85635. Fax: 520/459-6052. **Terms:** [CP] meal plan; 15 day cancellation notice; small pets only, $10 extra charge, dogs only. **Facility:** 52 rooms. 2 stories; exterior corridors. **Cards:** AE, CB, DI, DS, MC, VI.   (icons)

THUNDER MOUNTAIN INN
Phone: (520)458-7900
(AAA) (SAVE)   All Year   1P: $55-$70   2P: $60-$75   XP: $5   F18
◆ ◆ ◆
Motor Inn   **Location:** SR 92, 1 mi s of jct SR 90. 1631 S Hwy 92 85635. Fax: 520/458-7900. **Terms:** Package plans; pets, $20 dep req. **Facility:** 102 rooms. Five miles e of Fort Huachuca. 2 stories; interior corridors; whirlpool. **Dining:** Restaurant; 6:30 am-9 pm; $8-$20; cocktails. **All Rooms:** extended cable TV. **Some Rooms:** Fee: VCR. **Cards:** AE, DI, DS, MC, VI. **Special Amenities:** Free local telephone calls and preferred room (subject to availability with advanced reservations).   (icons)

WESTERN MOTEL
Phone: (520)458-4303
(AAA) (SAVE)   All Year   1P: $30-$35   2P: $35-$38   XP: $5   F12
◆
Motel   **Location:** 0.4 mi e of main entrance to Fort Huachuca. 43 W Fry Blvd 85635. Fax: 520/459-4197. **Terms:** 5 day cancellation notice. **Facility:** 25 rooms. Some small rooms. 1 story; exterior corridors. **All Rooms:** extended cable TV. **Cards:** AE, CB, DI, DS, MC, VI. **Special Amenities: Early check-in/late check-out and free local telephone calls.**   (icons)

WINDEMERE HOTEL & CONFERENCE CENTER
Phone: (520)459-5900
(AAA) (SAVE)   All Year   1P: $78-$86   2P: $86   XP: $8   F17
◆ ◆ ◆
Motor Inn   **Location:** SR 92, 1.5 mi s of jct SR 90. 2047 S Hwy 92 85635. Fax: 520/458-1347. **Terms:** [BP] meal plan; check-in 4 pm; 3 day cancellation notice; pets, $50 dep req. **Facility:** 149 rooms. Large rooms. Attractive public areas. 3 stories; interior corridors; heated pool, whirlpool. **Dining:** Schooners Restaurant, see separate listing. **Services:** complimentary evening beverages. **Recreation:** in-room video games. **All Rooms:** extended cable TV. **Cards:** AE, CB, DI, DS, JC, MC, VI. **Special Amenities: Free breakfast and free local telephone calls.**   (icons)

──────── RESTAURANTS ────────

THE GRILLE AT PUEBLO DEL SOL COUNTRY CLUB
Lunch: $5-$9   **Dinner:** $11-$21   **Phone:** 520/378-2476
◆ ◆ ◆
American   **Location:** From jct SR 90, take SR 92 s 2.4 mi, then 0.5 mi w. 2770 St Andrews Dr 85635. **Hours:** 7 am-8:30 pm. Closed: 12/25. **Reservations:** suggested. **Features:** Sunday brunch; cocktails & lounge. Attractive Southwestern decor with view of golf course. Smoke free premises. **Cards:** AE, CB, DI, DS, MC, VI.   (icon)

THE MESQUITE TREE RESTAURANT
Dinner: $10-$16   **Phone:** 520/378-2758
◆ ◆
American   **Location:** SR 92, 7 mi s of jct SR 90. 6398 S Hwy 92 85635. **Hours:** 5-9 pm, Sun & Mon-8 pm. Closed major holidays. **Reservations:** suggested. **Features:** cocktails & lounge. Casual dining; nice selection of steaks, prime rib, barbecue, seafood, chicken and pasta. Patio dining, weather permitting. **Cards:** AE, DS, MC, VI.   (icon)

SCHOONERS RESTAURANT
Lunch: $5-$9   **Dinner:** $7-$17   **Phone:** 520/459-6870
◆ ◆
American   **Location:** SR 92, 1.5 mi s of jct SR 90; in Windemere Hotel and Conference Center. 2047 S Hwy 92 85635. **Hours:** 6 am-2 & 5-9 pm. Closed: Sun for dinner. **Features:** casual dress; Sunday brunch; children's menu; senior's menu; cocktails & lounge. A contemporary, colorfully decorated dining room. Lunch buffet also available. Smoke free premises. **Cards:** AE, CB, DI, DS, JC, MC, VI.   (icon)

SOAP CREEK

──────── LODGING ────────

CLIFF DWELLERS LODGE
Phone: (520)355-2228
(AAA) (SAVE)   5/1-9/30   1P: $60-$80   2P: $60-$80   XP: $7
◆   4/1-4/30   1P: $50-$70   2P: $50-$70   XP: $7
Motor Inn   2/1-3/31 & 10/1-1/31   1P: $40-$60   2P: $40-$60   XP: $7
Location: 9 mi w of Navajo Bridge on US 89A, towards North Rim. 86036 (HC 67-30, Hwy 89A, MARBLE CANYON). Fax: 520/355-2229. **Terms:** Cancellation fee imposed. **Facility:** 21 rooms. At base of Vermillion Cliffs. Small, rustic rooms in original stone buildings to modern motel units in new section. Convenience store and gas station. Exterior corridors. **Dining:** Restaurant; 6 am-9 pm; $8-$20; cocktails. **All Rooms:** combo or shower baths. **Cards:** DS, MC, VI. *(See color ad p 195)*   (icons)

SONOITA pop. 100

——— RESTAURANTS ———

ER PASTARO
◆ ◆ ◆
Italian
Dinner: $12-$15   **Phone:** 520/455-5821
Location: On SR 82, just e of jct SR 83. 3084 Hwy 82 85637. **Hours:** Open 2/1-6/1 & 9/14-1/31; 4 pm-9 pm. Closed major holidays, Mon & Tues. **Features:** casual dress; cocktails; a la carte. Small, popular and charming. Outdoor patio dining avail. Reservations not accepted.

KAREN'S WINE COUNTRY CAFE
◆ ◆ ◆
American
Lunch: $7-$9   **Dinner:** $11-$18   **Phone:** 520/455-5282
Location: SR 82, just e of jct SR 83. 3266 Hwy 82 85637. **Hours:** 11 am-4 pm, Thurs-Sat 11 am-4 & 5-8 pm. Closed major holidays. **Reservations:** suggested. **Features:** casual dress; cocktails; a la carte. Delightful dining in a colorful country atmosphere. Gift shop features their own wines, jellies and condiments. Smoke free premises. **Cards:** MC, VI.

SPRINGERVILLE pop. 1,800

——— LODGING ———

SUPER 8 MOTEL
AAA SAVE
◆
Motel
Phone: (520)333-2655
All Year   1P: $37-$50   2P: $41-$60   XP: $5   F12
Location: Just w on Main St (US 60/180). 138 W Main St 85938 (PO Box 1568). Fax: 520/333-5450. **Terms:** Weekly rates avail; pets, $25, prior approval required dep req. **Facility:** 41 rooms. Some small units. 1 large suite $88.88; 2 stories; exterior corridors. **All Rooms:** extended cable TV. **Cards:** AE, CB, DI, DS, MC, VI. **Special Amenities:** Free local telephone calls and preferred room (subject to availability with advanced reservations).

SUN CITY/SUN CITY WEST —See Phoenix p. 280.

SURPRISE —See Phoenix p. 280.

TAYLOR

——— LODGING ———

SILVER CREEK INN
AAA SAVE
◆ ◆
Motel
Phone: (520)536-2600
All Year   1P: $46-$56   2P: $55-$65   XP: $10   F16
Location: 0.6 mi n on SR 77. 825 N Main St 85939 (PO Box 980). Fax: 520/536-3250. **Terms:** [ECP] meal plan; pets. **Facility:** 42 rooms. 2 stories; exterior corridors; sauna, whirlpool. **Cards:** AE, DI, DS, MC, VI. **Special Amenities:** Free breakfast.

TEMPE —See Phoenix p. 281.

TOLLESON —See Phoenix p. 289.

TOMBSTONE pop. 1,200

——— LODGINGS ———

BEST WESTERN LOOKOUT LODGE
AAA SAVE
◆ ◆ ◆
Motel
Phone: (520)457-2223
12/24-1/31   1P: $67-$85   2P: $68-$85   XP: $7   F12
2/1-12/23   1P: $65-$80   2P: $68-$85   XP: $7   F12
Location: 1 mi n on SR 80. (PO Box 787, 85638). Fax: 520/457-3870. **Terms:** [CP] meal plan; cancellation fee imposed. **Facility:** 40 rooms. In a quiet desert setting overlooking the Dragoon Mountains. 2 stories; exterior corridors; heated pool. **All Rooms:** extended cable TV. **Cards:** AE, CB, DI, DS, MC, VI. **Special Amenities:** Free breakfast and free local telephone calls. (See ad below)

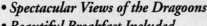

TOMBSTONE MOTEL
◆
Motel

| | 2/1-5/27 | 1P: $45-$65 | 2P: $55-$70 | XP: $5 | F12 |
| | 5/28-1/31 | 1P: $35-$55 | 2P: $45-$70 | XP: $5 | F12 |

Phone: (520)457-3478

Location: On SR 80, in center of town. 502 E Fremont St 85638 (PO Box 0837). Fax: 520/457-9017. **Terms:** Cancellation fee imposed; small pets only, $25 dep req. **Facility:** 13 rooms. Cozy, comfortable rooms, some in a building dating back to the late 1800's. 1 small unit. 1 story; exterior corridors. **All Rooms:** combo or shower baths. **Cards:** AE, DS, MC, VI.

(ASK) 🐾 ✕ 🖥

TRAIL RIDERS INN
(AAA)
◆ ◆
Motel

| | 2/1-6/1 & 9/1-1/31 | 1P: $35 | 2P: $45 | XP: $5 | F9 |
| | 6/2-8/31 | 1P: $35 | 2P: $40 | XP: $5 | F9 |

Phone: 520/457-3573

Location: 13 N 7th St 85638 (PO Box 182). Fax: 520/457-3049. **Terms:** Pets. **Facility:** 13 rooms. 1 story; exterior corridors. **All Rooms:** combo or shower baths, extended cable TV. **Cards:** MC, VI.

🐾 ✕

──────── RESTAURANT ────────

THE LONGHORN RESTAURANT   **Lunch:** $6-$10   **Dinner:** $12-$30   **Phone:** 520/457-3405
◆
American

Location: In historic district. 501 E Allen at Fifth 85638. **Hours:** 7 am-8 pm. Closed: 11/23 & 12/25. **Features:** casual dress; children's menu; carryout; beer & wine only; street parking. Good selection of steak, sandwiches and Mexican entrees. Old West decor. **Cards:** MC, VI.

✕

TUBAC pop. 300

──────── LODGINGS ────────

TUBAC GOLF RESORT
◆ ◆ ◆
Resort

	2/1-4/16	1P: $135-$145	2P: $135-$145	XP: $15	F12
	4/17-5/14	1P: $95-$105	2P: $95-$105	XP: $15	F12
	10/1-1/31	1P: $90-$100	2P: $90-$100	XP: $15	F12
	5/15-9/30	1P: $75-$85	2P: $75-$85	XP: $15	F12

Phone: (520)398-2211

Location: E of I-19 between exits 34 and 40. 1 Otero Rd 85646 (PO Box 1297). Fax: 520/398-9261. **Terms:** 7 day cancellation notice; cancellation fee imposed; package plans; pets, $5 extra charge, in designated rooms. **Facility:** 46 rooms. Restful setting on several acres of nicely landscaped grounds. Nicely furnished rooms and suites, some with fireplace. 1 story; exterior corridors; putting green; heated pool. Fee: 18 holes golf; 1 tennis court. **Cards:** AE, DS, MC, VI.

🐾 🍴 🍸 ⚒ ⛰ ✕ 🖨 💻 🖥 🔌 🏊 ✕

VALLE VERDE RANCH BED & BREAKFAST   **Phone: 520/398-2246**
◆ ◆ ◆
Bed &
Breakfast

| | 2/1-5/31 & 11/1-1/31 | 1P: $80-$135 | 2P: $80-$135 | | |

Location: I-19 exit 34, then just s on e Frontage Rd. 2149 E Frontage Rd 85640 (PO Box 157, TUMACACORI). Fax: 520/398-2246. **Terms:** Open 2/1-5/31 & 11/1-1/31; [BP] meal plan; 15 day cancellation notice; cancellation fee imposed. **Facility:** 5 rooms. Beautifully decorated mission style ranch home on tree-shaded grounds. Full breakfast served to guests staying in main house; expanded continental breakfast for guests staying in outside units. 1 story; interior/exterior corridors; smoke free premises. **All Rooms:** combo or shower baths. **Some Rooms:** efficiency, kitchen.

✕ (VCR) 💻 🖥 🔌

──────── RESTAURANT ────────

MONTURA RESTAURANT   Historical   **Lunch:** $7-$9   **Dinner:** $12-$20   **Phone:** 520/398-2678
◆ ◆ ◆
American

Location: E of I-19 between exits 34 and 40; at Tubac Golf Resort. 1 Otero Rd 85646. **Hours:** 7-11 am, 11:30-2:30 & 5-8:30 pm, Fri & Sat-9 pm, Sun 7 am-8:30 pm. **Reservations:** suggested. **Features:** casual dress; carryout; cocktails & lounge. Attractive dining room with ranch decor built in original Otero Ranch stables. Varied selection of beef, chicken, fish, pasta and Mexican dishes. **Cards:** AE, DS, MC, VI.

✕

TUBA CITY pop. 7,300

──────── LODGING ────────

QUALITY INN TUBA CITY
◆ ◆
Motor Inn

| | 4/1-10/31 | 1P: $85-$130 | 2P: $90-$135 | XP: $5 | F18 |
| | 2/1-3/31 & 11/1-1/31 | 1P: $70-$100 | 2P: $75-$105 | XP: $5 | F18 |

Phone: (520)283-4545

Location: On Main St (US 160), 1 mi n of jct US 160 and SR 264, adjacent to historic Tuba Trading Post. Main & Moenave (PO Box 247, 86045). Fax: 520/283-4144. **Terms:** Small pets only, $20 dep req. **Facility:** 80 rooms. 2 stories; interior corridors. **Services:** gift shop. **Cards:** AE, CB, DI, DS, JC, MC, VI.

(SAVE) 🐾 🍴 ⚒ ⛰ ✕ 🎥 🖨 💻 🖥 🔌

AAA members
can reserve a room
with us *anytime,
anywhere* - from a
rest stop, cell phone, or
even at
the hotel counter
and *always get
the special AAA
discount.*

If you're looking for great
lodging, we have over 2,000
hotels to choose from across
North America. Best of all, as
AAA members, you always
enjoy at least a 10% discount,
100% satisfaction guarantee,
and kids always stay free!
And you'll find our familiar
brands in 40 countries worldwide too.

For reservations, call
1-800-228-1AAA, visit
www.choicehotels.com, or
contact your local AAA club.

 TourBookMark

Lodging Listing Symbols

Member Values

- Ⓐ Official Appointment
- SAVE Offers minimum 10% discount
- SAVE SYC&S chain partners
- A$K May offer discount
- S𝐷 Offers senior discount
- fyi Informational listing only

Member Services

- Airport transportation
- Pets allowed
- Restaurant on premises
- Restaurant off premises (walking distance)
- 24 hour room service
- Cocktail lounge

Special Features

- Business services
- Valet parking
- Laundry service
- Child care
- Fully accessible
- Semi-accessible
- Roll-in showers
- Hearing impaired

In-Room Amenities

- Non-smoking rooms
- No air conditioning
- No telephones
- No cable TV
- Movies
- VCR
- Radio
- Coffee maker
- Microwave
- Refrigerator
- Data port/modem line

Sports/Recreation

- Outdoor pool
- Indoor Pool
- Indoor/outdoor pool
- Fitness center
- Recreational facilities

Call property for detailed information about fees & restrictions relating to the lodging listing symbols.

CHOICE HOTELS
INTERNATIONAL

Destination Tucson

*V*isitors searching for variety will find it in Tucson.

*N*estled in a dry valley surrounded by four mountain ranges, Tucson is a magnet for lovers of the outdoors thanks to its various recreation options. What's more, preservation of the local environment is taken seriously here. Tohono Chul Park and Tucson Mountain Park are just two of the protected sites that show off the area's distinctive desert setting.

Tucson skyline. Looking at its modern skyline, Tucson's nickname, "the Old Pueblo," hardly seems appropriate.

Skiing on Mt. Lemmon. High in the Catalina Mountains, snowy Mt. Lemmon, site of the country's southernmost ski area, is a world apart from Tucson just 30 miles away. (See listing page 110)

Oracle

*P*laces included in this AAA Destination City:
Green Valley.......348
Oracle................349

See Downtown map page 323

Tucson

See Vicinity map page 324

Green Valley

Hiking. Hikers pick their way carefully along one of the numerous scenic trails that thread through the rugged mountains surrounding Tucson.

Tennis. Tucson's sunny, dry climate serves up great weather for tennis players.

Tucson pop. 405,400

This index helps you "spot" where approved accommodations are located on the detailed maps that follow. Rate ranges are for comparison only and show the property's high season. Turn to the listing page for more detailed information and consult display ads for special promotions. Restaurant rate range is for dinner unless only lunch (L) is served.

✈ Airport Accommodations

Spotter/Map Page Number	OA	TUCSON	Diamond Rating	Rate Range High Season	Listing Page
81 / p. 324		Baymont Inn & Suites-Tucson Airport, just n of entrance	◆◆	$70-$110	327
71 / p. 324		Best Western Inn At The Airport, at airport entrance	◆◆◆	$98-$126	328
44 / p. 324		Clarion Hotel Tucson Airport, Just n of airport	◆◆◆	$95-$115	329
49 / p. 324		Courtyard by Marriott-Tucson Airport, 0.6 mi n of airport entrance	◆◆◆	$119-$129	332
46 / p. 324	ⒶⒶ	**Embassy Suites Hotel - Airport, at airport entrance**	◆◆◆	$95-$139	334
45 / p. 324		Hampton Inn Airport, , just n of airport	◆◆◆	$119-$129	335
48 / p. 324		Holiday Inn Express-Airport, 1 mi ne of airport	◆◆	Failed to provide	336
74 / p. 324	ⒶⒶ	**La Quinta Inn & Suites Airport, Just n of airport**	◆◆◆	$89-$109 [SAVE]	338

DOWNTOWN TUCSON

Spotter/Map Page Number	OA	DOWNTOWN TUCSON - Lodgings	Diamond Rating	Rate Range High Season	Listing Page
1 / p. 323		Holiday Inn-City Center - see color ad p 330	◆◆◆	$107-$127	325
2 / p. 323	ⒶⒶ	**La Quinta Inn-West - see color ad p 242, p 339**	◆◆	$79-$99 [SAVE]	325
3 / p. 323		Inn Suites Hotel & Resort - see color ad p 328, p 325	◆◆	$75-$125	325
5 / p. 323		El Presidio Bed & Breakfast Inn	◆◆◆	$85-$125	325
6 / p. 323	ⒶⒶ	**Days Inn I-10/Convention Center**	◆◆	$109-$149 [SAVE]	325
7 / p. 323		Clarion Santa Rita Hotel & Suites - see color ad p 330	◆◆◆	$99-$159	324
8 / p. 323		Four Points Hotel By Sheraton	◆◆◆	$89-$99	325
9 / p. 323		The Royal Elizabeth Bed & Breakfast Inn	◆◆◆	$130-$180	326
		DOWNTOWN TUCSON - Restaurants			
1 / p. 323		Janos	◆◆◆◆	$22-$32	326
2 / p. 323		El Charro Cafe	◆	$8-$17	326
4 / p. 323		Cafe Poca Cosa	◆◆	$11-$17	326

TUCSON

Spotter/Map Page Number	OA	TUCSON - Lodgings	Diamond Rating	Rate Range High Season	Listing Page
11 / p. 324		Hampton Inn & Suites	◆◆◆	$119-$159	336
12 / p. 324	ⒶⒶ	**Westward Look Resort - see color ad p 344**	◆◆◆◆	$200-$299 [SAVE]	345
13 / p. 324	ⒶⒶ	**Best Western InnSuites-Catalina - see color ad p 328, p 325**	◆◆◆	$119-$189 [SAVE]	328
14 / p. 324	ⒶⒶ	**Loews Ventana Canyon Resort**	◆◆◆◆	$221-$320 [SAVE]	339
16 / p. 324		Sheraton Tucson Hotel & Suites	◆◆◆	$129-$179	343
17 / p. 324	ⒶⒶ	**Wayward Winds Lodge - see color ad p 343**	◆◆◆	$69-$99 [SAVE]	345
18 / p. 324	ⒶⒶ	**Ghost Ranch Lodge - see color ad p 335**	◆◆	$69-$99 [SAVE]	334
19 / p. 324	ⒶⒶ	**Rodeway Inn I-10 & Grant Rd - see ad p 341**	◆◆	$50-$89 [SAVE]	342
20 / p. 324		Hacienda Bed & Breakfast	◆◆	$75-$125	335
21 / p. 324		Best Western Executive Inn	◆◆	$65-$85	328
22 / p. 324	ⒶⒶ	**Econo Lodge**	◆	$79-$110 [SAVE]	333
23 / p. 324	ⒶⒶ	**Best Western A Royal Sun Inn & Suites - see color ad p 57, p 327, p 198**	◆◆◆	$79-$99 [SAVE]	328

Spotter/Map Page Number	OA	TUCSON - Lodgings (continued)	Diamond Rating	Rate Range High Season	Listing Page
24 / p. 324		Arizona Inn	◆◆◆◆	$195-$2500	326
25 / p. 324		Plaza Hotel	◆◆◆	$119-$149	340
26 / p. 324		Hawthorn Suites LTD - see color ad p 230	◆◆◆	$99-$139	336
27 / p. 324		Casa Tierra	◆◆◆	$135-$300	329
28 / p. 324		DoubleTree Guest Suites-Tucson - see ad p 333	◆◆◆	$127	333
29 / p. 324		Residence Inn By Marriott	◆◆◆	$149-$189	341
30 / p. 324	AAA	**Smuggler's Inn Hotel - see color ad p 342**	◆◆◆	$99-$119 SAVE	344
31 / p. 324		Hilton-Tucson East - see color ad p 41 & ad p 337	◆◆◆	$135-$199	336
32 / p. 324	AAA	**La Quinta Inn-East - see color ad p 339**	◆◆◆	$75-$95 SAVE	338
33 / p. 324		Viscount Suite Hotel	◆◆◆	Failed to provide	345
34 / p. 324	AAA	**Comfort Inn**	◆	$85-$120 SAVE	331
35 / p. 324		Casa Alegre Bed & Breakfast Inn	◆◆◆	$80-$125	329
36 / p. 324		Doubletree Hotel at Reid Park - see ad p 333	◆◆◆	$119-$139	333
37 / p. 324	AAA	**Windmill Inn at St. Philip's Plaza - see ad p 343**	◆◆◆	$145 SAVE	345
38 / p. 324	AAA	**Rodeway Inn-Park Ave at I-10 - see ad p 341**	◆	$99-$120 SAVE	342
39 / p. 324	AAA	**Holiday Inn-Palo Verde**	◆◆◆	$87 SAVE	338
40 / p. 324	AAA	**Red Roof Inn-Tucson South**	◆◆	$66-$91	341
41 / p. 324	AAA	**Ramada-Palo Verde**	◆◆◆	$149-$159 SAVE	340
42 / p. 324		The SunCatcher	◆◆◆	$140-$165	344
43 / p. 324		La Posada Del Valle Bed & Breakfast	◆◆◆	$78-$148	338
44 / p. 324		Clarion Hotel Tucson Airport - see ad p 331	◆◆◆	$95-$115	329
45 / p. 324		Hampton Inn Airport	◆◆◆	$119-$129	335
46 / p. 324	AAA	**Embassy Suites Hotel - Airport - see color ad p 332**	◆◆◆	$95-$139	334
47 / p. 324	AAA	**Sumner Suites**	◆◆◆	$129-$139 SAVE	344
48 / p. 324		Holiday Inn Express-Airport	◆◆	Failed to provide	336
49 / p. 324		Courtyard by Marriott-Tucson Airport - see color ad p 332	◆◆◆	$119-$129	332
51 / p. 324		The Peppertrees Bed & Breakfast Inn	◆◆◆	$98-$135	340
53 / p. 324	AAA	**Sheraton El Conquistador**	◆◆◆◆	$354-$469 SAVE	343
54 / p. 324		Omni Tucson National Golf Resort & Spa	◆◆◆◆	$265-$355	340
55 / p. 324	AAA	**Lazy K Bar Guest Ranch**	◆◆	$157-$298	339
56 / p. 324		Country Inn & Suites By Carlson - see color ad p 229	◆◆	$129	331
57 / p. 324		Car-Mar's Southwest Bed & Breakfast	◆◆◆	$60-$125	329
58 / p. 324		Coyote Crossing Bed & Breakfast	◆◆◆	$95-$120	332
59 / p. 324	AAA	**Super 8 Central East**	◆◆	$79-$85 SAVE	345
60 / p. 324	AAA	**Howard Johnson Hotel**	◆◆	$89-$129 SAVE	338
61 / p. 324		Adobe Rose Inn	◆◆◆	$95-$140	326
62 / p. 324		Catalina Park Inn	◆◆◆	$75-$124	329
63 / p. 324	AAA	**Ramada Inn Foothills - see color ad p 340**	◆◆	$89-$135 SAVE	340
64 / p. 324	AAA	**Lazy 8 Motel**	◆	$39-$47 SAVE	339
65 / p. 324		Baymont Inn - see color ad p 327	◆◆◆	$44-$109	326
66 / p. 324		Fairfield Inn By Marriott	◆◆◆	$95-$125	334
67 / p. 324		Comfort Inn I-10 & Ina	◆◆	$100-$125	331
68 / p. 324	AAA	**Embassy Suites Hotel-Broadway - see ad p 334**	◆◆◆	$109-$159 SAVE	334
69 / p. 324	AAA	**Hampton Inn North - see color ad p 336**	◆◆◆	$69-$130 SAVE	336
70 / p. 324		Holiday Inn Express-Marana	◆◆	Failed to provide	336
71 / p. 324		Best Western Inn At The Airport	◆◆◆	$98-$126	328
72 / p. 324	AAA	**Holiday Inn Express-Starr Pass Blvd**	◆◆◆	$119 SAVE	338
73 / p. 324		Clarion Hotel-Randolph Park - see color ad p 330	◆◆	$89-$129	329
74 / p. 324	AAA	**La Quinta Inn & Suites Airport - see color ad p 339**	◆◆◆	$89-$109 SAVE	338
75 / p. 324		The Lodge At Ventana Canyon	◆◆◆◆	$389-$499	339

Spotter/Map Page Number	OA	TUCSON - Lodgings (continued)	Diamond Rating	Rate Range High Season	Listing Page
76 / p. 324		Marriott University Park Hotel	◆◆◆	$149-$189	339
77 / p. 324	⊕	**Red Roof Inn Tucson North**	◆◆	$66-$91	341
78 / p. 324		Super 8 Motel - see color ad p 342	◆	$79-$99	345
79 / p. 324		Courtyard By Marriott-Tucson Williams Centre - see color ad p 332	◆◆◆	$99-$119	332
80 / p. 324	⊕	**Days Inn**	◆◆	$89-$100 ⊡	332
81 / p. 324		Baymont Inn & Suites-Tucson Airport - see color ad p 327	◆◆	$70-$110	327
82 / p. 324		Comfort Suites	◆◆◆	$130	331
84 / p. 324		Jeremiah Inn Bed & Breakfast	◆◆◆	$90-$120	338
85 / p. 324	⊕	**Studio 6**	◆◆	Failed to provide	344
87 / p. 324		Shoney's Inn	◆◆	Failed to provide	343
89 / p. 324		Agave Grove Bed & Breakfast Inn	◆◆	$95-$165	326
90 / p. 324		Candlelight Suites	◆	$65-$70	328
92 / p. 324	⊕	**The Golf Villas at Oro Valley - see color ad p 335**	◆◆◆◆	$489 ⊡	334
94 / p. 324	⊕	**Knights Inn**	◆	$99-$119 ⊡	338
		TUCSON - Restaurants			
⑨ / p. 324	⊕	**La Fuente Restaurant**	◆◆	$8-$18	346
⑩ / p. 324		Cafe Terra Cotta	◆◆	$9-$22	346
⑪ / p. 324		Le Rendez-vous	◆◆◆	$19-$30	347
⑬ / p. 324		Pinnacle Peak Restaurant	◆	$8-$14	347
⑭ / p. 324	⊕	**The Tack Room**	◆◆◆◆◆	$25-$35	347
⑮ / p. 324		Kingfisher	◆◆	$12-$20	346
⑯ / p. 324		The Last Territory	◆◆	$13-$21	347
⑰ / p. 324		Lotus Garden	◆◆	$9-$20	347
⑱ / p. 324		Keaton's Arizona Grill	◆◆	$10-$19	346
⑲ / p. 324	⊕	**Triple C Chuckwagon Suppers**	◆	$16-$21	348
⑳ / p. 324		Olive Tree Restaurant	◆◆◆	$18-$30	347
㉒ / p. 324		The Gold Room	◆◆◆◆	$19-$29	346
㉓ / p. 324		Michelangelo Ristorante Italiano	◆◆◆	$9-$22	347
㉔ / p. 324		El Corral	◆	$9-$13	346
㉕ / p. 324		Fuego	◆◆◆	$14-$24	346
㉗ / p. 324		Scordato's Restaurant	◆◆◆	$15-$21	347
㉙ / p. 324		Anthony's In The Catalinas	◆◆◆◆	$20-$33	346
㉚ / p. 324		Cottonwood Cafe	◆◆◆	$12-$20	346
㉛ / p. 324		Cibaria Cucina Italiana	◆◆	$10-$20	346
㉜ / p. 324		Daniel's	◆◆◆◆	$17-$28	346
㉝ / p. 324		Main Dining Room at the Arizona Inn	◆◆◆	$19-$25	347
㉞ / p. 324		The Ventana Room	◆◆◆◆	$28-$50	348
㊱ / p. 324		Ovens Restaurant	◆◆	$9-$18	347
㊳ / p. 324		Keaton's Arizona Grill	◆◆	$10-$20	346
㊵ / p. 324		Vivace Restaurant	◆◆	$12-$20	348
㊷ / p. 324		McMahon's Steakhouse	◆◆◆	$25-$50	347
㊺ / p. 324		Metropolitan Grill	◆◆◆	$9-$16	347

© AAA

DOWNTOWN TUCSON ACCOMMODATIONS

Scale in Miles 0 0.3
Scale in Kilometers 0 0.5

1813-G

DOWNTOWN TUCSON   (See map p. 323; index p. 320)

——— LODGINGS ———

CLARION SANTA RITA HOTEL & SUITES

◆◆◆

Motel

2/1-3/31	1P: $99-$149	2P: $109-$159	XP: $10
4/1-5/31 & 10/1-1/31	1P: $69-$99	2P: $79-$109	XP: $10
6/1-9/30	1P: $59-$89	2P: $69-$99	XP: $10

Phone: (520)622-4000   **7**

F18
F18
F18

Location: Downtown, 0.6 mi e of I-10, Broadway/Congress exit 258. 88 E Broadway 85701. Fax: 520/620-0376. **Terms:** [CP] meal plan; 7 day cancellation notice; cancellation fee imposed; small pets only, $25 dep req. **Facility:** 161 rooms. 8 stories; interior corridors; heated pool. **Cards:** AE, CB, DI, DS, MC, VI. *(See color ad p 330)*

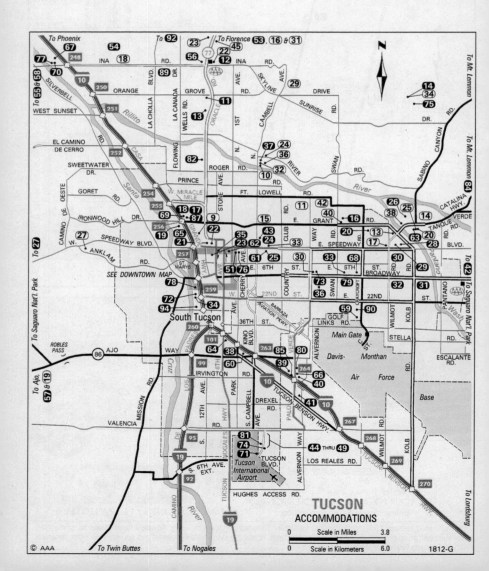

TUCSON
ACCOMMODATIONS

© AAA

1812-G

(See map p. 323)

DAYS INN I-10/CONVENTION CENTER

AAA SAVE
◆◆
Motel

Phone: (520)791-7511 **6**

2/1-2/29	1P: $109-$129	2P: $129-$149	XP: $10	F12
3/1-6/1 & 10/1-1/31	1P: $69-$89	2P: $79-$99	XP: $10	F12
6/2-9/30	1P: $32-$42	2P: $42-$52	XP: $5	F12

Location: W side of I-10, exit Congress St/Broadway. 222 S Freeway 85745. Fax: 520/622-3481. **Terms:** [CP] meal plan; 7 day cancellation notice, During special events. **Facility:** 122 rooms. 2 stories; exterior corridors; whirlpool. **Recreation:** barber shop, beauty & nail salon. **All Rooms:** combo or shower baths. **Cards:** AE, DI, DS, MC, VI. **Special Amenities: Early check-in/late check-out and free breakfast.**

EL PRESIDIO BED & BREAKFAST INN

◆◆◆
Historic Bed
& Breakfast

Phone: (520)623-6151 **5**

2/1-5/31 & 9/1-1/31	1P: $85-$110	2P: $95-$125	XP: $25	F12
6/1-8/31	1P: $75-$95	2P: $80-$110	XP: $20	F12

Location: Downtown, in the El Presidio Historic District, just n of Congress St/Broadway Blvd. 297 N Main Ave 85701. Fax: 520/623-3860. **Terms:** [BP] meal plan; check-in 4 pm; 14 day cancellation notice; 2 night min stay. **Facility:** 4 rooms. An 1886 Victorian adobe with beautiful courtyard and garden. Very nicely decorated and well equipped rooms and suites. Within walking distance of museums and art district. Curb parking with permit provided. 1 story; interior/exterior corridors; smoke free premises. **Recreation:** bicycles. **All Rooms:** combo or shower baths. **Some Rooms:** 2 kitchens.

FOUR POINTS HOTEL BY SHERATON

◆◆◆
Motor Inn

Phone: (520)622-6611 **8**

2/1-3/31	1P: $89-$99	2P: $89-$99	XP: $10	F18
4/1-5/31 & 10/1-1/31	1P: $69-$79	2P: $69-$79	XP: $10	F18
6/1-9/30	1P: $65-$75	2P: $65-$75	XP: $10	F18

Location: Adjacent to I-10, exit 258 (Congress St). 350 S Freeway 85745. Fax: 520/622-8143. **Terms:** [CP] meal plan; 5 day cancellation notice; pets, $50 cleaning fee. **Facility:** 174 rooms. 2 stories; interior/exterior corridors; heated pool. **All Rooms:** combo or shower baths. **Some Rooms:** Fee: refrigerators. **Cards:** AE, CB, DI, DS, JC, MC, VI.

HOLIDAY INN-CITY CENTER

◆◆◆
Hotel

Phone: (520)624-8711 **1**

2/1-5/15 & 1/1-1/31	1P: $107-$127	2P: $107-$127	XP: $10	F18
10/1-12/31	1P: $79-$99	2P: $79-$99	XP: $10	F18
5/16-9/30	1P: $61-$81	2P: $61-$81	XP: $10	F18

Location: Just e of I-10, Congress St/Broadway exit 258. 181 W Broadway 85701. Fax: 520/623-8121. **Terms:** Pets, $25 dep req. **Facility:** 311 rooms. Adjacent to Tucson Convention Center. 14 stories; interior corridors; heated pool. **Services:** gift shop. **Some Rooms:** color TV. **Cards:** AE, CB, DI, DS, JC, MC, VI. *(See color ad p 330)*

INN SUITES HOTEL & RESORT

◆◆
Motor Inn

Phone: (520)622-3000 **3**

2/1-5/31	1P: $75-$125	2P: $75-$125
10/1-1/31	1P: $69-$119	2P: $69-$119
6/1-9/30	1P: $55-$95	2P: $55-$95

Location: Adjacent and just e of I-10, St Mary's Rd exit. 475 N Granada Ave 85701. Fax: 520/623-8922. **Terms:** [BP] meal plan; cancellation fee imposed; pets, $50 dep req. **Facility:** 277 rooms. Spacious grounds. 2-4 stories; interior/exterior corridors; heated pool; playground. **Services:** gift shop. **All Rooms:** combo or shower baths. **Cards:** AE, CB, DI, DS, JC, MC, VI. *(See color ad p 328 & below)*

LA QUINTA INN-WEST

AAA SAVE
◆◆
Motel

Phone: (520)622-6491 **2**

2/1-3/31	1P: $79-$99	2P: $79-$99
4/1-1/31	1P: $59-$79	2P: $59-$79

Location: W side of I-10, St Mary's Rd exit. 665 N Frwy 85745. Fax: 520/798-3669. **Terms:** [CP] meal plan; small pets only. **Facility:** 133 rooms. 2 one-bedroom suites; suites avail; 2 stories; exterior corridors; heated pool. **Dining:** Coffee shop nearby. **Some Rooms:** Fee: microwaves. **Cards:** AE, CB, DI, DS, JC, MC, VI. **Special Amenities: Free breakfast and free local telephone calls.** *(See color ad p 242 & p 339)*

(See map p. 323)

THE ROYAL ELIZABETH BED & BREAKFAST INN   Phone: (520)670-9022   **9**
◆◆◆   2/1-5/31 & 9/1-1/31   1P: $130-$180   2P: $130-$180   XP: $20
Historic Bed   6/1-8/31   1P: $95-$125   2P: $95-$125   XP: $20
& Breakfast   **Location:** Downtown, in the El Presidio Historic District, just s of Congress St/Broadway. 204 S Scott Ave 85701. Fax: 520/629-9710. **Terms:** [BP] meal plan; 14 day cancellation notice; cancellation fee imposed; 2 night min stay, weekends in season. **Facility:** 6 rooms. Built in 1878. Beautifully restored and decorated in antiques. Check-in 3 pm-6 pm. 1 story; interior corridors; designated smoking area. **All Rooms:** combo or shower baths. **Cards:** AE, DS, MC, VI.

------ **RESTAURANTS** ------

CAFE POCA COSA   **Lunch:** $8-$10   **Dinner:** $11-$17   Phone: 520/622-6400   **4**
◆◆   **Location:** Downtown, 0.6 mi e of I-10, Broadway/Congress exit 258; at Clarion Santa Rita Hotel and Suites.
Mexican   88 E Broadway 85701. **Hours:** 11 am-9 pm. Closed major holidays& Sun. **Reservations:** suggested. **Features:** casual dress; cocktails. Colorfully decorated. Serves an interesting variety of Mexican cuisine. Menu changes daily. Smoke free premises. **Cards:** MC, VI.

EL CHARRO CAFE   **Lunch:** $5-$10   **Dinner:** $8-$17   Phone: 520/622-1922   **2**
◆   **Location:** Downtown; in the El Presidio Historic District. 311 N Court Ave 85701. **Hours:** 11 am-9 pm, Fri &
Mexican   Sat-10 pm. Closed major holidays. **Features:** casual dress; children's menu; cocktails & lounge; street parking. A busy, popular restaurant operated by the same family since 1922. Several small dining areas and an outdoor cantina. Smoke free premises. **Cards:** AE, DI, DS, MC, VI.

JANOS   Historical   **Dinner:** $22-$32   Phone: 520/615-6100   **1**
◆◆◆◆   **Location:** 1.3 mi e of Campbell Ave via Skyline Dr; in The Westin La Paloma, Tucson. 3770 Sunrise Dr
Regional   85718. **Hours:** 5:30 pm-9 pm, Fri & Sat-9:30 pm. Closed major holidays, Sun & also Mon 5/16-11/14.
American   **Reservations:** suggested. **Features:** casual dress; cocktails & lounge; a la carte. Innovative French-inspired Southwestern cuisine. **Cards:** AE, CB, DI, MC, VI.

TUCSON pop. 405,400   (See map p. 324; index p. 320)

------ **LODGINGS** ------

ADOBE ROSE INN   Phone: (520)318-4644   **61**
◆◆◆   2/1-5/31 & 12/16-1/31   1P: $95-$115   2P: $105-$140   XP: $15
Bed &   9/1-12/15   1P: $75   2P: $85-$95   XP: $15
Breakfast   6/1-8/31   1P: $60   2P: $70   XP: $15
Location: Just s of Speedway Blvd on se corner of Olsen Ave and 2nd St., just e of University of Arizona. 940 N Olsen Ave 85719. Fax: 520/325-0055. **Terms:** [BP] meal plan; 14 day cancellation notice. **Facility:** 7 rooms. 2 rooms with woodburning fireplace and 2 with private entrance. Adobe home built in 1933. 1-2 stories; interior/exterior corridors; smoke free premises. **All Rooms:** combo or shower baths. **Some Rooms:** 2 efficiencies. **Cards:** CB, DI, MC, VI.

AGAVE GROVE BED & BREAKFAST INN   Phone: (520)797-3400   **89**
◆◆   2/1-4/30 & 10/1-1/31   1P: $95-$165   2P: $95-$165   XP: $15   D18
Bed &   5/1-9/30   1P: $70-$125   2P: $70-$125   XP: $15   D18
Breakfast   **Location:** I-10, exit 250 (Orange Grove Rd), 3 mi e to La Canada, then 0.4 mi s to Panorama Rd, then 0.6 mi e. 800 W Panorama Rd 85704. Fax: 520/797-0980. **Terms:** 14 day cancellation notice; cancellation fee imposed. **Facility:** 4 rooms. Common area with movies, stereo system, pool table and VCR. Phones avail. 1 story; interior/exterior corridors; designated smoking area. **All Rooms:** combo or shower baths. **Cards:** AE, DS, MC, VI.

ARIZONA INN   Phone: (520)325-1541   **24**
◆◆◆◆   2/1-4/15   1P: $195-$2500   2P: $195-$2500   XP: $15   F9
Historic   4/16-5/31   1P: $170-$2500   2P: $170-$2500   XP: $15   F9
Complex   9/15-1/31   1P: $130-$2500   2P: $130-$2500   XP: $15   F9
   6/1-9/14   1P: $86-$1500   2P: $98-$1500   XP: $15   F9
Location: 0.5 mi n of Speedway Blvd, just e of Campbell Ave. 2200 E Elm St 85719. Fax: 520/881-5830. **Terms:** 3 day cancellation notice; cancellation fee imposed. **Facility:** 86 rooms. Several acres of beautifully landscaped grounds. Atmosphere of gracious charm with southwest syle adobe buildings. Originally built in 1930. Many rooms furnished with antiques and original furnishings. 2 stories; exterior corridors; heated pool; 2 lighted tennis courts. **Services:** gift shop. Fee: massage. **Some Rooms:** Fee: VCR. **Cards:** AE, CB, DI, MC, VI.

BAYMONT INN   Phone: (520)624-3200   **65**
◆◆◆   2/1-3/31   1P: $84-$90   2P: $84-$90
Motel   4/1-1/31   1P: $49   2P: $49
   Location: Just w of I-10, exit 256 (Grant Rd). 1560 W Grant Rd 85745. Fax: 520/622-3212. **Terms:** [CP] meal plan; 7 day cancellation notice; pets. **Facility:** 66 rooms. 3 stories; interior corridors; heated pool. **Cards:** AE, CB, DI, DS, MC, VI. *(See color ad p 327)*

(See map p. 324)

BAYMONT INN & SUITES-TUCSON AIRPORT   **Phone:** (520)889-6600   [81]

◆◆
Motel

	1/1-1/31	1P: $70-$100	2P: $80-$110
	2/1-4/15	1P: $68-$98	2P: $78-$108
	9/16-12/31	1P: $60-$70	2P: $68-$98
	4/16-9/15	1P: $55-$85	2P: $65-$95

Location: Just n of entrance to Tucson International Airport. 2548 E Medina Rd 85706. Fax: 520/889-6168. **Terms:** [CP] meal plan; cancellation fee imposed; small pets only, $20 refundable dep req. **Facility:** 98 rooms. 3 stories; interior corridors; heated pool. **Cards:** AE, CB, DI, DS, MC, VI. *(See color ad below)*

(See map p. 324)

BEST WESTERN A ROYAL SUN INN & SUITES   Phone: (520)622-8871   [23]
[AAA] [SAVE]   2/1-4/29 & 9/8-1/31   1P: $79-$99   2P: $79-$99   XP: $10   F12
◆ ◆ ◆   4/30-9/7   1P: $59-$79   2P: $59-$79   XP: $10   F12
Motor Inn   **Location:** 0.8 mi w of I-10, exit Speedway Blvd, just s on Stone. 1015 N Stone Ave 85705. Fax: 520/623-2267.
Terms: [CP] meal plan; 14 day cancellation notice; cancellation fee imposed. **Facility:** 79 rooms. 0.7 mi n of
downtown, 0.8 mi w of University of Arizona. Attractive landscaping. Nicely decorated rooms and one-bedroom
suites in a contemporary southwest motif. 20 whirlpool rooms, $89-$169; suites, $89-$169; 2 stories; exterior corridors; heated
pool, whirlpool. **Dining:** Restaurant; 6 am-9 pm; $6-$15. **Cards:** AE, CB, DI, DS, MC, VI. **Special Amenities: Free breakfast
and free local telephone calls.** (See color ads p 57, p 198, & p 327)

BEST WESTERN EXECUTIVE INN   Phone: (520)791-7551   [21]
◆ ◆   2/1-4/22   1P: $65-$80   2P: $70-$85   XP: $10   F18
Motor Inn   4/23-5/31 & 10/1-1/31   1P: $45-$60   2P: $50-$65   XP: $8   F18
6/1-9/30   1P: $39-$49   2P: $42-$52   XP: $6   F18
Location: I-10, Speedway Blvd exit; 0.5 mi e to Main St, then 0.3 mi n. 333 W Drachman St 85705. Fax: 520/623-7803.
Terms: Cancellation fee imposed; small pets only. **Facility:** 129 rooms. Main building and annex section across side street.
Large, contemporary style rooms. 2 stories; interior corridors; heated pool. **Some Rooms:** 5 efficiencies. Fee: refrigerators,
VCR. **Cards:** AE, CB, DI, DS, MC, VI.

BEST WESTERN INN AT THE AIRPORT   Phone: 520/746-0271   [71]
◆ ◆ ◆   2/1-4/1   1P: $98-$116   2P: $108-$126   XP: $10   F
Motor Inn   4/2-5/31 & 9/13-1/31   1P: $80   2P: $90   XP: $10   F
6/1-9/12   1P: $62   2P: $72   XP: $10   F
Location: 7060 S Tucson Blvd 85706. Fax: 520/889-7391. **Terms:** [CP] meal plan. **Facility:** 149 rooms. Poolside rooms have
balcony or patio. 2-3 stories; interior corridors; heated pool. **Some Rooms:** Fee: VCR. **Cards:** AE, CB, DI, DS, MC, VI.

BEST WESTERN INNSUITES-CATALINA   Phone: (520)297-8111   [13]
[AAA] [SAVE]   2/1-3/16   1P: $119-$189   2P: $119-$189   XP: $8   F19
8/16-1/31   1P: $109-$149   2P: $109-$149
◆ ◆ ◆   3/17-5/25   1P: $109-$149   2P: $109-$149   XP: $8   F19
Motel   5/26-8/15   1P: $79-$109   2P: $79-$109
Location: On Oracle Rd (SR 77), just s of Orange Grove Rd. 6201 N Oracle Rd 85704. Fax: 520/297-2935.
Terms: [CP] meal plan; weekly & monthly rates avail; small pets only, $25 dep req. **Facility:** 159 rooms. 42 one-bedroom
suites with efficiency. 3 units with private, full sized indoor whirlpool. 8 whirlpool rooms, $109-$189; 2 stories; exterior corri-
dors; heated pool, whirlpool; 2 lighted tennis courts. **Dining:** Light meals avail lunch & dinner; coffee shop nearby.
Services: complimentary evening beverages; area transportation, within 5 mi. **Recreation:** in-room video games.
All Rooms: extended cable TV. **Cards:** AE, CB, DI, DS, MC, VI. **Special Amenities: Free breakfast and free local telephone calls.** (See color ad below & p 325)

CANDLELIGHT SUITES   Phone: 520/747-1440   [90]
◆   2/1-3/31   1P: $65   2P: $70   XP: $5   F12
Suite Motel 10/1-1/31   1P: $50-$60   2P: $50-$60   XP: $5   F12
4/1-5/31   1P: $50   2P: $50   XP: $5   F12
6/1-9/30   1P: $45   2P: $50   XP: $5   F12
Location: Just s of 22nd St. 1440 S Craycroft Rd 85711. Fax: 520/750-0144. **Terms:** Pets, $50 dep req. **Facility:** 68 rooms.
2 stories; exterior corridors. **All Rooms:** efficiencies. **Cards:** AE, CB, DI, DS, MC, VI.

(See map p. 324)

CAR-MAR'S SOUTHWEST BED & BREAKFAST
◆◆◆   All Year   1P: $60-$120   2P: $65-$125
Bed &   **Location:** From I-19 exit Ajo Way (SR 86), 7.1 mi w to Camino Verde, n to Old Ajo Rd, just e to Camino Verde
Breakfast again, n to Oklahoma St, then w. 6766 W Oklahoma St 85746. Fax: 520/578-7272. **Terms:** [BP] meal plan; 14
day cancellation notice. **Facility:** 4 rooms. Southwestern style home located in a residential desert area. Nicely
landscaped pool area. 3 rooms with private patio. Telephone avail. 1 story; interior corridors; smoke free premises.
Some Rooms: shower baths, shared bathrooms, color TV. **Cards:** MC, VI.
Phone: (520)578-1730   **57**
XP: $15   D15

CASA ALEGRE BED & BREAKFAST INN   Phone: 520/628-1800   **35**
◆◆◆   2/1-5/31   1P: $80-$115   2P: $80-$125   XP: $10   F18
            9/1-1/31   1P: $70-$115   2P: $80-$125   XP: $10   F18
Bed &   6/1-8/31   1P: $50-$65   2P: $60-$75   XP: $10   F18
Breakfast **Location:** Just e of Stone Ave, at se corner of Speedway and 5th Ave. 316 E Speedway Blvd 85705.
Fax: 520/792-1800. **Terms:** [BP] meal plan; check-in 4 pm; 7 day cancellation notice; cancellation fee imposed. **Facility:** 7
rooms. 7 blocks w of University of Arizona. Attractive rooms in 1915 and 1923 Craftsman bungalows. 1 room with woodburning
fireplace. Telephone jacks in all rooms. 1 story; interior corridors; designated smoking area. **All Rooms:** combo or shower
baths. **Cards:** AE, DS, MC, VI.

CASA TIERRA   Phone: 520/578-3058   **27**
◆◆◆   2/1-5/31 & 9/1-1/31   1P: $135-$300   2P: $135-$300
            6/1-8/31   1P: $95-$200   2P: $95-$200
Bed &   **Location:** I-10, take Speedway and Gates Pass 9.5 mi w, 3 mi nw on Kinney, 1.5 mi w on Milewide, 0.7 mi s
Breakfast on unpaved road. 11155 W Calle Pima 85743. Fax: 520/578-8445. **Terms:** [BP] meal plan; age restrictions may
apply; check-in 4 pm; 14 day cancellation notice; cancellation fee imposed. **Facility:** 4 rooms. Charming adobe home, in an
isolated desert location. 3.5 mi w of Arizona-Sonora Desert Museum. Lovely courtyard and fountain. Telephones avail. Full
vegetarian breakfast. Exterior corridors; smoke free premises. **All Rooms:** combo or shower baths. **Cards:** MC, VI.

CATALINA PARK INN   Phone: 520/792-4541   **62**
◆◆◆   2/1-6/30 & 8/1-1/31   1P: $75-$124   2P: $75-$124
Bed &   **Location:** Just s of Speedway Blvd, ne corner of 5th Ave and 1st St, in the West University Historic District.
Breakfast 309 E 1st St 85705. Fax: 520/792-4541. **Terms:** Open 2/1-6/30 & 8/1-1/31; [BP] meal plan; age restrictions
may apply; check-in 4 pm; 14 day cancellation notice. **Facility:** 6 rooms. Nicely decorated rooms in a 1927
residence. 2 rooms with a separate entrance in the garden area. Closed in July for vacation. 1-2 stories; interior/exterior corridors; designated smoking area. **All Rooms:** combo or shower baths. **Cards:** AE, DS, MC, VI.

CLARION HOTEL-RANDOLPH PARK   Phone: (520)795-0330   **73**
◆◆   2/1-4/30   1P: $89-$109   2P: $97-$129   XP: $5   F18
Motel   1/1-1/31   1P: $97-$109   2P: $103-$119   XP: $5   F18
            9/16-12/31   1P: $72-$79   2P: $77-$86   XP: $5   F18
            5/1-9/15   1P: $58-$69   2P: $65-$74   XP: $5   F18
Location: Just n of Broadway. 102 N Alvernon 85711. Fax: 520/326-2111. **Terms:** [BP] meal plan; 3 day cancellation notice;
cancellation fee imposed. **Facility:** 157 rooms. 1 two-bedroom unit. 3 stories; interior/exterior corridors. **Cards:** AE, CB, DI,
DS, JC, MC, VI. *(See color ad p 330)*

CLARION HOTEL TUCSON AIRPORT   Phone: (520)746-3932   **44**
◆◆◆   2/1-3/31 & 1/1-1/31   1P: $95-$115   2P: $95-$115   XP: $10   F18
Motor Inn 9/5-12/31   1P: $69-$79   2P: $69-$79   XP: $10   F18
            4/1-9/4   1P: $55-$79   2P: $55-$79   XP: $10   F18
Location: Just n of Tucson International Airport. 6801 S Tucson Blvd 85706. Fax: 520/889-9934. **Terms:** [BP] meal plan; cancellation fee imposed. **Facility:** 189 rooms. Nicely landscaped courtyard and pool area. 2 stories; interior corridors; heated
pool. **Services:** gift shop. **Cards:** AE, CB, DI, DS, MC, VI. *(See ad p 331)*

(See map p. 324)

COMFORT INN   Phone: (520)791-9282   **34**
AAA SAVE   2/1-3/31 & 1/1-1/31   1P: $85-$95   2P: $90-$120   XP: $5   F17
◆   4/1-4/30 & 5/1-12/31   1P: $39-$44   2P: $44-$59   XP: $5   F17
Motel   **Location:** Just w of I-10, 22nd St/Starr Pass Rd exit 259. 715 W Starr Pass Rd 85713. Fax: 520/798-1458.
Terms: [CP] meal plan. **Facility:** 68 rooms. 2 stories; exterior corridors; whirlpool. **Dining:** Restaurant nearby.
All Rooms: extended cable TV. **Cards:** AE, DI, DS, MC, VI. **Special Amenities: Free breakfast and free
local telephone calls.**

COMFORT INN I-10 & INA   Phone: 520/579-7202   **67**
◆◆   2/1-2/29   1P: $100   2P: $110-$125   XP: $10   F12
Motel   3/1-3/31   1P: $90-$110   2P: $100-$120   XP: $10   F12
       1/1-1/31   1P: $70-$80   2P: $80-$90   XP: $10   F12
       4/1-12/31   1P: $60-$70   2P: $70-$80   XP: $10   F12
Location: W side of I-10, Ina Rd exit 248. 4930 W Ina Rd 85743. Fax: 520/579-3894. **Terms:** 7 day cancellation notice.
Facility: 60 rooms. 3 stories; interior corridors. **Cards:** AE, CB, DI, DS, MC, VI.

COMFORT SUITES   Phone: (520)888-6676   **82**
◆◆◆   2/1-3/31 & 1/1-1/31   1P: $90-$130
Motel   10/1-12/31   1P: $71-$130
        4/1-9/30   1P: $61-$100
Location: Just w of SR 77 (Oracle Rd) and Tucson Mall. 515 W Auto Mall Dr 85705. Fax: 520/888-6617. **Terms:** [CP] meal
plan; $1 service charge; pets, $10. **Facility:** 87 rooms. 3 stories; interior corridors; heated pool. **Cards:** AE, CB, DI, DS, JC,
MC, VI.

COUNTRY INN & SUITES BY CARLSON   Phone: (520)575-9255   **56**
◆◆   2/1-4/30   1P: $129   2P: $129   XP: $10   F18
Motel   5/1-5/31 & 10/1-1/31   1P: $89   2P: $89   XP: $10   F18
       6/1-9/30   1P: $69   2P: $69   XP: $10   F18
Location: On SR 77 (Oracle Rd), just n of Ina Rd. 7411 N Oracle Rd 85704. Fax: 520/575-8671. **Terms:** [CP] meal plan; cancellation fee imposed. **Facility:** 157 rooms. Close to Tohono Chul Park which has desert nature trails, demonstration garden
and gift shops. 2-3 stories; exterior corridors; putting green; heated pool. **Some Rooms:** 65 efficiencies, 92 kitchens.
Cards: AE, CB, DI, DS, MC, VI. *(See color ad p 229)*

(See map p. 324)

COURTYARD BY MARRIOTT-TUCSON AIRPORT Phone: (520)573-0000 [49]
◆◆◆ 2/1-5/31 1P: $119-$129 2P: $119-$129
Motor Inn 10/1-1/31 1P: $79-$109 2P: $79-$109
6/1-9/30 1P: $49-$69 2P: $49-$69
Location: On Tucson Blvd 0.6 mi n of Tucson International Airport entrance. 2505 E Executive Dr 85706. Fax: 520/573-0470.
Terms: Cancellation fee imposed. **Facility:** 149 rooms. Attractivly landscaped courtyard. 3 stories; interior corridors; heated
pool. **Cards:** AE, CB, DI, DS, MC, VI. *(See color ad below)*

ASK SD ⊞ ♀ ⤢ ⊠ ☒ ⊠ VCR ⊟ ⬛ ⬚ ⊟ DATA PORT ⤢ (♦)

COURTYARD BY MARRIOTT-TUCSON WILLIAMS CENTRE Phone: (520)745-6000 [79]
◆◆◆ 2/1-3/25 1P: $99-$119 2P: $99-$119
Motor Inn 3/26-5/20 & 9/10-1/31 1P: $79-$99 2P: $79-$99
5/21-9/9 1P: $49-$69 2P: $49-$69
Location: Just s of Broadway between Swan and Craycroft. 201 S Williams Blvd 85711. Fax: 520/745-2393. **Terms:** Cancellation fee imposed. **Facility:** 153 rooms. Nicely landscaped courtyard and pool area. 3 stories; interior corridors; heated pool.
Services: area transportation. **Cards:** AE, CB, DI, DS, MC, VI. *(See color ad below)*

ASK SD ♀ ⤢ ⤢ ♁ ⤢ ☒ ☒ ⊟ ⬛ ⬚ ⊟ DATA PORT ⤢ (♦)

COYOTE CROSSING BED & BREAKFAST Phone: (520)744-3285 [58]
◆◆◆ 2/1-5/31 & 10/1-1/31 1P: $95-$115 2P: $100-$120 XP: $15 F6
Bed & 8/1-9/30 1P: $70-$90 2P: $75-$95 XP: $5 F6
Breakfast 6/1-6/30 1P: $70-$90 2P: $75-$95 XP: $15 F6
Location: 10 mi nw on I-10 to exit 248, 2.3 w on Ina Rd, then 0.2 mi s on Camino Verde. 6985 N Camino Verde
85743. Fax: 520/744-5161. **Terms:** Open 2/1-6/30 & 8/1-1/31; [CP] meal plan; check-in 4 pm; 2 night min stay, weekends.
Facility: 4 rooms. A comfortable, modern Arizona ranch home in a desert setting. 1 story; interior/exterior corridors; designated
smoking area; heated pool. **All Rooms:** combo or shower baths.

SD ⊠ ☎ VCR ⬛ ⬚ ⊟ ⤢

DAYS INN Phone: (520)747-8988 [80]
AAA SAVE 2/1-2/15 1P: $89-$95 2P: $95-$100 XP: $6 F12
◆◆ 2/16-4/30 1P: $59-$69 2P: $69-$79 XP: $6 F12
Motel 11/1-1/31 1P: $49-$59 2P: $59-$69 XP: $6 F12
5/1-10/31 1P: $42-$48 2P: $48-$54 XP: $6 F12
Location: Just n of I-10, westbound exit 264, eastbound exit 264B. 4855 S Palo Verde 85714.
Fax: 520/747-8428. **Facility:** 65 rooms. 2 stories; exterior corridors; whirlpool. **All Rooms:** combo or shower baths.
Cards: AE, CB, DI, DS, MC, VI. **Special Amenities:** Free breakfast and free local telephone calls.

SD ⤢ ⊠ ☒ ⊟ ⬚ ⊟ DATA PORT ⤢ (♦)

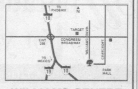

(See map p. 324)

DOUBLETREE GUEST SUITES-TUCSON   Phone: (520)721-7100   28

◆ ◆ ◆

	2/1-4/2	1P: $127	2P: $127	XP: $10 F18
Suite Motor	4/3-5/14 & 9/26-1/31	1P: $99	2P: $99	XP: $10 F18
Inn	5/15-9/25	1P: $60	2P: $60	XP: $10 F18

Location: Just e of Wilmot Rd. 6555 E Speedway Blvd 85710. Fax: 520/721-1991. **Terms:** [BP] meal plan; small pets only, $25. **Facility:** 304 rooms. Nicely landscaped, tree-shaded courtyard areas. 1-bedroom suites with living room, wet bar and refrigerator; some with microwave. 5 stories; exterior corridors; heated pool. **Services:** gift shop. **Cards:** AE, CB, DI, DS, JC, MC, VI. *(See ad below)*

DOUBLETREE HOTEL AT REID PARK   Phone: (520)881-4200   36

◆ ◆ ◆

	2/1-4/15	1P: $119-$139	2P: $119-$139	XP: $20 F17
Hotel	9/25-1/31	1P: $79-$99	2P: $79-$99	XP: $20 F17
	4/16-5/13	1P: $79-$89	2P: $79-$89	XP: $20 F17
	5/14-9/24	1P: $54-$69	2P: $54-$69	XP: $20 F17

Location: Just s of Broadway Blvd. 445 S Alvernon Way 85711. Fax: 520/323-5225. **Terms:** Small pets only, $50 dep req. **Facility:** 295 rooms. Across street from Randolph Golf Course. 2-9 stories; interior/exterior corridors; heated pool; 3 lighted tennis courts. **Services:** gift shop. **Some Rooms:** honor bars. Fee: refrigerators. **Cards:** AE, CB, DI, DS, JC, MC, VI. *(See ad below)*

ECONO LODGE   Phone: (520)622-7763   22

AAA SAVE

◆

	2/1-2/17	1P: $79-$100	2P: $89-$110	XP: $6 F18
	12/20-1/31	1P: $49-$79	2P: $59-$89	XP: $6 F18
Motel	2/18-5/31	1P: $55-$65	2P: $65-$75	XP: $6 F18
	6/1-12/19	1P: $39-$49	2P: $45-$55	XP: $6 F18

Location: 1 mi e of I-10, exit Speedway Blvd; just n on Stone. 1165 N Stone Ave 85705. Fax: 520/792-0776. **Facility:** 43 rooms. Located on busy commercial strip. Rooms with 2 beds somewhat crowded. 2 stories; exterior corridors. **Cards:** AE, CB, DI, DS, JC, MC, VI. **Special Amenities:** Free breakfast and free local telephone calls.

(See map p. 324)

EMBASSY SUITES HOTEL - AIRPORT
Phone: (520)573-0700   **46**

AAA   9/7-1/31   1P: $95-$139   2P: $95-$139   XP: $10   F

◆◆◆   2/1-3/31   1P: $139   2P: $139   XP: $10   F

            4/1-5/31   1P: $109   2P: $109   XP: $10   F

Suite Motor   6/1-9/6   1P: $72   2P: $72   XP: $10   F

Inn   **Location:** At entrance to Tucson International Airport. 7051 S Tucson Blvd 85706. Fax: 520/741-9645. **Terms:** Cancellation fee imposed. **Facility:** 204 rooms. 3 stories; exterior corridors; heated pool, whirlpool. **Dining:** Restaurant; 6 am-10 pm, Fri & Sat-11 pm; $8-$16; cocktails. **Services:** gift shop; complimentary evening beverages. **Recreation:** in-room video games. **All Rooms:** efficiencies. **Some Rooms:** Fee: VCR. **Cards:** AE, CB, DI, DS, JC, MC, VI. *(See color ad p 332)*

EMBASSY SUITES HOTEL-BROADWAY
Phone: (520)745-2700   **68**

AAA SAVE   2/1-3/16   1P: $109-$149   2P: $119-$159   XP: $10   F18

◆◆◆   9/18-1/31   1P: $85-$129   2P: $85-$139   XP: $10   F18

            3/17-5/31   1P: $89-$109   2P: $99-$119   XP: $10   F18

Suite Motel   6/1-9/17   1P: $79-$89   2P: $79-$99   XP: $10   F18

     Location: 5335 E Broadway 85711. Fax: 520/790-9232. **Terms:** [BP] meal plan; monthly rates avail; pets, $25 extra charge. **Facility:** 142 rooms. Nicely landscaped pool area. Spacious 1-bedroom suites. 3 stories; exterior corridors; heated pool, whirlpool. **Cards:** AE, DI, DS, MC, VI. **Special Amenities:** Free breakfast and free newspaper. *(See ad below)*

FAIRFIELD INN BY MARRIOTT
Phone: (520)747-7474   **66**

◆◆◆   2/1-4/1   1P: $95-$115   2P: $105-$125

Motel   4/2-5/31 & 9/1-1/31   1P: $60-$85   2P: $70-$95

            6/1-8/31   1P: $45-$55   2P: $45-$60

Location: 5 mi se on I-10, exit Palo Verde Rd, westbound exit 264, eastbound exit 264B; just e of Palo Verde Rd. 4850 S Hotel Dr 85714. Fax: 520/747-5468. **Terms:** [CP] meal plan; cancellation fee imposed. **Facility:** 66 rooms. 3 stories; interior corridors; heated pool. **Cards:** AE, CB, DI, DS, MC, VI.

GHOST RANCH LODGE
Phone: (520)791-7565   **18**

AAA SAVE   2/1-4/15   1P: $69-$94   2P: $76-$99   XP: $8   F12

◆◆   4/16-6/3 & 10/6-1/31   1P: $48-$72   2P: $54-$79   XP: $8   F12

Motor Inn   6/4-10/5   1P: $39-$60   2P: $39-$68   XP: $8   F12

     Location: 1 mi e of I-10, exit 255, Miracle Mile; just w of Oracle Rd (SR77). 801 W Miracle Mile 85705. Fax: 520/791-3898. **Terms:** [CP] meal plan; pets. **Facility:** 83 rooms. Long-established, with attractively landscaped grounds and cactus garden. Most rooms surround the garden area. Some smaller rooms at back. 13 rooms with private, walled-in yards. 1 story; exterior corridors; heated pool, whirlpool. **Dining:** Dining room; 6:30 am-2 & 5-9 pm; $8-$15; cocktails. **Recreation:** barbecue pit, shuffleboard court, video library. **Some Rooms:** 6 efficiencies, 12 kitchens. Fee: VCR. **Cards:** AE, CB, DI, DS, JC, MC, VI. **Special Amenities:** Early check-in/late check-out and free breakfast. *(See color ad p 335)*

THE GOLF VILLAS AT ORO VALLEY
Phone: (520)498-0098   **92**

AAA SAVE   2/1-4/16   1P: $269-$489

◆◆◆◆   9/12-1/31   1P: $189-$399

            4/17-5/25   1P: $189-$369

Condominium   5/26-9/11   1P: $99-$219

     Location: I-10, exit Ina Rd E, 4 mi to La Canada, then 4.5 mi n. 10950 N La Canada 85737. Fax: 520/498-3988. **Terms:** Monthly rates avail; check-in 4 pm; 10 day cancellation notice; cancellation fee imposed; package plans; pets. **Facility:** 67 rooms. Each guest unit with washer and dryer. 46 two-bedroom units, 9 three-bedroom units. Nine 3-bedroom villas, $199-$449; 67 whirlpool rooms, $99-$489; 2 stories; exterior corridors; smoke free premises; 2 heated pools, whirlpools. **Services:** area transportation. **Recreation:** full range of guest services & recreation facilities at El Conquistador Country Club, free video rentals. **All Rooms:** kitchens, extended cable TV, honor bars. **Cards:** AE, CB, DI, DS, MC, VI. **Special Amenities:** Free local telephone calls and free newspaper. *(See color ad p 335)*

(See map p. 324)

HACIENDA BED & BREAKFAST Phone: (520)290-2224 **20**
◆◆ 2/1-5/31 & 9/1-1/31 1P: $75-$115 2P: $85-$125
Bed & 6/1-8/31 1P: $57-$87 2P: $64-$94
Breakfast **Location:** Just e of Craycroft Rd. 5704 E Grant Rd 85712. Fax: 520/721-9066. **Terms:** [BP] meal plan; 14 day cancellation notice; cancellation fee imposed. **Facility:** 4 rooms. Two large living areas with TV, videos, baby grand piano and library. Cozy, comfortable rooms. 2 stories; interior corridors; smoke free premises. **All Rooms:** shower baths. **Some Rooms:** color TV. **Cards:** AE, DS, MC, VI.

HAMPTON INN AIRPORT Phone: (520)889-5789 **45**
◆◆◆ 2/1-3/31 & 1/1-1/31 1P: $119 2P: $129
Motel 10/1-12/31 1P: $69 2P: $79
4/1-9/30 1P: $59 2P: $69
Location: Just n of Tucson International Airport. 6971 S Tucson Blvd 85706. Fax: 520/889-4002. **Terms:** [CP] meal plan. **Facility:** 126 rooms. 4 stories; interior corridors; heated pool. **Services:** area transportation. **Cards:** AE, CB, DI, DS, MC, VI.

(See map p. 324)

HAMPTON INN & SUITES　　　　　　　　　　　　　　　　　　　Phone: 520/618-8000 　⓫
◆◆◆　　2/1-4/14　　　　　　　　　　　1P: $119-$149　　2P: $129-$159
Motel　　9/8-1/31　　　　　　　　　　　1P: $89-$139　　2P: $99-$159
　　　　　4/15-9/7　　　　　　　　　　　1P: $89-$109　　2P: $99-$119
Location: I-10, Orange Grove e exit, 4 mi to Oracle, then right 0.5 mi s. 5950 N Oracle Rd 85704. Fax: 520/618-8055.
Terms: [CP] meal plan. **Facility:** 110 rooms. 3 stories; interior corridors; heated pool. **Services:** area transportation.
Some Rooms: 40 kitchens. **Cards:** AE, DI, DS, MC, VI.

HAMPTON INN NORTH　　　　　　　　　　　　　　　　　　　Phone: (520)206-0602 　⓺⓽
(AAA) [SAVE]　　2/1-4/30　　　　　　　　　1P: $69-$130　　2P: $79-$130
　　　　　10/1-1/31　　　　　　　　　　1P: $79-$89　　2P: $89-$99
◆◆◆　　5/1-9/30　　　　　　　　　　　1P: $59-$89　　2P: $69-$99
Motel　　　　　**Location:** Grant Rd, just w of I-10, exit 256. 1375 W Grant Rd 85745. Fax: 520/206-0610. **Terms:** [CP] meal
plan; small pets only. **Facility:** 91 rooms. 4 whirlpool rooms, $89-$125; 5 stories; interior corridors; heated pool,
whirlpool. **Dining:** Restaurant nearby. **All Rooms:** extended cable TV. **Cards:** AE, CB, DI, DS, JC, MC, VI. **Special Amenities:**
Free breakfast and free local telephone calls. *(See color ad below)*

HAWTHORN SUITES LTD　　　　　　　　　　　　　　　　　　　Phone: (520)298-2300 　⓶⓺
◆◆◆　　2/1-3/31　　　　　　　　1P: $99-$139　　2P: $99-$139　　XP: $10　　F16
Motel　　10/1-1/31　　　　　　　　1P: $79-$109　　2P: $79-$109　　XP: $10　　F16
　　　　　4/1-5/31　　　　　　　　1P: $69-$89　　2P: $69-$89　　XP: $10　　F16
　　　　　6/1-9/30　　　　　　　　1P: $59-$69　　2P: $59-$69　　XP: $10　　F16
Location: Just w of Sabino Canyon Rd. 7007 E Tanque Verde Rd 85715. Fax: 520/298-6756. **Terms:** [BP] meal plan; cancellation fee imposed; pets, $25 non-refundable dep req. **Facility:** 90 rooms. Rooms surround tree-shaded courtyards. 2 stories;
exterior corridors; heated pool. **Some Rooms:** 60 efficiencies. **Cards:** AE, DI, DS, MC, VI. *(See color ad p 230)*

HILTON-TUCSON EAST　　　　　　　　　　　　　　　　　　　Phone: (520)721-5600 　⓷⓵
◆◆◆　　2/1-4/15　　　　　　　　1P: $135-$185　　2P: $149-$199　　XP: $14　　F18
Hotel　　9/16-1/31　　　　　　　　1P: $89-$185　　2P: $103-$199　　XP: $14　　F18
　　　　　4/16-5/31　　　　　　　　1P: $89-$139　　2P: $103-$153　　XP: $14　　F18
　　　　　6/1-9/15　　　　　　　　1P: $59-$109　　2P: $73-$123　　XP: $14　　F18
Location: 0.6 mi e of Kolb Rd. 7600 E Broadway 85710. Fax: 520/721-5696. **Facility:** 233 rooms. Large atrium area and attractive public areas. 7 stories; interior corridors; heated pool. **Services:** gift shop. **Some Rooms:** honor bars. Fee: refrigerators. **Cards:** AE, CB, DI, DS, JC, MC, VI. *(See color ad p 41 & ad p 337)*

HOLIDAY INN EXPRESS-AIRPORT　　　　　　　　　　　　　　Phone: 520/294-2500 　⓸⓼
◆◆　　　　　　　　　　　　Property failed to provide current rates
Motel　　**Location:** 1 mi ne of Tucson International Airport; just e of Tucson Blvd. 2803 E Valencia Rd 85706.
Fax: 520/741-0851. **Terms:** [CP] meal plan. **Facility:** 97 rooms. 3 stories; interior corridors; heated pool.
Some Rooms: Fee: refrigerators. **Cards:** AE, CB, DI, DS, JC, MC, VI.

HOLIDAY INN EXPRESS-MARANA　　　　　　　　　　　　　　Phone: 520/744-3382 　�7⓿
◆◆　　　　　　　　　　　　Property failed to provide current rates
Motel　　**Location:** 10 mi nw on I-10, Ina Rd exit 248. 4910 W Ina Rd 85743. Fax: 520/744-4116. **Facility:** 69 rooms.
2 stories; exterior corridors. **All Rooms:** combo or shower baths. **Cards:** AE, CB, DI, DS, MC, VI.

7600 E. Broadway
Tucson, AZ 85710
520-721-5600

Hilton
Tucson East

Expect **more value** at Hilton.

Hilton offers special room rates to all AAA members.

From
$55-$122
per room
per night

Whenever you travel to Arizona, the Hilton Tucson East is waiting to serve you. Complete with fitness center, outdoor heated pool and spa. We're just minutes from shopping, historic

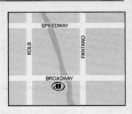

downtown and the Tuscon International Airport. To receive your special rate, just call your AAA travel office or Hilton's private AAA number at **1-800-916-2221** and request "Plan Code AA"

It happens at the Hilton.

(See map p. 324)

HOLIDAY INN EXPRESS-STARR PASS BLVD
Phone: (520)624-4455 **72**

AAA SAVE
◆◆◆
Motel

2/1-3/15	1P: $119	2P: $119	XP: $10 F18
3/16-5/25	1P: $89	2P: $89	XP: $10 F18
10/1-1/31	1P: $79	2P: $79	XP: $10 F18
5/26-9/30	1P: $64	2P: $64	XP: $10 F18

Location: just w of I-10, exit 259 (22nd St). 750 Starr Pass Blvd 85713. Fax: 520/624-3172. **Terms:** [CP] meal plan; cancellation fee imposed. **Facility:** 98 rooms. 2 stories; interior corridors; heated pool, saunas, whirlpool. **Dining:** Restaurant nearby. **All Rooms:** extended cable TV, safes. **Cards:** AE, CB, DI, DS, MC, VI. **Special Amenities: Free breakfast and free newspaper.**

HOLIDAY INN-PALO VERDE
Phone: (520)746-1161 **39**

AAA SAVE
◆◆◆
Motor Inn

All Year   1P: $87   2P: $87   XP: $8   F12

Location: 0.5 mi n of I-10, exit Palo Verde, westbound exit 264, eastbound exit 264B. 4550 S Palo Verde Blvd 85714. Fax: 520/741-1170. **Facility:** 301 rooms. 51 1-bedroom suites with wetbar, refrigerator and microwave. 3-6 stories; interior/exterior corridors; heated pool, sauna, whirlpool; 1 lighted tennis court. **Dining:** Restaurant; 6 am-2 & 5-10 pm; $6-$18; cocktails. **Services:** gift shop. **Cards:** AE, CB, DI, DS, MC, VI. **Special Amenities: Free newspaper and free room upgrade (subject to availability with advanced reservations).**

HOWARD JOHNSON HOTEL
Phone: (520)623-7792 **60**

AAA SAVE
◆◆
Motor Inn

2/1-3/31	1P: $89-$129	2P: $89-$129	XP: $5 F17
4/1-5/31 & 10/1-1/31	1P: $59-$79	2P: $59-$79	XP: $5 F17
6/1-9/30	1P: $39-$69	2P: $39-$69	XP: $5 F17

Location: Adjacent and just s of I-10, exit 262(Park Ave/Benson Hwy). 1025 E Benson Hwy 85713. Fax: 520/620-1556. **Terms:** 14 day cancellation notice; cancellation fee imposed. **Facility:** 136 rooms. Attractive pool area. 2 stories; interior corridors; heated pool, saunas, whirlpool. **Dining:** Coffee shop; 5 am-11 pm; $6-$10; wine/beer only. **Cards:** AE, CB, DI, DS, MC, VI. **Special Amenities: Free local telephone calls and free newspaper.**

JEREMIAH INN BED & BREAKFAST
Phone: (520)749-3072 **84**

◆◆◆
Bed & Breakfast

2/1-5/31 & 10/1-1/31	1P: $90-$115	2P: $95-$120	XP: $15 F3
6/1-9/30	1P: $75-$95	2P: $80-$100	XP: $15 F3

Location: Ne area of town; from Tanque Verde Rd, take Catalina Hwy 3.7 mi ne, then just w on Synder. 10921 E Snyder Rd 85749. **Terms:** [BP] meal plan. **Facility:** 4 rooms. Modern Arizona home in a desert setting at foot of Catalina Mountains. 1 story; interior corridors; smoke free premises. **Cards:** AE, MC, VI.

KNIGHTS INN
Phone: (520)624-8291 **94**

AAA SAVE
◆
Motel

2/1-2/15	1P: $99-$119	2P: $109-$119	XP: $5 F12
2/16-1/31	1P: $35-$65	2P: $40-$70	XP: $5 F12

Location: W side I-10, exit 22nd St (exit 259) then 0.5 mi s, then just w on 29th St. 720 W 29th St 85713. Fax: 520/884-1624. **Terms:** Small pets only, $3 fee. **Facility:** 94 rooms. 1 story; exterior corridors; whirlpool. **Cards:** AE, CB, DI, DS, MC, VI. **Special Amenities: Free breakfast and free local telephone calls.**

LA POSADA DEL VALLE BED & BREAKFAST
Phone: (520)795-3840 **43**

◆◆◆
Bed & Breakfast

9/1-1/31	1P: $78-$128	2P: $95-$148	XP: $25 F3
2/1-5/31	1P: $88-$138	2P: $95-$138	XP: $25 F3
6/1-6/30 & 8/1-8/31	1P: $58-$98	2P: $68-$98	XP: $25 F3

Location: 0.5 mi n of Speedway Blvd, on se corner of Campbell Ave and Elm St. 1640 N Campbell Ave 85719. Fax: 520/795-3840. **Terms:** Open 2/1-6/30 & 8/1-1/31; [BP] meal plan; 14 day cancellation notice; cancellation fee imposed. **Facility:** 5 rooms. Beautifully decorated guest quarters in a charming southwest adobe style building. Check in 3 pm-6 pm. Attractive garden area. 1 story; exterior corridors; smoke free premises. **Cards:** MC, VI.

LA QUINTA INN & SUITES AIRPORT
Phone: (520)573-3333 **74**

AAA SAVE
◆◆◆
Motel

2/1-3/31	1P: $89-$109	2P: $89-$109
4/1-1/31	1P: $79-$99	2P: $79-$99

Location: Just n of Tucson International Airport. 7001 S Tucson Blvd 85706. Fax: 520/573-7710. **Terms:** [CP] meal plan; small pets only. **Facility:** 143 rooms. Spacious, very nicely decorated rooms. Interior corridors; heated pool, whirlpool. **Dining:** Restaurant nearby. **Services:** area transportation, within 5 mi. **Recreation:** in-room video games. **All Rooms:** extended cable TV. **Cards:** AE, CB, DI, DS, MC, VI. **Special Amenities: Free breakfast and free local telephone calls.** (See color ad p 339)

LA QUINTA INN-EAST
Phone: (520)747-1414 **32**

AAA SAVE
◆◆◆
Motel

2/1-3/31	1P: $75-$95	2P: $75-$95
4/1-1/31	1P: $65-$85	2P: $65-$85

Location: Just e of Wilmot Rd. 6404 E Broadway 85710. Fax: 520/745-6903. **Terms:** [CP] meal plan; small pets only. **Facility:** 141 rooms. Tree-shaded courtyard and pool area. 2 stories; exterior corridors; heated pool, whirlpool. **Dining:** Restaurant nearby. **All Rooms:** extended cable TV. **Some Rooms:** Fee: refrigerators, microwaves. **Cards:** AE, CB, DI, DS, JC, MC, VI. **Special Amenities: Free breakfast and free local telephone calls.** (See color ad p 339)

(See map p. 324)

LAZY 8 MOTEL　　　　　　　　　　　　　　　　　　　　　　　　　Phone: (520)622-3336　64

2/1-4/1	1P: $39-$44	2P: $47	XP: $5　F12
10/2-1/31	1P: $31-$36	2P: $41	XP: $5　F12
4/2-6/1	1P: $33-$37	2P: $40	XP: $5　F12
6/2-10/1	1P: $27-$33	2P: $37	XP: $5　F12

AAA SAVE ◆ Motel

Location: S side of I-10, exit 261 (6th Ave); on Frontage Rd, just e of 6th Ave. 314 E Benson Hwy 85713. Fax: 520/882-5496. **Terms:** Weekly rates avail. **Facility:** 48 rooms. 1-2 stories; exterior corridors. **All Rooms:** combo or shower baths. **Cards:** AE, DS, MC, VI. **Special Amenities:** Free breakfast and free local telephone calls.

LAZY K BAR GUEST RANCH　　　　　　　　　　　　　　　　　　Phone: (520)744-3050　55

12/18-1/31	1P: $157-$189	2P: $260-$298	XP: $73　D17
2/1-4/30	1P: $150-$180	2P: $248-$284	XP: $70　D17
9/15-12/17	1P: $141-$173	2P: $229-$260	XP: $73　D17
5/1-6/18	1P: $118-$149	2P: $190-$210	XP: $70　D17

AAA ◆◆ Ranch

Location: 13 mi nw on I-10, exit 246; 1 mi w on Cortaro Rd, then 1.3 mi nw on Silverbell Rd and 1.5 mi w on Pima Farms Rd. 8401 N Scenic Dr 85743. Fax: 520/744-7628. **Terms:** Open 2/1-6/18 & 9/15-1/31; [AP] meal plan; weekly rates avail; age restrictions may apply; 30 day cancellation notice; cancellation fee imposed; 16% service charge. **Facility:** 23 rooms. Secluded setting at foot of Tucson Mountains on landscaped desert terrain. Many recreational facilities and activities. Some rooms with private patio. Four suites with fireplaces. Daily rate includes horseback riding twice daily; 1 story; exterior corridors; heated pool, whirlpool; 2 lighted tennis courts; playground. **Services:** gift shop. **Recreation:** horseshoe pit, shuffleboard court. Fee: bicycles. **Cards:** AE, DS, MC, VI.

THE LODGE AT VENTANA CANYON　　　　　　　　　　　　　　Phone: (520)577-1400　75

2/1-4/8	1P: $389-$499	2P: $389-$499	XP: $25　F16
10/1-1/31	1P: $289-$499	2P: $289-$499	XP: $25　F16
4/9-5/25	1P: $189-$399	2P: $189-$399	XP: $25　F16
5/26-9/5	1P: $89-$199	2P: $89-$199	XP: $25　F16

◆◆◆◆ Resort

Location: Just e of Kolb Rd, 0.6 mi n of Sunrise Dr. 6200 N Clubhouse Ln 85750. Fax: 520/577-4065. **Terms:** Check-in 4 pm; 21 day cancellation notice; cancellation fee imposed; package plans; 15% service charge. **Facility:** 50 rooms. In northeast area of town at foot of Catalina Mountains. Spacious rooms decorated in a Southwest motif. 13 two-bedroom units. 2 stories; interior/exterior corridors; beachfront; heated pool; 12 lighted tennis courts. Fee: 36 holes golf. **Services:** Fee: massage. **Recreation:** Fee: bicycles. **All Rooms:** efficiencies, combo or shower baths, honor bars. **Some Rooms:** Fee: VCR. **Cards:** AE, CB, DI, DS, MC, VI.

LOEWS VENTANA CANYON RESORT　　　　　　　　　　　　　Phone: (520)299-2020　14

9/6-1/31	1P: $221-$320	2P: $221-$320	XP: $25　F18
2/1-5/20	1P: $198-$275	2P: $198-$275	XP: $25　F18
5/21-9/5	1P: $99-$126	2P: $99-$126	XP: $25　F18

AAA SAVE ◆◆◆ Resort

Location: 13 mi ne; 2 mi e of Craycroft Rd on Sunrise Dr, 1.5 mi n on Kolb Rd. 7000 N Resort Dr 85750. Fax: 520/299-6832. **Terms:** 7 day cancellation notice; cancellation fee imposed; package plans. **Facility:** 398 rooms. Beautiful location at foot of Catalina Mountains. 12 whirlpool rooms; 3-4 stories; interior/exterior corridors; 2 heated pools, saunas, steamrooms, whirlpools; playground. Fee: 18 holes golf; 8 lighted tennis courts. **Dining:** Dining room, 2 restaurants; 6 am-11 pm; $15-$50; cocktails; afternoon tea; also, The Ventana Room, see separate listing; entertainment. **Services:** gift shop. Fee: massage, area transportation, within 5 mi. **Recreation:** hiking trails, par course. Rental: bicycles. **All Rooms:** honor bars. **Some Rooms:** Fee: microwaves, VCR. **Cards:** AE, CB, DI, DS, JC, MC, VI.

MARRIOTT UNIVERSITY PARK HOTEL　　　　　　　　　　　　Phone: 520/792-4100　76

2/1-4/24	1P: $149-$189	2P: $149-$189	XP: $15　F18
9/8-1/31	1P: $114-$189	2P: $114-$189	XP: $15　F18
4/25-6/24	1P: $99-$159	2P: $99-$159	XP: $15　F18
6/25-9/7	1P: $77-$129	2P: $77-$129	XP: $15　F18

◆◆◆ Hotel

Location: Just w of University of Arizona; just s of Speedway Blvd. 880 E 2nd St 85719. Fax: 520/882-4100. **Terms:** 5 day cancellation notice. **Facility:** 250 rooms. Contemporary hotel with atrium lobby. 9 stories; interior corridors; heated pool. Fee: parking. **Services:** gift shop. **Cards:** AE, CB, DI, DS, JC, MC, VI.

(See map p. 324)

OMNI TUCSON NATIONAL GOLF RESORT & SPA   **Phone:** (520)297-2271   54
◆◆◆◆   1/1-1/31   1P: $265-$355   2P: $265-$355   XP: $20   F17
Resort   2/1-5/27   1P: $260-$350   2P: $260-$350   XP: $20   F17
            9/10-12/31   1P: $170-$260   2P: $170-$260   XP: $20   F17
            5/28-9/9   1P: $100-$160   2P: $100-$160   XP: $20   F17
Location: I-10, exit 246 (Cortaro Rd); 3.5 mi e, then n on Shannon Rd. 2727 W Club Dr 85741. **Fax:** 520/742-2452.
Terms: 7 day cancellation notice; cancellation fee imposed; package plans. **Facility:** 167 rooms. On several acres of nicely
landscaped grounds. Extensive health spa facilities. Spacious, nicely furnished rooms, suites and haciendas; many overlooking
the golf course. 1-2 stories; exterior corridors; 2 heated pools; 4 lighted tennis courts. Fee: 27 holes golf. **Services:** gift shop.
Fee: massage. **All Rooms:** honor bars. **Some Rooms:** 28 efficiencies, 24 kitchens. Fee: VCR. **Cards:** AE, CB, DI, DS,
MC, VI.

THE PEPPERTREES BED & BREAKFAST INN   **Phone:** 520/622-7167   51
◆◆◆   9/2-1/31   1P: $98-$115   2P: $108-$135
Bed &   2/1-5/31   1P: $88-$115   2P: $108-$135
Breakfast 6/1-9/1   1P: $75-$85   2P: $85-$95
            Location: Just w of University of Arizona. 724 E University Blvd 85719. **Fax:** 520/622-7167. **Terms:** [BP] meal
plan; 14 day cancellation notice; 2 night min stay, weekends. **Facility:** 6 rooms. Two charming territorial homes built in the early
1900's and southwestern style guest houses. TV in common rooms and studio unit. 1-2 stories; interior/exterior corridors;
smoke free premises. **All Rooms:** combo or shower baths. **Some Rooms:** 2 efficiencies. **Cards:** DS, MC, VI.

PLAZA HOTEL   **Phone:** (520)327-7341   25
◆◆◆   2/1-4/1   1P: $119-$149   2P: $119-$149   XP: $15   F18
Hotel   9/8-1/31   1P: $99-$149   2P: $99-$149   XP: $15   F18
            4/2-5/20   1P: $99-$129   2P: $99-$129   XP: $15   F18
            5/21-9/7   1P: $79-$99   2P: $79-$99   XP: $15   F18
Location: Se corner of Speedway Blvd and Campbell Ave. 1900 E Speedway Blvd 85719. **Fax:** 520/327-0276. **Terms:** Can-
cellation fee imposed. **Facility:** 150 rooms. Just east of University of Arizona. 7 stories; interior corridors; heated pool.
Cards: AE, CB, DI, DS, JC, MC, VI.

RAMADA INN FOOTHILLS   **Phone:** (520)886-9595   63
ⓐⓐⓐ SAVE   2/1-4/23   1P: $89-$125   2P: $99-$135   XP: $10   F18
            10/1-1/31   1P: $60-$125   2P: $60-$135   XP: $10   F18
◆◆   4/24-5/31   1P: $60-$80   2P: $60-$100   XP: $10   F18
Motel   6/1-9/30   1P: $45-$70   2P: $50-$80   XP: $10   F18
            Location: Just w of Sabino Canyon Rd. 6944 E Tanque Verde Rd 85715. **Fax:** 520/721-8466. **Terms:** [CP]
meal plan. **Facility:** 113 rooms. 2 stories; exterior corridors; heated pool, saunas, whirlpool. **Dining:** Restaurant nearby.
Services: complimentary evening beverages. **All Rooms:** extended cable TV. **Cards:** AE, CB, DI, DS, JC, MC, VI.
Special Amenities: Free breakfast and free local telephone calls. *(See color ad below)*

RAMADA-PALO VERDE   **Phone:** (520)294-5250   41
ⓐⓐⓐ SAVE   2/1-2/20   1P: $149   2P: $159   XP: $10   F18
            2/21-4/30   1P: $99   2P: $99   XP: $10   F18
◆◆◆   1/1-1/31   1P: $89   2P: $99   XP: $10   F18
Motor Inn 5/1-12/31   1P: $79   2P: $89   XP: $10   F18
            Location: Just s of I-10,Palo Verde Rd, exit 264A. 5251 S Julian Dr 85706. **Fax:** 520/295-1058. **Terms:** [BP]
meal plan. **Facility:** 173 rooms. 20 suites with wetbar, refrigerator & microwave, $89-$169; 2 stories; exterior corridors; heated
pool, whirlpools. **Dining:** Restaurant; 6 am-10 pm; $7-$13; cocktails. **Services:** complimentary evening beverages; area transportation, within 5 mi. **Recreation:** in-room video games. **Cards:** AE, CB, DI, DS, MC, VI. **Special Amenities:** Free breakfast
and free room upgrade (subject to availability with advanced reservations).

(See map p. 324)

RED ROOF INN TUCSON NORTH

				Phone: (520)744-8199	77
	2/1-4/4	1P: $66-$86	2P: $71-$91	XP: $5	F18
	1/1-1/31	1P: $46-$66	2P: $51-$71	XP: $5	F18
◆ ◆	4/5-5/9	1P: $36-$56	2P: $41-$61	XP: $5	F18
Motel	5/10-12/31	1P: $31-$51	2P: $36-$56	XP: $5	F18

Location: Just w of I-10, Ina Rd exit 248. 4940 W Ina Rd 85743. Fax: 520/744-7782. **Terms:** Pets, in smoking rooms only. **Facility:** 133 rooms. 4 stories; interior corridors; heated pool. **Dining:** Restaurant nearby. **Cards:** AE, CB, DI, DS, MC, VI.

RED ROOF INN-TUCSON SOUTH

				Phone: (520)571-1400	40
	2/1-4/4	1P: $66-$86	2P: $71-$91	XP: $5	F18
	1/1-1/31	1P: $46-$66	2P: $51-$71	XP: $5	F18
◆ ◆	4/5-5/9	1P: $36-$56	2P: $41-$61	XP: $5	F18
Motor Inn	5/10-12/31	1P: $31-$51	2P: $36-$56	XP: $5	F18

Location: 5 mi se on I-10, exit Palo Verde Rd; westbound exit 264, eastbound exit 264B, just e of Palo Verde Rd. 3700 E Irvington Rd 85714. Fax: 520/519-0051. **Terms:** Small pets only. **Facility:** 118 rooms. 2 stories; exterior corridors; heated pool, whirlpool. **Dining:** Coffee shop nearby. **Recreation:** in-room video games. **Cards:** AE, CB, DI, DS, MC, VI.

RESIDENCE INN BY MARRIOTT

				Phone: (520)721-0991	29
◆ ◆ ◆	2/1-4/30	1P: $149-$189	2P: $149-$189		
Apartment	10/1-12/31 & 1/1-1/31	1P: $109-$149	2P: $109-$149		
	5/1-9/30	1P: $79-$104	2P: $79-$104		

Location: Just e of Wilmot Rd. 6477 E Speedway Blvd 85710. Fax: 520/290-8323. **Terms:** [CP] meal plan; check-in 4 pm; cancellation fee imposed; pets, $8 extra charge, $50-$75 cleaning fee. **Facility:** 128 rooms. Attractive studios and 1 bedroom suites; some fireplaces. 32 two-bedroom units. 2 stories; exterior corridors; heated pool. **Recreation:** sports court. **All Rooms:** kitchens. **Cards:** AE, CB, DI, DS, JC, MC, VI.

(See map p. 324)

RODEWAY INN I-10 & GRANT RD Phone: (520)622-7791 **19**

	9/1-1/31	1P: $50-$79	2P: $55-$89
	2/1-3/31	1P: $79	2P: $89
◆◆	4/1-5/31	1P: $59	2P: $69
Motor Inn	6/1-8/31	1P: $45	2P: $49

Location: Just w of I-10, Grant Rd exit 256. 1365 W Grant Rd 85745. Fax: 520/629-0201. **Terms:** Small pets only, $10 extra charge, in smoking rooms only. **Facility:** 147 rooms. 2 stories; exterior corridors; heated pool, whirlpool. **Dining:** Restaurant; 7 am-2 & 5-9 pm; $5-$10. **All Rooms:** extended cable TV. **Cards:** AE, CB, DI, DS, MC, VI. **Special Amenities:** Free newspaper and free room upgrade (subject to availability with advanced reservations). *(See ad p 341)*

RODEWAY INN-PARK AVE AT I-10 Phone: (520)884-5800 **38**

	2/1-2/15	1P: $99	2P: $120	XP: $5	F18
	2/16-3/31 & 1/1-1/31	1P: $55-$65	2P: $61-$69	XP: $5	F18
◆	4/1-12/31	1P: $42-$48	2P: $46-$52	XP: $5	F18

Motel **Location:** Just s of I-10, Park Ave/Benson Hwy exit 262. 810 E Benson Hwy 85713. Fax: 520/624-2681. **Terms:** [CP] meal plan; small pets only, $25 dep req. **Facility:** 99 rooms. 2 stories; exterior corridors; heated pool. **Dining:** Restaurant nearby. **Some Rooms:** Fee: refrigerators, microwaves. **Cards:** AE, CB, DI, DS, JC, MC, VI. **Special Amenities:** Free breakfast and free local telephone calls. *(See ad p 341)*

(See map p. 324)

SHERATON EL CONQUISTADOR   Phone: (520)544-5000   53

AAA SAVE	2/1-3/31	1P: $354-$469	2P: $354-$469	XP: $20	F17
	9/18-1/31	1P: $309-$469	2P: $309-$469	XP: $20	F17
◆◆◆◆	4/1-5/25	1P: $269-$369	2P: $269-$369	XP: $20	F17
Resort	5/26-9/17	1P: $159-$234	2P: $159-$234	XP: $20	F17

Location: SR 77, 3.5 mi n of Ina Rd. 10000 N Oracle Rd 85737. Fax: 520/544-1222. **Terms:** Check-in 4 pm; 7 day cancellation notice; cancellation fee imposed; package plans; small pets only, $50 dep req. **Facility:** 428 rooms. On several acres of nicely landscaped grounds in a desert area at foot of the Catalina Mountains. Spacious, nicely decorated rooms surround a large, landscaped pool area. Some rooms located in a more private casita area. Casita suites with separate bedroom & living room, wet bar & fireplace $35-$45 extra; 2 whirlpool rooms; 1-3 stories; interior/exterior corridors; 4 heated pools, whirlpools. Fee: 45 holes golf; racquetball courts, 31 lighted tennis courts. **Dining:** Dining room, 4 restaurants; 7 am-10 pm; $8-$30; cocktails; also, The Last Territory, see separate listing; entertainment. **Services:** gift shop; area transportation. **Recreation:** Fee: horseback riding. Rental: bicycles. **All Rooms:** extended cable TV, safes, honor bars. **Some Rooms:** Fee: refrigerators, microwaves. **Cards:** AE, CB, DI, DS, JC, MC, VI. **Special Amenities: Preferred room (subject to availability with advanced reservations).**

SHERATON TUCSON HOTEL & SUITES   Phone: (520)323-6262   16

◆◆◆	2/1-4/15	1P: $129-$179	2P: $129-$179	XP: $10	F18
Motor Inn	10/1-1/31	1P: $109-$169	2P: $109-$169	XP: $10	F18
	4/16-5/21	1P: $99-$159	2P: $99-$159	XP: $10	F18
	5/22-9/30	1P: $69-$109	2P: $69-$109	XP: $10	F18

Location: 0.5 mi e of Swan Rd. 5151 E Grant Rd 85712. Fax: 520/325-2989. **Terms:** [BP] meal plan; cancellation fee imposed. **Facility:** 216 rooms. Standard units and 1-bedroom suites with living room. Located in area with many health care facilities. 4 stories; interior/exterior corridors; heated pool. **Services:** gift shop. **Some Rooms:** Fee: microwaves, VCR. **Cards:** AE, CB, DI, DS, MC, VI.

SHONEY'S INN   Phone: 520/620-6500   87

◆◆   Property failed to provide current rates

Motel   **Location:** 0.3 mi w of I-10, exit 256. 1550 W Grant Rd 85745. Fax: 520/903-0225. **Terms:** [CP] meal plan; $1
             service charge. **Facility:** 65 rooms. 2 stories; exterior corridors. **Some Rooms:** Fee: VCR. **Cards:** AE, CB, DI,
DS, MC, VI.

(See map p. 324)

SMUGGLER'S INN HOTEL
Phone: (520)296-3292 **30**

	2/1-3/31	1P: $99-$119	2P: $99-$119	XP: $10	F16
	4/1-5/15	1P: $89-$109	2P: $89-$109	XP: $10	F16
	10/1-1/31	1P: $79-$89	2P: $79-$89	XP: $10	F16
Motor Inn	5/16-9/30	1P: $69-$79	2P: $69-$79	XP: $10	F16

Location: Se corner of Speedway Blvd and Wilmot Rd. 6350 E Speedway Blvd 85710. Fax: 520/722-3713. **Terms:** [CP] meal plan. **Facility:** 149 rooms. Beautifully landscaped grounds with streams and ponds. Large units with patio or balcony. 28 larger rooms with efficiency & sitting area, $135; 5/11-1/11, $96; 2 stories; exterior corridors; putting green; heated pool, whirlpool. **Dining:** Restaurant; 6:30 am-10:30 & 4-9 pm; $8-$12; cocktails. **Services:** gift shop. **Cards:** AE, CB, DI, DS, JC, MC, VI. **Special Amenities:** Free breakfast and free newspaper. *(See color ad p 342)*

STUDIO 6
Phone: 520/746-0030 **85**

Property failed to provide current rates

Location: Adjacent to I-10; exit 264 eastbound, exit 264B; just w of Palo Vere Rd and s of Irvington Rd. 4950 S Outlet Center Rd 85706. Fax: 520/741-7403. **Terms:** Weekly rates avail; pets, $25 extra charge. **Facility:** 120 rooms. 2 stories; exterior corridors; heated pool. **All Rooms:** efficiencies. **Cards:** AE, CB, DI, DS, MC, VI.

SUMNER SUITES
Phone: (520)295-0405 **47**

	2/1-5/12 & 9/11-1/31	1P: $129-$139	2P: $129-$139	XP: $10	F17
Suite Motel	5/13-9/10	1P: $89-$99	2P: $89-$99	XP: $10	F17

Location: Just n of Tucson International Airport. 6885 S Tucson Blvd 85706. Fax: 520/295-9140. **Terms:** [CP] meal plan. **Facility:** 122 rooms. 5 stories; interior corridors; heated pool. **Dining:** Restaurant nearby. **Services:** area transportation, within 5 mi. **All Rooms:** extended cable TV. **Cards:** AE, CB, DI, DS, JC, MC, VI. **Special Amenities:** Free breakfast and free local telephone calls.

THE SUNCATCHER
Phone: (520)885-0883 **42**

Bed &	2/1-4/30 & 12/1-1/31	1P: $140-$165	2P: $140-$165
Breakfast	9/15-11/30	1P: $125-$145	2P: $125-$145
	5/1-9/14	1P: $80-$100	2P: $80-$100

Location: 16.5 mi e of downtown via Broadway; 2.6 mi e of Houghton Rd, just n on Avenida Javalina (gravel road). 105 N Avenida Javalina 85748. Fax: 520/885-0883. **Terms:** [BP] meal plan; 14 day cancellation notice; cancellation fee imposed. **Facility:** 4 rooms. Contemporary home in a quiet desert setting. Guest rooms furnished in style of four of the famous hotels of the world. 1 story; interior/exterior corridors; designated smoking area; heated pool. **All Rooms:** combo or shower baths. **Cards:** AE, DI, DS, MC, VI.

(See map p. 324)

SUPER 8 CENTRAL EAST
(AAA) [SAVE] — Phone: (520)790-6021 [59]

◆ ◆	2/1-2/15	1P: $79		2P: $85	XP: $5	F12
	2/16-3/31	1P: $59		2P: $69	XP: $5	F12
Motel	1/1-1/31	1P: $49		2P: $55		F12
	4/1-12/31	1P: $45		2P: $49	XP: $5	F12

Location: 0.5 mi n of Main Gate to Davis Monthan Air Force Base; 0.5 mi s of 22nd St. 1990 S Craycroft Rd 85711. Fax: 520/790-6074. **Terms:** [CP] meal plan; cancellation fee imposed. **Facility:** 42 rooms. 2 stories; exterior corridors; small pool, seasonal pool. **Some Rooms:** color TV. **Cards:** AE, CB, DI, DS, JC, MC, VI. **Special Amenities: Free breakfast and free local telephone calls.**

SUPER 8 MOTEL
◆ — Phone: 520/622-8089 [78]

Motel	2/1-2/29	1P: $79-$89	2P: $99	XP: $8	F10
	10/1-1/31	1P: $49-$59	2P: $59-$69	XP: $5	F10
	3/1-3/31	1P: $49-$59	2P: $69	XP: $8	F10
	4/1-9/30	1P: $39-$49	2P: $49	XP: $5	F10

Location: W side of I-10, just n of 22nd St exit. 1000 S Freeway 85745. Fax: 520/798-3940. **Facility:** 42 rooms. 2 stories; interior corridors. **Cards:** AE, CB, DI, DS, MC, VI. *(See color ad p 342)*

VISCOUNT SUITE HOTEL
◆ ◆ ◆ — Phone: (520)745-6500 [33]
Suite Hotel
Property failed to provide current rates
Location: 5 mi e; just e of Swan Rd. 4855 E Broadway 85711. Fax: 520/790-5114. **Terms:** [BP] meal plan. **Facility:** 216 rooms. Large attractive atrium area. 2 two-bedroom units. 4 stories; interior corridors; heated pool. **Services:** gift shop. **Some Rooms:** Fee: VCR. **Cards:** AE, DI, DS, MC, VI.

WAYWARD WINDS LODGE
(AAA) [SAVE] — Phone: (520)791-7526 [17]

◆ ◆ ◆	2/1-3/31	1P: $69-$99	2P: $69-$99	XP: $10	F12
	1/1-1/31	1P: $59-$89	2P: $59-$89	XP: $10	F12
Motel	4/1-5/31	1P: $49-$89	2P: $49-$89	XP: $10	F12
	6/1-12/31	1P: $39-$69	2P: $39-$69	XP: $10	F12

Location: 1.2 mi e of I-10, exit 255, Miracle Mile; just w of Oracle Rd (SR 77). 707 W Miracle Mile 85705. Fax: 520/791-9502. **Terms:** [CP] meal plan; weekly & monthly rates avail, in summer; 3 day cancellation notice; small pets only. **Facility:** 40 rooms. Nicely landscaped lawn and pool area. 8 two-bedroom units. 1 story; exterior corridors; heated pool. **Recreation:** barbecue, pool slide, shuffleboard courts. **All Rooms:** extended cable TV. **Some Rooms:** 9 efficiencies, 9 kitchens. **Cards:** AE, DI, DS, MC, VI. **Special Amenities: Free local telephone calls and preferred room (subject to availability with advanced reservations).** *(See color ad p 343)*

WESTWARD LOOK RESORT
(AAA) [SAVE] — Phone: (520)297-1151 [12]

◆ ◆ ◆ ◆	2/1-4/30		2P: $200-$299	XP: $25	F17
	9/7-1/31		2P: $109-$199	XP: $25	F17
Resort	5/1-5/31		2P: $129-$189	XP: $25	F17
	6/1-9/6		2P: $99-$139	XP: $25	F17

Location: 0.5 mi e on Ina Rd from Oracle Rd (SR 77), just n on Westward Look Dr. 245 E Ina Rd 85704. Fax: 520/297-9023. **Terms:** 7 day cancellation notice; cancellation fee imposed; package plans; small pets only. **Facility:** 244 rooms. Attractive desert setting on several acres of grounds. 1-2 stories; exterior corridors; 3 heated pools, whirlpools. Fee: 8 tennis courts (5 lighted). **Dining:** Dining room, restaurant; 6:30 am-11:30 pm; $9-$30; cocktails; also, The Gold Room, see separate listing. **Services:** gift shop. **Recreation:** hiking trails, jogging, massage therapy & body treatments in the Wellness Center. **All Rooms:** honor bars. **Some Rooms:** Fee: VCR. **Cards:** AE, CB, DI, DS, MC, VI. **Special Amenities: Early check-in/late check-out and free newspaper.** *(See color ad p 344)*

WINDMILL INN AT ST. PHILIP'S PLAZA
(AAA) [SAVE] — Phone: (520)577-0007 [37]

◆ ◆ ◆	2/1-4/15 & 4/16-5/31	1P: $135-$145	XP: $10	F18
Suite Motel	6/1-9/15 & 9/16-1/31	1P: $65-$80	XP: $10	F18

Location: Se corner Campbell Ave and River Rd. 4250 N Campbell Ave 85718. Fax: 520/577-0045. **Terms:** [CP] meal plan; check-in 4 pm; pets. **Facility:** 122 rooms. All units are one bedroom suites. 5 presidential suites with whirlpool, $200-$400; 3 stories; interior corridors; heated pool, whirlpool. **Dining:** Continental breakfast served to room; restaurant nearby. **Recreation:** bicycles, lending library. **All Rooms:** extended cable TV. **Cards:** AE, CB, DI, DS, MC, VI. **Special Amenities: Free breakfast and free local telephone calls.** *(See ad p 343)*

(See map p. 324)

—————— RESTAURANTS ——————

ANTHONY'S IN THE CATALINAS   **Lunch:** $8-$14   **Dinner:** $20-$33   **Phone:** 520/299-1771   29
◆◆◆◆   **Location:** Just n of Skyline Dr. 6440 N Campbell Ave 85718. **Hours:** 11:30 am-2:30 & 5:30-10 pm, Sun from
Continental   5:30 pm. Closed major holidays. **Reservations:** suggested. **Features:** semi-formal attire; cocktails & lounge;
valet parking. Desert setting with city or mountain views. Beautifully decorated dining room. Extensive wine
selections. Fine dining. **Cards:** AE, CB, DI, MC, VI.

CAFE TERRA COTTA   **Lunch:** $9-$22   **Dinner:** $9-$22   **Phone:** 520/577-8100   10
◆◆   **Location:** Se corner Campbell Ave and River Rd; in St Philips Plaza. 4310 N Campbell Ave 85718.
Southwest   **Hours:** 11 am-9:30 pm, Fri & Sat-10 pm. Closed: 11/23 & 12/25. **Reservations:** suggested.
American   **Features:** casual dress; children's menu; carryout; cocktails; a la carte. Casual indoor or outdoor patio
dining. Interesting selection of contemporary Southwestern cuisine and gourmet wood-fired pizza. Regional
ingredients. Flavorful dishes created by chef/owner. Gourmet takeout section. Smoke free premises. **Cards:** AE, CB, DI, DS,
MC, VI.

CIBARIA CUCINA ITALIANA   **Lunch:** $6-$9   **Dinner:** $10-$20   **Phone:** 520/825-2900   31
◆◆   **Location:** On SR 77; in Oro Valley; 8 mi n of Ina Rd in Rancho Vista Plaza. 12985 N Oracle Rd 85737.
Italian   **Hours:** 11 am-2:30 & 4:30-9 pm. Closed major holidays & Sun. **Reservations:** suggested. **Features:** casual
dress; children's menu; carryout; cocktails. Features a large variety of pasta entrees. Also a selection of veal,
seafood and chicken. Smoke free premises. **Cards:** AE, CB, DI, DS, MC, VI.

COTTONWOOD CAFE   **Lunch:** $5-$9   **Dinner:** $12-$20   **Phone:** 520/326-6000   30
◆◆◆   **Location:** Just n of Broadway. 60 N Alvernon Way 85711. **Hours:** 11:15 am-10 pm, Fri & Sat-11 pm. Limited
Southwest   menu available until midnight in the club. Closed: 11/23 & 12/25. **Reservations:** suggested.
American   **Features:** casual dress; children's menu; carryout; cocktails & lounge; entertainment; a la carte. Very
attractive Southwestern restaurant with a large outdoor patio dinner area. **Cards:** AE, DI, DS, MC, VI.

DANIEL'S   **Dinner:** $17-$28   **Phone:** 520/742-3200   32
◆◆◆◆   **Location:** Se corner Campbell Ave and River Rd; in St Philips Plaza. 4340 N Campbell Ave, #107 85718.
Northern   **Hours:** 5 pm-9 pm, Fri & Sat-10 pm. Closed major holidays. **Reservations:** suggested. **Features:** dressy
Italian   casual; cocktails & lounge; a la carte. An elegant restaurant featuring a nice selection of veal, lamb, seafood
and pasta. **Cards:** AE, CB, DI, DS, MC, VI.

EL CORRAL   Historical   **Dinner:** $9-$13   **Phone:** 520/299-6092   24
◆   **Location:** Just e of Campbell Ave on the n side of River Rd. 2201 E River Rd 85718. **Hours:** 5 pm-10 pm,
Steakhouse   Fri, Sat & Sun 4:30 pm- 10 pm. Closed: 11/23 & 12/25. **Features:** casual dress; children's menu; carryout;
cocktails & lounge. Casual dining in a historic adobe ranch house built in the late 1800s. Reservations not
accepted. **Cards:** AE, DI, DS, MC, VI.

FUEGO   **Dinner:** $14-$24   **Phone:** 520/886-1745   25
◆◆◆   **Location:** Just w of Sabino Canyon Rd. 6958 E Tanque Verde Rd 85715. **Hours:** 5:30 pm-9 pm, Fri &
Southwest   Sat-10 pm. Closed major holidays. **Reservations:** suggested. **Features:** casual dress; children's menu;
American   cocktails & lounge; a la carte. Menu features a nice variety of contemporary Southwestern cuisine. Some
game dishes. **Cards:** AE, MC, VI.

THE GOLD ROOM   **Lunch:** $8-$16   **Dinner:** $19-$29   **Phone:** 520/297-1151   22
◆◆◆◆   **Location:** 0.5 mi e on Ina Rd from Oracle Rd (SR 77), just n on Westward Look Dr; in Westward Look
Continental   Resort. 245 E Ina Rd 85704. **Hours:** 7-10 am, 11-2 & 5-10 pm, Sun brunch available 9/16-6/9.
Reservations: suggested. **Features:** casual dress; Sunday brunch; cocktails & lounge; valet parking; a la
carte. Fine dining with a view of the city. Menu features a nice variety of classic and contemporary cuisine. Sun brunch
9/16-6/9. Smoke free premises. **Cards:** AE, CB, DI, DS, MC, VI.

KEATON'S ARIZONA GRILL   **Lunch:** $7-$14   **Dinner:** $10-$19   **Phone:** 520/297-1999   18
◆◆   **Location:** 2.2 mi w of Oracle Rd (SR 77) via Ina Rd; west side of Foothills Mall. 7401 N La Cholla 85741.
American   **Hours:** 11 am-10 pm. Closed: 5/31, 11/23 & 12/25. **Reservations:** suggested. **Features:** casual dress;
Sunday brunch; children's menu; carryout; cocktails & lounge. Selections include steak, seafood, pasta and
chicken entrees. **Cards:** AE, CB, DI, DS, MC, VI.

KEATON'S ARIZONA GRILL   **Lunch:** $7-$11   **Dinner:** $10-$20   **Phone:** 520/721-1299   38
◆◆   **Location:** Between Pima and Grant rds. 6464 E Tanque Verde Rd 85715. **Hours:** 11 am-10 pm. Closed:
American   11/23 & 12/25. **Features:** casual dress; children's menu; carryout; cocktails & lounge. Menu features a nice
variety of seafood, steaks, veal and chicken. **Cards:** AE, CB, DI, DS, MC, VI.

KINGFISHER   **Lunch:** $7-$10   **Dinner:** $12-$20   **Phone:** 520/323-7739   15
◆◆   **Location:** Just e of Tucson Blvd. 2564 E Grant Rd 85716. **Hours:** 11 am-midnight, Sat & Sun from 5 pm,
Regional   late menu after 10 pm. **Reservations:** suggested. **Features:** casual dress; children's
American   menu; carryout; cocktails & lounge; a la carte. Large selection of fresh fish. Also pasta, beef and chicken.
Summer menu features Regional cuisine. **Cards:** AE, DI, DS, MC, VI.

LA FUENTE RESTAURANT   **Lunch:** $5-$8   **Dinner:** $8-$18   **Phone:** 520/623-8659   9
AAA   **Location:** 0.5 mi s of Grant Rd. 1749 N Oracle Rd 85705. **Hours:** 11:30 am-10 pm, Fri-11 pm, Sat noon-11
◆◆   pm. Closed major holidays. **Features:** casual dress; children's menu; cocktails & lounge; entertainment.
Mexican   Colorful decor. Sun champagne brunch 11 am-2 pm. Mariachi music nightly. **Cards:** AE, DI, MC, VI.

(See map p. 324)

THE LAST TERRITORY   Dinner: $13-$21   Phone: 520/544-5000   ⑯
◆◆   **Location:** SR 77, 3.5 mi n of Ina Rd; in Sheraton El Conquistador. 10000 N Oracle Rd 85737. **Hours:** 5
Steakhouse   pm-10 pm. Closed: Sun & Mon. **Features:** children's menu; cocktails. Casual, informal Western decor.
     Selection of steak, chicken and barbeque ribs. Western entertainment. Lively atmosphere. **Cards:** AE, CB,
DI, DS, JC, MC, VI.   ✕

LE RENDEZ-VOUS   Lunch: $8-$12   Dinner: $19-$30   Phone: 520/323-7373   ⑪
◆◆◆   **Location:** Just w of Alvernon Way on s side of Ft Lowell Rd. 3844 E Ft Lowell Rd 85716. **Hours:** 11:30
French   am-2 & 6-10 pm, Sat & Sun from 6 pm. Closed: 1/1, 11/23, 12/25 & Mon. **Reservations:** suggested.
     Features: casual dress; cocktails; a la carte. A small, charming restaurant. **Cards:** AE, CB, DI, DS, MC, VI.

LOTUS GARDEN   Lunch: $6-$7   Dinner: $9-$20   Phone: 520/298-3351   ⑰
◆◆   **Location:** 0.4 mi w of Wilmot Rd. 5975 E Speedway Blvd 85712. **Hours:** 11:30 am-11 pm, Fri &
Chinese   Sat-midnight. Closed: 11/23 & 12/25. **Reservations:** suggested. **Features:** casual dress; carryout; cocktails;
     a la carte. Specializing in Cantonese and Szechuan cuisine. Contemporary decor. Smoke free premises.
Cards: AE, CB, DI, MC, VI.   ✕

MAIN DINING ROOM AT THE ARIZONA INN   Lunch: $7-$16   Dinner: $19-$25   Phone: 520/325-1541   ㉝
◆◆◆   **Location:** 0.5 mi n of Speedway Blvd, just e of Campbell Ave. 2200 E Elm St 85719. **Hours:** 6:30-10 am,
Continental   11:30-2 & 6-10 pm, Sun 7-10 am, 11-2 & 6-10 pm. **Reservations:** suggested. **Features:** semi-formal attire;
     Sunday brunch; children's menu; cocktails & lounge; entertainment; a la carte. Refined dining in a historic
Inn. Outside dining weather permitting. Smoke free premises. **Cards:** AE, CB, DI, MC, VI.   ✕

MCMAHON'S STEAKHOUSE   Lunch: $7-$15   Dinner: $25-$50   Phone: 520/327-7463   ㊷
◆◆◆   **Location:** Swan Rd at Fort McDowell Rd. 2959 N Swan Rd 85712. **Hours:** 11:30 am-10 pm, Fri-11 pm, Sat
Steakhouse   5 pm-11 pm, Sun 5 pm-10 pm. Closed major holidays. **Reservations:** suggested. **Features:** casual dress;
     children's menu; health conscious menu; cocktails & lounge; entertainment; valet parking; a la carte.
Excellent selection of choice steaks, chops and appetizers. Upscale decor. Smoke free premises. **Cards:** AE, CB, DI, DS,
MC, VI.   ✕

METROPOLITAN GRILL   Lunch: $7-$10   Dinner: $9-$16   Phone: 520/531-1212   ㊺
◆◆◆   **Location:** In Plaza Escondida Shopping Center, at Magee Rd. 7892 N Oracle Rd 85704. **Hours:** 11 am-10
American   pm, Fri & Sat-10:30 pm. Closed: 7/4 & 12/25. **Reservations:** suggested. **Features:** casual dress; children's
     menu; early bird specials; health conscious menu; carryout; cocktails & lounge. Very nice selection of meats,
poultry, seafood and pasta dishes. **Cards:** AE, DS, MC, VI.   ✕

MICHELANGELO RISTORANTE ITALIANO   Lunch: $5-$9   Dinner: $9-$22   Phone: 520/297-5775   ㉓
◆◆◆   **Location:** just w of Oracle Rd (SR 77) and 1 mi n of Ina Rd. 420 W Magee Rd 85704. **Hours:** 11 am-10
Italian   pm. Closed: 12/25 & Sun. **Features:** casual dress; children's menu; carryout; cocktails & lounge.
     Family-owned and operated restaurant serving a large selection of pasta, chicken, veal, seafood and pizza.
Patio seating avail. **Cards:** AE, MC, VI.   ✕

OLIVE TREE RESTAURANT   Dinner: $18-$30   Phone: 520/298-1845   ⑳
◆◆◆   **Location:** Just w of Sabino Canyon Rd, in Santa Fe Square. 7000 E Tanque Verde Rd 85715. **Hours:** 5
Greek   pm-9:30 pm, Fri & Sat-10 pm. Closed: 7/4, 11/23 & 12/25. **Reservations:** suggested. **Features:** casual
     dress; children's menu; carryout; cocktails & lounge. Nice selection of lamb, seafood, chicken and pasta in
addition to traditional Greek dishes. **Cards:** AE, CB, DI, MC, VI.   ✕

OVENS RESTAURANT   Lunch: $9-$18   Dinner: $9-$18   Phone: 520/577-9001   ㊱
◆◆   **Location:** SE corner Campbell Ave at River Rd; in St Philips Plaza. 4280 N Campbell Ave #37 85718.
American   **Hours:** 11 am-9:30 pm, Fri & Sat-10 pm. Closed: 11/23 & 12/25. **Reservations:** suggested.
     Features: casual dress; carryout; cocktails & lounge; a la carte. Varied selection of pasta, wood-fired pizza,
seafood, beef and chicken entrees. **Cards:** AE, DI, MC, VI.   ✕

PINNACLE PEAK RESTAURANT   Dinner: $8-$14   Phone: 520/296-0911   ⑬
◆   **Location:** Between Pima and Grant rds. 6541 E Tanque Verde Rd 85715. **Hours:** 5 pm-10 pm, Sat & Sun
Steakhouse   from 4:30 pm. Closed: 11/23 & 12/25. **Features:** casual dress; children's menu; carryout; cocktails & lounge.
     Popular, informal Western atmosphere. Reservations not accepted. **Cards:** AE, DI, DS, MC, VI.   ✕

SCORDATO'S RESTAURANT   Dinner: $15-$21   Phone: 520/624-8946   ㉗
◆◆◆   **Location:** 4.6 mi w of I-10. 4405 W Speedway Blvd 85745. **Hours:** 5 pm-9 pm, Sun 5 pm-8:30 pm. Closed
Italian   major holidays, Mon, Sun & Mon in summer. **Reservations:** suggested. **Features:** semi-formal attire;
     carryout; cocktails; a la carte. Elegant decor. Nice selection of veal, seafood, chicken and pasta. **Cards:** AE,
CB, DI, DS, MC, VI.   ✕

THE TACK ROOM   Dinner: $25-$35   Phone: 520/722-2800   ⑭
ⒶⒶⒶ   **Location:** 10 mi ne; 0.5 mi n of Tanque Verde Rd. 7300 E Vactor Ranch Trail 85715. **Hours:** 6 pm-9:30 pm.
◆◆◆◆◆   Closed: 11/25, 7/01-7/18, Mon 5/15-1/15 & Tues 7/19-9/30. **Reservations:** suggested. **Features:** semi-formal
Southwest   attire; cocktails; valet parking; a la carte. Expertly prepared American southwest cuisine. Sophisticated dining
American   in an elegant spanish ranch atmosphere. **Cards:** AE, CB, DI, DS, JC, MC, VI.   ✕

(See map p. 324)

TRIPLE C CHUCKWAGON SUPPERS   Dinner: $16-$21   Phone: 520/883-2333 ⑲
🔺🔺🔺 **Location:** From I-19, 5 mi w on SR 86 (Ajo Way), 0.5 mi n on Kinney Rd, 4.3 mi w on Bopp Rd. 8900 W
◆ Bopp Rd 85746. **Hours:** Open 2/1-4/15 & 12/27-1/31; One seating at 7 pm. Children 12 & under $9-$14.
American Closed major holidays. **Reservations:** suggested. **Features:** No A/C; casual dress. Located in desert area.
Ranch-style chuckwagon suppers served indoors. Western entertainment after supper. Smoke free premises.
Cards: DS, MC, VI.   ✖️

THE VENTANA ROOM   Dinner: $28-$50   Phone: 520/299-2020 ㉞
◆◆◆◆ **Location:** 2 mi e of Craycroft Rd on Sunrise Dr 1.5 mi n on Kolb Rd; in Loews Ventana Canyon Resort.
Continental 7000 N Resort Dr 85715. **Hours:** 6 pm-9 pm, Fri & Sat-10 pm. **Reservations:** suggested.
Features: semi-formal attire; cocktails; valet parking; a la carte. Beautifully appointed room with spectacular
city view. Sophisticated dining in an elegant setting. Smoke free premises. **Cards:** AE, CB, DI, DS, JC, MC, VI. ♿ ✖️

VIVACE RESTAURANT   Lunch: $8-$12   Dinner: $12-$20   Phone: 520/795-7221 ㊵
◆◆ **Location:** Grant Rd at Swan, in the Crossroads Festival. 4811 E Grant Rd Suite 155 85712. **Hours:** 11:30
Italian am-9 pm, Fri & Sat-10 pm, Sun 5 pm-9 pm. Closed: 11/23 & 12/25. **Reservations:** suggested.
Features: cocktails & lounge; a la carte. A popular, contemporary bistro style restaurant. **Cards:** AE, DI,
MC, VI.   ♿ ✖️

The Tucson Vicinity

GREEN VALLEY pop. 13,200

——— LODGINGS ———

BEST WESTERN GREEN VALLEY   Phone: (520)625-2250
🔺🔺🔺 SAVE 2/1-4/30   1P: $79-$129   2P: $89-$129   XP: $10   F17
◆◆◆ 10/1-1/31   1P: $79-$95   2P: $79-$95   XP: $10   F17
Motor Inn 5/1-5/31   1P: $79-$89   2P: $79-$89   XP: $10   F17
6/1-9/30   1P: $59-$69   2P: $69-$75   XP: $10   F17
Location: 0.5 mi sw of I-19, exit 65, Esperanza Rd. 111 S La Canada Dr 85614. Fax: 520/625-0215.
Terms: [BP] meal plan; cancellation fee imposed; package plans; pets, $25 dep req. **Facility:** 108 rooms. 2 stories; interior
corridors; heated pool, whirlpool. **Dining:** Dining room; 6 am-2 & 5-8 pm, Sun 6 am-2 pm; $7-$14; cocktails. **All Rooms:** extended cable TV. **Cards:** AE, CB, DI, DS, MC, VI. **Special Amenities:** Free breakfast and free local telephone calls.
(See ad below)   🔲 🛏️ 🍽️ 🐾 🏊 ✖️ 📹 🖨️ 💻 📠 📱 (DATA PORT) 🚗

HOLIDAY INN EXPRESS   **Phone:** (520)625-0900
◆◆   2/1-4/15   1P: $119-$129   2P: $129-$139
Motel   12/17-1/31   1P: $89-$99   2P: $99-$109
              9/27-12/16   1P: $69-$79   2P: $79-$89
              4/16-9/26   1P: $59-$69   2P: $69-$79
Location: Adjacent to I-19, exit 69, Duval Mine Rd. 19200 S I-19 Frontage Rd 85614. Fax: 520/393-0522. **Terms:** [CP] meal plan; 5 day cancellation notice; pets. **Facility:** 60 rooms. 3 stories; interior corridors; heated pool. **Cards:** AE, CB, DI, DS, MC, VI.

ORACLE pop. 3,000

———— **LODGING** ————

BIOSPHERE 2 HOTEL & CONFERENCE CENTER   **Phone:** (520)896-6222
🛆🛆🛆 SAVE   2/1-12/24 & 12/26-1/31   1P: $67-$109   2P: $67-$109   XP: $25   F12
◆◆   **Location:** 5 mi ne on SR 77 from jct SR 79, then 2 mi s. 85623 (PO Box 689). Fax: 520/896-6471.
Motor Inn   **Terms:** Open 2/1-12/24 & 12/26-1/31; cancellation fee imposed; package plans. **Facility:** 27 rooms. Located
              on bluff above Biosphere. Large rooms with balcony have view of the Catalina Mountains. 1 story; exterior cor-
              ridors. **Dining:** Restaurant; 7 am-7 pm; hrs vary by season; $6-$15; cocktails. **Services:** gift shop.
All Rooms: extended cable TV. **Some Rooms:** honor bars. **Cards:** AE, DI, DS, MC, VI.

This ends listings for the Tucson Vicinity.
The following page resumes the alphabetical listings of
cities in Arizona.

WICKENBURG pop. 4,500

LODGINGS

AMERICINN
◆◆
Motor Inn

11/1-1/31	1P: $61-$74	2P: $67-$80	XP: $6	F16
2/1-5/31	1P: $61-$72	2P: $67-$78	XP: $6	F16
6/1-10/31	1P: $52-$62	2P: $52-$68	XP: $6	F16

Phone: (520)684-5461

Location: 1.3 mi se on US 60. 850 E Wickenburg Way 85358 (PO Box 1359). Fax: 520/684-5461. **Terms:** [CP] meal plan. **Facility:** 29 rooms. Some balconies and patios. 2 stories; interior corridors; heated pool. **All Rooms:** combo or shower baths. **Cards:** AE, CB, DI, DS, MC, VI.

BEST WESTERN RANCHO GRANDE
ⒶⒶⒶ ⓈⒶⓋⒺ
◆◆
Motel

All Year   1P: $66-$91   2P: $69-$101   XP: $3   F12

Phone: (520)684-5445

Location: Center on Wickenburg Way (US 60). 293 E Wickenburg Way 85390. Fax: 520/684-7380. **Terms:** Cancellation fee imposed; pets. **Facility:** 80 rooms. Good to very good rooms. 1-2 stories; exterior corridors; heated pool, whirlpool; 1 lighted tennis court; playground. **Dining:** Restaurant nearby. **All Rooms:** combo or shower baths. **Some Rooms:** 16 efficiencies, 11 kitchens. Fee: VCR. **Cards:** AE, CB, DI, DS, JC, MC, VI. **Special Amenities:** Free local telephone calls and free newspaper. *(See ad below)*

LOS VIAJEROS INN
◆◆◆
Motel

All Year   1P: $72-$85   2P: $90-$110   XP: $10   F12

Phone: (520)684-7099

Location: 1 mi n of jct US 60/US 93. 1000 N Tegner Rd 85390. Fax: 520/684-7112. **Facility:** 57 rooms. All rooms have patio or balcony. 2 stories; exterior corridors; heated pool. **Cards:** AE, CB, DI, DS, MC, VI.

MERV GRIFFIN'S WICKENBURG INN AND DUDE RANCH
◆◆
Resort

All Year   1P: $125-$340   2P: $215-$430   XP: $89   F5

Phone: (520)684-7811

Location: 6 mi n on Hwy 93, 2 mi n on Hwy 89. 34801 N Hwy 89 85390. Fax: 520/684-2981. **Terms:** [AP] meal plan; 30 day cancellation notice; cancellation fee imposed. **Facility:** 63 rooms. A true Western experience, remote location with unpaved access and parking. Rustic lodge, casitas with fireplace, some with rooftop patio. 1-2 stories, no elevator; interior corridors; 2 heated pools; 9 tennis courts. **Services:** gift shop. Fee: massage, area transportation. **Recreation:** hiking trails, horseback riding. Fee: bicycles. **Some Rooms:** 54 efficiencies. Fee: VCR. **Cards:** AE, DS, MC, VI.

SUPER 8 MOTEL
◆◆
Motel

10/1-1/31	1P: $55-$70	2P: $60-$75	XP: $5	F12
2/1-9/30	1P: $50-$65	2P: $55-$70	XP: $5	F12

Phone: 520/684-0808

Location: 1 mi n of US 60, on Hwy 93. 925 N Tegner 85390. Fax: 520/684-0878. **Terms:** [CP] meal plan; 3 day cancellation notice; pets, $5 extra charge. **Facility:** 40 rooms. 2 stories; interior/exterior corridors; **Cards:** AE, CB, DI, DS, JC, MC, VI.

RESTAURANT

HOMESTEAD RESTAURANT   **Lunch:** $5-$8   **Dinner:** $9-$17   **Phone:** 520/684-0648
◆◆
American

Location: Center, on Wickenburg Way (US 60) just se of jct US 60 and US 93. 222 E Wickenburg Way 85390. **Hours:** 6 am-9 pm. **Features:** casual dress; children's menu; carryout; cocktails & lounge. Coffee shop and dining rooms in turn-of-the-century decor. Entrees include beef, chicken and fish. **Cards:** AE, CB, DI, DS, MC, VI.

WILLCOX pop. 3,100

——— LODGINGS ———

BEST WESTERN PLAZA INN   Phone: (520)384-3556
All Year   1P: $59   2P: $59   XP: $10   F12
Location: Just s of I-10, exit 340. 1100 W Rex Allen Dr 85643. Fax: 520/384-2679. **Terms:** [BP] meal plan; 10
day cancellation notice; pets, $8 extra charge. **Facility:** 92 rooms. Nicely landscaped courtyard/pool area. 6
Motor Inn   whirlpool rooms, $79; 2 stories; exterior corridors; heated pool. **Dining:** Dining room; 6 am-9 pm, Fri & Sat-10
pm; $7-$15; cocktails. **All Rooms:** extended cable TV. **Cards:** AE, CB, DI, DS, MC, VI. **Special Amenities:**
Free breakfast and free local telephone calls.

DAYS INN   Phone: (520)384-4222
All Year   1P: $40-$45   2P: $50-$55   XP: $5   F12
Location: Adjacent to I-10, exit 340. 724 N Bisbee Ave 85643. Fax: 520/384-3785. **Terms:** [CP] meal plan;
pets, $5 extra charge. **Facility:** 73 rooms. Adjacent to shopping center. 2 stories; exterior corridors.
Motel   **Dining:** Restaurant nearby. **Cards:** AE, CB, DI, DS, MC, VI. **Special Amenities: Free breakfast and free
local telephone calls.**

SUPER 8 MOTEL   Phone: (520)384-0888
                                  Property failed to provide current rates
Motel   **Location:** Just n of I-10, exit 340. 1500 W Ft Grant Rd 85643. Fax: 520/384-4485. **Terms:** [CP] meal plan.
Facility: 53 rooms. 2 stories; interior corridors; heated pool. **Cards:** AE, CB, DI, DS, MC, VI.

WILLIAMS pop. 2,500—See also GRAND CANYON NATIONAL PARK.

——— LODGINGS ———

ARIZONA WELCOME INN & SUITES   Phone: (520)635-9127
5/16-9/7   1P: $45-$49   2P: $45-$59   XP: $5   F12
4/1-5/15   1P: $30-$38   2P: $35-$40   XP: $4   F12
9/8-1/31   1P: $20-$38   2P: $35-$40   XP: $3   F12
Motel   2/1-3/31   1P: $20-$25   2P: $24-$28   XP: $3   F12
Location: Just s of I-40, exit 163. 750 N Grand Canyon Blvd 86046. Fax: 520/635-9801. **Terms:** Cancellation
fee imposed; pets, $10, $5 dep req. **Facility:** 19 rooms. 1 two-bedroom unit. 2 stories; interior corridors. **Some Rooms:**
Fee: refrigerators, microwaves. **Cards:** AE, CB, DI, DS, JC, MC, VI. **Special Amenities:** Early check-in/late check-out and
free local telephone calls. *(See ad p 197 & below)*

BEST WESTERN INN OF WILLIAMS   Phone: (520)635-4400
8/1-8/31   1P: $99-$129   2P: $99-$129   XP: $10   F12
5/1-7/31   1P: $79-$99   2P: $79-$99   XP: $10   F12
2/1-4/30 & 9/1-1/31   1P: $59-$89   2P: $59-$89   XP: $10   F12
Motel   **Location:** On I-40 business loop; from I-40 exit 161, just s. 2600 W Rt 66 Ave 86046. Fax: 520/635-4488.
Terms: [CP] meal plan; 14 day cancellation notice. **Facility:** 78 rooms. Hillside location in a forest setting.
Large lobby area with nice views. Spacious, tastefully decorated rooms. 2 stories; interior corridors; heated pool, whirlpool.
Dining: Restaurant nearby. **Services:** gift shop. **All Rooms:** combo or shower baths, extended cable TV. **Cards:** AE, CB, DI,
DS, JC, MC, VI. **Special Amenities:** Early check-in/late check-out and free newspaper.
(See color ads p 57, p 198, & p 327)

BUDGET HOST INN　　　　　　　　　　　　　　　　　　　　　　　　Phone: (520)635-4415

AAA SAVE	5/16-10/31	1P: $30-$42	2P: $32-$48	XP: $5　F12
◆	4/1-5/15	1P: $30-$32	2P: $32-$35	XP: $4　F12
Motel	2/1-3/31	1P: $18-$20	2P: $20-$30	XP: $3　F12
	11/1-1/31	1P: $18-$20	2P: $20-$24	XP: $3　F12

Location: On I-40 Business Loop; 1 mi e of I-40 exit 161. 620 W Route 66 86046. Fax: 520/635-4781.
Terms: Small pets only, $5. **Facility:** 26 rooms. Family unit, $69; 2 stories; exterior corridors. **Dining:** Restaurant nearby.
Cards: CB, DI, JC, MC, VI. **Special Amenities:** Early check-in/late check-out and free local telephone calls.
(See color ad p 194 & below)　　　　　　　　　　　　　　　　[S⊘] [🐾] [🍴] [✕] [📹] [🔌]

CANYON COUNTRY INN BED & BREAKFAST　　　　　　　　　　　Phone: (520)635-2349

AAA SAVE	5/16-9/15	1P: $55-$70	2P: $60-$75	
◆◆◆	2/1-5/15	1P: $45-$60	2P: $50-$70	XP: $5　F18
Motel	9/16-12/31	1P: $40-$60	2P: $45-$65	
	1/1-1/31	1P: $35-$55	2P: $45-$55	XP: $5　F18

Location: On I-40 business loop; from I-40, exit 163, 0.5 mi s, just w on Railroad Ave. 442 W Rt 66 Ave 86046.
Fax: 520/635-9898. **Terms:** [CP] meal plan; 3 day cancellation notice, in summer. **Facility:** 13 rooms. Cozy to large rooms attractively decorated in an Early American/country motif. 2 stories; interior/exterior corridors; designated smoking area.
All Rooms: extended cable TV. **Cards:** AE, DS, MC, VI. **Special Amenities:** Free breakfast and free local telephone calls.　　　　　　　　　　　　　　　　　　　　　　　　　　[S⊘] [✕] [📹]

COURTESY INN　　　　　　　　　　　　　　　　　　　　　　　　Phone: (520)635-2619

AAA SAVE	5/15-9/10	1P: $35-$39	2P: $39-$47	XP: $3　F16
◆◆	3/21-5/14	1P: $30-$34	2P: $34-$38	XP: $3　F16
Motel	9/11-3/34	1P: $19-$34	2P: $21-$38	XP: $3　F16
	2/1-3/20	1P: $19-$21	2P: $21-$29	XP: $3　F16

Location: On I-40 business loop; from I-40 exit 163, 0.6 mi s, then just e. 334 E Rt 66 86046.
Fax: 520/635-2610. **Terms:** [CP] meal plan. **Facility:** 24 rooms. Some small rooms. 1 two-bedroom unit. 1-2 stories; exterior corridors. **Cards:** AE, DI, DS, MC, VI. **Special Amenities:** Free breakfast and free local telephone calls.
(See color ad p 353)　　　　　　　　　　　　　　　　　　　　　　[✕] [📷] [🔌]

DAYS INN　　　　　　　　　　　　　　　　　　　　　　　　　　　Phone: (520)635-4051

◆◆	3/16-9/14	1P: $68-$88	2P: $78-$98
Motel	9/15-10/31	1P: $58-$78	2P: $68-$88
	2/1-3/15 & 11/1-1/31	1P: $39-$52	2P: $46-$68

Location: On I-40 business loop, 0.3 mi e of I-40 exit 161. 2488 W Rt 66 Ave 86046. Fax: 520/635-4411. **Terms:** Cancellation fee imposed. **Facility:** 73 rooms. 2 stories; interior corridors; heated pool. **All Rooms:** safes. **Some Rooms:** Fee: VCR.
Cards: AE, CB, DI, DS, MC, VI. *(See color ad p 353)*　　[SAVE] [S⊘] [🍴] [📶] [△] [✕] [📹] [VCR] [DATA PORT]

ECONO LODGE

Phone: (520)635-4085

4/1-9/9	1P: $45-$79	2P: $45-$109	XP: $5	F17
9/10-10/31	1P: $45-$69	2P: $45-$89	XP: $5	F17
2/1-3/31 & 11/1-1/31	1P: $25-$45	2P: $25-$55	XP: $5	F17

Motel
Location: I-40, exit 163; 0.5 mi s, 0.3 mi e on Rt 66. 302 E Rt 66 86046. **Fax:** 520/635-1326. **Facility:** 40 rooms. 2 one-bedroom suites, $45-$110; 2 stories; exterior corridors. **Dining:** Restaurant nearby.
All Rooms: combo or shower baths, extended cable TV. **Cards:** AE, CB, DI, DS, JC, MC, VI.

EL RANCHO MOTEL

Phone: (520)635-2552

5/22-9/4	1P: $52-$63	2P: $52-$72	XP: $5	F12
9/5-10/31	1P: $40-$50	2P: $40-$55	XP: $5	F12
2/1-5/21	1P: $26-$43	2P: $26-$48	XP: $5	F12
11/1-1/31	1P: $26-$30	2P: $26-$35	XP: $5	F12

Motel
Location: On I-40 business loop, from I-40 exit 163, 0.8 mi s, then just e on Rt 66. 617 E Rt 66 86046. **Fax:** 520/635-4173. **Terms:** Cancellation fee imposed; small pets only, in limited rooms. **Facility:** 25 rooms. 2 two-bedroom units. 2 stories; exterior corridors; heated pool, seasonal pool. **Dining:** Restaurant nearby. **All Rooms:** extended cable TV. **Cards:** AE, DS, MC, VI. **Special Amenities:** Free local telephone calls and free room upgrade (subject to availability with advanced reservations). *(See color ad below)*

FAIRFIELD INN BY MARRIOTT
Phone: (520)635-9888

◆◆

Motel

5/1-9/30	1P: $59-$79	2P: $59-$79
10/1-1/31	1P: $39-$69	2P: $39-$69
2/1-4/30	1P: $39-$59	2P: $39-$59

Location: Adj to I-40, exit 163. 1029 N Grand Canyon Blvd 86046. Fax: 520/635-2235. **Terms:** [ECP] meal plan. **Facility:** 80 rooms. 2 stories; interior corridors; heated pool. **All Rooms:** combo or shower baths. **Cards:** AE, DI, DS, MC, VI.
(See color ad p 352)

(ASK) (S/D) (TI•) (🛗) (🐕) (👤) (👤) (🌀) (✕) (📺) (🖨) (DATA PORT) (🚭)

FRAY MARCOS HOTEL
Phone: (520)635-4010

◆◆◆

Motor Inn

3/16-10/14	1P: $119	2P: $119	XP: $10	F16
10/15-1/31	1P: $79	2P: $79	XP: $10	F16
2/1-3/15	1P: $69	2P: $69	XP: $10	F16

Location: 0.5 mi s of I-40, exit 163; Grand Canyon Blvd. 235 N Grand Canyon Blvd 86046. Fax: 520/635-2180. **Terms:** Package plans. **Facility:** 89 rooms. At the historic Williams Depot, starting point of the Grand Canyon Railway. 2 stories; interior corridors. **Services:** gift shop. **All Rooms:** combo or shower baths. **Cards:** AE, DS, MC, VI. *(See ad p 55)*

(ASK) (TI) (T) (👤) (🌀) (✕) (📺) (🖨) (DATA PORT)

HIGHLANDER MOTEL
Phone: (520)635-2541

(AAA) (SAVE)

◆

Motel

5/13-9/5	1P: $40	2P: $40-$45	XP: $5	F12
9/6-10/31	1P: $25	2P: $30-$35	XP: $5	F12
2/1-5/12	1P: $15-$25	2P: $20-$35	XP: $5	F12
11/1-1/31	1P: $15	2P: $20-$25	XP: $3	F12

Location: On I-40 business loop; 1.2 mi e of I-40, exit 161. 533 W Route 66 86046. Fax: 520/635-0609. **Terms:** Cancellation fee imposed; small pets only, $5 extra charge. **Facility:** 12 rooms. Small, cozy units. 1 story; exterior corridors. **Dining:** Restaurant nearby. **All Rooms:** extended cable TV. **Cards:** AE, DS, MC, VI. **Special Amenities:** Early check-in/late check-out and free local telephone calls.

(S/D) (🐕) (TI•) (✕)

HOLIDAY INN
Phone: (520)635-4114

(AAA) (SAVE)

◆◆◆

Motor Inn

6/1-10/15	1P: $79-$119	2P: $79-$119
4/1-5/31	1P: $59-$99	2P: $59-$99
2/1-3/31 & 10/16-1/31	1P: $49-$69	2P: $49-$69

Location: Adjacent to I-40, exit 163. 950 N Grand Canyon Blvd 86046. Fax: 520/635-2700. **Terms:** Pets. **Facility:** 127 rooms. 7 two-bedroom units. 2 whirlpool rooms; suites, $79-$159; 2 stories; interior corridors; heated pool, sauna, whirlpool. **Dining:** Restaurant; 6 am-10 & 5-10 pm; to 9 pm, in winter; $7-$20; cocktails. **Services:** gift shop. **All Rooms:** extended cable TV. **Some Rooms:** color TV. **Cards:** AE, CB, DI, DS, MC, VI.

(🐕) (TI) (T) (🛗) (👤) (👤) (👤) (🌀) (✕) (🖨) (💳) (📺) (🖨) (🔌) (DATA PORT) (🚭)

HOWARD JOHNSON EXPRESS INN
Phone: (520)635-9561

(AAA) (SAVE)

◆

Motel

5/1-8/31	1P: $47-$64	2P: $59-$89	XP: $6	F12
9/1-10/31	1P: $45-$59	2P: $59-$89	XP: $6	F12
2/1-4/30 & 11/1-1/31	1P: $32-$49	2P: $39-$69	XP: $6	F12

Location: Just s of I-40, exit 163. 511 N Grand Canyon Blvd 86046. Fax: 520/635-9565. **Terms:** [CP] meal plan. **Facility:** 56 rooms. 2 stories; interior corridors; heated pool, whirlpool. **All Rooms:** extended cable TV. **Cards:** AE, DI, DS, MC, VI. **Special Amenities:** Free breakfast and free local telephone calls. *(See color ad below)*

(✕) (📺) (💳) (🔌) (🚭)

MOTEL 6 COUNTRYSIDE
Phone: (520)635-4464

◆◆

Motel

4/1-8/15	1P: $36-$61	2P: $42-$67	XP: $6	F18
8/16-10/31	1P: $47-$57	2P: $53-$63	XP: $6	F18
2/1-3/31	1P: $33-$37	2P: $37-$40	XP: $4	F18
11/1-1/31	1P: $29-$33	2P: $33-$37	XP: $4	F18

Location: On I-40 business loop; 1.2 mi e of I-40 exit 161. 710 W Route 66 86046. Fax: 520/635-1058. **Terms:** Small pets only. **Facility:** 48 rooms. 2 stories; interior corridors. **Cards:** AE, CB, DI, DS, MC, VI.

(ASK) (S/D) (🐕) (✕)

MOTEL 6-4010
♦♦ Motel

			Phone: (520)635-9000
4/1-8/15	1P: $38-$63	2P: $44-$69	XP: $6	F18
8/16-10/31	1P: $49-$59	2P: $55-$65	XP: $6	F18
2/1-3/31	1P: $35-$39	2P: $39-$42	XP: $4	F18
11/1-1/31	1P: $31-$35	2P: $35-$39	XP: $4	F18

Location: On I-40 business loop, 1 mi e of I-40 exit 161. 831 W Rt 66 Ave 86046. Fax: 520/635-2300. **Terms:** Small pets only. **Facility:** 51 rooms. Rooms decorated in light, contemporary colors. 2 stories; interior corridors; heated pool. **Cards:** AE, CB, DI, DS, MC, VI.

MOUNTAIN COUNTRY LODGE BED & BREAKFAST
♦♦ Bed & Breakfast

			Phone: (520)635-4341
5/26-9/17	1P: $65-$90	2P: $65-$90	XP: $10	F8
1/1-1/31	1P: $55-$80	2P: $55-$80		
2/1-5/25 & 9/18-12/31	1P: $55-$80	2P: $55-$80	XP: $10	F8

Location: Downtown, Historic Rt 66. 437 W Rt 66 86046. **Terms:** Cancellation fee imposed; package plans. **Facility:** 8 rooms. 2 stories; interior/exterior corridors. **All Rooms:** combo or shower baths. **Cards:** AE, MC, VI.

MOUNTAIN SIDE INN
♦♦♦ Motor Inn

			Phone: 520/635-4431
4/2-5/27	1P: $76-$86	2P: $76-$86	XP: $10	F18
5/28-10/31	1P: $86	2P: $86	XP: $10	F18
2/1-4/1	1P: $66-$76	2P: $66-$76	XP: $10	F18
11/1-1/31	1P: $66	2P: $66	XP: $10	F18

Location: On I-40 business loop, from I-40 exit 163, 0.6 mi s, then just e on Rt 66. 642 E RT 66 86046. Fax: 520/635-2292. **Terms:** Package plans; pets. **Facility:** 96 rooms. Attractively decorated rooms. 2 stories; exterior corridors. **Dining:** entertainment. **Recreation:** hiking trails. **Cards:** AE, DI, DS, MC, VI. *(See ad p 198)*

NORRIS MOTEL
🔺🔺🔺 [SAVE]
♦♦ Motel

			Phone: (520)635-2202
5/15-9/7	1P: $55	2P: $55-$67	XP: $5	F12
2/1-5/14 & 9/8-10/31	1P: $42	2P: $44-$54	XP: $5	F12
11/1-1/31	1P: $24	2P: $28-$36	XP: $5	F12

Location: On w side of I-40 business loop; 0.9 mi e of I-40 exit 161. 1001 W Route 66 Ave 86046 (PO Box 388). Fax: 520/635-9202. **Terms:** Cancellation fee imposed. **Facility:** 33 rooms. Family unit, $42-$89; suites, $46-$107; 1 story; interior/exterior corridors; heated pool, whirlpool. **All Rooms:** combo or shower baths, extended cable TV. **Cards:** AE, DS, MC, VI. **Special Amenities:** Free local telephone calls and preferred room (subject to availability with advanced reservations). IMA. *(See color ad below)*

QUALITY INN-MOUNTAIN RANCH
🔺🔺🔺 [SAVE]
♦♦♦ Motor Inn

			Phone: (520)635-2693
5/16-9/30	1P: $89-$109	2P: $89-$109	XP: $10	F12
4/2-5/15 & 10/1-11/1	1P: $69-$99	2P: $69-$99	XP: $10	F12
3/1-4/1	1P: $58-$88	2P: $59-$89	XP: $10	F12

Location: 8 mi e, adjacent to I-40, Deer Farm Rd, exit 171. 6701 E Mountain Ranch Rd 86046. Fax: 520/635-4188. **Terms:** Open 3/1-11/1; [BP] meal plan; package plans; small pets only, $20 extra charge. **Facility:** 73 rooms. On spacious grounds in a scenic country location. 2 stories; exterior corridors; heated pool, whirlpool, seasonal pool; 2 tennis courts. **Dining:** Dining room, coffee shop; 6 am-10 pm; $10-$19; cocktails. **Services:** gift shop. **Recreation:** sports court, video rentals. Fee: horseback riding. **All Rooms:** combo or shower baths. **Some Rooms:** Fee: refrigerators, microwaves, VCR. **Cards:** AE, CB, DI, DS, JC, MC, VI. **Special Amenities:** Free breakfast and free local telephone calls.

ROUTE 66 INN
Phone: (520)635-4791

(AAA) [SAVE]

Motel

5/15-9/15	1P: $40-$55	2P: $48-$70	XP: $5	F10
2/1-5/14	1P: $30-$45	2P: $35-$65	XP: $5	F10
9/16-10/31	1P: $38-$45	2P: $42-$60	XP: $5	F10
11/1-1/31	1P: $25-$32	2P: $30-$45	XP: $5	F10

Location: I-40 exit 163, then .5 mi to Route 66, then .1 mi e. 128 E Route 66 86046. Fax: 520/635-4993. **Terms:** Weekly rates avail; small pets only, $5 extra charge. **Facility:** 19 rooms. 1 two-bedroom unit, 1 three-bedroom unit. Two 1-bedroom suite & one 2-bedroom suite, $50-$130; 2 stories; exterior corridors. **Dining:** Restaurant nearby. **Services:** gift shop. **All Rooms:** combo or shower baths, extended cable TV. **Some Rooms:** Fee: refrigerators. **Cards:** AE, CB, DI, DS, MC, VI. **Special Amenities:** Early check-in/late check-out and free local telephone calls.

THE SHERIDAN HOUSE INN
Phone: (520)635-9441

◆◆◆

Bed &
Breakfast

All Year	1P: $110-$225	2P: $110-$225	XP: $15	F14

Location: 460 E Sheridan Ave 86046. Fax: 520/635-1005. **Terms:** [BP] meal plan; 7 day cancellation notice; cancellation fee imposed. **Facility:** 7 rooms. 1 two-bedroom unit. 3 stories, no elevator; interior corridors; smoke free premises. **All Rooms:** combo or shower baths. **Cards:** AE, DS, MC, VI.

SUPER 8 MOTEL
Phone: (520)635-4045

◆◆

Motel

4/15-10/3	1P: $59-$89	2P: $59-$89
10/4-1/31	1P: $49-$79	2P: $49-$79
2/1-4/14	1P: $39-$59	2P: $39-$59

Location: On w side of I-40 business loop; 1 mi e of I-40 exit 161. 911 W RT 66 Ave 86046. Fax: 520/635-9060. **Terms:** [CP] meal plan; small pets only, $10 extra charge. **Facility:** 74 rooms. 2 stories; interior corridors; heated pool. **All Rooms:** combo or shower baths. **Cards:** AE, CB, DI, DS, JC, MC, VI.

SUPER 8 MOTEL
Phone: (520)635-4700

◆◆

Motel

6/2-8/31	1P: $52-$60	2P: $60-$75		
2/1-6/1	1P: $45-$55	2P: $50-$65	XP: $5	F14
9/1-12/31	1P: $48-$55	2P: $54-$62		
1/1-1/31	1P: $35-$45	2P: $45-$50	XP: $5	F14

Location: I-40, exit 165, 1 mi s. 2001 E Rte 66 86046. Fax: 520/635-4700. **Facility:** 40 rooms. 2 stories; interior corridors. **Cards:** AE, CB, DI, JC, MC, VI.

TERRY RANCH BED & BREAKFAST
Phone: (520)635-4171

◆◆◆

Bed &
Breakfast

4/1-9/30 & 1/1-1/31		2P: $110-$140	XP: $15
2/1-3/31 & 10/1-12/31		2P: $100-$130	XP: $15

Location: I-40, exit 165 Grand Canyon exit, 1 mi s on Business Loop 40, then 0.3 mi w on Rodeo Rd at Quarterhorse Rd and Rodeo Rd. 701 Quarterhorse Rd 86046. Fax: 520/635-2488. **Terms:** [BP] meal plan; check-in 4 pm; 7 day cancellation notice, Handling fee imposed; cancellation fee imposed. **Facility:** 4 rooms. Beautifully decorated log cabin style residence nicely furnished rooms and public areas. Three rooms with fireplace. 1 story; interior/exterior corridors; smoke free premises. **Some Rooms:** color TV. **Cards:** AE, DS, MC, VI.

THE WESTERNER MOTEL
Phone: (520)635-4312

(AAA) [SAVE]

Motel

5/15-9/15	1P: $38-$44	2P: $38-$48	XP: $5	F10
9/16-10/31	1P: $24-$28	2P: $28-$32	XP: $5	F10
2/1-5/14 & 11/1-1/31	1P: $22-$28	2P: $24-$30	XP: $5	F10

Location: On I-40 business loop; 1.3 mi e of I-40, exit 161. 530 W Rt 66 86046 (PO Box 426). Fax: 520/635-9313. **Terms:** Small pets only. **Facility:** 24 rooms. 4 small rooms. Charming property. Three 2-bedroom units for up to 6 persons, $38-$68; 1-2 stories; exterior corridors. **All Rooms:** combo or shower baths, extended cable TV. **Cards:** AE, DS, MC, VI. **Special Amenities:** Early check-in/late check-out and free local telephone calls.

------ **RESTAURANTS** ------

CRUISERS CAFE 66
Lunch: $6-$13　　Dinner: $7-$13　　Phone: 520/635-2445

◆◆

American

Location: Downtown on Historic Rt 66. 233 W Rt 66 86046. **Hours:** 11 am-10 pm, winter from 3 pm. **Features:** casual dress; children's menu; early bird specials; carryout; cocktails & lounge. Outdoor dining avail in summer. Pleasant family dining in the spirit of Rt 66. **Cards:** AE, DS, MC, VI.

PANCHO MCGILLICUDDY'S
Lunch: $5-$13　　Dinner: $7-$13　　Phone: 520/635-4150

◆◆

Mexican

Location: I-40, exit 163; 0.5 mi s. 141 Railroad Ave 86046. **Hours:** 11 am-10 pm in summer; 3 pm-10 pm in winter; outdoor dining avail in summer. Closed: 11/23 & 12/25. **Features:** No A/C; casual dress; children's menu; early bird specials; carryout; cocktails & lounge. **Cards:** AE, DS, MC, VI.

PINE COUNTRY RESTAURANT
Lunch: $4-$7　　Dinner: $6-$10　　Phone: 520/635-9718

◆

American

Location: Downtown; Cross street Rt 66. 107 N Grand Canyon Blvd 86046. **Hours:** 5:30 am-9:30 pm; to 9 pm in winter. Closed: 11/23, 12/25. **Features:** No A/C; carryout. Casual relaxed dining, homestyle cooking, homemade pies. **Cards:** AE, DS, MC, VI.

WINDOW ROCK

──── LODGING ────

NAVAJO NATION INN
◆◆ All Year   1P: $57   2P: $62   Phone: (520)871-4108
                                                                              XP: $5   F12
Motel   **Location:** 34 mi e of SR 191 on SR 264. 48 W Hwy 264 86515 (PO Box 2340). Fax: 520/871-5466.
           Terms: Small pets only, $50 extra charge. **Facility:** 56 rooms. 2 stories; exterior corridors. **Services:** gift shop.
Cards: AE, DI, MC, VI. *(See ad below)*   🛏 🍽 🕳 ✕ 🎦 🔌 ▦

WINSLOW pop. 9,100

──── LODGINGS ────

BEST WESTERN ADOBE INN   Phone: (520)289-4638
🅰🅰🅰 SAVE   6/1-9/30   1P: $50-$60   2P: $57-$67   XP: $6
           5/1-5/31   1P: $48-$58   2P: $53-$63   XP: $6
◆◆◆   2/1-4/30 & 10/1-1/31   1P: $44-$54   2P: $48-$58   XP: $6
Motor Inn **Location:** Adjacent to I-40, exit 253. 1701 North Park Dr 86047. Fax: 520/289-5514. **Terms:** Small pets only.
           Facility: 72 rooms. Large atrium area includes heated pool and whirlpool. 2 stories; interior corridors; heated
pool. **Dining:** Dining room; 6 am-2 & 4-10 pm, Sun-9 pm; 7 am-2 & 4-10 pm, in winter; $6-$14; cocktails. **All Rooms:** combo
or shower baths. **Cards:** AE, CB, DI, DS, MC, VI. **Special Amenities: Early check-in/late check-out and free local telephone calls.** *(See color ad below)*   S𝐃 🛏 🍽 🕳 ⛱ 🔥 ✕ 🎦 📺 🔌 🏊

DAYS INN   Phone: (520)289-1010
🅰🅰🅰 SAVE   All Year   1P: $39-$75   2P: $45-$95   XP: $5   F12
◆◆◆   **Location:** Just s of I-40, exit 252. 2035 W Hwy 66 86047. Fax: 520/289-5778. **Terms:** [CP] meal plan; pets,
Motel $3 extra charge. **Facility:** 63 rooms. 2 stories; interior corridors; heated pool, whirlpool. **Some Rooms:**
           Fee: VCR. **Cards:** AE, CB, DI, DS, MC, VI. **Special Amenities: Free breakfast and free local telephone
calls.**   S𝐃 🛏 ⛱ ✕ 🎦 VCR 🔌 🏊

ECONO LODGE   Phone: (520)289-4687
◆   5/1-10/31   1P: $45-$64   2P: $49-$79   XP: $5   F18
Motel   2/1-4/30 & 11/1-1/31   1P: $39-$54   2P: $44-$59   XP: $5   F18
           Location: Adjacent to I-40, exit 253. 1706 N Park Dr 86047. Fax: 520/289-9377. **Terms:** 5 day cancellation
notice; small pets only, $5 extra charge. **Facility:** 72 rooms. 2 stories; exterior corridors. **Cards:** AE, CB, DI, DS, JC, MC, VI.
                              SAVE S𝐃 🛏 🍽 ⛱ 🌀 ✕ 🎦 🔌 🔌 🏊

HOLIDAY INN EXPRESS
◆◆ **Phone:** 520/289-2960
Motel   Property failed to provide current rates
Location: From I-40 n side at exit 255. 816 Transcon Ln 86047. Fax: 520/289-2947. **Terms:** [ECP] meal plan; small pets only, $20 dep req. **Facility:** 53 rooms. 2 stories; interior corridors; heated pool. **All Rooms:** combo or shower baths. **Cards:** AE, DI, DS, MC, VI.

LA POSADA HOTEL
◆◆◆   **Phone:** (520)289-4366
            All Year   1P: $69-$99   2P: $69-$99   XP: $5   D
Historic Hotel **Location:** I-40, exit 252, s to Rt 66 (2nd St), then 0.5 mi e at jct SR 87 and Historic Rt 66. 303 E 2nd St 86047. Fax: 520/289-3873. **Terms:** [CP] meal plan; 7 day cancellation notice; small pets only, $5 extra charge. **Facility:** 23 rooms. Beautifully restored historic hotel. Tastefully decorated. Spacious grounds. 2 stories; interior corridors. **Cards:** AE, CB, DI, DS, JC, MC, VI.

MOTEL 6 WINSLOW
◆◆   **Phone:** (520)289-9581
            5/1-7/31   1P: $40-$45   2P: $45-$50   XP: $5   F12
Motel   8/1-10/15   1P: $38-$43   2P: $43-$48   XP: $5   F12
            2/1-4/30 & 10/16-1/31   1P: $35-$40   2P: $40-$45   XP: $5   F12
Location: Just w on North Park Dr, just s of I-40, exit 253. 520 W Desmond St 86047. Fax: 520/289-5642. **Terms:** [CP] meal plan; small pets only, in smoking rooms only. **Facility:** 55 rooms. Rooms decorated in light southwestern colors, across from shopping center. 2 stories; interior corridors; heated pool. **All Rooms:** combo or shower baths. **Some Rooms:** Fee: VCR. **Cards:** AE, CB, DI, DS, MC, VI.

SUPER 8 MOTEL
(AAA) (SAVE)   **Phone:** (520)289-4606
            6/1-9/30   1P: $46-$52   2P: $50-$58   XP: $4   F12
            2/1-5/31 & 10/1-1/31   1P: $36-$42   2P: $40-$48   XP: $4   F12
◆◆   **Location:** Just e of I-40, exit 252. 1916 W Third St 86047. Fax: 520/289-4606. **Terms:** Pets, $20 dep req, in
Motel   smoking rooms only. **Facility:** 46 rooms. 2 stories; interior corridors. **Dining:** Restaurant nearby. **All Rooms:** combo or shower baths. **Cards:** AE, CB, DI, DS, MC, VI. **Special Amenities:** Free local telephone calls and free room upgrade (subject to availability with advanced reservations).

TOWN HOUSE LODGE
◆◆ **Phone:** (520)289-4611
Motor Inn   Property failed to provide current rates
Location: 0.5 mi e of I-40 exit 252. 1914 W Third St 86047. Fax: 520/289-4611. **Terms:** Pets. **Facility:** 68 rooms. Ranch style buildings on spacious grounds. Some small rooms in original section. 5 two-bedroom units. 1 story; exterior corridors; heated pool. **All Rooms:** combo or shower baths. **Cards:** AE, CB, DI, DS, JC, MC, VI.

YOUNGTOWN —See Phoenix p. 289.

YUMA pop. 57,000

——— LODGINGS ———

AIRPORT TRAVELODGE
◆◆   **Phone:** (520)726-4721
            10/1-1/31   1P: $54-$64   2P: $74-$84   XP: $5   F17
Motor Inn   2/1-3/31   1P: $59-$64   2P: $69-$79   XP: $10   F17
            4/1-9/30   1P: $45-$54   2P: $59-$64   XP: $5   F17
Location: I-8 Business Loop; 2.3 mi se of jct US 95. 711 E 32nd St 85365. Fax: 520/344-0452. **Terms:** [CP] meal plan; age restrictions may apply; pets, on approval, $25 dep req. **Facility:** 80 rooms. Palm shaded pool area. Exterior corridors; heated pool. **Some Rooms:** 6 efficiencies. **Cards:** AE, DI, DS, JC, MC, VI.

BEST WESTERN CORONADO

Phone: (520)783-4453

(AAA) [SAVE]
◆◆◆
Motor Inn

| | 1/1-1/31 | 1P: $72-$120 | 2P: $89-$150 | XP: $8 | F12 |
| | 2/1-12/31 | 1P: $62-$99 | 2P: $69-$120 | XP: $8 | F12 |

Location: I-8 business loop; From I-8, eastbound exit 4th Ave, 0.5 mi s; westbound exit 1 (Giss Pkwy), 0.5 mi w. 233 4th Ave 85364. Fax: 520/782-7487. **Terms:** [BP] meal plan; weekly & monthly rates avail; 7 day cancellation notice; small pets only. **Facility:** 86 rooms. Long established motel with a variety of accommodations from cozy to spacious, nicely furnished rooms. Museum and gift shop. 32 two-bedroom units. 7 kitchens, $10 extra charge.; 12 whirlpool rooms, $69-$120; 1-2 stories; exterior corridors; 2 pools, 1 heated, whirlpool. **Dining:** Restaurant; 6 am-10 pm, Fri & Sat-11 pm; $5-$13; cocktails. **Services:** gift shop. **All Rooms:** combo or shower baths, safes. **Cards:** AE, CB, DI, DS, JC, MC, VI. **Special Amenities:** Free breakfast and free newspaper. *(See ad p 358)*

BEST WESTERN INNSUITES HOTEL & SUITES

Phone: (520)783-8341

(AAA) [SAVE]
◆◆◆
Motel

	2/1-3/31 & 1/1-1/31	1P: $99	2P: $99	XP: $5	F18
	9/1-12/31	1P: $89	2P: $89	XP: $5	F18
	4/1-8/31	1P: $76	2P: $76	XP: $5	F18

Location: Just ne of I-8, at jct SR 95 (16th St). 1450 Castle Dome Ave 85365. Fax: 520/783-1349. **Terms:** [BP] & [CP] meal plans; cancellation fee imposed; pets, $25 dep req. **Facility:** 166 rooms. A variety of rooms and suites decorated in a southwest motif. 11 whirlpool rooms, $119-$159; 2-3 stories; exterior corridors; heated pool, whirlpool; 2 lighted tennis courts; playground. **Dining:** Small restaurant open 6 am-2 & 5-10 pm; $8-$15; cocktails. **Services:** complimentary evening beverages. **Recreation:** basketball court. **Some Rooms:** 80 efficiencies. **Cards:** AE, CB, DI, DS, MC, VI. **Special Amenities:** Free breakfast and free local telephone calls. *(See color ad below)*

COMFORT INN

Phone: (520)782-1200

(AAA) [SAVE]
◆◆◆
Motel

| | 2/1-4/15 & 1/1-1/31 | 1P: $70-$99 | 2P: $70-$99 | XP: $5 | F18 |
| | 4/16-12/31 | 1P: $55-$85 | 2P: $55-$85 | XP: $5 | F18 |

Location: 0.5 mi w of I-8, exit US 95 (16th St). 1691 S Riley Ave 85365. Fax: 520/782-0744. **Terms:** [CP] meal plan; pets, $5 extra charge. **Facility:** 81 rooms. 3 stories; interior corridors; heated pool, whirlpool. **Dining:** Restaurant nearby. **Cards:** AE, CB, DI, DS, MC, VI. **Special Amenities:** Free breakfast and free local telephone calls.

DAYS INN

Phone: (520)329-7790

(AAA) [SAVE]
◆◆
Motel

	2/1-3/31	1P: $80-$100	2P: $90-$100	XP: $10	F12
	1/1-1/31	1P: $70-$80	2P: $80-$90	XP: $10	F12
	4/1-12/31	1P: $55-$60	2P: $60-$70	XP: $10	F12

Location: US 95, just e of jct I-8. 1671 E 16th St 85365. Fax: 520/329-7790. **Terms:** [CP] meal plan. **Facility:** 65 rooms. 4 whirlpool rooms, $100-$150; 2 stories; exterior corridors; small pool, whirlpool. **Dining:** Restaurant nearby. **All Rooms:** combo or shower baths. **Cards:** AE, CB, DI, DS, JC, MC, VI. **Special Amenities:** Free breakfast and free local telephone calls.

HOLIDAY INN EXPRESS

Phone: (520)344-1420

◆◆◆
Motel

	2/1-4/30 & 1/1-1/31	1P: $72-$82	2P: $72-$82	XP: $10	F19
	9/1-12/31	1P: $56-$66	2P: $56-$66	XP: $10	F19
	5/1-8/31	1P: $49-$59	2P: $49-$59	XP: $10	F19

Location: On I-8 business loop, 2 mi s of jct US 95, at 32nd St. 3181 S 4th Ave 85364. Fax: 520/341-0158. **Terms:** [CP] meal plan; small pets only. **Facility:** 120 rooms. Across from shopping centers. 2 stories; exterior corridors; heated pool. **Cards:** AE, DI, DS, MC, VI.

LA FUENTE INN

Phone: (520)329-1814

(AAA) [SAVE]
◆◆◆
Motel

| | 2/1-4/30 & 1/1-1/31 | 1P: $88-$99 | 2P: $88-$99 | XP: $10 | F12 |
| | 5/1-12/31 | 1P: $78-$88 | 2P: $78-$88 | | |

Location: On US 95, just e of I-8. 1513 E 16th St 85365. Fax: 520/343-2671. **Terms:** [CP] meal plan. **Facility:** 96 rooms. Attractive grounds with large pool surrounded by grass, shrubs and many trees. Nicely furnished rooms and 1-bedroom suites. Whirlpool room; 2 stories; exterior corridors; heated pool, whirlpool. **Dining:** Restaurant nearby. **Services:** complimentary evening beverages. **Cards:** AE, CB, DI, DS, MC, VI. **Special Amenities:** Free breakfast and free local telephone calls. *(See color ad p 360)*

RADISSON SUITES INN YUMA   Phone: (520)726-4830

◆◆◆	2/1-3/31 & 1/15-1/31	1P: $119-$179	2P: $129-$179	XP: $10	F16
Suite Motel	9/1-1/14	1P: $109-$129	2P: $119-$129	XP: $10	F16
	4/1-8/31	1P: $99-$119	2P: $109-$119	XP: $10	F16

Location: I-8 business loop; 1.2 mi s of jct US 95. 2600 S 4th Ave 85364. Fax: 520/341-1152. **Terms:** [CP] meal plan; small pets only. **Facility:** 164 rooms. All units are 1-bedroom suites with wet bar. 3 stories; exterior corridors; heated pool. **Cards:** AE, CB, DI, DS, JC, MC, VI. *(See color ad p 330)*

SHILO CONFERENCE HOTEL
◆◆◆ All Year 1P: $79-$150 2P: $79-$150 XP: $12 F12
Phone: (520)782-9511
Motor Inn **Location:** Just ne of I-8, at jct SR 95 (16th St). 1550 S Castle Dome Ave 85365. Fax: 520/783-1538.
Terms: [BP] meal plan; pets, $7 extra charge. **Facility:** 134 rooms. A contemporary, full service hotel on nicely landscaped grounds. 4 stories; interior corridors; heated pool. **Some Rooms:** 15 kitchens. **Cards:** AE, CB, DI, DS, JC, MC, VI. *(See color ad p 360)* (ASK) (SD) (⊞) (🛏) (🍴) (🐕) (🛋) (✕) (🎥) (🖥) (💻) (📠) (🔌) (DATA PORT) (🛁) (♿)

YUMA CABANA MOTEL
Phone: (520)783-8311
(AAA) (SAVE) 2/1-2/29 1P: $56-$64 2P: $63-$74 XP: $6 F12
11/1-1/31 1P: $36-$57 2P: $42-$66 XP: $6 F12
◆◆ 3/1-4/15 1P: $42-$54 2P: $52-$62 XP: $6 F12
Motel 4/16-10/31 1P: $32-$42 2P: $40-$50 XP: $6 F12
Location: I-8 business loop; 0.6 mi s of jct US 95. 2151 S 4th Ave 85364. Fax: 520/783-1126. **Terms:** [CP] meal plan; cancellation fee imposed; pets, $6 extra charge. **Facility:** 63 rooms. Some units with balcony. 4 one-bedroom suites with efficiency & 7 kitchens, $12 extra charge; 2 stories; interior corridors; heated pool. **Dining:** Restaurant nearby. **Recreation:** shuffleboard court. **All Rooms:** combo or shower baths. **Some Rooms:** Fee: refrigerators, microwaves. **Cards:** AE, CB, DI, DS, JC, MC, VI. **Special Amenities:** Free breakfast and free local telephone calls. *(See color ad p 360)* (SD) (🛏) (🍴) (🛋) (✕) (🎥) (📠) (🔌) (🛁)

YUMA 4TH AVE TRAVELODGE
Phone: (520)782-3831
(AAA) (SAVE) 2/1-2/29 1P: $62 2P: $72-$82 XP: $5 F15
◆◆ 3/1-3/31 & 1/1-1/31 1P: $42 2P: $52-$62 XP: $5 F15
Motel 4/1-12/31 1P: $32 2P: $42-$52 XP: $5 F15
Location: I-8 business loop; 0.5 mi s of jct US 95. 2050 S 4th Ave 85364. Fax: 520/783-4616. **Terms:** Weekly rates avail; cancellation fee imposed. **Facility:** 48 rooms. Small picnic area with barbeque and tables. 3 rooms with kitchen, 1 week min rental $35 extra charge; 4 two-room units, $5 extra charge; 2 stories; exterior corridors; heated pool. **Dining:** Coffee shop nearby. **All Rooms:** combo or shower baths, extended cable TV. **Cards:** AE, CB, DI, DS, MC, VI. **Special Amenities:** Free local telephone calls and free newspaper. (SD) (🛏) (🛋) (✕) (🎥) (💻) (🔌) (🛁)

YUMA SUPER 8 MOTEL
Phone: (520)782-2000
◆◆ 2/1-4/15 & 1/1-1/31 1P: $73-$88 2P: $78-$93
Motel 4/16-12/31 1P: $55-$75 2P: $60-$80
Location: Just w of I-8, exit US 95 (16th St). 1688 S Riley Ave 85365. Fax: 520/782-6657. **Terms:** Pets, $5 extra charge. **Facility:** 82 rooms. 3 stories; interior corridors; heated pool. **Cards:** AE, CB, DI, DS, MC, VI. (ASK) (SD) (🛏) (🍴) (🛋) (🐕) (♿) (✕) (🎥) (📠) (🔌) (DATA PORT) (🛁)

── **RESTAURANTS** ──

EL PAPPAGALLO MEXICAN RESTAURANT Lunch: $4-$6 Dinner: $9-$14 Phone: 520/343-9451
◆ **Location:** Just n of 16th St (SR 95); 1.5 mi w of I-8 business loop. 1401 S Avenue B 85364. **Hours:** 11
Mexican am-9 pm, Fri & Sat-9:30 pm. Closed: 11/23 & 12/25. **Features:** carryout; cocktails. A small, casual restaurant. Family recipes used in food preparation. **Cards:** AE, CB, DI, DS, JC, MC, VI.

THE GARDEN CAFE & COFFEE COMPANY Lunch: $5-$8 Phone: 520/783-1491
◆ **Location:** Downtown, just w of I-8, adjacent to Arizona Historical Society Museum. 250 Madison Ave 85364.
American **Hours:** 9 am-2:30 pm, Sat & Sun from 8 am. Closed major holidays, Mon & 6/1-9/30. **Features:** casual dress; Sunday brunch. Delightful dining in a terraced, outdoor, tree shaded patio area in building complex that dates to 1887. Nice variety of salad, sandwiches, soup, quiche and dessert. Indoor dining also avail. **Cards:** AE, MC, VI. (✕)

JULIEANNA'S PATIO CAFE Lunch: $5-$11 Dinner: $16-$23 Phone: 520/317-1961
◆◆◆ **Location:** 1 mi w of 4th Ave Via 24th St, just s on 19th Ave at Pichacho Mountain Medical Center. 1951 W
American 25th St 85364. **Hours:** 11 am-3 & 5-9 pm, Sat 5 pm-9 pm. Closed: 4/23, 11/23 & 12/25. **Reservations:** suggested. **Features:** casual dress; cocktails & lounge. Colorfully decorated dining room and large outdoor patio. **Cards:** AE, CB, DI, DS, MC, VI. (✕)

MANDARIN PALACE Lunch: $6-$8 Dinner: $8-$14 Phone: 520/344-2805
◆◆ **Location:** I-8 business loop; 2.4 mi se of jct US 95. 350 E 32nd St 85364. **Hours:** 11 am-10 pm, Fri &
Chinese Sat-11 pm. Lunch buffet Mon-Fri 11 am-2 pm. **Features:** casual dress; early bird specials; carryout; cocktails & lounge; a la carte. Mandarin and Szechuan cuisine; complete dinners $12-$13.50. A limited selection of American entrees. **Cards:** AE, DI, MC, VI. (✕)

Precautions Can Save A Vacation!

Travelers are faced with the task of protecting themselves while in a strange environment. Although there is no way to guarantee absolute protection from crime, the experts—law enforcement officials—advise travelers to take a proactive approach to securing their property and ensuring their safety.

- Make sure the hotel desk clerk does not announce your room number; if he does, quietly request a new room assignment.

- Ask front desk personnel which areas of town to avoid and what, if any, special precautions should be taken when driving a rental car (some criminals target tourists driving rental cars).

- Never open the door to a stranger; use the peephole and request identification. If you are still unsure, call the front desk to verify the identity of the person and the purpose of his/her visit.

- Carry money separately from credit cards or use a "fanny pack." Carry your purse close to your body and your wallet in an inside coat or front trouser pocket. Never leave luggage unattended, and use your business address, if possible, on luggage tags.

- Beware of distractions staged by would-be scam artists, especially groups of children that surround you, or a stranger who accidentally spills something on you. They may be lifting your wallet.

- If using an automatic teller machine (ATM), choose one in a well-lit area with plenty of foot traffic, such as one at a grocery store. Law enforcement officials suggest that machines inside establishments are generally safer to use.

- Use room safes or safety deposit boxes provided by the hotel. Store all valuables out of sight, even when you are in the room.

- Law enforcement agencies consider card-key (electronic) door locks the most secure.

New Mexico

Albuquerque... 365

Carlsbad........ 393

Gallup 403

Santa Fe........ 425

Taos............. 446

ALAMOGORDO pop. 27,600

———— LODGINGS ————

ALL AMERICAN INN
AAA SAVE
◆◆
Motel
All Year   1P: $30-$34   2P: $34-$38   XP: $4   F12
Phone: (505)437-1850
Location: 1 mi s on US 54, 70 and 82. 508 S White Sands Blvd 88310. **Terms:** Small pets only. **Facility:** 28 rooms. 2 stories; exterior corridors; heated pool. **Dining:** Restaurant nearby. **All Rooms:** combo or shower baths, extended cable TV. **Some Rooms:** Fee: refrigerators, microwaves. **Cards:** AE, CB, DI, MC, VI. **Special Amenities:** Free local telephone calls.

BEST WESTERN DESERT AIRE MOTOR HOTEL   **Phone:** (505)437-2110
AAA SAVE
◆◆◆
Motel
5/1-9/30   1P: $57   2P: $62
2/1-4/30 & 10/1-1/31   1P: $52   2P: $57
Location: 1.5 mi s on US 54, 70 and 82. 1021 S White Sands Blvd 88310. Fax: 505/437-1898. **Terms:** [CP] meal plan; monthly rates avail; age restrictions may apply; 3 day cancellation notice; cancellation fee imposed; pets, $50 dep req. **Facility:** 100 rooms. Located in a commercial area. 12 whirlpool rooms, $79-$109; 2 stories; exterior corridors; heated pool, sauna, whirlpool. **Recreation:** Game Room, Pool Table. **Some Rooms:** 9 kitchens. Fee: microwaves, VCR. **Cards:** AE, CB, DI, DS, MC, VI. **Special Amenities:** Free breakfast and free local telephone calls. *(See ad below)*

DAYS INN   **Phone:** (505)437-5090
◆◆◆
Motel
MC, VI.
All Year   1P: $50-$70   2P: $55-$100   XP: $8   F12
Location: 1.5 mi s on US 54, 70 and 82. 907 S White Sands Blvd 88310. Fax: 505/434-5667. **Terms:** Cancellation fee imposed. **Facility:** 40 rooms. 2 stories; exterior corridors; heated pool. **Cards:** AE, CB, DI, DS, JC, MC, VI.

HOLIDAY INN EXPRESS-ALAMOGORDO   **Phone:** (505)437-7100
◆◆◆
Motel
DI, DS, MC, VI.
All Year   1P: $65   2P: $65   XP: $8   F19
Location: US 70, 0.6 mi n of jct US 70, 54 and 82. 1401 S White Sands Blvd 88310. Fax: 505/437-7100. **Terms:** [ECP] meal plan; cancellation fee imposed; small pets only, $50 dep req. **Facility:** 106 rooms. 2 stories; interior corridors; designated smoking area; heated pool. **Some Rooms:** Fee: refrigerators, microwaves. **Cards:** AE, CB, DI, DS, MC, VI.

MOTEL 6 - 368   **Phone:** 505/434-5970
AAA
◆◆
Motel
All Year   1P: $34-$54   2P: $50-$60   XP: $3   F17
Location: US 70, 0.6 mi n of jct US 70, 54 and 82. 251 Panorama Blvd 88310. Fax: 505/437-5491. **Terms:** Small pets only. **Facility:** 97 rooms. 2 stories; exterior corridors; heated pool. **Dining:** Restaurant nearby. **All Rooms:** shower baths. **Cards:** AE, CB, DI, DS, MC, VI.

SUPER 8 MOTEL   **Phone:** 505/434-4205
◆◆
Motel
Property failed to provide current rates
Location: US 54, 70 and 82, 2 mi n. 3204 N White Sands Blvd 88310. Fax: 505/434-4205. **Terms:** [CP] meal plan; small pets only. **Facility:** 57 rooms. Across from mall and adjacent to fairgrounds. 2 stories; interior corridors. **Some Rooms:** Fee: refrigerators. **Cards:** AE, CB, DI, DS, MC, VI.

WESTERN MOTEL

(AAA) (SAVE)
◆
Motel

All Year   1P: $30-$35   2P: $40-$50

Phone: (505)437-2922
XP: $5   D12

Location: 1.5 mi s on US 54, 70 and 82. 1101 S White Sands Blvd 88310. Fax: 505/443-8365. **Terms:** Weekly rates avail; 3 day cancellation notice. **Facility:** 25 rooms. 2 two-bedroom units. 1 story; exterior corridors. **All Rooms:** combo or shower baths. **Cards:** AE, CB, DI, DS, MC, VI. **Special Amenities:** Early check-in/late check-out and free local telephone calls.

WHITE SANDS INN

(AAA) (SAVE)
◆ ◆ ◆
Motel

All Year   1P: $46-$54   2P: $55-$60

Phone: (505)434-4200
XP: $5   F12

Location: 1.5 mi s on US 54 and 70. 1020 S White Sands Blvd 88310. Fax: 505/434-8872. **Terms:** [CP] meal plan. **Facility:** 92 rooms. 2 stories; exterior corridors; heated pool, whirlpool. **All Rooms:** extended cable TV. **Some Rooms:** 18 efficiencies, kitchen. Fee: VCR. **Cards:** AE, DI, DS, MC, VI. **Special Amenities:** Free breakfast and free local telephone calls.

ALBUQUERQUE pop. 384,600 (See map p. 369; index below)

This index helps you "spot" where approved accommodations are located on the detailed maps that follow. Rate ranges are for comparison only and show the property's high season. Turn to the listing page for more detailed rate information and consult display ads for special promotions. Restaurant rate range is for dinner unless only lunch (L) is served.

✈ Airport Accommodations

Spotter/Map Page Number	OA	ALBUQUERQUE	Diamond Rating	Rate Range High Season	Listing Page
68 / p. 369		Baymont Inn Airport, 1 mi nw	◆◆◆	$65-$75	372
26 / p. 369	(AAA)	Best Western Airport Inn, 0.5 mi nw	◆◆◆	$79-$99 SAVE	373
50 / p. 369	(AAA)	Comfort Inn-Airport, at airport, 0.5 mi nw	◆◆◆	$55-$95 SAVE	374
45 / p. 369		Courtyard by Marriott (Airport), 1 mi nw	◆◆◆	$125	376
41 / p. 369	(AAA)	Fairfield Inn Airport, 1 mi nw	◆◆◆	$55-$78 SAVE	377
24 / p. 369		La Quinta Inn-Airport, 1 mi nw	◆◆◆	$75-$95	380
28 / p. 369	(AAA)	Radisson Inn Hotel Albuquerque-Airport, 1 mi nw	◆◆◆	$109-$119 SAVE	381
70 / p. 369	(AAA)	Ramada Limited (Airport), 1 mi nw	◆◆◆	$63-$81 SAVE	382
27 / p. 369	(AAA)	Wyndham Hotel, at airport, 0.3 mi w	◆◆◆	$59-$99 SAVE	384

ALBUQUERQUE

Spotter/Map Page Number	OA	ALBUQUERQUE - Lodgings	Diamond Rating	Rate Range High Season	Listing Page
1 / p. 369	(AAA)	Amberley Suite Hotel - see color ad p 371	◆◆◆	$89-$99 SAVE	371
2 / p. 369		La Quinta Inn North - see color ad p 380	◆◆◆	$69-$89	380
3 / p. 369	(AAA)	Barcelona Suites Hotel	◆◆	$69-$79 SAVE	372
4 / p. 369		Crowne Plaza Pyramid Hotel	◆◆◆	$122	376
5 / p. 369		Albuquerque Hilton - see color ad p 41	◆◆◆	$92	370
6 / p. 369		Holiday Inn-Mountain View - see ad p 378	◆◆◆	$90-$119	379
7 / p. 369	(AAA)	Travelodge - see ad p 383	◆◆◆	$55-$64 SAVE	384
8 / p. 369	(AAA)	Radisson Hotel & Conference Center - see ad p 382	◆◆◆	$99 SAVE	381
9 / p. 369		La Quinta Inn San Mateo - see color ad p 380	◆◆◆	$65-$85	380
10 / p. 369		AmeriSuites - see color ad opposite title page	◆◆◆	$69-$107 SAVE	372
11 / p. 369	(AAA)	Best Western Winrock Inn - see color ad p 375	◆◆◆	$65-$85 SAVE	373
12 / p. 369		The Albuquerque Marriott Hotel	◆◆◆	$169	370
13 / p. 369	(AAA)	Howard Johnson Express Inn - see color ad p 379, p 368	◆◆◆	$55-$69 SAVE	379
14 / p. 369		Howard Johnson Hotel & Convention Center - see color ad p 368	◆◆◆	$53-$71	379
15 / p. 369	(AAA)	Econo Lodge Midtown	◆◆	$65-$75 SAVE	377
16 / p. 369	(AAA)	Best Western American Motor Inn & RV Park - see color ad p 371	◆◆◆	$69-$99 SAVE	373
17 / p. 369	(AAA)	Comfort Inn East - see color ad p 376	◆◆◆	$49-$61 SAVE	375
18 / p. 369	(AAA)	Econo Lodge	◆◆	$55-$76 SAVE	377
19 / p. 369	(AAA)	Days Inn-East	◆◆	$50-$65 SAVE	376
20 / p. 369	(AAA)	Brittania & W E Mauger Estate Bed & Breakfast - see color ad p 372	◆◆◆	$89-$199 SAVE	373
21 / p. 369	(AAA)	Bottger-Koch Mansion Bed & Breakfast in Old Town	◆◆◆	$99-$109 SAVE	373

Spotter/Map Page Number	OA	ALBUQUERQUE - Lodgings (continued)	Diamond Rating	Rate Range High Season	Listing Page
22 / p. 369		Howard Johnson	◆◆◆	$40-$67	379
24 / p. 369		La Quinta Inn-Airport - see color ad p 380	◆◆◆	$75-$95	380
25 / p. 369		Days Inn Eubank	◆◆◆	$45-$70	377
26 / p. 369	⊕	**Best Western Airport Inn**	◆◆◆	$79-$99 🆂	373
27 / p. 369	⊕	**Wyndham Hotel - see color ad p 383**	◆◆◆	$59-$99 🆂	384
28 / p. 369	⊕	**Radisson Inn Hotel Albuquerque-Airport**	◆◆◆	$109-$119 🆂	381
29 / p. 369		Econo Lodge	◆◆	Failed to provide	377
30 / p. 369		Plaza Inn Albuquerque - see color ad p 381	◆◆◆	$80-$92	381
31 / p. 369	⊕	**Lorlodge Motel East**	◆	$38-$56 🆂	380
32 / p. 369	⊕	**Hacienda Antigua B & B**	◆◆◆	$99-$179 🆂	378
33 / p. 369	⊕	**Albuquerque Doubletree Hotel - see color ad p 370**	◆◆◆	$129-$155	370
34 / p. 369		Ramada Inn Mountainview	◆◆◆	$55-$105	382
35 / p. 369	⊕	**Monterey Non Smokers Motel**	◆◆◆	$42-$56	381
36 / p. 369		Sheraton Old Town Hotel	◆◆◆	$115-$135	383
37 / p. 369	⊕	**Best Western Rio Grande Inn - see color ad p 374**	◆◆◆	$99-$115 🆂	373
38 / p. 369	⊕	**Motel 6 - 1349**	◆◆	$38-$54	381
39 / p. 369		Albuquerque Holiday Inn Express	◆◆◆	$79-$89	370
40 / p. 369		Super 8 Motel of Albuquerque	◆◆	$45-$50	384
41 / p. 369	⊕	**Fairfield Inn Airport**	◆◆◆	$55-$78 🆂	377
42 / p. 369	⊕	**Comfort Inn Mid-Town**	◆◆◆	$49-$110 🆂	376
43 / p. 369	⊕	**Hyatt Regency - see color ad p 368**	◆◆◆◆	$159 🆂	380
45 / p. 369		Courtyard by Marriott (Airport)	◆◆◆	$125	376
46 / p. 369		**Hampton Inn-North - see ad p 378**	◆◆◆	$60-$110	378
47 / p. 369		Baymont Inn & Suites Albuquerque North - see color ad p 372	◆◆◆	$61-$66	373
48 / p. 369		Homestead Village Guest Studios	◆◆	$59	379
49 / p. 369		Residence Inn by Marriott	◆◆◆	$126	382
50 / p. 369	⊕	**Comfort Inn-Airport - see color ad p 370**	◆◆◆	$55-$95 🆂	374
51 / p. 369	⊕	**AmeriSuites - see color ad opposite title page**	◆◆◆	$85-$107 🆂	372
52 / p. 369		Ramada Inn-Downtown	◆◆◆	$73-$81	382
53 / p. 369		La Quinta Inn-West - see color ad p 380	◆◆◆	$75-$95	380
54 / p. 369		Red Roof Inns Midtown	◆◆◆	$45-$67	382
55 / p. 369		Days Inn West	◆◆◆	Failed to provide	377
56 / p. 369	⊕	**Holiday Inn Express-West**	◆◆◆	$70-$87 🆂	379
57 / p. 369		Holiday Inn Express	◆◆◆	$95-$100	378
58 / p. 369		ClubHouse Inn & Suites - see ad p 375	◆◆◆	$89-$133	374
59 / p. 369		Fairfield Inn by Marriott	◆◆◆	$62-$69	378
61 / p. 369	⊕	**Econo Lodge Old Town**	◆◆◆	$50-$95 🆂	377
62 / p. 369		Super 8 Motel East	◆◆	$45-$50	384
63 / p. 369	⊕	**Motel 6 Premiere - 741**	◆◆	$34-$50	381
64 / p. 369	⊕	**Luxury Inn**	◆◆	$40-$65 🆂	380
65 / p. 369	⊕	**Motel 6 - 1145**	◆◆	$32-$48	381
66 / p. 369	⊕	**Best Inn**	◆◆	$35-$80 🆂	373
67 / p. 369	⊕	**Wyndham Garden Hotel**	◆◆◆	$59-$120 🆂	384
68 / p. 369		Baymont Inn Airport - see color ad p 372	◆◆◆	$65-$75	372
69 / p. 369		Comfort Inn & Suites	◆◆◆	$65-$89	375
70 / p. 369	⊕	**Ramada Limited (Airport)**	◆◆◆	$63-$81 🆂	382
71 / p. 369	⊕	**Comfort Inn West**	◆◆◆	$99-$109 🆂	376
72 / p. 369		Courtyard by Marriott Journal Center	◆◆◆	$92	376
73 / p. 369	⊕	**Ramada Limited**	◆◆◆	$69-$79 🆂	382
75 / p. 369		Homestead Village Guest Studios	◆◆	$39-$44	379
76 / p. 369		Sheraton Albuquerque Uptown	◆◆◆	$79-$185	382
77 / p. 369	⊕	**Sleep Inn Airport**	◆◆	$89-$99 🆂	383
78 / p. 369	⊕	**Sumner Suites**	◆◆◆	$115-$125 🆂	383

Spotter/Map Page Number	OA	ALBUQUERQUE - Restaurants	Diamond Rating	Rate Range High Season	
1 / p. 369		Garduno's of Mexico Restaurant & Cantina	◆◆	$8-$15	386
2 / p. 369	🔷	Cervantes	◆◆	$7-$15	385
3 / p. 369		Quarters Bar-B-Que	◆◆	$10-$24	388
4 / p. 369	🔷	High Finance	◆◆	$16-$42	386
5 / p. 369		Christy Mae's	◆◆	$6-$10	385
6 / p. 369		The County Line of Albuquerque	◆◆	$8-$17	385
7 / p. 369		M & J Restaurant/Sanitary Tortilla Factory	◆	$5-$8(L)	387
8 / p. 369		La Esquina Restaurante	◆◆	$6-$14	387
9 / p. 369	🔷	High Noon Restaurant & Saloon	◆◆	$10-$25	386
10 / p. 369		Classic Grill	◆◆	$6-$15	385
11 / p. 369		Maria Teresa Restaurant	◆◆◆	$13-$24	387
13 / p. 369		Antiquity	◆◆	$15-$23	385
14 / p. 369		Eloy's Mexican Restaurant	◆◆	$5-$10	386
15 / p. 369		Monte Vista Fire Station Restaurant	◆◆◆	$11-$21	387
18 / p. 369	🔷	Barry's Oasis Restaurant	◆◆	$7-$20	385
19 / p. 369		Rancher's Club of New Mexico	◆◆◆	$16-$32	388
20 / p. 369		Scalo Northern Italian Grill	◆◆◆	$8-$19	388
21 / p. 369		Fresh Choices	◆◆	$5-$7	386
22 / p. 369		McGrath's Restaurant & Bar	◆◆◆	$6-$12(L)	387
23 / p. 369		Stephens An American Cafe	◆◆◆	$18-$25	389
24 / p. 369	🔷	Trattoria Trombino	◆◆◆	$10-$20	389
25 / p. 369		Ragin' Shrimp	◆◆	$6-$13	388
26 / p. 369		Rudy's Country Store & Bar-B-Q	◆	$7-$8	388
29 / p. 369		Assets Grille & Brewery Co.	◆◆	$6-$18	385
30 / p. 369		Cafe Spoleto	◆◆	$11-$18	385
31 / p. 369		Ragin Shrimp	◆◆	$8-$14	388
32 / p. 369		Double Rainbow Bakery Cafe	◆◆	$6-$10	385
33 / p. 369		El Norteno	◆◆	$6-$12	385
36 / p. 369		Emilie's Bakery & Cafe	◆◆	$8-$21	386
37 / p. 369		Garcia's Kitchen	◆	$3-$7	386
38 / p. 369		Gin Mill Restaurant & Tavern	◆◆	$6-$16	386
40 / p. 369		Grandma's K&I Diner	◆	$5-$9(L)	386
42 / p. 369		Great American Land & Cattle Company	◆◆	$10-$22	386
43 / p. 369		Los Cuates del Norte	◆	$6-$10	387
45 / p. 369		Manhattan on the Rio Grande	◆	$7-$9	387
46 / p. 369		O'Niell's Pub	◆◆	$6-$10	387
47 / p. 369		Owl Cafe	◆	$4-$9	387
49 / p. 369		Paul's Monterey Inn	◆	$9-$24	387
50 / p. 369		Powdrell's Barbecue House	◆	$6-$10	387
51 / p. 369		Robb's Ribbs	◆	$5-$15	388
53 / p. 369		Sadie's Dining Room	◆◆	$8-$15	388
54 / p. 369		Scarpas	◆◆	$5-$8	388
55 / p. 369		Seasons Rotisserie & Grill	◆◆◆	$11-$26	389
58 / p. 369		Tomato Cafe	◆◆	$8	389
59 / p. 369		Vivace	◆◆	$9-$17	389
62 / p. 369		Yesterdave's Grill	◆◆	$7-$15	389
63 / p. 369		Ribs In Uptown	◆◆	$7-$18	388

Nearby Accommodations

Spotter/Map Page Number	OA	RIO RANCHO - Lodgings	Diamond Rating	Rate Range High Season	Listing Page
82 / p. 369	🔷	Days Inn	◆◆	$75-$90 📼	421
83 / p. 369		Ramada Limited Hotel	◆◆◆	$45-$50	421
84 / p. 369	🔷	Best Western Inn at Rio Rancho - see color ad p 421	◆◆◆	$79-$129 📼	421
85 / p. 369		Rio Rancho Super 8 Motel	◆◆	Failed to provide	421
86 / p. 369	🔷	Hilton Garden Inn	◆◆◆	$69-$139 📼	421
88 / p. 369	🔷	Wellesley Inn & Suites	◆◆◆	$49-$99 📼	422

Spotter/Map Page Number	OA	RIO RANCHO - Restaurant	Diamond Rating	Rate Range High Season	
67 / p. 369		Wine & Roses Restaurant	◆◆	$9-$15	422
		BERNALILLO - Lodgings			
89 / p. 369		La Hacienda Grande - see ad p 377	◆◆◆	$95-$129	393
		BERNALILLO - Restaurant			
72 / p. 369		Prairie Star	◆◆◆	$15-$32	393

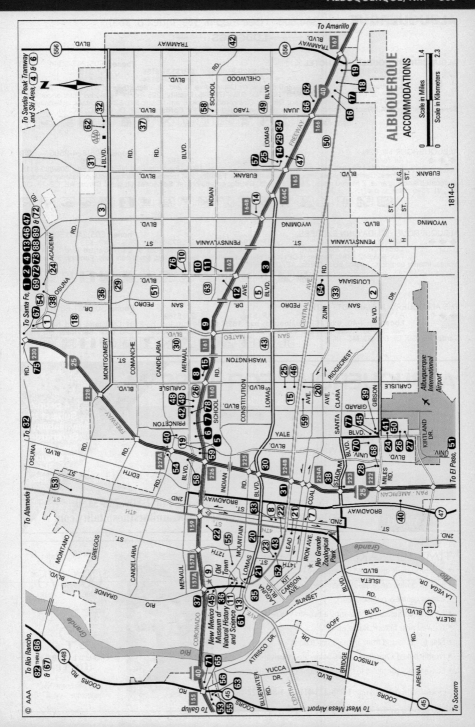

ALBUQUERQUE
ACCOMMODATIONS

Scale in Miles
Scale in Kilometers

1814-G

ALBUQUERQUE pop. 384,600 (See map p. 369; index p. 365)

——— LODGINGS ———

ALBUQUERQUE DOUBLETREE HOTEL
Phone: (505)247-3344 **33**
2/1-5/26 & 9/5-11/17   1P: $129-$150   2P: $134-$155   XP: $10   F17
5/27-9/4 & 11/18-1/31   1P: $99-$129   2P: $104-$134   XP: $10   F17
Hotel
Location: I-25, Central Ave exit, 0.8 mi w on Central Ave to 2nd St, then 2 blks n; adjacent to convention center. 201 Marquette Ave NW 87102. Fax: 505/247-7025. **Facility:** 295 rooms. 16 stories; interior corridors; small heated pool. Fee: parking. **Dining:** Dining room, deli; 6 am-11 pm; $12-$21; cocktails; entertainment.
Services: gift shop. **All Rooms:** combo or shower baths, extended cable TV. **Cards:** AE, CB, DI, DS, JC, MC, VI.
(See color ad below)

ALBUQUERQUE HILTON
Phone: (505)884-2500 **5**
All Year   1P: $92   2P: $92   XP: $10   F18
Hotel
Location: I-40, exit 160, just n to Menaul Blvd, 1 mi w. 1901 University Blvd NE 87102. Fax: 505/889-9118.
Terms: Cancellation fee imposed; package plans. **Facility:** 264 rooms. 2-12 stories; interior/exterior corridors; designated smoking area; 2 heated pools; 2 tennis courts. **Dining:** entertainment. **Services:** gift shop. **Cards:** AE, CB, DI, DS, MC, VI. *(See color ad p 41)*

ALBUQUERQUE HOLIDAY INN EXPRESS
Phone: (505)247-1500 **39**
All Year   1P: $79-$89   2P: $79-$89   XP: $5   F18
Motel
Location: I-25, exit 222A, 1 mi e to Yale Blvd, just n, then just e. 2331 Centre Ave SE 87106.
Fax: 505/842-8881. **Terms:** [ECP] meal plan; cancellation fee imposed; small pets only. **Facility:** 58 rooms. 3 stories; interior corridors; heated pool. **Cards:** AE, DI, DS, MC, VI.

THE ALBUQUERQUE MARRIOTT HOTEL
Phone: 505/881-6800 **12**
All Year   1P: $169   2P: $169
Hotel
Location: I-40, exit 162 westbound; exit 162B eastbound; just n. 2101 Louisiana Blvd NE 87110.
Fax: 505/881-1780. **Facility:** 411 rooms. 17 stories; interior corridors; heated pool. **Services:** gift shop.
Cards: AE, CB, DI, DS, JC, MC, VI.

(See map p. 369)

AMBERLEY SUITE HOTEL

Phone: (505)823-1300 ❶

All Year	1P: $89-$99	2P: $89-$99	XP: $10 F18

Location: I-25, exit 231, 0.8 mi n on frontage road. 7620 Pan American Frwy NE 87109. Fax: 505/823-2896. **Terms:** [BP] meal plan; monthly rates avail; check-in 4 pm; cancellation fee imposed; pets, $5 extra charge. **Facility:** 168 rooms. 3 stories; interior corridors; small heated pool, sauna, whirlpool. **Dining:** Restaurant; 6 am-9:30 & 5-9 pm, Sat & Sun 7 am-10:30 & 5-9 pm; $10-$15; cocktails. **Services:** gift shop; complimentary evening beverages; area transportation, within 3 mi. **Recreation:** game room. **All Rooms:** combo or shower baths. **Some Rooms:** 60 efficiencies. **Cards:** AE, CB, DI, DS, JC, MC, VI. **Special Amenities:** Free breakfast and free local telephone calls. (See color ad below)

(See map p. 369)

AMERISUITES
Phone: (505)872-9000 **10**
All Year 1P: $69-$98 2P: $69-$107 XP: $10 F18
Suite Motel **Location:** I-40, exit 162 westbound; exit 162B eastbound, 0.7 mi n. 6901 Arvada Ave NE 87110. Fax: 505/872-3829. **Terms:** [CP] meal plan; pets, $25 extra charge. **Facility:** 128 rooms. 6 stories; interior corridors; heated pool. **Recreation:** Fee: in-room video games. **All Rooms:** combo or shower baths. **Cards:** AE, CB, DI, DS, JC, MC, VI. **Special Amenities:** Free breakfast and free newspaper.
(See color ad opposite title page)

AMERISUITES
Phone: (505)242-9300 **51**
All Year 1P: $85-$98 2P: $94-$107 XP: $10 F18
Motel **Location:** I-25, exit 221, 0.3 mi e to University Blvd exit, just n to Woodward Rd. 1400 Sunport Place SE 87106. Fax: 505/242-0998. **Terms:** Cancellation fee imposed; small pets only, $25 fee. **Facility:** 128 rooms. 6 stories; interior corridors; heated pool. **Services:** area transportation, within 3 mi. **All Rooms:** combo or shower baths, extended cable TV. **Cards:** AE, CB, DI, DS, JC, MC, VI. **Special Amenities:** Free breakfast and free newspaper. *(See color ad opposite title page)*

BARCELONA SUITES HOTEL
Phone: (505)255-5566 **3**
All Year 1P: $69 2P: $79 XP: $5
Motel **Location:** I-40, exit 162, 0.5 mi s. 900 Louisiana Blvd NE 87110. Fax: 505/266-6644. **Terms:** [BP] meal plan; 3 day cancellation notice; cancellation fee imposed. **Facility:** 164 rooms. All rooms have separate sitting area. 4 whirlpool rooms; 3 stories; interior/exterior corridors; 2 pools, 1 indoor heated, sauna, whirlpool. **Services:** complimentary evening beverages. **All Rooms:** extended cable TV. **Cards:** AE, CB, DI, DS, MC, VI. **Special Amenities:** Free breakfast.

BAYMONT INN AIRPORT
Phone: (505)242-1555 **68**
2/1-6/30 1P: $65-$75 2P: $65-$75 XP: $5 F18
Motel 7/1-1/31 1P: $60-$70 2P: $60-$70 XP: $5 F18
Location: I-25, exit 222 (Gibson Blvd) northbound; exit 222A southbound, just e. 1511 Gibson Blvd SE 87106. Fax: 505/242-8801. **Terms:** [CP] meal plan; cancellation fee imposed; pets. **Facility:** 109 rooms. 4 stories; interior corridors; heated pool. **Services:** gift shop; area transportation. **All Rooms:** combo or shower baths. **Cards:** AE, CB, DI, DS, MC, VI.
(See color ad below)

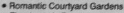

(See map p. 369)

BAYMONT INN & SUITES ALBUQUERQUE NORTH

◆◆◆
Motel

5/26-1/31	1P: $61	2P: $66
2/1-5/25	1P: $55	2P: $60

Phone: (505)345-7500 47
XP: $5 F18
XP: $5 F18

Location: I-25, exit 231, just w. 7439 Pan American Frwy NE 87109. Fax: 505/345-1616. **Terms:** [CP] meal plan; pets. **Facility:** 101 rooms. 3 stories; interior corridors. **Cards:** AE, CB, DI, DS, MC, VI. *(See color ad p 372)*

[icons]

BEST INN

⬥⬥⬥ SAVE
◆◆
Motel

All Year	1P: $35-$75	2P: $40-$80

Phone: (505)293-4444 66
XP: $15 F12

Location: I-40, exit 166, just n to Cooper, just s. 601 Paisano NE 87123. Fax: 505/293-9441. **Terms:** [CP] meal plan; weekly rates avail. **Facility:** 65 rooms. 2 stories; exterior corridors; heated pool, whirlpool. **Some Rooms:** Fee: refrigerators. **Cards:** AE, CB, DI, DS, JC, MC, VI. **Special Amenities:** Free breakfast and free local telephone calls.

[icons]

BEST WESTERN AIRPORT INN

⬥⬥⬥ SAVE
◆◆◆
Motel

10/4-10/31	1P: $79-$89	2P: $89-$99
2/1-10/3	1P: $59-$69	2P: $64-$74
11/1-1/31	1P: $49-$59	2P: $59-$64

Phone: (505)242-7022 26
XP: $10 F12
XP: $5 F12
XP: $5 F12

Location: I-25, exit 222 (Gibson Blvd) northbound; exit 222A southbound, 1 mi e, just s. 2400 Yale Blvd SE 87106. Fax: 505/243-0620. **Terms:** [CP] meal plan; weekly & monthly rates avail; cancellation fee imposed; pets, $10 fee. **Facility:** 118 rooms. 2 stories; interior corridors; heated pool, whirlpool. **Dining:** Restaurant nearby. **Recreation:** Fee: in-room video games. **All Rooms:** extended cable TV. **Some Rooms:** Fee: refrigerators. **Cards:** AE, DI, DS, JC, MC, VI. **Special Amenities:** Free breakfast and free local telephone calls.

[icons]

BEST WESTERN AMERICAN MOTOR INN & RV PARK

⬥⬥⬥ SAVE
◆◆◆
Motor Inn

10/1-10/15	1P: $69-$89	2P: $79-$99
5/26-9/30	1P: $59-$79	2P: $69-$79
2/1-5/25	1P: $59-$69	2P: $65-$79
10/16-1/31	1P: $49-$59	2P: $59-$69

Phone: (505)298-7426 16
XP: $4 F12
XP: $4 F12
XP: $4 F12
XP: $4 F12

Location: I-40, exit 167, 0.3 mi w on Central Ave westbound; exit 166 right on Juan Tabo, left on Central Ave, then 0.5 mi eastbound. 12999 Central Ave NE 87123. Fax: 505/298-0212. **Terms:** [BP] meal plan; pets, $3 extra charge. **Facility:** 77 rooms. In a commercial area. 4 efficiencies, $5-$6 extra charge, up to 6 persons; whirlpool room; 2 stories; exterior corridors; heated pool, whirlpool. **Dining:** Restaurant; 6 am-9:30 pm; $4-$11. **Cards:** AE, CB, DI, DS, MC, VI. **Special Amenities:** Free breakfast and free local telephone calls. *(See color ad p 371)*

[icons]

BEST WESTERN RIO GRANDE INN

⬥⬥⬥ SAVE
◆◆◆
Motor Inn

10/6-10/15	1P: $99-$107	2P: $105-$115
6/1-10/5	1P: $75-$85	2P: $85-$95
2/1-5/31	1P: $70-$80	2P: $80-$90
10/16-1/31	1P: $59-$69	2P: $69-$79

Phone: (505)843-9500 37
XP: $6 F12
XP: $6 F12
XP: $6 F12
XP: $6 F12

Location: I-40, exit 157A, just s. 1015 Rio Grande Blvd NW 87104. Fax: 505/843-9238. **Terms:** Monthly rates avail; cancellation fee imposed. **Facility:** 174 rooms. 4 stories; interior corridors; heated pool, whirlpool; pool & whirlpool domed in winter. **Dining:** Restaurant; 6 am-9:30 pm; $6-$15; cocktails. **All Rooms:** extended cable TV. **Some Rooms:** Fee: VCR. **Cards:** AE, DI, JC, MC, VI. **Special Amenities:** Free local telephone calls and free newspaper. *(See color ad p 374)*

[icons]

BEST WESTERN WINROCK INN

⬥⬥⬥ SAVE
◆◆◆
Motel

All Year	1P: $65-$75	2P: $75-$85

Phone: (505)883-5252 11
XP: $10 F17

Location: I-40, exit 162 westbound; exit 162B eastbound, just n via Americas Pkwy. 18 Winrock Center NE 87110. Fax: 505/889-3206. **Terms:** [BP] & [ECP] meal plans; 30 day cancellation notice. **Facility:** 173 rooms. 2 stories; interior/exterior corridors; heated pool. **Dining:** Restaurant nearby. **Recreation:** Fee: health club privileges. **Cards:** AE, CB, DI, DS, MC, VI. **Special Amenities:** Free breakfast and free room upgrade (subject to availability with advanced reservations). *(See color ad p 375)*

[icons]

BOTTGER-KOCH MANSION BED & BREAKFAST IN OLD TOWN

⬥⬥⬥ SAVE
◆◆◆
Historic Bed
& Breakfast

All Year	1P: $99	2P: $109

Phone: (505)243-3639 21
XP: $10 F6

Location: I-40, Rio Grande Blvd exit, 1.5 mi s on Rio Grande, just e off Central. 110 San Felipe NW 87104. Fax: 505/243-4378. **Terms:** [BP] & [CP] meal plans; monthly rates avail; 20 day cancellation notice; cancellation fee imposed. **Facility:** 8 rooms. 2 two-bedroom units. 2 bedroom suite avail; whirlpool room, $149; 2 stories; interior corridors; smoke free premises; street parking only. **All Rooms:** combo or shower baths. **Cards:** AE, DI, MC, VI. **Special Amenities:** Free breakfast and free local telephone calls.

[icons]

BRITTANIA & W E MAUGER ESTATE BED & BREAKFAST

⬥⬥⬥ SAVE
◆◆◆
Historic Bed
& Breakfast

All Year	1P: $89-$199	2P: $89-$199

Phone: (505)242-8755 20
XP: $20 F5

Location: I-25, exit 225 (Lomas Ave), 1 mi w, just s on 7th Ave. 701 Roma Ave NW 87102. Fax: 505/842-8835. **Terms:** [BP] meal plan; weekly & monthly rates avail; check-in 4 pm; 10 day cancellation notice; cancellation fee imposed; pets, $30 extra charge. **Facility:** 8 rooms. Renovated 1897 Old West victorian mansion listed on National Register. Voice mail avail. 1 two-bedroom unit. 3 stories, no elevator; interior corridors; smoke free premises. **All Rooms:** shower baths. **Cards:** AE, DI, DS, MC, VI. **Special Amenities:** Free breakfast and free local telephone calls. *(See color ad p 372)*

[icons]

(See map p. 369)

CLUBHOUSE INN & SUITES
♦♦♦
Motel

All Year

Phone: (505)345-0010 **58**

| 1P: $89-$123 | 2P: $99-$133 | XP: $10 | F12 |

Location: I-25, exit 227A, just e to University Blvd, 0.5 mi s to Menual Blvd, 0.5 mi w. 1315 Menaul Blvd NE 87107. Fax: 505/344-3911. **Terms:** [BP] meal plan; cancellation fee imposed; pets. **Facility:** 137 rooms. 2 stories; interior corridors; heated pool. **Cards:** AE, CB, DI, DS, MC, VI. *(See ad p 375)*

COMFORT INN-AIRPORT
〔AAA〕 〔SAVE〕
♦♦♦
Motel

Phone: (505)243-2244 **50**

6/1-8/31	1P: $55-$85	2P: $65-$95	XP: $10	F17
2/1-5/31 & 9/1-11/19	1P: $45-$65	2P: $55-$75	XP: $10	F17
11/20-1/31	1P: $40-$60	2P: $45-$65	XP: $10	F17

Location: I-25, exit 222A (Gibson Blvd) southbound; exit 222 northbound, 1 mi n, just s. 2300 Yale Blvd SE 87106. Fax: 505/247-2925. **Terms:** [CP] meal plan; cancellation fee imposed; pets, $7 extra charge. **Facility:** 118 rooms. Traditional room decor. 3 stories; interior/exterior corridors; small heated pool, whirlpool. **Dining:** Coffee shop nearby. **Some Rooms:** color TV. **Cards:** AE, CB, DI, DS, JC, MC, VI. **Special Amenities:** Early check-in/late checkout. *(See color ad p 370)*

(See map p. 369)

COMFORT INN & SUITES
◆◆◆ 6/2-9/6
Motel 2/1-6/1 & 9/7-1/31
1P: $65-$79 2P: $75-$89 **Phone:** (505)822-1090 [69]
1P: $55-$69 2P: $65-$79 XP: $10 F18
XP: $5 F18
Location: I-25, exit 233, just e via Alameda. 5811 Signal Ave NE 87113. Fax: 505/822-1154. **Terms:** [CP] meal plan; check-in 3:30 pm; pets, $10 extra charge. **Facility:** 69 rooms. Well appointed rooms. Inviting pool and spa area. 3 stories; interior corridors; heated pool. **All Rooms:** combo or shower baths. **Cards:** AE, CB, DI, DS, JC, MC, VI.

COMFORT INN EAST
(AAA) All Year
◆◆◆ Motor Inn
1P: $49-$56 2P: $55-$61 **Phone:** (505)294-1800 [17]
XP: $6 F17
Location: I-40, exit 167, just w. 13031 Central Ave NE 87123. Fax: 505/293-1088. **Terms:** [BP] meal plan; small pets only, $3 extra charge. **Facility:** 122 rooms. In a commercial area. 2 stories; exterior corridors; heated pool, whirlpool. **Dining:** Cafeteria; 6 am-10 & 5-8 pm, Sat & Sun 6-11 am; $6-$13; wine/beer only. **Some Rooms:** Fee: refrigerators. **Cards:** AE, CB, DI, DS, JC, MC, VI. **Special Amenities:** Free breakfast and free local telephone calls. (See color ad p 376)

(See map p. 369)

COMFORT INN MID-TOWN
Phone: (505)881-3210 **42**
All Year 1P: $49-$110 2P: $49-$110 XP: $5 F18
Location: I-25, exit 227A, just s on University Ave. 2015 Menaul Blvd NE 87107. Fax: 505/888-1196. **Terms:** [CP] meal plan; pets, $10 extra charge, in smoking rooms. **Facility:** 147 rooms. 3 stories; exterior corridors; small heated pool, whirlpool. **Dining:** Restaurant nearby. **Services:** gift shop. **All Rooms:** combo or shower baths, extended cable TV. **Some Rooms:** kitchen. **Cards:** AE, DI, DS, MC, VI. **Special Amenities:** Free breakfast and free newspaper.

COMFORT INN WEST
Phone: (505)836-0011 **71**
10/1-10/10 1P: $99 2P: $109 XP: $5 F12
5/1-9/30 1P: $59-$69 2P: $69-$79 XP: $5 F12
2/1-4/30 & 10/11-1/31 1P: $49-$59 2P: $59-$69 XP: $5 F12
Location: I-40, exit 155, just s on Coors Rd, just e. 5712 Iliff Rd NW 87120. Fax: 505/833-5295. **Terms:** [CP] meal plan. **Facility:** 65 rooms. 4 whirlpool rooms; 2 stories; exterior corridors; heated pool, whirlpool. **All Rooms:** combo or shower baths. **Cards:** AE, CB, DI, DS, JC, MC, VI.

COURTYARD BY MARRIOTT (AIRPORT)
Phone: (505)843-6600 **45**
10/6-10/15 1P: $125 2P: $125
2/1-10/5 & 10/16-1/31 1P: $59-$95 2P: $59-$105 XP: $10 F18
Location: I-25, exit 222 (Gibson Blvd) northbound; exit 222A southbound, 1 mi e, just n. 1920 Yale Blvd SE 87106. Fax: 505/843-8740. **Terms:** Check-in 4 pm; cancellation fee imposed. **Facility:** 150 rooms. 4 stories; interior corridors; heated pool. **Some Rooms:** Fee: VCR. **Cards:** AE, DI, DS, MC, VI.

COURTYARD BY MARRIOTT JOURNAL CENTER
Phone: 505/823-1919 **72**
All Year 1P: $72-$92
Location: I-25, exit 222, just s on Pan American NE. 5151 Journal Center Blvd NE 87109. Fax: 505/823-1918. **Facility:** 150 rooms. Attractive public areas, well appointed contemporary rooms. Southwestern motif with lodge type atmosphere to public areas. 4 stories; interior corridors; heated pool. **Services:** gift shop. **All Rooms:** combo or shower baths. **Some Rooms:** Fee: refrigerators. **Cards:** AE, DI, DS, MC, VI.

CROWNE PLAZA PYRAMID HOTEL
Phone: (505)821-3333 **4**
All Year 1P: $122 2P: $122 XP: $20 F12
Location: I-25, exit 232 (Paseo del Norte), just w, 1 mi s on Pan American NE. 5151 San Francisco Rd NE 87109. Fax: 505/828-0230. **Terms:** Cancellation fee imposed; package plans. **Facility:** 311 rooms. 10 stories; interior corridors; heated pool. **Dining:** nightclub. **Services:** gift shop. **All Rooms:** combo or shower baths. **Some Rooms:** Fee: VCR. **Cards:** AE, CB, DI, DS, JC, MC, VI.

DAYS INN-EAST
Phone: (505)294-3297 **19**
2/1-9/30 1P: $50-$60 2P: $55-$65 XP: $10 F8
10/1-1/31 1P: $45-$55 2P: $45-$55 XP: $10 F8
Location: I-40, exit 167, just s. 13317 Central Ave NE 87123. Fax: 505/293-3973. **Terms:** [CP] meal plan; small pets only, $5 extra charge. **Facility:** 72 rooms. 2 stories; exterior corridors; heated pool, sauna, whirlpool. **Dining:** Restaurant nearby. **Cards:** AE, DI, DS, JC, MC, VI. **Special Amenities:** Free breakfast and free local telephone calls.

(See map p. 369)

DAYS INN EUBANK
◆◆◆   All Year   1P: $45-$65   2P: $50-$70   XP: $5   **25**
Motel   **Location:** I-40, exit 165, just n on Eubank Ave. 10321 Hotel Cir NE 87123. Fax: 505/275-0245. **Terms:** [CP]   F17
               meal plan; pets, $5 extra charge. **Facility:** 76 rooms. Some rooms have mountain view. 2 stories; exterior cor-
               ridors; heated pool. **All Rooms:** Fee: safes. **Cards:** AE, DI, DS, MC, VI.

DAYS INN WEST   **Phone:** 505/836-3297   **55**
◆◆◆   Property failed to provide current rates
Motel   **Location:** I-40, exit 155, just s on Coors Rd, just w. 6031 Iliff Rd NW 87121. Fax: 505/836-1214. **Terms:** [CP]
               meal plan; pets, $5 extra charge. **Facility:** 81 rooms. 2 stories; exterior corridors; heated pool.
All Rooms: combo or shower baths. Fee: safes. **Cards:** AE, CB, DI, DS, JC, MC, VI.

ECONO LODGE   **Phone:** (505)292-7600   **18**
AAA SAVE   10/1-10/17   1P: $55-$65   2P: $66-$76   XP: $10   F12
              7/1-9/30   1P: $41-$46   2P: $48-$58   XP: $10   F12
◆◆   2/1-6/30   1P: $33-$38   2P: $41-$46   XP: $10   F12
Motel   10/18-1/31   1P: $31-$36   2P: $41-$46   XP: $10   F12
              Location: I-40, exit 167, just s. 13211 Central Ave NE 87123. Fax: 505/298-4536. **Terms:** [CP] meal plan; 5
day cancellation notice; cancellation fee imposed; small pets only, $5 extra charge. **Facility:** 60 rooms. 3 stories, no elevator;
exterior corridors. **Dining:** Coffee shop nearby. **Cards:** AE, CB, DI, DS, VI. **Special Amenities:** Free breakfast and free local
telephone calls.

ECONO LODGE   **Phone:** 505/271-8500   **29**
◆◆   Property failed to provide current rates
Motel   **Location:** I-40, exit 165 (Eubank Ave), 2 blks n. 10331 Hotel Ave 87123. Fax: 505/296-5984. **Terms:** [CP] meal
               plan. **Facility:** 50 rooms. 2 stories; interior corridors. **Cards:** AE, CB, DI, DS, MC, VI.

ECONO LODGE MIDTOWN   **Phone:** (505)880-0080   **15**
AAA SAVE   9/29-10/15   1P: $65-$70   2P: $70-$75   XP: $5   F12
              4/1-9/28   1P: $45-$50   2P: $50-$55   XP: $5   F12
◆◆   2/1-3/31 & 10/16-1/31   1P: $40-$45   2P: $45-$50   XP: $5   F12
Motel   **Location:** I-40, exit 160, just n. 2412 Carlisle Blvd NE 87110. Fax: 505/880-0053. **Terms:** [CP] meal plan.
               Facility: 38 rooms. 2 stories; exterior corridors. **Cards:** AE, CB, DI, DS, JC, MC, VI. **Special Amenities:** Free
breakfast and free local telephone calls.

ECONO LODGE OLD TOWN   **Phone:** (505)243-8475   **61**
AAA SAVE   9/8-10/15   1P: $50-$90   2P: $55-$95   XP: $5   F18
              4/28-9/7   1P: $50-$70   2P: $55-$75   XP: $5   F18
◆◆◆   2/1-4/27 & 10/16-1/31   1P: $45-$55   2P: $50-$60   XP: $5   F18
Motel   **Location:** I-40, exit 157A, 0.6 mi s on Rio Grande Blvd, 0.4 mi w. 2321 Central Ave NW 87104.
               Fax: 505/243-4205. **Terms:** [CP] meal plan; pets, 1 room avail. **Facility:** 44 rooms. 7 whirlpool rooms, $60-
$100; 2 stories; exterior corridors; heated pool, whirlpool. **Dining:** Restaurant nearby. **All Rooms:** extended cable TV.
Cards: AE, DI, DS, MC, VI.

FAIRFIELD INN AIRPORT   **Phone:** (505)247-1621   **41**
AAA SAVE   All Year   1P: $55-$70   2P: $55-$78   XP: $3   F18
◆◆◆   **Location:** I-25, exit 222 (Gibson Blvd) northbound; exit 222A southbound, 1 mi e to Yale Blvd, ne jct of Gibson
Motel   and Yale blvds. 2300 Centre Ave SE 87106. Fax: 505/247-9719. **Terms:** [CP] meal plan; cancellation fee im-
               posed. **Facility:** 118 rooms. Suites, $75-$148; 4 stories; interior corridors; heated pool, whirlpool. **Dining:** Res-
taurant nearby. **All Rooms:** combo or shower baths, extended cable TV. **Cards:** AE, CB, DI, DS, MC, VI.
Special Amenities: Early check-in/late check-out and free local telephone calls.

(See map p. 369)

FAIRFIELD INN BY MARRIOTT
◆◆◆ All Year   1P: $62   2P: $69   **Phone: (505)889-4000** 🏢59
Motel   **Location:** I-40, exit 160, just n on Menaul Blvd, then 1 mi w. 1760 Menaul Blvd NE 87107. Fax: 505/872-3094.   XP: $69   F21
   Terms: 7 day cancellation notice; cancellation fee imposed. **Facility:** 188 rooms. 3 stories; interior corridors; 2
pools, 1 indoor heated; 2 tennis courts. **Services:** gift shop. **Some Rooms:** Fee: refrigerators. **Cards:** AE, DI, DS, MC, VI.

HACIENDA ANTIGUA B & B
🆑🆑🆑 SAVE   All Year   1P: $99-$179   2P: $119-$179   **Phone: (505)345-5399** 🏢32
   Location: I-25, exit 230 (Osuna Dr), 2 mi w, just n. 6708 Tierra Dr 87107. Fax: 505/345-3855.   XP: $25   F12
◆◆◆   **Terms:** [BP]
Historic Bed   meal plan; check-in 4 pm; 10 day cancellation notice; cancellation fee imposed. **Facility:** 5 rooms. Adobe ha-
& Breakfast   cienda dating back to the 1700s set in residential area. 4 units with working fireplace and 1 with wood stove.
   Authentic setting with modern amenities. 1 two-bedroom unit. 1 story; interior/exterior corridors; smoke free
premises; whirlpool. **All Rooms:** combo or tub baths. **Cards:** AE, DS, MC, VI. **Special Amenities:** Free break-
fast and free local telephone calls. (See color ad p. 372)

HAMPTON INN-NORTH
🆑🆑🆑   10/1-1/31   1P: $60-$110   2P: $64-$110   **Phone: (505)344-1555** 🏢46
   5/2-9/30   1P: $64-$80   2P: $69-$85
◆◆◆   2/1-5/1   1P: $60-$75   2P: $64-$79
Motel   **Location:** I-25, exit 231, just w. 5101 Ellison NE 87109. Fax: 505/345-2216. **Terms:** [CP] meal plan; pets.
   Facility: 124 rooms. 3 stories; exterior corridors; heated pool. **Recreation:** in-room video games. **Cards:** AE,
CB, DI, DS, JC, MC, VI. (See ad below)

HOLIDAY INN EXPRESS
◆◆◆   10/1-10/16   1P: $95   2P: $100   **Phone: (505)275-8900** 🏢57
Motel   5/1-9/30   1P: $55   2P: $60   XP: $5   F17
   2/1-4/30 & 10/17-1/31   1P: $45   2P: $50   XP: $5   F17
                                      XP: $5   F17
Location: I-40, exit 165, 2 blks n on Eubank Ave. 10330 Hotel Ave NE 87123. Fax: 505/275-6000. **Terms:** [CP] meal plan; 30
day cancellation notice; cancellation fee imposed; pets, $5 extra charge. **Facility:** 104 rooms. 2 stories; exterior corridors;
heated pool. **All Rooms:** combo or shower baths, safes. **Cards:** AE, DI, DS, JC, MC, VI.

(See map p. 369)

HOLIDAY INN EXPRESS-WEST

Phone: (505)836-8600 **56**

(AAA) (SAVE) All Year 1P: $70-$82 2P: $75-$87 XP: $5 F17
◆ ◆ ◆ **Location:** I-40, exit 155, just sw. 6100 Iliff Rd 87121. Fax: 505/836-8600. **Terms:** [CP] meal plan; pets.
Motel **Facility:** 103 rooms. 15 whirlpool rooms; 3 stories; interior/exterior corridors; heated pool, sauna, whirlpool.
Cards: AE, CB, DI, DS, JC, MC, VI. **Special Amenities: Free breakfast and free local telephone calls.**

HOLIDAY INN-MOUNTAIN VIEW

Phone: (505)884-2511 **6**

◆ ◆ ◆ All Year 1P: $90-$109 2P: $100-$119 XP: $10 F18
Motor Inn **Location:** I-40, exit 160 (Carlisle Blvd), 0.3 mi n to Menaul Blvd, 1 mi w. 2020 Menaul Blvd NE 87107.
Fax: 505/884-5720. **Terms:** Cancellation fee imposed; pets, $25 extra charge, $100 dep req. **Facility:** 363
rooms. 2-5 stories; interior corridors; heated pool. **Services:** gift shop; area transportation. **All Rooms:** combo or shower
baths. **Some Rooms:** Fee: refrigerators. **Cards:** AE, CB, DI, DS, JC, MC, VI. *(See ad p 378)*

HOMESTEAD VILLAGE GUEST STUDIOS

Phone: (505)883-8888 **48**

◆ ◆ All Year 1P: $39-$59 XP: $5 F5
Apartment **Location:** I-40, exit 160, just n to Menaul Blvd, just w, just s. 2401 Wellsley Dr NE 87110. Fax: 505/883-2830.
Terms: 30 day cancellation notice; cancellation fee imposed; small pets only, $75 fee. **Facility:** 138 rooms. 2
stories; exterior corridors. **All Rooms:** efficiencies, combo or shower baths. **Cards:** AE, CB, DI, DS, JC, MC,.

HOMESTEAD VILLAGE GUEST STUDIOS

Phone: (505)344-7744 **75**

◆ ◆ All Year 1P: $39 2P: $44 XP: $5 F16
Apartment **Location:** I-25, exit 230, just w of jct. 4441 Osuna Rd NE 87109. Fax: 505/345-9214. **Terms:** Small pets only,
$75 fee. **Facility:** 141 rooms. 2 stories; exterior corridors. **All Rooms:** efficiencies, combo or shower baths.
Cards: AE, CB, DI, DS, JC, MC, VI.

HOWARD JOHNSON

Phone: (505)242-5228 **22**

◆ ◆ ◆ All Year 1P: $40-$60 2P: $47-$67 XP: $4 F18
Motel **Location:** I-40, exit 159A, just s via 4th St N. 411 McKnight Ave NW 87102. Fax: 505/766-9218. **Terms:** Can-
MC, VI. cellation fee imposed. **Facility:** 100 rooms. 4 stories; interior corridors; heated pool. **Cards:** AE, CB, DI, DS,

HOWARD JOHNSON EXPRESS INN

Phone: (505)828-1600 **13**

(AAA) (SAVE) All Year 1P: $55-$65 2P: $59-$69 XP: $5 F9
◆ ◆ ◆ **Location:** I-25, exit 231, 0.8 mi n on Frontage Rd. 7630 Pan American Frwy 87109. Fax: 505/856-6446.
Motel **Terms:** [CP] meal plan; check-in 4 pm; pets, $5 extra charge. **Facility:** 85 rooms. 3 stories; interior corridors;
heated pool; playground. **Dining:** Restaurant nearby. **All Rooms:** combo or shower baths. **Cards:** AE, CB, DI,
DS, MC, VI. **Special Amenities: Early check-in/late check-out and free room upgrade (subject to avail-
ability with advanced reservations).** *(See color ad below & p 371)*

HOWARD JOHNSON HOTEL & CONVENTION CENTER

Phone: (505)296-4852 **14**

◆ ◆ ◆ All Year 1P: $53-$71 2P: $53-$71 XP: $5 F17
Motor Inn **Location:** I-40, exit 165 (Eubank Blvd), 2 blks n. 15 Hotel Cir NE 87123. Fax: 505/293-9072. **Terms:** [CP] meal
DI, DS, JC, MC, VI. *(See color ad p 371)* plan; package plans, 11/1-3/31. **Facility:** 150 rooms. 2 stories; interior corridors; heated pool. **Cards:** AE, CB,

(See map p. 369)

HYATT REGENCY
Hotel | AAA SAVE | ◆◆◆◆
Phone: (505)842-1234 **43 F18**
All Year 1P: $159 XP: $25
Location: Downtown; I-24, exit 224B, 0.5 mi w near the Convention Center. 330 Tijeras Ave NW 87102. Fax: 505/766-6710. **Terms:** Cancellation fee imposed. **Facility:** 395 rooms. 2 whirlpool rooms; 20 stories; interior corridors; heated pool, saunas, whirlpools. Fee: parking. **Dining:** Cocktails; also, McGrath's Restaurant & Bar, see separate listing; entertainment. **Services:** gift shop. Fee: massage. **Some Rooms:** Fee: VCR. **Cards:** AE, CB, DI, DS, JC, MC, VI. *(See color ad p 368)*

LA QUINTA INN-AIRPORT
◆◆◆ Motel
Phone: (505)243-5500 **24**
All Year 1P: $75-$95 2P: $75-$95
Location: I-25, exit 222A (Gibson Blvd) southbound; exit 222 (Gibson Blvd) northbound, 1 mi e. 2116 Yale Blvd SE 87106-4233. Fax: 505/247-8288. **Terms:** [CP] meal plan; small pets only. **Facility:** 105 rooms. 3 stories; interior/exterior corridors; heated pool. **All Rooms:** combo or shower baths. **Some Rooms:** Fee: refrigerators. **Cards:** AE, CB, DI, DS, MC, VI. *(See color ad below)*

LA QUINTA INN NORTH
◆◆◆ Motel
Phone: (505)821-9000 **2**
All Year 1P: $69-$89 2P: $69-$89
Location: I-25, exit 231, just e. 5241 San Antonio Dr NE 87109. Fax: 505/821-2399. **Terms:** [CP] meal plan; small pets only. **Facility:** 130 rooms. 2 stories; exterior corridors; heated pool. **All Rooms:** combo or shower baths. **Some Rooms:** Fee: refrigerators. **Cards:** AE, CB, DI, DS, MC, VI. *(See color ad below)*

LA QUINTA INN SAN MATEO
◆◆◆ Motel
Phone: (505)884-3591 **9**
All Year 1P: $65-$85 2P: $65-$85
Location: I-40, exit 161 westbound; exit 161B eastbound, just n. 2424 San Mateo Blvd NE 87110-4053. Fax: 505/881-3065. **Terms:** Small pets only. **Facility:** 106 rooms. 7 two-bedroom units. 2 stories; exterior corridors; heated pool. **All Rooms:** combo or shower baths. **Some Rooms:** Fee: refrigerators. **Cards:** AE, CB, DI, DS, MC, VI. *(See color ad below)*

LA QUINTA INN-WEST
◆◆◆ Motel
Phone: (505)839-1744 **53**
All Year 1P: $75-$95 2P: $75-$95
Location: I-40, exit 155, just sw. 6101 Iliff Rd NW 87121. Fax: 505/839-1797. **Terms:** [CP] meal plan. **Facility:** 118 rooms. 5 stories; interior corridors; heated pool. **All Rooms:** combo or shower baths. **Cards:** AE, CB, DI, DS, MC, VI. *(See color ad below)*

LORLODGE MOTEL EAST
AAA SAVE | ◆ | Motel
Phone: (505)243-2891 **31**
9/7-10/15 1P: $38 2P: $46-$56 XP: $8 F11
4/20-9/5 1P: $26 2P: $34-$40 XP: $4 F11
2/1-4/19 1P: $22 2P: $30-$34 XP: $4 F11
10/16-1/31 1P: $22 2P: $28-$34 XP: $4 F11
Location: I-25, exit 224B, just e. 801 Central Ave NE 87102. **Terms:** [CP] meal plan; weekly rates avail, off season; cancellation fee imposed. **Facility:** 33 rooms. In a commercial area near hospitals. 2 stories; exterior corridors. **Dining:** Restaurant nearby. **Cards:** AE, DS, JC, MC, VI. **Special Amenities:** Early check-in/late check-out and free local telephone calls.

LUXURY INN
AAA SAVE | ◆◆ | Motel
Phone: (505)255-5900 **64**
9/1-9/30 1P: $40 2P: $65 XP: $8 F12
2/1-8/31 & 10/1-1/31 1P: $30-$36 2P: $36-$50 XP: $6 F12
Location: I-40, exit 162 westbound; exit 162A eastbound; 1.5 mi s, then just w. 6718 Central SE 87108. Fax: 505/256-4915. **Terms:** Cancellation fee imposed. **Facility:** 58 rooms. 2 stories; exterior corridors; heated pool, whirlpool. **Dining:** Restaurant nearby. **All Rooms:** extended cable TV. **Cards:** AE, CB, DI, DS, JC, MC, VI. **Special Amenities:** Free breakfast and free local telephone calls.

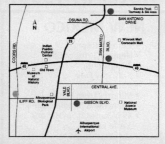

(See map p. 369)

MONTEREY NON SMOKERS MOTEL Phone: 505/243-3554 [35]
(AAA)
| 4/1-10/31 | 1P: $42-$48 | 2P: $44-$56 | XP: $6 | D12 |
| 2/1-3/31 & 11/1-1/31 | 1P: $38-$45 | | XP: $6 | D12 |

◆◆◆ Motel
Location: I-40, exit 157A, 0.5 mi s on Rio Grande Blvd, 0.3 mi w. 2402 Central Ave SW 87104. Fax: 505/243-9701. **Facility:** 15 rooms. Walking distance to Historic Old Town and botanical gardens. 1 story; exterior corridors; smoke free premises; heated pool. **Dining:** Restaurant nearby. **All Rooms:** extended cable TV. **Cards:** AE, MC, VI.

MOTEL 6 - 1145 Phone: 505/831-8888 [65]
(AAA)
| 5/25-1/31 | 1P: $32-$42 | 2P: $38-$48 | XP: $3 | F17 |
| 2/1-5/24 | 1P: $30-$40 | 2P: $36-$46 | XP: $3 | F17 |

◆◆ Motel
Location: I-40, exit 155, just s on Coors Blvd, just e. 5701 Iliff Rd NW 87105. Fax: 505/831-6296. **Terms:** Small pets only. **Facility:** 109 rooms. 3 stories; exterior corridors; heated pool. **Dining:** Restaurant nearby. **All Rooms:** combo or shower baths. **Cards:** AE, CB, DI, DS, MC, VI.

MOTEL 6 - 1349 Phone: 505/243-8017 [38]
(AAA)
5/25-10/25	1P: $38-$48	2P: $44-$54	XP: $3	F17
10/26-1/31	1P: $36-$46	2P: $42-$52	XP: $3	F17
2/1-5/24	1P: $35-$45	2P: $41-$51	XP: $3	F17

◆◆ Motel
Location: I-25, exit 223, just w. 1000 Avenida Cesar Chavez 87102. Fax: 505/242-5137. **Terms:** Small pets only. **Facility:** 95 rooms. 2 stories; exterior corridors; heated pool. **Cards:** AE, CB, DI, DS, MC, VI.

MOTEL 6 PREMIERE - 741 Phone: 505/831-3400 [63]
(AAA)
| 5/25-9/27 & 9/28-1/31 | 1P: $34-$44 | 2P: $40-$50 | XP: $3 | F17 |
| 2/1-5/24 | 1P: $32-$42 | 2P: $38-$48 | XP: $3 | F17 |

◆◆ Motel
Location: I-40, exit 155, just s on Coors Blvd, just w. 6015 Iliff Rd NW 87121. Fax: 505/831-3609. **Terms:** Small pets only. **Facility:** 130 rooms. 2 stories; exterior corridors. **Dining:** Restaurant nearby. **All Rooms:** combo or shower baths. **Some Rooms:** Fee: refrigerators, microwaves. **Cards:** AE, CB, DI, DS, MC, VI.

PLAZA INN ALBUQUERQUE Phone: (505)243-5693 [30]
◆◆◆ Motor Inn
| 2/1-10/6 & 10/7-1/31 | 1P: $80 | 2P: $92 | XP: $7 | F18 |

Location: I-25, exit 225, just e. 900 Medical Arts NE 87102. Fax: 505/843-6229. **Terms:** [CP] meal plan; cancellation fee imposed; small pets only. **Facility:** 120 rooms. 5 stories; interior corridors; heated pool. **Some Rooms:** Fee: refrigerators. **Cards:** AE, CB, DI, DS, JC, MC, VI. *(See color ad below)*

RADISSON HOTEL & CONFERENCE CENTER Phone: (505)888-3311 [8]
(AAA) [SAVE]
4/1-11/30	1P: $99	2P: $99	XP: $10	F18
2/1-3/31	1P: $89	2P: $89	XP: $10	F18
12/1-1/31	1P: $82	2P: $82	XP: $10	F18

◆◆◆ Hotel
Location: I-40, exit 160, just n. 2500 Carlisle Blvd NE 87110. Fax: 505/881-7452. **Terms:** Cancellation fee imposed; pets, $50 dep req. **Facility:** 366 rooms. 4 whirlpool rooms, $189; 2-4 stories; interior/exterior corridors; 2 pools, 1 indoor heated, whirlpool. **Dining:** Restaurant; 6 am-11 pm; $7-$16; cocktails. **Services:** gift shop. **All Rooms:** combo or shower baths, extended cable TV. **Some Rooms:** Fee: refrigerators, microwaves. **Cards:** AE, CB, DI, DS, MC, VI. **Special Amenities:** Free breakfast and free newspaper. *(See ad p 382)*

RADISSON INN HOTEL ALBUQUERQUE-AIRPORT Phone: (505)247-0512 [28]
(AAA) [SAVE]
| All Year | 1P: $109-$119 | 2P: $119 | XP: $10 | F18 |

◆◆◆ Motor Inn
Location: I-25, exit 222A (Gibson Blvd) southbound; exit 222 northbound, just e to University Blvd SE. 1901 University Blvd SE 87106. Fax: 505/843-7148. **Terms:** 30 day cancellation notice; package plans. **Facility:** 148 rooms. 2-3 stories; interior corridors; heated pool, whirlpool. **Dining:** Restaurant; 6 am-10 pm; $8-$18; cocktails. **Cards:** AE, DI, DS, JC, MC, VI. **Special Amenities:** Free breakfast and free newspaper.

(See map p. 369)

RAMADA INN-DOWNTOWN
◆◆◆   2/1-10/5 & 10/6-1/31   1P: $73   2P: $81
Motor Inn   **Location:** Center, 7th and Central Ave. 717 Central Ave NW 87102. Fax: 505/924-2465. **Terms:** [CP] meal plan; package plans. **Facility:** 135 rooms. 6 stories; exterior corridors. **Services:** gift shop; area transportation.
All Rooms: combo or shower baths. **Cards:** AE, DI, DS, JC, MC, VI.
Phone: (505)924-2400   52
XP: $10   F18

RAMADA INN MOUNTAINVIEW
◆◆◆   7/1-1/31   1P: $55-$95   2P: $69-$105
Motor Inn   2/1-6/30   1P: $55-$69   2P: $65-$85
     Location: I-40, exit 165, just n via Hotel Cir. 25 Hotel Cir NE 87123-1298. Fax: 505/291-9028. **Terms:** 14 day cancellation notice; package plans; pets. **Facility:** 205 rooms. 2 stories; interior/exterior corridors; heated pool. **Cards:** AE, CB, DI, DS, JC, MC, VI.
Phone: (505)271-1000   34
XP: $10   F18
XP: $10   F18

RAMADA LIMITED
(AAA) (SAVE)   All Year   1P: $69   2P: $79
◆◆◆   **Location:** I-25, exit 233, just w. 5601 Alameda Blvd NE 87113. Fax: 505/858-3298. **Terms:** [CP] meal plan; 7
Motel   day cancellation notice; cancellation fee imposed. **Facility:** 80 rooms. 10 whirlpool rooms; 2 stories; interior corridors; heated pool, sauna, whirlpool. **All Rooms:** combo or shower baths, extended cable TV. **Cards:** AE, CB, DI, DS, MC, VI. **Special Amenities:** Free breakfast and free local telephone calls.
Phone: (505)858-3297   73
XP: $10   F18

RAMADA LIMITED (AIRPORT)
(AAA) (SAVE)   All Year   1P: $63-$81   2P: $63-$81
◆◆◆   **Location:** I-25, exit 222 (Gibson Blvd) northbound; exit 222A southbound, 1 mi e, just n. 1801 Yale Blvd SE
Motel   87106. Fax: 505/242-0068. **Terms:** [CP] meal plan. **Facility:** 76 rooms. 3 stories; interior corridors; heated pool, sauna, whirlpool. **All Rooms:** extended cable TV. **Cards:** AE, DI, DS, JC, MC, VI. **Special Amenities:** Free breakfast and free local telephone calls.
Phone: (505)242-0036   70
XP: $5   F17

RED ROOF INNS MIDTOWN
◆◆◆   6/1-9/30   1P: $45-$60   2P: $52-$67
Motel   4/1-5/31   1P: $40-$55   2P: $47-$62
     2/1-3/31 & 10/1-1/31   1P: $35-$50   2P: $42-$57
Location: I-25, exit 227A, just w. 1635 Candelaria 87107. Fax: 505/343-9370. **Terms:** [CP] meal plan. **Facility:** 87 rooms. 2 stories; interior corridors; heated pool. **All Rooms:** combo or shower baths, safes. **Cards:** AE, CB, DI, DS, MC, VI.
Phone: (505)344-5311   54
XP: $7   F18
XP: $7   F18
XP: $7   F18

RESIDENCE INN BY MARRIOTT
◆◆◆   All Year   1P: $126
Apartment   **Location:** I-40, exit 160, just n to Menaul Blvd, just w, just s on Wellesley Dr NE. 3300 Prospect NE 87107.
     Fax: 505/884-5551. **Terms:** [CP] meal plan; cancellation fee imposed; pets, $25 extra charge. **Facility:** 112 rooms. Complex of 14 buildings. All rooms with fireplace and private balcony. 2 stories; exterior corridors; heated pool. **Recreation:** sports court. **All Rooms:** kitchens. **Cards:** AE, CB, DI, DS, JC, MC, VI.
Phone: (505)881-2661   49

SHERATON ALBUQUERQUE UPTOWN
◆◆◆   All Year   1P: $79-$175   2P: $89-$185
Hotel   **Location:** I-40, exit 162, 0.8 mi n. 2600 Louisiana Blvd NE 87110. Fax: 505/881-3736. **Terms:** 3 day cancellation notice; cancellation fee imposed. **Facility:** 294 rooms. Well appointed public areas. 7 stories; interior corridors; heated pool. **Dining:** entertainment. **Services:** gift shop; area transportation. **All Rooms:** combo or shower baths. **Cards:** AE, CB, DI, DS, MC, VI.
Phone: (505)881-0000   76

(See map p. 369)

SHERATON OLD TOWN HOTEL   Phone: (505)843-6300   [36]
◆◆◆   All Year   1P: $115-$125   2P: $125-$135   XP: $10   F18
Hotel   **Location:** I-40, exit 157A (Rio Grande Blvd), 0.4 mi s. 800 Rio Grande Blvd NW 87104. Fax: 505/842-9863. **Terms:** 5 day cancellation notice; cancellation fee imposed. **Facility:** 188 rooms. 11 stories; interior corridors; heated pool. **Services:** gift shop. **Some Rooms:** honor bars. **Cards:** AE, CB, DI, DS, MC, VI.

SLEEP INN AIRPORT   Phone: (505)244-3325   [77]
(AAA) [SAVE]   10/6-10/14   1P: $89   2P: $99   XP: $10   F16
         5/1-10/5   1P: $69-$79   2P: $79-$89   XP: $5   F16
◆◆   2/1-4/30 & 10/15-1/31   1P: $49-$69   2P: $59-$79   XP: $5   F16
Motel   **Location:** I-25, exit 222 northbound; exit 222A southbound, 1 mi e to Yale Blvd, just n. 2300 International Ave SE 87106. Fax: 505/244-3312. **Terms:** [ECP] meal plan; cancellation fee imposed. **Facility:** 105 rooms. 1-3 stories; interior corridors; heated pool, whirlpool. **Services:** area transportation, within 5 mi. **All Rooms:** combo or shower baths, extended cable TV. **Cards:** AE, CB, DI, DS, MC, VI. **Special Amenities:** Free breakfast and free local telephone calls.

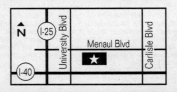

SUMNER SUITES   Phone: (505)881-0544   [78]
(AAA) [SAVE]   10/6-10/15   1P: $115-$125   2P: $115-$125   XP: $10   F17
         2/1-10/5 & 10/16-1/31   1P: $99-$109   2P: $99-$109   XP: $10   F17
◆◆◆   **Location:** I-40, exit 160, just n to Menaul Blvd, 0.6 mi w. 2500 Menaul Blvd NE 87107. Fax: 505/881-0381.
Apartment   **Terms:** [CP] meal plan. **Facility:** 125 rooms. 6 stories; interior corridors. **Dining:** Cocktails. **All Rooms:** combo or shower baths. **Cards:** AE, CB, DI, DS, MC, VI. **Special Amenities:** Free breakfast and free local telephone calls.

(See map p. 369)

SUPER 8 MOTEL EAST
◆◆
Motel

7/1-10/31	1P: $45	2P: $50		**Phone: (505)271-4807**	62
4/1-6/30	1P: $44	2P: $49		XP: $3	F12
2/1-3/31	1P: $43	2P: $48			
11/1-1/31	1P: $43	2P: $48		XP: $3	F12

Location: I-40, exit 166, just n to Cooper, just s. 450 Paisano NE 87123. Fax: 505/271-4807. **Terms:** Pets, $5 extra charge. **Facility:** 100 rooms. 4 two-bedroom units. 3 stories; interior corridors. **All Rooms:** combo or shower baths. **Cards:** AE, DI, DS, MC, VI.

SUPER 8 MOTEL OF ALBUQUERQUE
◆◆
Motel

7/1-10/31	1P: $45	2P: $50		**Phone: (505)888-4884**	40
4/1-6/30	1P: $44	2P: $49		XP: $3	F12
2/1-3/31 & 11/1-1/31	1P: $43	2P: $48		XP: $3	F12
				XP: $3	F12

Location: I-25, exit 227A, just s. 2500 University Blvd NE 87107. Fax: 505/888-4884. **Terms:** Pets, $5 extra charge. **Facility:** 243 rooms. 3 stories; interior corridors. **Services:** area transportation. **Cards:** AE, CB, DI, DS, MC, VI.

TRAVELODGE AAA SAVE
◆◆◆
Motel

All Year   1P: $55   2P: $55-$64   **Phone: (505)884-0250** 7
XP: $10   F17
Location: I-40, exit 160, just n to Menaul Blvd, 0.8 mi w. 2120 Menaul Blvd NE 87107. Fax: 505/883-0594. **Terms:** [CP] meal plan; cancellation fee imposed. **Facility:** 200 rooms. 2 stories; exterior corridors; heated pool. **Dining:** Restaurant nearby. **All Rooms:** extended cable TV. **Some Rooms:** safes. **Cards:** AE, DI, DS, MC, VI. **Special Amenities:** Free breakfast and free newspaper. (See ad p 383)

WYNDHAM GARDEN HOTEL AAA SAVE
◆◆◆
Hotel
breakfast.

All Year   1P: $59-$120   2P: $69-$120   **Phone: (505)798-3900** 67
XP: $20   F18
Location: I-25, exit 230 (San Mateo Blvd), just e. 6000 Pan American Frwy NE 87109. Fax: 505/798-4305. **Terms:** Cancellation fee imposed. **Facility:** 151 rooms. 5 stories; interior corridors; heated pool, sauna, whirlpool. **Dining:** Restaurant; 6:30 am-2 & 5-10 pm; $7-$22; cocktails. **Some Rooms:** Fee: refrigerators. **Cards:** AE, CB, DI, DS, JC, MC, VI. **Special Amenities:** Early check-in/late check-out and free

WYNDHAM HOTEL AAA SAVE
◆◆◆
Hotel

All Year   1P: $59-$99   2P: $59-$99   **Phone: (505)843-7000** 27
XP: $20   F18
Location: I-25, exit 222 (Gibson Blvd) northbound; exit 222A southbound, 1 mi e on Gibson Blvd, 0.5 mi s. 2910 Yale Blvd SE 87106. Fax: 505/843-6307. **Terms:** Cancellation fee imposed; package plans; small pets only. **Facility:** 276 rooms. 15 stories; interior corridors; heated pool; 2 tennis courts. **Dining:** Restaurant; 6 am-10 pm; $8-$25; cocktails. **Services:** gift shop. **Recreation:** Fee: in-room video games. **All Rooms:** combo or shower baths. **Cards:** AE, CB, DI, DS, JC, MC, VI. **Special Amenities:** Early check-in/late check-out and preferred room (subject to availability with advanced reservations). (See color ad p 383)

———— *The following lodging was either not inspected or did not* ————
meet AAA rating requirements but is listed for your information only.

HAMPTON INN UNIVERSITY-MIDTOWN fyi
Motel
All Year   1P: $59   2P: $69   **Phone: 505/837-9300**
Too new to rate, opening scheduled for August 1999. **Location:** 2300 Carlisle NE 87110. Fax: 505/837-2211. **Amenities:** 131 rooms, radios, coffeemakers, pool. **Cards:** AE, CB, DI, DS, MC, VI. (See ad below)

(See map p. 369)

─── RESTAURANTS ───

ANTIQUITY   Dinner: $15-$23   Phone: 505/247-3545 ⑬
◆ ◆
Continental
Location: In Old Town; I-40, exit 157A (Rio Grande Blvd), 0.5 mi s to Romero, just n of Central Ave. 112 Romero NW 87104. **Hours:** 5 pm-9 pm, Fri & Sat-9:30 pm. Closed major holidays. **Reservations:** suggested. **Features:** casual dress; beer & wine only; street parking. Antiquity's intimate, adobe-style dining has a Southwestern flair enhanced by a candelit ambiance. Entrees include veal filet, fresh salmon and chicken accompanied by a good variety of appetizers and salads. Desserts are especially creative. Smoke free premises. **Cards:** AE, DI, DS, MC, VI. ✕

ASSETS GRILLE & BREWERY CO.   Lunch: $6-$15   Dinner: $6-$18   Phone: 505/889-6400 ㉙
◆ ◆
American
Location: At Louisiana and Montgomery blvds. 6910 Montgomery Blvd NE 87109. **Hours:** 11:30 am-10 pm, Fri & Sat-10:30 pm, Sun 5 pm-9 pm. Closed major holidays. **Reservations:** suggested. **Features:** casual dress; carryout; cocktails; a la carte. Be sure to try this restaurant's beer sampler offering several tasty brews made in their on-site microbrewery. Its innovative cuisine includes gourmet mini-pizzas and pasta dishes. The setting features a brass rail and dark wood atmosphere. **Cards:** AE, CB, DI, DS, MC, VI. ✕

BARRY'S OASIS RESTAURANT   Lunch: $4-$10   Dinner: $7-$20   Phone: 505/884-2324 ⑱
ⒶⒶⒶ
◆ ◆
Continental
Location: I-25, exit 230, 0.8 mi s; in Sun West Center. 5400 San Mateo Blvd NE 87109. **Hours:** 11 am-3 & 5-9 pm, Fri & Sat-10 pm, Sun 5 pm-9 pm. Closed: 11/23 & 12/25. **Reservations:** accepted. **Features:** casual dress; children's menu; carryout; cocktails & lounge. Lamb and seafood specialties, appetizing vegetarian dishes, and yummy desserts such as homemade chocolate baklava and fudge pie highlight this restaurant's eclectic menu. Its small, cozy interior is dressed in candlelight and white linen on weekends. **Cards:** DI, DS, MC, VI. ✕

CAFE SPOLETO   Dinner: $11-$18   Phone: 505/880-0897 ㉚
◆ ◆
Ethnic
Location: 0.5 mi n of jct Menaul Blvd. 2813 San Mateo Blvd NE 87110. **Hours:** 11 am-2 & 5:30-9:30 pm, Sat from 5:30 pm. Closed major holidays, Sun & Mon. **Reservations:** suggested. **Features:** dressy casual; health conscious menu items; beer & wine only; a la carte. You'll appreciate this restaurant's small, intimate dining rooms and its delicious California cuisine prepared with a touch of northern Italy. The menu offers fresh focaccio, pasta with caramelized artichokes, homemade grilled sausage, and chicken. Smoke free premises. **Cards:** AE, DS, MC, VI. ✕

CERVANTES   Lunch: $6-$13   Dinner: $7-$15   Phone: 505/262-2253 ②
ⒶⒶⒶ
◆ ◆
Regional
American
Location: San Pedro Blvd. 5801 Gibson Rd 87108. **Hours:** 11 am-2 & 4:30-10 pm; Sun from noon. Closed: 4/23 & 12/25. **Features:** casual dress; children's menu; carryout; cocktails & lounge; a la carte. Well-prepared Mexican dishes, including excellent chili rellenos and homemade tamales, are featured at this locally popular restaurant, close to the Atomic Museum/Kirtland Air Force Base. Its large dining area and covered patio offer a casual atmosphere. **Cards:** AE, CB, DI, DS, MC, VI. ✕

CHRISTY MAE'S   Lunch: $4-$8   Dinner: $6-$10   Phone: 505/255-4740 ⑤
◆ ◆
American
Location: I-40, exit 162 westbound; exit 162A eastbound, 0.5 mi s on Louisiana Blvd to Lomas Blvd, w on Lomas 0.5 mi to San Pedro Dr, 2 blks. 1400 San Pedro Dr NE 87110. **Hours:** 11 am-8 pm. Closed major holidays & Sun. **Features:** casual dress; children's menu; carryout; a la carte. Christy Mae's is an unpretentious family operation offering home-style cooking and a very good selection of soups, salads, sandwiches and pot pies. Breads and desserts such as carrot cake are prepared in house. The restaurant is smoke-free during lunch. **Cards:** AE, DI, DS, MC, VI. ✕

CLASSIC GRILL   Lunch: $6-$15   Dinner: $6-$15   Phone: 505/881-0000 ⑩
◆ ◆
American
Location: I-40, exit 162, 0.8 mi n; in Sheraton Albuquerque Uptown. 2600 Louisiana Blvd NE 87110. **Hours:** 6 am-2 & 5-11 pm, Sat & Sun from 6:30 am. **Reservations:** suggested. **Features:** dressy casual; children's menu; senior's menu; cocktails & lounge. This locally popular restaurant has a warm and inviting atmosphere that's enhanced by rich dark woods and decorative architecture. Creative artwork intensifies its appeal. The varied menu offers sandwiches, pizza, pork, fish and steak. **Cards:** AE, CB, DI, DS, MC, VI. ✕

THE COUNTY LINE OF ALBUQUERQUE   Dinner: $8-$17   Phone: 505/856-7477 ⑥
◆ ◆
American
Location: I-25, Tramway Blvd exit, 5 mi e. 9600 Tramway Blvd NE 87122. **Hours:** 5 pm-9 pm, Fri & Sat-10 pm, Sun 4 pm-9 pm. **Features:** casual dress; children's menu; carryout; cocktails. While you sip your aperitif and nibble your hors d'oeuvres, you can enjoy the view of the city from Sandia Peak. Although the specialties are barbecue you can order steak and seafood. Homemade bread, ice cream and cobbler round out the meal. **Cards:** AE, DI, DS, MC, VI. ✕

DOUBLE RAINBOW BAKERY CAFE   Lunch: $6-$10   Dinner: $6-$10   Phone: 505/275-8311 ㉜
◆ ◆
American
Location: Just n of jct Montgomery. 4501 Juan Tabo Blvd NE 87111. **Hours:** 6:30 am-midnight, Sun-11 pm. Closed: 11/23 & 12/25. **Features:** casual dress; children's menu; health conscious menu items; carryout; a la carte. The Double Rainbow has a trendy coffee-shop setting with an area for reading magazines while enjoying quiche, pizza, salad, stir-fry, sandwiches, baguettes and dessert. They have a good range of coffees and Italian soda, and seating on the outside deck. Smoke free premises. **Cards:** AE, DS, MC, VI. ✕

EL NORTENO   Lunch: $5-$7   Dinner: $6-$12   Phone: 505/255-2057 ㉝
◆
Mexican
Location: Just w of jct Louisiana. 6416 Zuni Rd SE 87108. **Hours:** 11 am-9 pm. Closed major holidays. **Reservations:** suggested. **Features:** casual dress; children's menu; health conscious menu; carryout; beer & wine only; a la carte. This unpretentious eatery, festooned in Mexican beer flags and Juarez wares, serves a Baja cuisine. Its menu includes a savory selection of tacos including tongue and goat, chicken enchiladas, spicy sauteed shrimp, pollo, mole, cerveza and steamers. **Cards:** AE, DS, MC, VI. ✕

(See map p. 369)

ELOY'S MEXICAN RESTAURANT **Lunch:** $5-$10 **Dinner:** $5-$10 **Phone:** 505/293-6018 (14)
◆◆
Mexican
Location: I-40, exit 164B, 2 blks n; in Bellhaven Commercial Center. 1508 Wyoming Blvd NE 87112. **Hours:** 11 am-8 pm, Fri & Sat-9 pm. Closed major holidays & Sun. **Features:** casual dress; children's menu; carryout; beer & wine only. A friendly, attentive staff greets you at this unpretentious family operation, and the restaurant's good selection of home-style recipes from Mexico and northern New Mexico will not disappoint your appetite. They also serve a wide choice of beer and wine. **Cards:** MC, VI.

EMILIE'S BAKERY & CAFE **Lunch:** $3-$8 **Dinner:** $8-$21 **Phone:** 505/881-8104 (36)
◆◆
French
Location: 6209 Montgomery NE 87109. **Hours:** 11 am-2 & 5-9 pm, Fri & Sat-10 pm. Closed: 7/4, 11/23 & Sun. **Reservations:** accepted. **Features:** carryout; beer & wine only. The flavors of Provence—olive oil, anchovies, warm breads, fresh seafood, tomatoes and herbs—waft through the small, simply decorated dining area. The bakery offers a good selection of desserts, pastries and crusty, crunchy baguettes of French bread. Smoke free premises. **Cards:** AE, CB, DI, DS, MC, VI.

FRESH CHOICES **Lunch:** $5-$7 **Dinner:** $5-$7 **Phone:** 505/242-6447 (21)
◆◆
Italian
Location: Downtown; I-25, exit 224B, 1 mi w. 402 Central SW 87102. **Hours:** 11 am-9 pm. Closed major holidays & Sun. **Features:** casual dress; street parking; buffet, a la carte. Fresh Choices has a quaint bistro atmosphere with brick walls and hardwood floors. The buffet offers many items, such as salads, pizza, Italian meatballs, beef stroganoff, herb chicken, muffins, pudding, fresh pies and cakes, to choose from. **Cards:** AE, DS, MC, VI.

GARCIA'S KITCHEN **Lunch:** $3-$7 **Dinner:** $3-$7 **Phone:** 505/275-5812 (37)
◆
Mexican
Location: Sw corner of Juan Tabo Blvd and Comanche. 3601 Juan Tabo Blvd NE 87111. **Hours:** 6:30 am-10 pm. Closed: 12/25. **Features:** casual dress; children's menu; early bird specials; carryout; beer & wine only; a la carte. Green chili and carne adovada addictions have been born at Garcia's Kitchen. And many tortilla worshipers make pilgrimages here on a regular basis. This bright and flashy restaurant serves breakfast at any time of the day. **Cards:** AE, DS, MC, VI.

GARDUNO'S OF MEXICO RESTAURANT & CANTINA **Lunch:** $8-$11 **Dinner:** $8-$15 **Phone:** 505/821-3030 (1)
◆◆
Mexican
Location: I-25, exit 230, just e on San Mateo Blvd, just n. 5400 Academy Rd NE 87109. **Hours:** 11 am-10 pm, Fri & Sat-10:30 pm, Sun 10:30 am-10 pm. Closed: 11/23 & 12/25. **Reservations:** accepted. **Features:** casual dress; children's menu; carryout; cocktails & lounge; a la carte. Garduno's has much to offer: an extensive menu, hearty portions of burritos, nachos, tacos, fajitas and enchiladas, and mariachi music Thurs-Sat 6-9 pm and Sun noon-3 pm. This restaurant looks like a Mexican cantina inside and a hacienda outside. **Cards:** AE, DI, DS, MC, VI.

GIN MILL RESTAURANT & TAVERN **Lunch:** $5-$8 **Dinner:** $6-$16 **Phone:** 505/821-6300 (38)
◆◆
American
Location: At jct Academy Rd; in Far North Shopping Center. 6300 San Mateo Blvd NE 87109. **Hours:** 11 am-midnight, Fri & Sat from 10 am, Sun 10 am-11 pm. Closed: 11/23, 12/25 & Easter. **Reservations:** accepted. **Features:** casual dress; Sunday brunch; health conscious menu items; carryout; cocktails & lounge; a la carte. This cozy pub offers several variations of beefy burgers and traditional fiery New Mexican food. Offerings spotlight turkey, huge salads, meatloaf and green chili chicken stew. Their hearty sandwiches include fried egg as well as tuna and red onion. **Cards:** AE, DI, DS, MC, VI.

GRANDMA'S K&I DINER **Lunch:** $5-$9 **Phone:** 505/243-1881 (40)
◆
Mexican
Location: I-25, exit 222 (Gibson Blvd) northbound; exit 222A southbound, 0.5 mi w on Gibson, 0.5 mi s. 2500 Broadway Blvd SE 87102. **Hours:** 6 am-3 pm. Closed major holidays, Sat & Sun. **Reservations:** suggested. **Features:** casual dress; children's menu; carryout. Grandma's has been a local favorite for 40 years. It's a knotty-pine diner that serves big breakfasts, big sandwiches, slabs of corn bread, meatloaf with fixings, ham hocks with lima beans, fried chicken and Travis, and a massive burrito platter.

GREAT AMERICAN LAND & CATTLE COMPANY **Lunch:** $5-$13 **Dinner:** $10-$22 **Phone:** 505/292-1510 (42)
◆◆
Steak and
Seafood
Location: At jct Indian School Rd; in the Skyview Center. 1550 Tramway Blvd NE 87112. **Hours:** 11 am-2 & 5-9 pm, Fri-10 pm, Sat 5 pm-10 pm, Sun 5 pm-9 pm. Closed: 11/23 & 12/25. **Features:** casual dress; children's menu; carryout; cocktails. This friendly restaurant has beef so tasty and succulent that it vanishes from your plate to a chorus of "mmmms." It's home to a two-pound T-bone. Cole slaw, ranch-style beans, salad, baked potato and a sparkling view of the city will complete your meal. **Cards:** AE, CB, DI, DS, MC, VI.

HIGH FINANCE **Lunch:** $6-$20 **Dinner:** $16-$42 **Phone:** 505/243-9742 (4)
AAA
◆◆
American
Location: I-25, exit 234, 0.5 mi w. 40 Tramway Rd 87122. **Hours:** 11 am-3 & 4:30-9 pm. Closed: 12/25. **Reservations:** suggested. **Features:** casual dress; cocktails & lounge; fee for parking; a la carte. High Finance offers its cuisine on top of the 10,378-foot Sandia Peak—you'll enjoy a great view of the city. You reach this restaurant only by aerial tramway, with reduced ticket prices when you make reservations. Be prepared for a time-consuming meal. Smoke free premises. **Cards:** AE, DI, DS, MC, VI.

HIGH NOON RESTAURANT & SALOON Historical **Lunch:** $5-$7 **Dinner:** $10-$25 **Phone:** 505/765-1455 (9)
AAA
Regional
American
Location: In Old Town; I-40, exit 57A (Rio Grande Blvd), 0.5 mi s to Mountain Rd, just e. 425 San Felipe NW 87104. **Hours:** 11 am-9:30 pm, Fri & Sat-10 pm, Sun noon-9 pm. Closed: 1/1 & 12/25. **Reservations:** suggested. **Features:** casual dress; carryout; cocktails & lounge. High Noon's eclectic menu offers selections of wild game, steak, seafood and New Mexican cuisine. Its decor features northern New Mexico, and part of its structure is the original 250-year-old adobe building. You'll find leisurely paced dining here. **Cards:** AE, DI, DS, MC, VI.

(See map p. 369)

LA ESQUINA RESTAURANTE Lunch: $5-$7 Dinner: $6-$14 Phone: 505/242-3432 ⑧
◆◆
Mexican Location: 3rd St and Tijeras Ave, lower level. 1st Plaza, Galeria 60 87102. Hours: 11 am-2:30 pm, Fri 11 am-4 & 5-8:30 pm. Closed major holidays, Sat & Sun. Features: casual dress; cocktails. Locals love the Southwestern cuisine served in a comfortable atmosphere. Known best for its blue corn enchiladas, this Mexican restaurant also has a nice dessert selection. Located downtown in the lower level of a high-rise, it has ample garage parking. Cards: AE, CB, DI, MC, VI. ✕

LOS CUATES DEL NORTE Lunch: $4-$8 Dinner: $6-$10 Phone: 505/255-5079 ㊸
◆
Regional American Location: Just w of San Mateo Blvd. 4901 Lomas Blvd NE 87110. Hours: 11 am-9 pm, Sun from noon. Closed: 11/23 & 12/25. Features: casual dress; children's menu; carryout; cocktails & lounge. This is a large and locally popular restaurant, and you may experience a wait before you can sample its New Mexican cuisine of fajitas, dark red and spicy salsa, hefty burger-filled burritos, chicken enchiladas on corn tortilla, refried beans and rice. Cards: AE, CB, DI, DS, MC, VI. ✕

M & J RESTAURANT/SANITARY TORTILLA FACTORY Lunch: $5-$8 Phone: 505/242-4890 ⑦
◆
Mexican Location: Downtown, just s of jct Central Ave. 403 2nd St SW 87102. Hours: 9 am-4 pm. Closed major holidays, Sat & Sun. Features: casual dress; children's menu; carryout. Authentic Mexican recipes are used to create this restaurant's homemade flour and corn tortillas, the specialties of the house. The menu offers daily specials. Watercolors and other paintings by various local artists complement the decor. Smoke free premises. ✕

MANHATTAN ON THE RIO GRANDE Lunch: $7-$9 Dinner: $7-$9 Phone: 505/248-1514 ㊺
◆
American Location: I-40, exit 157A, just s; in Rio Grande Plaza. 901 Rio Grande Blvd NW 87104. Hours: 11 am-8 pm, Fri & Sat-9 pm, Sun 10 am-5 pm. Features: casual dress; Sunday brunch; health conscious menu items; carryout; cocktail lounge; beer & wine only. This deli-style restaurant features burgers, pizza, pastas and homemade desserts in addition to sandwiches, which are packed with quality meats and cheeses. Its Southwestern surroundings have a touch of New York and offer a relaxed dining experience. Smoke free premises. Cards: AE, MC, VI. ✕

MARIA TERESA RESTAURANT Historical Lunch: $6-$11 Dinner: $13-$24 Phone: 505/242-3900 ⑪
◆◆◆
American Location: I-40, exit 157A, just s. 618 Rio Grande Blvd NW 87104. Hours: 11 am-2:30 & 5-9 pm. Closed: 12/25. Reservations: suggested. Features: dressy casual; children's menu; cocktails & lounge. Maria Teresa's is a restored 1850s adobe hacienda with decor from that period. It features quaint dining rooms as well as relaxed K19courtyard dining, and its menu has a good variety that includes steak, rabbit, veal, duck, shrimp, salmon and fajitas. Cards: AE, DI, MC, VI. ✕

MCGRATH'S RESTAURANT & BAR Lunch: $6-$12 Phone: 505/842-1234 ㉒
◆◆◆
Continental Location: Downtown; I-24, exit 224B, 0.5 mi w near the Convention Center; in Hyatt Regency. 330 Tijeras Ave NW 87102. Hours: 6:30 am-10:30 pm. Reservations: suggested; dinner. Features: dressy casual; Sunday brunch; cocktails & lounge; fee for valet parking; a la carte. You'll have a comfortable dining experience in McGrath's contemporary, upscale setting. Try the tasty wild-boar soup with hominy and spicy broth or one of the many other appetizers. They also have an extensive selection of poultry, seafood and steak. Cards: AE, CB, DI, DS, JC, MC, VI. ✕

MONTE VISTA FIRE STATION RESTAURANT Historical Lunch: $6-$10 Dinner: $11-$21 Phone: 505/255-2424 ⑮
◆◆◆
Nouvelle American Location: I-25, Central Ave exit, 2.5 mi e. 3201 Central Ave NE 87106. Hours: 11 am-2:30 & 5-10:30 pm, Fri-11 pm, Sat 5 pm-11 pm, Sun 5 pm-10:30 pm. Closed major holidays. Reservations: suggested. Features: casual dress; children's menu; cocktails & lounge. Built in an old fire station, this fine-dining restaurant is famous for crab cakes with roasted garlic vinaigrette, and grilled filet with red chili and crumbled feta cheese. The trendy upstairs bar has a great view of the mountains. Scrumptious desserts. Cards: AE, DI, DS, MC, VI. ✕

O'NIELL'S PUB Lunch: $6-$10 Dinner: $6-$10 Phone: 505/256-0564 ㊻
◆◆
American Location: Nob Hill, at jct Brynn Mawr. 3211 Central Ave NE 87106. Hours: 11:30 am-midnight, Sun 11 am-11 pm. Closed major holidays. Reservations: accepted. Features: casual dress; cocktails & lounge; street parking; a la carte. Locals love this place for its burgers, beer, and live music. Its friendly servers dish up salads, soups, mini-loaves of homemade bread, pasta, and creative sandwiches such as grilled provolone, eggplant, tomato and basil on green-chili cheese bread. Cards: DS, MC, VI.

OWL CAFE Lunch: $4-$9 Dinner: $4-$9 Phone: 505/291-4900 ㊼
◆
American Location: I-40, exit 165, just w. 800 Eubank Ave NE 87123. Hours: 7 am-10 pm, Fri & Sat-11 pm. Closed: 11/23 & 12/25. Features: casual dress; children's menu; early bird specials; health conscious menu items; carryout; beer & wine only; a la carte. The Owl Cafe delivers its unique green-chili cheeseburgers in a '50s diner setting complete with tableside jukeboxes and soda-jerk malts. It also offers a wide-ranging menu of stir-fry veggies, red-chili pork tamales and chicken-fried steak. Cards: AE, DI, DS, MC, VI. ✕

PAUL'S MONTEREY INN Lunch: $6-$10 Dinner: $9-$24 Phone: 505/294-1461 ㊾
◆
American Location: Just n of jct Lomas Blvd. 1000 Juan Tabo Blvd NE 87112. Hours: 11 am-2:30 & 5-10 pm, Fri & Sat-11 pm. Closed major holidays & Sun. Reservations: suggested. Features: casual dress; cocktails & lounge; a la carte. Thick and juicy steaks, prime rib, surf and turf, ribs and shrimp—all served in ample portions—make Paul's Monterey Inn a favorite with the locals. The ambience and dark upholstery and wall coverings may remind you of a lounge from the 1960s. Cards: AE, CB, DI, MC, VI. ✕

POWDRELL'S BARBECUE HOUSE Lunch: $6-$10 Dinner: $6-$10 Phone: 505/298-6766 ㊿
◆
American Location: 0.5 mi e of jct Eubank. 11301 Central Ave NE 87123. Hours: 11 am-9 pm, Fri & Sat-9:30 pm. Closed major holidays & Sun. Reservations: accepted. Features: casual dress; children's menu; senior's menu; carryout. You'll enjoy this popular Barbecue House with its deep, smoky, hickory flavors. Sample the pork, ribs, beef, Polish and hot links, or chicken, by the pound or the platter. Meals are served in a casual setting, where napkins are, thankfully, plentiful. Smoke free premises. Cards: AE, CB, DI, DS, MC, VI. ✕

(See map p. 369)

QUARTERS BAR-B-QUE   **Lunch:** $4-$8   **Dinner:** $10-$24   **Phone:** 505/299-9864   ③
◆◆
Regional
American
Location: I-40, exit 164B eastbound, 3 mi n; exit I-640 westbound, 0.5 mi w on Lomas Blvd, 3.3 mi n. 4516 Wyoming Blvd NE 87111. **Hours:** 11 am-9 pm, Fri & Sat-10 pm. Closed major holidays & Sun. **Reservations:** accepted; for 6 or more. **Features:** casual dress; carryout; cocktails. Quarters is widely known for baebecued spare ribs, beef and hot links, but don't pass up the chance to try the Alaskan King crab legs. Plan to save room for dessert, especially tempting to those with a sweet tooth are their mud pie and cheesecake. **Cards:** AE, MC, VI.   ☒

RAGIN SHRIMP   **Lunch:** $7-$8   **Dinner:** $8-$14   **Phone:** 505/323-6035   ㉛
◆◆
American
Location: Just e of jct Eubank in Paradise Square. 9800 Montgomery Blvd NE 87111. **Hours:** 11 am-9 pm, Sat & Sun from 11:30 am, Fri & Sat-10 pm. Closed major holidays. **Features:** casual dress; children's menu; carryout; beer & wine only. This Ragin' Shrimp has a trendy decor with outdoor patio seating. They serve a variety of spicy sauces with large, delicious, Gulf shrimp, and the jambalaya is as good as you'll find in New Orleans. Chicken and pork tenderloin are also good choices. Smoke free premises. **Cards:** AE, DS, MC, VI.   ☒

RAGIN' SHRIMP   **Lunch:** $6-$9   **Dinner:** $6-$13   **Phone:** 505/254-1544   ㉕
◆◆
American
Location: I-40, exit 160, 1 mi s on Carlisle Blvd at jct Copper Ave. 3619 Copper Ave NE 87108. **Hours:** 11 am-9 pm, Fri & Sat 11:30 am-10 pm. Closed major holidays. **Features:** casual dress; children's menu; health conscious menu items; carryout; beer & wine only; a la carte. This chic, small, Nob Hill eatery specializes in huge Gulf shrimp served over rice with a Jamaican sauce. Or try the delicious chicken breast, pork tenderloin, or pasta and French bread. Ragin' dipping sauce complements the entrees. Excellent jambalaya. **Cards:** AE, MC, VI.   ☒

RANCHER'S CLUB OF NEW MEXICO   **Lunch:** $6-$14   **Dinner:** $16-$32   **Phone:** 505/884-2500   ⑲
◆◆◆
Steak and
Seafood
Location: I-40, exit 160 (Carlisle Blvd), 0.3 mi n to Menaul Blvd, 1 mi w; in Albuquerque Hilton. 1901 University NE 87102. **Hours:** 11:30 am-2 & 5:30-10 pm, Sat 5:30 pm-10 pm, Sun 10 am-2 & 5:30-9 pm. **Reservations:** accepted. **Features:** casual dress; Sunday brunch; cocktails & lounge. An attractive, well-appointed dining room surrounds you in this restaurant specializing in steak and seafood entrees grilled over a variety of hardwoods. Live music in the lounge and a uniformed staff complement the congenial atmosphere. **Cards:** AE, DI, DS, MC, VI.   ☒

RIBS IN UPTOWN   **Lunch:** $7-$18   **Dinner:** $7-$18   **Phone:** 505/883-7427   ㉓
◆◆
American
Location: I-40, exit 162, just w on Louisiana, just s; in Uptown Plaza. 6601 Uptown Blvd NE 87110. **Hours:** 11 am-9 pm. Closed: 7/4, 11/23 & 12/25. **Features:** casual dress; health conscious menu items; carryout; cocktails & lounge; a la carte. You'll discover more than barbecue ribs here. You'll find a good selection of dishes—barbecue chicken, turkey, beef, burgers, sandwiches, fish and more—plus microbrews to choose from as well. The bustling atmosphere has a rustic and sports-theme decor. **Cards:** AE, DI, DS, MC, VI.   ☒

ROBB'S RIBBS   **Lunch:** $5-$15   **Dinner:** $5-$15   **Phone:** 505/884-7422   �51
◆
Southwest
American
Location: At jct Candelaria. 3000 San Pedro Rd NE 87110. **Hours:** 11 am-8 pm, Fri & Sat-9 pm, Sun noon-8 pm. Closed major holidays, 8/31, 9/1, 12/24 & Mon. **Reservations:** suggested; weekends. **Features:** casual dress; children's menu; health conscious menu items; carryout; beer & wine only; a la carte. Oak, apple and pecan wood fires help create flavorful meats and sauces at Robb's Ribbs. The fragrant, sweet and spicy sauces are fueled by yellow hots, chili pequin and red chili. Try the homemade spicy beer sausage or tasty smoked chicken. Smoke free premises. **Cards:** AE, DI, DS, MC, VI.   ☒

RUDY'S COUNTRY STORE & BAR-B-Q   **Lunch:** $7-$8   **Dinner:** $7-$8   **Phone:** 505/884-4000   ㉖
◆
American
Location: I-40, exit 160, just n. 2321 Carlisle Blvd NE 87110. **Hours:** 10 am-10 pm. Closed: 11/23 & 12/25. **Features:** health conscious menu items; carryout; beer & wine only. You'll enjoy a picnic-style, fun-filled visit to Rudy's, where they specialize in slow-smoked, tender, flavorful brisket, and serve meals on butcher paper and bread. The open-air patio offers a great view of the Sandia and Manzano mountains. **Cards:** AE, DI, DS, MC, VI.   ☒

SADIE'S DINING ROOM   **Lunch:** $4-$10   **Dinner:** $8-$15   **Phone:** 505/345-5339   ㉓
◆◆
Southwest
American
Location: 0.5 mi s of jct Osuna. 6230 4th St NW 87107. **Hours:** 11 am-10 pm, Sun-9 pm. Closed: 11/23 & 12/25. **Reservations:** accepted. **Features:** casual dress; children's menu; cocktails & lounge; a la carte. Sadie's is a popular restaurant, with some of the hottest New Mexican food you'll find, so expect a wait to be seated here. The chicken enchilada on corn shell is wonderful. The interior is decorated in the traditional Southwestern pink and turquoise. **Cards:** AE, CB, DI, DS, MC, VI.   ☒

SCALO NORTHERN ITALIAN GRILL   **Lunch:** $5-$12   **Dinner:** $8-$19   **Phone:** 505/255-8782   ⑳
◆◆◆
Northern
Italian
Location: I-25, Central Ave exit, 2 mi e; in Nob Hill Shopping Center. 3500 Central Ave SE 87106. **Hours:** 11:30 am-2:30 & 5-11 pm, Sun 5 pm-9 pm. Closed: 7/4, 11/23 & 12/25. **Reservations:** accepted. **Features:** casual dress; children's menu; cocktails & lounge. This locally popular restaurant prepares its pasta in-house and offers a good selection of pasta dishes and other entrees. The black-and-white linguine with scallops is especially good. Desserts are tempting too. Patio dining is available. **Cards:** AE, DI, DS, MC, VI.   ☒

SCARPAS   **Lunch:** $5-$8   **Dinner:** $5-$8   **Phone:** 505/821-1885   ㉔
◆◆
American
Location: Just e of jct San Mateo Blvd. 5500 Academy Rd NE 87109. **Hours:** 11 am-10 pm, Sun noon-9 pm. Closed: 12/25. **Features:** casual dress; health conscious menu items; beer & wine only. At Scarpas, pizza is a vehicle for gourmet musings. Each is a individual-size pizza with smoky crust, mozzarella and fontina cheese, served with toppings such as artichoke hearts, pancetta, shiitake mushrooms, smoked salmon and grilled chicken. Smoke free premises. **Cards:** AE, MC, VI.   ☒

(See map p. 369)

SEASONS ROTISSERIE & GRILL   **Lunch:** $6-$9   **Dinner:** $11-$26   **Phone:** 505/766-5100   55
◆◆◆   **Location:** In San Felipe Plaza, just n of Old Town. 2031 Mountain Rd NW 87104. **Hours:** 11:30 am-2:30 &
Continental   5-10 pm, Fri & Sat-11 pm. Closed: 12/25. **Reservations:** suggested. **Features:** dressy casual; cocktails &
lounge; a la carte. Food is creatively prepared, plentiful and earthy at Seasons. The menu offers garlic
mashed potatoes, rosemary-roasted chicken, rock shrimp fritters, and clams in a vodka marinara sauce. This two-level bistro
has outdoor seating on the second floor. **Cards:** AE, DI, DS, MC, VI.

STEPHENS AN AMERICAN CAFE   **Dinner:** $18-$25   **Phone:** 505/842-1773   23
◆◆◆   **Location:** I-25, Central Ave exit, 2.5 mi w at 14th and Central Ave. 1311 Tijeras Ave NW 87102. **Hours:** 5:30
American   pm-9:30 pm, Fri & Sat-10 pm. Closed major holidays. **Reservations:** suggested. **Features:** cocktails &
lounge. Stephens maintains its status as one of Albuquerque's finer restaurants. Its casual, elegant dining
features fresh ingredients, professionally prepared entrees and an attentive, friendly staff. Delightful desserts such as creme
brulee are made in-house. **Cards:** AE, DI, MC, VI.

TOMATO CAFE   **Lunch:** $6   **Dinner:** $8   **Phone:** 505/293-5100   58
◆◆   **Location:** Just n of jct Indian School Rd; in Fashion Villa Shops. 1930 Juan Tabo Blvd NE 87112.
Italian   **Hours:** 11:15 am-2 & 5-8:30 pm, Fri-9 pm, Sat noon-2 & 5-9 pm, Sun noon-2 & 5-8:30 pm. Closed: 11/23 &
12/25. **Features:** casual dress; children's menu; senior's menu; carryout; beer & wine only; buffet. You'll be
able to have a feast from the Tomato Cafe's all-you-can-eat gourmet array of pastas, handmade pizzas, meatballs, soups,
sauces, salads and breads. Then you may choose from their good selection of Italian wines, espressos and tiramisu. Smoke
free premises. **Cards:** AE, DS, MC, VI.

TRATTORIA TROMBINO   **Lunch:** $6-$10   **Dinner:** $10-$20   **Phone:** 505/821-5974   24
AAA   **Location:** I-25, exit 230 (San Mateo Blvd), just s on San Mateo Blvd to Academy Rd, then e. 5415 Academy
◆◆◆   Rd NE 87109. **Hours:** 11 am-2:30 & 5-10 pm, Fri-10:30 pm, Sat 11 am-10:30 pm, Sun 4 pm-9 pm. Closed:
Italian   11/23 & 12/25. **Reservations:** suggested; for dinner. **Features:** casual dress; children's menu; carryout;
cocktails & lounge; a la carte. Well-prepared and delicious entrees, including yellowfin tuna on bowtie pasta,
are served amid this locally popular restaurant's Mediterranean ambience. Fresh ingredients, tasty breads,
steak and chicken choices, and tempting desserts complete the menu. **Cards:** AE, DI, DS, MC, VI.

VIVACE   **Lunch:** $7-$10   **Dinner:** $9-$17   **Phone:** 505/268-5965   59
◆◆   **Location:** Nob Hill area, just e of jct Richmond. 3118 Central Ave SE 87106. **Hours:** 11:30 am-2:30 & 5:30-9
Italian   pm, Fri-10 pm, Sat & Sun 5:30 pm-10 pm. **Reservations:** suggested. **Features:** dressy casual; health
conscious menu; carryout; beer & wine only; street parking; a la carte. Vivace's is a small, nicely appointed
trattoria offering a bounty of pasta, panini and grilled beef and chicken. Or you may want to sample the robust bistecca
fiorentina, grilled yellowfin tuna, spaghetti carbonara or mussels steamed in Pernod. Smoke free premises. **Cards:** AE, CB,
DI, DS, MC, VI.

YESTERDAVE'S GRILL   **Lunch:** $6-$13   **Dinner:** $7-$15   **Phone:** 505/293-0033   62
◆◆   **Location:** Just w of jct Juan Tabo Blvd. 10601 Montgomery Blvd NE 87111. **Hours:** 11 am-10 pm, Fri &
American   Sat-10:30 pm, Sun 10 am-9:30 pm. Closed: 11/23 & 12/25. **Reservations:** accepted. **Features:** casual
dress; Sunday brunch; children's menu; carryout; cocktails & lounge; entertainment; a la carte. Here you'll
discover a mountain of fountain delights—mighty green-chili cheeseburgers, nachos and fajitas—served amid '50s and '60s
nostalgia. Servers wear poodle skirts or carhop suspenders. They also have a DJ, motorcycles and an auto museum.
Cards: AE, CB, DI, DS, MC, VI.

The following restaurants have not been inspected by AAA
but are listed for your information only.

THE ARTICHOKE CAFE   **Phone:** 505/243-0200
fyi   Not inspected. **Location:** 424 Central Ave SE 87048. **Features:** A mixed blend of spices and herbs flavor
dishes served in an eclectic setting. Moderate prices.

CAPO'S HIDE AWAY   **Phone:** 505/898-2002
fyi   Not inspected. **Location:** 8938 4th St NW 87111. **Features:** Menu offerings include a variety of pizzas,
ravioli, calzones and fettuccine dishes.

CAPO'S RISTORANTE ITALIANO   **Phone:** 505/242-2007
fyi   Not inspected. **Location:** 722 Lomas NW 87111. **Features:** Established in 1954, this restaurant offers
fireside dining in a cozy setting with a menu of veal, spaghetti, pizzas and calzones.

CHINA GARDEN RESTAURANT   **Phone:** 505/883-4455
fyi   Not inspected. **Location:** 4615 Menaul Blvd NE 87110. **Features:** Specialties include Mongolian barbecue
as well as Mandarin and Szechwan style cuisine.

COOPERAGE RESTAURANT   **Phone:** 505/255-1657
fyi   Not inspected. **Location:** 7220 Lomas Blvd NE 87110. **Features:** Famous for prime rib, the menu includes a
variety of steak and lobster entrees served in a rustic barrel-shaped setting.

COUNTRY HARVEST BUFFET RESTAURANT   **Phone:** 505/881-7479
fyi   Not inspected. **Location:** 3901 Menaul Blvd NE 87110. **Features:** Featuring home-style cooking, this
restaurant offers a wide variety of items, including soup, salad bar, fish, barbecue, poultry, lasagna and ribs.

GIOVANNI'S PIZZA   **Phone:** 505/255-1233
fyi   Not inspected. **Location:** 921 San Pedro Dr SE 87108. **Features:** Specialties of New York-style pizzas,
calzones, vegetarian pizzas and pesto are featured.

INDIAN PALACE   **Phone:** 505/271-5009
fyi   Not inspected. **Location:** 4410 Q Wyoming NE 87111. **Features:** Select from a wide variety of Indian dishes
such as lamb tikka kebab, vegetable buryani, chicken korma and sag paneer.

(See map p. 369)

JR'S BAR-B-Q & SEAFOOD
Phone: 505/268-1676
[fyi] Not inspected. **Location:** 6501 Gibson 87111. **Features:** A variety of seafood and barbecue platters include beef brisket, ribs, burritos, catfish and sandwiches.

JR'S BAR-B-Q & SEAFOOD
Phone: 505/242-4400
[fyi] Not inspected. **Location:** 1306 Rio Grande Blvd NW 87111. **Features:** Choose from a variety of seafood and barbecue platters. The menu features beef brisket, ribs, burritos, catfish and sandwiches.

LUIGI'S ITALIAN RESTAURANT & PIZZERIA
Phone: 505/343-0466
[fyi] Not inspected. **Location:** 6225 4th St NW 87111. **Features:** Fare includes pizzas, pasta, antipasto, shrimp scampi, chicken Florentine and eggplant as well as sandwiches and desserts.

MIMMO'S RISTORANTE & PIZZERIA
Phone: 505/831-4191
[fyi] Not inspected. **Location:** 3301 Coors Rd NW 87111. **Features:** The menu includes a variety of Italian fare, such as antipasto, pasta, pizzas, veal, calzones, seafood and chicken.

ORTEGA'S MEXICAN RESTAURANT & GRILL
Phone: 505/298-0223
[fyi] Not inspected. **Location:** 3617 Wyoming NE 87111. **Features:** A variety of menu choices includes chili rellenos, enchiladas, burritos, tamales, tacos and fajitas.

PACIFIC PEARL
Phone: 505/888-1157
[fyi] Not inspected. **Location:** 5411 Osuna Rd NE 87109. **Features:** Menu offerings include a variety of pork, beef, poultry, seafood, salads and appetizers.

PELICAN'S RESTAURANT
Phone: 505/298-7678
[fyi] Not inspected. **Location:** 9800 Montgomery Blvd NE 87111. **Features:** Steak, seafood, prime rib, lobster and king crab are just a few selections from the menu.

RONNEY J'S
Phone: 505/890-6890
[fyi] Not inspected. **Location:** At jct Ronney J's and Irving, 0.5 mi n of Paseo del Norte. 9401 Coors Blvd NW 87114. **Features:** Eclectic cuisine, including sandwiches, burritos, nachos and burgers, is served in a nouveau warehouse-chic atmosphere.

RUDY'S COUNTRY STORE & BAR-B-Q
Phone: 505/890-7113
[fyi] Not inspected. **Location:** 10136 Coors Blvd NW 87114. **Features:** The Texas-style barbecue featured here includes brisket, pork loin, chopped beef, prime rib, chicken, baby back ribs, ham, trout and much more.

SALSA LATIN GRILL & CANTINA
Phone: 505/822-0403
[fyi] Not inspected. **Location:** At the Tram Launch Site. 38 Tramway Rd NE 87048. **Features:** Fun and a whimsical decor blend with traditional entrees served by a friendly staff. A good family value.

SCALO NORTHERN ITALIAN GRILL
Phone: 505/255-8781
[fyi] Not inspected. **Location:** 3500 Central Ave SE 87048. **Features:** You'll find all the homemade favorites here in a comfortable, warm atmosphere. Enjoy ample portions at moderate prices.

SEAGULL STREET FISH MARKET
Phone: 505/821-0020
[fyi] Not inspected. **Location:** 5410 Academy Rd NE 87109. **Features:** Mesquite-grilled fish, steak, lobster and crab legs are features on this menu.

SHALIMAR EAST INDIAN RESTAURANT
Phone: 505/275-7949
[fyi] Not inspected. **Location:** 8405 Montgomery Blvd NE 87109. **Features:** The cuisine includes a range of choices such as basmati rice, curried dishes and traditional entrees of India.

STUART ANDERSON'S BLACK ANGUS
Phone: 505/292-1911
[fyi] Not inspected. **Location:** 2290 Wyoming Blvd 87109. **Features:** Dine on a variety of choice steak, prime rib, chicken and seafood entrees.

TAJ MAHAL CUISINE OF INDIA
Phone: 505/255-1994
[fyi] Not inspected. **Location:** 1930 Carlisle Blvd NE 87110. **Features:** Enjoy the cuisine of India, such as tandoori, curries, masalas, kormas and saegs.

TEXAS LAND & CATTLE STEAK HOUSE
Phone: 505/343-9800
[fyi] Not inspected. **Location:** 4949 Pan American Frwy NE 87048. **Features:** A variety of finger foods and entrees are included on the menu. Bring your appetite, as this eatery is known for its large portions.

VILLA DI CAPO
Phone: 505/242-2006
[fyi] Not inspected. **Location:** 722 Central SW 87111. **Features:** The menu includes pizzas, ravioli, calzones, fettuccine and veal dishes.

(See map p. 369)

ALGODONES pop. 450

―――― LODGING ――――

HACIENDA VARGAS BED AND BREAKFAST INN　　　　　　　**Phone:** (505)867-9115
◆◆◆　　All Year　　　　　　　　　　　　　　2P: $79-$149　　　　　XP: $15　　　　F3
Historic Bed　**Location:** I-25, exit 248, 0.5 mi w. 1431 SR 313 (El Camino Real) 87001 (PO Box 307). Fax: 505/867-1902.
& Breakfast　**Terms:** [BP] meal plan; age restrictions may apply; check-in 4 pm; 10 day cancellation notice; cancellation fee
imposed. **Facility:** 8 rooms. 18th century hacienda. 1 story; interior corridors; smoke free premises.
Services: gift shop. **All Rooms:** combo or shower baths. **Cards:** MC, VI.

ALTO pop. 850

―――― LODGING ――――

HIGH COUNTRY LODGE　　　　　　　　　　　　　　　**Phone:** 505/336-4321
◆◆　　　All Year　　　　　　　　1P: $79-$139　　　　2P: $79-$139　　　　XP: $10　　　　F13
Cottage　　**Location:** Center. Hwy 48 88312 (PO Box 137). Fax: 505/336-8205. **Terms:** 7 day cancellation notice; cancel-
lation fee imposed; pets, $10 extra charge. **Facility:** 32 rooms. Rustic cabins with fireplace. 12 mi s of Ski
Apache. 1 story; exterior corridors; heated pool; 1 tennis court; playground. **Recreation:** sports court. **All Rooms:** kitchens.
Cards: AE, CB, DI, DS, MC, VI.

ANGEL FIRE

―――― LODGING ――――

ANGEL FIRE RESORT　　　　　　　　　　　　　　　　**Phone:** (505)377-6401
◆◆　　　12/16-1/5　　　　　　　1P: $195-$315　　　2P: $195-$315
Resort　　2/1-3/20　　　　　　　　1P: $135-$260　　　2P: $135-$260
　　　　　1/6-1/31　　　　　　　　1P: $119-$185　　　2P: $119-$185
　　　　　3/21-12/15　　　　　　　1P: $85-$100　　　　2P: $85-$100
Location: From US 64, 2.6 mi s on SR 434, then 0.4 mi. 1 N Angel Fire Rd 87710 (PO Box Drawer B). Fax: 505/377-4200.
Terms: Check-in 4 pm; 2 night min stay, weekends; package plans; pets, in summer. **Facility:** 139 rooms. Large rooms and
spacious public areas. 18 two-bedroom units. 5 stories; interior corridors; small heated indoor pool; 4 tennis courts; playground.
Fee: 18 holes golf, miniature golf. **Services:** gift shop. **Recreation:** downhill & cross country skiing, snow-
mobiling; bicycles, horseback riding. **Some Rooms:** 18 kitchens. **Cards:** AE, CB, DI, DS, MC, VI.

ARROYO HONDO pop. 300—See also TAOS.

―――― LODGING ――――

LITTLE TREE BED & BREAKFAST　　　　　　　　　　　**Phone:** (505)776-8467
◆◆　　　All Year　　　　　　　　1P: $80-$100　　　　2P: $85-$105　　　　XP: $15　　　　F12
Bed &　　**Location:** Jct SR 150 and US 64 W, 2.7 mi e on SR 150, 1.9 mi nw on SR 230, 2 mi w on Arroyo Hondo Rd,
Breakfast　follow signs. 226 County Rd B-143 87514 (PO Drawer II, TAOS, 87571). **Terms:** [BP] meal plan; check-in 4
pm; 10 day cancellation notice; 2 night min stay, weekends; pets on premises. **Facility:** 4 rooms. Gorgeous
rural setting. Located out of Taos toward the ski area at Taos Mountain. Authentic adobe style. 2 rooms with Kiva fireplaces. 1
story; exterior corridors; smoke free premises; mountain view. **All Rooms:** combo or shower baths. **Some Rooms:** color TV.
Cards: AE, DI, DS, MC, VI.

ARROYO SECO pop. 300—See also TAOS.

―――― LODGINGS ――――

ADOBE AND STARS B & B　　　　　　　　　　　　　　**Phone:** (505)776-2776
◆◆◆　　All Year　　　　　　　　1P: $105-$170　　　2P: $115-$180　　　　XP: $40　　　　D4
Bed &　　**Location:** 1.1 mi ne on SR 150 at Valdez Rd. 584 SR 150 87514 (PO Box 2285, TAOS, 87571).
Breakfast　Fax: 505/776-2872. **Terms:** [BP] meal plan; check-in 4 pm; 14 day cancellation notice; cancellation fee im-
posed; small pets only, $50 dep req. **Facility:** 8 rooms. Stylish contemporary home with a Southwestern flair.
Large rooms and baths with some luxury details, including fireplace and radiant-heat floors. Astronomy-buff owner encourages
star-gazing. 1-2 stories; interior/exterior corridors; smoke free premises. **All Rooms:** combo or shower baths. **Cards:** AE, DS,
MC, VI.

COTTONWOOD INN BED & BREAKFAST　　　　　　　　**Phone:** (505)776-5826
◆◆◆　　All Year　　　　　　　　1P: $90-$170　　　　2P: $95-$190　　　　XP: $20　　　　D18
Bed &　　**Location:** SR 150 at jct SR 230. 02 SR 230 87514 (HCR 74 Box 24609, EL PRADO, 87529).
Breakfast　Fax: 505/776-1141. **Terms:** [BP] meal plan; check-in 4 pm; 14 day cancellation notice; cancellation fee im-
posed; package plans. **Facility:** 7 rooms. Adobe style building set in rolling country side. 5 rooms with fire-
places, decks and patios. 1 room with large hot tub. 2 stories; interior/exterior corridors; smoke free premises; playground.
Services: Fee: massage. **Recreation:** hiking trails, jogging. **All Rooms:** combo or shower baths. **Cards:** DS, MC, VI.

QUAIL RIDGE INN RESORT
◆ ◆ ◆

	12/22-1/31	1P: $89-$150	2P: $89-$150	XP: $10	F18
Cottage	2/1-3/18	1P: $89-$110	2P: $89-$110	XP: $10	F18
	3/19-4/9	1P: $79-$89	2P: $79-$89	XP: $10	F18
	4/10-12/21	1P: $59-$89	2P: $59-$89	XP: $10	F18

Phone: (505)776-2211

Location: 1 mi ne from jct US 64. SR 150 Taos Ski Valley Rd (#88) 87571 (PO Box 707, TAOS). Fax: 505/776-2949. **Terms:** [BP] meal plan; check-in 4 pm; 4 day cancellation notice; cancellation fee imposed; package plans. **Facility:** 110 rooms. In cluster buildings on extensive natural grounds. All rooms with fireplace. 1 three-bedroom unit, 20 two-bedroom units. 1-2 stories; exterior corridors; heated pool; racquetball courts, 8 tennis courts (2 indoor, 2 lighted). **Services:** Fee: massage. **Some Rooms:** 64 kitchens. **Cards:** AE, DI, DS, MC, VI.

——— RESTAURANT ———

CASA FRESEN BAKERY   **Lunch:** $6-$9   **Dinner:** $6-$9   Phone: 505/776-2969
◆
American   **Location:** Center on SR 150. 482 SR 150 87514. **Hours:** 7 am-3 pm, Fri & Sat-5 pm; 7:30 am-5 pm 5/1-10/31. Closed major holidays & Sun. **Features:** No A/C; casual dress; carryout; a la carte. This small, rustic deli/bakery offers homemade breads and pastries as well as premium-quality cheeses and deli meats. You may find the menu's sandwiches, soups and salads a bit pricey, but they would be ideal for a gourmet picnic. **Cards:** DS, MC, VI.

ARTESIA pop. 10,600

——— LODGINGS ———

ARTESIA INN
AAA SAVE   Phone: (505)746-9801
◆ ◆   **Location:** 1.5 mi s on US 285. 1820 S 1st St 88210. **Terms:** 3 day cancellation notice; pets, $10 extra charge.
Motel   All Year   1P: $38-$48   2P: $45-$55   XP: $7   F12
Facility: 34 rooms. Well kept older property. 1 story; exterior corridors. **All Rooms:** combo or shower baths, extended cable TV. **Cards:** AE, CB, DI, DS, JC, MC, VI. **Special Amenities:** Free local telephone calls and free room upgrade (subject to availability with advanced reservations).

BEST WESTERN PECOS INN
AAA SAVE   All Year   1P: $55-$75   2P: $65-$85   XP: $10   F12
◆ ◆ ◆   Phone: (505)748-3324
Motor Inn   **Location:** 1.5 mi w on US 82. 2209 W Main 88210. Fax: 505/748-2868. **Terms:** [BP] meal plan; 3 day cancellation notice. **Facility:** 82 rooms. Large rooms. 3 two-bedroom units. 2 stories; interior corridors; heated pool, sauna, whirlpool. **Dining:** Dining room; 6-10 am, 11-2 & 5-9 pm, Sun-8 pm; $6-$12. **All Rooms:** extended cable TV. **Some Rooms:** kitchen. Fee: microwaves, VCR. **Cards:** AE, CB, DI, DS, MC, VI. **Special Amenities:** Free breakfast and free local telephone calls.

HERITAGE INN BED & BREAKFAST
AAA   Phone: 505/748-2552
◆ ◆ ◆   All Year   1P: $45-$55   2P: $55-$65   XP: $10
Historic Bed & Breakfast   **Location:** Downtown on US 82. 1211 W Main St 88210. Fax: 505/746-3407. **Terms:** [CP] meal plan; weekly & monthly rates avail. **Facility:** 9 rooms. Simple, elegant colonial American style decor. 2 stories; interior corridors; designated smoking area; street parking only. **Dining:** Restaurant nearby. **All Rooms:** combo or shower baths, extended cable TV. **Cards:** AE, DS, MC, VI.

HOLIDAY INN EXPRESS-ARTESIA
◆ ◆ ◆   All Year   1P: $58   XP: $8   F19
Motel   Phone: 505/748-3904
MC, VI.   **Location:** 1.6 mi w of jct US 82 and 285. 2210 W Main 88210. Fax: 505/748-3796. **Facility:** 40 rooms. 2 stories; interior corridors; heated pool. **All Rooms:** combo or shower baths. **Cards:** AE, CB, DI, DS, JC,

——— RESTAURANT ———

LA FONDA RESTAURANT   **Lunch:** $5-$16   **Dinner:** $5-$16   Phone: 505/746-9411
◆ ◆   **Location:** Center. 206 W Main 88210. **Hours:** 11 am-2 & 5-9 pm, Sat & Sun 11 am-9 pm. Closed: 7/4, 11/23
Mexican   & 12/25. **Reservations:** accepted. **Features:** casual dress; children's menu; carryout; salad bar. La Fonda is family-type restaurant offering a Southwestern ambience with American fare in addition to the regional and Mexican selections, including flautas, chimichangas and tacos. They serve large portions, and also feature a luncheon buffet. **Cards:** AE, DS, MC, VI.

AZTEC pop. 5,500

——— LODGING ———

THE STEP BACK INN
AAA SAVE   Phone: (505)334-1200
◆ ◆ ◆   5/16-11/15   1P: $68-$72   2P: $68-$72   XP: $8   F17
Motel   11/16-1/31   1P: $58-$60   2P: $60-$68   XP: $6   F17
    2/1-5/15   1P: $58-$60   2P: $58-$60   XP: $6   F17
Location: Jct US 550 and NM 544. 103 W Aztec Blvd 87410. Fax: 505/334-9858. **Terms:** [CP] meal plan. **Facility:** 39 rooms. Rooms with a Victorian flair, each themed after the town's founding families. Beauty salon on site. 2 stories; interior corridors. **Dining:** Health conscious menu items; restaurant nearby. **All Rooms:** shower baths. **Cards:** AE, MC, VI. **Special Amenities:** Free local telephone calls and preferred room (subject to availability with advanced reservations).

BELEN pop. 6,500

------ LODGING ------

BEST WESTERN
◆ ◆ ◆   All Year   1P: $59-$69   2P: $64-$74   XP: $5   F18
Motel   **Location:** I-25, exit 191, just w of jct. 2111 Sosimo Padilla Blvd 87002. Fax: 505/864-7364. **Terms:** Pets, $20
                 dep req. **Facility:** 50 rooms. 2 stories; interior/exterior corridors; designated smoking area; heated pool.
All Rooms: combo or shower baths. **Cards:** AE, DI, DS, JC, MC, VI.

Phone: (505)861-3181

BERNALILLO pop. 6,000   (See map p. 369; index p. 368)—

------ LODGING ------

LA HACIENDA GRANDE   **Phone:** (505)867-1887   89
◆ ◆ ◆   All Year   1P: $95-$125   2P: $99-$129   XP: $15   D18
Historic Bed   **Location:** I-25, exit 242, 0.3 mi w to Camino del Pueblo, 0.5 mi n on Camino del Pueblo. 21 Barros Ln 87004.
& Breakfast   Fax: 505/771-1436. **Terms:** [BP] meal plan; check-in 4 pm; 11 day cancellation notice; cancellation fee im-
                 posed. **Facility:** 6 rooms. Restored 250 year old hacienda. TV and VCR avail upon request. 1 story;
interior/exterior corridors. **All Rooms:** combo or shower baths. **Some Rooms:** color TV. Fee: VCR. **Cards:** AE, DI, DS,
MC, VI. *(See ad p 377)*

------ RESTAURANT ------

PRAIRIE STAR   **Dinner:** $15-$32   **Phone:** 505/867-3327   72
◆ ◆ ◆   **Location:** I-25, exit 242, 2.2 mi w on NM 44 to Jemez Canyon Dam Rd, then 0.5 mi n. 255 Prairie Star Rd
American   87026. **Hours:** 5:30 pm-9 pm, Fri & Sat-10 pm, Sun 5:30 pm-9 pm. Closed: 12/25 & Mon.
                 Reservations: suggested. **Features:** casual dress; cocktails & lounge. The cuisine at Prairie Star is
American—a combination of pasta, fresh seafood, steak and chicken—with a Mexican flair. The rambling, old adobe
mansion ambience is perfect for a couple's romantic night out. They also offer a good dessert selection. **Cards:** AE, DI, DS,
MC, VI.

BLOOMFIELD pop. 5,200

------ LODGING ------

SUPER 8 MOTEL   **Phone:** (505)632-8886
◆ ◆   All Year   1P: $40   2P: $44
Motel   **Location:** Jct of US 64 and SR 44. 525 W Broadway Blvd 87413. Fax: 505/632-8886. **Terms:** [CP] meal plan;
                 pets, $20 dep req. **Facility:** 42 rooms. Modern rooms for the budget conscious. 2 extra large family rooms with
third bed or pull-out sleeper sofa. 2 stories; interior corridors. **Cards:** AE, DS, MC, VI.

CANONCITO pop. 100

------ LODGING ------

APACHIE CANYON RANCH BED & BREAKFAST COUNTRY INN   **Phone:** 505/836-7220
◆ ◆ ◆   All Year   1P: $90-$200   2P: $90-$265   XP: $20
Bed &   **Location:** I-40, exit 131, 3 mi n on Canonieto Hwy. 4 Canyon Dr 87026. Fax: 505/836-2922. **Terms:** [BP] meal
Breakfast   plan; 14 day cancellation notice; cancellation fee imposed. **Facility:** 4 rooms. Located on Ranch Land near
                 Native American settlements. Well appointed rooms and common areas. 1 two-bedroom unit. 1 story;
interior/exterior corridors; smoke free premises. **Services:** Fee: massage. **Recreation:** hiking trails, jogging.
Some Rooms: kitchen. **Cards:** AE, MC, VI.

CARLSBAD pop. 25,000

------ LODGINGS ------

BEST WESTERN MOTEL STEVENS   **Phone:** (505)887-2851
                 All Year   1P: $54   2P: $59   XP: $5   F12
◆ ◆ ◆   **Location:** 1 mi s on US 62, 180 and 285. 1829 S Canal St 88220 (PO Box 580). Fax: 505/887-6338.
Motor Inn   **Terms:** 3 day cancellation notice; small pets only. **Facility:** 202 rooms. On main hwy. Variety of rooms, family
                 ambiance. 18 whirlpool rooms, $69-$79; 1-2 stories; exterior corridors; wading pool; playground.
                 Dining: Coffee shop; 5:30 am-10 pm, Sun-9 pm; $6-$13; cocktails; also, The Flume Restaurant, see separate
listing; entertainment. **All Rooms:** combo or shower baths, extended cable TV. **Some Rooms:** 22 efficiencies, 16 kitchens.
Fee: VCR. **Cards:** AE, DI, DS, MC, VI. **Special Amenities:** Free local telephone calls and free newspaper.

CARLSBAD INN

	6/1-9/15	1P: $32-$36	2P: $38-$45	XP: $5 F12
	3/2-5/31	1P: $30-$35	2P: $34-$42	XP: $5 F12
	2/1-3/1 & 9/16-1/31	1P: $28-$32	2P: $32-$40	XP: $5 F12

Phone: (505)887-1171

Motel **Location:** 1.5 mi s on US 62, 180 and 285. 2019 S Canal St 88220. Fax: 505/887-6577. **Terms:** Weekly rates avail. in winter; cancellation fee imposed; small pets only. **Facility:** 30 rooms. Large rooms with contemporary decor. 2 stories; exterior corridors; heated pool; playground. **Dining:** Restaurant nearby. **All Rooms:** extended cable TV. **Some Rooms:** Fee: VCR. **Cards:** AE, DI, DS, MC, VI. **Special Amenities:** Free local telephone calls and free room upgrade (subject to availability with advanced reservations).

CONTINENTAL INN

	5/1-9/15	1P: $35-$40	2P: $45-$55	XP: $5 F14
	2/1-4/30 & 9/16-1/31	1P: $30-$35	2P: $40-$50	XP: $5 F14

Phone: (505)887-0341

Motel **Location:** 3.5 mi sw on US 62 and 180. 3820 National Parks Hwy 88220. Fax: 505/885-1186. **Terms:** Pets, $10 dep req. **Facility:** 60 rooms. On main hwy. 2 stories; exterior corridors; heated pool. **Some Rooms:** Fee: refrigerators. **Cards:** AE, CB, DI, DS, MC, VI.

DAYS INN OF CARLSBAD

	All Year	1P: $50-$55	2P: $57-$62	XP: $7 F12

Phone: (505)887-7800

Motel **Location:** 3.5 mi sw on US 62 and 180. 3910 National Parks Hwy 88220. Fax: 505/885-9433. **Terms:** [CP] meal plan; 7 day cancellation notice; cancellation fee imposed; small pets only, $5 extra charge. **Facility:** 50 rooms. 2 stories; exterior corridors; small heated indoor pool, whirlpool. **Dining:** Restaurant nearby. **All Rooms:** extended cable TV. **Cards:** AE, CB, DI, DS, MC, VI. **Special Amenities:** Free breakfast and preferred room (subject to availability with advanced reservations).

HOLIDAY INN CARLSBAD

	6/16-8/15	1P: $80-$104	2P: $86-$104	XP: $6 F18
	2/1-4/30 & 8/16-1/31	1P: $75-$104	2P: $81-$104	XP: $6 F18

Phone: (505)885-8500

Motor Inn **Location:** Center on US 62, 180 and 285, Canal St at Lee St. 601 S Canal 88220. Fax: 505/887-5999. **Terms:** [BP] meal plan; pets, $25 dep req. **Facility:** 100 rooms. Large rooms done in regional style. Extremely well kept property. 5 whirlpool rooms, $104-$150; 2 stories; exterior corridors; heated pool, whirlpool; playground. **Dining:** Dining room; 6 am-10 & 5-11:30 pm; $8-$16; cocktails; also, Ventanas', see separate listing. **All Rooms:** combo or shower baths, extended cable TV. **Some Rooms:** Fee: refrigerators, microwaves. **Cards:** AE, CB, DI, DS, MC, VI. **Special Amenities:** Free breakfast and free local telephone calls.

QUALITY INN

AAA SAVE
◆ ◆ ◆
Motor Inn

Phone: (505)887-2861

All Year   1P: $49-$59   2P: $59-$69   XP: $10   F18
Location: 3 mi sw on US 62 and 180. 3706 National Park Hwy 88220 (PO Box 5037). Fax: 505/887-2861.
Terms: [ECP] meal plan; 7 day cancellation notice; cancellation fee imposed; small pets only. **Facility:** 122
rooms. 2 stories; exterior corridors; whirlpool. **Dining:** Dining room; 5 pm-10 pm; $8-$16; cocktails; entertainment, nightclub. **Recreation:** video game room. **All Rooms:** extended cable TV. **Cards:** AE, CB, DI, DS, JC,
MC, VI. **Special Amenities:** Free breakfast and free room upgrade (subject to availability with advanced reservations). *(See color ad p 394)*

STAGECOACH INN

AAA SAVE
◆
Motel

Phone: (505)887-1148

All Year   1P: $36-$40   2P: $40-$46   XP: $5   D
Location: 1 mi s on US 62, 180 and 285. 1819 S Canal 88220. Fax: 505/887-1148. **Terms:** Weekly rates avail;
cancellation fee imposed; pets. **Facility:** 55 rooms. Rates for up to 4 persons; 1 story; exterior corridors;
wading pool, whirlpool; playground. **Dining:** Restaurant nearby. **All Rooms:** combo or shower baths, extended
cable TV. **Some Rooms:** 4 kitchens, no utensils. **Cards:** AE, CB, DI, DS, JC, MC, VI. **Special Amenities:** Free
local telephone calls and free room upgrade (subject to availability with advanced reservations).

─────── RESTAURANTS ───────

THE FLUME RESTAURANT

AAA
◆ ◆
American

Lunch: $6-$12   **Dinner:** $9-$20   **Phone:** 505/887-2851

Location: 1 mi s on US 62, 180 and 285; in Best Western Motel Stevens. 1829 S Canal St 88220.
Hours: 5:30 am-10 pm, Sun-9 pm. **Reservations:** accepted. **Features:** casual dress; children's menu;
carryout; salad bar; cocktails. Prime rib is the specialty at the Flume, which also has a nice selection of
seafood dishes such as lobster tail and filet, and Mexican dishes to choose from, with vegetable side dishes
to accompany the entrees. **Cards:** AE, DI, DS, MC, VI.

VENTANAS'

AAA
◆ ◆ ◆
American

Dinner: $12-$20   **Phone:** 505/885-8500

Location: Center on US 62, 180 and 285, Canal St at Lee St; in Holiday Inn Carlsbad. 601 S Canal 88220.
Hours: 5:30 pm-9:30 pm. Closed: 12/25 & Sun. **Reservations:** accepted. **Features:** casual dress; health
conscious menu; cocktails. You'll receive prompt, attentive, friendly service from Ventanas' professional,
uniformed staff. They have an attractive dining area, and entrees that are cooked to order and well-prepared
with fresh ingredients. The filet mignon is cooked to perfection. **Cards:** AE, CB, DI, DS, MC, VI.

─────── *The following restaurant has not been inspected by AAA* ───────
but is listed for your information only.

LUCY'S

[fyi]

Phone: 505/887-7714

Not inspected. **Location:** 701 S Canal St 88220. **Features:** Enjoy hand-made Mexican fare such as tamales,
enchiladas and chili rellenos. Informal, casual dining.

CHAMA pop. 1,000

─────── LODGINGS ───────

BRANDING IRON MOTEL

AAA SAVE
◆ ◆
Motor Inn

Phone: 505/756-2162

4/15-10/31   1P: $69-$79   2P: $79-$89   XP: $10   F12
2/1-4/14 & 11/1-1/31   1P: $53-$65   2P: $65-$75   XP: $10   F12
Location: 0.5 mi s. 1511 W Main 87520 (PO Box 557). Fax: 505/756-2912. **Facility:** 41 rooms. 2 stories; exterior corridors. **Dining:** Restaurant; 6 am-10 pm; $3-$17; cocktails. **All Rooms:** combo or shower baths.

THE GANDY DANCER BED & BREAKFAST

AAA SAVE
◆ ◆ ◆
Historic Bed
& Breakfast

Phone: (505)756-2191

5/1-10/31   1P: $75-$85   2P: $95-$125   XP: $15
2/1-4/30 & 11/1-1/31   1P: $65-$75   2P: $85-$95   XP: $15
Location: Just w of SR 17 via 3rd St. 299 Maple Ave 87520 (PO Box 810). Fax: 505/756-9110. **Terms:** [BP]
meal plan; age restrictions may apply; 10 day cancellation notice; cancellation fee imposed; package plans.
Facility: 7 rooms. Quaint Victorian home circa 1913. Hearty breakfasts; friendly informal hosts. Common
phone avail. Lava lounge fireplace area. 2 stories; interior corridors; smoke free premises; whirlpool.
Dining: Breakfast terrace in summer; picnic lunch by reservation; dinner by reservation 11/1-5/31. **Recreation:** 1 blk from
scenic railroad station, limited exercise equipment. **All Rooms:** combo or shower baths, extended cable TV. **Cards:** AE, CB,
DI, DS, JC, MC, VI. **Special Amenities:** Free breakfast and free local telephone calls.

POSADA ENCANTO

AAA SAVE
◆ ◆ ◆
Bed &
Breakfast

Phone: 505/756-1048

2/1-10/31   1P: $79   2P: $85   XP: $15
11/1-1/31   1P: $65   2P: $75   XP: $15
Location: Just w of Hwy 17 via 3rd St to Maple. 277 Maple Ave 87520 (PO Box 536). Fax: 505/756-1843.
Terms: [BP] meal plan; 7 day cancellation notice; cancellation fee imposed. **Facility:** 4 rooms. Pleasant Southwestern flair to decor to rooms in former converted church building. 1 story; interior corridors; smoke free premises. **All Rooms:** shower baths. **Cards:** AE, CB, DI, DS, JC, MC, VI.

RIVER BEND LODGE

Phone: (505)756-2264

5/1-11/30	1P: $63-$73	2P: $68-$78	XP: $10	F12
12/1-1/31	1P: $57-$67	2P: $68-$78	XP: $10	F12
2/1-4/30	1P: $57-$67	2P: $63-$73	XP: $10	F12

Motel

Location: 0.5 mi s of SR 17. 2625 Hwy 64/84 87520 (PO Box 593). Fax: 505/756-2664. **Terms:** Cancellation fee imposed; pets, $10 extra charge. **Facility:** 18 rooms. 4 with electric fireplace. 4 cabins avail, $99-$119, 1 with fireplace; 1 story; exterior corridors; whirlpool. **Dining:** Restaurant nearby. **Services:** area transportation. **All Rooms:** combo or shower baths, extended cable TV. **Some Rooms:** 4 kitchens. **Cards:** AE, DI, DS, MC, VI. **Special Amenities:** Free local telephone calls and preferred room (subject to availability with advanced reservations).

VISTA DEL RIO LODGE

Phone: (505)756-2138

All Year	1P: $65-$75	2P: $71-$81	XP: $5	F5

Motel

Location: 0.5 mi s of SR 17. 2595 US Hwy 84/64 87520 (HC 75 Box 37). Fax: 505/756-1872. **Facility:** 19 rooms. Modern motel with a strong Western flair, from the log cabin-style exterior to handcrafted pine furnishings in rooms. Small pond and stream in back. 1 story; exterior corridors; whirlpool; playground. **Recreation:** fishing. **All Rooms:** extended cable TV. **Cards:** AE, DI, DS, MC, VI. **Special Amenities:** Free breakfast and free local telephone calls.

------- RESTAURANT -------

HIGH COUNTRY RESTAURANT

Lunch: $4-$10   **Dinner:** $8-$22   Phone: 505/756-2384

Steak and Seafood

Location: SR 17, just n of jct US 64 and 84. Hwy 84 87520. **Hours:** 7 am-10 pm. Closed: 4/23, 11/23 & 12/25. **Reservations:** accepted. **Features:** casual dress; children's menu; carryout; cocktails & lounge; buffet. High Country features casual dining and New Mexican favorites. An interesting turn-of-the-century saloon adjoins the dining room. They offer outdoor seating in the beer garden during the summer, and a weekend breakfast buffet is served 7-11 am. **Cards:** AE, DS, MC, VI.

CHIMAYO

------- LODGING -------

CASA ESCONDIDA

Phone: 505/351-4805

11/1-1/31	1P: $60-$135	2P: $70-$145		F7
4/2-10/31	1P: $70-$130	2P: $80-$140	XP: $15	F7
2/1-4/1	1P: $60-$100	2P: $70-$120	XP: $15	F7

Bed & Breakfast

Location: From SR 68, 7.1 mi e on SR 76; then 0.5 mi on CR 0100 (dirt road) following signs. 64 Rd 0100 87522 (PO Box 142). Fax: 505/351-2575. **Terms:** [BP] meal plan; check-in 4 pm; cancellation fee imposed; pet on premises. **Facility:** 8 rooms. Located in rural area. Rooms with modest decor and furnishings. 2 stories; interior/exterior corridors; designated smoking area. **All Rooms:** combo or shower baths. **Some Rooms:** kitchen. **Cards:** AE, MC, VI.

CIMARRON pop. 800

------- LODGINGS -------

CASA DEL GAVILAN

Phone: 505/376-2246

All Year	1P: $75-$125	2P: $75-$125	XP: $20	F4

Historic Bed & Breakfast

Location: SR 21, 5.7 mi s of US 64. Hwy 21 S 87714 (PO Box 518). Fax: 505/376-2247. **Terms:** [BP] meal plan; 7 day cancellation notice. **Facility:** 5 rooms. Hacienda style ranch house, circa 1905. In secluded area with vistas. 1 story; interior corridors; designated smoking area. **Recreation:** hiking trails. **Cards:** AE, DS, MC, VI.

CIMARRON INN & RV PARK

Phone: (505)376-2268

All Year	1P: $40-$44	2P: $44-$50	XP: $6	F8

Motel

Location: US Hwy 64. 212 E 10th St 87714. Fax: 505/376-2724. **Terms:** Monthly rates avail, off season; cancellation fee imposed. **Facility:** 12 rooms. Some individually decorated rooms. 1 story; exterior corridors. **Dining:** Restaurant nearby. **All Rooms:** combo or shower baths. **Cards:** AE, DS, JC, MC, VI. **Special Amenities:** Early check-in/late check-out and free local telephone calls.

CLAYTON pop. 2,500

------- LODGINGS -------

BEST WESTERN KOKOPELLI LODGE

Phone: (505)374-2589

All Year	1P: $59-$89	2P: $59-$89

Motel

Location: US 87, 0.5 mi se of jct US 56 and 64. 702 S 1st St 88415. Fax: 505/374-2554. **Terms:** [ECP] meal plan; small pets only, $5 extra charge, with prior approval. **Facility:** 47 rooms. Southwestern decor. 8 rooms with hair dryer. 2 whirlpool rooms, $79-$109; 2 stories; exterior corridors; heated pool. **Recreation:** picnic area, shuffleboard. **Some Rooms:** Fee: refrigerators. **Cards:** AE, CB, DI, DS, MC, VI. **Special Amenities:** Free breakfast and free local telephone calls.

SUPER 8 MOTEL   **Phone:** (505)374-8127
◆◆   4/1-9/30 & 10/1-1/31   1P: $50-$55   2P: $60-$65   XP: $6   F12
Motel   2/1-3/31   1P: $45-$50   2P: $55-$60   XP: $6   F12
           Location: US 87, 1 mi se of jct US 56 and 64. 1425 S 1st St 88415. Fax: 505/374-2598. **Terms:** [CP] meal
plan; pets, $7 extra charge. **Facility:** 31 rooms. 2 stories; interior corridors. **Cards:** AE, CB, DI, DS, MC, VI. *(See ad below)*

──────── **RESTAURANT** ────────

THE EKLUND DINING ROOM & SALOON   **Lunch:** $6-$11   **Dinner:** $8-$19   **Phone:** 505/374-2551
◆◆   **Location:** Center on US 56, just s of jct US 64 and 87. 15 Main St 88415. **Hours:** 10:30 am-9 pm. Closed:
American   11/23 & 12/25. **Reservations:** accepted. **Features:** casual dress; children's menu; carryout; cocktails &
           lounge. You can relive history in this 1892 hotel with its original saloon and historic memorabilia. The dining
room, richly decorated in Victorian style, offers the ambiance of yesteryear. Steak, burgers and homemade Mexican dishes
are featured. **Cards:** MC, VI.

CLOUDCROFT pop. 600

──────── **LODGING** ────────

THE LODGE   **Phone:** (505)682-2566
           All Year   1P: $95-$215   2P: $95-$215   XP: $10   F12
Classic Hotel **Location:** US 82, 0.3 mi s. 1 Corona Pl 88317 (PO Box 497). Fax: 505/682-2715. **Terms:** [CP] meal plan;
◆◆◆   check-in 4 pm; 14 day cancellation notice; cancellation fee imposed; package plans. **Facility:** 61 rooms. Re-
           stored hotel constructed 1899. Variety of room types. 4 suites with common area with kitchen, pavillion, $79-
           $109; 11 whirlpool rooms, $145-$225; suites, $145-$225; 3 stories, no elevator; interior corridors; heated pool,
sauna, whirlpool. Fee: 9 holes golf. **Dining:** Dining room; cocktails; afternoon tea; also, Rebecca's, see separate listing.
Services: gift shop. Fee: massage. **Recreation:** winter tubing; hiking trails, jogging, community park & playground, croquet,
horseshoes, volleyball. Fee: cross country skiing, snowmobiling; bicycles. **All Rooms:** combo or shower baths, extended cable
TV. **Some Rooms:** kitchen. **Cards:** AE, DI, JC, MC, VI. *(See ad below)*

------ RESTAURANT ------

REBECCA'S
American

Lunch: $7-$14   Dinner: $16-$31   Phone: 505/682-2566
Location: US 82, 0.3 mi s; in The Lodge. 1 Corona Pl 88317. **Hours:** 7-10:30 am, 11:30-2:30 & 5:30-10 pm; to 9 pm in winter. **Features:** casual dress; Sunday brunch; children's menu; health conscious menu; carryout; cocktails & lounge; entertainment. Located in a lovely hotel that dates back to 1899, Rebecca's wonderful stained-glass porch windows enhance the mountain views. Lunch offers sandwiches or pasta. Dinner is formal, with piano music, steaks, seafood, and well-known, tasty fruit cobbler. Smoke free premises. **Cards:** AE, CB, DI, DS, MC, VI.

CLOVIS pop. 31,000

------ LODGINGS ------

BEST WESTERN LA VISTA INN
Motel

All Year   1P: $41-$54   2P: $46-$59   XP: $4   F12
Location: 1 mi e on US 60, 70 and 84. 1516 Mabry Dr 88101. Fax: 505/762-1422. **Terms:** [CP] meal plan. **Facility:** 47 rooms. 1 story; exterior corridors; heated pool. **Dining:** Restaurant nearby. **All Rooms:** combo or shower baths, extended cable TV. **Some Rooms:** Fee: refrigerators. **Cards:** AE, CB, DI, DS, MC, VI. **Special Amenities: Free local telephone calls.**
Phone: (505)762-3808

CLOVIS INN
Motel

All Year   1P: $46   2P: $53   XP: $5   F12
Location: 1.8 mi e on US 60, 70 and 84. 2912 Mabry Dr 88101. Fax: 505/762-6803. **Terms:** [CP] meal plan. **Facility:** 97 rooms. Contemporary room appointments. Very well kept. 2 stories; exterior corridors; whirlpool. **All Rooms:** extended cable TV. **Cards:** AE, CB, DI, DS, MC, VI. **Special Amenities: Free breakfast and free local telephone calls.**
Phone: (505)762-5600

COMFORT INN
Motel

All Year   1P: $40-$45   2P: $52-$65   XP: $10   F18
Location: 1 mi e on US 60, 70 and 84. 1616 Mabry Dr 88101. Fax: 505/763-6747. **Terms:** [CP] meal plan; small pets only, in smoking rooms. **Facility:** 50 rooms. 2 stories; exterior corridors; heated pool. **Dining:** Restaurant nearby. **All Rooms:** extended cable TV. **Some Rooms:** Fee: refrigerators. **Cards:** AE, CB, DI, DS, JC, MC, VI. **Special Amenities: Early check-in/late check-out and free breakfast.**
Phone: (505)762-4591

DAYS INN
Motel

All Year   1P: $39-$45   2P: $48-$53   XP: $5   F12
Location: 1 mi e on US 60, 70 and 84. 1720 Mabry Dr 88101. Fax: 505/762-2735. **Terms:** [CP] meal plan; 7 day cancellation notice; small pets only, $6 dep req. **Facility:** 94 rooms. 1-2 stories; exterior corridors; heated pool; 1 lighted tennis court. **Some Rooms:** Fee: refrigerators. **Cards:** AE, CB, DI, DS, JC, MC, VI.
Phone: (505)762-2971

HOLIDAY INN
Motor Inn

All Year   1P: $55-$100   2P: $60-$105   XP: $5   F18
Location: 1.5 mi e on US 60, 70 and 84. 2700 Mabry Dr 88101 (PO Box 973). Fax: 505/769-0564. **Terms:** 7 day cancellation notice; small pets only. **Facility:** 120 rooms. All rooms with hair dryer, iron and ironing board. 2 stories; exterior corridors; 2 pools, 1 indoor heated; racquetball court. **All Rooms:** combo or shower baths. **Cards:** AE, CB, DI, DS, JC, MC, VI.
Phone: (505)762-4491

------ RESTAURANT ------

POOR BOY'S STEAKHOUSE
Steakhouse

Lunch: $4-$13   Dinner: $8-$18   Phone: 505/763-5222
Location: 1.5 mi n on SR 209. 2115 N Prince St 88101. **Hours:** 11 am-9 pm, Fri & Sat-10 pm. Closed: 11/23 & 12/25. **Features:** casual dress; children's menu; carryout; salad bar. You'll find traditional American cuisine at this restaurant, which offers steak, seafood, chicken, burger and sandwich selections served in a casual, family-oriented atmosphere. The salad bar has a variety of toppings, pasta and fresh fruit. **Cards:** AE, DS, MC, VI.

CORRALES pop. 5,500

------ LODGINGS ------

THE CHOCOLATE TURTLE BED & BREAKFAST
Bed & Breakfast

All Year   1P: $60-$80   2P: $80-$100   XP: $10   F13
Location: I-25, exit 233 (Alameda Blvd), w on Alameda Blvd, 4 mi to Corrales Rd, 1 mi n to Meadowlark Ln, then 2 mi w. 1098 W Meadowlark Ln 87048. Fax: 505/898-5328. **Terms:** [BP] meal plan; age restrictions may apply; check-in 4 pm; 7 day cancellation notice; cancellation fee imposed; package plans. **Facility:** 4 rooms. Territorial exterior, Southwest decor. 1 story; interior corridors; smoke free premises. **All Rooms:** combo or shower baths. **Some Rooms:** color TV. **Cards:** AE, DI, DS, MC, VI.
Phone: (505)898-1800

THE SANDHILL CRANE BED & BREAKFAST
Bed & Breakfast

All Year   1P: $90   2P: $90
Location: I-25, exit 233 (Alameda Blvd), 4 mi w on Alameda Blvd to Corralos Rd, 3 mi n on Corralos Rd, 0.5 mi w. 389 Camino Hermosa 87048. Fax: 505/898-1189. **Terms:** [BP] meal plan; check-in 4 pm; cancellation fee imposed. **Facility:** 3 rooms. Located in a small village a short drive from Albuquerque. Renovated hacienda. 1 story; interior corridors; smoke free premises. **All Rooms:** combo or shower baths. **Some Rooms:** kitchen, color TV. **Cards:** AE, MC, VI.
Phone: (505)898-2445

THE AREA'S TOP 19 TOURIST DESTINATIONS.

(IN OUR OPINION.)

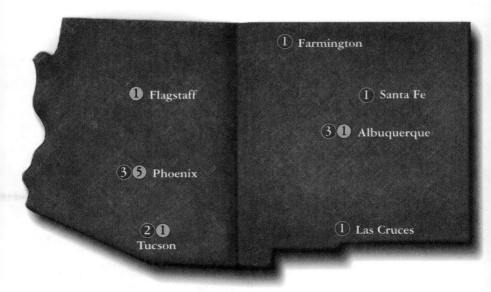

1 Farmington

1 Flagstaff

1 Santa Fe

3 1 Albuquerque

3 5 Phoenix

2 1 Tucson

1 Las Cruces

For Reservations and Information, Call

1-800-221-4731

19 LOCATIONS IN ARIZONA AND NEW MEXICO.

With so many locations in the area, AAA members can enjoy La Quinta® hospitality in all the best places.

So wherever the road takes you, you can be sure to find a relaxing place to stay, filled with all the thoughtful amenities you would expect. And more.

AAA
preferred partner
since 1987

- 100% Satisfaction Guarantee
- Guaranteed lowest rate
- 100% AAA 3 Diamond rating

- Free breakfast and local calls
- Coffee makers and 25" TVs with movies on-demand and Nintendo®
- Sparkling pools
- Inn & Suites also offer spas, fitness centers, guest laundry facilities, plus king rooms and 2-room suites with microwaves and refrigerators
- Kids 18 and under stay free with parents

www.laquinta.com

For reservations nationwide, call 1-800-221-4731

YOUR'S TRULY BED & BREAKFAST
Phone: (505)898-7027
All Year　　　　　　　1P: $98-$135　　　　2P: $98-$135　　　XP: $15　　　　D18
Bed &
Breakfast
Location: From jct SR 528 and SR 448, 1.7 mi n on Corrales Rd/SR 448, left on Meadowlark 1 mi, just right on Loma Largo. 160 Paseo de Cerrales 87048 (PO Box 2263). Fax: 505/898-9022. **Terms:** [BP] meal plan; age restrictions may apply; 3 day cancellation notice. **Facility:** 4 rooms. A contemporary adobe home sitting on hill with panoramic views of the mountains, the valleys and the city lights of Albuquerque. 1 story; interior corridors. **All Rooms:** combo or shower baths. **Cards:** AE, DI, DS, MC, VI.

DEMING pop. 11,000

─────── LODGINGS ───────

ANSELMENT'S BUTTERFIELD STAGE MOTEL
Phone: (505)544-0011
All Year　　　　　　　1P: $29-$38　　　　2P: $36-$38　　　XP: $3　　　　F12
Motel
Location: Center. 309 W Pine 88030. Fax: 505/544-0614. **Terms:** 3 day cancellation notice; small pets only. **Facility:** 13 rooms. Large rooms. 1 story; exterior corridors. **Dining:** Restaurant nearby. **Some Rooms:** efficiency. Fee: microwaves. **Cards:** AE, DS, MC, VI. **Special Amenities: Free local telephone calls and free room upgrade (subject to availability with advanced reservations).**

BEST WESTERN MIMBRES VALLEY INN
Phone: (505)546-4544
All Year　　　　　　　1P: $39-$49　　　　2P: $44-$49　　　XP: $5　　　　F12
Motel
Location: I-10, exit 81. 1500 W Pine 88030 (PO Box 1159). Fax: 505/546-9875. **Terms:** [CP] meal plan; 7 day cancellation notice; pets. **Facility:** 40 rooms. Family ambiance. 1 story; exterior corridors; heated pool. **Cards:** AE, CB, DI, JC, VI. **Special Amenities: Free breakfast and free local telephone calls.**

DAYS INN
Phone: (505)546-8813
All Year　　　　　　　1P: $36-$40　　　　2P: $40-$48　　　XP: $5　　　　F12
Motor Inn
Location: 1.3 mi e on US 70 and 80 city route and I-10 business loop. 1601 E Pine St 88030. Fax: 505/546-7095. **Terms:** [CP] meal plan; weekly & monthly rates avail; pets, $5 extra charge. **Facility:** 57 rooms. In a commercial area. 4 two-bedroom units. 2 stories; exterior corridors; heated pool. **Cards:** AE, CB, DI, DS, MC, VI. **Special Amenities: Free breakfast and free local telephone calls.**

THE DEMING MOTEL
Phone: (505)546-2737
(AAA) [SAVE]   All Year   1P: $28-$34   2P: $32-$38   XP: $4   F12
◆◆   **Location:** I-10, exit 82, 4 blks w on Motel Dr/Pine St. 500 W Pine St 88030. Fax: 505/546-8556. **Terms:** [CP]
Motel   meal plan; weekly rates only; small pets only, $3 extra charge. **Facility:** 29 rooms. Near center of town. 1 two-
bedroom unit. 2 stories; exterior corridors; small pool. **All Rooms:** combo or shower baths, extended cable TV.
Some Rooms: color TV. **Cards:** AE, DS, MC, VI. **Special Amenities:** Free local telephone calls and preferred room (subject to availability with advanced reservations).
[icons]

GRAND MOTOR INN
Phone: (505)546-2632
(AAA) [SAVE]   All Year   1P: $38   XP: $6   F13
◆◆◆   **Location:** 1.3 mi e on US 70 and 80 city route and I-10 business loop. 1721 E Spruce St 88030 (PO Box 309,
Motor Inn   88031). Fax: 505/546-4446. **Terms:** Weekly & monthly rates avail; small pets only. **Facility:** 60 rooms. 2 sto-
ries; exterior corridors; heated pool, wading pool. **Dining:** Grand Restaurant, see separate listing. **Cards:** AE,
CB, DI, DS, MC, VI. *(See color ad p 399)*
[icons]

HOLIDAY INN
Phone: (505)546-2661
◆◆◆   All Year   1P: $50-$60   2P: $50-$60   XP: $10   F18
Motor Inn   **Location:** I-10, exit 85. (PO Box 1138, 88031). Fax: 505/546-6308. **Terms:** Pets. **Facility:** 120 rooms. 2 sto-
ries; exterior corridors; heated pool. **Cards:** AE, CB, DI, DS, JC, MC, VI.
[icons]

MOTEL 6 - 285
Phone: 505/546-2623
(AAA)   5/25-1/31   1P: $34-$44   2P: $40-$50   XP: $3   F17
◆◆   2/1-5/24   1P: $32-$42   2P: $38-$48   XP: $3   F17
Motel   **Location:** I-10 and Country Club Dr. (PO Box 970, 88031). Fax: 505/546-0934. **Terms:** Small pets only.
Facility: 80 rooms. 2 stories; exterior corridors; heated pool. **All Rooms:** shower baths. **Cards:** AE, CB, DI,
DS, MC, VI.
[icons]

WAGON WHEEL MOTEL
Phone: (505)546-2681
(AAA) [SAVE]   All Year   1P: $24-$26   2P: $26-$29   XP: $3   F16
◆   **Location:** 1 mi w on US 70 and 80 city route, just e of exit 81, off I-10. 1109 W Pine St 88030.
Motel   Fax: 505/546-7020. **Terms:** Monthly rates avail; small pets only. **Facility:** 19 rooms. In a commercial area. 1
story; exterior corridors. **Dining:** Restaurant nearby. **All Rooms:** combo or shower baths. **Cards:** DS, MC, VI.
Special Amenities: Free local telephone calls and free room upgrade (subject to availability with advanced reservations).
[icons]

——— **RESTAURANTS** ———

FAT EDDIES AT THE INN   **Lunch:** $5-$8   **Dinner:** $5-$16   Phone: (505)546-2661
◆◆   **Location:** I-10, exit 85; in Holiday Inn. **Hours:** 6 am-2 & 4-9 pm, Fri & Sat-10 pm. **Features:** casual dress;
American   Sunday brunch; children's menu; carryout; salad bar; cocktails. Fat Eddie's prepares buffets every day and
offers home-style cooking as well as Italian and seafood dishes. Its dessert selection of cobblers and pie
also is good. The casual dining room within the hotel features a Southwestern motif. **Cards:** AE, CB, DI, DS, JC, MC, VI.
[icon]

GRAND RESTAURANT   **Lunch:** $5-$7   **Dinner:** $7-$15   Phone: 505/546-2632
(AAA)   **Location:** 1.3 mi e on US 70 and 80 city route and I-10 business loop; in Grand Motor Inn. 1721 E Spruce
◆◆   St 88031. **Hours:** 6 am-10 pm, 10/1-3/1 to 9 pm. **Features:** children's menu; cocktails. This locally popular
Steak and   restaurant is also attractive to visitors to the area. It features steak, seafood, homemade soups and pies,
Seafood   salad bar, authentic Mexican dishes and weekly specials in a casual, family-style setting within the hotel.
Cards: AE, DI, DS, MC, VI. *(See color ad p 399)*
[icon]

ELEPHANT BUTTE

——— **LODGING** ———

QUALITY INN
Phone: (505)744-5431
(AAA) [SAVE]   3/16-9/15   1P: $75-$80   2P: $80-$85   XP: $7   F12
◆◆◆   2/1-3/15 & 9/16-1/31   1P: $55-$60   2P: $60-$65   XP: $7   F12
Motor Inn   **Location:** I-25, exit 83, 4 mi e. SR 195 87935 (PO Box 996). Fax: 505/744-5044. **Terms:** Cancellation fee im-
MC, VI.   posed; package plans; pets, $5-$10 extra charge. **Facility:** 48 rooms. Near marina. 2 stories; exterior corridors;
heated pool; 1 tennis court. **Dining:** Restaurant; 7 am-9:30 pm; $8-$20; cocktails. **Cards:** AE, DI, DS,
[icons]

EL PRADO —See TAOS.

ESPANOLA pop. 8,400

——— **LODGINGS** ———

COMFORT INN
Phone: (505)753-2419
(AAA) [SAVE]   5/1-9/30   1P: $58-$64   2P: $64-$68   XP: $7   F18
◆◆◆   2/1-4/30 & 10/1-1/31   1P: $49-$54   2P: $54-$58   XP: $7   F18
Motel   **Location:** US 84 and 285, just s of jct SR 68. 604-B S Riverside Dr 87532. Fax: 505/753-5131. **Terms:** [CP]
meal plan; 14 day cancellation notice; pets, $5 extra charge. **Facility:** 41 rooms. 2 stories; interior corridors;
heated pool, whirlpool. **Dining:** Restaurant nearby. **All Rooms:** extended cable TV. **Cards:** AE, DI, DS,
MC, VI. **Special Amenities:** Free breakfast and free local telephone calls.
[icons]

ESPANOLA DAYS INN
Phone: (505)747-1242
	5/1-10/31	1P: $60-$75	2P: $66-$80	XP: $6	F13
	11/1-1/31	1P: $45-$60	2P: $50-$65	XP: $6	F13
	2/1-4/30	1P: $45	2P: $50	XP: $6	F13

Motel   **Location:** US 84 and 285, 0.7 mi s of jct SR 68. 807 S Riverside Dr 87532. Fax: 505/753-8089. **Facility:** 40 rooms. Contemporary room appointments. 2 stories; exterior corridors. **Dining:** Restaurant nearby. **All Rooms:** extended cable TV. **Cards:** AE, CB, DI, DS, MC, VI.   🅂🄳 🍴 ✕ 🎬

INN AT THE DELTA
Phone: (505)753-9466
◆◆◆
 Bed &   Property failed to provide current rates
Breakfast   **Location:** US 84 and 285 (Chama Hwy), 1 mi n of jct SR 68, 0.3 mi n of jct SR 30. 304 Paseo de Onate 87532. Fax: 505/753-5057. **Terms:** [BP] meal plan. **Facility:** 10 rooms. Spacious rooms individually decorated with original art work. Specially commissioned handcrafted furnishings. All rooms with kiva fireplaces. Coffee makers in rooms on request. 1-2 stories; exterior corridors. **Cards:** AE, DI, DS, MC, VI.   🍴 🆓 ✕ 🎬 📠

SUPER 8 MOTEL
Phone: (505)753-5374
	5/26-9/4	1P: $45-$95	2P: $45-$110	XP: $10	F12
	9/5-10/15	1P: $40-$85	2P: $40-$95	XP: $10	F12
	2/1-5/25 & 10/16-1/31	1P: $38-$75	2P: $38-$75	XP: $10	F12

Motel   **Location:** US 84 and 285, 0.5 mi s of jct SR 68. 811 S Riverside Dr 87532. Fax: 505/753-5339. **Terms:** [CP] meal plan. **Facility:** 48 rooms. 1-2 stories; interior corridors. **Dining:** Restaurant nearby. **All Rooms:** extended cable TV. **Cards:** AE, CB, DI, DS, MC, VI. **Special Amenities:** Free breakfast and free local telephone calls.   🍴 ✕ 🎬 DATA PORT

---------- **RESTAURANT** ----------

ANTHONY'S AT THE DELTA
Dinner: $13-$25
Phone: 505/753-4511
◆◆◆
Steak and   **Location:** US 84 and 285 (Chama Hwy), 1 mi n of jct SR 68, 0.3 mi n of jct SR 30. 228 Paseo Onate NW
Seafood   87532. **Hours:** 5 pm-10 pm; to 9 pm, 9/4-5/29. Closed: 1/1, 11/23, 12/25 & Mon. **Reservations:** suggested. **Features:** casual dress; carryout; salad bar; cocktails & lounge. Anthony's has comfortable, Colonial-style dining rooms adorned with local art, hand-carved wood accents, fresh plants and flowers. You'll enjoy their traditional preparation of quality steak, fresh seafood, as well as a good selection of vegetarian items. **Cards:** AE, DI, DS, MC, VI.   ✕

FARMINGTON pop. 34,000

---------- **LODGINGS** ----------

BEST WESTERN INN & SUITES
Phone: (505)327-5221
	5/16-10/15	1P: $79-$99	2P: $89-$109	XP: $10	F12
	2/1-5/15 & 10/16-1/31	1P: $60-$79	2P: $70-$89	XP: $10	F12

Motor Inn   **Location:** 0.8 mi e on US 64 at Bloomfield Blvd and Scott Ave. 700 Scott Ave 87401. Fax: 505/327-1565. **Terms:** Package plans; small pets only. **Facility:** 192 rooms. Atrium-style indoor recreation center. Suites with sleeper sofa and wet bar area. All rooms with hair dryer. Suites $107-$125; 3 stories; interior corridors; heated pool, saunas, whirlpool. **Dining:** Restaurant; 6-10 am, 11:30-2 & 5-10 pm, Fri & Sat-11 pm, Sun 6 am-2 & 5-10 pm; Sun brunch avail; $7-$18; cocktails. **Recreation:** video game room. **Cards:** AE, CB, DI, DS, MC, VI. **Special Amenities:** Free breakfast and preferred room (subject to availability with advanced reservations). *(See color ad below)*
🅂🄳 🐾 🍴 🍸 🆓 ♿ 🏊 ✕ 🎬 📠 💻 🛅 🎒 🦽

THE CASA BLANCA INN
Phone: (505)327-6503
◆◆◆
	All Year	1P: $68-$128	2P: $68-$128	XP: $15	F3

Bed &   **Location:** US 550, just n on Butler, just w. 505 E LaPlata St 87401. Fax: 505/326-5680. **Terms:** [BP] meal plan;
Breakfast   check-in 4 pm; 7 day cancellation notice; package plans. **Facility:** 6 rooms. 1950s mission-style home perched on a bluff overlooking the community and surrounding cliffs. Tastefully decorated rooms with some charming details. 2 stories; interior corridors; smoke free premises. **All Rooms:** combo or shower baths. **Cards:** AE, DS, MC, VI.   ASK 🆓 🆓 ✕ VCR 📠

COMFORT INN

AAA SAVE
◆◆◆
Motel

All Year — 1P: $50-$64 — 2P: $56-$70

Phone: (505)325-262x
XP: $6
F
[C

Location: 0.8 mi e on US 64 (Bloomfield Blvd), just n. 555 Scott Ave 87401. Fax: 505/325-7675. **Terms:** [C meal plan; pets, $5 extra charge. **Facility:** 60 rooms. Very nice looking rooms. 2 stories; interior corrido heated pool. **Dining:** Restaurant nearby. **Cards:** AE, CB, DI, DS, JC, MC, VI. **Special Amenities:** Free brea fast and free local telephone calls.

FARMINGTON EAST SUPER 8 MOTEL

◆◆◆
Motel

4/1-1/31 — 1P: $50 — 2P: $54-$58 — XP: $4 — F
2/1-3/31 — 1P: $45 — 2P: $49-$53 — XP: $4 — F

Location: US 550 at jct Cortez Way. 4751 Cortez Way 87402. Fax: 505/564-8103. **Terms:** [CP] meal pla cancellation fee imposed. **Facility:** 67 rooms. Nice looking newer rooms in commercial/shopping area. 3 stories; interior ce ridors; heated pool. **All Rooms:** combo or shower baths. **Cards:** AE, CB, DI, DS, MC, VI.

HOLIDAY INN EXPRESS

◆◆◆
Motel

2/1-2/29 — 1P: $69 — 2P: $75 — XP: $6 — F
3/1-1/31 & 9/6-1/31 — 1P: $62 — 2P: $68 — XP: $6 — F
5/21-9/5 — 1P: $59 — 2P: $65 — XP: $6 — F

Location: 1.6 mi e on US 64. 2110 Bloomfield Blvd 87401. Fax: 505/325-3262. **Terms:** [CP] meal plan; pets, $50 dep re **Facility:** 66 rooms. Some rooms with extra sleeper sofa. 3 stories; interior corridors; heated pool. **All Rooms:** combo shower baths. **Cards:** AE, CB, DI, DS, JC, MC, VI.

HOLIDAY INN OF FARMINGTON

◆◆◆
Motor Inn

5/25-9/5 — 1P: $75 — 2P: $81 — XP: $6 — F
2/1-5/24 — 1P: $65-$69 — 2P: $71-$75 — XP: $6 — F
9/6-10/31 — 1P: $69 — 2P: $75 — XP: $6 — F
11/1-1/31 — 1P: $71 — 2P: $71 — XP: $6 — F

Location: 0.8 mi e on US 64 at Bloomfield Blvd and Scott Ave. 600 E Broadway 87401. Fax: 505/325-228 **Terms:** Package plans; pets, $50 dep req. **Facility:** 149 rooms. All rooms with hair dryer. 2 stories; interior corridors; heate pool. **Cards:** AE, CB, DI, DS, JC, MC, VI.

KNIGHT'S INN

AAA SAVE
◆
Motel

All Year Wkly — 1P: $27-$32 — 2P: $29-$35

Phone: (505)325-506x
XP: $5
F

Location: 0.5 mi n from US 550 (Main St), just e of jct US 550 and 64. 701 Airport Dr 8740 Fax: 505/325-5061. **Facility:** 21 rooms. Set back from the road at the base of a small mesa. 1 story; exterix corridors. **All Rooms:** extended cable TV. **Cards:** AE, DS, MC, VI. **Special Amenities:** Free local telephor calls.

LA QUINTA INN

◆◆◆
Motel

All Year — 1P: $69-$89 — 2P: $69-$89

Phone: (505)327-470C

Location: 0.8 mi e on US 64 at Bloomfield Blvd and Scott Ave. 675 Scott Ave 87401. Fax: 505/325-658 **Terms:** [CP] meal plan; small pets only. **Facility:** 106 rooms. 2 rooms with interior hall entrance, upstairs fro lobby. Contemporary room decor. 2 stories; exterior corridors; heated pool. **Some Rooms:** Fee: refrigerators. **Cards:** AE, CB DI, DS, MC, VI.

RAMADA INN

◆◆◆
Motor Inn

4/1-9/30 — 1P: $69-$74 — 2P: $69-$74 — XP: $10 — F1
2/1-3/31 & 10/1-1/31 — 1P: $65-$70 — 2P: $65-$70 — XP: $10 — F1

Phone: (505)325-119x

Location: 0.8 mi e on US 64 at Bloomfield Blvd and Scott Ave. 601 E Broadway 87401. Fax: 505/325-122x **Facility:** 75 rooms. Sharp looking rooms in newer facility. 3 stories; interior corridors; heated pool. **Services:** gift shop; are transportation. **All Rooms:** combo or shower baths. **Cards:** AE, CB, DI, DS, JC, MC, VI.

SUPER 8 MOTEL

AAA [SAVE]
◆◆
Motel

	6/1-9/30	1P: $48-$54	2P: $58-$64	XP: $6	F12
	4/1-5/31	1P: $46-$50	2P: $56-$60	XP: $10	F12
	2/1-3/31 & 10/1-1/31	1P: $40-$42	2P: $45-$52	XP: $6	F12

Phone: (505)325-1813

Location: Just n of jct SR 44. 1601 E Broadway 87401. Fax: 505/325-1813. **Terms:** [CP] meal plan; 3 day cancellation notice; cancellation fee imposed; pets, $5 extra charge. **Facility:** 60 rooms. Whirlpool room; suites, $80-$90; 3 stories; interior corridors. **Recreation:** game room. Fee: health club privileges. **All Rooms:** combo or shower baths, extended cable TV. **Cards:** AE, MC, VI. **Special Amenities:** Free breakfast and free local telephone calls.

TRAVELODGE

AAA [SAVE]
◆
Motel

All Year   1P: $39-$59   2P: $45-$65   XP: $5   F11

Phone: (505)327-0242

Location: 1.1 mi e on US 64 past intersection of Bloomfield Blvd and Scott Ave. 510 Scott Ave 87401. Fax: 505/327-5617. **Terms:** [CP] meal plan; 3 day cancellation notice. **Facility:** 98 rooms. 3 stories; exterior corridors; heated pool. **All Rooms:** extended cable TV. Fee: refrigerators, microwaves. **Cards:** AE, DI, DS, JC, MC, VI. **Special Amenities:** Free breakfast and free local telephone calls.

(See ad p 402)

─── RESTAURANT ───

K B DILLON'S

◆◆
American

Lunch: $5-$10   Dinner: $14-$25   Phone: 505/325-0222

Location: Downtown on US 64. 101 W Broadway 87401. **Hours:** 11 am-10 pm, Sat 5 pm-10 pm. Closed major holidays & Sun. **Reservations:** accepted. **Features:** casual dress; carryout; cocktails & lounge. You'll find that this restaurant has rustic surroundings on the outside, and a cozy and warm atmosphere on the inside. Their menu offers steak, poultry, fish and veal choices with several seafood selections as well. Save room for dessert. **Cards:** AE, MC, VI.

GALISTEO

─── LODGING ───

THE GALISTEO INN

◆◆◆
Historic
Country Inn

All Year   1P: $75-$190   2P: $115-$190   XP: $25

Phone: (505)466-4000

Location: SR 41, La Vega St exit. 9 La Vega St 87540 (HC 75, Box 4). Fax: 505/466-4008. **Terms:** [BP] meal plan; age restrictions may apply; check-in 4 pm; 14 day cancellation notice; cancellation fee imposed; 2 night min stay, 5/1-10/31. **Facility:** 12 rooms. Tranquil setting of the 250 year old hacienda. 1 story; exterior corridors; smoke free premises; heated pool. **Services:** Fee: massage. **Recreation:** bicycles. Fee: horseback riding. **Some Rooms:** color TV. **Cards:** DS, MC, VI.

GALLUP pop. 19,200

─── LODGINGS ───

AMBASSADOR MOTEL

AAA
◆
Motel

All Year   1P: $25   2P: $31   XP: $35   F5

Phone: 505/722-3843

Location: I-40, exit 20, 0.5 mi s to US 66, just w. 1601 W Hwy 66 87301. **Terms:** Small pets only. **Facility:** 45 rooms. Well-kept 1950s motel. 1-2 stories; exterior corridors; heated pool; playground. **All Rooms:** shower baths, extended cable TV. **Cards:** AE, CB, DI, DS, MC, VI.

BEST WESTERN INN & SUITES

AAA [SAVE]
◆◆◆
Motor Inn

	5/1-10/31	1P: $69-$89	2P: $79-$99	XP: $10	F12
	2/1-4/30	1P: $49-$69	2P: $59-$79	XP: $10	F12
	11/1-1/31	1P: $49-$64	2P: $59-$79	XP: $10	F12

Phone: (505)722-2221

Location: I-40, exit 16, 1 mi e. 3009 US 66 W 87301. Fax: 505/722-7442. **Terms:** [BP] meal plan; small pets only. **Facility:** 126 rooms. Spacious rooms well-appointed with a Western flair. Large, indoor recreation area trimmed with live plants and water fountains. 22 suites with king bed, wet bar, mini-fridge & microwave $72-$105; 2 stories; interior corridors; heated pool, sauna, whirlpool. **Dining:** Restaurant; 6 am-10 & 5-9:30 pm, Fri & Sat-10 pm; $7-$17; cocktails. **Services:** gift shop. **Recreation:** game room. **All Rooms:** extended cable TV. **Cards:** AE, DI, DS, MC, VI. **Special Amenities:** Free breakfast and preferred room (subject to availability with advanced reservations).

(See color ad below)

BEST WESTERN RED ROCK INN

AAA SAVE

◆◆◆
Motel

| 5/1-10/31 | 1P: $55-$129 | 2P: $60-$149 | XP: $7 | F12 |
| 2/1-4/30 & 11/1-1/31 | 1P: $45-$109 | 2P: $50-$129 | XP: $7 | F12 |

Location: I-40, exit 26, 1 mi w on US 66. 3010 US 66 E 87301. Fax: 505/722-9770. **Terms:** [CP] meal plan; cancellation fee imposed. **Facility:** 77 rooms. Some with balcony and view of surrounding red mesas. 4 whirlpool rms, $125; 2 stories; interior corridors; heated pool, sauna, whirlpool. **Dining:** Restaurant nearby. **All Rooms:** extended cable TV. **Some Rooms:** Fee: VCR. **Cards:** AE, CB, DI, DS, JC, MC, VI. **Special Amenities:** Early check-in/late check-out and free breakfast.

Phone: (505)722-7600

🔟 🛏 🍴 ⊛ ⛱ 🐕 ✕ 🎿 VCR 🖨 📠 🛏 🔌 🏊 ♿

BEST WESTERN ROYAL HOLIDAY MOTEL

AAA SAVE

◆◆◆
Motel

| 5/1-10/31 | 1P: $55-$129 | 2P: $60-$149 | XP: $7 | F12 |
| 2/1-4/30 & 11/1-1/31 | 1P: $45-$99 | 2P: $50-$109 | XP: $7 | F12 |

Location: I-40, exit 20, 0.5 mi s to US 66, 0.8 mi w. 1903 US 66W 87301. Fax: 505/863-9952. **Terms:** [CP] meal plan; small pets only. **Facility:** 50 rooms. Nice rooms in close proximity to train activity. 4 two-bedroom units. 2 stories; interior/exterior corridors; heated pool, sauna, whirlpool. **Dining:** Restaurant nearby. **All Rooms:** extended cable TV. **Cards:** AE, CB, DI, DS, MC, VI. **Special Amenities:** Early check-in/late check-out and free breakfast.

Phone: (505)722-4900

🛏 🍴 ✕ 🎿 🖨 📠 🛏 🔌 🏊

BLUE SPRUCE LODGE

AAA SAVE

◆
Motel

| All Year | 1P: $24-$28 | 2P: $26-$32 | XP: $3 | F12 |

Location: I-40, exit 22, just s to US 66, then just e. 1119 US 66E 87301. Fax: 505/863-6104. **Terms:** 3 day cancellation notice; small pets only, $10 dep req, in designated rooms. **Facility:** 20 rooms. Older motor court with basic exterior, some rooms with modern improvements. 6 two-bedroom units. 1 story; exterior corridors. **Dining:** Restaurant nearby. **All Rooms:** combo or shower baths, extended cable TV. **Cards:** AE, DI, DS, MC, VI. **Special Amenities:** Free local telephone calls and preferred room (subject to availability with advanced reservations).

Phone: (505)863-5211

🔟 🛏 🍴 ✕ 🎿 🔌

BUDGET INN

AAA SAVE

◆
Motel

| 5/1-10/31 | 1P: $26-$36 | 2P: $34-$49 | XP: $9 | D12 |
| 2/1-4/30 & 11/1-1/31 | 1P: $20-$30 | 2P: $25-$40 | XP: $5 | D12 |

Location: I-40, exit 16, 0.8 mi e. 3150 US 66 W 87301. **Terms:** Pets, limited rooms. **Facility:** 40 rooms. Decent economy rooms. 2 stories; exterior corridors. **All Rooms:** extended cable TV. **Cards:** AE, DS, MC, VI. **Special Amenities:** Free local telephone calls and preferred room (subject to availability with advanced reservations).

Phone: (505)722-6631

🔟 🛏 ✕

COMFORT INN

AAA SAVE

◆◆◆
Motel

| All Year | 1P: $46-$59 | 2P: $50-$62 | XP: $6 | F18 |

Location: I-40, exit 16, 0.3 mi e. 3208 US 66 W 87301 (PO Box 219, 87305). Fax: 505/722-2404. **Terms:** [CP] meal plan; pets, $5 extra charge. **Facility:** 51 rooms. Adobe-style exterior. Good-sized rooms with some Southwestern touches. 2 stories; interior corridors; heated pool. **Dining:** Restaurant nearby. **All Rooms:** extended cable TV. **Some Rooms:** Fee: refrigerators, microwaves. **Cards:** AE, CB, DI, DS, JC, MC, VI. **Special Amenities:** Free breakfast and free local telephone calls.

Phone: (505)722-0982

🔟 🛏 🍴 ⊛ ✕ 🎿 🖨 📠 🛏 🔌 🏊

DAYS INN EAST

AAA SAVE

◆◆
Motel

| 5/1-8/31 | 1P: $45-$55 | 2P: $50-$60 | XP: $5 | F18 |
| 2/1-4/30 & 9/1-1/31 | 1P: $30-$40 | 2P: $40-$50 | XP: $5 | F18 |

Location: I-40, exit 20, 0.5 mi s to US 66, just w. 1603 W Hwy 66 87301. Fax: 505/863-3891. **Terms:** [CP] meal plan; small pets only, $5 extra charge. **Facility:** 78 rooms. Large rooms, modern furnishings. Paved RV/truck parking adjacent. 2 stories; exterior corridors; heated pool; playground. **All Rooms:** extended cable TV. **Cards:** AE, DS, MC, VI. *(See ad below)*

Phone: (505)863-3891

🔟 🛏 ⛱ ✕ 🎿 🛏 🏊 ✕

DAYS INN WEST
Phone: (505)863-6889
AAA SAVE
5/1-8/31 & 9/1-1/31   1P: $45-$55   2P: $50-$65   XP: $5   F18
2/1-4/30 & 9/1-1/31   1P: $35-$45   2P: $40-$50   XP: $5   F18
◆◆◆
Motel   **Location:** I-40, exit 16, 0.3 mi e. 3201 W Hwy 66 87301. **Fax:** 505/863-6889. **Terms:** [CP] meal plan; pets, $5 extra charge. **Facility:** 74 rooms. Paved RV/truck parking adjacent. Whirlpool room; 2 stories; exterior corridors; heated pool, whirlpool. **Dining:** Restaurant nearby. **All Rooms:** extended cable TV. **Cards:** AE, DS, MC, VI. *(See ad p 404)*

ECONO LODGE GALLUP INN
Phone: (505)722-3800
◆◆
5/1-10/31   1P: $44-$99   2P: $49-$109   XP: $7   F12
Motel   2/1-4/30 & 11/1-1/31   1P: $34-$79   2P: $39-$89   XP: $7   F12
Location: I-40, exit 16, 0.8 mi e. 3101 US 66 W 87301. **Terms:** Pets, $10 dep req. **Facility:** 51 rooms. Well kept rooms off wide corridors. 2 stories; interior corridors. **Cards:** AE, CB, DI, DS, MC, VI.

ECONOMY INN
Phone: (505)863-9301
AAA SAVE
All Year   1P: $20-$25   2P: $25-$29   XP: $5   F12
◆
Motel   **Location:** I-40, exit 20, s to US 66, 0.5 mi w. 1709 US 66 W 87301. **Fax:** 505/722-9112. **Terms:** Weekly rates avail; cancellation fee imposed; small pets only. **Facility:** 50 rooms. 2 two-bedroom units. 1-2 stories; exterior corridors. **Dining:** Restaurant nearby. **All Rooms:** combo or shower baths. **Cards:** AE, DS, MC, VI. **Special Amenities:** Free local telephone calls and preferred room (subject to availability with advanced reservations).

EL CAPITAN MOTEL
Phone: 505/863-6828
AAA SAVE
5/1-10/31   1P: $25-$29   2P: $30-$35   XP: $3   F10
2/1-4/30 & 11/1-1/31   1P: $20-$24   2P: $26-$32   XP: $3   F10
◆
Motel   **Location:** I-40, exit 22, just s to US 66. 1300 US 66 E 87301. **Fax:** 505/722-7580. **Terms:** Small pets only, $5 fee. **Facility:** 42 rooms. Older-style motel with updated room decor. 2 two-bedroom units, 3 three-bedroom units. 1 story; exterior corridors. **Dining:** Restaurant nearby. **All Rooms:** extended cable TV. **Cards:** AE, DI, DS, MC, VI.

GALLUP TRAVELODGE
Phone: (505)722-2100
AAA SAVE
5/1-8/31 & 9/1-1/31   1P: $35-$55   2P: $50-$60   XP: $5   F18
2/1-4/30 & 9/1-1/31   1P: $35-$45   2P: $35-$50   XP: $5   F18
◆◆◆
Motel   **Location:** I-40, exit 16, just e. 3275 US 66 W 87301. **Fax:** 505/722-2100. **Terms:** [CP] meal plan; pets, $5 extra charge. **Facility:** 50 rooms. Nicely appointed rooms. 2 stories; interior corridors; heated pool, whirlpool. **Dining:** Restaurant nearby. **All Rooms:** combo or shower baths, extended cable TV. **Cards:** AE, DS, MC, VI. *(See ad below)*

HOLIDAY INN EXPRESS-GALLUP
Phone: (505)726-1000
AAA SAVE
5/1-10/31   1P: $70-$140   2P: $80-$150   XP: $9   F12
2/1-4/30 & 11/1-1/31   1P: $60-$100   2P: $70-$110   XP: $9   F12
◆◆◆
Motel   **Location:** I-40, exit 20, just n on Munoz Dr, just w. 1500 W Maloney Ave 87301. **Fax:** 505/722-4954. **Terms:** [CP] meal plan; small pets only. **Facility:** 70 rooms. Tastefully appointed rooms within walking distance to shopping mall. 5 whirlpool rooms, $70-$150; 2 stories; interior/exterior corridors; heated pool, sauna, whirlpool. **Dining:** Restaurant nearby. **All Rooms:** combo or shower baths. **Cards:** AE, CB, DI, DS, MC, VI. **Special Amenities:** Early check-in/late check-out and free breakfast.

HOLIDAY INN HOLIDOME
Phone: (505)722-2201

AAA [SAVE]
◆◆◆
Motor Inn

5/28-8/26	1P: $65-$87	2P: $70-$105	XP: $5	F18
2/1-5/27 & 8/27-10/31	1P: $56-$72	2P: $61-$82	XP: $5	F18
11/1-1/31	1P: $54-$70	2P: $59-$75	XP: $5	F18

Location: I-40, exit 16, s to US 66, then 1 mi e. 2915 US 66 W 87301. **Fax:** 505/722-9616. **Terms:** [BP] meal plan; weekly & monthly rates avail; pets. **Facility:** 212 rooms. Nicely decorated spacious rooms and facility. 2 stories; interior/exterior corridors; putting green; heated pool, sauna, whirlpool. **Dining:** 2 restaurants; 6 am-10 pm; $10-$16; cocktails. **Services:** gift shop; area transportation, train & bus station. **Recreation:** game room, ping pong, pool table. **All Rooms:** extended cable TV. **Cards:** AE, CB, DI, DS, JC, MC, VI. **Special Amenities:** Free breakfast and free local telephone calls.

MICROTEL INN
Phone: (505)722-2600

AAA [SAVE]
◆◆
Motel

5/1-10/31	1P: $29-$40	2P: $38-$55	XP: $9	F12
2/1-4/30 & 11/1-1/31	1P: $26-$40	2P: $33-$55	XP: $9	F12

Location: I-40, exit 16, just e. 3270 US 66 W 87301. **Fax:** 505/726-2444. **Facility:** 53 rooms. Effective use of space in rooms. 2 stories; interior corridors. **Dining:** Restaurant nearby. **All Rooms:** combo or shower baths, extended cable TV. **Cards:** AE, DS, MC, VI. **Special Amenities:** Free local telephone calls and preferred room (subject to availability with advanced reservations).

RED ROOF INN
Phone: (505)722-7765

AAA [SAVE]
◆◆
Motel

All Year	1P: $29-$49	2P: $36-$56	XP: $4	F18

Location: I-40, exit 16, just se. 3304 W Hwy 66 87301. **Fax:** 505/722-4752. **Terms:** Cancellation fee imposed. **Facility:** 105 rooms. Paved truck/RV parking adjacent. 4 suites with separate living room, wet bar, & mini-fridge, 5/15-10/15 $51-$75; 10/16-4/30, $43-$62; 2 stories; exterior corridors; heated pool, whirlpool. **All Rooms:** extended cable TV. **Cards:** AE, DI, DS, MC, VI. **Special Amenities:** Early check-in/late check-out and free local telephone calls.

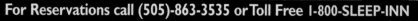

OAD RUNNER MOTEL Phone: 505/863-3804
All Year   1P: $26-$32   2P: $32-$36   XP: $4   F12
Location: I-40, exit 26, 1 mi w o. 3012 Hwy 66 E 87301. Fax: 505/863-3805. **Terms:** 3 day cancellation notice; cancellation fee imposed; small pets only, $20 dep req. **Facility:** 31 rooms. 1960s style motor court; odest rooms. Vintage exterior signage adds a Route 66 feel. 2 stories; exterior corridors; small heated pool. **Services:** gift op. **Some Rooms:** Fee: refrigerators. **Cards:** AE, CB, DI, DS, MC, VI.

OSEWAY INN Phone: (505)863-9385
All Year   1P: $29-$39   2P: $35-$39   XP: $3   F12
Location: I-40, exit 20, 1 mi w. 2003 US 66 W 87301. Fax: 505/863-6532. **Terms:** Weekly & monthly rates avail; 3 day cancellation notice; pets, $20 dep req. **Facility:** 92 rooms. Good sized rooms, very basic decor. 2 stories; interior corridors; heated pool, sauna, whirlpool. **Dining:** Restaurant, coffee shop; 6 am-10 pm; $5-$9; cocktails. **Cards:** AE, DI, DS, JC, MC, VI. **Special Amenities:** Early check-in/late check-out and free local lephone calls. *(See color ad p 406)*

LEEP INN Phone: (505)863-3535
6/1-10/31   1P: $53-$60   2P: $60-$65   XP: $5   F
2/1-5/31 & 11/1-1/31   1P: $45-$50   2P: $50-$65   XP: $5   F
Location: I-40, exit 26, just e. 3820 E US 66 87301. Fax: 505/722-3737. **Terms:** [CP] meal plan; pets, $5 extra charge, $150 dep req. **Facility:** 61 rooms. Compact modern rooms. 2 stories; interior corridors; heated pool, whirlpool. **Dining:** Restaurant nearby. **All Rooms:** combo or shower baths, extended cable TV. me **Rooms:** Fee: refrigerators, microwaves. **Cards:** AE, DI, DS, MC, VI. **Special Amenities:** Free breakfast and free local lephone calls. *(See color ad p 406)*

UPER 8 MOTEL Phone: (505)722-5300
5/1-1/31   1P: $46-$53   2P: $48-$56   XP: $7   F12
2/1-4/30   1P: $41-$48   2P: $45-$52   XP: $7   F12
Location: I-40, exit 20, s to US 66, 0.5 mi w. 1715 US 66 W 87301. Fax: 505/722-5300. **Terms:** [CP] meal plan; 3 day cancellation notice. **Facility:** 75 rooms. Budget oriented, with limited amenities and facilities. 2 stories; interior corridors; heated pool, sauna, whirlpool. **Dining:** Restaurant nearby. **All Rooms:** extended cable V. **Cards:** AE, CB, DI, DS, MC, VI. **Special Amenities:** Early check-in/late check-out and free breakfast.

--- **RESTAURANTS** ---

ARL'S FAMILY RESTAURANT   **Lunch:** $4-$8   **Dinner:** $6-$10   Phone: 505/863-4201
Location: I-40, exit 22, just s to US 66, then e. 1400 E Hwy 66 87301. **Hours:** 6 am-9:30 pm, Sun from 7 am. Closed major holidays. **Reservations:** accepted. **Features:** casual dress; children's menu; carryout; salad bar. You'll feel like you're one of the family at Earl's, which has served customers since 1947. It has a bustling atmosphere, and a menu that offers Mexican favorites as well as standard American fare such as steaks, burgers, liver and onions, homemade pies. **Cards:** AE, MC, VI.
merican

L SOMBRERO   **Lunch:** $5-$14   **Dinner:** $5-$14   Phone: 505/863-4554
Location: I-40, exit 20, just w. 1201 US 66 W 87301. **Hours:** 7 am-11 pm. Closed: 1/1, 11/23 & 12/25.
outhwest **Features:** casual dress; children's menu; carryout; beer & wine only; a la carte. You'll appreciate the decor exican of this restaurant, which is reminiscent of old U.S. Route 66—with an added Southwestern flair. American dishes are available, but the number-K41one seller is the sombrero special, and the stuffed sopaipilla is a ose second. **Cards:** MC, VI.

NG DRAGON   **Lunch:** $5-$10   **Dinner:** $7-$10   Phone: 505/863-6300
Location: I-40, exit 20, just n; in American Heritage Shopping Center. 828 N Hwy 66 87301. **Hours:** 11 am-9 pm, Fri & Sat-10 pm. Closed: 11/23 & 12/25. **Features:** casual dress; children's menu; carryout; beer & hinese wine only. Specializing in Mandarin, Szechwan and Hunan favorites with a selection of beef, pork and icken and a good choice of soups, this restaurant also offers a popular buffet at lunch. They serve up large portions, fresh egetables and tasty dishes. **Cards:** AE, DI, DS, MC, VI.

HE RANCH KITCHEN   **Lunch:** $5-$8   **Dinner:** $7-$15   Phone: 505/722-2537
Location: I-40, exit 16, 1 mi se. 3001 US 66 W 87301. **Hours:** 7 am-10 pm; to 9 pm 10/1-3/31. Closed: 4/23 & 12/25. **Reservations:** accepted. **Features:** casual dress; children's menu; carryout; beer & wine only. Serving the area for more than 40 years, the Ranch Kitchen features American and Mexican food in a merican Southwestern atmosphere. The "Navajo tacos" with fried bread and mild or spicy chili are a perennial favorite. Steaks are prepared on a pit barbecue. **Cards:** AE, DI, DS, MC, VI.

GLENWOOD pop. 300

--- **LODGING** ---

OS OLMOS GUEST RANCH Phone: 505/539-2311
All Year   1P: $60-$78   2P: $72-$103   XP: $18
istoric **Location:** US 180. 1 Los Olmos Rd 88039 (PO Box 127). Fax: 505/539-2312. **Terms:** [BP] meal plan; 4 day ottage cancellation notice; small pets only, $5 extra charge. **Facility:** 13 rooms. Stone cottages. Advance reservations required 12/1-2/28. 2 two-bedroom units. 1 story; exterior corridors; smoke free premises; playground. ervices: gift shop. **Recreation:** fishing; hiking trails. Fee: horseback riding. **All Rooms:** combo or shower baths. ards: AE, DS, MC, VI.

GRANTS pop. 8,600

―――― LODGINGS ――――

BEST WESTERN INN & SUITES OF GRANTS   **Phone:** (505)287-79⬛
AAA SAVE
◆◆◆   5/21-10/20   1P: $59-$79   2P: $69-$89   XP: $10   F
Motor Inn   2/1-5/20 & 10/21-1/31   1P: $39-$59   2P: $49-$69   XP: $10   F
Location: I-40, exit 85. 1501 E Santa Fe Ave 87020. Fax: 505/285-5751. **Terms:** [BP] meal plan; small pe
only. **Facility:** 126 rooms. Suites with kitchenettes $70-$97, extra person $10; 2 stories; interior corrido⬛
heated pool, sauna, whirlpool. **Dining:** Dining room, coffee shop; 6 am-9 & 5-9 pm; $7-$16; cocktai
Services: gift shop. **Recreation:** indoor recreation area. **All Rooms:** extended cable TV. **Cards:** AE, CB, DI, DS, MC, ⬛
Special Amenities: Free breakfast and preferred room (subject to availability with advanced reservations).
(See color ad below)

DAYS INN   **Phone:** (505)287-88⬛
AAA SAVE
◆◆◆   2/1-10/31   1P: $50-$70   2P: $60-$90   XP: $10   F
Motel   11/1-1/31   1P: $50-$60   2P: $60-$80   XP: $10   F
Location: I-40, exit 85, 0.3 mi n of e interchange. 1504 E Santa Fe Ave 87020 (PO Box 29). Fax: 505/287-777⬛
Terms: [CP] meal plan; pets. **Facility:** 55 rooms. In a commerical area. Contemporary room decor. 2 stories; e⬛
terior corridors. **Dining:** Restaurant nearby. **All Rooms:** extended cable TV. **Cards:** AE, DI, DS, MC, ⬛
Special Amenities: Free breakfast and free local telephone calls. *(See color ad below)*

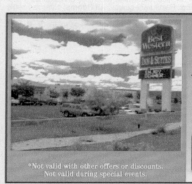

GRANTS TRAVELODGE

(AAA) (SAVE)
◆◆◆
Motel

			Phone: (505)287-7800
5/1-8/31	1P: $35-$55	2P: $50-$60	XP: $5 F18
2/1-4/30 & 9/1-1/31	1P: $35-$45	2P: $35-$50	XP: $5 F18

Location: I-40, exit 85. 1608 E Santa Fe Ave 87020. Fax: 505/287-7800. **Terms:** [CP] meal plan; pets, $5 fee. **Facility:** 60 rooms. Well appointed rooms. 2 stories; exterior corridors; heated pool, whirlpool. **Dining:** Restaurant nearby. **All Rooms:** combo or shower baths, extended cable TV. **Cards:** AE, DS, MC, VI. *(See ad below)*

HOLIDAY INN EXPRESS

(AAA) (SAVE)
◆◆◆
Motel

			Phone: (505)285-4676
3/1-10/31	1P: $59-$69	2P: $69-$79	XP: $10 F19
11/1-1/31	1P: $49-$59	2P: $59-$69	XP: $10 F19
2/1-2/29	1P: $49-$59	2P: $54-$69	XP: $10 F19

Location: I-40, exit 85, 0.3 mi n of e interchange. 1496 E Sante Fe Ave 87020 (PO Box 29). Fax: 505/285-6998. **Terms:** [CP] meal plan; 7 day cancellation notice; small pets only. **Facility:** 58 rooms. Contemporary room decor. Large rooms. 2 stories; interior/exterior corridors; heated pool, whirlpool. **Dining:** Restaurant nearby. **All Rooms:** extended cable TV. **Cards:** AE, CB, DI, DS, MC, VI. **Special Amenities:** Free breakfast and free local telephone calls. *(See color ad below)*

LEISURE LODGE

(AAA) SAVE

◆◆
Motel

| All Year | 1P: $28 | 2P: $32 | XP: $4 | F |

Phone: (505)287-2991

Location: I-40, exit 85, 0.8 mi w on Business Loop 40. 1204 E Santa Fe Ave 87020. **Terms:** Cancellation fee imposed; small pets only. **Facility:** 32 rooms. Modest rooms between downtown and interstate. 2 stories; exterior corridors; heated pool. **Dining:** Restaurant nearby. **All Rooms:** combo or shower baths, extended cable TV. **Cards:** AE, DS, MC, VI. **Special Amenities:** Free local telephone calls.

SANDS MOTEL

(AAA) SAVE

◆◆
Motel

| All Year | 1P: $35-$40 | 2P: $42-$50 | XP: $4 | F18 |

Phone: (505)287-2996

Location: I-40, exit 85, 1.5 mi w on Business Loop 40. 112 McArthur St 87020 (PO Box 1437). Fax: 505/287-2107. **Terms:** [CP] meal plan; pets, $10 extra charge. **Facility:** 24 rooms. A well kept and maintained property. 1 story; exterior corridors. **All Rooms:** extended cable TV. **Cards:** AE, CB, DI, DS, MC, VI. **Special Amenities:** Free breakfast and free local telephone calls.

─────── *The following lodging was either not inspected or did not* ───────
meet AAA rating requirements but is listed for your information only.

COMFORT INN

[fyi]

Motel

| 5/1-9/30 | 1P: $55 | 2P: $65 | XP: $5 |
| 2/1-4/30 & 10/1-1/31 | 1P: $50 | 2P: $55 | XP: $5 |

Phone: 505/797-9347

Too new to rate, opening scheduled for May 1999. **Location:** I-40, exit 85. 1551 E Santa Fe Ave 87020. **Terms:** [CP] meal plan. **Amenities:** 51 rooms, pets, coffeemakers, microwaves, refrigerators, pool. **Cards:** AE, CB, DI, DS, MC, VI.

─────── **RESTAURANTS** ───────

4 B'S RESTAURANT

(AAA)
◆
Southwest
American

| Lunch: $4-$11 | Dinner: $4-$11 | Phone: 505/285-6697 |

Location: I-40, exit 85, 0.3 mi n. 1516 Santa Fe Ave 87020. **Hours:** 24 hrs. Closed: 11/23 & 12/25. **Features:** casual dress; children's menu; senior's menu; carryout; salad bar. **Cards:** AE, DI, DS, MC, VI.

GRANTS STATION RESTAURANT

(AAA)
◆
Southwest
American

| Lunch: $6-$10 | Dinner: $6-$10 | Phone: 505/287-2334 |

Location: I-40, exit 85, 2 mi n. 200 W Santa Fe Ave 87020. **Hours:** 6 am-10 pm. Closed: 12/25. **Features:** casual dress; Sunday brunch; children's menu; carryout; salad bar; a la carte. Train travel and antiques predominate at this restaurant offering casual dining and American and Mexican food. You may want to try the burrito grande or the fajitas, which will be served sizzling hot by a friendly server. Breakfast is served all day. **Cards:** AE, DI, DS, MC, VI.

HOUSE OF PANCAKES

(AAA)
◆
American

| Lunch: $4-$8 | Dinner: $4-$8 | Phone: 505/287-2946 |

Location: I-40, exit 85, just n of exit. 1508 E Santa Fe Ave 87020. **Hours:** 5:30 am-10 pm, to 9 pm in winter. **Features:** casual dress; children's menu; carryout. You'll discover traditional fare and attentive service at the House of Pancakes. Expect to have a hard time deciding between breakfast offerings and lunch and dinner items. Try the Mexican combo plate with mild red-chili sauce—it's tasty. **Cards:** DI, MC, VI.

HERNANDEZ

─────── **LODGING** ───────

CASA DEL RIO

(AAA)
◆◆◆
Bed &
Breakfast

| All Year | 1P: $95-$125 | 2P: $95-$125 | XP: $20 |

Phone: (505)753-2035

Location: 2.3 mi n from jct US 285, then just e on gated drive. Hwy 84, MM 199.46 87532 (PO Box 702, ABIQUIU, 87510). Fax: 505/753-9490. **Terms:** [BP] meal plan; age restrictions may apply; check-in 4 pm; 21 day cancellation notice; pets, horses only. **Facility:** 2 rooms. Set peacefully among Georgia O'Keefe's pink cliffs. A modern residence built in traditional adobe style and garden casita are decorated with local handmade crafts. Tranquil natural setting along the Rio Chama. 1 story; interior/exterior corridors; smoke free premises. **Services:** gift shop. **Recreation:** Fee: stables. **All Rooms:** shower baths. **Cards:** MC, VI.

HOBBS pop. 29,100

─────── **LODGINGS** ───────

BEST INN

(AAA) SAVE

◆◆
Motor Inn

| All Year | 1P: $42 | 2P: $47 | XP: $5 | F17 |

Phone: (505)397-3251

Location: 2.5 mi e on US 62 and 180. 501 N Marland Blvd 88240. Fax: 505/393-3065. **Terms:** [CP] meal plan; 3 day cancellation notice; small pets only, $20 dep req. **Facility:** 72 rooms. 2 stories; interior/exterior corridors. **Services:** area transportation. **All Rooms:** extended cable TV. **Cards:** AE, CB, DI, DS, JC, MC. **Special Amenities:** Free breakfast and free local telephone calls.

DAYS INN

(AAA) SAVE

◆◆
Motel

| All Year | 1P: $32-$35 | 2P: $42-$45 | XP: $5 | F12 |

Phone: (505)397-6541

Location: 2 mi e on US 62 and 180. 211 N Marland Blvd 88240. Fax: 505/397-6544. **Terms:** [CP] meal plan; small pets only, $10 dep req. **Facility:** 57 rooms. Contemporary room appointments. 2 stories; exterior corridors. **Dining:** Restaurant nearby. **All Rooms:** combo or shower baths, extended cable TV. Fee: safes. **Cards:** AE, CB, DI, DS, MC, VI. **Special Amenities:** Free breakfast and free local telephone calls.

ECONO LODGE
AAA SAVE
◆◆
Motel

All Year   1P: $28-$33   2P: $34-$43
Phone: (505)397-3591   XP: $5   F12
Location: 2.5 mi e on US 62 and 180. 619 N Marland Blvd 88240. Fax: 505/397-3591. **Terms:** [CP] meal plan; cancellation fee imposed; pets. **Facility:** 38 rooms. Contemporary room appointments. 2 stories; exterior corridors; designated smoking area; small heated pool. **Dining:** Cafeteria nearby. **All Rooms:** extended cable TV. **Cards:** CB, DI, DS, JC, MC, VI. **Special Amenities:** Free breakfast and free local telephone calls.

HOLIDAY INN EXPRESS
◆◆◆
Motel
JC, MC, VI.

All Year   1P: $65-$95   2P: $65-$95
Phone: (505)392-8777   XP: $5   F18
Location: Jct SR 18 and Business 19, 1.2 mi n. 3610 N Lovington Hwy 88240. Fax: 505/392-9321. **Terms:** [CP] meal plan. **Facility:** 65 rooms. 3 stories; interior corridors; heated pool. **Cards:** AE, CB, DI, DS,

INNKEEPERS
◆◆
Motel

5/31-9/5   1P: $40-$45   2P: $45-$50
9/6-1/31   1P: $38-$45   2P: $43-$50
2/1-5/30   1P: $36-$40   2P: $40-$44
Phone: (505)397-7171   XP: $5   F12   XP: $5   F12
Location: 2 mi e on US 62 and 180. 309 N Marland Blvd 88240. Fax: 505/391-9276. **Terms:** [CP] meal plan; pets, $20 dep req. **Facility:** 63 rooms. 2 stories; exterior corridors; heated pool. **Cards:** AE, DI, DS, MC, VI.

TRAVELODGE HOBBS
AAA SAVE
◆◆
Motel

All Year   1P: $40-$65   2P: $45-$70
Phone: (505)393-4101   XP: $6   F12
Location: 2 mi e on US 62 and 180. 1301 E Broadway 88240. Fax: 505/393-4101. **Terms:** [BP] meal plan; small pets only. **Facility:** 72 rooms. Carport at some rooms. 1 story; exterior corridors. **Dining:** Restaurant nearby. **All Rooms:** combo or shower baths, extended cable TV. **Cards:** AE, CB, DI, MC, VI. **Special Amenities:** Free breakfast and free local telephone calls.

JEMEZ SPRINGS pop. 400

—— LODGING ——

RIVERDANCER INN
◆◆◆
Bed & Breakfast

3/16-11/1   1P: $89-$109   2P: $109-$129
2/1-3/15 & 11/2-1/31   1P: $79-$99   2P: $99-$117
Phone: 505/829-3262   XP: $20   F3   XP: $20   F3
Location: 1 mi s of center. 16445 Hwy 4 87025. Fax: 505/829-3262. **Terms:** [BP] meal plan; age restrictions may apply; 10 day cancellation notice; cancellation fee imposed; pet on premises. **Facility:** 6 rooms. Enchanting, remote mountain setting. Cozy rooms. 1 story; interior corridors; smoke free premises. **Services:** Fee: massage. **Cards:** DS, MC, VI.

LAS CRUCES pop. 62,100

—— LODGINGS ——

BAYMONT INN & SUITES LAS CRUCES
◆◆◆
Motel

5/1-1/31   1P: $38   2P: $43
2/1-5/25   1P: $36   2P: $41
Phone: (505)523-0100   XP: $5   F18   XP: $5   F18
Location: I-10, exit 140, just se of jct I-25 and Avenida de Mesilla. 1500 Hickory Dr 88005. Fax: 505/523-0707. **Terms:** [CP] meal plan; pets, in limited rooms. **Facility:** 88 rooms. Contemporary style rooms and public areas. 4 stories; interior corridors; heated pool. **Cards:** AE, CB, DI, DS, MC, VI. *(See color ad below)*

BEST WESTERN MESILLA VALLEY INN
AAA SAVE — ◆◆◆ Motor Inn

Phone: (505)524-8603

All Year — 1P: $59-$69 — 2P: $59-$79 — XP: $8 — F13

Location: I-10, exit 140 (Mesilla). 901 Avenida de Mesilla 88004 (PO Drawer 849). Fax: 505/526-8437. **Terms:** Weekly & monthly rates avail; pets. **Facility:** 160 rooms. Near historic Mesilla. 2 stories; exterior corridors; heated pool, whirlpool. **Dining:** Restaurant; 6 am-10 pm; $5-$14; entertainment. **Some Rooms:** kitchen. Fee: refrigerators. **Cards:** AE, CB, DI, DS, JC, MC, VI. **Special Amenities:** Free local telephone calls and free room upgrade (subject to availability with advanced reservations). *(See ad below)*

BEST WESTERN MISSION INN
AAA SAVE — ◆◆◆ Motor Inn

Phone: (505)524-8591

All Year — 1P: $45-$55 — 2P: $55-$65 — XP: $8 — F12

Location: I-10, exit 142, 1 mi n. 1765 S Main St 88005. Fax: 505/523-4740. **Terms:** [BP] meal plan; weekly rates avail; small pets only, in smoking rooms. **Facility:** 68 rooms. In a commerical area. 2 stories; exterior corridors; heated pool; playground. **Dining:** Restaurant; 6 am-2 & 5-9 pm; $5-$12. **Cards:** AE, CB, DI, DS, MC, VI. **Special Amenities:** Free breakfast and free local telephone calls.

COMFORT INN OF LAS CRUCES
AAA SAVE — ◆◆◆ Motel

Phone: (505)527-2000

All Year — 1P: $50-$75 — 2P: $55-$95 — XP: $5 — F18

Location: I-10, exit 142 (University Ave). 2585 S Valley Dr 88005. Fax: 505/527-0966. **Terms:** [CP] meal plan; weekly rates avail. **Facility:** 38 rooms. 2 stories; interior corridors; heated pool, whirlpool. **Some Rooms:** Fee: VCR. **Cards:** AE, CB, DI, DS, JC, MC, VI. **Special Amenities:** Free newspaper and free room upgrade (subject to availability with advanced reservations).

COMFORT SUITES
◆◆◆ Motel — MC, VI.

Phone: (505)522-1300

All Year — 1P: $59-$69 — 2P: $69-$79 — XP: $10 — F18

Location: I-25, exit 1. 2101 S Triviz 88001. Fax: 505/522-1313. **Terms:** [CP] meal plan; pets, $15 extra charge, in designated rooms. **Facility:** 61 rooms. 3 stories; interior corridors; heated pool. **Cards:** AE, DI, DS,

DAYS END LODGE
AAA SAVE — ◆ Motel

Phone: (505)524-7753

All Year — 1P: $28-$30 — 2P: $36-$40 — XP: $3 — F15

Location: I-10, exit 139, 1.5 mi e on Amador Ave, 0.8 mi n on Valley Dr; I-25, exit 6B, 2.5 mi sw on US 70 and 82, 1 mi w on Picacho St, just s. 755 N Valley Dr 88005. Fax: 505/541-0732. **Terms:** Weekly rates avail; cancellation fee imposed. **Facility:** 31 rooms. In commercial area. 4 two-bedroom units. 2 stories; exterior corridors. **All Rooms:** combo or shower baths. **Some Rooms:** Fee: refrigerators. **Cards:** AE, DS, MC, VI. **Special Amenities:** Early check-in/late check-out and free local telephone calls.

DAYS INN
AAA SAVE — ◆◆◆ Motor Inn

Phone: (505)526-4441

All Year — 1P: $60 — 2P: $55 — XP: $5 — F18

Location: I-10, exit 142 (University Ave). 2600 S Valley Dr 88005. Fax: 505/526-1980. **Terms:** [AP], [BP] & [CP] meal plans; weekly & monthly rates avail; pets, $10 extra charge. **Facility:** 130 rooms. 2 stories; interior corridors; heated pool, sauna. **Dining:** Restaurant; 6 am-10 & 5-10 pm, Sun-11 am; $4-$10; cocktails. **Cards:** AE, DS, MC, VI. **Special Amenities:** Free breakfast and free local telephone calls.

DESERT LODGE MOTEL
AAA — ◆ Motel

Phone: (505)524-1925

All Year — 1P: $24-$28 — 2P: $28-$32 — XP: $5 — D12

Location: I-10, exit 139, 1 mi n, 0.8 mi e on Picacho St (I-10 business route); I-25, exit 6A, 2 mi sw on (US 70 W), 2 mi w. 1900 W Picacho St 88005. **Terms:** Small pets only. **Facility:** 10 rooms. In commercial area. 1 story; exterior corridors. **All Rooms:** combo or shower baths. **Cards:** AE, DS, MC, VI.

THE FAIRFIELD INN
◆◆◆ Motel

Phone: 505/522-6840

Property failed to provide current rates

Location: I-25, exit 6A, then 2 blks e to Telshore Dr, 0.8 mi s on Telshore Dr. 2101 Summit Ct 88011. Fax: 505/522-9784. **Terms:** [CP] meal plan. **Facility:** 78 rooms. 3 stories; interior corridors; heated pool. **Cards:** AE, DI, DS, MC, VI.

HAMPTON INN

◆◆◆ Motel

All Year   1P: $52-$64   2P: $57-$69   XP: $5

Phone: (505)526-8311

Location: I-10, exit 140 (Mesilla). 755 Avenida de Mesilla 88005. Fax: 505/527-2015. **Terms:** [CP] meal plan; pets. **Facility:** 117 rooms. 2 stories; exterior corridors. **Cards:** AE, CB, DI, DS, MC, VI.

HILLTOP HACIENDA B & B

◆◆◆ Bed & Breakfast

All Year   1P: $75-$85   2P: $75-$85   XP: $15

Phone: (505)382-3556

Location: I-25, exit 6A, just e to Del Rey St, 3 mi n to Westmoreland St, then 1 mi e. 2600 Westmoreland St 88012. Fax: 505/382-3536. **Terms:** [BP] meal plan; age restrictions may apply; 10 day cancellation notice; cancellation fee imposed; pets. **Facility:** 3 rooms. 20 acres located on a hilltop, desert setting with a panoramic view of the mountains and the valley. Kitchen avail. 2 stories; interior corridors; smoke free premises. **Recreation:** bicycles, hiking trails. **All Rooms:** combo or shower baths. **Cards:** AE, DS, MC, VI.

HOLIDAY INN DE LAS CRUCES

(AAA) [SAVE]
◆◆◆ Motor Inn

All Year   1P: $49-$65   2P: $49-$65   XP: $5   F17

Phone: (505)526-4411

Location: 2.8 mi s on US 80, 85 and 180 at jct I-10, exit 142. 201 E University Ave 88005. Fax: 505/524-0530. **Terms:** Small pets only, $20 dep req. **Facility:** 114 rooms. Beauty salon. 2 stories; interior corridors; heated pool, wading pool. **Dining:** Restaurant; 6 am-10 pm; $7-$15; cocktails. **Services:** gift shop. **All Rooms:** combo or shower baths. **Cards:** AE, CB, DI, DS, JC, MC, VI. **Special Amenities:** Early check-in/late check-out and free newspaper.

HOLIDAY INN EXPRESS

◆◆◆ Motel

Property failed to provide current rates

Phone: (505)527-9947

Location: I-10, exit 142, then 2 blks w. 2200 S Valley Dr 88005. Fax: 505/647-4988. **Terms:** [CP] meal plan; small pets only, $5-$20 extra charge. **Facility:** 53 rooms. 2 stories; exterior corridors; designated smoking area. **Some Rooms:** Fee: refrigerators. **Cards:** AE, CB, DI, MC, VI. *(See color ad below)*

LA QUINTA INN-LAS CRUCES

◆◆◆ Motel

All Year   1P: $59-$79   2P: $59-$79

Phone: (505)524-0331

Location: I-10, exit 140 (Mesilla). 790 Avenida de Mesilla 88005. Fax: 505/525-8360. **Terms:** [CP] meal plan; small pets only. **Facility:** 139 rooms. Spanish design. 2 stories; interior corridors; heated pool. **Cards:** AE, CB, DI, DS, MC, VI.

LAS CRUCES HILTON INN

◆◆◆ Hotel

All Year   1P: $77   2P: $77   XP: $10   F12

Phone: (505)522-4300

Location: I-25, exit 3 (Lohman Dr). 705 S Telshor Blvd 88011. Fax: 505/522-7657. **Terms:** Pets. **Facility:** 203 rooms. 7 stories; interior corridors; heated pool. **Dining:** entertainment. **Services:** gift shop. **Some Rooms:** Fee: refrigerators. **Cards:** AE, CB, DI, DS, MC, VI. *(See color ad p 41)*

LUNDEEN'S INN OF THE ARTS

◆◆◆ Historic Bed & Breakfast

All Year   1P: $53-$72   2P: $58-$150   XP: $15

Phone: (505)526-3326

Location: Center. 618 S Alameda Blvd. Fax: 505/647-1334. **Terms:** 3 day cancellation notice; cancellation fee imposed; small pets only, $15 dep req. **Facility:** 22 rooms. 100 year old restored adobe. Office opens at 3 pm. 2 stories; interior corridors; smoke free premises. **Services:** Fee: massage. **All Rooms:** combo or shower baths. **Some Rooms:** 9 kitchens, color TV. **Cards:** AE, CB, DI, DS, MC, VI.

MOTEL 6 - 363

(AAA)
◆◆ Motel

5/25-1/31   1P: $36-$46   2P: $42-$52   XP: $3   F17
2/1-5/24   1P: $34-$44   2P: $40-$50   XP: $3   F17

Phone: 505/525-1010

Location: 2.8 mi s on US 80, 85 and 180 at jct I-10 exit 142. 235 La Posada Ln 88001. Fax: 505/525-0139. **Terms:** Small pets only. **Facility:** 118 rooms. Extended stay rooms, $40-$46; 2 stories; exterior corridors; heated pool. **All Rooms:** shower baths. **Some Rooms:** 10 efficiencies. **Cards:** AE, CB, DI, DS, MC, VI.

ROYAL HOST MOTEL
Phone: (505)524-8536

AAA SAVE

◆◆

Motel

All Year   1P: $27-$30   2P: $34-$38   XP: $4   F12

Location: I-10, exit 139, 1 mi n, then 0.5 mi e on Picacho St (I-10 business route). 2146 W Picacho St 88005. **Terms:** Weekly rates avail; pets, $5 extra charge. **Facility:** 26 rooms. In commercial area. 1 story; exterior corridors; heated pool. **Dining:** Restaurant nearby. **All Rooms:** combo or shower baths. **Cards:** DS, MC, VI.

Special Amenities: Free local telephone calls and free room upgrade (subject to availability with advanced reservations).

SLEEP INN
Phone: (505)522-1700

◆◆◆

Motel

All Year   1P: $49-$59   2P: $59-$69   XP: $5   F18

Location: I-25, exit 1. 2121 S Triviz 88001. Fax: 505/522-1515. **Terms:** [CP] meal plan; pets, $15 extra charge. **Facility:** 63 rooms. 3 stories; interior corridors; designated smoking area; heated pool. **All Rooms:** shower baths. **Cards:** AE, DI, DS, MC, VI.

SPRINGHILL SUITES BY MARRIOTT
Phone: (505)541-8887

◆◆◆

Motel

All Year   1P: $59-$79   XP: $5   F

Location: I-10, exit 140. 1611 Hickory Loop 88005. Fax: 505/541-8837. **Terms:** [ECP] meal plan; 7 day cancellation notice. **Facility:** 101 rooms. 3 stories; interior corridors; heated pool. **Cards:** AE, DI, DS, MC, VI.

SUPER 8 MOTEL
Phone: 505-523-8695

◆◆

Motel

All Year   1P: $34   2P: $34

Location: 2.8 mi s on US 80, 85 and 180 at jct I-10, exit 142. 245 La Posada Ln 88005. Fax: 505/523-8695. **Terms:** 14 day cancellation notice; small pets only, $25 dep req. **Facility:** 60 rooms. 3 stories; interior corridors. **Cards:** AE, CB, DI, DS, MC, VI.

TRH SMITH BED & BREAKFAST
Phone: (505)525-2525

◆◆◆

Bed &
Breakfast

MC, VI.

All Year   1P: $56-$132   2P: $56-$132   XP: $15   F4

Location: Center. 909 N Alameda Blvd 88005. Fax: 505/524-8227. **Terms:** [BP] meal plan; 7 day cancellation notice; small pets only. **Facility:** 4 rooms. Constructed in 1914 designed by architect Henry C Trost. 3 stories, no elevator; interior corridors; smoke free premises. **Some Rooms:** shared bathrooms. **Cards:** AE, DS,

─────── **RESTAURANTS** ───────

BRASS CACTUS BISTRO

AAA

◆◆◆

American

Lunch: $6-$10   **Dinner:** $9-$16   **Phone:** 505-527-4656

Location: I-10, exit 140, 0.8 mi s. 1800 B Avenida de Mesilla 88005. **Hours:** 11:30 am-2 & 5:30-9 pm, Sun 5 pm-8 pm. **Reservations:** suggested; for dinner. **Features:** casual dress; beer & wine only. This restaurant's European-trained chef/owner prepares a varied menu featuring fresh seafood, pasta, prime steaks, grilled veggies and desserts. Sample the Cajun bread pudding with peaches. It's yummy. You'll be able to view the open kitchen and grill. Smoke free premises. **Cards:** DS, MC, VI.

CASA LUNA

◆

Italian

Lunch: $4-$6   **Dinner:** $7-$9   **Phone:** 505-523-0111

Location: I-25 exit 3, 1 mi e. 1340 E Lohman 88001. **Hours:** 11 am-9 pm, Fri & Sat-10 pm. **Features:** casual dress; children's menu; senior's menu; carryout; beer & wine only. Casa Lung is a small family-oriented restaurant serving homemade calzones, sausage, pizza, minestrone soup, chicken-fried steak and desserts. They also have lots of finger foods, sandwiches and salads. The lunch buffet is served Mon-Fri 11 am-2 pm. Smoke free premises. **Cards:** AE, DS, MC, VI.

THE DYNASTY CHINESE CUISINE

◆

Chinese

Lunch: $6-$8   **Dinner:** $7-$11   **Phone:** 505-525-8116

Location: I-10 exit 140 (Mesilla), 0.5 mi e; in El Paseo Place. 1210 El Paseo 88005. **Hours:** 11 am-4 pm. **Features:** casual dress; children's menu; health conscious menu; carryout. The Dynasty features a very good buffet of appetizers, soups and a selection of pork, chicken, beef and seafood. They also prepare cooked-to-order meals and four-course family dinners. The fried dumplings and shrimp lo mein are both excellent. **Cards:** CB, DI, DS, MC, VI.

FARLEY'S

◆◆

American

Lunch: $5-$8   **Dinner:** $6-$13   **Phone:** 505-552-0466

Location: I-25 exit 3 (Lohman Dr). 3499 Foothills Blvd 88011. **Hours:** 11 am-9 pm, Fri & Sat-10 pm. **Features:** casual dress; children's menu; carryout; cocktails & lounge. Your entire family will have fun at Farley's. They have an arcade area to entertain the kids, plus hot dogs, pizza and grilled cheese, and choices for Mom and Dad too, such as ribs, sandwiches, steak, fajitas, soups, salads, beer and fantastic margaritas. **Cards:** AE, DS, MC, VI.

THE HACIENDA RESTAURANT

◆◆

Mexican

Lunch: $6-$9   **Dinner:** $6-$9   **Phone:** 505/522-6380

Location: I-10, exit 142, 1 mi e on University Ave; I-25, exit 1, 1 mi w on University Ave. 2605 S Espina 88001. **Hours:** 11 am-2:30 & 4:30-9 pm, Sat from 4:30 pm. Closed major holidays. **Features:** children's menu; cocktails. You'll enjoy the Hacienda's New Mexican specialties including their fresh seafood and award-winning chili. Daily specials and a wide selection of margaritas and beer make this a lovely, casual dining experience. It's near New Mexico State University. Smoke free premises. **Cards:** AE, DI, DS, MC, VI.

LORENZO'S

◆◆

Italian

Lunch: $5-$8   **Dinner:** $6-$10   **Phone:** 505-521-3505

Location: I-25 exit 1 s. 1753 University 88005. **Hours:** 11 am-9 pm, Fri & Sat-9:30. **Features:** casual dress; carryout; beer & wine only. Authentic Sicilian dishes are served at Lorenzo's, which offers imported pastas, varied sauces, hand-tossed pizza with unusual combinations, appetizers, cannelloni, eggplant parmigiana, calamari and seafood. Finish with tiramisu, spumoni or cheesecake. **Cards:** AE, MC, VI.

RED MOUNTAIN CAFE   **Lunch:** $5-$8   **Dinner:** $6-$9   **Phone:** 505/522-7584
◆
Southwest   **Location:** I-25, exit 6A, 2 blks e to Telshor Dr, then s. 1120A Commerce Dr 88011. **Hours:** 7 am-7 pm, Thur
American   & Fri-11 pm. Closed: Sun. **Features:** casual dress; health conscious menu; carryout; beer & wine only. Red
                 Mountain Cafe offers many wonderful gourmet sandwiches and salads as well as box lunches, coffee, tea
and espresso. They also serve fresh breads and pastries, homemade soups and desserts, and a good
selection of beer and other beverages. Smoke free premises. **Cards:** DS, MC, VI.   ☒

LAS VEGAS pop. 14,800

———— **LODGINGS** ————

COMFORT INN   **Phone:** (505)425-1100
🆋🆋🆋 SAVE   5/1-9/30   1P: $65-$75   2P: $65-$75   XP: $5   F18
◆◆◆   2/1-4/30 & 10/1-1/31   1P: $60-$70   2P: $60-$70   XP: $5   F18
Motel   **Location:** US 85 and I-25 business route, just sw of jct I-25, exit 347. 2500 N Grand Ave 87701.
             Fax: 505/454-8404. **Terms:** [ECP] meal plan; small pets only, in smoking rooms. **Facility:** 101 rooms. 2 sto-
ries; interior corridors; small heated indoor pool, whirlpool. **Cards:** AE, CB, DI, DS, JC, MC, VI.
                                                         🆂🅳 🛏 ⊗ ⟨ ☒ 📺 🖨 🅿 ⟰ ⟰

DAYS INN-LAS VEGAS   **Phone:** (505)425-1967
◆◆   5/1-9/30   1P: $60-$70   2P: $70-$75   XP: $6   F13
Motel   2/1-4/30 & 10/1-1/31   1P: $50-$55   2P: $55-$60   XP: $6   F13
             Location: US 85 and I-25 business route, 0.8 mi sw of jct I-25, exit 347. 2000 N Grand Ave 87701.
Fax: 505/425-3837. **Terms:** [CP] meal plan. **Facility:** 36 rooms. 2 stories; interior corridors; heated pool. **Cards:** AE, CB, DI,
DS, MC, VI. *(See ad below)*
                                               SAVE 🆂🅳 ⊞ ☒ 📺 🖨 ⬚ 🔌 🅿 ⟰

EL CAMINO MOTEL   **Phone:** (505)425-5994
🆋🆋🆋 SAVE   5/1-9/30   1P: $40-$50   2P: $50-$60   XP: $6   D12
◆   10/1-1/31   1P: $35-$45   2P: $45-$50
Motor Inn   2/1-4/30   1P: $35-$45   2P: $45-$50   XP: $6   D12
             Location: US 85 and I-25 business route, 0.3 mi w of jct I-25, exit 345; SR 65, 0.5 mi n. 1152 N Grand Ave
             87701. **Fax:** 505/425-5447. **Terms:** Small pets only, $6 extra charge, $20 dep req; smoking rm. **Facility:** 23
rooms. 1-2 stories; exterior corridors. **Dining:** Restaurant; 6 am-9 pm; $5-$10. **Services:** winter plug-ins. **Cards:** AE, CB, DI,
DS, MC, VI. **Special Amenities:** Free local telephone calls. *(See ad below)*
                                                         🆂🅳 🛏 ⊞ ☒ 📺

INN ON THE SANTA FE TRAIL

Phone: (505)425-6791

(AAA) [SAVE]

◆ ◆
Motor Inn

4/16-10/15	1P: $64-$74	2P: $69-$79	XP: $5
10/16-1/31	1P: $44-$54	2P: $54-$59	XP: $5
2/1-4/15	1P: $44-$54	2P: $49-$59	XP: $5

Location: I-25 business route and US 84, 0.3 mi w from jct; I-25, exit 345, 0.5 mi n. 1133 N Grand Ave 87701. Fax: 505/425-0417. **Terms:** [CP] meal plan; weekly & monthly rates avail; pets, $5 extra charge. **Facility:** 42 rooms. 1937 hacienda style on shady grounds. Rooms appointed with locally handcrafted Southwestern furniture. 1 story; exterior corridors; heated pool, whirlpool. **Dining:** Restaurant; seasonal patio dining; 5:30 pm-9 pm Tues-Sun; $8-$16; wine/beer only. **Some Rooms:** Fee: VCR. **Cards:** AE, DS, MC, VI. **Special Amenities:** Free breakfast and free local telephone calls. *(See color ad p 415)*

PLAZA HOTEL

Phone: (505)425-3591

(AAA) [SAVE]

◆ ◆ ◆
Historic Hotel

5/1-10/31	1P: $63-$91	2P: $69-$97	XP: $6 F17
2/1-4/30 & 11/1-1/31	1P: $59-$81	2P: $65-$87	XP: $6 F17

Location: I-25, exit 343; w following signs to Old Town Plaza. 230 Plaza 87701. Fax: 505/425-9659. **Terms:** [ECP] meal plan; package plans; pets, $10 extra charge. **Facility:** 36 rooms. 1882 historic Western Victorian hotel. 3 stories; interior corridors; street parking only. **Dining:** Landmark Grill, see separate listing. **Some Rooms:** Fee: refrigerators, VCR. **Cards:** AE, DI, DS, MC, VI. **Special Amenities:** Free breakfast.

SUPER 8 MOTEL-LAS VEGAS

Phone: (505)425-5288

◆ ◆
Motor

4/1-1/31	1P: $50	2P: $55-$57	XP: $3 F12
2/1-3/31	1P: $43	2P: $48-$51	XP: $3 F12

Location: US 85 and I-25 business route, 0.8 mi sw of jct I-25, exit 347. 2029 N Grand Ave 87701. Fax: 505/454-8481. **Terms:** [CP] meal plan. **Facility:** 36 rooms. Traditional room decor. Ample paved parking. 2 stories; interior corridors. **Cards:** AE, CB, DI, DS, MC, VI.

——— RESTAURANT ———

LANDMARK GRILL Historical

Lunch: $4-$8   **Dinner:** $6-$18   **Phone:** 505/425-3591

◆ ◆
American

Location: From I-25 exit 343; w following signs to Old Town Plaza; in Plaza Hotel. 230 Plaza 87701. **Hours:** 7 am-2 & 5-9 pm. **Reservations:** suggested; for dinner. **Features:** casual dress; Sunday brunch; children's menu; carryout; cocktails & lounge; street parking. The Landmark Grill offers a mix of Italian dishes, a selection of Mexican, New Mexican and Southwestern meals as well as grilled items. Begin with a good quality appetizer. This restaurant serves guests in a small dining room in a Victorian-era hotel. **Cards:** AE, CB, DI, DS, MC, VI.

LINCOLN pop. 12,450

——— LODGING ———

CASA DE PATRON BED & BREAKFAST INN

Phone: (505)653-4676

◆ ◆ ◆
Historic Bed
& Breakfast

4/1-10/31	1P: $79-$107	2P: $89-$117	XP: $20

Location: Center. Hwy 380 E 88338 (PO Box 27). Fax: 505/653-4671. **Terms:** Open 4/1-10/31; [BP] meal plan; 7 day cancellation notice. **Facility:** 6 rooms. Principal structure is a single-story adobe home built circa 1860. Elevation of 5,700 ft allows for natural cooling during summer months. 1 story; interior/exterior corridors; smoke free premises. **Cards:** MC, VI.

LORDSBURG pop. 3,000

——— LODGINGS ———

BEST WESTERN AMERICAN MOTOR INN

Phone: (505)542-3591

(AAA) [SAVE]

◆ ◆ ◆
Motor Inn

All Year	1P: $39	2P: $44	XP: $5 F17

Location: 1.5 mi e on US 70 and 80, 1 mi w of exit 24 off I-10. 944 E Motel Dr 88045. Fax: 505/542-3572. **Terms:** Small pets only. **Facility:** 88 rooms. In commercial and railroad area. 1-2 stories; exterior corridors; wading pool; playground. **Dining:** Restaurant; 6:30 am-9:30 pm, closed 12/25; $4-$13; cocktails. **Some Rooms:** Fee: VCR. **Cards:** AE, CB, DI, DS, MC, VI. **Special Amenities:** Early check-in/late check-out and free local telephone calls.

BEST WESTERN WESTERN SKIES

Phone: (505)542-8807

◆ ◆ ◆
Motor Inn

All Year	1P: $53	2P: $58	XP: $5 F17

Location: I-10, exit 22. 1303 S Main St 88045. Fax: 505/542-8895. **Terms:** Small pets only. **Facility:** 40 rooms. 1 story; exterior corridors; designated smoking area; heated pool. **Cards:** AE, CB, DI, DS, MC, VI.

DAYS INN

Phone: (505)542-3600

◆ ◆ ◆
Motel

All Year	1P: $55-$65	2P: $65-$75	XP: $10 F17

Location: I-10, exit 20. 1100 W Motel Dr 88045. **Terms:** [CP] meal plan; small pets only, $7 dep req. **Facility:** 56 rooms. Designated smoking area; heated pool. **Cards:** AE, CB, DI, DS, MC, VI.

HOLIDAY INN EXPRESS

Phone: (505)542-3666

◆ ◆ ◆
Motel

All Year	1P: $59	2P: $59

Location: I-10, exit 22. 1408 S Main 88045. Fax: 505/542-3665. **Terms:** [ECP] meal plan; small pets only, $50 dep req. **Facility:** 40 rooms. 2 stories; exterior corridors; heated pool. **Cards:** AE, CB, DI, DS, MC, VI.

SUPER 8 MOTEL
All Year   1P: $39   2P: $43   XP: $5   F12
Phone: (505)542-8882
Location: I-10, exit 22. 110 E Maple 88045. Fax: 505/542-8882. **Facility:** 41 rooms. 2 stories; interior corridors. **Dining:** Restaurant nearby. **Cards:** AE, DS, MC, VI. **Special Amenities:** Free breakfast and free local telephone calls.

LOS ALAMOS pop. 11,500

──────── LODGING ────────

BEST WESTERN HILLTOP HOUSE HOTEL & LA SUITES
Phone: (505)662-2441
5/1-10/31   1P: $79-$82   2P: $89-$92   XP: $10   F12
Motor Inn   2/1-4/30 & 11/1-1/31   1P: $77-$80   2P: $87-$90   XP: $10   F12
Location: Just e. 400 Trinity Dr 87544. Fax: 505/662-5913. **Facility:** 92 rooms. 1 two-bedroom unit. 3 stories; interior corridors; heated pool. **All Rooms:** combo or shower baths. **Some Rooms:** 31 efficiencies, kitchen. **Cards:** AE, DI, DS, JC, MC, VI.

LOS BRAZOS

──────── LODGING ────────

CASA DE MARTINEZ BED & BREAKFAST
Phone: 505/588-7858
2/14-10/25   1P: $90-$115   2P: $90-$125   D13
Location: On CR 334, just n of jct US 64/84, 9 mi s from SR 17 and Chama. Old US 84 87520 (PO Box 96, LOS OJOS, 87551). **Terms:** Open 2/14-10/25; [BP] meal plan; weekly rates avail; age restrictions may apply; check-in 4 pm; 10 day cancellation notice; cancellation fee imposed. **Facility:** 5 rooms. Small village location. Beautifully converted adobe residence built in 1859 and operated by same family. Very extensive common areas. Rooms furnished with original antiques. Infants to 1 yr & children 13 & older accepted; 2 stories; interior/exterior corridors; smoke free premises. **Dining:** Breakfast served 8:30 am. **All Rooms:** combo or shower baths. **Cards:** MC, VI.
Historic Bed & Breakfast

LOS LUNAS pop. 6,000

──────── LODGING ────────

DAYS INN
Phone: (505)865-5995
All Year   1P: $48-$50   2P: $58-$60   XP: $6   F12
Motel
Location: I-25, exit 203, just s to entrance at se corner. 1919 Main St NW 87031. Fax: 505/865-9490. **Terms:** [CP] meal plan. **Facility:** 46 rooms. 2 stories; interior corridors; heated pool. **Cards:** AE, DS, MC, VI.

──────── RESTAURANT ────────

LUNA MANSION   Historical   **Dinner:** $9-$20   Phone: 505/865-7333
Location: I-25, exit 203, then 1.5 mi e on SR 6. Jct SR 314 & 6 87031. **Hours:** 5 pm-9 pm, Fri & Sat-9:30 pm. Closed: 12/25, Mon & Tues. **Features:** casual dress; children's menu; cocktails & lounge. The Continental cuisine at Luna Mansion offers a complete menu of shrimp won ton, oysters Rockefeller, pasta, home-style meals, salads, Mexican dishes, choice beef, fresh seafood and desserts. It's located in a restored adobe mansion constructed in 1881. **Cards:** AE, DS, MC, VI.
Continental

MESILLA pop. 2,000

──────── LODGING ────────

MESON DE MESILLA
Phone: (505)525-9212
All Year   1P: $45-$145   2P: $45-$145
Country Inn
Location: I-10, exit 142, Mesilla and SR 28, 0.8 mi s. 1803 Avenida de Mesilla 88046 (PO Box 1212). Fax: 505/527-4196. **Terms:** [BP] meal plan. **Facility:** 15 rooms. Many rooms with view of Organ Mountains. Rooms nicely decorated and furnished with some modern American antiques. 2 stories; interior corridors; smoke free premises. **Services:** gift shop. **Cards:** AE, CB, DI, DS, MC, VI.

──────── RESTAURANTS ────────

DOUBLE EAGLE RESTAURANT   Historical   **Lunch:** $5-$9   **Dinner:** $9-$15   Phone: 505/523-6700
Location: On Historic Plaza. **Hours:** 11 am-10 pm, Sun-9 pm. **Reservations:** suggested. **Features:** casual dress; Sunday brunch; carryout; cocktails & lounge. Listed on the National Register of Historic Places, this restaurant is decorated with baccarat crystal and 19th-K33century art. Their regional cuisine includes delicious grilled chicken Mesilla and banana enchiladas, served indoors or on the garden patio. **Cards:** AE, DI, DS, MC, VI.
Steak and Seafood

LA POSTA DE MESILLA   Historical   **Lunch:** $7-$12   **Dinner:** $9-$16   Phone: 505/524-3524
Location: I-10 exit 142, Mesilla and SR 28, 0.8 mi s; in the Meson de Mesilla. 2410 Calle de Parian 88046. **Hours:** 11 am-9 pm, Fri & Sat-9:30 pm. Closed: Mon. **Features:** casual dress; children's menu; carryout; cocktails; street parking. This 1840s adobe structure was once a stagecoach stop. It now houses an atrium of shops and Southwestern gourmet foods. The restaurant serves traditional Mexican meals, all cooked to order. You may have to wait a bit, but it's well worth it!. Smoke free premises. **Cards:** AE, DI, DS, MC, VI.
Mexican

MESON DE MESILLA RESTAURANT   **Lunch:** $10-$15   **Dinner:** $22-$30   **Phone:** 505/525-9211
♦♦♦   **Location:** I-10 exit 142, Mesilla and SR 28, 0.8 mi s; in the Meson de Mesilla. 1803 Avenida de Mesilla
Regional   88046. **Hours:** 11 am-1:45 & 5:30-9 pm, Fri & Sat-10 pm. Closed: 12/25. **Reservations:** suggested; dinner
Continental   **Features:** casual dress; cocktails & lounge; a la carte. This adobe restaurant has the warmth and hospitality
     of traditional European styling. The menu changes to reflect the freshest ingredients available. The chef
working on the cutting edge of preparation methods, creates the desserts, dressings and sauces. Smoke free premises.
Cards: AE, DI, DS, MC, VI.   ☒

OLD MESILLA PASTRY CAFE   **Lunch:** $5-$9   **Phone:** 505/525-2636
♦   **Location:** I-10 exit 142, 2 mi s. 2790 Avenida de Mesilla 88005. **Hours:** 7:30 am-2:30 pm, bakery-4 pm
Mexican   Closed: Mon & Tues. **Features:** casual dress; carryout; street parking. This wonderful bakery offers such
     vegetarian delights as garden burgers and grilled eggplant sandwiches. The wood-burning oven produces
pizza, calzone and bread. Breakfast offerings range from huevos rancheros and eggs benedict to pancakes and omelets.
Smoke free premises. **Cards:** AE, MC, VI.   ☒

MILAN pop. 1,900

———— **LODGING** ————

CROSSROADS MOTEL   **Phone:** 505/287-9264
♦   All Year   1P: $24   2P: $27
Motel   **Location:** I-40, exit 79. 1600 W US 66 87021 (PO Box 2202). **Terms:** Pets. **Facility:** 14 rooms. Older, well
     kept roadside motel with sliding glass entry door. 1 story; exterior corridors. **Cards:** AE, DS, MC, VI.
                                                            (ASK) 🔲 🐄 ☒ ⓩ 📠 🔳

MORIARTY pop. 1,400

———— **LODGINGS** ————

DAYS INN   **Phone:** (505)832-4451
(AAA) (SAVE)   4/1-9/30 & 10/1-10/31   1P: $43-$54   2P: $48-$59   XP: $5   F17
♦♦   2/1-3/31 & 11/1-1/31   1P: $38-$49   2P: $43-$54   XP: $5   F17
Motel   **Location:** I-40, exit 194. US 66 W & I-40 87035 (PO Box 367). Fax: 505/832-6464. **Terms:** [CP] meal plan;
     pets, $5 extra charge. **Facility:** 41 rooms. In a commercial area. 2 stories; interior corridors. **Cards:** AE, CB,
     DI, DS, MC, VI. **Special Amenities:** Free breakfast and free local telephone calls.
                                                            🔲 🐄 ☒ 🎬 📠 🔳 (DATA PORT)

HOWARD JOHNSON   **Phone:** (505)832-4457
(AAA) (SAVE)   All Year   1P: $40   2P: $42   XP: $6   F12
♦♦   **Location:** 0.5 mi se on US 66 and I-40 business loop from I-40, exit 194. 1316 Central Ave 87035 (PO Box
Motel   1610). Fax: 505/832-4965. **Terms:** [CP] meal plan; pets, $10 extra charge. **Facility:** 29 rooms. Commercial lo-
     cation. 2 stories; interior corridors. **All Rooms:** extended cable TV. **Cards:** AE, CB, DI, DS, MC, VI.
     Special Amenities: Free breakfast and free local telephone calls. *(See color ad p 371)*
                                                            🔲 🐄 ☒ 🎬 📠 💻 🔲 🔳

MOTEL 6   **Phone:** 505/832-6666
♦♦   All Year   1P: $40-$50   2P: $46-$56   XP: $3   F17
Motel   **Location:** 0.5 mi e on US 66, 1 mi e of I-40, exit 197. 109 Rt 66 E 87035 (PO Box 280). Fax: 505/832-1282.
     Terms: Small pets only. **Facility:** 69 rooms. 2 stories; interior corridors; designated smoking area; heated pool.
Cards: AE, CB, DI, DS, MC, VI.   🐄 🛏 ♿ 🐄 ☒ 🎬 🔲

SUNSET MOTEL   **Phone:** (505)832-4234
(AAA) (SAVE)   All Year   1P: $39-$43   2P: $43-$47   XP: $2   F12
♦♦   **Location:** 0.5 mi e on US 66, 1 mi w of e interchange I-40, exit 197. 501 Old Rt 66 87035 (PO Box 36).
Classic Motel   **Terms:** Pets, $5 extra charge. **Facility:** 18 rooms. Classic property located along historic Rt 66, built by owner
     in 1949. 1 story; exterior corridors. **Dining:** Restaurant nearby. **All Rooms:** extended cable TV. **Cards:** DI, DS,
     MC, VI.   🔲 🔲 🐄 🍴 ☒ 🎬 💻 📠 🔳

SUPER 8 MOTEL   **Phone:** (505)832-6730
(AAA) (SAVE)   10/15-1/31   1P: $50-$60   2P: $60-$70   XP: $6   F12
♦♦   2/1-10/14   1P: $50-$60   2P: $55-$65   XP: $6   F12
Motel   **Location:** I-40, exit 194, then 0.5 mi e on Central Ave. 1611 W Old Rt 66 87035 (PO Box 1127).
     Fax: 505/832-6730. **Terms:** [CP] meal plan; pets, $20 dep req. **Facility:** 70 rooms. 1 two-bedroom unit. 2 sto-
     ries; interior corridors. **All Rooms:** combo or shower baths, extended cable TV. **Cards:** AE, CB, DI, DS,
MC, VI. **Special Amenities:** Free breakfast and free local telephone calls.
                                                            🔲 🐄 🛏 🔲 🐄 ☒ 🎬 📠 🔳 (DATA PORT)

PLACITAS pop. 1,650

———— **LODGING** ————

HACIENDA DE PLACITAS INN OF THE ARTS   **Phone:** (505)867-0082
♦♦♦   All Year   2P: $99-$199   XP: $20
Bed &   **Location:** 1-25, exit 242, 4.9 mi e. 491 Hwy 165 87043. Fax: 505/867-3775. **Terms:** [BP] meal plan; check-in
Breakfast   4 pm; 14 day cancellation notice; cancellation fee imposed; pets, $50 dep req. **Facility:** 7 rooms. 2 stories; ex-
     terior corridors; smoke free premises. **Services:** gift shop. **All Rooms:** combo or shower baths.
Some Rooms: 3 kitchens. **Cards:** AE, DS, MC, VI.   🔲 🔲 🔲 (VCR) 📠 🔲 🔳 (DATA PORT)

───── RESTAURANT ─────

CAFE DE PLACITAS   **Lunch:** $5-$11   **Dinner:** $13-$25   **Phone:** 505/867-1610
◆◆◆   **Location:** I-25, exit 242, 6.4 mi e. 664 Hwy 165 87043. **Hours:** 11:30 am-2:30 & 6-9 pm, Fri-9:30, Sat
American   6-9:30 pm. Closed major holidays & Sun. **Reservations:** suggested; for dinner. **Features:** beer & wine only.
          Cafe de Placitas has attractive Southwestern architecture and decor. Its menu offers an eclectic American
cuisine with Italian and French influences, homemade bread, and fresh salads containing local ingredients. Patio dining is
available. **Cards:** AE, DS, MC, VI.   ☒

RANCHOS DE TAOS pop. 2,000—*See also TAOS.*

───── LODGING ─────

THE TAOS MOTEL   **Phone:** (505)758-2524
(AAA) [SAVE]   All Year   1P: $39-$49   2P: $45-$55   XP: $5   F6
◆   **Location:** Center, on SR 68. 1798 Paseo Del Pueblo Sur Ave 87557. Fax: 505/758-1989. **Terms:** [CP] meal
Motel   plan; pets. **Facility:** 27 rooms. 2 stories; exterior corridors; whirlpool. **Dining:** Restaurant nearby.
          Special Amenities: Free breakfast and free local telephone calls.   [S◇] 🛏 [ⓘ] ☒ [♨]

───── RESTAURANTS ─────

THE STAKEOUT GRILL & BAR   **Dinner:** $14-$28   **Phone:** 505/758-2042
◆◆◆   **Location:** 4 mi sw on SR 68, 1.3 mi e on gravel road at sign. 101 Stakeout Dr 87557. **Hours:** 5 pm-9:30
Steak and   pm. Closed: 11/1-11/30. **Reservations:** suggested. **Features:** casual dress; children's menu; health
Seafood   conscious menu; cocktails & lounge; a la carte. This restaurant has a unique setting on Outlaw Hill and
          offers good views of the mountain and sunsets. You can dine on the patio in summer. Specialty dishes
include lamb, veal and duck. The menu also has beef, seafood, fresh veggies and homemade desserts. **Cards:** AE, CB, DI,
DS, MC, VI.   ☒

─────── *The following restaurant has not been inspected by AAA* ───────
but is listed for your information only.

TRADING POST CAFE   **Phone:** 505/758-5089
[fyi]   Not inspected. **Location:** 4179 Paseo del Pueblo Sur 87557. **Features:** This is a bustling establishment
          where contemporary American and Italian fare come highly recommended. A local favorite, the restaurant is
visually appealing, with local art and sculpture on display.

RATON pop. 7,400

───── LODGINGS ─────

BEST WESTERN SANDS   **Phone:** (505)445-2737
(AAA) [SAVE]   5/11-9/3   1P: $79-$99   2P: $79-$99   XP: $5   F17
          9/4-10/14   1P: $59-$79   2P: $59-$79   XP: $5   F17
◆◆◆   2/1-5/10 & 10/15-1/31   1P: $49-$69   2P: $49-$69   XP: $5   F17
Motor Inn   **Location:** US 64 and 87, just w of jct I-25, exit 451. 300 Clayton Rd 87740. Fax: 505/445-4053. **Terms:** 7 day
          cancellation notice. **Facility:** 50 rooms. Large rooms. 1 story; interior/exterior corridors; heated pool; whirlpool;
playground. **Dining:** Restaurant; 6 am-9 pm; $5-$15. **Services:** gift shop. **All Rooms:** combo or shower baths.
Some Rooms: Fee: refrigerators, VCR. **Cards:** AE, DI, DS, MC, VI. **Special Amenities: Early check-in/late check-out and
free room upgrade (subject to availability with advanced reservations).** *(See color ad below)*
[S◇] [ⓘ] [⟨] [◎] ☒ [♨] [VCR] [▤] [▭] [▣] [█] [DATA PORT] [◿] ☒

BUDGET HOST MELODY LANE MOTEL

Phone: (505)445-3655

5/16-9/15	1P: $44	2P: $49	XP: $5	F8
2/1-5/15 & 9/16-1/31	1P: $36	2P: $41	XP: $5	F8

Motel

Location: I-25, exit 454, 0.8 mi s on I-25 business loop. 136 Canyon Dr 87740. Fax: 505/445-3461. **Terms:** [CP] meal plan; small pets only, $1 extra charge. **Facility:** 27 rooms. Convenient to historic downtown, exceptionally well-maintained and clean rooms. 1 two-bedroom unit. 1 story; exterior corridors; beachfront. **Recreation:** 8 rooms with steambaths; free movies in some rooms. **All Rooms:** combo or shower baths. **Cards:** AE, CB, DI, DS, MC, VI. **Special Amenities:** Free breakfast and free local telephone calls. *(See color ad p 374)*

🛇 🐾 🏠 ⊠

COMFORT INN
◆◆

Phone: (505)445-4200

All Year	1P: $53-$58	2P: $58-$63	XP: $5	F18

Motel

Location: US 64 and 87, just w of jct I-25, exit 451. 533 Clayton Rd 87740. Fax: 505/445-7144. **Terms:** [ECP] meal plan. **Facility:** 47 rooms. 2 stories; interior corridors. **Cards:** AE, CB, DI, DS, MC, VI.

SAVE 🛇 ⊠ ⊠ ⊠ ⊠ ⊠ ⊠ ⊠ ⊠

RATON SUPER 8
◆

Phone: (505)445-2355

4/2-9/3	1P: $48-$52	2P: $52-$58	XP: $6	F12
9/4-1/31	1P: $43-$49	2P: $47-$53	XP: $6	F12
2/1-4/1	1P: $42-$48	2P: $46-$52	XP: $6	F12

Motel

Location: I-25, exit 451. 1610 Cedar 87740. Fax: 505/445-2355. **Terms:** 14 day cancellation notice; small pets only, $25 dep req. **Facility:** 48 rooms. 3 stories, no elevator; interior corridors. **Some Rooms:** Fee: VCR. **Cards:** AE, DI, DS, MC, VI.

ASK 🛇 ⊠ ⊠ ⊠ ⊠ ⊠ VCR ⊠

——— RESTAURANTS ———

GRAPEVINE RESTAURANT AND PIZZERIA

Lunch: $5-$11   Dinner: $7-$20   Phone: 505/445-0969

Italian

Location: Center. 120 N 2nd St 87740. **Hours:** 11 am-9 pm. Closed: 12/25. **Reservations:** accepted. **Features:** casual dress; children's menu; senior's menu; health conscious menu; carryout; beer & wine only. Dine in a casual atmosphere at Grapevine Restaurant and Pizzeria, where the experienced chef/owner has produced a very good selection of freshly prepared Continental dishes including steak, seafood and pasta. Dishes have a Mediterranean influence. Smoke free premises. **Cards:** AE, CB, DI, DS, JC, MC, VI.

⊠

PAPPAS SWEET SHOP RESTAURANT

Lunch: $6-$9   Dinner: $9-$25   Phone: 505/445-9811

American

Location: 0.5 mi w on US 64 and 87 from jct I-25, exit 451; then just s on US 64. 1201 S Second St 87740. **Hours:** 9 am-2 & 5-9 pm. Closed: 1/1, 12/25 & Sun 9/1-5/31. **Reservations:** suggested; in season. **Features:** casual dress; children's menu; cocktails. This restaurant's well-rounded menu offers spaghetti, steak, seafood, sandwiches and Mexican meals. You'll also find displays of antiques, collectibles and items related to the family-owned restaurant and its early years of candy and ice cream making. **Cards:** AE, DS, MC, VI.

⊠

SHANG HAI RESTAURANT

Lunch: $4-$11   Dinner: $6-$14   Phone: 505/445-2933

Chinese

Location: I-25 exit 451 (Clayton Rd), 0.5 mi w jct. 1156 S 2nd St 87740. **Hours:** 11 am-9:30 pm, Fri-10 pm, Sat 11:30 am-10 pm, Sun 11:30 am-9:30 pm. **Features:** casual dress; a la carte. The locally popular Shang Hai specializes in Cantonese, Szechuan and Hunan cuisines featuring a variety of beef, pork, seafood and chicken, complemented by soups and appetizers. The buffet is a good choice for lunch; the staff is friendly and attentive. **Cards:** AE, DS, MC, VI.

⊠

RED RIVER pop. 400

——— LODGINGS ———

ALPINE LODGE
◆◆

Phone: (505)754-2952

2/1-4/2 & 11/22-1/31	1P: $52-$88	2P: $52-$88	XP: $10
4/3-11/21	1P: $35-$72	2P: $35-$72	XP: $8

Motor Inn

Location: Just nw of center on SR 38. 417 W Main St 87558 (PO Box 67). Fax: 505/754-6421. **Terms:** 30 day cancellation notice; cancellation fee imposed; 2 night min stay, weekends in season. **Facility:** 45 rooms. Variety of rooms in several buildings along the Red River. Some rooms with gas fireplace. 1 three-bedroom unit. 1 two-bedroom apartments, $55-$106 for up to 4 persons; 1-3 stories, no elevator; interior/exterior corridors; whirlpools; playground. **Dining:** Coffee shop; 7 am-2 pm; closed 10/15-11/27 & 4/1-5/22; cocktails. **Recreation:** fishing. Fee: downhill skiing. **All Rooms:** combo or shower baths. **Some Rooms:** 2 efficiencies. **Cards:** AE, DS, MC, VI. **Special Amenities:** Free local telephone calls.

🛇 ⊠ ⊠ ⊠ ⊠ ⊠ ⊠ ⊠ ⊠ ⊠ ⊠

LAZY MINER LODGE
◆

Phone: 505/754-6444

2/1-3/31	1P: $59-$139	2P: $59-$139	XP: $10
11/22-1/31	1P: $54-$139	2P: $54-$139	XP: $10
4/1-9/4	1P: $30-$105	2P: $30-$105	XP: $10
9/5-11/21	1P: $30-$75	2P: $30-$75	XP: $5

Motel

Location: SR 38 just w of jct SR 578. 505 E Main St 87558 (PO Box 836). Fax: 505/754-6479. **Terms:** 5 day cancellation notice; cancellation fee imposed; 2 night min stay, weekends, in season; package plans. **Facility:** 12 rooms. Modest accommodations. Most rooms with gas log fireplace. 1 three-bedroom unit, 5 two-bedroom units. 2 stories; exterior corridors; playground. **Recreation:** fishing. Fee: downhill skiing. **Some Rooms:** 7 kitchens. **Cards:** AE, DS, MC, VI.

ASK ⊠ ⊠ ⊠ ⊠ ⊠ ⊠ ⊠ ⊠ ⊠

——— RESTAURANT ———

TEXAS REDS STEAKHOUSE

Dinner: $10-$35   Phone: 505/754-2964

West American

Location: Center on SR 38. 111 E Main St 87558. **Hours:** 5 pm-9:30 pm. Closed: Mon-Thurs 4/1-5/15. **Features:** casual dress; children's menu; cocktails & lounge. This Old West saloon-style restaurant, with its rustic decor and peanut shells on the floor, is very popular, especially on weekends. The upstairs dining room serves a good selection of steaks, chops, chicken and burgers. The service is fast and friendly. **Cards:** AE, DI, DS, MC, VI.

RIO RANCHO pop. 32,500   (See map p. 369; index p. 367)—

──── LODGINGS ────

BEST WESTERN INN AT RIO RANCHO   Phone: (505)892-1700   **84**
🆑 ⒮ⓐⓥⓔ   5/1-10/14   1P: $79-$109   2P: $89-$129   XP: $6   F17
◆◆◆   2/1-4/30   1P: $69-$99   2P: $79-$109   XP: $6   F17
Motor Inn   10/15-1/31   1P: $59-$89   2P: $69-$99   XP: $6   F17
          Location: I-25, exit 233, 6.5 mi w on Alameda Blvd; I-40, exit 155, 10 mi n on Coors Rd/Coors Bypass to Hwy
          528, 1 mi n. 1465 Rio Rancho Blvd 87124. Fax: 505/892-4628. **Terms:** Weekly & monthly rates avail; pets, $25
extra charge. **Facility:** 118 rooms. 6 whirlpool rooms; 1-2 stories; exterior corridors; whirlpool. **Dining:** Dining room, coffee
shop; 6:30 am-10 pm; $3-$14; cocktails; also, Wine & Roses Restaurant, see separate listing; entertainment. **Services:** gift
shop. **Some Rooms:** Fee: VCR. **Cards:** AE, CB, DI, DS, JC, MC, VI. **Special Amenities:** Free breakfast and free local telephone calls. *(See color ad below)*

DAYS INN   Phone: (505)892-8800   **82**
🆑 ⒮ⓐⓥⓔ   10/1-10/15   1P: $75-$85   2P: $85-$90   XP: $12   F12
◆◆   5/1-9/30   1P: $50-$60   2P: $60-$65   XP: $8   F12
Motel   2/1-4/30 & 10/16-1/31   1P: $45-$55   2P: $55-$60   XP: $8   F12
          Location: I-25, exit 233 (Alameda Blvd), then 8 mi w on NM 528; I-40, exit 155, then 8 mi n on Coors Rd (NM
          448). 4200 Crestview Dr 87124. Fax: 505/896-3321. **Terms:** [CP] meal plan; small pets only. **Facility:** 46
rooms. 2 stories; exterior corridors; heated pool, whirlpool. **All Rooms:** extended cable TV. **Some Rooms:** Fee: refrigerators,
microwaves. **Cards:** AE, CB, DI, DS, MC, VI. **Special Amenities:** Free breakfast and free local telephone calls.

HILTON GARDEN INN   Phone: (505)896-1111   **86**
🆑 ⒮ⓐⓥⓔ   All Year   1P: $69-$139   2P: $69-$139   XP: $5   F18
◆◆◆   **Location:** I-25 N to Alameda Dr becomes Hwy 528/Rio Rancho Blvd. 1771 Rio Rancho Blvd 87124.
Hotel   Fax: 505/896-2100. **Facility:** 129 rooms. All rooms with hair dryer, iron and ironing board. 4 stories; interior
          corridors; heated pool, whirlpool. **Dining:** 6 am-1 & 5-10 pm; restaurant nearby. **Recreation:** in-room video
games. **Cards:** AE, DI, DS, MC, VI.

RAMADA LIMITED HOTEL   Phone: (505)892-5998   **83**
◆◆◆   All Year   1P: $45   2P: $50   XP: $6   F17
Motel   **Location:** I-25, exit 233, then 8 mi w on Alameda Blvd (NM 528); I-40, exit 155, 8 mi n on Coors Rd (NM 448).
          4081 High Resort Blvd 87124. Fax: 505/892-9131. **Terms:** [CP] meal plan; 3 day cancellation notice; small pets
only. **Facility:** 57 rooms. 2 stories; interior corridors; heated pool. **Some Rooms:** Fee: refrigerators, microwaves. **Cards:** AE,
CB, DI, DS, MC, VI.

RIO RANCHO SUPER 8 MOTEL   Phone: 505/896-8888   **85**
◆◆   Property failed to provide current rates
Motel   **Location:** I-25, exit 233, 0.5 mi w on Alameda Blvd, 3.8 mi nw on 528, just e. 4100 Barbara Loop 87124.
          Fax: 505/896-2665. **Terms:** Pets, $6 fee. **Facility:** 48 rooms. 2 stories; interior corridors. **Some Rooms:**
Fee: refrigerators. **Cards:** AE, DI, DS, MC, VI.

(See map p. 369)

WELLESLEY INN & SUITES

All Year   1P: $49-$99   2P: $49-$99   XP: $10

Phone: (505)892-7900   88

F18

Extended Stay
Motel

Location: I-25, exit 233 6 mi w on Alameda Blvd, turns into Rio Rancho Blvd/SR 528. 2221 Rio Rancho Blvd 87124. Fax: 505/892-7999. **Terms:** [CP] meal plan; pets, $150 fee, $100 dep req. **Facility:** 109 rooms. 3 stories; interior corridors; heated pool. **Recreation:** barbecue facility, basketball court. **All Rooms:** kitchens, extended cable TV. **Cards:** AE, CB, DI, DS, JC, MC, VI. **Special Amenities:** Free breakfast and free newspaper.

——— RESTAURANT ———

WINE & ROSES RESTAURANT   **Lunch:** $5-$9   **Dinner:** $9-$15   **Phone:** 505/892-1700   67

Continental

Location: I-25, exit 233, 6.5 mi w on Alameda Blvd; I-40, exit 155, 10 mi n on Coors Rd/Coors Bypass to Hwy 528, 1 mi n; in Best Western Inn at Rio Rancho. 1465 Rio Rancho Dr 87124. **Hours:** 6:30 am-10 pm. **Features:** casual dress; children's menu; senior's menu; cocktails & lounge. You may want to consider dining on the patio in its lovely courtyard setting while sampling the spicy, fresh seafood, served daily. The menu also features German specialties, finger foods for appetizers, and good-size steaks for hearty appetites. **Cards:** AE, DI, DS, MC, VI.

ROSWELL pop. 44,700

——— LODGINGS ———

BEST WESTERN EL RANCHO PALACIO MOTOR LODGE

All Year   1P: $42-$60   2P: $46-$65   XP: $5

Phone: (505)622-2721

F12

Motel

Location: 1.8 mi n on US 70 and 285. 2205 N Main St 88201. Fax: 505/622-2725. **Terms:** [ECP] meal plan; pets. **Facility:** 44 rooms. Contemporary room appointments. 2 stories; exterior corridors; heated pool, whirlpool. **Dining:** Restaurant nearby. **All Rooms:** extended cable TV. **Cards:** AE, CB, DI, DS, MC, VI. **Special Amenities:** Free breakfast and free local telephone calls.

BEST WESTERN SALLY PORT INN & SUITES

All Year   1P: $69-$89   2P: $79-$99   XP: $10

Phone: (505)622-6430

F12

Motor Inn

Location: 1.5 mi n on US 70 and 285. 2000 N Main St 88201. Fax: 505/623-7631. **Terms:** Small pets only. **Facility:** 124 rooms. 2 stories; interior corridors; golf proshop; heated pool, saunas, whirlpool; 1 tennis court. **Dining:** Restaurant; 6 am-10 & 5-9 pm, Sat & Sun 6 am-11 & 5-10 pm; $10-$17; cocktails. **Recreation:** hair salon, indoor recreation area, video game room. **All Rooms:** extended cable TV. **Cards:** AE, CB, DI, DS, MC, VI. **Special Amenities:** Free breakfast and free room upgrade (subject to availability with advanced reservations). *(See color ad below)*

BUDGET INN-NORTH

5/2-9/1   1P: $30-$40   2P: $35-$50
9/2-1/31   1P: $28-$32   2P: $32-$45
2/1-5/1   1P: $28-$32   2P: $32-$45   XP: $4

Phone: (505)623-6050

F12

Motel

Location: 1.8 mi n on US 70 and 285. 2101 N Main St 88201. Fax: 505/623-8546. **Terms:** Weekly rates avail; cancellation fee imposed; small pets only, $2 extra charge. **Facility:** 42 rooms. Mature property. 2 stories; exterior corridors; small pool, whirlpool. **Dining:** Restaurant nearby. **All Rooms:** extended cable TV. **Cards:** AE, CB, DI, DS, MC, VI. **Special Amenities:** Free local telephone calls.

BUDGET INN WEST

All Year   1P: $27-$37   2P: $48   XP: $5

Phone: (505)623-3811

F14

Motel

Location: 2 mi w on US 70 and 380. 2200 W 2nd St 88201. Fax: 505/623-7030. **Terms:** Weekly rates avail; small pets only, $2 extra charge. **Facility:** 29 rooms. Mature property. 2 stories; exterior corridors; small pool, whirlpool. **All Rooms:** extended cable TV. **Some Rooms:** kitchen. **Cards:** AE, DS, MC, VI. **Special Amenities:** Free local telephone calls.

DAYS INN
AAA SAVE
◆◆
Motor Inn

Phone: (505)623-4021
All Year   1P: $44-$60   2P: $52-$65   XP: $5   F12
Location: 0.8 mi n on US 70 and 285. 1310 N Main St 88201. Fax: 505/623-0079. **Terms:** [BP] meal plan; pets. **Facility:** 62 rooms. In a commercial area. At-door parking. 2 stories; exterior corridors; whirlpool. **Dining:** Restaurant, coffee shop; 6:30 am-10 pm; $6-$21; cocktails. **All Rooms:** extended cable TV. **Cards:** AE, CB, DI, DS, MC, VI.

FRONTIER MOTEL
AAA
◆◆
Motel

Phone: (505)622-1400
All Year   1P: $28-$40   2P: $32-$48   XP: $4
Location: 2.5 mi n on US 70 and 285. 3010 N Main St 88201. Fax: 505/622-1405. **Terms:** [CP] meal plan; pets. **Facility:** 38 rooms. Well kept older property. 2 two-bedroom units. 1 story; exterior corridors. **Dining:** Restaurant nearby. **All Rooms:** combo or shower baths, extended cable TV. **Cards:** AE, CB, DI, DS, MC, VI. (See color ad below)

LEISURE INN
AAA SAVE
◆◆
Motel

Phone: (505)622-2575
All Year   1P: $32-$42   2P: $36-$46   XP: $5   F12
Location: 2.5 mi w on US 70 and 380. 2700 W 2nd St 88201. Fax: 505/622-2575. **Terms:** [CP] meal plan; weekly & monthly rates avail; small pets only. **Facility:** 90 rooms. Large rooms and attractive courtyard. 2 bedroom unit, $65 for up to 6 persons; 2 stories; exterior corridors. **Dining:** Restaurant nearby. **Services:** winter plug-ins. **Recreation:** sports court. **Some Rooms:** 5 efficiencies, 2 kitchens, no utensils. **Cards:** AE, DS, MC, VI. **Special Amenities:** Early check-in/late check-out and free local telephone calls.

MOTEL 6 OF ROSWELL - 4075
◆◆
Motel
MC, VI.

Phone: 505/625-6666
Property failed to provide current rates
Location: 3307 N Main St 88201. Fax: 505/625-6741. **Terms:** Pets, $30 dep req. **Facility:** 83 rooms. 3 stories; interior corridors; small heated indoor pool. **All Rooms:** combo or shower baths. **Cards:** AE, CB, DI,

NATIONAL 9 INN
AAA SAVE
◆◆
Motel

Phone: (505)622-0110
All Year   1P: $29-$35   2P: $32-$38   XP: $6   F17
Location: 1.5 mi n on US 285 and 70. 2001 N Main St 88201. Fax: 505/622-6011. **Terms:** Weekly & monthly rates avail; pets, $5 extra charge. **Facility:** 65 rooms. Mature property. 2 stories; exterior corridors. **All Rooms:** extended cable TV. **Cards:** AE, DI, DS, MC, VI. **Special Amenities:** Free local telephone calls.

RAMADA INN
AAA SAVE
◆◆◆
Motor Inn

Phone: (505)623-9440
All Year   1P: $64-$74   2P: $68-$78   XP: $5   F17
Location: 2.5 mi w on US 70 and 380. 2803 W 2nd 88202. Fax: 505/622-9708. **Terms:** Pets, $50 dep req. **Facility:** 59 rooms. 2 stories; interior/exterior corridors; heated pool. **Dining:** Restaurant; 7 am-2 & 5-8 pm; $9-$13. **All Rooms:** extended cable TV. **Cards:** AE, CB, DI, DS, JC, MC, VI. **Special Amenities:** Free local telephone calls.

——— RESTAURANTS ———

KWAN DEN
◆
Chinese

Lunch: $5-$6   Dinner: $6-$8   Phone: 505/622-4192
Location: 0.8 mi w on US 385/70, corner of 2nd St and Union Ave. 1000 W 2nd St 88201. **Hours:** 11 am-2 & 5-9 pm, Sun 11 am-8 pm. Closed: 11/23 & 12/25. **Features:** casual dress; children's menu; carryout; salad bar. Lunch and dinner buffets offer the best value at this restaurant featuring Chinese dishes with beef, shrimp, chicken and pork. They also have a limited number of American dishes with chicken and seafood. You'll receive prompt, friendly service here. **Cards:** AE, DS, MC, VI.

PASTA CAFE
◆◆
Italian

Lunch: $6-$9   Dinner: $8-$13   Phone: 505/624-1111
Location: US 70/285; in Roswell Mall. 4501 N Main St 88201. **Hours:** 11:30 am-9 pm. Closed: 4/23, 11/23 & 12/25. **Features:** casual dress; children's menu; carryout; beer & wine only; a la carte. You'll enjoy a good selection of tasty pasta dishes, pizza selections and hot appetizers as well as a limited number of steak, seafood and pork entrees at the Pasta Cafe. Two types of fresh baked bread offered. A small bar area is off the dining room. **Cards:** AE, DI, DS, MC, VI.

PEPPERS GRILL & BAR   **Lunch:** $5-$8   **Dinner:** $6-$14   **Phone:** 505/623-1700
◆
American   **Location:** US 70/285, corner of Main and 6th St. 500 N Main St 88201. **Hours:** 11 am-10 pm. Closed major holidays & Sun. **Features:** casual dress; children's menu; carryout; cocktails & lounge; a la carte. This restaurant offers a good variety of appetizers, burgers, salads, pasta, sandwiches and traditional Mexican dishes for lunch and dinner. Live entertainment is presented on the outdoor patio on Fridays and Saturdays during the summer. **Cards:** AE, CB, DI, DS, MC, VI.

The following restaurant has not been inspected by AAA but is listed for your information only.

CATTLE BARON STEAK & SEAFOOD   **Phone:** 505/622-2465
(fyi)   Not inspected. **Location:** 1113 Main St 88201. **Features:** A ranch-like atmosphere, hand-cut steaks and a huge salad bar highlight this highly popular eatery.

RUIDOSO pop. 4,600

——— LODGINGS ———

DAN DEE CABINS-RESORT   **Phone:** (505)257-2165

6/15-9/6	1P: $94-$109	2P: $94-$109	XP: $10
2/1-4/15	1P: $84-$94	2P: $84-$94	XP: $10
9/7-1/31	1P: $74-$94	2P: $74-$94	XP: $5
4/16-6/14	1P: $74-$84	2P: $74-$84	XP: $5

Cottage **Location:** 0.8 mi w on Upper Canyon Rd. 310 Main Rd 88345 (PO Box 844, 88355). **Terms:** Weekly rates avail; 14 day cancellation notice; cancellation fee imposed; package plans. **Facility:** 13 rooms. 1- to 3-bedroom housekeeping cabins with fireplace. 5-acre pine forest. 6 two-bedroom units, 2 three-bedroom units. 3-bedroom cabins, $103-$142 for up to 7 persons; 1 story; exterior corridors; playground. **Recreation:** fishing. **All Rooms:** kitchens, combo or shower baths, extended cable TV. **Cards:** DS, MC, VI. **Special Amenities: Free local telephone calls and preferred room (subject to availability with advanced reservations).**

ENCHANTMENT INN   **Phone:** 505-378-4051
◆◆
Motor Inn   All Year   1P: $89-$185   2P: $89-$185   XP: $10   F
Location: US 70 at jct Sudderth Dr and US 70. 307 W Hwy 70 88345 (PO Box 8060). Fax: 505/378-5427. **Terms:** Package plans. **Facility:** 81 rooms. Commercial location. Short drive to race track. 2 two-bedroom units. 2 stories; interior corridors; heated pool. **Dining:** entertainment. **Some Rooms:** 29 efficiencies. Fee: VCR. **Cards:** AE, DI, DS, MC, VI.

HOLIDAY INN EXPRESS   **Phone:** (505)257-3736
◆◆◆
Motel   All Year   1P: $59-$139   2P: $59-$139   XP: $10   F18
Location: US 70, just w of jct with Sudderth Dr. 400 W Hwy 70 88355 (PO Box 7310). Fax: 505/257-5202. **Terms:** [ECP] meal plan; cancellation fee imposed. **Facility:** 104 rooms. Large, well appointed rooms in Southwestern style. 3 stories; interior corridors; small heated pool. **All Rooms:** combo or shower baths. **Cards:** AE, CB, DI, DS, JC, MC, VI.

RUIDOSO LODGE CABINS   **Phone:** 505-257-2510
◆◆◆
Cottage   All Year   1P: $99   2P: $109   XP: $20
Location: 0.7 mi w on Upper Canyon Rd. 300 Main Rd 88345. **Terms:** 14 day cancellation notice. **Facility:** 9 rooms. All cabins with fireplace. Lovely grounds. 1 story; exterior corridors. **Recreation:** fishing.
All Rooms: kitchens. **Cards:** DS, MC, VI.

SHADOW MOUNTAIN LODGE   **Phone:** (505)257-4886

6/1-10/21	1P: $82-$97	2P: $82-$97	XP: $10
2/1-5/31 & 10/22-1/31	1P: $67-$82	2P: $67-$82	XP: $10

Motel **Location:** Just w on Upper Canyon Rd. 107 Main Rd 88345. Fax: 505/257-2000. **Terms:** Weekly rates avail; age restrictions may apply; 7 day cancellation notice; package plans. **Facility:** 19 rooms. Nicely landscaped grounds. All units with fireplace hair dryer, iron and ironing board. 1 story; exterior corridors; whirlpool. **Dining:** Restaurant nearby. **All Rooms:** extended cable TV. **Some Rooms:** 10 kitchens. **Cards:** AE, CB, DI, DS, MC, VI. **Special Amenities: Free local telephone calls.**

STORY BOOK CABINS   **Phone:** 505-257-2115

2/1-5/21 & 11/1-1/31	1P: $89-$109	2P: $89-$109	XP: $10
5/22-10/31	1P: $109	2P: $109	XP: $10

Cottage **Location:** 1 mi w on Upper Canyon Rd. 410 Main Rd 88345 (PO Box 472, 88355). Fax: 505/257-7512. **Terms:** Weekly rates avail; 14 day cancellation notice; package plans. **Facility:** 10 rooms. 1- to 3-bedroom housekeeping cabins with fireplace; in pine forest. 2-bedroom $119, 3-bedroom $159 in season; 1 story; exterior corridors. **Recreation:** fishing; hiking trails. **All Rooms:** kitchens, extended cable TV. **Cards:** AE, DS, MC, VI.

VILLAGE LODGE   **Phone:** 505-258-5442
◆◆◆
Apartment   All Year   1P: $79-$129   2P: $79-$129   XP: $10
Location: 2 mi n on SR 48. 1000 Mechem Dr 88345. Fax: 505/258-3127. **Terms:** 7 day cancellation notice; small pets only, $10 fee, dogs only. **Facility:** 24 rooms. 1-bedroom suites with fireplace. 2 stories; exterior corridors. **All Rooms:** kitchens. **Cards:** AE, DS, MC, VI.

——— RESTAURANTS ———

CASA BLANCA
◆◆
Mexican
Lunch: $6-$12   **Dinner:** $6-$12   **Phone:** 505/257-2495
Location: 1 mi n on SR 48. 501 Mechem St 88345. **Hours:** 11 am-10 pm. Closed: 11/23 & 12/25.
Reservations: accepted; 5 persons. **Features:** casual dress; children's menu; cocktails; a la carte. This popular restaurant serves up sumptuous and plentiful portions of its Mexican and New Mexican influenced cuisine. The tasty salsa and tortilla chips provide a wonderful warm-up for favorites such as the green-chili chicken enchiladas. **Cards:** AE, MC, VI.   ✕

CATTLE BARON STEAK & SEAFOOD
◆◆
Steak and
Seafood
Lunch: $5-$8   **Dinner:** $9-$23   **Phone:** 505/257-9355
Location: 1.3 mi s. 657 Sudderth Dr 88355. **Hours:** 11 am-10 pm, Fri & Sat-10:30 pm. **Features:** casual dress; children's menu; carryout; salad bar; cocktails & lounge. The bustling, casual, Western-style atmosphere at Cattle Baron's proves the popularity of its menu, which offers steak, seafood, prime rib, filet mignon and shrimp scampi in satisfying portions. It also has one of the most extensive salad bars imaginable. **Cards:** AE, DI, DS, MC, VI.   ✕

LA LORRAINE
(AAA)
◆◆◆
French
Lunch: $7-$12   **Dinner:** $14-$30   **Phone:** 505/257-2954
Location: Center. 2523 Sudderth Dr 88345. **Hours:** 11:30 am-2 & 5:30-9 pm, Fri & Sat-9:30 pm. Closed: Mon & Tues for lunch & Sun. **Reservations:** suggested. **Features:** casual dress; carryout; beer & wine only; street parking; a la carte. The French Provincial decor and excellent food are hallmarks of this little Parisian oasis in the middle of New Mexico. Their specialties are Long Island duckling and rack of lamb. The pates, bisques, salads and homemade desserts are mouth-watering. **Cards:** AE, DI, DS, MC, VI.   ✕

——— *The following restaurant has not been inspected by AAA* ———
but is listed for your information only.

CAFE RIO
[fyi]
of beer.
Phone: 505/257-7746
Not inspected. **Location:** 2547 Sudderth Dr 88345. **Features:** This unpretentious establishment features excellent deep-dish pizza, calzones and a variety of Mediterranean dishes as well as an extensive selection

RUIDOSO DOWNS pop. 900

——— LODGINGS ———

BESTWAY INN
(AAA) [SAVE]
◆◆
Motel
Phone: (505)378-8000

5/23-9/30	1P: $110-$140	2P: $126-$185	XP: $9	F17
10/1-1/31	1P: $45-$65	2P: $65-$85	XP: $9	F17
3/15-5/22	1P: $65-$70	2P: $70-$80	XP: $9	F17
2/1-3/14	1P: $45-$55	2P: $55-$65	XP: $9	F17

Location: US 70, 0.5 mi e of jct US 70 and SR 48. (PO Box 89, 88346). Fax: 505/378-1010. **Terms:** Cancellation fee imposed; pets. **Facility:** 19 rooms. 2 stories; exterior corridors. **All Rooms:** combo or shower baths, extended cable TV, safes. **Some Rooms:** Fee: VCR. **Cards:** AE, CB, DI, DS, MC, VI. **Special Amenities:** Early check-in/late check-out and free local telephone calls.   [S/D] 🛏 △ ✕ 🍴 [VCR] 📺 📞

DAYS INN
(AAA) [SAVE]
◆◆◆
Motel
Phone: (505)378-4299

9/5-1/31	1P: $46-$96	2P: $56-$146	XP: $10	F17
2/1-5/20	1P: $46-$96	2P: $56-$145	XP: $10	F17
5/21-9/4	1P: $56-$116	2P: $56-$116	XP: $10	F17

Location: US 70, 0.5 mi e of jct US 70 and SR 48. 2088 Hwy 70 W 88346 (HCR 46, Box 608). Fax: 505/378-1010. **Terms:** [CP] meal plan; cancellation fee imposed. **Facility:** 50 rooms. Contemporary style rooms. 7 whirlpool rooms; 2 stories; exterior corridors; small heated indoor pool, whirlpool. **Dining:** Restaurant nearby. **All Rooms:** extended cable TV, safes. **Some Rooms:** Fee: VCR. **Cards:** AE, CB, DI, DS, MC, VI. **Special Amenities:** Free breakfast and free local telephone calls.   [S/D] 🍴 △ ✕ 🍴 [VCR] 📺 📞 [DATA PORT] 🔒 🔒

SANTA FE pop. 55,900 (See map p. 428; index below)

This index helps you "spot" where approved accommodations are located on the detailed maps that follow. Rate ranges are for comparison only and show the property's high season. Turn to the listing page for more detailed rate information and consult display ads for special promotions. Restaurant rate range is for dinner unless only lunch (L) is served.

SANTA FE

Spotter/Map Page Number	OA	SANTA FE - Lodgings	Diamond Rating	Rate Range High Season	Listing Page
① / p. 428	(AAA)	Sunterra Resorts Villas de Santa Fe	◆◆◆	$170-$190 [SAVE]	440
③ / p. 428	(AAA)	Casa de la Cuma B & B	◆◆◆	$85-$145 [SAVE]	429
④ / p. 428		Spencer House Bed & Breakfast Inn	◆◆◆	$105-$150	440
⑥ / p. 428		Territorial Inn - see color ad p 433	◆◆◆	$120-$180	440
⑦ / p. 428		Fort Marcy Hotel Suites - see color ad p 433	◆◆◆	$219-$285	432
⑧ / p. 428		RIO VISTA SUITES - see color ad p 433	◆◆◆	$135-$165	439
⑨ / p. 428		Las Palomas	◆◆◆	Failed to provide	438
⑩ / p. 428	(AAA)	Eldorado Hotel - see color ad p 431	◆◆◆◆	$239-$269 [SAVE]	431
⑪ / p. 428		Casapueblo Inn	◆◆◆	$159-$269	430

SANTA FE, NM (426)

Spotter/Map Page Number	OA	SANTA FE - Lodgings (continued)	Diamond Rating	Rate Range High Season	Listing Page
12 / p. 428		Hilton of Santa Fe - see color ad 41, p 433	♦♦♦	$199-$289	433
13 / p. 428		Otra Vez en Santa Fe	♦♦♦	Failed to provide	438
14 / p. 428	(A)	Radisson Hotel & Suites on the Plaza Santa Fe	♦♦♦	$179 SAVE	438
15 / p. 428		Inn of the Anasazi	♦♦♦♦♦	$265-$415	435
16 / p. 428		Hacienda Nicholas	♦♦♦	$160	432
17 / p. 428	(A)	The Hotel Loretto - see color ad p 434	♦♦♦	$215-$520 SAVE	434
18 / p. 428	(A)	Inn of the Governors - see color ad p 436	♦♦♦	$189-$199 SAVE	436
19 / p. 428		The Madeleine	♦♦	$80-$160	438
20 / p. 428	(A)	La Fonda Hotel - see color ad p 437	♦♦♦	$199-$249 SAVE	437
21 / p. 428		Hotel St Francis - see color ad p 435	♦♦♦	$98-$353	434
22 / p. 428		Adobe Abode	♦♦♦	$120-$170	429
23 / p. 428		Seret's 1001 Nights - see color ad p 433	♦♦	$219-$269	440
24 / p. 428	(A)	Inn On The Alameda - see color ad p 436	♦♦♦	$147-$342 SAVE	437
25 / p. 428	(A)	El Farolito Bed & Breakfast Inn	♦♦♦	$140-$175	431
26 / p. 428	(A)	Santa Fe Motel - see color ad p 433	♦♦	$110-$159 SAVE	440
27 / p. 428	(A)	Hotel Santa Fe - see color ad p 435	♦♦♦	$169-$259 SAVE	434
28 / p. 428	(A)	El Paradero Bed & Breakfast	♦♦♦	$65-$125	432
29 / p. 428	(A)	Alexander's Inn	♦♦♦	$90-$160	429
30 / p. 428	(A)	Santa Fe Plaza Travelodge	♦♦	$89-$125 SAVE	440
32 / p. 428	(A)	Santa Fe Budget Inn	♦♦	$82-$94	439
34 / p. 428		Four Kachinas Inn	♦♦♦	$112-$160	432
38 / p. 428		The Bishop's Lodge	♦♦♦	$271-$408	429
39 / p. 428		Cities of Gold Casino Hotel	♦♦♦	$85	430
40 / p. 428	(A)	Radisson Santa Fe - see ad p 439	♦♦♦	$89-$139 SAVE	438
41 / p. 428	(A)	Motel 6 - 150	♦	$52-$68	438
42 / p. 428	(A)	El Rey Inn - see color ad p 432	♦♦♦	$75-$155	432
43 / p. 428		Residence Inn by Marriott	♦♦♦	Failed to provide	439
44 / p. 428		Days Inn of Santa Fe	♦♦	$69-$85	431
45 / p. 428	(A)	Cactus Lodge Motel	♦	$48-$88	429
46 / p. 428	(A)	Quality Inn	♦♦♦	$95-$105 SAVE	438
47 / p. 428		Comfort Suites	♦♦♦	$79-$119	430
48 / p. 428		Santa Fe Courtyard by Marriott	♦♦♦	$99-$139	439
50 / p. 428		Cerrillos Road Travelodge	♦♦♦	$79-$119	430
51 / p. 428		Holiday Inn Express	♦♦♦	$89-$129	434
55 / p. 428		Best Western of Santa Fe - see color ad p 429	♦♦♦	$65-$125	429
56 / p. 428	(A)	Luxury Inn - see color ad p 437	♦♦	$55-$90 SAVE	438
57 / p. 428		Howard Johnson Express - see ad p 436	♦♦	$50-$89	435
58 / p. 428	(A)	Holiday Inn	♦♦♦	$129 SAVE	434
59 / p. 428	(A)	Sleep Inn	♦♦	$84-$129 SAVE	440
60 / p. 428		Fairfield Inn by Marriott	♦♦♦	$85-$93	432
61 / p. 428	(A)	La Quinta Inn	♦♦♦	$95-$115 SAVE	437
62 / p. 428	(A)	Comfort Inn - see color ad p 430	♦♦♦	$75-$125 SAVE	430
		SANTA FE - Restaurants			
1 / p. 428		Osteria d'Assisi	♦♦	$14-$25	442
3 / p. 428	(A)	Santacafe	♦♦♦	$17-$27	442
5 / p. 428		The Old House	♦♦♦♦	$17-$31	441
7 / p. 428		Plaza Restaurant	♦	$8-$12	442
8 / p. 428		Ore House on the Plaza	♦♦	$13-$27	441
9 / p. 428	(A)	The Palace & Saloon	♦♦♦	$16-$25	442
10 / p. 428		Paul's Restaurant of Santa Fe	♦♦	$15-$20	442
12 / p. 428		Anasazi Restaurant	♦♦♦	$17-$32	440
14 / p. 428		San Francisco Street Bar & Grill	♦	$7-$13	442
15 / p. 428		India Palace	♦♦	$10-$18	441
16 / p. 428	(A)	Coyote Cafe	♦♦♦	$40	441
18 / p. 428		The Shed	♦♦	$9-$15	442
20 / p. 428	(A)	La Casa Sena Restaurant	♦♦♦	$19-$57	441
22 / p. 428		Tomasita's Santa Fe Station	♦	$8-$11	442

Spotter/Map Page Number	OA	SANTA FE - Restaurants (continued)	Diamond Rating	Rate Range High Season	Listing Page
㉓ / p. 428		Pranzo Italian Grill	◆◆	$7-$20	442
㉔ / p. 428	⊕	**Upper Crust Pizza**	◆	$5-$14	443
㉕ / p. 428		The Pink Adobe	◆◆	$10-$25	442
㉖ / p. 428		El Comedor	◆◆	$5-$12	441
㉘ / p. 428		The Dining Room at The Bishop's Lodge	◆◆◆	$19-$29	441
㉙ / p. 428		Bistro 315	◆◆◆	$17-$29	441
㉚ / p. 428		Geronimo	◆◆◆	$18-$30	441
㉞ / p. 428		Old Mexico Grill	◆◆	$9-$18	441
㊱ / p. 428	⊕	**Tortilla Flats**	◆◆	$6-$10	443
㊳ / p. 428		Harry's Road House Cafe	◆	$8-$12	441
㊵ / p. 428		Steaksmith at El Gancho	◆◆	$9-$25	442

Rules of the Road Can Change at State Borders

*S*peed limits are usually posted at state lines, but adherence to less known traffic regulations also is important for safe and enjoyable travel between states.

To assist traveling motorists, AAA publishes the *Digest of Motor Laws*–a comprehensive description of the laws that govern motor vehicle operation in the United States and Canada.

Examples of laws that differ in neighboring states include:

- In Oklahoma, police can only cite motorists for not wearing seat belts if they are stopped for another infraction. In neighboring Texas–and in 12 other states–police can stop motorists solely for failure to wear a seat belt.

- Drivers in Michigan are permitted to wear headsets, but not when they cross the border into Ohio or travel to 14 other states.

- Radar detectors are legal in Maryland–and 48 other states–but can't be used in Virginia and Washington, D.C.

To obtain a copy of the *Digest of Motor Laws*, contact your local AAA club or the traffic safety department of AAA's national office at 1000 AAA Drive, Heathrow, FL 32746-5063. The glove-compartment-size book retails for $8.95.

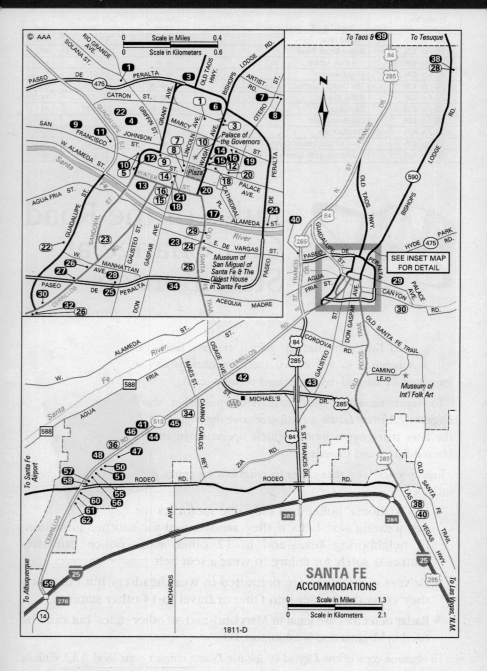

© AAA

RIO GRANDE AVE.
SOLANA ST.
PASEO DE 475 PERALTA
CATRON ST.
22
4 GRIFFIN ST. GRANT AVE.
SAN
9 MARCY AVE.
11 FRANCISCO JOHNSON ST.
W. ALAMEDA ST.
Santa
10 12 9
5
13
AGUA FRIA ST.
16
15
21
18
17
22
23 23
24
26 W. MANHATTAN AVE.
27 28
30 PASEO DE 25 PERALTA
32 26 34

OLD TAOS HWY.
BISHOPS LODGE RD.
ARTIST RD.
3
1 6
OTERO ST.
7
8
3
Palace of the Governors
7
8 10
14
16
19
12
20
18
20
Plaza
PALACE AVE.
CATHEDRAL PL.
E. ALAMEDA
24
29 E. DE VARGAS ST.
River
Museum of San Miguel of Santa Fe & The Oldest House in Santa Fe
25
ACEQUIA MADRE

To Taos & 39   To Tesuque
84
285
38
28
590
OLD TAOS HWY.
BISHOPS LODGE RD.
84
HYDE 475 PARK RD.
40
285
SEE INSET MAP FOR DETAIL
PASEO DE PERALTA
AGUA FRIA ST.
29
CANYON
30
PALACE AVE. RD.

ALAMEDA River
W.
Santa
AGUA
588
FRIA
588
OSAGE AVE.
MAES ST.
CERRILLOS RD.
510
CAMINO CARLOS REY
42
MICHAEL'S
43
CORDOVA RD.
GALISTEO ST.
DON GASPAR RD.
OLD SANTA FE TRAIL
CAMINO LEJO
Museum of Int'l Folk Art
34
41 45
46 44
36
48 47
50
57 51
58
RODEO RD.
60
61
62
To Santa Fe Airport
CERRILLOS RD.
S. ST. FRANCIS DR.
84
RD.
ZIA
RODEO RD.
282
284
25
OLD SANTA FE TRAIL
38
40
LAS VEGAS HWY.
25
To Las Vegas, N.M.

To Albuquerque
25
278
14
59

RICHARDS AVE.

SANTA FE
ACCOMMODATIONS
0   Scale in Miles   1.3
0   Scale in Kilometers   2.1

1811-D

SANTA FE pop. 55,900 (See map p. 428; index p. 425)

—— LODGINGS ——

ADOBE ABODE
Phone: (505)983-3133 　**22**
◆◆◆　All Year　1P: $120-$160　2P: $130-$170　XP: $20
Historic Bed　**Location:** At McKenzie St. 202 Chapelle 87501. Fax: 505/424-3027. **Terms:** [BP] meal plan; 14 day cancella-
& Breakfast　tion notice; cancellation fee imposed. **Facility:** 6 rooms. Adobe home circa 1907, rooms vary in size from cozy
to spacious. Eclectic decor, with themes varying from "English Garden" to "Bronco". 1 story; interior/exterior
corridors; smoke free premises. **All Rooms:** combo or shower baths. **Cards:** DS, MC, VI.

ALEXANDER'S INN
Phone: (505)986-1431 　**29**
🅰🅰🅰　3/15-11/15　1P: $90-$160　2P: $90-$160　XP: $20
　2/1-3/14 & 11/16-1/31　1P: $80-$145　2P: $80-$145　XP: $20
◆◆◆　**Location:** 6 blks e of Plaza. 529 E Palace Ave 87501. Fax: 505/982-8572. **Terms:** [BP] & [ECP] meal plans;
Historic Bed　weekly & monthly rates avail; age restrictions may apply; 14 day cancellation notice; pets, $20 extra charge.
& Breakfast　**Facility:** 9 rooms. Victorian bungalow home built in 1903. Decorated with antiques. Some guest rooms with
fireplace. Whirlpool room, $140-$160; 2 stories; interior/exterior corridors; smoke free premises; whirlpool.
Services: Fee: massage. **All Rooms:** extended cable TV. **Some Rooms:** 3 kitchens, color TV. **Cards:** DS, MC, VI.

BEST WESTERN OF SANTA FE
Phone: 505/438-3822 　**55**
◆◆◆　5/26-9/10　1P: $65-$115　2P: $65-$125　XP: $10　F18
Motel　9/11-10/11　1P: $40-$115　2P: $45-$125　XP: $10　F18
　2/1-5/25 & 10/12-1/31　1P: $40-$75　2P: $45-$85　XP: $10　F18
Location: I-25, exit 278B, 2.8 mi n. 3650 Cerrillos Rd 87505. Fax: 505/438-3795. **Terms:** [CP] meal plan; small pets only.
Facility: 97 rooms. Many suites avail. Some rooms with balcony. 3 stories; interior corridors; heated pool. **All Rooms:** safes.
Cards: AE, CB, DI, DS, MC, VI. *(See color ad below)*

THE BISHOP'S LODGE
Phone: (505)983-6377 　**38**
◆◆◆　5/26-8/31　1P: $271-$408　2P: $271-$408　XP: $15　F3
Resort　3/17-5/25 & 9/1-1/31　1P: $165-$265　2P: $165-$265　XP: $15　F3
　2/1-3/16　1P: $110-$185　2P: $110-$185　XP: $15　F3
Location: 3.5 mi n. N Bishop's Lodge Rd 87501 (PO Box 2367, 87504). Fax: 505/989-8739. **Terms:** Check-in 4 pm; 14 day
cancellation notice; cancellation fee imposed; package plans. **Facility:** 112 rooms. 1917 ranch resort on 1,000 acres in the
Sangre de Cristo Mountains. Variety of room types, many rooms with Kiva fireplace. 2 two-bedroom units. 1-3 stories, no el-
evator; interior/exterior corridors; 2 heated pools; playground. Fee: 4 tennis courts. **Services:** gift shop; area transportation.
Fee: massage. **Recreation:** fishing; hiking trails. Fee: horseback riding. **All Rooms:** safes. **Cards:** AE, DI, DS, MC, VI.

CACTUS LODGE MOTEL
Phone: (505)471-7699 　**45**
🅰🅰🅰 [SAVE]　3/15-10/31　1P: $48-$75　2P: $68-$88　XP: $5　F5
　2/1-3/14 & 11/1-1/31　1P: $32-$48　2P: $38-$58　XP: $5　F5
◆　**Location:** 3.8 mi sw on US 85. 2864 Cerrillos Rd 87505. **Terms:** Weekly rates avail, in winter; cancellation fee
Motel　imposed; pets, dogs only. **Facility:** 25 rooms. On main hwy. 4 two-bedroom units. 1 story; exterior corridors.
All Rooms: combo or shower baths, extended cable TV. **Some Rooms:** Fee: refrigerators, microwaves.
Cards: AE, DS, MC, VI. **Special Amenities:** Free local telephone calls and preferred room (subject to availability with
advanced reservations).

CASA DE LA CUMA B & B
Phone: (505)983-1717 　**3**
🅰🅰🅰 [SAVE]　6/1-10/31　1P: $85-$145　2P: $85-$145　XP: $10　F3
　2/1-5/31 & 11/1-1/31　1P: $75-$115　2P: $75-$115　XP: $10　F3
◆◆◆　**Location:** Just w off Old Taos Hwy. 105 Paseo de la Cuma 87501. Fax: 505/983-2241. **Terms:** [CP] meal plan;
Bed &　weekly rates avail; 10 day cancellation notice; 2 night min stay, weekends; package plans, seasonal; pet on
Breakfast　premises. **Facility:** 4 rooms. Circa 1950s, adobe style near Cross of the Martyrs. Patio with fire pit. Children
in suite only. 1 unit with wood burning fireplace. 1 story; interior/exterior corridors; smoke free premises; whirlpool. **Dining:** Restaurant nearby. **Cards:** MC, VI. **Special Amenities:** Early check-in/late check-out and free local telephone calls.

(See map p. 428)

CASAPUEBLO INN — Phone: (505)988-4455 — 11

◆◆◆	6/29-10/28	1P: $159-$269	2P: $159-$269	XP: $20	F18
Bed &	10/29-1/31	1P: $129-$269	2P: $129-$269	XP: $20	F18
Breakfast	4/7-6/28	1P: $159-$179	2P: $159-$179	XP: $20	F18
	2/1-4/6	1P: $119-$179	2P: $119-$179	XP: $20	F18

Location: Center intersection Guadalupe and Park. 138 Park Ave 87501. Fax: 505/983-6003. **Terms:** Check-in 4 pm; 3 day cancellation notice; cancellation fee imposed; pets. **Facility:** 21 rooms. Sophisticated and beautifully deocrated adobe in the heart of exciting "Old Santa Fe". Enjoy a romantic stroll to the plaza and historic district. 1-2 stories; exterior corridors. **All Rooms:** efficiencies, safes, honor bars. **Cards:** AE, DI, DS, MC, VI.

CERRILLOS ROAD TRAVELODGE — Phone: 505/471-4000 — 50

◆◆◆	5/26-10/31	1P: $79-$119	2P: $79-$119	XP: $10	F17
Motel	2/1-5/25 & 11/1-1/31	1P: $49-$69	2P: $49-$69	XP: $10	F17

Location: I-25, exit 278, then 3 mi n. 3450 Cerrillos Rd 87501. Fax: 505/474-4394. **Terms:** [CP] meal plan; cancellation fee imposed; small pets only, $10 extra charge. **Facility:** 76 rooms. Well appointed rooms. 3 stories; interior corridors; heated pool. **All Rooms:** combo or shower baths. **Cards:** AE, DI, DS, MC, VI.

CITIES OF GOLD CASINO HOTEL — Phone: (505)455-0515 — 39

◆◆◆	5/16-1/31	1P: $85	2P: $85	XP: $10	F18
Motor Inn	2/1-5/15	1P: $75	2P: $75	XP: $10	F18

Location: 15 mi n on US 84/285. Rt 11 Box 21B 87501. Fax: 505/455-3060. **Terms:** Pets, $25 dep req. **Facility:** 124 rooms. Contemporary Southwestern style lodging on Pueblo reservation. Casino adjacent. 2 stories; interior corridors. **Services:** gift shop. **All Rooms:** combo or shower baths.

COMFORT INN — Phone: (505)474-7330 — 62

AAA SAVE	6/1-9/1	1P: $75-$125	2P: $75-$125	XP: $5	F18
◆◆◆	9/2-1/31	1P: $45-$125	2P: $45-$125	XP: $5	F18
Motel	3/1-5/31	1P: $45-$105	2P: $45-$105	XP: $5	F18
	2/1-2/29	1P: $45-$85	2P: $45-$85	XP: $5	F18

Location: I-25, exit 278, 1.6 mi n. 4312 Cerrillos Rd 87505. Fax: 505/474-7330. **Terms:** [ECP] meal plan; cancellation fee imposed; small pets only, in smoking rooms. **Facility:** 83 rooms. 10 whirlpool rooms; 3 stories; interior corridors; heated pool, whirlpool. **Dining:** Restaurant nearby. **All Rooms:** combo or shower baths, extended cable TV. **Cards:** AE, CB, DI, DS, JC, MC, VI. **Special Amenities:** Free breakfast and free local telephone calls. *(See color ad below)*

COMFORT SUITES — Phone: (505)473-9004 — 47

◆◆◆	5/16-9/15	1P: $79-$99	2P: $99-$119	XP: $10	F18
Motel	2/1-5/15 & 9/16-1/31	1P: $59-$79	2P: $69-$89	XP: $5	F18

Location: I-25, exit 278B, 2 mi n. 1435 Avenida de las Americas 87505. Fax: 505/438-4627. **Terms:** [CP] meal plan. **Facility:** 60 rooms. Contemporary room decor, some Santa Fe influences. 3 stories; interior corridors; heated pool. **All Rooms:** combo or shower baths. **Cards:** AE, DI, DS, MC, VI.

(See map p. 428)

DAYS INN OF SANTA FE

◆◆ Motel

Phone: (505)424-3297 [44]

	1P	2P	XP	
6/25-10/21	1P: $69-$85	2P: $69-$85	XP: $6	F16
5/25-6/24	1P: $50-$79	2P: $55-$79	XP: $6	F16
10/22-1/31	1P: $40-$69	2P: $45-$69	XP: $6	F16
2/1-5/24	1P: $40-$55	2P: $45-$60	XP: $6	F16

Location: I-25, exit 278, 4 mi n at Siler Rd. 2900 Cerrillos Rd 87505. Fax: 505/424-3297. **Terms:** [CP] meal plan; pets, $10 extra charge. **Facility:** 83 rooms. 2 stories; exterior corridors. **Services:** gift shop. **Cards:** AE, CB, DI, DS, MC, VI.

ELDORADO HOTEL

(AAA) SAVE
◆◆◆◆ Hotel

Phone: (505)988-4455 [10]

	1P	2P	XP	
4/7-8/26	1P: $239-$269	2P: $239-$269	XP: $20	F18
8/27-12/21	1P: $189-$239	2P: $189-$239	XP: $20	F18
2/1-4/6 & 12/22-1/31	1P: $149-$199	2P: $149-$199	XP: $20	F18

Location: Just w of The Plaza, at Sandoval St. 309 W San Francisco 87501. Fax: 505/995-4543. **Terms:** Check-in 4 pm; 3 day cancellation notice; cancellation fee imposed; package plans, skiing; pets. **Facility:** 219 rooms. Large rooms, Santa Fe-style. Many balconies and some suites. Deluxe and above rooms offer butler service. Many rooms with mountain and downtown views. Some rooms with fireplace. Presidential suite, $690-$975.; whirlpool room; 5 stories; interior corridors; small heated pool, saunas, whirlpool. **Dining:** Restaurant; 6:30 am-11 pm; espresso stand; $12-$18; cocktails; also, The Old House, see separate listing; entertainment. **Services:** gift shop. Fee: massage. **Recreation:** beauty salon. **All Rooms:** safes, honor bars. **Cards:** AE, DI, DS, MC, VI. *(See color ad below)*

EL FAROLITO BED & BREAKFAST INN

(AAA)
◆◆◆
Historic Bed & Breakfast

Phone: (505)988-1631 [25]

	1P	2P	XP
5/1-10/31	1P: $140-$175	2P: $140-$175	XP: $15
2/1-4/30	1P: $110-$155	2P: $110-$155	XP: $15
11/1-1/31	1P: $105-$140	2P: $105-$140	XP: $15

Location: From Cerrillos Rd (SR 510) just e on DePeralta to Galisteo St. 514 Galisteo St 87501. Fax: 505/988-4589. **Terms:** [CP] meal plan; weekly rates avail; check-in 4 pm; 14 day cancellation notice; cancellation fee imposed; 2 night min stay, weekends; pet on premises. **Facility:** 7 rooms. Individual rooms in a courtyard like surrounding. All rooms nicely decorated in various Southwestern New Mexico decor each with a kiva fireplace. 1 story; exterior corridors; smoke free premises. **Dining:** Restaurant nearby. **All Rooms:** extended cable TV. **Cards:** AE, DS, MC, VI.

(See map p. 428)

EL PARADERO BED & BREAKFAST　　　　　　　　　　　　　　　　**Phone:** (505)988-1177　**28**
- 4/15-10/31　　　　　1P: $65-$115　　2P: $75-$125　　XP: $15　　F12
- 2/1-4/14 & 11/1-1/31　1P: $65-$95　　2P: $75-$105　　XP: $15　　F12

Historic Bed & Breakfast
◆◆◆
Location: 0.3 mi s on Cerrillos Rd, 1/2 blk on E Manhattan Ave. 220 W Manhattan Ave 87501. Fax: 505/988-3577. **Terms:** [BP] meal plan; daily rates avail; age restrictions may apply; 10 day cancellation notice; pets, in some rooms. **Facility:** 14 rooms. Originally a Spanish farmhouse built between 1800-1820 in downtown area. Some rooms with skylights and bancos. 1-2 stories; interior/exterior corridors; smoke free premises. **Dining:** Restaurant nearby. **All Rooms:** extended cable TV. **Some Rooms:** 2 efficiencies, color TV.
Cards: MC, VI.

EL REY INN　　　　　　　　　　　　　　　　　　　　**Phone:** 505/982-1931　**42**
- 5/1-10/31　　　1P: $75-$135　　2P: $75-$155
- 11/1-1/31　　　1P: $65-$135　　2P: $65-$155
- 2/1-4/30　　　　1P: $60-$125　　2P: $60-$145

Motel
◆◆◆
Location: 2.5 mi sw on I-25 business route. 1862 Cerrillos Rd 87505 (PO Box 4759, 87502). Fax: 505/989-9249. **Terms:** [CP] meal plan. **Facility:** 86 rooms. A lovely property which captures the Santa Fe charm with white adobe buildings, lush landscaping and Southwestern style room decor. 8 two-bedroom units. Some rooms with fireplace, $10 extra charge; suites, $100-$200; 2 stories; exterior corridors; smoke free premises; heated pool, sauna, whirlpools, seasonal; playground. **Dining:** Restaurant nearby. **All Rooms:** combo or shower baths, extended cable TV. **Some Rooms:** 5 efficiencies, safes. **Cards:** AE, DI, DS, MC, VI. *(See color ad below)*

FAIRFIELD INN BY MARRIOTT　　　　　　　　　　　　　**Phone:** (505)474-4442　**60**
◆◆◆
- 6/10-9/4　　　　　1P: $85　　　2P: $93
Motel
- 5/5-6/9　　　　　1P: $65　　　2P: $74
- 2/1-5/4 & 9/5-1/31　1P: $55　　　2P: $65

Location: I-25, exit 278 (Cerrillos Rd), 2 mi n. 4150 Cerrillos Rd 87505. Fax: 505/474-7569. **Terms:** [ECP] meal plan. **Facility:** 56 rooms. 2 stories; interior corridors; no parking; heated pool. **Cards:** AE, DI, DS, MC, VI.

FORT MARCY HOTEL SUITES　　　　　　　　　　　　　**Phone:** (505)982-6636　**7**
◆◆◆
- 5/1-10/31　　　　　　1P: $219-$285　2P: $219-$285　XP: $20　F16
Condominium
- 2/1-4/30 & 11/1-1/31　1P: $159-$211　2P: $159-$211　XP: $20　F16

Terms: [CP] meal plan; check-in 4 pm; 3 day cancellation notice; cancellation fee imposed; package plans, skiing. **Facility:** 94 rooms. Spacious condominiums, some with washer/dryer. Quiet setting on 10 acres. 68 two-bedroom units, 8 three-bedroom units. 1-2 stories; exterior corridors; heated pool. **Services:** area transportation. **All Rooms:** kitchens. **Cards:** AE, DI, MC, VI. *(See color ad p 433)*

FOUR KACHINAS INN　　　　　　　　　　　　　　　　**Phone:** (505)982-2550　**34**
◆◆◆
- 3/31-10/31　　　1P: $112-$160　2P: $112-$160　XP: $30
Bed & Breakfast
- 2/1-3/30　　　　1P: $80-$140　　2P: $80-$140　　XP: $25
- 11/1-1/31　　　1P: $80-$140　　2P: $80-$140　　XP: $30

Location: 0.3 mi s on Cerrillos Rd to Paseo de Peralta, 4 blks e on Paseo de Peralta. 512 Webber St 87501. Fax: 505/989-1323. **Terms:** [ECP] meal plan; check-in 4 pm; 14 day cancellation notice; cancellation fee imposed. **Facility:** 6 rooms. Attractive, well-kept property. 2 stories; exterior corridors; smoke free premises. **Cards:** DS, MC, VI.

HACIENDA NICHOLAS　　　　　　　　　　　　　　　　**Phone:** (505)986-1431　**16**
◆◆◆
- 3/15-11/15　　　1P: $110-$160
Bed & Breakfast
- 2/1-3/14 & 11/16-1/31　1P: $95-$140

Location: 4 blks e of the Plaza. 320 E Marcy St 87501 (106 E Marcy St). Fax: 505/982-8572. **Terms:** [BP] meal plan; 30 day cancellation notice; pets, $20 extra charge. **Facility:** 7 rooms. 1 story; interior/exterior corridors; smoke free premises. **Services:** Fee: massage. **All Rooms:** combo or shower baths. **Cards:** DS, MC, VI.

(See map p. 428)

HILTON OF SANTA FE
◆◆◆
Hotel

6/23-8/19	1P: $199-$289	2P: $199-$289	XP: $20	F18
4/28-6/22 & 8/20-1/31	1P: $179-$269	2P: $179-$269	XP: $20	F18
2/1-4/27	1P: $169-$249	2P: $169-$249	XP: $20	F18

Phone: (505)988-2811 🔢12

Location: Just sw of The Plaza, between San Francisco and Water sts. 100 Sandoval St 87501 (PO Box 25104, 87504). **Fax:** 505/986-6435. **Terms:** Check-in 4 pm; 3 day cancellation notice; cancellation fee imposed. **Facility:** 157 rooms. Upscale property built around the historic home of one of the city's prominent early families. Extensive public areas. Some rooms facing inner courtyard with swimming pool. 1 two-bedroom unit. 3 stories; interior corridors; heated pool. Fee: parking. **Services:** gift shop; area transportation. **Some Rooms:** 3 efficiencies. **Cards:** AE, CB, DI, DS, JC, MC, VI. *(See color ad 41 & below)*

[icon row]

(See map p. 428)

HOLIDAY INN

Phone: (505)473-4646 **58**

Hotel

6/1-8/31	1P: $106-$129	XP: $10	F18
10/15-1/31	1P: $59-$129	XP: $10	F18
9/1-10/14	1P: $89-$109	XP: $10	F18
2/1-5/31	1P: $59-$89	XP: $10	F18

Location: I-25, exit 278B, 2.3 mi n just n of Rodeo Dr. 4048 Cerrillos Rd 87505. Fax: 505/473-2186. **Terms:** 3 day cancellation notice; cancellation fee imposed; pets, $25 extra charge (1st floor only). **Facility:** 130 rooms. Adobe-style exterior; public areas with a strong Southwestern flair. Most rooms with private balcony. All rooms with hair dryer, iron and ironing board. 4 stories; interior corridors; heated pool, saunas, whirlpool. **Dining:** Restaurant; 6:30 am-1:30 & 4-10 pm, Sat & Sun -10:30 pm; $9-$21; cocktails. **Services:** gift shop; area transportation, plaza only. **Recreation:** video game room. **All Rooms:** extended cable TV. **Cards:** AE, CB, DI, DS, JC, MC, VI.

HOLIDAY INN EXPRESS

Phone: 505/474-7570 **51**

Motel

5/28-10/31	1P: $89-$129	2P: $89-$129	XP: $10	F18
2/1-5/27 & 11/1-1/31	1P: $59-$89	2P: $59-$89	XP: $10	F18

Location: I-25, exit 278, 3 mi n. 3470 Cerrillos Rd 87501. Fax: 505/474-6342. **Terms:** [ECP] meal plan. **Facility:** 79 rooms. 2 stories; interior corridors; heated pool. **All Rooms:** combo or shower baths. **Cards:** AE, CB, DI, DS, JC, MC, VI.

THE HOTEL LORETTO

Phone: (505)988-5531 **17**

Motor Inn

11/1-1/31	1P: $215-$250	2P: $215-$520	XP: $15	F17
6/1-10/31	1P: $279-$329	2P: $279-$329	XP: $15	F17
2/1-5/31	1P: $215-$260	2P: $215-$260	XP: $15	F17

Location: Just s of The Plaza. 211 Old Santa Fe Tr 87501. Fax: 505/984-7988. **Terms:** Monthly rates avail; check-in 4 pm; 3 day cancellation notice; cancellation fee imposed. **Facility:** 140 rooms. Unique Pueblo-style architecture. Most rooms with balcony. 5 stories; interior corridors; heated pool. Fee: parking. **Dining:** Dining room, deli; 6:30 am-9:30 pm; from 7 am, 11/1-5/1; $14-$22; cocktails; entertainment. **Services:** gift shop. **Cards:** AE, CB, DI, DS, MC, VI. *(See color ad below)*

HOTEL ST FRANCIS

Phone: (505)983-5700 **21**

Historic Hotel

5/1-10/31	1P: $98-$353	2P: $98-$353		F12
11/1-1/31	1P: $78-$353	2P: $78-$353	XP: $15	F12
3/1-4/30	1P: $88-$278	2P: $88-$278	XP: $15	F12
2/1-2/29	1P: $78-$278	2P: $78-$278	XP: $15	F12

Location: Just s of The Plaza. 210 Don Gaspar 87501. Fax: 505/989-7690. **Terms:** 3 day cancellation notice; cancellation fee imposed. **Facility:** 83 rooms. Listed on the National Register of Historic Places. Hotel was built in 1920. 1 two-bedroom unit. 3 stories; interior corridors. **All Rooms:** combo or shower baths, safes. **Some Rooms:** kitchen. **Cards:** AE, CB, DI, DS, MC, VI. *(See color ad p 435)*

HOTEL SANTA FE

Phone: (505)982-1200 **27**

Hotel

6/16-8/26	1P: $169-$259	2P: $169-$259	XP: $15	F17
10/29-1/31	1P: $109-$239	2P: $109-$239	XP: $15	F17
8/27-10/28	1P: $149-$229	2P: $149-$229	XP: $15	F17
2/1-6/15	1P: $119-$209	2P: $119-$209	XP: $15	F17

Location: At Cerrillos Rd, 0.6 mi s of the Plaza. 1501 Paseo de Peralta 87501. Fax: 505/984-2211. **Terms:** Check-in 4 pm; cancellation fee imposed; package plans; pets, $50 dep req. **Facility:** 129 rooms. Comfortable lodgings with a strong Native American influence, including public areas and grounds featuring paintings and sculptures by prominent artists. Most rooms with extra-long king beds, many suites avail. 3 stories; interior corridors; heated pool, whirlpool. **Dining:** Restaurant; 7 am-10 pm; live classical guitar & flute music Wed-Sat evenings; $12-$24; cocktails. **Services:** gift shop; area transportation. **Recreation:** Native American dance demonstrations weekends in season. **All Rooms:** honor bars. **Some Rooms:** safes. **Cards:** AE, CB, DI, DS, JC, MC, VI. *(See color ad p 435)*

(See map p. 428)

HOWARD JOHNSON EXPRESS
◆◆
Motel

			Phone: (505)438-8950	57
5/1-12/31	1P: $50-$69	2P: $55-$89	XP: $6	F18
2/1-4/30 & 1/1-1/31	1P: $44-$52	2P: $48-$65	XP: $6	F18

Location: I-25, Cerrillos Rd exit, 1.5 mi n. 4044 Cerrillos Rd 87505. Fax: 505/471-9129. **Terms:** [CP] meal plan. **Facility:** 47 rooms. 2 stories; interior corridors; small pool. **Cards:** AE, CB, DI, DS, MC, VI. *(See ad p 436)*

INN OF THE ANASAZI
◆◆◆◆
Hotel

			Phone: (505)988-3030	15
6/29-10/31	1P: $265-$415	2P: $265-$415	XP: $20	F12
3/30-6/28	1P: $249-$409	2P: $249-$409	XP: $20	F12
2/1-3/29 & 11/1-1/31	1P: $205-$355	2P: $205-$355	XP: $20	F12

Location: Just ne of The Plaza. 113 Washington Ave 87501. Fax: 505/988-3277. **Terms:** 3 day cancellation notice; cancellation fee imposed; 2 night min stay, weekends; package plans, 1/2-3/31; pets, $30 extra charge. **Facility:** 59 rooms. Intimate luxury hotel with outstanding interior design themed to ancient Pueblo cultures. Cozy but elegant rooms with viga ceilings, gas-lit Kiva fireplaces and quality furnishings. 3 stories; interior corridors. **Services:** Fee: massage. **All Rooms:** safes, honor bars. **Cards:** AE, CB, DI, DS, JC, MC, VI.

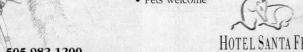

(See map p. 428)

INN OF THE GOVERNORS

				Phone: (505)982-4333	**18**
	7/1-10/23	1P: $189	2P: $199	XP: $15	F18
	5/14-6/30	1P: $175	2P: $185	XP: $15	F18
Motor Inn	2/1-5/13 & 10/24-1/31	1P: $155	2P: $165	XP: $15	F18

Location: Center. 234 Don Gaspar Ave 87501. Fax: 505/989-9149. **Terms:** Check-in 4 pm; cancellation fee imposed. **Facility:** 100 rooms. Many rooms with fireplace and private patio or balcony. 2-3 stories; interior/exterior corridors; heated pool. **Dining:** Dining room; 6:30 am-9 pm; $9-$19; cocktails; entertainment. **All Rooms:** honor bars. **Cards:** AE, CB, DI, DS, MC, VI. **Special Amenities:** Free newspaper. *(See color ad below)*

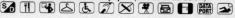

(See map p. 428)

INN ON THE ALAMEDA
Phone: (505)984-2121 [24] F17

AAA SAVE ◆◆◆ Motel
All Year
1P: $147-$342   2P: $147-$342   XP: $15
Location: 4 blks e of The Plaza. 303 E Alameda Blvd 87501. Fax: 505/986-8325. **Terms:** [CP] meal plan; check-in 4 pm; 3 day cancellation notice; cancellation fee imposed; pets, $20 extra charge. **Facility:** 69 rooms. Pueblo-style architecture. Rooms with unique decor and Southwest furnishings. Many rooms with kiva fireplace, balcony or private courtyard. Whirlpool room; 1-3 stories, no elevator; interior/exterior corridors; whirlpools. **Dining:** Cocktails. **Services:** Fee: massage. **All Rooms:** combo or shower baths, extended cable TV. **Some Rooms:** Fee: VCR. **Cards:** AE, CB, DI, DS, MC, VI. **Special Amenities:** Free breakfast and free newspaper. *(See color ad p 436)*

LA FONDA HOTEL
Phone: (505)982-5511 [20] F

AAA SAVE ◆◆◆ Historic Hotel
6/1-1/31   1P: $199-$249   2P: $199-$249   XP: $15
2/1-5/31   1P: $189-$249   2P: $189-$249   XP: $15
Location: On the Santa Fe Plaza. 100 E San Francisco St 87501. Fax: 505/988-2952. **Terms:** 48 day cancellation notice; cancellation fee imposed. **Facility:** 167 rooms. Many units with fireplace. There has been an inn on this site since 1620. Present building dates back to the 1920s. Whimsically hand-painted furnishings and accents. 3 two-bedroom units. 4 two-bedroom units; 3 whirlpool rooms; 5 stories; interior corridors; heated pool, whirlpools. Fee: parking. **Dining:** Dining room; 7 am-10 pm; $11-$20; cocktails; entertainment. **Services:** gift shop. Fee: massage. **All Rooms:** safes. **Some Rooms:** 3 kitchens. **Cards:** AE, CB, DI, DS, MC, VI. **Special Amenities:** Free room upgrade and preferred room (each subject to availability with advanced reservations). *(See color ad below)*

LA QUINTA INN
Phone: (505)471-1142 [61]

AAA SAVE ◆◆◆ Motel
4/1-9/30   1P: $95-$115   2P: $95-$115
2/1-3/31 & 10/1-1/31   1P: $69-$89   2P: $69-$89
Location: I-25, Cerrillos Rd exit, 1.8 mi n. 4298 Cerrillos Rd 87505. Fax: 505/438-7219. **Terms:** [ECP] meal plan; small pets only. **Facility:** 130 rooms. 3 stories; exterior corridors; heated pool. **Dining:** Restaurant nearby. **All Rooms:** combo or shower baths. **Some Rooms:** Fee: refrigerators, microwaves. **Cards:** AE, CB, DI, DS, MC, VI. **Special Amenities:** Free breakfast and free local telephone calls.

(See map p. 428)

LAS PALOMAS
◆ ◆ ◆
Historic Motel
Phone: 505/988-4455 **9**
Property failed to provide current rates
Location: 4 blks w of the Plaza. 119 Park Ave 87501. Fax: 505/995-4543. **Terms:** [CP] meal plan; check-in 4 pm; 3 day cancellation notice; pets. **Facility:** 20 rooms. Restored adobe casitas which provide excellent Southwestern ambiance and extras including cappucino/expresso maker, CD player and a kiva fireplace. 1 story; exterior corridors. **All Rooms:** combo or shower baths, safes. **Some Rooms:** 10 efficiencies, 10 kitchens. **Cards:** AE, MC, VI.

LUXURY INN
(AAA) [SAVE]
◆ ◆
Motel
Phone: (505)473-0567 **56**

5/1-10/31	1P: $55-$69	2P: $70-$90	XP: $6
2/1-4/30 & 11/1-1/31	1P: $38-$55	2P: $50-$70	XP: $6

Location: I-25, Cerrillos Rd exit, 1.8 mi n. 3752 Cerrillos Rd 87505. Fax: 505/471-9139. **Terms:** [CP] meal plan; weekly rates avail. **Facility:** 51 rooms. 2 stories; interior corridors; heated pool, whirlpool. **Cards:** AE, DS, MC, VI. **Special Amenities: Free breakfast and free local telephone calls.** *(See color ad p 437)*

THE MADELEINE
◆ ◆
Historic Bed
& Breakfast
Phone: (505)982-3465 **19**

3/16-11/15	1P: $80-$160	2P: $80-$160	XP: $20
2/1-3/15 & 11/16-1/31	1P: $70-$145	2P: $70-$145	XP: $20

Location: 3 blks e of the Plaza (Palace to Faithway). 106 Faithway 87501. Fax: 505/982-8972. **Terms:** [BP] meal plan; age restrictions may apply; 14 day cancellation notice; cancellation fee imposed; pets, $20 extra charge. **Facility:** 8 rooms. 3 stories, no elevator; interior/exterior corridors; smoke free premises.

MOTEL 6 - 150
(AAA)
◆
Motel
Phone: 505/473-1380 **41**

6/15-10/18	1P: $52-$62	2P: $58-$68	XP: $3	F17
5/25-6/14	1P: $42-$52	2P: $48-$58	XP: $3	F17
10/19-1/31	1P: $40-$50	2P: $46-$56	XP: $3	F17
2/1-5/24	1P: $37-$47	2P: $43-$53	XP: $3	F17

Location: I-25, exit 278, 3.8 mi n. 3007 Cerrillos Rd 87505. Fax: 505/473-7784. **Terms:** Small pets only. **Facility:** 104 rooms. 2 stories; exterior corridors; heated pool. **All Rooms:** shower baths. **Cards:** AE, DI, DS, MC, VI.

OTRA VEZ EN SANTA FE
◆ ◆ ◆
Condominium
Phone: (505)988-2244 **13**
Property failed to provide current rates
Location: Center. 202 Galisteo St 87501 (PO Box 2927, 87504). Fax: 505/989-5094. **Terms:** 3 day cancellation notice. **Facility:** 18 rooms. Well appointed rooms in Santa Fe style. Some with fireplace. 8 two-bedroom units. 2-3 stories; interior corridors. **All Rooms:** kitchens. **Cards:** AE, MC, VI.

QUALITY INN
(AAA) [SAVE]
◆ ◆ ◆
Motor Inn
Phone: (505)471-1211 **46**

8/1-9/15	1P: $95-$105	2P: $95-$105	XP: $10	F18
9/16-1/31	1P: $60-$90	2P: $60-$95	XP: $10	F18
5/1-7/31	1P: $75-$90	2P: $75-$90	XP: $10	F18
2/1-4/30	1P: $60-$75	2P: $60-$75	XP: $10	F18

Location: I-25, exit 278B, 3.8 mi n. 3011 Cerrillos Rd 87505. Fax: 505/438-9535. **Terms:** [CP] meal plan; pets. **Facility:** 99 rooms. Many rooms with balcony and patio. 2 stories; interior corridors; heated pool. **Dining:** Restaurant; 6:30 am-9 pm; $6-$8; cocktails. **Services:** area transportation, Lamy train station. **All Rooms:** extended cable TV. **Cards:** AE, CB, DI, DS, JC, MC, VI. **Special Amenities: Free local telephone calls and free newspaper.**

RADISSON HOTEL & SUITES ON THE PLAZA SANTA FE
(AAA) [SAVE]
◆ ◆ ◆
Suite Hotel
Phone: (505)988-4900 **14**

5/26-10/31 & 12/21-1/31	1P: $179	2P: $179	XP: $10	F17
2/1-5/25 & 11/1-12/20	1P: $116	2P: $116	XP: $10	F17

Location: Center; just ne of The Plaza. 125 Washington Ave 87501. Fax: 505/983-9322. **Terms:** 3 day cancellation notice; cancellation fee imposed. **Facility:** 56 rooms. Unique territorial-style design, with most rooms facing a sunny brick courtyard accented by wood balcony and chile ristras. Most rooms are suites; many have fireplace. Suites, $189-$219; 3 whirlpool rooms; 2-3 stories; exterior corridors. Fee: parking. **Dining:** Restaurant, coffee shop; seasonal patio cafe 11 am-4 pm; espresso bar 7-10:30 am; cocktails. **Recreation:** recreation facilities avail at Radisson Hotel Santa Fe. **All Rooms:** extended cable TV. **Some Rooms:** efficiency, kitchen. **Cards:** AE, CB, DI, DS, MC, VI.

RADISSON SANTA FE
(AAA) [SAVE]
◆ ◆ ◆
Complex
Phone: (505)992-5800 **40**

10/17-1/31	1P: $89-$139	2P: $89-$139	XP: $10	F17
6/1-10/16	1P: $139	2P: $139	XP: $10	F17
4/1-5/31	1P: $109	2P: $109	XP: $10	F17
2/1-3/31	1P: $89	2P: $89	XP: $10	F17

Location: 1.5 mi nw off US 64, 84 and 285. 750 N St Francis Dr 87501. Fax: 505/992-5865. Check-in 4 pm; 3 day cancellation notice; cancellation fee imposed. **Facility:** 161 rooms. Large rooms, attractive pool 3 two-bedroom units. Condos, $109-$349; 6 whirlpool rooms; 1-2 stories; interior/exterior corridors; heated pool, whirl-ning: Dining room; 6:30 am-10 pm; $9-$18; cocktails; entertainment. **Services:** area transportation, Plaza & Opera. ms: extended cable TV. **Some Rooms:** 33 kitchens. **Cards:** AE, CB, DI, DS, JC, MC, VI. *(See ad p 439)*

(See map p. 428)

RESIDENCE INN BY MARRIOTT
◆◆◆
Apartment
Phone: 505/988-7300   **43**
Property failed to provide current rates
Location: I-25, exit 282, 1 mi n on St Francis Dr to St Michaels Dr, just e. 1698 Galisteo St 87505. Fax: 505/988-3243. **Terms:** [CP] meal plan; pets, $10 extra charge, $150 dep req. **Facility:** 120 rooms. Large housekeeping units with fireplace, iron and ironing board, dishwasher. 30 bi-level 'penthouses' with sleeping loft and second bedroom separated by privacy curtain. 2 stories; exterior corridors; heated pool. **Recreation:** sports court. **All Rooms:** kitchens. **Cards:** AE, CB, DI, DS, JC, MC, VI.

RIO VISTA SUITES
◆◆◆
Condominium
Phone: (505)982-6636   **8**
5/29-9/5	1P: $135-$165	2P: $135-$165	XP: $20	F18
2/1-5/28 & 9/6-1/31	1P: $115-$165	2P: $115-$165	XP: $20	F18
Location: 527 E Alameda St, 0.5 mi e of center. 320 Artist Rd 87501. Fax: 505/984-8682. **Terms:** [CP] meal plan; check-in 4 pm; 3 day cancellation notice; cancellation fee imposed; pets, $50 extra charge. **Facility:** 11 rooms. 1 story; exterior corridors. **All Rooms:** kitchens. **Cards:** AE, MC, VI. *(See color ad p 433)*

SANTA FE BUDGET INN
ⒶⒶⒶ
◆ ◆
Motel
Phone: (505)982-5952   **32**
7/4-10/21	1P: $82-$94	2P: $82-$94	XP: $9
5/1-7/3	1P: $69-$89	2P: $78-$89	XP: $8
2/1-4/30 & 10/22-1/31	1P: $54-$72	2P: $58-$72	XP: $8
Location: 0.4 mi ne of St Francis Dr (US 84). 725 Cerrillos Rd 87501. Fax: 505/984-8879. **Terms:** Cancellation fee imposed. **Facility:** 160 rooms. Modest but functional decor. 2 stories; exterior corridors; small pool. **Dining:** Restaurant nearby. **All Rooms:** extended cable TV. **Cards:** AE, DI, MC, VI.

SANTA FE COURTYARD BY MARRIOTT
◆◆◆
Motor Inn
Phone: (505)473-2800   **48**
5/1-10/15	1P: $99-$139	2P: $99-$139	XP: $10	F17
2/1-4/30 & 10/16-1/31	1P: $79-$99	2P: $79-$99	XP: $10	F17
Location: I-25, exit 278B (Cerrillos Rd), 3.2 mi n. 3347 Cerrillos Rd 87505. Fax: 505/473-4905. **Terms:** Check-in 4 pm; 30 day cancellation notice; cancellation fee imposed; package plans. **Facility:** 213 rooms. Attractive courtyard and public areas. Rooms are most handsomely appointed in a contemporary Southwestern style. Entire property has an upscale feel. 1 three-bedroom unit. 3 stories; interior/exterior corridors; heated pool. **Services:** gift shop; area transportation. Fee: massage. **All Rooms:** combo or shower baths. **Some Rooms:** 7 efficiencies. **Cards:** AE, CB, DI, DS, MC, VI.

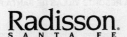

(See map p. 428)

SANTA FE MOTEL   Phone: (505)982-1039 26

| (AAA) (SAVE) | 5/1-10/31 | 1P: $110-$159 | 2P: $110-$159 | XP: $10 | F10 |
| | 2/1-4/30 & 11/1-1/31 | 1P: $79-$109 | 2P: $79-$109 | XP: $10 | F10 |

◆◆
Motel   **Location:** 4 blks sw of The Plaza. 510 Cerrillos Rd 87501. Fax: 505/986-1275. **Terms:** [CP] meal plan; check-in 4 pm; 3 day cancellation notice; cancellation fee imposed. **Facility:** 23 rooms. Variety of room types, all done in Southwestern style. Regular type motel units and casitas avail. 1-2 stories; exterior corridors. **All Rooms:** combo or shower baths. **Some Rooms:** 5 efficiencies. **Cards:** AE, DI, MC, VI. **Special Amenities: Free breakfast and preferred room (subject to availability with advanced reservations).** (See color ad p 433)

SANTA FE PLAZA TRAVELODGE   Phone: (505)982-3551 30

(AAA) (SAVE)	8/1-9/30	1P: $89-$125	2P: $125	XP: $6	F17
	5/1-7/31	1P: $79-$125	2P: $125	XP: $6	F17
	10/1-1/31	1P: $49-$69	2P: $69		F17
◆◆	2/1-4/30	1P: $49-$69	2P: $69	XP: $6	F17

Motel   **Location:** 0.8 mi sw of The Plaza on I-25 business route. 646 Cerrillos Rd 87501. Fax: 505/983-8624. **Facility:** 49 rooms. 2 stories; interior/exterior corridors; heated pool. **Dining:** Restaurant nearby. **All Rooms:** combo or shower baths. **Cards:** AE, CB, DI, DS, MC, VI. **Special Amenities: Free local telephone calls and free newspaper.**

SERET'S 1001 NIGHTS   Phone: (505)982-6636 23

| ◆◆ | 5/1-10/31 | 1P: $219-$269 | 2P: $219-$269 | XP: $20 | F16 |
| | 2/1-4/30 & 11/1-1/31 | 1P: $159-$199 | 2P: $159-$199 | XP: $20 | F16 |

Historic Bed & Breakfast **Location:** 0.5 mi s of the Plaza at "Old Santa Fe Trail". 147 E DeVargas St 87501. Fax: 505/984-8682. **Terms:** [ECP] meal plan; 3 day cancellation notice; cancellation fee imposed; package plans. **Facility:** 18 rooms. Charming, authentic "Old Santa Fe" bed and breakfast full of fascinating antique and imported furnishings near the Historic Plaza De Santa Fe. 1 two-bedroom unit. 2 stories; interior/exterior corridors; smoke free premises. **All Rooms:** combo or shower baths. **Some Rooms:** efficiency, 17 kitchens. **Cards:** AE, DI, DS, MC, VI. (See color ad p 433)

SLEEP INN   Phone: (505)474-9500 59

(AAA) (SAVE)	6/1-8/31	1P: $84-$114	2P: $89-$129	XP: $10	F18
	9/1-1/31	1P: $76-$96	2P: $81-$101	XP: $10	F18
◆◆	3/1-5/31	1P: $74-$94	2P: $79-$99	XP: $10	F18
Motel	2/1-2/29	1P: $66-$86	2P: $69-$89	XP: $10	F18

Location: I-25, exit 278, 0.3 mi n. 8376 Cerrillos Rd 87505. Fax: 505/474-9535. **Terms:** [ECP] meal plan; cancellation fee imposed. **Facility:** 99 rooms. A nicely done property which is adjacent to the Santa Fe Premium Outlet stores. 3 stories; interior corridors; whirlpool. **Recreation:** exercise equipment. **All Rooms:** combo or shower baths, extended cable TV. **Cards:** AE, CB, DI, DS, JC, MC, VI. **Special Amenities: Free breakfast and free local telephone calls.**

SPENCER HOUSE BED & BREAKFAST INN   Phone: (505)988-3024 4

| ◆◆◆ | 5/1-10/31 | 1P: $105-$150 | 2P: $105-$150 | XP: $20 | |
| | 2/1-4/30 & 11/1-1/31 | 1P: $99-$140 | 2P: $99-$140 | XP: $20 | |

Historic Bed & Breakfast **Location:** At Chappelle St. 222 McKenzie St 87501. Fax: 505/984-9862. **Terms:** [BP] meal plan; age restrictions may apply; check-in 4 pm; 14 day cancellation notice; cancellation fee imposed. **Facility:** 5 rooms. Cozy 1923 adobe home. Rooms carefully appointed with quality English, Welsh and Colonial-American antiques. 1 suite with kiva fireplace. 1 story; interior/exterior corridors; smoke free premises. **Some Rooms:** kitchen, color TV. **Cards:** AE, MC, VI.

SUNTERRA RESORTS VILLAS DE SANTA FE   Phone: (505)988-3000 1

(AAA) (SAVE)	5/1-3/31	1P: $170-$190	2P: $170-$190		
	3/1-4/30	1P: $135-$160	2P: $135-$160		
◆◆◆	2/1-2/29 & 11/1-1/31	1P: $115-$135	2P: $115-$135		

Suite Motel   **Location:** St Francis US 84 and 285, 0.6 mi n on Paseo de Peralta, w on Griffin St. 400 Griffin St 87501. Fax: 505/988-4700. **Terms:** [CP] meal plan; weekly & monthly rates avail; check-in 4 pm; 3 day cancellation notice; cancellation fee imposed. **Facility:** 100 rooms. Spacious housekeeping suites with pull-out sofa, dishwasher, iron and ironing board; most with private balcony, some with fireplace. 5 two-bedroom units. Rates for up to 4 persons, 2 bedroom, 2 bath suites $255-310, for up to 6 persons; 3-4 stories; interior corridors; small heated pool, whirlpools. **Dining:** Restaurant nearby. **Services:** area transportation, Plaza. **All Rooms:** efficiencies, combo or shower baths, extended cable TV. **Cards:** AE, DI, DS, MC, VI. **Special Amenities: Free breakfast and free newspaper.**

TERRITORIAL INN   Phone: (505)989-7737 6

| ◆◆◆ | 5/1-10/31 | 1P: $120-$180 | 2P: $120-$180 | XP: $15 | |
| | 2/1-4/30 & 11/1-1/31 | 1P: $95-$150 | 2P: $95-$150 | XP: $15 | |

Bed & Breakfast **Location:** 3 blks from the Santa Fe Plaza. 215 Washington Ave 87501. Fax: 505/986-9212. **Terms:** [ECP] meal plan; age restrictions may apply; 3 day cancellation notice; cancellation fee imposed. **Facility:** 10 rooms. Territorial style house built in 1826. Near the Santa Fe Plaza. 2 stories; interior corridors; smoke free premises. **Cards:** AE, DI, MC, VI. (See color ad p 433)

——— **RESTAURANTS** ———

ANASAZI RESTAURANT   **Lunch:** $7-$14   **Dinner:** $17-$32   Phone: 505/988-3236 12
◆◆◆   **Location:** Just ne of The Plaza; in Inn of the Anasazi. 113 Washington St 87501. **Hours:** 7-10:30 am, Regional   11:30-2:30 & 5:30-10 pm. **Reservations:** suggested. **Features:** dressy casual; Sunday brunch; children's American   menu; carryout; cocktails & lounge; valet parking; a la carte, also prix fixe. You'll be treated to superior food preparation and presentation and an upscale-casual dining experience at Anasazi's. The chef offers innovative preparation methods of stylish Western cuisine, featuring organic produce, free-range meats and fresh fish. Smoke free premises. **Cards:** AE, CB, DI, DS, MC, VI.

(See map p. 428)

BISTRO 315   **Lunch:** $8-$12   **Dinner:** $17-$29   **Phone:** 505/986-9190   (29)
◆ ◆ ◆   **Location:** 0.5 mi s of the Plaza at De Vargas. 315 Old Santa Fe Tr 87501. **Hours:** 11:30 am-2 & 5:30-9:30
French   pm, to 9 pm in winter. **Closed:** Sun in winter. **Reservations:** suggested. **Features:** dressy casual; beer &
                     wine only; street parking; a la carte. The service is warm, casual and friendly at Bistro 315, where excellent
French and American preparations and a seasonal menu generally feature pate, steak frites and warm tarte tatin with creme
fraiche. Outdoor dining is also available. **Cards:** AE, MC, VI.

COYOTE CAFE   **Lunch:** $8-$14   **Dinner:** $40   **Phone:** 505/983-1615   (16)
(AAA)   **Location:** Just sw of The Plaza, between Ortiz and Galisteo sts. 132 W Water St 87501. **Hours:** 6 pm-9:30
                     pm, Sat & Sun 11:30 am-2:30 & 6-9:30 pm; casual rooftop cantina with lighter fare 11:30 am-9:30 pm
◆ ◆ ◆   4/1-10/31. **Reservations:** suggested. **Features:** dressy casual; children's menu; cocktails; prix fixe. This
Regional   renowned trend-setter has a well-deserved reputation for fine New American-Southwestern cuisine and an
American   excellent wine selection. Its lively, laid-back ambiance suits families or couples. The rooftop cantina is open
                     11:30 am-9 pm, A+K41pril-October. Smoke free premises. **Cards:** AE, DI, DS, MC, VI.   ✖

THE DINING ROOM AT THE BISHOP'S LODGE   **Lunch:** $7-$13   **Dinner:** $19-$29   **Phone:** 505/983-6377   (28)
◆ ◆ ◆   **Location:** 3.5 mi n; in The Bishop's Lodge. 87504. **Hours:** 7:30-10 am, 11:30-2 & 6-10 pm, Sun 7:30-10 am,
Regional   11-2 & 6-9 pm. **Reservations:** suggested. **Features:** casual dress; Sunday brunch; children's menu; senior's
American   menu; cocktails; a la carte. This restaurant features upscale dining in a relaxed Southwestern atmosphere.
                     Specialties include very good New American and Southwestern cuisine selections. The outdoor patio/lounge
has a fireplace and overlooks the Sangre de Christo Mountains. Smoke free premises. **Cards:** AE, DI, DS, MC, VI.

EL COMEDOR   **Lunch:** $5-$12   **Dinner:** $5-$12   **Phone:** 505/989-7575   (26)
◆ ◆   **Location:** 0.4 mi ne of St Francis Dr (US 84). 727 Cerrillos Rd 87501. **Hours:** 7 am-9 pm. **Closed:** 11/23 &
Regional   12/25. **Features:** casual dress; children's menu; carryout; beer & wine only. The authentic New Mexican
American   dishes here are some of the best in town. House specialties include the fajitas and the carne adovado. The
                     homemade salsa is excellent and hot! The+K73 decor is traditional Southwestern, and patio dining is
available. **Cards:** AE, CB, DI, MC, VI.   ✖

GERONIMO   **Lunch:** $8-$14   **Dinner:** $18-$30   **Phone:** 505/982-1500   (30)
◆ ◆ ◆   **Location:** 0.5 mi e on Canyon Rd from Paseo de Peralta. 724 Canyon Rd 87501. **Hours:** 11:30 am-2:30 &
Regional   6-10 pm, Mon from 6 pm. **Reservations:** suggested. **Features:** casual dress; Sunday brunch; cocktails; a la
American   carte. Geronimo's features new Southwestern cuisine that is creatively simple with fresh pasta, meat and fish
                     entrees. The Colorado smoked lamb chops with garlic mashed potatoes are very good, and the cheesecake
in citrus sauce is wonderful and light. **Cards:** AE, MC, VI.   ✖

HARRY'S ROAD HOUSE CAFE   **Lunch:** $5-$7   **Dinner:** $8-$12   **Phone:** 505/989-4629   (38)
◆   **Location:** I-25, exit 284 (Old Pecos Tr); 0.8 mi se on Frontage Rd (Old Las Vegas Hwy). Rt 19 87505.
American   **Hours:** 7 am-9:30 pm. **Closed:** 1/1, 11/23 & 12/25. **Features:** No A/C; casual dress; Sunday brunch;
                     carryout; a la carte. Harry's has an eclectic menu that features creative twists on traditional New Mexican
cuisine as well as standard favorites. Desserts such as the lemon meringue pie are prepared fresh on the premises. The
staff is cordial and attentive. Smoke free premises. **Cards:** MC, VI.   ✖

INDIA PALACE   **Lunch:** $8   **Dinner:** $10-$18   **Phone:** 905/986-9859   (15)
◆ ◆   **Location:** At rear of Water St parking lot. 227 Don Gaspar 87501. **Hours:** 11:30 am-2:30 & 5-10 pm.
Indian   **Closed:** Super Bowl Sun. **Features:** casual dress; carryout; cocktails; a la carte. This restaurant offers
                     authentic northern Indian cuisine expertly prepared. Specialties are vindaloo and tandoori; the tandoori mixed
grill with shrimp, seabass, lamb and chicken is excellent. Lunch buffet has vegetarian dishes. Patio dining available.
Cards: AE, DI, DS, MC, VI.

LA CASA SENA RESTAURANT   Historical   **Lunch:** $8-$13   **Dinner:** $19-$57   **Phone:** 505/988-9232   (20)
(AAA)   **Location:** Just e of Taos Plaza. 125 E Palace Ave 87501. **Hours:** 11:30 am-3 & 5:30-10 pm, Fri & Sat-10
                     pm, Sun 11 am-3 & 5:30-10 pm. **Reservations:** suggested. **Features:** dressy casual; Sunday brunch;
◆ ◆ ◆   cocktails & lounge; entertainment; street parking; a la carte, also prix fixe. La Casa Sena features excellent
Regional   regional preparation of traditional menu selections. You'll find that the servers are attentive and
American   knowledgeable, and a large outdoor dining area is available. They also have an extensive wine list.
                     Cards: AE, CB, DI, DS, MC, VI.   ✖

THE OLD HOUSE   **Dinner:** $17-$31   **Phone:** 505/988-4455   (5)
◆ ◆ ◆ ◆   **Location:** Just w of The Plaza at Sandoval St; in Eldorado Hotel. 309 W San Francisco 87501. **Hours:** 5:30
Regional   pm-11 pm. **Reservations:** suggested. **Features:** dressy casual; cocktails & lounge; valet parking; a la carte.
American   Experience sophisticated, innovative Southwestern cuisine at this elegant restaurant built on the preserved
                     foundation of an early Santa Fe house. Creative menu renditions—miso ahi tuna, veal chops, rack of lamb—
are specialties, as is the creme brulee. Smoke free premises. **Cards:** AE, CB, DI, DS, MC, VI.   ✖

OLD MEXICO GRILL   **Lunch:** $6-$11   **Dinner:** $9-$18   **Phone:** 505/473-0338   (34)
◆ ◆   **Location:** I-25, exit 278, 4 mi n; in College Plaza South. 2434 Cerrillos Rd 87505. **Hours:** 11:30 am-2:30 &
Mexican   5:30-9 pm, Fri & Sat-9:30 pm. **Closed:** 11/23, 12/25 & Super Bowl Sun. **Features:** casual dress; senior's
                     menu; carryout; cocktails. Enjoy the authentic traditional entrees or unique and creative variations on
Mexican cuisine at this festive facility. Great salsas, moles and specialties such as carne asada a la tampiquena are
prepared by chefs you can see in the exhibition kitchen. **Cards:** DS, MC, VI.   ✖

ORE HOUSE ON THE PLAZA   **Lunch:** $5-$9   **Dinner:** $13-$27   **Phone:** 505/983-8687   (8)
◆ ◆   **Location:** 50 Lincoln Ave 87501. **Hours:** 11:30 am-10 pm, Sun from noon. **Closed:** 11/23 & 12/25.
Regional   **Reservations:** suggested; for dinner. **Features:** casual dress; children's menu; carryout; cocktails;
American   entertainment. You'll enjoy the casual, quiet dining at Ore House, as well as its good selection of
                     Southwestern specialties such as red-chili pesto stuffed in a steak or blackened prime rib with garlic sauce.
The attractive patio overlooks the plaza. **Cards:** AE, MC, VI.   ✖

(See map p. 428)

OSTERIA D'ASSISI　　　　**Lunch:** $12-$16　　　**Dinner:** $14-$25　　　**Phone:** 505/986-5858　　①
◆◆
Northern
Italian
Location: 1 blks n of The Plaza. 58 S Federal Place 87501. **Hours:** 11 am-9 pm, Fri & Sat-10 pm. Closed major holidays & Sun. **Reservations:** suggested. **Features:** carryout; beer & wine only; a la carte. You'll find a relaxed, comfortable, casual atmosphere as well as indoor and patio dining at this Santa Fe style restaurant. The menu features northern Italian selections and includes a variety of microbrewery beers. Smoking is allowed on the patio only. **Cards:** AE, DI, MC, VI.

THE PALACE & SALOON　　　**Lunch:** $4-$11　　　**Dinner:** $16-$25　　　**Phone:** 505/982-9891　　⑨
ⒶⒶⒶ
◆◆◆
Continental
Location: Just w of The Plaza. 142 W Palace Ave 87504. **Hours:** 11:30 am-3 & 5:30-10 pm. Closed: 12/25 & Sun for lunch. **Reservations:** accepted. **Features:** cocktails & lounge; a la carte. Classic Victorian is the decor at the cozy Palace, perhaps the town's oldest restaurant. The menu features fresh pasta dishes as well as seafood and veal. The family-owned restaurant offers courtyard dining on the outdoor patio, weather permitting. **Cards:** AE, DI, DS, MC, VI.

PAUL'S RESTAURANT OF SANTA FE　　**Lunch:** $7-$8　　**Dinner:** $15-$20　　**Phone:** 505/982-8738　　⑩
◆◆
Nouvelle
American
Location: Just n of The Plaza, between Lincoln and Washington sts. 72 W Marcy St 87501. **Hours:** 11:30 am-2 & 5:30-9 pm, Fri & Sat-9:30 pm, Sun 6 pm-9:30 pm. Closed: 12/25. **Reservations:** suggested; for dinner. **Features:** casual dress; beer & wine only; a la carte. Paul's Restaurant is a simple, cheerful bistro with an imaginative cuisine that reflects a variety of influences, including French Provencal and Southwestern tastes. Try the baked salmon with pecan and herb topping. The desserts are excellent. Smoke free premises. **Cards:** AE, DS, MC, VI.
⊠

THE PINK ADOBE　　　　**Lunch:** $6-$8　　　**Dinner:** $10-$25　　　**Phone:** 505/983-7712　　㉕
◆◆
Continental
Location: 2 blks s of The Plaza. 406 Old Santa Fe Tr 87501. **Hours:** 11:30 am-2 & 5:30-9:30 pm. Closed major holidays. **Reservations:** suggested. **Features:** casual dress; children's menu; cocktails & lounge; entertainment; a la carte. A tradition for 55 years, the Pink Adobe has casual dining, Continental and New Mexican cuisine and an attractive decor in a 350-year-old home. Each intimate room has a fireplace. Live classical guitar entertainment every evening except Sun, Mon and Fri. Smoke free premises. **Cards:** AE, CB, DI, DS, MC, VI.
⊠

PLAZA RESTAURANT　Historical　　**Lunch:** $6-$10　　**Dinner:** $8-$12　　**Phone:** 505/982-1664　　⑦
◆
American
Location: W side of The Plaza. 54 Lincoln Ave 87501. **Hours:** 7 am-10 pm. Closed: 11/23 & 12/25. **Features:** No A/C; casual dress; children's menu; carryout; beer & wine only; a la carte. You'll receive a good basic meal for not very much money at the Plaza, which has provided continuous service since 1918. It's a cozy diner with a variety of classic favorites. They also have New Mexican specialties and a few Greek dishes. **Cards:** DS, MC, VI.
⊠

PRANZO ITALIAN GRILL　　**Lunch:** $7-$10　　**Dinner:** $7-$20　　**Phone:** 505/984-2645　　㉓
◆
Italian
Location: 3 blks s of the Plaza; in Sanbusco Center. 540 Montezuma St 87501. **Hours:** 11:30 am-3 & 5-10 pm. **Reservations:** accepted. **Features:** casual dress; carryout; cocktails. Located in a renovated warehouse and dressed in a contemporary art-deco theme, Pranzo's is popular with locals, who recommend its grilled favorites of smoked chicken, steak and seafood dishes. The pasta and thin-crust pizza are popular also. **Cards:** AE, CB, DI, DS, MC, VI.

SAN FRANCISCO STREET BAR & GRILL　**Lunch:** $6-$7　**Dinner:** $7-$13　**Phone:** 505/982-2044　⑭
◆
American
Location: Just sw of The Plaza, at Plaza Mercado. 114 W San Francisco St 87501. **Hours:** 11 am-11 pm. Closed: 1/1, 11/23 & 12/25. **Features:** casual dress; carryout; cocktails & lounge; a la carte. You may discover the best burger in town at San Francisco's, a casual, family-style cafe with excellent sandwiches and light fare. All breads, pastas, dressings and soups are baked or prepared in-house. They have a good selection of wine by the glass. Smoke free premises. **Cards:** AE, DI, DS, MC, VI.
⊠

SANTACAFE　Historical　　　**Lunch:** $8-$10　　**Dinner:** $17-$27　　**Phone:** 505/984-1788　　③
ⒶⒶⒶ
◆◆◆
Nouvelle
American
Location: Just ne of The Plaza, between Marcy St and Paseo de Peralta. 231 Washington Ave 87501. **Hours:** 11:30 am-2 & 5:30-11 pm; 11:30 am-2 & 6-10 pm, in winter. **Reservations:** suggested. **Features:** casual dress; cocktails & lounge; a la carte. A refined but relaxed atmosphere can be found at Santacafe, located in a restored 1854 home. The restaurant features sophisticated preparation methods, excellent flavors and quality ingredients. A lovely courtyard for patio dining is available in season. **Cards:** AE, MC, VI.
⊠

THE SHED　Historical　　　**Lunch:** $5-$10　　**Dinner:** $9-$15　　**Phone:** 505/982-9030　　⑱
◆◆
Regional
American
Location: Just e of The Plaza. 113 1/2 E Palace 87501. **Hours:** 11 am-2:30 pm, Wed-Sat also 5:30 pm-9 pm. Closed: 1/1, 11/23, 12/25 & Sun. **Features:** casual dress; carryout; cocktails. Red and green chili enchiladas and mocha cake are the specialties at The Shed, located in a 17th-century fortified hacienda. Its casual dining features northern New Mexican dishes. It has been owned/operated by three generations of the Carswell family. Smoke free premises. **Cards:** AE, DS, MC, VI.
⊠

STEAKSMITH AT EL GANCHO　　　　　**Dinner:** $9-$25　　　**Phone:** 505/988-3333　　㊵
◆◆
Steak and
Seafood
Location: I-25, exit 284 (Old Pecos Tr), 1 mi se on Frontage Rd (Old Las Vegas Hwy). 87505. **Hours:** 5:30 pm-10 pm, Sun 5 pm-9 pm. Closed major holidays. **Reservations:** suggested. **Features:** casual dress; children's menu; carryout; cocktails & lounge. A contemporary, Santa Fe decor and warm, cozy ambiance combine to set the tone for this restaurant. The menu features aged beef and seafood specials such as stuffed trout with shrimp, local favorites and a few fresh entrees. **Cards:** AE, CB, DI, DS, MC, VI.
⊠

TOMASITA'S SANTA FE STATION　　**Lunch:** $7-$9　　**Dinner:** $8-$11　　**Phone:** 505/983-5721　　㉒
◆
Regional
American
Location: 500 S Guadalupe 87501. **Hours:** 11 am-10 pm. Closed: 1/1, 11/23, 12/25 & Sun. **Features:** No A/C; casual dress; children's menu; carryout; cocktails & lounge. A restored train station is the setting for this busy, bustling restaurant, which serves large portions of traditional New Mexican cuisine including its specialty burritos, blue corn enchiladas and rellenos. Locals and visitors alike dine here. **Cards:** MC, VI. ⊠

(See map p. 428)

TORTILLA FLATS
AAA
◆ ◆
Regional
American

| | Lunch: $5-$9 | Dinner: $6-$10 | Phone: 505/471-8685 | (36) |

Location: I-25, exit 278, 3.5 mi ne. 3139 Cerrillos Rd 87505. **Hours:** 7 am-9 pm, Fri & Sat-10 pm; 7 am-10 pm 5/31-9/4, Sun-9 pm. Closed: 11/23 & 12/25. **Features:** casual dress; children's menu; carryout; cocktails; a la carte. The New Mexican specialties at Tomasita's include chicken and vegetarian quesadillas, chili rellenos, enchiladas, carne adovada and filling platters. Its comfortable, casual and inviting atmosphere appeals to young professionals and executives. **Cards:** DS, MC, VI.

UPPER CRUST PIZZA
AAA
◆
American

| | Lunch: $3-$14 | Dinner: $5-$14 | Phone: 505/982-0000 | (24) |

Location: 0.5 mi s of The Plaza at De Vargas. 329 Old Santa Fe Trail 87505. **Hours:** 11 am-10 pm, Fri & Sat-11 pm; noon-11 pm, 6/1-9/30. Closed: 9/4, 11/23 & 12/25. **Features:** No A/C; casual dress; carryout; beer & wine only; a la carte. This eatery provides a good value for light appetites or lean budgets. The fresh ingredients lend to its excellent pizza, stromboli and calzone—all made on-site. They have several small dining rooms, great patio dining, and live music in the summer. Smoke free premises. **Cards:** MC, VI.

──────── *The following restaurants have not been inspected by AAA* ────────
but are listed for your information only.

BLUE CORN CAFE
[fyi]
Phone: 505/984-1800
Not inspected. **Location:** 133 Water St 87501. **Features:** A fun and upbeat eatery serving New Mexican food, this restaurant also offers its own brewery and stays open later than most.

THE BURRITO COMPANY
[fyi]
Phone: 505/982-4453
Not inspected. **Location:** 111 Washington Ave 87501. **Features:** On the plaza, this restaurant is open for breakfast, lunch and dinner. A very good value.

CAFE PASQUAL'S
[fyi]
Phone: 505/983-9340
Not inspected. **Location:** 121 Don Gaspar Ave 87501. **Features:** This popular establishment features creative regional American dishes in a festive atmosphere with hand-painted murals adorning the walls.

COWGIRL HALL OF FAME
[fyi]
Phone: 505/982-2565
Not inspected. **Location:** 319 S Guadalupe St 87501. **Features:** A fun, hip eatery and bar which offers some form of entertainment most nights. Cowgirl memorabilia is abundant, and the food features regional, Cajun and barbecue favorites.

GUADALUPE CAFE
[fyi]
Phone: 505/982-9762
Not inspected. **Location:** 422 Old Santa Fe Tr 87501. **Features:** This tried and true restaurant, adjacent to the state capitol, provides good value on New Mexican favorites. Breakfast, lunch and dinner are served.

IL PIATTO
[fyi]
Phone: 505/984-1091
Not inspected. **Location:** 95 W Marcy St 87501. **Features:** This local favorite has a country-Italian appeal. Fresh pastas and other authentic Italian cuisine are offered.

JACK'S
[fyi]
Phone: 505/983-7220
Not inspected. **Location:** 135 W Palace Ave 87501. **Features:** Experience contemporary American cuisine and decor at this establishment, where menu choices include creative steak, salmon and chicken entrees.

JULIAN'S
[fyi]
Phone: 505/988-2355
Not inspected. **Location:** 221 Shelby St 87501. **Features:** Enjoy visiting this sophisticated Northern Italian restaurant. Specialties such as piccata de vittello and pollo al agro dolci are served in a romantic atmosphere.

MODU NOODLES
[fyi]
Phone: 505/983-1411
Not inspected. **Location:** 1494 Cerrillos Rd 87505. **Features:** Pacific Rim cuisine, featuring Malaysian laksa and Pad Thai, is served in a simple, spare and somewhat cozy atmosphere. Friendly service.

PAUL'S
[fyi]
Phone: 505/982-8738
Not inspected. **Location:** 72 W Marcy St. **Features:** Contemporary French cuisine features creative versions of seafood, duck and lamb. Very popular and a good value.

RISTRA
[fyi]
Phone: 505/982-8608
Not inspected. **Location:** 548 Agua Fria 87501. **Features:** Innovative New American, French and Southwestern creations, such as rack of lamb, filet mignon and Alaskan halibut, highlight this eatery in a historic home.

SANTA ROSA pop. 2,300

──────── **LODGINGS** ────────

BEST WESTERN ADOBE INN
AAA SAVE
◆ ◆
Motel

				Phone: (505)472-3446
5/16-9/30	1P: $45-$55	2P: $49-$65	XP: $4	F12
2/1-5/15 & 10/1-1/31	1P: $42-$52	2P: $46-$58	XP: $4	F12

Location: I-40, exit 275. 1501 Will Rogers Dr 88435 (PO Box 410). Fax: 505/472-5759. **Terms:** [ECP] meal plan; small pets only. **Facility:** 58 rooms. 2 stories; exterior corridors; heated pool. **Cards:** AE, CB, DI, DS, MC, VI. **Special Amenities:** Free breakfast and free local telephone calls.

BEST WESTERN SANTA ROSA INN
AAA SAVE
◆ ◆ ◆
Motel

				Phone: (505)472-5877
10/1-1/31	1P: $50-$55	2P: $60-$65	XP: $5	
2/1-9/30	1P: $45-$50	2P: $55-$60	XP: $5	

Location: I-40, exit 277, 0.5 mi w on Will Rogers Dr (US 66). 3022 Will Rogers Dr 88435 (PO Box 501). Fax: 505/472-5880. **Terms:** [ECP] meal plan; 14 day cancellation notice; small pets only. **Facility:** 44 rooms. 1 story; exterior corridors; heated seasonal pool. **Dining:** Restaurant nearby. **Cards:** AE, CB, DI, DS, MC, VI. **Special Amenities:** Free breakfast and free newspaper.

COMFORT INN
◆◆◆
Motel
All Year · 1P: $69-$89 · 2P: $56-$99 · XP: $5 · F11
Phone: (505)472-5570
Location: US 84, just w of I-40, exit 277. 3343 E Will Rogers Dr 88435. Fax: 505/472-5575. **Terms:** [ECP] meal plan; pets. **Facility:** 45 rooms. 2 stories; exterior corridors; heated pool. **Cards:** AE, CB, DI, DS, MC, VI.

DAYS INN OF SANTA ROSA
(AAA) (SAVE)
◆◆
Motel
5/1-8/31 · 1P: $45-$50 · 2P: $50-$55 · XP: $5 · F13
9/1-1/31 · 1P: $40-$45 · 2P: $50-$55 · XP: $5 · F13
2/1-4/30 · 1P: $40-$45 · 2P: $45-$50 · XP: $5 · F13
Phone: (505)472-5985
Location: I-40, exit 275, then 2 blks e. 1830 Will Rogers Dr 88435. Fax: 505/472-5989. **Terms:** [CP] meal plan; pets, $3 extra charge. **Facility:** 52 rooms. 2 stories; exterior corridors. **Dining:** Restaurant nearby. **Cards:** AE, CB, DI, DS, JC, MC, VI. **Special Amenities:** Free breakfast and free local telephone calls.

HOLIDAY INN EXPRESS
(AAA) (SAVE)
◆◆◆
Motel
2/1-7/1 · 1P: $45-$55 · 2P: $60-$70 · XP: $10 · F18
7/2-1/31 · 1P: $40-$50 · 2P: $55-$65 · XP: $10 · F18
Phone: (505)472-5411
Location: I-40, exit 277, then 0.3 mi w on Will Rogers Dr (US 66). 3300 Will Rogers Dr 88435 (PO Box 304). Fax: 505/472-3537. **Terms:** [ECP] meal plan; 5 day cancellation notice; small pets only, in smoking rooms. **Facility:** 78 rooms. Southwestern design. All rooms with hair dryer, iron and ironing board. 2 stories; interior corridors; heated pool, whirlpool. **Dining:** Restaurant nearby. **Cards:** AE, CB, DI, DS, JC, MC, VI. **Special Amenities:** Free breakfast and free local telephone calls. *(See color ad below)*

MOTEL 6 - 273
(AAA)
◆
Motel
5/25-9/4 · 1P: $42-$52 · 2P: $48-$58 · XP: $3 · F17
2/1-5/24 & 9/5-1/31 · 1P: $36-$46 · 2P: $42-$52 · XP: $3 · F17
Phone: 505/472-3045
Location: I-40, exit 277, then 0.3 mi w on Will Rogers Dr (US 66). 3400 Will Rogers Dr 88435. Fax: 505/472-5923. **Terms:** Weekly rates avail; small pets only. **Facility:** 90 rooms. Exterior corridors; heated pool. **All Rooms:** shower baths. **Cards:** AE, CB, DI, DS, MC, VI.

RAMADA LIMITED
(AAA) (SAVE)
◆◆
Motel
All Year · 1P: $50-$60 · 2P: $65-$80 · XP: $10 · F
Phone: (505)472-4800
Location: I-40, exit 275, just e. 1701 Will Rogers Dr 88435. Fax: 505/472-4809. **Terms:** [ECP] meal plan; small pets only, $10 extra charge. **Facility:** 60 rooms. 2 stories; interior corridors; heated pool, whirlpool. **Recreation:** exercise bicycle. **All Rooms:** safes. **Some Rooms:** Fee: VCR. **Cards:** AE, CB, DI, DS, JC, MC, VI. **Special Amenities:** Free breakfast and free local telephone calls.

SUPER 8 MOTEL-SANTA ROSA
◆◆
Motel
Property failed to provide current rates
Phone: 505/472-5388
Location: I-40, exit 275, 2 blks w. 1201 Will Rogers Dr 88435. Fax: 505/472-5388. **Terms:** [CP] meal plan; pets, $20 dep req. **Facility:** 88 rooms. Exceptionally clean rooms. 2 stories; interior corridors. **Some Rooms:** Fee: VCR. **Cards:** AE, CB, DI, DS, MC, VI.

------ **RESTAURANT** ------

SILVER MOON RESTAURANT
◆
American
Lunch: $4-$14   **Dinner:** $5-$16   **Phone:** 505/472-3162
Location: I-40 exit 277, just n. 3620 Will Rogers 88435. **Hours:** 6:30 am-9:30 pm. Closed: 11/23 & 12/25.
Features: casual dress; children's menu; carryout. Established in 1959, the restaurant is located on and is part of the old Route 66 nostalgia. Neon window signs and a very relaxed family style environment add to the charm of this yesteryear establishment. **Cards:** MC, VI.

SILVER CITY pop. 10,700 ------ LODGINGS ------

THE CARTER HOUSE
◆◆◆
Bed &
Breakfast
Phone: 505/388-5485
All Year   1P: $62-$72   2P: $70-$80   XP: $10   D10
Location: Historic downtown; adjacent to Grant County Court House, corner of Broadway and N Copper sts, 0.3 mi w of SR 90. 101 N Cooper St 88061. Fax: 505/388-5485. **Terms:** [BP] meal plan; check-in 4 pm; 7 day cancellation notice. **Facility:** 5 rooms. Located in residential area. Handsome oak trimmed home, main part of home built in 1906. Separate youth hostel on ground floor. 1 story; interior corridors; smoke free premises. **All Rooms:** combo or shower baths. **Cards:** AE, MC, VI.

COMFORT INN
(AAA) (SAVE)
◆◆◆
Motel
Phone: (505)534-1883
All Year   1P: $57-$150   2P: $62-$150   XP: $5   F18
Location: 1.5 mi e on US 180 and SR 90. 1060 E Hwy 180 88061. Fax: 505/534-0778. **Terms:** [CP] meal plan. **Facility:** 52 rooms. Large rooms. Contemporary decor. 2 stories; interior corridors; heated pool, whirlpool. **Dining:** Restaurant nearby. **All Rooms:** extended cable TV. **Cards:** AE, CB, DI, DS, MC, VI. **Special Amenities: Free breakfast and free local telephone calls.**

COPPER MANOR MOTEL
(AAA) (SAVE)
◆◆◆
Motor Inn
Phone: (505)538-5392
All Year   1P: $43-$54   2P: $47-$58   XP: $4   F14
Location: 1.3 mi ne on US 180 and SR 90. 710 Silver Heights Blvd 88062 (PO Box 1405). Fax: 505/538-5830. **Terms:** [CP] meal plan; small pets only. **Facility:** 68 rooms. Very nicely decorated and furnished rooms. 2 stories; exterior corridors; 2 pools, 1 indoor heated, whirlpool. **Dining:** Restaurant; 5:45 am-10 pm; $6-$15; cocktails; entertainment. **All Rooms:** extended cable TV. **Some Rooms:** kitchen. Fee: VCR. **Cards:** AE, CB, DI, DS, MC, VI. **Special Amenities: Free breakfast and free local telephone calls.**

THE DRIFTER MOTEL
(AAA) (SAVE)
◆◆
Motor Inn
Phone: (505)538-2916
All Year   1P: $41-$47   2P: $45-$50   XP: $4   F14
Location: 1.3 mi ne on US 180 and SR 90. 711 Silver Heights Blvd 88062 (PO Box 1288). Fax: 505/538-5703. **Terms:** [CP] meal plan; small pets only. **Facility:** 69 rooms. 2 stories; exterior corridors; 2 pools, 1 indoor heated, whirlpool. **Dining:** Restaurant; 5:45 am-10 pm; $6-$25; cocktails; entertainment. **All Rooms:** extended cable TV. **Cards:** AE, CB, DI, DS, JC, MC,. **Special Amenities: Free breakfast and free local telephone calls.**

ECONOLODGE SILVER CITY
(AAA) (SAVE)
◆◆
Motel
Phone: (505)534-1111
5/1-9/30   1P: $40-$65   2P: $40-$70   XP: $7   F18
2/1-4/30 & 10/1-1/31   1P: $40-$59   2P: $40-$67   XP: $7   F18
Location: 1.5 mi on US 180 and SR 90. 1120 Hwy 180 E 88061. Fax: 505/534-2222. **Terms:** [CP] meal plan; 7 day cancellation notice; small pets only, $25 dep req. **Facility:** 63 rooms. 3 stories; interior corridors; heated pool, whirlpool. **Dining:** Restaurant nearby. **All Rooms:** combo or shower baths, extended cable TV. **Cards:** AE, CB, DI, DS, MC, VI. **Special Amenities: Free breakfast and free local telephone calls.**

HOLIDAY MOTOR HOTEL
◆◆
Motor Inn
Phone: (505)538-3711
All Year   1P: $47-$53   2P: $53-$59   XP: $4   F12
Location: 2 mi ne on jct SR 180 and 90. 3420 Hwy 180E 88061. Fax: 505/538-3711. **Terms:** Small pets only, in designated rooms. **Facility:** 79 rooms. 2 stories; exterior corridors; heated pool. **Some Rooms:** Fee: refrigerators, microwaves. **Cards:** AE, DI, DS, MC, VI.

SUPER 8 MOTEL
(AAA) (SAVE)
◆◆
Motel
Phone: (505)388-1983
All Year   1P: $39-$50   2P: $49-$60   XP: $5   F12
Location: 1.5 mi ne on US 180 and SR 90. 1040 E Hwy 180 88061. Fax: 505/388-1983. **Terms:** Weekly rates avail; small pets only, $10 fee. **Facility:** 69 rooms. 2 stories; interior corridors. **All Rooms:** extended cable TV. **Some Rooms:** Fee: VCR. **Cards:** AE, CB, DI, DS, MC, VI. **Special Amenities: Free breakfast and free local telephone calls.**

SOCORRO pop. 8,200 ------ LODGINGS ------

ECONO LODGE
(AAA) (SAVE)
◆◆◆
Motel
Phone: (505)835-1500
All Year   1P: $32-$44   2P: $36-$58   XP: $5   F18
Location: 1 mi s of I-25, exit 150. 713 California Ave NW 87801 (PO Box 977). Fax: 505/835-1500. **Terms:** [CP] meal plan; small pets only, $5 extra charge. **Facility:** 64 rooms. Mini suites avail; 1-2 stories; exterior corridors; 2 heated pools, sauna, whirlpools. **Dining:** Restaurant nearby. **Some Rooms:** Fee: VCR. **Cards:** AE, CB, DI, DS, MC, VI. **Special Amenities: Free breakfast and free local telephone calls.**

HOLIDAY INN EXPRESS
◆◆◆
Motel
All Year · 1P: $79-$99 · 2P: $84-$104 · XP: $5 · F19
Phone: (505)838-0556
Location: Center. 1100 California Ave NE 87801. Fax: 505/838-0598. **Terms:** [CP] meal plan; 14 day cancellation notice; small pets only, $5 extra charge. **Facility:** 80 rooms. Well appointed rooms. Ample at-door parking. 2 stories; interior/exterior corridors; heated pool. **Cards:** AE, CB, DI, DS, JC, MC, VI.

MOTEL 6
AAA
◆◆
Motel
5/25-1/31 · 1P: $36-$46 · 2P: $42-$52 · XP: $3 · F19
2/1-5/24 · 1P: $34-$44 · 2P: $40-$50 · XP: $3 · F19
Phone: (505)835-4300
Location: Exit 147. 807 S US 85 87801. **Terms:** Small pets only. **Facility:** 95 rooms. 2 stories; exterior corridors; heated pool. **All Rooms:** shower baths. **Cards:** AE, DI, DS, MC, VI.

------ **RESTAURANTS** ------

VAL VERDE STEAK HOUSE Historical · **Lunch:** $7-$10 · **Dinner:** $13-$22 · **Phone:** 505/835-3380
◆◆
Steakhouse
Location: Center. 203 Manzanares 87801. **Hours:** 11 am-2 & 5-9 pm, Sun noon-9 pm. Closed: 12/25. **Features:** casual dress; cocktails & lounge. Located in a historic hotel constructed in 1919, Val Verde's site was a place of aid, they say, for the 1598 expedition of Juan de Onate. The restaurant features prime cuts of beef, plus chicken, ham, fish, enchiladas, chili and traditional sandwiches. **Cards:** AE, DI, DS, MC, VI.

------ *The following restaurants have not been inspected by AAA* ------
but are listed for your information only.

EL COMINO FAMILY RESTAURANT
[fyi]
Phone: 505/835-1180
Not inspected. **Location:** 715 California Ave NW 87801. **Features:** This local favorite is open 24 hours.

EL SOMBRERO
[fyi]
Phone: 505/835-3945
Not inspected. **Location:** 210 Mesquite NE 87801. **Features:** Specialties include steaks and homemade Mexican food.

TAOS pop. 4,100—*See also ARROYO HONDO, ARROYO SECO, EL PRADO, RANCHOS DE TAOS & TAOS SKI VALLEY.*

------ **LODGINGS** ------

AMERICAN ARTISTS GALLERY HOUSE BED & BREAKFAST
◆◆◆
Bed & Breakfast
All Year · 1P: $75-$165 · 2P: $75-$165 · XP: $25
Phone: (505)758-4446
Location: SR 68, 1 mi sw of jct US 64 & Taos Plaza, 0.3 mi e. 132 Frontier Ln 87571 (PO Box 584). Fax: 505/798-0497. **Terms:** [BP] meal plan; age restrictions may apply; 14 day cancellation notice; cancellation fee imposed; pet on premises. **Facility:** 10 rooms. "Gallery" style rooms, done in tasteful Southwestern style, feature works by local artists. The area's three diverse cultures are displayed throughout. 1 story; smoke free premises. **All Rooms:** combo or shower baths. **Some Rooms:** kitchen.

BEST VALUE INDIAN HILLS INN DE TAOS
AAA [SAVE]
◆◆
Motel
All Year · 1P: $49-$79 · 2P: $54-$84 · XP: $10 · F6
Phone: (505)758-4293
Location: SR 68, just s of Taos Plaza. 233 Paseo del Pueblo Sur 87571 (PO Box 1229). Fax: 505/758-4293. **Terms:** 3 day cancellation notice; cancellation fee imposed. **Facility:** 55 rooms. Within walking distance to Taos Plaza. 2 stories; exterior corridors; heated pool. **Dining:** Restaurant nearby. **Services:** gift shop. **All Rooms:** extended cable TV. **Cards:** AE, DI, DS, MC, VI. **Special Amenities:** Free breakfast and free local telephone calls. IMA. *(See color ad p 447)*

BEST WESTERN KACHINA LODGE & MEETINGS CENTER

Phone: (505)758-2275

10/26-1/31	1P: $49-$139	2P: $59-$149	XP: $10	F12
5/25-10/25	1P: $69-$109	2P: $79-$119	XP: $10	F12
2/1-4/1	1P: $59-$99	2P: $69-$109	XP: $10	F12
4/2-5/24	1P: $49-$89	2P: $59-$99	XP: $10	F12

Motor Inn

Location: US 64, 0.5 mi n of jct SR 68 and Taos Plaza. 413 Paseo del Pueblo Norte 87571. Fax: 505/758-9207. **Facility:** 118 rooms. 1-2 stories; interior/exterior corridors; heated pool, whirlpool. **Dining:** Dining room, coffee shop; 6 am-10 pm; $7-$22; cocktails; entertainment. **Services:** gift shop; area transportation, within 5 mi. **Recreation:** Native American dance performances daily, 5/15-10/31. **All Rooms:** extended cable TV. **Some Rooms:** kitchen. **Cards:** AE, DI, DS, MC, VI. **Special Amenities:** Early check-in/late check-out and free newspaper. *(See color ad below)*

THE BROOKS STREET INN

Phone: (505)758-1489

All Year	1P: $88-$121	2P: $88-$121	XP: $25

Bed & Breakfast

Location: 0.5 mi n on US 64 from jct SR 68 and Taos Plaza, just e. 119 Brooks St 87571 (PO Box 4954, 119 Brooks St). **Terms:** [BP] meal plan; age restrictions may apply; check-in 4 pm; 10 day cancellation notice; cancellation fee imposed; pets on premises. **Facility:** 6 rooms. Cozy adobe home in residential neighborhood on quiet wooded grounds. Individually furnished rooms with beamed ceilings and polished wood floors. 3 garden casita rooms with fireplace. 1 story; interior/exterior corridors; smoke free premises. **All Rooms:** combo or shower baths. **Cards:** MC, VI.

CASA BENAVIDES BED & BREAKFAST INN

Phone: (505)758-1772

All Year	1P: $80-$125	2P: $85-$225	XP: $15

Bed & Breakfast

Location: Center; on US 64 E just e of jct SR 68 and Taos Plaza. 137 Kit Carson Rd 87571. Fax: 505/758-5738. **Terms:** [BP] meal plan; 10 day cancellation notice; cancellation fee imposed. **Facility:** 33 rooms. Out-sized bed and breakfast, wide variety of building and room types. 2 two-bedroom units. 2 stories; interior/exterior corridors; smoke free premises. **All Rooms:** combo or shower baths. **Some Rooms:** 3 kitchens. **Cards:** AE, MC, VI.

CASA DE LAS CHIMENEAS BED & BREAKFAST

Phone: (505)758-4777

All Year	1P: $165-$315	2P: $175-$325	XP: $15

Bed & Breakfast

Location: Center; s from jct US 68 and 64, 0.3 mi on US 68, e on Los Pandos to Cordoba Rd, s follow signs. 405 Cordoba Rd 87571 (Box 5303). Fax: 505/758-3976. **Terms:** [BP] meal plan; 14 day cancellation notice; cancellation fee imposed. **Facility:** 8 rooms. Luxurious hacienda with rooms facing impressive formal garden. Traditional rooms with beamed ceilings, hand-painted tile, and fireplaces. 4 whirlpool rooms, $190-$325; 1 story; exterior corridors; smoke free premises; whirlpool. **Services:** Fee: massage. **All Rooms:** combo or shower baths, extended cable TV. **Cards:** AE, DI, MC, VI. **Special Amenities:** Free breakfast and free local telephone calls.

CASA ENCANTADA
Phone: (505)758-7477
◆◆◆ All Year 1P: $95-$140 2P: $95-$140 XP: $15 F6
Bed & **Location:** 0.6 mi e on US 64 from jct SR 68 and Taos Plaza, just s. 416 Liebert St 87571 (6460 NDCBU).
Breakfast Fax: 505/737-5085. **Terms:** [BP] meal plan; check-in 4 pm; 10 day cancellation notice; cancellation fee imposed; pets on premises. **Facility:** 10 rooms. Lovely courtyard behind adobe walls; cheerful breakfast area. Variety of rooms in main house and adobe out-buildings, half with fireplace. Children welcome. 3 two-bedroom units. 1-2 stories; exterior corridors; smoke free premises. **All Rooms:** combo or shower baths. **Some Rooms:** 2 kitchens. **Cards:** AE, MC, VI.

CASA EUROPA
Phone: (505)758-9798
◆◆◆ All Year 1P: $95-$135 2P: $105-$145 XP: $20
Historic Bed **Location:** 1.7 mi s from jct SR 64. 840 Upper Ranchitos Rd 87571 (HC 68, Box 3F). Fax: 505/758-9798.
& Breakfast **Terms:** [BP] meal plan; 14 day cancellation notice; cancellation fee imposed. **Facility:** 7 rooms. 17th century restored home with Spanish and European influence. 1 unit with full hot tub and steambath shower. 7 units with fireplace. 2 stories; interior/exterior corridors; smoke free premises. **Services:** area transportation. **All Rooms:** combo or shower baths. **Some Rooms:** kitchen, color TV. **Cards:** MC, VI.

COMFORT SUITES
Phone: (505)751-1555
(AAA) (SAVE) All Year 1P: $69-$149 2P: $69-$149
◆◆◆ **Location:** SR 68, 3 mi sw of jct US 64. 1500 Paseo Del Pueblo Sur 87571. Fax: 505/751-1991.
Motel **Terms:** [CP] meal plan; 3 day cancellation notice; cancellation fee imposed; package plans. **Facility:** 60 rooms. Suites with separate living room all with very nice Southwest decor. 2 stories; interior corridors; heated pool, whirlpool. **Dining:** Restaurant nearby. **All Rooms:** combo or shower baths, extended cable TV. **Cards:** AE, DI, DS, JC, MC, VI. **Special Amenities:** Free breakfast and free local telephone calls. *(See color ad below)*

DAYS INN
Phone: (505)758-2230
◆◆ All Year 1P: $49-$69 2P: $59-$79 XP: $6 F17
Motel **Location:** SR 68, 2.5 mi sw of jct US 64 and Taos Plaza. 1333 Paseo del Pueblo Sur 87571 (PO Box 6004). Fax: 505/758-8929. **Terms:** [CP] meal plan. **Facility:** 37 rooms. 2 stories; interior corridors. **Cards:** AE, CB, DI, DS, MC, VI. *(See ad below)*

DREAM CATCHER BED & BREAKFAST
◆◆◆
Bed &
Breakfast

Phone: (505)758-0613

All Year 1P: $79-$104 2P: $89-$119 XP: $20
Location: From Plaza Don Fernando W to La Loma, s on San Antonio, then 0.4 mi. 416 La Lomita Rd 87571 (PO Box 2069). Fax: 505/751-0115. **Terms:** [BP] meal plan; check-in 4 pm; 14 day cancellation notice; cancellation fee imposed; package plans. **Facility:** 7 rooms. Beautiful secluded, romantic bed & breakfast located in a rural setting, yet near the excitement of Taos' Central Plaza. 1 two-bedroom unit. 1 story; exterior corridors. **All Rooms:** combo or shower baths. **Cards:** AE, DS, MC, VI.

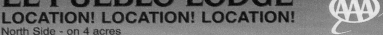

EL MONTE LODGE
(AAA) [SAVE]
◆◆
Motel

Phone: (505)758-3171

All Year 1P: $55-$85 2P: $75-$125 XP: $10
Location: US 64, 0.5 mi e of jct SR 68 and Taos Plaza. 317 Kit Carson Rd 87571 (PO Box 22). Fax: 505/758-1536. **Terms:** 7 day cancellation notice; pets, $6 extra charge. **Facility:** 13 rooms. Adobe-style cottage units, a few with mountain views; some with fireplaces. Rustic furnishings. Tranquil site on wooded grounds, large patio area off registration. 4 two-bedroom units. 4 kitchens, $10 extra charge; whirlpool room; 1 story; exterior corridors; whirlpool. **All Rooms:** extended cable TV. **Cards:** AE, DS, MC, VI. **Special Amenities:** Early check-in/late check-out and free local telephone calls.

EL PUEBLO LODGE
(AAA) [SAVE]
◆◆
Motel

Phone: (505)758-8700

All Year 1P: $50-$125 2P: $68-$125 XP: $7
Location: US 64, 0.5 mi n of jct SR 68 and Taos Plaza. 412 Paseo del Pueblo Norte 87571. Fax: 505/758-7321. **Terms:** [CP] meal plan; cancellation fee imposed; package plans; pets, $10 extra charge. **Facility:** 60 rooms. Fairly standard room decor; one wing more modern, with larger units and contemporary furnishings; second wing features a few Mexican antiques in rooms. A few units with mountain views; a few with fireplace. 6 two-bedroom units. 3 bedroom, $105-$235; 1-2 stories; exterior corridors; heated pool, whirlpool. **Dining:** Restaurant nearby. **Recreation:** patio with barbecue area. **All Rooms:** combo or shower baths. **Some Rooms:** 11 efficiencies. **Cards:** AE, DS, MC, VI. **Special Amenities:** Free breakfast. *(See color ad below)*

FECHIN INN
(AAA) [SAVE]
◆◆◆
Motel

Phone: (505)751-1000

All Year 1P: $109-$169 2P: $109-$169 XP: $15 F18
Location: Center; just n on US 64 of jct SR 68 and Taos Plaza. 227 Paseo Del Pueblo Norte 87571. Fax: 505/751-7338. **Terms:** [CP] meal plan; 7 day cancellation notice; cancellation fee imposed; pets, $50 dep req. **Facility:** 85 rooms. Adjacent to Kit Carson Park. Many rooms have kiva fireplace, balcony and patio. Built on the grounds of the Fechin Institute, Russian-born painter, builder and master woodcarver. Weekends $10 extra charge, seasonal; 2 stories; interior corridors; whirlpool. **Dining:** Cocktails; restaurant nearby. **Services:** Fee: massage. **All Rooms:** combo or shower baths, extended cable TV. **Cards:** AE, CB, DI, DS, MC, VI. *(See color ad below)*

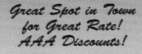

HAMPTON INN
Phone: (505)737-5700
◆◆◆ Motel
All Year   1P: $76   2P: $81
Location: SR 68, 3 mi s of Taos Plaza. 1515 Paseo del Pueblo Sur 87571. Fax: 505/737-5701. **Terms:** [CP] meal plan. **Facility:** 71 rooms. Southwest adobe stucco while maintaining Hampton character; inviting enclosed pool. 2 stories; interior corridors; heated pool. **All Rooms:** combo or shower baths. **Cards:** AE, CB, DI, DS, MC, VI.

THE HISTORIC TAOS INN
Phone: 505-758-2233
(AAA) [SAVE]
◆◆◆
Classic Motor Inn
All Year   1P: $85-$165   2P: $85-$165
Location: Center; on US 64, just n of jct SR 68 and Taos Plaza. 125 Paseo del Pueblo Norte 87571. Fax: 505/758-5776. **Terms:** 14 day cancellation notice; cancellation fee imposed. **Facility:** 36 rooms. Main building dates from late 1800s. Some compact rooms, some with patio courtyard, most with fireplace. Strong Southwestern ambiance with Spanish-Colonial antiques, locally made furnishings and hand-woven coverings. 3 two-bedroom units. 3 suites, $225; 1-2 stories; interior/exterior corridors; heated pool, whirlpool. **Dining:** Doc Martin's At The Historic Taos Inn, see separate listing; entertainment. **All Rooms:** extended cable TV. **Cards:** AE, DI, MC, VI.

HOLIDAY INN DON FERNANDO DE TAOS
Phone: (505)758-4444
(AAA) [SAVE]
◆◆◆
Motor Inn
2/1-10/13 & 1/1-1/31   1P: $100-$130   2P: $100-$130   XP: $10   F19
10/14-12/31   1P: $84-$100   2P: $84-$100   XP: $10   F19
Location: SR 68, 1.8 mi sw of jct US 64 and Taos Plaza. 1005 Paseo del Pueblo Sur 87571 (PO Drawer V). Fax: 505/758-0055. **Terms:** [BP] meal plan; cancellation fee imposed; package plans; pets, $75 dep req. **Facility:** 126 rooms. Hand carved furnishings add a regional touch. Also offers 24 suites with separate living room and fireplace. 2 stories; exterior corridors; heated pool, whirlpool, atrium style pool area with retractable roof; 1 tennis court. **Dining:** Restaurant; 6:30 am-2 & 5-10 pm; $7-$18; cocktails. **Services:** area transportation, within 5 mi. **All Rooms:** extended cable TV. **Cards:** AE, CB, DI, DS, JC, MC, VI. **Special Amenities:** Early check-in/late check-out and free room upgrade (subject to availability with advanced reservations).

INN ON LA LOMA PLAZA
Phone: (505)758-1717
(AAA)
◆◆◆
Historic Bed & Breakfast
2/1-10/31   1P: $115-$225   2P: $125-$235   XP: $20   F6
11/1-1/31   1P: $85-$170   2P: $85-$180   XP: $20   F6
Location: 0.3 mi sw on Ranchitos Rd, just w of Toas Plaza. 315 Ranchotos Rd 87571 (Box 4159). Fax: 505/751-0155. **Terms:** [BP] meal plan; check-in 4 pm; 10 day cancellation notice; cancellation fee imposed; pets on premise. **Facility:** 7 rooms. All units with fireplace. 2 studio suites, $160-$195; 2 stories; interior/exterior corridors; smoke free premises; whirlpool; playground. **Dining:** Afternoon tea. **Services:** Fee: massage. **All Rooms:** combo or shower baths, extended cable TV. **Some Rooms:** 2 efficiencies. **Cards:** AE, MC, VI. (See color ad p 446)

INN ON THE RIO
Phone: (505)758-7199
(AAA) [SAVE]
◆◆◆
Motel
All Year   1P: $69-$99   2P: $79-$129   XP: $10   F4
Location: US 64, 1.5 mi e of jct SR 68 and Taos Plaza. 910 E Kit Carson Rd 87571 (Box 6529 NDCBU). Fax: 505/751-1816. **Terms:** [CP] meal plan; weekly rates avail, off season; 14 day cancellation notice; cancellation fee imposed; pets, $10 extra charge, small dogs only. **Facility:** 12 rooms. Cozy lobby; breakfast area trimmed with gallery-quality art, Navajo blankets, and impressive kiva fireplace. Picnic area with barbecue grill. Homemade light breakfast, hearty on weekends and holidays. 1 story; exterior corridors; designated smoking area; mountain view; heated pool, whirlpool. **Recreation:** bicycles. **All Rooms:** shower or tub baths, extended cable TV. **Cards:** DS, MC, VI. **Special Amenities:** Free breakfast and free local telephone calls. (See color ad below)

LA POSADA DE TAOS
Phone: (505)758-8164
◆◆◆
Historic Bed & Breakfast
All Year   1P: $85-$140   2P: $95-$150   XP: $15   D
Location: Taos Plaza 2 blks w on Don Fernando to Manzanares, just s on Manzanares to Juanita Ln, just w. 309 Juanita Ln 87571 (PO Box 1118). Fax: 505/751-3294. **Terms:** [BP] meal plan; age restrictions may apply; 10 day cancellation notice; cancellation fee imposed. **Facility:** 6 rooms. Century-old adobe home quietly located on a dead-end lane in the historic district. Elegant but informal, 19th century antiques and hand-woven rugs. All rooms ground-floor level, 5 rooms with fireplace, private patio. 2 stories; interior/exterior corridors; smoke free premises. **All Rooms:** combo or shower baths. **Cards:** AE, DI, MC, VI.

QUALITY INN
Phone: (505)758-2200
All Year   1P: $59-$89   2P: $59-$99   XP: $7   F17
Location: SR 68, 2 mi sw of jct US 64 and Taos Plaza. 1043 Paseo del Pueblo Sur 87571 (PO Box 2319).
Fax: 505/758-9009. **Terms:** [BP] meal plan; 3 day cancellation notice; cancellation fee imposed; package plans; pets, $5 extra charge. **Facility:** 99 rooms. Standard rooms with a few regional touches. Some rooms with second entry for at-door parking. 2 stories; interior/exterior corridors; heated pool, whirlpool. **Dining:** Restaurant; 6:30 am-2 & 5:30-9 pm; $8-$12; cocktails. **All Rooms:** extended cable TV. **Some Rooms:** 2 efficiencies, safes. **Cards:** AE, DI, DS, MC, VI. **Special Amenities:** Free breakfast and free local telephone calls. *(See color ad below)*

RAMADA INN DE TAOS
Phone: (505)758-2900
12/21-1/5   1P: $79-$110   2P: $89-$120   XP: $10   F17
2/1-3/31, 4/1-12/20 & 1/6-1/31   1P: $59-$79   2P: $69-$89   XP: $10   F17
Location: SR 68, 1 mi sw of jct US 64 and Taos Plaza. 615 Paseo del Pueblo Sur 87571 (Box 6257 NDCBU).
Fax: 505/758-1662. **Terms:** [CP] meal plan; package plans; small pets only, $25 dep req. **Facility:** 124 rooms. Good-sized rooms, average decor. 4 rooms with gas fireplace. 2 stories; exterior corridors; heated pool. **Some Rooms:** Fee: refrigerators. **Cards:** AE, CB, DI, DS, MC, VI.

SAGEBRUSH INN
Phone: (505)758-2254
5/26-10/29 & 12/17-1/31   1P: $85-$115   2P: $85-$115   XP: $10   F17
2/1-5/25   1P: $70-$115   2P: $70-$115   XP: $10   F17
10/30-12/16   1P: $70-$105   2P: $70-$105   XP: $10   F17
Location: SR 68, 3 mi sw of jct US 64 and Taos Plaza. 1508 Paseo del Pueblo Sur 87571 (PO Box 557).
Fax: 505/758-5077. **Terms:** [BP] meal plan; 3 day cancellation notice; cancellation fee imposed; package plans; pets. **Facility:** 100 rooms. Pueblo-style exterior; main building circa 1929, once frequented by Georgia O'Keefe. Public areas and rooms with a strong Southwestern atmosphere, including some rooms with kiva fireplace. 70 with fireplace. Suite with separate living room & extra Murphy bed, $105-$130 rates for 2 persons; 1-2 stories; exterior corridors; heated pool, whirlpools. **Dining:** 2 dining rooms; 6:30 am-11 & 5:30-10 pm; $10-$18; cocktails; entertainment. **All Rooms:** extended cable TV. **Cards:** AE, CB, DI, DS, JC, MC, VI. **Special Amenities:** Free breakfast. *(See color ad below)*

SAN GERONIMO LODGE

Phone: (505)751-3776

(AAA) (SAVE)
◆◆◆
Historic
Lodge

All Year   1P: $95-$150   2P: $95-$150   XP: $10   F6

Location: Center; jct US 64 and 68, 1.3 mi e on US 64 E (Kit Carson Rd), 0.6 mi s. 1101 Witt Rd 87571 (PO Box 2950, RANCHOS DE TAOS, 87557). Fax: 505/751-1493. **Terms:** [BP] meal plan; 10 day cancellation notice; cancellation fee imposed; 3 night min stay, 3/1-4/9; package plans. **Facility:** 18 rooms. 1925 adobe lodge in a quiet country setting. Large rooms nicely appointed with locally-made furnishings and art; some with gas or wood burning fireplace. 2 stories; interior/exterior corridors; smoke free premises; mountain view; heated pool, whirlpool. **Dining:** Murder Mystery Night. **Services:** gift shop; complimentary evening beverages. **Fee:** massage. **Recreation:** yoga workshops, poetry, knitting workshops, library. **All Rooms:** combo or shower baths, extended cable TV. **Cards:** AE, DI, DS, MC, VI. **Special Amenities: Free breakfast and free local telephone calls.**

SUN GOD LODGE

Phone: (505)758-3162

(AAA) (SAVE)
◆◆
Motel

2/1-4/23 & 5/29-10/31	1P: $75-$100	2P: $80-$105	XP: $10 F17
11/1-1/31	1P: $55-$85	2P: $65-$90	XP: $10 F17
4/24-5/28	1P: $50-$70	2P: $55-$75	XP: $10 F17

Location: SR 68, 1.8 mi sw of jct US 64 and Taos Plaza. 919 Paseo del Pueblo Sur 87571 (PO Box 1713). Fax: 505/758-1716. **Terms:** 3 day cancellation notice; package plans; small pets only, $50 dep req. **Facility:** 55 rooms. One wing of 'economy rooms' very compact. Some units with fireplace. Most rooms fairly contemporary, with some charming local touches. 1-2 stories; exterior corridors; whirlpool. **Dining:** Restaurant nearby. **All Rooms:** extended cable TV. **Some Rooms:** 4 efficiencies. **Cards:** AE, DS, MC, VI. **Special Amenities: Early check-in/late check-out and free newspaper.**

TOUCHSTONE BED & BREAKFAST

Phone: (505)758-0192

(AAA) (SAVE)
◆◆◆
Historic Bed
& Breakfast

All Year   1P: $90-$100   2P: $250   XP: $30

Location: N from jct US 64 and 68 (center of town) 1.1 mi, on e side of road, follow signs. 110 Mabel Dodge Ln 87571 (PO Box 1885). Fax: 505/758-3498. **Terms:** [BP] meal plan; age restrictions may apply; 14 day cancellation notice; cancellation fee imposed; 2 night min stay, weekends; small pets only, $10 extra charge, in one room only. **Facility:** 9 rooms. Charming adobe hacienda circa 1795 with lushly overgrown garden bordering Pueblo lands. Artist/owner has filled the rooms and common areas with a tasteful and unusual display of art and Southwestern furnishings. Cozy rooms. 4 whirlpool rooms, $150-$250; suites, $250-$300; 1-2 stories; interior/exterior corridors; smoke free premises; whirlpool. **Dining:** Restaurant nearby. **Services:** Fee: massage. **All Rooms:** combo or shower baths, extended cable TV. **Cards:** MC, VI. **Special Amenities: Free breakfast and free local telephone calls.**

——— **RESTAURANTS** ———

APPLE TREE RESTAURANT

Lunch: $4-$10   **Dinner:** $12-$19   **Phone:** 505/758-1900

◆◆
Southwest
American

Location: Just n of Taos Plaza, just w of US 64. 123 Bent St 87571. **Hours:** 11:30 am-9 pm, Sun from 10 am. Closed: 11/29-12/12. **Reservations:** suggested. **Features:** casual dress; Sunday brunch; children's menu; health conscious menu; carryout; beer & wine only; street parking. Grilled filet mignon with mushroom sauce or mango carnitas enchiladas would make a superb choice here, where in the summer you can sit on the patio under a 50-year-old apple tree. The menu also has New Mexican and seafood meals and an excellent wine list. Smoke free premises. **Cards:** CB, DI, DS, MC, VI.

DOC MARTIN'S AT THE HISTORIC TAOS INN

Historical   **Lunch:** $6-$9   **Dinner:** $14-$29   **Phone:** 505/758-1977

(AAA)
◆◆◆
Regional
American

Location: Center; on US 64, just n of jct SR 68 and Taos Plaza; in The Historic Taos Inn. 125 Paseo del Pueblo Norte 87571. **Hours:** 7:30 am-2:30 & 5:30-9:30 pm. **Reservations:** suggested. **Features:** casual dress; Sunday brunch; cocktails; a la carte. Doc Martin's has stylish preparation and presentation of contemporary Southwestern cuisine, including beef, chicken, pork and venison specialties. It has a cozy setting in an 1800s structure. The noteworthy wine list has international standard. Smoke free premises. **Cards:** AE, DI, MC, VI.

LA LUNA RISTORANTE

Dinner: $8-$20   **Phone:** 505/751-0023

◆◆◆
Italian

Location: SR 68, 0.3 mi sw of jct US 64 and Taos Plaza. 223 Paseo del Pueblo Sur 87571. **Hours:** 5 pm-10 pm. **Reservations:** accepted. **Features:** casual dress; carryout; beer & wine only; a la carte. You can view the preparation and baking of pizza in a wood-burning oven at this cozy Southwestern-style bistro. The menu also features fresh ingredients and nice presentation of heaping bowls of pasta, fresh seafood, grilled steak and delicious desserts. **Cards:** AE, DS, MC, VI.

LAMBERT'S OF TAOS

Dinner: $10-$20   **Phone:** 505/758-1009

◆◆◆
American

Location: SR 68, 0.4 mi sw of jct US 64 and Taos Plaza. 309 Paseo del Pueblo Sur 87571. **Hours:** 5:30 pm-9 pm, Fri-9:30 pm. **Reservations:** suggested; dinner. **Features:** No A/C; casual dress; children's menu; beer & wine only; a la carte. Lambert's has relaxed fine dining with a straightforward, skilled preparation of fresh, seasonal ingredients. They offer lighter-size entrees, a well-rounded wine list and a very good selection of homemade desserts. The attentive staff does a fine job. **Cards:** AE, DI, MC, VI.

MICHAEL'S KITCHEN
◆◆
American

Lunch: $5-$7   **Dinner:** $8-$13   **Phone:** 505/758-4178
Location: US 64, 0.3 mi n of jct SR 68 and Taos Plaza. 304C Paseo del Pueblo Norte 87571. **Hours:** 7 am-8:30 pm. Closed major holidays & 11/1-11/30. **Features:** casual dress; children's menu; carryout. Michael's Kitchen is a bustling eatery that has a rustic atmosphere and an extensive menu of casual offerings such as nachos, chicken tacos, tamales and enchiladas. Breakfast is served at any time of the day. The pastries are baked on the premises. **Cards:** AE, DS, MC, VI.

VILLA FONTANA RESTAURANT
(AAA)
◆◆◆
Northern
Italian

Dinner: $20-$28   **Phone:** 505/758-5800
Location: SR 522, 0.8 mi n of jct US 64. 71 SR 522 87529. **Hours:** 5:30 pm-9 pm. Closed: Sun-Tues. **Reservations:** suggested. **Features:** No A/C; dressy casual; health conscious menu items; beer & wine only. Villa Fontana has dining rooms with an intimate feel within its country-style Southwestern adobe exterior. This restaurant offers a classic cuisine that uses fresh ingredients and wild mushrooms gathered locally. **Cards:** AE, CB, DI, DS, MC, VI.   ✕

——— *The following restaurants have not been inspected by AAA* ———
but are listed for your information only.

BENT STREET DELI & CAFE
fyi

Phone: 505/758-5787
Not inspected. **Location:** 120 Bent St 87571. **Features:** Enjoy breakfast, lunch or dinner at this establishment a block off the plaza. An array of deli sandwiches and breakfast burritos is offered. Sophisticated dinner entrees are included on the menu.

ESKE'S BREW PUB & EATERY
fyi

Phone: 505/758-1517
Not inspected. **Location:** 106 Des Georges Ln. **Features:** Handcrafted beers and wholesome food are featured at this establishment in the historic district. A fun place with live entertainment.

FRED'S PLACE
fyi

Phone: 505/758-0514
Not inspected. **Location:** 332 Paseo del Pueblo Sur 87571. **Features:** A new Mexican eatery popular with the locals offers dining in a picturesque environment with an array of crucifixes and artistic murals adorning the walls and ceilings.

GUADALAJARA GRILL
fyi

Phone: 505/751-0063
Not inspected. **Location:** 1384 Paseo del Pueblo Sur 87571. **Features:** This Mexican restaurant features tacos, burritos and seafood.

TAOS SKI VALLEY pop. 350—*See also TAOS.*

——— **LODGING** ———

CHALET MONTESANO
(AAA) (SAVE)
◆◆◆
Lodge

Phone: (505)776-8226

12/19-1/31	1P: $148-$200	2P: $185-$280
2/1-5/24	1P: $144-$196	2P: $180-$276
11/20-12/18	1P: $109-$145	2P: $135-$210
5/25-11/19	1P: $70-$95	2P: $86-$140

Location: Walking distance to village center and ski lifts. O.E. Pattison Loop #3 87525 (PO Box 77). Fax: 505/776-8760. **Terms:** Weekly rates avail; age restrictions may apply; 45 day cancellation notice, in winter; cancellation fee imposed. **Facility:** 7 rooms. Swiss Alpine style chalet in woodland setting. Individually decorated rooms have locally made furniture. Some with fireplace. Elevation 9400 ft. Closed 4/11-5/24 & 10/2-11/19; 2 stories; interior corridors; smoke free premises; whirlpool, indoor heated lap pool. **Services:** winter plug-ins. **Recreation:** Fee: downhill skiing. **Some Rooms:** 4 kitchens. **Cards:** AE, DS, MC, VI. **Special Amenities:** Free local telephone calls and preferred room (subject to availability with advanced reservations).   🛎 ✕ 🎦 VCR 📠 💻 🖨 📱 ᴅᴀᴛᴀ ᴘᴏʀᴛ 🐾 ✕

TESUQUE pop. 1,500

——— **RESTAURANT** ———

——— *The following restaurant has not been inspected by AAA* ———
but is listed for your information only.

TESUQUE VILLAGE MARKET
fyi

Phone: 505/988-8848
Not inspected. **Location:** Rt 4 Box 70a 87504. **Features:** Just north of Santa Fe, this market, deli and restaurant offers breakfast, lunch and dinner. American and Southwestern favorites accompany very good beer, wine and tequila selections.

THOREAU pop. 150

——— **LODGING** ———

ZUNI MOUNTAIN LODGE
◆◆
Country Inn

Phone: (505)862-7769
All Year	1P: $55	2P: $85	XP: $20
			F6

Location: From I-40 exit 53, 13 mi s on SR 612, then w. 40 W Perch Dr 87323 (PO Box 5114). Fax: 505/862-7616. **Terms:** [BP] meal plan; 3 day cancellation notice; cancellation fee imposed; pets, with prior approval. **Facility:** 8 rooms. Secluded location on the edge of a small community amidst the Zuni Mountains; some rooms with views of Bluewater Lake. 1-3 stories, no elevator; interior/exterior corridors; designated smoking area. **All Rooms:** combo or shower baths.   ASK 🛏 🛎 ✕ 🎦 ☎

TINNIE pop. 150

------ RESTAURANT ------

TINNIE SILVER DOLLAR RESTAURANT   Historical   **Lunch:** $9-$13   **Dinner:** $9-$29   **Phone:** 505/653-4425
Location: US 70, 3.5 mi e of jct US 380. 88351. **Hours:** 11 am-11 pm. **Reservations:** suggested.
Features: casual dress; children's menu; carryout; cocktails & lounge. Tinnie Silver Dollar's is a restored
19th-century general store that now has a Victorian decor. Steak, seafood, chicken, chops and trout—all with
American   Southwestern influence cooked in—are featured on the menu. The margarita chicken is unusual and
delicious. **Cards:** AE, DI, DS, MC, VI.   ⊠

TRUTH OR CONSEQUENCES pop. 6,200

------ LODGINGS ------

BEST WESTERN HOT SPRING MOTOR INN   **Phone:** (505)894-6665
[AAA] [SAVE]   4/1-9/30   1P: $55   2P: $60   XP: $5   F13
2/1-3/31 & 10/1-1/31   1P: $52   2P: $57   XP: $5   F13
Motor Inn   **Location:** I-25, exit 79. 2270 N Date St 87901. Fax: 505/894-6665. **Terms:** Small pets only. **Facility:** 40
rooms. 1 story; exterior corridors; heated pool. **Dining:** Restaurant; 7 am-8 pm, Fri & Sat-9 pm; $6-$12;
wine/beer only. **Cards:** AE, CB, DI, DS, MC, VI. **Special Amenities:** Free local telephone calls and free
room upgrade (subject to availability with advanced reservations).   [icons]

SUPER 8 MOTEL   **Phone:** (505)894-7888
[AAA] [SAVE]   2/1-9/30   1P: $50-$58   2P: $53-$61   XP: $3   F12
10/1-1/31   1P: $47-$55   2P: $51-$58   XP: $3   F12
Motel   **Location:** I-25, exit 79, just s. 2151 N Date St 87901 (PO Box 347). Fax: 505/894-7883. **Terms:** Pets, $15 dep
req. **Facility:** 40 rooms. 2 stories; interior corridors. **Dining:** Restaurant nearby. **Cards:** AE, CB, DI, DS,
MC, VI. **Special Amenities:** Free breakfast and free local telephone calls.   [icons]

TUCUMCARI pop. 6,800

------ LODGINGS ------

AMERICANA MOTEL   **Phone:** (505)461-0431
[AAA] [SAVE]   6/1-8/31   1P: $24-$32   2P: $32-$42   XP: $4
2/1-5/31 & 9/1-1/31   1P: $20-$28   2P: $28-$38   XP: $4
Motel   **Location:** I-40, exit 332, 1.5 mi n on SR 18, 0.5 mi e on US 66. 406 E Tucumcari Blvd 88401. **Terms:** Weekly
rates avail; small pets only. **Facility:** 14 rooms. 1 story; exterior corridors. **Dining:** Restaurant nearby.
All Rooms: combo or shower baths. **Cards:** AE, DS, MC, VI. **Special Amenities:** Free local telephone
calls.   [icons]

BEST WESTERN DISCOVERY INN   **Phone:** (505)461-4884
[AAA] [SAVE]   5/1-10/31   1P: $69-$74   2P: $69-$74   XP: $5   F12
2/1-4/30 & 11/1-1/31   1P: $53-$58   2P: $53-$58   XP: $5   F12
Motel   **Location:** I-40, exit 332. 200 E Estrella 88401. Fax: 505/461-2463. **Terms:** Small pets only, $5 extra charge.
Facility: 107 rooms. 2 stories; exterior corridors; heated pool, whirlpool. **Dining:** Restaurant; 6 am-10 pm; $7-
$12. **Services:** gift shop. **Some Rooms:** Fee: VCR. **Cards:** AE, CB, DI, DS, JC, MC, VI. **Special Amenities:**
Free local telephone calls and free newspaper. *(See color ad p 455)*   [icons]

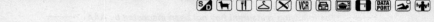

BEST WESTERN POW WOW INN
Phone: (505)461-0500
All Year 1P: $46-$56 2P: $59-$79 XP: $6 F12
Location: I-40, exit 332, 1.5 mi n on SR 18, 0.5 mi w on US 66. 801 W Tucumcari Blvd 88401 (PO Box 1146).
Fax: 505/461-0135. **Terms:** 7 day cancellation notice; pets, $10 extra charge. **Facility:** 64 rooms. Attractive
Southwestern decor. 1 two-bedroom unit. 1 story; exterior corridors; heated pool; playground. **Dining:** Restaurant; 6 am-10 pm; $8-$18; cocktails; entertainment. **Services:** gift shop. **Some Rooms:** kitchen, no utensils.
Fee: VCR. **Cards:** AE, CB, DI, DS, JC, MC, VI. **Special Amenities:** Early check-in/late check-out and free local telephone
calls.

COMFORT INN
Phone: (505)461-4094
5/1-8/31 1P: $59-$75 2P: $69-$89 XP: $6 F16
2/1-4/30 & 9/1-1/31 1P: $49-$69 2P: $55-$75 XP: $6 F16
Location: I-40, exit 335, then 0.5 mi w. 2800 E Tucumcari Blvd 88401 (PO Box 1424). Fax: 505/461-4099.
Terms: [CP] meal plan; 7 day cancellation notice; pets, $6 extra charge. **Facility:** 59 rooms. 2 stories; exterior corridors; small
heated pool. **Cards:** AE, CB, DI, DS, JC, MC, VI.

HOLIDAY INN
Phone: (505)461-3780
5/14-10/15 1P: $65-$85 2P: $70-$95 XP: $8 F17
2/1-5/13 1P: $60-$85 2P: $70-$95 XP: $8 F17
10/16-1/31 1P: $60-$80 2P: $65-$90 XP: $8 F17
Location: I-40, exit 335, 0.3 mi w on US 66. 3716 E Tucumcari Blvd 88401 (PO Box 808). Fax: 505/461-3931.
Terms: [BP] meal plan; cancellation fee imposed; package plans; pets, $6 dep req, in smoking rooms.
Facility: 100 rooms. 2 stories; exterior corridors; heated pool, whirlpool; playground. **Dining:** Restaurant; 6 am-2 & 4:30-9:30
pm; Fri & Sat-10 pm; $7-$16; cocktails. **Services:** gift shop. **Cards:** AE, CB, DI, DS, MC, VI. **Special Amenities:** Free breakfast and free local telephone calls. *(See color ad below)*

Holiday Inn

Tucumcari
3716 E. Tucumcari Blvd.

Tucumcari NM

- Kids Eat & Stay Free* (all year round)
- Priority Club® Worldwide Rewards Program
- Newly Renovated • Fitness Room, Heated Pool and Spa
- Quality Restaurant and Lounge
- Local Airport and Shuttle Service • Parking for Large Vehicles
- Gardens with Children's Playground
- Top Scoring Hotel in New Mexico for Guest Service

For Reservations Call 505-461-3780 or 1-800-HOLIDAY
*Restrictions apply. Call for details.
www.holiday-inn.com

HOWARD JOHNSON
Phone: (505)461-2747
AAA SAVE
◆◆
Motel
All Year   1P: $40-$60   2P: $50-$70   XP: $10   F16
Location: I-40, exit 335, then 0.5 mi w. 3604 E Tucumcari Blvd 88401 (PO Box 809). Fax: 505/461-2259. **Terms:** [ECP] meal plan; small pets nearby. **Facility:** 32 rooms. 2 stories; interior corridors. **Dining:** Restaurant nearby. **Cards:** AE, CB, DI, DS, JC, MC, VI. **Special Amenities:** Free breakfast and free local telephone calls.

MICROTEL INN
Phone: (505)461-0600
AAA SAVE
◆◆
Motel
5/16-8/31	1P: $40-$56	2P: $40-$56	XP: $6 F12
3/1-5/15	1P: $38-$53	2P: $38-$53	XP: $6 F12
9/1-1/31	1P: $35-$53	2P: $35-$53	XP: $6 F12
2/1-2/29	1P: $35-$50	2P: $35-$50	XP: $6 F12

Location: I-40, exit 332, just n. 2420 S First St 88401. Fax: 505/461-0900. **Terms:** [CP] meal plan; small pets only, $6 fee. **Facility:** 53 rooms. 2 stories; interior corridors; heated pool, whirlpool. **Dining:** Restaurant nearby. **All Rooms:** combo or shower baths. **Cards:** AE, DI, DS, MC, VI. **Special Amenities:** Free breakfast and free local telephone calls.

RODEWAY INN EAST
Phone: (505)461-0360
AAA SAVE
◆◆
Motel
All Year   1P: $24-$47   2P: $30-$68   XP: $6   F18
Location: I-40, exit 333 to Tucumcari Blvd, 0.6 mi w. 1023 E Tucumcari Blvd 88401. Fax: 505/461-0360. **Terms:** [CP] meal plan; cancellation fee imposed; small pets only, in designated rooms. **Facility:** 46 rooms. 2 stories; exterior corridors; heated pool. **Dining:** Restaurant nearby. **All Rooms:** combo or shower baths. **Cards:** AE, DS, MC, VI. **Special Amenities:** Free breakfast and free local telephone calls.

SAFARI MOTEL
Phone: (505)461-3642
AAA SAVE
◆◆
Motel
All Year   1P: $26-$29   2P: $36-$40   XP: $4   F12
Location: I-40, exit 332; 1.5 mi n on 1st St, 0.4 mi e on US 66. 722 E Tucumcari Blvd 88401. **Terms:** Pets, $3 extra charge. **Facility:** 23 rooms. 1 story; exterior corridors; small heated pool. **Cards:** AE, DS, MC, VI. **Special Amenities:** Free local telephone calls and preferred room (subject to availability with advanced reservations).

SUPER 8 MOTEL
Phone: (505)461-4444
◆◆
Motel
5/29-8/31	1P: $40-$60	2P: $45-$69	XP: $4 F12
3/16-5/28	1P: $40-$50	2P: $40-$55	XP: $4 F12
2/1-3/15 & 9/1-1/31	1P: $35-$45	2P: $40-$50	XP: $4 F12

Location: I-40, exit 335, just w. 4001 E Tucumcari Blvd 88401 (PO Box 1223). Fax: 505/461-4320. **Terms:** [ECP] meal plan; small pets only, $25 dep req. **Facility:** 64 rooms. 2 stories; interior corridors; heated pool. **Services:** winter plug-ins. **Cards:** AE, DI, DS, MC, VI.

TUCUMCARI TRAVELODGE
Phone: (505)461-1401
AAA SAVE
◆◆
Motel
All Year   1P: $30-$35   2P: $40-$50   XP: $4   F12
Location: I-40, exit 333, 1.5 mi n on Mountain Rd, then 0.5 mi w. 1214 E Tucumcari Blvd 88401. Fax: 505/461-3741. **Terms:** [CP] meal plan; small pets only, $5 dep req. **Facility:** 38 rooms. 2 stories; exterior corridors; small pool. **Dining:** Restaurant nearby. **All Rooms:** combo or shower baths. **Cards:** AE, CB, DI, DS, MC, VI. **Special Amenities:** Free breakfast and free local telephone calls.

——— RESTAURANTS ———

DEL'S RESTAURANT   **Lunch:** $5-$13   **Dinner:** $5-$13   Phone: 505/461-1740
◆◆
American
Location: I-40, exit 333, 1.5 mi n on Mountain Rd, 0.5 mi w. 1202 E Tucumcari Blvd 88401. **Hours:** 6 am-9 pm. Closed: 12/25 & Sun. **Reservations:** accepted. **Features:** casual dress; children's menu; senior's menu; carryout; salad bar. The casual, family dining atmosphere at Del's features authentic, homemade American and Mexican cuisine that includes steak, fajitas and chimichangas served up in a Southwestern and floral decor. The salad bar offers fresh ingredients. **Cards:** DS, MC, VI.

EL TORO CAFE   **Lunch:** $5-$8   **Dinner:** $5-$8   Phone: 505/461-3328
◆
Mexican
Location: I-40, exit 332, 1.8 mi n on SR 18 (1st St). 107 S 1st St 88401. **Hours:** 11 am-7 pm. Closed major holidays, Sat & Sun. **Features:** casual dress; carryout. El Toro offers a back-to-basics casual, family atmosphere. Its friendly, hometown staff serves well-prepared and nicely presented American favorites and red or green chili Mexican dishes amid a pleasant home-style decor. The chilis are home-grown. **Cards:** MC, VI.

VAUGHN pop. 600

——— LODGINGS ———

BEL-AIR MOTEL
Phone: 505/584-2241
AAA
◆◆
Motel
All Year   1P: $30-$36   2P: $36-$40   XP: $3
Location: 1 mi e on US 54, 60 and 285. (PO Box 68, 88353). **Terms:** Pets. **Facility:** 21 rooms. 1 story; exterior corridors. **Dining:** Restaurant nearby. **Services:** winter plug-ins. **All Rooms:** combo or shower baths, extended cable TV. **Cards:** AE, CB, DI, JC, MC, VI.

OAK TREE INN
Phone: (505)584-8733
◆◆
Motel
All Year   1P: $49-$59   2P: $54-$64   XP: $5   F12
Location: 1.5 mi e on US 54, 60 & 285. (PO Box 559, 88353). Fax: 505/584-9601. **Terms:** 10 day cancellation notice. **Facility:** 60 rooms. Crew lounge 24 hr. 2 stories; interior/exterior corridors; smoke free premises. **Cards:** AE, DS, MC, VI.

WHITE ROCK

———— LODGING ————

BANDELIER INN **Phone:** (505)672-3838

All Year 1P: $62 2P: $69 XP: $7 F10

Location: 132 SR 4 87544. Fax: 505/672-3537. **Terms:** [CP] meal plan; weekly & monthly rates avail; small pets only, $7 extra charge. **Facility:** 50 rooms. 2 stories; exterior corridors; designated smoking area; indoor whirlpool. **Dining:** Restaurant nearby. **All Rooms:** extended cable TV. **Some Rooms:** 14 efficiencies. **Cards:** AE, CB, DI, MC, VI. **Special Amenities:** Free breakfast and free local telephone calls.

(See color ad p. 137)

WHITES CITY pop. 100

———— LODGINGS ————

BEST WESTERN CAVERN INN **Phone:** (505)785-2291

5/15-9/14 1P: $65-$85 2P: $65-$85 XP: $6 F12

2/1-5/14 & 9/15-1/31 1P: $55-$75 2P: $55-$75 XP: $6 F12

Location: US 62 and 180 at jct SR 7. 17 Carlsbad Caverns Hwy 88268 (PO Box 128). Fax: 505/785-2283. **Terms:** Cancellation fee imposed; small pets only, $10 extra charge. **Facility:** 63 rooms. Near the entrance to Carlsbad Caverns. Desert surroundings. 61 whirlpool rooms; 2 stories; exterior corridors; 2 heated pools, whirlpools; playground. **Dining:** Restaurant nearby. **Services:** gift shop. **Recreation:** hiking trails. **Cards:** AE, CB, DI, DS, MC, VI. **Special Amenities:** Early check-in/late check-out and free local telephone calls. *(See color ad p 394)*

BEST WESTERN GUADALUPE INN **Phone:** (505)785-2291

5/15-9/14 1P: $65-$85 2P: $65-$85 XP: $6 F12

2/1-5/14 & 9/15-1/31 1P: $55-$75 2P: $55-$75 XP: $6 F12

Location: US 62 and 180 at jct SR 7. 17 Carlsbad Caverns Hwy 88268 (PO Box 128). Fax: 505/785-2283. **Terms:** Cancellation fee imposed. **Facility:** 42 rooms. Near entrance to Carlsbad Caverns. Southwest design. 1 story; exterior corridors; 2 heated pools, whirlpools; playground. **Dining:** Restaurant nearby. **Services:** gift shop. **Recreation:** hiking trails. **Cards:** AE, CB, DI, DS, MC, VI. **Special Amenities:** Early check-in/late check-out and free local telephone calls. *(See color ad p 394)*

458

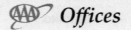 *Offices*

Cities with main offices are listed in **BOLD TYPE** and toll-free member service numbers in *ITALIC TYPE*.
All are closed Saturdays, Sundays and holidays unless otherwise indicated.
The type of service provided is designated below the name of the city where the office is located:
Auto travel services, including books/maps, marked maps and on-demand Triptik maps ✛
Auto travel services, including books/maps, marked maps, but no on-demand Triptik maps ●
Provides books/maps only. No marked maps or on-demand Triptik maps available ■
Travel agency services ▲

ARIZONA

MESA—AAA ARIZONA, 262 E UNIVERSITY DR, 85201.
MON-FRI 8-5:30, SAT 9-1. (602) 274-1116.✛▲

PEORIA—AAA ARIZONA, 7380 W OLIVE AVE, 85345. MON-FRI
8-5:30, SAT 9-1. (602) 274-1116.✛▲

PHOENIX—AAA ARIZONA, 3144 N 7TH AVE, 85013. MON-FRI
8-5:30. (602) 274-1116.✛▲

PHOENIX—AAA ARIZONA, 4046 E GREENWAY RD,
85032-4749. MON-FRI 8-5:30, SAT 9-1. (602) 274-1116.✛▲

PRESCOTT—AAA ARIZONA, 3767 KARITCIO LN #1-D,
86303-6829. MON-FRI 8:30-5, SAT 9-1. (520) 776-4222.●▲

SCOTTSDALE—AAA ARIZONA, 701 N SCOTTSDALE RD, 85257.
MON-FRI 8-5:30. (602) 274-1116.✛▲

SUN CITY WEST—AAA ARIZONA, 13940 W MEEKER BLVD
#141, 85375. MON-FRI 8:30-5. (602) 274-1116.●▲

TUCSON—AAA ARIZONA, 6950 N ORACLE RD, 85704.
MON-FRI 8-5:30, SAT 9-1. (520) 885-0694.✛▲

TUCSON—AAA ARIZONA, 8204 E BROADWAY, 85710.
MON-FRI 8-5:30. (520) 296-7461.✛▲

YUMA—AAA ARIZONA, 1045 S 4TH AVE, 85364. MON-FRI
8:30-5. (520) 783-3339.✛▲

NEW MEXICO

ALBUQUERQUE—AAA NEW MEXICO, 10501 MONTGOMERY
NE, 87111. MON-FRI 8:30-5, SAT 9-1. *(800) 846-0377.*✛▲

ALBUQUERQUE—AAA NEW MEXICO, 9231 COORS RD NW STE
5&6, 87114. MON-FRI 8:30-5, SAT 9-1. (505) 792-1938, *(800)
846-0377.*✛▲

LAS CRUCES—AAA NEW MEXICO, 225 E IDAHO #21, 88005.
MON-FRI 8:30-5. (505) 523-5681, *(877) 862-0002.*✛▲

SANTA FE—AAA NEW MEXICO, 1644 ST MICHAEL DR, 87505.
MON-FRI 8:30-5, SAT 9-1. (505) 471-6620, *(800) 881-7585.*✛▲

 For Hassle-Free
International Travel...

Put AAA First on Your Itinerary

*W*hen traveling south of the border, carry an **Inter-American Driving Permit...** even if you're not planning to drive. Should you need to communicate with foreign authorities, this recognizable form of identification can help you get on your way more quickly. Valid in more than 15 countries, the permit contains your name, photo, and driver information translated into three foreign languages.

Before you travel the world, travel to any AAA office for your Inter-American Driving Permit. Bring your valid U.S. driver's license, $10, and two passport -size photos (also available at AAA offices).

Travel With Someone You Trust®

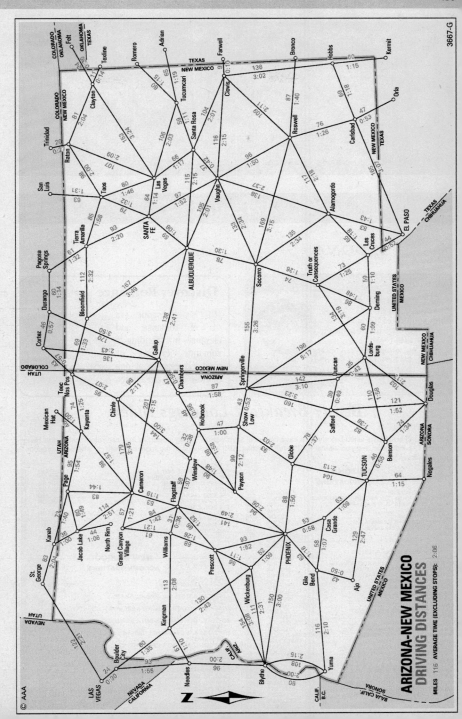

ARIZONA-NEW MEXICO
DRIVING DISTANCES

MILES 116 AVERAGE TIME (EXCLUDING STOPS): 2:06

© AAA

3667-G

Arizona

SEDONA

Bed & Breakfast Lodgings Index

Some bed and breakfasts listed below might have historical significance. Those properties are also referenced in the Historical index. The indication that continental [CP] or full breakfast [BP] is included in the room rate reflects whether a property is a Bed-and-Breakfast facility.

ARIZONA
ACCOMMODATIONS

A SUNSET CHATEAU B&B INN ....SEDONA 312
A TERRITORIAL HOUSE OLD WEST BED & BREAKFAST.......SEDONA 298
"A TOUCH OF SEDONA"-BED & BREAKFAST..........SEDONA 298
ADOBE HACIENDA ....SEDONA 297
ADOBE ROSE INN ....TUCSON 326
ADOBE VILLAGE & THE GRAHAM INN ....SEDONA 297
AGAVE GROVE BED & BREAKFAST INN ....TUCSON 326
ALMA DE SEDONA INN ....SEDONA 297
AMADO TERRITORY INN ....AMADO 172
APPLE ORCHARD INN ....SEDONA 298
BARTRAM'S WHITE MOUNTAIN BED &
  BREAKFAST ....PINETOP-LAKESIDE 290
BED & BREAKFAST AT SADDLE ROCK RANCH ....SEDONA 300
BOOTS & SADDLES BED & BREAKFAST ....SEDONA 301
CANYON VILLA BED & BREAKFAST INN ....SEDONA 301
CAR-MAR'S SOUTHWEST BED & BREAKFAST ....TUCSON 329
CASA ALEGRE BED & BREAKFAST INN..........TUCSON 329
CASA SEDONA ....SEDONA 302
CASA TIERRA ....TUCSON 329
CATALINA PARK INN ....TUCSON 329
COYOTE CROSSING BED & BREAKFAST ....TUCSON 332
COZY CACTUS BED & BREAKFAST ....SEDONA 303
CREEKSIDE INN AT SEDONA ....SEDONA 303
DOLLS & ROSES BED & BREAKFAST ....PRESCOTT 292
EL PRESIDIO BED & BREAKFAST INN..........DOWNTOWN TUCSON 325
GOTLAND'S INN CAVE CREEK ....CAVE CREEK 256
HACIENDA BED & BREAKFAST ....TUCSON 335
JEANETTE'S BED & BREAKFAST ....FLAGSTAFF 186
JEREMIAH INN BED & BREAKFAST ....TUCSON 338
LA POSADA DEL VALLE BED & BREAKFAST ....TUCSON 338
LYNX CREEK FARM BED & BREAKFAST ....PRESCOTT 293
MARICOPA MANOR BED & BREAKFAST INN ....PHOENIX 243
MOUNTAIN COUNTRY LODGE BED & BREAKFAST ....WILLIAMS 355
PLEASANT STREET INN ....PRESCOTT 293
PRESCOTT PINES INN BED & BREAKFAST ....PRESCOTT 293
TERRY RANCH BED & BREAKFAST ....WILLIAMS 356
THE FOUNTAIN INN ....PAYSON 213

THE GUEST HOUSE INN ....AJO 172
THE INN AT 410 BED & BREAKFAST ....FLAGSTAFF 185
THE INN ON OAK CREEK ....SEDONA 305
THE LODGE AT SEDONA ....SEDONA 308
THE MINE MANAGER'S HOUSE INN ....AJO 172
THE PEPPERTREES BED & BREAKFAST INN ....TUCSON 340
THE ROYAL ELIZABETH BED &
  BREAKFAST INN ....DOWNTOWN TUCSON 326
THE SHERIDAN HOUSE INN ....WILLIAMS 356
THE SUNCATCHER ....TUCSON 344
VALLE VERDE RANCH BED & BREAKFAST ....TUBAC 318
WISHING WELL BED & BREAKFAST ....SEDONA 312

NEW MEXICO
ACCOMMODATIONS

ADOBE ABODE ....SANTA FE 429
ADOBE AND STARS B & B ....ARROYO SECO 391
ALEXANDER'S INN ....SANTA FE 429
AMERICAN ARTISTS GALLERY HOUSE BED &
  BREAKFAST ....TAOS 446
APACHIE CANYON RANCH BED & BREAKFAST COUNTRY
  INN ....CANONCITO 393
BOTTGER-KOCH MANSION BED & BREAKFAST IN OLD
  TOWN ....ALBUQUERQUE 373
BRITTANIA & W E MAUGER ESTATE BED &
  BREAKFAST ....ALBUQUERQUE 373
CASA BENAVIDES BED & BREAKFAST INN ....TAOS 447
CASA DE LA CUMA B & B ....SANTA FE 429
CASA DE LAS CHIMENEAS BED & BREAKFAST ....TAOS 447
CASA DE MARTINEZ BED & BREAKFAST ....LOS BRAZOS 417
CASA DE PATRON BED & BREAKFAST INN ....LINCOLN 416
CASA DEL GAVILAN ....CIMARRON 396
CASA DEL RIO ....HERNANDEZ 410
CASA ENCANTADA ....TAOS 448
CASA ESCONDIDA ....CHIMAYO 396
CASA EUROPA ....TAOS 448
CASAPUEBLO INN ....SANTA FE 430

BED & BREAKFAST LODGINGS (CONT'D)

COTTONWOOD INN BED & BREAKFAST .... ARROYO SECO 391
DREAM CATCHER BED & BREAKFAST .... TAOS 449
EL FAROLITO BED & BREAKFAST INN .... SANTA FE 431
EL PARADERO BED & BREAKFAST .... SANTA FE 432
FOUR KACHINAS INN .... SANTA FE 432
HACIENDA ANTIGUA B & B .... ALBUQUERQUE 378
HACIENDA DE PLACITAS INN OF THE ARTS .... PLACITAS 418
HACIENDA NICHOLAS .... SANTA FE 432
HACIENDA VARGAS BED AND BREAKFAST
  INN .... ALGODONES 391
HERITAGE INN BED & BREAKFAST .... ARTESIA 392
HILLTOP HACIENDA B & B .... LAS CRUCES 413
INN AT THE DELTA .... ESPANOLA 401
INN ON LA LOMA PLAZA .... TAOS 450
LA HACIENDA GRANDE .... BERNALILLO 393
LA POSADA DE TAOS .... TAOS 450
LITTLE TREE BED & BREAKFAST .... ARROYO HONDO 391

LUNDEEN'S INN OF THE ARTS .... LAS CRUCES 413
POSADA ENCANTO .... CHAMA 395
RIVERDANCER INN .... JEMEZ SPRINGS 411
SERET'S 1001 NIGHTS .... SANTA FE 440
SPENCER HOUSE BED & BREAKFAST INN .... SANTA FE 440
TERRITORIAL INN .... SANTA FE 440
THE BROOKS STREET INN .... TAOS 447
THE CARTER HOUSE .... SILVER CITY 445
THE CASA BLANCA INN .... FARMINGTON 401
THE CHOCOLATE TURTLE BED &
  BREAKFAST .... CORRALES 398
THE GANDY DANCER BED & BREAKFAST .... CHAMA 395
THE MADELEINE .... SANTA FE 438
THE SANDHILL CRANE BED & BREAKFAST .... CORRALES 398
TOUCHSTONE BED & BREAKFAST .... TAOS 452
TRH SMITH BED & BREAKFAST .... LAS CRUCES 414
YOUR'S TRULY BED & BREAKFAST .... CORRALES 399

Country Inns Index

Some of the following country inns can also be considered as bed-and-breakfast operations. The indication that continental [CP] or full breakfast [BP] is included in the room rate reflects whether a property is a Bed-and-Breakfast facility.

NEW MEXICO
ACCOMMODATIONS

MESON DE MESILLA .... MESILLA 417
THE GALISTEO
  INN .... GALISTEO 403

ZUNI MOUNTAIN
  LODGE .... THOREAU 453

Historical Lodgings & Restaurants Index

Some of the following historical lodgings can also be considered as bed-and-breakfast operations. The indication that continental [CP] or full breakfast [BP] is included in the room rate reflects whether a property is a Bed-and-Breakfast facility.

ARIZONA
ACCOMMODATIONS

ARIZONA INN .... TUCSON 326
BED & BREAKFAST AT SADDLE ROCK RANCH .... SEDONA 300
DOLLS & ROSES BED & BREAKFAST .... PRESCOTT 292
EL PRESIDIO BED & BREAKFAST INN .... DOWNTOWN TUCSON 325
EL TOVAR HOTEL .... GRAND CANYON NP 192
HASSAYAMPA INN .... PRESCOTT 292
HOTEL VENDOME, A CLARION CARRIAGE
  HOUSE INN .... PRESCOTT 293
LA POSADA HOTEL .... WINSLOW 358
THE INN AT 410 BED & BREAKFAST .... FLAGSTAFF 185
THE MINE MANAGER'S HOUSE INN .... AJO 172
THE ROYAL ELIZABETH BED & BREAKFAST
  INN .... DOWNTOWN TUCSON 326

RESTAURANTS

CAFE ROKA .... BISBEE 173
EL CORRAL .... TUCSON 346
EL TOVAR HOTEL DINING
  ROOM .... GRAND CANYON NP 199
GURLEY ST GRILL .... PRESCOTT 294
JANOS .... DOWNTOWN TUCSON 326
MONTURA RESTAURANT .... TUBAC 318
MURPHY'S RESTAURANT .... PRESCOTT 294
PEACOCK ROOM .... PRESCOTT 295

NEW MEXICO
ACCOMMODATIONS

ADOBE ABODE .... SANTA FE 429
ALEXANDER'S INN .... SANTA FE 429
BOTTGER-KOCH MANSION BED & BREAKFAST IN OLD
  TOWN .... ALBUQUERQUE 373
BRITTANIA & W E MAUGER ESTATE BED &
  BREAKFAST .... ALBUQUERQUE 373
CASA DE MARTINEZ BED & BREAKFAST .... LOS BRAZOS 417
CASA DE PATRON BED & BREAKFAST INN .... LINCOLN 416
CASA DEL GAVILAN .... CIMARRON 396

CASA EUROPA .... TAOS 448
EL FAROLITO BED & BREAKFAST INN .... SANTA FE 431
EL PARADERO BED & BREAKFAST .... SANTA FE 432
HACIENDA ANTIGUA B & B .... ALBUQUERQUE 378
HACIENDA VARGAS BED AND BREAKFAST INN .... ALGODONES 391
HERITAGE INN BED & BREAKFAST .... ARTESIA 392
THE HISTORIC TAOS INN .... TAOS 450
HOTEL ST FRANCIS .... SANTA FE 434
INN ON LA LOMA PLAZA .... TAOS 450
LA FONDA HOTEL .... SANTA FE 437
LA HACIENDA GRANDE .... BERNALILLO 393
LA POSADA DE TAOS .... TAOS 450
LAS PALOMAS .... SANTA FE 438
THE LODGE .... CLOUDCROFT 397
LOS OLMOS GUEST RANCH .... GLENWOOD 407
LUNDEEN'S INN OF THE ARTS .... LAS CRUCES 413
PLAZA HOTEL .... LAS VEGAS 416
SAGEBRUSH INN .... TAOS 451
SAN GERONIMO LODGE .... TAOS 452
SERET'S 1001 NIGHTS .... SANTA FE 440
SPENCER HOUSE BED & BREAKFAST INN .... SANTA FE 440
SUNSET MOTEL .... MORIARTY 418
THE GALISTEO INN .... GALISTEO 403
THE GANDY DANCER BED & BREAKFAST .... CHAMA 395
THE MADELEINE .... SANTA FE 438
TOUCHSTONE BED & BREAKFAST .... TAOS 452

RESTAURANTS

DOC MARTIN'S AT THE HISTORIC TAOS INN .... TAOS 452
DOUBLE EAGLE RESTAURANT .... MESILLA 417
HIGH NOON RESTAURANT & SALOON .... ALBUQUERQUE 386
LA CASA SENA RESTAURANT .... SANTA FE 441
LA POSTA DE MESILLA .... MESILLA 417
LANDMARK GRILL .... LAS VEGAS 416
LUNA MANSION .... LAS LUNAS 417
MARIA TERESA RESTAURANT .... ALBUQUERQUE 387
MONTE VISTA FIRE STATION RESTAURANT .... ALBUQUERQUE 387
PLAZA RESTAURANT .... SANTA FE 442
SANTACAFE .... SANTA FE 442
THE SHED .... SANTA FE 442
TINNIE SILVER DOLLAR RESTAURANT .... TINNIE 454
VAL VERDE STEAK HOUSE .... SOCORRO 446

Resorts Index

Many establishments are located in resort areas; however, the following places have extensive on-premises recreational facilities:

ARIZONA
ACCOMMODATIONS

ARIZONA GOLF RESORT & CONFERENCE CENTER .... MESA 261
BLUE WATER RESORT & CASINO .... PARKER 212
DOUBLETREE LA POSADA RESORT -
  SCOTTSDALE .... SCOTTSDALE 268
DOUBLETREE PARADISE VALLEY RESORT .... SCOTTSDALE 268
ENCHANTMENT RESORT .... SEDONA 304

FOUR SEASONS RESORT SCOTTSDALE AT TROON
  NORTH .... SCOTTSDALE 277
HYATT REGENCY SCOTTSDALE AT GAINEY
  RANCH .... SCOTTSDALE 272
LAKE MOHAVE RESORT .... BULLHEAD CITY 174
LOEWS VENTANA CANYON RESORT .... TUCSON 339
MARRIOTT'S CAMELBACK INN RESORT, GOLF CLUB &
  SPA .... SCOTTSDALE 273
MARRIOTT'S MOUNTAIN SHADOWS RESORT AND GOLF
  CLUB .... SCOTTSDALE 273

RESORTS (CONT'D)

MERV GRIFFIN'S WICKENBURG INN AND DUDE RANCH	WICKENBURG	350
OMNI TUCSON NATIONAL GOLF RESORT & SPA	TUCSON	340
POCO DIABLO RESORT	SEDONA	309
POINTE HILTON SOUTH MOUNTAIN RESORT	PHOENIX	244
POINTE HILTON SQUAW PEAK RESORT	PHOENIX	244
POINTE HILTON TAPATIO CLIFFS RESORTS	PHOENIX	244
RADISSON RESORT & SPA SCOTTSDALE	SCOTTSDALE	278
REGAL MCCORMICK RANCH	SCOTTSDALE	274
RENAISSANCE COTTONWOODS RESORT	SCOTTSDALE	275
RIO RICO RESORT & COUNTRY CLUB	RIO RICO	296
SCOTTSDALE PRINCESS	SCOTTSDALE	276
SHERATON EL CONQUISTADOR	TUCSON	343
THE BOULDERS RESORT	CAREFREE	256
THE BUTTES-A WYNDHAM RESORT	TEMPE	288
THE LODGE AT VENTANA CANYON	TUCSON	339
THE PHOENICIAN	SCOTTSDALE	274
THE SCOTTSDALE PLAZA RESORT	SCOTTSDALE	276
THE WESTIN LA PALOMA, TUCSON	TUCSON	345
THE WIGWAM RESORT	LITCHFIELD PARK	260
TUBAC GOLF RESORT	TUBAC	318
WAHWEAP LODGE	PAGE	211
WESTWARD LOOK RESORT	TUCSON	345

NEW MEXICO ACCOMMODATIONS

ANGEL FIRE RESORT	ANGEL FIRE	391
THE BISHOP'S LODGE	SANTA FE	429

Savings for all Seasons

Hertz rents Fords and other fine cars.
® REG. U.S. PAT. OFF. © HERTZ SYSTEM INC., 1999/2006-99.

No matter the season, Hertz offers AAA members exclusive discounts and benefits.

With a fleet of more than 550,000 vehicles and over 6,100 rental locations worldwide, Hertz makes traveling more convenient and efficient wherever and whenever you go. Hertz offers AAA members discounts up to 20% on car rentals worldwide. **T**o receive your exclusive AAA member discounts and benefits, mention your AAA membership card at time of reservation and present it at time of rental. **F**or reservations and program details, call your AAA travel office or the Hertz/AAA Desk at **1-800-654-3080.**

Show Your Card & Save

exactly.

Points of Interest Index

AMUSEMENTS & THEME PARKS
BIG SURF...TEMPE, AZ   87
GOLDFIELD GHOST TOWN & MINE TOURS.....APACHE JUNCTION, AZ   82
GOLFLAND/SUNSPLASH......................................MESA, AZ   84
THE ICE CHALET.......................................PHOENIX, AZ   80
OLD TUCSON STUDIOS.....................................TUCSON, AZ   106
RAWHIDE..SCOTTSDALE, AZ   85
ROCKIN' R RANCH...MESA, AZ   84
SURFSIDE SKATELAND..................................PHOENIX, AZ   80
WATERWORLD SAFARI...................................PHOENIX, AZ   78

AMPHITHEATERS
ECHO AMPHITHEATER.................................CARSON NF, NM   141
THE LION'S WILDERNESS PARK......................FARMINGTON, NM   148

ANTIQUES
HISTORIC CATLIN COURT SHOPS DISTRICT.............GLENDALE, AZ   83
OLD TOWNE GLENDALE.................................GLENDALE, AZ   83

AQUARIUMS
THE ALBUQUERQUE AQUARIUM.................ALBUQUERQUE, NM   134

ARBORETUMS
*BOYCE THOMPSON ARBORETUM SP ....SUPERIOR, AZ   97

ART GALLERIES
ARIZONA STATE UNIVERSITY ART MUSEUM................TEMPE, AZ   87
BRANIGAN CULTURAL CENTER .... LAS CRUCES, NM   152
CARLSBAD MUSEUM AND ART CENTER..............CARLSBAD, NM   139
CENTER FOR THE ARTS.........................ALBUQUERQUE, NM   136
CHIRICAHUA GALLERY ....RODEO, NM   156
COBRE VALLEY CENTER FOR THE ARTS ....GLOBE, AZ   52
DE GRAZIA GALLERY IN THE SUN.....................TUCSON, AZ   105
ERNEST L. BLUMENSCHEIN HOME.......................TAOS, NM   166
THE FECHIN HOUSE AND STUDIO........................TAOS, NM   167
FLEISCHER MUSEUM...............................SCOTTSDALE, AZ   85
FULLER LODGE ART CENTER.......................LOS ALAMOS, NM   154
HARWOOD FOUNDATION....................................TAOS, NM   167
HISTORICAL MUSEUM AND ART CENTER ....ARTESIA, NM   137
INSTITUTE OF AMERICAN INDIAN ARTS MUSEUM:
  COLLECTION OF CONTEMPORARY INDIAN ART.......SANTA FE, NM   161
JONSON GALLERY ....ALBUQUERQUE, NM   136
KOLB STUDIO .... GRAND CANYON NP, AZ   56
MUSEUM OF FINE ARTS ....SANTA FE, NM   161
PHIPPEN MUSEUM ....PRESCOTT, AZ   89
PHOENIX ART MUSEUM ....PHOENIX, AZ   78
*ROSWELL MUSEUM AND ART CENTER.................ROSWELL, NM   156
SAN JUAN COLLEGE FINE ARTS CENTER.........FARMINGTON, NM   148
SCOTTSDALE CENTER FOR THE ARTS.............SCOTTSDALE, AZ   85
SHEMER ART GALLERY.................................PHOENIX, AZ   78
STABLES ART GALLERY ....TAOS, NM   167
TUCSON MUSEUM OF ART AND HISTORIC BLOCK ....TUCSON, AZ   107
UNIVERSITY OF ARIZONA MUSEUM OF ART ....TUCSON, AZ   108

ARTS & CRAFTS
*AMERIND FOUNDATION MUSEUM....................DRAGOON, AZ   48
ARTS AND CRAFT MUSEUM ....DULCE, NM   146
BIEN MUR INDIAN MARKET CENTER ....ALBUQUERQUE, NM   132
CHIMAY ....NM   143
CORDOVA ....CHIMAY, NM   143
GILA RIVER CULTURAL CENTER.......................SACATON, AZ   91
*HEARD MUSEUM ....PHOENIX, AZ   76
HOPI CULTURAL CENTER MUSEUM ....SECOND MESA, AZ   92
INDIAN PUEBLO CULTURAL CENTER ....ALBUQUERQUE, NM   134
MOHAVE MUSEUM OF HISTORY AND ARTS ....KINGMAN, AZ   60
MUSEUM OF INDIAN ARTS AND CULTURE ....SANTA FE, NM   161
THE MYSTERY CASTLE...............................PHOENIX, AZ   77
OLD AZTEC MILL MUSEUM ....CIMARRON, NM   144
THE PUEBLO GRANDE MUSEUM AUXILIARY INDIAN
  MARKET ....PHOENIX, AZ   81
RED ROCK MUSEUM.................................GALLUP, NM   149
TRUCHAS ....CHIMAY, NM   143
VISITOR CENTER ....GANADO, AZ   50
WHEELWRIGHT MUSEUM OF THE AMERICAN
  INDIAN..SANTA FE, NM   163

ATOMIC ENERGY INSTALLATIONS & NUCLEAR PLANTS
PALO VERDE NUCLEAR GENERATING STATION ...... PALO VERDE, AZ   84

AUDITORIUMS
SUNDOME .... SUN CITY/SUN CITY WEST, AZ   86
TAOS COMMUNITY AUDITORIUM ....TAOS, NM   166

BATTLEFIELDS
VALVERDE BATTLEFIELD ....SAN ANTONIO, NM   158

BATTLE RE-ENACTMENTS
PIONEER ARIZONA LIVING HISTORY MUSEUM........... PHOENIX, AZ   78

BRIDGES
AGATE BRIDGE .... PETRIFIED FOREST NP, AZ   69
CATWALK..GILA NF, NM   150
GLEN CANYON BRIDGE ....GLEN CANYON NRA, AZ   51
LONDON BRIDGE .... LAKE HAVASU CITY, AZ   61
NAVAJO BRIDGE .... GRAND CANYON NP, AZ   58
RIO GRANDE GORGE ....TAOS, NM   166

BUILDINGS, OFFICE
ARCOSANTI.....................................CORDES JUNCTION, AZ   46

BUILDINGS, PUBLIC; CAPITOL; CITY HALL
ARCOSANTI.....................................CORDES JUNCTION, AZ   46
*ARIZONA STATE CAPITOL MUSEUM....................PHOENIX, AZ   76
STATE CAPITOL ....SANTA FE, NM   163

CANYONS
APACHE-SITGREAVES NFS ....AZ   40
ARAVAIPA CANYON.................................WINKELMAN, AZ   116
BLACK CANYON ....LAKE MEAD NRA, AZ   62
BONITA CANYON ....CHIRICAHUA NMO, AZ   45
CANYON BONITO .... FORT DEFIANCE, AZ   50
CANYON DE CHELLY ....CANYON DE CHELLY NMO, AZ   44
CANYON DEL MUERTO ....CANYON DE CHELLY NMO, AZ   44
CAVE CREEK CANYON.................................PORTAL, AZ   88
COCONINO NF ....AZ   46
DEVIL'S CANYON ....GLOBE, AZ   52
DOG CANYON ....LINCOLN NF, NM   153
FISH CREEK CANYON ....APACHE JUNCTION, AZ   81
*GRAND CANYON NP...................................AZ   52
*HAVASU CANYON ....SUPAI, AZ   97
KEAMS CANYON ....AZ   59
MARBLE CANYON .... GRAND CANYON NP, AZ   58
*OAK CREEK CANYON ....SEDONA, AZ   94
PALM CANYON ....QUARTZSITE, AZ   91
RAMSEY CANYON PRESERVE ....SIERRA VISTA, AZ   96
RUCKER CANYON ROAD ....CORONADO NF, AZ   46
SABINO CANYON ....TUCSON, AZ   106
SALT RIVER CANYON ....GLOBE, AZ   52
SOUTH MOUNTAIN PARK ....PHOENIX, AZ   78
SUGARITE CANYON SP ....RATON, NM   156
TOPOCK GORGE .... LAKE HAVASU CITY, AZ   61
WHITEWATER CANYON ....GILA NF, NM   150

CAROUSELS
MCCORMICK-STILLMAN RAILROAD PARK .... SCOTTSDALE, AZ   85
SPRING RIVER PARK AND ZOO ....ROSWELL, NM   157

CASINO AND RIVERBOAT GAMBLING
BUCKY'S CASINO ....PRESCOTT, AZ   89
CASINO OF THE SUN...................................TUCSON, AZ   109
COCOPAH CASINO.................................SOMERTON, AZ   96
DESERT DIAMOND CASINO...............................TUCSON, AZ   109
HARRAH'S PHOENIX AK-CHIN CASINO ....MARICOPA, AZ   63
HON-DAH RESORT CASINO AND CONFERENCE
  CENTER.......................................PINETOP-LAKESIDE, AZ   88
ISLETA GAMING PALACE ....ALBUQUERQUE, NM   136
MAZATZAL CASINO ....PAYSON, AZ   68
SAN FELIPE'S CASINO HOLLYWOOD ...... SAN FELIPE PUEBLO, NM   134

CAVES
*CARLSBAD CAVERN........... CARLSBAD CAVERNS NP, NM   140
*CARLSBAD CAVERNS NP.................................NM   139
COLOSSAL CAVE...VAIL, AZ   112
CORONADO CAVE ....CORONADO NME, AZ   47
GRAND CANYON CAVERNS ....PEACH SPRINGS, AZ   68
ICE CAVE AND BANDERA VOLCANO ....GRANTS, NM   150
SLAUGHTER CANYON CAVE .... CARLSBAD CAVERNS NP, NM   141

CEMETERIES
BOOTHILL GRAVEYARD ....TOMBSTONE, AZ   98
KIT CARSON PARK ....TAOS, NM   167
SANTA FE NC ....SANTA FE, NM   162
SUNSET CEMETERY ....WINSLOW, AZ   116

CHILDREN'S ATTRACTIONS
ARIZONA MUSEUM FOR YOUTH ....MESA, AZ   84
GOLFLAND/SUNSPLASH ....MESA, AZ   84
OCEANSIDE ICE ARENA...............................PHOENIX, AZ   80
PHOENIX ZOO ....PHOENIX, AZ   77
ROCKIN' R RANCH ....MESA, AZ   84
SANTA FE CHILDREN'S MUSEUM ....SANTA FE, NM   161

INDEX ABBREVIATIONS

NB............................... national battlefield
NBP.......................... national battlefield park
NC................................. national cemetery
NF...................................national forest
NHM............... national historic(al) monument
NHP................. national historic(al) park
NHS................. national historic(al) site
NL................................. national lakeshore
NME.............................national memorial
NMO............................. national monument
NMP........................ national military park
NP...............................national park
NRA.......................national recreation area

NR..............................national river
NS............................ national seashore
NWR........................... national wildlife refuge
PHP.................provincial historic(al) park
PHS.................provincial historic(al) site
PP............................ provincial park
SF................................ state forest
SHM............... state historic(al) monument
SHP................. state historic(al) park
SHS.................state historic(al) site
SME......................... state memorial
SP................................ state park
SRA................. state recreation area

TUCSON CHILDREN'S MUSEUM .... TUCSON, AZ 107
WATERWORLD SAFARI .... PHOENIX, AZ 78
WILDLIFE WORLD ZOO .... LITCHFIELD PARK, AZ 83

CHURCHES, CATHEDRALS & BASILICAS
CATHEDRAL OF ST. FRANCIS OF ASSISI .... SANTA FE, NM 160
CHURCH OF THE PUEBLO OF SANTO DOMINGO .... DOMINGO, NM 146
CRISTO REY CHURCH .... SANTA FE, NM 160
NUESTRA SENORA DE LA PURISIMA CONCEPCION DE CUARAC .... SALINAS PUEBLO MISSIONS NMO, NM 157
ST. PAUL'S EPISCOPAL CHURCH .... TOMBSTONE, AZ 97
SAN BUENAVENTURA .... SALINAS PUEBLO MISSIONS NMO, NM 157
SAN FELIPE DE NERI CHURCH .... ALBUQUERQUE, NM 135
SAN FRANCISCO DE ASIS CHURCH .... TAOS, NM 167
SAN GREGORIO DE ABO .... SALINAS PUEBLO MISSIONS NMO, NM 157
SAN ISIDRO .... SALINAS PUEBLO MISSIONS NMO, NM 157

CHURCHES-CHAPELS
CHAPEL OF THE HOLY CROSS .... SEDONA, AZ 93
EL SANTUARIO DE NUESTRO SENOR DE ESQUIPULAS .... CHIMAY, NM 143
*VIETNAM VETERANS NME .... ANGEL FIRE, NM 136

CHURCHES-MISSONS
MISSION OF SAN AGUSTIN DE ISLETA .... ALBUQUERQUE, NM 134
MISSION OF SAN LORENZO .... PENASCO, NM 155
*MISSION OF SAN MIGUEL OF SANTA FE .... SANTA FE, NM 161
MISSION OF THE PUEBLO OF LAGUNA .... LAGUNA, NM 151
MISSION OF THE PUEBLO OF TESUQUE .... SANTA FE, NM 161
MISSION SAN JOSE DE TUMACACORI .... TUMACACORI NHP, AZ 113
*MISSION SAN XAVIER DEL BAC .... TUCSON, AZ 106
SAN ESTEBAN DEL REY MISSION .... ACOMA (SKY CITY), NM 131
SAN JOSE DE LOS JEMEZ MISSION .... JEMEZ PUEBLO, NM 151
SAN MIGUEL MISSION .... SOCORRO, NM 165
*TUMACACORI NHP .... AZ 113
ZIA PUEBLO AND MISSION .... BERNALILLO, NM 138

CHURCHES-SHRINES
SANTUARIO DE GUADALUPE .... SANTA FE, NM 162
SHRINE OF ST. JOSEPH OF THE MOUNTAINS .... YARNELL, AZ 117

CHURCHES-TEMPLES & SYNAGOGUES
ARIZONA TEMPLE VISITOR CENTER .... MESA, AZ 84
SCOTTISH RITE TEMPLE .... SANTA FE, NM 162

CONVENTS & MONASTERIES
NUESTRA SENORA DE LA PURISIMA CONCEPCION DE CUARAC .... SALINAS PUEBLO MISSIONS NMO, NM 157

COURTHOUSES
LINCOLN COUNTY COURTHOUSE .... LINCOLN, NM 153

CULTURAL CENTERS & CIVIC CENTERS
BRANIGAN CULTURAL CENTER .... LAS CRUCES, NM 152
COMMUNITY CENTER .... TUCSON, AZ 101
FARMINGTON CIVIC CENTER .... FARMINGTON, NM 148
THE FECHIN HOUSE AND STUDIO .... TAOS, NM 167
GAMMAGE CENTER FOR THE PERFORMING ARTS .... TEMPE, AZ 86
HOPI CULTURAL CENTER .... KEAMS CANYON, AZ 59
INDIAN PUEBLO CULTURAL CENTER .... ALBUQUERQUE, NM 134
PLAN B EVOLVING ARTS .... SANTA FE, NM 160
SCOTTSDALE CIVIC CENTER AND MALL .... SCOTTSDALE, AZ 85

DAMS
COOLIDGE DAM .... SAN CARLOS, AZ 92
DAVIS DAM .... LAKE MEAD NRA, AZ 62
GLEN CANYON DAM .... GLEN CANYON NRA, AZ 50
*HOOVER DAM .... LAKE MEAD NRA, AZ 62
PARKER DAM AND POWER PLANT .... PARKER, AZ 66
THEODORE ROOSEVELT DAM AND LAKE .... ROOSEVELT, AZ 91
WADDELL DAM .... PEORIA, AZ 84

DUNES
*WHITE SANDS NMO .... NM 169

EVENTS-GENERAL
BATTLE OF GLORIETA PASS .... SANTA FE, NM 160
POSADAS .... PHOENIX, AZ 81
YAQUI EASTER CEREMONY .... TUCSON, AZ 111

EVENTS-DANCES
DANCE OF THE MATACHINES .... ESPANOLA, NM 147
SOUTHERN ARIZONA SQUARE AND ROUND DANCE FESTIVAL .... TUCSON, AZ 111

EVENTS-EXPOSITIONS
COWBOY ARTISTS OF AMERICA EXHIBITION .... PHOENIX, AZ 81

EVENTS-FAIRS
ARIZONA STATE FAIR .... PHOENIX, AZ 81
MARICOPA COUNTY FAIR .... PHOENIX, AZ 81
PIMA COUNTY FAIR .... TUCSON, AZ 111

EVENTS-FESTIVALS
ARIZONA RENAISSANCE FESTIVAL .... APACHE JUNCTION, AZ 81
CINCO DE MAYO FESTIVAL .... PHOENIX, AZ 81
LUMINARIA NIGHT .... TUCSON, AZ 111
OCTOBERFEST .... TUCSON, AZ 111
US WEST NATIONAL FESTIVAL OF THE WEST .... SCOTTSDALE, AZ 85
VALLEY OF THE SUN ANNUAL SQUARE AND ROUND DANCE FESTIVAL .... PHOENIX, AZ 81

EVENTS-FIESTAS
KODAK ALBUQUERQUE INTERNATIONAL BALLOON FIESTA .... ALBUQUERQUE, NM 133

EVENTS-PAGEANTS, PARADES, DAYS
FIESTA BOWL PARADE .... PHOENIX, AZ 81
PARADA DEL SOL .... PHOENIX, AZ 81

EVENTS-POWWOWS
POW WOW ROCK AND MINERAL SHOW .... QUARTZSITE, AZ 90

EVENTS-RODEOS
LA FIESTA DE LOS VAQUEROS RODEO .... TUCSON, AZ 111

EVENTS-SHOWS
ALL-ARABIAN HORSE SHOW .... PHOENIX, AZ 81
INDIAN FAIR AND MARKET .... PHOENIX, AZ 81
POW WOW ROCK AND MINERAL SHOW .... QUARTZSITE, AZ 90
THUNDERBIRD BALLOON CLASSIC AND AIR SHOW .... PHOENIX, AZ 81
TUCSON INTERNATIONAL GEM & MINERAL SHOW .... TUCSON, AZ 111

EVENTS-SPORTS
ALL-AMERICAN FUTURITY .... RUIDOSO DOWNS, NM 157
FIESTA BOWL .... PHOENIX, AZ 78
FIESTA BOWL FOOTBALL CLASSIC .... TEMPE, AZ 86
INSIGHT.COM BOWL .... TUCSON, AZ 111
LPGA STANDARD REGISTER PING .... PHOENIX, AZ 81
NASCAR .... PHOENIX, AZ 79
NRA WHITTINGTON CENTER .... RATON, NM 156
PHOENIX OPEN GOLF TOURNAMENT .... PHOENIX, AZ 81
RAINBOW FUTURITY .... RUIDOSO DOWNS, NM 157
RUIDOSO QUARTER HORSE FUTURITY .... RUIDOSO DOWNS, NM 157
TOUCHSTONE ENERGY CHAMPIONSHIP LPGA TUCSON OPEN .... TUCSON, AZ 111
WINTERNATIONALS .... PHOENIX, AZ 81

EXHIBITS & COLLECTIONS-GENERAL
ALAN BIBLE VISITOR CENTER .... LAKE MEAD NRA, AZ 62
ARCOSANTI .... CORDES JUNCTION, AZ 46
ARIZONA HALL OF FAME .... PHOENIX, AZ 71
ARIZONA MINING AND MINERAL MUSEUM .... PHOENIX, AZ 76
ARIZONA TEMPLE VISITOR CENTER .... MESA, AZ 84
THE BEAD MUSEUM .... GLENDALE, AZ 83
BULLFROG VISITOR CENTER .... GLEN CANYON NRA, AZ 51
CARL HAYDEN VISITOR CENTER .... GLEN CANYON NRA, AZ 51
CENTER FOR CREATIVE PHOTOGRAPHY .... TUCSON, AZ 107
EXHIBIT BUILDING .... LAKE MEAD NRA, AZ 62
FORT HUACHUCA MUSEUM .... FORT HUACHUCA, AZ 50
GILA VISITOR CENTER .... GILA NF, NM 150
GOLDFIELD GHOST TOWN & MINE TOURS .... APACHE JUNCTION, AZ 82
*HALL OF FLAME MUSEUM OF FIREFIGHTING .... PHOENIX, AZ 76
HUBBARD MUSEUM OF THE AMERICAN WEST .... RUIDOSO DOWNS, NM 157
HUBBELL TRADING POST NHS .... GANADO, AZ 50
THE LITTLE HOUSE MUSEUM .... EAGAR, AZ 48
MARTINEZ HACIENDA .... TAOS, NM 167
MASSAI POINT .... CHIRICAHUA NMO, AZ 45
MAXWELL MUSEUM OF ANTHROPOLOGY .... ALBUQUERQUE, NM 136
MILLICENT ROGERS MUSEUM .... TAOS, NM 167
MOHAVE MUSEUM OF HISTORY AND ARTS .... KINGMAN, AZ 60
MUHEIM HERITAGE HOUSE .... BISBEE, AZ 43
*MUSEUM OF INTERNATIONAL FOLK ART .... SANTA FE, NM 161
MUSEUM OF NEW MEXICO .... SANTA FE, NM 161
NAVAJO BRIDGE INTERPRETIVE CENTER .... GLEN CANYON NRA, AZ 51
*PALACE OF THE GOVERNORS .... SANTA FE, NM 161
*PETRIFIED FOREST NP .... AZ 68
RAINBOW FOREST MUSEUM .... PETRIFIED FOREST NP, AZ 69
*SPACE CENTER .... ALAMOGORDO, NM 132
TOY TRAIN DEPOT .... ALAMOGORDO, NM 132
UNIVERSITY MUSEUM .... LAS CRUCES, NM 152
*VISITOR CENTER .... GRAND CANYON NP, AZ 55

EXHIBITS & COLLECTIONS-ANIMALS & BIRDS
GHOST RANCH LIVING MUSEUM .... ABIQUIU, NM 131
INTERNATIONAL WILDLIFE MUSEUM .... TUCSON, AZ 105
LAS CRUCES MUSEUM OF NATURAL HISTORY .... LAS CRUCES, NM 152

EXHIBITS & COLLECTIONS-AVIATION
AIR MUSEUM PLANES OF FAME .... VALLE, AZ 113
CHAMPLIN FIGHTER AIRCRAFT MUSEUM .... MESA, AZ 84
CONFEDERATE AIR FORCE—ARIZONA WING .... MESA, AZ 84
FLYING MUSEUM .... HOBBS, NM 150
NATIONAL ATOMIC MUSEUM .... ALBUQUERQUE, NM 134
PIMA AIR AND SPACE MUSEUM .... TUCSON, AZ 106
*WAR EAGLES AIR MUSEUM .... SANTA TERESA, NM 164

EXHIBITS & COLLECTIONS-DOLLS & TOYS
ARIZONA DOLL AND TOY MUSEUM .... PHOENIX, AZ 77
GOLDEN ERA TOY AND AUTO MUSEUM .... COOLIDGE, AZ 46
MILLION DOLLAR MUSEUM .... WHITES CITY, NM 169

EXHIBITS & COLLECTIONS-HISTORICAL
THE ALBUQUERQUE MUSEUM OF ART & HISTORY .... ALBUQUERQUE, NM 134
*AMERIND FOUNDATION MUSEUM .... DRAGOON, AZ 48
APACHE COUNTY HISTORICAL SOCIETY MUSEUM .... ST. JOHNS, AZ 91
ARIZONA HISTORICAL SOCIETY CENTURY HOUSE MUSEUM AND GARDENS .... YUMA, AZ 117
THE ARIZONA HISTORICAL SOCIETY MUSEUM .... TEMPE, AZ 87
ARIZONA HISTORICAL SOCIETY/TUCSON MUSEUM .... TUCSON, AZ 104
AZTEC MUSEUM AND PIONEER VILLAGE .... AZTEC, NM 137
BESH-BA-GOWAH ARCHAEOLOGICAL PARK .... GLOBE, AZ 52
BISBEE MINING AND HISTORICAL MUSEUM .... BISBEE, AZ 43
BISBEE RESTORATION MUSEUM .... BISBEE, AZ 43
CARLSBAD MUSEUM AND ART CENTER .... CARLSBAD, NM 139
CASA GRANDE VALLEY HISTORICAL SOCIETY AND MUSEUM .... CASA GRANDE, AZ 44
CITY OF LAS VEGAS MUSEUM AND ROUGHRIDER MEMORIAL COLLECTION .... LAS VEGAS, NM 152
COLORADO RIVER INDIAN TRIBES MUSEUM AND LIBRARY .... PARKER, AZ 66
DEMING LUNA MIMBRES MUSEUM .... DEMING, NM 146
DESERT CABALLEROS WESTERN MUSEUM .... WICKENBURG, AZ 114
EL RANCHO DE LAS GOLONDRINAS .... SANTA FE, NM 160
FORT SELDEN STATE MONUMENT .... LAS CRUCES, NM 152
FORT UNION NMO .... NM 148
FORT VERDE SHP .... CAMP VERDE, AZ 44
GADSDEN MUSEUM .... MESILLA, NM 154
GERONIMO SPRINGS MUSEUM .... TRUTH OR CONSEQUENCES, NM 168
GHOST RANCH LIVING MUSEUM .... ABIQUIU, NM 131
GOVERNOR'S MANSION .... PRESCOTT, AZ 89
HERITAGE AND SCIENCE PARK .... PHOENIX, AZ 77
HISTORICAL MUSEUM AND ART CENTER .... ARTESIA, NM 137
JEROME SHP .... JEROME, AZ 59
JOHN WESLEY POWELL MUSEUM AND VISITOR INFORMATION CENTER .... PAGE, AZ 66
KIT CARSON HOME AND MUSEUM .... TAOS, NM 167
LA CASA CORDOVA .... TUCSON, AZ 107
LAS CRUCES MUSEUM OF NATURAL HISTORY .... LAS CRUCES, NM 152
LEA COUNTY COWBOY HALL OF FAME AND WESTERN HERITAGE CENTER .... HOBBS, NM 151
LINCOLN STATE MONUMENT .... LINCOLN, NM 153
LOS ALAMOS COUNTY HISTORICAL MUSEUM .... LOS ALAMOS, NM 154
LUTES CASINO .... YUMA, AZ 117
MESA SOUTHWEST MUSEUM .... MESA, AZ 84
METEOR CRATER .... WINSLOW, AZ 116
MILLION DOLLAR MUSEUM .... WHITES CITY, NM 169
MINE MUSEUM .... JEROME, AZ 59
*MISSION SAN XAVIER DEL BAC .... TUCSON, AZ 106
MUSEO CHICANO (CHICANO MUSEUM) .... PHOENIX, AZ 77
OLD AZTEC MILL MUSEUM .... CIMARRON, NM 144
OLD FORT SUMNER MUSEUM .... FORT SUMNER, NM 148
OLIVER LEE MEMORIAL SP .... ALAMOGORDO, NM 132
*PALACE OF THE GOVERNORS .... SANTA FE, NM 161
PECOS NHP .... NM 155
PHILMONT SCOUT RANCH .... CIMARRON, NM 145

PHOENIX MUSEUM OF HISTORY ... PHOENIX, AZ 77
PINAL COUNTY HISTORICAL MUSEUM ... FLORENCE, AZ 49
PINOS ALTOS HISTORICAL MUSEUM ... PINOS ALTOS, NM 155
PIONEER ARIZONA LIVING HISTORY MUSEUM ... PHOENIX, AZ 78
THE POSTAL HISTORY FOUNDATION ... TUCSON, AZ 106
QUARAI ... SALINAS PUEBLO MISSIONS NMO, NM 157
RATON MUSEUM ... RATON, NM 156
RAWHIDE ... SCOTTSDALE, AZ 85
REX ALLEN ARIZONA COWBOY MUSEUM ... WILLCOX, AZ 114
ROOSEVELT COUNTY MUSEUM ... PORTALES, NM 155
ROSE TREE MUSEUM AND BOOKSTORE ... TOMBSTONE, AZ 98
*ROSWELL MUSEUM AND ART CENTER ... ROSWELL, NM 156
ST. MICHAELS HISTORICAL MUSEUM ... WINDOW ROCK, AZ 116
SAN BERNARDINO RANCH NATIONAL HISTORIC LANDMARK (SLAUGHTER RANCH MUSEUM) ... DOUGLAS, AZ 48
THE SANTA FE TRAIL MUSEUM ... SPRINGER, NM 166
SANTUARIO DE GUADALUPE ... SANTA FE, NM 162
SCOTTSDALE HISTORICAL MUSEUM ... SCOTTSDALE, AZ 85
*SHARLOT M. HALL MUSEUM ... PRESCOTT, AZ 89
SILVER CITY MUSEUM ... SILVER CITY, NM 165
SOSA-CARILLO-FREMONT HOUSE ... TUCSON, AZ 107
STEINS RAILROAD GHOST TOWN ... STEINS, NM 166
THELMA WEBBER SOUTHWEST HERITAGE ROOM ... HOBBS, NM 150
TOMBSTONE COURTHOUSE SHP ... TOMBSTONE, AZ 98
TUBAC PRESIDIO SHP ... TUBAC, AZ 99
TUCSON MUSEUM OF ART AND HISTORIC BLOCK ... TUCSON, AZ 107
TUCUMCARI HISTORICAL MUSEUM ... TUCUMCARI, NM 168
TULAROSA BASIN HISTORICAL SOCIETY MUSEUM ... ALAMOGORDO, NM 131
WESTERN NEW MEXICO UNIVERSITY MUSEUM ... SILVER CITY, NM 165
YAVAPAI OBSERVATION STATION ... GRAND CANYON NP, AZ 57
YUMA CROSSING SHP ... YUMA, AZ 118

EXHIBITS & COLLECTIONS-INDIAN
*AMERIND FOUNDATION MUSEUM ... DRAGOON, AZ 48
*ARIZONA STATE MUSEUM ... TUCSON, AZ 105
AZTEC MUSEUM AND PIONEER VILLAGE ... AZTEC, NM 137
*AZTEC RUINS NMO ... NM 137
*BANDELIER NMO ... NM 137
BESH-BA-GOWAH ARCHAEOLOGICAL PARK ... GLOBE, AZ 52
CARLSBAD MUSEUM AND ART CENTER ... CARLSBAD, NM 139
*CASA GRANDE RUINS NMO ... AZ 44
COLORADO RIVER INDIAN TRIBES MUSEUM AND LIBRARY ... PARKER, AZ 66
DEER VALLEY ROCK ART CENTER ... PHOENIX, AZ 76
DEMING LUNA MIMBRES MUSEUM ... DEMING, NM 146
DESERT CABALLEROS WESTERN MUSEUM ... WICKENBURG, AZ 114
FORT SUMNER STATE MONUMENT ... FORT SUMNER, NM 148
GADSDEN MUSEUM ... MESILLA, NM 154
GERONIMO SPRINGS MUSEUM ... TRUTH OR CONSEQUENCES, NM 168
GILA RIVER CULTURAL CENTER ... SACATON, AZ 91
GRAN QUIVIRA ... SALINAS PUEBLO MISSIONS NMO, NM 157
*HEARD MUSEUM ... PHOENIX, AZ 76
HOPI CULTURAL CENTER MUSEUM ... SECOND MESA, AZ 92
HUBBELL TRADING POST NHS ... GANADO, AZ 50
INDIAN PUEBLO CULTURAL CENTER ... ALBUQUERQUE, NM 134
INSTITUTE OF AMERICAN INDIAN ARTS MUSEUM: NATIONAL COLLECTION OF CONTEMPORARY INDIAN ART ... SANTA FE, NM 161
JOHN WESLEY POWELL MUSEUM AND VISITOR INFORMATION CENTER ... PAGE, AZ 66
KIT CARSON HOME AND MUSEUM ... TAOS, NM 167
LEA COUNTY COWBOY HALL OF FAME AND WESTERN HERITAGE CENTER ... HOBBS, NM 151
LINCOLN STATE MONUMENT ... LINCOLN, NM 153
MESA SOUTHWEST MUSEUM ... MESA, AZ 84
MILLION DOLLAR MUSEUM ... WHITES CITY, NM 169
*MONTEZUMA CASTLE NMO ... AZ 63
MUSEUM OF INDIAN ARTS AND CULTURE ... SANTA FE, NM 161
MUSEUM OF NORTHERN ARIZONA ... FLAGSTAFF, AZ 49
THE MYSTERY CASTLE ... PHOENIX, AZ 77
NAVAJO NATION MUSEUM ... WINDOW ROCK, AZ 115
OLD AZTEC MILL MUSEUM ... CIMARRON, NM 144
PECOS NHP ... NM 155
PICURIS PUEBLO ... PENASCO, NM 155
PINAL COUNTY HISTORICAL MUSEUM ... FLORENCE, AZ 49
PUEBLO BONITO ... CHACO CULTURE NHP, NM 142
PUEBLO GRANDE MUSEUM AND ARCHAEOLOGICAL PARK ... PHOENIX, AZ 78
RED ROCK MUSEUM ... GALLUP, NM 149
ST. MICHAELS HISTORICAL MUSEUM ... WINDOW ROCK, AZ 116
SALMON RUIN ... BLOOMFIELD, NM 138
*SHARLOT M. HALL MUSEUM ... PRESCOTT, AZ 89
SILVER CITY MUSEUM ... SILVER CITY, NM 165
SMOKI MUSEUM ... PRESCOTT, AZ 89
THELMA WEBBER SOUTHWEST HERITAGE ROOM ... HOBBS, NM 150
TUCUMCARI HISTORICAL MUSEUM ... TUCUMCARI, NM 168
*TUSAYAN RUIN AND MUSEUM ... GRAND CANYON NP, AZ 57
*TUZIGOOT NMO ... AZ 113
VISITOR CENTER ... CHACO CULTURE NHP, NM 142
*WALNUT CANYON NMO ... AZ 113
WESTERN NEW MEXICO UNIVERSITY MUSEUM ... SILVER CITY, NM 165
WHEELWRIGHT MUSEUM OF THE AMERICAN INDIAN ... SANTA FE, NM 163

EXHIBITS & COLLECTIONS-SCIENCE
THE ALBUQUERQUE MUSEUM OF ART & HISTORY ... ALBUQUERQUE, NM 134
ARIZONA SCIENCE CENTER ... PHOENIX, AZ 77
ARIZONA STATE UNIVERSITY MUSEUM OF GEOLOGY ... TEMPE, AZ 87
*ARIZONA-SONORA DESERT MUSEUM ... TUCSON, AZ 104
*BRADBURY SCIENCE MUSEUM ... LOS ALAMOS, NM 154
DOME THEATER ... TUCSON, AZ 108
FLANDRAU SCIENCE CENTER & PLANETARIUM ... TUCSON, AZ 108
INTERNATIONAL WILDLIFE MUSEUM ... TUCSON, AZ 105
KITT PEAK NATIONAL OBSERVATORY ... TUCSON, AZ 105
LOWELL OBSERVATORY ... FLAGSTAFF, AZ 49
METEOR CRATER ... WINSLOW, AZ 116
METEORITE MUSEUM ... ALBUQUERQUE, NM 136
MINERAL MUSEUM ... TUCSON, AZ 108
MUSEUM OF ASTROGEOLOGY ... WINSLOW, AZ 116
MUSEUM OF NORTHERN ARIZONA ... FLAGSTAFF, AZ 49
*ROSWELL MUSEUM AND ART CENTER ... ROSWELL, NM 156
*SPACE CENTER ... ALAMOGORDO, NM 132
TUCSON CHILDREN'S MUSEUM ... TUCSON, AZ 107
WHIPPLE OBSERVATORY ... CORONADO NF, AZ 46

EXHIBITS & COLLECTIONS-VEHICLES
DEMING LUNA MIMBRES MUSEUM ... DEMING, NM 146
GOLDEN ERA TOY AND AUTO MUSEUM ... COOLIDGE, AZ 46
GOVERNOR'S MANSION ... PRESCOTT, AZ 89
HUBBARD MUSEUM OF THE AMERICAN WEST ... RUIDOSO DOWNS, NM 157
MILLION DOLLAR MUSEUM ... WHITES CITY, NM 169
*SPACE CENTER ... ALAMOGORDO, NM 132
*WAR EAGLES AIR MUSEUM ... SANTA TERESA, NM 164

EXHIBITS & COLLECTIONS-WARS
CHAMPLIN FIGHTER AIRCRAFT MUSEUM ... MESA, AZ 84
CONFEDERATE AIR FORCE—ARIZONA WING ... MESA, AZ 84
*WAR EAGLES AIR MUSEUM ... SANTA TERESA, NM 164

EXHIBITS & COLLECTIONS-WEAPONS
LOS ALAMOS COUNTY HISTORICAL MUSEUM ... LOS ALAMOS, NM 154
NATIONAL ATOMIC MUSEUM ... ALBUQUERQUE, NM 134
TITAN MISSILE MUSEUM ... GREEN VALLEY, AZ 111

FARMS
GRAND CANYON DEER FARM ... WILLIAMS, AZ 115

FISH HATCHERIES
ALCHESAY NATIONAL FISH HATCHERY ... WHITERIVER, AZ 114
PAGE SPRINGS FISH HATCHERY ... SEDONA, AZ 94
ROCK LAKE TROUT HATCHERY ... SANTA ROSA, NM 164
WILLIAMS CREEK HATCHERY ... WHITERIVER, AZ 114

FORESTS, NATIONAL; STATE
APACHE-SITGREAVES NFS ... AZ 40
CARSON NF ... NM 141
CIBOLA NF ... NM 144
COCONINO NF ... AZ 46
CORONADO NF ... AZ 46
GILA NF ... NM 149
KAIBAB NF ... AZ 59
LINCOLN NF ... NM 153
PRESCOTT NF ... AZ 90
SANTA FE NF ... NM 163
TONTO NF ... AZ 98

FORTS & MILITARY INSTALLATIONS
CANNON AIR FORCE BASE ... CLOVIS, NM 145
FORT APACHE HISTORIC PARK ... FORT APACHE, AZ 49
FORT DEFIANCE ... AZ 50
FORT HUACHUCA ... AZ 50
FORT VERDE SHP ... CAMP VERDE, AZ 44
HOLLOMAN AIR FORCE BASE ... ALAMOGORDO, NM 131
KIRTLAND AIR FORCE BASE ... ALBUQUERQUE, NM 132
OLD FORT BOWIE NHS ... WILLCOX, AZ 114
WHITE SANDS MISSILE RANGE ... LAS CRUCES, NM 152

FOSSILS
ARIZONA STATE UNIVERSITY MUSEUM OF GEOLOGY ... TEMPE, AZ 87
DESERT CABALLEROS WESTERN MUSEUM ... WICKENBURG, AZ 114
MINERAL MUSEUM ... SOCORRO, NM 165
*PETRIFIED FOREST NP ... AZ 68
RAINBOW FOREST MUSEUM ... PETRIFIED FOREST NP, AZ 69

FOUNTAINS
THE FOUNTAIN ... FOUNTAIN HILLS, AZ 82

GAPS & PASSES
RATON PASS ... RATON, NM 155
SCHULTZ PASS ROAD ... FLAGSTAFF, AZ 49

GARDENS
ARIZONA HISTORICAL SOCIETY CENTURY HOUSE MUSEUM AND GARDENS ... YUMA, AZ 117
*ARIZONA-SONORA DESERT MUSEUM ... TUCSON, AZ 104
*BOYCE THOMPSON ARBORETUM SP ... SUPERIOR, AZ 97
*DESERT BOTANICAL GARDEN ... PHOENIX, AZ 77
HERITAGE AND SCIENCE PARK ... PHOENIX, AZ 77
PANCHO VILLA SP ... COLUMBUS, NM 145
THE RIO GRANDE BOTANIC GARDEN ... ALBUQUERQUE, NM 135
SANTUARIO DE GUADALUPE ... SANTA FE, NM 162
*SHARLOT M. HALL MUSEUM ... PRESCOTT, AZ 89
TUCSON BOTANICAL GARDENS ... TUCSON, AZ 107

GEOLOGICAL FORMATIONS
AGATE BRIDGE ... PETRIFIED FOREST NP, AZ 69
ANGEL PEAK RECREATION AREA ... FARMINGTON, NM 148
APACHE LEAP CLIFF ... SUPERIOR, AZ 97
BATTLESHIP ROCK ... JEMEZ PUEBLO, NM 151
BIG ROOM ... CARLSBAD CAVERNS NP, NM 140
BISTI/DE-NA-ZIN WILDERNESS ... FARMINGTON, NM 148
BLACK HILLS BACK COUNTRY BYWAY ... SAFFORD, AZ 91
*CAPULIN VOLCANO NMO ... NM 139
CAVE CREEK CANYON ... PORTAL, AZ 88
*CHIRICAHUA NMO ... AZ 45
CITY OF ROCKS SP ... DEMING, NM 146
DEVIL'S CANYON ... GLOBE, AZ 52
EL MALPAIS NMO AND NATIONAL CONSERVATION AREA ... GRANTS, NM 150
ENCHANTED MESA ... ACOMA (SKY CITY), NM 131
GRAND CANYON CAVERNS ... PEACH SPRINGS, AZ 68
*GRAND CANYON NP ... AZ 52
GRANITE DELLS ... PRESCOTT, AZ 89
HALL OF THE WHITE GIANT ... CARLSBAD CAVERNS NP, NM 141
KAIBAB NF ... AZ 59
KING'S PALACE ... CARLSBAD CAVERNS NP, NM 141
LEFT HAND TUNNEL ... CARLSBAD CAVERNS NP, NM 141
LOWER CAVE ... CARLSBAD CAVERNS NP, NM 141
METEOR CRATER ... WINSLOW, AZ 116
MONTEZUMA WELL ... MONTEZUMA CASTLE NMO, AZ 63
MYSTERY VALLEY ... MONUMENT VALLEY NAVAJO TRIBAL PARK, AZ 63
NATURAL ENTRANCE ... CARLSBAD CAVERNS NP, NM 140
NEWSPAPER ROCK ... PETRIFIED FOREST NP, AZ 69
*OAK CREEK CANYON ... SEDONA, AZ 94
*PETRIFIED FOREST NP ... AZ 68
RAINBOW BRIDGE NMO ... GLEN CANYON NRA, AZ 51
RAINBOW FOREST MUSEUM ... PETRIFIED FOREST NP, AZ 69
ROUND MOUNTAIN ROCKHOUND AREA ... SAFFORD, AZ 91
SALT RIVER CANYON ... GLOBE, AZ 52
SAN FRANCISCO PEAKS ... FLAGSTAFF, AZ 48
SHIPROCK ... SHIPROCK, NM 164
SODA DAM ... JEMEZ PUEBLO, NM 151
SOUTH MOUNTAIN PARK ... PHOENIX, AZ 78
SPIDER CAVE ... CARLSBAD CAVERNS NP, NM 141
SUNSET CRATER VOLCANO ... SUNSET CRATER VOLCANO NMO, AZ 96
TENT ROCKS ... DOMINGO, NM 146
THUMB BUTTE ... PRESCOTT, AZ 89
TOROWEAP OVERLOOK ... GRAND CANYON NP, AZ 58
VALLE GRANDE ... LOS ALAMOS, NM 153
VALLEY OF FIRES RECREATION AREA ... CARRIZOZO, NM 141

VULCAN'S THRONE .... GRAND CANYON NP, AZ 58
*WHITE SANDS NMO .... NM 169

GHOST TOWNS
GHOST TOWNS .... KINGMAN, AZ 60
GHOST TOWNS AND MINING CAMPS .... DOUGLAS, AZ 47
GOLDFIELD GHOST TOWN & MINE TOURS .... APACHE JUNCTION, AZ 82
OATMAN .... KINGMAN, AZ 60
STEINS RAILROAD GHOST TOWN .... STEINS, NM 166
TYRONE .... SILVER CITY, NM 165
WHITE OAKS .... CARRIZOZO, NM 141

GRAVES & TOMBS
ARCHBISHOP J.B. LAMY .... SANTA FE, NM 160
BILLY THE KID .... FORT SUMNER, NM 148
D.H. LAWRENCE .... TAOS, NM 166
FRAY GERONIMO DE LA LAMA .... SANTA FE, NM 160
FRAY ZARATE .... SANTA FE, NM 160
KIT CARSON .... TAOS, NM 167
PADRE MARTINEZ .... TAOS, NM 167

HALLS OF FAME
ARIZONA HALL OF FAME .... PHOENIX, AZ 71
LEA COUNTY COWBOY HALL OF FAME AND WESTERN HERITAGE CENTER .... HOBBS, NM 151
NATIONAL FIREFIGHTING HALL OF HEROES .... PHOENIX, AZ 76

HISTORIC BUILDINGS & HOUSES
*ARIZONA STATE CAPITOL MUSEUM .... PHOENIX, AZ 76
CAMILLUS FLY STUDIO .... TOMBSTONE, AZ 98
CLOUDCROFT PIONEER VILLAGE .... CLOUDCROFT, NM 145
CRYSTAL PALACE .... TOMBSTONE, AZ 97
EL PRESIDIO HISTORIC DISTRICT .... TUCSON, AZ 107
EL RANCHO DE LAS GOLONDRINAS .... SANTA FE, NM 160
ERNEST L. BLUMENSCHEIN HOME .... TAOS, NM 166
FARAWAY RANCH .... CHIRICAHUA NMO, AZ 45
GADSDEN HOTEL .... DOUGLAS, AZ 47
GAMMAGE CENTER FOR THE PERFORMING ARTS .... TEMPE, AZ 86
GOVERNOR'S MANSION .... PRESCOTT, AZ 89
HERITAGE AND SCIENCE PARK .... PHOENIX, AZ 77
JEROME SHP .... JEROME, AZ 59
JOHN C. FREMONT HOUSE .... PRESCOTT, AZ 89
KIT CARSON HOME AND MUSEUM .... TAOS, NM 167
KOLB STUDIO .... GRAND CANYON NP, AZ 56
LA CASA CORDOVA .... TUCSON, AZ 107
LUTES CASINO .... YUMA, AZ 117
MARTINEZ HACIENDA .... TAOS, NM 167
MUHEIM HERITAGE HOUSE .... BISBEE, AZ 43
THE MYSTERY CASTLE .... PHOENIX, AZ 77
O.K. CORRAL .... TOMBSTONE, AZ 98
OLD MAIN .... TUCSON, AZ 107
THE OLDEST HOUSE IN SANTA FE .... SANTA FE, NM 161
OLIVER LEE MEMORIAL SP .... ALAMOGORDO, NM 132
ORPHEUM THEATRE .... PHOENIX, AZ 80
PALACE HOTEL .... RATON, NM 156
*PALACE OF THE GOVERNORS .... SANTA FE, NM 161
PRESCOTT .... AZ 88
RIORDAN MANSION SHP .... FLAGSTAFF, AZ 49
ROSSON HOUSE .... PHOENIX, AZ 77
ST. JAMES HOTEL .... CIMARRON, NM 144
SAN FRANCISCO DE ASIS CHURCH .... TAOS, NM 167
SCHIEFFELIN HALL .... TOMBSTONE, AZ 98
SCOTTISH RITE TEMPLE .... SANTA FE, NM 162
SOSA-CARILLO-FREMONT HOUSE .... TUCSON, AZ 107
TALIESIN WEST .... SCOTTSDALE, AZ 85
TOMBSTONE EPITAPH BUILDING .... TOMBSTONE, AZ 97
TUNSTALL MUSEUM .... LINCOLN, NM 153
*VISITOR CENTER .... GRAND CANYON NP, AZ 55
WILLIAM C. BASHFORD HOUSE .... PRESCOTT, AZ 89
YUMA CROSSING SHP .... YUMA, AZ 118
YUMA TERRITORIAL PRISON SHP .... YUMA, AZ 118

HISTORIC DOCUMENTS, MANUSCRIPTS & RARE BOOKS
BISBEE MINING AND HISTORICAL MUSEUM .... BISBEE, AZ 43

HISTORIC SITES
BESH-BA-GOWAH ARCHAEOLOGICAL PARK .... GLOBE, AZ 52
CANYON DEL MUERTO .... CANYON DE CHELLY NMO, AZ 44
CHACO CULTURE NHP .... NM 142
FORT BURGWIN .... TAOS, NM 166
FORT LOWELL MUSEUM .... TUCSON, AZ 105
FORT SELDEN STATE MONUMENT .... LAS CRUCES, NM 152
FORT SUMNER STATE MONUMENT .... FORT SUMNER, NM 148
FORT VERDE SHP .... CAMP VERDE, AZ 44
HUBBELL TRADING POST NHS .... GANADO, AZ 50
JEROME SHP .... JEROME, AZ 59
LINCOLN STATE MONUMENT .... LINCOLN, NM 153
MCFARLAND SHP .... FLORENCE, AZ 49
OLD FORT BOWIE NHS .... WILLCOX, AZ 114
OLIVER LEE MEMORIAL SP .... ALAMOGORDO, NM 132
RUINS OF THE MISSION SAN GERONIMO DE TAOS .... TAOS, NM 168
SALINAS PUEBLO MISSIONS NMO .... NM 157
SAN BERNARDINO RANCH NATIONAL HISTORIC LANDMARK (SLAUGHTER RANCH MUSEUM) .... DOUGLAS, AZ 48
SANTA CRUZ DE TERRENATE PRESIDIO NHS .... AZ 92
*TOMBSTONE .... AZ 97
TUBAC PRESIDIO SHP .... TUBAC, AZ 99

INDIAN MOUNDS, REMAINS & RUINS
ABO .... SALINAS PUEBLO MISSIONS NMO, NM 157
ANTELOPE HOUSE .... CANYON DE CHELLY NMO, AZ 44
*AZTEC RUINS NMO .... NM 137
*BANDELIER NMO .... NM 137
BESH-BA-GOWAH ARCHAEOLOGICAL PARK .... GLOBE, AZ 52
BETATAKIN AREA .... NAVAJO NMO, AZ 64
BLACKWATER DRAW ARCHAEOLOGICAL SITE .... PORTALES, NM 155
*CANYON DE CHELLY NMO .... AZ 44
CASA GRANDE .... CASA GRANDE RUINS NMO, AZ 44
CHACO CULTURE NHP .... NM 142
CORONADO STATE MONUMENT .... BERNALILLO, NM 138
EL MALPAIS NMO AND NATIONAL CONSERVATION AREA .... GRANTS, NM 150
EL MORRO NMO .... NM 146
FORT APACHE HISTORIC PARK .... FORT APACHE, AZ 49
GILA CLIFF DWELLINGS NMO .... NM 149
GRAN QUIVIRA .... SALINAS PUEBLO MISSIONS NMO, NM 157
GUISEWA PUEBLO .... JEMEZ PUEBLO, NM 151
HERITAGE PARK .... BLOOMFIELD, NM 138
HOMOLOVI RUINS SP .... WINSLOW, AZ 116
KEET SEEL AREA .... NAVAJO NMO, AZ 64
KINISHBA RUINS .... WHITERIVER, AZ 114
LOS ALAMOS COUNTY HISTORICAL MUSEUM .... LOS ALAMOS, NM 154
MONTEZUMA CASTLE .... MONTEZUMA CASTLE NMO, AZ 63
MONTEZUMA WELL .... MONTEZUMA CASTLE NMO, AZ 63
MUMMY CAVE .... CANYON DE CHELLY NMO, AZ 44
*NAVAJO NMO .... AZ 64
PECOS NHP .... NM 155
PUEBLO BONITO .... CHACO CULTURE NHP, NM 142
PUEBLO GRANDE MUSEUM AND ARCHAEOLOGICAL PARK .... PHOENIX, AZ 78
PUERCO PUEBLO .... PETRIFIED FOREST NP, AZ 69
PUYE CLIFF DWELLINGS AND COMMUNAL HOUSE RUINS .... ESPANOLA, NM 147
QUARAI .... SALINAS PUEBLO MISSIONS NMO, NM 157
RAVEN SITE RUIN .... SPRINGERVILLE, AZ 96
SALINAS PUEBLO MISSIONS NMO .... NM 157
SALMON RUIN .... BLOOMFIELD, NM 138
SAN PEDRO RIPARIAN CONSERVATION AREA .... SIERRA VISTA, AZ 96
STANDING COW .... CANYON DE CHELLY NMO, AZ 44
TONTO NMO .... AZ 98
*TUSAYAN RUIN AND MUSEUM .... GRAND CANYON NP, AZ 57
*TUZIGOOT NMO .... AZ 113
*WALNUT CANYON NMO .... AZ 113
WHITE HOUSE .... CANYON DE CHELLY NMO, AZ 44
*WUPATKI NMO .... AZ 117

INDIAN PICTOGRAPHS & PETROGLYPHS
ANTELOPE HOUSE .... CANYON DE CHELLY NMO, AZ 44
DEER VALLEY ROCK ART CENTER .... PHOENIX, AZ 76
FORT APACHE HISTORIC PARK .... FORT APACHE, AZ 49
HOMOLOVI RUINS SP .... WINSLOW, AZ 116
INSCRIPTION ROCK .... EL MORRO NMO, NM 146
NEWSPAPER ROCK .... PETRIFIED FOREST NP, AZ 69
PETROGLYPH NMO .... ALBUQUERQUE, NM 132
PETROGLYPHS .... PETRIFIED FOREST NP, AZ 68
PICTOGRAPHS .... CANYON DE CHELLY NMO, AZ 44
PUERCO PUEBLO .... PETRIFIED FOREST NP, AZ 69
RAVEN SITE RUIN .... SPRINGERVILLE, AZ 96
*SAGUARO NP .... AZ 111
THREE RIVERS PETROGLYPH SITE .... THREE RIVERS, NM 168
*TUCSON MOUNTAIN PARK .... TUCSON, AZ 107

INDIAN RESERVATIONS & VILLAGES
ACOMA .... ACOMA (SKY CITY), NM 131
CASA GRANDE .... CASA GRANDE RUINS NMO, AZ 44
COCHITI PUEBLO .... DOMINGO, NM 146
COLORADO RIVER INDIAN TRIBES MUSEUM AND LIBRARY .... PARKER, AZ 66
FORT APACHE RESERVATION .... WHITERIVER, AZ 114
GANADO .... AZ 50
GILA RIVER CULTURAL CENTER .... SACATON, AZ 91
HAVASUPAI INDIAN RESERVATION .... SUPAI, AZ 97
HOPI RESERVATION .... KEAMS CANYON, AZ 59
HOPI RESERVATION .... SECOND MESA, AZ 92
HUALAPAI INDIAN RESERVATION .... PEACH SPRINGS, AZ 68
HUBBELL TRADING POST NHS .... GANADO, AZ 50
ISLETA INDIAN RESERVATION .... ALBUQUERQUE, NM 132
JEMEZ PUEBLO .... NM 151
JICARILLA APACHE INDIAN RESERVATION .... DULCE, NM 146
LAGUNA PUEBLO .... LAGUNA, NM 151
MESCALERO APACHE RESERVATION .... MESCALERO, NM 154
*MONUMENT VALLEY NAVAJO TRIBAL PARK .... AZ 63
NAVAJO AND HOPI INDIAN RESERVATIONS .... TUBA CITY, AZ 99
NAVAJO INDIAN RESERVATION .... FARMINGTON, NM 148
NAVAJO RESERVATION .... FORT DEFIANCE, AZ 50
NAVAJO RESERVATION .... KEAMS CANYON, AZ 59
NAVAJO RESERVATION .... SECOND MESA, AZ 92
OLD ORAIBI .... KEAMS CANYON, AZ 59
PICURIS PUEBLO .... PENASCO, NM 155
PIMA RESERVATION .... SACATON, AZ 91
PIPE SPRING NMO .... AZ 88
POJOAQUE AND NAMBE PUEBLOS .... ESPANOLA, NM 147
SAN CARLOS APACHE RESERVATION .... GLOBE, AZ 52
SAN ILDEFONSO PUEBLO .... ESPANOLA, NM 147
SAN JUAN PUEBLO .... ESPANOLA, NM 147
SANDIA RESERVATION .... ALBUQUERQUE, NM 132
SANTA CLARA INDIAN PUEBLO .... ESPANOLA, NM 147
SANTO DOMINGO PUEBLO .... DOMINGO, NM 146
TAOS PUEBLO .... TAOS, NM 167
TOHONO O'ODHAM INDIAN RESERVATION .... SELLS, AZ 95
WALPI .... KEAMS CANYON, AZ 59
ZIA PUEBLO AND MISSION .... BERNALILLO, NM 138
ZUNI .... NM 169

INDUSTRIAL TOURS
CARL HAYDEN VISITOR CENTER .... GLEN CANYON NRA, AZ 51
CLAYTON LIVESTOCK RESEARCH CENTER .... CLAYTON, NM 145
*HOOVER DAM .... LAKE MEAD NRA, AZ 62
PALO VERDE NUCLEAR GENERATING STATION .... PALO VERDE, AZ 84
VERY LARGE ARRAY (VLA)—RADIO TELESCOPE .... SOCORRO, NM 165

LAKES, PONDS & RESERVOIRS
ABIQUIU LAKE .... ABIQUIU, NM 131
APACHE LAKE .... APACHE JUNCTION, AZ 81
CABALLO LAKE .... TRUTH OR CONSEQUENCES, NM 168
CANYON LAKE .... APACHE JUNCTION, AZ 82
COCHITI LAKE .... DOMINGO, NM 146
CONCHAS LAKE .... TUCUMCARI, NM 168
ELEPHANT BUTTE LAKE .... TRUTH OR CONSEQUENCES, NM 168
GRANITE BASIN .... PRESCOTT, AZ 89
GRANITE DELLS .... PRESCOTT, AZ 89
LAKE CARLSBAD .... CARLSBAD, NM 139
LAKE HAVASU .... LAKE HAVASU CITY, AZ 60
LAKE LUCERO .... WHITE SANDS NMO, NM 169
LAKE MARY .... COCONINO NF, AZ 46
LAKE MEAD .... LAKE MEAD NRA, AZ 62
LAKE MOHAVE .... LAKE MEAD NRA, AZ 62
LAKE PLEASANT .... PEORIA, AZ 84
LAKE POWELL .... GLEN CANYON NRA, AZ 51
MORGAN LAKE .... FARMINGTON, NM 148
MORPHY LAKE .... LAS VEGAS, NM 152
NAVAJO RESERVOIR .... BLOOMFIELD, NM 138
PARK LAKE .... SANTA ROSA, NM 164
PERCH LAKE .... SANTA ROSA, NM 164
SANTA CRUZ LAKE .... ESPANOLA, NM 147
SANTA ROSA LAKE SP .... SANTA ROSA, NM 164
STORRIE LAKE .... LAS VEGAS, NM 152
THEODORE ROOSEVELT DAM AND LAKE .... ROOSEVELT, AZ 91
UTE LAKE .... TUCUMCARI, NM 168

LIBRARIES, ARCHIVES
CENTER FOR CREATIVE PHOTOGRAPHY ... TUCSON, AZ 107
COLORADO RIVER INDIAN TRIBES MUSEUM AND LIBRARY ... PARKER, AZ 66
SAN JUAN COUNTY ARCHAEOLOGICAL RESEARCH CENTER AND LIBRARY ... BLOOMFIELD, NM 138
SCARBOROUGH MEMORIAL LIBRARY ... HOBBS, NM 150
SETON MEMORIAL LIBRARY ... CIMARRON, NM 145
WHEELWRIGHT MUSEUM OF THE AMERICAN INDIAN ... SANTA FE, NM 163

MARKETS
BIEN MUR INDIAN MARKET CENTER ... ALBUQUERQUE, NM 132
HUBBELL TRADING POST NHS ... GANADO, AZ 50
THE PUEBLO GRANDE MUSEUM AUXILIARY INDIAN MARKET ... PHOENIX, AZ 81

MEMORIALS
CITY OF LAS VEGAS MUSEUM AND ROUGHRIDER MEMORIAL COLLECTION ... LAS VEGAS, NM 152
CORONADO NME ... AZ 47
HI JOLLY MEMORIAL ... QUARTZSITE, AZ 90
★SPACE CENTER ... ALAMOGORDO, NM 132
★VIETNAM VETERANS NME ... ANGEL FIRE, NM 136

MINES & MINERALS
ARIZONA MINING AND MINERAL MUSEUM ... PHOENIX, AZ 76
ASARCO MINERAL DISCOVERY CENTER ... SAHUARITA, AZ 112
CARLSBAD MUSEUM AND ART CENTER ... CARLSBAD, NM 139
CHINO MINES CO. ... SILVER CITY, NM 165
DEMING LUNA MIMBRES MUSEUM ... DEMING, NM 146
GEOLOGY MUSEUM OF THE UNIVERSITY OF NEW MEXICO ... ALBUQUERQUE, NM 136
GOLDFIELD GHOST TOWN & MINE TOURS ... APACHE JUNCTION, AZ 82
LITTLE FLORIDA ... DEMING, NM 146
MINE MUSEUM ... JEROME, AZ 59
MINERAL MUSEUM ... SOCORRO, NM 165
MINERAL MUSEUM ... TUCSON, AZ 108
NAVAJO MINE ... FARMINGTON, NM 147
NEW CORNELIA OPEN PIT MINE ... AJO, AZ 40
NEW MEXICO MINING MUSEUM ... GRANTS, NM 150
POW WOW ROCK AND MINERAL SHOW ... QUARTZSITE, AZ 90
QUEEN MINE ... BISBEE, AZ 43
RAY MINE ... SUPERIOR, AZ 97
ROCKHOUND SP ... DEMING, NM 146
SURFACE MINE AND HISTORIC DISTRICT VAN TOUR ... BISBEE, AZ 43

MONUMENTS, GENERAL
BUCKY O'NEILL MONUMENT ... PRESCOTT, AZ 89
JACOB WALTZ ... APACHE JUNCTION, AZ 81
LEOPOLD VISTA HISTORICAL MONUMENT ... GILA NF, NM 149

MONUMENTS, NATIONAL; STATE
★AZTEC RUINS NMO ... NM 137
★BANDELIER NMO ... NM 137
★CANYON DE CHELLY NMO ... AZ 44
★CAPULIN VOLCANO NMO ... NM 139
★CASA GRANDE RUINS NMO ... AZ 44
★CHIRICAHUA NMO ... AZ 45
CORONADO NME ... AZ 47
CORONADO STATE MONUMENT ... BERNALILLO, NM 138
EL MALPAIS NMO AND NATIONAL CONSERVATION AREA ... GRANTS, NM 150
EL MORRO NMO ... NM 146
FORT SELDEN STATE MONUMENT ... LAS CRUCES, NM 152
FORT SUMNER STATE MONUMENT ... FORT SUMNER, NM 148
FORT UNION NMO ... NM 148
FOUR CORNERS MONUMENT ... WINDOW ROCK, AZ 116
GILA CLIFF DWELLINGS NMO ... NM 149
JEMEZ STATE MONUMENT ... JEMEZ PUEBLO, NM 151
LA MESILLA STATE MONUMENT ... MESILLA, NM 154
LINCOLN STATE MONUMENT ... LINCOLN, NM 153
★MONTEZUMA CASTLE NMO ... AZ 63
★NAVAJO NMO ... AZ 64
★ORGAN PIPE CACTUS NMO ... AZ 66
PETROGLYPH NMO ... ALBUQUERQUE, NM 132
PIPE SPRING NMO ... AZ 88
SALINAS PUEBLO MISSIONS NMO ... NM 157
SUNSET CRATER VOLCANO NMO ... AZ 96
TONTO NMO ... AZ 98
★TUZIGOOT NMO ... AZ 113
★WALNUT CANYON NMO ... AZ 113
★WHITE SANDS NMO ... NM 169
★WUPATKI NMO ... AZ 117

MOUNTAINS
BRADSHAW MOUNTAINS ... CORDES JUNCTION, AZ 46
BROKEOFF MOUNTAINS ... LINCOLN NF, NM 153
GUADALUPE MOUNTAINS ... LINCOLN NF, NM 153
HUACHUCA MOUNTAINS ... SIERRA VISTA, AZ 96
JEMEZ MOUNTAINS ... SANTA FE NF, NM 163
LITTLE FLORIDA ... DEMING, NM 146
MOUNT AGASSIZ ... COCONINO NF, AZ 46
MOUNT HUMPHREYS ... COCONINO NF, AZ 46
ORGAN MOUNTAINS ... LAS CRUCES, NM 152
RABBIT EAR MOUNTAINS ... CLAYTON, NM 145
SACRAMENTO MOUNTAINS ... CLOUDCROFT, NM 145
SACRAMENTO MOUNTAINS ... RUIDOSO, NM 157
SANDIA CREST ... CIBOLA NF, NM 144
SANGRE DE CRISTO RANGE ... SANTA FE NF, NM 163
SUPERSTITION MOUNTAINS ... APACHE JUNCTION, AZ 82
TUCUMCARI MOUNTAIN ... TUCUMCARI, NM 168
WHEELER PEAK ... CARSON NF, NM 141

MURALS & MOSAICS
DEMING LUNA MIMBRES MUSEUM ... DEMING, NM 146

MUSEUMS
AIR MUSEUM PLANES OF FAME ... VALLE, AZ 113
THE ALBUQUERQUE MUSEUM OF ART & HISTORY ... ALBUQUERQUE, NM 134
AMERICAN INTERNATIONAL RATTLESNAKE MUSEUM ... ALBUQUERQUE, NM 134
★AMERIND FOUNDATION MUSEUM ... DRAGOON, AZ 48
APACHE COUNTY HISTORICAL SOCIETY MUSEUM ... ST. JOHNS, AZ 91
ARIZONA DOLL AND TOY MUSEUM ... PHOENIX, AZ 77
ARIZONA HALL OF FAME ... PHOENIX, AZ 71
ARIZONA HISTORICAL SOCIETY CENTURY HOUSE MUSEUM AND GARDENS ... YUMA, AZ 117
THE ARIZONA HISTORICAL SOCIETY MUSEUM ... TEMPE, AZ 87
ARIZONA HISTORICAL SOCIETY/TUCSON MUSEUM ... TUCSON, AZ 104
ARIZONA MINING AND MINERAL MUSEUM ... PHOENIX, AZ 76
ARIZONA MUSEUM FOR YOUTH ... MESA, AZ 84
ARIZONA SCIENCE CENTER ... PHOENIX, AZ 77
★ARIZONA STATE CAPITOL MUSEUM ... PHOENIX, AZ 76
★ARIZONA STATE MUSEUM ... TUCSON, AZ 105
ARIZONA STATE UNIVERSITY MUSEUM OF GEOLOGY ... TEMPE, AZ 87
★ARIZONA-SONORA DESERT MUSEUM ... TUCSON, AZ 104
ARTS AND CRAFT MUSEUM ... DULCE, NM 146
AZTEC MUSEUM AND PIONEER VILLAGE ... AZTEC, NM 137
THE BEAD MUSEUM ... GLENDALE, AZ 83
BESH-BA-GOWAH ARCHAEOLOGICAL PARK ... GLOBE, AZ 52
BISBEE MINING AND HISTORICAL MUSEUM ... BISBEE, AZ 43
BISBEE RESTORATION MUSEUM ... BISBEE, AZ 43
BLACKWATER DRAW ARCHAEOLOGICAL SITE ... PORTALES, NM 155
BLACKWATER DRAW MUSEUM ... PORTALES, NM 155
★BRADBURY SCIENCE MUSEUM ... LOS ALAMOS, NM 154
CARLSBAD MUSEUM AND ART CENTER ... CARLSBAD, NM 139
CASA GRANDE VALLEY HISTORICAL SOCIETY AND MUSEUM ... CASA GRANDE, AZ 44
CENTER FOR THE ARTS ... ALBUQUERQUE, NM 136
CHAMPLIN FIGHTER AIRCRAFT MUSEUM ... MESA, AZ 84
CITY OF LAS VEGAS MUSEUM AND ROUGHRIDER MEMORIAL COLLECTION ... LAS VEGAS, NM 152
COLORADO RIVER INDIAN TRIBES MUSEUM AND LIBRARY ... PARKER, AZ 66
COLUMBUS HISTORICAL SOCIETY ... COLUMBUS, NM 145
CONFEDERATE AIR FORCE—ARIZONA WING ... MESA, AZ 84
DEER VALLEY ROCK ART CENTER ... PHOENIX, AZ 76
DEMING LUNA MIMBRES MUSEUM ... DEMING, NM 146
DESERT CABALLEROS WESTERN MUSEUM ... WICKENBURG, AZ 114
EL RANCHO DE LAS GOLONDRINAS ... SANTA FE, NM 160
THE FECHIN HOUSE AND STUDIO ... TAOS, NM 167
FLEISCHER MUSEUM ... SCOTTSDALE, AZ 85
FLYING MUSEUM ... HOBBS, NM 150
FORT HUACHUCA MUSEUM ... FORT HUACHUCA, AZ 50
FORT LOWELL MUSEUM ... TUCSON, AZ 105
FORT SELDEN STATE MONUMENT ... LAS CRUCES, NM 152
FORT UNION NMO ... NM 148
FORT VERDE SHP ... CAMP VERDE, AZ 44
GADSDEN MUSEUM ... MESILLA, NM 154
GATEWAY MUSEUM AND VISITORS CENTER ... FARMINGTON, NM 148
GEOLOGY MUSEUM OF THE UNIVERSITY OF NEW MEXICO ... ALBUQUERQUE, NM 136
GERONIMO SPRINGS MUSEUM ... TRUTH OR CONSEQUENCES, NM 168
GHOST RANCH LIVING MUSEUM ... ABIQUIU, NM 131
GILA RIVER CULTURAL CENTER ... SACATON, AZ 91
GOLDEN ERA TOY AND AUTO MUSEUM ... COOLIDGE, AZ 46
★HALL OF FLAME MUSEUM OF FIREFIGHTING ... PHOENIX, AZ 76
★HEARD MUSEUM ... PHOENIX, AZ 76
HISTORICAL MUSEUM AND ART CENTER ... ARTESIA, NM 137
HOPI CULTURAL CENTER MUSEUM ... SECOND MESA, AZ 92
HUBBARD MUSEUM OF THE AMERICAN WEST ... RUIDOSO DOWNS, NM 157
INDIAN PUEBLO CULTURAL CENTER ... ALBUQUERQUE, NM 134
INSTITUTE OF AMERICAN INDIAN ARTS MUSEUM: NATIONAL COLLECTION OF CONTEMPORARY INDIAN ART ... SANTA FE, NM 161
INTERNATIONAL UFO MUSEUM & RESEARCH CENTER ... ROSWELL, NM 156
INTERNATIONAL WILDLIFE MUSEUM ... TUCSON, AZ 105
JEMEZ STATE MONUMENT ... JEMEZ PUEBLO, NM 151
JEROME SHP ... JEROME, AZ 59
JOHN WESLEY POWELL MUSEUM AND VISITOR INFORMATION CENTER ... PAGE, AZ 66
KIT CARSON HOME AND MUSEUM ... TAOS, NM 167
LAS CRUCES MUSEUM OF NATURAL HISTORY ... LAS CRUCES, NM 152
LEA COUNTY COWBOY HALL OF FAME AND WESTERN HERITAGE CENTER ... HOBBS, NM 151
THE LITTLE HOUSE MUSEUM ... EAGAR, AZ 48
LOS ALAMOS COUNTY HISTORICAL MUSEUM ... LOS ALAMOS, NM 154
LT. GEN. DOUGLAS L. MCBRIDE MUSEUM ... ROSWELL, NM 156
MAXWELL MUSEUM OF ANTHROPOLOGY ... ALBUQUERQUE, NM 136
MESA SOUTHWEST MUSEUM ... MESA, AZ 84
METEOR CRATER ... WINSLOW, AZ 116
METEORITE MUSEUM ... ALBUQUERQUE, NM 136
MILLICENT ROGERS MUSEUM ... TAOS, NM 167
MILLION DOLLAR MUSEUM ... WHITES CITY, NM 169
MINE MUSEUM ... JEROME, AZ 59
MINERAL MUSEUM ... SOCORRO, NM 165
MINERAL MUSEUM ... TUCSON, AZ 108
MOHAVE MUSEUM OF HISTORY AND ARTS ... KINGMAN, AZ 60
MUHEIM HERITAGE HOUSE ... BISBEE, AZ 43
MUSEO CHICANO (CHICANO MUSEUM) ... PHOENIX, AZ 77
MUSEUM OF ASTROGEOLOGY ... WINSLOW, AZ 116
MUSEUM OF FINE ARTS ... SANTA FE, NM 161
MUSEUM OF INDIAN ARTS AND CULTURE ... SANTA FE, NM 161
★MUSEUM OF INTERNATIONAL FOLK ART ... SANTA FE, NM 161
MUSEUM OF NEW MEXICO ... SANTA FE, NM 161
MUSEUM OF NORTHERN ARIZONA ... FLAGSTAFF, AZ 49
NATIONAL ATOMIC MUSEUM ... ALBUQUERQUE, NM 134
NAVAJO NATION MUSEUM ... WINDOW ROCK, AZ 115
NEW MEXICO MINING MUSEUM ... GRANTS, NM 150
★NEW MEXICO MUSEUM OF NATURAL HISTORY & SCIENCE ... ALBUQUERQUE, NM 135
OLD AZTEC MILL MUSEUM ... CIMARRON, NM 144
OLD COAL MINE MUSEUM ... MADRID, NM 154
OLD FORT SUMNER MUSEUM ... FORT SUMNER, NM 148
OLD PUEBLO MUSEUM ... TUCSON, AZ 110
PHILMONT SCOUT RANCH ... CIMARRON, NM 145
PHIPPEN MUSEUM ... PRESCOTT, AZ 89
PHOENIX ART MUSEUM ... PHOENIX, AZ 78
PHOENIX MUSEUM OF HISTORY ... PHOENIX, AZ 77
PICURIS PUEBLO ... PENASCO, NM 155
PIMA AIR AND SPACE MUSEUM ... TUCSON, AZ 106
PINAL COUNTY HISTORICAL MUSEUM ... FLORENCE, AZ 49
PINOS ALTOS HISTORICAL MUSEUM ... PINOS ALTOS, NM 155
PIONEER ARIZONA LIVING HISTORY MUSEUM ... PHOENIX, AZ 78
THE POSTAL HISTORY FOUNDATION ... TUCSON, AZ 106
PUEBLO GRANDE MUSEUM AND ARCHAEOLOGICAL PARK ... PHOENIX, AZ 78
QUARAI ... SALINAS PUEBLO MISSIONS NMO, NM 157
RAINBOW FOREST MUSEUM ... PETRIFIED FOREST NP, AZ 69
RATON MUSEUM ... RATON, NM 156
RAWHIDE ... SCOTTSDALE, AZ 85
RED ROCK MUSEUM ... GALLUP, NM 149
REX ALLEN ARIZONA COWBOY MUSEUM ... WILLCOX, AZ 114
ROOSEVELT COUNTY MUSEUM ... PORTALES, NM 155
ROSE TREE MUSEUM AND BOOKSTORE ... TOMBSTONE, AZ 98

*ROSWELL MUSEUM AND ART CENTER ... ROSWELL, NM 156
SACRAMENTO MOUNTAINS HISTORICAL MUSEUM ... CLOUDCROFT, NM 145
ST. MICHAELS HISTORICAL MUSEUM ... WINDOW ROCK, AZ 116
SANTA FE CHILDREN'S MUSEUM ... SANTA FE, NM 161
THE SANTA FE TRAIL MUSEUM ... SPRINGER, NM 166
SCOTTSDALE HISTORICAL MUSEUM ... SCOTTSDALE, AZ 85
*SHARLOT M. HALL MUSEUM ... PRESCOTT, AZ 89
SILVER CITY MUSEUM ... SILVER CITY, NM 165
SMOKI MUSEUM ... PRESCOTT, AZ 89
TINKERTOWN MUSEUM ... ALBUQUERQUE, NM 135
TITAN MISSILE MUSEUM ... GREEN VALLEY, AZ 111
TUCSON CHILDREN'S MUSEUM ... TUCSON, AZ 107
TUCSON MUSEUM OF ART AND HISTORIC BLOCK ... TUCSON, AZ 107
TUCUMCARI HISTORICAL MUSEUM ... TUCUMCARI, NM 168
TULAROSA BASIN HISTORICAL SOCIETY MUSEUM ... ALAMOGORDO, NM 131
*TUMACACORI NHP ... AZ 113
TUNSTALL MUSEUM ... LINCOLN, NM 153
THE TURQUOISE MUSEUM ... ALBUQUERQUE, NM 136
*TUSAYAN RUIN AND MUSEUM ... GRAND CANYON NP, AZ 57
*TUZIGOOT NMO ... AZ 113
UNIVERSITY MUSEUM ... LAS CRUCES, NM 152
UNIVERSITY OF ARIZONA MUSEUM OF ART ... TUCSON, AZ 108
VISITOR CENTER ... CHACO CULTURE NHP, NM 142
*VISITOR CENTER ... GRAND CANYON NP, AZ 55
*WALNUT CANYON NMO ... AZ 113
*WAR EAGLES AIR MUSEUM ... SANTA TERESA, NM 164
WESTERN NEW MEXICO UNIVERSITY MUSEUM ... SILVER CITY, NM 165
WHEELWRIGHT MUSEUM OF THE AMERICAN INDIAN ... SANTA FE, NM 163
YAVAPAI OBSERVATION STATION ... GRAND CANYON NP, AZ 57
YUMA TERRITORIAL PRISON SHP ... YUMA, AZ 118

MUSIC HALLS & OPERA HOUSES
CENTENNIAL HALL ... TUCSON, AZ 111
SANTA FE OPERA ... SANTA FE, NM 162

NATURAL BRIDGES
RAINBOW BRIDGE NMO ... GLEN CANYON NRA, AZ 51
TONTO NATURAL BRIDGE SP ... PAYSON, AZ 67

NATURAL PHENOMENA
AIRPORT HILL ... SEDONA, AZ 93
ARIZONA STATE UNIVERSITY MUSEUM OF GEOLOGY ... TEMPE, AZ 87
BELL ROCK ... SEDONA, AZ 93
BOYNTON CREEK ... SEDONA, AZ 93
CATHEDRAL ROCK ... SEDONA, AZ 93

NATURE CENTERS
RIO GRANDE NATURE CENTER SP ... ALBUQUERQUE, NM 135

NATURE TRAILS
BOSQUE DEL APACHE NWR ... SAN ANTONIO, NM 158
*BOYCE THOMPSON ARBORETUM SP ... SUPERIOR, AZ 97
BRIGHT ANGEL TRAIL ... GRAND CANYON NP, AZ 56
*CARLSBAD CAVERNS NP ... NM 139
LAS VEGAS NWR ... LAS VEGAS, NM 152
NORTH KAIBAB TRAIL ... GRAND CANYON NP, AZ 58
NORTH MOUNTAIN PARK ... PHOENIX, AZ 77
OLIVER LEE MEMORIAL SP ... ALAMOGORDO, NM 132
PANCHO VILLA SP ... COLUMBUS, NM 145
PAPAGO PARK ... PHOENIX, AZ 77
RIM TRAIL ... GRAND CANYON NP, AZ 57
SANDIA CREST ... CIBOLA NF, NM 144
SANTA ROSA LAKE SP ... SANTA ROSA, NM 164
SMOKEY BEAR HISTORICAL SP ... CAPITAN, NM 138
SOUTH KAIBAB TRAIL ... GRAND CANYON NP, AZ 57
SUNSET CRATER VOLCANO NMO ... AZ 96
TOHONO CHUL PARK ... TUCSON, AZ 107

OBSERVATORIES
FLANDRAU SCIENCE CENTER & PLANETARIUM ... TUCSON, AZ 108
KITT PEAK NATIONAL OBSERVATORY ... TUCSON, AZ 105
LOWELL OBSERVATORY ... FLAGSTAFF, AZ 49
NATIONAL SOLAR OBSERVATORY ... SUNSPOT, NM 166
VERY LARGE ARRAY (VLA)—RADIO TELESCOPE ... SOCORRO, NM 165
WHIPPLE OBSERVATORY ... CORONADO NF, AZ 46

PAINTINGS
*ROSWELL MUSEUM AND ART CENTER ... ROSWELL, NM 156
THE SHADOW OF THE CROSS ... TAOS, NM 167

PARKS, CITY; STATE; PROVINCIAL
ALAMEDA PARK AND ZOO ... ALAMOGORDO, NM 132
ALAMO LAKE SP ... WENDEN, AZ 114
ANGEL PEAK RECREATION AREA ... FARMINGTON, NM 148
BILL WILLIAMS RIVER NWR ... LAKE HAVASU CITY, AZ 61
BOTTOMLESS LAKES SP ... ROSWELL, NM 156
BUCKSKIN MOUNTAIN SP & RIVER ISLAND UNIT ... PARKER, AZ 66
CATALINA SP ... TUCSON, AZ 105
CATTAIL COVE SP ... LAKE HAVASU CITY, AZ 61
CITY OF ROCKS SP ... DEMING, NM 146
CLAYTON LAKE SP ... CLAYTON, NM 145
COCHITI LAKE ... DOMINGO, NM 146
DEAD HORSE RANCH SP ... COTTONWOOD, AZ 47
ENCANTO PARK ... PHOENIX, AZ 76
ESTRELLA MOUNTAIN REGIONAL PARK ... GOODYEAR, AZ 83
FOOL HOLLOW LAKE RECREATION AREA ... SHOW LOW, AZ 96
FORT VERDE SHP ... CAMP VERDE, AZ 44
GENE C. REID PARK ... TUCSON, AZ 105
HILLCREST PARK ... CLOVIS, NM 145
HUALAPAI MOUNTAIN PARK ... KINGMAN, AZ 60
HYDE MEMORIAL SP ... SANTA FE, NM 160
JANES-WALLACE MEMORIAL PARK ... SANTA ROSA, NM 164
JEROME SHP ... JEROME, AZ 59
KIT CARSON PARK ... TAOS, NM 167
LAKE HAVASU SP ... LAKE HAVASU CITY, AZ 61
LAKE PLEASANT REGIONAL PARK ... PEORIA, AZ 84
LIVING DESERT ZOO & GARDENS ... CARLSBAD, NM 139
LOST DUTCHMAN SP ... APACHE JUNCTION, AZ 82
LYMAN LAKE SP ... ST. JOHNS, AZ 92
MCFARLAND SHP ... FLORENCE, AZ 49
*MONUMENT VALLEY NAVAJO TRIBAL PARK ... AZ 63
MORPHY LAKE ... LAS VEGAS, NM 152
NAMBE FALLS RECREATION AREA ... ESPANOLA, NM 147
NAVAJO LAKE SP ... BLOOMFIELD, NM 138
NORTH MOUNTAIN PARK ... PHOENIX, AZ 77
OASIS SP ... PORTALES, NM 155
OLIVER LEE MEMORIAL SP ... ALAMOGORDO, NM 132
PANCHO VILLA SP ... COLUMBUS, NM 145
PAPAGO PARK ... PHOENIX, AZ 77
PATAGONIA LAKE SP ... PATAGONIA, AZ 67
PERCH LAKE ... SANTA ROSA, NM 164
PICACHO PEAK SP ... PICACHO, AZ 88
RED ROCK SP ... GALLUP, NM 149
RED ROCK SP ... SEDONA, AZ 94
RIO GRANDE NATURE CENTER SP ... ALBUQUERQUE, NM 135
RIORDAN MANSION SHP ... FLAGSTAFF, AZ 49
ROCKHOUND SP ... DEMING, NM 146
ROPER LAKE SP ... SAFFORD, AZ 91
SANTA ROSA LAKE SP ... SANTA ROSA, NM 164
SENTINEL PEAK PARK ... TUCSON, AZ 107
SLIDE ROCK SP ... SEDONA, AZ 95
SMOKEY BEAR HISTORICAL SP ... CAPITAN, NM 138
SOUTH MOUNTAIN PARK ... PHOENIX, AZ 78
*SPACE CENTER ... ALAMOGORDO, NM 132
SPRING RIVER PARK AND ZOO ... ROSWELL, NM 157
STORRIE LAKE ... LAS VEGAS, NM 152
SUGARITE CANYON SP ... RATON, NM 156
TOHONO CHUL PARK ... TUCSON, AZ 107
TOMBSTONE COURTHOUSE SHP ... TOMBSTONE, AZ 98
TONTO NATURAL BRIDGE SP ... PAYSON, AZ 67
TUBAC PRESIDIO SHP ... TUBAC, AZ 99
*TUCSON MOUNTAIN PARK ... TUCSON, AZ 107
VALLE VIDAL PARK ... CIMARRON, NM 144
VALLEY OF FIRES RECREATION AREA ... CARRIZOZO, NM 141
YUMA CROSSING SHP ... YUMA, AZ 118
YUMA TERRITORIAL PRISON SHP ... YUMA, AZ 118

PARKS, NATIONAL
*CARLSBAD CAVERNS NP ... NM 139
CHACO CULTURE NHP ... NM 142
*GLEN CANYON NRA ... AZ 50
*GRAND CANYON NP ... AZ 52
*LAKE MEAD NRA ... AZ 61
PECOS NHP ... NM 155
*PETRIFIED FOREST NP ... AZ 68
*SAGUARO NP ... AZ 111
SANTA CRUZ DE TERRENATE PRESIDIO NHS ... AZ 92
*TOMBSTONE ... AZ 97
*TUMACACORI NHP ... AZ 113

PLANETARIUMS
CLYDE W. TOMBAUGH IMAX DOME THEATER AND PLANETARIUM ... ALAMOGORDO, NM 132
DOME THEATER ... TUCSON, AZ 108
FLANDRAU SCIENCE CENTER & PLANETARIUM ... TUCSON, AZ 108

RACETRACKS-AUTO
FIREBIRD RACEWAY ... PHOENIX, AZ 79
PHOENIX INTERNATIONAL RACEWAY ... PHOENIX, AZ 79

RACETRACKS-DOGS
PHOENIX GREYHOUND PARK ... PHOENIX, AZ 79
TUCSON GREYHOUND PARK ... TUCSON, AZ 110

RACETRACKS-HORSE
PRESCOTT DOWNS ... PRESCOTT, AZ 89
RUIDOSO DOWNS ... RUIDOSO DOWNS, NM 157
TURF PARADISE ... PHOENIX, AZ 79

RAILROADS
*CUMBRES AND TOLTEC SCENIC RAILROAD ... CHAMA, NM 142
DENVER AND RIO GRANDE WESTERN RAILROAD ... ESPANOLA, NM 147
GRAND CANYON RAILWAY ... WILLIAMS, AZ 115
SAN PEDRO & SOUTHWESTERN RAILROAD ... BENSON, AZ 41
SANTA FE SOUTHERN RAILWAY ... SANTA FE, NM 162
VERDE CANYON RAILROAD ... CLARKDALE, AZ 45

RAILROADS-LOCOMOTIVES & CARS
GRAND CANYON RAILWAY ... WILLIAMS, AZ 115
MCCORMICK-STILLMAN RAILROAD PARK ... SCOTTSDALE, AZ 85
TOY TRAIN DEPOT ... ALAMOGORDO, NM 132

RAILROADS & SKI LIFTS, CABLE; COG; INCLINE; NARROW GAUGE
GOLDFIELD GHOST TOWN & MINE TOURS ... APACHE JUNCTION, AZ 82
MCCORMICK-STILLMAN RAILROAD PARK ... SCOTTSDALE, AZ 85
*SANDIA PEAK AERIAL TRAMWAY ... CIBOLA NF, NM 144

RANCHES
DOUBLE D RANCH AND WAGON TRAIN CO. ... PAULDEN, AZ 67
KIOWA RANCH ... TAOS, NM 166
PHANTOM RANCH ... GRAND CANYON NP, AZ 57
PHILMONT SCOUT RANCH ... CIMARRON, NM 145
ROCKIN' R RANCH ... MESA, AZ 84

RECREATION-SUMMER ACTIVITIES
ABIQUIU LAKE ... ABIQUIU, NM 131
ANGEL FIRE ... NM 136
APACHE STABLES ... GRAND CANYON NP, AZ 56
APACHE-SITGREAVES NFS ... AZ 40
BOTTOMLESS LAKES SP ... ROSWELL, NM 156
CANYON LAKE ... PHOENIX, AZ 79
CARSON NF ... NM 141
CLOUDCROFT ... NM 145
COCHITI LAKE ... DOMINGO, NM 146
CONCHAS LAKE ... TUCUMCARI, NM 168
CORONADO NF ... AZ 46
DESERT JEEP AND BIKE RENTALS ... SEDONA, AZ 95
EL MALPAIS NMO AND NATIONAL CONSERVATION AREA ... GRANTS, NM 150
ENCANTO PARK ... PHOENIX, AZ 76
ESTRELLA MOUNTAIN REGIONAL PARK ... GOODYEAR, AZ 83
FAR FLUNG ADVENTURES ... PILAR, NM 155
GILA NF ... NM 149
IMPERIAL NWR ... YUMA, AZ 118
LAKE CARLSBAD ... CARLSBAD, NM 139
LAKE MEAD ... LAKE MEAD NRA, AZ 62
*LAKE MEAD NRA ... AZ 61
LAKE MOHAVE ... LAKE MEAD NRA, AZ 62
LOS RIOS RIVER RUNNERS ... TAOS, NM 168
MORPHY LAKE ... LAS VEGAS, NM 152
NATIVE SONS ADVENTURES ... TAOS, NM 168
NEW WAVE RAFTING CO. ... SANTA FE, NM 163
PAPAGO PARK ... PHOENIX, AZ 77
RIO GRANDE RAPID TRANSIT ... PILAR, NM 155
RUIDOSO ... NM 157
SAGUARO LAKE ... PHOENIX, AZ 79
SALT RIVER RECREATION ... MESA, AZ 84
SALT RIVER TUBING & RECREATION ... PHOENIX, AZ 79
SAN PEDRO RIPARIAN CONSERVATION AREA ... SIERRA VISTA, AZ 96

SANTA FE RAFTING CO. ... SANTA FE, NM 163
SEDONA JEEP RENTALS ... SEDONA, AZ 95
STORRIE LAKE ... LAS VEGAS, NM 152
TONTO NF ... AZ 98
UTE LAKE ... TUCUMCARI, NM 168
WATER SPORT CENTER INC. ... LAKE HAVASU CITY, AZ 61
WHEELER PEAK WILDERNESS AREA ... TAOS, NM 166

RECREATION-WINTER ACTIVITIES
ANGEL FIRE ... NM 136
APACHE-SITGREAVES NFS ... AZ 40
BILL WILLIAMS MOUNTAIN ... WILLIAMS, AZ 115
CARSON NF ... NM 141
CORONADO NF ... AZ 46
GILA NF ... NM 149
MOUNT LEMMON SKI VALLEY ... TUCSON, AZ 110
RUIDOSO ... NM 157
SANDIA CREST ... CIBOLA NF, NM 144
SANTA FE BASIN ... SANTA FE NF, NM 163
SKI APACHE ... RUIDOSO, NM 157
SNOWBOWL ... FLAGSTAFF, AZ 49
SUNRISE SKI AREA ... PINETOP-LAKESIDE, AZ 88
TAOS SKI VALLEY ... TAOS, NM 168

RESEARCH ORGANIZATIONS
BIOSPHERE 2 CENTER ... ORACLE, AZ 111
CLAYTON LIVESTOCK RESEARCH CENTER ... CLAYTON, NM 145
COSANTI FOUNDATION ... SCOTTSDALE, AZ 85
INTERNATIONAL UFO MUSEUM & RESEARCH CENTER ... ROSWELL, NM 156
LOS ALAMOS NATIONAL LABORATORY ... LOS ALAMOS, NM 153
RAVEN SITE RUIN ... SPRINGERVILLE, AZ 96
SAN JUAN COUNTY ARCHAEOLOGICAL RESEARCH CENTER AND LIBRARY ... BLOOMFIELD, NM 138

RESTORED VILLAGES & SETTLEMENTS
CASA MALPAIS PUEBLO ... SPRINGERVILLE, AZ 96
GILA RIVER CULTURAL CENTER ... SACATON, AZ 91
OLD TUCSON STUDIOS ... TUCSON, AZ 106
PIONEER ARIZONA LIVING HISTORY MUSEUM ... PHOENIX, AZ 78
RAWHIDE ... SCOTTSDALE, AZ 85

RIVERS
SALT RIVER ... APACHE JUNCTION, AZ 81
SAN JUAN RIVER ... FARMINGTON, NM 148

ROCKS
ARIZONA STATE UNIVERSITY MUSEUM OF GEOLOGY ... TEMPE, AZ 87
INSCRIPTION ROCK ... EL MORRO NMO, NM 146
METEORITE MUSEUM ... ALBUQUERQUE, NM 136
MINERAL MUSEUM ... SOCORRO, NM 165
*PETRIFIED FOREST NP ... AZ 68
ROCKHOUND SP ... DEMING, NM 146

RUINS
ANTELOPE HOUSE ... CANYON DE CHELLY NMO, AZ 44
*AZTEC RUINS NMO ... NM 137
*BANDELIER NMO ... NM 137
BESH-BA-GOWAH ARCHAEOLOGICAL PARK ... GLOBE, AZ 52
BETATAKIN AREA ... NAVAJO NMO, AZ 64
CANYON DE CHELLY ... CANYON DE CHELLY NMO, AZ 44
*CASA GRANDE RUINS NMO ... AZ 44
CASA MALPAIS PUEBLO ... SPRINGERVILLE, AZ 96
CHACO CULTURE NHP ... NM 142
CORONADO STATE MONUMENT ... BERNALILLO, NM 138
EL MALPAIS NMO AND NATIONAL CONSERVATION AREA ... GRANTS, NM 150
FORT APACHE HISTORIC PARK ... FORT APACHE, AZ 49
FORT UNION NMO ... NM 148
HOMOLOVI RUINS SP ... WINSLOW, AZ 116
KEET SEEL AREA ... NAVAJO NMO, AZ 64
KINISHBA RUINS ... WHITERIVER, AZ 114
LOS ALAMOS COUNTY HISTORICAL MUSEUM ... LOS ALAMOS, NM 154
MISSION SAN JOSE DE TUMACACORI ... TUMACACORI NHP, AZ 113
MONTEZUMA CASTLE ... MONTEZUMA CASTLE NMO, AZ 63
*MONTEZUMA CASTLE NMO ... AZ 63
MONTEZUMA WELL ... MONTEZUMA CASTLE NMO, AZ 63
MUMMY CAVE ... CANYON DE CHELLY NMO, AZ 44
*NAVAJO NMO ... AZ 64
PECOS NHP ... NM 155
PUEBLO GRANDE MUSEUM AND ARCHAEOLOGICAL PARK ... PHOENIX, AZ 78
PUERCO PUEBLO ... PETRIFIED FOREST NP, AZ 69
PUYE CLIFF DWELLINGS AND COMMUNAL HOUSE RUINS ... ESPANOLA, NM 147
RAVEN SITE RUIN ... SPRINGERVILLE, AZ 96
SALINAS PUEBLO MISSIONS NMO ... NM 157
SALMON RUIN ... BLOOMFIELD, NM 138
STANDING COW ... CANYON DE CHELLY NMO, AZ 44
TONTO NMO ... AZ 98
TUBAC PRESIDIO SHP ... TUBAC, AZ 99
*TUSAYAN RUIN AND MUSEUM ... GRAND CANYON NP, AZ 57
*TUZIGOOT NMO ... AZ 113
*WALNUT CANYON NMO ... AZ 113
WHITE HOUSE ... CANYON DE CHELLY NMO, AZ 44
*WUPATKI NMO ... AZ 117

SCENIC DRIVES
APACHE TRAIL ... APACHE JUNCTION, AZ 81
APACHE TRAIL (SR 88) ... GLOBE, AZ 52
APACHE TRAIL (SR 88) ... TONTO NF, AZ 98
APACHE-SITGREAVES NFS ... AZ 40
BAJADA LOOP DRIVE ... SAGUARO NP, AZ 112
BEELINE HIGHWAY (SR 87) ... TONTO NF, AZ 98
BLACK HILLS BACK COUNTRY BYWAY ... SAFFORD, AZ 91
CACTUS FOREST DRIVE ... SAGUARO NP, AZ 112
COCONINO NF ... AZ 46
CORONADO TRAIL SCENIC BYWAY ... APACHE-SITGREAVES NFS, AZ 40
DUNES DRIVE ... WHITE SANDS NMO, NM 169
ENCHANTED CIRCLE SCENIC BYWAY ... CARSON NF, NM 141
HIGH ROAD TO TAOS ... CHIMAY, NM 143
HISTORIC ROUTE 66 ... KINGMAN, AZ 60
I-25 ... ALBUQUERQUE, NM 133
I-40 ... ALBUQUERQUE, NM 133
INDIAN ROUTE 33 ... SHIPROCK, NM 164
INNER LOOP/GILA CLIFF DWELLINGS SCENIC BYWAY ... GILA NF, NM 150
INNER LOOP/GILA CLIFF DWELLINGS SCENIC BYWAY ... SILVER CITY, NM 165
KAIBAB PLATEAU-NORTH RIM SCENIC BYWAY ... KAIBAB NF, AZ 59
KELVIN HIGHWAY ... FLORENCE, AZ 49
LITTLE TESUQUE CANYON ... SANTA FE, NM 160
ONION SADDLE ROAD ... CORONADO NF, AZ 46
*PAINTED DESERT ... PETRIFIED FOREST NP, AZ 69
PINAL PIONEER PARKWAY ... FLORENCE, AZ 49
PRESCOTT NF ... AZ 90
ROUND MOUNTAIN ROCKHOUND AREA ... SAFFORD, AZ 91
RUBY ROAD ... CORONADO NF, AZ 46
RUCKER CANYON ROAD ... CORONADO NF, AZ 46
SANDIA CREST ROAD SCENIC BYWAY ... CIBOLA NF, NM 144
THE SANTA FE SCENIC BYWAY ... SANTA FE, NM 160
SCHULTZ PASS ROAD ... FLAGSTAFF, AZ 49
SKY ISLAND SCENIC BYWAY ... CORONADO NF, AZ 46
SOUTH MOUNTAIN PARK ... PHOENIX, AZ 78
SR 14 ... ALBUQUERQUE, NM 133
SR 44 ... ALBUQUERQUE, NM 133
SR 44 ... JEMEZ PUEBLO, NM 151
SR 63 ... SANTA FE NF, NM 163
SR 85 ... ORGAN PIPE CACTUS NMO, AZ 66
SR 89/89A ... FLAGSTAFF, AZ 49
SR 89A ... FLAGSTAFF, AZ 48
SR 89A ... JEROME, AZ 59
SR 91 ... SANTA ROSA, NM 164
SR 522 ... TAOS, NM 166
SRS 82 AND 83 ... CORONADO NF, AZ 46
SUNSPOT HIGHWAY ... LINCOLN NF, NM 153
SWIFT TRAIL ... CORONADO NF, AZ 46
TURQUOISE TRAIL ... ALBUQUERQUE, NM 133
TURQUOISE TRAIL ... CIBOLA NF, NM 144
TURQUOISE TRAIL ... SANTA FE, NM 160
US 60 ... GLOBE, AZ 52
US 60 ... SUPERIOR, AZ 97
US 64 ... CIMARRON, NM 144
US 64 ... TAOS, NM 166
US 163 ... KAYENTA, AZ 59
WALNUT CANYON DESERT DRIVE ... CARLSBAD CAVERNS NP, NM 140
WHITE MOUNTAINS SCENIC BYWAY ... APACHE-SITGREAVES NFS, AZ 40
YOUNG HIGHWAY (SR 288) ... TONTO NF, AZ 98

SCHOOL BUILDINGS
GAMMAGE MEMORIAL AUDITORIUM ... TEMPE, AZ 87

SCHOOLS
TALIESIN WEST ... SCOTTSDALE, AZ 85

SCHOOLS-COLLEGES & UNIVERSITIES
ARIZONA STATE UNIVERSITY ... TEMPE, AZ 86
ARIZONA STATE UNIVERSITY ... TEMPE, AZ 87
COLLEGE OF THE SOUTHWEST ... HOBBS, NM 150
EASTERN NEW MEXICO UNIVERSITY ... PORTALES, NM 155
EASTERN NEW MEXICO UNIVERSITY ... ROSWELL, NM 156
NEW MEXICO STATE UNIVERSITY ... LAS CRUCES, NM 152
SOUTHERN METHODIST UNIVERSITY ... TAOS, NM 166
THUNDERBIRD, THE AMERICAN GRADUATE SCHOOL OF INTERNATIONAL MANAGEMENT ... GLENDALE, AZ 83
UNIVERSITY OF ARIZONA ... TUCSON, AZ 107
UNIVERSITY OF NEW MEXICO ... ALBUQUERQUE, NM 136
WESTERN NEW MEXICO UNIVERSITY ... SILVER CITY, NM 165

SCHOOLS-INSTITUTES
NEW MEXICO INSTITUTE OF MINING AND TECHNOLOGY ... SOCORRO, NM 165
NEW MEXICO MILITARY INSTITUTE ... ROSWELL, NM 156

SELF-GUIDING TOURS
ABO ... SALINAS PUEBLO MISSIONS NMO, NM 157
ALBUQUERQUE ... NM 132
BITTER LAKE NWR ... ROSWELL, NM 156
*CARLSBAD CAVERNS NP ... NM 139
DOUGLAS ... AZ 47
FLAGSTAFF ... AZ 48
FORT UNION NMO ... NM 148
GILA CLIFF DWELLINGS NMO ... NM 149
*GLEN CANYON NRA ... AZ 50
GRAN QUIVIRA ... SALINAS PUEBLO MISSIONS NMO, NM 157
HOLBROOK ... AZ 58
LAS VEGAS ... NM 152
METROPOLITAN TUCSON CONVENTION AND VISITORS BUREAU ... TUCSON, AZ 109
NOGALES ... AZ 65
OLD TOWN ... SCOTTSDALE, AZ 85
*ORGAN PIPE CACTUS NMO ... AZ 66
ORPHEUM THEATRE ... PHOENIX, AZ 80
PRESCOTT ... AZ 88
PUEBLO GRANDE MUSEUM AND ARCHAEOLOGICAL PARK ... PHOENIX, AZ 78
QUARAI ... SALINAS PUEBLO MISSIONS NMO, NM 157
SCOTTSDALE ... AZ 85
SOCORRO ... NM 165
YUMA ... AZ 117

SHOPS, FIRMS & STORES
4TH AVENUE ... TUCSON, AZ 110
ARCADIA CROSSING ... PHOENIX, AZ 80
ARIZONA CENTER ... PHOENIX, AZ 80
ARIZONA FACTORY SHOPS ... PHOENIX, AZ 80
ARIZONA WILDWEAR ... TUCSON, AZ 11
ARROWHEAD TOWNE CENTER ... PHOENIX, AZ 80
ATKINSON'S HERMAN INDIAN TRADING POST ... PHOENIX, AZ 80
BILTMORE FASHION SQUARE ... PHOENIX, AZ 80
BORGATA OF SCOTTSDALE ... SCOTTSDALE, AZ 85
CANYON ROAD ... SANTA FE, NM 16
CHRIS-TOWN SHOPPING CENTER ... PHOENIX, AZ 80
CORONADO CENTER ... ALBUQUERQUE, NM 13
COTTONWOOD MALL ... ALBUQUERQUE, NM 13
DESERT SKY MALL ... PHOENIX, AZ 8
EL CON MALL ... TUCSON, AZ 11
EL MERCADO DE BOUTIQUES ... TUCSON, AZ 11
EL PEDREGAL ... CAREFREE, AZ 8
THE ENGLISH VILLAGE ... LAKE HAVASU CITY, AZ 6
FASHION SQUARE ... SCOTTSDALE, AZ 8
FIESTA MALL ... MESA, AZ 8
FIFTH AVENUE ... SCOTTSDALE, AZ 8
FLAGSTAFF MALL ... FLAGSTAFF, AZ 4
FOOTHILLS MALL ... TUCSON, AZ 11
GALLERIA PLAZA DEL CERRO ... CHIMAY, NM 14
GILBERT ORTEGA'S ... PHOENIX, AZ 8
GREY WOLF ... PHOENIX, AZ 8
HEARD MUSEUM SHOP ... PHOENIX, AZ 8
HISTORIC CATLIN COURT SHOPS DISTRICT ... GLENDALE, AZ 8
INDIAN PUEBLO CULTURAL CENTER ... ALBUQUERQUE, NM 13
ISLAND FASHION MALL ... LAKE HAVASU CITY, AZ 6

LA MESILLA STATE MONUMENT ... MESILLA, NM 154
LONDON SHOPPING CENTER ... LAKE HAVASU CITY, AZ 61
LOS PORTALES ... CAREFREE, AZ 82
MESA MARKET PLACE AND SWAP MEET ... MESA, AZ 83
METROCENTER ... PHOENIX, AZ 80
OAK CREEK FACTORY OUTLET ... SEDONA, AZ 93
OLD BISBEE ... BISBEE, AZ 43
OLD PUEBLO MUSEUM ... TUCSON, AZ 110
OLD TOWN ... SCOTTSDALE, AZ 85
OLD TOWN ARTISANS ... TUCSON, AZ 110
OLD TOWN TEMPE ... TEMPE, AZ 87
OLD TOWNE GLENDALE ... GLENDALE, AZ 83
PARADISE VALLEY MALL ... PHOENIX, AZ 80
PARK MALL ... TUCSON, AZ 110
PARK 'N' SWAP ... PHOENIX, AZ 80
SANTA FE FACTORY STORES ... SANTA FE, NM 160
SANTO DOMINGO TRADING POST ... DOMINGO, NM 146
SHAMBLES VILLAGES ... LAKE HAVASU CITY, AZ 61
SPANISH VILLAGE ... CAREFREE, AZ 82
SUPERSTITION SPRINGS CENTER ... MESA, AZ 83
SWAPMART ... PHOENIX, AZ 80
TANQUE VERDE SWAP MEET ... TUCSON, AZ 110
TLAQUEPAQUE ... SEDONA, AZ 92
TLAQUEPAQUE ... SEDONA, AZ 93
TOWER PLAZA ... PHOENIX, AZ 80
TOWN & COUNTRY SHOPPING CENTER ... PHOENIX, AZ 80
TUCSON MALL ... TUCSON, AZ 110
VF FACTORY OUTLET MALL ... MESA, AZ 83
WARREN MALL ... CAREFREE, AZ 82
WHISKEY ROW/COURTHOUSE SQUARE ... PRESCOTT, AZ 89
WIGWAM OUTLET STORES ... PHOENIX, AZ 80

SIGHTSEEING-AIRCRAFT RIDES & TOURS
A AEROZONA ADVENTURE INC. ... PHOENIX, AZ 80
AIR GRAND CANYON ... GRAND CANYON NP, AZ 54
AIRSTAR HELICOPTERS ... GRAND CANYON NP, AZ 54
ARIZONA HELICOPTER ADVENTURES ... SEDONA, AZ 93
GRAND CANYON AIRLINES ... GRAND CANYON NP, AZ 54
★GRAND CANYON NP ... AZ 52
HOT AIR EXPEDITIONS ... PHOENIX, AZ 80
KENAI HELICOPTERS GRAND CANYON ... GRAND CANYON NP, AZ 54
NORTHERN LIGHT BALLOON EXPEDITIONS ... SEDONA, AZ 93
PAGE ... AZ 66
PAPILLON GRAND CANYON HELICOPTERS ... GRAND CANYON NP, AZ 54
RED ROCK BALLOON ADVENTURES ... SEDONA, AZ 93
RED ROCK BI-PLANE TOURS AND AIR SAFARI ... SEDONA, AZ 94
SKY HIGH BALLOON ADVENTURES ... COTTONWOOD, AZ 47
SUNRISE AIRLINES ... PHOENIX, AZ 78
UNICORN BALLOON CO. ... PHOENIX, AZ 80

SIGHTSEEING TOURS
ABOOT ABOUT/SANTA FE WALKS ... SANTA FE, NM 160
AFOOT IN SANTA FE ... SANTA FE, NM 160
AJO STAGE LINES ... AJO, AZ 40
APACHE STABLES ... GRAND CANYON NP, AZ 56
ARIZONA DESERT MOUNTAIN JEEP TOURS ... PHOENIX, AZ 78
ASARCO MINERAL DISCOVERY CENTER ... SAHUARITA, AZ 112
BIG RED JEEP TOURS ... PHOENIX, AZ 78
★CANYON DE CHELLY NMO ... AZ 44
★CUMBRES AND TOLTEC SCENIC RAILROAD ... CHAMA, NM 142
DESERT JEEP AND BIKE RENTALS ... SEDONA, AZ 95
DON DONNELLY HORSEBACK VACATIONS AND STABLES ... APACHE JUNCTION, AZ 82
DOUBLE D RANCH AND WAGON TRAIN CO. ... PAULDEN, AZ 67
FLAGSTAFF ... AZ 48
★GLEN CANYON NRA ... AZ 50
GOLDFIELD GHOST TOWN & MINE TOURS ... APACHE JUNCTION, AZ 82
GRAND CANYON JEEP TOURS & SAFARIS ... GRAND CANYON NP, AZ 55
★GRAND CANYON NP ... AZ 52
GRAND CANYON RAILWAY ... WILLIAMS, AZ 115
GRAND CANYON TOURS ... PHOENIX, AZ 78
GRAND CANYON WILD WEST TOURS ... SEDONA, AZ 93
GRAY LINE ... FLAGSTAFF, AZ 48
GRAY LINE TOURS ... TUCSON, AZ 109
GREAT VENTURES CHARTER TOURS ... SEDONA, AZ 93
GUIDED CAVE TOURS ... CARLSBAD CAVERNS NP, NM 140
★HOOVER DAM ... LAKE MEAD NRA, AZ 62
KAYENTA ... AZ 59
LORETTO LINE ... SANTA FE, NM 160
★MONUMENT VALLEY NAVAJO TRIBAL PARK ... AZ 63
MULEBACK TRIPS ... GRAND CANYON NP, AZ 55
NORTH RIM ... GRAND CANYON NP, AZ 55
OLD PUEBLO TOURS ... TUCSON, AZ 109
★ORGAN PIPE CACTUS NMO ... AZ 66
OUTBACK OFF-ROAD ADVENTURES INC. ... LAKE HAVASU CITY, AZ 61
PINK JEEP TOURS ... SEDONA, AZ 93
RAWHIDE LAND AND CATTLE COMPANY JEEP TOURS ... CAREFREE, AZ 82
SABINO CANYON TOURS ... TUCSON, AZ 106
★SAGUARO NP ... AZ 111
SAN PEDRO & SOUTHWESTERN RAILROAD ... BENSON, AZ 41
SANTA FE SOUTHERN RAILWAY ... SANTA FE, NM 162
SCOTTSDALE JEEP RENTALS ... SCOTTSDALE, AZ 86
SEDONA ADVENTURES ... SEDONA, AZ 93
SEDONA JEEP RENTALS ... SEDONA, AZ 95
SEDONA RED ROCK JEEP TOURS ... SEDONA, AZ 93
SEDONA TROLLEY ... SEDONA, AZ 93
SOUTH RIM ... GRAND CANYON NP, AZ 55
SOUTHWEST SAFARIS ... SANTA FE, NM 162
SURFACE MINE AND HISTORIC DISTRICT VAN TOUR ... BISBEE, AZ 43
TAOS HISTORIC WALKS ... TAOS, NM 166
VERDE CANYON RAILROAD ... CLARKDALE, AZ 45
WAYWARD WIND TOURS INC. ... PHOENIX, AZ 78

SIGHTSEEING TOURS-BOATS
BLUE WATER CHARTERS ... LAKE HAVASU CITY, AZ 60
DESERT PRINCESS ... LAKE MEAD NRA, AZ 62
LONDON BRIDGE WATERCRAFT TOURS ... LAKE HAVASU CITY, AZ 60
PAGE ... AZ 66

SIGHTSEEING TOURS-HOUSE & GARDEN
HOME TOUR ... JEROME, AZ 59

SIGHTSEEING TOURS-RAFTING & CANOEING
MAE'S MILD TO WILD RAFTING ... CAMP VERDE, AZ 44
MAE'S MILD TO WILD RAFTING ... GLOBE, AZ 52
FAR FLUNG ADVENTURES ... GLOBE, AZ 52
★GRAND CANYON NP ... AZ 52
PAGE ... AZ 66
RAFT TRIPS ... GRAND CANYON NP, AZ 56

SOUND & LIGHT PRESENTATIONS
CLYDE W. TOMBAUGH IMAX DOME THEATER AND PLANETARIUM ... ALAMOGORDO, NM 132
★WHITE SANDS NMO ... NM 169

SPORTS ARENAS
AMERICA WEST ARENA ... PHOENIX, AZ 79
ARIZONA STADIUM ... TUCSON, AZ 110
ARIZONA VETERAN'S MEMORIAL COLISEUM ... PHOENIX, AZ 79
COMMUNITY CENTER ... TUCSON, AZ 101
HO HO KAM PARK ... PHOENIX, AZ 79
MARYVALE SPORTS COMPLEX ... PHOENIX, AZ 79
MCKALE CENTER ... TUCSON, AZ 110
PEORIA SPORTS COMPLEX ... PHOENIX, AZ 79
PHOENIX MUNICIPAL STADIUM ... PHOENIX, AZ 79
SCOTTSDALE STADIUM ... PHOENIX, AZ 79
SUN DEVIL STADIUM ... TEMPE, AZ 87
TEMPE DIABLO STADIUM ... PHOENIX, AZ 79
TUCSON ELECTRIC PARK ... TUCSON, AZ 110
U S WEST SPORTS COMPLEX AT HI CORBETT FIELD ... TUCSON, AZ 110

SPRINGS
BLUE HOLE ... SANTA ROSA, NM 163
OJO CALIENTE ... OJO CALIENTE, NM 154

STREETS, PLAZAS, SQUARES, CITY AREAS
ARCOSANTI ... CORDES JUNCTION, AZ 46
EL PRESIDIO HISTORIC DISTRICT ... TUCSON, AZ 107
HERITAGE AND SCIENCE PARK ... PHOENIX, AZ 77
LA PLACITA VILLAGE ... TUCSON, AZ 101
OLD BISBEE ... BISBEE, AZ 43
★OLD TOWN ... ALBUQUERQUE, NM 135
OLD TOWN PLAZA PARK ... LAS VEGAS, NM 152
SAN BUENAVENTURA DE CHIMAYO ... CHIMAY, NM 143
SUN CITY WEST ... SUN CITY/SUN CITY WEST, AZ 86
TLAQUEPAQUE ... SEDONA, AZ 92

THEATERS-BUILDINGS
ARIZONA THEATER CO. ... PHOENIX, AZ 80
BIRD CAGE THEATRE ... TOMBSTONE, AZ 97
CLYDE W. TOMBAUGH IMAX DOME THEATER AND PLANETARIUM ... ALAMOGORDO, NM 132
DOME THEATER ... TUCSON, AZ 108
GAMMAGE MEMORIAL AUDITORIUM ... TEMPE, AZ 87
GASLIGHT THEATRE ... TUCSON, AZ 110
GRAND CANYON IMAX THEATER ... GRAND CANYON NP, AZ 56
HERBERGER THEATER ... PHOENIX, AZ 80
IMAX THEATER ... SCOTTSDALE, AZ 85
IMAX THEATER AT ARIZONA MILLS ... TEMPE, AZ 87
THE INVISIBLE THEATRE ... TUCSON, AZ 110
ORPHEUM THEATRE ... PHOENIX, AZ 80
PHOENIX THEATRE ... PHOENIX, AZ 80
SEDONA SUPERVUE THEATER ... SEDONA, AZ 95
STAGEBRUSH THEATER ... PHOENIX, AZ 80
TEMPLE OF MUSIC AND ART ... TUCSON, AZ 110
THEATERWORKS ... PHOENIX, AZ 80

THEATERS-PLAYS, DRAMAS & MUSICALS
BLACK RIVER TRADERS ... FARMINGTON, NM 148
HISTORAMA ... TOMBSTONE, AZ 98
PASSION PLAY ... MESA, AZ 84

TOWERS
WATCHTOWER ... GRAND CANYON NP, AZ 57

TREES
CORONADO NF ... AZ 46
MESQUITE JAIL TREE ... WICKENBURG, AZ 114

VIEWS
BRIGHT ANGEL TRAIL ... GRAND CANYON NP, AZ 56
CAPE ROYAL ... GRAND CANYON NP, AZ 58
CORONADO PEAK ... CORONADO NME, AZ 47
DOBBINS LOOKOUT ... PHOENIX, AZ 78
FIVE POINTS VISTA ... LINCOLN NF, NM 153
★GRAND CANYON NP ... AZ 52
KACHINA POINT ... PETRIFIED FOREST NP, AZ 68
LIPAN POINT ... GRAND CANYON NP, AZ 57
MARBLE CANYON ... GRAND CANYON NP, AZ 58
MASSAI POINT ... CHIRICAHUA NMO, AZ 45
MONTEZUMA PASS ... CORONADO NME, AZ 47
NORTH RIM ... GRAND CANYON NP, AZ 57
PARKER DAM AND POWER PLANT ... PARKER, AZ 66
PINTADO POINT ... PETRIFIED FOREST NP, AZ 68
POINT IMPERIAL ... GRAND CANYON NP, AZ 58
ROSE PEAK ... APACHE-SITGREAVES NFS, AZ 40
SANDIA CREST ... CIBOLA NF, NM 144
SENTINEL PEAK PARK ... TUCSON, AZ 107
SOUTH KAIBAB TRAIL ... GRAND CANYON NP, AZ 57
SOUTH RIM ... GRAND CANYON NP, AZ 56
SWIFT TRAIL ... SAFFORD, AZ 91
TOROWEAP OVERLOOK ... GRAND CANYON NP, AZ 58
★VIETNAM VETERANS NME ... ANGEL FIRE, NM 136
VISTA ENCANTADA ... GRAND CANYON NP, AZ 58
WATCHTOWER ... GRAND CANYON NP, AZ 57
YAVAPAI OBSERVATION STATION ... GRAND CANYON NP, AZ 57

VISITOR CENTERS
ALAN BIBLE VISITOR CENTER ... LAKE MEAD NRA, AZ 62
APACHE-SITGREAVES NFS ... AZ 40
ARIZONA TEMPLE VISITOR CENTER ... MESA, AZ 84
BOSQUE DEL APACHE NWR ... SAN ANTONIO, NM 158
BULLFROG VISITOR CENTER ... GLEN CANYON NRA, AZ 51
★CANYON DE CHELLY NMO ... AZ 44
CARL HAYDEN VISITOR CENTER ... GLEN CANYON NRA, AZ 51
★CASA GRANDE RUINS NMO ... AZ 44
CASA MALPAIS PUEBLO ... SPRINGERVILLE, AZ 96
★CHIRICAHUA NMO ... AZ 45
EL MALPAIS NMO AND NATIONAL CONSERVATION AREA ... GRANTS, NM 150
FORT UNION NMO ... NM 148
GILA VISITOR CENTER ... GILA NF, NM 150
★GRAND CANYON NP ... AZ 52
HOMOLOVI RUINS SP ... WINSLOW, AZ 116
HOOVER DAM VISITOR CENTER ... LAKE MEAD NRA, AZ 62
METEOR CRATER ... WINSLOW, AZ 116
★MONTEZUMA CASTLE NMO ... AZ 63
★MONUMENT VALLEY NAVAJO TRIBAL PARK ... AZ 63
NAVAJO BRIDGE INTERPRETIVE CENTER ... GLEN CANYON NRA, AZ 51
★NAVAJO NMO ... AZ 64
OLD FORT BOWIE NHS ... WILLCOX, AZ 114

OLIVER LEE MEMORIAL SP ... ALAMOGORDO, NM 132
*ORGAN PIPE CACTUS NMO ... AZ 66
PAINTED DESERT VISITOR CENTER ... PETRIFIED FOREST NP, AZ 69
*SAGUARO NP ... AZ 111
SALINAS PUEBLO MISSIONS NMO ... NM 157
SMOKEY BEAR HISTORICAL SP ... CAPITAN, NM 138
SUNSET CRATER VOLCANO NMO ... AZ 96
TONTO NMO ... AZ 98
UNIVERSITY OF ARIZONA ... TUCSON, AZ 107
*VIETNAM VETERANS NME ... ANGEL FIRE, NM 136
VISITOR CENTER ... CHACO CULTURE NHP, NM 142
VISITOR CENTER ... GANADO, AZ 50
*VISITOR CENTER ... GRAND CANYON NP, AZ 55
*WALNUT CANYON NMO ... AZ 113
*WUPATKI NMO ... AZ 117

VISITOR INFORMATION
AJO ... AZ 40
ALAMOGORDO ... NM 131
ALBUQUERQUE ... NM 132
ANGEL FIRE ... NM 136
APACHE JUNCTION ... AZ 81
ARTESIA ... NM 136
AZTEC ... NM 137
BERNALILLO ... NM 138
BISBEE ... AZ 43
BLOOMFIELD ... NM 138
BULLHEAD CITY ... AZ 43
CAMP VERDE ... AZ 43
CAPITAN ... NM 138
CAREFREE ... AZ 82
CARLSBAD ... NM 139
CARRIZOZO ... NM 141
CASA GRANDE ... AZ 44
CHAMA ... NM 142
CIMARRON ... NM 144
CLAYTON ... NM 145
CLOUDCROFT ... NM 145
CLOVIS ... NM 145
COTTONWOOD ... AZ 47
DEMING ... NM 146
DOUGLAS ... AZ 47
FARMINGTON ... NM 147
FLAGSTAFF ... AZ 48
FLORENCE ... AZ 49
FORT SUMNER ... NM 148
FOUNTAIN HILLS ... AZ 82
GALLUP ... NM 149
GILA BEND ... AZ 50
GLENDALE ... AZ 83
GLOBE ... AZ 52
GOODYEAR ... AZ 83
*GRAND CANYON NP ... AZ 52
GRANTS ... NM 150
GREEN VALLEY ... AZ 111
HOBBS ... NM 150
HOLBROOK ... AZ 58
JEROME ... AZ 58
KINGMAN ... AZ 59
LAKE HAVASU CITY ... AZ 60
LAS CRUCES ... NM 152
LAS VEGAS ... NM 152
LOS ALAMOS ... NM 153
MARICOPA ... AZ 63
MESA ... AZ 83
NAVAJOLAND ... AZ 64
NOGALES ... AZ 65
PAGE ... AZ 66
PARKER ... AZ 66
PAYSON ... AZ 67
PEARCE ... AZ 68
PINETOP-LAKESIDE ... AZ 88
PINOS ALTOS ... NM 155
PORTALES ... NM 155
PRESCOTT ... AZ 88
QUARTZSITE ... AZ 90
RATON ... NM 155
ROSWELL ... NM 156
RUIDOSO ... NM 157
SAFFORD ... AZ 91
SANTA FE ... NM 158
SANTA ROSA ... NM 163
SCOTTSDALE ... AZ 85
SEDONA ... AZ 92
SHOW LOW ... AZ 96
SIERRA VISTA ... AZ 96
SILVER CITY ... NM 165
SOCORRO ... NM 165
SPRINGER ... NM 166
SPRINGERVILLE ... AZ 96
SUN CITY/SUN CITY WEST ... AZ 86
SUPERIOR ... AZ 97
TAOS ... NM 166
TEMPE ... AZ 86
*TOMBSTONE ... AZ 97
TRUTH OR CONSEQUENCES ... NM 168
TUBAC ... AZ 99
TUCUMCARI ... NM 168
WICKENBURG ... AZ 114
WILLCOX ... AZ 114
WILLIAMS ... AZ 115
WINDOW ROCK ... AZ 115
WINSLOW ... AZ 116
YARNELL ... AZ 117
YUMA ... AZ 117

WALKING TOURS
ARIZONA STATE UNIVERSITY ... TEMPE, AZ 87
CORONADO NME ... AZ 47
FLAGSTAFF ... AZ 48
*GLEN CANYON NRA ... AZ 50
METROPOLITAN TUCSON CONVENTION AND VISITORS BUREAU ... TUCSON, AZ 109
NOGALES ... AZ 65
OLD TOWN ... SCOTTSDALE, AZ 85
PRESCOTT ... AZ 88
SCOTTSDALE ... AZ 85
SOSA-CARILLO-FREMONT HOUSE ... TUCSON, AZ 107

WATERFALLS
HAVASU FALLS ... SUPAI, AZ 97
NAMBE FALLS ... ESPANOLA, NM 147
SITTING BULL FALLS PICNIC AREA ... LINCOLN NF, NM 153

WATER PARKS
BIG SURF ... TEMPE, AZ 87
GOLFLAND/SUNSPLASH ... MESA, AZ 84
WATERWORLD SAFARI ... PHOENIX, AZ 78

WILDERNESS AREAS
ALDO LEOPOLD ... GILA NF, NM 149
APACHE KID ... CIBOLA NF, NM 144
BIOSPHERE 2 CENTER ... ORACLE, AZ 111
BISTI/DE-NA-ZIN WILDERNESS ... FARMINGTON, NM 148
BLUE RANGE ... GILA NF, NM 149
CHAMA WILDERNESS ... SANTA FE NF, NM 163
CRUCES BASIN ... CARSON NF, NM 141
DOME WILDERNESS ... SANTA FE NF, NM 163
EL MALPAIS NMO AND NATIONAL CONSERVATION AREA ... GRANTS, NM 150
GILA WILDERNESS ... GILA NF, NM 149
HAVASU WILDERNESS AREA ... LAKE HAVASU CITY, AZ 61
LATIR PEAK ... CARSON NF, NM 141
MANZANO ... CIBOLA NF, NM 144
PAINTED DESERT ... PETRIFIED FOREST NP, AZ 69
PATAGONIA-SONOITA CREEK PRESERVE ... PATAGONIA, AZ 67
PECOS AND CHAMA ... CARSON NF, NM 141
PECOS WILDERNESS ... SANTA FE NF, NM 163
RIO GRANDE WILD RIVER ... CARSON NF, NM 141
SALT CREEK WILDERNESS ... ROSWELL, NM 156
SAN PEDRO PARKS WILDERNESS ... SANTA FE NF, NM 163
SANDIA ... CIBOLA NF, NM 144
TUWEEP AREA ... GRAND CANYON NP, AZ 58
WHEELER PEAK ... CARSON NF, NM 141
WHEELER PEAK WILDERNESS AREA ... TAOS, NM 166
THE WITHINGTON ... CIBOLA NF, NM 144

WILDLIFE SANCTUARIES
BILL WILLIAMS RIVER NWR ... LAKE HAVASU CITY, AZ 61
BITTER LAKE NWR ... ROSWELL, NM 156
BOSQUE DEL APACHE NWR ... SAN ANTONIO, NM 158
BUENOS AIRES NWR ... SASABE, AZ 92
CABEZA PRIETA NWR ... AJO, AZ 40
GRAND CANYON NATIONAL GAME PRESERVE ... KAIBAB NF, AZ 59
HAVASU NWR ... LAKE HAVASU CITY, AZ 61
IMPERIAL NWR ... YUMA, AZ 118
KOFA NWR ... QUARTZSITE, AZ 91
LAS VEGAS NWR ... LAS VEGAS, NM 152
MAXWELL NWR ... CIMARRON, NM 144
RAMSEY CANYON PRESERVE ... SIERRA VISTA, AZ 96
RIO GRANDE NATURE CENTER SP ... ALBUQUERQUE, NM 135
SAN PEDRO RIPARIAN CONSERVATION AREA ... SIERRA VISTA, AZ 96

WINERIES
ANDERSON VALLEY VINEYARDS ... ALBUQUERQUE, NM 136
ARIZONA VINEYARDS ... NOGALES, AZ 65
DARK MOUNTAIN BREWERY AND WINERY ... VAIL, AZ 112
SANDIA SHADOWS VINEYARD AND WINERY ... ALBUQUERQUE, NM 136
SONOITA VINEYARDS ... ELGIN, AZ 48

ZOOLOGICAL PARKS & EXHIBITS
ALAMEDA PARK AND ZOO ... ALAMOGORDO, NM 132
*ARIZONA-SONORA DESERT MUSEUM ... TUCSON, AZ 104
GENE C. REID PARK ... TUCSON, AZ 105
GRAND CANYON DEER FARM ... WILLIAMS, AZ 115
HERITAGE PARK ZOO ... PRESCOTT, AZ 89
HILLCREST PARK ZOO ... CLOVIS, NM 145
LIVING DESERT ZOO & GARDENS ... CARLSBAD, NM 139
OUT OF AFRICA WILDLIFE PARK ... FOUNTAIN HILLS, AZ 82
PAYSON ZOO ... PAYSON, AZ 67
PHOENIX ZOO ... PHOENIX, AZ 77
REID PARK ZOO ... TUCSON, AZ 105
*RIO GRANDE ZOOLOGICAL PARK ... ALBUQUERQUE, NM 135
SAHATI CAMEL FARM AND DESERT ANIMAL BREEDING CENTER ... YUMA, AZ 118
SPRING RIVER PARK AND ZOO ... ROSWELL, NM 157
WILD WEST NATURE PARK ... EDGEWOOD, NM 146
WILDLIFE WORLD ZOO ... LITCHFIELD PARK, AZ 83

ZOOLOGICAL PARKS & EXHIBITS-CHILDREN'S ZOOS
OUT OF AFRICA WILDLIFE PARK ... FOUNTAIN HILLS, AZ 82
PHOENIX ZOO ... PHOENIX, AZ 77
WILD WEST NATURE PARK ... EDGEWOOD, NM 146

SAVE *Attraction Admission Discount Index*

ARIZONA

A AEROZONA ADVENTURE INC. ... PHOENIX 80
AMERIND FOUNDATION MUSEUM ... DRAGOON 48
ARIZONA HELICOPTER ADVENTURES ... SEDONA 93
ARIZONA MUSEUM FOR YOUTH ... MESA 84
ARIZONA SCIENCE CENTER ... PHOENIX 77
ASARCO MINERAL DISCOVERY CENTER ... SAHUARITA 112
BIOSPHERE 2 CENTER ... ORACLE 111
CHAMPLIN FIGHTER AIRCRAFT MUSEUM ... MESA 84
CONFEDERATE AIR FORCE—ARIZONA WING ... MESA 84
DARK MOUNTAIN BREWERY AND WINERY ... VAIL 112
DEER VALLEY ROCK ART CENTER ... PHOENIX 76
DESERT BOTANICAL GARDEN ... PHOENIX 77
DESERT CABALLEROS WESTERN MUSEUM ... WICKENBURG 114
DON DONNELLY HORSEBACK VACATIONS AND STABLES ... APACHE JUNCTION 82
FAR FLUNG ADVENTURES ... GLOBE 52
GOLDEN ERA TOY AND AUTO MUSEUM ... COOLIDGE 46

ATTRACTION ADMISSION DISCOUNT (CONT'D)

GOLDFIELD GHOST TOWN & MINE TOURS	APACHE JUNCTION	82
GRAND CANYON AIRLINES	GRAND CANYON NP	54
GRAND CANYON CAVERNS	PEACH SPRINGS	68
GRAND CANYON DEER FARM	WILLIAMS	115
GRAND CANYON RAILWAY	WILLIAMS	115
GRAY LINE	FLAGSTAFF	48
GRAY LINE TOURS	TUCSON	109
GREAT VENTURES CHARTER TOURS	SEDONA	93
HEARD MUSEUM	PHOENIX	76
HERITAGE PARK ZOO	PRESCOTT	89
HOT AIR EXPEDITIONS	PHOENIX	80
IMAX THEATER AT ARIZONA MILLS	TEMPE	87
INTERNATIONAL WILDLIFE MUSEUM	TUCSON	105
LONDON BRIDGE WATERCRAFT TOURS	LAKE HAVASU CITY	60
LOWELL OBSERVATORY	FLAGSTAFF	49
MESA SOUTHWEST MUSEUM	MESA	84
MUSEUM OF NORTHERN ARIZONA	FLAGSTAFF	49
THE MYSTERY CASTLE	PHOENIX	77
OLD PUEBLO TOURS	TUCSON	109
OLD TUCSON STUDIOS	TUCSON	106
PHIPPEN MUSEUM	PRESCOTT	89

PHOENIX MUSEUM OF HISTORY	PHOENIX	77
PIMA AIR AND SPACE MUSEUM	TUCSON	106
PIONEER ARIZONA LIVING HISTORY MUSEUM	PHOENIX	78
PUEBLO GRANDE MUSEUM AND ARCHAEOLOGICAL PARK	PHOENIX	78
RAVEN SITE RUIN	SPRINGERVILLE	96
RED ROCK BI-PLANE TOURS AND AIR SAFARI	SEDONA	94
ROCKIN' R RANCH	MESA	84
ROSE TREE MUSEUM AND BOOKSTORE	TOMBSTONE	98
ROSSON HOUSE	PHOENIX	77
SAN BERNARDINO RANCH NATIONAL HISTORIC LANDMARK (SLAUGHTER RANCH MUSEUM)	DOUGLAS	48
SCOTTSDALE CENTER FOR THE ARTS	SCOTTSDALE	85
SCOTTSDALE JEEP RENTALS	SCOTTSDALE	86
SEDONA ADVENTURES	SEDONA	93
SEDONA SUPERVUE THEATER	SEDONA	95
TITAN MISSILE MUSEUM	GREEN VALLEY	111
TUCSON BOTANICAL GARDENS	TUCSON	107
TUCSON CHILDREN'S MUSEUM	TUCSON	107
UNICORN BALLOON CO.	PHOENIX	80
WATER SPORT CENTER INC.	LAKE HAVASU CITY	61
WILDLIFE WORLD ZOO	LITCHFIELD PARK	83

Comprehensive City Index

Here is an alphabetical list of all cities appearing in this TourBook® guide. Cities are presented by state/province. Page numbers under the POI column indicate where points of interest text begins. Page numbers under the L&R column indicate where lodging and restaurant listings begin.

ARIZONA

	POI	L&R
AJO	40	172
AMADO	N/A	172
APACHE JUNCTION	81	255
APACHE-SITGREAVES NFS	40	N/A
BENSON	41	172
BISBEE	43	173
BUCKEYE	N/A	255
BULLHEAD CITY	43	173
CAMP VERDE	43	175
CANYON DE CHELLY NMO	44	N/A
CAREFREE	82	256
CASA GRANDE RUINS NMO	44	N/A
CASA GRANDE	44	176
CAVE CREEK	82	256
CHAMBERS	N/A	176
CHANDLER	N/A	256
CHINLE	N/A	176
CHIRICAHUA NMO	45	N/A
CLARKDALE	45	N/A
COCONINO NF	46	N/A
COOLIDGE	46	N/A
CORDES JUNCTION	46	N/A
CORONADO NF	46	N/A
CORONADO NME	47	N/A
COTTONWOOD	47	177
DOUGLAS	47	N/A
DOWNTOWN TUCSON	N/A	324
DRAGOON	48	N/A
EAGAR	48	177
EHRENBERG	N/A	178
ELGIN	48	N/A
ELOY	N/A	178
FLAGSTAFF	48	178
FLORENCE	49	190
FOREST LAKES	N/A	190
FORT APACHE	49	N/A
FORT DEFIANCE	50	N/A
FORT HUACHUCA	50	N/A
FOUNTAIN HILLS	82	259
GANADO	50	N/A
GILA BEND	50	190
GLEN CANYON NRA	50	N/A
GLENDALE	83	260
GLOBE	52	191
GOLD CANYON	N/A	192
GOODYEAR	83	260
GRAND CANYON NP	52	192
GREEN VALLEY	111	348
HEBER	N/A	199
HOLBROOK	58	199
JEROME	58	N/A
KAIBAB NF	59	N/A
KAYENTA	59	202
KEAMS CANYON	59	N/A
KINGMAN	59	202
LAKE HAVASU CITY	60	204
LAKE MEAD NRA	61	N/A
LAKE MONTEZUMA	N/A	207
LITCHFIELD PARK	83	260
MARICOPA	63	N/A

	POI	L&R
MESA	83	261
MIAMI	N/A	207
MONTEZUMA CASTLE NMO	63	N/A
MONUMENT VALLEY NAVAJO TRIBAL PARK	63	N/A
MONUMENT VALLEY, UTAH	N/A	208
MORMON LAKE	N/A	208
MUNDS PARK	N/A	208
NAVAJO NMO	64	N/A
NAVAJOLAND	64	N/A
NOGALES	65	208
ORACLE	111	349
ORGAN PIPE CACTUS NMO	66	N/A
PAGE	66	209
PALO VERDE	84	N/A
PARADISE VALLEY	N/A	265
PARKER	66	212
PATAGONIA	67	N/A
PAULDEN	67	N/A
PAYSON	67	213
PEACH SPRINGS	68	215
PEARCE	68	N/A
PEORIA	84	265
PETRIFIED FOREST NP	68	N/A
PHOENIX	70	216
PICACHO	88	N/A
PINETOP-LAKESIDE	88	290
PIPE SPRING NMO	88	N/A
PORTAL	88	N/A
PRESCOTT NF	90	N/A
PRESCOTT VALLEY	N/A	295
PRESCOTT	88	291
QUARTZSITE	90	295
RIO RICO	N/A	296
ROOSEVELT	91	N/A
SACATON	91	N/A
SAFFORD	91	296
SAGUARO NP	111	N/A
SAHUARITA	112	N/A
SAN CARLOS	92	N/A
SANTA CRUZ DE TERRENATE PRESIDIO NHS	92	N/A
SASABE	92	N/A
SCOTTSDALE	85	266
SECOND MESA	92	N/A
SEDONA	92	297
SELIGMAN	N/A	314
SELLS	95	N/A
SHOW LOW	96	314
SIERRA VISTA	96	315
SOAP CREEK	N/A	316
SOMERTON	96	N/A
SONOITA	N/A	317
SPRINGERVILLE	96	317
ST. JOHNS	91	296
ST. MICHAELS	N/A	296
SUN CITY/SUN CITY WEST	86	280
SUNSET CRATER VOLCANO NMO	96	N/A
SUPAI	97	N/A
SUPERIOR	97	N/A
SURPRISE	N/A	280
TAYLOR	N/A	317

COMPREHENSIVE CITY INDEX (CONT'D)

	POI	L&R
TEMPE	86	281
TOLLESON	N/A	289
TOMBSTONE	97	317
TONTO NF	98	N/A
TONTO NMO	98	N/A
TUBA CITY	99	318
TUBAC	99	318
TUCSON	100	318
TUMACACORI NHP	113	N/A
TUZIGOOT NMO	113	N/A
VAIL	112	N/A
VALLE	113	N/A
WALNUT CANYON NMO	113	N/A
WENDEN	114	N/A
WHITERIVER	114	N/A
WICKENBURG	114	350
WILLCOX	114	351
WILLIAMS	115	351
WINDOW ROCK	115	357
WINKELMAN	116	N/A
WINSLOW	116	357
WUPATKI NMO	117	N/A
YARNELL	117	N/A
YOUNGTOWN	N/A	289
YUMA	117	358
ABIQUIU	131	N/A
ACOMA (SKY CITY)	131	N/A
ALAMOGORDO	131	N/A

NEW MEXICO	POI	L&R
ALAMOGORDO	N/A	364
ALBUQUERQUE	132	365
ALGODONES	N/A	391
ALTO	N/A	391
ANGEL FIRE	136	391
ARROYO HONDO	N/A	391
ARROYO SECO	N/A	391
ARTESIA	136	392
AZTEC RUINS NMO	137	N/A
AZTEC	137	392
BANDELIER NMO	137	N/A
BELEN	N/A	393
BERNALILLO	138	393
BLOOMFIELD	138	393
CANONCITO	N/A	393
CAPITAN	138	N/A
CAPULIN VOLCANO NMO	139	N/A
CARLSBAD CAVERNS NP	139	N/A
CARLSBAD	139	393
CARRIZOZO	141	N/A
CARSON NF	141	N/A
CHACO CULTURE NHP	142	N/A
CHAMA	142	395
CHIMAY	143	N/A
CHIMAYO	N/A	396
CIBOLA NF	144	N/A
CIMARRON	144	396
CLAYTON	145	396
CLOUDCROFT	145	397
CLOVIS	145	398
COLUMBUS	145	N/A
CORRALES	N/A	398
DEMING	146	399
DOMINGO	146	N/A
DULCE	146	N/A
EDGEWOOD	146	N/A
EL MORRO NMO	146	N/A
ELEPHANT BUTTE	N/A	400
ESPAÑOLA	147	N/A
ESPAÑOLA	N/A	400

	POI	L&R
FARMINGTON	147	401
FORT SUMNER	148	N/A
FORT UNION NMO	148	N/A
GALISTEO	N/A	403
GALLUP	149	403
GILA CLIFF DWELLINGS NMO	149	N/A
GILA NF	149	N/A
GLENWOOD	N/A	407
GRANTS	150	408
HERNANDEZ	N/A	410
HOBBS	150	410
JEMEZ PUEBLO	151	N/A
JEMEZ SPRINGS	N/A	411
LAGUNA	151	N/A
LAS CRUCES	152	411
LAS VEGAS	152	415
LINCOLN NF	153	N/A
LINCOLN	153	416
LORDSBURG	N/A	416
LOS ALAMOS	153	417
LOS BRAZOS	N/A	417
LOS LUNAS	N/A	417
MADRID	154	N/A
MESCALERO	154	N/A
MESILLA	154	417
MILAN	N/A	418
MORIARTY	N/A	418
OJO CALIENTE	154	N/A
PEÑASCO	155	N/A
PECOS NHP	155	N/A
PILAR	155	N/A
PINOS ALTOS	155	N/A
PLACITAS	N/A	418
PORTALES	155	N/A
RANCHOS DE TAOS	N/A	419
RATON	155	419
RED RIVER	N/A	420
RIO RANCHO	N/A	421
RODEO	156	N/A
ROSWELL	156	422
RUIDOSO DOWNS	157	425
RUIDOSO	157	424
SALINAS PUEBLO MISSIONS NMO	157	N/A
SAN ANTONIO	158	N/A
SAN FELIPE PUEBLO	158	N/A
SANTA FE NF	163	N/A
SANTA FE	158	425
SANTA ROSA	163	443
SANTA TERESA	164	N/A
SHIPROCK	164	N/A
SILVER CITY	165	445
SOCORRO	165	445
SPRINGER	166	N/A
STEINS	166	N/A
SUNSPOT	166	N/A
TAOS SKI VALLEY	N/A	453
TAOS	166	446
TESUQUE	N/A	453
THOREAU	N/A	453
THREE RIVERS	168	N/A
TINNIE	N/A	454
TRUTH OR CONSEQUENCES	168	454
TUCUMCARI	168	N/A
TUCUMC,ARI	N/A	454
VAUGHN	N/A	456
WHITE ROCK	N/A	457
WHITE SANDS NMO	169	N/A
WHITES CITY	169	457
ZUNI	169	N/A

Photo Credit Index

Superstition Mountains / AZ
  © David Muench .... Cover, Title,
                                          Table of Contents

Wickenburg, AZ
  © Mark E. Gibson .... Cover

TOURBOOK NAVIGATOR

Hotel / Hotel Royal Plaza, Lake Buena Vista, FL 20
Motel / Sea Gull Motel, Virginia Beach, VA 20
Country Inn / Greenville Inn, Greenville, ME 20
Resort / Turnberry Isle Resort & Club, Aventura, FL 20
B&B / Harbour Town Inn, Boothbay Harbor, ME 20
Condo / Sands of Kahana, Kahana, Maui, HI 20
Motor Inn / Days Inn-Hwy 192, Kissimmee, FL 20
Complex / The Beachmere Inn, Ogunquit, ME 21
Lodge / Frankenmuth Bavarian Inn,
  Frankenmuth, MI 21
Apartment / Coral Beach Motel, Daytona Beach, FL 21
Cottage / Desert Rose Inn, Bluff, UT 21
Ranch / C Lazy U Ranch, Granby, CO 21

ARIZONA

Monument Valley, AZ /
  © David Muench 27, 33, 163, 171
Kachina Peaks Wilderness, AZ /
  © David Muench .... 28, Table of Contents
Phoenix / Downtown skyline /
  G.L. French / H. Armstrong Roberts 70
Phoenix / Papago Park/
  © Mark E. Gibson ...... 71, 87, 289, Table of Contents
Tucson / Overview of city / A. Jackamets /
  H. Armstrong Roberts 100
Tucson / Old Tucson /
  © Mark E. Gibson ... 101, 112, 349, Table of Contents

NEW MEXICO

Pecos River, NM /
  © David Muench .... 119, 125, 363, Table of Contents
Sangre de Cristo Range, NM /
  © David Muench .... 120, Table of Contents

*A special thank you to the following organizations for
their photo contributions throughout the TourBook:
Archive Photos™
Tucson Convention & Visitors Bureau
Greater Phoenix Convention & Visitors Bureau*

One Above The Rest

*A*s a AAA member, you know how AAA can simplify your life. Now simplify it even more with **AAA Plus**.

AAA Plus gives you more of what you joined AAA for.

In addition to the benefits of basic membership, **AAA Plus** members get:

- Extended towing up to 100 miles
- Locksmith reimbursement
- Enhanced extrication service
- Reimbursement for non-AAA emergency road services
- Free fuel if you run out of gas

Simplify your life even more–upgrade your AAA basic membership to AAA Plus. Call or stop by your nearest AAA office today. And make AAA the one for you.

476

Tours for Only $15.00

MEMBERS SAVE $9.95!
(Retail $24.95)

Embark on a journey of learning and adventure, open the door to history, culture, geography, sightseeing opportunities and more with AAA TRAVEL VIDEOS.

478

Call on the names you trust.

Call 1-800-HOLIDAY for special AAA Rates at more than 1,000 Holiday Inn® hotels across the U.S., where kids always eat and stay free.* You'll enjoy all the amenities of a full-service hotel, along with dependable AT&T communications at most locations. AT&T helps you keep in touch with the ones who matter most.

Experience today's Holiday Inn hotels, building on a reputation you've come to trust. For AAA Rates or special discounts, visit our Web site at www.holiday-inn.com.

For reservations, call
1-800-HOLIDAY

To learn more about
AT&T services, dial
1-800 CALL ATT
or visit www.att.com

Guests with hearing impairments please call 1-800-238-5544 (TDD only).